THE *unofficial* GUIDE®

TO Walt Disney World®

2024

BOB SEHLINGER *and* LEN TESTA

(Walt Disney World is officially known as Walt Disney World Resort.)

Please note that prices fluctuate in the course of time and that travel information changes under the impact of many factors that influence the travel industry. We therefore suggest that you email or call ahead for confirmation when making your travel plans. Every effort has been made to ensure the accuracy of information throughout this book, and the contents of this publication are believed to be correct at the time of printing. Nevertheless, the publishers cannot accept responsibility for errors or omissions, for changes in details given in this guide, or for the consequences of any reliance on the information provided by the same. Assessments of attractions and so forth are based upon the authors' own experiences; therefore, descriptions given in this guide necessarily contain an element of subjective opinion, which may not reflect the publisher's opinion or dictate a reader's own experience on another occasion. Readers are invited to write the publisher with ideas, comments, and suggestions for future editions. There is a risk of contracting COVID-19 in any public space. The Unofficial Guides are not liable for any illness or injury. Consult a physician regarding your risk factors before booking travel.

The Unofficial Guides
An imprint of AdventureKEEN
2204 First Ave. S., Ste. 102
Birmingham, AL 35233

To contact us from within the United States, please call 800-678-7006 or fax 877-374-9016. You may also email us at info@theunofficialguides.com. Reach us on social media at TheUnofficialGuides on Facebook, Instagram, and Pinterest; @TheUGSeries on Twitter; and TheUnofficialGuideSeries on YouTube.

AdventureKEEN also publishes its books in a variety of electronic formats. Some content that appears in print may not be available in electronic formats.

Unofficial Guide is a registered trademark of Keen Communications, LLC, in the United States and other countries and may not be used without written permission. All other trademarks are the property of their respective owners. Keen Communications, LLC, is not associated with any product or vendor mentioned in this book.

Cover design by Scott McGrew
Text design by Vertigo Design

ISBN: 978-1-62809-143-4 (pbk.); eISBN: 978-1-62809-144-1 (ebook)

Distributed by Publishers Group West

Manufactured in the United States of America

5 4 3 2 1

COME CHECK US OUT!

Supplement your valuable guidebook with tips, news, and deals by visiting our websites:

theunofficialguides.com
touringplans.com

Sign up for the Unofficial Guide newsletter for even more travel tips and special offers.

Join the conversation on social media:

 @TheUGSeries

 TheUnofficialGuides

 @TheUnofficialGuides

 TheUnofficialGuides

 TheUnofficialGuideSeries

Other Unofficial Guides

The Disneyland Story: The Unofficial Guide to the Evolution of Walt Disney's Dream

Universal vs. Disney: The Unofficial Guide to American Theme Parks' Greatest Rivalry

The Unofficial Guide to Disney Cruise Line

The Unofficial Guide to Disneyland

The Unofficial Guide to Las Vegas

The Unofficial Guide to Universal Orlando

The Unofficial Guide to Walt Disney World with Kids

The Unofficial Guide to Washington, D.C.

LIST *of* MAPS *and* DIAGRAMS

CONTENTS

INTRODUCTION

FOR *the* LOVE *of* DISNEY

DEAR READER, we've been writing *The Unofficial Guide to Walt Disney World* since 1986. You've really got to love a place to cover it for that long—and we do. Millions of you do too. Comments like these arrive at our office every day:

> *"Disney World was definitely the most magical and the best family vacation we ever had."*

> *"Holiday of a lifetime. Meticulous planning required, but amazing."*

> *"We've already booked another trip."*

Disney's theme parks are among the world's greatest man-made vacation destinations. At their best, they combine unparalleled imagination and storytelling with new technologies, all presented with optimism and an unwavering faith in humanity. Walt Disney World in particular is essentially a purpose-built city: a place designed to entertain, amaze, and inspire.

WHY DISNEY WORLD NEEDS *a* 744-PAGE GUIDEBOOK

WE KNOW WHAT YOU'RE THINKING. The child-rearing classic *What to Expect When You're Expecting* clocks in at 656 pages, and a typical version of the King James Bible is around 1,200. Does the advice needed for Walt Disney World really fall somewhere between childbirth and God's manual for living?

If it's your first time, yes.

The thing that surprises most new visitors to Walt Disney World is that a Disney vacation requires much more planning and effort than most other vacations they've had.

Why? The main reason is capacity. Around 60,000 people visit Disney World's Magic Kingdom theme park in a normal day. Most of them would eat at its most popular restaurant—Be Our Guest—if they could get in. But the restaurant can serve only a tiny fraction of those who want to dine there. Visitors who can't get into Be Our Guest often end up at restaurants with worse food, higher prices, or both.

Capacity also affects Disney World's popular rides: For some rides, there are far more people who want to ride than the ride can handle. As a result, some visitors will wait just 10 minutes to experience a ride, and others will wait 2 hours or more for the same attraction on the same day. A reader from Hessmer, Louisiana, explains:

> I don't know how people do Disney without this information. I felt sorry seeing people so excited to get into the parks and only then realize that a little homework beforehand would've saved their trip.

Don't panic. If you love theme parks, Disney World is as good as it gets—the best in the small-*w* world. If you arrive without knowing a thing about the place and make every possible mistake, chances are about 90% that you'll have a wonderful vacation anyway.

The job of a guidebook is to give you a heads-up regarding opportunities and potential problems. We're certain we can help you turn a great vacation into an absolutely fabulous one.

A mom from Streator, Illinois, who was amazed at the size of the *Unofficial Guide,* came back saying this:

> It had been 10 years since we'd been to WDW, and I was shocked by how much your book grew. After going, I'm surprised that it's so small.

WHAT MAKES THIS BOOK DIFFERENT?

THE ADVICE IN THIS BOOK is different from what you'll find on the internet or in other books, in three important ways.

First, the team that produces this book is totally independent of the Walt Disney Company, Walt Disney World, and all other members of the Disney corporate family. We don't accept free trips, gifts, special favors, or other compensation from Disney in exchange for our coverage; we pay for everything we review. Disney doesn't request, influence, edit, or approve anything you'll read here.

In this guide, we represent and serve you, the reader. If a restaurant serves bad food, a gift item is overpriced, or a ride isn't worth the wait, we say so. In the process, we hope to make your visit more fun and rewarding.

Second, we use data, science, and technology to help solve problems that you'll encounter in Walt Disney World. In many ways, the Disney theme parks are the quintessential system: the ultimate in mass-produced entertainment, the most planned and programmed environment anywhere. Lines for rides and restaurants form in predictable ways at predictable times, for example. That makes it possible for us to study them.

You may be surprised that Disney-related questions like "How can I wait less in line?" or "What rides should my kids try?" are active areas of research in schools around the world; similar problems pop up in businesses every day. The authors and researchers who write this book have years—some have decades—of academic and professional experience in these areas and use them to benefit you.

The third way this book is different is the amount of time and money that goes into making it. Disney research is the full-time job of most of our core team. Over the years, we've spent millions of dollars reviewing and analyzing Disney World's hotels, rides, lines, and restaurants. No other book or website commits the people, skills, or budget to do anything like the research you'll find in these pages. The only other organization that does comparable analysis of Disney World is Disney itself. And we will tell you what it won't.

HOW *to* USE THIS BOOK

THE BEST WAY TO USE THIS BOOK is to read in order the first few pages of each chapter, to get a feel for the kinds of questions the chapter answers. Then read in depth the chapters most important to you.

We've organized the chapters so that they appear in the same sequence and timeline that you'll use to plan and take your trip. For example, Part 2 contains advice on what you need to know to start planning your trip. The next few chapters guide you through choosing a hotel, finding good places to eat, and picking the best rides and entertainment in the parks.

KEY QUESTIONS ANSWERED IN THIS CHAPTER

- Where can I find a planning checklist and timeline? (*pages 24–28*)

- What are the six most important tips for avoiding lines at Disney World? (*pages 47–67*)

- What is the Genie+ ride reservation system, and how do I use it? (*pages 60–64*)

Each chapter starts with **Key Questions,** a list of the most common and important queries that visitors have about Walt Disney World (and Universal Orlando). For each question, we've listed where in the chapter to find the answers. Here's an example:

If you don't recognize a term such as *Genie+*, you should read that section of the chapter—it's probably important.

Of course, each chapter answers many more questions than the ones shown on the first page. We suggest skimming each chapter's boldfaced section headings to see if a particular topic is relevant to your family.

Some subjects, such as how Disney accommodates guests in wheelchairs, are relevant across multiple parts of your vacation. These subjects are usually covered in depth in one chapter (in this case, Part 8, "Tips for Varied Circumstances"), with cross-references in other chapters when they're needed.

Many topics are discussed in depth. For example, Disney World has hundreds of attractions, from simple spinning things you find at your local town carnival to massive super-headliners, the likes of which you've never seen. Understanding the scale of these rides, and how they're run, will help you decide what's worth your time. And if you visit another theme park later, you'll know what to look for when planning that trip too.

If you use the guide like an encyclopedia or dictionary—say, you look something up in one of the indexes then go to the cited page—you may overlook information presented in previous sections that is vital to understanding the subject. Likewise, if you skip or skim over explanatory material in the introductory chapters, that might lead to a misunderstanding later on.

THE *UNOFFICIAL GUIDE* TEAM

ALLOW US TO INTRODUCE THE PEOPLE who work on this book, except for our dining critic, who shall remain anonymous:

- **BOB SEHLINGER** Author and publisher
- **LEN TESTA** Coauthor
- **FRED HAZELTON** Statistician
- **DAVID DAVIES** Webmaster, TouringPlans.com
- **JIM HILL** Disney Dish contributor
- **TRAVIS BRYANT** Webmaster, TheUnofficialGuides.com
- **KAREN TURNBOW, PhD** Child psychologist

DATA COLLECTORS
Chantale Brazeau
Shane Grizzard
Christine Harrison
Giovanna Harrison
Cliff Myers
Ivonne Ramos
Darcie Vance
Rich Vosburgh
Kelly Whitman

CONTRIBUTORS
Rich Bernato
Christina Harrison

Seth Kubersky
Brian McNichols
Liliane J. Opsomer
Sue Pisaturo
Laurel Stewart
Mary Waring
Deb Wills

HOTEL INSPECTORS
Kristen Helmstetter
Lillian Macko
Richard Macko
Darcie Vance

EDITORIAL, ART, AND PRODUCTION
- **KATE JOHNSON** Managing editor
- **ANNIE LONG** Layout
- **JENNA BARRON, EMILY BEAUMONT, RITCHEY HALPHEN, ANDREW MOLLENKOF** Proofreaders
- **SCOTT McGREW** Cover design
- **STEVE JONES, CASSANDRA POERTNER** Cartography
- **TAMI KNIGHT, CHRIS ELIOPOULOS** Illustration
- **POTOMAC INDEXING** Indexing (**Joanne Sprott**, team leader)

YOUR UNOFFICIAL WALT DISNEY WORLD TOOLBOX

WHEN IT COMES TO WALT DISNEY WORLD, a couple with two toddlers in diapers needs different advice than a party of seniors going to the EPCOT International Flower & Garden Festival. Likewise, adults touring without children, families with kids of varying ages, and honeymooners all require their own special guidance.

To meet the needs of our diverse readers, we've created the comprehensive guide before you. We call *The Unofficial Guide to Walt Disney World*, at 760 pages, the "Big Book." It provides the detailed information that anyone traveling to Walt Disney World needs in order to have a super vacation. It's our cornerstone.

As thorough as we try to make the main guide, though, there just isn't sufficient space for all the tips and resources that may be useful to certain readers. Therefore, we've developed three additional guides that provide information tailored to specific visitors.

Here's what's in the toolbox:

The Unofficial Guide to Disney Cruise Line, by Erin Foster with Len Testa and Ritchey Halphen, presents advice for first-time cruisers; money-saving tips for booking your cruise; and detailed profiles for restaurants, shows, and nightclubs, along with deck plans and thorough coverage of the ports visited by Disney Cruise Line.

The Unofficial Guide to Walt Disney World with Kids, by Bob Sehlinger and Liliane J. Opsomer with Len Testa, presents detailed planning and touring tips for a family vacation, along with more than 20 family touring plans not included in the Big Book.

The Unofficial Guide to Universal Orlando, by Seth Kubersky, is the most comprehensive guide to Universal Orlando Resort in print. At more than 400 pages, it's the perfect tool for understanding and enjoying Universal's ever-expanding complex of theme parks, a water park, resort hotels, nightclubs, and restaurants. The guide includes field-tested touring plans that will save you hours of standing in line.

CORRECTIONS, UPDATES, AND BREAKING NEWS

WE EXPECT THIS 2024 EDITION to be available through fall 2024. The first set of updates was started in the spring of 2023 and incorporates Disney's current operating procedures at press time. An up-to-date summary of book changes is available at tinyurl.com/wdwupdates.

LETTERS AND COMMENTS FROM READERS

MANY USERS OF *The Unofficial Guide to Walt Disney World* write us to comment or share their own strategies for visiting Disney World. Their feedback is frequently incorporated into future editions of the *Guide* and has contributed immeasurably to its ongoing improvement. If you write us or complete our reader survey, rest assured that we won't release your name or address to any mailing-list companies, direct-marketing advertisers, or other third parties. If you're up for having your comments quoted in the Guide, be sure to tell us where you're from.

Speaking of comments, from the thousands of letters, emails, and surveys we receive, only about one in eight contains comments. Of these, only a small percentage are substantive and well stated. In other words, quotable comments are like gold to us. If a comment on a particular subject hits the nail on the head, it's unlikely (though it happens) that we'll receive a more well-written and more incisive one. If a better comment isn't forthcoming, the older one remains in the next edition because it best serves our readers.

Online Reader Survey

Our website hosts a questionnaire you can use to express opinions about your Walt Disney World visit. Access it here: touringplans.com /walt-disney-world/survey. This questionnaire lets every member of your party, regardless of age, tell us what they think about attractions, hotels, restaurants, and more.

You can also print out the reader survey and mail it to us at the following address:

Reader Survey
The Unofficial Guide to Walt Disney World
2204 First Ave. S., Ste. 102
Birmingham, AL 35233

Finally, if you'd like to review this book on Amazon, go to tinyurl .com/wdw2023reviews.

How to Contact the Authors

Bob Sehlinger and Len Testa
The Unofficial Guide to Walt Disney World
2204 First Ave. S., Ste. 102
Birmingham, AL 35233
info@theunofficialguides.com
Facebook: TheUnofficialGuides | Twitter: @TheUGSeries

When you write, please put your mailing address on both your letter and your envelope—the two sometimes get separated. It's also a good idea to include your phone number. If you email us, please tell us where you're from.

Steve Bloom and Becky Gandillon contributed much of the statistical analysis for this book. Gerelyn Reaves answers email better than we could and generally keeps everyone in line. Seth Kubersky is our Universal Orlando guru, assisted by food consigliere Derek Burgan. Brad Huber developed the latest version of our Lines app. Todd Perlmutter, Bryan Klinck, and EJJ skillfully debugged our touring plan software. Lines's chat is moderated by the fabulous Weasus, missoverexcited, and PrincipalTinker.

We'd like to say thanks to these folks for their assistance with fact-checking and research: Robert Bloom, Shannon Bohn, Dani Dennison, Anne Densk, Alyssa Drake, Erin Foster, Scott Gustin, Jennifer Heymont, Erin Jenkins, Lauren Macvane, David McDonough, Bethany Vinton, and Carlye Wisel. Thanks also to Jamie Holding and his GitHub repository (github.com/cubehouse/themeparks). Thanks to John Tierney, who, as far as we know, did not acquire his "data collection" skills during stints in Eastern Europe working for three-letter US government agencies.

Finally, to everyone at Walt Disney Parks and Resorts who follows our research from a distance in this special, weird relationship, even if they can't say it: We love you too.

THE IMPORTANCE OF BEING SERIOUS

SOME READERS ARE ASTONISHED that seemingly intelligent adults would spend so much time on critical analyses of theme park rides. If you've ever heard "You're going to Disney *again?*" from a relative, try explaining to complete strangers your theory that Mrs. Potts is an unreliable narrator. But most of us wouldn't think twice about reading *Consumer Reports* before buying a car or a major appliance. And Disney World costs more than a dishwasher.

Beyond that, the Disney corporation is immensely powerful—it has enough money, talent, and time to do almost anything its executives desire. When Disney's marketing says its theme parks and restaurants are "world-class" and its artists are "legends," it's important to hold it accountable for those words, if they are to mean anything at all.

The best way to do that is to point out whether the things Disney wants to sell you meet the standards it has set for itself. When we say that Rise of the Resistance in Disney's Hollywood Studios is the best theme park ride Disney has made in at least 30 years, it's because we believe it meets the highest of Disney's ideals dating back to Walt himself. Likewise, if you read us kvetching about a cartoon-based roller coaster in EPCOT, or that the adjective *regal* means "fit for a king" and absolutely shouldn't be used in the name of a post-Colonial American restaurant next to an attraction literally dedicated to the republic, it's because those things don't make sense in the stories that Disney has already established. And as Disney says, it all begins with a story.

THE IMPORTANCE OF BEING GOOFY

AT BREAKFAST at Disney's Old Key West Resort, four Disney execs were celebrating all the ways they made a Disney World visit more complicated and expensive. Said Tom, "We've saved a pot of money by chunking free bus service to and from the airport."

"Cutting regular maid service at the resorts was another good one," John added.

"You said it," responded Earl. "Also we launched Genie+ and Individual Lightning Lane—real money makers—and got rid of that stupid free FastPass+. What a coup that was. All the guests hate it, but what can they do, go to Wacky Golf?"

"I love making guests call in at exactly 7 a.m. to get a boarding group for Tron," Scott chimed in. "We set it up so that guests need to be fast and lucky. Boarding groups are often completely allocated for the entire day within 10 seconds of 7 a.m. Whoever thought you should be able to sleep late on vacation?"

"My favorite is having a half-hour Early Entry period at all four parks every day for Disney resort guests," John commented.

"Yeah," Tom followed up, "that means guests who don't stay in Disney resorts don't get in until all the parks are packed with Disney resort guests."

"I love it," said Earl. "Who says we can't stiff the day guests while giving our resort guests some extra sugar."

"Exactly," Tom inserted. "The day guests are boiling mad, but what can they do?"

"Go to Wacky Golf!" shouted Scott. Everybody laughed.

As breakfast was wrapping up, all the theme parks were opening Early Entry for Disney resort guests. While waiting for the check, John's cell phone rang. He answered and listened for about 30 seconds. "It's security, and we have a situation at the Studios."

"Put security on speaker," Earl said.

"This is Captain Rogers at the Studios. Hundreds of day guests arrived about an hour before we commenced Early Entry and before resort guests began arriving. They clogged security checkpoints, ticket windows, and the areas fronting the turnstiles. They were able to pass through security given that security doesn't check for tickets or Disney resort ID."

"Where are our resort guests?" Tom asked.

"All the way at the back of the mob. They can't even see the turnstiles," reported Captain Rogers. "At Early Entry time, the day guests proceeded to the turnstiles and tried to enter using their tickets. When cast members asked for Disney Resort ID, of course the day guests didn't have any. Refused admittance, they became very upset and carried on about how much they paid for their admission and how unfair it was not being admitted. Each day guest ate up about 10 minutes acting out while a cast member tried to calm them down. Some were very loud and even demanded to speak to a supervisor. Our security folks tried to intervene, but they were so outnumbered that the entire entrance area was clogged almost immediately.

"With day guests stacking up at every turnstile, and more guests arriving at the back of the crowd," Captain Rogers continued, "an admission problem is turning into a public relations and safety problem. Local news organizations were clued in, and within minutes they descended, filming the event and interviewing guests. There was a lot of ranting and frayed tempers, but I'm happy to report no physical confrontations."

Meanwhile the Disney execs were reviewing their options. Earl suggested letting them through the turnstiles and setting up a secondary checkpoint inside the park. Captain Rogers opined that doing that would just move the logjam into the park.

"Also," Scott said, "we'll be inundated with resort guests soon, and if they're in the park, we won't be able to tell them apart from the day guests."

"This did not happen spontaneously," Tom insisted. "How was it organized?"

"We've been working on that," said Captain Rogers. "Evidently there were hundreds of posts on social media. They said if you're going to Disney's Hollywood Studios tomorrow, stand by for an important message that will make your day a lot better. Also, go to bed early."

"So, what was the important message?" asked John.

"As far as we can tell, it was never sent," Captain Rogers replied. (Fourteen organizers checked into the largest non-Disney hotels. Everyone staying there by definition would be considered day guests. About 10 p.m., two organizers in each hotel slipped notes under hotel room doors with instructions for the next morning.)

"That's nuts!" Earl exclaimed. "What's next?"

"I hate we were outfoxed," said Captain Rogers, "but the easiest and safest way to end this is to just let everybody in."

The execs looked glumly at each other and said to Captain Rogers: "Just do it."

Wacky Golf anyone?

And so it goes . . .

What makes writing about Walt Disney World so much fun is that the Disney people take everything so seriously. Day to day, they debate momentous decisions with far-ranging consequences: Will Pluto look silly in a silver cape? Have we gone too far with the Little Mermaid's cleavage? With the nation's drug problem a constant concern, should we have a dwarf named Dopey?

Unofficially, we think having a sense of humor is important. This guidebook has one, and it's probably necessary that you do too—not to use this book but to have the most fun possible at Walt Disney World. Think of *The Unofficial Guide* as your private trainer getting your sense of humor in shape. It will help you understand the importance of being goofy.

WALT DISNEY WORLD:
An Overview

WHAT IS DISNEY WORLD?

WE MAY BE BIASED, but we think Walt Disney World (WDW), in Orlando, Florida, is the best collection of theme parks on Earth. Its combined size, quality, and ambition go far beyond that of any other amusement park or theme park you may have seen.

If this is your first visit, you're probably familiar with Disney World through Disney's theme park advertising. It's great at showing families enjoying exciting rides and meeting its famous characters. But 30-second ads don't convey where to find those rides and characters, how long you'll stand in line, or how much money the visit will cost.

Walt Disney World has four theme parks. If you're familiar with any of them, it's probably the **Magic Kingdom**—the first one built and the one most people think of when they hear the words *Disney World*. The other three theme parks are **EPCOT, Disney's Hollywood Studios,** and **Disney's Animal Kingdom.**

Walt Disney World also contains two water parks, **Blizzard Beach** and **Typhoon Lagoon.** But there's more: over three dozen hotels and a campground; more than 100 restaurants; a massive year-round sports center; an outdoor mall/entertainment/hotel complex called **Disney Springs;** six convention centers; four golf courses; and an array of spas, recreation options, and other activities.

HOW BIG IS WALT DISNEY WORLD?

WALT DISNEY WORLD IS HUGE—around 43 square miles, about double the size of Manhattan and slightly smaller than Miami.

For easy reference, we (and Disney) use the theme parks as rough guides to locations within Walt Disney World. For example, the **Magic Kingdom Resort Area** is about 7 square miles and contains the Magic Kingdom theme park and nearby hotels, restaurants, golf courses, and entertainment. The **EPCOT Resort Area** is roughly 1.5 square miles and contains EPCOT and nearby hotels, restaurants, and so on. Most of these areas are separated by miles of barely developed Central Florida swampland.

The areas are so far apart that it's not possible to walk between them. Instead, you'll usually get around via the Walt Disney World transportation system's fleet of buses, boats, vans, monorail trains (monorails), and aerial trams. Disney World's bus system is the third largest in Florida, behind Jacksonville's and Miami's. Its transportation system is so large that Part 9 of this book is dedicated to it.

Because of Walt Disney World's size, it would probably take around two weeks to explore most of it. Most families don't have two weeks to spare, so we'll tell you the best things to see in the time you have.

THE MAJOR THEME PARKS

The Magic Kingdom

When most people think of Walt Disney World, they think of the Magic Kingdom, opened in 1971. It consists of **Cinderella Castle** and adventures, rides, and shows featuring the Disney cartoon characters. It's only one element of Disney World, but it remains the heart.

The Magic Kingdom is divided into six "lands" arranged around a central hub. First you come to **Main Street, U.S.A.,** which connects the Magic Kingdom entrance with the hub. Arranged clockwise around the hub are **Adventureland, Frontierland, Liberty Square, Fantasyland,** and **Tomorrowland.** The Magic Kingdom has more rides, shows, and entertainment than any other WDW theme park. A comprehensive tour takes two days; a tour of the highlights can be done in one full day.

Six hotels—**Bay Lake Tower,** the **Contemporary** and **Grand Floridian Resorts, Polynesian Village** (and an upcoming, **separate tower wing**), and **The Villas at the Grand Floridian**—are connected to the Magic Kingdom by monorail and boat. Three other hotels—**Shades of Green** (for the US military and their families), **Wilderness Lodge** (incorporating the **Boulder Ridge Villas** and **Copper Creek** time-share units), and **Fort Wilderness Resort & Campground**—are located nearby but are served by boat and bus instead of monorail.

EPCOT

Opened in October 1982, EPCOT is twice as big as the Magic Kingdom and comparable in scope. The "front" (southern) part consists of three areas (**World Discovery, World Celebration,** and **World Nature**) holding giant pavilions concerning human creativity, technological advancement, the natural world, and—increasingly—cartoon characters; **World Showcase,** the "back" (northern) part, is arranged around a 40-acre lagoon and presents the architectural, social, and cultural heritages of almost a dozen nations, each country represented by replicas of famous landmarks and settings familiar to world travelers.

The EPCOT resorts—the **BoardWalk Inn & Villas, Dolphin, Swan, Swan Reserve, Yacht & Beach Club Resorts,** and **Beach Club Villas**— are within a 5- to 15-minute walk of the International Gateway, the World Showcase entrance to the theme park. The hotels are also linked to EPCOT and Disney's Hollywood Studios by boat and walkway. EPCOT is connected to the Magic Kingdom and its hotels by monorail. An elevated ski lift–like gondola system called the **Skyliner** links EPCOT and Disney's Hollywood Studios to Disney's Pop Century, Art of Animation, Caribbean Beach, and Riviera Resorts.

Disney's Hollywood Studios

Opened in 1989 in an area a little larger than the Magic Kingdom, Disney's Hollywood Studios (DHS) has two main sections. One area, occupying about 50% of the Studios, is a theme park focused on the motion picture, music, and television industries. Park highlights include a re-creation of Hollywood and Sunset Boulevards from Hollywood's Golden Age, several rides and musical shows, and a movie stunt show.

The other half of DHS is two immersive lands based on popular Disney film franchises: **Toy Story Land** opened in 2018 with three highly themed rides for children. **Star Wars: Galaxy's Edge**, opened in 2019, has two state-of-the-art, large rides for older children, teens, and adults.

DHS is connected to other Walt Disney World areas by highway, boat, and Skyliner but not by monorail. Guests can park in DHS's pay parking lot or commute by bus; guests at EPCOT resort hotels can reach DHS by boat, on foot, or by Skyliner.

Disney's Animal Kingdom

About five times the size of the Magic Kingdom, Disney's Animal Kingdom combines zoological exhibits with rides, shows, and live entertainment. The park is arranged in a hub-and-spoke configuration somewhat like the Magic Kingdom. A lush tropical rainforest serves as Main Street, funneling visitors to **Discovery Island,** the park's hub. Dominated by the park's central icon, the 14-story-tall, hand-carved **Tree of Life,** Discovery Island offers services, shopping, and dining. From there, guests can access the themed areas: **Africa, Asia, DinoLand U.S.A.,** and **Pandora.** Discovery Island, Africa, and DinoLand U.S.A. opened in 1998, followed by Asia in 1999. Africa, the largest themed area at 100 acres, is home to free-roaming herds in a re-creation of the Serengeti Plain.

Pandora—The World of Avatar, based on James Cameron's *Avatar* film franchise, is the most significant recent expansion. Its biggest draws may be the animals and scenery—including "floating mountains" and glow-in-the-dark plants—which Disney has replicated from the movie. See Part 13 for full details.

Disney's Animal Kingdom has its own parking lot and is connected to other Walt Disney World destinations by the Disney bus system. Although no hotels lie within Animal Kingdom proper, the **All-Star Resorts, Animal Kingdom Lodge & Villas,** and **Coronado Springs Resort** are all nearby.

continued on page 16

South Orlando

Walt Disney World

N

Reedy Lake

THE MAGIC KINGDOM

Bay Lake Tower

Seven Seas Lagoon

Contemporary Resort

Bay Lake

Grand Floridian Resort & Spa, Villas

Wilderness Lodge
Boulder Ridge Villas
Copper Creek Villas & Cabins

Magnolia Golf Course

Floridian Way

Polynesian Village Resort & Villas

Fort Wilderness Resort & Campground

Oak Trail Golf Course

7 Seas Dr.

Shades of Green

P P

World Dr.

Palm Golf Course

Vista Blvd.

Magic Kingdom tollbooths

toll road

429

World Dr.

Flamingo Crossings

Western Way

Yacht & Beach Club Resorts

BoardWalk Inn & Villas

Gran Destino Tower

Dolphin

Swan Reserve

Swan

W. Savannah Cir.

E. Savannah Cir.

Western Way

Coronado Springs Resort

Fantasia Gardens

P

Western Expwy. (toll road)

DISNEY'S ANIMAL KINGDOM

DISNEY'S HOLLYWOOD STUDIOS

Animal Kingdom Lodge & Villas

Buena Vista Dr.

Blizzard Beach & Winter Summerland

Star Wars Galactic Starcruiser Hotel

toll road

P

Osceola Pkwy.

Publix

W. Irlo Bronson Memorial Hwy.

192

530

Sherberth Rd.

All-Star Resorts

World Dr.

ESPN Wide World of Sports Complex

Victory Way

Formosa Gardens Blvd.

429

Funie Steed Rd.

530

W. Irlo Bronson Memorial Hw

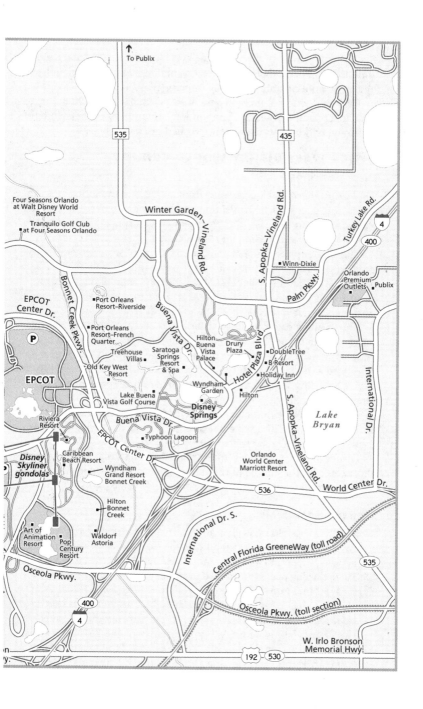

continued from page 11

THE WATER PARKS

DISNEY WORLD HAS TWO MAJOR WATER PARKS: **Typhoon Lagoon** and **Blizzard Beach.** Opened in 1989, Typhoon Lagoon is distinguished by a wave pool capable of making 6-foot waves. Blizzard Beach opened in 1995 and features more slides. Both parks pay great attention to atmosphere and aesthetics. Typhoon Lagoon and Blizzard Beach have their own parking lots and can be reached by Disney bus.

OTHER WALT DISNEY WORLD VENUES

Disney Springs

Themed to evoke a Florida waterfront town, Disney Springs encompasses four areas, each with shopping, dining, and entertainment: the **Marketplace,** on the east; the **West Side,** on (surprise!) the west; **The Landing,** on the waterfront; and **Town Center.**

The Marketplace contains the country's largest store selling Disney-character merchandise; upscale resort-wear and specialty shops; and numerous restaurants. The West Side is a diverse mix of nightlife, shopping, dining, and notable entertainment. That entertainment includes a dedicated **Cirque du Soleil** show found only at Disney World.

The Landing offers additional shopping and arguably the best dining options in Disney Springs. These include **The Boathouse,** an upscale waterfront seafood eatery with better steaks than anything nearby; **Morimoto Asia,** a high-quality, midpriced table-service restaurant from Iron Chef Masaharu Morimoto; **Chef Art Smith's Homecomin',** a restaurant from celebrity chef and Florida native Art Smith that features local farm-to-table ingredients, traditional Southern cooking, and excellent cocktails; and **Wine Bar George,** serving tasty Mediterranean small plates and a well-curated list of affordable wines.

Disney Springs includes three multistory parking garages, with short walks to the middle of the action. It is also accessible via Disney transportation from Disney resort hotels and theme parks.

Disney's BoardWalk

Near EPCOT, the BoardWalk is an idealized replication of a 1930s East Coast waterfront resort. Open all day, the BoardWalk features upscale restaurants, shops and galleries, and a brewpub. In the evening, a nightclub with dueling pianos and a DJ dance club join the lineup. Both are for guests age 21 and up only. There's no admission fee for the BoardWalk, but the piano bar levies a cover charge at night. This area is anchored by the **BoardWalk Inn & Villas,** along with its adjacent convention center.

The BoardWalk is within walking distance of the EPCOT resorts, EPCOT's International Gateway, and Disney's Hollywood Studios. Boat transportation is available to and from EPCOT and Disney's Hollywood Studios, the Skyliner connects the BoardWalk to the Studios and the hotels on its route, and buses serve other Walt Disney World locations.

Disney Cruise Line: The Mouse at Sea

Disney launched (literally) its own cruise line in 1998 with the 2,400-passenger *Disney Magic.* Four more ships were added, and three more will join the soon-to-be eight-ship fleet in a few years. Most cruises depart from Port Canaveral, Florida (about a 90-minute drive from Walt Disney World), or from Miami on three-, four-, and seven-night itineraries. Bahamian and Caribbean cruises include a day at **Castaway Cay,** Disney's 1,000-acre private island since 1998, or **Lighthouse Point,** a 750-acre private resort for Disney cruise guests, scheduled to open in 2024. Cruises can be packaged with a stay at Disney World. Disney offers a free online video at disneycruiseline.com to help familiarize you with Disney Cruise Line cruises.

To get the most out of your cruise, check out *The Unofficial Guide to Disney Cruise Line,* by Erin Foster with Len Testa and Ritchey Halphen.

WHAT'S NEW AT WALT DISNEY WORLD

Disneyland is something that will never be finished. It's something that I can keep developing. It will be a live, breathing thing that will need change.

—Walt Disney

WHAT WALT SAID OF DISNEYLAND is also true of Disney World. The table on pages 18–19 shows all the major changes that have taken place at Walt Disney World in the last 2, 5, and 10 years.

THE PEOPLE OF WALT DISNEY WORLD

DISNEY'S EMPLOYEES are called **cast members.** How you're treated by the ones you encounter can make or break a vacation. Fortunately, Disney staff often go the extra mile to make your visit special, as the following three readers report.

First, from a family from Pawnee, Illinois, who was assisted in a health emergency:

On our first day at the resort, our 6-year-old grandson woke up with a deep cough, fever, and kind of wheezing. Our daughter-in-law contacted the desk and found that WDW provided a shuttle to a local prompt-care facility. As it turned out, the shuttle wasn't available, so they called a cab instead and covered the cost! Our grandson was able to be seen by a physician and received medication that allowed him to get better and salvage the trip. We can't say enough about what the staff and WDW did for us that day! They were terrific!

A family from St. Joseph, Michigan, had this to relate:

We had a very unexpected and wonderful surprise waiting in our stroller after the Country Bear Jamboree. *Out of nearly 30 strollers, ours had been visited by Santa Mickey while we were in the show. We came out to a stroller decorated with silly bands, Christmas ornaments, and a snowman Mickey plush toy. Our 5-year-old son, not to mention the rest of our party, were delighted. Just another way that WDW goes one more step to make a magical experience.*

continued on page 19

WHAT'S NEW AT WALT DISNEY WORLD

COMING IN LATE 2023 OR 2024

- EPCOT's **Journey of Water, Inspired by Moana** should open in late 2023.
- A new nighttime fireworks show for **EPCOT** has also been announced.
- A major expansion of the **Polynesian Village Resort,** for Disney Vacation Club members, should open on the Seven Seas Lagoon in 2024.
- **Tiana's Bayou Adventure,** a retheming of the Splash Mountain log flume ride, will open in Frontierland in 2024.

LAST 2 YEARS

- **Tron Lightcycle/Run,** an outdoor roller-coaster, opened in the Magic Kingdom's Tomorrowland in April 2023.
- **Guardians of the Galaxy: Cosmic Rewind,** the world's longest indoor roller-coaster, opened in EPCOT in 2022.
- Disney's paid **Genie+** and **Individual Lightning Lane** ride reservation systems debuted, replacing FastPass+.
- Disney's **Early Theme Park Entry** and **Extended Evening Theme Park Hours** debuted, replacing the previous Extra Magic Hours program.
- EPCOT opened a new nighttime show, *Harmonious,* in October 2021 (since closed), along with **Remy's Ratatouille Adventure,** a ride based on the Pixar film *Ratatouille*.
- The **Magic Kingdom** debuted a new nighttime show, *Disney Enchantment,* featuring fireworks and digital projection technology that extends special effects from Cinderella Castle to Main Street, U.S.A. It has since been closed.
- The **Star Wars: Galactic Starcruiser** hotel opened in 2022. The innovative two-day role-playing experience will close in September 2023.

LAST 5 YEARS

- The land **Star Wars: Galaxy's Edge** opened in Disney's Hollywood Studios (DHS), with two new state-of-the-art rides (**Star Wars: Rise of the Resistance** and *Millennium Falcon:* **Smugglers Run**), and *Star Wars*–themed dining options.
- DHS opened **Mickey and Minnie's Runaway Railway,** an immersive 3-D ride through the new Mickey Mouse cartoon universe.
- **Disney's Riviera Resort,** a Disney Vacation Club property, opened in 2019 adjacent to the Caribbean Beach Resort. Connecting the Riviera to EPCOT and DHS is the new **Disney Skyliner** elevated gondola system, which also links Disney's Pop Century, Art of Animation, and Caribbean Beach Resorts with each other and those theme parks.
- **Disney's Coronado Springs Resort** opened the 15-story **Gran Destino Tower** in 2019, with more-upscale guest rooms and dining options.
- DHS opened **Toy Story Land,** with two new rides: **Alien Swirling Saucers,** a variation on an amusement park spinning ride, and **Slinky Dog Dash,** a mild roller coaster that's more fun than it might seem at first glance.
- Disney introduced the **Disability Access Service (DAS)** to help guests with disabilities better navigate the parks' lines.

LAST 10 YEARS

- EPCOT unveiled the food-and-arts-themed **Festival of the Arts,** which takes plan in January and February.
- The remodeling of Disney's Animal Kingdom is complete with the park's sixth "land," **Pandora—The World of Avatar.** It features two attractions (**Avatar Flight of Passage,** a thrilling flight simulator, and **Na'vi River Journey,** a gentle boat ride) and glowing "bioluminescent" plants. The adventurous restaurant **Tiffins** opened with the accompanying **Nomad Lounge.**
- **Copper Creek Villas & Cabins** at **Disney's Wilderness Lodge Resort** opened, adding refurbished Disney Vacation Club rooms and two-bedroom cabins along Bay Lake, as well as the **Geyser Point Bar & Grill.**

WHAT'S NEW AT WALT DISNEY WORLD

LAST 10 YEARS *(continued)*

- The Magic Kingdom opened **New Fantasyland,** an expanded area with **Seven Dwarfs Mine Train; Under the Sea: Journey of the Little Mermaid;** *Enchanted Tales with Belle;* and **Be Our Guest Restaurant.** In Adventureland, **Jungle Navigation Co. Ltd. Skipper Canteen** offers table-service dining with all the whimsy of the Jungle Cruise. **Festival of Fantasy** became the new daytime parade.

- **MagicBands** (flexible, RFID-enabled bracelets) were introduced as a form of admission and a way to use ride reservations, pay for food and merchandise, and more.

- EPCOT saw the opening of **Frozen Ever After,** a ride based on the popular film *Frozen,* in World Showcase's Norway Pavilion.

continued from page 17

Finally, from a suburban Philadelphia family:

At Expedition Everest, I witnessed expert handling of a group of teenage line-jumpers by Disney staff. Once they reached the loading area, cast members ushered them aside in a very calm and friendly fashion, causing no apparent disruption. I didn't see where they were ushered or what happened next, but I did not see them board the ride. It was as if they were never there.

UNIVERSAL ORLANDO

LIKE WALT DISNEY WORLD, Universal Orlando Resort consists of two theme parks, a water park, several hotels, dozens of restaurants, and other entertainment venues. A third theme park is set to open in 2025. It sits about 14 miles east of Walt Disney World, just off I-4. Both resorts are owned by media companies: Comcast owns Universal, and the Walt Disney Company owns Walt Disney World. Thus, admission tickets bought for Disney World can't be used at Universal, and vice versa.

Because they're owned by different companies, Disney and Universal are generally viewed as direct competitors—the time and money you spend in one place are time and money not spent in the other. We think the Disney and Universal parks complement each other; if you're in Orlando for themed entertainment, it's worth visiting both.

Universal's major claims to fame are its two spectacular lands themed to the *Harry Potter* film franchise: **The Wizarding World of Harry Potter—Hogsmeade** at Universal's Islands of Adventure (IOA) and **Diagon Alley** at Universal Studios Florida (USF). Both are highly detailed areas with amazing technology and beloved characters. (Len has never seen the films or read the books yet happily spent 6 hours exploring just Diagon Alley.) And Universal continues to expand, adding more hotels and rides to its almost 1,000 acres of land. Its latest high-speed coaster, **VelociCoaster,** is the best of its kind in Orlando.

Universal is a high-quality alternative to Walt Disney World, so we cover its basics in this guide. For an in-depth guide to everything Universal has to offer, try **The Unofficial Guide to Universal Orlando,** by Seth Kubersky.

POCKET TRANSLATOR FOR COMMON DISNEY AND UNIVERSAL ABBREVIATIONS

IT MAY COME AS A SURPRISE to many, but Walt Disney World has its own somewhat peculiar language. Here are some abbreviations and slang you're likely to encounter, both in this guide and in the larger Disney (and Universal) community.

COMMON ABBREVIATIONS AND WHAT THEY STAND FOR	
ADR Advance Dining Reservation	**I-DRIVE** International Drive (a major Orlando thoroughfare)
BG Boarding group (for newer rides such as Tron Lightcycle/Run)	**IOA** Universal's Islands of Adventure theme park
CM Cast member	**MDE** My Disney Experience mobile app
DCL Disney Cruise Line	**ROTR** Star Wars: Rise of the Resistance ride
DDV Disney Deluxe Villas	**TTC** Ticket and Transportation Center
DHS Disney's Hollywood Studios	**USF** Universal Studios Florida theme park
DSRA Disney Springs Resort Area	**WDI** Walt Disney Imagineering
DTS Disney Transportation System	**WDTC** Walt Disney Travel Company
DVC Disney Vacation Club	**WDW** Walt Disney World
ETPE Early Theme Park Entry (formerly Morning Extra Magic Hours, or Morning EMH)	
EETPH Extended Evening Theme Park Hours (formerly Evening Extra Magic Hours, or Evening EMH)	

THE DISNEY LEXICON IN A NUTSHELL
ADVENTURE Ride | **ATTRACTION** Ride or theater show
ATTRACTION HOST Ride operator | **AUDIENCE** Crowd
BACKSTAGE Behind the scenes, out of view of customers
CAST MEMBER Employee
CHARACTER Disney character impersonated by an employee
COSTUME Work attire or uniform | **DARK RIDE** Indoor ride
DAY GUEST Any customer not staying at a Disney resort
DRC Disney Reservation Center
FACE CHARACTER A character who doesn't wear a head-covering costume (Snow White, Cinderella, Jasmine, and the like)
GENERAL PUBLIC Same as day guest
GREETER Employee positioned at an attraction entrance | **GUEST** Customer
HIDDEN MICKEYS Frontal silhouette of Mickey's head worked subtly into the design of buildings, railings, golf greens, attractions, and just about anything else
OFF-SITE HOTEL A hotel located outside of Walt Disney World's boundaries
ON-SITE HOTEL A hotel located inside Walt Disney World's boundaries and served by Disney's transportation network
ONSTAGE In full view of customers
PRESHOW Entertainment at an attraction before the feature presentation
RESORT GUEST A customer staying at a Disney resort
ROLE A cast member's job
SOFT OPENING The opening of a park or attraction before its stated opening date
TRANSITIONAL EXPERIENCE An element of the queuing area and/or preshow that provides information essential to understanding the attraction

PART 2

PLANNING *before* YOU LEAVE HOME

KEY QUESTIONS ANSWERED IN THIS CHAPTER

- Where can I find a planning checklist and timeline? *(pages 24-28)*
- What is My Disney Experience, and how do I use it? *(pages 28-31)*
- When is Disney World least crowded and most crowded? *(pages 32-36)*
- What are Early Theme Park Entry and Extended Evening Theme Park Hours, and how do I use them? *(pages 36-39)*
- What special events are scheduled while I'm at Walt Disney World? *(pages 39-42)*
- How can I contact someone at Disney with questions? *(pages 41-43)*

Visiting Walt Disney World is a bit like childbirth—you never really believe what people tell you, but once you have been through it yourself, you know exactly what they were saying!

—Hilary Wolfe, a mother and
Unofficial Guide reader from Swansea, Wales

GATHERING INFORMATION

IN ADDITION TO USING THIS GUIDE, we recommend that you visit our sister website, **TouringPlans.com.** The companion blog posts breaking news for Walt Disney World, Universal Orlando, Disney Cruise Line, and Disneyland.

TouringPlans.com complements and augments the information in our books, and it provides real-time personal services that are impossible to build into a book. The book is your comprehensive reference source; TouringPlans.com is your personal concierge. Sign up for free here: touringplans.com/walt-disney-world/join/basic.

With that free access, you'll be able to create custom touring plans, follow them in the parks, and get updates to them if conditions change while you're there. You'll also find tools for saving money on tickets, plus up-to-the-minute information on attractions, shows, restaurants, crowds, park hours, and more.

A few parts of the site require a small subscription fee to access, such as a detailed, day-by-day crowd calendar and a service that sends your hotel room request directly to Disney. That fee covers the costs of the extra people, technology, and external services it takes to provide them, beyond what's needed for the books.

Below is a brief rundown of some things you'll find on the site. If this looks like a long advertisement, it's because we still receive many requests each year asking us for tools and information—such as where to find ticket discounts—that are already available on the site for free.

TICKET DISCOUNTS A free, customizable search helps you find the cheapest tickets for your specific trip dates and needs. A typical family of four saves around $130 on average by purchasing admission from one of our recommended ticket wholesalers.

CUSTOM TOURING PLANS The best and most efficient touring plans are found in these guidebooks. They've been used by millions of families over the years, usually with excellent results. They depend, however, on your arriving at the park before opening. For some families with children, and for those who bristle at rising early, being on hand for park opening is a nonstarter. In those cases, and for others with unique circumstances, we provide custom touring plans online.

If getting up early isn't an issue, you can customize the plans in this book by simply skipping any attractions that don't interest you.

Like the plans in this book, the free online plans will also identify which Genie+ reservations to obtain, and when, to minimize your wait in line throughout the day. Online plans also work with Disney's Disability Access Service system (pages 405–407).

A DETAILED 365-DAY CROWD CALENDAR FOR EACH THEME PARK Subscribers can see which parks will be the least crowded every day of their trip, using a 1–10 scale. You can also view historical crowd data and check the accuracy of our predictions.

HOTEL-ROOM VIEWS AND ROOM-REQUEST SERVICE We have photos of the views from every Disney-owned hotel room in Walt Disney World—more than 35,000 images in all—and we'll give you the exact wording to use for requesting a specific room. For subscribers, we'll even automatically email your request to Disney 30 days before you arrive. A mother who used the service writes:

> *The send-ahead feature was wonderful! We got a room with a GORGEOUS river view! My husband's jaw dropped when he saw what our view was like! He immediately gave me a big high-five. Thanks!*

Disney tries to accommodate your request, but its ability to do that depends on variables we can't control. Most of the requests we send on behalf of readers are honored in full or partially, but sometimes Disney just can't make it work. Feel fortunate if you get what you asked for.

GENIE+/INDIVIDUAL LIGHTNING LANE INFORMATION The site shows which reservations are the most useful and will automatically suggest the best ones for your touring plans.

ANSWERS TO YOUR TRIP-PLANNING QUESTIONS Our online community includes tens of thousands of Disney experts and fans willing to help with your vacation plans. Ask questions and offer your own helpful tips.

LINES APP Our in-park app is available on the Apple App Store and the Google Play Store. For years, Lines has been one of the highest-rated Disney World apps for Apple and Android devices—higher than even Disney's own apps. Designed to accompany you in the park, Lines has lots of interesting, free features and provides ride and park information that Disney doesn't, including

- **Posted and actual wait times at attractions.** Lines is the only Disney-parks app that displays both posted wait times and the actual times you'll wait in line. The wait time you see posted outside of a ride is sometimes much longer than the real wait time, often because Disney's trying to do crowd control. With Lines, you can make better decisions about what to see.

- **"Ride now or wait" recommendations.** Lines shows you whether ride wait times are likely to get longer or shorter. If you find a long line at a particular attraction, Lines tells you the best time to come back.

- **Real-time touring plan updates while you're in a park.** Lines automatically updates your custom touring plan to reflect actual crowd conditions at a given moment. You can also restart your plan and add or change attractions, breaks, meals, and more.

Seeing actual wait times can also help set kids' expectations about how long they'll be in line, as this family from Mount Holly, New Jersey, found:

The Lines app had the actual wait time nailed almost every single time we consulted it. My kids used Lines on their phones and felt like they were in on a huge adult secret.

The *Unofficial Guide* and TouringPlans.com, along with the Lines app, are designed to work together as a comprehensive planning and touring resource.

This mom from St. Louis used all of the tools in our toolbox:

The Unofficial Guide *was the perfect place to start planning our vacation (actually our honeymoon). After reading the book, I had a good idea of what hotels I was interested in, and I had must-do and must-eat places somewhat picked out. I then took the knowledge from the book and switched to the website to personalize our touring plans and use as a reference when needed. The book and the website together made our trip INCREDIBLE.*

A mother from Lexington, South Carolina, echoes the sentiments of the mom above:

The Lines app and the personalized touring plans were unbeatable! If we missed a step or took extra time on something, it was so easy to catch right back up. The book allowed me to preplan our entire trip, from what to pack to what to see and eat. It was priceless. We traveled during Thanksgiving week, so the parks were at very high crowd levels. The planning allowed us to maximize the use of our time and quietly rejoice that we weren't the ones standing in line for hours.

Our other website, **TheUnofficialGuides.com,** is dedicated to news about our guidebooks and features a blog with posts from *Unofficial Guide* authors. You can also sign up for the **"Unofficial Guides Newsletter,"** which contains even more travel tips and special offers. Next, we recommend that you obtain the following:

1. **WALT DISNEY WORLD RESORT VACATION-PLANNING VIDEOS**
Disney has online videos advertising Walt Disney World's offerings at disneyplanning.com. You can access videos about Disney Cruise Line and other Disney destinations from the same website.

2. **GUIDE FOR GUESTS WITH DISABILITIES** An overview of services and options for guests with disabilities is available at disneyworld.disney .go.com/guest-services/guests-with-disabilities; at Guest Relations when entering the parks; at resort front desks; and at wheelchair-rental areas (locations are listed in each theme park chapter).

YOUR DISNEY TRIP-PLANNING TIMELINE: THE QUICK-START GUIDE TO USING THE *GUIDE*

AS YOU GO THROUGH THIS BOOK, you'll see many references to date-specific planning milestones for your trip: As we went to press, you could make Disney park reservations for dates through mid-January 2024 (see page 30) and dining reservations 60 days before your arrival. You might be wondering about other important dates for your Disney trip.

Starting on the opposite page is a comprehensive timeline that represents the major research, decisions, and tasks that come into play when preparing for a typical Walt Disney World vacation. Next to each milestone, we've put a reference to the section in this book that has the information you need for that milestone, and/or links to our website and blog for additional material like photos or videos.

Most Disney trips involve about a dozen important dates to remember. If you've started planning more than 11 months before your trip, you'll have plenty of time to do research ahead of those dates. If you've decided to visit Disney World within the next couple of months, you'll want to move a bit quicker.

Do you really need to do this? Absolutely—the demand for park reservations and restaurants can easily outstrip their capacity, and you may not get to experience them without planning and reservations. In past years, for example, Disney's Hollywood Studios and Magic Kingdom showed no available park reservations for several days around Thanksgiving, Christmas, and New Year's Eve—four to five months in advance. And a hot restaurant such as Be Our Guest, running at full speed, can serve lunch to only a tiny percentage of people who want to eat there.

Making park and dining reservations as soon as possible is vital if you want to eat at nice restaurants and avoid hours-long waits at popular rides. Other reservations, such as those for spas or recreational activities, can often be made when you arrive in Orlando, especially if you're visiting during a slower time of year or if you're flexible with the date or time of your appointment. But your best bet is to research early and make reservations as soon as Disney allows.

How to Plan in a Hurry

We get variations on this email a lot:

OMG! Our first Disney trip is in three weeks, and I just found out about the Unofficial Guide. *I had no idea about all the preparation I should have done! What do I do?*

Three weeks is plenty of time. You'll still want to go through the following timeline, because those steps are important, if not mandatory—you'll just have a more compressed schedule.

If your preferred places to eat are already booked, ch
guide on page 277 that shows highly rated alternatives to
restaurants. Also check **TouringPlans.com** for advice.

You'll also want to follow the touring plans starting on
they're your insurance against long waits in line. The pl
which ride reservations to get and when. If our recommendations
aren't available, our free touring plan software can make alternative
suggestions and work with whatever ride reservations you can get.

12–9 Months Before Your Trip

You may already have a general idea of when you want to visit Disney
World. What the trip will cost you, however, can be a surprise. Take a
couple of evenings to plan a budget and an approximate time of year to
travel, and to narrow down your hotel choices.

- **Establish a budget.** See pages 70–72 for an idea of how much Disney vacation you can get for $1,500–$4,000, for various family sizes. More information is available at tinyurl.com/1500-disney-vacation.

- **Figure out when to go and where to stay.** Begin researching resorts (see Part 5) and the best times of year to visit to avoid crowds (see page 32). Our own Erin Foster has devised an excellent method for finding the best vacation dates for your family; see tinyurl.com/planningwdw.

- **Brush up on discounts.** Disney releases certain discounts around the same time every year. Check mousesavers.com for a list of these regular discounts, when they're usually announced, and the travel dates they cover at tinyurl.com/wdw-historic-discounts. Also see our section on hotel discounts beginning on page 96 in Part 5.

- **Create an account at My Disney Experience** (see page 29). You'll need it to make park, hotel, dining, and ride reservations later.

- **Make a preliminary hotel reservation.** This typically requires a deposit equal to one night's cost and guarantees you a room. Staying at a Disney resort gets you early and late access to the theme parks, offering a substantial advantage in avoiding long lines (see page 36). It also opens up a separate pool of park reservations (see page 30) for you. You can change or cancel without penalty for several months while you continue your research.

- **Disney Vacation Club** (DVC) members can make reservations at their home resorts starting 11 months before their trip. See page 98 for information on how to rent points from a DVC member.

- **Investigate whether trip insurance makes sense for your situation.** If you'll be traveling to Disney World during peak hurricane season (August and September), it might be worthwhile. Third-party policies, such as those from insuremytrip.com, are usually cheaper than Disney's trip insurance and are often more comprehensive. We think almost all trips should be insured for trip cancellation or interruption, and for medical emergencies.

- **If you're not a US citizen, make sure your family's passports and visas are in order.** Passports typically need to be valid for six months beyond your travel dates. An electronic US visa is typically good for two years from the date of issue, if you need one. See esta.cbp.dhs.gov/esta to check whether your country participates in the US's visa waiver program. As of 2023, you must apply for a visa (or waiver) at least 72 hours prior to arrival.

9–7 Months Before Your Trip

Now is the time to start thinking about where you'll be eating and what
you want to do in the theme parks.

- **Purchase your park admission** at least this far in advance (see pages 74–75 for ticket and add-on details). Our Least Expensive Ticket Calculator will find you the best discounts on Disney tickets: touringplans.com /walt-disney-world/ticket-calculator.

- **Link your tickets to your My Disney Experience account,** so you can make park reservations now (see next item) and dining reservations at the 60-day mark.

- **Make theme park reservations.** Disney World requires certain ticket holders to make park reservations in addition to purchasing admission (see page 30). At press time, reservations were available through mid-January 2024. Visit disneyworld.disney.go.com/park-reservations to get started.

- **Disney Vacation Club** members can make resort reservations outside their home resorts starting seven months before their trip.

- **Check the best days to visit each park.** Use our Disney World Crowd Calendar to select the parks you'll visit on each day of your trip: touringplans .com/walt-disney-world/crowd-calendar.

6–4 Months Before Your Trip

Get familiar with Disney's rides, shows, and attractions, and start planning what you'll see each day. This will help identify potential bottlenecks, which you can address using our touring plans and Disney's Genie+ and Individual Lightning Lane programs.

- **Review the attractions and shows** in the Magic Kingdom (page 469), EPCOT (page 516), Disney's Animal Kingdom (page 552), and Disney's Hollywood Studios (page 582).

- **Make a list of must-see attractions in each park.** If you're unsure whether your child should experience a particular attraction, see our Small-Child Fright-Potential Table on pages 390–392. Every attraction is listed. A table on page 394 lists height requirements for the attractions. Finally, you can preview attractions on YouTube at tinyurl.com/wdw-ride-videos.

- **Review our touring plans** (see page 713) and use them to begin putting together a touring strategy for each park. You can also use our touring plan software: See touringplans.com/walt-disney-world/touring-plans. By starting now, you'll be able to see what attractions would benefit from Genie+ and Individual Lightning Lane reservations (if available; see pages 468, 514, 551, and 581). You'll also see whether you'll need to add the Park Hopper option to your theme park tickets (which can be done later).

180 Days Before Your Trip

Use this time to research Disney's restaurants and dining options.

- **Get familiar with Disney World restaurants** (see Part 6) so you're ready when Disney's dining reservation system opens at your 60-day mark. See touringplans.com/walt-disney-world/dining for current restaurant ratings, menus, and prices at every Disney restaurant, all searchable.

- **Also get familiar with the Disney Dining Plan** (returning in 2024; see page 272). If you're planning to stay at a Disney hotel, you'll need to figure out if the plan will save you money on the restaurants you're interested in.

120 Days Before Your Trip

As your vacation approaches, it's time to make concrete arrangements for your days in the theme parks.

- **Save money on stroller rentals in the parks** (if needed) by renting from a third-party company; see page 385 for our recommendations. You can also **save on wheelchair and ECV rentals** this way; see page 407 for details and recommendations.

60 Days Before Your Trip

Now you can start making restaurant, tour, spa, and other reservations.

- **Make reservations for sit-down dining** beginning at 5:45 a.m. Eastern time online at disneyworld.disney.go.com/dining, or at 6:45 a.m. by phone (see page 273 for tips): ☎ 407-WDW-DINE (939-3463). If you're staying at a Walt Disney World resort, you can make reservations for up to 10 days of your trip today. You have a better chance of getting what you want if you use the website instead of calling.

- **Make reservations for the following:**
    Theme park tours: ☎ 407-WDW-TOUR (939-8687)
    Recreational activities such as boating: ☎ 407-WDW-PLAY (939-7529)
    Spa treatments: ☎ 407-WDW-SPAS (939-7727)
    Bibbidi Bobbidi Boutique (page 665): ☎ 407-WDW-STYL (939-7895)

- **Revisit the economics of the Disney Dining Plan** (returning in 2024; see page 272) after you've made your dining reservations, to verify it's still worth the money. If you determine that it's not, call Disney to remove it from your reservation.

- **Start a walking regimen** to prepare for the 7–10 miles per day you may be walking in the parks. See page 375 for more on that.

- **Try a ride-hailing app** like Lyft or Uber. These services are often the fastest way to get between your hotel and the airport or theme parks, and they're cheaper than taxis. Download one of these apps to your smartphone, create an account, and take a short trip in your hometown to become familiar with how they work.

- **If you decide not to go to Disney World,** you typically have 30 days to cancel most Disney vacation packages without a penalty; room-only reservations can be canceled without a penalty until six days before your trip. See page 93 for a review of Disney's cancellation policies. Otherwise, you can start your online check-in at Disney resorts 60 days before you arrive.

- **Start online check-in** at disneyworld.disney.go.com/trip/online-check-in, if you're staying at a Disney-owned hotel. Doing this in advance means you'll be able to head directly to your hotel room upon arrival, without having to stop at the front desk.

45 Days Before Your Trip

- **Final payment for room-only reservations** is due if you book online within 45 days of arrival (payment of room-only reservations booked farther out isn't due until check-in).

- **Order your MagicBands** (page 81) if desired.

- **If you're flying,** make arrangements for your transfer between the airport and your hotel (see page 421).

- **If you want to switch resorts** or make more dining reservations, now is a good time to check, because people sometimes cancel at the last minute.

30 Days Out

- **Send your room request to Disney.** We can do this for you automatically. See tinyurl.com/wdw-hotel-fax for details.

- **Final payment is due for Disney vacation packages.**

- **Sign up for Disney's Disability Access Service** (see page 405) 2–30 days before your trip. You'll be able to make two ride reservations in advance. See tinyurl.com/get-wdw-das for more details.

- **Confirm park hours** and finish preliminary touring plans.

- Download our **Lines** app so you can follow your touring plan and get updates in the parks: touringplans.com/disney-world-app.
- **Arrange to stop delivery of mail and newspapers.**
- **Arrange for pet or house sitters.**

2 Weeks Out

- **Arrange grocery delivery to your resort** (see page 458).
- If you're flying to the US from another country, complete the **Advance Passenger Information and Secure Flight (APIS)** process at least 72 hours before your flight. You should be able to do this through your airline's website; otherwise, make sure your travel agent has your information. You'll need to provide the address where you'll be staying in the United States, so have that information handy when you complete this form.
- **Check that you have enough prescription medication.**
- **If staying at a Disney Good Neighbor hotel,** ensure your hotel reservation appears in the "Resort Hotel" section of the My Disney Experience app or website. This is how Disney knows you're eligible for Early Theme Park Entry (see pages 36–37).

6 Days Out

- This is typically your last chance to **cancel Disney room-only reservations booked online** without a penalty. Call ☎ W-DISNEY (407-934-7639).
- **Check the weather forecast** for Orlando: tinyurl.com/wdw-weather.
- **Start packing.** See touringplans.com/blog/tag/packing-tips for our tips.

5 Days Out

- This is typically your last chance to **cancel Disney room-only reservations booked by phone or travel agent** without a penalty. Call ☎ 407-W-DISNEY.

4 Days Out

- **Purchase Disney's Memory Maker photo package** (see page 455) at least three days in advance to ensure that all photos are linked as soon as you arrive. You'll also get a discount if you buy your package in advance.

The Day Before

- **Check in for your flight online.**
- **Finish your Disney resort online check-in,** if you haven't already done so, at disneyworld.disney.go.com/trip/online-check-in.
- **Cancel any unneeded dining or baby- or pet-sitting reservations.**
- **Do one last check of park hours and weather.**

DISNEY ONLINE: OFFICIAL AND OTHERWISE

A SET OF HIGH-TECH ENHANCEMENTS to Disney's theme parks and hotels, known as **MyMagic+,** includes optional rubber wristbands (**MagicBands**) that function as admission tickets, hotel keys, and charge cards; MyMagic+ also encompasses Disney's dining and ride reservation systems. It requires you to make detailed decisions about every day of your trip, sometimes months in advance, if you want to visit popular parks and avoid long waits (see page 25 for a complete trip-planning timeline). Disney's theme park reservation requirement means you must decide in advance which park you want to visit on each day of your trip, and dining reservations require you to know the exact time you want to eat, and where, two months before you arrive.

The Walt Disney World website (disneyworld.disney.go.com) and the **My Disney Experience** mobile app are the glue that binds all of this together. Because you must plan so much before you leave home, we cover the basics of both the website and the app in the next section. While we may provide navigational instructions here, note that Disney's web designers move things around all the time, so you may have to hunt around to find some features. More information about theme park reservations is on page 30; MagicBands starts on page 81. Details on Disney's ride reservation systems—**Genie+** and **Individual Lightning Lane**—and Disney's other new way of waiting in lines, called **boarding groups** or **virtual queues,** start on page 60. Finally, Disney's **Genie** itinerary-planning service, which you absolutely should *not* use, is profiled on page 64.

My Disney Experience on the Disney World Website

In this area of the Disney website (disneyworld.disney.go.com/plan), you can make park, hotel, dining, ride, and some recreation reservations; buy admission; and get park hours, attraction information, and much more.

TECHNICAL PROBLEMS Disney World's website is so unreliable that a Google search for "My Disney Experience issues" returns *millions* of results. Likewise, Disney's app frequently doesn't work as intended. If you run into technical issues on Disney's website, the first thing to do is to use your web browser's private or incognito mode to do what you want. Disney's website often places so many tracking cookies on your computer that it appears to break its own systems. If that doesn't work and human intervention is required, call ☎ 407-939-4357 in the US or ☎ 0800 169 0749 in the UK for help.

Set aside a full day to get these issues resolved. We're not kidding. Disney's phone systems have been understaffed since the pandemic, and stories abound of multihour waits for support, only for the call to be disconnected when the caller has been on hold for a certain number of hours.

BEFORE YOU BEGIN Set aside at least 30–40 minutes to complete this process. Make sure you have the following items on hand:

- A valid admission ticket or confirmation number for everyone in your group
- Your hotel reservation number, if you're staying on-site (including the Swan, Swan Reserve, Dolphin, and Disney Springs hotels)
- A computer, smartphone, or tablet connected to the Internet
- An email account that you can access easily while traveling
- A schedule of the parks you'll be visiting each day, including arrival and departure times and the times of any midday breaks
- The dates, times, and confirmation numbers of any dining or recreation reservations you've made

If you're coordinating travel plans with friends or family who live elsewhere, you'll also need the following information:

- The names and (optional) email addresses of the people you're traveling with
- A schedule of the parks they are visiting on each day of their trip, including their arrival, departure, and break times
- The dates and times of any dining or recreation reservations they've made

GETTING STARTED Go to disneyworld.disney.go.com/plan and click "Create Account." You'll be asked for your email address, along with your name, billing address, and birth date. (Disney uses your billing address to send your hotel reservation information, if applicable, and to charge your credit card for anything you purchase.)

Once you've created an account, the website will display a page with links to other steps in the planning process. These steps are described next. It's worth noting that these steps apply only to the first time you sign into Disney's website—for some reason, the website shows you different screens and options when you sign in after that. In those cases, click the "My Disney Experience" icon in the upper-right corner of the page, and look for wording like that below.

DISNEY HOTEL INFORMATION If you're staying at a Disney hotel, select "Resort Hotel" and then "Link Reservation." Enter your reservation number. This associates your My Disney Experience (MDE) account with your hotel stay in Disney's computer systems. If you've booked a travel package that includes theme park admission, Disney computers will automatically link the admission to your MDE account, allowing you to skip the "Linking Tickets" step. If you've booked a Disney hotel through a third-party site like Expedia, that site should send you a Disney reservation number to use here. Note that it can take up to a week for third-party sites to send Disney your booking information, so plan ahead accordingly.

REGISTER FRIENDS AND FAMILY Click the "Family & Friends" icon; then enter the names and ages of everyone traveling with you. You can do this later, too, but you'll need this information when you make your park and dining reservations.

LINKING TICKETS You will need to have purchased theme park tickets for each member of your group and linked them to each member's MDE profile before making some reservations.

If you haven't purchased your tickets, do so now. Disney's website doesn't have the cheapest prices for theme park tickets of three or more days. See page 78 for where to find better deals. Once purchased, you can add these tickets to MDE just like tickets bought directly from Disney.

If you've already purchased tickets but have not linked them, click the "Park Tickets" widget, then click on "Link Tickets," and follow the instructions.

MAKING PARK RESERVATIONS Disney has announced it will be removing the park-reservation requirement for date-based tickets with a start date of January 9, 2024, or later. Until then, you'll need to make a park reservation in addition to purchasing a ticket: Once you've linked your park tickets to your My Disney Experience account, click on "Park Reservations." If you're buying 1- to 10-day tickets, you'll be able to make park reservations for as many days as you have admission. Annual Pass holders who have booked a Disney hotel can make reservations for each day of their hotel stay, while Pass holders staying off-site can make five at a time. They can make an additional reservation once an existing reservation's day is done.

MAKING DINING RESERVATIONS In My Disney Experience, click the "Dining" icon, then the "Make a Reservation" link. (You may have to reenter your travel dates.) A list of every Walt Disney World eatery will be displayed. Use the filtering criteria at the top of the page to narrow the list. Once you've settled on a restaurant, click its name to check availability. If space is available and you want to make a reservation, you'll need to indicate which members of your party will be joining you. You'll also need to enter a credit card number to hold your reservation. If you want to make other dining reservations, you'll need to repeat this process for each one.

My Disney Experience Mobile App

unofficial **TIP**
Some features of My Disney Experience, including mobile ordering, may not be available on older devices.

In addition to its website, Disney offers a companion app called My Disney Experience, available on the Apple App Store and Google Play Store. It includes park hours, attraction operating hours and descriptions, wait times for buses, restaurant hours with descriptions and menus, the ability to make dining and ride reservations online, GPS-based directions, counter-service meal ordering, the locations of park photographers, and more.

Our Recommended Websites

Searching online for Disney information is like navigating an immense maze for a tiny piece of cheese: You may find a lot of dead ends before you get what you want. Our picks follow.

BEST Q&A SITE planDisney, formerly Walt Disney World's Mom's Panel, consists of Disney World veterans chosen from among more than 10,000 applicants. The panelists have a website, plandisney .disney.go.com, where they offer tips and discuss how to plan a Disney World vacation. Several panelists have specialized experience in areas such as Disney Cruise Line, runDisney, and traveling with sports groups. Some speak Spanish, French, and Portuguese too.

BEST MONEY-SAVING SITE MouseSavers (mousesavers.com) keeps an updated list of discounts for use at Disney World resorts, separated into categories such as "For the general public" and "For residents of certain states." Anyone who calls or books online can use a current discount. The savings can be considerable—as much as 40%. The site also offers deals on rental cars and non-Disney hotels in the area, along with a calendar showing when Disney sales typically launch.

BEST SITE FOR CAR-RENTAL DEALS AutoSlash (autoslash.com) will use every available discount code for every car company in Orlando to find you the best car-rental deal. See page 424 for more on car rentals.

SOCIAL MEDIA YouTube is an excellent place to find videos of Disney World and other Central Florida attractions. **Facebook, Twitter,** and **Instagram** are popular places for Disneyphiles to gather online and share tips and photos. Walt Disney World's official social media outlets are facebook.com/waltdisneyworld, twitter.com/waltdisneyworld, and instagram.com/waltdisneyworld.

BEST DISNEY DISCUSSION BOARDS There are tons of these; among the most active boards are **disboards.com; forums.wdwmagic.com;** our own **forum.touringplans.com;** and, for Brits, **thedibb.co.uk** (*DIBB* stands for "Disney Information Bulletin Board").

WHEN *to* GO *to* WALT DISNEY WORLD

SELECTING THE TIME OF YEAR FOR YOUR VISIT

WALT DISNEY WORLD IS BUSIEST from the weekend before Christmas Day until the first weekend in January. Next busiest are spring break (early March–early April, plus the week before Easter when Easter is later); Thanksgiving week; and February during Presidents' Day and Mardi Gras. You'll also see shorter bursts of crowds in early June as public-school summer vacations start, and on three-day weekends, such as Columbus Day.

The least busy time *historically* is Labor Day through the beginning of October. In addition, the last two weeks of October and the first week of November are usually less crowded than average, as are the weeks after Thanksgiving and before Christmas. The weeks between late April and Memorial Day have lower crowds than the weeks on either side. Aside from being asphalt-melting hot, July normally brings throngs of tourists from South America who are on their winter holiday; summer crowds in 2022 were highest between July and the first week of August.

Late February and early April are dicey. Crowds ebb and flow according to school vacation schedules and the timing of Mardi Gras and Presidents' Day weekend.

The rule of thumb is that Walt Disney World is less crowded (and less expensive) when kids are in school. That said, Disney has become adept at loading off-peak periods with special events, conventions, food festivals, and the like; discounts on rooms and dining during slower periods also figure in, as does the number of employees Disney decides to use in the parks.

New rides and Disney's theme park reservation system (see page 30) also affect crowds. In the weeks immediately after Disney opens a new ride, expect getting reservations for that park to be more difficult than normal; the park may also halt park-hopping.

In short: The World can be packed at any time, and you'll need to look beyond the time of year to pinpoint the least crowded dates. For a calendar of scheduled Disney events, see tinyurl.com/wdwevents.

Off-Season Touring

We strongly recommend going to Disney World in the fall, winter, or spring because of the milder weather, generally smaller crowds, and deeper discounts. However, these benefits come with some trade-offs.

The parks often close early during the off-season because of lower crowds. This drastically reduces touring hours. Even when crowds are small, it's difficult to see big parks such as the Magic Kingdom between 9 a.m. and 7 p.m. Early closing may mean no evening entertainment. And because these are slow times, some rides and attractions may be closed. Finally, Central Florida temperatures fluctuate wildly during late fall, winter, and early spring; daytime highs in the 40s and 50s aren't uncommon. Still, it's so much easier to see the parks during the off-season that we'd advise taking children out of school for a Disney World visit. See page 373 for the pros and cons of this approach.

If this isn't possible, we want to make it clear that you can have a wonderful experience regardless of when you go. Our advice, irrespective of season, is to arrive early at the parks and use one of our touring plans. If lines are low, kick back and forget the plans.

DON'T FORGET AUGUST Kids go back to school pretty early in Florida (and in a lot of other places too). This makes mid- to late August a good time for families who can't vacation during the off-season.

A New Jersey mother of two school-age children spells it out:

The end of August is the PERFECT time to go (just watch out for hurricanes; it's the season). There were virtually no wait times, 20 minutes at the most.

A family from Roxbury, New Jersey, agrees:

I recommend the last two weeks of August for anyone traveling there during the summer. We have visited twice during this time of year and have had great success touring the parks.

PLANNING FOR FLORIDA WEATHER

Why is the world's best theme park in the world's worst climate?

—A reader from Clackamas, Oregon

LONG BEFORE WALT DISNEY WORLD, tourists visited Florida year-round to enjoy the temperate tropical and subtropical climates. The best weather months are generally November through March (see the table on page 35). Fall is usually dry, whereas spring and summer are wet. Rain is possible anytime, usually in the form of scattered thunderstorms. An entire day of rain is unusual.

Y'all need to give statistical weight to rides with outdoor waits in the heat (we went in August). For instance, just because the Guide says to get in line for Runaway Railway at 1 p.m., I'm not going to do that because it's too hot at that time of day.

—A reader from Sugar Land, Texas

SUMMER TEMPERATURES CAN FEEL LIKE 120°F Did you know that air temperature is measured in the shade? So, if your phone's weather app says it's 95°F in Orlando, it's warmer if you're standing in the sun, and hotter still if you're wearing dark-colored clothing.

Florida's humidity makes the heat feel worse because it prevents your perspiration from evaporating to cool you off. Meteorologists use something called the Heat Index to express the combined effect of heat and humidity as a temperature reading we can understand. During summer in the Magic Kingdom, you'll commonly feel Heat Index temperatures above 110°F, and we've measured highs of up to 122°F. How hot is that? A steak cooked rare is considered done at 130°F.

CROWD CALENDAR

DISNEY WORLD'S ATTENDANCE is approaching its pre-pandemic "normals" of almost 59 million guests per year—an average of around 161,000 guests per day. Tips for avoiding crowds are what our readers are most interested in. Besides which month or week to visit, readers want to know the best park to visit on each day of their stay.

Expect Disney to regularly adjust things like resort discounts, park capacity, and park hours. Because of that, it's not possible to include an accurate calendar in this book. To make things easier for you (and us), we provide at TouringPlans.com a calendar covering the next year (click "Crowd Calendar" on the home page). For each date, we offer a crowd-level index based on a 1–10 scale, with 1 being least crowded and 10 being most crowded. Our calendar is based on how long you'll wait in line and takes into account all holidays, special events, and more, as described in the next section.

Keeping the online Crowd Calendar updated requires year-round work. Thus, we have to charge a modest subscription fee. Much of the rest of the website is free, and owners of the current edition of this guide are eligible for a substantial discount on the subscription. See pages 21–24 for more information about TouringPlans.com.

Even on a "slow" day, you may see waits of 60 minutes or more for popular rides such as Seven Dwarfs Mine Train in the Magic Kingdom, Flight of Passage in Disney's Animal Kingdom, Test Track in EPCOT, and Mickey and Minnie's Runaway Railway in DHS.

A Braintree, Massachusetts, woman cautions:

> It should be emphasized that parks can still feel really crowded on a low-crowd day, especially the Magic Kingdom. But you will notice the difference when you see the wait times for the rides. Anyone expecting to have room to roam freely in certain parts of the Magic Kingdom on a low-attendance day will be disappointed. The same is true for Animal Kingdom: We went there on a "low" attendance day in the afternoon, and it was extremely congested and difficult to walk through some areas of the park.

HOW WE DETERMINE CROWD LEVELS AND BEST DAYS A number of factors contribute to the models we use to predict both crowd levels and the best days to visit each theme park.

Data we use to predict crowd levels:

- Recent wait times, which are given higher importance
- Historical theme park hours from the same time period in past years
- Future hotel-room bookings in the Orlando area
- Disney's special-events calendar (for example, the Magic Kingdom's Halloween and Christmas parties)
- Legal holidays in the United States
- Public-school schedules, weighted by distance from Florida and tourism rates

We also collect thousands of wait times from every ride in every Disney park every day, including posted and actual times. *Popular Science* did a nice article on the data science behind our predictions; read it at popsci.com/touring-plan-app-disney-lines.

WALT DISNEY WORLD CLIMATE

	JAN	FEB	MAR	APR	MAY	JUN	JUL	AUG	SEP	OCT	NOV	DEC
AVERAGE DAILY HIGH												
	72°F	75°F	79°F	84°F	88°F	91°F	92°F	91°F	89°F	85°F	78°F	75°F
AVERAGE DAILY MAX HEAT INDEX (COMBINED EFFECT OF HEAT AND HUMIDITY)												
	72°F	75°F	81°F	92°F	106°F	119°F	121°F	120°F	111°F	96°F	79°F	75°F
AVERAGE DAILY TEMPERATURE												
	62°F	64°F	68°F	74°F	79°F	82°F	84°F	83°F	82°F	77°F	69°F	65°F
AVERAGE DAILY HUMIDITY												
	71%	68%	65%	64%	65%	75%	79%	80%	80%	73%	71%	73%
AVERAGE RAINFALL PER MONTH												
	2.1"	1.9"	2.5"	2.2"	2.7"	6.1"	6.0"	6.6"	5.5"	2.4"	1.2"	1.6"
NUMBER OF DAYS OF RAIN PER MONTH												
	4	4	5	4	6	12	13	14	11	5	3	4

Source: climate-data.org

SUMMER AND HOLIDAY CROWDS

MANY FOLKS HAVE NO CHOICE regarding the time of year they visit Disney World. Much of this book, in fact, is dedicated to helping readers who visit during busier times enjoy the experience. Armed with knowledge and some strategy, you can have a great time whenever you go.

To put things in perspective, early summer (up to about June 8) and late summer (after August 15) are not as crowded as midsummer. Disney World experiences its highest demand during holiday periods. If you visit during spring break or a major holiday, the first thing you need to know is that the theme parks' guest capacity is not infinite. Disney allocates park capacity so that guests staying at its hotels and those who have bought date-specific tickets in advance have priority for park reservations (see page 30). We're reasonably sure that Disney cuts off

ANNUAL ATTENDANCE PATTERNS IN THE MAGIC KINGDOM

Visitors Per Day (*Thousands*)

park reservations at the Magic Kingdom (for example) if it sees too few guests choosing Animal Kingdom on their own. If you're not staying in the World, you may find yourself on the outside looking in, as did this Dahlonega, Georgia, family:

> *Because we planned our July visit late, there were no park reservations available for the Magic Kingdom or Hollywood Studios on any of the five days of our trip. We couldn't get a Rise of the Resistance reservation because of that. We didn't have park-hopping tickets, so we ended up at EPCOT and Animal Kingdom every. single. day.*

The reader might have done well by purchasing the Park Hopper option and by checking each morning whether day-of park reservations were available for the Magic Kingdom and Studios. The point is to be sure to obtain park reservations well in advance, if they're required for the dates of your trip.

Christmas and New Year's at the Theme Parks

Don't expect to see all the attractions in a single day of touring at any park. That said, Disney's Animal Kingdom is usually the least crowded park during the winter holidays, especially on New Year's Eve. EPCOT is a good choice, too, because it has about twice the land and typically lower crowds than the Magic Kingdom. (It also has fewer attractions, but many of them are high-capacity shows and rides.)

New Year's Eve is the busiest day of the year in the Magic Kingdom. The park stages New Year's Eve fireworks on both December 30 and December 31 for those who either wish to see fireworks in multiple parks or don't wish to be caught in the crowds. If you stay until midnight, expect it to take 1–3 hours to get back to your hotel by bus or car. We suggest getting a room at a Magic Kingdom monorail resort (the **Contemporary, Bay Lake Tower, Grand Floridian,** or **Polynesian Village**), which have walking paths as well. If you're visiting EPCOT or the Studios for New Year's Eve, we suggest the **BoardWalk Inn, BoardWalk Villas, Yacht Club, Beach Club, Swan, Swan Reserve,** or **Dolphin** resorts, all within walking distance of those parks.

EARLY THEME PARK ENTRY

EARLY THEME PARK ENTRY (aka Early Entry or ETPE) is a perk for families staying at Disney resort hotels, including the Swan, Dolphin, Swan Reserve, Shades of Green, Four Seasons, Disney Springs hotels, and Hilton hotels in Bonnet Creek. Those guests can enter any of Disney's theme parks 30 minutes earlier than official park operating hours any day of the week. This perk replaced Extra Magic Hours.

WHAT'S REQUIRED? A valid ticket or MagicBand, along with a reservation for that theme park on that day, are required to enter the park. If you haven't yet checked into your Disney hotel, make sure you have your reservation linked to your My Disney Experience account.

DISNEY SPRINGS AND GOOD NEIGHBOR HOTELS The Early Entry benefit is offered to guests staying at Disney Springs hotels and select Disney Good Neighbor hotels (page 89). But Disney's computer systems don't always know this, as this reader from Swarthmore, Pennsylvania, found out:

Some of my [Disney Springs hotel] reservations never appear in My Disney Experience, so there's really no way for me to know whether Disney knows I get Early Entry until I get to the park turnstiles. Most of the time, the kind cast member that stops me from entering has no idea about the policy and needs to ask a supervisor.

On my most recent trip, the cast members actually had to Google the Disney World Good Neighbor hotels list. To make it even more complex, at the time, the Holiday Inn name was listed on the Disney website incorrectly, leaving me trying to explain that the hotel I was staying at was in fact the Disney Springs location.

We're told that the computer systems of Disney and the Good Neighbor hotels are supposed to communicate these details through Disney's My Disney Experience (MDE) system. If you're staying at a Good Neighbor hotel eligible for Early Entry, ensure two weeks before you arrive that your reservation number appears in MDE. (If you booked your hotel room through a third-party website such as Expedia, it can take up to a week for the third-party's system to talk to the hotel and Disney.)

If these computer systems don't communicate properly before your trip, you'll have to find a hotel manager who knows what to do, as this reader from San Francisco found out:

For some reason, our Hilton reservation never showed up in MDE. After asking about a dozen people how I could make sure I'd be able to get into the park for Early Entry (including Disney Guest Relations at Disney Springs, who said they could not help), we ended up back at the Hilton concierge desk. After talking to several staff members who'd never heard of Early Theme Park Entry, we got to a manager who could help.

Believe it or not, the answer is that they give you what is essentially a business card. For each guest, the manager writes down a bunch of numbers (basically a confirmation code), the dates of your stay, and each guest's name on little paper cards with Disney branding on them, and those are what you show to the park cast members for Early Entry. To my understanding, this is the "backup" process for all of the third-party Disney hotels.

WHEN IS EARLY ENTRY OFFERED? Early Entry is offered every day at all four Disney theme parks.

HOW DOES EARLY ENTRY WORK? Eligible resort guests (see above) are invited to enter any theme park 30 minutes before the general public. During this time, guests should be able to enjoy select attractions. In the Magic Kingdom, for example, you should find some attractions open in Fantasyland and Tomorrowland at least.

In practice, we think on-site guests should arrive at their chosen park's entrance about an hour before official opening. That gets you at the very front of the crowd, ready to go to your first attraction as soon as the park opens. And on days of high attendance, Disney might open the park a bit earlier than 30 minutes in advance, giving you even more of a bonus.

During holidays and other busy times, the Magic Kingdom opens to regular guests at 8 a.m. and Early Entry begins at 7:30 a.m., so you'll need to be at the park entrance no later than 7 a.m. You won't be alone, but because relatively few people are willing to get up that early for a theme park, your first few hours in the parks will be (pardon us) magical.

How Early Entry Affects Attendance at the Theme Parks

Early Entry affects theme park attendance much less than the previous EMH program because EMH was offered only at one or two parks a day. When Animal Kingdom offered morning EMH sessions on Monday, for example, rides at that park had longer waits throughout the day because of the additional guests who arrived early to take advantage of their perk and stayed all day.

That incentive to visit a specific park on a specific day is removed with Early Entry because it's offered at every park, every day. That spreads out Disney resort guests more evenly among the parks, while still providing an on-site benefit for Disney to dangle in front of potential hotel customers.

If you're staying at a Disney resort, remember these three things about Early Entry:

1. The Magic Kingdom has more attractions open for Early Entry than any other park. We think the Magic Kingdom's Early Entry, coupled with a good touring plan, is the most worthwhile of any park's.

2. Early Entry is especially useful when Disney opens new rides.

3. Early Entry is a big advantage when using the standby line at popular attractions such as Star Wars: Rise of the Resistance in Disney's Hollywood Studios; Guardians of the Galaxy: Cosmic Rewind and Remy's Ratatouille Adventure in EPCOT; and Tron Lightcycle/Run in the Magic Kingdom.

WHAT'S THE CATCH? The disadvantage of Early Entry for on-site guests is that they must now get up a half hour earlier to beat the crowds.

Off-site guests are considerably disadvantaged by the Early Entry program. With the old EMH schedule, off-site guests could level the playing field by simply avoiding the park that offered morning EMH. If that park was EPCOT, then it was still possible to stay at an inexpensive hotel, get up early, and be at the front of the pack when the Magic Kingdom's rides opened.

With Early Entry, off-site guests are guaranteed to have thousands of on-site guests already in front of them at any theme park they visit on any day. When the Magic Kingdom opens a new ride, such as Tron Lightcycle/Run, it's a safe bet that its line will be hours long well before the first off-site guest even sets foot inside the park.

To mitigate the effect of Early Entry on off-site guests, we've added off-site versions of our touring plans to this book. Be aware, however, that even with an optimal touring plan, off-site guests may wait several more hours in line per day than on-site guests, due to the head start those on-site guests have.

EXTENDED EVENING THEME PARK HOURS

EXTENDED EVENING THEME PARK HOURS (EETPH) is the limited revival of the former Evening Extra Magic Hours program, which was discontinued in 2020. Typically held on one night per week and, for now, only for certain parks, EETPH allows guests staying at Disney's Deluxe and DVC resorts—and only those guests—2 extra hours in that park after official closing. Thus, if the Magic Kingdom closes at 9 p.m. to regular guests, the park will operate Extended Hours from 9 to 11 p.m. for guests at a Disney Deluxe or DVC resort only.

The Magic Kingdom typically schedules extended hours on Wednesdays, and EPCOT schedules them on Mondays. Don't count on the Studios or Animal Kingdom to offer them consistently.

During EETPH, Disney sets up checkpoints throughout the park, such as the entrance to each land, to verify that guests entering the area are eligible for the program. Disney scans your MagicBand or plastic ticket to verify your resort.

Most theme park attractions are open during EETPH, although brand-new rides are often excluded for maintenance.

The advantage to EETPH is that so few guests qualify that lines are exceptionally short. In late December 2022, we managed to see 10 attractions in the Magic Kingdom during EETPH, waiting a total of 31 minutes in line. In comparison, those same 10 attractions would've taken almost 7 hours to see during that day. In EPCOT, the lines are so short that the limiting factor to how many rides you can ride is the walking distance between them.

THE WALT DISNEY WORLD CALENDAR

DISNEY CELEBRATES SPECIAL EVENTS throughout the year. Some events commemorate major holidays, while others are designed by Disney to boost attendance during otherwise-slow times of year.

JANUARY Usually held the second weekend after New Year's (though it's January 3–7 in 2024), the **Walt Disney World Marathon** pulls in more runners and their families every year. Information on all Disney running events can be found at rundisney.com.

Another winter event is the **EPCOT International Festival of the Arts.** Running from the first full week of January until the third full week of February, the festival, which is included as part of your park admission, features art (some of it Disney-themed), food, entertainment, and workshops to further your creative skills. See page 290 for more information.

FEBRUARY **Black History Month** is celebrated throughout Walt Disney World with displays, artisans, storytellers, and entertainers.

In 2024, **Presidents' Day** is Monday, February 19, and **Mardi Gras** is Tuesday, February 13. These holidays should substantially increase attendance starting the weekend before.

MARCH At the **EPCOT International Flower & Garden Festival,** which runs March–July, expert horticulturists showcase exotic floral displays and share gardening tips. The 30 million blooms from some 1,200 species will make your eyes pop. The festival features food and beverage kiosks, making it more like fall's International Food & Wine Festival (see page 290), only with flowers. **Easter** is March 31, 2024. Expect peak spring break season to be mid-March through the week of April 7, 2024.

WALT DISNEY WORLD PHONE NUMBERS

General Information ☎ 407-824-4321 or 407-824-2222

General Information for the Hearing-Impaired (TTY) ☎ 407-827-5141

Accommodations/Central Reservations ☎ 407-934-7639

Advance Dining Reservations ☎ 407-939-3463

Advent Health Centra Care (urgent-care clinic) ☎ 407-390-1888 (Kissimmee); ☎ 407-934-2273 (Lake Buena Vista); ☎ 407-291-8975 (Universal–Dr. Phillips)

All-Star Movies Resort ☎ 407-939-7000

All-Star Music Resort ☎ 407-939-6000

All-Star Sports Resort ☎ 407-939-5000

AMC Movies at Disney Springs ☎ 407-827-1308

Animal Kingdom Lodge & Villas Jambo House ☎ 407-938-3000 Kidani Village ☎ 407-938-7400

Art of Animation Resort ☎ 407-938-7000

Beach Club Resort ☎ 407-934-8000

Beach Club Villas ☎ 407-934-8000

Blizzard Beach Information ☎ 407-560-3400

BoardWalk Inn & Villas ☎ 407-939-6200

Caribbean Beach Resort ☎ 407-934-3400

Car Rentals ☎ 407-824-3470, ext. 1

Contemporary Resort & Bay Lake Tower ☎ 407-824-1000

Convention Information ☎ 321-939-7129

Coronado Springs Resort ☎ 407-939-1000

Disabled Guests Special Requests ☎ 407-939-7807

Disney Institute ☎ 321-939-4600

Disney Springs Information ☎ 407-939-5277

ESPN Wide World of Sports Complex ☎ 407-939-1500

Fantasia Gardens Miniature Golf ☎ 407-560-4870

Fort Wilderness Resort & Campground ☎ 407-824-2900

Golf Reservations and Information ☎ 407-939-4653

Grand Floridian Resort & Spa/Grand Floridian Villas ☎ 407-824-3000

Group Camping ☎ 407-939-7807

APRIL In the past, Disney has announced a **"free" Disney Dining Plan** promotion in mid- to late April for travel dates usually starting in August. Dining plans are scheduled to return in 2024; no word on when or if the Free Dining promotion will return. Check tinyurl.com /wdwupdates for more information as it becomes available.

JUNE Gay Days, an unofficial gathering of LGBTQ people from around the world, has been happening annually since 1991. Organizers say previous Gay Days have attracted close to 200,000 visitors and their friends and families. For additional information, visit gaydays.com.

Those who say Christmas is the most wonderful time of year have never been to the **EPCOT International Food & Wine Festival.** Usually

WALT DISNEY WORLD PHONE NUMBERS

Guided-Tour Information ☎ 407-939-8687

Guided VIP Solo Tours ☎ 407-560-4033

House of Blues Tickets & Information ☎ 407-934-2583

Lost and Found *(for articles lost yesterday or before; for same day, go to Guest Relations, front desk, or disneyworld.com/lostandfound)* ☎ 407-824-4245

Merchandise Guest Services ☎ 877-560-6477

Old Key West Resort ☎ 407-827-7700

Outdoor Recreation Reservations & Information ☎ 407-939-7529

Polynesian Village Resort ☎ 407-824-2000

Polynesian Village Villas ☎ 407-824-3500

Pop Century Resort ☎ 407-938-4000

Port Orleans Resort–French Quarter ☎ 407-934-5000

Port Orleans Resort–Riverside ☎ 407-934-6000

Riviera Resort ☎ 407-828-7030

Resort Dining ☎ 407-939-3463

Saratoga Springs Resort & Spa, Treehouse Villas ☎ 407-827-1100

Security ☎ 407-560-7959 (routine); ☎ 407-560-1990 (urgent)

Shades of Green Resort ☎ 407-824-3400 or 407-824-3600

Star Wars: Galactic Starcruiser ☎ 407-939-1800

Telecommunication for the Deaf Reservations (TTY) ☎ 407-827-5141

Walt Disney Travel Company ☎ 407-939-6244

Walt Disney World Dolphin ☎ 407-934-4000

Walt Disney World Swan ☎ 407-934-3000

Walt Disney World Swan Reserve ☎ 407-934-3000

Walt Disney World Ticket Inquiries ☎ 407-939-7679

Weather Information ☎ 407-827-4545

Wilderness Lodge/Boulder Ridge & Copper Creek Villas ☎ 407-824-3200

Winter Summerland Miniature Golf ☎ 407-560-3000

Wrecker Service (7 a.m.–11 p.m.; if closed, call Security) ☎ 407-824-0976

Yacht Club Resort ☎ 407-934-7000

held in the World Showcase from July to late November, the celebration represents 25 nations and cuisines. The event may include demonstrations, wine seminars, tastings, and opportunities to see some of the world's top chefs. Many of these activities are included in EPCOT admission, though some workshops and tastings are by reservation only and cost more than $100. See page 290 for more information about the festival.

AUGUST As far as Walt Disney World is concerned, fall begins in mid-August. **Mickey's Not So Scary Halloween Party,** in the Magic Kingdom, is typically held on select nights between mid-August and November 1, 7 p.m.–midnight. (In 2022 it was August 12–October 31.) Ticket

IMPORTANT WALT DISNEY WORLD ADDRESSES

GENERAL INFORMATION
WDW Guest Communications, PO Box 10040, Lake Buena Vista, FL 32830-0040
☎ 407-560-2544; wdw.guest.communications@disneyworld.com or
guest.services@disneyworld.com
General online help: disneyworld.disney.go.com/help/email

CONVENTION AND BANQUET INFORMATION (aka Group Sales)
Walt Disney World Resort South, PO Box 10000, Lake Buena Vista, FL 32830-1000
☎ 321-939-7129; disneymeetings.com

DISNEY IMAGINATION CAMPUS (youth programs)
☎ 321-939-7560; disneycampus.com

WALT DISNEY WORLD TICKET MAIL ORDER
☎ 407-566-4985; ticket.inquiries@disneyworld.com

holders can get into the park starting at 4 p.m. In 2022, tickets cost $116–$212, with October dates being the most expensive. The festivities include trick-or-treating in costume, parades, live music, storytelling, and a fireworks show. See page 84 for more information.

NOVEMBER The **Wine and Dine Half-Marathon** early in this month revolves around a 13.1-mile race that ends with a nighttime party amid the EPCOT International Food & Wine Festival. The 2022 event was the weekend of November 3–6.

DECEMBER The annual **Disney Parks Christmas Day Parade,** televised on December 25, is usually taped in the Magic Kingdom in November or the first week of December. The parade ties up pedestrian traffic on Main Street, U.S.A., all day.

EPCOT's holiday celebration, **EPCOT International Festival of the Holidays,** typically runs late November–late December and includes food booths similar to those present in World Showcase during the Festival of the Arts, Food & Wine, and Flower & Garden Festivals.

Disney's Very Merry Christmas Party takes place on select evenings in November and December, 7 p.m.–midnight (after regular hours; ticketed guests can get into the park starting at 4 p.m.). In 2022, tickets were $159–$212 per person. The event includes attractions; stage shows featuring Disney characters; an unlimited supply of complimentary snacks and drinks; a holiday-themed fireworks show; carolers; "a magical snowfall on Main Street"; white lights on Cinderella Castle; and live entertainment.

PART 3

MAKING *the* MOST *of* YOUR TIME

KEY QUESTIONS ANSWERED IN THIS CHAPTER

- How long does it take to see Walt Disney World? *(see below)*
- What are standby queues, boarding groups, Disney's Genie/Genie+, and Individual Lightning Lane, and how do I use them? *(pages 59–67)*
- What are the six most important tips for avoiding lines at Disney World? *(page 47)*
- What are touring plans, and how do I use them? *(pages 50–59)*

ALLOCATING TIME

THE VACATION THAT FIGHTS BACK

A WHIRLWIND TOUR of Disney's four theme parks and two water parks takes at least **six full days** and a level of stamina more often associated with running a marathon. A British gentleman, thinking we exaggerated, measured how far he walked and found this:

> Our visits to the theme parks were spread over five days, during which my wife and I (ages 51 and 55) walked a total of 68 miles for an average of 13 miles per day!

At Walt Disney World, less is more. Take the World in small doses, with plenty of swimming, napping, reading, and relaxing in between. If you don't see everything, you can always come back.

An articulate Anchorage, Alaska, teen and her family found out the hard way the importance of building in time to decompress:

> We crammed our schedule a little too full, with seven parks—Disney, Universal, and SeaWorld—in eight full days. My older sisters would speed-walk from attraction to attraction while my parents straggled behind trying to keep up, while I was caught in the middle, both wanting to get to the next ride as fast as I could and wanting just to spend some quality time with my parents. No family should spend more than two consecutive days at the parks without a low-key day in the middle. I wish I'd known this going in.

It's exhausting to rise at dawn and run around a theme park for 8–10 hours day after day. Sooner or later (usually sooner), you hit the wall. To avoid that, use these two tips alone or in combination:

1. Take at least a morning off (preferably an entire day) after two consecutive days in the parks.

2. Return to your hotel for a 3- to 5-hour break each day you're in the parks.

The keys to those sleep-in days are to set up a touring plan (see page 50) and visit over multiple days. To get you started, we've created **late-start touring plans** for Animal Kingdom. Check them out at tinyurl.com/sleepin-animalkingdom.

This Arlington, Virginia, family recommends taking it slow and easy:

We spent eight days in Disney, and it was totally worth it. A longer trip, believe it or not, eliminates the happy death march—we cut our stress by 90%. Each day, we took some sort of break: a morning swim, an afternoon nap, a sit-down snack in a restaurant. The end result was that the kids got to see/ride everything they wanted without exhausting themselves (or us)—or spending most of their days in line. And we had almost zero tantrums (really!).

The rest of this section will help you decide which park to see first, when to arrive, how to build breaks and naps into your schedule, and what to do on the first and last days of your trip.

WHICH PARK SHOULD YOU SEE FIRST?

THIS QUESTION IS LESS OBVIOUS than it appears, especially if your party includes children or teenagers. If kids see the Magic Kingdom first, they expect the same experience at the other parks. In EPCOT, they're often disappointed (as are many adults) by the educational orientation of the older Future World attractions. And children may not find Animal Kingdom as exciting as the Magic Kingdom or Hollywood Studios—real animals, after all, can't be programmed to entertain on cue.

First-time visitors should see **Animal Kingdom** first; it's educational, but the animals provide a change of pace. See **EPCOT** second. Like Animal Kingdom, most of EPCOT's experiences are not based on Disney's film and TV characters, so you'll be able to enjoy it without having been preconditioned to think of Disney entertainment as solely fantasy or adventure. Next, see **Disney's Hollywood Studios** (**DHS**), which helps you transition from the educational EPCOT and Animal Kingdom to the fanciful Magic Kingdom. We recommend saving the **Magic Kingdom** for last, although we recognize that for many readers the Magic Kingdom is synonymous with Walt Disney World.

OPERATING HOURS

THE DISNEY WORLD WEBSITE typically publishes park hours around 60–75 days in advance, but schedule adjustments can happen at any time, including the day of your visit. Check disneyworld.disney .go.com or call ☎ 407-939-5277 for the exact hours before you arrive. Off-season, parks may be open as few as 11 hours (8 a.m.–7 p.m.), while at busy times (particularly holidays) they may operate for more than 12 hours. Animal Kingdom usually opens first, typically at 8 or 8:30 a.m., followed by Disney's Hollywood Studios (8:30 a.m.), EPCOT (8:30 or 9 a.m.), and the Magic Kingdom (9 a.m.).

Opening Time

When you search online or call for park hours, Disney usually quotes the times at which the park is available to the general public: For example, when it says, "The Magic Kingdom is open from 9 a.m. to 9 p.m." that means the gates open to all ticket holders at 9 a.m. However, Early Entry (page 36) means it opens at 8:30 a.m. for Disney hotel guests.

On days of very high attendance, Disney may open the parks to Disney hotel guests even earlier, say 8:15 a.m. That extra 15 minutes might save 30 minutes standing in line over the course of your day. But because Disney advertises the 8:30–9 a.m. time as exclusive to its hotel guests, off-site guests are likely to be held at the park entrance until official opening at 9 a.m.

Closing Time

Attractions shut down at approximately the official closing time. Some shopping venues, such as Main Street, U.S.A., in the Magic Kingdom, stay open 30 minutes to an hour after the rest of the park has closed.

THE PRACTICALITY OF RETURNING TO YOUR HOTEL FOR REST

MANY READERS WRITE ABOUT the practicality of departing the theme park for a nap and swim at the hotel.

A dad from Sequim, Washington, made the following request:

I would like to see nearness to the parks emphasized in your accommodation guide. We tried going back to the hotel for midday breaks, but it was too time-consuming. By the time you got to the car, negotiated traffic, rested, and reversed the process to get back to the park, it took 2–3 hours for a short rest and was not worth it!

In Part 5, you'll find a table (pages 254–265) that lists the commuting times to each of the Disney theme parks from many popular hotels within 20 miles of Walt Disney World.

How long will it take you to get from a theme park to your hotel by car? At Animal Kingdom, Hollywood Studios, and EPCOT, you can get to your car in the parking lot in about 15–20 minutes. From the Magic Kingdom, it will take you 40–50 minutes. Obviously, if you're at the farthest point from the park entrance when you decide to return to the hotel, it will take longer. But from most places in the parks, the times above are correct. Once in your car, you'll be able to commute to most US 192 hotels, all Disney World hotels, all Lake Buena Vista hotels, and most hotels along the I-4 corridor and south International Drive (I-Drive) in 20 minutes or less. It will take about the same time to reach hotels on I-Drive north of Sand Lake Road and in the Universal Orlando area. So, for most people, the one-way commute will average 35–40 minutes.

ARRIVAL AND DEPARTURE DAYS: WHAT TO DO WHEN YOU HAVE ONLY HALF A DAY

ON ARRIVAL AND DEPARTURE DAYS, you will probably have only part of a day for touring or other recreational pursuits. It's a common problem: You roll into the World about 1 p.m., excited and ready to go—but where?

The first question: Do you feel comfortable using a full day's admission when you have less than a full day to tour? The incremental cost to add another day is under $20 if you're visiting for four or more days but $90 and up for one to three days (see table on pages 76–77 for the breakdown). The availability of park reservations, your arrival time, and the parks' closing times are also considerations. If you even think you might want to visit a park on your first or last day, make a theme park reservation (if required for the dates of your visit; see page 30) just in case. There's no charge to do so, and you can cancel at any time.

Opting for a Partial Day at the Theme Parks

If you decide to use one day's admission on a half day or less, refer to our **Lines** app for the least crowded park to visit and to see which parks have park reservations and Genie+ reservations available.

One option—if you can reach the park before 1 p.m. and stay until closing (usually 7 p.m.)—is Disney's Animal Kingdom, which requires the least amount of time to tour. You'll find shorter lines for Avatar Flight of Passage, Kilimanjaro Safaris, and Expedition Everest in the late afternoon on all but the busiest days of the year.

Another option is to experience Disney's Hollywood Studios' secondary attractions, such as Star Tours—The Adventures Continue, any live shows and entertainment, and shopping on your partial day, leaving your full day for the park's headliner attractions.

Whenever you arrive at a theme park after noon, you should go to higher-capacity attractions where waiting time is relatively brief, even during the most crowded part of the day. Our clip-out Touring Plan Companions in the back of the book list attractions in each of the Disney parks that require the least waiting during the most crowded part of the day. Although the lines for these attractions may seem humongous, they move quickly.

Alternatives to the Theme Parks on Arrival Day

Before you head out for fun on arrival day, you must check in, unpack, and buy admissions, and you will probably detour to the grocery or convenience store to buy snacks, drinks, and breakfast food. At all Disney resorts and many non-Disney hotels, you can't occupy your room until after 3 p.m. (4 p.m. for DVC resorts); however, many properties will check you in, sell you tickets, and store your luggage before that.

The least expensive way to spend your arrival day is to check in, unpack, do your chores, and relax at your hotel swimming pool.

Another daytime option is a trip to a **water park** (see Part 16 for details). Any one that stays open past 5 p.m. is worth a look because the crowds at all parks clear out substantially after 4 p.m. If the park is open late and you get hungry, you'll find ample fast food.

If none of the above options sound appealing, consider minigolf (expensive in Walt Disney World, more reasonable outside it) or the entertainment lineup at Disney Springs (see Part 17, page 673).

In the Evening

Dinner provides a great opportunity to plan the next day's activities. If you're hungry for entertainment, too, consider **Disney Springs**. It includes

Cirque du Soleil (page 664) and **Raglan Road** (page 334), an Irish pub with live music and good food, both best appreciated by adults.

Departure Days

Departure days don't seem to cause as much consternation as arrival days. If you want to visit a theme park on your departure day, Animal Kingdom is usually the first to open, and it's easier to get into and out of than the Magic Kingdom. Get up early and be at the park when it opens. If you have plenty of time, check out and store your luggage with the bell desk or in your car. Or, if you can arrange a late checkout, you might want to return to your hotel for a shower and change of clothes before your trip home.

HOW *to* AVOID LONG WAITS *in* LINE

LONG LINES ARE USUALLY THE TOP COMPLAINT among theme park guests—not the quality of the rides, the cost to get in, or the food. It's fair to say that the *Unofficial Guide* was written to save you time in line. It's what the book is most famous for, and what most of our day-to-day work revolves around.

Disney's on record saying the average Magic Kingdom guest experiences around 10 of that park's 50-ish attractions in a one-day visit, about one ride per hour. Disney considers everything from headliner rides, like Seven Dwarfs Mine Train, to the Main Street, U.S.A., piano player as one of those 10. Using the advice and touring plans in this book, we're confident you'll see 20 or more attractions in the same time. And the way to see so much is to minimize waiting.

There are six keys to avoiding long lines at Disney World. We elaborate on each these in the remainder of this chapter.

1. Decide in advance what you really want to see (see below).
2. Arrive early (see page 48).
3. Know what to expect when you arrive (see page 49).
4. Use a touring plan (see page 50).
5. Understand how standby queues, boarding groups, Genie+, and Individual Lightning Lane work to supplement the touring plans (see page 59).
6. Use the single-rider line if one is available (see page 67).

DECIDE IN ADVANCE WHAT YOU REALLY WANT TO SEE

DISNEY'S ATTRACTIONS RANGE from midway-type rides like you'd find at your local carnival to high-tech extravaganzas found nowhere else on earth. To help you decide which to see, we describe the theme parks and their attractions in detail. In each description, we include our evaluation of the attraction and give it an overall star rating; the opinions of Disney World guests are also expressed as star ratings, with five stars being the highest rating. Our evaluation also uses the following hierarchy of categories to compare the size and scope of the different attractions:

SUPER-HEADLINERS The best attractions the theme park has to offer. Mind-boggling in size, scope, and imagination, they represent the cutting edge of attraction technology and design. When you get back from Walt Disney World and people ask, "Did you go on so-and-so?" this is what they'll be talking about.

HEADLINERS Multimillion-dollar, full-scale, themed adventures and theater presentations that are modern in technology and design and employ a full range of special effects.

MAJOR ATTRACTIONS More modestly themed adventures that incorporate state-of-the-art technologies. Or larger-scale attractions of older design.

MINOR ATTRACTIONS Midway-type rides, small "dark" rides (cars on a track, zigzagging through the dark), small theater presentations, transportation rides, and elaborate walk-through attractions.

DIVERSIONS Exhibits, both passive and interactive, including playgrounds, video arcades, and street theater.

Not every attraction fits neatly into these descriptions, but it's a handy way to compare any two. Remember that bigger and more elaborate doesn't always mean better. Peter Pan's Flight, a minor attraction in the Magic Kingdom, continues to be one of the park's most beloved rides. Likewise, for many young children, no attraction, regardless of size, surpasses Dumbo.

A Word About Disney Thrill Rides

Readers of all ages should try to be open-minded about Disney "thrill rides." Compared to those at other theme parks, the Disney attractions are quite tame, with more emphasis on sights, atmosphere, and special effects than on the motion, speed, or feel of the ride. While we suggest you take Disney's pre-ride warnings seriously, we can tell you that guests of all ages report enjoying rides such as Big Thunder Mountain, Guardians of the Galaxy: Cosmic Rewind, Soarin' Around the World, and The Twilight Zone Tower of Terror.

Expedition Everest, Rock 'n' Roller Coaster, and Tron Lightcycle/ Run, however, are a different story. These are serious coasters that are faster and more intense than Space Mountain or Big Thunder Mountain.

Mission: Space, a high-tech simulation ride in EPCOT, is a toss-up (pun intended)—it absolutely has the potential to make you sick, as do the Star Tours simulator and the spinning Guardians of the Galaxy: Cosmic Rewind.

ARRIVE EARLY! ARRIVE EARLY! ARRIVE EARLY!

THIS IS THE MOST IMPORTANT KEY to efficient touring and avoiding long lines. First thing in the morning, there are no lines and fewer people. The same four rides you experience in 1 hour in the early morning in the Magic Kingdom can take as long as 3 hours after 10:30 a.m.

Eat breakfast before you arrive; don't waste prime touring time sitting in a restaurant.

You gain a big advantage if you're already past the turnstiles when the park opens. While everyone else is stuck in line waiting for the people ahead to find their admission media and figure out how the turnstiles work, the lucky few (hundreds) already in the park will be in line for their first attraction. You'll probably be done and on your way to your second before many of them are even in the park, and the time savings accrue throughout the rest of the day.

The earlier a park opens, the greater your advantage. This is because most vacationers won't make the effort to rise early and get to a park before it opens. Fewer people are willing to make an 8 a.m. opening than a 9 a.m. opening. If you visit during midsummer and are staying at a Disney resort, arrive at the turnstiles 60 minutes before official opening (to take advantage of the Early Theme Park Entry benefit for Disney hotel guests). If you're staying off-site, arrive 30 minutes before official opening to get into the park as soon as it officially opens.

During holiday periods, Disney resort guests should arrive 60–70 minutes early, and off-site guests, 40–50 minutes early. By arriving, we mean be at the turnstiles at the recommended time. Consider that you'll have to clear security before advancing to the turnstiles.

Many readers share their experiences about getting to the parks before opening. From a Pennsylvania mom of two:

> *Be there at rope drop [park opening]. I went during one of the slowest times of the year, and the morning I didn't wake up for rope drop I was able to experience less than half of what I did the other days.*

A reader from Ohiopyle, Pennsylvania, notes that this secret was becoming more widely known before the shutdown:

> *We found that Early Theme Park Entry increased the number of people getting up early. We used to be able to get several rides in at rope drop, but now we were lucky to get a couple.*

Even with more people rope-dropping, it's still the best free strategy for seeing the most popular attractions with minimal waits.

Some readers note that Disney's new Early Theme Park Entry program (page 36) greatly reduces the early-morning advantage for off-site guests. A family from Minnesota found that staying late helped:

> *Going to the park first thing only works if you are staying at a Disney property. If you are not, then it's much better to arrive later in the day and stay until the evening. And get in line for the busiest ride right before park close. We tried Rise of the Resistance at 8:55 p.m. and were through the line and out of the ride by 9:15 p.m.*

If getting the kids up earlier than usual makes for rough sailing, don't despair. You'll have a great time no matter when you get to the park. Many families with young children have found that it's better to accept the relative inefficiencies of arriving at the park a bit late than to jar the children out of their routine. In our guide especially for families, *The Unofficial Guide to Walt Disney World with Kids,* we provide several special touring plans (including touring plans for sleepyheads) that we don't have room for in this guide.

KNOW WHAT TO EXPECT WHEN YOU ARRIVE

BECAUSE MOST OF THE TOURING PLANS hinge on being present when the theme park opens, you need to know about opening procedures. Disney transportation to the parks begins 1–1½ hours before official opening. The parking lots open about an hour before the park does. Each park has an entrance plaza outside the turnstiles, where you'll remain until the parks open.

Disney typically allows Disney hotel guests into the parks roughly 30–60 minutes before official opening time (off-site guests may be directed to a holding area outside the park until official opening). This prevents dense crowds from forming around the admission turnstiles. Once inside, guests are typically held at various points in the park until it opens, a process called rope drop for historical reasons. Once the park is open, you can walk immediately to your first attraction.

USE A TOURING PLAN

WE KNOW FROM RESEARCH that theme park patrons base their overall satisfaction on the number of attractions they're able to experience. Thus, we developed field-tested touring plans: step-by-step itineraries that allow readers to experience as many attractions as possible with the least amount of waiting.

unofficial **TIP**
The facts and figures in our books come from years of data collection and analysis by expert statisticians, programmers, field researchers, and life-long Disney enthusiasts.

We're confident that the touring plans in this book can save you up to 4 hours or more of standing in line, and they allow you to see more attractions. How do they do this? The answer is *science*.

You may be surprised to learn that avoiding lines in theme parks is like everyday situations faced by companies around the world. For example, it's almost the exact problem FedEx and UPS have when trying to deliver packages efficiently (you're the driver; the rides you want to ride are the customers that need to be visited; and the time you spend walking and waiting in line is the travel time to the next customer).

Because this kind of problem is common, it gets studied widely in schools and corporations, mainly in the fields of mathematics, operations research, and computer science. Bob used his experience teaching college operations research to come up with the first Disney touring plans in this book. Years later, Bob helped Len while Len was writing his master's thesis on efficient computer techniques for this kind of problem. It was their chocolate-and-peanut-butter moment.

In the years since, we've assembled a full-time team of data scientists, programmers, and researchers, and spent millions of dollars, to figure out how to avoid lines at Disney World.

This research has been recognized by both the travel industry and academe, having been cited by such diverse sources as *Popular Science, The Atlanta Journal-Constitution, The Dallas Morning News,* the Mathematical Association of America, *Money, The New York Times,* Operations Research Forum, *Travel Weekly, USA Today,* and *Wired,* along with the BBC, CBS News, Fox News, and the Travel Channel. The methodology behind our touring plans was also used as a case study in the book *Numbers Rule Your World,* by Kaiser Fung, an expert in business analytics and data visualization.

So that's a touring plan: a step-by-step guide to avoiding lines, just for you, that is supported by a team of well-funded, obsessive, Disney science–y types with lots and lots of computers.

We get a ton of reader mail—98% of it positive—commenting on our touring plans. First, from a mother who planned a last-minute trip:

We rode all of the main attractions in EPCOT, Magic Kingdom, and Hollywood Studios over a three-day period, and we didn't wait more than 10 minutes for any ride—and this was during spring break!

An Ohio family felt the wind in their sails:

The whole time we were in the Magic Kingdom, following the touring plan, it seemed that we were traveling in front of a hurricane—we'd wait 10 minutes or so for an attraction (or less—sometimes we just walked right on), but when we got out and started moving on to the next one, we could see the line building for what we just did.

From a Noblesville, Indiana, couple:

LOVE the touring plans. They work. I was skeptical.

A family of four from Louisville, Kentucky, had this to say:

If there is one cult in this world I could join, it would be the staff of the Unofficial Guide. *I tell everyone going to Disney to use this book and the awesome app. Years ago, we tried to convince friends to use the book, but they were scared off by the highly structured nature of the touring plans. We happened to see them at Disney during a late summer afternoon. Our family had enjoyed a full day with lots of rides and no more than a 20-minute wait. They had been on two total rides, standing in line over 1½ hours each time. They were miserable, and already considering escaping back to the hotel.*

A mom from Warren, Arkansas, gave the touring plans a shot:

This is our fifth family trip to WDW, and this was my first time to use a touring plan. I have read the books and been a member of Lines for years. However, I never bought into the demands of the touring plan. After this last trip, I am officially a fan! I cannot express to you how much better our trip was since we followed a plan. We accomplished more in the first hour of Magic Kingdom than we used to accomplish in 3 hours. My family will use touring plans from now on.

From a Monroe, Michigan, family of 10:

I have always read the Unofficial Guide *but never paid much mind to the touring plan section. This trip there were 10 of us in total going to the parks! We decided to give the plans a try so that we weren't standing around saying, "What do you want to do next?" Oh, my goodness! How have we survived without the plans? We got to do every attraction that everyone in the group wanted, with minimal crying from the 2- and 4-year-old nieces.*

A woman from Westminster, Colorado, chimed in with this:

I love the Unofficial Guides. *I love the humor, and I feel like I get a real idea of what to expect. When I first told my family I wanted to use the touring plans to maximize our theme park experience, they thought I was crazy. I secretly cut the plans out of the book and stowed them in my day pack, then urged us in the direction of the plans. After the first day they were shocked at how much we got done and how few huge lines we had to wait in. When I told them that we had actually followed your touring plans, they happily followed them the rest of the trip. It made a huge difference with the crowds and heat of summer!*

A 30-something mom of two from Oconomowoc, Wisconsin, found that the touring plans fanned the flames of *amour:*

> My husband was a bit doubtful about using a touring plan, but on our first day at Magic Kingdom, after we'd done all the Fantasyland attractions and ridden Splash Mountain [now Tiana's Bayou Adventure] twice before lunch, he looked at me with amazement and said, "I've never been so attracted to you."

A woman from Smithville, Tennessee, used the touring plans as a litmus test for her fiancé:

> Your book has helped me plan two amazing trips to Disney World. My first trip there, I went in blind. My second trip, I discovered your book and used your touring plans. My third trip, I used the app you created and had the best trip of my life! My fiancé just informed me that we can't go "every year." I think I'm going to have to break it off with him.

Finally, from an Edmonds, Washington, family who used the touring plans for Universal's Islands of Adventure:

> This trip was the first time we were actually going to leave the property (gasp!) and go to Universal, and I was very happy that you included a touring plan for Islands of Adventure. It worked like a charm! I've always wondered how it feels to follow your plans not ever having seen the park before, and now I know—it was easy!

Variables That Affect the Success of the Touring Plans

The success of the plans will be affected by how early you arrive at the parks; how quickly you move from attraction to attraction; when and how many breaks you take; when, where, and how you eat (counter service vs. table service); and whether you have young children in your tour group, among other factors. **Rider Switch** (page 396), also known as "baby swap," among other things, inhibits families with little ones from moving expeditiously among attractions. Plus, some folks simply cannot conform to the plans' "early to rise" conditions, as this reader from Cleveland Heights, Ohio, recounts:

> Our touring plans were thrown totally off by one member who could not be on time for opening. Even in October, this made a huge difference in our ability to see attractions without waiting.

UNEXPECTED RIDE CLOSURES Some things are beyond your control. Tops among these are rides that don't open on time or stop running suddenly during the day. For example, Test Track, an automobile-based thrill ride in EPCOT, can run about 30 cars at a time. But it's a decades-old outdoor ride with fragile technology that doesn't seem to handle Florida's humid mornings very well.

Test Track has unscheduled stoppages about 9 days out of every 10, for ride breakdowns and weather. On average, it's unavailable to guests for around 2 hours per day. (Set aside the question "Why does Chevrolet sponsor a car ride that is this unreliable?") To get Test Track running again, the staff might begin the ride with 10 or 20 cars before going to full capacity; on these days, you'll have a long wait even if you're among the first to get back in line.

ATTRACTIONS THAT FREQUENTLY EXPERIENCE OUTAGES		
ATTRACTION AND THEME PARK	**AVERAGE DOWNTIME PER DAY (IN MINUTES)**	**LIKELIHOOD RIDE IS DOWN AT SOME POINT DURING THE DAY**
Test Track *(EPCOT)*	115	90%
Star Wars: Rise of the Resistance *(Hollywood Studios)*	110	90%
Expedition Everest *(Animal Kingdom)*	72	55%
Remy's Ratatouille Adventure *(EPCOT)*	65	85%
Rock 'n' Roller Coaster *(Hollywood Studios)*	65	65%
Big Thunder Mountain Railroad *(Magic Kingdom)*	65	50%
Frozen Ever After *(EPCOT)*	60	63%
Seven Dwarfs Mine Train *(Magic Kingdom)*	60	60%
Pirates of the Caribbean *(Magic Kingdom)*	60	50%

Breakdowns have more impact at parks with fewer attractions, such as Hollywood Studios and EPCOT. At the Studios, Rise of the Resistance averages nearly 2 hours of downtime per day; Rock 'n' Roller Coaster, over an hour; Slinky Dog Dash and Mickey and Minnie's Runaway Railway, over 45 minutes; and Tower of Terror, over 35. So, the Studios has nine rides, and five of them are unreliable. It's not better at EPCOT, where, in addition to the problems at Test Track, Remy, and Frozen Ever After noted in the table above, Spaceship Earth averages over 50 minutes of downtime per day; Guardians of the Galaxy and Journey into Imagination, nearly 30. Half the park's rides are unreliable. On bad days, multiple headliner attractions break down simultaneously, as this reader from Connecticut experienced:

What took tons of time was down attractions. It seems like almost everything was down: Kilimanjaro Safaris at Animal Kingdom; Soarin', Spaceship Earth, and Remy's Ratatouille Adventure when we visited EPCOT; and Rise of the Resistance and Smugglers Run at the Studios.

At least Smugglers Run handled it well. They gave us a pass to re-ride without waiting. In the welcome video when we re-rode, the guy said, "Oh, I didn't expect you to come back after the incident. Good to see you again." That was amazing.

RIDE BREAKDOWNS AND LIGHTNING LANE All of Disney's least reliable rides use Lightning Lane. The combination of Lightning Lane and breakdowns makes standby waits substantially worse. When a ride like Test Track breaks down for 2 hours, thousands of guests who would've ridden it end up going to another attraction. We estimate around half those guests were using Lightning Lane, and Disney gives them the opportunity to use that reservation at another attraction. But those other attractions are almost certainly already running at full capacity. The only way to fit the displaced Test Track guests into those Lightning Lanes is to put them ahead of standby guests. This makes the standby guests wait longer because another ride broke down.

Of course, some of those standby guests will end up purchasing Individual Lightning Lane to avoid these suddenly longer lines. That makes the problem of subsequent ride breakdowns larger, because more people will be using Lightning Lane. The extra revenue Disney earns from these "because of downtime" Lightning Lane purchases can be a perverse incentive not to fix the original problem.

We nevertheless recommend purchasing Individual Lightning Lane for Rise of the Resistance to guests who really want to experience it. As noted above, Rise breaks down for about 2 hours per day. We think it has around two outages per day, with each outage lasting about an hour. When Rise breaks down, Disney usually kicks out everyone in line and tells them to try back "later" when the ride is running again. (This process is called "dumping the queue.") If you're a particularly unlucky standby guest, you can waste hours waiting in line for an attraction you never get to ride.

Our touring plans consider ride reliability when choosing which attraction to visit first each morning. The EPCOT plans usually visit Guardians of the Galaxy or Remy's Ratatouille Adventure first, for example, because there's a decent chance that walking to Test Track or Frozen Ever After would be a waste of time and effort. If you're following a touring plan on our Lines app, you can tap "Optimize" to have the plan adjust automatically to avoid the problem areas.

If you're following a printed touring plan, it's safe to assume that a ride outage will affect your plan at some point during the day. Our advice is to check the My Disney Experience app or the Lines app for current wait times throughout the rest of the park and then adjust your plan accordingly.

WEATHER AND STAFFING Two other variables we can't predict are the weather and how Disney will staff its rides. When lightning or heavy rains are close, Disney will close many (if not all) outdoor rides for safety. The effect on ride wait times when this happens is similar to a set of unexpected ride breakdowns, as described above.

Also, Disney will occasionally cut a ride's staffing or hourly capacity, typically to save money. We're pretty sure—because we've counted how many people exited the attractions per hour—that this has happened many times over the past few years; it's likely to keep happening, too, but it's unpredictable.

THEATER SHOWS Another variable is your arrival time for a theater show: You'll wait from the time you arrive until the end of the presentation in progress. The sooner you arrive after the show in progress has started, the longer you'll wait; conversely, the later you arrive, the shorter your wait will be.

Customize Your Touring Plans

The attractions included in our touring plans are the most popular, as determined by more than 1 million reader surveys. If you've never been to Walt Disney World, we suggest using the plans in this book. Not only are they the best our program can produce, but they've also been field-tested by millions of families. They'll ensure that you see the best Disney attractions with as little waiting in line as possible.

If you are a return visitor, your favorite attractions may be different. One way to customize the plans is to go to **TouringPlans.com** to create personalized versions. Tell the software the date, time, and park you've chosen to visit, along with the attractions you want to see.

Your custom plan will tell you, for your specific travel date and time, the exact order in which you should visit attractions to minimize your waits in line. If you decide to purchase Disney's Genie+ ride reservation system, the plans will tell you which reservations are most worthwhile to obtain for your plan and incorporate whichever ones you get into the itinerary. (Likewise for Individual Lightning Lane purchases.) The touring plans also support Rider Switch on thrill rides (see page 396). Besides attractions, you can schedule meals, breaks, character greetings, and more. You can even tell the software how fast you plan to walk, and it'll make the necessary adjustments.

Our custom touring plans get rave reviews from readers and TouringPlans.com subscribers. From an Edmonton, Alberta, reader:

We love the ability to personalize the touring plans! Because we rarely arrive at park opening, we can't use the ones printed in the book. The personalized plans let us reduce wait times and eliminate arguing about what we are going to do next. Everyone can see their "big" attraction coming up on the plan, and we know we'll get to them all.

From a mother of two from Halifax, Nova Scotia:

I was hesitant to pay additional money to get the TouringPlans.com membership, but boy, am I glad I did! My husband was hesitant about needing to have a plan for the park, but when we got there and he saw how we beat all the lines by following it and using the [suggested ride reservations] in the book, he was happy we had the plan. We also used the Lines app in the park to see the waiting times for rides, which were much more accurate than the Disney posted times. Next time we go to Disney World, the very first thing we will do is get a website membership!

(As a reminder, you can create touring plans for free on the website. See page 22 for details.)

From an Alexandria, Virginia, mom:

The touring plans helped make our vacation perfect! We visited WDW over spring break, the week before Easter. It was CROWDED. We saw signs for 90- to 120-minute waits on some of the rides. Using our touring plans, we only waited for 30 minutes once. Other than that, our longest wait was 20 minutes, and most of our other waits were 0–10 minutes. We would have had a completely different vacation without the touring plans. They were lifesavers!

From a couple across the pond in London:

The personalized touring plans and the Lines app worked really well. In our five days at the parks, we managed to ride everything we wanted to multiple times. Even though there were posted waits of up to and over 120 minutes for some rides at peak times, we very rarely waited more than 15 minutes, and most times we just walked straight up to the rides.

Finally, from a Chelsea, Alabama, reader:

The book and the personal touring plans are like a one–two punch. Between them we were completely covered.

Alternatively, some changes are simple enough to make on your own. If a plan calls for an attraction you're not interested in, simply skip it and move on to the next one. You can also substitute similar attractions in the same area of the park. If a plan calls for, say, riding Dumbo and you'd rather not, but you would enjoy the Mad Tea Party (which is not on the plan), then go ahead and substitute that for Dumbo. As long as the substitution is a similar attraction (substituting a show for a ride won't work) and is near the attraction called for in the touring plan, you won't compromise the overall effectiveness of the plan.

A family of four from South Slocan, British Columbia, found they could easily tailor the touring plans to meet their needs:

We amended your touring plans by taking out the attractions we didn't want to do and just doing the remainder in order. It worked great, and by arriving before the parks opened, we got to see everything we wanted, with virtually no waits!

A Jacksonville, Florida, family found the same:

We used a combination of the Two-Day Touring Plan for Parents with Small Children and the Two-Day Touring Plan for Adults. We were able to get on almost everything with a 10-minute wait or less.

What the Touring Plans Assume

Millions of families have used our touring plans. For an audience that large, we have to make some assumptions around what most guests can reasonably do. For example, we know that only around 25% of theme park guests arrive in time for park opening. If we assumed everyone was going to show up that early, we'd be wrong 75% of the time. So when we have to make these decisions, we often look at the benefits of being right as compared to the consequences of being wrong.

For example, our EPCOT plans that start at International Gateway might not direct you to Remy's Ratatouille Adventure first thing in the morning. This reader from Sudbury, Massachusetts, ignored that advice and had a better experience:

The custom touring plans we made said to skip Remy when arriving at International Gateway, because it's going to be an hour no matter what time you go and Soarin' and other rides had shorter waits and we'd get a lot of them in. But in reality we were the 30th people in line for Remy, which opened early, while Soarin' and other rides didn't.

The reader did a bunch of things right here: Being one of the first people in line for park opening, noticing that Remy was opening extra-early, and realizing that Remy's line was never going to be shorter.

We wouldn't want to assume, however, that everyone reading this book will be among the first 50 people in line for a park's opening—we'd be wrong hundreds of times for every one time we were right. We'll tell you the benefits of being at the front of the pack, but we assume that you'll be somewhere in the middle to back of the initial wave of guests. That's the more realistic scenario for most readers.

The good news is that no matter what you ride first, the touring plan software can handle it. Just tell the software which ride you've completed and ask it to reoptimize your plan. The rest of your day will be planned out, no matter where you first went.

What to Do If You Lose the Thread

If unforeseen events interrupt a plan:

1. If you're following a touring plan in our Lines app (touringplans.com /lines), just tap "Optimize" when you're ready to start touring again. The app will figure out the best possible plan for the remainder of your day.

2. If you're following a printed touring plan, skip a step on the plan for every 20 minutes' delay. For example, if you lose your phone and spend an hour hunting for it, skip three steps and pick up from there.

3. Forget the plan and organize the remainder of your day using the standby wait times listed in Lines or the Clip-Out Touring Plan Companions in the back of this book.

"Bouncing Around"

Disney generally tries to place its popular rides on opposite sides of the park. In the Magic Kingdom, for example, the most popular attractions are positioned as far apart as possible—in the north, east, and west corners of the park—so that guests are more evenly distributed throughout the day.

It's often possible to save a lot of time in line by walking across the park to catch one of these rides when crowds are low. Some readers object to this crisscrossing. A woman from Decatur, Georgia, told us she "got dizzy from all the bouncing around." Believe us, we empathize.

In general, our touring plans recommend crossing the park only if you'll save more than 1 minute in line for every 1 minute of extra walking. (If you prefer some other trade-off, our touring plan software can help.)

We sometimes recommend crossing the park to see a newly opened ride; in these cases, a special trip to visit the attraction early avoids much longer waits later. Also, live shows, especially at the Studios, sometimes have performance schedules so at odds with each other (and the rest of the park's schedule) that orderly touring is impossible.

If you want to experience headliner attractions in one day without long waits, you can see those first (requires crisscrossing the park) or squeeze in visits during the last 2 hours the park is open (may not work).

If you have two days to visit the Magic Kingdom, use its Two-Day Touring Plan (see page 719–720). It spreads the popular attractions over two mornings and works great even when the parks close early.

Touring Plan Rejection

We suggest sticking to the plans religiously, especially in the mornings, if you're visiting during busy times. The consequence of touring spontaneity in peak season is hours of standing in line. However, some folks don't respond well to the regimentation of a touring plan. If you encounter this problem with someone in your party, roll with the punches, as this Maryland couple did:

The rest of the group was not receptive to the use of the touring plans. I think they all thought I was being a little too regimented about planning this vacation. Rather than argue, I left the touring plans behind as we ventured off for the theme parks. You can guess the outcome.

A reader from Royal Oak, Michigan, ran into trouble by not getting her family on board ahead of time:

The one thing I will suggest is if one member of the family is doing most of the research and planning (like I did), that they communicate what the book/touring plans suggest. I failed to do this and it led to some, shall we say, tense moments between my husband and me on our first day. However, once he realized how much time we were saving, he understood why I was so bent on following the touring plans.

That said, if you're a type-A planner, relax and be prepared for surprises and setbacks. It's easy to get overwhelmed with all of this, as this woman from Trappe, Pennsylvania reflected:

I had been planning for this trip for two years and researching it using guidebooks, websites, videos, and information from WDW. On night three of our trip, I ended up taking an unscheduled trip to the ER. When the doctor asked what seemed to be the problem, I responded, "I don't know—but I can't stop shaking and I can't stay here very long, because I have to get up in a couple hours to go to Disney's Hollywood Studios." Diagnosis: an anxiety attack caused by my excessive itinerary.

One of our all-time favorite letters came from an Omaha, Nebraska, couple. One of them was a planner, and one clearly wasn't. They were both experienced negotiators, as their letter shows:

We created our own 4.25-by-5.5-inch guidebook for our trip that included a number of pages from the TouringPlans.com website. This was the first page:

THE TYPE-A SPOUSE'S BILL OF RIGHTS
1. We will not see everything in one vacation, and any attempt to do so may be met with blunt trauma.
2. Len Testa will not be vacationing with us. His plans don't schedule time for benches. Ours may.
3. We may deviate from the touring plans at some point. Really.
4. Even if it isn't on the Disney Dining Plan, a funnel cake or other snack may be purchased without a grouchy face from the nonpurchasing spouse.
5. Sometimes, sitting by the pool may sound more fun than going to a park, show, or other scheduled event. On this vacation, that will be fine.
6. "But I thought we were going to . . ." is a phrase that must be stricken from the discussion of any plans that had not been previously discussed as a couple.
7. Other items may be added as circumstances dictate at the parks.

It was a much happier vacation with these generally understood principles in writing.

How Early Theme Park Entry, Extended Evening Theme Park Hours, and Special Events Work with the Touring Plans

With Early Theme Park Entry, Disney resort guests are admitted to all four Disney theme parks 30 minutes before official park opening. Off-site resort guests who enter the parks at official opening will find thousands of on-site guests already ahead of them in lines.

To mitigate the effect of Early Entry on off-site guests, we've added off-site versions of our touring plans to this book. And our free touring plan software (see touringplans.com/walt-disney-world/touring-plans) will optimize touring plans that begin up to an hour before official park opening.

During Extended Evening Theme Park Hours (page 38), crowds are so low that a touring plan isn't needed—just head to the nearest attraction that interests you. However, that's not true for most special events, including the Halloween and Christmas parties (page 84). (We get lots of reader comments about how crowded Halloween and Christmas parties are.)

STANDBY QUEUES, BOARDING GROUPS, GENIE+, INDIVIDUAL LIGHTNING LANE, AND GENIE (MINUS THE PLUS)

PRIOR TO 2021, Disney ran a *free* ride reservation system called Fast-Pass+ that allowed you to reserve a spot on an attraction for a specific day and time. You could book a reservation at a specific ride, for a specific 1-hour time window, up to two months before your trip. When your reservation arrived, you went to the attraction, got in a line separate from the regular (standby) line, and were given priority access to get on the ride. In practice, the wait to use a FastPass+ was often around 20% of the wait in the standby line. All free of charge.

The original goal of FastPass+ was to increase guest satisfaction—Disney knew that guests who used it were more satisfied than guests who didn't. That increase in guest satisfaction was apparently so important that Disney reportedly spent over $1 billion on the implementation of FastPass+ and related technology. The problem, from Disney's perspective, was that it was hard to translate an increase in guest satisfaction into more money for shareholders.

In 2021 Disney decided to make this trade-off much clearer, by charging money to wait less. The result is an unprecedented, unpopular, unwieldy system for navigating Disney's theme parks. There are now at least four different Disney processes for waiting in line at rides. Each method has its own set of rules, often put in place for Disney's benefit, not yours. We think that this complexity is intentional—some guests will simply give up trying to figure out how it all works and throw money at Disney to make it simpler.

Here are the ways you can wait in line at Walt Disney World:

STANDBY QUEUES This is the way most people are familiar with: You get in a line for a ride, and you wait until it's your turn to ride. It doesn't cost anything, and the wait-time sign in front of the attraction gives you some idea of how long you're going to be waiting.

As we went to press, it was rare for any Walt Disney World ride not to operate a standby queue. The last two not to operate one were Tron Lightcycle/Run in the Magic Kingdom and Guardians of the Galaxy: Cosmic Rewind in EPCOT, which used boarding groups (see next page) exclusively when they opened and for some time afterward.

COST: Standby queues are free with park admission.

BOARDING GROUPS/VIRTUAL QUEUES A boarding group, or virtual queue, is a virtual line without a specific return time. They're typically used at new, popular rides, so it's possible you'll see them at Tiana's Bayou Adventure when it opens in the Magic Kingdom. Here's how it works: You first make a park reservation (if required) for whatever park holds the ride you want to ride. At exactly 7 a.m. on the day of your visit, you'll use My Disney Experience (MDE) to request a boarding group. If you're successful, you'll get a boarding group number and a rough estimate of how long you must wait until your group is called.

You need to be fast and lucky: Boarding groups for Rise of the Resistance were often fully allocated for the entire day within 10 seconds of 7 a.m. So many people tried to get a boarding group that it was essentially a lottery as to who got in. And if anything went wrong, your chance to experience the ride was almost certainly gone. (A second group of reservations is available at 1 p.m., using the same process; however, these reservations were less likely to be called to ride.)

If the ride is running smoothly, boarding groups typically start getting called within 30 minutes of park opening, beginning with boarding group 1. The MDE app will display the current range of boarding groups that are able to ride. When your group is called, the app will alert you so you can return.

Boarding groups are used at rides that Disney thinks are likely to break down often. Because new rides may not have worked out all their bugs, Disney isn't confident that it can give guests a specific time to return and ride. For example, suppose Disney gave you a specific time of 1–2 p.m. to ride Tron. If Tron breaks down and is unavailable between 1 and 2 p.m., then at 2 p.m., the ride must accommodate everyone who didn't get to ride between 1 and 2, plus everyone who was scheduled to ride between 2 and 3 p.m. There's not enough ride capacity to do that (and Disney doesn't want to run the ride at half capacity in anticipation of it either). Boarding groups solve this problem by not attaching a specific return time to your virtual wait.

An issue with boarding groups (when used) is that you are not able to ride Guardians or Tron unless your first park of the day is EPCOT or the Magic Kingdom—at press time, you must have a park reservation before you attempt to get a boarding group. So, if you plan to park-hop to EPCOT or the Magic Kingdom, you have almost no chance of riding those parks' headliner rides for free. The same is likely to be true of any ride that uses boarding groups, in any park.

COST: Boarding groups are free with park admission and reservations.

GENIE+ AND LIGHTNING LANE *(aka paid FastPass+)* Genie+ is a paid version of Disney's former FastPass+ system. Built as a feature in the My Disney Experience app, using it costs $16–$31 per person, per day. The price varies by day, and Genie+ costs more on busier days.

As we went to press, you could only purchase Genie+ on the day of your park visit. That means you have to make separate, daily purchases for each day you plan to use it. (Disney has said it's working on changing this aspect of the system in 2024.)

Disney can limit the number of guests who purchase Genie+. While that doesn't happen open, if you want to be absolutely certain you

RIDE RESERVATION SYSTEM DEFINITIONS	
LIGHTNING LANE	An alternative to the standby line at some rides. Comes in two flavors: Genie+ and Individual.
GENIE+	A way of using the Lightning Lane at most (but not all) of the popular rides in each park, for a single additional upcharge per person per day.
INDIVIDUAL LIGHTNING LANE (ILL)	Another way of using the Lighting Lane that's available, for a per-attraction fee, for the two most popular rides in each park. It's a way of charging more than Genie+ to get shorter lines at a park's top two attractions.

have it, you can purchase Genie+ at midnight on the day of your park visit to guarantee you have reservations. You must also be back online at 6:55 a.m. to start making Genie+ reservations at 7 a.m.

Paying for Genie+ allows you to make reservations that work like the old FastPass+ system: At participating rides, Genie+ will show you the next available return time at each attraction, such as 1–2 p.m. or 1:15–2:15 p.m. You'll pick the attraction whose return time works best for your day. (This is another difference from the old FastPass+ system, where Disney gave you several times to choose from.)

When you return to ride, you'll use the Lightning Lane—a separate line that's shorter than the standby line. Guests in this line are given priority to board. Almost all the attractions and character greetings that offered FastPass+ offer Lightning Lane.

The number of Lightning Lane reservations available is limited, so Lightning Lane doesn't eliminate the need to arrive early. With Fast Pass+, Disney would normally allocate 75%–80% of a ride's hourly capacity to FastPass+ riders. In practice, that meant Disney put three or four people from the FastPass+ line on the ride for every one person it took from the standby line. But even with a separate line for Fast Pass+ riders, people often waited 30 minutes or more in the FastPass+ line once they returned to ride.

We think that Disney is reserving around 50% of each ride's capacity for Genie+ as well. But because Genie+ costs real money, we believe Disney has set an upper goal on how long people will wait in the Lightning Lane—something like "no more than 10 minutes." And that means that if the Genie+ gets backed up, Disney will take up to 99 guests from the Genie+ line for every 1 guest it takes from the standby line. Put another way, if there are 30 people in front of you in line at Rise of the Resistance, you might have a 2-hour wait.

Because Lightning Lane passes are offered only on the day of your visit, it's possible for a ride to run out of Lightning Lane passes or desirable return times before you arrive at the park.

Guests staying at Disney resorts can make reservations starting at 7 a.m., while off-site guests can make reservations when the park they're visiting opens officially. As we went to press, 7 a.m. was also the time at which you needed to purchase Individual Lightning Lane access and make (when they're offered) boarding group reservations. We're not sure why Disney scheduled these critical, mutually exclusive tasks for the exact same time of day—we suspect it's that nobody who made the decision ever had to do this for themselves. We're hoping staggering the times is on the list of changes it's making to Genie+ for 2024.

Speaking of boarding groups, Genie+ isn't available on rides that use boarding groups. For those, you'll need Individual Lightning Lane.

IS GENIE+ WORTH THE COST? In general, yes. We recommend using Genie+ in the Magic Kingdom, Hollywood Studios, and Animal Kingdom, in conjunction with a touring plan. We're not ready to say that a family of four should spend $124 on Genie+ in EPCOT, though: EPCOT has fewer rides and they're spaced far apart, limiting the amount of time you'd save using Genie+ beyond what you'd get just by showing up early and hitting the key attractions first. For specific advice on how best to use Genie+ at each park, read the Genie+ section in that park's chapter.

Most reader comments we get on Genie+ are negative, focusing on the cost and the constant need to use smartphones:

Genie+ makes everyone miserable. If you don't have it, you resent all the people flying by you, the unpredictable wait times, and the feeling that you're somehow less than everyone else. If you have it, you sacrifice any sense of being "in the moment" because your face is constantly buried in your phone working to plan your next Lightning Lane. And when there's a wait in the LL line, you feel like you just wasted all your money. The whole system has added a level of sadness to the Happiest Place on Earth. You end up feeling like everyone's out for themselves and just gross.
—A reader from Cincinnati

Genie+ is a money shakedown and we refused to buy it. Everyone seemed angry and the crowds were awful.
—A reader from Vancouver, Washington

Disney is doing a lot to cause us to vacation elsewhere. The [former] CEO's statements about Annual Pass holders [being less profitable than infrequent guests], the lack of [free] FastPass+, and Disney's taking away benefits and raising prices makes other bucket list trips more attractive. We will be selling our DVC and moving on. Raising prices and cutting amenities is a poor way to control crowds.
—A family from Port Jefferson, New York

Disney World is still magical but far less enjoyable with Genie+. We visited during a relatively off-peak time, and had we not bought Lightning Lane reservations, our waits for the popular rides would've been over an hour within 30–60 minutes of park opening on most days.
—A family from Missouri

And regarding phone usage, a visitor from North Wales, Pennsylvania, says:

Vacation was less than magical this time. I'm not entirely sure why, but I think it had something to do with working my phone so much. I am not high-tech, but I was able to do mobile ordering, Genie+, and ILL with few problems. But my phone became the focus too many times during the day instead of the park.

These folks from Cincinnati agree:

I don't need an app or map to know how to navigate the parks, and I still spent 22 hours MORE TIME on my phone during our

VACATION. An entire day, staring at MDE and mobile ordering. Something's gotta give.

Remember that we're not printing just the negative comments— this is a representative sample of what we get every day. A reader from Charleston, South Carolina adds:

I refuse to pay that much extra for something that was once included, so we just walked around and hung out at bars. It was still fun but very different.

And a reader from Erdenheim, Pennsylvania, declares:

Disney Genie+ and Lightning Lane purchases are another way for Disney to extract money from visitors who already pay plenty for park tickets.

The bad news: Disney is saying that somewhere between 33% and 50% of park guests are using these reservations, throwing tens of millions of dollars per year into its coffers. So prices aren't going down (or away) anytime soon.

Genie+ Guidelines

- Park tickets are required to obtain Lightning Lane return times.
- Before 2 p.m., you can make Genie+ reservations only for the park where you have a reservation. If you try to make a reservation at another park, Genie+ will only offer you return times after 2 p.m.
- You may hold only one Genie+ Lightning Lane reservation at a time (unless 2 hours have elapsed since you obtained a Genie+ reservation for a ride whose return-time window has not yet started), and/or up to two reservations for Individual Lightning Lane attractions. The only other exceptions to this rule are that (1) there is no limit to the number of Replacement Lightning Lane reservations (see next page) you can simultaneously hold and (2) users of Disney's Disability Access Service (DAS) can make two Genie+ reservations at the start of each day.
- Don't make a Genie+ reservation unless it can save you 30 minutes or more at an attraction or if the ride is distributing immediate return times.
- If you arrive after a park opens, obtain a return time for your preferred Genie+ attraction first thing.
- Always check the return period before obtaining your reservation. Keep an eye out for attractions whose Lightning Lane return time is immediate, or at least sooner than the standby wait.
- Don't depend on Lightning Lane being available for popular attractions after noon during busier times of the year. This especially applies to Guardians of the Galaxy, Rise of the Resistance, Remy's Ratatouille Adventure, Tiana's Bayou Adventure (when it opens), and Tron.
- Make sure everyone in your party has their own Lightning Lane return time. Reservations are tied to each individual admission pass and may not be transferred.
- You can obtain a second Genie+ return time (1) as soon as you use your first, (2) 2 hours after you obtained your last Genie+ reservation, or (3) when your unused Genie+ return-time window has expired. You can maximize efficiency by always obtaining a new Lightning Lane return time for the next attraction while waiting to board the previous one.
- Be mindful of your Lightning Lane return time, and plan intervening activities accordingly. You may use your Genie+ Lightning Lane entry 5 minutes

before its start time and up to 15 minutes after it expires. This unadvertised grace period is typically the only exception to your return window.

- Attractions may not dispense Lightning Lane reservations while they are closed for technical difficulties or special events.

- If an attraction is unavailable due to technical difficulties during your return window, your Lightning Lane automatically converts to a Replacement Lightning Lane pass. Replacement passes remain valid for use until closing time at that attraction (if it reopens) or at selected other Lightning Lane attractions in the same park. If the original return window was near closing time, the Replacement pass may be valid the next day.

- You may want to pick one member of your party to handle everyone's tickets and Lightning Lane reservations on their phone. This gives your group the option of splitting up while retaining access to each other's plans; however, each person must still use their own ticket to enter the park or redeem Lightning Lane reservations.

COST: Genie+ is $16–$31 per person per day.

INDIVIDUAL LIGHTNING LANE (ILL) The idea here is that you'll pay more to get on a new or popular ride. If Tron offers boarding groups but you didn't get one, or if you want to avoid a 2-hour wait, Disney will offer you a chance to ride at a price, using ILL.

Purchasing an ILL in MDE is straightforward. Passes are sold per-person, and guests are limited to two per day. When it's your time to ride, you'll be directed to the Lightning Lane to board.

Individual Lightning Lane is separate from Genie+; you don't need to purchase Genie+ to purchase ILL. Likewise, purchasing ILL does not get you access to the other attractions in the Genie+ portfolio.

At press time, these were the Individual Lightning Lane attractions in each park:

- **Magic Kingdom** Seven Dwarfs Mine Train and Tron Lightcycle/Run

- **EPCOT** Guardians of the Galaxy: Cosmic Rewind

- **Hollywood Studios** Star Wars: Rise of the Resistance

- **Animal Kingdom** Avatar Flight of Passage

COST: Varies by attraction, day of year, and time of day. The lowest cost we've seen so far for an ILL is $7, at Space Mountain. The highest cost (so far) is $27 at Rise of the Resistance. We expect these prices to increase.

IS ILL WORTH THE COST? For certain rides. The table on the opposite page shows how much time you're likely to save at each ILL attraction on a busy day, along with the maximum cost we've seen for that ILL.

As a rough estimate, the highest-priced one-day park ticket costs about $15 per hour you're in the park (assuming $170 for the ticket over 11 hours). So, any ILL that costs less than around $15.40 per hour saved is a good deal. Only Avatar Flight of Passage meets that criterion.

DISNEY GENIE Disney announced the Genie itinerary-planning feature of the MDE app in 2019 and said little more about it for the next two years. Originally, Genie sounded a lot like our computer-optimized touring plans: You'd tell Genie what rides you want to ride, and Genie would plan your day to minimize your wait in line.

But that's not at all what Genie does. In fact, Genie is one of the worst products Disney has ever produced. Its real purpose isn't to plan

INDIVIDUAL LIGHTNING LANE (ILL) SAVINGS ANALYSIS			
ATTRACTION	**AVERAGE MINUTES IN LINE SAVED ON A VERY BUSY DAY**	**HIGHEST COST**	**COST PER SAVED MINUTE/HOUR**
Avatar Flight of Passage *Animal Kingdom*	91	$16	$0.18/$11
Individual Lightning Lanes below this line are often not a good use of money			
Seven Dwarfs Mine Train *Magic Kingdom*	57	$16	$0.27/$17
Star Wars: Rise of the Resistance* *Hollywood Studios*	69	$27	$0.39/$23
Guardians of the Galaxy *EPCOT*	27	$18	$0.67/$40
Tron Lightcycle/Run *Magic Kingdom*	Not enough data at press time		

Note: ILL prices (at press time) include tax and are rounded to the nearest dollar.

*We recommend that readers determined to ride Rise of the Resistance purchase an ILL for it. As noted on page 53, Rise breaks down often enough that using the standby line risks wasting too much time and never riding.

your day—because it doesn't. It's to serve Disney's park management needs. To understand why requires some background.

Around 2010, Disney's guest survey data indicated that people who used the original, free Fastpass system were more satisfied than those who used it less. To encourage more use (and get higher satisfaction), Disney launched FastPass+ as a free service and allowed guests to grab three ride reservations before they set foot in the park.

A lot of ride capacity is needed to give each guest at least three FastPasses per day. Think about it—if there are 60,000 people in the Magic Kingdom, up to 180,000 individual rides were the bare minimum needed to give each of them three FastPasses. To get that capacity, Disney had to offer FastPass+ at many attractions that guests wouldn't normally ride if they had to wait in the standby line, such as Mad Tea Party in the Magic Kingdom or Journey into Imagination with Figment in EPCOT.

Making that many FastPasses available, at rides located around the park, turned FastPass+ into a very effective crowd-distribution tool; you had to move around the park to use those FastPasses.

As we said in previous editions, spreading guests throughout the park made the waits at the headliner rides slightly lower. It was a classic win–win: Guests were more satisfied, and Disney's ride-utilization numbers improved. We considered FastPass+ to be one of the great industrial engineering achievements of its decade, and we still believe that.

So, FastPass+ lowered wait times at headliner attractions by (1) giving guests at least three free reservations and (2) using less popular attractions around the park as additional system capacity to provide those three rides per guest.

Genie, Minus the Plus

Now consider the Genie+ ride reservation system. It costs money, so fewer people use it than used FastPass+. That means Disney loses the all-important crowd-distribution mechanism that FastPass+ provided. The risk to Disney's park operations is that guests just queue up for Disney's best, most popular rides, resulting in long lines, while other attractions sit underused.

That's where Genie comes in—it sends guests to lower-rated, less popular attractions that they wouldn't have otherwise visited and directs crowds away from the parks' most popular attractions. That's a bold claim, but it has been borne out in our field-testing. For example, we tested Genie one day in Hollywood Studios. Arriving at 8:30 a.m., in time for Early Entry, Len fired up the Genie app to get Genie's recommendations. Here was the morning itinerary that Genie suggested:

9:30 a.m. Ride Toy Story Mania!

10:20 a.m. Buy a droid in Galaxy's Edge.

11:10 a.m. Eat lunch at Ronto Roasters.

That's right, reader: Genie knew Len was in the park at 8:30 a.m. At that hour, waits at Tower of Terror, Rock 'n' Roller Coaster, and Toy Story Mania! were well below 5 minutes (we had another researcher ride them to check). Despite no lines at these headliners, Genie suggested just one ride in the first 3½ hours Len was in the park.

Genie also tried to upsell Len on the benefits of Genie+ and Individual Lightning Lane purchases, and suggested he buy a $100 *Star Wars* droid. All told, Genie immediately suggested three ways for Len to spend money before noon, but only one ride.

It got worse. When Len declined Genie's invitation to buy a droid at 10:20 a.m., Genie suggested these four attractions instead:

Walt Disney Presents

Disney Junior Play and Dance!

Lightning McQueen's Racing Academy

Alien Swirling Saucers

Let us point out that Genie suggested that Len—a middle-aged man in the park by himself—see two stage shows designed expressly for small children or go on a midway-style ride also designed for small children. Setting aside the ick factor, these are also four of the lowest-rated attractions in the park.

The afternoon portion of Len's Genie's itinerary looked like this:

12:10 p.m. Ride *Millennium Falcon:* Smugglers Run.

2:00 p.m. Experience Star Tours—The Adventures Continue.

2:35 p.m. Ride Star Wars: Rise of the Resistance (using standby line).

4:30 p.m. Ride Alien Swirling Saucers.

5:35 p.m. See *Muppet-Vision 3-D.*

6:00 p.m. Eat dinner at ABC Commissary.

6:40 p.m. See the *Vacation Fun* Mickey Mouse movie.

7:30 p.m. Ride The Twilight Zone Tower of Terror.

8:45 p.m. Watch the *Wonderful World of Animation* projection show.

Rise of the Resistance broke down before Len could ride it, and Genie swapped Rise out for Slinky Dog Dash. While Rise resumed operation shortly after, Genie never suggested it to Len again that day.

It's worth noting that Genie's initial 12½-hour plan didn't include Mickey and Minnie's Runaway Railway, Slinky Dog Dash, or Rock 'n' Roller Coaster—some of the park's highest-rated attractions for his age group. And while Len eventually got on Slinky, he missed out on Rise of the Resistance. So in a full day in the park, with plenty of time, Len experienced just three of the top five rides.

Other readers have chimed in with experiences like Len's. Here's one from a family from Green Bay, Wisconsin:

> We were VERY disappointed with the new Genie app. It was tedious to use, not intuitive, and showed us things we could care less about and could not remove from our screens. How many times in a day must we tell the app that we don't want to go to Swiss Family Treehouse?

A family from Chicago chimes in with this:

> We only did one Disney park—Hollywood Studios—and it was such a train wreck, with ride closures and a Genie system that never worked to offer a reservation slot all day, that we cut our losses, ate the mistake of $140 each for tickets, and left at 4 p.m., having done only THREE rides. Never again would any of us give a single dollar to Disney parks.

What happened in the Studios isn't unusual: In every park where we've tried Genie, it asked us what rides we wanted to ride and produced an itinerary that ignored all or some of those choices. In the Magic Kingdom, for example, we've told Genie that we want to ride Big Thunder Mountain and Splash Mountain, only to have Genie suggest Swiss Family Treehouse, *Walt Disney's Enchanted Tiki Room*, and *Country Bear Jamboree* instead.

Another odd Genie behavior is that there doesn't seem to be a way to tell it when you want to leave the park. The only way it works right now is by assuming you'll be in the park until it closes. Obviously, it's harder to make an itinerary with a time constraint. But it's also safe to say that Disney wants you in the park all day, so you'll spend as much money as possible.

We've heard that guest satisfaction survey results for Genie are terrible. One insider described them as "disastrous" and "far below even the lowest expectations." That's not surprising.

As we see it, Genie is two parts crowd control for Disney park operations, two parts upselling engine, and one part planning app. Genie is unlikely to get you to all of a park's highest-rated attractions. Needless to say, we don't think it's a substitute for our touring plans. We don't think it's good, period.

COST: The basic version of Genie is free. It is not worth that.

---

6. USE THE SINGLE-RIDER LINE *(if available)*

THIS TIME-SAVER, a line for individuals riding alone, is available at **Test Track** in EPCOT, **Expedition Everest** in Animal Kingdom, and **Rock 'n' Roller Coaster Starring Aerosmith** and *Millennium Falcon:* **Smugglers Run** at Hollywood Studios. The objective is to fill odd spaces left by groups that don't quite fill the ride vehicle. Because there aren't many singles and most groups are unwilling to split up, single-rider lines are usually shorter.

MAKING *the* MOST *of* YOUR MONEY

When you're immersed in it and not paying attention to how you're being fleeced, it's still amazing.

—A reader from Baltimore, Maryland

ALLOCATING MONEY

HOW MUCH DOES A DISNEY VACATION COST?

EVERY YEAR, WE HEAR FROM tens of thousands of families who are either planning or just back from a Disney vacation, and we talk with travel agents who hear from thousands more. The thing that surprises these families the most is how expensive their trip turned out to be.

So that you know what you're dealing with up front, we've created the table on pages 70–72. It shows how much Disney vacation you get for $1,500, $2,000, $3,000, and $4,000, for families of various sizes. Most cells contain a list of options, such as the type of hotel (off-site budget, Disney Value, Disney Moderate, or Disney Deluxe) or the type of restaurant (counter-service or sit-down). These options illustrate the trade-offs you should consider when planning your trip—and there *will* be trade-offs. Here's an example for a family of two adults and one child with a $2,000 budget, excluding transportation:

OPTION A Two full days at a Disney's theme park, two days of counter-service meals, and one night at a Disney Deluxe resort

OPTION B Three full days at a Disney's theme parks, three days of counter-service meals, and three nights at a budget off-site motel

In this case, and in general, your choice is between (1) a nicer hotel or (2) a longer trip (meaning more time in the parks) at a cheaper hotel. You may also get better meals every day.

If you'd like to plug in your own numbers, you can download our spreadsheet at tinyurl.com/wdwyouget2024. Ticket prices are based on Disney's February 2023 costs and include tax. All hotel prices are quoted for summer nights in 2023 and include tax. These prices include a summer 2023 discount of around 15%–25%. What you'll pay later in the year may be higher.

Here are the assumptions we made to go along with actual prices from Disney's website:

- Children are ages 3-9; adults are ages 10 and up.
- One night at a non-Disney budget hotel—the Rodeway Inn Kissimmee Maingate West—booked through the hotel, costs $67.
- One night at any of Disney's All-Star Resorts (all had the cheapest Disney Value resort rates at press time) costs $176 on the WDW website.
- One night at Disney's Coronado Springs Resort (the cheapest Disney Moderate resort at the time) costs $241 using Disney's website.
- One night in a studio at Disney's Old Key West (the cheapest Disney Deluxe/ Disney Vacation Club resort at press time) costs $390 using Disney's website.
- A day's worth of counter-service meals, plus one snack, costs $59 for adults and $44 for kids.
- A counter-service breakfast and lunch, a snack, and a table-service meal costs $90 per adult and $57 per child.

In most places in the table, theme park admission ranges from 35% to 60% of the cost of a trip, regardless of family size. If you're not staying at a Deluxe resort, it's safe to assume that ticket costs will take half of your budget (again, excluding transportation).

It's a different story for off-site hotels, which lack services like free shuttles and extra time in the theme parks. Excellent third-party resorts, such as the **Sheraton Vistana** and **Marriott's Harbour Lake,** offer *two-bedroom* rates up to 65% less than those of Disney's cheapest one-bedroom Deluxe hotels. It helps considerably if you have a car, even if you factor in the cost of gas.

How to Save Over $500 on Your Trip

This guide describes many techniques for saving money on a Walt Disney World vacation, including finding an inexpensive hotel, discounts on third-party admission tickets, and budget-friendly restaurants. But sometimes you can do all of that and *still* need to cut your budget.

TouringPlans.com blogger **Kristi Fredericks** offers six simple ways to save over $500 on your Disney vacation.

For each of these tips, assume a family of four traveling to Walt Disney World for a one-week (six-day, seven-night) vacation. Our sample family includes two adults and two children ages 3 and 9.

continued on page 73

WHAT YOU PAY AND WHAT YOU GET AT WDW

2 ADULTS/$4,000	2 ADULTS, 2 KIDS/$4,000
BUDGET OPTION ($4,182) • 10 days theme park admission, parking • 10 nights at a budget off-site motel • 10 sit-down dinners	**BUDGET OPTION ($3,978)** • 5 days theme park admission, parking • 5 nights at a budget off-site motel • 5 counter-service meals
VALUE OPTION ($3,958) • 8 days theme park admission • 9 nights at a Disney Value resort • 8 counter-service meals	**VALUE OPTION ($3,976)** • 4 days theme park admission • 5 nights at a Disney Value resort • 4 counter-service meals
MODERATE OPTION ($3,890) • 7 days theme park admission • 7 nights at a Disney Moderate resort • 7 counter-service meals	**MODERATE OPTION ($4,063)** • 4 days theme park admission • 4 nights at a Disney Moderate resort • 4 counter-service meals
DELUXE OPTION ($3,819) • 5 days theme park admission • 5 nights at a Disney Deluxe resort • 5 counter-service meals	**DELUXE OPTION ($3,927)** • 3 days theme park admission • 4 nights at a Disney Deluxe resort • 3 counter-service meal

2 ADULTS, 1 KID/$4,000	3 ADULTS/$4,000
BUDGET OPTION ($4,187) • 8 days theme park admission, parking • 9 nights at a budget off-site motel • 8 counter-service meals	**BUDGET OPTION ($3,914)** • 7 days theme park admission, parking • 7 nights at a budget off-site motel • 7 counter-service meals
VALUE OPTION ($4,185) • 6 days theme park admission • 7 nights at a Disney Value resort • 6 counter-service meals	**VALUE OPTION ($4,123)** • 6 days theme park admission • 6 nights at a Disney Value resort • 6 counter-service meals
MODERATE OPTION ($3,911) • 5 days theme park admission • 5 nights at a Disney Moderate resort • 5 counter-service meals	**MODERATE OPTION ($4,194)** • 5 days theme park admission • 5 nights at a Disney Moderate resort • 3 counter-service meals, 2 sit-down dinners
DELUXE OPTION ($3,925) • 4 days theme park admission • 4 nights at a Disney Deluxe resort • 4 sit-down dinners	**DELUXE OPTION ($3,927)** • 3 days theme park admission • 4 nights at a Disney Deluxe resort • 3 counter-service meals

3 ADULTS, 1 KID/$4,000	
BUDGET OPTION ($4,076) • 5 days theme park admission, parking • 5 nights at a budget off-site motel • 5 counter-service meals	**MODERATE OPTION ($4,143)** • 4 days theme park admission • 4 nights at a Disney Moderate resort • 4 counter-service meals
VALUE OPTION ($3,988) • 4 days theme park admission • 4 nights at a Disney Value resort • 3 counter-service meals, 1 sit-down dinner	**DELUXE OPTION ($3,988)** • 3 days theme park admission • 4 nights at a Disney Deluxe resort • 3 counter-service meals

2 ADULTS/$3,000	2 ADULTS, 2 KIDS/$3,000
BUDGET OPTION ($3,077) • 8 days theme park admission, parking • 8 nights at a budget off-site motel • 8 counter-service meals	**BUDGET OPTION ($2,901)** • 3 days theme park admission, parking • 4 nights at a budget off-site motel • 4 counter-service meals
VALUE OPTION ($3,100) • 6 days theme park admission • 6 nights at a Disney Value resort • 6 counter-service meals	**VALUE OPTION ($3,071)** • 3 days theme park admission • 3 nights at a Disney Value resort • 1 counter-service meal, 2 sit-down dinners
MODERATE OPTION ($3,074) • 5 days theme park admission • 5 nights at a Disney Moderate resort • 5 counter-service meals	**MODERATE OPTION ($3,090)** • 3 days theme park admission • 3 nights at a Disney Moderate resort • 3 counter-service meals
DELUXE OPTION ($2,800) • 4 days theme park admission • 3 nights at a Disney Deluxe resort • 4 counter-service meals	**DELUXE OPTION ($2,929)** • 2 days theme park admission • 3 nights at a Disney Deluxe resort • 2 sit-down dinners

WHAT YOU PAY AND WHAT YOU GET AT WDW *(continued)*

2 ADULTS, 1 KID/$3,000	3 ADULTS/$3,000
BUDGET OPTION ($3,142) • 5 days theme park admission, parking • 5 nights at a budget off-site motel • 5 counter-service meals	**BUDGET OPTION ($2,861)** • 4 days theme park admission, parking • 5 nights at a budget off-site motel • 4 counter-service meals
VALUE OPTION ($3,142) • 4 days theme park admission • 4 nights at a Disney Value resort • 3 counter-service meals, 1 sit-down dinner	**VALUE OPTION ($3,147)** • 4 days theme park admission • 4 nights at a Disney Value resort • 4 counter-service meals
MODERATE OPTION ($3,088) • 4 days theme park admission • 3 nights at a Disney Moderate resort • 4 counter-service meals	**MODERATE OPTION ($2,831)** • 3 days theme park admission • 4 nights at a Disney Moderate resort • 3 counter-service meals
DELUXE OPTION ($2,812) • 3 days theme park admission • 2 nights at a Disney Deluxe resort • 3 sit-down dinners	**DELUXE OPTION ($3,037)** • 3 days theme park admission • 3 nights at a Disney Deluxe resort • 3 counter-service meals

3 ADULTS, 1 KID/$3,000	
BUDGET OPTION ($3,009) • 3 days theme park admission, parking • 3 nights at a budget off-site motel • 3 sit-down dinners	**MODERATE OPTION ($3,016)** • 3 days theme park admission • 2 nights at a Disney Moderate resort • 2 counter-service meals, 1 sit-down dinner
VALUE OPTION ($2,954) • 3 days theme park admission • 3 nights at a Disney Value resort • 3 counter-service meals	**DELUXE OPTION ($3,005)** • 2 days theme park admission • 3 nights at a Disney Deluxe resort • 2 sit-down dinners

2 ADULTS/$2,000	2 ADULTS, 2 KIDS/$2,000
BUDGET OPTION ($2,047) • 4 days theme park admission, parking • 5 nights at a budget off-site motel • 4 counter-service meals	**BUDGET OPTION ($2,001)** • 2 days theme park admission, parking • 3 nights at a budget off-site motel • 2 sit-down dinners
VALUE OPTION ($1,946) • 3 days theme park admission • 4 nights at a Disney Value resort • 3 counter-service meals	**VALUE OPTION ($2,020)** • 2 days theme park admission • 2 nights at a Disney Value resort • 1 counter-service meal, 1 sit-down dinner
MODERATE OPTION ($1,967) • 3 days theme park admission • 3 nights at a Disney Moderate resort • 3 counter-service meals	**MODERATE OPTION ($2,062)** • 2 days theme park admission • 2 nights at a Disney Moderate resort • 2 counter-service meals
DELUXE OPTION ($1,735) • 2 days theme park admission • 2 nights at a Disney Deluxe resort • 2 sit-down meals	**DELUXE OPTION ($2,059)** • 2 days theme park admission • 1 night at a Disney Deluxe resort • 1 counter-service meal, 1 sit-down dinner

2 ADULTS, 1 KID/$2,000	3 ADULTS/$2,000
BUDGET OPTION ($2,067) • 3 days theme park admission, parking • 3 nights at a budget off-site motel • 3 counter-service meals	**BUDGET OPTION ($2,061)** • 3 days theme park admission, parking • 2 nights at a budget off-site motel • 3 counter-service meals
VALUE OPTION ($2,045) • 2 days theme park admission • 3 nights at a Disney Value resort • 1 counter-service meal, 2 sit-down dinners	**VALUE OPTION ($1,773)** • 2 days theme park admission • 3 nights at a Disney Value resort • 2 counter-service meals
MODERATE OPTION ($1,929) • 2 days theme park admission • 3 nights at a Disney Moderate resort • 2 counter-service meals	**MODERATE OPTION ($2,062)** • 2 days theme park admission • 2 nights at a Disney Moderate resort • 2 counter-service meals
DELUXE OPTION ($1,986) • 2 days theme park admission • 2 nights at a Disney Deluxe resort • 2 counter-service meals	**DELUXE OPTION ($2,059)** • 2 days theme park admission • 1 night at a Disney Deluxe resort • 1 counter-service meal, 1 sit-down dinner

continued on next page

continued from previous page

WHAT YOU PAY AND WHAT YOU GET AT WDW *(continued)*

3 ADULTS, 1 KID/$2,000

BUDGET OPTION ($2,076)
• 2 days theme park admission, parking
• 3 nights at a budget off-site motel
• 2 sit-down dinners

VALUE OPTION ($2,079)
• 2 days theme park admission
• 2 nights at a Disney Value resort
• 1 counter-service meal, 1 sit-down dinner

MODERATE OPTION ($1,862)
• 2 days theme park admission
• 1 night at a Disney Moderate resort
• 2 counter-service meals

DELUXE OPTION ($2,011)
• 2 days theme park admission
• 1 night at a Disney resort
• 2 counter-service meals

2 ADULTS/$1,500

BUDGET OPTION ($1,574)
• 3 days theme park admission, parking
• 4 nights at a budget off-site motel
• 3 counter-service meals

VALUE OPTION ($1,182)
• 2 days theme park admission
• 2 nights at a Disney Value resort
• 2 counter-service meals

MODERATE OPTION ($1,437)
• 2 days theme park admission
• 2 nights at a Disney Moderate resort
• 2 sit-down dinners

DELUXE OPTION ($1,345)
• 2 days theme park admission
• 1 night at a Disney Deluxe resort
• 2 sit-down dinners

2 ADULTS, 2 KIDS/$1,500

BUDGET OPTION (984)
• 1 day theme park admission, parking
• 2 night at a budget off-site motel
• 1 counter-service meal

VALUE OPTION ($1,269)
• 1 day theme park admission
• 2 nights at a Disney Value resort
• 1 sit-down dinner

MODERATE OPTION ($1,517)
• 1 day theme park admission
• 2 nights at a Disney Moderate resort
• 2 counter-service meals

DELUXE OPTION ($1,219)
• 1 day theme park admission
• 1 night at a Disney Deluxe resort
• 1 counter-service meal

2 ADULTS, 1 KID/$1,500

BUDGET OPTION ($1,523)
• 2 days theme park admission, parking
• 3 nights at a budget off-site motel
• 1 counter-service meal, 1 sit-down dinner

VALUE OPTION ($1,381)
• 2 days theme park admission
• 1 night at a Disney Value resort
• 2 counter-service meals

MODERATE OPTION ($1,522)
• 2 days theme park admission
• 1 night at a Disney Moderate resort
• 1 counter-service meal, 1 sit-down dinner

DELUXE OPTION ($1,413)
• 1 day theme park admission
• 2 nights at a Disney Deluxe resort
• 1 counter-service meal

3 ADULTS/$1,500

BUDGET OPTION ($1,488)
• 2 days theme park admission, parking
• 3 nights at a budget off-site motel
• 2 counter-service meals

VALUE OPTION ($1,515)
• 2 days theme park admission
• 1 night at a Disney Value resort
• 1 counter-service meal, 1 sit-down dinner

MODERATE OPTION ($1,487)
• 2 days theme park admission
• 1 night at a Disney Moderate resort
• 2 counter-service meals

DELUXE OPTION ($1,433)
• 1 day theme park admission
• 2 nights at a Disney Deluxe resort
• 1 counter-service meal

3 ADULTS, 1 KID/$1,500

BUDGET OPTION ($1,111)
• 1 day theme park admission, parking
• 2 nights at a budget off-site motel
• 1 sit-down dinner

VALUE OPTION ($1,528)
• 1 day theme park admission
• 2 nights at a Disney Value resort
• 1 counter-service meal, 1 sit-down dinner

MODERATE OPTION ($1,439)
• 1 day theme park admission
• 2 nights at a Disney Moderate resort
• 1 sit-down dinner

DELUXE OPTION ($1,240)
• 1 day theme park admission
• 1 night at a Disney Deluxe resort
• 1 counter-service meal

continued from page 69

TIP #1: BRING YOUR OWN RAINGEAR

Disney World can be a rainy place no matter what time of year you visit. Bring your own rain ponchos instead of buying at the parks to save some dough.

DON'T Buy 2 adult ponchos x $10 and 2 kids' ponchos x $9 = **$38**
DO Buy 4 ponchos at local dollar store = **$4**
SAVINGS $38 – $4 = **$34**

TIP #2: BUY TICKETS IN ADVANCE

Disney adds a $21.30 surcharge to every ticket of three days or longer that is bought at its theme parks. Why? Because it can; Disney knows that you're not likely to turn the kids around and leave once you're that close.

DON'T Wait until you get to the parks to buy tickets.
DO Buy tickets in advance either from Disney or from one of our recommended ticket wholesalers (see page 78).
SAVINGS $21.30 x 4 tickets = **$85**

TIP #3: BRING YOUR OWN STROLLER

Our sample family will need a stroller for their 3-year-old in the parks, and it's handy to have a stroller for the airport and resort areas as well. Remember that most airlines will gate-check your stroller for free.

DON'T Rent a stroller for $15 per day (length-of-stay rate) x 6 days = **$90**
DO Buy 1 umbrella stroller on Amazon = **$32**
SAVINGS $90 – $32 = **$58**

TIP #4: DRINK FREE WATER

All Disney restaurants will give you a free cup of ice water. Instead of wasting money and calories on sugary drinks, this is an easy way to save some cash. For our sample family, let's assume that everyone wants to drink something other than water at breakfast and that the kids' meals will include a drink at lunch and dinner. Only the adults will drink free water, and only at lunch and dinner.

DON'T Buy 1 beverage at $4.29 each x 2 adults x 2 meals x 6 days = **$103**
DO Drink free water = **$0**
SAVINGS $110 – $0 = **$103**

TIP #5: BRING YOUR OWN SNACKS

It's amazing how much you can save by bringing your own nonperishable snacks into the park. A zip-top plastic bag filled with cereal bars, granola, raisins, and crackers goes a long way toward staving off hunger.

DON'T Buy 1 snack at $4 each x 4 people x 2 times x 6 days = **$192**
DO Bring your own snacks = **$60**
SAVINGS $192 – $60 = **$132**

TIP #6: EAT BREAKFAST IN YOUR ROOM

This saves you time and a small fortune. Let's assume our family will grab two coffees and two milks from their hotel's food court each morning, so we won't include beverages in either cost.

DON'T Buy one $13 breakfast platter + one $7 yogurt parfait + two $8 kids' Mickey waffle meals x 6 days = **$216**
DO Bring your own breakfast, including paper bowls, napkins, plastic spoons, cereal, breakfast pastries, mini doughnuts, and cereal bars = **$90**
SAVINGS $216 – $90 = **$126**

TOTAL SAVINGS **$538** *(about $90 per day)*

FOUR MORE TIPS FROM BOB

1. Buy your admission online from one of the sellers on page 78. Get tickets only for the number of days you plan to visit, skipping any add-ons.

2. Book a hotel outside of Walt Disney World. Hotels on US 192 (Irlo Bronson Memorial Highway) are usually the least expensive. Or consider renting a vacation home (see discussion starting on page 223) if you have four or more people in your group.

3. Avoid parking fees by using your hotel's shuttle service or by taking a Disney bus from the water parks or Disney Springs (where—for the moment—parking is free) to a Disney hotel, then to your chosen theme park. This suggestion takes a lot of time, so do it only if you're budgeting to the penny.

4. Buy discounted Disney-brand apparel and souvenirs from one of Orlando's two **Disney Character Warehouse** outlets (tinyurl.com/disneyoutlets).

WALT DISNEY WORLD ADMISSION TICKETS

DISNEY OFFERS THOUSANDS of theme park ticket options, ranging from the humble **1-Day Base Ticket,** which is good for a single day's entry into one Disney theme park, to the blinged-out **Incredi-Pass,** good for 365 days of admission into every Disney theme park and more attractions. See pages 76–77 for a summary of the most common admission types.

For date-based tickets with a start date before January 9, 2024, a theme park reservation is required for each day you plan to use your tickets (see page 30). Make reservations using the **Disney Park Pass** system as far in advance as possible. Capacity is limited, and buying tickets, even directly from Disney and for specific dates, doesn't guarantee you a reservation. Thus, there's a risk you could purchase tickets that cannot be used, especially during busier dates.

If you purchased tickets and were planning to use them between March 12 and July 11, 2020, Disney automatically extended those tickets to be used on any date through September 26, 2021. If you didn't visit before September 26, 2021, you can apply the value of the unused portion of your tickets to new tickets bought after that date. To speak to Disney about your specific situation, call ☎ 407-939-1289. Set aside at least 4 hours to wait on hold for this call.

DATE-BASED PRICING AND OTHER SURCHARGES

DISNEY USES DATE-BASED PRICING for theme park tickets, meaning prices fluctuate depending on the date, similar to the way hotel rooms and airline flights are priced. Likewise, 1-day tickets for the Magic Kingdom usually cost more than for the other parks.

Tickets are now generally most expensive when children are out of school: Christmas and other holidays, spring break, and summer vacation. Less-expensive tickets are generally available during non-holiday periods when children are in school and during months subject to inclement weather: January and February, for example, and peak hurricane season in September.

You must tell Disney the first date you plan to visit a theme park or water park. Your ticket price will be based on that starting date, the number of days you plan to visit theme parks or water parks, and whether you plan to visit more than one theme park per day.

If you need to move your vacation dates from more-expensive to less-expensive days, Disney will not refund the difference in ticket prices—but they will charge you the incremental cost if you need to move from less-expensive to more-expensive days.

TICKET ADD-ONS

THREE TICKET ADD-ON OPTIONS are available with your park admission, each at an additional cost:

PARK HOPPER Lets you visit more than one theme park per day. The cost is about $90–$100 on top of the base ticket price. The longer your stay, the more affordable it is: As an add-on to a 7-Day Base Ticket, for example, the flat fee works out to around $14 a day for park-hopping privileges; as an add-on to a 2-Day Base Ticket, the fee can be $45 a day. If you want to visit the Magic Kingdom in the morning and eat in EPCOT in the evening, this is the feature to request.

If you are park hopping, you must make a reservation for the first park you wish to visit *and* must enter that park first. While you don't need to make a reservation for your second park, you will not be allowed to hop to that park until 2 p.m. (The 2 p.m. time was strictly enforced at press time, but that's subject to change.) As mentioned, you must enter the park for which you made your reservation before you enter a second park. Thus, if you made park reservation for the Magic Kingdom but did not go, you have two options:

- Cancel your Magic Kingdom park reservation and obtain a day-of park reservation for EPCOT.
- Go to the Magic Kingdom and tap in to enter. Then turn around and go to EPCOT.

WATER PARK AND SPORTS This $75 (including tax) option provides daily entry to Disney's two water parks (Blizzard Beach and Typhoon Lagoon), the Oak Trail Golf Course, Fantasia Gardens and Winter Summerland minigolf, and the ESPN Wide World of Sports Complex.

PARK HOPPER PLUS The Park Hopper Plus (PHP) option combines the Park Hopper and Water Park and Sports add-ons. This option costs $90–$122 more than a Base Ticket, including tax, which is cheaper than the combined cost of the two options purchased separately.

You can't change how many Park Hopper/Water Park/PHP admissions you can buy with either option; the number is fixed, and unused days aren't refundable. You can, however, skip Park Hopper/Water Park/PHP entirely and buy an individual admission to any of the above venues—that's frequently the best deal if you're not park-hopping and want to visit just Typhoon Lagoon and/or Blizzard Beach once.

If you buy a ticket but then decide later that you want to add the Park Hopper/PHP option, you can do so. Disney doesn't prorate the cost: If you add Park Hopper/PHP on the last day of your trip, you'll pay the same price as if you'd bought it before you left home.

WDW THEME PARK TICKET OPTIONS

	1-DAY	2-DAY	3-DAY	4-DAY	5-DAY
USE WITHIN: 1 DAY	4 DAYS	5 DAYS	7 DAYS	8 DAYS
BASE TICKET AGES 3–9					
ALL PARKS: $111–$196	$227–$348	$347–$513	$466–$654	$503–$734
—	($114–$174/day)	($116–$171/day)	($116–$164/day)	($101–$147/day)
BASE TICKET AGE 10+					
ALL PARKS: $116–$169	$236–$358	$362–$528	$485–$673	$524–$755
—	($118–$179/day)	($121–$176/day)	($121–$168/day)	($105–$151/day)

Base Ticket admits guest to one theme park each day of use. Tickets must be used within the number of days shown in the "Use Within" row above.

PARK HOPPER					
AGES 3–9: $190–$263 AGE 10+: $195–$268	$306–$439 $316–$449	$427–$604 $442–$619	$556–$755 $575–$775	$594–$835 $614–$856

Park Hopper option entitles guest to visit more than one theme park on each day of use. See page 75 for details.

WATER PARK AND SPORTS					
AGES 3–9: NOT SOLD AGE 10+: NOT SOLD	$301–$423 $311–$433	$422–$588 $437–$603	$540–$729 $559–$748	$578–$808 $598–$830

Water Park and Sports entitles you to a specified number of visits (between 1 and 10) to a choice of entertainment and recreation venues. It's a flat $75 fee to add to any ticket for any age and any ticket length.

PARK HOPPER PLUS					
AGES 3–9: $211–$284 AGE 10+: $216–$290	$327–$460 $338–$470	$449–$625 $463–$640	$578–$777 $597–$796	$615–$856 $636–$877
1 visit	2 visits	3 visits	4 visits	5 visits

Park Hopper Plus option entitles guest to a specified number of visits (1–10) to a choice of entertainment and recreation venues, plus the Park Hopper option above. PHP tickets expire 1 day later than the "Use Within" days above.

WHEN TICKETS EXPIRE
(for tickets dated August 13, 2021, and later)

ALONG WITH IMPLEMENTING date-based pricing, Disney has shortened the amount of time you have to use your tickets. Whereas previously all tickets expired 14 days from the date of first use, ticket expiration is now based on how many days you're visiting the theme parks and water parks, as shown in the table on page 78.

For example, if you purchase a basic 4-Day Base Ticket and specify that you'll start using it on June 1, 2023, you must complete your four theme park visits by midnight June 7, 2023. *Once you start using your ticket, any unused admissions expire even if you don't use them.*

If you purchase a ticket and don't use any of it before it expires, you can apply the amount paid for that ticket toward the purchase of a new ticket at current prices, provided the new ticket's price is the same cost (or more) of the expired ticket.

ANNUAL PASSES

ANNUAL PASSES PROVIDE UNLIMITED USE of the major theme parks for one year. Pass holders can add on a year of water park access

NOTE: ALL TICKET AND ADD-ON PRICES INCLUDE 6.5% SALES TAX.

6-DAY	7-DAY	8-DAY	9-DAY	10-DAY
9 DAYS	10 DAYS	12 DAYS	13 DAYS	14 DAYS
BASE TICKET AGES 3–9				
$519–$777	$524–$797	$570–$817	$593–$830	$614–$845
($87–$130/day)	($76–$114/day)	($71–$102/day)	($66–$92/day)	($61–$85/day)
BASE TICKET AGE 10+				
$540–$800	$556–$820	$593–$841	$617–$855	$638–$870
($90–$133/day)	($79–$117/day)	($74–$105/day)	($69–$95/day)	($64–$87/day)
Park choices are Magic Kingdom, EPCOT, Disney's Hollywood Studios, or Disney's Animal Kingdom.				
PARK HOPPER				
$610–$878 $630–$901	$624–$898 $646–$921	$661–$919 $684–$943	$684–$931 $708–$956	$704–$946 $728–$971
Park choices are any combination of Magic Kingdom, EPCOT, Disney's Hollywood Studios, or Disney's Animal Kingdom on each day of use.				
WATER PARK AND SPORTS				
$593–$852 $614–$874	$609–$872 $631–$895	$645–$892 $668–$916	$668–$905 $692–$929	$688–$919 $712–$945
Choices are Disney's Blizzard Beach water park, Disney's Typhoon Lagoon water park, Oak Trail Golf Course, ESPN Wide World of Sports Complex (if open), and Fantasia or Winter Summerland minigolf.				
PARK HOPPER PLUS				
$630–$900 $652–$922	$646–$919 $668–$943	$682–$940 $705–$964	$705–$953 $729–$977	$725–$967 $750–$992
6 visits	7 visits	8 visits	9 visits	10 visits
Choices are Disney's Blizzard Beach water park, Disney's Typhoon Lagoon water park, Oak Trail Golf Course, ESPN Wide World of Sports Complex (if open), or Fantasia Gardens or Winter Summerland minigolf.				

for an additional $105. Four versions are available (prices are for age 3 and up and include tax):

- The **Pixie Dust Pass** ($425; Florida residents only) lets you have up to three simultaneous park reservations. The Pixie Dust Pass has the most blockout dates, or dates when the pass cannot be used (almost all weekends are off-limits, plus a week or two around every major holiday and chunks of time around minor holidays).

- The **Pirate Pass** ($744; Florida residents only) includes four simultaneous park reservations. Has fewer weekend blockout dates than the Pixie Dust Pass. Retains blockout dates for every major and minor holiday.

- The **Sorcerer Pass** ($957; Florida residents and Disney Vacation Club members only) includes five simultaneous park reservations. The only blockout dates are the Wednesday to Saturday around Thanksgiving, and December 20–January 3 in 2023.

- The **Incredi-Pass** ($1,383; available to everyone) includes five simultaneous park reservations and has no blockout dates.

Holders of all Annual Passes also get perks, including free parking; hotel, dining, and merchandise discounts; and seasonal offers such as a dedicated entrance line at the parks. They can also visit the parks

EXPIRE										
TICKET	1	2	3	4	5	6	7	8	9	10
TICKET EXPIRES ... USE (WITHOUT ...PPER PLUS)	Expires after first use	4	5	7	8	9	10	12	13	14
DAYS TILL TICKET EXPIRES FROM FIRST USE (WITH PARK HOPPER PLUS)	1	5	6	8	9	10	11	13	14	15

after 2 p.m. without needing a reservation (except on Saturdays and Sundays in the Magic Kingdom). Annual Passes are not valid for special events. See disneyworld.disney.go.com/passes for details.

Note: A theme park reservation is required for each day you plan to use your tickets; Annual Passes don't guarantee you a park reservation. In 2024, Disney plans to offer select days on which Pass holders may visit the theme parks without needing a park reservation.

WHERE TO PURCHASE DISNEY WORLD TICKETS

TICKETS ARE AVAILABLE at Disney resorts and theme parks, Disney Stores, and disneyworld.disney.go.com for the prices shown on pages 76–77. (If you purchase on arrival, you will incur a $21.30-per-ticket surcharge for tickets of three days or longer.)

unofficial **TIP**
If you order physical tickets in advance, allow enough time for them to be mailed to your home.

If you're trying to keep your vacation costs to an absolute minimum, consider using an online wholesaler such as **Tripster** (☎ 888-590-5910; tripster.com) or **Boardwalk Ticketing** (boardwalkticketing.com), especially for trips of three or more days in the parks. All tickets are brand new, and the savings can easily exceed $200 for a family of four. Vendors will provide you with electronic tickets just like Disney does, so you'll be able to make park reservations immediately through the My Disney Experience website.

You might be wondering why Disney gives third-party wholesalers such large discounts on tickets. The answer is volume. Disney knows most visitors will pay full price for tickets, so there's no incentive to offer them a discount. However, Disney also knows that there are lots of shoppers who will visit only if they can get a deal. Disney uses third-party wholesalers to offer discounted tickets to those shoppers, so it doesn't have to offer discounts to the general public. It's a win–win–win: The discount shoppers get their deal, Disney maximizes its revenue, and third-party companies earn a little bit too.

Tripster offers discount tickets for almost all Central Florida attractions, including Disney, Universal, and SeaWorld. Boardwalk Ticketing offers them only for Disney. Discounts for the major theme parks range from about 6% to 12%; tickets for other attractions are more deeply discounted.

Finally, tickets are available at some non-Disney hotels and shopping centers and through independent ticket brokers. Because Disney admissions are only marginally discounted in the Walt Disney World–Orlando area, the chief reason for you to buy from an independent broker is convenience. Offers of free or heavily discounted tickets abound, but the catch is they generally require you to attend a time-share sales presentation.

Where *Not* to Buy Tickets and Passes

In addition to the many authorized resellers of Disney admissions, a number of unauthorized ones exist. They buy unused days on legitimately purchased park passes and resell them as if they were brand new.

unofficial TIP
Also steer clear of passes offered on eBay and Craigslist.

These resellers insist that you specify the exact days you plan to use the ticket. They already know, of course, how many days are left on the pass and when it expires. If you tell them that you plan to use it tomorrow and the next two days, then they'll sell you a ticket that has three days left on it and expires in three days. Naturally, because they don't tell you this, you assume that the usual five-day expiration period applies from the date of first use. In the case of your tickets, however, the original purchaser triggered the five-day expiration period. Skip a day instead of using the pass on the next three consecutive days, and you'll discover to your chagrin that it has expired.

HOW TO SAVE MONEY ON DISNEY WORLD TICKETS

DISNEY'S DATE-BASED PRICING SCHEME is the most compli-cated system it has ever used for ticket purchases—so complicated, in fact, that we wrote a computer program to analyze all the options and to look for loopholes in the new pricing rules. Visit **TouringPlans.com** and try our **Ticket Price Comparison Tool** (tinyurl.com/ug-ticketcalcu lator). It aggregates ticket prices from Disney and a number of online ticket vendors. Answer a few questions relating to the size of your party and the parks you intend to visit, and the calculator will identify your four cheapest ticket options. It will also show you how much you'll save versus buying at the gate.

The program will also make recommendations for considerations other than price. For example, Annual Passes might cost more, but Disney often offers substantial resort discounts and other deals to Annual Pass holders. These resort discounts, especially during the off-season, can more than offset the price of the pass.

Our Ticket Calculator will automatically use all of the tips below, and more. If you'd rather do the heavy lifting yourself (please don't), here's what you'll need to consider:

1. BUY PARK TICKETS BEFORE YOU GET TO THE PARKS. As mentioned previously, if you buy at the theme parks, Disney adds a surcharge of $21.30 to park tickets with three or more days of admission.

2. BUY FROM A THIRD-PARTY WHOLESALER. As we've noted, Disney contracts with third-party ticket vendors to offer discounts to con-sumers who'll visit only if they can get a deal. By using other compa-nies, Disney doesn't have to offer those discounts directly to people who'd visit anyway. These vendors sign contracts with Disney and provide the same tickets you'd purchase at Walt Disney World. See opposite page for vendors we recommend.

3. MEMBERS OF THE US MILITARY AND FLORIDA RESIDENTS GET SPECIAL DISCOUNTS. Disney's recent deal for US military personnel included a 4-Day Park Hopper for $350, substantially less than the $719 regular price. Florida resident discounts aren't as steep, but they're better than anything the general public gets.

4. SET YOUR TICKET'S START DATE EARLIER THAN YOUR ARRIVAL DATE. Suppose you're visiting for a long weekend (Thursday–Sunday) and you're buying four-day tickets. You'd naturally pick Thursday as your ticket's start date. But remember that four-day park tickets are valid for seven days. If you're visiting at the start of a busy (i.e., expensive) season, setting your ticket start date to Monday or Tuesday can save around $9 per ticket.

5. BUY A SEPARATE WATER PARK TICKET INSTEAD OF THE WATER PARK AND SPORTS ADD-ON IF YOU'RE VISITING ONLY ONE WATER PARK. The break-even point on the Water Park and Sports option is two water-park visits.

6. VISIT A WATER PARK ON YOUR FIRST OR LAST DAY. Say your trip starts at the end of a busy period and you're already planning one water park visit. Visiting the water park on your first day allows you to set your theme park start date one day later, saving around $4 per ticket. The same advice works in reverse: If your trip ends at the beginning of a busy season, go to the water park on the last day of your trip.

Ticket Deals for Canada Residents

Disney often discounts theme park admission for Canada residents by setting the Canadian dollar at par with the US dollar. The exchange rate as of this writing is $1 CAD equals $0.74 USD, so this deal effectively boosts the value of the Loonie by around 33%. Visit disneyworld.disney.go.com/en_CA/special-offers to see the latest offers.

Ticket Deals for United Kingdom Residents

In the UK, Disney offers advance-purchase tickets that aren't available in the United States. As we went to press, you can get 14-Day **Ultimate Tickets** starting at £519 for adults and £499 for kids—the same price as a 7-Day Ultimate Ticket. Ultimate Tickets provide unlimited admission to major and minor parks along with park-hopping privileges to the major parks. Ultimate Tickets expire 14 days after first use. To find out more, call ☎ 0800-169-0730 UK or 407-566-4985 US (Monday–Friday, 9 a.m.–8 p.m.; Saturday, 9 a.m.–7 p.m.; and Sunday, 10 a.m.–4 p.m.), or see disneyholidays.co.uk/walt-disney-world or the **Disney Information Bulletin Board** (thedibb.co.uk).

Discounts Available to Certain Groups and Individuals

DISNEY VACATION CLUB Members get a discount on Annual Passes.

CONVENTION-GOERS Disney World, Universal Orlando, SeaWorld, and other Orlando-area parks sometimes set up a web link cited in convention materials allowing you to purchase discounted afternoon and evening admissions.

DISNEY CORPORATE SPONSORS If you work for one of these, you may be eligible for discounted admissions or perks at the parks. Check with your workplace's employee-benefits office.

FLORIDA RESIDENTS get substantial savings on virtually all tickets. You'll need to prove Florida residency with a valid driver's license or state identification card.

MILITARY, DEPARTMENT OF DEFENSE, CIVIL SERVICE Active-duty and retired military, Department of Defense (DOD) civilian employees, some civil-service employees, and dependents of these groups can buy Disney multiday admissions at a 9%–10% discount. Military personnel can buy discounted admission for nonmilitary guests if the military member accompanies the nonmilitary guest. If a group seeks the discount, at least half of the group's members must be eligible.

DISNEY IMAGINATION CAMPUS Disney runs educational programs for K–12 students; these programs also offer substantial ticket discounts (but with substantial restrictions). See disneycampus.com.

DISNEY TICKET PRICE INCREASES

DISNEY USUALLY RAISES TICKET PRICES once or twice a year. Hikes were announced in February and December 2022, February 2020, March 2019, February and September 2018, and February 2014–2017.

> *unofficial* **TIP**
> Save money on tickets by planning ahead—buy them before the next price increase.

Prices on all tickets went up an average of almost 9% in 2022, 6% in 2020, 4% in 2019, 9% in 2018, and 7% in 2017. If you're putting together a budget, assume an increase of around 10% per year to be safe.

FOR ADDITIONAL INFORMATION ON TICKETS

IF YOU HAVE A QUESTION regarding admissions that can be addressed only with a person-to-person conversation, call **Disney Ticket Inquiries** at ☎ 407-566-4985 or email ticket.inquiries@disney world.com. If you call, be aware that you may spend considerable time on hold; if you email, that it can take up to three days to get a response. In contrast, the ticket section of the Disney World website, disney world.disney.go.com/tickets, is refreshingly straightforward in showing how ticket prices break down.

TICKETS AND MAGICBANDS

WE'VE USED THE WORD *TICKET* to describe that thing you carry around as proof of your admission to the park. In fact, Disney admission media come in three forms—none of which is a ticket.

One admission medium is a rubber wristband about the size and shape of a small wristwatch. Called a **MagicBand,** it contains a tiny radio frequency identification (RFID) chip, on which is stored a link to the record of your admission purchase in Disney's computers. Your MagicBand also functions as your Disney hotel-room key, and it can (optionally) work as a credit card for most food and merchandise purchases. MagicBands are available for purchase for about $13 each if you're staying off-site, or about $5 if you're staying on-site.

Each member of your family gets their own MagicBand, each with a unique serial number. The wristbands are removable, resizable, and waterproof, and they have ventilation holes for cooling. Eleven colors are available: black, blue, green, mint green, orange, pink, purple, red, yellow, dark gray, and gray (the default). You can choose your colors and personalize your bands when you order them at the Disney World website. More customized bands are available throughout the parks.

Some guests, particularly those with hand- or wrist-mobility issues, find using the MagicBand physically challenging. To help with this, the center portion of the band (essentially a puck the size of a quarter) is removable. The puck can then be placed on a lanyard or clipped on a bag, making it easier to maneuver.

Along with the wristband, each family member will be asked to select a four-digit personal-identification number (PIN) for purchases. See below for details.

If you don't want a MagicBand, you're staying off-property, or you bought your admission from a third-party vendor, your second "ticket" option is a **Key to the World (KTTW) Card,** which is a flexible, credit card–size piece of plastic with an embedded RFID chip.

Your third option is to use the **My Disney Experience** (MDE) app on your Bluetooth-enabled smartphone. This option allows you to "tap" your smartphone for admission at park entrances, in the same way you tap your phone for payments at stores and restaurants.

Of these three options, we think the MagicBands and KTTW Cards are the fastest and easiest to use. The main problem with using the MDE app is that it's far slower to take out your phone, open the app, and find the right screen to do what you want. And that's assuming you don't have to connect to Wi-Fi, log into the app, or remember the password you used.

RFID for Payment, Genie+, Hotel-Room Access, and Photos

Disney's hotel-room doors have RFID readers, allowing you to enter your room simply by tapping your wristband or KTTW Card against the reader, or by telling the MDE app to open the door. RFID readers are also installed at virtually every Disney cash register on-property, allowing you to pay for food, drinks, Genie+ and Individual Lightning Lane reservations, and souvenirs by tapping your MagicBand/KTTW Card against the reader. For in-person purchases, you'll be asked to verify your identity by entering your PIN on a small keypad.

The MDE app requires that you enable Bluetooth transmitting and receiving for tickets, photos, ride reservations, and payments. (Note that doing so will allow your location to be tracked while you're using the app.)

*un**official*** **TIP**
Disney strongly encourages guests to use contactless methods of payment throughout the World. These include MagicBands, ApplePay, Google Pay, credit cards, and debit cards.

If you're using Disney's **Memory Maker** service (see page 455), your MagicBand/KTTW Card serves as the link between your photos and your family. Each photographer carries a small RFID reader, against which you tap your MagicBand, KTTW Card, or (eventually) your phone after having your photo taken. The computers that run the Memory Maker system will link your photos to you, and you'll be able to view them on the Disney World website.

Disney's onboard ride-photo computers incorporate RFID technology too. As you begin down the big drop near the finale of Tiana's Bayou Adventure, for example, sensors read the serial number on your MagicBand (or detect the Bluetooth signal sent from the MDE app on your phone) and pass it to Tiana's cameras. When those cameras snap your family plunging into the briar patch, they attach your MagicBands' serial number to the photo, allowing you to see your ride photos together after you've returned home. Because ride sensors may not pick up the signal from an RFID card or a phone sitting in a wallet or purse, we think onboard ride photos require MagicBands.

PRIVACY CONCERNS Many people are understandably wary of multinational corporations tracking their movements. As noted earlier, guests who prefer not to wear MagicBands or not to download the MDE app can instead obtain KTTW Cards, which are somewhat harder to track (RFID-blocking wallets are available online). Disney says guests who opt out of MagicBands and the MDE app don't get the full range of ride experiences, though, so there's a trade-off.

OPTIONAL EXPENSES

WHICH SPECIAL EVENTS ARE WORTH THE MONEY?

AS A WAY TO "SELL" THE SAME THEME PARK RIDES multiple times per day, Disney constantly experiments with offers of extra time in the parks that require buying separate admission. For example, before the pandemic, the Magic Kingdom hosted a preopening event, regular park hours, and then another event after the park closed to regular guests, all on the same day.

The scope of the events varies: Morning events usually include access to all the rides in just one land, plus breakfast. Evening events typically include most of a park's attractions. Holiday-themed events are held in the evening and include special entertainment, parades, fireworks, and decorations in addition to access to almost all the park's rides; complimentary snacks are also offered. (Guests with tickets to evening events are usually admitted to the parks starting around 4 p.m., allowing them to catch a few extra hours in the parks too.)

Disney restricts the number of tickets sold for these events, from a few hundred at the morning events to less than 30,000 (we've heard) for the Halloween and Christmas events. As a result, wait times for rides at most of these are usually 15 minutes or less. Hyperpopular rides, such as Seven Dwarfs Mine Train or Mickey and Minnie's Runaway Railway, will undoubtedly have longer waits, but nothing like those during the day. The trade-off for the money, therefore, is shorter lines (and often unique entertainment). We think all the events have some value to guests with limited time. To help you decide whether they are worth the cost, we've summarized each below, in the (rough) order we think they're worth. In addition, each theme park chapter includes a table showing which attractions are best experienced during these events.

Finally, as we discuss in Part 7, children rate character greetings and these events' parades and fireworks higher than almost every ride in these parks. If you're looking for good entertainment with short lines for your children, start here.

1. MICKEY'S NOT SO SCARY HALLOWEEN PARTY (Magic Kingdom; select days mid-August–November 1, 7 p.m.–midnight, with ticketed guests allowed into the park starting at 4 p.m.; ticket prices were $116–$212 per person in 2022). With holiday-themed characters and performers, the Magic Kingdom's Halloween parade is the best in Walt Disney World. The event also includes decorations throughout the park; special (often rare) character sightings; fireworks; and occasional, light retheming of a few attractions, plus a boatload of candy if you're interested.

3. DISNEY'S VERY MERRY CHRISTMAS PARTY (Magic Kingdom; select days early November–late December, 7 p.m.–midnight, with ticketed guests allowed into the park starting at 4 p.m.; 2023 prices not available at press time but were $159–$212 per person in 2022). Like the Halloween party, the Christmas party offers holiday decorations and a special parade and fireworks, plus unique shows and live performances by the Disney characters. We like the Halloween parade and character greetings better.

2. MAGIC KINGDOM AFTER HOURS (Magic Kingdom; 3 hours after regular park closing; select Mondays and Thursdays; $159–$169 per person). Yes, it's $170 for 3 hours in the park, but the high cost keeps crowds low. Most rides will have wait times of 5 minutes or less, meaning that the number of rides you can visit depends largely on how fast you can walk between them and how long the rides last.

5. EPCOT AFTER HOURS (EPCOT; 3 hours after regular park closing; typically Thursday but days of week vary; $159 per person). Like at Hollywood Studios, this is the way to see the park's headliners without long lines. Waits are usually so short that the limiting factor to how many rides you'll experience is likely to be the walking distance between Remy's and Guardians of the Galaxy.

4. DISNEY'S HOLLYWOOD STUDIOS AFTER HOURS (Disney's Hollywood Studios; 3 hours after regular park closing; typically Wednesday but days of week vary; $148–$159 per person). If you can't get up early for Rise of the Resistance and you're visiting during a busy time of year, this is the most direct way to experience the ride (multiple times!) with short waits. Plus, nighttime rides on Tower of Terror and Slinky Dog Dash are vastly different than during the day.

5. DISNEY H2O GLOW AFTER HOURS (Typhoon Lagoon; 3 hours after regular park closing; typically Saturday from mid-May through early September; days vary; $75 to $80 per person). During the months with warmer nights, Disney offers after-hours admission to Typhoon Lagoon. Besides the glow-in-the-dark visuals at the wave pool, this event offers some of the shortest lines you'll likely find at a Disney water park.

PART 5

ACCOMMODATIONS

KEY QUESTIONS ANSWERED IN THIS CHAPTER

The BASIC CONSIDERATIONS

LOCATING A SUITABLE HOTEL OR CONDO is critical to planning any Walt Disney World vacation. The basic question is whether to stay at a hotel located inside Disney World ("on-site") or not ("off-site").

unofficial **TIP**
We recommend that most readers' first choice for lodging be an on-site hotel at Walt Disney World (or Universal Orlando). The incremental extra cost is generally more than offset by the room quality, amenities, transportation, and theme park benefits.

Around 86% of *Unofficial Guide* readers stay on-site during their trips. Beyond the convenience and the amenities, readers say they enjoy "being in the Disney bubble"— that is, the special magic and peace of mind associated with staying inside the World. "I feel more a part of everything and less like a visitor," one guest writes. We agree.

The primary reasons to stay off-site are cost and space. Walt Disney World room rates vary from about $150 on a slow weeknight at what Disney calls its Value resorts to over $2,000 per night during the holidays at its Deluxe properties. Outside the World, clean, bare-bones motel rooms can be had for as little as $70 a night. Lodging prices can change, but it's possible to get a hotel room comparable to one at a midtier Disney resort for half the cost during holidays, or a room twice the size for the same money, all within a 15-minute drive of the parks.

There are advantages to staying outside Disney World and driving or taking a hotel shuttle to the theme parks. Meals can be less expensive, and rooming outside the World makes you more receptive to other Orlando-area attractions and eating spots. **Universal Studios** and **Universal's Islands of Adventure, Kennedy Space Center Visitor Complex, SeaWorld,** and **Gatorland** are well worth your attention.

Because Walt Disney World is so large, some off-property hotels are actually closer in both time and distance to many of the theme parks than some Disney resorts are. Check our Hotel Information Table on pages 254–265, which lists commuting times from both Disney and non-Disney hotels.

If you have young children, read Part 7, "Walt Disney World with Kids," before choosing lodging. Seniors, couples on a honeymoon or romantic holiday, and disabled guests should read the applicable sections of Part 8, "Tips for Varied Circumstances," before booking.

Finally, if you're looking for the cheapest room possible on the premise that "it's just a place to sleep," please read our discussion on page 247 first. Our research indicates that most people are happier *not* booking the cheapest room, even when they take the extra cost into account.

THE LATEST IN LODGING

AS WE WERE GOING TO PRESS, Disney was offering limited hotel discounts in the summer of 2023. With only one new attraction opening in the next few years (Tiana's Bayou Adventure in late 2024), Disney may need to discount hotel rooms to give people a reason to visit. So there may be opportunities to stretch your lodging budget.

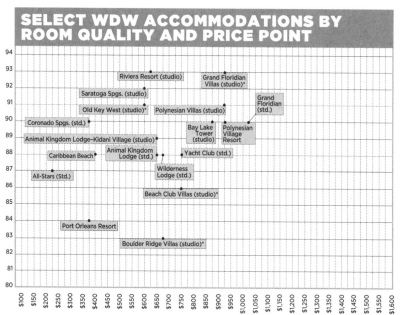

SELECT WDW ACCOMMODATIONS BY ROOM QUALITY AND PRICE POINT

PRICE PER NIGHT

*Disney Vacation Club properties

Speaking of stretching your vacation budget, if you're planning to stay at a Disney Moderate or Deluxe resort, it's possible to get an equivalent or superior room by renting **Disney Vacation Club** (**DVC**) points instead of paying cash (see page 98). In the table on page 97, for example, note that it can be less expensive to rent a one-bedroom villa in Animal Kingdom Lodge than it is to pay cash for a standard room. Likewise, a two-bedroom villa at the Grand Floridian is often less expensive than a standard room at one of the resort's outer buildings. If renting DVC points is outside your budget, see "The Best Off-Site Hotels for Families," page 229, for the best alternatives.

THE BENEFITS OF STAYING IN THE WORLD

GUESTS WHO STAY on Disney property enjoy privileges and amenities unavailable to those staying off-site. Though some of these perks are advertising gimmicks, others are real and potentially valuable. Here are the benefits and what they mean:

1. CONVENIENCE Commuting to the theme parks using the Disney transportation system is easy, especially if you stay in a hotel connected by monorail, boat, or Skyliner.

2. EARLY ACCESS TO ATTRACTION AND RESTAURANT RESERVATIONS Guests at Disney resorts can make **Genie+** reservations (see page 60) starting at 7 a.m.; off-site guests must wait until the park opens. Guests staying on-property can also make dining reservations 60 days before they arrive and then an additional 10 days into their trip.

3. EARLY THEME PARK ENTRY Disney resort guests—along with guests of the **Swan, Dolphin, Swan Reserve, Shades of Green, Signia by Hilton Orlando Bonnet Creek, Waldorf Astoria Orlando, Four Seasons,** and **Disney Springs Resort Area** hotels—enjoy extra time in the theme parks not available to the general public. In many cases, this means shorter waits in line for Disney's most popular rides. See page 36 for details.

4. EXTENDED EVENING THEME PARK HOURS Guests staying at Disney Deluxe resorts and DVC properties, plus the Dolphin, Swan, Swan Reserve, and Shades of Green, get 2 extra hours in the theme parks after they close to regular guests. At the time of this writing, Extended Evening Theme Park Hours were offered one day per week in the Magic Kingdom and EPCOT only. See page 38 for details.

5. SEPARATE POOL OF PARK RESERVATIONS The **Disney Park Pass** reservation system holds a certain number of reservation slots to be used only by Disney resort guests. Thus, even if no park reservations remain for (off-site) Annual Pass holders or (off-site) guests with dated tickets, Disney resort guests might still be able to get reservations. This is a big advantage, especially if you're trying to get into the parks during busier times of the year. See page 30 for more on park reservations.

6. FREE PARKING Disney resort guests pay nothing to park in theme park lots—this saves you $25 per day. Likewise, Disney doesn't charge a fee for overnight parking at its resorts, as most hotels do.

7. GOLFING PRIVILEGES Disney guests get priority tee times at the on-property golf courses.

WDW RESORT PRIVILEGES AT A GLANCE

HOTEL	GENIE+ RESERVATIONS	RESTAURANT RESERVATIONS	EARLY THEME PARK ENTRY	EXTENDED EVENING HOURS
Disney resort hotels and Disney Vacation Club (DVC) properties	Starting at 7 a.m.	Up to 70 days out	Yes	Deluxe, DVC only
Disney Springs Resort Area (DSRA) hotels*	Park opening	60 days out	Yes	No
Four Seasons Orlando	Park opening	60 days out	Yes	No
Shades of Green	Starting at 7 a.m.	60 days out	Yes	Yes
Signia by Hilton Orlando Bonnet Creek	Park opening	60 days out	Yes	No
Swan, Dolphin, and Swan Reserve	Starting at 7 a.m.	60 days out	Yes	Yes
Waldorf Astoria Orlando	Park opening	60 days out	Yes	No
Non-Disney hotels	Park opening	60 days out	No	No

*B Resort & Spa, DoubleTree Suites by Hilton, Drury Plaza Hotel Orlando, Hilton Orlando Buena Vista Palace, Hilton Orlando Lake Buena Vista, Holiday Inn Orlando–Disney Springs, and Wyndham Garden Lake Buena Vista

Note: All table-service restaurants at Disney Springs and the Swan, Dolphin, and Swan Reserve are independently owned and run, as are a handful of other restaurants around the parks (such as Patina Restaurant Group's Tutto Italia and Via Napoli in EPCOT). These non-Disney-owned restaurants take Advance Dining Reservations, but many also accept reservations directly or through OpenTable.com, meaning 1) they may have tables available even when Disney says they don't and 2) depending on the restaurant, you may not have to prebook with a credit card or pay a no-show fee when you make reservations outside of the Disney system.

8. NO RESORT FEES Unlike many hotels outside of Walt Disney World, the on-site hotels don't charge a nebulous nightly resort fee (on top of a parking fee) on top of their advertised rates.

THE PROS AND CONS OF STAYING ON-SITE

1. COST Realistically, you should expect to pay **$150–$175 per night** (including taxes and fees), depending on time of year, for a clean, safe, well-maintained hotel room near Disney World. In this price range, on-site hotels come out ahead. Rooms at the **Pop Century Resort,** for example, cost $195–$365 (before discounts) throughout the year. *Plus* on-site resorts have convenient transportation and perks such as a separate pool of park reservations (see opposite page). In addition, Pop Century has completed a major stylish refurbishment. For an incremental cost of around $45–$100 per night (most times of the year and before discounts), we think Pop is the best Value choice for most readers.

Off-site hotels and homes are often better deals for families looking for more space, or high-end lodging and service, for the same money. For instance, Disney's cheapest family suite, at the **Art of Animation Resort,** sleeps six and costs $460–$840 per night. A comparable room at the **Sonesta ES Suites Lake Buena Vista** costs around $200–$325 per night, depending on the time of year. Renting a three-bedroom condo in Kissimmee is even cheaper: around $160–$260 per night. You can afford a longer trip with those savings—a fact that more than offsets the advantage of park reservations. Similarly, the cheapest room at Disney's flagship **Grand Floridian Resort & Spa** costs about $780–$1,280. The cheapest room at the **Four Seasons Resort Orlando** (adjacent to Walt Disney World) is at the upper end of that range. But the Four Seasons room is larger and better in every way, with restaurants generally as good as or better than the Grand Flo's, along with superior customer service.

While we think Disney's least expensive hotels are worth the incremental cost versus staying off-site, we continue to receive more negative reader comments than ever. The vast majority are decidedly negative about the value of Disney's more expensive hotels. A reader from Noblesville, Indiana, explains:

> We have stayed on-property for every visit, but our next trip will be off-property. The on-property value-added benefits are significantly less than the price increases they've implemented, meaning they've jacked up room rates and are no longer including the 180-day [free] FastPass+ perks, free Magical Express bus service to the airport, etc.

A reader from Colleyville, Texas, stayed at Disney's Art of Animation (a Value resort) and had this to say:

> I chose Art of Animation because we were three adults and wanted two bedrooms and two bathrooms. This was our first budget resort. Our six nights cost almost $4,000—a shocking amount for what we got. Hallways and pool were very noisy from inside the room.
>
> The refrigerator was noisy and designed only for drinks. It could not reach a safe temperature to store food. The food court opened at 7 a.m., so eating before getting to the parks for rope drop was difficult.
>
> The bathroom had a very bright night light whose beam slipped through the cracks of the door. Mounted near the toilet was a motion sensor in the loud fan that flashed a green light as you were in there in the dark. That was a creepy surprise!

This mom from Indiana had similar thoughts about Disney's Caribbean Beach Resort, a Moderate:

> There is no way I would stay at Caribbean Beach again until it has had a major refurbishment. The rooms had one Disney touch that was only visible if the fifth sleeper was open. The air-conditioning didn't work at night, and every room had leaks outside. The shower had about as much water pressure as a garden hose, and the beds didn't allow luggage underneath. Buses were few and far between (but access to the Skyliner was amazing).

It's the same story at Disney's Deluxe resorts, according to this reader from Amarillo, Texas:

> We stayed at the Grand-freaking-Floridian, were on the app at 6:59 every morning, and still had a tough time getting the ride reservations we wanted. As Disney veterans, after two or three days we had figured out what works and what doesn't, but a novice family would walk away from a WDW vacation today with a very bad taste in their mouths.
>
> Dining reservations were impossible to get via normal channels, but the two of us had a lot of luck simply walking up and asking for a table. We were always surrounded by empty tables, so I suspect they're limiting dining reservations because of staffing issues. Service at the hotel was better than last time, but still not worth $770 a night for a lagoon-view room.

Our takeaway from this vacation is that Disney is now officially in the nickel-and-diming business. It's a great product that is incredibly overpriced.

We agree that Disney's Deluxe hotels, and the Grand Floridian and Contemporary in particular, have neither the room quality nor the amenities of comparably priced hotels (that is, they're overpriced). As at the Contemporary, what you're paying for at the Grand Flo is the ability to walk to the Magic Kingdom.

Our ratings of hotel quality, cost, and commuting times to the theme parks include hotels both in and out of the World (see How the Hotels Compare, pages 250–253, and the Hotel Information Table, pages 254–265).

2. EASE OF ACCESS   Even if you do stay in Walt Disney World, you're dependent on some mode of transportation. It may be less stressful to use the Disney transportation system, but with the single exception of commuting to the Magic Kingdom, the fastest, most efficient, and most flexible way to get around is usually a car. If you're in EPCOT, for example, and you want to take your cranky kids back to Disney's Contemporary Resort for a nap, forget the monorail. You'll get back much faster by car.

A Raynham, Massachusetts, reader who stayed at Caribbean Beach Resort writes:

> Even though the resort is on the Disney bus line, I recommend renting a car if it fits your budget. The buses don't go directly to many destinations, and often you have to switch buses. Getting a bus back to the hotel after a hard day can mean a long wait in line.

Readers complain about problems with the Disney transportation system more than most topics. The following comment from a Columbus, Ohio, reader is typical:

> Sometimes it felt like we were visiting Mass Transit World instead of Walt Disney World. More and more of our energy was devoted to planning for getting from point A to point B than there had been in the past. I've never rented a car on-property, but after this trip I might have to consider it.

Although it exists exclusively for the use and benefit of Walt Disney World guests, the Disney transportation system is nonetheless public, and users must expect inconveniences: conveyances that arrive and depart on *their* schedule, not yours; the occasional need to transfer; multiple stops; time lost loading and unloading passengers; and, generally, the challenges of using and managing a large, complex transportation network.

If you plan to have a car, consider this: Walt Disney World is so large that some destinations within the World can be reached more quickly from off-property hotels than from Disney hotels. For example, lodgings on US 192 (near the so-called Walt Disney World Maingate) are closer to Disney's Hollywood Studios, Animal Kingdom, and Blizzard Beach water park than many hotels inside Disney World.

Traffic on I-4 is the largest potential problem with staying at an off-site hotel, especially if you're coming or going during rush hours. Thus, the closer your off-site hotel is to Disney property, the less risk there is in being stuck in I-4 traffic. Secondary roads, such as Turkey

Lake Road, Palm Parkway, International Drive, and Universal Boulevard, can help get you around that traffic; look for shortcuts in Part 9.

A Kentucky dad overruled his family about staying at a Disney resort and is glad he did:

> *My wife read in another guidebook that it can take 2 hours to commute to the parks if you stay outside Walt Disney World. I guess it could take 2 hours if you stayed in Tampa, but from our hotel on US 192, we could commute to any of the parks except the Magic Kingdom and have at least one ride under our belt in about an hour.*

For commuting times from specific non-WDW hotels, see our Hotel Information Table on pages 254–265.

3. FOOD COSTS Many off-site hotels' prices include some sort of free (often prepackaged) breakfast, ranging from fruit and pastries to pancakes, microwavable waffles, bacon, and eggs. The Disney hotels don't. Depending on how hungry your family is in the morning, eating breakfast at your off-site hotel can save you a minimum of $6–$16 per person per day versus breakfast in the parks.

Beyond breakfast, if you have a large family that chows down like cattle on a finishing lot, you may likewise do better staying outside the World, where food is a lot less expensive.

4. YOUNG CHILDREN Although the hassle of commuting to most non-World hotels is only slightly (if at all) greater than that of commuting to Disney hotels, a definite peace of mind results from staying in the World. Regardless of where you stay, make sure you get your young children back to the hotel for a nap each day.

5. SPLITTING UP If you're in a party that will probably split up to tour (as frequently happens in families with teens or children of widely varying ages), staying in the World offers more transportation options and, thus, more independence. Mom and Dad can take the car and return to the hotel for a relaxed dinner and early bedtime while the teens remain in the park for extra rides.

6. VISITING OTHER ORLANDO-AREA ATTRACTIONS If you also plan to visit Universal Orlando, SeaWorld, Kennedy Space Center, or other area attractions, it may be more convenient to stay outside of Walt Disney World.

The DISNEY RESORTS

DISNEY RESORTS 101

BEFORE YOU MAKE ANY DECISIONS, understand these basics regarding Disney resorts.

unofficial **TIP**
Understand that Disney Reservation Center and Walt Disney Travel Company representatives don't have detailed personal knowledge of the resorts.

Disney has four main categories of resorts: **Value, Moderate, Deluxe,** and **Deluxe Villa.** It's a handy system that we'll use in discussing both Disney and off-site hotels. A fifth category, **Campground,** is exclusive to the campsites at **Fort Wilderness Resort.** (*Star Wars:* **Galactic Starcruiser** [see page 196] isn't classified as a hotel; Disney calls it an experience.)

Value resorts have the lowest rates of any Disney-owned hotels, along with the smallest rooms and most limited amenities.

Moderate resorts are a step up from the Values in guest-room quality, amenities, and cost. Disney also classifies **The Cabins at Fort Wilderness Resort** as a Moderate resort.

Deluxe resorts are Disney's top-of-the-line hotels, boasting extensive theming; luxurious rooms; and superior on-site dining, recreation, and services.

Disney Deluxe Villa (DDV) resorts, also known as **Disney Vacation Club (DVC) resorts,** offer suites, some with full kitchens. DDV/DVC resorts, several of which are attached to Deluxe resorts, equal or surpass Deluxe resorts in quality. They can also be a better value.

MAKING RESERVATIONS Whether you book your hotel room through Disney, a travel agent, the internet, a tour operator, or an organization like AAA, you can frequently save by reserving the room exclusive of any vacation package. This is known as a **room-only reservation.** Though later on in this chapter we'll scrutinize the advantages and disadvantages of buying a package (see page 210), we'll go ahead and tell you now that Disney World packages at list price rarely save you any money (although they can certainly be convenient).

We recommend that you book your trip at the Walt Disney World website (disneyworld.disney.go.com) instead of calling the Disney Reservation Center (DRC) at ☎ 407-W-DISNEY (934-7639). Not only is booking online much faster than booking by phone, but DRC reservationists are also focused on selling you a Walt Disney Travel Company package. Even if you insist that all you want is the room, they'll try to persuade you to bundle it

*un*official **TIP**
If you must book by phone, call before 11 a.m. or after 3 p.m. Eastern.

with some small extra, like a minigolf pass, so that your purchase can be counted as a package—this lets Disney apply various restrictions and cancellation policies that you wouldn't be saddled with if you bought just the room by itself.

CANCELLATION POLICIES Regarding cancellation, know that there are some trade-offs. If you book a package and then cancel 2–29 days before arrival, you lose your $200 deposit. If you cancel a day or less before arrival, you lose the entire package cost, including your airfare and insurance. If you reserve only a room and cancel fewer than five days before arrival (six days if you booked through Disney's website), you lose your deposit of one night's room charge, which can easily be more than $200 if you booked at a Moderate, Deluxe, or DDV resort. Further, Disney imposes a $50 fee, plus a $15 processing fee, for changing your package's details—such as adjusting travel dates, moving to a cheaper resort, or adding a discount code—30 days or fewer before your trip.

If you have to book by phone rather than online, tell the agent up front what you want in terms of lodging, and make sure to get a *room-only rate quote.* Then tell the agent what you're looking for in terms of park admissions. When you've pinned down your room selection and lodging costs, ask the agent if there are any deals that beat the à la carte prices. But don't be swayed by little sweeteners included in a package unless they have real value for you. If the first agent you speak to isn't accommodating, hang up and call back—DRC has hundreds of agents, some more helpful than others.

When dealing with Disney reservations, a careful shopper from West Lafayette, Indiana, advises both wariness and toughness:

> *Making reservations through 407-W-DISNEY is like buying a car: You need to know the sales tricks, have a firm idea of what you want, and be prepared to walk away if you don't get it at a price you're willing to pay.*

If you need specific information, call the resort directly, ask for the front desk, and pose your question before phoning the DRC (the person who answers your call almost certainly won't be at the hotel's front desk, but they'll know who to ask). If your desired dates aren't available, keep calling back or checking online. Something might open up.

YOUR HOTEL-ROOM VIEW Rates at Disney hotels vary by season (see page 74) and from room to room according to view. Furthermore, each Disney resort has its own seasonal calendar that varies depending on the resort instead of that tired old 12-months-of-the-year thing the rest of us use. But as confusing as Disney seasons can be, they're logic personified compared with the panoply of guest-room views the resorts offer. Depending on the resort, you can choose standard views, courtyard views, water views, pool views, lagoon views, nature views, garden views, theme park views, or savanna views, among others.

Standard view, the most ambiguous category, crops up at about three-fourths of Disney resorts. It's usually interpreted as a view of infrastructure or unremarkable scenery. In Animal Kingdom Lodge, for example, you have savanna views, pool views, and standard views. Savanna views overlook the replicated African veldt, pool views overlook the swimming pool, and value and standard views offer stunning vistas of . . . rooftops and parking lots.

With a standard view, however, you can at least pinpoint what you *won't* be seeing. Every resort defines views of water differently. At the Grand Floridian Resort & Spa, for example, rooms with views of Seven Seas Lagoon are sensibly called lagoon-view rooms, while those with views of the marina or pools are known as garden-view rooms.

Zip over to the Yacht Club Resort, another Deluxe property. Like the Grand Floridian, it's on a lake and has a pool and a marina. Views of all three are lumped into one big "water" category—anything wet counts! But wait, what's the view of the lake, pool, or waterfall called at the Wilderness Lodge? You guessed it: courtyard.

Our favorite water views are at the Contemporary Resort's South Garden Wing, which extends toward Bay Lake to the east of the giant A-frame. Rooms in this three-story structure, such as room 6109, afford some of the best lake vistas in Disney World (see tinyurl.com /contemporary6109 for a view from one of these rooms). Many rooms are so near the water, in fact, that you could spit a prune pit into the lake from your window. And their category? Garden views.

For many readers, a good view is essential to enjoying their hotel room. Getting the view you want, however, doesn't necessarily mean that you'll have the *experience* you want, as a Rochester, New York, couple points out:

We stayed in the Conch Key building at the Grand Floridian. The view was lovely, but we could hear the boat's horn blasting every 20 minutes, 7 a.m.–midnight. It was obnoxious and kept us up.

It's worth noting that scoring a Grand Floridian room with a view of the Magic Kingdom can require excruciatingly specific verbiage, as a mom from Pontefract, England, attests:

We stayed at the Grand Floridian and paid extra for a Magic Kingdom view. I was soooo disappointed when all I could see from the balcony was Space Mountain. I was so looking forward to sitting on the balcony with a glass of wine and watching the fireworks. Next time I'll ask for a view of Cinderella Castle—not just a Magic Kingdom view.

We could go on, but pinning Disney down on precisely what will be outside your window is the point. In our discussion of individual resorts later in this chapter, we'll tell you which rooms have the best views.

unofficial **TIP**
Disney will guarantee connecting rooms if your party includes more kids than adults. (In Disney terms, *adjoining rooms* are next to each other, and *connecting rooms* have a door between them.)

Our website's **Hotel Room Views** project uses more than 35,000 photos to show the view you get from every Disney-owned hotel room in Walt Disney World, plus instructions on how to request each room. It also has interactive maps for every building in every resort, so you can search for rooms by cost, view, walking distance, noise, accessibility, and more. Visit touringplans.com/walt-disney-world/hotels to see photos of the rooms we recommend.

HOW TO GET THE ROOM YOU WANT Disney won't guarantee a specific room when you book but will post your request on your reservation record. The easiest way to make a request is to use our Hotel Room Views tool, described above. Select the room you want, and we'll automatically email your request to Disney 30 days before you arrive.

Our experience indicates that making a request with just a single room number confuses Disney's reservationists; as a result, they're unsure where to place you if the room you've asked for is unavailable. To increase your odds of getting the room you want, tell the reservationist (or your travel agent) *to the letter* what characteristics and amenities you desire.

Be politely assertive when speaking to the Disney agent. At Port Orleans Riverside, for example, rooms with king beds have options for standard-, garden-, pool-, preferred-, and river-view rooms. If you want to overlook the river, say so; likewise, if you want a pool view, speak up. Similarly, state clearly such preferences as a particular floor, a room near restaurants, or a room away from elevators and ice machines. If

unofficial **TIP**
A week or two before you arrive, call your resort's front desk. Call late in the evening when they're not so busy and reconfirm the requests that by now should be appearing in their computers.

you have a long list of preferences, type it in order of importance and email, fax, or snail-mail it to the hotel. Include your contact information and your reservation-confirmation number. Be brief, though: We're told that Disney's reservation system has a limited amount of space to store what you write.

It will be someone from Disney's Centralized Inventory Management team, or the resort itself, who assigns your room. Call back in a few days to make sure your preferences were posted to your record.

We'll provide the information needed for each resort to frame your requests, including a resort map and our recommendations for specific rooms or buildings. A dash (–) indicates a range of rooms.

Readers say our hotel-request service works about two out of three times. Disney's room assigners tell us that the most common reasons for not getting the exact room requested are as follows:

- **Someone is already in the requested room.** This is common during holidays and other busy times. It helps to list several alternatives.

- **Asking to get into your room early (before 3 or 4 p.m.).** Unless you say otherwise, the front desk will assume that any room currently available overrides your earlier requests.

- **Listing only rooms that are more expensive than the one you paid for.** It doesn't hurt to ask for an upgrade, but make sure you've given the room assigners a fallback option based on what you've bought.

- **Unclear requests.** We've read multipage requests with sentences about room preferences embedded in paragraphs relating the life stories of everyone in the group, and requests with enough picky stuff to rule out every room in the hotel. Make sure that your requests are *succinct* and *realistic.*

HOW TO GET DISCOUNTS ON LODGING

THERE ARE SO MANY GUEST ROOMS IN AND AROUND Disney World that competition is brisk, and everyone, including Disney, wheels and deals to fill them. Disney, however, has its own atypical way of managing its room inventory. To uphold the brand integrity of its hotels, Disney prefers to use inducements rather than discounts per se. For example, in the past Disney has included a Free Dining benefit if you reserved a certain number of nights at rack rate and has offered special deals only by email to returning guests. Consequently, many of the strategies for obtaining discounted rates in most cities and destinations don't work well for Disney hotels. We'll explore these strategies in-depth when we discuss booking non-Disney hotels near Walt Disney World; for the moment, though, here are some tips for getting price breaks at Disney properties.

One of our ongoing major research projects is to identify sellers with the steepest discounts on Disney hotel rooms. Those best discounts are almost certainly found through sites that offer last-minute, one- to four-night DVC deals—where *last-minute* typically means "within 90 days." If you're willing to stay at any Disney hotel as long as it's a great deal, see "Rent Disney Vacation Club Points" on page 98 for details.

Note: Discounts may be limited to a certain number of rooms or certain dates. Rooms at deep discounts tend to get snatched up quickly, so don't take too long to decide what you want to do.

1. LOOK FOR SEASONAL SAVINGS Save 15%–35% per night or more on a Disney hotel room by visiting during the slower times of year. However, Disney has so many seasons in its calendar that it's hard to keep up; plus, the dates for each "season" vary among resorts. Disney

2023 COST PER NIGHT OF DISNEY HOTEL ROOMS (rack rates)

Rates are for standard rooms except as noted.

ALL-STAR RESORTS	$148-$290
ALL-STAR MUSIC RESORT FAMILY SUITES	$338-$658
ANIMAL KINGDOM LODGE	$474-$842
ANIMAL KINGDOM VILLAS (studio, Jambo House/Kidani Village)	$475-$838
ART OF ANIMATION FAMILY SUITES	$428-$839
ART OF ANIMATION RESORT	$231-$392
BAY LAKE TOWER AT CONTEMPORARY RESORT (studio)	$641-$1,110
BEACH CLUB RESORT	$534-$982
BEACH CLUB VILLAS (studio)	$534-$982
BOARDWALK INN	$597-$1,044
BOARDWALK VILLAS (studio)	$597-$1,044
BOULDER RIDGE VILLAS (studio)	$453-$916
CARIBBEAN BEACH RESORT	$310-$479
CONTEMPORARY RESORT (Garden Wing)	$559-$988
COPPER CREEK VILLAS & CASCADE CABINS (studio)	$453-$914
CORONADO SPRINGS RESORT	$294-$446
DOLPHIN (Sheraton)	$222-$367
FORT WILDERNESS RESORT & CAMPGROUND (cabins)	$448-$872
GRAN DESTINO TOWER	$398-$608
GRAND FLORIDIAN RESORT & SPA	$780-$1,279
GRAND FLORIDIAN VILLAS (studio)	$794-$1,279
OLD KEY WEST RESORT (studio)	$457-$744
POLYNESIAN VILLAGE RESORT	$672-$1,184
POLYNESIAN VILLAS & BUNGALOWS (studio)	$672-$1,184
POP CENTURY RESORT	$195-$367
PORT ORLEANS RESORT (French Quarter and Riverside)	$299-$451
RIVIERA RESORT (studio)	$443-$814
SARATOGA SPRINGS RESORT & SPA (studio)	$451-$770
SHADES OF GREEN	$163-$184
STAR WARS: GALACTIC STARCRUISER (rate is for a 2-night stay)	$5,000+
SWAN (Westin)	$222-$367
SWAN RESERVE (Autograph Collection)	$322-$485
TREEHOUSE VILLAS	$1,114-$2,134
WILDERNESS LODGE	$453-$916
YACHT CLUB RESORT	$537-$986

also changes the price of its hotel rooms with the day of the week, charging more for the same room on Friday and Saturday nights. The rate hikes can range from $13 to over $100 per room, per night.

2. ASK ABOUT SPECIALS If you're booking by phone, ask the reservationist what special deals or discounts are available at Disney hotels during the time of your visit. Being specific and assertive paid off for a Warren Township, New Jersey, dad:

> Your tip on asking Disney employees about discounts was invaluable. They will not volunteer this information, but by asking, we saved almost $500 on our hotel room.

A family from West Springfield, Massachusetts, discovered that continuing to shop after you've booked can really pay off:

> I booked our trip online with Disney using a special-offer discount we had received in the mail. Two months before our trip, and after I had already paid in full, Disney ran a special that was even better than the one I had booked. I gave them a call, and they politely, quickly, and efficiently credited the difference.

Be aware that specials can include discounts on vacation packages in addition to discounts on rooms. Discounts on park admission or dining packages (see "Disney Lodging for Less," pages 212–213) can be substantial, depending on the number of people in your traveling party or where you're staying.

3. READ THE BANNERS ON DISNEY'S WEBSITE As we went to press, Disney's website listed all the discounts running for the general public. The trick is knowing where to look: In Disney's case, visit disney world.disney.go.com/resorts. The link to the discounts page is found in the banner near the top of the page—exactly where we've been trained not to look, as these are usually ads.

4. INVESTIGATE INTERNET SELLERS Expedia (expedia.com), **Hotwire** (hotwire.com), **Priceline** (priceline.com) and its **Express Deals** section (tinyurl.com/priceline-express), and **Travelocity** (travelocity.com) offer discounted rooms at Disney hotels, but usually at a price approximating the rate obtainable from the Walt Disney Travel Company or Walt Disney World Central Reservations. Most breaks are in the 7%–25% range. *Always check these websites' prices against Disney's.*

5. RENT DISNEY VACATION CLUB POINTS The **Disney Vacation Club** (**DVC**) is Disney's time-share program. DVC members buy a number of "points" annually that they use to pay for their Disney accommodations. Sometimes members elect to "rent" (sell) their points instead of using them in a given year. Though Disney is not involved in the transaction, it allows DVC members to make these points available to the general public.

The going rental rate for points is $15–$19 per point, depending on the resort and time of year, when you deal with members directly; third-party brokers charge $18–$21 per point for hosting the buying-and-selling market and offering credit card payments.

Last-minute deals can bring the price down to the $8–$12 range. For example, in mid-2023 we saw last-minute offers for a standard-view, two-bedroom Grand Floridian Villa for around $500 per night, all-in. Disney's rack rate for the room was $1,960, so the DVC points represented a 75% discount.

Renting a studio for six nights during summer 2023 in Animal Kingdom Lodge & Villas currently costs $3,210 if you're paying with cash. The same room costs a DVC member 57 points. If you rented those points at $21 per point, that studio would cost you $1,197—a savings of more than $2,000.

We think renting a one-bedroom villa is a good alternative for families looking for extra space, at not much more cost than a regular hotel room. For example, a 344-square-foot standard room in Animal Kingdom Lodge also cost around $3,210 for six nights during summer 2023. It consists of one main room for everyone and a bathroom.

A one-bedroom villa in Animal Kingdom Lodge, however, is around 629 square feet, with a full kitchen and separate bedroom, living room, and bath. It rents for 127 points, or $2,667 at $21 per point. That's a savings of $543 with 80% more space, a private bedroom, two bathrooms, and a full kitchen.

Likewise, if you're a family of six people or more, a two-bedroom villa in Animal Kingdom Lodge sleeps eight. While it costs around $620 per night (at $21 per point), a family suite at Art of Animation costs $630 (without discounts). For $10 *less* per night, you get more than double the space—1,170 square feet in Animal Kingdom versus 565 at Art of Animation—and better amenities.

As mentioned previously, you have two options when renting points: Go through a third-party broker or deal directly with a DVC member. For a fixed rate of around $18–$21 per point, **David's Vacation Club Rentals** (dvcrequest.com) will match your request for a specific resort and dates to its available supply. David's per-point rate is higher than if you did the legwork yourself, but they take requests months in advance, and they notify you as soon as something becomes available; plus, they take credit cards. We've used David's for huge New Year's Eve events and last-minute trips, and it's tops.

In addition to David's, some readers, like this one from St. Louis, have had good results with the **DVC Rental Store** (dvcrentalstore.com):

We rented DVC points for this trip through the DVC Rental Store, and we had a wonderful experience. Unlike David's, they don't make you pay the entire cost upon booking. For our stay at Boulder Ridge Villas, we paid just over half what we were planning to pay for the Wilderness Lodge.

LAST-MINUTE DVC DEALS The website **DVCReservations.com** emails a newsletter roughly every week with steeply discounted DVC rooms available within the next 90 days. These discounts are, by a wide margin, the best generally available deals you can find on Disney hotel rooms: typically 35%–60% off Disney's rates. We've seen instances where the least expensive room on-property was a 376-square-foot DVC rental villa at Old Key West or Saratoga Springs, not a 260-square-foot Value resort room such as Pop Century or the All-Stars.

The best last-minute discounts are on one- and two-bedroom villas at **Old Key West** and **Saratoga Springs Resorts**: as low as $310 per night for a 714-square-foot one-bedroom and $520 per night for 1,075-square-foot two-bedrooms. Those are better rates than Disney was offering for a standard room at its Moderate and Deluxe resorts, which have less than half the space of the DVC units.

You're most likely to find these last-minute rentals for stays of one to four nights. If you're willing to switch resorts every couple of nights, though, you can easily make a week of it.

When you deal directly with the selling DVC member, you pay the member directly, such as by certified check (few members take credit cards). The member makes a reservation in your name and pays Disney the requisite number of points. Arrangements vary, but again, the going rate is around $15–$19 per point. Trust is required from both parties. Usually, your reservation is documented by a confirmation sent from Disney to the owner and then passed along to you. Though the deal you cut is strictly up to you and the owner, you should always insist on receiving the aforementioned confirmation before making more than a one-night deposit.

We suggest checking online at one of the various Disney discussion boards (such as MouseOwners.com or Disboards.com) if you're not picky about where you stay and when you go and you're willing to put in the effort to ask around. If you're trying to book a particular resort, especially during a busy time of year, there's something to be said for the low-hassle approach of a points broker.

When you're looking at these sites, keep in mind that Disney World has 12 DVC resorts, also known as Disney Deluxe Villas (DDV): **Animal Kingdom Villas, Bay Lake Tower at the Contemporary Resort, Beach Club Villas, BoardWalk Villas, Boulder Ridge Villas, Copper Creek Villas & Cascade Cabins, Grand Floridian Villas, Old Key West Resort, Polynesian Villas & Bungalows, Riviera Resort, Saratoga Springs Resort & Spa,** and **Treehouse Villas at Saratoga Springs.** Construction on a 13th resort, a new DVC tower for the **Polynesian Village,** should be complete by the end of 2024.

6. CRACK THE (PIN) CODE Disney maintains a list of recent Walt Disney World visitors as well as those who have inquired about a Disney World vacation. During slow times of the year, Disney will send these folks personalized discounts by direct mail and email. Each offer is uniquely identified by a long string of letters and numbers called a PIN code. This code is required to get the discount—thus, it can't be shared—and Disney will verify that the street or email address that the code was sent to is yours.

To get your name into the Disney system for a PIN code, call ☎ 407-W-DISNEY (934-7639) and request written info. If you've been to Disney World before, your name and address will, of course, already be on record, but you won't be as likely to receive a PIN-code offer as you would by calling and requesting that information be mailed to you.

unofficial **TIP**
To enhance your chances of receiving a PIN-code offer, you need to get your name and street or email address into the Disney system.

Or go to disneyworld.disney.go.com and sign up to automatically be sent offers and news at your email address. You might also consider getting a **Disney Rewards Visa Card,** which entitles you to exclusive discounts (visit disneyrewards.com for details).

7. DISNEY-SPECIALIST TRAVEL AGENTS Disney vacations are so popular that entire travel agencies specialize in just Disney theme park trips and cruises. Even large, general-travel agencies such as AAA often have dedicated agents with specialized, up-to-date knowledge of what's going on at the parks.

Three obvious situations where it makes sense to engage a travel agent are as follows:

1. This is one of your first trips to Walt Disney World and you'd like to talk to someone objective in person.

2. You're looking to save time in evaluating several different scenarios, such as which of two discounts saves the most money.

3. You want someone else to keep checking for a better deal than what you already have.

We can't emphasize enough how much time (and money) a travel agent will save you in those last two scenarios. If you're trying to compare, say, the cost difference between a Value and a Moderate resort with a particular discount that may not be available at all resorts on all dates, you could easily spend an hour working through different combinations to find the best deal. We think most people give up far before finishing, potentially wasting a lot of money. Good travel agents will do this for you at no charge (because they'll earn a commission from Disney when you book through them). Travel agents save so much time in these scenarios that we use them ourselves. Even if the agent can't beat a deal that we've found on our own, we let them book it anyway if it's commissionable, to nurture the relationship.

Our reader-survey results indicate that for Walt Disney World, you'll be much more satisfied using a travel agent who specializes in Disney and will be much more likely to recommend those agents to a friend. We suggest asking your travel agency if it has agents who specialize in Disney vacations.

8. ORGANIZATIONS AND AUTO CLUBS Disney has developed time-limited programs with some auto clubs and organizations. AAA, for example, can often offer discounts on hotels and packages comparable to those Disney offers its Annual Pass holders. Such deals come and go, but the market suggests there will be more. If you're a member of AARP, AAA, or any travel or auto club, ask whether the group has a program before shopping elsewhere.

9. ROOM UPGRADES Sometimes a room upgrade is as good as a discount. If you're visiting Disney World during a slower time, book the least expensive room your discounts will allow. When checking in, ask politely about being upgraded to a water-view or pool-view room. A fair percentage of the time, you'll get one at no additional charge or at a deep discount. Understand, however, that a room upgrade should be considered a favor. Hotels are under no obligation to upgrade you, so if your request is not met, accept the decision graciously. Also, note that suites at Deluxe resorts are exempt from discount offers.

10. MILITARY DISCOUNTS **Shades of Green Armed Forces Recreation Center,** near the Grand Floridian Resort & Spa, offers luxury accommodations at rates based on a service member's rank, as well as attraction tickets to the theme parks (see profile on page 144). For rates and other information, call ☎ 888-593-2242 or visit shadesof green.org.

11. YEAR-ROUND DISCOUNTS AT THE SWAN AND DOLPHIN RESORTS Government workers, teachers, nurses, military, and AAA and *Entertainment Coupon Book* members can save on rooms at the Dolphin or Swan (when space is available, of course). Call ☎ 888-828-8850 or visit swandolphin.com and click on "Special Offers."

CHOOSING A WALT DISNEY WORLD HOTEL

IF YOU WANT TO STAY IN THE WORLD but don't know which hotel to choose, the most important factors to consider are as follows:

1. Room quality (page 102)
2. Transportation (page 104)
3. Cost (page 105)
4. Pools and amenities (page 108)
5. Location/distance from parks (page 109)
6. Theme (page 110)
7. Dining options (page 111)
8. The size of your room vs. the size of your group (page 112)

1. ROOM QUALITY Many Disney hotel rooms are among the best designed and appointed anywhere. Plus, they're maintained much better than the average hotel room in Orlando. All rooms, for instance, have minifridges and free, reliable Wi-Fi, along with coffee makers in the DVC units.

As Disney refurbishes its hotel rooms, it also reexamines how modern families use these spaces. As a simple example, new rooms have 5–10 built-in USB charging ports to accommodate everyone's cell phones and tablets. Other changes are much more substantial.

Not surprisingly, many readers rate Disney's Deluxe and DVC rooms highest for quality, but some Value and Moderate rooms rate even higher than some Deluxe and DVC rooms. The text that follows provides context for these room-quality ratings. In addition, the table on the opposite page shows how the Walt Disney World hotels stack up as far as room quality.

VALUE RESORTS Room quality is highest at **Pop Century** and the **All-Star Resorts,** where the entire room configuration has changed in the last few years. Carpet has been replaced with vinyl plank flooring. Queen beds are now standard, and king beds are still available. More interesting is that in rooms with two queen beds, one bed folds into the wall during the day, exposing a desk. That frees up around 36 square feet of space in these 260-square-foot rooms—around 14% in all. In addition, bathrooms are brighter and more open, and more storage is available in the living areas.

Art of Animation's room quality is in the middle of the pack for the Disney Value resorts. Rooms are clean and functional, but because the resort opened in 2012, they're not yet old enough to need the updates that Pop and the All-Stars have gotten.

MODERATE RESORTS Readers rate the rooms at **Coronado Springs** the highest of any Moderate resort. These rooms have been modernized

HOTEL	ROOM-QUALITY RATING		
GRAND FLORIDIAN VILLAS	93		FORT WILDERNESS CABINS	88
RIVIERA RESORT	93		WILDERNESS LODGE	88
SARATOGA SPRINGS RESORT & SPA (studio)	92		YACHT CLUB RESORT	88
SHADES OF GREEN	92		CARIBBEAN BEACH RESORT (renovated rooms)	88
OLD KEY WEST RESORT	91		ALL-STAR RESORTS (standard rooms)	87
POLYNESIAN VILLAS & BUNGALOWS (studio)	91		BEACH CLUB RESORT	87
BAY LAKE TOWER	90		POP CENTURY RESORT	87
BOARDWALK INN	90		BEACH CLUB VILLAS (studio)	86
CORONADO SPRINGS RESORT	90		SWAN	86
GRAND FLORIDIAN RESORT & SPA	90		SWAN RESERVE	86
POLYNESIAN VILLAGE RESORT	90		ANIMAL KINGDOM LODGE-JAMBO HOUSE (studio)	85
ANIMAL KINGDOM LODGE-KIDANI VILLAGE (studios)	89		DOLPHIN	85
BOARDWALK VILLAS (studio)	89		PORT ORLEANS RESORT-FRENCH QUARTER	85
TREEHOUSE VILLAS	89		PORT ORLEANS RESORT-RIVERSIDE	84
ANIMAL KINGDOM LODGE	88		BOULDER RIDGE VILLAS (studio)	83
CONTEMPORARY RESORT	88		ART OF ANIMATION RESORT (standard room)	82
COPPER CREEK VILLAS & CASCADE CABINS	88		

Star Wars: Galactic Starcruiser did not have enough surveys to rate.

with vinyl plank flooring, plenty of desk space, excellent lighting, and doors separating the bathroom area from the main living space.

Readers rate the rooms at **The Cabins at Fort Wilderness Resort** the second-highest and rooms at **Port Orleans French Quarter** the third-highest. The cabins are more like small mobile homes, with a separate living room, kitchen, and bedroom. Rooms at French Quarter have flooring similar to that at Coronado Springs but don't have the newest storage or bathroom makeovers. We think French Quarter's rooms are rated highly because this resort is the smallest and most intimate of the Moderates, and that atmosphere carries over to the room ratings.

Port Orleans Riverside and **Caribbean Beach** have the lowest-rated Moderate rooms. All rooms in Riverside have vinyl flooring. One section, Alligator Bayou, has an updated bathroom design and a new drop-down twin bed for a fifth child. However, the furniture design in these rooms is rustic (to fit the theming) and lacks the modern conveniences found in the updated Value resorts.

Caribbean Beach is undergoing a welcome upgrade, starting with a conversion of its *Pirates of the Caribbean*–themed rooms in the Trinidad section to a *Finding Nemo* theme. These updates use lighter, brighter color schemes and bring foldout and drop-down bed options to rooms that used to have two fixed beds. Like the renovations at the Value resorts, this update will modernize and increase the functionality of the rooms at Caribbean Beach. Our one word of caution is that, because of its size, many Caribbean Beach reno efforts get stopped before all rooms are finished. A quick walk-through in the spring of 2023, for example, identified around four different room themes spread out over various sections. If you're booking here, ask specifically for a refurbished room.

Disney's most recent addition to the Moderate category is **Gran Destino Tower** at Coronado Springs, which offers some of the best-designed bathrooms in this category. Even better, Gran Destino's Club Level rooms—with access to the fabulous private **Chronos Club** lounge—are the cheapest Club Level rooms on-property. If you're looking to try one of these rooms, Gran Destino is a great place to start.

DELUXE RESORTS Rooms at the **Grand Floridian Resort & Spa** are rated the highest in this category. These are among the largest and best appointed anywhere on Disney property. Rooms include textured carpeting along with plenty of storage, desk, and bathroom space.

Other above-average Deluxe rooms are found at the **Contemporary** and **Yacht Club Resorts, Polynesian Village,** and **Disney's BoardWalk Inn.** Those at **Animal Kingdom Lodge–Jambo House** are rated average. The lowest-rated rooms are found at the Swan and Dolphin.

Animal Kingdom Lodge & Villas, BoardWalk Inn, and **Wilderness Lodge,** along with the **Contemporary, Grand Floridian, Polynesian Village,** and **Yacht & Beach Club Resorts** and **Gran Destino Tower** at Coronado Springs, boast **Club Level** (concierge) floors. Benefits include personalized trip planning and a lounge stocked with small bites to graze on. This Basking Ridge, New Jersey, reader, however, found the snacks on the skimpy side:

> We found the Club Level food offerings limited and carefully metered out. Tiny plates were replenished slowly. Given that Club Level is a significant extra expense, we didn't appreciate being told how much we could eat and when.

DVC RESORTS Disney's highest-rated rooms are found at its time-share resorts. Topping the list are **Old Key West, Riviera Resort, Shades of Green,** and **The Villas at Disney's Grand Floridian Resort & Spa.** Opened in late 2019, the Riviera is Disney's newest DVC resort. With above-average on-site dining and Skyliner access to EPCOT and Hollywood Studios, it's a positive (if pricey) addition to Disney's resort lineup. The large, stylish rooms are, in our opinion, the best of any Disney-owned hotel. Old Key West's rooms are large, very functional, and quiet, plus they've been updated recently.

Almost all other DVC resorts have rooms rated above average: **Bay Lake Tower, Animal Kingdom Lodge–Kidani Village, Copper Creek Villas & Cascade Cabins at Wilderness Lodge, Treehouse Villas at Saratoga Springs,** and **BoardWalk Villas.**

Readers continue to rate the rooms at **Boulder Ridge Villas at Wilderness Lodge** as below average. We agree that they're not as good as rooms at other DVC resorts—in particular, the room layout, decor, and furnishings at Boulder Ridge suffer compared with the other DVC complexes at Wilderness Lodge (the **Copper Creek Villas** and **Cascade Cabins**). The **BoardWalk Villas** were getting ready to start an upgrade as we went to press; ask for a renovated room when you book.

2. TRANSPORTATION If you'll be driving, your Disney hotel's transportation isn't especially important unless you plan to spend most of your time in the Magic Kingdom. (In this case, Disney transportation is usually more efficient than your car because it bypasses the Transportation and Ticket Center, the Magic Kingdom's transportation hub, and deposits you at the theme park entrance.) If you haven't decided whether you want a car for your Disney vacation, see "How to Travel Around the World" (page 430).

The hotels our readers rate highest for Disney transportation are **Polynesian Village, Grand Floridian, Riviera, Art of Animation,** and **Pop Century.** The Polynesian and Grand Floridian connect to the Magic Kingdom and EPCOT by monorail. These resorts use buses to get to other destinations on-property. The Riviera's and Pop Century's transportation is primarily bus service to most destinations on-property; the Skyliner connects these two resorts with Caribbean Beach and Art of Animation Resorts, Disney's Hollywood Studios, and EPCOT.

unofficial **TIP**
If you plan to use Disney transportation to visit all four theme parks and one or both water parks, book a centrally located resort that has good transportation connections, such as the EPCOT resorts (page 147) or the **Polynesian Village, Caribbean Beach, Art of Animation, Pop Century,** or **Port Orleans Resorts.**

The resorts our readers rated as below average for transportation are the **Swan, Swan Reserve,** and **Dolphin; Port Orleans Riverside;** and the **Treehouse Villas** at Saratoga Springs. The bus service at Port Orleans and Saratoga Springs makes multiple stops at these resorts, which increases the time it takes to get where you're going. The non-Disney bus service at the Swan, Swan Reserve, and Dolphin runs less often than Disney's own buses and drops guests off at the Transportation and Ticket Center, not the Magic Kingdom park entrance.

3. COST Hotel rooms start as low as $148 a night at the All-Stars and top out above $2,100 at the Grand Floridian. The table on page 97 shows the cost per night for various Disney hotel rooms.

Disney's **Value resorts** are the least expensive on-site hotels. Because they're popular, they have four separate, unofficial price categories:

- The **All-Star Resorts** are Disney's oldest and least expensive Value resorts.

- **Pop Century Resort** sits in the middle of the Value price range—about 20% per night more than the All-Stars. It's the most popular Disney World resort among *Unofficial Guide* readers.

- **Art of Animation Resort** has the largest rooms, best food court, and best pools in this category. Standard rooms cost about $100 per night more than those at the All-Stars.

- Two-room **Family Suites** are available at the All-Star Music and Art of Animation Resorts, from around $340 to $840 per night with tax.

While the All-Stars and Pop Century are older and less expensive than AOA, they've had extensive room renovations that make them among the most attractive and functional on-property. In terms of room quality, they're better and cheaper than AOA's standard rooms.

The next most expensive tier includes Disney's **Moderate resorts.** Like the Values, these have different price points:

- **Coronado Springs Resort** ($294–$446 per night) has the cheapest rooms in the moderate category. It's large, with multiple bus stops, and has low-rated on-site dining.

- **Port Orleans Riverside** and **Port Orleans French Quarter** ($299–$451 per night) are only slightly more expensive. They lack the newness of Gran Destino Tower and the Skyliner access found at Caribbean Beach.

- **Caribbean Beach Resort** ($310–$479 per night) got a bump in popularity (and prices) when it got a Skyliner station.

- **Gran Destino Tower** ($398–$608 per night) is the newest entry in the Moderate category. The 15-story tower is located on the grounds of Coronado Springs Resort. Its Club Level rooms are the least expensive in Walt Disney World.

- **The Cabins at Fort Wilderness Resort** ($481–$779 per night) are unique in the Moderate category. These small, mobile home–like accommodations sleep up to six and include a small kitchen.

Rates at Disney's **Deluxe resorts** vary depending on room size and the hotel's location relative to the theme parks:

- The **Walt Disney World Swan, Walt Disney World Dolphin,** and **Swan Reserve** are usually the least expensive Deluxe hotel rooms on-property. They're not owned by Disney, and they cater to convention traffic as much as families, giving them a different feel from the other hotels. These hotels are within walking distance of EPCOT and Disney's Hollywood Studios.

- The smallest and least expensive Disney-owned Deluxe hotel rooms are found at **Wilderness Lodge** and **Animal Kingdom Lodge.** Both hotels have excellent theming; Animal Kingdom Lodge has excellent dining as well.

- The next tier of Deluxe prices applies to the EPCOT resorts: the **Yacht Club, Beach Club,** and **BoardWalk Inn**. These are arranged around Crescent Lake, with a short walk to EPCOT and a slightly longer walk to Disney's Hollywood Studios.

- Slightly more expensive are the **Polynesian Village** and **Contemporary Resorts.** Both opened in 1971 and are a short walk or monorail ride from the Magic Kingdom and EPCOT. The Polynesian Village has excellent theming. Along with its easy access to two theme parks, its location makes it easy to visit any hotel restaurant along the Magic Kingdom monorail loop.

- Finally, Disney's most expensive standard hotel rooms are found at the **Grand Floridian Resort & Spa,** Disney World's flagship hotel.

IS IT MORE THAN A PLACE TO SLEEP? Many families headed to Walt Disney World opt for the Value resorts, not so much because of the lower cost but because, in their words, "it's just a place to sleep." But do those families feel the same way at the end of their trip? We put together an experiment to find out.

Since 2019, we've surveyed more than 24,000 families about the brand of hotel they typically stay at when *not* vacationing at Walt Disney World. We categorized those hotels as follows:

- **Budget:** Days Inn, Motel 6, Super 8, etc.
- **Moderate:** Best Western, Hampton Inn, Holiday Inn Express, etc.
- **Upscale:** Crowne Plaza, Radisson, SpringHill Suites, Wyndham, etc.
- **Luxury:** Four Seasons, Ritz-Carlton, Waldorf Astoria, etc.

We grouped Disney's hotels into Disney's own Value, Moderate, Deluxe, and DVC categories. Then we asked the families three questions, each on a five-point scale:

- How satisfied were you with your Disney hotel?
- Would you recommend this hotel to a friend?
- Would you stay at this hotel again?

Here's how the results shook out among those families who were "very satisfied" with their Disney hotel, would recommend it to a friend, and would stay at that hotel again:

TYPE OF HOTEL TYPICALLY CHOSEN	DISNEY VALUE (% Positive Responses)	DISNEY MODERATE (% Positive Responses)	DISNEY DELUXE (% Positive Responses)	DVC/DDV (% Positive Responses)
BUDGET	79%	71%	76%	78%
MODERATE	73%	66%	78%	80%
UPSCALE	72%	67%	79%	81%
LUXURY	76%	72%	81%	79%

The takeaway? No matter what kind of hotel you stay at outside of Walt Disney World, **you'll probably be most satisfied at a Disney Deluxe or DVC resort.** So even if you stay at a low-cost Microtel Inn on other trips, you'll still be happier if you stay in Animal Kingdom Lodge instead of Port Orleans.

After doing these surveys for 30 years, we're convinced that most people add the words "for the money I paid" to the end of every question we ask. So, when you read the survey results on pages 122–123,

DISNEY RESORT POOL RATINGS

1. YACHT & BEACH CLUB RESORTS & BEACH CLUB VILLAS (*shared complex*) ★★★★★

2. GRAND FLORIDIAN RESORT & SPA, VILLAS ★★★★½

3. ANIMAL KINGDOM VILLAS (*Kidani Village*) ★★★★½

4. SARATOGA SPRINGS RESORT & SPA/TREEHOUSE VILLAS ★★★★½

5. WILDERNESS LODGE & BOULDER RIDGE/COPPER CREEK VILLAS ★★★★½

6. ANIMAL KINGDOM LODGE & VILLAS (*Jambo House*) ★★★★

7. PORT ORLEANS RESORT ★★★★

8. CORONADO SPRINGS RESORT/GRAN DESTINO TOWER ★★★★

9. DOLPHIN ★★★★

10. SWAN ★★★★

11. POLYNESIAN VILLAGE, VILLAS & BUNGALOWS ★★★★

12. BAY LAKE TOWER ★★★★

13. CARIBBEAN BEACH RESORT ★★★★

14. RIVIERA RESORT ★★★★

15. BOARDWALK INN & VILLAS ★★★½

16. CONTEMPORARY RESORT ★★★½

17. SWAN RESERVE ★★★½

18. ALL-STAR RESORTS ★★★

19. ART OF ANIMATION RESORT ★★★

20. OLD KEY WEST RESORT ★★★

21. FORT WILDERNESS RESORT & CAMPGROUND ★★★

22. POP CENTURY RESORT ★★★

23. SHADES OF GREEN ★★★

Star Wars: Galactic Starcruiser doesn't have a pool.

DISNEY RESORT AMENITIES					
RESORT	SUITES	CONCIERGE FLOOR	NUMBER OF ROOMS	ROOM SERVICE (full)	FITNESS CENTER
ALL-STAR RESORTS	●	—	5,406	—	—
ANIMAL KINGDOM LODGE	●	●	972	●	●
ANIMAL KINGDOM VILLAS	●	●*	458	●	●
ART OF ANIMATION RESORT	●	—	1,984	—	—
BAY LAKE TOWER	●	—	295	●	●
BEACH CLUB VILLAS	●	—	282	●	●
BOARDWALK INN	●	●	378	●	●
BOARDWALK VILLAS	●	—	532	●	●
CARIBBEAN BEACH RESORT	—	—	1,536	—	—
CONTEMPORARY RESORT	●	●	655	●	●
CORONADO SPRINGS RESORT	●	●	1,839	●	●
DOLPHIN	●	—	1,509	●	●
FORT WILDERNESS CABINS	—	—	409	—	—
GRAN DESTINO TOWER	●	●	545	●	—
GRAND FLORIDIAN RESORT & SPA, VILLAS	●	●	1,016	●	●
OLD KEY WEST RESORT	●	—	761	—	●
POLYNESIAN VILLAGE, VILLAS & BUNGALOWS	●	●	866	●	—
POP CENTURY RESORT	—	—	2,880	—	—
PORT ORLEANS RESORT	—	—	3,056	—	—
RIVIERA RESORT	—	—	300	●	●
SARATOGA SPRINGS RESORT & SPA	●	—	1,260	—	●
SHADES OF GREEN	●	—	586	●	●
STAR WARS: GALACTIC STARCRUISER	●	—	100	●	—
SWAN	●	—	758	●	●
SWAN RESERVE	●	—	349	●	●
TREEHOUSE VILLAS	●	—	60	—	●
WILDERNESS LODGE & BOULDER RIDGE/COPPER CREEK VILLAS	●	●	889	●	●
YACHT & BEACH CLUB RESORTS	●	●	1,211	●	●

*Jambo House only

it's safe to assume that they take into account the higher cost of the hotel rooms. If you have the budget, we think you'll have a better trip by booking a Deluxe hotel or DVC.

4. POOLS AND AMENITIES Disney's **Yacht & Beach Club Resorts** share the highest-rated pool in Walt Disney World. Called **Stormalong Bay,** it includes a lazy river with a sand bottom and an elaborate waterslide that begins from a pirate ship beached on Crescent Lake. Stormalong Bay is so popular that guests must show proof they're staying at the resort before being admitted to the pool area.

The **Riviera**'s pools also get top marks from readers. With two pools and a child's water-play area, there's plenty of space for guests to relax. In the middle of the pools (and conveniently located next to the water-play area) is **Bar Riva,** with shade and beverages for adults.

The pools at **Art of Animation** are also rated above average. These are well themed and have convenient bar and food options.

Readers rate the pools as below average at these resorts: **Contemporary, Pop Century,** and **Fort Wilderness.** Of these, our opinion is that all but Pop have relatively generic pool offerings; all are often crowded.

See the table on page 107 for specific resort pool ratings and the table on the opposite page for a summary of the amenities at each resort.

5. LOCATION AND DISTANCE FROM THE THEME PARKS Once you've determined your budget, think about what you want to do at Walt Disney World. Will you go to all four theme parks or concentrate on one or two?

The resorts closest to the Magic Kingdom include the **Grand Floridian** and its **Villas;** the **Contemporary** and **Bay Lake Tower;** and the **Polynesian Village, Villas & Bungalows.** All are served by the monorail and walking paths, so staying at one of these resorts also gets you access to more dining options, many of which are among Disney World's best.

Next closest to the Magic Kingdom, **Wilderness Lodge & Boulder Ridge/Copper Creek Villas,** along with **Fort Wilderness Resort & Campground,** are linked to the Magic Kingdom by boat and to everywhere else in the World by rather convoluted bus service.

The most centrally located hotels in Walt Disney World are the EPCOT resorts—the **BoardWalk Inn, BoardWalk Villas, Yacht & Beach Club Resorts, Beach Club Villas, Swan, Dolphin,** and **Swan Reserve**— and **Coronado Springs/Gran Destino Tower,** near Disney's Animal Kingdom. The EPCOT resorts are within easy walking distance of Disney's Hollywood Studios and EPCOT's International Gateway. Besides giving you easy theme park access, staying at one of these hotels gets you access to a wide variety of restaurants. EPCOT hotels are best for guests planning to spend most of their time in EPCOT or DHS. Coronado Springs is convenient for driving to EPCOT, Hollywood Studios, Animal Kingdom, or Blizzard Beach water park.

Caribbean Beach, Riviera, Pop Century, and **Art of Animation Resorts** are just south and east of EPCOT and DHS. All are connected to EPCOT and DHS by the Skyliner and to everything else by bus.

The Disney resorts along Bonnet Creek, which offer quick access to Disney Springs and its top restaurants, include **Old Key West Resort, Saratoga Springs Resort & Spa** and its **Treehouse Villas,** and the two **Port Orleans Resorts.** On an adjacent 70-acre parcel of non-Disney land called **Bonnet Creek Resort** are the **Waldorf Astoria Orlando;** the **Signia by Hilton Orlando Bonnet Creek;** and two **Wyndham** properties, **Club Wyndham Bonnet Creek** and its more luxurious sibling, the **Wyndham Grand Orlando Resort Bonnet Creek.**

The Bonnet Creek Resort area walks the line between on- and off-property: The hotels are as close to the theme parks as Disney's own, offer transportation to the parks and Disney Springs, and are every bit as good as Disney's best—often at around half the price. Further muddying the waters, guests of the Signia and Waldorf Astoria get Early Theme Park Entry privileges (as do guests of the **Four Seasons Resort Orlando,** adjacent to Fort Wilderness Resort). We profile the Signia and the Waldorf in "Hotels Outside Walt Disney World" (pages 240 and 241, respectively).

DISNEY HOTELS BY THEME

ALL-STAR RESORTS	Movies, music, and sports
ANIMAL KINGDOM LODGE & VILLAS	African game preserve
ART OF ANIMATION RESORT	Disney's animated films
BAY LAKE TOWER	Upscale, ultramodern urban hotel
BEACH CLUB RESORT & VILLAS	New England beach club of the 1870s
BOARDWALK INN	East Coast boardwalk hotel of the early 1900s
BOARDWALK VILLAS	East Coast beach cottage of the early 1900s
CARIBBEAN BEACH RESORT	Caribbean islands
CONTEMPORARY RESORT	The future as perceived by past and present generations
CORONADO SPRINGS RESORT	Northern Mexico and the American Southwest
DOLPHIN	"Modern" (read: early-1990s-vintage) Florida resort
GRAN DESTINO TOWER	Spanish/Moorish influences
GRAND FLORIDIAN RESORT & SPA, VILLAS	Turn-of-the-20th-century luxury hotel
OLD KEY WEST RESORT	Relaxed Florida Keys vibe
POLYNESIAN VILLAGE RESORT, VILLAS & BUNGALOWS	Hawaii–South Seas
POP CENTURY RESORT	Popular-culture icons from various decades of the 20th century
PORT ORLEANS RESORT-FRENCH QUARTER	Turn-of-the-19th-century New Orleans
PORT ORLEANS RESORT-RIVERSIDE	Old Louisiana bayou-side retreat
RIVIERA RESORT	Mediterranean beach resort in the South of France
SARATOGA SPRINGS RESORT & SPA	1880s Victorian lake
STAR WARS: GALACTIC STARCRUISER	*Star Wars*-themed adventure
SWAN	What modern looked like 30 years ago
SWAN RESERVE	Brand-new resort with a true 21st-century design aesthetic
TREEHOUSE VILLAS	Disney-rustic vacation homes with modern amenities
WILDERNESS LODGE & BOULDER RIDGE/COPPER CREEK VILLAS	Grand national park lodge of the early 1900s
YACHT CLUB RESORT	New England seashore hotel of the 1880s

6. THEME With a few exceptions, each Disney resort is designed to evoke a special place or period of history. Some resorts carry off their theming better than others, and some themes are more exciting. See the table above for a summary of each resort's theme.

Readers rate the resorts in the next four paragraphs tops for theming:

Animal Kingdom Lodge & Villas replicates grand safari lodges of Kenya and Tanzania and overlooks its own African-style game preserve. By far the most exotic Disney resort, it's made to order for couples on romantic getaways and for families with children.

Wilderness Lodge & Boulder Ridge/Copper Creek Villas is visually extraordinary, reminiscent of a grand early-20th-century national park lodge. The lobby opens eight stories to a timbered ceiling supported by giant columns of bundled logs. One look eases you into the woodsy wilderness theme. Wilderness Lodge is a great choice for couples and seniors and is heaven for children.

Likewise dramatic, the **Polynesian Village Resort, Villas & Bungalows** convey the feeling of the Pacific Islands. They're great for romantics and families. Many waterfront rooms on upper floors offer a perfect view of Cinderella Castle and the Magic Kingdom fireworks across Seven Seas Lagoon.

Port Orleans Resort–French Quarter does a good (albeit sanitized) job of capturing the architectural essence of its New Orleans inspiration. **Port Orleans Resort–Riverside** likewise succeeds with its early-19th-century Louisiana bayou setting.

Unofficial Guide readers rate the following resorts as below average for theming: the **All-Star Resorts; Pop Century; Saratoga Springs** and **Treehouse Villas;** the **Contemporary Resort** and **Bay Lake Tower;** and the **Swan, Swan Reserve,** and **Dolphin.**

The **All-Star Resorts** have 15 themed areas: 5 celebrate sports (surfing, basketball, tennis, football, and baseball), 5 recall Hollywood films, and 5 have musical motifs. The resort's design, with entrances shaped like giant Dalmatians, Coke cups, footballs, and the like, is somewhat adolescent, sacrificing grace and beauty for energy and novelty. Guest-room decor is reminiscent of a teenage boy's bedroom.

unofficial **TIP**
The best resort lounges are the DVC-only **Top of the World** at Bay Lake Tower (cozy up to an owner for access), **Victoria Falls** in Animal Kingdom Lodge, and **Trader Sam's** at the Polynesian. Honorable mention goes to the **Territory Lounge** at Wilderness Lodge and **Crew's Cup** at the Yacht Club.

Pop Century Resort is pretty much a clone of the All-Star Resorts, only here the giant icons symbolize decades of the 20th century (Big Wheels, 45-rpm records, silhouettes of people doing period dances, and such), and period memorabilia decorates the rooms.

Saratoga Springs Resort & Spa, supposedly representative of an upstate New York country retreat, looks like what you'd get if you crossed the Beach Club with the Wilderness Lodge. When it comes to the resorts inspired by Northeastern hotels (including the **Yacht and Beach Clubs**), thematic distinctions are subtle and thus lost on many guests.

The **Contemporary, Bay Lake Tower, Swan, Swan Reserve,** and **Dolphin** are essentially themeless though architecturally interesting. The original Contemporary Resort is a 15-story A-frame building with monorails running through the middle. An update in 2021 added characters from Pixar's *The Incredibles.* The Swan and Dolphin are massive yet whimsical; designed by Michael Graves, they're excellent examples of early-1990s "entertainment architecture," but they lack any references to Disney theme parks, films, or characters.

7. DINING OPTIONS The best resorts for dining quality are **Animal Kingdom Lodge & Villas** and the **Grand Floridian Resort & Villas.** Three of Walt Disney World's top sit-down restaurants are found in Animal Kingdom Lodge: **Jiko—The Cooking Place, Sanaa,** and **Boma—Flavors of**

unofficial **TIP**
If you stay at an EPCOT resort, you have more than 30 restaurants within a 5- to 12-minute walk.

Africa. The Grand Floridian holds Walt Disney World's very best restaurant, **Victoria & Albert's,** and five of its other restaurants all place near the top of our reader surveys. The Grand Floridian is also a short monorail ride from the **California Grill** at the Contemporary Resort, another top venue. If high-quality dining is a top priority for your Walt Disney World trip and these two resorts fit in your budget, we think they're excellent choices.

The best resorts for dining quality *and* selection are the EPCOT resorts: the **Beach Club Villas, BoardWalk Inn & Villas, Dolphin, Swan,** and **Yacht and Beach Club Resorts.** (The exception is the **Swan Reserve,** which has one restaurant for the entire hotel.) Each has decent sit-down restaurants, and each is within easy walking distance of the others as well as the dining options available in World Showcase. However, on-site quick-service options are limited for all but the BoardWalk Inn & Villas, and readers rate these hotels below average for quick-service options. If quick, simple breakfasts and lunches are what you're after, stay elsewhere.

The only other hotels in Disney World with similar access to a con-centrated area of good restaurants comprise the **Disney Springs Resort Area.** In addition to restaurants in the hotels themselves, **B Resort & Spa, DoubleTree Suites, Drury Plaza Hotel, Hilton Orlando Buena Vista Palace, Hilton Orlando Lake Buena Vista, Holiday Inn Orlando, Sara-toga Springs Resort & Spa,** and **Wyndham Garden Lake Buena Vista** are all within walking distance of restaurants in Disney Springs. As with the EPCOT resorts, though, many readers complain about the difficulty they have finding quick, tasty breakfast and lunch options at these hotels.

Hotels rated as below average for dining include **Fort Wilderness Resort & Campground,** all the **Value resorts, Coronado Springs,** and **Shades of Green.** Because Fort Wilderness caters primarily to guests who are cooking for themselves, on-site dining options are limited, and not just in terms of the menu selections: The restaurants' remote location, near the shore of Bay Lake, makes them a hassle to get to from most parts of the resort—so unless you've brought a car or you're renting a bike or golf cart, count on a *long* walk or bus ride to get something to eat. Coronado Springs probably needs a complete dining rethink—since it's never been rated highly for food. Disney's operation of the Value resort restaurants indicates that they want you to eat in the parks.

8. ROOM SIZE How much space you get inside a Disney hotel room almost always depends on how much you pay. The size of a standard (or studio) room at Disney's resorts varies from 260 square feet at the Value resorts to 440 square feet at the Deluxe **Grand Floridian Resort** to 460 square feet for a studio at the **Polynesian Villas** DVC resort. The diagrams on pages 114–119 show the size and layout of typical rooms at each Disney property.

It's no surprise that readers rate larger rooms better than smaller ones. At the top of this list are rooms at **Old Key West,** Disney's first DVC resort, which are larger than most. Also scoring well are the rooms at the **Grand Floridian Villas**—we're not kidding when we say that the showers here are large enough that you can hear an echo. And although they don't score well in most other categories, the rooms at the **Fort Wilderness Cabins** and Saratoga Springs' **Treehouse Villas** are popular with readers in terms of sheer space.

There are two exceptions to the "more money, more space" mantra: Standard rooms in the main buildings of **Animal Kingdom Lodge** and **Wilderness Lodge** are 344 square feet—the smallest of any Deluxe resort, and closer in size to the rooms at many Moderate resorts than Deluxes. Readers rate these among the lowest for space. The other rooms rated lowest for space are at Disney's Value resorts.

Standard rooms at the **Riviera** include a two-person, 225-square-foot option that's small enough to necessitate a fold-down bed. They're almost certainly the worst rooms on Disney property, and we recommend skipping them.

STANDARD ROOMS THAT SLEEP FIVE (plus one child under age 3 in a crib) are found at the following resorts:

- **DELUXE** Beach Club, BoardWalk Inn, Contemporary, Grand Floridian, Polynesian, Yacht Club
- **MODERATE** Caribbean Beach, Port Orleans Riverside (Alligator Bayou only)

FAMILY SUITES sleep six people and are found exclusively at **All-Star Music** and **Art of Animation Resorts.** The All-Star versions are basically two Value rooms stuck together; those at Art of Animation, however, were designed from the ground up and are slightly larger (and nicer). Family Suites at both resorts have two bathrooms.

The **Fort Wilderness Cabins** also sleep six, but they have just one bathroom each.

HOW WE INSPECT HOTELS

WE EVALUATE SEVERAL HUNDRED hotels in the Walt Disney World area to compile the *Unofficial Guide*'s list of lodging choices. If a hotel has been renovated or has refurbished its guest rooms, we reinspect it, along with any new hotels, for the next edition of the *Guide.* Hotels reporting no improvements are rechecked every two years. We inspect most Disney-owned hotels every 6–12 months, and no less than once every couple of years.

Pipe Down Out There!

The most common complaint that Walt Disney World–area hotel guests make regarding their rooms is excessive noise. A well-designed room blocks noise coming from both your neighbor's television and the pool across the resort.

The hotels with the best exterior soundproofing are **Saratoga Springs, Riviera, Contemporary, Grand Floridian, Gran Destino Tower,** and **Yacht Club.**

Hotels with the least exterior soundproofing are **Caribbean Beach, All-Star Movies,** both **Port Orleans Resorts, Art of Animation**'s *Little Mermaid* rooms, and **Polynesian Village** (but not the Villas).

The **Riviera** and **Gran Destino Tower** are newer resorts, and it looks like Disney specifically addressed soundproofing when installing those exterior doors. At the other end of the list, the **Polynesian Village** and **Port Orleans Resorts** have performed consistently poorly in our tests over the years. Your best bet here might be to ask for a remote corner room without a connecting interior door.

Illustration: Chris Eliopoulos

continued on page 118

DISNEY DELUXE RESORTS

CONTEMPORARY RESORT
Typical room, 394 square feet;
accommodates 5 guests
plus 1 child under age 3 in a crib

POLYNESIAN VILLAGE RESORT
Typical room, 415 square feet;
accommodates 5 guests
plus 1 child under age 3 in a crib

BOARDWALK INN
Typical room, 371 square feet;
accommodates 5 guests
plus 1 child under age 3 in a crib

GRAND FLORIDIAN RESORT & SPA
Typical room, 440 square feet;
accommodates 5 guests
plus 1 child under age 3 in a crib

BEACH CLUB RESORT
Typical room, 381 square feet;
accommodates 5 guests
plus 1 child under age 3 in a crib

YACHT CLUB RESORT
Typical room, 381 square feet;
accommodates 5 guests
plus 1 child under age 3 in a crib

WILDERNESS LODGE
Typical room, 344 square feet;
accommodates 4 guests
plus 1 child under age 3 in a crib

ANIMAL KINGDOM LODGE
Typical room, 344 square feet;
accommodates 4 guests
plus 1 child under age 3 in a crib

COPPER CREEK VILLAS & CASCADE CABINS
Studio (sleeps 4): 345 square feet (*gray area*)
1-bedroom (sleeps 4): 761 square feet
2-bedroom (sleeps 8): 1,105 square feet
Cabin (2 bedrooms; sleeps 8):
1,737 square feet
Grand Villa (3 bedrooms; sleeps 12):
3,204 square feet

DISNEY DELUXE VILLA RESORTS

OLD KEY WEST RESORT
Studio: 376 square feet (*gray area*);
1-bedroom: 942 square feet; **2-bedroom:** 1,333
square feet; **Grand Villa:** 2,202 square feet

BAY LAKE TOWER AT CONTEMPORARY RESORT
Studio: 339 square feet (*gray area*);
1-bedroom: 803 sf; **2-bedroom:** 1,152 sf
Grand Villa: 2,044 square feet

TREEHOUSE VILLAS AT SARATOGA SPRINGS RESORT & SPA
3-bedroom:
1,074 square feet

BOARDWALK VILLAS
Studio: 412 square feet (*gray area*);
1-bedroom: 814 square feet; **2-bedroom:** 1,236
square feet; **Grand Villa:** 2,491 square feet

THE VILLAS AT GRAND FLORIDIAN RESORT & SPA
Studio: 374 square feet (*gray area*)
1-bedroom: 844 square feet
2-bedroom lock-off: 1,232 square feet

DDV GUEST-OCCUPANCY LIMITS

Studios: 4 at all but Boulder Ridge Villas (5),
Grand Floridian (5), Polynesian (5),
and Riviera (2 for Tower Studios,
5 for Deluxe Studios)

- **1-bedroom villas:** 4 at Beach Club,
Saratoga Springs, and Boulder Ridge;
4 or 5 in Animal Kingdom Lodge
(Jambo House); 5 everywhere else

- **2-bedroom villas and bungalows:**
8 or 9 in Animal Kingdom Lodge
(Jambo House); 9 in Animal Kingdom
Lodge (Kidani Village), Bay Lake Tower,
BoardWalk, Old Key West, and Riviera; 9 or
10 at Grand Floridian; 8 everywhere else

- **3-bedroom and Grand Villas:**
9 at Treehouse Villas; 12 everywhere else

  Note: To all these limits you may add
  1 child under age 3 in a crib.

DISNEY DELUXE VILLA RESORTS
(continued)

ANIMAL KINGDOM VILLAS–JAMBO HOUSE
Studio: 316–365 square feet *(gray area)*
1-bedroom: 629–710 sf; **2-bedroom:** 945–1,075 sf
Grand Villa: 2,349 square feet

ANIMAL KINGDOM VILLAS–KIDANI VILLAGE
Studio: 366 square feet *(gray area)*
1-bedroom: 807 square feet
2-bedroom: 1,173 square feet
Grand Villa: 2,201 square feet

SARATOGA SPRINGS RESORT & SPA
Studio: 355 square feet *(gray area)*
1-bedroom: 714 square feet
2-bedroom: 1,075 square feet
Grand Villa: 2,113 square feet

POLYNESIAN VILLAGE BUNGALOWS
1,650 square feet

BOULDER RIDGE VILLAS
Studio: 356 square feet *(gray area)*
1-bedroom: 727 square feet
2-bedroom: 1,080 square feet

BEACH CLUB VILLAS
Studio: 356 square feet *(gray area)*
1-bedroom: 726 square feet
2-bedroom: 1,083 square feet

POLYNESIAN VILLAGE VILLAS
Studio: 460 square feet

DISNEY DELUXE VILLA RESORTS
(continued)

DISNEY'S RIVIERA RESORT
Deluxe Studio:
423 square feet (*gray area*)
1-bedroom: 813 square feet
2-bedroom lock-off:
1,246 square feet
3-bedroom: 2,530 square feet

DISNEY'S RIVIERA RESORT,
TOWER STUDIO
225 square feet;
accommodates 2 guests
plus 1 child under age 3 in a crib

DISNEY MODERATE RESORTS

CORONADO SPRINGS RESORT
Typical room, 314 square feet;
accommodates 4 guests
plus 1 child under age 3 in a crib

CARIBBEAN BEACH RESORT
Typical room, 314 square feet;
accommodates 5 guests
plus 1 child under age 3 in a crib

PORT ORLEANS RESORT–
FRENCH QUARTER
Typical room, 314 square feet;
accommodates 4 guests
plus 1 child under age 3 in a crib

PORT ORLEANS RESORT–RIVERSIDE
Typical room, 314 square feet;
accommodates 5 guests
plus 1 child under age 3 in a crib.
Alligator Bayou has trundle bed for
child (54" long) at no extra charge.

CORONADO SPRINGS RESORT,
GRAN DESTINO TOWER
Typical room, 375 square feet;
accommodates 4 guests plus
1 child under age 3 in a crib

DISNEY VALUE RESORTS

ART OF ANIMATION RESORT, *LITTLE MERMAID* STANDARD ROOM
Typical room, 277 square feet; accommodates 4 guests plus 1 child under age 3 in a crib

ART OF ANIMATION RESORT, *FINDING NEMO* FAMILY SUITE
Typical suite, 565 square feet; accommodates 6 guests plus 1 child under age 3 in a crib

ALL-STAR RESORTS (MUSIC AND SPORTS)
Typical room, 260 square feet; accommodates 4 guests plus 1 child under age 3 in a crib

ALL-STAR RESORTS FAMILY SUITE
Typical suite, 520 square feet; accommodates 6 guests plus 1 child under age 3 in a crib

ALL-STAR MOVIES RESORT
Typical room, 260 square feet; accommodates 4 guests plus 1 child under age 3 in a crib

POP CENTURY RESORT
Typical room, 260 square feet; accommodates 4 guests plus 1 child under age 3 in a crib

continued from page 113

Room soundproofing, however, is only half of the story; the other half, as any good real estate agent knows, is location, particularly as it relates to guest traffic. A pool-view room at any resort, for instance, is likely to pick up a lot more noise than an upper-floor corner room.

With all of these factors in mind, we set out to determine the amount of external noise affecting every single room at Walt Disney World. We took into account factors including the floor level, pedestrian traffic, proximity to public spaces, and number of nearby rooms.

Take the northwest-facing rooms in buildings 4 and 5 of Disney's **All-Star Music Resort:** They overlook the extreme end of a parking lot, well away from most public spaces. There's little pedestrian traffic here, and the rooms themselves are well soundproofed—a recipe for quiet, or so we thought. But as it turns out, the remoteness of this location isn't lost on Disney: It's where the diesel buses are warmed up in the morning before servicing the three All-Stars.

Our research indicates that quiet rooms can be found in almost any resort, regardless of price point. For readers who put peace and quiet

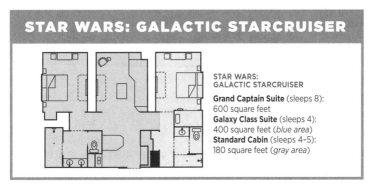

at the top of their lists, we've listed the 12 quietest spots among all WDW resorts in the table below.

Let There Be Light!

In addition to sound, we measure the amount of light available in three key areas of each hotel room: at the bathroom vanity or sink, at the desk or work area, and in bed. The good news is that Disney has been steadily improving the lighting throughout most of its resorts. The **Contemporary Resort** sets the standard: Light at the desk measures well above the

QUIETEST ROOMS AT WALT DISNEY WORLD
All-Star Music Buildings 5 and 6, rooms facing west
All-Star Sports Building 3, rooms facing west; building 2, rooms facing north
Bay Lake Tower Any room is good here—rooms are the quietest in WDW
Beach Club Easternmost hallways, rooms facing east
Beach Club Villas Rooms facing southeast
BoardWalk Inn All rooms facing courtyard, just east of main lobby
Caribbean Beach Trinidad South, buildings 35 and 38, rooms facing lake
Port Orleans Riverside Alligator Bayou, buildings 26 and 28, rooms facing east; Acadian House, north wings, rooms facing west
Port Orleans French Quarter Building 1, rooms facing water; building 7, north wing, rooms facing water; building 6, north wing, rooms facing water
Treehouse Villas Any room is good
Wilderness Lodge/Copper Creek Villas Middle of northernmost wing, rooms facing northwest (woods)
Boulder Ridge Villas Southernmost part of the building, water-view rooms facing east

recommended level for office or school work. Light at the bathroom vanity is brighter than normal daylight. Other resorts with good lighting include the **Riviera, Polynesian Village, Wilderness Lodge,** and the **All-Stars.** Resorts that didn't do well in our lighting test include **BoardWalk Villas** (before its 2023 redo) and **Port Orleans Riverside.** If you think you'll need to get work done while vacationing at Walt Disney World, consider staying at a hotel with good lighting.

Check-In and Checkout

Up to 60 days before you arrive, you can log on to mydisneyexperience .com to complete the check-in process, make room requests and dining reservations, and note events such as birthdays and anniversaries that you're celebrating during your trip. Depending on how much information you provide to the site before your trip, your resort check-in can be eliminated or streamlined considerably in a variety of ways.

DIRECT-TO-ROOM CHECK-IN If you provide the website with a credit card number, a PIN for purchases, and your arrival and departure times, Disney will send you an email or text confirmation that your check-in is complete. Next, Disney will email or text you with your room number a few hours before you arrive at your resort, allowing you to go straight to your room without stopping at the front desk.

unofficial **TIP**
Check the My Disney Experience app before you get in a long check-in line—sometimes the app will be updated with your room number even if you didn't get a text or email alert.

ONLINE CHECK-IN If you've checked in online but you haven't added a credit card or PIN to your account, you'll still be able to bypass the regular check-in desk and head for the Online Check-In Desk to finish the check-in process. *Note:* Online check-in should be completed at least 24 hours before you arrive.

AT THE FRONT DESK At the Value resorts, such as All-Star Sports, which get lots of tour and sports-team traffic, Disney has separate check-in areas for those groups, leaving the huge main check-in desk free for regular travelers. A cast member also roams the lobby and can issue an "all hands on deck" alert when lines develop. The arrival of a busload of guests can sometimes overwhelm the front desk of Deluxe resorts, which have smaller front desks and fewer agents, but this is the exception rather than the rule. If your room is unavailable when you arrive, Disney will either give you a phone number to call to check on the room or will offer to call or text you when it's ready.

On your checkout day, your bill will be prepared and emailed or available in My Disney Experience. If everything is in order, you have only to pack up and depart.

A Kutztown, Pennsylvania, reader jumped through the hoops, to no avail:

> We did online check-in, but when we got to the resort, there was no separate line for this—we had to stand in line with people doing regular check-in.

EARLY CHECK-IN Official check-in time is 3 p.m. at Disney hotels and 4 p.m. for DVC time-shares. Note that if you check in early and you ask for a room that's ready, that request will cancel out any previous one you've made.

HOUSEKEEPING SERVICE As of 2023, Disney's housekeeping service visits rooms every other day at Value and Moderate resorts and daily at the Deluxe resorts.

PARKING POLICIES Disney dropped its overnight parking fees in 2023. Guests staying at the campground section of **Disney's Fort Wilderness Resort** get a parking space for one vehicle. Day guests who visit the Disney resorts to eat, shop, use recreational facilities, and the like can park there for free (again, valet parking costs extra). Day parking in the theme parks is also free for guests staying on-property.

READERS' DISNEY RESORT REPORT CARD

EACH YEAR, SEVERAL THOUSAND READERS send in responses to our surveys. The Readers' 2023 Disney Resort Report Card, on pages 122–123, documents their opinions of the Walt Disney World resorts as well as the Swan, Dolphin, and Swan Reserve Resorts.

In the **% Stay Again** and **% Rec to Friends** columns, we list the percentage of readers responding "Definitely" to the questions "Would you stay at this hotel again?" and "Would you recommend this hotel to a friend?" Percentages of 97 or above in response to the first question and 94 or above in response to the second are considered **Above Average;** percentages of 82 or below in response to the first question and 79 or below in response to the second are considered **Below Average.** In the hotel profiles on the subsequent pages, we include these two percentages, plus the overall reader rating expressed as a letter grade, from the Report Card.

Room Quality reflects readers' satisfaction with their rooms, while **Check-In Efficiency** rates the speed and ease of check-in. **Quietness of Room** measures how well, in the guests' perception, their rooms are insulated from external noise. **Shuttle Service** rates Disney bus, boat, Skyliner, and/or monorail service to and from the hotels. **Pool** reflects readers' satisfaction with the resorts' swimming pools. **Staff** measures the friendliness and helpfulness of the resort's employees, and **Dining** rates the overall food quality and value.

Readers have ranked Disney resorts about the same over the past seven years, with most properties receiving an overall B rating. Also for a seventh consecutive year, bus transportation and dining options are the areas where Disney scores lowest. Check-in processing is an area where they do better than most.

Off-site hotels are, on average, rated slightly lower than Disney hotels, with problems noted in food courts and transportation. As noted earlier in this chapter, we think these ratings justify the premium that Disney charges at many of its hotels.

continued on page 124

READERS' 2023 DISNEY RESORT REPORT CARD

RESORT	PAGE	NO. OF SURVEYS	% STAY AGAIN	% REC TO FRIENDS	
VALUE					
ALL-STAR MOVIES	186	142	89	84	
ALL-STAR MUSIC	186	131	90	89	
ALL-STAR SPORTS	186	45	84	87	
ART OF ANIMATION	194	240	87	81	
CAMPSITES AT FORT WILDERNESS	205	47	98	90	
POP CENTURY	191	771	97	93	
MODERATE					
CABINS AT FORT WILDERNESS	205	48	85	79	
CARIBBEAN BEACH	160	299	92	87	
CORONADO SPRINGS	182	231	92	87	
PORT ORLEANS FRENCH QUARTER	172	276	94	88	
PORT ORLEANS RIVERSIDE	172	249	84	81	
DELUXE					
ANIMAL KINGDOM LODGE	177	154	92	90	
ANIMAL KINGDOM VILLAS–JAMBO HOUSE	177	65	91	89	
BEACH CLUB	147	173	95	91	
BEACH CLUB VILLAS	147	105	93	89	
BOARDWALK INN	152	134	90	85	
CONTEMPORARY	140	148	89	79	
GRAND FLORIDIAN	125	128	90	88	
POLYNESIAN VILLAGE	129	179	90	86	
POLYNESIAN VILLAS & BUNGALOWS	129	161	94	91	
WALT DISNEY WORLD DOLPHIN	156	97	92	80	
WALT DISNEY WORLD SWAN	156	92	93	83	
WALT DISNEY WORLD SWAN RESERVE	156	34	88	80	
WILDERNESS LODGE	135	128	94	90	
YACHT CLUB	147	194	96	95	
DELUXE VILLA (DVC)					
ANIMAL KINGDOM VILLAS–KIDANI VILLAGE	177	173	82	77	
BAY LAKE TOWER AT THE CONTEMPORARY	140	182	94	91	
BOARDWALK VILLAS	152	152	96	90	
BOULDER RIDGE VILLAS	135	47	91	85	
COPPER CREEK VILLAS & CASCADE CABINS	135	84	96	92	
OLD KEY WEST	170	157	94	84	
RIVIERA	163	148	97	93	
SARATOGA SPRINGS	165	223	92	88	
SHADES OF GREEN	144	56	100	92	
VILLAS AT THE GRAND FLORIDIAN	125	43	93	89	
Average for Disney Hotels			**91**	**87**	
Average for Off-Site Hotels			**84**	**74**	

Treehouse Villas at Disney's Saratoga Springs Resort and Star Wars: Galactic Starcruiser did not have enough surveys to rate for this edition.

ROOM QUALITY	CHECK-IN EFFICIENCY	QUIETNESS OF ROOM	PARK SHUTTLE SERVICE	POOL	STAFF	FOOD COURT	OVERALL
B-	B+	C-	B-	B-	B	D	C
B	B	B	C	B	B	C-	B
B-	B	C	C+		B	C	B-
B	B+	C	B	B	B	D	B
A	A	B	B	C+	B	C+	B
B	A	C+	B+	C-	C	D	B
B	B	A	B	C+	C	C	B
B	B+	B	B	B-	B	C	B
A	B	B	C	B	B	C	B
B	B+	B	B	B	B	D	B
B	B	B	C	B-	B	C	B-
A-	A-	B	C	B	B	B	B
B	A	B	C	B	B	B-	B
B	B	B	B	B+	B	C-	B
B+	B	B	C	A-	B	C	B
A	A	B	C	C+	B	D+	B
A	B	B	B-	B	B	C	B
A	B+	C	B	B	B	B	B
A	B	C	B+	B	B	C+	B
A-	B	B	B	B	B	C	B
B	B-	B	D	B	B	C	C+
B	B	B	D	B-	B	C	B
B	B	B	D	B	B	C	B
A	B+	B	B	B	B	C	B
A-	A-	B	B-	B+	B	C	B
A	B+	B+	C	B	B	C	B
A	A-	B+	B	B	B	B	B
A	A	B	B	B	B	C-	B
B	A	B	B	A-	A	C-	B
A	B	B	B	B	B	B	B
A	B	B	C	B	B	C	B
A	A-	A	B	B	B	B	A-
A	B+	B	C	B	B	C	B
A	A-	B	C+	B+	B	C	B
A	B+	B	B	B	B	B	B
B	**B+**	**B**	**B-**	**B**	**B**	**C-**	**B**
B	**B-**	**C**	**F**	**D**	**D**	**F**	**C**

UNOFFICIAL PICKS FOR DISNEY ON-SITE RESORTS

ADULTS

VALUE: Pop Century For the nostalgic decor and new room designs

MODERATE: Port Orleans French Quarter For its theming and small, intimate size

DELUXE: Grand Floridian For excellent service and access to good sit-down restaurants

GROUPS OF 5 OR MORE

VALUE: Art of Animation Newest suites with two baths

MODERATE: Port Orleans Riverside One or two connecting rooms in Alligator Bayou

DELUXE: Old Key West Two-bedroom villa (booked with DVC rental points)

FAMILIES WITH YOUNG KIDS

VALUE: Art of Animation Kids will delight in the architecture and themed pools.

MODERATE: Port Orleans French Quarter Kid-friendly, smaller-scale resort

DELUXE: Animal Kingdom Lodge Fantastic scenery and chances to see animals

FAMILIES WITH OLDER KIDS

VALUE: Pop Century A lively pool scene means meeting new friends. Very teen-friendly food court, with Art of Animation's within walking distance.

MODERATE: Fort Wilderness There's plenty of opportunity to independently explore this massive resort, and having a kitchen means you won't have to take out a second mortgage to feed the bottomless pits that are teen stomachs.

DELUXE: Yacht & Beach Clubs For Stormalong Bay and easy access to EPCOT and Disney's Hollywood Studios

continued from page 121

Putting It All Together: Reader Picks for Best and Worst Resorts

Disney's **Riviera Resort** takes top honors in this year's survey, for the first time ever. The Riviera is highly rated in every category except food, where it gets a solid B score. Ignoring cost, we'd probably agree that this is Disney's top resort. Just behind the Riviera are **Bay Lake Tower** and **The Villas at Disney's Grand Floridian Resort & Spa.** The Grand Flo Villas took the top spot in our reader survey for the previous seven years. Both resorts get room quality and quietness.

The highest-rated Disney Moderate resorts are **Caribbean Beach** and **Coronado Springs.** We think readers really like the Skyliner transportation option at Caribbean Beach and the price at Coronado relative to other Moderates. All Disney Value resorts are rated about the same.

The lowest-rated Disney resorts remain the **Swan, Swan Reserve,** and **Dolphin.** All are rated low for transportation to the parks and for dining options. We think readers are spot-on with those assessments.

WALT DISNEY WORLD HOTEL PROFILES

FOR MORE INFORMATION on the Disney resorts, including photos and videos, check out our website, **TouringPlans.com.**

One of our readers' top concerns is getting quickly to the parks using Disney's transportation network. The simplest way to reduce your transportation wait is to walk—for example, from the Polynesian, Grand Floridian, or Contemporary to the Magic Kingdom, or from any EPCOT resort to EPCOT or Disney's Hollywood Studios. The next best alternative is to get a taxi or ride-hailing service to drop you off at the closest resort to the park you're visiting and walk over. Driving your own car or taking a Disney bus is the next best option. Boats and the Skyliner may take the longest to get you to the parks.

THE MAGIC KINGDOM RESORTS
Disney's Grand Floridian Resort & Spa

(See map on page 126; see **tinyurl.com/ug-grandfloridian** *for extended coverage.)*

STRENGTHS	WEAKNESSES
• High staff-to-guest ratio	• Most expensive WDW resort
• Excellent dining options for adults	• Public areas often blocked by wedding parties
• Large rooms with daybeds	
• Very good on-site spa	• Noise from Magic Kingdom, boat horns, and whistles
• Fantastic kids' *Alice in Wonderland*-themed splash area	
• Boat and monorail transportation to the Magic Kingdom, plus a pedestrian walkway	• Bus transportation to DHS, Animal Kingdom, water parks, and Disney Springs is shared by the other monorail resorts
• Diverse recreational options	
• Close to Palm, Magnolia, and Oak Trail Golf Courses	

Unofficial Guide **Reader-Survey Results**

Percentage of readers who'd stay here again	90% *(Average)*
Percentage of readers who'd recommend this resort to a friend	88% *(Average)*
Overall reader rating	B

QUICK TAKE: *The Villas at Disney's Grand Floridian Resort & Spa (page 128) is one of the highest-rated resorts in Walt Disney World. It also has many sit-down restaurants that are rated near the top of our reader surveys. If the Villas are within your budget, your only big decision is whether to stay there or in Animal Kingdom Lodge & Villas (see page 177).*

WALT DISNEY WORLD'S FLAGSHIP HOTEL was inspired by grand Victorian resorts such as the Hotel del Coronado in San Diego and Mount Washington Resort in New Hampshire. A complex of four- and five-story white-frame buildings, the Grand Floridian integrates verandas, intricate latticework, dormers, and turrets beneath a red-shingle roof to capture the most distinctive elements of 19th-century ocean-resort architecture. Covering 40 acres along Seven Seas Lagoon, the Grand Floridian offers lovely pools, white-sand beaches, and a marina.

The 867 guest rooms, with wood trim and soft goods (curtains, linens, towels, and the like) in tones of deep red, gold, and tan, are luxurious, though the mocha-colored walls are a little dreary at night. The woodwork, marble-topped sinks, and ceiling fans amplify the Victorian theme. Large by any standard, the typical room is 440 square feet (dormer rooms are smaller) and furnished with two queen beds,

Grand Floridian Resort & Spa and Grand Floridian Villas

a daybed, and a small desk with chair. Many rooms have a balcony. All rooms have a Keurig coffee maker, a large dresser with minifridge, and a wall-mounted TV.

Bathrooms are large, with plenty of counter space and fluffy towels. Two shelves under the sink provide a small amount of storage. A 1,500-watt, wall-mounted hair dryer is provided, but it's not very powerful, so bring your own if you have lots of hair. Water pressure in the shower is probably less than what you get at home but still enough to rinse out shampoo suds. A separate dressing area next to the bathroom includes two sinks and enough counter space to fit most of your toiletries. Combined with the bathroom, this allows three people to get dressed at the same time.

With a high ratio of staff to guests, service is outstanding. The hotel is connected directly to the Magic Kingdom by monorail, boat, and a pedestrian walkway, and to other Disney World destinations by bus. Walking time to the monorail-, boat-, and bus-loading areas from the most remote guest rooms is about 7–10 minutes. It takes about 15–20 minutes on the pedestrian walkway to get to the Magic Kingdom turnstiles from the farthest points of the Grand Floridian.

The resort has several full-service restaurants, including **Victoria & Albert's.** Others are a short monorail ride or walk away.

The Grand Floridian's **Senses Spa,** modeled after the spas on the Disney Cruise Line ships, is one of the best in the Orlando area. In addition, the resort's pools are among the nicest on Disney property. The **Courtyard Pool,** large enough that local waterfowl mistake it for a lake, has a zero-entry ramp for small children to splash in. Cabanas are available to rent here too. An *Alice in Wonderland*–themed splash area sits between the main building and the Villas. If your kids like water, this is the place to be.

The rest of the Grand Floridian's grounds are maintained to an extremely high standard. It's a lovely place to walk around during the evening, with romantic light levels and charming background music. A stroll from the marina, past the resort's main buildings, and over to the Polynesian Village for a nightcap is a nice way to end the evening.

Most reader comments concerning the Grand Floridian are positive. First, from a Durham, North Carolina, mother of two preschoolers:

> *The Grand Floridian pool with the waterslide was a big hit with our kids. They also loved taking the boat across the lagoon to return from the Magic Kingdom.*

Speaking of pools, a father of two from Minneapolis had this specific concern:

> *The concrete surrounding the Grand Floridian's beach pool gets very hot. Walking from pool chair to pool was a very painful experience and one that could have been avoided with proper materials [for example, heat-reducing concrete].*

GOOD (AND NOT-SO-GOOD) ROOMS AT THE GRAND FLORIDIAN *(See* tinyurl.com/gfroomviews *for photos.)* The resort is spread over a peninsula that juts into Seven Seas Lagoon. In addition to the main building, there are five dispersed rectangular buildings. Most of the rooms have a balcony, and most balconies are enclosed by a rail that affords good visibility. Dormer rooms, just beneath the roof in each building, have smaller enclosed balconies that limit visibility when you're seated. Most dormer rooms, however, have vaulted ceilings and a coziness that compensates for the less-desirable balconies.

The main building displays life-size gingerbread houses at Christmas, which brings noise and crowds to the lobby.

If you want to be near the bus and monorail, most of the restaurants, and shopping, ask for a room in the main building (all Club Level rooms). The best rooms are **4322–4329** and **4422–4429,** which have full balconies and overlook the lagoon in the direction of the beach and the Polynesian Village. Other excellent main-building rooms are **4401–4409,** with full balconies overlooking the marina and an unobstructed view of Cinderella

unofficial **TIP**
In 2022, the Grand Floridian converted all 200 guest rooms in its Big Pine Key building to DVC studios. This reduced the number of rooms available for cash-paying guests and likely increased cost too.

Castle across the lagoon. The main building is, not surprisingly, the highest-rated building at the Grand Flo (Sugar Loaf Key is second).

Of the four lodges, two—**Boca Chica** and **Conch Key**—have one long side facing the lagoon and the other facing inner courtyards and swimming pools. At Conch Key, full-balcony rooms **7229–7231, 7328, 7329, 7331, 7425–7429,** and **7431** offer vistas across the lagoon to the Magic Kingdom and castle. Room **7427** is just about perfect. Less-expensive rooms in the same building that offer good marina views are **7212, 7312, 7412–7415, 7417, 7419, 7421, 7513–7515,** and **7517.** (Grand Floridian room numbers are coded. Take room 7213: 7 is the building number, 2 is the floor, and 13 is the room number.) In Boca Chica, ask for a lagoon-view room on the first, second, or third floor. A few garden-view rooms in Boca Chica have views obstructed by a poolside building. These are the worst views from any Grand Floridian room.

The two remaining buildings, **Sugar Loaf Key** (Club Level) and **Sago Key,** face each other across the marina. The opposite side of Sugar Loaf Key faces a courtyard, while the other side of Sago Key faces a finger of the lagoon and a forested area. These views are pleasant but not in the same league as those from the rooms listed previously. Exceptions are end rooms in Sago Key that have a view of the lagoon and Cinderella Castle (rooms **5139, 5144, 5145, 5242–5245,** and **5342–5345**).

THE VILLAS AT DISNEY'S GRAND FLORIDIAN RESORT & SPA

(See map on page 126; see **tinyurl.com/ug-gfvillas** *for extended coverage.)*

Unofficial Guide **Reader-Survey Results**

Percentage of readers who'd stay here again	**93%** *(Average)*
Percentage of readers who'd recommend this resort to a friend	**89%** *(Average)*
Overall reader rating	**B**

THIS DISNEY DELUXE VILLA PROPERTY opened in the fall of 2013. Readers consistently rate it as one of the three best resorts in Walt Disney World, and it's the absolute favorite of many.

Decorated in neutral tones, with mostly green and red accent colors, the rooms are the nicest at any DDV property. Most have vaulted living-room ceilings and faux-wood balconies or porches. Those balconies stretch the entire length of the room, giving everyone enough space for a good view.

Studios have a kitchenette with minifridge, sink, and drip coffee maker, while the larger rooms have full kitchens. Those feature a stainless steel oven range, with the dishwasher and refrigerator tucked behind white wood panels that match the glass-door cabinets. Other amenities in the full kitchens include a full-size drip coffee maker, a toaster, frying pans, and the usual set of plates, glasses, cups, and cutlery. Also in the kitchen are a banquette seat and a table with room for six.

The living room has a sofa that seats three comfortably, an upholstered chair and ottoman, a coffee table, and a large flat-screen TV. The sofa converts into a bed that sleeps two; a cabinet below the TV hides a small pull-down bed. We'd use these beds for kids, not adults.

Studio rooms have a queen bed in addition to the folding options listed above. One-bedroom villas have a king bed along with the folding options; two-bedroom villas have a king bed in one room and two queen beds in the other, plus the folding options; the Grand Villa's third bedroom has an additional two queen beds.

The one- and two-bedroom units and the Grand Villa bedrooms are outfitted with a large writing desk, a flat-screen TV with DVD player, two nightstands with convenient electric plugs, and a side chair. They also have large walk-in closets.

Bathrooms are large, with marble tile and flat-screen TVs built into the mirrors. Studio bathrooms have a separate toilet and shower area; in the one-bedroom configuration, a tub and dressing area sit adjacent to the bedroom. The bathroom and shower are connected by a pocket door, allowing two groups of people to get dressed at the same time. The tiled shower looks as if it could comfortably hold eight people should the need arise. It also has a rain showerhead mounted in the ceiling in addition to a wall-mounted faucet.

The villas have their own parking lot next to the building but no on-site dining. Within walking distance, however, are the restaurants of both the main Grand Floridian and the Polynesian Village, giving you a bit more variety than at other Magic Kingdom resorts. Room service is available from the Grand Floridian's in-room dining menu. Rates are high, as you might expect, but renting DVC points helps in that regard.

GOOD (AND NOT-SO-GOOD) ROOMS AT THE GRAND FLORIDIAN VILLAS *(See* tinyurl.com/gfvillaviews *for photos.)* Rooms **1X14**, **1X16**, and **1X18** face the Magic Kingdom and have views of Space Mountain and the castle; **1X14** has probably the best views of any room in all of the Villas. (*X* indicates a floor number.)

Even-numbered rooms **1X02–1X12** face west, toward the Polynesian Village and Seven Seas Lagoon, and afford a good view of the nightly water pageant as it floats by.

Rooms **1X15, 1X17, 1X19–1X22, 1X24, 1X26,** and **1X28** face Disney's Wedding Pavilion, the parking lot, the monorail, and landscaping. Odd-numbered rooms **1X03–1X13** and **1X25, 1X27,** and **1X29** look out onto the pool facilities and landscaping.

South-facing rooms in Big Pine Key look out over the Seven Seas Lagoon, although mature trees and landscaping partially block those views from many upper-floor rooms. Rooms **9X41–9X47** may have views of the Magic Kingdom fireworks.

Note: Rooms at the Villas will be affected by construction noise at the Polynesian Village's DVC tower next door through most of 2024.

Disney's Polynesian Village Resort, Villas & Bungalows
(See map on page 130; see tinyurl.com/ug-poly *for extended coverage.)*

STRENGTHS	WEAKNESSES
• Walking distance to EPCOT monorail	• Close to Palm, Magnolia, and Oak Trail Golf Courses
• Most family-friendly dining on the monorail loop	**WEAKNESSES**
• Fun South Seas theme	• No spa or exercise facilities (guests must use those at the Grand Floridian)
• Boat and monorail transportation to the Magic Kingdom	• Noise from boat horns and whistles
• Among the best Club Levels of the Deluxe resorts	• Construction noise through 2024
	• Bus transportation to DHS, Animal Kingdom, water parks, and Disney Springs

Polynesian Village Resort, Villas & Bungalows

Unofficial Guide **Reader-Survey Results**
(resort only; see page 133 for villa/bungalow ratings)

Percentage of readers who'd stay here again	**90%** *(Average)*
Percentage of readers who'd recommend this resort to a friend	**86%** *(Average)*
Overall reader rating	**B**

SOUTH PACIFIC TROPICS ARE RE-CREATED at this Deluxe resort, which consists of two- and three-story Hawaiian longhouses situated around the four-story **Great Ceremonial House,** which contains restaurants, shops, and an atrium lobby with slate floors and many species of tropical plants. Buildings feature wood accents, including exposed roof beams and tribal-inspired geometric inlays in the cornices.

Spread across 39 acres along Seven Seas Lagoon, the resort, which has fewer than 500 standard hotel rooms, has three white-sand beaches, some with volleyball courts. Its pool complex likewise captures the South Pacific theme. There is no dedicated fitness center, but guests are welcome to use the Grand Floridian's facilities, just a quarter-mile walk or 2-minute monorail ride away. Landscaping is superb—garden-view rooms are generally superior to equivalent rooms at other resorts.

The Polynesian Village's **Moorea, Pago Pago,** and **Tokelau** buildings are part of Disney's time-share program (described in the next section).

Except for the three aforementioned buildings, the resort opened with the Magic Kingdom in 1971. The most recent room refurbishments were completed in summer 2021, adding bright, island-themed murals and subtle references to characters from Disney's *Moana*.

We're always suspicious when Disney adds characters to anything, as it's often an attempt to distract from something else. But this is one of Disney's better room-renovation projects in recent memory, and the *Moana* additions work well with the resort's theme. As before, most rooms have two queen beds, a sofa, a reading chair, a large dresser with plenty of shelf space, and a wall-mounted TV. A minifridge and coffee maker sit between two large closets near the doorway and opposite the bathroom area. The closets are spacious and light. Lighting throughout the room, including that for the desk and beds, has improved.

The Poly's bathrooms have also been redone. Two large sinks offer plenty of counter space. A spacious, glass-enclosed shower provides good-to-excellent water pressure. (*Note:* We're pretty sure that most bathrooms have only showers, not bathtubs, so if a tub is important to you, ask your travel agent or Disney about it when booking.) The new bathroom layout includes a door between the toilet and sink area, plus another separating the entire bathroom from the rest of the room. This allows three people to get dressed at once—an improvement over the old bathroom design.

The Polynesian Village has an on-site monorail station, and all rooms are within easy walking distance of the monorail station at the Transportation and Ticket Center with access to the EPCOT monorail. Easily accessible by monorail are full-service restaurants at the Grand Floridian and Contemporary Resorts, as well as restaurants in the Magic Kingdom. Bus service is available to other Disney destinations, and boat service takes you to the Magic Kingdom. Walking time to the bus and on-site monorail stations from the most remote rooms is

8–11 minutes. The pedestrian walkway between the Poly and Grand Floridian continues to the Magic Kingdom—it's about 1.5 miles from the farthest point at the Poly to the Magic Kingdom turnstiles.

The Poly's transportation options are a major draw for some readers:

We stay at the Polynesian Village because it offers the best transportation. You can walk to a direct monorail to both the Magic Kingdom and EPCOT, the water taxi can be a fast option, and the bus service to other parks is fairly direct.

A Maryland family found the room soundproofing lacking, confirming our own research:

We took towels from the pool and stuffed them under the door to deaden the noise coming from the connecting room.

Unofficial Guide correspondents Dawn and Taylor gave us this scoop about self-parking:

The parking situation here was INSANE! People were circling like vultures—like what you'd see at the mall on Black Friday.

The Polynesian Village has two lounges, with **Trader Sam's Grog Grotto** being the more themed. Modeled after the famed bar of the same name at the Disneyland Hotel, Trader Sam's serves whimsical (and potent) cocktails and tasty appetizers, along with interactive art and "artifacts" stuffed into every available inch of space. We love it ourselves, although in this Hartford, Wisconsin, reader's eyes, it's not special enough to warrant a stay at the resort:

unofficial **TIP**
During busier times of the year, it can take several hours to get a table at Trader Sam's.

After I stayed in Animal Kingdom Lodge in a savanna-view room, the Polynesian Village was a letdown. The proximity to the Magic Kingdom is nice, and Trader Sam's was awesome, but otherwise it was nothing extraordinary. They need to step it up for what they charge.

GOOD (AND NOT-SO-GOOD) ROOMS AT POLYNESIAN VILLAGE RESORT *(See tinyurl.com/polyroomviews for photos.)* The Polynesian Village's 11 guest room buildings, or longhouses, are spread over a long strip of land bordered by the monorail on one side and Seven Seas Lagoon on the other. All buildings have first-floor patios and third-floor balconies. The older buildings, which comprise more than half of the resort's rooms, have faux balconies on their second floors. (The newer buildings offer full balconies on both the second and third floors, and patios on the first.) Although mature vegetation blocks the views from a small number of patios, they provide more room than the balconies on the third floor. If views are important and you're staying in one of the eight older longhouses, ask for a third-floor room.

The Great Ceremonial House contains most of the restaurants and shops, as well as the resort lobby, guest services, and bus and monorail stations. The longhouses most convenient to the Great Ceremonial House—**Fiji**, the **Tonga suites, Rarotonga, Niue,** and **Samoa**—offer views of the swimming complex, a small marina, or inner gardens (possibly with the monorail). There are no lagoon views except for oblique views from the upper floors of Fiji, Samoa, and Tuvalu; Aotearoa; and a tunnel view from Tonga. Samoa, however, by virtue of its proximity to the main swimming complex, is a good choice for families who plan to spend time at the pool. If your children are under age 8, request a first-floor room on the volcano-pool side of Samoa. The 22-room Niue is the highest-rated building at the Polynesian. You're not going to get views of the Magic Kingdom, but Niue is centrally located between both pools and the Great Ceremonial House. (It should also be well insulated from construction noise.)

You can specifically request a lagoon- or Magic Kingdom–view room at the Polynesian Village, provided you're willing to pay extra. The best of these rooms are on the third floor in **Tuvalu** and, if you're staying in a Club Level (concierge) room, the third floor in **Hawaii.**

In addition to second-floor rooms in the older buildings (the ones with fake balconies), we also advise against booking the monorail-side (south-facing) rooms in **Rarotonga** and **Aotearoa.** Garden-view rooms here are especially nice, but the monorail, though quiet, runs within spitting distance.

Many first-floor rooms in **Hawaii (1501–1518)** are garden- or lagoon-view rooms; their scenery is blocked by the over-the-water bungalows. These rooms still offer a chance to see the evening fireworks, however, and are a little less expensive than similar rooms on higher floors.

Tuvalu, Fiji, and **Aotearoa** are the most distant accommodations from the bus stop. For large strollers or wheelchair access, take the ferry to the Magic Kingdom.

POLYNESIAN VILLAS & BUNGALOWS

Unofficial Guide Reader-Survey Results

Percentage of readers who'd stay here again	94% (*Average*)
Percentage of readers who'd recommend this resort to a friend	91% (*Average*)
Overall reader rating	B

THE TOKELAU, MOOREA, AND PAGO PAGO longhouses hold DVC studio rooms that sleep five and are the largest studios in Walt Disney World's DVC inventory. They also have two bathrooms: The smaller bath has a small sink and step-in shower; the larger has a toilet, sink, and bath/shower combination. This allows three people to get ready simultaneously. The studios also include kitchenettes.

While these studios are functionally similar to the Poly's standard rooms, they have enough small touches to make them different, including recessed ceilings, more stone and tile work in the baths, and a slightly darker color scheme.

The Polynesian's 20 over-the-water **Bora Bora Bungalows** sit in front of Hawaii, Tokelau, and Moorea. Connected to land by a wood walkway, these two-bedroom bungalows offer stunning views of the Magic Kingdom fireworks and of Seven Seas Lagoon and its nightly Electrical Water Pageant. Not surprisingly, those stunning views come with stunning prices—up to $6,100 per night.

Let's start with the positives: The bungalows are well built, with top-notch design elements from top to bottom. The bedrooms are spacious, the beds are the best on Disney property, the bathrooms are gorgeous, and the showers will make you feel as happy as anything nonsentient can. The open kitchen design works wonderfully, and you could easily host a good-size party inside. The floors are spotlessly clean, with interesting slate and rug textures, so you'll want to run around barefoot. Hell, the doorbell plays a different chime every time you ring it. And yeah, the views are spectacular.

The bungalows' two fatal flaws: price and location. First of all, 115 DVC points for a one-night stay is equivalent to about $2,300 in cash at the time of this writing. Check-in is at 4 p.m. and checkout at 11 a.m., so a 19-hour stay costs about $121 an hour.

During our first stay, we couldn't check in at 4—we never got our room assignment by text, email, or phone. It wasn't until we walked back to the front desk at 5 p.m. that we finally got our bungalow. The 75 minutes we couldn't use it amounted to about $150 in lost time—almost enough to pay for an entire night at Saratoga Springs. And nobody said a word about it.

The first "Are you out of the room yet?" knock on our door came before 9 a.m. We're not kidding.

Then there's the ferry horn. We were in 7019, the second-closest bungalow to the Transportation and Ticket Center (TTC) ferry dock. A ferry leaves here about every 12 minutes, from about 30–45 minutes before the park opens until an hour after closing. Every time a ferry departs, it has to sound a warning horn so that nearby craft know it's coming.

The sound of the horn is akin to an air-raid siren: loud enough to stop indoor conversation in its tracks. Reading, watching TV, getting a baby to nap? Forget it. You simply can't hear or think above the noise.

If the bungalows were on the other side of the Poly's marina, we could *almost* justify selling a gently used organ to stay here again, but between the stratospheric prices and that hellish horn, we just can't. If you're determined to stay here anyway, shoot for one of **bungalows 7001–7005,** which are farthest from the TTC.

The Polynesian Villas have a separate parking lot close to their longhouses. Dining and transportation are shared with the main resort.

NEW DVC BUILDING Disney is in the midst of construction of a large new DVC building for the Polynesian. This new tower, which concept art suggests is at least eight stories high, will sit on the northwest side of the Polynesian's land, between the existing Aotearoa and Fiji buildings, and Disney's Wedding Pavilion at the Grand Floridian. A new pool complex is also planned between those existing buildings and the new tower.

The project has an aggressive construction schedule, with an expected opening in 2024. This construction is significantly affecting the view and noise level at Aotearoa and Fiji buildings, and at Tuvalu and Tonga to a lesser extent. The walkway between the Polynesian and the Grand Floridian (and, thus, the Magic Kingdom) may be closed for parts of this construction, though plans show the walkway again once work is complete.

GOOD (AND NOT-SO-GOOD) ROOMS AT THE POLYNESIAN VILLAS Because there are a few quirks in the way Disney categorizes room views here, it's possible to snag a Magic Kingdom view from a garden-view room. The second- and third-floor rooms in **Tokelau** (**2901–2928, 2939–2948, 3901–3928,** and **3939–3948**) offer the best shot at getting side views of Cinderella Castle and the fireworks, although readers report that palm trees may block some second-floor views. First-floor rooms (**1901–1913** and **1939–1948**) may also have landscaping blocking some views; on the upside, the patios provide room to move to find a better spot. Overall, Tokelau is the highest-rated DVC building at the Polynesian.

The second and third floors in **Moorea** have rooms with lagoon and Magic Kingdom views; those that face north see the Magic Kingdom. Avoid **Pago Pago**'s southeast-facing rooms (**1X01–1X12**)—these look onto the parking lot and monorail.

If you plan to spend a lot of time in EPCOT, **Moorea** and **Pago Pago** are good choices because they're within easy walking distance of the TTC and the EPCOT monorail. Even if you're going to the Magic Kingdom, it's a shorter walk from Moorea and Pago Pago to the TTC and Magic Kingdom monorail than to the monorail station at the Great Ceremonial House.

Disney's Wilderness Lodge, Boulder Ridge Villas, and Copper Creek Villas & Cascade Cabins

(See map on page 136; see tinyurl.com/ug-wlodge *for extended coverage.)*

STRENGTHS	WEAKNESSES
• National park lodge theme is a favorite of kids and adults alike	• Transportation to Magic Kingdom is by bus or boat only
• Along with Animal Kingdom Lodge, it's the least expensive Disney Deluxe resort	• Noise from main building's lobby can be heard inside nearby rooms
• Excellent lounge for adults	• Bus transportation to Magic Kingdom sometimes shared with Fort Wilderness
• Close to recreational options at Fort Wilderness	• Smallest rooms and baths of Disney's Deluxe resorts
• Great views from guest rooms	
• Exceptionally peaceful location and public areas (Villas)	

Unofficial Guide **Reader-Survey Results** *(Wilderness Lodge only; see page 138 for Copper Creek Villas and Cascade Cabins and page 139 for Boulder Ridge Villas)*

Percentage of readers who'd stay here again	**94%** *(Average)*
Percentage of readers who'd recommend this resort to a friend	**90%** *(Average)*
Overall reader rating	**B**

QUICK TAKE: *Hotel rooms at the lodge, DVC rooms at Copper Creek Villas, and (if it's in your budget) the Cascade Cabins are our picks.*

THIS DELUXE RESORT is inspired by grand, rustic Arts and Crafts lodges of the early 20th century—think The Ahwahnee in Yosemite National Park and the Grove Park Inn in Asheville, North Carolina. Situated on the shore of Bay Lake, the lodge consists of an eight-story central building augmented by two seven-story guest wings, a wing of studio and one- and two-bedroom condominiums, and 26 lakeside cabins. The hotel features exposed timber columns, log cabin–style facades, and dormer windows, along with an 82-foot-tall stone fireplace in the lobby. Outside, there's a beach and a delightful pool modeled on a mountain stream.

We use the admittedly clunky "Wilderness Lodge & Boulder Ridge/ Copper Creek Villas" to refer to the entire complex, including its

Wilderness Lodge & Boulder Ridge/Copper Creek Villas

Bay Lake

Cascade Cabins

Geyser Point Bar & Grill

Copper Creek Villas

Boulder Ridge Villas

Wilderness Lodge

Cascade Cabins

time-share units, which are available to the general public when not being used by DVC members. (The full name is Disney's Wilderness Lodge, Boulder Ridge Villas, and Copper Creek Villas & Cascade Cabins, which is what happens when you pay a marketing team by the pound.) Here's what the various names mean:

- **Disney's Wilderness Lodge** refers to the hotel (that is, the non-time-share) component of the main building (the lodge), which opened in 1994.

- **Boulder Ridge Villas** (Boulder Ridge for short) refers to time-share rooms in an adjacent building that opened in 2000.

- **Copper Creek Villas & Cascade Cabins** (Copper Creek for short) refers to DVC time-share rooms in the main building (Copper Creek Villas) and the lakeside Cascade Cabins, both opened in 2017.

The lodge's guest rooms were last refurbished in 2012. Darkly stained Mission-style furniture is complemented by soft goods in burnt umber and blue, accented with American Indian–inspired patterns. Carved-wood headboards, rough-hewn armoires, and rustic light fixtures create a log cabin atmosphere.

Typical rooms have two queen beds. Single king rooms are also available. All rooms have a table and chairs, a dresser, a TV, a double vanity just outside the bathroom, a minifridge, and a coffee maker. Rooms on the ground floor have patios; rooms above have balconies.

The pool area features a children's water-play area and a pool bar.

Dining choices consist of two full-service restaurants plus the outdoor **Geyser Point Bar & Grill.** More dining options are available via a short boat ride to the Contemporary or Fort Wilderness.

The resort is connected to the Magic Kingdom by boat and to other parks by bus. Your best bet for catching the first boat is to send someone out to the boat dock about 90 minutes before the Magic Kingdom's official opening time. If a line has started to form but has fewer than 30 people, get in line. If the line is longer than that, consider taking a bus or using a ride-hailing app. Boat service may be suspended during storms, so if it's raining or rain looks likely, Disney will provide buses. Walking time to buses and boats from the most remote rooms is 5–8 minutes.

A Boone County, Indiana, reader thinks transportation is a weak spot:

> To paraphrase Mark Twain, rumors that Wilderness Lodge's transportation problems have been resolved are greatly exaggerated—it's an easy boat ride to the Magic Kingdom, but bus trips to the Studios and Animal Kingdom take nearly an hour, which is just inexcusable.

A mom from Oklahoma City concurs:

> During our most recent stay, transportation from Wilderness Lodge to the parks was the worst we have ever experienced in all our trips to WDW. We waited more than an hour for a boat to the Magic Kingdom; then, after it finally showed up and loaded, we made an unexplained trip to Fort Wilderness and loaded 26 more people. It took 90 minutes to get to the Magic Kingdom! The bus system wasn't much better—it's nearly impossible to get to the parks before opening.

GOOD (AND NOT-SO-GOOD) ROOMS AT WILDERNESS LODGE *(See tinyurl.com/wlroomviews for photos.)* The lodge is shaped like a very blocky letter V. The main entrance and lobby are at the closed end of the V. Next are middle wings that connect the lobby to the parallel end sections, which extend to the open part of the V. The V's open end flanks pools and gardens and overlooks Bay Lake directly or obliquely. Avoid rooms on the fourth, fifth, and sixth floors numbered 67–99; these overlook the main lobby and pick up any noise there.

The better rooms are on floors four, five, and six, toward the V's open end. On the very end of the northernmost V, rooms **4000–4003,**

5000–5003, and **6000–6003** offer a direct frontal view of Bay Lake through some tall trees. Toward the end of the *V* on the parallel wings but facing inward, odd-numbered rooms **4005–4023, 5005–5023,** and **6005–6023** face the courtyard but have excellent oblique lake views. Even-numbered rooms **5004–5034** and **6004–6034** face the Cascade Cabins; the woodlands northwest of the lodge; and, beyond the woodlands, the Magic Kingdom.

Odd-numbered rooms **5035–5041** and **6035–6041,** on the lake end of the parallel middle wings, offer a direct but distant view of the lake, with pools and gardens in the foreground.

Standard-view rooms **X042–X066** are some of the cheapest in the main building, with views of parking lots, service areas, and such, and the Cascade Cabins in the foreground. Avoid these on the fourth floor. On the fifth and sixth floors, however, these rooms afford views of the Magic Kingdom fireworks and are more expensive. (Seventh-floor rooms are Club Level—that is, expensive. These rooms aren't recommended because only those facing the Magic Kingdom have nice views, and even those have a service area in the foreground.)

The rooms listed previously afford the most desirable views, but if you can't score one, you're pretty much assured of a woodland view or a room fronting the faux rocks and creek in the *V*'s inner courtyard. Almost all rooms at Wilderness Lodge have balconies.

COPPER CREEK VILLAS & CASCADE CABINS

Unofficial Guide Reader-Survey Results

Percentage of readers who'd stay here again	96% (*Average*)
Percentage of readers who'd recommend this resort to a friend	82% (*Average*)
Overall reader rating	B

SOME ROOMS IN THE LODGE'S MAIN BUILDING are DVC units—Disney calls these Copper Creek Villas. Options include studios and one-, two-, and three-bedroom villas. The studios have kitchenettes, while most one- and two-bedroom villas have full kitchens (the one-bedroom we stayed in had a galley kitchen). All rooms have vinyl plank flooring; modern furniture, including a table and chairs; a coffee maker; and a microwave. Bathrooms are spacious, although sink space is limited; storage is plentiful otherwise.

Copper Creek rooms have less theming than those in the rest of the lodge—with another color of paint and different knickknacks, they could be rooms at Saratoga Springs or Animal Kingdom Lodge. Nonetheless, they're so well appointed and comfortable that they highlight the need for refurbishments at the older Boulder Ridge Villas.

We've stayed multiple times at the lakeside Cascade Cabins. Their floor plan (page 114) is similar to that of the Bora Bora Bungalows at Polynesian Village. Room quality and views are excellent—and they'd better be at these prices—around $4,900 per night in peak season.

We prefer the cabins over the bungalows, as does this Iowa City, Iowa, reader:

Loved the cabin at Copper Creek—better value than the Polynesian bungalows. Quiet and well arranged, but close to everything.

GOOD (AND NOT-SO-GOOD) ROOMS AT COPPER CREEK VILLAS These rooms are in the main building's southeast wing. Avoid rooms **X100–X106,** which overlook the lobby. Odd-numbered rooms **X107–X133** face the interior courtyard and pool. Studios **X119** have a nice view of the lake in the distance. Even-numbered rooms **X108–X134** face the Boulder Ridge Villas, a garden area, and woods. Rooms on the sixth floor are high enough for you to see the lake past Boulder Ridge and the Cascade Cabins in the foreground.

GOOD ROOMS AT CASCADE CABINS Guests in cabins **8001–8006** get to watch boats glide to the Magic Kingdom, while cabins **8023–8026** offer excellent fireworks views.

BOULDER RIDGE VILLAS

Unofficial Guide Reader-Survey Results

Percentage of readers who'd stay here again	91% (*Average*)
Percentage of readers who'd recommend this resort to a friend	85% (*Average*)
Overall reader rating	B

ALSO PART OF THE DVC TIME-SHARE PROGRAM, the 136 Boulder Ridge Villas are studio and one- and two-bedroom units in a freestanding building to the right of the lodge. Studios have kitchenettes; one- and two-bedroom villas have full kitchens. The rustic decor features pine furniture, textured rugs, curtains, and woodland creatures from Disney's *Bambi* decorating the pillows and bedding. Boulder Ridge has its own pool but shares restaurants and other amenities with the main lodge.

The villas' studios have fold-down sleeper sofas. All villas have armoires and flat-screen TVs, and one- and two-bedroom units have stainless steel kitchen appliances. We think more updates are needed. This reader from Buffalo, New York, agrees:

> *Absolutely hated the room at Boulder Ridge—any Hampton Inn I've ever stayed at for half the price had better rooms. The furniture was mismatched and outdated, the rugs were worn, and the pullout sofa bed was worse than the one we owned in the 1970s! Most upsetting, there were no grab bars in the showers, which are a hotel-industry safety standard. Perhaps because the bathroom was so small, Disney figured we could just hold on to the walls?*

A Plymouth, Massachusetts, family found a way to make the room more comfortable:

> *The sofa bed was improved greatly after we requested an additional mattress for it. We couldn't use the sofa, but the extra mattress made for a much better night's sleep.*

GOOD (AND NOT-SO-GOOD) ROOMS AT BOULDER RIDGE VILLAS Except for a few rooms overlooking the pool, these rooms offer woodland views. The best are odd-numbered rooms **X531–X563** on floors three through five, which open to the lake (northeast) side of the resort (you usually can't see the lake, though). Rooms on the opposite side of the same wing offer similar views, but with some roads and parking lots visible, and with traffic noise.

Disney's Contemporary Resort & Bay Lake Tower

(See map on page 141; see tinyurl.com/ug-contemporary *for extended coverage.)*

THIS 655-ROOM DELUXE RESORT ON BAY LAKE is unique in that its A-frame design permits the Magic Kingdom monorail to pass through the structure's cavernous atrium. A 90-foot mosaic depicts American Indian children and nature. The off-white central tower is augmented by a three-story Garden Wing fronting Bay Lake to the south and by Bay Lake Tower, a 295-room, 15-story Disney Deluxe Villa development, to the north.

STRENGTHS	WEAKNESSES
• Iconic architecture; the only hotel that the monorail goes *through*	• Overpriced, especially so-called Magic Kingdom–view rooms that mostly look out onto parking lots
• Large rooms with views of Bay Lake	• Refurbished rooms are a downgrade, with decor that's lazy and uninspired
• Bay Lake Tower rooms are the quietest in all of Walt Disney World	• Very small studios in Bay Lake Tower sleep no more than 2 people comfortably
• Easy walk to the Magic Kingdom	• Hallway decor at Bay Lake Tower can feel institutional
• Excellent staff/service	
• Convenient parking	• Bus transportation to Hollywood Studios, Animal Kingdom, the water parks, and Disney Springs is shared with the other monorail resorts
• Best lounge at Walt Disney World (Top of the World, Bay Lake Tower)	
• Recreation options on Bay Lake	

Unofficial Guide Reader-Survey Results *(Contemporary Resort only; see page 142 for Bay Lake Tower ratings)*

Percentage of readers who'd stay here again	89% *(Average)*
Percentage of readers who'd recommend this resort to a friend	79% *(Below Average)*
Overall reader rating	B

Standard rooms in the A-frame afford fantastic views of Bay Lake or the Magic Kingdom, and all have balconies. At 394 square feet each, they're only slightly smaller than equivalent rooms at the Grand Flo.

Rooms in the Contemporary's main building were refurbished in the summer of 2021, adding characters from Pixar's *The Incredibles* films. Off-white walls, bedspreads, and flooring are joined by carpets and couches in bold reds and other accent colors. All rooms include a mini-fridge and coffee maker. There's plenty of storage space and spots to plug in device chargers. The beds in our room were Sealy Posturepedic pillow-tops, which were very comfortable. The Contemporary's refurbishment also includes a new iteration of a foldout kid's bed. Another touch we liked in the main living area was that the new tile floors had rugs around the beds. Soundproofing from outdoor noises has been improved.

Bathrooms have been remodeled as well, with a continuous counter-top featuring two sinks and plenty of storage. The shower/tub combination remains standard, and it's all enclosed by glass sliders. It's quite possibly the best bathroom in any Disney Deluxe resort. Likewise, the bathroom door is a midcentury-appropriate (and space-saving) slider. References to *The Incredibles* are found on soft goods and posters and in hidden spots around the room. If you're looking at photos of these rooms online, note that we think they look much better in person.

Our main criticism of the Contemporary's refurbishment is that it's devoid of style, taste, and imagination. It's no secret that Disney tries

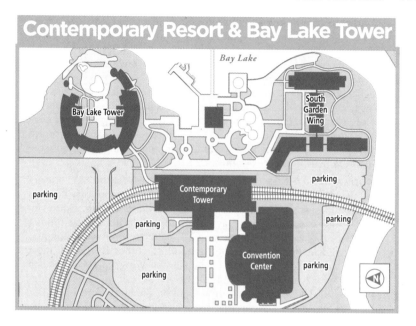

Contemporary Resort & Bay Lake Tower

to shoehorn characters into every available space around the World, whether they're needed or not. It's also not a secret that Disney cuts corners by standardizing everything, from the same white bedspreads in every room in every resort to common bathroom designs. In some cases, like the new rooms at Disney's Polynesian Village Resort, those two forces can still produce interesting rooms whose design melds with the resort's overall look and feel.

In the case of the Contemporary, Disney had a chance to make this into one of America's great midcentury-themed hotels, and they didn't—even though there are plenty of places they could have drawn inspiration from. Take the TWA Hotel at New York City's JFK International Airport, for instance: Its rooms are miniature masterpieces of midcentury-modern design in small spaces. And a 2-hour drive from Disney's headquarters in Burbank puts you in Palm Springs, the spiritual home of the midcentury-modern aesthetic, where you can't walk a block without running into fabulous retro architecture and furniture.

What Disney has put in the Contemporary is just lazy—it's the same generic ideas they've been putting into every recent hotel. Compare the look of the Contemporary's restyled rooms with those of the TWA Hotel (twahotel.com) or even the Motel 6 Anaheim Maingate, near Disneyland (tinyurl.com/anaheim-motel6), and ask yourself if the Contemporary is $400–$600 better per night. If you ask us, it's not. What Disney's *really* selling these days at the Contemporary is walking-distance access to the Magic Kingdom (under 14 minutes from our room to standing inside the park). But what's the point of being a company worth $270 billion if you're not swinging for the fences at your flagship hotels?

Dining options abound at the Contemporary. On the first floor is **Steakhouse 71,** specializing in grilled meats. The counter-service

Contempo Cafe on the fourth floor's Grand Canyon Concourse serves upscale sandwiches, salads, and flatbread pizzas. **Chef Mickey's,** also on the fourth floor, hosts a popular character buffet. On the 15th floor, the award-winning **California Grill** serves sophisticated contemporary American cuisine.

The pool has slides for kids and cabanas for rent. The resort also has a few shops. The Contemporary is within easy walking distance of the Magic Kingdom; monorail transportation is available to both the Magic Kingdom and EPCOT. Other destinations can be accessed by bus or boat. Walking time to transportation loading areas from the most remote rooms is 6–9 minutes.

GOOD (AND NOT-SO-GOOD) ROOMS AT THE CONTEMPORARY RESORT
(See tinyurl.com/crroomviews *for photos.)* The Contemporary has two hotel buildings: the A-frame tower and the **Garden Wing.** Rooms in the A-frame overlook either Bay Lake and the marina and swimming complex on one side or the parking lot, with Seven Seas Lagoon and the Magic Kingdom in the background on the other. Except for most second- and third-floor rooms in the Garden Wing, each room has a balcony with two chairs and a table. If you stay on the Magic Kingdom side of the A-frame, ask for a room on the ninth floor or higher. The parking lot and connecting roads are less distracting there (see tinyurl.com/cr-room4848 as an example). On the Bay Lake side, the view is fine from all floors, though higher floors are preferable.

In the Garden Wing, all ground-floor rooms have patios. Only end rooms on the second and third floors facing Bay Lake have full balconies; all other rooms have balconies only a foot deep. Also, keep in mind that the Garden Wing is a fair walk from the restaurants, shops, front desk, guest services, and monorail station in the A-frame.

There's a lot of boat traffic in the lake and canal alongside the Garden Wing. Nearest the lake, and quietest, are rooms **6116–6123, 6216–6223,** and **6316–6323.** At the water's edge, but noisier, are rooms **6107–6115, 6207–6215,** and **6307–6315.** Flanking the canal connecting Bay Lake and Seven Seas Lagoon are rooms **5128–5151, 5228–5251,** and **5328–5351.** All of these have nice canal and lake views, which subject them to some daytime noise from passing watercraft, but the whole area is exceptionally quiet at night.

The Garden Wing also has rooms facing the marina, pool, and playground; these work well for families with kids. The views don't compare with views from the rooms previously listed, but ground-floor rooms **5105–5127** and **6124–6130** provide easy access to the pool.

In addition to offering some of the most scenic and tranquil guest rooms in Disney World, the Garden Wing likewise contains some of the most undesirable ones. Avoid rooms ending with numbers **52–70;** almost all of these look directly onto a parking lot.

BAY LAKE TOWER AT DISNEY'S CONTEMPORARY RESORT
(See map on page 141; see **tinyurl.com/ug-blt** *for extended coverage.)*

Unofficial Guide **Reader-Survey Results**

Percentage of readers who'd stay here again	94% *(Average)*
Percentage of readers who'd recommend this resort to a friend	91% *(Average)*
Overall reader rating	B

OPENED IN 2009, this 15-story, 295-unit DDV resort consists of studios and one- and two-bedroom villas, as well as two-story, three-bedroom Grand Villas with views of Bay Lake and the Magic Kingdom. Laid out in a semicircle, Bay Lake Tower is connected to the Contemporary by an elevated, covered outdoor walkway and shares the main resort's monorail service.

Rooms are well appointed, with flat-screen TVs, DVD players, mini-fridges, microwaves, and coffee makers. Brightly colored accessories, paintings, and accent walls complement an otherwise-neutral color scheme. Wood tables and granite countertops add a natural touch. Each room has a private balcony or patio. The rooms we've stayed in tested as the quietest on Disney property.

Studios sleep up to four people and include one queen-size bed and one double sleeper sofa. The part of the studio with the bed, sofa, and TV measures about 170 square feet and feels small with just two people; four would be an adventure.

One-bedroom villas sleep five people (the living room's chair and sofa fold out to sleep three) and provide a formal kitchen, a second bathroom, and a living room in addition to the studio bedroom.

The two-bedroom villas—our pick for the best of the standard rooms—sleep nine and include all the kitchen amenities found in a one-bedroom, plus an extra bathroom. One of the baths is attached to a second bedroom with two queen beds or a queen plus a sleeper-size sofa. As with the one-bedrooms, a sofa bed and sleeper chair in the living room provide extra places to snooze, though they're best suited for small children. Bathrooms in the two-bedroom villas are a bit more spacious than those in the one-bedrooms. One odd feature in the baths (also found at other DVC resorts) is a folding door separating the tub from the main bedroom.

The two-story Grand Villas sleep 12 and include four bathrooms, the same main-bedroom layout, and two bedrooms with two queen beds apiece. An upstairs seating area overlooking the main floor provides a sleeper sofa and chair. Two-story windows offer unparalleled views of Bay Lake or the Magic Kingdom—with prices to match.

Bay Lake Tower has its own check-in desk, as well as its own private pool and pool bar, plus a small fire pit on the beach. Its **Top of the World Lounge** is the best bar on Disney property, but, alas, it admits only DVC owners and their guests. If need be, offer to buy an owner a round of drinks in exchange for an invite.

A 1-mile jogging path loops around Bay Lake Tower and the Contemporary's Garden Wing. Dining, transportation, and other recreational activities are shared with the Contemporary Resort.

Readers give Bay Lake an A rating for its room quality. This Minnesota family of four loved the views:

> We had a studio with a Magic Kingdom view. The balcony was a private oasis where my husband and I would relax and watch the fireworks together after the kids were asleep. On our second night he looked at me and said, "We're always going to stay here."

GOOD (AND NOT-SO-GOOD) ROOMS AT BAY LAKE TOWER *(See* **tinyurl .com/blt-roomviews** *for photos.)* If you're paying for a Magic Kingdom view, request a room on an upper level—above the seventh floor, at least—if you don't want to look out on the parking lot. Even-numbered rooms **XX06–XX16** have the best viewing angle of the park. Rooms **XX24–XX30** may technically be described as having Magic Kingdom views, but they're oriented toward the Contemporary, and you have to turn the other way to see the park.

The rooms on the lake side of Bay Lake Tower have views of EPCOT's fireworks and more, as this longtime reader from Edmonds, Washington, found out:

> *I could watch the fireworks from our balcony (OK, the bed), and that was cool, but really the best part was being able to see Spaceship Earth lit up. Beautiful! More of this, please, Disney.*

Shades of Green

(See **tinyurl.com/ug-shades** *for extended coverage.)*

STRENGTHS	WEAKNESSES
• Large guest rooms	• No theming to speak of
• Discount tickets for military personnel with ID	• Room decor is nondescript
• Quiet setting	• Limited on-site dining
• Views of golf course from guest rooms	• Limited bus service
• Convenient self-parking	• Daily parking fee ($24)
• Swimming complex, fitness center	• No free parking at theme parks
• On-site car rental (Alamo; currently unavailable)	

Unofficial Guide **Reader-Survey Results**

Percentage of readers who'd stay here again	100% *(Above Average)*
Percentage of readers who'd recommend this resort to a friend	92% *(Average)*
Overall reader rating	B

ORIGINALLY OWNED BY DISNEY, Shades of Green was called The Golf Resort when it opened in 1973 and was renamed The Disney Inn in 1986. In 1994 Disney reached an agreement with the U.S. Army Family and Morale, Welfare, and Recreation Command (Army MWR) to lease the property as an official Armed Forces Recreation Center. In 1996 the Army MWR purchased the property outright; Disney, however, still owns the land on which the resort is located.

Shades of Green is open to active and retired US service members (including reservists) and their families, among other qualifying groups. Civilians may accompany eligible military personnel as their guests. (For details, see shadesofgreen.org/about-shades-green /eligibility.) If you're planning a holiday visit or a long weekend here, book as early as possible—up to seven months in advance. Guests at Shades of Green are eligible for Disney's Early Theme Park Entry and Extended Evening Hours.

Shades of Green consists of one three-story and one five-story building nestled among three golf courses that are open to Disney guests. At 455 square feet each, the 586 guest rooms at Shades of Green are larger than those at the Grand Floridian.

On its Frequently Asked Questions page, the resort's website states that Shades of Green would be comparable to the Disney Deluxe

Shades of Green

Ⓔ Elevator	🔲 Laundry
♿ Restroom	↖ Stairs
📞 Telephone	Ⓥ Vending/ice

1. AAFES Exchange
2. ATM
3. Attraction Ticket Sales
4. Bell stand and front desk
5. Bus stop
6. Evergreen's Sports Bar & Grille
7. Express Café
8. Fitness Center
9. The Garden Gallery Restaurant
10. Guest Services
11. Hot tub
12. Java Café
13. Kiddie Pool
14. Lobby
15. Magnolia Ballroom
16. Magnolia Pool Area
17. Magnolia Spa
18. Mangino's Bistro/Bistro To Go
19. Mill Pond Pool Area
20. Parking garage
21. Playground
22. Registration
23. Remember the Fun Walkway
24. Sales & Marketing
25. Tennis courts
26. Yoga room

To theme parks

resorts. While the rooms are certainly large, nicely appointed, and immaculately maintained—not to mention a great value for those who qualify to stay here—they are indistinguishable from the rooms at any number of decent midpriced hotels; there's no discernible theming or wow factor. The dining options and transportation are adequate. Service, on the other hand, is superb—definitely up to the Deluxe standard.

Standard rooms have two queen-size beds, a single sleeper sofa, a minifridge, a table and two chairs, and a TV. Junior suites sleep six with three queen beds, one in the living area. Family suites sleep eight with three queen sleeper sofas and a king bed; these suites also have two bathrooms. All rooms have a patio or balcony.

A military mom from Loganville, Georgia, wishes we loved Shades of Green as much as she does:

> We loved our stay at Shades of Green. I know it's only for military personnel, but I feel like you could say a little more about it. The rooms are huge. The pools are fantastic. Kids 4 and younger eat for less than $4, and the buffet is better than a typical chain—when I can feed my family of five for about $60, that's pretty awesome. They have fun themed nights all week and occasional kids' activities too.

Another mom, this one from Plainfield, Indiana, makes the case for exploring all of your lodging options:

> While it's true that SOG is often a good deal, military families should still do some comparison shopping. Room rates are tiered based on rank—the higher your rank, the higher the rate. Definitely check into military rates at Disney properties, and also check out the **Armed Forces Vacation Club** for condos near WDW [see afvclub.com for participating Orlando-area properties]. We rented a two-bedroom, two-bath condo with a full kitchen and pool for seven nights, and it cost us less than two nights at a Disney hotel.

Shades of Green has two pools. The **Mill Pond Pool** features a tiered waterslide, while the **Magnolia Pool** has a zero-entry feature as well as a splash-and-play area and hot tubs.

Restaurants include **Mangino's,** an Italian eatery; the **Garden Gallery** buffet; two quick-service options (**Express Café** and **Java Café**); and **Evergreen's,** a sports bar and grill. The **Army & Air Force Exchange Service,** comparable to a convenience store or hotel gift shop, sells Disney merchandise in addition to snacks, soft drinks, alcohol, tobacco, and over-the-counter medicines.

Transportation to all theme parks is by bus; a transfer is required to almost all destinations. Walking time to the bus-loading area from the most remote rooms is about 5 minutes. Readers such as this Lancaster, Ohio, woman report that bus service is a sore spot:

> Please, please, please stress to your readers how awful the transportation system is—there is no direct access to the Magic Kingdom or EPCOT, and the buses that go directly to the other parks run only once an hour. If you want to go back to your room midday, plan for an hour to an hour and a half of travel time there and then back to the park.

A Bloomington, Indiana, family advises that it's faster to just use Disney transportation:

> You can walk to the Polynesian Village to ride the monorail, bypassing the TTC to get to the Magic Kingdom.

Shades of Green has signs guiding guests to the Magic Kingdom walkways via the Polynesian Village and Grand Floridian Resorts.

You don't have to worry much about bad room views or locations here: Except for a small percentage that overlook the entrance road and parking lot, most offer views of the surrounding golf courses or the swimming area. Note, however, that a few rooms are located far from the elevators. When you reserve, make your preference known.

THE EPCOT RESORTS

THE EPCOT RESORTS ARE POSITIONED around Crescent Lake between EPCOT and Disney's Hollywood Studios (closer to EPCOT). Both theme parks are accessible by boat and on foot. No EPCOT resort offers transportation to EPCOT's main entrance, and it's 0.7–1.1 miles to walk, depending on the hotel and route. As a Greenville, South Carolina, mom reports, this can be a problem:

The only transportation to EPCOT is by boat or foot. There's no bus to take you to the front gates. We had to walk through the International Gateway and all the way to the front of EPCOT to ride Future World attractions. And if we finished EPCOT at the end of the day near the front entrance, the only way back home was a long hike through Future World and the International Gateway.

A reader from Emporia, Kansas, overcame this obstacle:

We had no transportation to the front gate of EPCOT for arrival before opening. So we decided to do early entry at Magic Kingdom (7 a.m.), take in one popular attraction, and then catch the monorail to EPCOT. Worked like a charm. We were at EPCOT by 8:20 a.m.

The **Skyliner** (see page 439) connects EPCOT's International Gateway with Disney's Hollywood Studios. If you're staying at the Beach Club, taking the Skyliner may be faster than walking.

Disney's Yacht & Beach Club Resorts and Beach Club Villas
(See map on page 149; see tinyurl.com/ug-yacht *and* tinyurl.com/ug-beach *for extended coverage.)*

STRENGTHS	WEAKNESSES
• Best pool complex of any WDW resort	• Villa parking is directly adjacent to the building
• Excellent staff/service	**WEAKNESSES**
• Walking distance to EPCOT's International Gateway	• Views and balcony size are hit-or-miss
• Close to BoardWalk and EPCOT dining	• Bus service to Magic Kingdom, Animal Kingdom, water parks, and Disney Springs is shared with other EPCOT resorts
• Well-themed public spaces	
• Bright and attractive guest rooms	• No three-bedroom Grand Villas at the Beach Club Villas
• Boat and Skyliner transportation to DHS	• Beach Club Villas have fewer baths per bedroom than newer DVC/DDV properties and have no lake views
• One-and two-bedroom Beach Club Villas offer laundry and kitchen facilities	

Unofficial Guide **Reader-Survey Results** *(resorts only; see page 151 for villa ratings)*

Percentage of readers who'd stay here again **Yacht: 96%; Beach: 95%** *(both Average)*	
Percentage of readers who'd recommend to a friend **Yacht: 95%** *(Above Average)*; **Beach: 91%** *(Average)*	
Overall reader rating **Yacht: B; Beach: B**	

THESE ADJOINING DELUXE RESORTS are similarly themed. Both have clapboard facades with whitewashed-wood trim. The Yacht Club is painted a subdued gray, the Beach Club a brighter blue. The Yacht Club has a nautical theme with model ships and antique navigational instruments in public areas. The Beach Club is embellished with beach scenes in seafoam green and white. Both have themed lobbies, with a giant globe in the Yacht Club's and sea horse fixtures in the Beach Club's. The resorts face the 25-acre Crescent Lake and share an elaborate swimming complex.

There are 635 rooms and 21 suites at the Yacht Club and 576 rooms at the Beach Club, plus 282 studio and one- and two-bedroom DVC units at the Beach Club Villas. Most rooms are 381 square feet and have two queen-size beds, a sofa, a desk and chair, a dresser, a wall-mounted TV, a minifridge, and a coffee maker (Yacht Club's is Keurig). The Yacht Club's rooms are decorated in white with blue and brass accents, while the Beach Club's are decked out in summery tans and blues. The most recent Yacht Club refurbishment also replaced carpeting with vinyl plank flooring, freshening the rooms' look; the Beach Club's redo kept the carpeted floors. Some rooms have full balconies; many rooms have mini balconies.

The Beach Club Villas evoke seaside Victorian cottages. Studio accommodations have kitchenettes; one- and two-bedroom villas have full kitchens. Like the Yacht Club (but unlike the Beach Club), the Villas got faux-hardwood laminate flooring in its most recent redo, as well as updated bathrooms. Other decor is like the Beach Club's.

As is the case with all DVC/DDV properties, the villas are available to the general public depending on availability. They share restaurants, pools, and other amenities with the main Yacht & Beach Club.

A Portsmouth, Rhode Island, reader with a big family likes the Villas' refresh:

> *The Beach Club Villas update was well done. Very nice-looking rooms, stylish baths, and plenty of accessible outlets, including 16 USB ports in a two-bedroom villa.*

A reader from Altadena, California, likewise appreciates the Yacht Club's upgrades:

> *The refurbished rooms at Yacht Club are lovely. The laminate floors are not noisy at all—if we had neighbors above us, we never heard them. Soundproofing on the balcony is good.*

As Deluxe resorts, both the Yacht Club and the Beach Club provide excellent service. Nine restaurants and lounges are within walking distance of EPCOT and the BoardWalk. Beach Club has an expanded grab-and-go area for quick snacks.

Transportation from these resorts to other destinations is by bus, boat, or Skyliner. Walking time to the transportation loading areas from the most remote rooms is 7 minutes.

Although the Yacht & Beach Club Resorts are situated along Crescent Lake, opposite Disney's BoardWalk, only a relatively small percentage of rooms actually overlook the lake dead-on—many additional rooms have lake views from the side but actually face a courtyard or garden. To complicate matters, the resorts don't differentiate between

Yacht & Beach Club Resorts and Beach Club Villas

a room with a lake view and one overlooking a swimming pool, pond, or canal. There's only one category for anything wet: lagoon or pool view. To see specific views from these rooms for yourself, go to tinyurl .com/yacht-roomviews or tinyurl.com/beach-roomviews.

The Beach Club consists of a long main building with several wings protruding toward Crescent Lake; viewed from the lake, the Beach Club adjoins the Yacht Club on the left and spreads toward EPCOT on the right. The main building and the various wings range from three to five stories. Most rooms have full or mini balconies or, on the ground floor, patios. Full balconies are big enough for a couple of chairs, while mini balconies are about 6 inches deep (stand at the rail or sit in a chair inside the room). Top-floor rooms often have enclosed balconies set into the roof. Unless you're standing, visibility is somewhat limited from these dormer balconies. Our **Hotel Room Views** describe each room's balcony type.

We receive a lot of mail about the Yacht & Beach Club. First, from a Wayland, Massachusetts, mom of two:

> *This was the first time we stayed at the Beach Club, and for us the amazing pool complex was worth the extra money. Several nights we climbed to the top of the waterslide as the sun was setting, and it was an incredible sight—truly a memorable experience!*

This family (no hometown given) got a chilly reception, however:

> *Families with kids should not stay at the Beach Club during the winter. Based on an experience at the Polynesian Village in December, we anticipated that Stormalong Bay would be warm enough to swim in—it was not. This was a terrible disappointment to our kids. The resort's location is divine (I loved walking to France for breakfast), but the pool situation made me bitter about the cost of this place.*

A reader from Danbury, Connecticut, advises that "standard" rooms at the Beach Club are anything but:

> *The term* standard rooms *at Beach Club means many things. Some standard rooms have one queen bed and one daybed, or two queen beds and a writing desk, two queen beds and a daybed, and so on. There are also variations in the sizes of the balconies: Some rooms have a full balcony with two chairs; others have a reduced-size balcony with two chairs squeezed in or a tiny, one-person balcony with just enough room to step outside.*

GOOD (AND NOT-SO-GOOD) ROOMS AT THE BEACH CLUB RESORT *(See* tinyurl.com/beach-roomviews *for photos.)* The Beach Club's better views are from rooms that have full balconies, and from those that overlook the lake. Other good rooms include those facing woods, with EPCOT in the background. The woods-facing rooms are the resort's most peaceful accommodations, both in terms of lack of noise and attractive scenery. These rooms are also the nearest to EPCOT's International Gateway entrance if you're walking, but the farthest from the resort's main pool area, lobby, and restaurants.

Of the remaining rooms, most face courtyards, with some of these providing oblique views of the lake and others overlooking parking lots and the resort's front entrance.

The following are our recommendations for good rooms at the Beach Club Resort. All room numbers are four digits, with the first digit specifying the floor and the remaining three digits specifying the room number.

Heads-up: The Beach Club will charge you for a water view if there's so much as a birdbath in sight. If you're going to spend the money, get a *real* water view.

WATER-VIEW ROOMS WITH FULL BALCONIES FACING THE LAKE Odd-numbered rooms **2641–2645**; suite **2647**; rooms **3501–3507**; odd-numbered rooms **4607–4623**, and odd-numbered Club Level rooms **5699–5725**

STANDARD-VIEW ROOMS WITH FULL BALCONIES FACING THE WOODS AND EPCOT   Even-numbered rooms **2528–2530, 2578–2596, 3512–3530,** and **4532–4596**

GOOD (AND NOT-SO-GOOD) ROOMS AT THE YACHT CLUB RESORT *(See* tinyurl.com/yacht-roomviews *for photos.)* When viewed from Crescent Lake, the resort is connected to the Beach Club on the right and angles toward the Dolphin hotel on the left. All Yacht Club rooms offer full balconies or, on the ground floor, patios. Rooms with the best views are as follows (the higher the last three digits in the room number, the closer to the lobby, main pool area, and restaurants):

ROOMS WITH FULL BALCONIES FACING THE LAKE, WITH THE BOARDWALK INN IN THE BACKGROUND   Odd-numbered rooms **2001–2009, 2043–2065, 2123–2137, 2157–2163; 3001–3009, 3043–3065, 3123–3137, 3157–3163; 4057–4065, 4123–4137, 4157–4163**; or Club Level rooms **5161, 5163,** or **5241**

FIFTH-FLOOR ROOMS DIRECTLY FACING EPCOT   Rooms **5195–5199** or **5153**

STANDARD-VIEW FOURTH-FLOOR ROOMS FACING EPCOT   Rooms **4195–4199** or **4153**

Some other rooms face the BoardWalk or EPCOT across Crescent Lake, but they're inferior to the rooms just listed.

Avoid standard-view rooms at either resort *except* for rooms **3512–3536** and **4578–4598** at the Beach Club; these overlook a dense pine thicket. In addition to offering a nice vista for a standard-view rate, these are the closest rooms to EPCOT available at any resort on Crescent Lake.

BEACH CLUB VILLAS

Unofficial Guide Reader-Survey Results

Percentage of readers who'd stay here again	**93%** *(Average)*
Percentage of readers who'd recommend this resort to a friend	**89%** *(Average)*
Overall reader rating	**B**

THIS DISNEY DELUXE VILLA PROPERTY is purportedly inspired by grand Atlantic seaside homes of the early 20th century. In point of fact, there's little to differentiate the Beach Club Villas from the Yacht & Beach Club Resorts, or from the parts of the BoardWalk Inn & Villas that don't front the BoardWalk.

Configured roughly in the shape of a fat Y or slingshot, the Beach Club Villas are set back away from the lake adjoining the front of the Beach Club Resort. Arrayed in connected four- and five-story taffy-blue sections topped with cupolas, the villas are festooned with white woodwork and slat-railed balconies. The effect is clean, breezy, and evocative . . . though of what exactly we're not sure.

Accommodations include studios, which have a kitchenette, a queen bed, a single pull-down bed, and a sleeper sofa, and one- and two-bedroom villas with full kitchens. The rooms are a bit small but attractively decorated in neutral shades accented by seashore-themed art.

A Springfield, Illinois, reader found her studio villa somewhat lacking in terms of space and amenities:

(1) There's very little space to unpack and store clothes. Drawer space is minimal, which left me living out of my suitcase. (2) No full-length mirror, which is inconvenient not to have when you have one at home. (3) The pullout vanity mirror is not height-adjustable.

Regarding her last point, we've also seen the vanity mirrors mounted at different heights in different bathrooms.

We don't like the Beach Club Villas as much as the Copper Creek Villas, which are newer and better appointed, or the villas of Old Key West Resort, which are roomier, more luxurious, and more private. The Beach Club Villas have their own modest swimming pool but otherwise share the restaurants, facilities, and transportation options of the adjoining Yacht & Beach Club Resorts. The villas' strengths and weaknesses include all of those listed for the Yacht & Beach Club Resorts. Additional strengths include laundry and kitchen facilities in the one- and two-bedroom units, and self-parking directly adjacent to the building. The villas' one additional weakness is that they offer no lake views.

GOOD (AND NOT-SO-GOOD) ROOMS AT THE BEACH CLUB VILLAS
(See **tinyurl.com/bcv-roomviews** for photos.) Although the studios and villas are attractive and livable, the location of the Beach Club Villas—between parking lots, roads, and canals—leaves much to be desired. Rooms facing the pool offer a limited view of a small canal but are subject to traffic noise. Ditto for the rooms on the northeast side, but they don't face the pool. Only southeast-facing rooms provide both a scenic landscape (woods) and relative relief from traffic noise. The nearby road is two lanes only, and traffic noise probably won't bother you if you're indoors with the balcony door closed, but for the bucks you shell out to stay at the villas, you can easily find nicer, quieter accommodations elsewhere on Disney property. If you elect to stay at the Beach Club Villas, go for odd-numbered rooms **225–251, 325–351, 425–451,** and **525–551.**

Disney's BoardWalk Inn & Villas

(See **tinyurl.com/ug-bwinn** for extended coverage.)

STRENGTHS	WEAKNESSES
• Walking distance to EPCOT's International Gateway and Disney's Hollywood Studios	• Long, confusing hallways
	• Some may find room theming overly fussy
• Excellent staff/service	• Limited quick-service dining options suitable for kids
• Unique garden suites	
• Vast selection of dining options for adults	• Not as many rooms overlook the BoardWalk as you might think
• Fitness center is larger than Yacht & Beach Club's	• Bus service to Magic Kingdom, Animal Kingdom, water parks, and Disney Springs is shared with other EPCOT resorts
• Refurbished rooms are on the schedule	
	• BoardWalk Villas have fewer baths per bedroom than newer DVC/DDV properties

Unofficial Guide **Reader-Survey Results** *(inn only; see page 155 for villa ratings)*

Percentage of readers who'd stay here again	90% *(Average)*
Percentage of readers who'd recommend this resort to a friend	85% *(Average)*
Overall reader rating	B

ON CRESCENT LAKE ACROSS from the Yacht & Beach Club, the BoardWalk Inn is another of Disney's Deluxe resorts. The complex is a detailed replica of an early-1900s East Coast beach boardwalk.

BoardWalk Inn & Villas

1. AbracadaBar
2. Atlantic Dance Hall
3. Belle Vue Lounge
4. Big River Grille & Brewing Works
5. BoardWalk Deli
6. BoardWalk Ice Cream
7. Disney's Character Carnival
8. Bus stop
9. Community Hall
10. Conference Center
11. DVC Sales Center
12. The Cake Bake Shop
13. Flying Fish
14. Muscles & Bustles Health Club
15. Jellyrolls
16. Lobby
17. Luna Park Pool
18. Quiet pool
19. Screen Door General Store
20. Seabreeze Point
21. Thimbles & Threads
22. Transportation dock
23. Trattoria Al Forno
24. Wyland Galleries

← To Swan and Dolphin

To → EPCOT

Crescent Lake

Disney's BoardWalk

BoardWalk Villas

BoardWalk Inn

To Disney's Hollywood Studios

To tennis courts

parking

Facades of hotels, diners, and shops create an inviting and exciting waterfront skyline.

In reality, the BoardWalk Inn & Villas comprise a single integrated structure behind the facades. Restaurants and shops occupy the boardwalk level, while accommodations rise to six stories above. The inn and villas share a pool featuring an old-fashioned amusement park theme; there are also two quiet pools for adults.

The BoardWalk Inn's 378 Deluxe rooms measure 371 square feet each. Most contain two queen-size beds, an upholstered daybed, a minifridge, a coffee maker, and ceiling fan. The inn's decor—updated in 2023—includes yellow wallpaper, vinyl flooring, and neutral curtains. Closet space exceeds that of rooms in other Deluxe resorts. Most rooms have balconies.

A new bakery, **The Cake Bake Shop** by Gwendolyn Rogers, will open in late 2023 along the lakefront boardwalk.

Readers continually give the inn high marks for room quality and check-in efficiency. Service is excellent. The complex is within walking distance of EPCOT and is connected to other destinations by bus and boat. Walking time to transportation loading areas from the most remote rooms is 5–6 minutes. It's about a 5-minute walk to the Skyliner's International Gateway station at EPCOT, if you'd rather use that to get to the Studios. If you're doing that, consider this note from a reader in Bolton, Ontario:

> When staying at BoardWalk, if you choose a room in the wing closest to the path to DHS, you have to walk back to the lobby to use the elevators. That negates the advantage of selecting a room close to DHS.

This Iowa City, Iowa, family stayed at the BoardWalk:

> We were surprised that so relatively few rooms at the BoardWalk Inn have interesting views. The one couple in our group who actually had a view of the boardwalk said it was noisy.

As is the case with several other Disney resorts, readers report that the BoardWalk's bus service is inefficient. This comment is typical:

> The bus to Animal Kingdom and Magic Kingdom was the worst. We almost missed a dinner reservation for which we'd left 1½ hours early.

GOOD (AND NOT-SO-GOOD) ROOMS AT THE BOARDWALK INN *(See* **tinyurl.com/bwi-roomviews** *for photos.)* The complex consists of several wings that radiate from the lobby area, in a rough H shape. Crescent Lake and the pedestrian BoardWalk itself are to the north, the entrance is to the south, and the canal that runs to Disney's Hollywood Studios is to the west. If you book a BoardWalk room through Disney's agents or website, *water view* means Crescent Lake and the BoardWalk area only; views of the canal or pool are considered standard view. But if you book a villa through a DVC member or the DVC website, the same canal and pool are called garden or pool view, and the view of the BoardWalk is cleverly called a BoardWalk view.

Most rooms have a balcony or patio, although balconies on the standard upper-floor rooms alternate between large and medium. The

BoardWalk Inn & Villas each share about half the frontage on the promenade, which overlooks Crescent Lake. The promenade's clubs, stores, and attractions are spread about equally between the two sections, leading to similar levels of noise and commotion. However, the inn side is closer to EPCOT and the nearby access road; this means easier access to that theme park, but also more road noise. Otherwise, the inn is actually less noisy than the more expensive villas; there's one tranquil, enclosed courtyard and another half-enclosed area with a quiet pool (where BoardWalk's Garden Suites are located).

There are many rooms to avoid at the inn, starting with rooms overlooking the access roads and parking lots, and rooms looking down onto the roof of the resort's adjacent conference center. And although the aforementioned quiet rooms face courtyards, the views are pretty ho-hum. When you get right down to it, the only rooms with decent views are those fronting the promenade and lake, specifically odd-numbered rooms **3213–3259** and **4213–4259**. We're told by Disney insiders that most of these rooms are reserved more than 10 months ahead.

BOARDWALK VILLAS

Unofficial Guide Reader-Survey Results

Percentage of readers who'd stay here again	96% (*Average*)
Percentage of readers who'd recommend this resort to a friend	90% (*Average*)
Overall reader rating	B

THE 532 BOARDWALK VILLAS are decorated in pastels—lots of green and pink, with neutral carpets—and bright tiles in the kitchens and baths. Villas measure 412–2,491 square feet (studio through three-bedroom) and sleep 4–12. Many villas have full kitchens, laundry rooms, and whirlpool tubs; most rooms have balconies. The studio and two-bedroom units tend to be more expensive than similar accommodations at Old Key West and Saratoga Springs—you're paying for the address. We expect that the BoardWalk Villas, like the BoardWalk Inn, will have their own refurbishment project, likely in late 2023.

GOOD (AND NOT-SO-GOOD) ROOMS AT THE BOARDWALK VILLAS Most villas overlook a canal to the west, with the Swan resort and its access road and parking lots on the far side. Worse are the rooms that front BoardWalk's entrance and car lots. As at the inn, the villas offer only a handful of rooms with good views. Odd-numbered rooms **3001–3047, 4001–4047,** and **5001–5047** afford dynamic views of the promenade and Crescent Lake, with EPCOT in the background. Rooms **X05, X07, X13, X15, X29,** and **X31** are studios. They're a little noisy if you open your balcony door but otherwise offer a glimpse of one of Walt Disney World's more happening places.

Promenade-facing villa rooms have the same noise issues as their inn counterparts. The midsection of the canal-facing villas looks out onto the **Luna Park Pool,** which gets extremely noisy during the day. Some quieter villas located away from the promenade have views of the canal and a partially enclosed quiet pool. Rooms on the opposite side of this wing are almost as quiet, but they face the parking lot.

The Walt Disney World Swan, Swan Reserve & Dolphin

(*See map on page 157;* see tinyurl.com/ug-swan *and* tinyurl.com/ug-dolphin *for extended coverage.*)

QUICK TAKE: *A respectable percentage of readers said they would stay at the Dolphin again; all things considered, however, it rates below average among Disney resorts (see pages 122–123). If you're spending your own money versus using Marriott points, we recommend almost any other Deluxe, Moderate, or DVC resort over the Dolphin.*

STRENGTHS	WEAKNESSES
• Best-priced location on Crescent Lake	• Conventioneers may be off-putting to vacationing families
• The hotels participate in the Marriott Loyalty program	• Daily resort ($43/night, plus tax) and parking fees ($37/night)
• Good on-site and nearby dining	• No Disney Dining Plan
• Only hotels within walking distance to minigolf (Fantasia Gardens)	• Non-Disney bus service runs less often than that of other resorts
• Large variety of upscale restaurants	• Architecture that was on the cutting edge decades ago now looks dated and cheesy (Swan, Dolphin)
• On-site car rental (Alamo, National)	• Self-parking is quite distant from the hotels' entrances
• Very nice pool complex	• Tiny bathrooms (Swan)
• Impressive public spaces	• Spotty front-desk service and housekeeping (Swan)
• Walking distance to both EPCOT International Gateway and DHS	

Unofficial Guide **Reader-Survey Results**

Percentage of readers who'd stay here again **Swan: 93%** (*Average*); **Dolphin: 92%** (*Average*); **Swan Reserve: 88%** (*Average*)
Percentage of readers who'd recommend this resort to a friend **Swan: 83%** (*Average*); **Dolphin: 80%** (*Average*); **Swan Reserve: 80%** (*Average*)
Overall reader rating **Swan: B; Dolphin: C+; Swan Reserve: B**

OPENED IN 1990, THE SWAN AND DOLPHIN face each other on either side of an inlet of Crescent Lake. The Swan Reserve is located across the street from the Swan and Dolphin. Although they're inside Walt Disney World and Disney handles their reservations, they are independently managed. As such, they can also be booked directly at swandolphin.com.

All three resorts are served by Disney transportation to the theme parks and participate in Early Entry and Extended Evening Hours, but they don't participate in the Disney Dining Plan (currently suspended).

The Dolphin's main building is a 27-story turquoise triangle. This central A-frame, with large wings extending from both sides and four smaller arms from its rear, is attached to a large conference center. Perched on the roof, at the edge of each main wing, are two 56-foot-tall dolphins balanced vertically, with their tails in the air.

Whereas the Dolphin is pointy, the Swan is rounded: Its gently arching main building rises 12 stories and is flanked by two 7-story towers, with two 47-foot-tall swans adorning its roof.

The last renovation of the hotels' guest rooms and lobby areas was completed in 2018. Key upgrades included new bedding and carpets, more electrical outlets, new AC units, and new TVs. In addition to

Swan, Swan Reserve & Dolphin

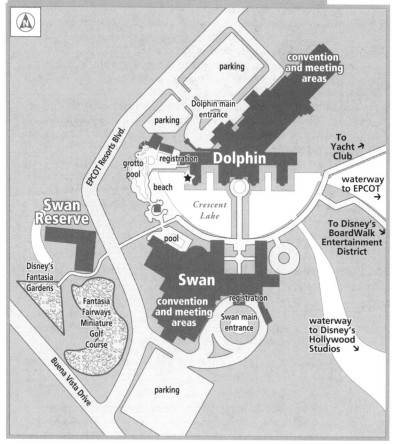

updated decor, the Dolphin lobby has a larger bar area, **Phins,** and a grab-and-go restaurant, **Fuel.**

The Dolphin's rooms incorporate light wood, gray carpeting, and taupe draperies. Oversize upholstered headboards buttress Westin's plush Heavenly Beds, and minimal art adorns the walls. A dresser and desk with desk chair round out the furnishings. One thing to note is that the Dolphin's beds are either doubles or kings, while the Swan has queens and kings. All rooms at the Dolphin have coffee makers, and some have balconies. The baths in most rooms have step-in showers.

The Swan's standard rooms are similar to but are, in our opinion, more attractive than the Dolphin's. Queen- or king-size Heavenly Beds make for ultracomfy sleeping. The reading light is great in or out of bed. A flat-screen TV sits on the dresser. The bathrooms, small for Disney, have step-in showers and limited counter space.

Because these hotels aren't run by Disney, service is less relentlessly cheerful than elsewhere on-property.

Be warned: Both resorts will nickel-and-dime you to death. Each tacks on a $43-per-day resort fee and another $37 per day for self-parking. Whatever rate you're quoted at either resort, count on another $100 per day in miscellaneous fees and higher-than-expected prices.

The two hotels collectively house more than a dozen restaurants and lounges and are within easy walking distance of EPCOT and the BoardWalk. They're also connected to other destinations by bus and boat. Walking time from the most remote rooms to the transportation loading areas is 7–9 minutes.

Regarding transportation, be warned that the Swan and Dolphin don't use Disney bus transportation between their hotels and Disney's theme parks and water parks. Buses going to the Magic Kingdom will drop you off at the Transportation and Ticket Center, where you'll have to take a boat, monorail, or bus to get to the Magic Kingdom (Disney buses will drop you off right at the park entrance). Likewise, bus service between the Swan/Dolphin and Disney Springs has changed, as this reader from Germantown, Maryland, found out:

> We were not aware that the Disney Springs bus service from the Dolphin dropped off at a location different from where the Disney buses dropped off, resulting in a much longer walk.

These readers from Houston say the Swan is the slightly easier of the two to navigate:

> While the Dolphin is closer to EPCOT, we prefer the Swan because it's easier and more straightforward to walk from the hotel to the park and vice versa. The Dolphin has a very narrow, winding sidewalk that doesn't look like it gets much traffic.

This Nashua, New Hampshire, couple gives the shared pool complex high marks:

> Neither the Disney nor the Swan and Dolphin website depicts how great the pool complex is. Not only are there multiple pools, a waterslide, and maybe the best poolside bar in all of Disney World, there's also a wonderfully green, restful grotto-in-tropical-forest theme.

SWAN RESERVE This 14-story hotel opened in 2021 and is adjacent to Disney's Fantasia Gardens minigolf course. The resort has 349 guest rooms and suites, some with views of either EPCOT or Hollywood Studios. Standard rooms sleep four and are around 330 square feet, 16 square feet larger than a Disney Moderate.

Our stays at the Swan Reserve have had mixed results. The beds are comfortable; the bathrooms are functional, with good water pressure; and it's possible to see theme park fireworks from some of the rooms. However, we could hear normal-volume conversations from a room next door, indicating the soundproofing here isn't great.

As a smaller resort, the Swan Reserve has just one full-service restaurant, **Amare**. That can be a problem on busy nights, since Amare handles its own restaurant orders, plus those from the bar, the pool, and room service.

The Swan Reserve has a stylish pool and a fitness center. Bus service is provided to Disney's theme parks, water parks, and Disney Springs, and the Swan and Dolphin are a short walk across the street. But the lack of amenities, coupled with the soundproofing issues, means you should consider another hotel for your vacation.

GOOD (AND NOT-SO-GOOD) ROOMS AT THE SWAN AND DOLPHIN
Note: The Swan and Dolphin are configured very differently, and because of their irregular shapes, it's easier to discuss groups of rooms in relation to exterior landmarks and compass directions rather than by room numbers. When speaking with a reservationist, use the following tips and descriptions.

THE SWAN East-facing rooms offer prime views, particularly in the upper half of the seven-story wing above Il Mulino New York restaurant. From this vantage point, you overlook a canal and Disney's BoardWalk, with EPCOT in the distance. Balcony rooms on floors five, six, and seven cost an additional $50 or more per night, versus the least expensive rooms.

On the downside, rooms in the wing nearest the main section have the southern portion of their views obscured by the building's easternmost portion, which juts east beyond the seven-story wing. There are some east-facing rooms on that portion of the main section, sans balconies. Lofty palm trees obscure the views from east-facing rooms below the fourth floor. The best rooms with views of EPCOT are **626** and **726**.

North-facing rooms afford views of the Dolphin and (generally) of the courtyard, except for those on the easternmost portion of the main section, which look across Crescent Terrace to the BoardWalk; these afford angled views of EPCOT and are buffered by palms on the lowest three floors.

The few north-facing rooms at the end of the Swan's two eight-story wings directly overlook Crescent Lake, while most of the north-facing rooms situated in the main section overlook the courtyard, which has greenery, fountains, and an indoor café in its center. Courtyard-facing rooms are subject to minor noise from below.

Above the eighth floor, north-facing rooms in the main section overlook roofs of the shorter wings. In these rooms, height enhances the vista from your window, but only near the center of the hotel is the view not seriously marred by rooftops below.

North-facing main-section rooms have more-direct views of the Dolphin across the lake than courtyard-facing rooms in either eight-story wing. Guests in most wing rooms, however, can see the lake at an angle.

Most courtyard-facing rooms have balconies; 224 rooms are so equipped, and these balconies offer panoramic 180-degree views. Of course, from most rooms at the Swan, part of any 180-degree view will include another section of the hotel.

The Swan's worst views are from the **west-facing rooms** above the fourth floor, which overlook the unsightly roof of the hotel's western wing. The northernmost rooms in the wing directly above Kimonos restaurant are an exception—their balconies overlook the pool and the beach on Crescent Lake's western shore. Rooms **680–691** offer nice pool views.

Above the Swan's main entrance, **south-facing rooms** overlook the parking lot, with forest and the Hollywood Studios in the distance. However, the canal is also visible to the east. These rooms lack balconies.

THE DOLPHIN If you want a room with easy access to shopping, dining, and transportation to and from the parks, almost any Dolphin room will do. The shuttle (outside the main entrance) and the boat dock are equidistant from the main front and rear exits. Restaurants and shopping are primarily on the first and third floors.

If, however, you also want a view of something besides parking-lot asphalt, your choices narrow considerably. Rooms in the Dolphin with pleasant views are in **the four arms on the rear of the building.** Rooms on all arms sport balconies from the first through fourth floors, then offer alternating balconies or windows on floors five through nine.

One of the Dolphin's best views overlooks the **Grotto Pool,** on the far west side of the building. An artificial beach with a small waterfall is visible from rooms at the very end of the large west wing. None of these rooms has a balcony. A better bet would be to ask for a room on the far west side of the first rear arm. These outer rooms have balconies and are more removed from the pool. Rooms on the inner, west part of that arm overlook a bladderwort-encrusted reflecting pool.

Between the second and third arms looms the monstrous **Dolphin fountain;** the better room choices here are located on the top two floors. Here, from arm two, you can see the BoardWalk (as well as nighttime fireworks in EPCOT), and from arm three you can see the Grotto Pool. Otherwise, you may "enjoy" a view of massive green-concrete fish scales.

Arms three and four are situated around a **reflecting pool.** A concern for rooms in this area is that the ferry toots its horn every time it approaches and departs the dock. Its path runs right by these rooms, and the horn blows just as it passes.

The **Crescent Lake** side of arm four, and the small jut of the large Dolphin wing perpendicular to it, offer arguably the best views. You have an unobstructed view of the lake and EPCOT fireworks; a fine BoardWalk view for people-watching; and, from higher floors, a view of the beach at Beach Club. There's ferry noise, but these rooms still have the most going for them. The best of the best in this arm are rooms **8015, 7015, 5015, 4015,** and **3015.**

Disney's Caribbean Beach Resort

(See map on page 162; see **tinyurl.com/ug-caribbean** *for extended coverage.)*

STRENGTHS	WEAKNESSES
• Colorful Caribbean theme; also pretty at night	• Check-in is far from rest of resort
• Updated rooms with new, modern layout and functionality (Trinidad)	• Dining gets low marks from readers
	• Multiple bus stops make it slow to go anywhere
• Lakefront setting	• Some "villages" are a good distance from restaurants and shops
• Large food court	
• Child-size Murphy beds in select rooms increase capacity to 5 people	• No elevators

Unofficial Guide Reader-Survey Results

Percentage of readers who'd stay here again	92% (*Average*)
Percentage of readers who'd recommend this resort to a friend	87% (*Average*)
Overall reader rating	B

CARIBBEAN BEACH WAS DISNEY'S first Moderate resort when it opened in 1998. It consists of two dozen colorful, two-story motel-style buildings, separated into five areas named for Caribbean islands: **Aruba, Barbados, Jamaica, Martinique,** and **Trinidad.**

Most of the 1,536 guest rooms measure 314 square feet and are outfitted with two queen beds; a fold-down Murphy bed is also available in select rooms. Except as noted below, decor is distinguished by neutral beach tones, bright tropical accent colors, and furnishings of dark wood and rattan. Sliding doors separate the grooming area from the main room. Together with the bathroom, this allows three people to get ready at once. All rooms have a dresser, small table with chairs, minifridge, coffee maker, TV, and plenty of storage. Rooms don't have balconies, but the access passageways are external and have railings.

Rooms in Trinidad were refurbished at the beginning of a resort-wide project. These rooms have lighter, brighter colors and a new room layout. Instead of two beds, these rooms have one fixed bed, one foldout sofa, and a fold-down child sleeper. This frees up space in the room during the day, making it appear larger (and making it easier to walk around in). Bathrooms, storage, and lighting have all been improved. If you're staying here, ask for an updated room.

The **Old Port Royale** building houses the check-in desk, restaurants, and shops. A food court has counter-service and grab-and-go options; **Sebastian's Bistro** is a sit-down restaurant with waterfront tables.

Caribbean Beach's on-site dining remains a weakness with readers. This Bismarck, North Dakota, reader, for example, thinks the counter-service dining logistics need work:

Not a fan of the queue area in the food court—who thought that was a good idea? Two checkout lanes for a resort that big? The grab-and-go area is way too small.

South and east of EPCOT and Hollywood Studios, Caribbean Beach offers transportation to all Disney World destinations by bus and to EPCOT and the Studios by **Skyliner.** Caribbean Beach has access to two Skyliner stations: one south of Jamaica and one north of Aruba at the Riviera Resort; bus service runs between the Skyliner stations and the resort villages.

Walking time to the transportation-loading area from Caribbean Beach's most remote rooms is 7–9 minutes, and readers rate Disney bus service here as below average. Seriously consider bringing a car—this 20-something couple from Kansas City, Missouri, wished they had:

Caribbean Beach's bus service is horrendous. It often felt like there was only one bus running at a time, and we experienced several 30-plus-minute waits. The bus circled the entire resort—which is huge—before it headed out, so if you were unlucky enough to be at one of the last

Caribbean Beach Resort & Riviera Resort

stops during a rush to the parks, the bus would pass right by if it was full. On multiple occasions, we arrived at the bus stop an hour or more before our dining reservations, but we still found ourselves running past the park gates to make it to the restaurant on time!

A mom from Fenton, Michigan, likewise found bus service lacking:

We recommend renting a car and/or paying for a preferred room location, especially during the hotter months. The buses just take way too long with all the stops, and it was a long hike to the food court and pools in the heat.

GOOD (AND NOT-SO-GOOD) ROOMS AT CARIBBEAN BEACH RESORT *(See* **tinyurl.com/cbrroomviews** *for photos.)* The five "islands," or groups of buildings clustered around Barefoot Bay, are identical. The two-story motel-style structures comprising each island are arranged in various ways to face courtyards, pools, the bay, and so forth. Except for the theme, the setup is very similar to the one at Coronado Springs Resort (page 182). The verdant landscaping features lots of ferns and palm trees, especially in the courtyards.

In general, corner rooms are preferable because they have more windows. Standard-view rooms face either parking lots or courtyards, and the usual broad interpretation of water views is in play here. Beyond that, your main choices will revolve around your preference for proximity to (or distance from) Old Port Royale's check-in desk and restaurants, pools, parking lots, pirates, or beaches on Barefoot Bay. Each island has direct access to at least one beach, playground, bus stop, and parking lot.

Martinique, next to the main pool and playground at Old Port Royale, is also closest to the Riviera, whose dining options are vastly superior to those at Caribbean Beach.

Aruba and **Jamaica** are similar to Martinique, but guests must cross a footbridge from here to Old Port Royale. Aruba buildings 54, 55, and 56, along with Jamaica building 41, are closest to the two Skyliner stations. Jamaica building 43, also close to the Skyliner, is the highest-rated building at Caribbean Beach.

With just three buildings, **Barbados** gets noise from surrounding roads and from rambunctious kids at Old Port Royale next door.

The quietest island, and the farthest from resort facilities, is **Trinidad.** It has its own playground, and its beach looks across Barefoot Bay onto wild, undeveloped Florida forest—a rarity on Disney property.

When it comes to the view from your room, avoid standard views: All look onto a parking lot, road, or tiny garden. Water views overlook swimming pools or Barefoot Bay; pool views are less than enchanting, not to mention the pools are noisy.

What you want are **bay views.** Rooms that fill the bill in Martinique, Barbados, and Trinidad catch the afternoon sun; bay-view rooms in Aruba and Jamaica catch the morning sun. Because we like the sun at our back in the evening, we always go for rooms **4246–4252** in **Jamaica** or **5256–5260** and **5541–5548** (but not 5542 or 5545) in **Aruba.** If you don't mind the sun in your eyes during cocktail time, rooms **2254–2256, 2413–2416,** and **2445–2448** in Martinique are good bets, as are lake-facing rooms **3533–3534, 3853–3858,** and **3949** in Trinidad. We're not crazy about any room in **Barbados.**

Disney's Riviera Resort

*(See **tinyurl.com/ug-drr** for extended coverage.)*

STRENGTHS	
• Stylish, well-appointed rooms	• Easy walk to Caribbean Beach and its pretty views
• Skyliner to EPCOT and Hollywood Studios	**WEAKNESSES**
• On-site dining and bar	• Expensive
• Children's play area near main pool	• Tower studios are small and dark

Unofficial Guide **Reader-Survey Results**

Percentage of readers who'd stay here again	**97%** *(Above Average)*
Percentage of readers who'd recommend this resort to a friend	**93%** *(Average)*
Overall reader rating	**A–**

THE RIVIERA IS THE TOP-RATED resort in Walt Disney World. Themed to evoke glamorous beach resorts in the South of France, it has 300 guest rooms, including studios and one-, two-, and three-bedroom villas, spread over nine floors. Though it's on land that used to belong to Caribbean Beach, a Moderate resort, Disney has positioned the Riviera to be as upscale as the Grand Floridian—with service, amenities, and prices to match.

Rooms at the Riviera are some of our favorite at Disney World, with white walls and off-white accents, beige carpets, and furniture in neutral tones. Laminate wood in a herringbone pattern covers the floors, except in the bedrooms, which have carpet. As with other DVC resorts, deluxe studio accommodations have kitchenettes, while the one-, two-, and three-bedroom villas have full kitchens. We like the villas quite a bit—they're bright, comfortable, and modern, even if the theme is understated.

The Riviera has a unique room type among DVC resorts that we like considerably less: the **tower studio,** which accommodates two guests. These rooms measure about 225 square feet—the smallest on Disney property, and small enough that they require the room's single bed to fold into the wall when not in use. Disney may have found a lower limit on how small it can make hotel rooms, and these are *too* small. In fact, when Len visited two friends who were staying in one of these rooms, one of them stood in the bathroom to maintain what felt like normal social distance—there's just not a lot of space here.

Beyond the size, the tower studio rooms are dim during the day and dismal at night. The most cheerful space in the studio is the bathroom because of the better lighting. There's little doubt that these are the worst rooms for the money in Walt Disney World.

In addition to otherwise-posh rooms and amenities and high-end restaurants, the Riviera boasts easy access to EPCOT and Disney's Hollywood Studios. The resort sits about 1,500 feet from World Showcase, affording park-facing rooms on high floors excellent views of both EPCOT's and the Studios' evening entertainment. The Riviera's restaurants have similar views.

Of course, Disney charges a premium for these views: Depending on date and view, rack rates run $443–$814 per night for tower studios; $665–$1,250 for deluxe studios; $934–$1,800 for one-bedroom villas; $1,477–$2,800 for two-bedroom units; and $2,956–$5,165 for three-bedroom villas.

The Riviera's restaurants include **Primo Piatto,** an excellent counter-service eatery with grab-and-go options; **Le Petit Café,** a morning-coffee-and-pastry bar that serves wine in the evening; and **Bar Riva,** a pool bar. **Topolino's Terrace,** the sit-down restaurant, is a Disney Signature venue that serves fixed-price character breakfasts for kids and upscale dinners for grown-ups.

Other amenities include two pools and a fitness center. The main **Riviera Pool** offers play areas for children, while the **Beau Soleil Pool** is the quiet pool. The Riviera Resort is connected to EPCOT and Disney's Hollywood Studios by **Skyliner** and to the rest of the World by bus.

THE BONNET CREEK RESORTS

Not to be confused with the Disney resorts that follow, the **Bonnet Creek Resort** *is a 70-acre hotel, golf, and convention complex located along Bonnet Creek. Although it's adjacent to and accessible from Walt Disney World, the resort is not owned by Disney. Two of its four hotels are reviewed in "Hotels Outside Walt Disney World" (the Signia, on page 240, and the Waldorf Astoria, on page 241).*

Disney's Saratoga Springs Resort & Spa
Treehouse Villas at Disney's Saratoga Springs Resort & Spa

(See maps on pages 166 and 169; see tinyurl.com/ug-ssr *for extended coverage.)*

STRENGTHS	WEAKNESSES
• Often available at discounted rates or as a DVC/DDV rental	• On-site dining is limited for a resort of this size
• Attractive main pool; multiple well-themed quiet pools with snack bars	• Theme is dull compared with those of other Disney resorts
• Closest resort to Disney Springs	• Fewer baths per bedroom than newer DVC/DDV properties
• Convenient parking	
• Only WDW-owned resort with dedicated golf (Lake Buena Vista Golf Course)	• Bus service can take some time to get out of the (huge) resort
• Grocery options in gift shop	
• Very nice spa and fitness center	

Unofficial Guide **Reader-Survey Results** *(resort & spa only; Treehouse Villas did not have enough surveys to rate for this edition)*

Percentage of readers who who'd stay here again	92% *(Average)*
Percentage of readers who'd recommend this resort to a friend	88% *(Average)*
Overall reader rating	B

QUICK TAKE: *The key issue at Saratoga Springs is bus transportation, which is extremely inconvenient to use due to the resort's remoteness.*

SARATOGA SPRINGS, A DDV RESORT, has a theme described by Disney as recalling a Victorian-era retreat in upstate New York. Its 1,260 studio and one-, two-, and three-bedroom villas are located across the lake from Disney Springs. Most buildings were constructed around 2004, while the fitness center and check-in building are older. An adjacent 60-unit DDV complex, **Treehouse Villas at Disney's Saratoga Springs Resort & Spa,** opened in 2009 (see profile on page 168).

The color scheme of the villas' renovated rooms tends toward neutral earth tones, with faux-teak vinyl floors in the living rooms and dark-brown patterned carpets in the bedrooms. Kitchen cabinets are white, while appliances are stainless steel. New furnishings and soft goods are more refined than the last iteration. Chairs, sofas, and tables are likewise more modern and less bulky, though you'd be hard-pressed to identify even the slightest bit of theming; this decor could be at any one of a dozen Disney hotels. A fold-down child's bed sits beneath the wall-mounted TV in the living room. Bathrooms, with color accent walls, are spacious in all but the studios, where they compare with those any other hotel room.

Saratoga Springs Resort & Spa

ACCOMMODATIONS
1. The Carousel (7101–7836)
2. Congress Park (1101–2836)
3. The Grandstand (8101–9836)
4. The Paddock (4501–6836)
5. The Springs (3101–4436)

AMENITIES
6. The Artist's Palette
7. Backstretch Pool Bar
8. BBQ Grill Area
9. On the Rocks Pool Bar
10. The Paddock Grill
11. Turf Club Bar & Grill

Broadway

Buena Vista Dr.

Union Ave.

Golf Dr.

Disney Vacation Club Way

← To
Treehouse Villas

Boat dock
Bus stop

Saratoga Springs guests can use Disney transportation, their cars, or an on-property walking path to get to Disney Springs.

Readers tend to be more critical of Saratoga Springs than other Disney resorts. The positive comments frequently mention the quiet rooms, proximity to Disney Springs, and quality of the spa and fitness center. Those were enough for this reader:

We loved Saratoga Springs! It was comfortable, beautiful, and quiet, with a quick walk to the dock for the boat to Disney Springs.

This reader from Mount Holly, New Jersey, agrees:

We were absolutely floored at how much we loved our stay at Saratoga Springs. Our first couple of days were in Congress Park, which was perfectly lovely. Then we moved (because we had two reservations) to a Paddock building immediately next to the pool, the bus stop, and the walkway to the main building. We truly enjoyed the time we spent there.

The fitness center is by far the best at Walt Disney World. **Senses Spa** (currently unavailable), like its counterpart at the Grand Floridian, echoes the spas of the same name on Disney Cruise Line's ships. Service is very good, plus this Senses location is easier to get to than the one at the Grand Floridian if you're staying east of the World.

Surrounded on three sides by a golf course, Saratoga Springs is the only Disney-owned resort that affords direct access to the links (the military-only **Shades of Green** also provides golf on-property).

The top reader complaints about Saratoga Springs have to do with transportation. These comments from an Arlington Heights, Illinois, family are typical:

Buses started running just 45 minutes before park opening. We had to make multiple stops inside the resort, and because of Saratoga's size and distance to the parks, we arrived at the park only about 15 minutes before opening. We faced instant 60-plus-minute waits for the top attractions despite our best efforts.

A couple from Peru, Indiana, had a variety of complaints:

Saratoga Springs is our least favorite resort. We didn't enjoy the theming, and unless you have a car, getting around by bus is a real hassle. The food court is very small and the food expensive. Also, checkout was very slow, and our room seemed smaller than comparable rooms at BoardWalk Villas and Old Key West.

GOOD (AND NOT-SO-GOOD) ROOMS AT SARATOGA SPRINGS RESORT & SPA *(See* tinyurl.com/ug-saratogasprings *for photos.)* This resort's sprawling size puts some of its best rooms very far away from the main lobby, restaurants, and shops. If you don't have a car, the best rooms are those in **The Springs,** numbered **3101–3436** and **3501–3836.** Ask for a room toward the northeast side of these buildings (away from the lobby), as the southwest rooms border a well-traveled road. Avoid rooms **4101–4436**—a pedestrian walkway running behind the patios gets a lot of use in the early morning from guests who are heading to breakfast.

If you have a car or don't mind a longer walk to the lobby, rooms **1101–1436** and **2501–2836** in **Congress Park** offer quietness, a view of Disney Springs, and a relatively short walk to the bus stop. Also good are rooms **4501–4826, 6101–6436,** and **6501–6836** in **The Paddock.** Also in The Paddock, avoid rooms on the northeast side of its

5101–5435 building, as well those as the northwest side of its **5501–5836** building—these border a swimming pool and bus stop.

In addition to being quiet, rooms **1101–1436** of **Congress Park** and rooms **6101–6436** and **6501–6836** of **The Paddock** afford the closest walks to Disney Springs.

If you're not concerned with the amenities of a specific room, ask for building 16 (**The Grandstand**). A short walk from the Carriage House, it's the top-rated building at Saratoga Springs.

TREEHOUSE VILLAS *(not enough surveys to rate)*

STRENGTHS	WEAKNESSES
• Spacious stand-alone three-bedroom villas	• Long distance from Saratoga Springs services such as check-in and dining
• Quiet location (but kids may find it boring)	• Lackluster pool
• Historical connection to the Treehouses from the 1970s	• Limited number of units makes them difficult to book
• Innovative round design feels more spacious than other villas with the same square footage	• Only two baths per villa
	• Bus travelers connect through Saratoga Springs

THIS COMPLEX OF 60 three-bedroom villas lies between Old Key West Resort and the Grandstand section of Saratoga Springs proper, with a separate entrance off Disney Vacation Club Way. The treehouses are bordered by Lake Buena Vista Golf Course to the northeast and a waterway to the southwest that feeds into Village Lake.

The villas stand on stilts 10 feet off the ground, with ramps providing wheelchair access. Surrounded by a densely wooded landscape, each villa is an eight-sided structure with three bedrooms and two full bathrooms covering about 1,074 square feet.

Villas hold nine people, about the same number as comparably sized rooms at other DDV resorts. The primary and second bedrooms have queen beds; the third bedroom has bunks; and the living room has a sofa bed and sleeper chair, both more appropriate for children than adults.

The interior of each villa is decorated with natural materials: stone floors in the kitchen, granite countertops, and stained-wood furniture. End tables, picture frames, and bunk beds are made from rustic logs. Bathrooms, outfitted in modern tile, have showers and tubs, along with a decent amount of counter space. Showers can be cramped, as noted below.

The three-bedroom Treehouses usually cost about $70–$350 more per night than a comparable two-bedroom villa and $600–$700 *less* than a standard three-bedroom villa elsewhere at Saratoga Springs. The trade-off for that third Treehouse bedroom is giving up some space elsewhere. In particular, beware the primary-bath shower, next to the tub in an enclosed glass wall: Tilt down to shave your legs or grab a bottle of shampoo, and you could bang your head on the side of the tub.

A Columbus, New Jersey, family thinks a stay at Treehouse Villas is money well spent:

Treehouse Villas at Saratoga Springs Resort & Spa

We give Treehouse Villas five stars for value. With nine people in our party, our villa saved us about $700–$1,000 per night. The three bedrooms and pullout couch comfortably slept our group, plus having a great eat-in kitchen helped us save money on breakfast.

A walking path connects the complex to the rest of Saratoga Springs; Treehouse guests can use all of the main resort's facilities. Two dedicated bus stops serve the Treehouses, but transportation is nevertheless a weakness. This Rhode Island reader felt stranded:

Transportation is abhorrent—and I actually had some idea what to expect (i.e., taking one bus at the villas to another bus at the main resort). The Treehouses are nice in and of themselves, but I would suggest not staying here if going to the parks is your main objective.

GOOD (AND NOT-SO-GOOD) ROOMS AT TREEHOUSE VILLAS Treehouses **7024–7034** and **7058–7060** are closest to one of the villas' two dedicated bus stops and the walkway to Saratoga Springs; **7026–7033** also have water views. Treehouses **7001–7011** and **7045–7054** are closest to the other bus stop; **7020–7023** are closest to the boat docks. Finally, Treehouses **7035–7037, 7055, 7056,** and **7060** surround the pool.

Disney's Old Key West Resort

*(See **tinyurl.com/ug-okwest** for extended coverage.)*

STRENGTHS	• Gift shop with grocery selection
• Largest villas of the DVC/DDV resorts	• Convenient parking
• Often available at discounted rates or as a DVC rental	**WEAKNESSES**
• Mature landscaping	• Multiple bus stops
• Homey, well-themed lounge (The Gurgling Suitcase)	• No elevators in many buildings
• Close to Lake Buena Vista Golf Course	• Highway noise
• Boat service to Disney Springs	• Fewer baths per bedroom than newer DVC/DDV properties
	• Mediocre on-site dining

Unofficial Guide Reader-Survey Results

Percentage of readers who'd stay here again	**94%** *(Average)*
Percentage of readers who'd recommend this resort to a friend	**84%** *(Average)*
Overall reader rating	**B**

OLD KEY WEST WAS THE FIRST Disney Vacation Club property. It's a favorite among readers and *Unofficial Guide* staff for its room quality and quiet surroundings. An Erie, Pennsylvania, reader thinks it's Walt Disney World's best-kept secret:

> *Old Key West has the most spacious rooms and the easiest access to your car—right outside your door! There are a number of small, almost private pools, so you don't have to go to the main pool to swim.*

The resort is a large aggregation of two- to three-story buildings modeled after Caribbean-style residences and guesthouses of the Florida Keys. Set subdivision-style around a golf course and along Bonnet Creek, the buildings are arranged in small, neighborhood-like clusters. They feature pastel facades, white trim, and shuttered windows. **Conch Flats Community Hall** houses the check-in area along with a full-service restaurant, fitness center, marina, and sundries shop. Each cluster of accommodations has a quiet pool; Conch Flats is home to the main pool, featuring a waterslide in the shape of a giant sandcastle.

Old Key West boasts some of the roomiest accommodations at Walt Disney World, with all rooms having been refurbished in 2018. Studios are 376 square feet; one-bedroom villas, 942; and two-bedroom villas, 1,333. Studios contain two queen-size beds, a table and two chairs, and an extra vanity outside the bathroom. One-bedroom villas have a king-size bed in the primary bedroom, a queen-size sleeper sofa in the living room, a laundry room, and a full kitchen with coffee

Old Key West Resort

maker. Two-bedroom villas feature a king-size bed in the primary bedroom, a queen-size sleeper sofa and foldout chair in the living room, and two queen beds in the second bedroom. Closets are large enough to hold your entire wardrobe.

Studios and villas are tastefully decorated. The latest refurbishment toned down the Key West beach theme while adding subtle Disney characters—we like it. Kitchen cabinets and TVs, along with the living room and bedroom furniture, were also upgraded. One-bedroom and larger villas have wood flooring instead of carpet.

Each villa has a private balcony that opens to views of the golf course, the landscape, or a waterway. The waterway views are among the best in Walt Disney World.

Transportation and lack of on-site dining options are Old Key West's main weaknesses with readers. This family from Basingstoke, England, also found that the groundskeepers often get started early in summer:

> We enjoyed our stay at Old Key West, but we would not return as we found it a bit noisy. Crews were leaf-blowing at 6:40 one morning, and the rooms are not soundproofed well at all. We also found the quick-service breakfast offerings very limited.

Old Key West is connected by boat to Disney Springs (and by bus when the boat isn't running). Transportation to other Disney destinations is by bus. Walking time to the transportation loading areas from the most remote rooms is about 6 minutes.

GOOD (AND NOT-SO-GOOD) ROOMS AT OLD KEY WEST RESORT (See tinyurl.com/oldkeywest-roomviews for photos.) Old Key West is huge, with 49 three-story villa buildings spread over about 100 acres. Views are nice from almost all villas; all multiroom villas and some studios have a large balcony furnished with a table and chairs.

Because the resort is bordered by busy Bonnet Creek Parkway and even busier Buena Vista Drive, the best villas are those located as far from the road noise as possible. For a lovely river view, ask for **building 45** or **46,** in that order (building 45 is the highest rated at Old Key West). For nice lake and golf-course views away from roads and close to restaurants, recreation, the marina, the main swimming complex, and shopping, ask for **building 13.** Nearby, **buildings 12** and **11** are likewise quiet and convenient; they offer primarily golf-course views. The next-best choices are **buildings 32** and **34;** the former looks onto a lake, with the golf course in the background, while the latter faces the golf course, with tennis courts to the left and a lake to the right. Avoid **buildings 19–22, 38, 39, 41, 42,** and **49–54,** which border Bonnet Creek Parkway and Buena Vista Drive and may get their attendant noise.

Finally, if you want to use your balcony without the sun in your face, use the map 171 to check out the position of your building relative to sunrise and sunset. If you want to enjoy a drink on your balcony in the afternoon or evening, ensure shade by asking for an east-facing building, and if you primarily want to use it in the morning, request a west-facing one.

Disney's Port Orleans Resort: French Quarter and Riverside

(See maps on pages 174 and 175; see tinyurl.com/ug-por and tinyurl.com/ug-pofq for extended coverage.)

A MODERATE RESORT, Port Orleans is divided into two sections. The smaller, southern part is called the **French Quarter;** the larger section is **Riverside.** French Quarter is this year's top Moderate, both overall and in terms of readers who said they'd stay there again, and it tied with another Moderate, the Fort Wilderness Cabins, regarding whether readers would recommend it to a friend.

PORT ORLEANS RESORT-FRENCH QUARTER

STRENGTHS	• Short walk to Riverside's restaurants
• Excellent staff/service	• Good place to walk or run for fitness
• Most compact of the Moderate resorts	**WEAKNESSES**
• One bus stop	• Ho-hum pool
• Live entertainment in Scat Cat's Club	• Shares bus service with Port Orleans
• Beignets in food court!	Riverside during slower times of year
• Attractively themed lobby	• No full-service dining

Unofficial Guide Reader-Survey Results

Percentage of readers who'd stay here again	94% *(Average)*
Percentage of readers who'd recommend this resort to a friend	88% *(Average)*
Overall reader rating	B

CONSISTING OF SEVEN THREE-STORY guest-room buildings next to the Sassagoula River, the 1,008-room French Quarter section is a sanitized Disney version of New Orleans's Vieux Carré. The prim pink-and-blue guest buildings are festooned with wrought iron filigree, shuttered windows, and old-fashioned iron lampposts.

The centrally located **Mint** contains the registration area and food court. The registration desk features a vibrant Mardi Gras mural and old-fashioned bank-teller windows. **Doubloon Lagoon** surrounds a colorful fiberglass creation depicting Neptune riding a sea serpent.

Rooms at Port Orleans French Quarter measure 314 square feet. Most are outfitted with two queen beds, a table and two chairs, a dresser–credenza, a minifridge, a coffee maker, and a vanity outside the bathroom. With their hardwood floors, cherry headboards, purple accent fabrics, and cherrywood credenzas, the rooms are themed but tasteful. A privacy curtain separates the dressing area from the rest of the room, allowing three people to get ready at once. No rooms have balconies, but iron-railed accessways on each floor provide a good (though less private) substitute.

Most readers really like Port Orleans French Quarter. Some, such as this Raleigh, North Carolina, family, rate it even higher than many Deluxe resorts:

We stayed at the Polynesian Village in 2017, but we loved French Quarter! The updated rooms were great and the resort was so easy to navigate.

Note that there's no full-service restaurant—just a food court that can get overwhelmed, as this Waxahachie, Texas, reader discovered:

The French Quarter food court was a disaster on the night we checked in. We waited 18 minutes for our order.

The closest full-service eatery is in the adjacent Riverside section, a 15-plus-minute walk away. The commute to restaurants in other hotels may be 40–60 minutes each way.

Port Orleans Resort–French Quarter

Disney buses link the French Quarter to all Disney World destinations. Walking time to bus-loading areas from the most remote French Quarter rooms is 5 minutes or less.

GOOD (AND NOT-SO-GOOD) ROOMS AT PORT ORLEANS RESORT–FRENCH QUARTER (*See* tinyurl.com/pofq-roomviews *for photos.*) Seven guest-room buildings flank the pool, Guest Relations building, and bus stop. The best views are from rooms facing the river and pine forest on the opposite bank. Wings of **buildings 1, 2, 5, 6,** and **7** flank the river and provide the best river views in all of Port Orleans. River-view rooms in **buildings 1, 6,** and **7** are a long walk from French Quarter public facilities, but they're the most tranquil. Families with children should request river-view rooms in **buildings 2** and **5,** nearest the swimming complex. Make sure the reservationist understands that you're requesting a room with a river view, not just a water view. All river-view rooms are also water-view rooms but not vice versa. Note that standard-view rooms look onto a courtyard or a parking lot.

The following are the best river-view rooms in each building:

BUILDING 1 Rooms 1127–1132, 1227–1232 (a tree blocks some of the view in 1229 and 1230), or 1327–1332

BUILDING 2 Rooms 2227–2232 (landscaping blocks some of the view in 2129 and 2130), or 2327–2332

BUILDING 5 Rooms 5118–5123, 5218–5225, or 5318–5325

BUILDING 6 Rooms 6123–6129, 6138–6139, 6145–6148, 6223–6226, 6233–6240, 6245–6248, 6323–6329, 6335–6340, or 6345–6348

BUILDING 7 Rooms 7142–7147, 7242–7247, or 7342–7347

Note that room **6X23** in building 6 is a corner room with two windows, one of which faces the river. But Disney puts it in the less expensive garden-view category.

If you're not overly concerned with the specific room you get, the highest-rated building at French Quarter is building 6—in fact, it's the fourth-highest-rated collection of rooms in Walt Disney World.

Port Orleans Resort-Riverside

PORT ORLEANS RESORT-RIVERSIDE

STRENGTHS

- Interesting narrative to theming
- Disney princess–themed rooms in Magnolia Bend
- Live entertainment in River Roost Lounge
- Rooms at Alligator Bayou can sleep five, the fifth in a Murphy bed
- Very nice feature pool
- Close driving distance to the Magic Kingdom
- Good place to walk or run for fitness
- Recreation options (bikes, boats)

WEAKNESSES

- Multiple bus stops; may share service with Port Orleans French Quarter during slower times of year

Unofficial Guide **Reader-Survey Results**

Percentage of readers who'd stay here again	**84%** *(Average)*
Percentage of readers who'd recommend this resort to a friend	**81%** *(Average)*
Overall reader rating	**B–**

THIS RESORT DRAWS ON THE LIFESTYLE and architecture of Mississippi River communities in early-19th-century Louisiana. Spread along the Sassagoula River, which encircles **Ol' Man Island** (the section's main swimming area), Riverside is subdivided into two more themed areas: **Magnolia Bend,** which features plantation-style architecture, and **Alligator Bayou,** featuring tin-roofed rustic (imitation) wooden buildings. "Mansions" in Magnolia Bend are three stories tall, while guesthouses in Alligator Bayou are a story shorter. Riverside's food court houses a working cotton press powered by a 32-foot waterwheel.

Each of Riverside's 2,048 rooms is 314 square feet. Most provide one king or two queen beds, a table and two chairs, a minifridge and coffee maker, and two pedestal sinks outside the bathroom.

Disney refurbished rooms in Alligator Bayou in 2019. These rooms, along with those at Caribbean Beach and the Fort Wilderness Cabins, are unique among Disney Moderates in that they sleep five people; the fifth bed is a Murphy-style fold-down, suitable for kids only. Rooms feature hickory-branch tables, and all have vinyl plank flooring. Bathrooms have increased shelf space and a curtain separator that allows three people to get ready at once.

Rooms in Magnolia Bend are more conventional, with light-green walls, chestnut-colored wood furnishings, and olive carpets. Bathroom lighting seems to have been improved, and a small shelf above the dual-sink countertop provides additional storage space.

Oak Manor and **Parterre Place** in Magnolia Bend contain exclusively Disney princess–themed rooms, similar in concept to the Disney-themed rooms at Caribbean Beach Resort. Port Orleans Riverside's rooms are themed to *The Princess and the Frog,* with appearances by Tiana's other princess friends. These rooms cost around up to $75 more per night than standard rooms.

Disney buses link Riverside to all Disney World destinations. Walking time to bus-loading areas from the most remote rooms is 5 minutes or less. Unfortunately, bus service is one of readers' biggest gripes about Riverside. First from a Scottsdale, Arizona, reader:

> *The buses were very crowded, hot, and sweaty. It was a fight just to get on in the morning, and we often had to wait for a second bus.*

Next, from a Delmar, Delaware, mom:

> *Port Orleans Riverside has some of the worst bus service on property. One day a bus to a park takes 20 minutes; two days later, going to the exact same park, you will experience a long, leisurely drive around the loop, then make a stopover at French Quarter, followed by finally getting to the park about 45 minutes later or more. Utter madness!*

A big fan of Port Orleans Riverside says she won't be going back:

> *I absolutely love Port Orleans Riverside and have stayed here four times. But as lovely as it is, I'm always very disappointed with the bus service to and from the Magic Kingdom. You have people trying to leave early enough to make it to their dining reservations, but whoever schedules the buses doesn't seem to care. And the service coming back from the park is nothing short of abominable: Every single night, I waited more than 35 minutes in a large crowd only to have to stand on the bus. It is for this reason that I will not go back to this beautiful resort.*

Don't throw Port Orleans Riverside under the bus (pun intended). Simply rent a car or use a ride-hailing app, and get off the bus, Gus.

Finally, the resort's size can be overwhelming to some guests, as this reader from Pensacola, Florida, writes:

> *It was our first extended stay at Port Orleans Riverside, and we found the resort to be too big and the pathways too confusing. We were situated 0.5 mile from the lobby/food court, which made taking advantage of our refillable mugs a somewhat-arduous task.*

GOOD (AND NOT-SO-GOOD) ROOMS AT PORT ORLEANS RIVERSIDE RESORT *(See* tinyurl.com/por-roomviews *for photos.)* Riverside is so large that we use bicycles whenever we visit there. All told, there are

20 guest-room buildings (not counting flanking wings on two buildings). Divided into two sections, **Alligator Bayou** and **Magnolia Bend,** the resort is arranged around two pine groves and a man-made watercourse that Disney calls the Sassagoula River.

Magnolia Bend consists of four three-story, grand plantation–style complexes named **Acadian House, Magnolia Terrace, Oak Manor,** and **Parterre Place.** Though Magnolia Bend is on the river, only about 15% of the guest rooms have an unobstructed view of the water. Most rooms overlook a courtyard or parking lot. Trees and other vegetation block the view of many rooms actually facing the river. The best views in Magnolia Bend are from the third-floor river side of Acadian House (building 80), which overlooks the river and Ol' Man Island: rooms **8414–8419.**

To the south are Magnolia Terrace (building 85) and Oak Manor (building 90), each in an H shape. They're nearer the front desk, restaurant, lounge, and shopping complex than Acadian House. Continuing south, Parterre Place (building 95) has a number of rooms facing the river, but most views are blocked by trees or extend to the parking lot on the opposite shore. Try **9537–9540, 9573–9576, 9737–9739,** and **9773–9776.** In general, with the few previous exceptions, if you want a nice river view, opt for Port Orleans French Quarter.

Alligator Bayou, the other part of Port Orleans Riverside, forms an arch around the resort's northern half. Sixteen smaller, two-story guest-room buildings, set among pine groves and abundant gardens, offer a cozy alternative to the more-imposing structures of the Magnolia Bend section of Riverside and of Port Orleans French Quarter. If you want a river view, ask for a second-story water-view room in **building 27** or **38.** (Building 27 is the second-highest-rated collection of rooms in the resort—keep reading.) **Building 14** also offers some river-view rooms and is convenient to shops, the front desk, and the restaurant, but it's in a noisy, high-traffic area. (That doesn't seem to deter readers, who rate building 14 as the best at the resort.) A good compromise for families is **building 18.** It's insulated from traffic and noise by landscaping, but it's also next to a satellite swimming pool and within an easy walk of the lobby and restaurant.

Disney's official Riverside map shows two green areas north of the river bend in Alligator Bayou—these are dried-up lakes that are now richly forested with pine. Though out of sight of water, these offer the most peaceful and serene accommodations in the entire Port Orleans Resort. In this area, we recommend **buildings 26, 25,** and **39,** in that order. Note that these buildings are somewhat distant from the resort's central facilities, and there's no adjacent parking. In Alligator Bayou, avoid **buildings 15, 16, 17,** and **24,** all of which are subject to traffic noise from nearby Bonnet Creek Parkway.

THE ANIMAL KINGDOM RESORTS

Disney's Animal Kingdom Lodge & Villas: Jambo House and Kidani Village

(See map on page 179; see tinyurl.com/ug-aklodge for extended coverage.)

QUICK TAKE: *Jambo House is rated among the highest of any Disney hotel. It also has easy access to three of the top sit-down restaurants in*

*our reader surveys. If it fits in your budget, Animal Kingdom Lodge &
Villas is the first on-property resort you should consider.*

IN THE SOUTHWESTERNMOST CORNER OF THE WORLD, adjacent to
the Animal Kingdom theme park, Animal Kingdom Lodge opened
in 2001. The resort is divided into **Jambo House,** which has regular
rooms and DVC/DDV studios and villas, and the all-DVC studios and
villas at **Kidani Village.** The section below describes Jambo House;
Kidani Village coverage follows.

ANIMAL KINGDOM LODGE–JAMBO HOUSE

STRENGTHS	WEAKNESSES
• Magnificent lobby	• Few counter-service dining options
• Excellent on-site sit-down dining options	• Most of the villas here are smaller than those at Kidani Village
• Large, beautiful feature pool	• Rooms are among the smallest of the Deluxe resorts
• On-site cultural and nature programs	• Erratic bus service
• Best theming of any Disney hotel	• No direct non-bus transportation to any theme park

Unofficial Guide **Reader-Survey Results** *(Lodge & Jambo House only;
see page 181 for Kidani Village)*

Percentage of readers who'd stay here again	**Lodge: 92%; Villas: 91%** *(both Average)*
Percentage of readers who'd recommend this resort to a friend	**Lodge: 90%; Villas: 89%** *(both Average)*
Overall reader rating	**Lodge: B; Villas: B**

DESIGNED BY PETER DOMINICK of Wilderness Lodge fame, Jambo
House fuses African tribal architecture with the rugged style of grand
East African national park lodges. Five-story thatched-roof guest-
room wings fan out from a vast central rotunda housing the lobby.
Public areas and about half of the rooms offer panoramic views of
a private 21-acre wildlife preserve, punctuated with streams and
elevated *kopje* (rock outcrops) and populated with some 200 free-
roaming hoofed animals and 130 birds.

Most of the lodge's 972 guest rooms measure 344 square feet and
boast hand-carved furnishings and richly colored soft goods. Standard amenities include a flat-screen TV, table with two chairs, ceiling
fan, minifridge, and coffee maker. Behind each headboard sits faux
mosquito netting. The bathrooms have animal-themed wallpaper, two
sinks, and a large mirror. Almost all rooms have full balconies.

Jambo House also has DDV studios and one-, two-, and three-
bedroom villas. Most are slightly smaller than at neighboring Kidani
Village—anywhere from 50 square feet smaller for a studio to more
than 200 square feet smaller for a two-bedroom villa. The three-
bedroom Grand Villas at Jambo House are an exception, larger than
those in Kidani by 148 square feet.

Jambo's lowest-priced one-bedroom rooms sleep four; standard,
savanna, and Club Level rooms sleep five. A Murfreesboro, Tennessee,
mom loved everything but the room size:

*We wanted to love staying in Animal Kingdom Lodge. We found
the setting unique, the staff exceptional, and the common areas*

Animal Kingdom Lodge & Villas

breathtakingly gorgeous. Loved all three table-service restaurants. Location wasn't an issue since we had a car, and the pool was fabulous. However, the rooms are really small for the price. We were especially dismayed at the commode/shower area—we had to sit on the commode in order to have room to shut the door. Unfortunately, the room size and bathrooms dropped us from "love" to "like."

From a New Jersey mom:

Animal Kingdom Lodge was wonderful, but the rooms were somewhat disappointing. While we loved the theme, ambience, staff, and amazing savanna view, the room was small and had terrible storage. There were only two dresser drawers for four people—the room could have used another dresser and under-sink storage. Even a few strategically placed shelves would have been helpful.

Besides theming, another of Jambo House's strengths is its upscale dining: Readers place all 3 of the sit-down restaurants in Animal Kingdom Lodge among Walt Disney World's top 10. At the top of the list is **Jiko—The Cooking Place.** Twin wood-burning ovens are the focal point of the restaurant, which serves meals inspired by the myriad cuisines of Africa. **Boma—Flavors of Africa,** the family restaurant, serves a buffet breakfast and dinner with food prepared in an exhibition kitchen featuring a wood-burning grill and rotisserie. Tables are under thatched roofs. (**Sanaa,** the third restaurant, is a short walk away at Kidani Village.) **Victoria Falls,** a delightful mezzanine lounge overlooking Boma, rounds out the hotel's sit-down service. **The Mara,** the lone quick-service place, can get crowded, even with extended hours. A family from New Canaan, Connecticut, found the resort's restaurants a draw:

> The restaurants in Animal Kingdom Lodge are great. We had lunch at Sanaa, which featured fantastic food and awesome views of the animals on the savanna. The Mara's counter-service options were way better than anything we found in the Magic Kingdom.

Uzima Springs serves drinks, salads, and snacks next to the resort's huge, elaborate pool. Other amenities include a village marketplace, outdoor movies shown nightly, and a nightly campfire.

The **Starlight Safari** wildlife tour is for guests age 8 and up. The 1-hour tour costs $81–$95 per person and takes place nightly at 8:30 and 10 p.m.

Jambo House is connected to the rest of Walt Disney World by bus, but because of the resort's remote location, you should seriously consider having a car if you stay there. This family from Downers Grove, Illinois, concurs:

> We stayed in Animal Kingdom Lodge knowing we were going to have minimal park time. The distance from the parks was noticeable— the buses were packed, with standing passengers the norm, and the posted wait times for the next bus were only a guide. We wouldn't recommend staying here if you were planning to go to the parks on a daily basis.

This Baltimore mom found transportation the resort's weakest aspect:

> Animal Kingdom Lodge was a calm oasis with peaceful hotel rooms, but it's too hard to access the Magic Kingdom from there, either by car or by bus.

GOOD (AND NOT-SO-GOOD) ROOMS AT JAMBO HOUSE (See **tinyurl .com/akl-roomviews** for photos.) A glance at the resort map tells you where the best rooms and villas are. **Kudu Trail** and **Zebra Trail,** two wings branching from the rear of Jambo House, form a semicircle around the central wildlife savanna. Along each wing are seven five-story buildings, with accommodations on floors two through five. Five buildings on each wing form the semicircle, while the remaining two buildings jut away from the center.

The best rooms—on floors three and four, facing into the circle— are high enough to survey the entire savanna yet low enough to let you appreciate the ground-level detail of this amazing wildlife exhibit; plus, these rooms offer the easiest access to the lobby and restaurants.

Second-floor rooms really can't take in the panorama, and fifth-floor rooms are a little too high for good views of the animals. Most of the fourth-floor rooms in Jambo House are reserved for Club Level guests, and the fifth and sixth floors house the DDV units.

Most rooms in the outward-jutting buildings, as well as rooms facing away from the interior, also survey a savanna, but one not as compelling as that of the inner circle. On the Zebra Trail, the first two buildings plus the first jutting building provide savanna views on one side and look onto the swimming complex on the other. Rooms in the Zebra Trail section are rated higher by readers, on average, than those in any other section of Jambo House.

Less attractive still are two smaller wings, **Ostrich Trail** and **Giraffe Trail,** branching from either side of the lodge near the main entrance. Some rooms on the left side of Ostrich Trail overlook a small savanna. Rooms on the opposite side of the same buildings overlook the front entrance. Least desirable is Giraffe Trail, extending from the right side of the lobby: Its rooms overlook either the pool (water view) or the resort entrance (standard view). A Portage, Indiana, family begs to differ with our assessment, however:

We stayed in a pool-view room in Giraffe Trail and loved it. The view was beautiful, even without animals (which you can see elsewhere). The proximity to the pool, lobby, and restaurants was great, and we saved about $500 over what we would've spent on a savanna view.

ANIMAL KINGDOM LODGE & VILLAS–KIDANI VILLAGE

STRENGTHS	
• Nice pool with excellent splash area	• Close to Jambo House amenities and restaurants
• Underground parking close to elevators	• Great fitness room
• Beautiful, understated lobby	**WEAKNESSES**
• Sanaa restaurant is an *Unofficial Guide* favorite	• Savanna views can be hit-or-miss
	• Erratic bus service
• Beautiful Grand Villas sleep 12	• No quick-service dining options other than pool bar

Unofficial Guide **Reader-Survey Results**

Percentage of readers who'd stay here again	**82%** (*Below Average*)
Percentage of readers who'd recommend this resort to a friend	**77%** (*Below Average*)
Overall reader rating	**B**

CONSISTING OF A SEPARATE BUILDING shaped like a backward 3, Kidani Village has 324 DDV units, a dedicated savanna, a well-themed pool and splash zone, and **Sanaa,** a top-rated sit-down restaurant combining Indian and African cuisines. Other amenities include a fitness center; an arcade; a gift shop; and tennis, shuffleboard, and basketball courts. Kidani Village is connected to Jambo House by a half-mile walking trail; DDV guests at either resort can use the facilities at both.

Kidani Village has studios and one-, two-, and three-bedroom villas. Except for the three-bedroom units, most rooms are larger than their counterparts at Jambo House by anywhere from 50 square feet (for a studio) to more than 200 square feet (for a two-bedroom unit). Kidani's villas also have one more bathroom for the one-, two-, and three-bedroom units. Because of the difference in area, one-bedroom units in Kidani Village can accommodate up to five people, and two-bedroom units can hold up to nine guests with a sleeper chair in the living room.

Kidani's rooms are scheduled for refurbishment in 2023. A family from Santa Fe, New Mexico, thinks it can't come soon enough:

> *Kidani Village is run-down and needs updating. Worst sleeper sofa we've ever encountered. Our son ended up sleeping on the floor.*

Having stayed at Kidani Village more than a dozen times, we think it's quiet and relaxed. The lobby and rooms have a smaller, more personal feel than Jambo House's. The exterior isn't anything special: It's basically a set of green rectangles with oversize African-themed decorations attached. Kidani's distance from Jambo House makes it feel especially remote. The bus stops are a fair distance from the main building, too, and it's easy to head in the wrong direction when you're coming back from the parks at night. This family from Mount Holly, New Jersey, agrees:

> *Kidani Village is gorgeous and comfortable, and we will never stay there again unless we have our own vehicle. Our room was a considerable hike from everything; that corridor seemed endless at the end of a long day! If we'd driven or rented a car it would have been easier, as our room was pretty close to an elevator. We did rent points knowing full well that Kidani was pretty far from everything except Animal Kingdom and that the only Disney transportation option was the bus, so it feels churlish to complain . . . but it turns out I like having multiple transportation options that don't rely on surge pricing.*

GOOD (AND NOT-SO-GOOD) UNITS AT AKL–KIDANI VILLAGE *(See* **tinyurl.com/kidani-roomviews** *for photos.)* The best views in Kidani Village are from the north-facing units near the bottom and middle of the backward 3. Try rooms **7X38–7X44, 7X46–7X52, 7X06–7X11, 7X68–7X82,** and **7X61–7X67** (*X* indicates numbers 0–9). These overlook the savanna next to Jambo House's Kudu Trail rooms and beyond into undeveloped woods. West- and south-facing units in the bottom half of Kidani Village overlook the parking lot; west-facing units in the top half have either pool or savanna views.

Disney's Coronado Springs Resort
(See **tinyurl.com/ug-coronado** *for extended coverage.)*

NEAR ANIMAL KINGDOM, Coronado Springs Resort is Disney's only midpriced convention property. Inspired by northern Mexico and the American Southwest, the resort is divided into four separately themed areas. The two- and three-story **Ranchos** call to mind Southwestern cattle ranches, while the two-story **Cabanas** are modeled after Mexican beach resorts. The multistory **Casitas** embody elements of Spanish architecture found in Mexico's great cities.

The **Gran Destino Tower** serves as the lobby for all of Coronado Springs, and the rooms in this 15-floor building are nicer than those

Coronado Springs Resort

STRENGTHS

- Most sophisticated room decor of the Moderate resorts
- Setting is beautiful at night
- Themed swimming area with waterslides
- Large feature pool
- On-site business center
- Best public Wi-Fi at any Disney resort

WEAKNESSES

- Dining options rated low by readers
- Conventioneers may be off-putting to vacationing families
- Some rooms are a long distance from check-in, lobby, and restaurants
- Multiple bus stops

Unofficial Guide Reader-Survey Results

Percentage of readers who'd stay here again	**92%** (*Average*)
Percentage of readers who'd recommend this resort to a friend	**87%** (*Average*)
Overall reader rating	**B**

in the rest of the resort. (The idea, we hear, is to appeal to companies reluctant to put their executives in Moderate hotel rooms.)

This vast resort, surrounding a 22-acre lake, has three small pools and one large swimming complex. The main pool features a reproduction of a Mayan step pyramid with a waterfall cascading down its side.

Most of the 1,839 rooms in the Ranchos, Cabanas, and Casitas measure 314 square feet and contain two queen beds, a desk with an excellent working area, a chair, a minifridge, a coffee maker, and a vanity outside the bathroom. Sliding doors divide the main living area from the sinks, allowing three people to get ready at the same time. Bathrooms have plenty of storage. Rooms are decorated with a subtle Southwestern theme, in a desert-landscape palette. None of the rooms have balconies.

The 545 rooms in Gran Destino Tower range from standard issue to deluxe, one-bedroom, and presidential suites. The public areas showcase a vibrant mix of Spanish and Moorish design, with bold colors and large, open spaces.

Gran Destino's standard rooms are almost 20% larger than those in the rest of the resort. They have vinyl plank flooring, large windows, good lighting, and lots of desk and storage space; rooms are also equipped with a minifridge and a Keurig coffee maker. Bathrooms have plentiful lighting and shelf space, two sinks, a huge shower, and separate areas for grooming and the toilet, allowing three people to get ready at the same time. Our one criticism is that there's little theming: The rooms barely differ from those at other Disney resorts.

Our favorite thing about Gran Destino is the relatively low cost of Club Level rooms, which get you access to the **Chronos Club** lounge. Standard rates for these rooms run $100–$300 per night less than the next-cheapest Club Level room on-property, and limited-time discounts can make the price even better. The Chronos Club has fantastic views, good food throughout the day, and a friendly staff. If you're looking for a little pampering on vacation, Gran Destino's Club Level rooms are probably the best value in Walt Disney World.

Perhaps because Coronado Springs is geared to conventions, getting actual work done here is easier than at any other Disney Moderate resort. Lighting above the desk provides excellent illumination of the work area. Wi-Fi is available throughout the resort.

Coronado Springs has four full-service restaurants and a food court, plus two bars. One of those full-service restaurants, **Toledo—Tapas, Steak & Seafood,** is in Gran Destino Tower. An over-water bar called **Three Bridges Bar & Grill** sits in the middle of the lake, connected to the resort by—drum roll—three bridges. Even with these additions, though, dining capacity, choices, quality, and value are not where they need to be for a resort this big. We suggest having a car to expand your options.

The resort is connected to other Disney destinations by bus only. Walking time from the most remote rooms to the bus stop is 8–10 minutes. Bus service is the other of Coronado Springs' weaknesses. This Oklahoma City family's comments are representative:

The buses took at least 30–45 minutes to arrive at the parks and/or resort. The queues for the bus would be filled with guests, and they still wouldn't send another.

Beyond transportation, reader opinions of Coronado Springs are split. A family from Cumming, Georgia, was disappointed:

The convention center really interferes with a family vacation— everyone we met there was working and wanted to talk about work while we were trying to get away from work!

A Chester, Virginia, mother had a very different experience:

Coronado Springs was absolutely fabulous. The staff was friendly, the kids loved the pool, and we all loved the market. It was nice and quiet at night. There were many convention guests, but they didn't interfere with our trip.

Coronado Springs was the Disney Moderate resort of choice for this Kansas City, Kansas, family:

On our previous three trips, we stayed at Pop Century, and I was curious if a Moderate resort was worth the extra money. At first the size of Coronado Springs was daunting, but we quickly settled into a routine and figured out the bus routes (bus service was really the only major drawback). The room was spacious, and the door separating the living area from the bath vanity was very useful because I was able to get ready in the morning without waking the kids. The kids really enjoyed the pool area, and I thought it was better themed than Pop Century. Overall, I thought the resort was worth the price difference.

A family from Indianapolis liked the swimming pools:

The pool at Coronado Springs was excellent—the kids loved the slide! We also utilized the smaller pool close to our room—it was good for the kids to relax before bedtime.

GOOD (AND NOT-SO-GOOD) ROOMS AT CORONADO SPRINGS RESORT *(See* **tinyurl.com/csr-roomviews** *for photos.)* As convention hotels go, Coronado Springs is kind of an odd duck. Whereas at comparable hotels everything is centrally located and the guest rooms are in close proximity to each other, the rooms here are spread around a huge lake called **Lago Dorado.** If you're assigned a room on the opposite side of the lake from the meeting area and restaurants, plan on an 11- to 15-minute hike every time you leave your room.

Coronado Springs' main lobby is inside **Gran Destino Tower.** To its west is **El Centro**, which contains shops, restaurants, and a conference center. There are three accommodation "communities": **Casitas, Ranchos,** and **Cabanas.** If you think of Coronado Springs as a clock face, El Centro is at the 6 o'clock position. Moving clockwise around the lake beyond El Centro, the Casitas are located near the lobby, restaurants, shops, and convention center, in the 7–9 o'clock positions. Standard-view rooms face parking lots or a courtyard. Water-view rooms cover pools, the lake, etc. For a good view of Lago Dorado, book one of these rooms:

3220-3223, 3241-3259, 3267-3273, or 3281-3287

3320-3383 (*except* 3324, 3330-3335, 3360-3365, 3374-3380, and 3384-3387)

3420-3423, 3425-3429, 3436-3459, 3466-3473, 3480-3482, or 3487

4461-4464

5202-5212

5303-5304 or 5311-5312

5400-5402, 5405-5410, 5413, or 5423-5463 (*except* 5450)

Next come the Ranchos, which are set back from the lake at the 11, 12, and 1 o'clock positions. The desert theme translates to lots of cactus and gravel, not much water or shade, and almost no good views. The Ranchos are a hike from everything but the main swimming area. Rooms **6X00-6X04** afford the best views.

The Cabanas are at 2, 3, and 4 o'clock. Lake-view rooms we recommend here include the following: **8129-8131** and **8142-8147; 8500-8510, 8550-8553,** and **8573** (*except* 8505, 8507, and 8509). Specific rooms aside, Cabanas **building 8C** (rooms **8800-8993**) is the highest-rated building at the resort.

Finally, Gran Destino Tower is at 5 o'clock, close to El Centro. Even-numbered rooms face EPCOT and Hollywood Studios, and guests on upper floors can see those parks' fireworks shows. Odd-numbered rooms at Gran Destino have a view of the resort's lake.

Disney's All-Star Resorts: Movies, Music, and Sports

(*See* tinyurl.com/ug-allstars *for extended coverage.*)

STRENGTHS	WEAKNESSES
• Least expensive of the Disney resorts	• Most likely Disney resorts to host large school groups
• Family suites at All-Star Music are less expensive than those at Art of Animation	• Room soundproofing is poor; bring a white-noise machine
• Convenient parking	
• Lots of pools	• No full-service dining; food courts often overwhelmed at mealtimes
• Lovely landscaping, if you know where to look (Music)	• All three resorts share buses during slower times of year; bus stops often crowded
• In-room pizza delivery (currently unavailable)	

Unofficial Guide **Reader-Survey Results**

Percentage of readers who'd stay here again **Movies: 89%** (*Average*); **Music: 90%** (*Average*); **Sports: 84%** (*Average*)
Percentage of readers who'd recommend this resort to a friend **Movies: 84%** (*Average*); **Music: 89%** (*Average*); **Sports: 87%** (*Average*)
Overall reader rating **Movies: C; Music: B; Sports: B–**

DISNEY'S ORIGINAL VERSION of a budget resort features three distinct themes executed in the same hyperbolic style. Spread over a vast expanse, the resorts comprise 30 three-story motel-style guest-room buildings. Although the three resorts are neighbors, each has its own lobby, food court, and registration area.

The facade of **All-Star Sports** features huge sports equipment: bright football helmets, tennis rackets, and baseball bats—all taller than the buildings they adorn. Similarly, **All-Star Music** features 40-foot guitars, maracas, and saxophones, while **All-Star Movies** showcases giant popcorn boxes and icons from Disney films.

All-Star Resorts

The food courts function well for their size and purpose. Lobbies are loud (in both decibels and brightness) and cartoonish, with checkerboard walls; photographs of famous athletes, musicians, or film stars; and a dedicated area for kids to watch Disney shows and movies while parents are checking in.

Each resort has two main pools; Music's are shaped like musical instruments (the **Piano Pool** and the guitar-shaped **Calypso Pool**), and one of Movies' is star-shaped. All six pools feature plastic replicas of Disney characters, some shooting water pistols.

At 260 square feet, standard rooms at the All-Star Resorts are very small—the same size as those at Pop Century Resort and slightly smaller than Art of Animation's standard rooms. The All-Star rooms are so small, in fact, that a family of four attempting to stay in one room might redefine *family values* by week's end. (*And just remember they give you 60 square feet per person in prison. —Len*)

All of the All-Star rooms have been refurbished. Each room includes vinyl plank flooring, sleek modern storage units, queen beds, 10 USB outlets (including USB-C), and a coffee maker. One of the beds folds into the wall when not being used, converting into a table; two chairs are included. Space has been freed under the fixed bed for storage. The bathroom remodel swaps out plastic shower curtains for sliding glass doors, new showerheads, and tile walls. The grooming area is vastly improved, with modular shelving, better lighting, and increased counter space. Another sliding door separates the bath from the main living space, allowing three people to get ready at the same time.

While we think the refurbishments are a big improvement overall, there's always an unexpected miss or two in a renovation. This reader from New Hampshire found a couple:

> *The updated rooms have a couple of downsides. One is zero water pressure in the shower. And the thermostat is behind the coffee station, so it's impossible to see the temperature or which buttons you're hitting.*

Due to the low staff-to-guest ratio, service is mediocre. Also, there are no full-service restaurants, and the bus ride from the remote All-Stars to a sit-down restaurant at another resort is about 45 minutes one-way (there is, however, a McDonald's about 0.25 mile away, with sidewalk access). Bus service to the theme and water parks is pretty efficient. Walking time to the bus stop from the most remote guest rooms is about 8 minutes.

If space is an important consideration, you may want to budget enough for a bigger room at another resort—Art of Animation's standard rooms, at least. Also, All-Star Sports and Music are the noisiest Disney resorts: We use a white-noise app when we stay here. Be aware, however, that while the All-Stars suffer compared with other Disney properties, you're better off here than at most hotels you'll find in Kissimmee or Lake Buena Vista for $150 per night or less.

We receive a lot of letters commenting on the All-Star Resorts. This family from Poplar Grove, Illinois, loved the renovated Movies rooms:

> *We stayed in a newly refurbished room at Pop Century; then we moved to All-Star Movies for two nights. Both were wonderful—we*

loved the new layouts, and there was plenty of space, even with all of our gear—but All-Star Movies felt a bit more upscale.

A Princeton, Indiana, family had a similarly positive experience:

Our hotel room had so many storage shelves! Even though it was super small, we could be organized with our stuff for the week. I wish all hotels were like that! Shelves next to each bed (along with plenty of outlets), shelves inside the bathroom, shelves in the main bedroom. It was great. The fridge should be called a cooler. It didn't really keep stuff cold but cool.

A Canadian family had a not-so-positive experience:

The Guide *didn't prepare us for the large groups of students who take over the resorts. They're very noisy and pushy when it comes to getting on buses. Our scariest experience was when we tried getting on a bus and got mobbed by about 100 students.*

ALL-STAR MUSIC FAMILY SUITES In the Jazz and Calypso Buildings, the 192 suites measure roughly 520 square feet, slightly larger than the Fort Wilderness Cabins but slightly smaller than Art of Animation's Family Suites. Each suite, formed from the combination of two formerly separate rooms, includes a kitchenette with full-size fridge, microwave, and coffee maker. Sleeping accommodations include a fold-down queen bed in the bedroom, plus a pullout sleeper sofa. We're not sure we'd let adult friends (ones we want to keep, anyway) sleep on the sofa bed, but it's fine for kids. A hefty door separates the two rooms.

> *unofficial* **TIP**
> Music 5654 may be the best room at the All-Star Resorts. This third-floor corner room overlooks a small pond in a wooded area behind the resort. See tinyurl.com/music5654 for a photo of the view.

The All-Star Music Family Suites have flat-screen TVs as well as two baths—one more than the Fort Wilderness Cabins. The suites cost up to 20% less than the cabins and about 15% less than Art of Animation's Family Suites, but they don't have the kitchen space or appliances to prepare anything more than rudimentary meals. If you're trying to save money by eating in your room, the cabins are your best bet. If you just want a little extra space and somewhere to nuke your Pop-Tarts in the morning, the All-Star suites are just fine.

Reader comments about the Family Suites are generally positive, albeit measured. First, from a North Carolina family of five:

It was so nice to have a place to unwind without the kids at night, along with two bathrooms and extra kitchen space. My only issue was that we weren't comfortable leaving the kids on the foldouts because they're right next to the front door; plus, my husband and I didn't want to be confined to the bedroom from the time we put the kids to bed, so we slept on a foldout.

From a Skokie, Illinois, family of five:

We found the All-Star Music Family Suite to be very roomy. Our teenagers and preteen were quite comfortable on the pullout sofa. Having the two bathrooms was a must, and the kitchen area had lots of shelf space for the food we had delivered from Garden Grocer [see page 458]. Our only complaint is that from 7:30 a.m. until midnight there's music playing. The rooms are soundproofed but not enough; we had to use earplugs.

GOOD (AND NOT-SO-GOOD) ROOMS AT THE ALL-STAR RESORTS *(See* tinyurl.com/asmo-roomviews, tinyurl.com/asmu-roomviews, *and* tinyurl.com/assp-roomviews *for photos.)* Although the layouts of the All-Star Resorts' Movies, Music, and Sports sections are different, the three buildings are identical T-shaped, three-story, three-winged structures. The buildings are further grouped into pairs, generally facing each other and sharing a common subtheme (for example, there's a *Toy Story* pair in the Movies section). In addition to being named by theme, such as *Fantasia,* the buildings are numbered 1–10 in each section. Rooms are accessed via a motel-style outdoor walkway, but each building has an elevator.

Parking is plentiful, all of it in sprawling lots buffering the three sections. A room near a parking lot means easier loading and unloading but also unsightly views of the lot. The resort offers a luggage service, but it often takes up to an hour for your bags to arrive.

To avoid a parking-lot vista, you can request a room facing a courtyard or pool. The trade-off is noise—the sound of cars starting in the parking lot pales in comparison to shrieking children and hooting teenagers in the pool. And don't count on a good view of the pool, even if your room faces it. The themed facade decorations are placed on the buildings' widest face—the top of the T—which is also the side facing the pool or courtyard. In some cases, as with the surfboards in the Sports section, these significantly obstruct the view. Floodlights are also trained on these facades, so if you step out of your room at night to view the action below, looking down may result in temporary blindness.

The sort of traveler you are should dictate the room you request. If you choose an All-Star Resort because you'd rather spend time and money at the parks, book a room near the bus stop, your link to the rest of the World. Note that buses leave from the central public buildings of each section, which are near the larger, noisier pools. If you're planning to return to your room for an afternoon nap, request a room farther from the pools. Also consider an upper-story room to minimize foot traffic past your door. If you're only concerned with the highest-rated building in each resort (as opposed to looking for the best rooms or for buildings with specific amenities), here are the top-rated buildings at the All-Stars, according to our reader surveys:

- **All-Star Movies** 10 (*Toy Story*); 7 and 6 (*Love Bug*)
- **All-Star Music** 1 (Calypso)
- **All-Star Sports** 10 and 7 (Touchdown!)

On the other hand, if you choose All-Star for its kid-friendly aspects, consider roosting near the action. A bottom-floor room provides easy pool access, and a room looking out on a courtyard or pool allows you to keep an eye on children playing outside.

For travelers without young children (infants excluded), the best bets for privacy and quiet are rooms in buildings that overlook the forest behind the resort: **buildings 2** and **3** in **All-Star Sports** and **buildings 5** and **6** in **All-Star Music.** Interior-facing rooms in these buildings (and their partners) also fill the bill because they overlook courtyards farthest from the large pools. The courtyards vary with theme but are generally only mildly amusing.

If you're traveling with kids, opt for a section and building with a theme that appeals to them. Often, that will be a film, but it might be a sport. If you're staying in Home Run Hotel, for instance, don't forget the ball and gloves to maximize the experience (just keep games of catch away from the pool). Older elementary- and middle-school children will probably want to spend hotel time in or near the bigger pools. Periodically, however, cadres of teenagers—too cool for their younger siblings—effectively commandeer the smaller secondary pools.

Playgrounds are tucked behind Cinema Hall, next to building 9, in **All-Star Movies;** between the backs of buildings 9 and 10 in **All-Star Music;** and between buildings 6 and 7 in **All-Star Sports.** Rooms facing these are ideal for families with children too young or timid for the often-chaotic larger pools. In All-Star Movies, the playground is nearer to the food court than to any rooms.

The following tip from a former All-Star Resorts cast member from Fayetteville, Georgia, illustrates just how big these resorts are:

Rooms at the far end of the Mighty Ducks building of All-Star Movies are closer to the All-Star Music food court, pool, and buses than to All-Star Movies' own facilities. Follow the walkway from the Ducks building north to All-Star Music's Melody Hall.

Disney's Pop Century Resort
(*See map on page 192;* see tinyurl.com/ug-popcentury *for extended coverage.*)

STRENGTHS	WEAKNESSES
• Theming is fun for anyone over 35	• Room soundproofing is poor; bring a white-noise machine
• Our favorite pool bar of the Value resorts	
• One bus stop	• Theming may be lost on kids and teens
• Skyliner connection to DHS and EPCOT	• Small rooms that are the same size as All-Stars' but slightly more expensive
• Stylish, modern room design	
• Convenient parking	• Bus stops at theme parks are a long distance from park entrances

Unofficial Guide Reader-Survey Results

Percentage of readers who'd stay here again	**97%** (*Above Average*)
Percentage of readers who'd recommend this resort to a friend	**93%** (*Average*)
Overall reader rating	**B**

NOTE: *More* Unofficial Guide *readers stay at Pop Century than any other Disney resort. Pop is tied with the Riviera as the resort with the highest percentage of readers saying they'd stay there again.*

ON CENTURY DRIVE, near the ESPN Wide World of Sports, is Pop Century Resort. A near-clone of the All-Star Resorts, it consists of four-story motel-style buildings arrayed around a central pool, food court, and registration area. Decorative touches make the difference: Where the All-Stars display larger-than-life icons from movies, music, and sports, and Art of Animation is inspired by Disney cartoons, Pop Century draws its icons from decades of the 20th century and their attendant fads and fancies: building-size Big Wheels, Hula-Hoops,

Pop Century Resort & Art of Animation Resort

and the like, punctuated by silhouettes of folks doing the jitterbug and the twist.

Running $195–$367 per night, guest rooms at Pop Century are small, at 260 square feet. For the third straight year, Pop is the No. 1 Value property among readers who say they would stay at a particular Disney resort again.

All rooms have been refurbished. The refurbishment replaced carpet with a modern hardwood-floor look. IKEA-style storage nooks and space-saving touches are everywhere. A particular feature we love is that the second bed in the room is a fold-down option, as at Art of Animation. When the bed isn't in use, it disappears into the wall, freeing floor space (and turning into a desk). The bulky armoire–TV stand has been replaced by built-in shelving and a wall-mounted monitor. The bathroom overhaul provides lots more shelf space, plenty of storage, and a modern shower.

The public areas at Pop Century feature 20th-century furniture and decor, rolled up in a saccharine "those were the days" theme. A food court, bar, playground, pools, and so on emulate the All-Star versions in size and location. A lake separating Pop Century from the Art of Animation Resort (AOA) offers water views not available at the All-Stars.

In another departure from the All-Stars, Pop Century has a combination dining–shopping area featuring merchandise retailers and fast-food concessions. As at the All-Stars and AOA, there's a bar but no full-service restaurant. AOA's food court is a short walk over a bridge from many Pop rooms; at press time, however, both food courts had the same selection. Because of the limited dining options, we recommend having a car.

Pop Century is connected to Walt Disney World by bus and the **Skyliner**. Readers rate Pop's bus service relatively low. Pop Century shares a Skyliner station with AOA. The Skyliner connects Pop and AOA with the Caribbean Beach and Riviera Resorts, and it's the main Disney transportation to Hollywood Studios and EPCOT. (Disney adds bus service to EPCOT and DHS during busy times and when the Skyliner isn't running.) On average, the Skyliner is more efficient than the bus system for getting between these resorts and theme parks. However, lines can form at Pop's Skyliner station anywhere from 90 minutes to 2 hours before opening at Hollywood Studios. We think it's far less hassle to drive, use a ridehailing app, or call a taxi.

unofficial **TIP**
We don't recommend Pop Century's so-called preferred rooms, which are closer to the main pool and lobby and cost about $15–$25 more than standard. They probably save only 5 minutes of walking per day and subject you to more noise from guests walking past your room.

Besides transportation, we receive many complaints from readers about poor soundproofing between Pop Century's rooms—something that the refurbishment didn't address. As with most hotel rooms, we recommend having a white-noise machine or app available.

A reader from Dublin, Georgia, likes Pop for several reasons:

(1) There's a lake and a view of fireworks. (2) The courtyards have Twister and neat pools for little children. (3) Pop's dinner entrées are among the best bargains and the best food anywhere. (4) The layout is convenient to the food court. (5) Bus transportation is better than anywhere else, including Grand Floridian! (6) Where else do the cast members do the shag to oldies?

From a Jackson, Mississippi, family:

We loved the newly remodeled rooms at Pop Century—they are very modern-looking and have loads of storage space. But while there was no noise from rooms next to or above us, the noise directly outside was disturbing.

A Beaver Dam, Wisconsin, family had the same "good room, bad soundproofing" experience:

The remodeled room was very nice. We liked the Murphy bed and extra bathroom counter space. The only downside was when we left the parks in the afternoon to take a nap—the loudspeaker in the pool area made it hard to rest in our room nearby.

A Springfield, Illinois, dad also gives Pop Century a mixed review:

We wanted something different from All-Star Movies, so we gave Pop Century a shot. Believe the noise complaints—it's like the walls were made of papier-mâché. Although the bus service was great and the pool was nice, we'll be back at All-Star Movies the next time around.

An Austin, Texas, couple doesn't sugarcoat their opinion of the food-court options:

The Pop Century food court at late-dinner time (9 p.m. and beyond) continues to be a hellscape and will drain any remaining life force in your body faster than you could ever imagine.

GOOD (AND NOT-SO-GOOD) ROOMS AT POP CENTURY RESORT *(See* tinyurl.com/pop-roomviews *for photos.)* The best rooms for both view and convenience are the lake-view rooms in **buildings 4** and **5** in the **1960s** area. Another option, though with a less compelling view, would be rooms in the same building facing east, toward the registration and food-court building. The next-best choices would be the east-facing rooms of **building 3** in the **1950s**, and of **building 6** in the **1970s**. Avoid south-facing rooms in the **1980s (building 7)** and the **1990s (building 8)**; both are echo chambers for noise from nearby Osceola Parkway.

If you're only concerned with the highest-rated building at Pop Century (as opposed to looking for the best rooms or for buildings with specific amenities), building 8 (the 1990s) is the highest-rated, but all of Pop's buildings' ratings are fairly close together.

Disney's Art of Animation Resort

(See map on page 192; see tinyurl.com/ug-artofanimation *for extended coverage.)*

STRENGTHS	WEAKNESSES
• Exceptional theming, particularly *Cars* and *Lion King* areas	• Most expensive Value resort
	• Terrible in-room mobile reception
• Best pool of the Value resorts	• The resort's standard rooms are rarely discounted
• Family Suites are innovatively designed and themed	
• Interior hallways in some buildings	• Poor soundproofing
• Skyliner connection to DHS and EPCOT	
• Walking trail around Hour Glass Lake and connecting bridge to Pop Century	
• Just one bus stop	

Unofficial Guide **Reader-Survey Results**

Percentage of readers who'd stay here again	87% (*Average*)
Percentage of readers who'd recommend this resort to a friend	81% (*Average*)
Overall reader rating	B

DISNEY'S ART OF ANIMATION is a Value resort across Hour Glass Lake from Pop Century. As at Pop Century, standard rooms are housed in four-story buildings and exterior-facing walkups, with themed swimming pools and a food court. Most of the resort's accommodations, however, are suites similar to those at Disney's All-Star Music Resort: There are 1,120 suites versus 864 standard rooms. The suite buildings have interior hallways to the rooms instead of the exterior walkways found at Disney's other Value resorts.

Art of Animation's suites are around 565 square feet, about what you'd get by combining two standard rooms. Each suite has a master bedroom, a living room, two full bathrooms, and a kitchenette with minifridge, microwave, and coffee maker. Sleeping arrangements are a queen bed in the bedroom, a sleeper sofa, and a living room table that converts into a full-size bed. The bedroom and living room have flat-screen TVs.

This family from McKinney, Texas, found that the suites' second bathroom sped things up in the morning:

> With two teenagers, the extra space and second bathroom were absolutely worth the additional cost. Imagine being able to get ready for a park day twice as fast!

Slightly larger than comparable rooms at other Value resorts, standard rooms are 277 square feet and include one king bed or two doubles, a flat-screen TV, a minifridge, and a table and chairs.

The theming incorporates characters from four Disney animated films: *Cars, Finding Nemo, The Lion King,* and *The Little Mermaid.* All but the *Little Mermaid*–themed rooms are suites. As at Pop Century, large, colorful icons stand in the middle of each group of buildings; here, though, they represent film characters rather than pop culture touchstones. Giant murals stretch the length of each exterior structure—the *Cars* buildings, for example, each display a four-story panoramic vista of the American desert, with the movie's iconic characters in the middle, while the *Lion King* buildings capture a single verdant jungle scene.

Readers complain, however, about the long walk from the *Little Mermaid*–themed buildings to the food court and front desk. A pooped reader from Illinois offered this:

> Only two reasons to stay in a Little Mermaid room at Art of Animation: (1) There is a die-hard Little Mermaid fan in your party who will make your trip miserable if you don't get this room. (2) You don't feel you will walk enough in the parks and you want to add an extralong trek to/from the bus, main pool, restaurant, gift shop, and front desk.

Three of the four sets of themed buildings have pools. Like the other Value resorts, Art of Animation has a central building—here called **Animation Hall**—for check-in and bus transportation; it also houses the resort's food court, **Landscape of Flavors;** a gift shop; and a video-game arcade.

Most of the comments concerning Art of Animation are positive. A Collingswood, New Jersey, reader says:

> I was skeptical about Art of Animation. From pics it looked like it was going to be a child's dream but not necessarily an adult's. I was wrong—it's incredible! For a Value resort, it feels more like a Deluxe. The room was awesome—great layout, and having two bathrooms was so nice. The Big Blue Pool and the Cozy Cone Pool are great. Landscape of Flavors impressed me too—so many options for fresh, delicious comfort food as well as exotic fare.

As is the case with many Disney resorts, readers give low marks to Art of Animation's bus transportation. This comment from an Ambler, Pennsylvania, family sums it up:

> Art of Animation was incredibly practical for a family of five. Only issues are with transportation, which was AWFUL! We were there during a busy week, but even on slower days, buses were impossible. We ended up driving almost everywhere.

As at Pop Century, the **Skyliner** is the main Disney transportation option from AOA to EPCOT and Disney's Hollywood Studios, and in the morning lines form to get to Hollywood Studios starting around 90 minutes to 2 hours before park opening. (Disney adds bus service to EPCOT and DHS during busy times and when the Skyliner isn't running.) Your best bet is to drive, use a ride-hailing app, or take a taxi to the Studios. Access to the rest of Walt Disney World is on buses.

Another issue specific to Art of Animation is slow Wi-Fi speeds. This Texas reader ran some tests:

> The Disney Wi-Fi speeds in the room (Lion King building 10) and by the pool were consistently around 25 Mbps download and 25 Mbps upload. When I stepped just outside our building, I got Disney Wi-Fi speeds of around 10 Mbps, but when I turned off Wi-Fi and used AT&T cellular, I actually got around 95 Mbps downloading.

The reader is right to be concerned: Network speed and reliability are absolutely critical when you're competing with thousands of other guests to make Genie+ and Individual Lightning Lane reservations at exactly 7 a.m.

Noise and soundproofing are likewise issues. A Guyton, Georgia, mom comments:

> The room was very poorly soundproofed. I heard snoring and bathroom noises from other rooms that I should not have been able to hear. One afternoon my toddler and I returned to the room for a nap—I suppose housekeeping was cleaning the room above ours, but it sounded like someone was bowling up there.

GOOD (AND NOT-SO-GOOD) ROOMS AT ART OF ANIMATION *(See* **tinyurl .com/animation-roomviews** *for photos.)* The quietest suites are south- and east-facing rooms in **buildings 3** (*Cars*), **4** (*Finding Nemo*), and **6** (*The Lion King*). The quietest standard rooms are east-facing rooms in **building 8** and south-facing rooms in **building 7** (both *The Little Mermaid*). Avoid northwest-facing rooms in **building 1** and southwest-facing rooms in **building 10,** which face the Disney bus route and Art of Animation's bus stops.

The *Little Mermaid* buildings are the lowest-rated buildings at the resort, probably in part because they also have the smallest rooms. Ratings for the all-suite buildings tend to be very close, with the *Lion King* buildings 6 and 10 rated slightly higher than the others.

Star Wars: Galactic Starcruiser *(not enough surveys to rate)*
(See **touringplans.com/walt-disney-world/hotels/star-wars-galactic-starcruiser** *for extended coverage.)*

STRENGTHS	WEAKNESSES
• The absolute best themed entertainment and story-telling available anywhere	• Expensive
• Good food on board	• No time for relaxation
	• Standard cabin mattresses are too firm for some guests

NOTE: *As we were going to press, Disney announced that the Starcruiser's final "voyage" will take place September 28–30, 2023. Prior to the announcement, Disney was having difficulty finding customers for the experience, and the number of voyages had been reduced by half for late*

Star Wars: Galactic Starcruiser

2023. Guests booked for voyages departing on or after September 30 will be contacted to discuss their options and modify their plans.

THE GALACTIC STARCRUISER is a live-action role-playing experience that happens to come with a hotel room. It's like being on a cruise ship that doesn't float. As on cruise ships, everyone checks in to and out of the starcruiser, called the *Halcyon,* on the same day, for the same two-day itinerary. Likewise, a daily schedule shows what you'll be doing at any given time, including assigned seating times for meals. Stays include all meals and nonalcoholic beverages, with plenty of upsell options.

We've experienced the Starcruiser twice. Having covered theme parks for more than 30 years, we can safely say that the Starcruiser is so far beyond the current state-of-the-art in themed entertainment that it deserves its own category: Starcruiser-like hotel experiences. It surely belongs on the short list of Disney firsts, along with *Steamboat Willie* and Disneyland.

It's also (pardon the pun) astronomically expensive, starting at just under $5,000 for two people for two days ($6,000 for a family of four). The cost makes Starcruiser worthwhile only to well-off, experienced travelers who enjoy both *Star Wars* and days-long role-playing. If that's you, then this is a chance to create your own *Star Wars* story that stays with you for the rest of your life.

For *Star Wars* fans, the story is set in the timeline of the last set of movies (*Episodes VII, VIII,* and *IX*). Characters referenced include Chewbacca, Kylo Ren, Rey, and Yoda, but not Luke Skywalker or Darth Vader. Aboard the *Halcyon,* seven live actors explain the plot and, in one-on-one conversations, ask you to perform tasks to help them and their cause.

As with a video game, you have some say in how events unfold. Your actions can't change how the story ultimately ends (one of our friends asked, "Can I kill Chewbacca?" to which a character replied, "No. And what's wrong with you, man?"), but what you do while playing will definitely influence what you get to see and do during the game.

Because interacting with the characters and other players is so important to the Galactic Starcruiser experience, introverts and those who prefer to watch from the sidelines should be willing to commit to the game play before making a reservation.

YOUR BACKSTORY AND WHY IT MATTERS Disney encourages guests to dress in *Star Wars*–appropriate clothing and to have a backstory (created before you arrive) that ties in, even tangentially, to the *Star Wars* universe. Your backstory doesn't have to be extensive, but we think it's mandatory for two reasons:

- It shows Disney that you want to participate actively in the game instead of just observing.
- It helps the characters improvise dialogue for you and determine which side you're supporting.

For example, if you're approached by a character who asks where you're from, and you say, "Pittsburgh," that might be taken as a sign that you're not willing to play along. If, however, your answer starts with something like "I was born to poor spice miners on the third moon of Endor," they know you're up for an adventure. All Disney cast members—not just the main actors—will remember your backstory throughout the voyage.

The actors who play the main characters are the heart and soul of the *Halcyon* experience. They benefit from a script and story that follow the *Star Wars* lore while allowing plenty of improvisation to include your specific details. A character named Saja led us through lightsaber training, but the experience began with an explanation of the Force's mystical properties; how it envelops and permeates everything around us; and how to "center" yourself physically, mentally, and spiritually in order to wield it. All of it is done with encouragement and emotional support that, frankly, none of us gets enough of in our daily lives. Let's put it this way: At the end of lightsaber training, Saja asks if you're willing to help the Resistance. Not only did we say yes through tears streaming down our faces, but if Saja had asked for a kidney instead, we would've said yes to that too. The acting and story are that good.

The second day of your Starcruiser experience includes a visit to the Galaxy's Edge land inside Disney's Hollywood Studios. You might be tempted to skip this part of the cruise, especially if you've already experienced the land. However, we think visiting is mandatory, along with riding both rides and completing all the tasks you're asked to do. Doing these unlocks special events for you to participate in back on the ship. Again, to get the most out of the experience: **Do *everything*.**

The Galactic Starcruiser has 100 rooms, by far the fewest of Disney World's hotels:

- **94 Standard Cabins** (many with accessibility options)
- **4 Galaxy Class Suites** (2 with accessibility options)
- **2 Grand Captain Suites** (1 with accessibility options)

We stayed in a standard cabin on both of our visits. That room is laid out in a familiar rectangle shape. Including the walls, storage, bath, and everything else, we think that rectangle is just under 250 square feet in size. Excluding space for walls and unwalkable space for those closets, the sink, and the like, we think these rooms measure around 180 square feet—by a wide margin the smallest rooms in Walt Disney World.

Standard rooms include a queen bed and two bunk beds, a walk-in shower, one sink, and a separate water closet. (We think some rooms have an optional fold-down bed for kids in one wall.) There's also a minifridge, a hair dryer, and a wall-mounted television, but no coffee maker or microwave. And no windows; instead, a video screen embedded in the wall emulates the view you'd see from space. Disney has taken this an extra step forward by syncing the video on your screen to the video that's displayed from other "windows" around the ship. So, for example, if a group of people launch the *Halcyon* into hyperspace during bridge training, your stateroom's video screen will also show the jump to light speed.

Despite its size and lack of windows, the room didn't feel small for two adults. We spoke, however, with groups of four adults who all said that two days was the upper limit on how long four people could get along in these small surroundings.

As far as the quality of the furnishings goes, we thought the queen and bunk mattresses were too firm—we like a soft pillow-top mattress with soft pillows. However, only a handful of people we spoke with shared my opinion, and several enjoyed the mattresses. At this price point, we'd like to see Disney offer different mattress and pillow options for guests.

Water pressure in the shower was good, and the bathroom setup is very functional. With doors separating the sink area from the rest of the room, and another door for the toilet, it's possible for three people to get ready at the same time. That's a smart use of space in a cabin of this size.

A couple of other items to note: There's plenty of storage space for your luggage and costumes. Air-conditioning is controlled through a modern digital thermostat. And there's an Alexa-like video-chat terminal in your room. It can't (we think) tell you about the weather, but interacting with it will help Disney figure out which side of the game you're on. Parents should note that it requires you to push a button and then scan a MagicBand to use, and we think it's unlikely to be in "always listening" mode.

DINING The Starcruiser has one dining location: the **Crown of Corellia Dining Room,** open for lunch immediately after you board on Day 1 and from 1 to 4 p.m. on day 2. Breakfast is served from 7 to 11 a.m.

on Day 2 and until checkout on day 3. Both breakfast and lunch are served cafeteria-style, where you walk through the kitchen and grab small plates of whatever strikes your fancy. Be forewarned that most food items come in unexpected or unusual shapes, and sometimes in exotic colors, which may be off-putting to picky eaters. For example, the waffles are round on the *Halcyon,* and the sliced fruit is amazingly translucent. It's all good—some of it quite good—and you can eat as much as you like.

Dinner each night is a full-blown, multicourse production, with live entertainment to go along with the food. If you're familiar with how other Disney World restaurants serve family-style meals, that's how dinner is run: Each night's dinner features a fixed menu. Unless you request otherwise, small plates of every item offered in every course are brought to your table. Eat as much as you like, and you're encouraged to ask for more of anything you particularly enjoyed. As with other cruises, the cost of meals is included in your fare; the cost of alcoholic beverages is not.

We found the dining room's dinner fare to be comparable in quality to **Boma,** the popular African-themed buffet at Disney's Animal Kingdom Lodge (see page 319). There's plenty of food, it's tasty, and it's visually appealing to boot. An optional $30 upcharge buys you seating at the Captain's Table for dinner. The primary benefit of this is that part of the story unfolds at that table, giving you a front-row seat for the action. We recommend booking the Captain's Table, preferably for dinner on day 2.

IS IT WORTH THE MONEY? At $5,000 for two nights, the Starcruiser experience makes sense only if you're willing to go all-in and play the game as it's intended. That means that for around 42 hours, you have to believe that the events in *Star Wars* actually happened, that the Force is real, and that you'll do absolutely anything anyone asks of you to further your cause.

Here's what we think you should do with $5,000 in travel money before you do the Galactic Starcruiser:

- If you haven't seen much of the United States—and that means Alaska; Hawaii; the Rocky Mountains; the Great Plains; the Pacific Northwest; and, you know, the spectacle of Las Vegas—do that first. Drive, don't fly, as much as you can, to get a sense of how big this country is. You'll find good people in every town, in every state, in every part of it, and it will restore your faith in America in a way that a theme park can't. Heck, Las Vegas even has its own interactive theater experience in Omega Mart.

- If you haven't been to the UK and Europe, do that next. Where the US has a couple hundred years of history, Europe has a couple thousand. Europe has its own unique way of doing things: the metric system, the social safety net, and different plumbing and electrical systems. By visiting Europe, you start to think about why they made these choices and what the advantages (and disadvantages) might be. And just like exploring the US, in Europe you'll find kind people everywhere.

- If your family history is from another part of the world, whether that's Africa, Asia, South America, or the North Pole, go see the homeland, for pretty much the same reasons.

After you've done all that, we would absolutely recommend spending $5,000 on the Starcruiser. It's a chance for your family to have two intense days together doing things that aren't possible anywhere else in the world. And you'll have your own personal *Star Wars* story for the rest of your life. That's as good as themed entertainment gets. Five stars out of five.

INDEPENDENT HOTELS OF THE DISNEY SPRINGS RESORT AREA

THE FIRST SIX HOTELS of the Disney Springs Resort Area (DSRA) were created back when Disney had far fewer of its own. These hotels— the **B Resort & Spa, DoubleTree Suites by Hilton Orlando–Disney Springs Area,** the **Hilton Orlando Buena Vista Palace,** the **Hilton Orlando Lake Buena Vista,** the **Holiday Inn Orlando–Disney Springs Area,** and the **Wyndham Garden Lake Buena Vista**—are chain affairs with minimal or nonexistent theming, though the Buena Vista Palace is fairly upscale. Several properties have shifted their focus to convention and business travelers. A seventh hotel, the **Drury Plaza Hotel Orlando,** opened in late 2022.

> *unofficial* **TIP**
> DSRA hotels do *not* have access to Extended Evening Hours, Disney bus transportation, or the Disney Dining Plan.

The main advantages to staying in the DSRA are as follows:

- The ability to pay for your stay with hotel rewards points instead of money
- The same Early Theme Park Entry benefits Disney resort guests get
- Being within walking distance of Disney Springs

The Wyndham Garden, Buena Vista Palace, and Holiday Inn are an easy 5- to 15-minute walk from the Marketplace, on the east side of Disney Springs. Guests at B Resort & Spa, DoubleTree Suites, an Drury Plaza are about 10 minutes farther.

Disney transportation can be accessed at Disney Springs, though the bus service is notoriously slow due to the number of stops throughout the resort complex. Although all of the DSRA hotels offer shuttles to the theme parks, the service is provided by private contractors and is somewhat inferior to Disney transportation in frequency of service, number of buses, and hours of operation. A Denver family of five, for example, found that the Hilton Orlando Lake Buena Vista's shuttle service fell short:

> *The transportation was unreliable. It did a better job of getting guests back to the hotel from the park than getting them to the park from*

AMENITIES AT THE DSRA RESORTS					
HOTEL	**CHILDREN'S PROGRAMS**	**DINING**	**KID-FRIENDLY**	**POOL(S)**	**RECREATION**
B RESORT & SPA	None	★★★½	★★½	★★½	★★★
DOUBLETREE SUITES	None	★★	★★★	★★½	★★½
DRURY PLAZA HOTEL ORLANDO	None	★★½	★★½	★★★	★★★
HILTON ORLANDO BUENA VISTA PALACE	★★★★	★★	★★★½	★★★½	★★★★
HILTON ORLANDO LBV	None	★★½	★★½	★★★	★★½
HOLIDAY INN ORLANDO	★★★	★★	★★	★★★	★★
WYNDHAM GARDEN LBV	★★½	★★½	★★★	★★★	★★★

WHAT IT COSTS TO STAY IN THE DISNEY SPRINGS RESORT AREA	
HOTEL	NIGHTLY RATE
B RESORT & SPA	$150–$175
DOUBLETREE SUITES BY HILTON ORLANDO	$124–$286
DRURY PLAZA HOTEL	$160–$375
HILTON ORLANDO BUENA VISTA PALACE	$270–$315
HILTON ORLANDO LAKE BUENA VISTA	$225–$290
HOLIDAY INN ORLANDO–DISNEY SPRINGS AREA	$145–$205
WYNDHAM GARDEN LAKE BUENA VISTA	$130–$210

ADDITIONAL FEES AT THE DSRA RESORTS (includes tax)				
HOTEL	SELF-PARKING	RESORT FEE	INTERNET	TOTAL PER DAY
B RESORT & SPA	$26	$42	Free	$68
DOUBLETREE SUITES	$23	$25	Free*	$48
DRURY PLAZA HOTEL	$25	None	Free	$25
HILTON ORLANDO BUENA VISTA PALACE	$27	$44	Free	$71
HILTON ORLANDO LBV	Free	$39	Free	$39
HOLIDAY INN ORLANDO	$22	$43	Free	$65
WYNDHAM GARDEN LBV	$23	$36	Free	$59

*After joining free Hilton Honors program

the hotel. Shuttles from the hotel were randomly timed and went repeatedly to the same parks—skipping others and leaving guests to wait for up to an hour.

All of these hotels are easily accessible by car and are only marginally farther from the Disney parks than several of the Disney resorts.

DSRA hotels, even the ones focused on business and convention travelers, try to appeal to families. Some have pool complexes rivaling the ones at the Disney resorts, while others offer a food court or all-suite rooms. A few sponsor character meals and organized kids' activities; all have counters for buying Disney tickets, and most have Disney gift shops. On the downside, the rooms in several of the hotels are outdated.

The Value Proposition

As noted previously, Disney extends some of the same benefits to the DSRA hotels as it does to its own hotels. Those benefits—such as Early Theme Park Entry—add to the DSRA value proposition. Some DSRA hotels, such as the **Drury,** offer free hot breakfast—that's a substantial savings for large families. That said, the lack of midday dining options and poor shuttle service means that many readers would be better off at **Disney's Pop Century.**

That said, if you're using a hotel's rewards-program points to pay for your stay, then the resorts with loyalty programs are a good value—you can save anywhere from $600 to $1,000 per week versus staying at Pop. That's a lot of money. Also, **DoubleTree**'s 540-square-foot suites cost considerably less than comparably sized Disney suites. If you can pay with points, the DoubleTree is a no-brainer.

Finally, when you're looking at room rates on the DSRA website, note that they don't include nightly self-parking, resort fees, or taxes. These can add $25–$71 per night to the cost of your room, as shown in the table on the opposite page.

B Resort & Spa ★★★½

1905 Hotel Plaza Blvd.
Lake Buena Vista
☎ 407-828-2828
bresortlbv.com

LOCATED WITHIN walking distance of shops and restaurants and situated 5 miles or less from the Disney parks, this 394-room resort targets couples, families, groups, and business travelers.

Decorated in cool blues, whites, and grays, guest rooms and suites afford views of downtown Orlando, area lakes, and theme parks. Along with B Resort's exclusive Blissful Beds, each room is outfitted with sleek modern furnishings and a large, interactive flat-screen TV. Additional touches include a minifridge and gaming consoles (available on request). Some rooms are also equipped with bunk beds, kitchenettes, or wet bars.

We enjoyed our most recent stay at B Resort quite a bit. Our standard room was spotlessly clean, and the room decor is fun without being faddish. The bathroom is spacious, with plenty of storage. The glass shower is well designed and has good water pressure.

A mom from Tennessee also likes the B Resort, especially when the rooms are on sale:

> The vibe of B Resort was great—like a knockoff of the W, very bright and modern. The restaurant was great, and the zero-entry pool was good. The resort has a more adult feel, but I never felt out of place with my son. I found a deal on Orbitz. If choosing between the B and Pop Century for a short stay, I'd take B Resort hands-down.

Amenities include free Wi-Fi and a fitness center. The main restaurant, **American Kitchen,** serves a modern-upscale take on classic comfort food. Guests can also choose from a poolside bar and grill; **The PickUp,** a grab-and-go shop off the lobby that serves breakfasts, snacks, picnic lunches, and ice cream; and in-room dining 6–11 a.m. and 5 p.m.–midnight.

Other perks: a zero-entry pool with interactive water features; a kids' area; loaner iPads for business guests; **Monscierge,** a touchscreen concierge and destination guide in the lobby; and more than 25,000 square feet of meeting and multiuse space. Though it's not served by Disney transportation, B Resort provides bus service to the parks and other Disney venues.

DoubleTree Suites by Hilton Orlando–Disney Springs Area ★★★½

2305 Hotel Plaza Blvd.
Lake Buena Vista
☎ 407-934-1000
doubletreeguestsuites.com

WITHIN WALKING DISTANCE of Disney Springs, this giant white bunker of a hotel is the only all-suite establishment on Disney property. What it lacks in atmosphere and creative attributes, it makes up for in convenience and comfort. The 229 suites are spacious for a family, although the decor is startling, with no apparent theme.

Amenities include a safe, a hair dryer, a minifridge, a microwave, a coffee maker, a foldout sofa bed, and two TVs (bedroom and living room).

Children will enjoy a free chocolate-chip cookie and a small playground. The heated pool, children's pool, and whirlpool spa are moderate in size; a minus is that traffic noise from I-4 can be heard faintly from the pool deck. The tiny fitness center, game room, four tennis courts, and outdoor bar are adjacent to the pool. High-speed internet and a business center in the lobby are convenient for those on working holidays. The **EverGreen Cafe** serves breakfast, lunch, and dinner.

The DoubleTree is the farthest DSRA hotel from Disney Springs—a little over 0.5 mile to the closest entrance and a mile to its center, so figure on a 15- to 20-minute walk each way. If you're headed to the Magic Kingdom, the DoubleTree's bus service may drop you off at the Transportation and Ticket Center instead of the Magic Kingdom bus stop, adding another 10 minutes or so each way to your commute. We recommend budgeting $15 each way for a Lyft or Uber to the Contemporary or Grand Floridian instead.

Drury Plaza Hotel Orlando

2000 Hotel Plaza Blvd. Lake Buena Vista
☎ 407-560-6111
druryplazahotel orlando.com

THE DRURY IS THE NEWEST HOTEL in Disney Springs, with 602 hotel rooms. Amenities include a large pool area, two restaurants and a grab-and-go store, and 24-hour fitness and business centers. Room types include king beds, queen beds, and two-room suites. All rooms have a microwave, a minifridge, a coffee maker, and an iron and ironing board. The Drury is around a half-mile walk to Disney Springs and offers complimentary transportation to the Disney parks and Disney Springs.

Hilton Orlando Buena Vista Palace ★★★

1900 E. Buena Vista Drive, Lake Buena Vista
☎ 407-827-2727
buenavistapalace.com

HILTON BOUGHT THIS PROPERTY in 2016 and has invested substantially in renovating it. That said, you should stay somewhere else. Rates approach $400 per night thanks to $71 in resort and parking fees; that's about the same as a Disney Moderate resort, only this Hilton isn't nearly as nice.

While some room features have been upgraded—an all-glass shower with decent water pressure, for example—the room layout and decor are dated, and the hotel's public-facing spaces show signs of wear and neglect.

The resort's key strength is its outdoor recreation: a float lagoon and two heated pools, as well as private cabanas. Two restaurants and a minimarket are on-site.

Hilton Orlando Lake Buena Vista– Disney Springs Area ★★★★

1751 Hotel Plaza Blvd. Lake Buena Vista
☎ 407-827-4000
hilton-wdwv.com

THE HILTON'S ROOMS are clean, comfortable, and nicer overall than those at some other DSRA hotels. On-site dining includes **Benihana,** part of the Japanese steakhouse–sushi chain, as well as a grab-and-go market and a poolside café. The Disney-character breakfast that was held here on Sundays pre-COVID remains temporarily suspended. The two heated pools are matched with a kids' spray pool. A fitness center and game room are also on-site, as is a 24-hour market. There are no organized kids' programs.

Rates at the Hilton can approach $430 per night—within $25 per night of Disney's Coronado Springs Resort. If you're paying in cash (rather than points), the Moderates are a better option.

Holiday Inn Orlando–Disney Springs Resort Area ★★★½

1805 Hotel Plaza Blvd. Lake Buena Vista
☎ 407-828-8888
hiorlando.com

LAST RENOVATED IN 2018, the Holiday Inn's rooms are clean and comfortable. The rest of the hotel looks like any midpriced hotel anywhere in the country, with tower rooms grouped around an atrium and wing rooms overlooking the pool. Disney Springs is a short walk away.

The totally upgraded 360-square-foot rooms feature pillow-top beds with triple sheeting and firm or soft pillows. Each room has a 49- or 55-inch flat-screen TV and free high-speed internet. The bathrooms are clean and well designed, the nicest in any DSRA resort; amenities include granite countertops and showerheads with a choice of comfort sprays.

Palm Breezes Restaurant serves breakfast and dinner at reasonable prices. The grab-and-go in the lobby sells quick snacks and sandwiches. Other amenities include a large and well-kept zero-entry pool, along with a whirlpool spa in the pool area. A separate entrance brings you into the convention center, ballroom, and meeting room areas, with a business center nearby.

If Disney's Value hotels are sold out, the Holiday Inn is worth considering.

Wyndham Garden Lake Buena Vista ★★★½

1850-B Hotel Plaza Blvd.
Lake Buena Vista
☎ 407-842-6644
wyndhamlakebuena
vista.com

THE MAIN REASON TO STAY at the Wyndham Garden is the short walk to Disney Springs. The lobby is bright and airy, and check-in service is friendly. Rooms are larger than most and have in-room refrigerators. Pool-facing rooms in the hotel's wings have exterior hallways that overlook the pool and center courtyard; these hallways can be noisy during summer. Elevators are unusually slow—it's probably faster to walk to the second and third floors, assuming you're up for the exercise.

The Wyndham Garden's pool and room soundproofing have gotten good marks in our reader surveys over the last few years. As with most off-site resorts, transportation and quick-service dining options score low. Also, readers rate staff service at the Wyndham Garden lower than that at any resort, Disney-owned or not, in Walt Disney World.

CAMPING AT WALT DISNEY WORLD
Fort Wilderness Resort & Campground

DISNEY'S FORT WILDERNESS RESORT & CAMPGROUND is a spacious area for tent and RV camping. Fully equipped, air-conditioned prefabricated log cabins are also available for rent.

Tent/Pop-Up campsites provide water, electricity, and cable TV and run $76–$199 a night depending on season. **Full Hook-Up** campsites have all of the amenities above, accommodate large RVs, and run $116–$242 per night. **Preferred** campsites for tents and RVs add sewer connections and run $128–$270 per night. **Premium** campsites add an extra-large concrete parking pad and run $138–$280 a night. Disney says all campsites accommodate up to 10 people. Parking for one vehicle is included in the nightly rate.

Sites are level and provide picnic tables, waste containers, grills, and free Wi-Fi. Fires are prohibited except in grills. Pets are permitted in some loops for a $5 fee per night but aren't allowed in tents or pop-up trailers.

Campsites are arranged on loops accessible from one of three main roads. There are 28 loops, with loops **100–2100** for tent and RV campers and loops **2200–2800** offering cabins at $481–$779 per night. The RV sites are roomy by Eastern US standards, with the Premium and Full Hook-Up campsites able to accommodate RVs more than 45 feet long, but tent campers will probably feel a bit cramped. (Note that tent stakes cannot be put into the concrete at the Premium sites.) On any given day, 90% or more of campers are RVers.

continued on page 208

Fort Wilderness Resort & Campground

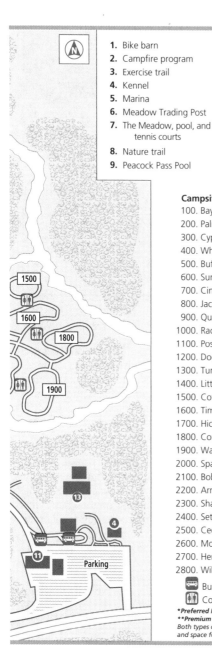

1. Bike barn
2. Campfire program
3. Exercise trail
4. Kennel
5. Marina
6. Meadow Trading Post
7. The Meadow, pool, and tennis courts
8. Nature trail
9. Peacock Pass Pool
10. Pioneer Hall
    Crockett's Tavern
    Guest Services
    Hoop-Dee-Doo
      Musical Revue
    Trail's End Restaurant
11. Reception Outpost
12. Settlement Trading Post
13. Tri-Circle-D Livery (horseback riding)
14. Tri-Circle-D Ranch

Campsite Loops
100. Bay Tree Lake*
200. Palmetto Path*
300. Cypress Knee Circle*
400. Whispering Pine Way**
500. Buffalo Bend**
600. Sunny Sage Way**
700. Cinnamon Fern Way**
800. Jack Rabbit Run**
900. Quail Trail**
1000. Raccoon Lane**
1100. Possum Path**
1200. Dogwood Drive**
1300. Tumblewood Turn**
1400. Little Bear Path and Big Bear Path**
1500. Cottontail Curl*
1600. Timber Trail*
1700. Hickory Hollow*
1800. Conestoga Trail*
1900. Wagon Wheel Way*
2000. Spanish Moss Lane
2100. Bobcat Bend
2200. Arrowhead Way
2300. Shawnee Bend
2400. Settler's Bend
2500. Cedar Circle
2600. Moccasin Trail
2700. Heron Hollow
2800. Willow Way

 Bus stop

Comfort station and laundry facility

*Preferred Hook-Up campsites
**Premium campsites
Both types of sites have power, water, sewer, cable TV, and space for large RVs.

FORT WILDERNESS RESORT AND CAMPGROUND

STRENGTHS	WEAKNESSES
• Informality	• Isolated location
• Children's play areas	• Complicated bus service
• Best recreational options at WDW	• Confusing campground layout
• Special day and evening programs	• Lack of privacy
• Campsite amenities	• Very limited on-site dining options
• Shower and toilet facilities	• Crowding at beaches and pools
• *Hoop-Dee-Doo Musical Revue* show	• Small baths in cabins
• Convenient self-parking	• Extreme distance to store and
• Off-site dining via boat at the Magic Kingdom	restaurant facilities from many cabins and campsites

Unofficial Guide **Reader-Survey Results**

Percentage of readers who'd stay here again **Cabins: 85%** (*Average*); **Campsites: 98%** (*Exceptional*)
Percentage of readers who'd recommend this resort to a friend **Cabins: 79%** (*Average*); **Campsites: 90%** (*Average*)
Overall reader rating **Cabins: B; Campsites: B**

continued from page 205

Fort Wilderness offers arguably the widest variety of recreational facilities and activities of any Disney resort. Among them are two arcades; nightly campfire programs; Disney movies; a dinner theater; two swimming pools; a beach; walking paths; bike, boat, canoe, golf-cart, and kayak rentals; horseback riding; wagon rides; and tennis, basketball, and volleyball courts. There are multiple dining options, including a full-service restaurant, a food truck, and a tavern. Comfort stations with toilets, showers, pay phones, ice machines, and laundry facilities are within walking distance of all campsites.

If you're in the mood to walk, paths within the resort are a great place to see deer and other woodland creatures.

Access to the Magic Kingdom is by boat from Fort Wilderness Landing and to EPCOT by bus, with a transfer at the Transportation and Ticket Center (TTC) to the EPCOT monorail. Boat service may be suspended during thunderstorms, in which case Disney will provide buses. An alternate route to the Magic Kingdom is by internal bus to the TTC, then by monorail or ferry to the park. Transportation to all other Disney destinations is by bus. Motor traffic within the campground is permitted only when entering or exiting. Get around within the campground by bus, golf cart, or bike, the latter two available for rent.

For tent and RV campers, there's a fairly stark trade-off between sites convenient to pools, restaurants, trading posts, and other amenities and those that are scenic, shady, and quiet. RVers who prefer to be near guest services, the marina, the beach, and the restaurant and tavern should go for loops **100, 200, 700,** and **400** (in that order—loop 100 is the highest rated at Fort Wilderness); note, however, that loops 100 and 400 are nearest ongoing hotel construction. Loops near the campground's secondary facility area with pool, trading post, bike and golf-cart rentals, and campfire program are **1400, 1300, 600, 1000,** and **1500,** in order of preference.

If you're looking for a tranquil, scenic setting among mature trees, we recommend loops **1800, 1900, 1700,** and **1600,** in that order, and the west-side sites on the **700** loop. The best loop of all—and the only one to offer both a lovely setting and proximity to key amenities—is **300.** The best loops for tents and pop-up campers are **1500** and **2000,** with 1500 being nearest a swimming pool, a convenience store, and the campfire program.

With the exception of loops **1800** and **1900,** avoid sites within 40 yards of the loop entrance—these are almost always flanked by one of the main traffic arteries within Fort Wilderness. Further, sites on the outside of the loop are almost always preferable to those in the center. RVers should note that all sites are back-ins and that the loop access roads are pretty tight and narrow.

Fort Wilderness Cabins

NOTE: DISNEY WILL CONVERT the Fort Wilderness Cabins to a DVC resort in 2024. All 364 cabins will be replaced. Concept art depicts these new structures as more like tiny modern houses, with lots of windows for light. Disney says the cabins' footprint will be about the same, with one bedroom, one bathroom, and sleeping accommodations for six. With this project comes the possibility of construction noise and limited cabin availability. **Loops 100** and **2200–2800** will be affected.

Existing cabins offer a queen bed and bunk bed in the bedroom and a sofa bed in the living room. The small bathroom has a shower and tub. The cabins are homey, but the stem-to-stern wood paneling and smallish windows make for rather dark accommodations at night. All cabins have air-conditioning, TVs, full kitchens, and dining tables. Housekeeping is provided every other day.

A Wappingers Falls, New York, family writes:

We stayed at Fort Wilderness in a cabin because (1) we wanted a separate bedroom area; (2) we wanted a kitchen; (3) our kids are very lively, and the cabins were apart from each other so we wouldn't disturb other guests; and (4) we thought the kids might meet other children to play with. The cabins worked out just right for us. The kids had a ball chasing the little lizards and frogs, kicking around pinecones, sitting on the deck to eat ice pops, and sleeping in bunk beds.

A mother of two from Albuquerque, New Mexico, offers this:

We liked having all the space and the full kitchen; however, the pool nearest our cabin (a quarter mile away!) never even had a lifeguard. I had hoped to be able to send the kids to swim when we needed some time to ourselves, but with the distance and lack of lifeguards, there was no way to do that.

A mother of two from Mechanicsville, Virginia, is a fan:

This is the only resort where you're encouraged to go outside and play! You can bike, swim, hike the nature trail, ride a horse, rent a boat, play volleyball, go to the beach, attend a character sing-along and marshmallow roast followed by a classic Disney movie, enjoy multiple playgrounds, play tennis, take a romantic carriage ride, take your first pony ride, and see a wild turkey. Don't forget the view of the fireworks from the beach or the up-close water light parade. With all of this stuff, much of it free or very affordable, who needs the parks?

Bus service at Fort Wilderness leaves much to be desired—so much, in fact, that we wouldn't stay there unless we had our own car. To go anywhere, you first have to catch an internal bus that makes many, many stops. If your destination is outside Fort Wilderness, you then must transfer to a second bus. To complicate things, buses serving destinations outside the campground depart from two locations, the **Reception Outpost** and **Pioneer Hall.** This means you must keep track of which destinations each transfer center serves.

A Washington, D.C., family of five writes:

We generally enjoyed our cabin at Fort Wilderness. It was spacious, with bunk beds for the kids, a separate room for the parents to sleep, and a kitchen. We were very surprised and disappointed, though, when we figured out that we couldn't get anywhere in the resort in a timely fashion without either bikes or a golf cart—otherwise, you spend your day waiting for buses. A quick trip to the pool or the counter-service diner was impossible.

A reader from Minneapolis found that feeding her crew was a bit of a challenge:

You really need to bring your own food. To get to the restaurants, it was over a mile on the bus, not to mention the choices were limited: The buffet looked pretty good but [was expensive], while the takeout place had just a few unhealthy options and nowhere to sit except outside. We were hoping the store would have something, but that was very limited as well—honestly, you'd have better luck at a gas station.

An Augusta, Georgia, family has this transportation tip:

Regular boat service to the Magic Kingdom from Fort Wilderness doesn't start until 30 minutes before park opening. We chose to ride a boat to the Contemporary and walk to the Magic Kingdom so we could get there earlier. (A boat captain did tell us that they send one boat at 7 a.m. to get people to the MK for early dining reservations.)

A number of independent campgrounds and RV parks are convenient to Walt Disney World. See **Camp Florida** (campflorida.com/regions/central-florida) for listings. If you rent a cabin or camp in a tent or RV, particularly in fall or spring, keep abreast of local weather conditions.

HOW *to* EVALUATE *a* WALT DISNEY WORLD TRAVEL PACKAGE

HUNDREDS OF WALT DISNEY WORLD package vacations are offered each year. Some are created by the Walt Disney Travel Company, others by airlines, independent travel agents, and wholesalers. Almost all include lodging at or near Disney World plus theme park admissions. Packages offered by airlines include air transportation.

Prices vary seasonally; mid-February through Easter, early summer, and holiday periods are the most expensive. Off-season, you can negotiate great discounts, especially at non-Disney properties. Airfares and car rentals are cheaper off-peak too.

Almost all package ads are headlined something to the effect of "5 Days at Walt Disney World from $845." The key word is *from:* The rock-bottom price includes the least desirable hotels; if you want better or more-convenient digs, you'll pay more—often much more.

Packages offer a wide selection of hotels. Some, like the Disney resorts, are very dependable. Others run the gamut of quality. Checking two or three independent sources is best. Also, before you book, ask how old the hotel is and when the guest rooms were last refurbished. Locate the hotel on a map to verify its proximity to Disney World. If you won't be driving a car, make sure the hotel has adequate shuttle service.

Packages with non-Disney lodging are much less expensive. But guests at Disney-owned properties (and several third-party hotels that operate inside Disney World's boundaries) get free parking and extra time at the parks and access to Disney transportation. See page 89 for a list of which benefits Disney extends to third-party hotels.

Packages should be a win–win proposition for both the buyer and the seller. The buyer makes just one phone call and deals with one salesperson to set up the whole vacation. The seller, likewise, deals with the buyer only once.

Because selling packages is efficient and the packager often can buy package components in bulk at discount, the seller's savings in operating expenses are sometimes passed on to the buyer. In practice, however, the seller may not pass on those savings: Packages are sometimes loaded with extras that cost the packager almost nothing but run the package's price sky-high.

Choose a package that includes features you're sure to use—you'll pay for all of them whether you use them or not. If price is more important than convenience, call around to see what the package would cost if you booked its components on your own. If the package price is less than the à la carte cost, the package is a good deal. If costs are about equal, the package probably is worth it for the convenience. Much of the time, however, you'll find you save significantly by buying the components individually.

WALT DISNEY TRAVEL COMPANY PACKAGES

DISNEY'S TRAVEL-PACKAGE PROGRAM mirrors the admission-ticket program. Here's how it works: You begin with a base package room and tickets. Tickets can be customized to match the number of days you intend to tour the theme parks and range in length from 2 to 10 days. (*Note:* The 1-Day Base Ticket isn't eligible for packages.) As with theme park admissions, the package program offers strong financial incentives to book a longer stay. "The longer you play, the less you pay per day," is the way Disney puts it, borrowing a page from Sam Walton's

unofficial **TIP**
Disney vacation packages may include dining plans as well as sweeteners such as a free round of minigolf and discounts on spa treatments, salon services, and recreational activities like water sports.

DISNEY LODGING FOR LESS

Sarah Stone, *the webmaster for* **MouseSavers** *(mousesavers.com), might know more about Disney hotel packages than anyone on the planet. Here are her money-saving suggestions.*

BOOK ROOM-ONLY. It's frequently a better deal to book a room-only reservation instead of buying a vacation package. Disney likes to sell vacation packages because they're easy and profitable. When you buy a package, you're typically paying a premium for the convenience, but you can often save money by putting together your own package. It's not hard—just book room-only at a resort and buy your passes, meals, and extras separately.

Disney doesn't break down the individual prices of the components of its packages, but direct comparison shows that Disney prices these components the same as if you'd purchased them separately at full price, plus a small extra "package fee." What Disney doesn't tell you, though, is that these components can often be purchased separately at a discount—and those discounts aren't always reflected in the prices of Disney's package. (Sometimes Disney offers package-only discounts, but those are relatively rare.)

Disney's packages often include coupons and sometimes small bits of merchandise like luggage tags, but the cash value of those extras is minimal. Also, packages require a $200 deposit and full payment 30 days in advance, and they have stringent change and cancellation policies. In contrast, booking room-only requires a deposit of one night's room rate with the remainder due at check-in. Your reservation can be changed or canceled for any reason until six days before check-in.

USE DISNEY'S DISCOUNTS TO REDUCE YOUR ROOM-ONLY OR PACKAGE RATE. Disney uses discount programs to push unsold rooms at certain times of year and occasionally offers packages that include resort discounts or value-added features. Check a website like MouseSavers to learn about discounts that may be available for your vacation dates. Some discounts are available to anyone, while others are just for Florida residents, Annual Pass holders, and so on.

concept of the universe. An adult 1-Day Base Ticket costs $116–$201 (including tax), depending on the day of your visit, whereas if you buy a 7-Day Base Ticket, the average cost per day drops to $79–$117 depending on which days you visit. You can purchase options to add to your Base Tickets, such as park hopping or visiting the water parks. (See page 74 for more details on ticket pricing.)

With Disney travel packages, you can avoid paying for features that you don't intend to use—you need not purchase a package with theme park tickets for the entire length of your stay. Rather, you can choose to purchase as many days of admission as you intend to use. On a one-week vacation, for example, you might want to spend only 5 days in the Disney parks, saving 1 day each for Universal Orlando and SeaWorld. (That is, even if your Disney hotel stay is 7 days, you can buy admission tickets lasting anywhere from 2 to 10 days; the ticket length doesn't need to match your hotel stay length.) Likewise, if you don't normally park-hop, you can purchase multiday admissions that don't include the

Discounts aren't always available from Disney for every hotel or every date, and they typically don't appear until two to six months in advance. The good news is that you can usually apply a discount to an existing reservation. Just call the Disney Reservation Center at ☎ 407-W-DISNEY (934-7639) or contact a Disney-savvy travel agent, and ask whether any rooms are available at your preferred hotel for your preferred dates using the discount.

In addition, other travel sellers sometimes tack on an additional discount on top of Disney's or offer a small discount on rooms that Disney doesn't typically discount. These offers vary constantly, but you can check MouseSavers for the latest ways to score additional stackable deals.

BE FLEXIBLE. Finding a discount on a room or package is a little like shopping for clothes at a discount store: If you wear a size extra-small or extra-large, or you like green when everyone else is wearing pink, you're a lot more likely to score a bargain. Likewise, resort discounts are available only when Disney has excess rooms to fill. You're more likely to get a discount during less popular times (such as value season) and at larger or less popular resorts—Animal Kingdom Lodge and Old Key West Resort, for instance, seem to have discounted rooms available more often than the other Disney resorts do. On the other hand, really popular resorts and room types, like the *Little Mermaid* rooms at Art of Animation and the Royal Rooms at Port Orleans Riverside, are often excluded from discounts because Disney can fill them at full price.

BE PERSISTENT. This is the most important tip. Disney allots a certain number of rooms for each discount. Once the discounted rooms are gone, you won't get that rate unless someone cancels. Fortunately, people change and cancel reservations all the time. If you can't get your preferred dates or hotel with one discount, try another one (if available) or keep checking back first thing in the morning for cancellations—the system resets overnight, and any reservations with unpaid deposits are automatically released for resale.

Park Hopper feature. Best of all, you can buy the various add-ons at any time during your vacation.

Before we inundate you with a boxcar of options and add-ons, let's begin by defining the basic components of a Disney travel package:

- One or more nights of accommodations at your choice of any Disney resort. Rates vary with lodging choice: The Grand Floridian is usually the most expensive, and the All-Stars, Pop Century, and Art of Animation are the least expensive.
- Base Ticket for the number of days you tour the theme parks (must be at least 2-Day Base Tickets for travel packages)
- Unlimited use of the Disney transportation system
- Free day parking at the theme parks

Booking Online vs. by Phone

It's much faster to book a Disney resort room online than it is to call Disney reservations (☎ 407-W-DISNEY [934-7639]). If you call, you'll be subjected to a minute or so of recordings covering recent park announcements—press *0* to skip this. Next, you'll go through about 5–10 minutes of answering more than a dozen recorded questions, asking you everything from your name and home address to the salutation you prefer. Slog on through, though, if you actually want to make a reservation. (When the question "How many times have you been to Walt Disney World?" pops up, answering "zero" may route you to an additional survey for "first-timers.") Unfortunately, there doesn't seem to be a way to bypass these questions by pressing *0*.

DOING THE MATH

COMPARING A DISNEY TRAVEL PACKAGE with purchasing the package components separately is a breeze.

1. Pick a Disney resort and decide how many nights you want to stay.

2. Next, work out a rough plan of what you want to do and see so you can determine the admission passes you'll require.

3. When you're ready, go online or call the Disney Reservation Center (DRC) at ☎ 407-W-DISNEY (934-7639) and price a package *with tax* for your selected resort and dates. The package will include both admissions and lodging. It's also a good idea to get a quote from a Disney-savvy travel agent (see page 100).

4. Now, to calculate the costs of buying your accommodations and admission passes separately, call the DRC a second time. This time, price a room-only rate for the same resort and dates. Be sure to ask about the availability of any special deals. While you're still on the line, obtain the prices, with tax, for the admissions you require. If you're not sure which of the various admission options will best serve you, consult our free Ticket Calculator at **TouringPlans.com.**

5. Add the room-only rates and the admission prices. Compare this sum to the DRC quote for the package.

6. Check for deals and discounts on packages and admission.

THROW ME A LINE!

IF YOU BUY A PACKAGE FROM DISNEY, don't expect the reservationists to help you sort out your options. Generally, they respond only to your specific questions, ducking queries that require an opinion. A reader from North Riverside, Illinois, complains:

> My wife made two phone calls, and the representatives from WDW were very courteous, but they answered only the questions posed and were not eager to give advice on what might be most cost-effective. I feel a person could spend 8 hours on the phone with WDW reps and not have any more input than you get from reading the literature.

If you can't get the information you need from Disney, get in touch with a travel agent to help you weigh your options.

WEIGHING THE COST OF CONVENIENCE

SUE PISATURO OF **Small World Vacations** (smallworldvacations.com), a travel agency that specializes in Walt Disney World, also thinks there's more involved in a package-purchase decision than just money.

> Should you purchase a Walt Disney World package or buy all the components of the package separately? There's no single answer to this confusing question.

A Walt Disney World package is like a store-bought prepackaged kids' meal, the kind with the little compartments filled with meat, cheese, crackers, drink, and dessert: You just grab the package and go. It's easy, and if it's on sale, why bother doing it yourself? If it's not on sale, it still may be worth the extra money for convenience.

Purchasing the components of your vacation separately is like buying each of the meal's ingredients, cutting them up into neat piles, and packaging the lunch yourself. Is it worth the extra time and effort to do it this way? Will you save money if you do it this way?

You have two budgets to balance when you plan your Disney World vacation: time and money. Satisfying both is your ultimate goal. Research and planning are paramount to realizing your Disney vacation dreams. Create your touring plans before making a final decision with regard to the number of days and options on your theme park passes. Create your dining itinerary (along with Advance Reservations, if possible) to determine if the Disney Dining Plan can save you some money.

HOTELS *outside* WALT DISNEY WORLD

SELECTING AND BOOKING A HOTEL OUTSIDE WALT DISNEY WORLD

LODGING COSTS OUTSIDE Disney World vary greatly. If you shop around, you can find a clean motel with a pool within 5–20 minutes of the World for as low as $70 a night with tax (but see our caveat on page 247). Discounts abound, particularly for AAA and AARP members.

There are four primary out-of-the-World areas to consider (see pages 216–219 for maps):

1. INTERNATIONAL DRIVE AREA This area, located about 15–25 minutes northeast of the World, parallels I-4 on its eastern side and offers a wide selection of hotels and restaurants. Prices range from $55 to over $400 per night. The chief drawbacks are terribly congested roads, countless traffic signals, and inadequate access to westbound I-4. While I-Drive's biggest bottleneck is its intersection with Sand Lake Road, the mile between Kirkman and Sand Lake Roads is almost always gridlocked, which increases the odds that you'll hit traffic going to a theme park in the morning, returning in the evening, or both.

Regarding traffic on International Drive (known locally as I-Drive), a conventioneer from Islip, New York, weighed in with this:

When I visited Disney World last summer, we wasted huge chunks of time in traffic on I-Drive. Our hotel was in the section between the big McDonald's at Sand Lake Road and Volcano Bay at Universal Boulevard. There are practically no left-turn lanes in this section, so anyone turning left can hold up traffic for a long time.

Traffic aside, a man from Ottawa, Ontario, sings the praises of his I-Drive experience:

continued on page 220

Lodging Areas Around Walt Disney World

1. International Drive
2. Lake Buena Vista and the I-4 Corridor
3. US 192
4. Universal Orlando

Lodging Areas 1 & 4: I-Drive & Universal

Lake Cane

Peregrine Ave.
Windhover Dr.

Florida's Turnpike (toll road)

4 — East to Downtown Orlando

Vineland Road

Universal Blvd.

435

77

Major Blvd.

Caravan Ct.

Orlando Premium Outlets

Universal Orlando

Hollywood Way

75AB — W. Oak Ridge Road

Turkey Lake Road

Adventure Way

74B

75B

American Way

75A

Grand National Dr.

International Dr.

Kirkman Road

Del Verde Way

International Dr.

Canada Ave.

Carrier Dr.

482 — Sand Lake Road

I-4 Exits

77	Florida's Turnpike
75A East	Universal Studios/International Drive
75AB West	FL 435 North/South
75B East	Kirkman Road
74B	Universal Studios
74A	Sand Lake Road
72	FL 528 (Beachline Expressway)
71	Central Florida Parkway

Official Visitor Center

74A

Universal Blvd.

Jamaican Ct.

Austrian Ct.

Austrian Row

International Dr.

Samoan Ct.

4

Pointe Plaza Ave.

Universal Blvd.

Orange County Convention Center

Destination Pkwy.

Hawaiian Ct.

To Orlando International Airport →

72

(no toll)

(no toll)

Aquatica

528

Beachline Expy. (toll road)

West to Walt Disney World Resort & Tampa ↙

Turkey Lake Road

71

Westwood Blvd.

Sea Harbor Dr.

International Dr.

Orangewood Blvd.

SeaWorld Orlando

Central Florida Parkway

Discovery Cove

Lodging Area 2: Lake Buena Vista & the I-4 Corridor

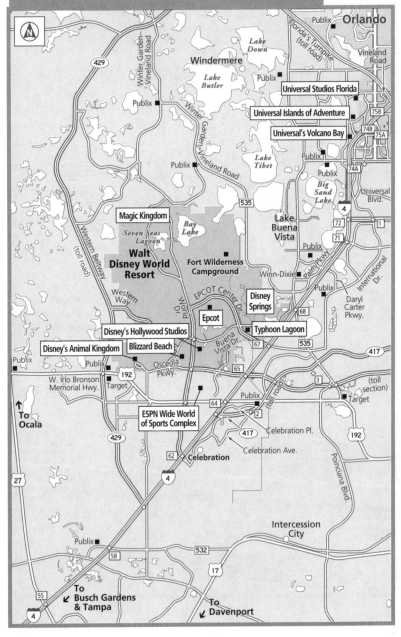

Lodging Area 3: US 192

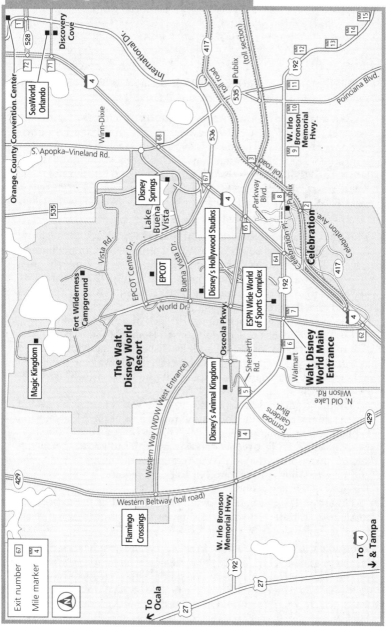

Exit number 67
Mile marker MM 4

continued from page 215

> *International Drive is the place to stay when going to Disney. There are plenty of discount stores, boutiques, restaurants, mini-putts, and other entertainment facilities, all within walking distance of remarkably inexpensive accommodations and a short drive away from Walt Disney World.*

I-Drive hotels are listed on the **Visit Orlando** website: visitorlando .com/places-to-stay (click "International Drive Area").

2. LAKE BUENA VISTA AND THE I-4 CORRIDOR A number of hotels are along FL 535 and west of I-4 between Disney World and I-4's intersection with Florida's Turnpike. They're easily reached from the interstate and are near many restaurants, including those on International Drive. The **Visit Orlando** website (visitorlando.com) lists most of them. For some traffic-avoidance tips, see our discussion on I-4 in Part 9, on page 427. This area includes Disney's value-priced **Flamingo Crossings** resort complex (see page 244).

3. US 192 (IRLO BRONSON MEMORIAL HIGHWAY) This is the highway to Kissimmee, to the southeast of Walt Disney World. In addition to large full-service hotels, some small, privately owned motels often offer a good value. Several dozen properties on US 192 are nearer Disney parks than are more expensive hotels inside the World. The number and variety of restaurants on US 192 is remarkable, compensating for the area's primary shortcoming: the lack of truly high-end resorts.

Locally, US 192 is called **Irlo Bronson Memorial Highway;** the section to the east and west of I-4 and the Disney Maingate is designated as Irlo Bronson Memorial Highway West. The highway has numbered mile markers that simplify navigation if you know which marker is closest to your destination.

Though traffic is heavy on Irlo Bronson west of the Maingate, it doesn't compare with the congestion found east of the Maingate and I-4 between mile markers 8 and 13. This section can—and should—be avoided by using **Osceola Parkway,** a partial toll road that parallels Irlo Bronson to the north and terminates in Disney World at the entrance to Animal Kingdom. No tolls are required to use Osceola Parkway on Disney property.

Hotels on US 192 and in Kissimmee are listed at the **Experience Kissimmee** website (experiencekissimmee.com); you can also order a copy of its newsletter by calling ☎ 407-569-4800.

4. UNIVERSAL ORLANDO AREA In the triangular area bordered by I-4 on the southeast, Vineland Road on the north, and Turkey Lake Road on the west are Universal Orlando and the hotels most convenient to it. Running north–south through the middle of the triangle is **Kirkman Road,** which connects to I-4. On the east side of Kirkman are several independent hotels and restaurants. Universal hotels, theme parks, and CityWalk are west of Kirkman. Traffic in this area is not nearly as congested as on nearby International Drive, and there are good interstate connections in both directions.

DRIVING TIME TO THE PARKS

OUR HOTEL INFORMATION TABLE on pages 254–265 shows the commuting time to the Disney theme parks from each hotel listed. Those commuting times represent an average of several test runs. Your actual time may be shorter or longer depending on traffic, road construction (if any), and delays at traffic signals.

The commuting times in our Hotel Information Table show conclusively that distance from the theme parks is not necessarily the dominant factor in determining commuting times. Among those we list, the hotels on Major Boulevard opposite the Kirkman Road entrance to Universal Orlando, for example, are the most distant (in miles) from the Disney parks. But because they're only one traffic signal from easy access to I-4, commuting time to the parks is significantly less than for many closer hotels.

Note that times in the table differ from those in the Door-to-Door Commuting Times table in Part 9. The latter compares using the Disney transportation system with driving your own car *inside* Walt Disney World. These times include actual transportation time plus tram, monorail, or other connections required to get from the parking lots to the entrance turnstiles. The hotel table's commuting times, in contrast, represent only the driving time to and from the entrance of the respective parking lot of each park, with no consideration for getting to and from the parking lot to the turnstiles.

Add to the commuting times in the Hotel Information Table a few minutes for paying your parking fee and parking. Once you park at the Transportation and Ticket Center (Magic Kingdom parking lot), it takes 20–30 minutes more to reach the Magic Kingdom via monorail or ferry, including security and health checks. To reach EPCOT from its parking lot, add 7–10 minutes. At Disney's Hollywood Studios and Animal Kingdom, the lot-to-gate transit is 5–15 minutes. If you haven't purchased your theme park admission in advance, tack on another 10–20 minutes.

If you're headed to the Magic Kingdom from off-site, you could put the park's standard $25 parking fee toward a Lyft or Uber that drops you off at **Disney's Contemporary Resort,** which is a 5-minute walk to the park. Doing that will save you 20–70 minutes of parking, trams, security checks, and monorails or ferries. It will save you almost as much time when leaving too. (If the security team at the Contemporary isn't allowing drop-offs, the area between Shades of Green and the Grand Floridian has ample spots.)

HOTEL SHOPPING

OTAs Online travel agencies (OTAs) sell travel products from a wide assortment of suppliers, often at deep discounts. These sites include such familiar names as **Travelocity, Orbitz, Priceline, Expedia, Hotels.com,** and **Hotwire.**

The better-known OTAs draw a lot more web traffic than a given hotel's (or even hotel chain's) website. Most hotels offer some sort of

*un*official **TIP**
Never click a pop-up that routes you to a third-party hotel site, regardless of how good the deal sounds or how slick the website looks.

"lowest-price guarantee" on their websites, offering to match or beat a price seen elsewhere for the same reservation.

More Hotel-Hunting Resources

NEW, INDEPENDENT, AND BOUTIQUE-HOTEL DEALS While chain hotels worry about sales costs and profit margins, independent and boutique hotels are concerned about making themselves known to the traveling public. The market is huge, and it's increasingly hard for such hotels to get noticed, especially when they're competing with major chains.

Independent and boutique hotels work on the premise that if they can get you through the front door, you'll become a loyal customer; thus, deep discounts are part of their marketing plan.

AIRBNB This service (airbnb.com) connects travelers with owner-hosted alternative lodging all over the world, from spare bedrooms in people's homes to private apartments, vacation homes, and even live-in boats.

We find Airbnb less useful in Orlando for a couple of reasons. First, Orlando has an enormous supply of vacation-home rentals and hotel rooms, which keeps prices down for lodging around Walt Disney World. Second, Disney's incentives for staying on-property are hard to beat. That said, Kissimmee appears to be a rapidly growing market for Airbnb. If you find a good property this way, let us know.

Be Careful Out There: Hotel Scams

In a very persuasive scam that's been metastasizing to hotels all over the country, a guest receives a phone call, purportedly from the front desk, explaining that a computer glitch has occurred and that the hotel needs the guest's credit card information again to expedite checkout.

Here's what you need to know: (1) A legit hotel won't ask you to provide sensitive information over the phone, and (2) a legit hotel *especially* won't call you in the middle of the night to get it out of you. If this happens to you, hang up and contact hotel security.

Another scam involves websites that look very polished and official and may even include the logos of well-known hotel brands. The scammers will happily sell you a room, paid for in advance with your credit card, and then email you credible-looking confirmation documents. Problem is, they never contacted the hotel to make the booking, *or* they made the booking but failed to pay the hotel.

Toll-Free Telephone Numbers

As we've stated, it's essential to communicate directly with the hotels when shopping for deals and stating your room preferences. Most toll-free numbers are routed to a hotel chain's central reservations office, where the customer-service agents typically have little or no detailed knowledge of the individual hotels in the chain or of any specials those hotels may be offering. In our Hotel Information Table on pages 254–265, therefore, we provide the hotels' local phone numbers rather than the toll-free numbers. You can also find these numbers in the Walt Disney World Phone Numbers table on pages 40–41, but note that rooms at Disney resorts must be booked through the Disney Reservation Center (☎ 407-W-DISNEY or 934-7639). After you've reserved your room, you can check online to make sure the reservation is in order.

CONDOMINIUMS AND VACATION HOMES

BECAUSE CONDOS TEND TO BE part of large developments (frequently time-shares), amenities such as swimming pools, playgrounds, game arcades, and fitness centers often rival those found in the best hotels. Generally speaking, condo developments don't have restaurants, lounges, or spas. In a condo, if something goes wrong, someone will be on hand to fix the problem. Vacation homes rented from a property-management company likewise will have someone to come to the rescue, although responsiveness tends to vary vastly from company to company. If you rent directly from an owner, correcting problems is often more difficult, particularly when the owner doesn't live in the same area as the rental home.

In a vacation home, all the amenities are self-contained (in planned developments, there may be community amenities available as well). Depending on the specific home, you might find a small swimming pool, hot tub, two-car garage, family room, game room, and even a home theater. Features found in both condos and vacation homes include full kitchens, laundry rooms, TVs, and DVD players. Interestingly, though almost all freestanding vacation homes have private pools, very few have backyards. This means that, except for swimming, the kids are pretty much relegated to playing in the house.

Time-share condos are clones when it comes to furniture and decor, but single-owner condos and vacation homes are furnished and decorated in a style that reflects the owner's taste. Vacation homes, usually one- to two-story houses in a subdivision, very rarely afford interesting views (though some overlook lakes or natural areas), while condos, especially the high-rise variety, sometimes offer exceptional ones.

How the Vacation-Home Market Works

In the Orlando–Walt Disney World area, just prior to the pandemic, there were more than 26,000 rental homes, including stand-alone homes, single-owner condos—that is, not time-shares—and townhomes. The same area had about 130,000 hotel rooms. Almost all the rental homes are occupied by their owners for at least a week or two each year; the rest of the year, owners make the homes available for rent. Some owners deal directly with renters, while others enlist the assistance of a property-management company.

Incredibly, about 700 property-management companies operate in the Orlando–Kissimmee–Walt Disney World market. Most are mom-and-pop outfits that manage an inventory of 10 homes or fewer (probably fewer than 70 companies manage an inventory of more than 100).

Some homes are made available to wholesalers, vacation packagers, and travel agents in deals negotiated either directly by the owners or by property-management companies on the owners' behalf. A wholesaler or vacation packager will occasionally drop its rates to

continued on page 226

Rental-Home Developments Near WDW

Abbey at West Haven 7
Acadia Estates 10
Ashley Manor 7
Aviana 7
Aylesbury 8
Bahama Bay 9
Bass Lake Estates 5
Bass Lake (US 27) 9
Bella Piazza 9
Bella Trae 7, 8
BellaVida 5
Bentley Oaks 7
Blue Heron Beach 1
Briargrove 7
Bridgewater
    Crossing 7
Bridgewater Town Ctr. 7
Buenaventura Lakes 4
Calabay Parc 9
Calabay Tower Lake 8
Calabria 9
Cane Island 5
ChampionsGate 7, 8
Chatham Park 5
Clear Creek 9
Club Cortile 5
Country Creek 5
Countryside Manor 6
Creekside 5
Crescent Lakes 6

Crystal Cove 5
Cumbrian Lakes 5
Cypress Lakes 3
Cypress Pointe Forest 7
Davenport Lakes 9
Doral Woods 6
Eagle Pointe 5
Emerald Island 10
Encantada 9
Esprit/Fairways 9
Fiesta Key 5
Flamingo Lakes 3
Florida Pines 9
Floridays 2
Formosa Gardens 10
Four Corners 9
Glenbrook 9
Golden Oaks 1
Grand Palms 9
Grand Reserve 7
Greater Groves 9
Hamilton Reserve 5
Hamlet at West Haven 7
Hampton Lakes 9
Happy Trails 9
Highgate Park 9
High Grove 9

Highland Park 10
Highlands Reserve 9
Hillcrest Estates 9
Indian Creek 10
Indian Point 5
Indian Ridge 10
Indian Ridge Oaks 10
Indian Wells 1
Island Club West 9
Laguna Bay 5
Lake Berkley 5
Lake Davenport 9
Lake Wilson
    Preserve 7
Lakeside 4
Legacy Dunes 9
Legacy Park 9
Liberty Village 5
Lighthouse Key Resort 9
Lindfields 9
Loma Linda 7
Loma Vista 4
Lucaya Village Resort 5
Magic Landings 4
Manors at Westridge 9
Marbella 8
Meadow Woods 4

Millbrook Manor 9
Mission Park 9
Montego Bay 5
Oak Island Cove 10
Oak Island Harbor 10
Oakpoint 7
Orange Lake 10
Orange Tree 9
The Palms 9
Paradise Woods 7
Pines West 8
Pinewood 7
Providence 4
Regal Palms 9
Remington Golf Club 4
Retreat at West Haven 7
Reunion 4
Remington Point 4
Ridgewood Lakes 8
Robbins Rest 7

Rolling Hills 10
Royal Oaks 5
Royal Palm Bay 9
Royal Palms 8
Runaway Beach Club 5
Sanctuary at
    West Haven 7
Sandy Ridge 10
Santa Cruz 7
Seasons 5
Shire at West Haven 7
Silver Creek 9
Solana 9
Southern Dunes 8
St. James Park 6

Lake Buena Vista

Walt Disney World

Citrus Ridge

Bunker Hill

Celebration

Zone 9

Zone 10

Zone 1

Zone 8

Zone 7

Zone 6

Western Way

Osceola Pkwy.

Intercession City

Loughman

535
536
192
27
429 (toll road)
545
4
417
17
27
4

0   3 mi
0   3 km

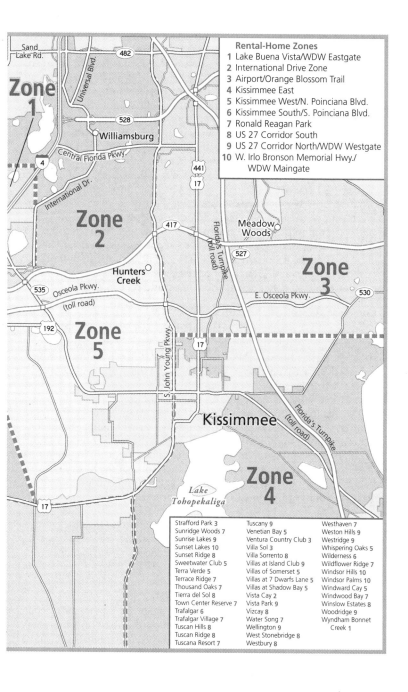

Rental-Home Zones
1 Lake Buena Vista/WDW Eastgate
2 International Drive Zone
3 Airport/Orange Blossom Trail
4 Kissimmee East
5 Kissimmee West/N. Poinciana Blvd.
6 Kissimmee South/S. Poinciana Blvd.
7 Ronald Reagan Park
8 US 27 Corridor South
9 US 27 Corridor North/WDW Westgate
10 W. Irlo Bronson Memorial Hwy./
   WDW Maingate

Zone 1
Zone 2
Zone 3
Zone 4
Zone 5

Sand Lake Rd.
Universal Blvd.
Williamsburg
Central Florida Pkwy.
International Dr.
Hunters Creek
Osceola Pkwy.
(toll road)
Meadow Woods
Florida's Turnpike (toll road)
E. Osceola Pkwy.
S. John Young Pkwy.
Kissimmee
Florida's Turnpike (toll road)
Lake Tohopekaliga

Strafford Park 3	Tuscany 9	Westhaven 7
Sunridge Woods 7	Venetian Bay 5	Weston Hills 9
Sunrise Lakes 9	Ventura Country Club 3	Westridge 9
Sunset Lakes 10	Villa Sol 3	Whispering Oaks 5
Sunset Ridge 8	Villa Sorrento 8	Wilderness 6
Sweetwater Club 5	Villas at Island Club 9	Wildflower Ridge 7
Terra Verde 5	Villas of Somerset 5	Windsor Hills 10
Terrace Ridge 7	Villas at 7 Dwarfs Lane 5	Windsor Palms 10
Thousand Oaks 7	Villas at Shadow Bay 5	Windward Cay 5
Tierra del Sol 8	Vista Cay 2	Windwood Bay 7
Town Center Reserve 7	Vista Park 9	Winslow Estates 8
Trafalgar 6	Vizcay 8	Woodridge 9
Trafalgar Village 7	Water Song 7	Wyndham Bonnet
Tuscan Hills 8	Wellington 9	Creek 1
Tuscan Ridge 8	West Stonebridge 8	
Tuscana Resort 7	Westbury 8	

continued from page 223

sell slow-moving inventory, but more commonly the cost to renters is higher than when dealing directly with owners or management companies: Because most wholesalers and packagers sell their inventory through travel agents, both the wholesaler/packager's markup and the travel agent's commission are passed along to the renter. These costs are in addition to the owner's cut and/or the fee for the property manager.

Along similar lines, logic may suggest that the lowest rate of all can be obtained by dealing directly with owners, thus eliminating an intermediary. Although this is sometimes true, it's more often the case that property-management companies offer the best rates. With their marketing expertise and larger customer base, these companies can produce a higher occupancy rate than can the owners themselves. What's more, management companies, or at least the larger ones, can achieve economies of scale unavailable to owners when it comes to maintenance, cleaning, linens, and even acquiring furniture and appliances (if a house is not already furnished). The combination of higher occupancy rates and economies of scale adds up to a win–win situation for owners, management companies, and renters alike.

Location, Location, Location

The best vacation home is one that's within easy commuting distance of the theme parks (see the map on pages 224–225). If you plan to spend some time at Universal, SeaWorld, and the like, you'll want something just northeast of Walt Disney World (between the World and Orlando). If you plan to spend most of your time in the World, the best selection of vacation homes is along **US 192,** south of the park.

Practically all of the vacation rentals in Orange County are in the **Floridays** and **Vista Cay** developments. By our reckoning, about half the rental homes in Osceola County and all the rental homes in Polk County are too far away for commuting to be practical. You might be able to save a few bucks by staying farther out, but the most desirable homes to be found are in **Vista Cay** and in developments no more than 10 miles south of Universal's main entrance, from west of John Young Parkway to east of FL 429/Western Beltway.

To get the most from a vacation home, you need to be close enough to commute in 20 minutes or less to your Orlando destination. This will allow for naps, quiet time, swimming, and dollar-saving meals you prepare yourself.

Shopping for a Vacation Home

There are three main types of websites in the home-rental game: those for property-management companies, which showcase a given company's homes and are set up for direct bookings; individual owner sites; and third-party listing sites, which advertise properties available through different owners and sometimes management companies as well. Sites in the last category will usually refer prospective renters to an owner's or management company's site for reservations.

We've found that most property-management sites are poorly designed and will test your patience. You can practically click yourself into old age trying to see all the homes available or figure out where on earth they are. Nearly all of them claim to be "just minutes from Disney." (By that reasoning, we should list our own homes: They're also just minutes from Disney—570 minutes, to be exact!)

Many websites list homes according to towns (such as Clermont, Lake Buena Vista, Windermere, and Winter Garden) or real estate developments (including Eagle Pointe, Floridays, Golden Oak, and Vista Cay) in the general Universal area, none of which you're likely to be familiar with. The information that counts is the distance of a vacation home or condo from Walt Disney World; for that, you often must look for something like "4 miles from Disney" embedded in the home's description.

The best websites provide the following:

- Numerous photos and in-depth descriptions of individual homes
- Detailed reviews of the homes that include dates of the reviewer's stay
- Overview maps or text descriptions that reflect how far specific homes or developments are from Walt Disney World
- The ability to actually book the rental home on the site
- An easy-to-find phone number for bookings and questions

The best sites are also easy to navigate, let you see what you're interested in without your having to log in or divulge any personal information, and list memberships in such organizations as the Better Business Bureau and the **Florida Vacation Rental Management Association** (VRMA; visit fvrma.org for the association's code of ethics).

Recommended Websites

After checking out dozens upon dozens of sites, here are the ones we recommend. All of them meet the criteria listed above. (For the record, we elected not to list some sites that met our criteria but whose homes are too far away from Walt Disney World.)

Florida Dream Homes (floridadreamhomes.com) has a good reputation for customer service and has photos of and information about the homes in its online inventory.

Vacation Rentals by Owner (vrbo.com) is a nationwide vacation-homes listing service that puts prospective renters in direct contact with owners. The site is straightforward and always lists a large number of rental properties in Celebration, Disney's planned community situated about 8–10 minutes from the theme parks. Similar listing services with good websites are **Vacation Rentals 411** (vacationrentals411.com) and **Last Minute Villas** (lastminutevillas.net).

Visit Orlando (visitorlando.com) is the website to check if you're interested in renting a condominium at one of the many time-share developments (click on "Places to Stay" at the site's home page). You can call the developments directly, but going through this site allows you to bypass sales departments and escape their high-pressure invitations to sit through sales presentations. The site also lists hotels, vacation homes, and campgrounds.

Making Contact

Once you've found a home you like, check the website for a FAQ page. If there isn't one, here are some of the things you'll want to ask.

1. How close is the property to Walt Disney World?
2. Is the home or condominium that I see on the internet the one I'll get?
3. Is the property part of a time-share development?
4. Are there any specials or discounts available?
5. Is everything included in the rental price, or are there additional charges?
6. How old is the property I'm interested in? Has it been refurbished recently?
7. What is the view from the property?
8. Is the property near any noisy roads?
9. What is your smoking policy?
10. What is your pet policy?
11. Is the pool heated? If yes, is there an extra charge for the heating?
12. Is there a fenced backyard where children can play?
13. How many people can be seated at the main dining table?
14. Is there a dedicated land phone line at the property to ensure a reliable connection to 911 and other emergency services?
15. Is high-speed internet available?
16. Are linens and towels provided?
17. How far are the nearest supermarket and drugstore?
18. Is childcare available?
19. Are there restaurants nearby?
20. Is transportation to the parks provided?
21. Will we need a car?
22. What is required to make a reservation?
23. What is your change/cancellation policy?
24. When is checkout time?
25. What will we be responsible for when we check out?
26. How will we receive our confirmation and arrival instructions?
27. What are your office hours?
28. What are the directions to your office?
29. What if we arrive after your office has closed?
30. Whom do we contact if something goes wrong during our stay?
31. How long have you been in business?
32. Are you licensed by the state of Florida?
33. Do you belong to the Better Business Bureau and/or the Florida VRMA?

We frequently receive letters from readers extolling the virtues of renting a condo or vacation home. This endorsement by a New Jersey family of five is typical:

> I cannot stress enough how important it is if you have a large family (more than two kids) to rent a house for your stay! We stayed at Windsor Hills Resort, 1.5 miles from the Disney Maingate. It took us about 10 minutes to drive there in the a.m., and we had no traffic issues at all.

THE BEST OFF-SITE HOTELS FOR FAMILIES

WHAT MAKES A SUPER FAMILY HOTEL? For starters, you should look for spacious rooms, free breakfast, an in-room fridge, a great pool, and activities for kids.

Narrowed from hundreds of properties, the hotels profiled in the next section, listed by zone and alphabetically, are the best we've found in each area of Orlando. Some of our picks are expensive, others are more reasonable, and some are a bargain. All understand a family's needs.

The best square footage for your lodging dollar is often found in a suite. Suites have the advantage of separate bedrooms, allowing tired family members to rest while others stay up.

Unofficial Guide readers give low ratings to most off-site hotels' park-transportation options. Though all hotels profiled in the following pages offer some type of shuttle to the theme parks, some offer very limited service, so be sure to call the hotel before you book and ask what the shuttle schedule will be when you visit. Likewise, most off-site hotels' restaurants won't meet the needs of a family staying for a week, so plan to go elsewhere for variety.

*un*official **TIP**
Check the resort's room photos to make sure you're booking an actual suite with multiple rooms. Some hotels with *suites* in their name or *all-suite* in their description are little more than slightly larger, single-space-for-everyone rooms with a microwave.

Ten Bangs for Your Hotel Buck

We have stayed at 10 villa-style resorts outside of Walt Disney World; 2 are profiled in the following section. Our goal was to assess the value for money paid, with a focus on space, amenities, and transportation to the parks. All 10 properties provided clean, comfortable rooms at reasonable prices for their size. We recommend the following 6 (see our caveat about the remaining 4 below):

- **Club Wyndham Cypress Palms**
- **Homewood Suites by Hilton** (Flamingo Crossings; page 244)
- **JW Marriott Orlando Bonnet Creek Resort & Spa**
- **Margaritaville Resort Orlando** (page 243)
- **Marriott's Cypress Harbour**
- **Marriott's Imperial Palm Villas**

Club Wyndham Cypress Palms, Marriott's Cypress Harbour, and **Marriott's Imperial Palms** are similar to **Marriott's Harbour Lake,** profiled on page 239.

The next four, while acceptable, are either more expensive than or not as nice as comparable off-site hotels, or they have marketing departments that hounded us repeatedly after our stay:

- **Aloft Orlando Lake Buena Vista**
- **Caribe Royale Orlando**
- **Grand Beach** (Diamond Resorts)
- **Home2Suites by Hilton** (Flamingo Crossings)

FIVE QUICK TIPS FOR BOOKING A HOTEL

1. START WITH GOOGLE MAPS Search for hotels close to your destination—for example, "hotels within 3 miles of Walt Disney World." (Google thinks the center of Walt Disney World is a patch of land to the right of World Drive as you pass EPCOT Center Drive. Most Disney resorts are within a 3-mile radius of that point.)

You can also search by walking distance, as in "hotels within a 10-minute walk of Disney Springs." A map will show nearby hotels, although it will also show a wider geographic area, so you'll have to zoom in to adequately differentiate the hotels and see where they are in relation to Disney Springs.

Once Google Maps knows you're looking for hotels, it will prompt you to enter your check-in and checkout dates.

2. IDENTIFY YOUR OPTIONS The hotels displayed on the map will show a blue block containing an advertised rate—look for the closest hotel with the best rate. Hovering your cursor over the block will bring up details including the name and star rating of the hotel. If you click on the block, a column will appear on the left side of the page with more information, including rate quotes from online travel agencies (OTAs) and other sites and the names of similar hotels nearby.

3. OPTIONAL: GET IN THE BLOCK If you're attending a meeting or event that has large numbers of reserved rooms managed by the event's sponsor, we recommend booking within that room block if you can afford it. Room blocks represent high-volume business for hotels, and sponsors can often leverage this volume for goodies such as catered events, hospitality suites, entertainment, and other extras that make your stay more enjoyable.

INTERNATIONAL DRIVE & UNIVERSAL AREAS

Hard Rock Hotel Orlando ★★★★

5800 Universal Blvd. Orlando
☎ 407-503-2000
hardrockhotels.com/orlando

Rate per night $406–$711. **Pool ★★★★. Fridge in room** Yes. **Shuttle to parks** Yes (Universal, SeaWorld, Discovery Cove, Aquatica, and Volcano Bay). **Maximum number of occupants per room** 4 (king)/5 (double queen). **Comments** Pets welcome ($100 flat fee, 2 max). Parking $28/day. **Survey results** 89% of *Unofficial Guide* readers would stay here again; 83% would recommend this resort to a friend.

FOR YOUNGER ADULTS AND FAMILIES WITH OLDER KIDS, the Hard Rock Hotel is the hippest place to lay your head. It's also the closest Universal Orlando resort to the theme parks. The exterior has a California Mission theme, with white stucco walls, arched entryways, and rust-colored roof tiles. Inside, the lobby's walls are decorated with enough concert posters, costumes, and musical instruments to start an outpost of the Rock and Roll Hall of Fame (ask the front desk about a self-guided memorabilia tour). The eight floors hold 650 rooms and 29 suites, with the rooms classified as Standard, Deluxe, and Club Level.

Standard rooms are 375 square feet, slightly larger than rooms at Disney's Moderate resorts and a bit smaller than most Disney Deluxe rooms. Neutral walls and linens are brightened by colorful retro-inspired chairs and accents.

If the rooms in the block are beyond your means, don't be afraid to book outside the block if you must; the sponsor will have anticipated at least a few such bookings in contracting with the hotel.

4. SEE IF THE HOTEL CAN BEAT ONLINE DEALS Every time a room is booked through a third party, whether that's an online travel agency, such as Expedia or Hotwire, or a content site like TripAdvisor, the hotel makes less money. Therefore, before you book a room, make a list of the best deals you've found online and call the hotel directly (don't call the toll-free national reservations number).

Ask for a rate quote for your selected travel dates—if it's higher than what you've found online, tell the hotel representative so, without quoting your best online rate: "I've found better rates online. Can you offer me a better rate for booking directly with you?" If the representative comes back in the affirmative, ask exactly what kind of room that rate gets you. Also get the representative's name and note the time of the call.

5. CHECK THE HOTEL'S WEBSITE Go to the website and investigate what kind of room you'll get at the quoted rate. If you're fine with what you see, call the hotel back and book. If you have any special room preferences, make sure they get noted on your reservation. We also usually ask about the age of the hotel, construction or renovations at or near the hotel, road noise, and Wi-Fi availability.

In addition, this is a good opportunity to ask about potential hidden charges such as taxes, resort fees, and fees for parking and internet. Hotels are notorious for tacking these on without disclosing them in their advertised rates.

Furnishings include two queen beds, along with a flat-screen TV, a refrigerator, a coffee maker, and an alarm clock with USB charging ports. A dresser and separate closet with sliding doors ensure plenty of storage space. In addition, most rooms have a reading chair and a small desk with two chairs. An optional rollaway bed, available at an extra charge, allows standard rooms to sleep up to five people.

Each room's dressing area features a sink and hair dryer. The bathroom is probably large enough for most adults to get ready in the morning while another person gets ready in the dressing area.

Deluxe rooms with king beds are around 400 square feet and can accommodate up to three people with an optional rollaway bed rental. These rooms feature a U-shaped sitting area in place of the second bed, and the rest of the amenities are the same as in standard rooms. Deluxe queen rooms are 500 square feet and can hold up to five people using a pullout sofa.

The 12,000-square-foot pool includes a 260-foot waterslide, a sand beach, and underwater speakers so you can hear the music while you swim. Adjacent to the pool are a fountain play area for small children, a sand-volleyball court, hot tubs, and a poolside bar. Private cabanas can be rented as well.

On-site dining includes **The Kitchen**, a casual full-service restaurant open for breakfast, lunch, and dinner, featuring American food such as burgers, steaks, and salads. **The Palm Restaurant** is an upscale steakhouse that's open for dinner only, while the lobby's **Velvet Bar** hosts nightly live entertainment.

And, of course, the world's largest **Hard Rock Cafe** is just a short distance away at Universal CityWalk.

While it's not exactly cheap—self-parking alone is $28 per night—the Hard Rock is a good value compared with, say, Disney's Yacht & Beach Clubs. What you're paying for here is a short walk to the theme parks and Universal Express Unlimited first, and the room second.

Hilton Grand Vacations Club SeaWorld Orlando ★★★★★

6924 Grand Vacations Way
Orlando
☎ 407-239-0100
tinyurl.com/seaworldhgv

Rate per night $210–$535. **Pool** ★★★★. **Fridge in room** Yes. **Shuttle to parks** Yes (Universal, SeaWorld). **Maximum number of occupants per room** 2 (studio)/8 (3-bedroom suite). **Comments** Guests get front-of-line access to some SeaWorld rides. **Survey results** 100% of *Unofficial Guide* readers would stay here again; 80% would recommend this resort to a friend.

ACROSS THE STREET FROM SEAWORLD, Hilton Grand Vacations is within a 15-minute drive of both Walt Disney World and Universal Orlando. While that means spending more time in a car, you get a lot more room for your money: one-bedroom suites are 878 square feet, compared with around 520 for Disney's Value Family Suites and Fort Wilderness Cabins. Grand Vacations' one-bedroom averages $240 per night in the summer—about $195 per night less than Disney's cheapest family suite, at All-Star Music. In fact, Grand Vacations' 1,225-square-foot, two-bedroom suite is often less than Disney's cheapest suite. Plus, Grand Vacations has free parking.

Unofficial Guide readers give this Hilton an A for room quality and a solid B for room quietness. Studios have kitchenettes. Suites come equipped with a washer and dryer; a kitchen with utensils, dishwasher, oven/range, microwave, and coffee maker; and flat-screen TVs. One-bedroom suites have a sofa bed and one bathroom, two-bedroom suites have two baths, and three-bedroom suites have three baths. The decor isn't the most modern, but it is bright, clean, functional, and comfortable.

Amenities include three pools with cabanas, a fitness center, a playground, basketball and tennis courts, and a business center. A sit-down restaurant is open noon-8 p.m., and a grab-and-go market and deli is open 8 a.m.–6 p.m.

Loews Portofino Bay Hotel at Universal Orlando ★★★★½

5601 Universal Blvd.
Orlando
☎ 407-503-1000
loewshotels.com
/portofino-bay-hotel

Rate per night $434–$762. **Pools** ★★★★. **Fridge in room** Yes. **Shuttle to parks** Yes (Universal, SeaWorld, Discovery Cove, Aquatica, Volcano Bay). **Maximum number of occupants per room** 3 (king)/5 (double queen). **Comments** Pets welcome ($100 flat fee, 2 max). Parking $28/day. **Survey results** 92% of *Unofficial Guide* readers would stay here again; 93% would recommend this resort to a friend.

UNIVERSAL'S TOP-OF-THE-LINE HOTEL evokes the Italian seaside city of Portofino, complete with a man-made bay past the lobby. To Universal's credit, the layout, color, and theming of the guest-room buildings are a good approximation of the architecture around the harbor in the real Portofino (with fewer yachts, of course).

Inside, the lobby is decorated with patterned marble floors, white columns, and arches. The space is airy and comfortable, with side rooms featuring seats and couches done in bold reds and deep blues.

Most guest rooms are 450 square feet, larger than most at Disney's Deluxe resorts, and have either one king bed or two queens. King rooms sleep up to three people with an optional rollaway bed; the same option allows queen rooms to sleep up to five. Two room-view options are available: Garden rooms look out over the landscaping and trees (many of these are the east-facing rooms in the resort's east wing; others face one of the three pools); bay-view rooms face either west or south and overlook Portofino Bay.

Rooms come furnished with a flat-screen TV, a minifridge, an alarm clock with USB charging ports, and a coffee maker. Other amenities include a small desk with two chairs, a comfortable reading chair with lamp, a chest of drawers, and a standing closet. As at all Universal on-site hotels, high-speed Wi-Fi access is free. Beds are large, plush, and comfortable.

The guest bathrooms are the best on Universal property. The shower has an adjustable spray nozzle that varies the water pulses to simulate everything from monsoon season in the tropics to the rhythmic thumps of wildebeest hooves during migrating season.

Portofino Bay has three pools, the largest of which, the **Beach Pool,** is on the west side of the resort. Two smaller quiet pools sit at the far end of the east wing and to the west of the main lobby. The Beach Pool has a zero-entry design and a waterslide themed after a Roman aqueduct, plus a children's play area, a sand beach, two hot tubs, and a poolside bar and grill. Three cabanas can be rented. The **Villa Pool** also has private cabanas for that Italian Riviera feeling. Rounding out the luxuries are the **Mandara Spa,** a complete fitness center, a business center, and a video arcade.

On-site dining includes three sit-down restaurants serving Italian cuisine, including **BiCE,** a sit-down, upscale dinner place; a deli that serves pizza; a Starbucks; and a gelateria. While we like BiCE quite a bit, some of the food prices at the other venues go well beyond what we'd consider reasonable, even for a theme park hotel.

Portofino Bay has some of Universal's best rooms, but the prices at the upper end put it on par with the Ritz-Carlton—something its good points can't quite justify. On the other hand, Portofino Bay is significantly cheaper than the resorts along Disney's monorail—and the Ritz isn't a short walk from The Wizarding World.

Loews Royal Pacific Resort at Universal Orlando ★★★★

Rate per night $406–$715. **Pools** ★★★★. **Fridge in room** Yes. **Shuttle to parks** Yes (Universal, SeaWorld, Discovery Cove, Aquatica, Volcano Bay). **Maximum number of occupants per room** 3 (king)/5 (double queen). **Comments** Microwaves available for $15/day. Pets welcome ($100 flat fee, 2 max). Parking $28/day. **Survey results** 94% of *Unofficial Guide* readers would stay here again; 90% would recommend this resort to a friend.

6300 Hollywood Way
Orlando
☎ 407-503-3000
loewshotels.com
/royal-pacific-resort

YOU MAY BE TEMPTED, as we were initially, to write off the Royal Pacific as a knockoff of Disney's Polynesian Village Resort. There are similarities, but the Royal Pacific is attractive enough, and has enough strengths of its own, for us to recommend that you try it for yourself.

Guests enter the lobby from a walkway two stories above an artificial stream that surrounds the resort. Once you're inside, dark teak accents contrast nicely with the enormous amount of light coming in from the windows and three-story A-frame roof. Palms line the walkway through the lobby, and through these you see that the whole lobby surrounds an enormous outdoor fountain.

The 1,000 rooms are spread among three Y-shaped wings attached to the main building. Standard rooms are 335 square feet—about the size of a room at Disney's Moderate resorts—and have one king or two queen beds. King rooms sleep up to three people with an optional rollaway bed; queen rooms sleep five with a rollaway. The beds, fitted with all-cotton linens, are very comfortable.

Rooms have modern monochrome wall treatments and carpets, accented with boldly colored floral graphics, and include a flat-screen TV, a minifridge, a coffee maker, an alarm clock, and several USB-equipped power outlets. Other amenities include a small desk with two chairs, a comfortable reading chair, a chest of drawers, and a large closet. A dressing area with sink is separated from the rest of the room by a wall. Next to the dressing area is the bathroom, with a tub, shower, and toilet. While they're acceptable, the bathroom and dressing areas at the Royal Pacific are our least favorite in the upscale Universal resorts.

As at the Hard Rock, the Royal Pacific's zero-entry pool includes a sand beach, a volleyball court, a play area for kids, a hot tub, and cabanas for rent, plus a poolside bar and grill.

Amenities include a 5,000-square-foot fitness facility, a business center, a video arcade, a full-service restaurant, a sushi bar, two bars, and a weekly luau (on Saturday). **Islands Dining Room,** serving Pacific Rim and traditional fare, is open for breakfast and dinner and has a play area for kids. **Jake's American Bar** is open for lunch, dinner, and late-night eats (until 1 a.m.), while the poolside **Bula Bar & Grille** offers wraps, sandwiches, burgers, salads, and fruity drinks.

Loews Sapphire Falls Resort at Universal Orlando ★★★★

6601 Adventure Way
Orlando
☎ 407-503-5000
loewshotels.com
/sapphire-falls-resort

Rate per night $219–$535. **Pools** ★★★★. **Fridge in room** Yes. **Shuttle to parks** Yes (Universal, SeaWorld, Discovery Cove, Aquatica, Volcano Bay). **Maximum number of occupants per room** 3 (king)/ 5 (double queen). **Comments** Microwaves available for $15/day. Pets welcome ($100 flat fee, 2 max). Parking $26/day. **Survey results** 86% of *Unofficial Guide* readers would stay here again, and 89% would recommend this resort to a friend.

UNIVERSAL'S FIFTH ON-SITE LOEWS HOTEL brought a sunny Caribbean vibe to the moderately priced market when its 1,000 rooms opened in 2016. Sandwiched between Royal Pacific and Cabana Bay—both physically and pricewise—Sapphire Falls sports all the amenities of Universal's three deluxe hotels, including water-taxi transportation to the parks, with the crucial exception of complimentary Universal Express privileges.

Water figures heavily here: The namesake falls form the scenic centerpiece of the resort. The 16,000-square-foot, zero-entry main pool features a white-sand beach, a waterslide, children's play areas, a fire pit, and cabanas for rent. A fitness room holds a sauna and hot tub.

For dinner, **Amatista Cookhouse** offers table-service Caribbean dining, with an open kitchen and waterfront views. **Drhum Club Kantine** serves tapas-style small plates near the pool bar's fire pit. **New Dutch Trading Co.** is an island-inspired grab-and-go marketplace. **Strong Water Tavern** in the lobby specializes in rum and deserves its own paragraph in this review. Strong Water serves tasty, island-inspired tapas from a menu longer than you'd expect. It's one of our favorite on-site restaurants and a great way to end your night. Try the ceviche.

Sapphire Falls also has 115,000 square feet of meeting space and a business center. Walkways connect to a parking structure that in turn connects to the meeting facilities at Royal Pacific, making these sister properties ideal for conventions. And that leads us to our main critique of the resort: Aside from the lobby and pool, the public areas feel like those of a standard convention hotel.

The rooms range from 364 square feet in a standard queen or king room to 529 square feet in the 36 Kids' Suites to up to 1,358 square feet in the 15

Hospitality Suites. All rooms have HDTVs, minifridges, and coffee makers. We like these a bit better than those at Aventura, but they're more expensive too.

Sheraton Vistana Villages Resort Villas, I-Drive/Orlando ★★★★½

Rate per night $159-$349. **Pool** ★★★★. **Fridge in room** Yes. **Shuttle to parks** No. **Maximum number of occupants per room** 6 (2-bedroom suite). **Survey results** 73% of *Unofficial Guide* readers would stay here again; 75% would recommend this resort to a friend.

12401 International Dr. Orlando
☎ 407-238-5000
tinyurl.com/vistana villagesresort

THIS IS ONE OF TWO SHERATON VISTANA properties in Orlando that are favorites of *Unofficial Guide* readers (the other is the **Sheraton Vistana Resort Villas** in Lake Buena Vista, profiled on page 239). The 1,100-square-foot, two-bedroom villas are the rooms to get. While that's double the size of a Disney one-bedroom Family Suite, rack rates are much less than Disney's, ranging from $239 per night in September to $349 per night at Christmas.

Suites have fully equipped kitchens and a washer and dryer. All rooms have a private balcony or patio. The resort has two pools, including one zero-entry for kids; a fitness center; and a business center.

This family from Bedford, Texas, really enjoyed their stay:

> I highly recommend Vistana Villages—it's the best value for the money. Plenty of space for everyone to spread out, great pools, and fantastic location—it was 10 minutes to EPCOT and Hollywood Studios and 5 minutes to Disney Springs, and lots of restaurants were nearby.

The Vistana Villages are about a 15-minute drive from Walt Disney World (and you don't have to take I-4!) and 20 minutes to Universal Orlando.

Universal's Aventura Hotel   ★★★★

Rate per night Standard rooms, $174-$309; Kids' Suites, $299-$533. **Pools** ★★★½. **Fridge in room** Yes. **Shuttle to parks** Yes (Universal, SeaWorld, Discovery Cove, Aquatica, Volcano Bay). **Maximum number of occupants per room** 4 (double queen or king with pullout)/6 (Kids' Suites). **Comments** Parking $18/day. **Survey results** 74% of *Unofficial Guide* readers would stay here again; 93% would recommend this resort to a friend.

6725 Adventure Way Orlando
☎ 407-503-6000
loewshotels.com/universals-aventura-hotel

OPENED IN SUMMER 2018, the Aventura Hotel is Universal Orlando's sixth resort and second so-called Prime Value–priced option. The curvilinear glass-and-steel tower evokes beachfront hotels of the 1950s. The 600 rooms range from 238 square feet for standard king rooms that sleep four to 575 square feet for Kids' Suites that sleep five. Decor is streamlined and minimalist, in keeping with the midcentury-modern architectural cues.

Aventura's standard rooms, about 22 square feet smaller than those at Disney's Value resorts, have vinyl plank flooring. Beds are comfortable and all the electronics work, but our shower curtain didn't extend far enough down, resulting in a wet floor every time someone showered.

Kids' Suites are distinguished by sleeping areas rather than special theming: Mom and Dad get a bedroom with a king bed, while kids get a separate room with two twin beds. Plus, the living room sofa converts to a deluxe bed with memory-foam mattress. All rooms have a coffee maker, iron and ironing board, flat-screen TV, and minifridge.

Reader ratings for Aventura lag behind in room quietness and food-court quality. We understand the food-court rating—it feels small and disjointed, with lots of small stations. We think Cabana Bay (see next profile) is a better value-priced option overall.

Food-and-drink options include **Bar 17 Bistro,** an expansive rooftop restaurant and lounge with fantastic views (great in the cooler months); the food court; lobby and pool bars; and a **Starbucks.** Rounding out the amenities are a pool with a separate kids' splash area, a fitness center, a gift shop with Universal-themed swag, and supervised children's activities.

Aventura guests enjoy early admission to The Wizarding World of Harry Potter at both theme parks as well as Volcano Bay (but not free Universal Express privileges).

Universal's Cabana Bay Beach Resort ★★★½

6550 Adventure Way
Orlando
☎ 407-503-4000
loewshotels.com
/cabana-bay-hotel

Rate per night Standard rooms, $158–$273; suites, $219–$369. **Pools** ★★★★. **Fridge in room** Yes. **Shuttle to parks** Yes (Universal, Sea-World, Discovery Cove, Aquatica, Volcano Bay). **Maximum number of occupants per room** 4 (standard)/6 (suite). **Comments** Parking $18/day. **Survey results** 90% of *Unofficial Guide* readers would stay here again; 87% would recommend this resort to a friend.

OPENED IN 2014, Cabana Bay was Universal's first on-site hotel aimed at the value and midpriced markets. But whereas Disney's Value resorts use kid-friendly, oversize characters and bright colors, Cabana Bay went with a sleek midcentury-modern theme. It was an instant hit, running at high occupancy levels from the day it opened. Disney's current redesign of its Value rooms is a direct result of Cabana Bay's success. The resort has proved so popular, in fact, that Universal has added two towers with 400 rooms that afford views of Universal's Volcano Bay water park.

Befitting a classy Rat Pack retreat in Palm Springs or Las Vegas, Cabana Bay's retro-hip 1950s style includes lots of windows, bright colors, and period-appropriate lighting and furniture. Kids will love the two large, well-themed pools (one with a lazy river), the video arcade, the bowling alley, and the vintage cars parked outside the lobby. Adults will appreciate the sophisticated kitsch of the decor, the multiple lounges, and the **Starbucks.** We think Cabana Bay is an excellent choice for price- and/or space-conscious families.

The hotel's closest competitor in the Orlando area is Disney's Art of Animation Resort (AOA), and the two share many similarities. Both have standard rooms and family suites. At 430 square feet per suite, Cabana Bay suites are about 135 square feet smaller than comparable suites at AOA and have just one bathroom. We found them well appointed for two to four people per room (though not for the six Loews claims as its capacity). Rack rates for the suites run about $210–$470 per night less than AOA's.

Each family suite has a small bedroom with two queen beds, divided from the living area and kitchenette by a sliding screen; a foldout sofa in the living area provides additional sleeping space. (Standard rooms also have two queen beds.) The bath is divided into three sections: toilet, sink area, and shower room with additional sink. The kitchenette has a microwave, coffee maker, and minifridge. A bar area provides extra seating for quick meals, and a large closet has enough space to store everyone's luggage. Built-in USB charging outlets for your devices are a thoughtful touch.

Recreational options include the 10-lane **Galaxy Bowl** ($15 per person with shoe rental; registered hotel guests only, same-day in-person reservations required), poolside table tennis and billiards, and a **Jack LaLanne Physical Fitness Studio.** (Fitness centers aren't found at any Disney Value or Moderate resort except Coronado Springs.) Outdoor movies are shown nightly near the pool.

In addition to the Starbucks, a food court with seating shows 1950s TV clips. **Swizzle Lounge** in the lobby, two pool bars, in-room pizza delivery, and Galaxy Bowl Restaurant round out the on-site dining options. The **Universal Studios Store** is the largest hotel store in the resort and stocks candy and apparel exclusive to Cabana Bay.

Unlike the pricier Universal resorts, Cabana Bay offers no watercraft service to the parks—it's either take the bus or walk. A pedestrian bridge connects Cabana Bay to CityWalk and the rest of Universal Orlando, but we recommend the bus for most visitors. Cabana Bay guests are eligible for Early Park Entry at Universal but not free Universal Express privileges.

The biggest complaints we hear about Cabana Bay are that wait times to check in during midafternoon are often excessive (try to arrive early or late) and that housekeeping services can sometimes be inconsistent. As the hotel reaches its 10th birthday, some rooms are starting to show their age, so ask to be moved to a refurbished room if your furnishings are unacceptably worn.

Universal's Endless Summer Resort ★★★★

Rate per night Standard rooms, $119–$229; suites, $171–$279. **Pool ★★★. Fridge in room** Yes. **Shuttle to parks** Yes (Universal, SeaWorld, Discovery Cove, Aquatica, Volcano Bay). **Maximum number of occupants per room** 4 (standard)/6 (suites). **Comments** Parking $15/day. **Survey results** Surfside remains the highest-rated value-priced resort at both Universal Orlando and Walt Disney World; 91% of *Unofficial Guide* readers would stay here again; 89% would recommend this resort to a friend.

Dockside Inn and Suites:
7125 Universal Blvd., Orlando
☎ 407-503-8000
loewshotels.com
/dockside-inn-and-suites

Surfside Inn and Suites:
7000 Universal Blvd. Orlando
☎ 407-503-7000
loewshotels.com
/surfside-inn-and-suites

UNIVERSAL'S LATEST HOTEL COMPLEX consists of two value-priced resorts: **Surfside Inn and Suites** opened in June 2019, and **Dockside Inn and Suites** opened in late 2020.

Surfside Inn has 360 standard rooms and 390 two-bedroom suites, while Dockside Inn has 577 standard rooms and 723 two-bedroom suites. With both hotels open, Universal has almost doubled the number of its on-site Value rooms. Both resorts' color schemes include pale blues and greens, with lots of white. Bright ocean- and surf-themed art hangs on the walls, and room soundproofing is excellent, which is a surprise at this price. Though there are plenty of under-shelf hooks on which to hang things, there are only a handful of drawers for stowing your clothes. Our biggest nitpick is the poor quality of the soft goods—foam pillows and polyester-blend bath towels should be illegal.

Standard rooms are around 313 square feet and have vinyl plank flooring, two queen beds, a chair, a minifridge, a coffee maker, and an iron and ironing board. They're about the size of a Disney Moderate room at Disney Value prices: about $180–$230 per night cheaper than a Moderate.

Two-bedroom suites are 440 square feet and include a kitchenette with picnic-style table and microwave, plus one bathroom. *Two-bedroom* is a misnomer, though: The suites have one main room with two beds and a separate room with another bed. That's about 65–80 square feet smaller—and one less bathroom—than Disney's Family Suites. Universal's suites, however, are roughly $160–$280 cheaper per night, which pays for a *lot* of park admission.

The pools are unusually shallow (maximum depth 4 feet) and lack waterslides. Unfortunately, Endless Summer guests are forbidden to crash the pools at the non-Value resorts. Each hotel includes a well-stocked, free fitness room, plus a **Universal Studios Store** and a video arcade.

Full-service dining isn't offered, but cafeteria-style food courts, lobby and pool bars, **Starbucks,** and pizza delivery are all available. Between the two hotels, we think Surfside has a slight edge owing to its smaller, more manageable size, but Dockside has a few improved amenities and food options.

Because Endless Summer is on the opposite side of International Drive and I-4 from the rest of Universal Orlando, walking to the parks from the resort isn't practical, so a fleet of free buses is provided, servicing both the parking hub (from which you walk to CityWalk and the theme parks) and direct to Volcano Bay. The ride from here is actually slightly shorter than the one from Cabana Bay; travel time is barely 5 minutes each way, and the entire trip (including walking and waiting to depart) takes about 15 minutes.

As at Cabana Bay, guests at Endless Summer get free early admission to Universal's theme parks but not free Universal Express.

LAKE BUENA VISTA & I-4 CORRIDOR

Four Seasons Resort Orlando at Walt Disney World Resort ★★★★★

10100 Dream Tree Blvd.
Lake Buena Vista
☎ 407-313-7777
fourseasons.com/orlando

Rate per night $970–$1,808. **Pools** ★★★★★. **Fridge in room** Yes. **Shuttle to parks** Yes (Disney). **Maximum number of occupants per room** 4 (3 adults or 2 adults + 2 children). **Comments** The best deluxe hotel rooms, staff service, and pool complex in Walt Disney World, if not Orlando. Character breakfast on Saturday (by reservation). **Survey results** 80% of *Unofficial Guide* readers would stay here again; 80% would recommend this resort to a friend.

WITH 444 GUEST ROOMS, THIS HOTEL is simultaneously the largest in the Four Seasons chain and the smallest on Disney property. It's also the best deluxe resort in the area, offering comfort, amenities, and personal service that far surpass anything that the Disney-branded Deluxe resorts offer.

Standard rooms average around 500 square feet and have either one king bed with a sleeper sofa or two double beds (a crib is available in double rooms). Amenities include two flat-screen TVs (one is in the mirror above the bathroom sink!), a coffee maker, a minifridge, a desk with two chairs, and Bluetooth speakers. In keeping with the room's gadget-friendly spirit, each nightstand has four electrical outlets and two USB ports. Bathrooms have glass-walled showers, a separate tub, marble vanities with two sinks, mosaic-tile floors, hair dryers, and lighted mirrors.

Most rooms have an 80-square-foot balcony with table and chairs—perfect for your morning coffee or an evening nightcap. Standard-view rooms look out onto the resort's lawns, gardens, and nearby homes in Golden Oak. Lake-view rooms—which overlook the lake, the Tom Fazio–designed Tranquilo Golf Club, or the pool—cost about $350 more per night than standard-view rooms. Park-view rooms, on floors 6–16, cost up to $800 *more* per night than standard-view rooms and offer views of the Magic Kingdom's nightly fireworks; EPCOT-view suites are available as well.

The 5-acre pool area is the best—and least crowded—on Disney property, with an adult pool, a family pool, an 11,000-square-foot lazy river, and a splash zone with two 242-foot waterslides. To put this in perspective, the Four Seasons' pool area is about twice as large as Stormalong Bay at the Yacht & Beach Club Resorts, but with only a third as many guests. Private cabanas rent for $500–$700 per day.

Capa, a one-Michelin-starred, Spanish-themed rooftop restaurant, serves seafood and steaks (open daily, 5–10 p.m.; dress is resort casual, and reservations are recommended). **Ravello,** on the first floor, serves American breakfasts (daily, 7–11 a.m.) and Italian dinners (daily, 5:30–10 p.m.; dress is smart casual, and reservations are recommended); it also offers a character breakfast on Saturday. **PB&G** (**Pool Bar and Grill**) serves barbecued meats and salads by the main pool (daily, 11 a.m.–6 p.m.).

At the hotel's Disney Planning Center, Four Seasons staff can help you with reservations or any other Disney needs. Disney will also deliver your in-park purchases to this resort, and staying here qualifies you for Early Theme Park Entry. The resort has a full-service spa and fitness center, as well as a beautiful late-checkout lounge that allows guests use of the showers and bathrooms in the spa.

Marriott's Harbour Lake   ★★★★½

Rate per night 1-bedroom villas, $229–$459; 2-bedroom villas, $259–$499. **Pool** ★★★★. **Fridge in room** Yes. **Shuttle to parks** No. **Maximum number of occupants per room** 4 (1-bedroom)/8 (2-bedroom). **Comments** Rated significantly higher than other suite hotels in Lake Buena Vista. **Survey results** 90% of *Unofficial Guide* readers would stay here again; 82% would recommend this resort to a friend.

7102 Grand Horizons Blvd. Orlando
☎ 407-465-6100
tinyurl.com/harbourlake

HARBOUR LAKE IS A FAVORITE of *Unofficial Guide* readers, with good deals on one- and two-bedroom villas within a 15-minute drive of both Disney World and Universal. The resort's theme seems to be a cross between Key West and Nantucket, with architectural elements and color palettes from both.

Room categories include studios and one- and two-bedroom villas, the latter being the ones to request. These include bedrooms separated from the living areas, a fully equipped kitchen, a sofa, a reading chair, a dining table and chairs, and a washer and dryer. The primary bedroom has a king bed, while the two-bedroom villa's second bedroom has two queens. The earth-toned decor isn't memorable, but it is modern and comfortable. Counter space around the bathroom sinks is a bit sparse, but there's plenty of storage elsewhere. Water pressure is acceptable. Most rooms have a balcony or patio.

Rates for the 1,082-square-foot two-bedroom villas are up to $340 per night cheaper than Disney's Art of Animation Family Suites during the off-season, with more than double the space. Rates for the 800-square-foot one-bedroom villas are even cheaper.

The pools here are top-notch, with a pirate ship, waterslides, and excellent play areas for smaller children. The resort also has an on-site fitness center and an 18-hole minigolf course.

On-site dining is limited to a bar and grill and a grab-and-go outpost, so be prepared to do some grocery shopping or eat out.

Sheraton Vistana Resort Villas   ★★★★

Rate per night 1-bedroom villas, $159–$329; 2-bedroom villas, $219–$389. **Pools** ★★★½. **Fridge in room** Yes. **Shuttle to parks** Yes (Disney). **Maximum number of occupants per room** 4 (1-bedroom)/8 (2-bedroom). **Comments** Though they're time-shares, the villas are rented nightly as well. **Survey results** 70% of *Unofficial Guide* readers would stay here again; 61% would recommend this resort to a friend.

8800 Vistana Centre Drive Orlando
☎ 407-239-3100
tinyurl.com/sheratonresortlbv

THE SHERATON VISTANA is deceptively large, stretching across both sides of Vistana Centre Drive. Because Sheraton's emphasis is on selling the time-shares, the rental angle is little known. But families should consider it; it's one of Orlando's best off–Disney World properties.

The spacious villas offer 850-square-foot one-bedroom and 1,025-square-foot two-bedroom models. Decorated in beachy pastels offset by dark wood finishes, each has a full kitchen (including fridge, microwave, oven/range, dishwasher, toaster, and coffee maker), with an option to have it stocked in advance with groceries and laundry products; a washer and dryer; TVs in the living room and each bedroom (one with DVD player); a stereo with CD player in some villas; a separate dining area; and a private patio or balcony in most villas.

The grounds feature seven swimming pools (three with bars); four playgrounds; three restaurants; game rooms; fitness centers; a minigolf course; sports-equipment rentals (including bikes); and courts for basketball, volleyball, tennis, and shuffleboard. The mind-boggling array of activities for kids (and adults) ranges from crafts to games and sports tournaments.

Of special note: Vistana is highly secure, with locked gates bordering all guest areas, so children can have the run of the place without parents worrying about them wandering off.

The one downside is the noise, both above (from the flight path of a helicopter-tour company) and below (from International Drive). Bring a white-noise machine or app for better sleep.

Signia by Hilton Orlando Bonnet Creek ★★★★

14100 Bonnet Creek Resort Ln.
Orlando
☎ 407-597-3600
hiltonbonnetcreek.com

Rate per night $251–$454. **Pool** ★★★★½. **Fridge in room** Yes. **Shuttle to parks** Yes (Disney). **Maximum number of occupants per room** 4. **Comments** $51/night resort fee. Parking $34/day. Guests are eligible for Early Theme Park Entry benefits. **Survey results** 80% of *Unofficial Guide* readers would stay here again; 83% would recommend this resort to a friend.

THE SIGNIA IS ONE of our favorite non-Disney hotels in Lake Buena Vista, and the value for the money beats anything in Disney's Deluxe category. Located behind Caribbean Beach and Pop Century Resorts, this Hilton property is much nicer than the two in the Disney Springs Resort Area.

Standard rooms measure around 414 square feet—comparable to Disney Deluxes. Mattresses and linens are very comfortable. Other features include a 37-inch TV, spacious desk, small reading chair with floor lamp, nightstand, and digital clock. A coffee maker, a minifridge, and an ironing board and iron are all standard, along with free Wi-Fi.

Bathrooms have tile floors, and some have glassed-in showers. Unfortunately, the layout isn't as up-to-date as other hotels'—where many upscale hotel bathrooms have two sinks, the Signia's have just one. And where modern bathroom configurations often include a dressing area separate from the bath and a separate water closet for the commode, everything is in the bathroom here.

Public areas are stylish and spacious. Families will enjoy the huge zero-entry pool, complete with waterslide, as well as the 3-acre lazy river. Even better, the staff runs arts-and-crafts activities poolside during the day, allowing parents to grab a quick swim and a cocktail. Pool-facing cabanas are also available for rent at around $300–$400 per day. A nice fitness center sits on the ground floor.

Children ages 5–12 can participate in the neighboring Waldorf Astoria's **WA Kids Club.** A daily program takes place 10:30 a.m.–1:30 p.m. and 2:30–5:30 p.m. An evening program is offered on Friday and Saturday, 6–9 p.m. The price for either program is $100 for one child, and $50 for each additional child.

The Signia and the Waldorf boast more than a dozen restaurants and bars between them, including **Bull & Bear,** an upscale steakhouse; **La Luce,** offering pizza, pasta, and other Italian favorites; **Zeta Asia** for sushi; tapas; a coffee bar, an American bistro; and a breakfast buffet. Reservations are recommended for the fancy places.

Sonesta ES Suites Lake Buena Vista

Rate per night 1-bedroom suites, $163–$254; 2-bedroom suites, $189–$304. **Pool** ★★★. **Fridge in room** Yes. **Shuttle to parks** Yes (Disney, Universal); fee applies. **Maximum number of occupants per room** 4 (1-bedroom suites)/8 (2-bedroom suites). **Comments** Parking $17/day. **Survey results** Not enough surveys to rate.

8751 Suiteside Drive
Orlando
☎ 407-238-0777
tinyurl.com/sonestalbv

WE FOUND THIS GEM back in 2016 through our reader surveys. Although it didn't receive many surveys this year, we still think it's one of the best off-site hotels near Walt Disney World. It's so inexpensive that we'd recommend the two-bedroom suites for families as small as two or three people.

The best values are the 750-square-foot two-bedroom suites, at rates less than you'd pay for a Disney Moderate resort. For that, you get two bedrooms on opposite ends of the suite. One bedroom has a king bed, the other two doubles. A sleeper sofa is standard in both the one- and two-bedroom layouts. The one-bedroom suites measure around 550 square feet.

Each bedroom has its own full bathroom. Between the bedrooms are a living room, dining area, and full kitchen with dishwasher, range, microwave, and fridge as well as plates, cups, glasses, cutlery, and basic pots and pans. There's a big-screen TV in the living room and smaller ones in each bedroom.

Other amenities include complimentary Wi-Fi, a small fitness center, and a pool. Service was excellent. Be aware that the Sonesta ES is so popular that it's unlikely your room will be ready much before the 4 p.m. check-in time.

Located about 0.5 mile from the Disney Springs Resort Area, just around the corner on South Apopka–Vineland Road, the hotel is about a 10-minute drive to the Disney Springs parking garages and about 19 minutes to the Magic Kingdom parking lot. Two shopping centers are in walking distance.

Waldorf Astoria Orlando   ★★★★½

Rate per night $407–$854. **Pool** ★★★★. **Fridge in room** Yes. **Shuttle to parks** Yes (Disney). **Maximum number of occupants per room** 4 plus child in crib. **Comments** Good alternative to Disney Deluxe resorts; $51/night resort fee. **Survey results** 100% of *Unofficial Guide* readers would stay here again; 66% would recommend this resort to a friend.

14200 Bonnet Creek
Resort Ln., Orlando
☎ 407-597-5500
waldorfastoriaorlando.com

THE WALDORF ASTORIA is between I-4 and Pop Century Resort, near the Signia by Hilton (profiled on opposite page) at the back of the Bonnet Creek Resort property. Getting here requires a GPS or good directions, so be prepared with those before you travel. Once you arrive, however, you'll know the trip was worth it. Beautifully decorated and appointed, the Waldorf is more elegant than any Disney resort. Service is excellent, and the staff-to-guest ratio is far higher than at Disney properties.

At just under 450 square feet, standard rooms feature either two queen beds or one king. A full-size desk allows you to get work done if it's absolutely necessary, and rooms also have flat-screen TVs, high-speed internet, and Wi-Fi (included with the resort fee). The bathrooms are spacious and gorgeous, with cool marble floors, glass-walled showers, separate tubs, and enough counter space for a Broadway makeup artist.

Amenities include a fitness center, a spa, a golf course, multiple restaurants, and two pools (including a zero-entry pool for kids). Shuttles service the Disney parks about every half hour (see www.bonnetshuttle.com for schedule). Runners will like the relative solitude—it's about 1 mile round-trip to the nearest busy road.

US 192 AREA

Gaylord Palms Resort & Convention Center ★★★½

6000 W. Osceola Pkwy. Kissimmee
☎ 407-586-0000
gaylordpalms.com

Rate per night $331–$854. **Pool** ★★★★. **Fridge in room** Yes. **Shuttle to parks** Yes (Disney, free; other parks, $21/person round-trip). **Maximum number of occupants per room** 4. **Comments** Along with a handful of other hotels, the Gaylord Palms is probably the closest you'll get to Disney-level extravagance outside of the World. $43/night resort fee. Parking $37/day. **Survey results** 100% of *Unofficial Guide* readers would stay here again; 50% would recommend this resort to a friend.

WITH ITS COLOSSAL CONVENTION FACILITY, this upscale resort caters to business clientele, but it's still a nice (if pricey) family resort. Hotel wings are defined by the three themed, glass-ceilinged atria they overlook. **Key West**'s design is reminiscent of island life in the Florida Keys; **Everglades** is an overgrown spectacle of shabby swamp chic; and the immense, central **St. Augustine** recalls Spanish Colonial Florida. Lagoons, streams, and waterfalls connect all three, and walkways and bridges abound. A fourth wing, **Emerald Bay Tower,** overlooks the Emerald Plaza shopping and dining area of the St. Augustine atrium. These rooms are the nicest and most expensive; they're mostly used by convention-goers. Although rooms have fridges, alarm clocks, and other perks such as high-speed internet, they work better as retreats for adults than for kids. However, children will enjoy the themed areas and the family pool (with water-squirting octopus). In-room childcare is available. The resort and parking fees add a whopping $80 to the room's nightly rate.

Holiday Inn Club Vacations at Orange Lake Resort

8505 W. Irlo Bronson Memorial Hwy. (US 192), Kissimmee
☎ 407-477-7025
tinyurl.com/holidayinn
orangelake

Rate per night $149–$215. **Pools** ★★★★. **Fridge in room** Yes. **Shuttle to parks** Yes, for a fee (varies based on destination). **Maximum number of occupants per room** Varies. **Comments** This is a time-share property, but if you rent directly through the resort instead of the sales office, you won't have to listen to any sales pitches. $22/night resort fee. **Survey results** Not enough surveys to rate.

YOU COULD SPEND YOUR ENTIRE VACATION never leaving this property about 6–10 minutes from the Disney theme parks. From its seven pools and mini water park to its golfing opportunities (36 holes of championship greens plus two 9-hole executive courses), Orange Lake offers an extensive menu of amenities and recreational opportunities. If you tire of lazing by the pool, try water-skiing, wakeboarding, tubing, fishing, and more on the 80-acre lake. There are also two fitness centers and an on-site trainer; tennis, basketball, racquetball, and volleyball courts; three arcades; a kids' activity center; and two minigolf courses. Other entertainment options may include live music and bingo.

The 2,478 units are tastefully decorated and comfortably furnished, ranging from suites and studios to three-bedroom villas, all with fully equipped kitchens. These rooms are massive and cheap: The 1,700-square-foot, three-bedroom villa sleeps 11 people and goes for as little as $320 a night. That's about the same as five—*five!*—Disney Moderate rooms, for less money.

If you'd rather not cook on vacation, try one of the eight restaurants scattered across the resort, offering everything from pizza to pub fare.

We reevaluated the resort after a reader noticed several negative reviews of the property on TripAdvisor, most mentioning room cleanliness. Our test room—a one-bedroom villa with washer and dryer and full kitchen for $136 per night including tax—was spotless, as were the rooms we got to peek into around the resort. As far as suites go, we like the **Sonesta ES Suites Lake Buena Vista** (see page 241) a bit better, but we'd stay at Orange Lake again.

Margaritaville Resort Orlando

Rate per night Hotel rooms, $201–$279; cottages (1–8 bedrooms), $249–$2,220. **Pool** ★★★★. **Fridge in room** Yes (full kitchen). **Shuttle to parks** No. **Maximum number of occupants per room** 2 for a standard room; 18 for an 8-bedroom cottage. **Comments** $50/night resort fee. $75/night pet fee (maximum charge of $300). **Survey results** Not enough surveys to rate.

8000 Fins Up Circle
Kissimmee
☎ 407-479-0950
tinyurl.com/margaritaville-fl

BEYOND OUR ABSOLUTE CERTAINTY that Margaritaville's restaurant would serve a Cheeseburger in Paradise, Jimmy Buffett's lyrics reveal few thoughts about hotel management. We were skeptical that this was going to be anything other than a standard hotel with some tropical prints and parrots. But Margaritaville is a well-designed, reasonably priced resort that's worth considering for large families and groups, especially those who aren't planning on going to Walt Disney World every day.

Located on an 300 acres of land, Margaritaville has two kinds of accommodations: The main building holds 265 standard rooms and suites, and another 187 one- to eight-bedroom cottages sit around a central lake.

As you might expect, an island/beach theme is consistent across the resort. Standard rooms are 470 square feet, larger than any standard Disney Deluxe room. Amenities include modern vinyl plank flooring, a microwave and coffee maker, and good lighting. Bathrooms are well lit and spacious, with walk-in showers and good water pressure.

Vacation cottages are freestanding homes, ranging from one-story, one-bedroom bungalows to three-story, eight-bedroom buildings that sleep up to 18 guests. The most notable thing about these cottages is that nothing feels cheap or underbuilt. The kitchen layout makes it easy to cook for large groups. The couches, chairs, and beds are comfortable. Bathrooms have good water pressure. The A/C blows cold. The lights and appliances work the way they're supposed to. And the homes we've stayed in have been spotlessly clean.

A 5-minute walk from the hotel lobby puts you in the middle of **Sunset Walk,** Margaritaville's dining and entertainment district, featuring more than 15 restaurants and bars with cuisines ranging from sushi to British pub to Memphis barbecue. We think it's worth visiting. There's also an on-site water park— **Island H2O**—but we consider Universal's Volcano Bay a better value. A Publix supermarket and a Target are less than a mile away. A free internal shuttle service links the hotel, cottages, and Sunset Walk.

If you're headed to Disney property from Margaritaville, you can avoid almost all of the US 192 traffic by taking Inspiration Drive to Black Lake Road to Osceola Parkway. That half-mile, traffic-free stretch of road puts you smack-dab between Animal Kingdom and Animal Kingdom Lodge, with clear, easy access to the rest of Walt Disney World.

Polynesian Isles Resort (Diamond Resorts) ★★★★

Rate per night 1-bedroom villas, $137–$306; 2-bedroom villas, $187–$364. **Pool** ★★★½. **Fridge in room** Yes (full kitchen). **Shuttle to parks** No. **Maximum number of occupants per room** 4 (1-bedroom)/6 (2-bedroom), plus child in crib. **Comments** $18/night resort fee. **Survey results** 100% of *Unofficial Guide* readers would stay here again; 75% would recommend this resort to a friend.

3045 Polynesian Isles Blvd.
Kissimmee
☎ 407-396-1622
polynesianisle.com

LET'S START BY SAYING that the Polynesian Isles' rooms aren't the most modern and could use a good interior decorator. And the location, a few miles east of I-4 in Kissimmee, isn't the most upscale. But there are few other places in Orlando where you can get 1,500–1,600 square feet of space for $200 a night. (Quantity, as they say, has a quality all its own.)

One-bedroom villas are 1,500 square feet and have one king bed and one sofa bed; two-bedroom villas are 1,600 square feet and have king, queen, and sofa beds. Both villa types are outfitted with a full kitchen, a dining room table with seating for six, upholstered chairs, and a TV. Bathrooms are large and clean, with decent water pressure and so-so lighting.

The resort's Polynesian theme is pulled off pretty well for something not in a theme park. Other amenities include tennis courts, a basketball half-court, a very small fitness room, a playground, and a heated outdoor pool.

FLAMINGO CROSSINGS

FLAMINGO CROSSINGS IS LOCATED at the intersection of US 429 and Western Way—we're not exaggerating when we say it's less than 60 seconds from Disney property by car. Follow Western Way for a bit, and you'll end up at Coronado Springs Resort. Five hotels are located in this area. Two are Hilton properties: **Home2Suites** and **Homewood Suites.** Three are Marriott brands: **Residence Inn**; **SpringHill Suites**; and the extended-stay **TownePlace Suites.** All have 220–300 rooms. In terms of value, we'd rate them in this order:

1. SpringHill Suites **2.** Residence Inn **3.** Homewood Suites

4. TownePlace Suites **5.** Home2Suites

The related hotels are adjacent and share parking, a huge pool complex, and gyms. Other amenities include practice fields and facilities—a nod to the sports groups that participate in events at the ESPN Wide World of Sports Complex. The lobbies are constantly abuzz with color-coordinated teens either preparing for or unwinding from some event.

Despite the potential for noise, our rooms were very quiet. They were also spotless. Our two-bedroom suite had a small, full kitchen, while our studio had a microwave and coffee maker. Both had only one bathroom, and we think the two-bedroom units could have used a second. Water pressure was better at the Marriott properties than the Hiltons.

In addition to being close to Disney property, the Flamingo Crossings hotels are about a 10-minute drive to a wide variety of retailers on US 192, including a Publix, a Super Target, and tons of restaurants. That said, if you have a car or aren't participating in anything at the ESPN complex, any of the other resorts in the preceding section offer better value for the money.

---

341 Flagler Ave.
Winter Garden
☎ 407-993-3999
tinyurl.com/fc-home2
suites

Home2Suites by Hilton

Rate per night $177–$280. **Pool** ★★★★. **Fridge in room** Yes. **Shuttle to parks** Yes (Magic Kingdom only, $5). **Maximum number of occupants per room** 6, plus child in crib. **Survey results** Not enough surveys to rate.

---

411 Flagler Ave.
Winter Garden
☎ 407-993-3011
tinyurl.com/hwdsuites
flamingo

Homewood Suites by Hilton ★★★★½

Rate per night $177–$280. **Pool** ★★★★. **Fridge in room** Yes. **Shuttle to parks** Yes (Magic Kingdom only, $5). **Maximum number of occupants per room** 4 (1-bedroom suite with king and pullout beds)–5 (1-bedroom suite with 2 queen and pullout beds), plus child in crib. **Survey results** Not enough surveys to rate.

Residence Inn

Rate per night Studios, $139–$209; 1-bedroom suites, $219–$343; 2-bedroom suites, $324–$433. **Pool** ★★★★. **Fridge in room** Yes. **Shuttle to parks** No. **Maximum number of occupants per room** 2 (studio)/ 6 (1-bedroom suite with pull-out sofa)/ 8 (2-bedroom suit with pull-out sofa). **Survey results** Not enough surveys to rate.

2111 Flagler Ave.
Winter Garden
☎ 407-993-3233
tinyurl.com
/resinnflamingo

WITH STUDIOS AND ONE- AND TWO-BEDROOM SUITES, a fitness center, free hot breakfast, and Disney-competitive peak-season rates for the two-bedroom units, this Residence Inn is a good option for large families. We're not fans of the foam pillows, but you can ask for feather pillows.

SpringHill Suites ★★★★

Rate per night $141–$285. **Pool** ★★★★. **Fridge in room** Yes. **Shuttle to parks** Yes (Magic Kingdom only, $5). **Maximum number of occupants per room** 6, plus child in crib. **Survey results** Not enough surveys to rate.

13279 Hartzog Rd.
☎ 407-507-1200
tinyurl.com
/fc-springhill

TownePlace Suites ★★★★

Rate per night $114–$189. **Pool** ★★★★. **Fridge in room** Yes. **Shuttle to parks** Yes (Magic Kingdom only, $5). **Maximum number of occupants per room** 3 (1-bedroom suite)/5 (2-bedroom suite with 2 queen and pull-out beds), plus child in crib. **Survey results** Not enough surveys to rate.

13295 Hartzog Rd.
Winter Garden
☎ 407-507-1300
tinyurl.com
/fc-towneplace

HOTEL *and* MOTEL ROOMS:
Rated and Ranked

IN THIS SECTION, WE COMPARE HOTEL ROOMS in four main lodging areas outside Walt Disney World (see page 215) with those inside the World. Additional hotels can be found at the intersection of US 27 and I-4, on US 441 (Orange Blossom Trail), and in downtown Orlando. Most of these require more than 30 minutes of commuting to Disney World and thus are not rated. We also haven't rated lodging east of Siesta Lago Drive on US 192. If a hotel isn't listed in this section, the most likely reason is that the ones that *are* listed are better choices in terms of quality and price.

WHAT'S IN A ROOM?

EXCEPT FOR CLEANLINESS, state of repair, and decor, many travelers pay little attention to hotel rooms. There is, of course, a certain standard of quality that differentiates Motel 6 from Holiday Inn, Holiday Inn from Marriott, and so on. But many guests don't fully appreciate that some rooms are better engineered than others. We've seen some beautifully appointed rooms that aren't well designed. Making the room usable for its occupants is an art that combines both form and function. Even more than decor, your room's details and layout will make you feel comfortable and at home.

ROOM RATINGS

TO CATEGORIZE PROPERTIES by their quality, tastefulness, state of repair, cleanliness, and size of their standard rooms, we have assigned the hotels and motels an **overall star rating.** These ratings are based on expected levels of quality established by specific American hotel corporations (see table below) and don't necessarily correspond to ratings awarded by *Frommer's*, TripAdvisor, AAA, or other travel critics.

OVERALL STAR RATINGS		
★★★★★	Superior rooms	Tasteful and luxurious by any standard
★★★★	Extremely nice rooms	What you'd expect at a Hyatt Regency or Marriott
★★★	Nice rooms	Holiday Inn or comparable quality
★★	Adequate rooms	Clean, comfortable, and functional without frills—like a Motel 6
★	Super-budget	These exist but are not included in our coverage

Overall star ratings apply only to room quality and describe the property's standard accommodations. For most hotels, a standard accommodation is a room with one king bed or two queen beds. In an all-suite property, a standard accommodation is either a studio or a one-bedroom suite. Ratings are assigned without regard to amenities such as restaurants, recreational facilities, and entertainment.

In addition to stars (which delineate broad categories), we use a numerical rating system—the **room-quality rating.** Our scale is 0–100, with 100 being the best possible rating and zero (0) the worst. Numerical ratings show the difference we perceive between one property and another. For instance, rooms at both **Liki Tiki Village** and **The Berkley Orlando** are rated three and a half stars (★★★½). The former has a room-quality rating of 77 and the latter an 80. This means that within the ★★★½ category, The Berkley has slightly nicer rooms.

The **location** column identifies the area around Walt Disney World where you'll find a particular property (key below).

LODGING AREAS (see maps on pages 216–219)	
WDW Inside Walt Disney World	
1 On or near International Drive	3 On or near US 192 (aka Irlo Bronson Memorial Highway, Vine Street, and Space Coast Parkway)
2 Lake Buena Vista, FL 535, and the I-4 Corridor and Vicinity	4 Universal Orlando Area

The names of properties along US 192 also designate location (for example, the Holiday Inn Maingate West). The consensus in Orlando seems to be that the main entrance to Walt Disney World is the broad interstate-type road that runs off US 192. This is called the **Maingate.** Properties along US 192 call themselves Maingate East or West to differentiate their positions along the highway. So, driving southeast from Clermont or Florida's Turnpike, the properties before you reach the Maingate turnoff are called Maingate West, while the properties after you pass the Maingate turnoff are called Maingate East.

Cost estimates are based on the hotel's published rack rates for standard rooms. Each **$** represents $50; amounts over $200 are indicated by **$ x 5** and so on.

We've focused on room quality and excluded location, services, recreation, or amenities. In some instances, a one- or two-room suite is available for around the same price as a single standard room. We add new properties and change ratings and rankings annually, based on factors such as room renovations or a change in maintenance or housekeeping. Conversely, lax housekeeping or poor maintenance can bring down ratings.

Before you shop for a hotel, consider this letter from a man in Hot Springs, Arkansas:

> *We canceled our room reservations to follow the advice in your book and reserved a hotel highly ranked by the* Unofficial Guide. *We wanted inexpensive, but clean and cheerful. We got inexpensive, but also dirty, grim, and depressing. The room spoiled the holiday for me aside from our touring.*

This letter was as unsettling to us as the bad room was to the reader—our integrity as travel journalists is based on the quality of the information we provide. When rechecking the hotel, we found our rating was representative, but the reader had been assigned one of a small number of threadbare rooms scheduled for renovation.

Be aware that some hotel chains use the same guest-room photo in promotional literature for all their hotels and that, consequently, the rooms at a specific property may bear no resemblance to the photo in question. When you or your travel agent calls, ask how old the property is and when the guest room you're being assigned was last renovated. If you're assigned a room that is inferior to your expectations, demand to be moved.

THE 30 BEST HOTEL VALUES

IN THE TABLE ON PAGE 249, we look at the best combinations of quality and value in a room. Rankings are calculated without consideration for location or the availability of restaurant(s), recreational facilities, entertainment, and/or amenities.

A reader wrote to complain that he had booked one of our top-ranked rooms in terms of value and had been very disappointed in the room. We noticed that the room the reader occupied had an overall quality rating of ★★½. Remember that the list of top deals is intended to give you some sense of value received for dollars spent. A ★★½ room at $60 may have the same *value* as a ★★★★ room at $120, but that doesn't mean the rooms will be of comparable *quality*. Regardless of whether it's a good deal, a ★★½ room is still a ★★½ room.

$120 IS THE NEW $70 One of our major research projects over the past few years has been to find hotels with clean, safe, functional rooms that we could recommend to you for around $70 per night with tax.

Gentle reader, we found exactly one for this edition (the Rodeway Inn Maingate, which did not have enough surveys to rate). And we learned something along the way: At the $70 price point, we frequently had to make compromises in either safety or functionality, or both. At one motel on International Drive, we were greeted with a sign advising that copies of our driver's licenses would be shared with local police! At another motel, our door lock was made of plastic and didn't include a dead bolt—we had to pack our belongings into the car every time we left the room. At a third, our game of "spot the meth lab" became "spot the one that's *not* a meth lab." We were too scared to stay the night. Most of the rooms we checked at this price point also had some sort of mechanical problem, from balky toilets to water shooting out of the faucet whenever you turned it on. On the upside, the staff we met were uniformly helpful, and most were downright cheerful.

Ultimately, we decided that **$120 per night** (with tax) is the bare minimum you should expect to pay for a clean, safe, not-sketchy hotel room near Disney property—the $70 room that made it into the book is a rare exception to the rule and isn't really representative when it comes to quality.

Not convinced? Here's the experience of a Rockton, Illinois, reader who booked a $75-per-night hotel for a solo trip, based on the hotel's internet photos—after he'd emailed us personally and we quoted the previous section:

> The TV remote looked so dirty that every time I used it, I grabbed my hand sanitizer. The dead bugs on the walls contributed to the "this place is definitely a dump" feeling. My biggest issue was with the front door—even with the dead bolt locked, the gaps between the door and the jamb meant that if someone had really wanted to kick the door in, they'd have had no problem. Every time I left the room, I locked my stuff in the car trunk. There's no way in hell my wife would stay here. I'd happily pay $100 a night for a better option.

If you find something cheaper than $100 per night that meets our criteria and isn't already listed here, please let us know.

THE TOP 30 BEST DEALS

	HOTEL	LODGING AREA	OVERALL QUALITY	ROOM QUALITY	COST ($ = $50)
1	Holiday Inn Orlando SW–Celebration Area	3	★★★★★	97	$$$+
2	Holiday Inn Resort Orlando–Lake Buena Vista	2	★★★★½	90	$$+
3	Mystic Dunes Resort & Golf Club (Diamond Resorts)	3	★★★★½	90	$$$+
4	Hilton Grand Vacations Club SeaWorld Orlando	1	★★★★★	97	$$$+
5	Homewood Suites by Hilton Orlando–International Drive/Convention Center	1	★★★★½	93	$$$
6	Best Western Plus Universal Inn	4	★★★★½	93	$$$
7	Holiday Inn Express & Suites/South Lake Buena Vista	2	★★★★½	90	$$$
8	Vacation Village at Parkway	3	★★★★	89	$$$-
9	Courtyard Orlando Lake Buena Vista at Vista Centre	2	★★★★	87	$$$-
10	Homewood Suites by Hilton Orlando Theme Parks	1	★★★★	87	$$$-
11	Galleria Palms Hotel	3	★★★★½	92	$$$+
12	Comfort Suites Maingate East	3	★★★★	87	$$$
13	Hilton Grand Vacations Club Tuscany Village	1	★★★★½	90	$$$+
14	Shades of Green	WDW	★★★★½	92	$$$+
15	Holiday Inn Orlando–Disney Springs Resort Area	WDW	★★★★½	90	$$$$-
16	Homewood Suites by Hilton Lake Buena Vista-Orlando	2	★★★★½	93	$$$$-
17	TownePlace Suites Orlando at Flamingo Crossings	2	★★★★	87	$$$
18	Marriott's Harbour Lake	2	★★★★½	94	$$$$-
19	Star Island Resort & Club	3	★★★★	82	$$$-
20	Homewood Suites by Hilton Orlando–Nearest to Universal Studios	1	★★★★	87	$$$
21	Extended Stay America Convention Center/Westwood	1	★★★★	87	$$
22	Hyatt Place Orlando/Lake Buena Vista	2	★★★★	88	$$$+
23	Hampton Inn Orlando/Lake Buena Vista	2	★★★★	86	$$$
24	B Resort & Spa	WDW	★★★★	85	$$$+
25	Cypress Pointe Resort	2	★★★★	88	$$$+
26	Universal's Endless Summer Resort: Surfside Inn & Suites	4	★★★★	86	$$$+
27	Westgate Vacation Villas Resort	3	★★★★	83	$$$
28	Delta Hotels Lake Buena Vista (Marriott)	2	★★★★½	90	$$$$
29	Universal's Endless Summer Resort: Dockside Inn & Suites	4	★★★★	85	$$$+
30	Silver Lake Resort	3	★★★★	87	$$$-

HOW THE HOTELS COMPARE

HOTEL	OVERALL QUALITY	LODGING AREA	ROOM QUALITY	COST ($ = $50)
Four Seasons Resort Orlando at Walt Disney World Resort	★★★★★	WDW	100	$ x 28
Omni Orlando Resort at ChampionsGate	★★★★★	2	97	$- x 7
Hilton Grand Vacations Club SeaWorld Orlando	★★★★★	1	97	$$$+
Holiday Inn Orlando SW-Celebration Area	★★★★★	3	97	$$$-
Wyndham Grand Orlando Resort Bonnet Creek	★★★★★	WDW	96	$ x 6
The Ritz-Carlton Orlando, Grande Lakes	★★★★½	1	95	$ x 17
Marriott Harbour Lake	★★★★½	2	94	$$$$-
Mi Casa Hotel Orlando	★★★★½	2	94	$$+
The Villas at Disney's Grand Floridian Resort & Spa	★★★★½	WDW	93	$- x 21
Disney's Riviera Resort	★★★★½	WDW	93	$- x 13
Homewood Suites by Hilton at Flamingo Crossings	★★★★½	2	93	$$$$$-
Homewood Suites by Hilton Lake Buena Vista-Orlando	★★★★½	2	93	$$$$-
Best Western Plus Universal Inn	★★★★½	4	93	$$$
Homewood Suites by Hilton Orlando-International Drive/Convention Center	★★★★½	1	93	$$$
Disney's Saratoga Springs Resort & Spa	★★★★½	WDW	92	$ x 12
Shades of Green	★★★★½	WDW	92	$$$+
Galleria Palms Hotel	★★★★½	3	92	$$$+
Disney's Polynesian Villas & Bungalows (studios)	★★★★½	WDW	91	$- x 19
Disney's Old Key West Resort	★★★★½	WDW	91	$ x 12
Disney's Grand Floridian Resort & Spa	★★★★½	WDW	90	$- x 21
Disney's Polynesian Village Resort	★★★★½	WDW	90	$- x 19
Disney's BoardWalk Inn	★★★★½	WDW	90	$+ x 16
Bay Lake Tower at Disney's Contemporary Resort (studios)	★★★★½	WDW	90	$+ x 16
Waldorf Astoria Orlando	★★★★½	WDW	90	$ x 16
Loews Portofino Bay Hotel at Universal Orlando	★★★★½	4	90	$ x 12
Disney's Coronado Springs Resort	★★★★½	WDW	90	$+ x 7
Sheraton Vistana Villages Resort Villas, I-Drive	★★★★½	1	90	$$$$$
Delta Hotels Lake Buena Vista (Marriott)	★★★★½	2	90	$$$$
Holiday Inn Orlando-Disney Springs Resort Area	★★★★½	WDW	90	$$$$-
Hilton Grand Vacations Club Tuscany Village	★★★★½	1	90	$$$+
Holiday Inn Express & Suites/South Lake Buena Vista	★★★★½	2	90	$$$
Mystic Dunes Resort & Golf Club (Diamond Resorts)	★★★★½	3	90	$$$-

HOW THE HOTELS COMPARE (continued)

HOTEL	OVERALL QUALITY	LODGING AREA	ROOM QUALITY	COST ($ = $50)
Holiday Inn Resort Orlando–Lake Buena Vista	★★★★½	2	90	$$+
Treehouse Villas at Disney's Saratoga Springs Resort & Spa	★★★★	WDW	89	$+ x 32
Disney's BoardWalk Villas	★★★★	WDW	89	$+ x 16
Disney's Animal Kingdom Villas (*Kidani Village, studios*)	★★★★	WDW	89	$ x 13
Hyatt Regency Grand Cypress	★★★★	2	89	$ x 6
Westgate Lakes Resort & Spa	★★★★	2	89	$$$$
Marriott's Grande Vista	★★★★	1	89	$$$$
Vacation Village at Parkway	★★★★	3	89	$$$-
Disney's Contemporary Resort	★★★★	WDW	88	$+ x 15
Disney's Yacht Club Resort	★★★★	WDW	88	$ x 15
Disney's Wilderness Lodge	★★★★	WDW	88	$- x 14
Copper Creek Villas & Cabins at Disney's Wilderness Lodge (*studios*)	★★★★	WDW	88	$- x 14
Disney's Animal Kingdom Lodge	★★★★	WDW	88	$ x 13
The Cabins at Disney's Fort Wilderness Resort	★★★★	WDW	88	$- x 13
Disney's Caribbean Beach Resort	★★★★	WDW	88	$- x 8
Sheraton Vistana Resort Villas, Lake Buena Vista	★★★★	2	88	$$$$$
Universal's Aventura Hotel	★★★★	4	88	$$$$$
SpringHill Suites Orlando at Flamingo Crossings	★★★★	2	88	$$$$+
Cypress Pointe Resort	★★★★	2	88	$$$+
Hyatt Place Orlando/Lake Buena Vista	★★★★	2	88	$$$+
Disney's Beach Club Resort	★★★★	WDW	87	$ x 15
Hard Rock Hotel Orlando	★★★★	4	87	$ x 13
Disney's Pop Century Resort	★★★★	WDW	87	$- x 6
Hilton Orlando	★★★★	1	87	$$$$$
Disney's All-Star Movies Resort	★★★★	WDW	87	$$$$+
Disney's All-Star Music Resort	★★★★	WDW	87	$$$$+
Disney's All-Star Sports Resort	★★★★	WDW	87	$$$$+
Signia by Hilton Orlando Bonnet Creek	★★★★	WDW	87	$$$$+
Residence Inn Near Universal Orlando	★★★★	1	87	$$$$+
Silver Lake Resort	★★★★	3	87	$$$$-
Extended Stay America Convention Center/Westwood	★★★★	1	87	$$#
Homewood Suites by Hilton Orlando–Nearest to Universal Studios	★★★★	1	87	$$$
TownePlace Suites Orlando at Flamingo Crossings	★★★★	2	87	$$$
Comfort Suites Maingate East	★★★★	3	87	$$$

HOW THE HOTELS COMPARE (continued)

HOTEL	OVERALL QUALITY	LODGING AREA	ROOM QUALITY	COST ($ = $50)
Courtyard Orlando Lake Buena Vista at Vista Centre	★★★★	2	87	$$$-
Hilton Orlando Buena Vista Palace	★★★★	WDW	87	$ x 6
Homewood Suites by Hilton Orlando Theme Parks	★★★★	1	87	$$$-
Disney's Beach Club Villas (studios)	★★★★	WDW	86	$ x 15
Loews Royal Pacific Resort at Universal Orlando	★★★★	4	86	$ x 11
Walt Disney World Swan Reserve	★★★★	WDW	86	$ x 8
Loews Sapphire Falls Resort at Universal Orlando	★★★★	4	86	$- x 8
Walt Disney World Swan	★★★★	WDW	86	$ x 6
DoubleTree Suites by Hilton Orlando–Disney Springs Area	★★★★	WDW	86	$$$$
Universal's Endless Summer Resort: Surfside Inn & Suites	★★★★	4	86	$$$+
Hampton Inn Orlando/Lake Buena Vista	★★★★	2	86	$$$
Disney's Animal Kingdom Villas (Jambo House, studios)	★★★★	WDW	85	$ x 13
Disney's Port Orleans Resort–French Quarter	★★★★	WDW	85	$- x 8
Walt Disney World Dolphin	★★★★	WDW	85	$ x 6
Universal's Endless Summer Resort: Dockside Inn & Suites	★★★★	4	85	$$$+
B Resort & Spa	★★★★	WDW	85	$$$+
Disney's Port Orleans Resort–Riverside	★★★★	WDW	84	$- x 8
Star Wars: Galactic Starcruiser	★★★★	WDW	83	$ x 80
Boulder Ridge Villas at Disney's Wilderness Lodge (studios)	★★★★	WDW	83	$- x 12
Westgate Vacation Villas Resort	★★★★	3	83	$$$
Polynesian Isles Resort (Diamond Resorts)	★★★★	3	88	$$$$+
Parkway International Resort	★★★½	3	88	$$$$-
Disney's Art of Animation Resort	★★★½	WDW	82	$ x 6
Universal's Cabana Bay Beach Resort	★★★½	4	82	$$$$+
Meliá Orlando Celebration	★★★½	3	82	$$$+
Star Island Resort & Club	★★★½	3	82	$$$-
Parc Corniche Resort	★★★½	1	80	$- x 10
Gaylord Palms Resort & Convention Center	★★★½	3	80	$+ x 8
Rosen Shingle Creek	★★★½	1	80	$ x 7
Drury Inn & Suites Near Universal Orlando	★★★½	1	80	$- x 7
The Berkley Orlando	★★★½	3	80	$$$$$-
SpringHill Suites Orlando Lake Buena Vista South	★★★½	3	80	$$$$

HOW THE HOTELS COMPARE *(continued)*

HOTEL	OVERALL QUALITY	LODGING AREA	ROOM QUALITY	COST ($ = $50)
Wyndham Garden Lake Buena Vista	★★★½	WDW	80	$$$$–
Holiday Inn & Suites Across from Universal Orlando	★★★½	4	80	$$$
DoubleTree by Hilton at the Entrance to Universal Orlando	★★★½	4	80	$$$
Hilton Orlando Lake Buena Vista–Disney Springs Area	★★★½	WDW	79	$$$$$
Liki Tiki Village	★★★½	3	77	$$$$$
Rosen Inn at Pointe Orlando	★★★½	1	77	$$$$–
Fairfield Inn & Suites Orlando Near Universal	★★★½	4	77	$$$+
Hawthorn Suites by Wyndham Lake Buena Vista	★★★½	2	77	$$$+
Wyndham Orlando Resort International Drive	★★★½	1	77	$$$+
Embassy Suites by Hilton Orlando Lake Buena Vista Resort	★★★½	2	77	$$$
Caribe Royale Orlando	★★★	2	67	$$$$$
Rosen Centre Hotel	★★★	1	67	$$$$+
Ramada by Wyndham Kissimmee Gateway	★★½	3	57	$$+

Hotels not listed did not have enough surveys to rate.

HOTEL INFORMATION TABLE

Aloft Orlando Lake Buena Vista
7950 Palm Pkwy.
Orlando, FL 32836
☎ 407-778-7600
tinyurl.com/aloftorlandofl

LOCATION	2
ROOM QUALITY	–
COST ($=$50)	$$$
DAILY RESORT FEE	None
COMMUTING TIMES TO PARKS *(in minutes):*	
MAGIC KINGDOM	15:00
EPCOT	14:00
ANIMAL KINGDOM	19:00
DHS	12:00

B Resort & Spa ★★★★
1905 Hotel Plaza Blvd.
Lake Buena Vista, FL 32830
☎ 407-828-2828
bresortlbv.com

LOCATION	WDW
ROOM QUALITY	85
COST ($=$50)	$$$+
DAILY RESORT FEE	$34
COMMUTING TIMES TO PARKS *(in minutes):*	
MAGIC KINGDOM	15:45
EPCOT	11:00
ANIMAL KINGDOM	15:00
DHS	12:45

Bay Lake Tower at Disney's Contemporary Resort
(studios) ★★★★½
4600 N. World Dr.
Lake Buena Vista, FL 32830
☎ 407-824-1000
tinyurl.com/baylaketower

LOCATION	WDW
ROOM QUALITY	90
COST ($=$50)	$+ x 16
DAILY RESORT FEE	None
COMMUTING TIMES TO PARKS *(in minutes):*	
MAGIC KINGDOM	on monorail
EPCOT	11:00
ANIMAL KINGDOM	17:15
DHS	14:15

The Cabins at Disney's Fort Wilderness Resort ★★★★
4510 N. Fort Wilderness Trl.
Lake Buena Vista, FL 32830
☎ 407-824-2900
tinyurl.com/ftwilderness

LOCATION	WDW
ROOM QUALITY	88
COST ($=$50)	$- x 13
DAILY RESORT FEE	None
COMMUTING TIMES TO PARKS *(in minutes):*	
MAGIC KINGDOM	13:15
EPCOT	08:30
ANIMAL KINGDOM	20:00
DHS	14:00

Caribe Royale Orlando ★★★
8101 World Center Dr.
Orlando, FL 32821
☎ 407-238-8000
cariberoyale.com

LOCATION	2
ROOM QUALITY	67
COST ($=$50)	$$$$$
DAILY RESORT FEE	$30
COMMUTING TIMES TO PARKS *(in minutes):*	
MAGIC KINGDOM	11:00
EPCOT	10:00
ANIMAL KINGDOM	17:00
DHS	09:00

Clarion Inn & Suites Across from Universal
5829 Grand National Dr.
Orlando, FL 32819
☎ 407-351-3800
tinyurl.com/clarionuniversal

LOCATION	4
ROOM QUALITY	–
COST ($=$50)	$$$$-
DAILY RESORT FEE	None
COMMUTING TIMES TO PARKS *(in minutes):*	
MAGIC KINGDOM	20:00
EPCOT	15:00
ANIMAL KINGDOM	18:00
DHS	17:00

Comfort Suites Near Universal Orlando Resort
5617 Major Blvd.
Orlando, FL 32819
☎ 407-363-1967
tinyurl.com/csuniversal

LOCATION	4
ROOM QUALITY	–
COST ($=$50)	$$$
DAILY RESORT FEE	None
COMMUTING TIMES TO PARKS *(in minutes):*	
MAGIC KINGDOM	17:00
EPCOT	16:00
ANIMAL KINGDOM	17:00
DHS	13:00

Copper Creek Villas & Cabins at Disney's Wilderness Lodge
(studios) ★★★★
901 Timberline Dr.
Lake Buena Vista, FL 32830
☎ 407-824-3200
tinyurl.com/wdwcoppercreek

LOCATION	WDW
ROOM QUALITY	88
COST ($=$50)	$- x 14
DAILY RESORT FEE	None
COMMUTING TIMES TO PARKS *(in minutes):*	
MAGIC KINGDOM	17:45
EPCOT	13:15
ANIMAL KINGDOM	16:15
DHS	15:15

Courtyard Orlando Lake Buena Vista at Vista Centre ★★★★
8501 Palm Pkwy.
Orlando, FL 32836
☎ 407-239-6900
tinyurl.com/courtyardlbv

LOCATION	2
ROOM QUALITY	87
COST ($=$50)	$$$-
DAILY RESORT FEE	$10
COMMUTING TIMES TO PARKS *(in minutes):*	
MAGIC KINGDOM	by ferry
EPCOT	10:00
ANIMAL KINGDOM	15:15
DHS	13:30

Disney's All-Star Music Resort ★★★★
1801 W. Buena Vista Dr.
Lake Buena Vista, FL 32830
☎ 407-939-6000
tinyurl.com/allstarmusicresort

LOCATION	WDW
ROOM QUALITY	87
COST ($=$50)	$$$$+
DAILY RESORT FEE	None
COMMUTING TIMES TO PARKS *(in minutes):*	
MAGIC KINGDOM	19:00
EPCOT	04:00
ANIMAL KINGDOM	10:00
DHS	09:00

Disney's All-Star Sports Resort ★★★★
1701 W. Buena Vista Dr.
Lake Buena Vista, FL 32830
☎ 407-939-5000
tinyurl.com/allstarsports

LOCATION	WDW
ROOM QUALITY	87
COST ($=$50)	$$$$+
DAILY RESORT FEE	None
COMMUTING TIMES TO PARKS *(in minutes):*	
MAGIC KINGDOM	19:00
EPCOT	04:00
ANIMAL KINGDOM	10:00
DHS	09:00

Disney's Animal Kingdom Lodge ★★★★
2901 W. Osceola Pkwy.
Lake Buena Vista, FL 32830
☎ 407-938-3000
tinyurl.com/aklodge

LOCATION	WDW
ROOM QUALITY	88
COST ($=$50)	$ x 13
DAILY RESORT FEE	None
COMMUTING TIMES TO PARKS *(in minutes):*	
MAGIC KINGDOM	06:15
EPCOT	05:45
ANIMAL KINGDOM	04:15
DHS	05:15

*Irlo Bronson Memorial Highway

The Berkley Orlando ★★★½
3545 W. US 192*
Kissimmee, FL 34747
☎ 321-329-7000 or
877-686-5259
theberkleyorlando.com

LOCATION	3
ROOM QUALITY	80
COST ($=$50)	$$$$$
DAILY RESORT FEE	None

COMMUTING TIMES TO PARKS
(in minutes):

MAGIC KINGDOM	20:00
EPCOT	21:00
ANIMAL KINGDOM	16:00
DHS	16:00

Best Western Plus Universal Inn ★★★★½
5618 Vineland Rd.
Orlando, FL 32819
☎ 407-226-9119
tinyurl.com/bwuniversal

LOCATION	4
ROOM QUALITY	93
COST ($=$50)	$$$
DAILY RESORT FEE	None

COMMUTING TIMES TO PARKS
(in minutes):

MAGIC KINGDOM	17:30
EPCOT	13:00
ANIMAL KINGDOM	16:00
DHS	15:30

Boulder Ridge Villas at Disney's Wilderness Lodge (studios) ★★★★
901 Timberline Dr.
Lake Buena Vista, FL 32830
☎ 407-824-3200
tinyurl.com/wlvillas

LOCATION	WDW
ROOM QUALITY	83
COST ($=$50)	$~ x 14
DAILY RESORT FEE	None

COMMUTING TIMES TO PARKS
(in minutes):

MAGIC KINGDOM	by ferry
EPCOT	10:00
ANIMAL KINGDOM	15:15
DHS	13:30

Club Wyndham Bonnet Creek
9560 Via Encinas
Orlando, FL 32830
☎ 407-238-3500
wyndhambonnetcreek.com

LOCATION	WDW
ROOM QUALITY	–
COST ($=$50)	$ x 7
DAILY RESORT FEE	$12

COMMUTING TIMES TO PARKS
(in minutes):

MAGIC KINGDOM	10:00
EPCOT	09:15
ANIMAL KINGDOM	07:00
DHS	09:00

Club Wyndham Cypress Palms
5324 Fairfield Lake Dr.
Kissimmee, FL 34746
☎ 407-397-1600
cypresspalms.com

LOCATION	3
ROOM QUALITY	–
COST ($=$50)	$$+
DAILY RESORT FEE	$28

COMMUTING TIMES TO PARKS
(in minutes):

MAGIC KINGDOM	08:00
EPCOT	06:00
ANIMAL KINGDOM	07:15
DHS	04:15

Comfort Suites Maingate East ★★★★
2775 Florida Plaza Blvd.
Kissimmee, FL 34746
☎ 407-397-7848
comfortsuitesfl.com

LOCATION	3
ROOM QUALITY	87
COST ($=$50)	$$$
DAILY RESORT FEE	None

COMMUTING TIMES TO PARKS
(in minutes):

MAGIC KINGDOM	15:15
EPCOT	15:00
ANIMAL KINGDOM	14:45
DHS	14:45

Cypress Pointe Resort ★★★★
8651 Treasure Cay Ln.
Orlando, FL 32836
☎ 407-597-2700
cypresspointe.net

LOCATION	2
ROOM QUALITY	88
COST ($=$50)	$$$+
DAILY RESORT FEE	$20

COMMUTING TIMES TO PARKS
(in minutes):

MAGIC KINGDOM	13:15
EPCOT	08:30
ANIMAL KINGDOM	11:30
DHS	11:00

Delta Hotels Lake Buena Vista (Marriott) ★★★★½
12490 S. Apopka-Vineland Rd.
Orlando, FL 32836
☎ 407-387-9999
tinyurl.com/deltaorlando

LOCATION	2
ROOM QUALITY	90
COST ($=$50)	$$$$
DAILY RESORT FEE	None

COMMUTING TIMES TO PARKS
(in minutes):

MAGIC KINGDOM	12:00
EPCOT	14:00
ANIMAL KINGDOM	13:00
DHS	12:00

Disney's All-Star Movies Resort ★★★★
1901 W. Buena Vista Dr.
Lake Buena Vista, FL 32830
☎ 407-939-7000
tinyurl.com/allstarmovies

LOCATION	WDW
ROOM QUALITY	87
COST ($=$50)	$$$$+
DAILY RESORT FEE	None

COMMUTING TIMES TO PARKS
(in minutes):

MAGIC KINGDOM	19:00
EPCOT	04:00
ANIMAL KINGDOM	10:00
DHS	09:00

Disney's Animal Kingdom Villas (Jambo House, studios) ★★★★
2901 W. Osceola Pkwy.
Lake Buena Vista, FL 32830
☎ 407-938-3000
tinyurl.com/akjambo

LOCATION	WDW
ROOM QUALITY	85
COST ($=$50)	$ x 13
DAILY RESORT FEE	None

COMMUTING TIMES TO PARKS
(in minutes):

MAGIC KINGDOM	08:15
EPCOT	06:15
ANIMAL KINGDOM	02:15
DHS	06:00

Disney's Animal Kingdom Villas (Kidani Village, studios) ★★★★
3701 W. Osceola Pkwy.
Bay Lake, FL 32830
☎ 407-938-7400
tinyurl.com/akkidani

LOCATION	WDW
ROOM QUALITY	89
COST ($=$50)	$ x 13
DAILY RESORT FEE	None

COMMUTING TIMES TO PARKS
(in minutes):

MAGIC KINGDOM	08:15
EPCOT	06:15
ANIMAL KINGDOM	02:15
DHS	06:00

Disney's Art of Animation Resort ★★★½
1850 Animation Way
Lake Buena Vista, FL 32830
☎ 407-938-7000
tinyurl.com/artofanimationresort

LOCATION	WDW
ROOM QUALITY	82
COST ($=$50)	$ x 6
DAILY RESORT FEE	None

COMMUTING TIMES TO PARKS
(in minutes):

MAGIC KINGDOM	08:15
EPCOT	06:15
ANIMAL KINGDOM	02:15
DHS	06:00

Hotels with no star rating did not have enough surveys to rate.

HOTEL INFORMATION TABLE *(continued)*

Disney's Beach Club Resort
★★★★
1800 EPCOT Resorts Blvd.
Lake Buena Vista, FL 32830
☎ 407-934-8000
tinyurl.com/disneybeachclub

LOCATION	WDW
ROOM QUALITY	87
COST ($=$50)	$ x 15
DAILY RESORT FEE	None

COMMUTING TIMES TO PARKS
(in minutes):

MAGIC KINGDOM	12:00
EPCOT	10:00
ANIMAL KINGDOM	12:00
DHS	03:00

Disney's Beach Club Villas *(studios)*
★★★★
1800 EPCOT Resorts Blvd.
Lake Buena Vista, FL 32830
☎ 407-934-8000
tinyurl.com/beachclubvillas

LOCATION	WDW
ROOM QUALITY	86
COST ($=$50)	$ x 15
DAILY RESORT FEE	None

COMMUTING TIMES TO PARKS
(in minutes):

MAGIC KINGDOM	07:15
EPCOT	05:15
ANIMAL KINGDOM	06:45
DHS	04:00

Disney's BoardWalk Inn ★★★★½
2101 N. EPCOT Resorts Blvd.
Lake Buena Vista, FL 32830
☎ 407-939-6200
tinyurl.com/boardwalkinn

LOCATION	WDW
ROOM QUALITY	90
COST ($=$50)	$+ x 16
DAILY RESORT FEE	None

COMMUTING TIMES TO PARKS
(in minutes):

MAGIC KINGDOM	07:15
EPCOT	05:15
ANIMAL KINGDOM	06:45
DHS	04:00

Disney's Coronado Springs Resort ★★★★½
1000 W. Buena Vista Dr.
Lake Buena Vista, FL 32830
☎ 407-939-1000
tinyurl.com/coronadosprings

LOCATION	WDW
ROOM QUALITY	90
COST ($=$50)	$+ x 7
DAILY RESORT FEE	None

COMMUTING TIMES TO PARKS
(in minutes):

MAGIC KINGDOM	on monorail
EPCOT	11:00
ANIMAL KINGDOM	17:15
DHS	14:15

Disney's Grand Floridian Resort & Spa ★★★★½
4401 Floridian Way
Lake Buena Vista, FL 32830
☎ 407-824-3000
tinyurl.com/grandflresort

LOCATION	WDW
ROOM QUALITY	90
COST ($=$50)	$- x 21
DAILY RESORT FEE	None

COMMUTING TIMES TO PARKS
(in minutes):

MAGIC KINGDOM	on monorail
EPCOT	04:45
ANIMAL KINGDOM	11:45
DHS	06:45

Disney's Old Key West Resort
★★★★½
1510 North Cove Rd.
Lake Buena Vista, FL 32830
☎ 407-827-7700
tinyurl.com/oldkeywest

LOCATION	WDW
ROOM QUALITY	91
COST ($=$50)	$ x 12
DAILY RESORT FEE	None

COMMUTING TIMES TO PARKS
(in minutes):

MAGIC KINGDOM	10:45
EPCOT	06:00
ANIMAL KINGDOM	14:30
DHS	10:30

Disney's Port Orleans Resort–French Quarter ★★★★
2201 Orleans Dr.
Lake Buena Vista, FL 32830
☎ 407-934-5000
tinyurl.com/portorleansfq

LOCATION	WDW
ROOM QUALITY	85
COST ($=$50)	$- x 8
DAILY RESORT FEE	None

COMMUTING TIMES TO PARKS
(in minutes):

MAGIC KINGDOM	12:00
EPCOT	08:00
ANIMAL KINGDOM	16:15
DHS	12:30

Disney's Port Orleans Resort–Riverside ★★★★
1251 Riverside Dr.
Lake Buena Vista, FL 32830
☎ 407-934-6000
tinyurl.com/portorleansriverside

LOCATION	WDW
ROOM QUALITY	84
COST ($=$50)	$- x 8
DAILY RESORT FEE	None

COMMUTING TIMES TO PARKS
(in minutes):

MAGIC KINGDOM	12:00
EPCOT	08:00
ANIMAL KINGDOM	16:15
DHS	12:30

Disney's Riviera Resort ★★★★½
1080 Esplanade Ave.
Lake Buena Vista, FL 32830
☎ 407-828-7030
tinyurl.com/disneyriviera

LOCATION	WDW
ROOM QUALITY	93
COST ($=$50)	$- x 13
DAILY RESORT FEE	None

COMMUTING TIMES TO PARKS
(in minutes):

MAGIC KINGDOM	08:00
EPCOT	06:00
ANIMAL KINGDOM	07:15
DHS	04:15

DoubleTree by Hilton at the Entrance to Universal Orlando
★★★½
5780 Major Blvd.
Orlando, FL 32819
☎ 407-351-1000
doubletreeorlando.com

LOCATION	4
ROOM QUALITY	80
COST ($=$50)	$$$
DAILY RESORT FEE	None

COMMUTING TIMES TO PARKS
(in minutes):

MAGIC KINGDOM	19:00
EPCOT	14:15
ANIMAL KINGDOM	17:15
DHS	16:45

DoubleTree Suites by Hilton Orlando–Disney Springs Area
★★★★
2305 Hotel Plaza Blvd.
Lake Buena Vista, FL 32830
☎ 407-934-1000
doubletreeguestsuites.com

LOCATION	WDW
ROOM QUALITY	86
COST ($=$50)	$$$$
DAILY RESORT FEE	$23

COMMUTING TIMES TO PARKS
(in minutes):

MAGIC KINGDOM	13:00
EPCOT	08:30
ANIMAL KINGDOM	12:30
DHS	10:00

Drury Inn & Suites Near Universal Orlando ★★★½
7301 W. Sand Lake Rd.
Orlando, FL 32819
☎ 407-354-1101
tinyurl.com/druryinnorlando

LOCATION	1
ROOM QUALITY	80
COST ($=$50)	$- x 7
DAILY RESORT FEE	None

COMMUTING TIMES TO PARKS
(in minutes):

MAGIC KINGDOM	18:30
EPCOT	15:30
ANIMAL KINGDOM	20:15
DHS	18:00

*Irlo Bronson Memorial Highway

Disney's BoardWalk Villas ★ ★ ★ ★
2101 N. EPCOT Resorts Blvd.
Lake Buena Vista, FL 32830
☎ 407-939-6200
tinyurl.com/boardwalkvillas

LOCATION	WDW
ROOM QUALITY	89
COST ($=$50)	$+ x 16
DAILY RESORT FEE	None
COMMUTING TIMES TO PARKS *(in minutes):*	
MAGIC KINGDOM	07:15
EPCOT	05:15
ANIMAL KINGDOM	06:45
DHS	04:00

Disney's Caribbean Beach Resort ★ ★ ★ ★
1114 Cayman Way
Lake Buena Vista, FL 32830
☎ 407-934-3400
tinyurl.com/caribbeanbeachresort

LOCATION	WDW
ROOM QUALITY	88
COST ($=$50)	$- x 8
DAILY RESORT FEE	None
COMMUTING TIMES TO PARKS *(in minutes):*	
MAGIC KINGDOM	07:15
EPCOT	05:30
ANIMAL KINGDOM	07:00
DHS	03:00

Disney's Contemporary Resort ★ ★ ★ ★
4600 N. World Dr.
Lake Buena Vista, FL 32830
☎ 407-824-1000
tinyurl.com/contemporarywdw

LOCATION	WDW
ROOM QUALITY	88
COST ($=$50)	$+ x 15
DAILY RESORT FEE	None
COMMUTING TIMES TO PARKS *(in minutes):*	
MAGIC KINGDOM	08:00
EPCOT	06:00
ANIMAL KINGDOM	07:15
DHS	04:15

Disney's Polynesian Village Resort ★ ★ ★ ★ ½
1600 Seven Seas Dr.
Lake Buena Vista, FL 32830
☎ 407-824-2000
tinyurl.com/wdwpolyvillage

LOCATION	WDW
ROOM QUALITY	90
COST ($=$50)	$- x 19
DAILY RESORT FEE	None
COMMUTING TIMES TO PARKS *(in minutes):*	
MAGIC KINGDOM	on monorail
EPCOT	08:00
ANIMAL KINGDOM	16:15
DHS	12:30

Disney's Polynesian Villas & Bungalows *(studios)* ★ ★ ★ ★ ½
1600 Seven Seas Dr.
Lake Buena Vista, FL 32830
☎ 407-824-2000
tinyurl.com/wdwpolyvillage

LOCATION	WDW
ROOM QUALITY	91
COST ($=$50)	$- x 19
DAILY RESORT FEE	None
COMMUTING TIMES TO PARKS *(in minutes):*	
MAGIC KINGDOM	on monorail
EPCOT	08:00
ANIMAL KINGDOM	16:15
DHS	12:30

Disney's Pop Century Resort ★ ★ ★ ★
1050 Century Dr.
Lake Buena Vista, FL 32830
☎ 407-938-4000
tinyurl.com/popcenturywdw

LOCATION	WDW
ROOM QUALITY	87
COST ($=$50)	$- x 6
DAILY RESORT FEE	None
COMMUTING TIMES TO PARKS *(in minutes):*	
MAGIC KINGDOM	08:30
EPCOT	06:30
ANIMAL KINGDOM	06:15
DHS	05:00

Disney's Saratoga Springs Resort & Spa ★ ★ ★ ½
1960 Broadway
Lake Buena Vista, FL 32830
☎ 407-827-1100
tinyurl.com/saratogawdw

LOCATION	WDW
ROOM QUALITY	92
COST ($=$50)	$ x 12
DAILY RESORT FEE	None
COMMUTING TIMES TO PARKS *(in minutes):*	
MAGIC KINGDOM	14:45
EPCOT	08:45
ANIMAL KINGDOM	18:15
DHS	14:30

Disney's Wilderness Lodge ★ ★ ★ ★
901 Timberline Dr.
Lake Buena Vista, FL 32830
☎ 407-824-3200
tinyurl.com/wildernesslodge

LOCATION	WDW
ROOM QUALITY	88
COST ($=$50)	$- x 14
DAILY RESORT FEE	None
COMMUTING TIMES TO PARKS *(in minutes):*	
MAGIC KINGDOM	by ferry
EPCOT	10:00
ANIMAL KINGDOM	15:15
DHS	13:30

Disney's Yacht Club Resort ★ ★ ★ ★
1700 EPCOT Resorts Blvd.
Lake Buena Vista, FL 32830
☎ 407-934-7000
tinyurl.com/yachtclubwdw

LOCATION	WDW
ROOM QUALITY	88
COST ($=$50)	$ x 15
DAILY RESORT FEE	None
COMMUTING TIMES TO PARKS *(in minutes):*	
MAGIC KINGDOM	07:15
EPCOT	05:15
ANIMAL KINGDOM	06:45
DHS	04:00

Drury Plaza Hotel Orlando
2000 Hotel Plaza Blvd.
Lake Buena Vista, FL 32830
☎ 407-560-6111
druryplazahotelorlando.com

LOCATION	WDW
ROOM QUALITY	—
COST ($=$50)	$$$$$+
DAILY RESORT FEE	None
COMMUTING TIMES TO PARKS *(in minutes):*	
MAGIC KINGDOM	12:45
EPCOT	08:00
ANIMAL KINGDOM	11:00
DHS	10:30

Embassy Suites by Hilton Orlando Lake Buena Vista Resort ★ ★ ★ ½
8100 Lake St.
Orlando, FL 32836
☎ 407-239-1144
tinyurl.com/embassylbv

LOCATION	2
ROOM QUALITY	77
COST ($=$50)	$$$
DAILY RESORT FEE	$25
COMMUTING TIMES TO PARKS *(in minutes):*	
MAGIC KINGDOM	17:30
EPCOT	12:45
ANIMAL KINGDOM	15:45
DHS	15:30

Extended Stay America Convention Center/Westwood ★ ★ ★ ★
6443 Westwood Blvd.
Orlando, FL 32821
☎ 407-351-1982
tinyurl.com/extendedstaywestwood

LOCATION	1
ROOM QUALITY	87
COST ($=$50)	$$$
DAILY RESORT FEE	None
COMMUTING TIMES TO PARKS *(in minutes):*	
MAGIC KINGDOM	18:00
EPCOT	11:00
ANIMAL KINGDOM	14:00
DHS	06:00

Hotels with no star rating did not have enough surveys to rate.

HOTEL INFORMATION TABLE *(continued)*

Fairfield Inn & Suites Orlando at SeaWorld
10815 International Dr.
Orlando, FL 32821
☎ 407-354-1139
tinyurl.com/fairfieldsw

LOCATION	1
ROOM QUALITY	–
COST ($=$50)	$$$
DAILY RESORT FEE	None

COMMUTING TIMES TO PARKS *(in minutes):*

MAGIC KINGDOM	17:30
EPCOT	12:45
ANIMAL KINGDOM	15:45
DHS	15:15

Fairfield Inn & Suites Orlando Kissimmee/Celebration
6073 US 192*
Kissimmee, FL 34747
☎ 407-390-1532
tinyurl.com/fairfieldinnkissimmee

LOCATION	3
ROOM QUALITY	–
COST ($=$50)	$$$-
DAILY RESORT FEE	None

COMMUTING TIMES TO PARKS *(in minutes):*

MAGIC KINGDOM	18:00
EPCOT	15:00
ANIMAL KINGDOM	17:00
DHS	15:00

Fairfield Inn & Suites Orlando Near Universal ★★★½
5614 Vineland Rd.
Orlando, FL 32819
☎ 407-581-5600
tinyurl.com/fairfielduniversal

LOCATION	4
ROOM QUALITY	77
COST ($=$50)	$$$+
DAILY RESORT FEE	None

COMMUTING TIMES TO PARKS *(in minutes):*

MAGIC KINGDOM	19:00
EPCOT	18:00
ANIMAL KINGDOM	22:00
DHS	18:00

Grand Beach *(Diamond Resorts)*
8317 Lake Bryan Beach Blvd.
Orlando, FL 32821
☎ 407-238-2500
diamondresortsandhotels.com /Resorts/Grand-Beach

LOCATION	2
ROOM QUALITY	–
COST ($=$50)	$ x 7
DAILY RESORT FEE	$17

COMMUTING TIMES TO PARKS *(in minutes):*

MAGIC KINGDOM	14:00
EPCOT	13:00
ANIMAL KINGDOM	16:00
DHS	11:00

Hampton Inn Orlando/ Lake Buena Vista ★★★★
8150 Palm Pkwy.
Orlando, FL 32836
☎ 407-465-8150
tinyurl.com/hamptoninnlbv

LOCATION	2
ROOM QUALITY	86
COST ($=$50)	$$$
DAILY RESORT FEE	None

COMMUTING TIMES TO PARKS *(in minutes):*

MAGIC KINGDOM	12:45
EPCOT	08:00
ANIMAL KINGDOM	11:00
DHS	10:30

Hampton Inn Universal
5621 Windhover Dr.
Orlando, FL 32819
☎ 407-351-6716
tinyurl.com/hamptonuniversal

LOCATION	4
ROOM QUALITY	–
COST ($=$50)	$+ x 6
DAILY RESORT FEE	None

COMMUTING TIMES TO PARKS *(in minutes):*

MAGIC KINGDOM	19:00
EPCOT	14:15
ANIMAL KINGDOM	17:15
DHS	16:45

Hilton Grand Vacations Club SeaWorld Orlando ★★★★★
6924 Grand Vacations Way
Orlando, FL 32821
☎ 407-239-0100
tinyurl.com/seaworldhgv

LOCATION	1
ROOM QUALITY	97
COST ($=$50)	$$$+
DAILY RESORT FEE	$25

COMMUTING TIMES TO PARKS *(in minutes):*

MAGIC KINGDOM	17:00
EPCOT	12:30
ANIMAL KINGDOM	16:30
DHS	15:30

Hilton Grand Vacations Club Tuscany Village ★★★★½
8122 Arrezzo Way
Orlando, FL 32821
☎ 407-465-2600
tinyurl.com/hgvtuscany

LOCATION	1
ROOM QUALITY	90
COST ($=$50)	$$$+
DAILY RESORT FEE	$25

COMMUTING TIMES TO PARKS *(in minutes):*

MAGIC KINGDOM	16:15
EPCOT	14:00
ANIMAL KINGDOM	17:00
DHS	16:30

Hilton Orlando ★★★★
6001 Destination Pkwy.
Orlando, FL 32819
☎ 407-313-4300
thehiltonorlando.com

LOCATION	1
ROOM QUALITY	87
COST ($=$50)	$$$$$
DAILY RESORT FEE	$40

COMMUTING TIMES TO PARKS *(in minutes):*

MAGIC KINGDOM	24:00
EPCOT	17:00
ANIMAL KINGDOM	16:00
DHS	14:00

Holiday Inn Club Vacations at Orange Lake Resort
8505 W. US 192*
Kissimmee, FL 34747
☎ 407-477-7025
tinyurl.com/holidayinnorangelake

LOCATION	3
ROOM QUALITY	–
COST ($=$50)	$$$
DAILY RESORT FEE	$20

COMMUTING TIMES TO PARKS *(in minutes):*

MAGIC KINGDOM	19:00
EPCOT	14:15
ANIMAL KINGDOM	17:15
DHS	16:45

Holiday Inn Express & Suites Orlando at SeaWorld
10771 International Dr.
Orlando, FL 32821
☎ 407-996-4100
tinyurl.com/holidaysw

LOCATION	1
ROOM QUALITY	–
COST ($=$50)	$ x 6
DAILY RESORT FEE	None

COMMUTING TIMES TO PARKS *(in minutes):*

MAGIC KINGDOM	08:45
EPCOT	08:30
ANIMAL KINGDOM	05:30
DHS	08:00

Holiday Inn Express & Suites/ South Lake Buena Vista ★★★★½
5001 Calypso Cay Way
Kissimmee, FL 34746
☎ 407-997-1400
hieorlando.com

LOCATION	2
ROOM QUALITY	90
COST ($=$50)	$$$
DAILY RESORT FEE	$25

COMMUTING TIMES TO PARKS *(in minutes):*

MAGIC KINGDOM	18:00
EPCOT	15:00
ANIMAL KINGDOM	17:00
DHS	15:00

*Irlo Bronson Memorial Highway

Four Seasons Resort Orlando at Walt Disney World Resort ★★★★★
10100 Dream Tree Blvd.
Lake Buena Vista, FL 32836
☎ 407-313-7777
fourseasons.com/orlando

LOCATION	WDW
ROOM QUALITY	100
COST ($=$50)	$ x 28
DAILY RESORT FEE	None

COMMUTING TIMES TO PARKS
(in minutes):

MAGIC KINGDOM	09:00
EPCOT	12:00
ANIMAL KINGDOM	15:00
DHS	08:00

Hard Rock Hotel Orlando ★★★★
5800 Universal Blvd.
Orlando, FL 32819
☎ 407-503-2000
hardrockhotels.com/orlando

LOCATION	4
ROOM QUALITY	87
COST ($=$50)	$ x 13
DAILY RESORT FEE	None

COMMUTING TIMES TO PARKS
(in minutes):

MAGIC KINGDOM	21:45
EPCOT	17:00
ANIMAL KINGDOM	20:00
DHS	19:30

Hilton Orlando Buena Vista Palace ★★★★
1900 E. Buena Vista Dr.
Lake Buena Vista, FL 32830
☎ 407-827-2727
buenavistapalace.com

LOCATION	WDW
ROOM QUALITY	87
COST ($=$50)	$ x 6
DAILY RESORT FEE	$39

COMMUTING TIMES TO PARKS
(in minutes):

MAGIC KINGDOM	08:00
EPCOT	06:00
ANIMAL KINGDOM	07:15
DHS	04:15

Holiday Inn Orlando SW–Celebration Area ★★★★★
5711 W. US 192*
Kissimmee, FL 34746
☎ 407-396-4222
hicelebration.com

LOCATION	3
ROOM QUALITY	97
COST ($=$50)	$$$-
DAILY RESORT FEE	$25

COMMUTING TIMES TO PARKS
(in minutes):

MAGIC KINGDOM	22:00
EPCOT	15:00
ANIMAL KINGDOM	16:00
DHS	10:00

Galleria Palms Hotel ★★★★½
3000 Maingate Ln.
Kissimmee, FL 34747
☎ 407-396-6300
gphkissimmee.com

LOCATION	3
ROOM QUALITY	92
COST ($=$50)	$$$+
DAILY RESORT FEE	$10

COMMUTING TIMES TO PARKS
(in minutes):

MAGIC KINGDOM	08:15
EPCOT	07:30
ANIMAL KINGDOM	05:15
DHS	07:15

Hawthorn Suites by Wyndham Lake Buena Vista ★★★½
8303 Palm Pkwy.
Orlando, FL 32836
☎ 407-597-5000
hawthornlakebuenavista.com

LOCATION	2
ROOM QUALITY	77
COST ($=$50)	$$$+
DAILY RESORT FEE	None

COMMUTING TIMES TO PARKS
(in minutes):

MAGIC KINGDOM	20:15
EPCOT	15:30
ANIMAL KINGDOM	18:30
DHS	18:00

Hilton Orlando Lake Buena Vista–Disney Springs Area ★★★½
1751 Hotel Plaza Blvd.
Lake Buena Vista, FL 32830
☎ 407-827-4000
hilton-wdwv.com

LOCATION	WDW
ROOM QUALITY	79
COST ($=$50)	$$$$$
DAILY RESORT FEE	$35

COMMUTING TIMES TO PARKS
(in minutes):

MAGIC KINGDOM	16:00
EPCOT	11:15
ANIMAL KINGDOM	15:15
DHS	13:00

Holiday Inn Orlando–Disney Springs Resort Area ★★★★½
1805 Hotel Plaza Blvd.
Lake Buena Vista, FL 32830
☎ 407-828-8888
hiorlando.com

LOCATION	WDW
ROOM QUALITY	90
COST ($=$50)	$$$$-
DAILY RESORT FEE	$30

COMMUTING TIMES TO PARKS
(in minutes):

MAGIC KINGDOM	12:15
EPCOT	12:00
ANIMAL KINGDOM	10:15
DHS	11:30

Gaylord Palms Resort & Convention Center ★★★½
6000 W. Osceola Pkwy.
Kissimmee, FL 34746
☎ 407-586-0000
gaylordpalms.com

LOCATION	3
ROOM QUALITY	80
COST ($=$50)	$+ x 8
DAILY RESORT FEE	$38

COMMUTING TIMES TO PARKS
(in minutes):

MAGIC KINGDOM	09:00
EPCOT	08:45
ANIMAL KINGDOM	07:00
DHS	08:15

High Point World Resort
2951 High Point Blvd.
Orlando, FL 34747
☎ 407-396-9600
highpointeresortorlando.com

LOCATION	3
ROOM QUALITY	–
COST ($=$50)	$$$
DAILY RESORT FEE	None

COMMUTING TIMES TO PARKS
(in minutes):

MAGIC KINGDOM	21:00
EPCOT	11:00
ANIMAL KINGDOM	08:00
DHS	09:00

Holiday Inn & Suites Across from Universal Orlando ★★★½
5916 Caravan Ct.
Orlando, FL 32819
☎ 407-351-3333
hiuniversal.com

LOCATION	4
ROOM QUALITY	80
COST ($=$50)	$$$
DAILY RESORT FEE	None

COMMUTING TIMES TO PARKS
(in minutes):

MAGIC KINGDOM	15:15
EPCOT	10:30
ANIMAL KINGDOM	14:30
DHS	12:15

Holiday Inn Resort Orlando–Lake Buena Vista ★★★★½
13351 FL 535
Orlando, FL 32821
☎ 407-239-4500
hiresortlbv.com

LOCATION	2
ROOM QUALITY	90
COST ($=$50)	$$+
DAILY RESORT FEE	$30

COMMUTING TIMES TO PARKS
(in minutes):

MAGIC KINGDOM	15:30
EPCOT	10:45
ANIMAL KINGDOM	12:30
DHS	14:45

Hotels with no star rating did not have enough surveys to rate.

HOTEL INFORMATION TABLE (continued)

Home2Suites by Hilton Orlando at Flamingo Crossings Town Center
341 Flagler Ave.
Winter Garden, FL 34787
☎ 407-993-3999
tinyurl.com/fc-home2suites

LOCATION	2
ROOM QUALITY	–
COST ($=$50)	$$$$$-
DAILY RESORT FEE	None

COMMUTING TIMES TO PARKS (in minutes):

MAGIC KINGDOM	10:45
EPCOT	06:00
ANIMAL KINGDOM	09:00
DHS	08:30

Homewood Suites by Hilton at Flamingo Crossings ★★★★½
411 Flagler Ave.
Winter Garden, FL 34787
☎ 407-993-3011
tinyurl.com/hwdsuitesflamingo

LOCATION	2
ROOM QUALITY	93
COST ($=$50)	$$$$$-
DAILY RESORT FEE	None

COMMUTING TIMES TO PARKS (in minutes):

MAGIC KINGDOM	18:00
EPCOT	16:00
ANIMAL KINGDOM	10:00
DHS	15:00

Homewood Suites by Hilton Lake Buena Vista–Orlando ★★★★½
11428 Marbella Palm Ct.
Orlando, FL 32836
☎ 407-239-4540
tinyurl.com/homewoodsuiteslbv

LOCATION	2
ROOM QUALITY	93
COST ($=$50)	$$$$-
DAILY RESORT FEE	None

COMMUTING TIMES TO PARKS (in minutes):

MAGIC KINGDOM	18:00
EPCOT	16:00
ANIMAL KINGDOM	10:00
DHS	15:00

Hyatt Place Orlando/ Lake Buena Vista ★★★★
8688 Palm Pkwy.
Orlando, FL 32836
☎ 407-778-5500
orlandolakebuenavista.place
.hyatt.com

LOCATION	2
ROOM QUALITY	88
COST ($=$50)	$$$+
DAILY RESORT FEE	None

COMMUTING TIMES TO PARKS (in minutes):

MAGIC KINGDOM	18:00
EPCOT	14:00
ANIMAL KINGDOM	20:00
DHS	20:00

Hyatt Regency Grand Cypress ★★★★
1 Grand Cypress Blvd.
Orlando, FL 32836
☎ 407-239-1234
grandcypress.hyatt.com

LOCATION	2
ROOM QUALITY	89
COST ($=$50)	$ x 6
DAILY RESORT FEE	$45

COMMUTING TIMES TO PARKS (in minutes):

MAGIC KINGDOM	18:00
EPCOT	13:00
ANIMAL KINGDOM	12:00
DHS	14:00

JW Marriott Orlando Bonnet Creek Resort & Spa
14900 Chelonia Pkwy.
Orlando, FL 32821
☎ 407-919-6300
tinyurl.com/jwmarriottorlandobc

LOCATION	WDW
ROOM QUALITY	–
COST ($=$50)	$- x 11
DAILY RESORT FEE	$35

COMMUTING TIMES TO PARKS (in minutes):

MAGIC KINGDOM	13:30
EPCOT	08:45
ANIMAL KINGDOM	11:45
DHS	11:15

Loews Royal Pacific Resort at Universal Orlando ★★★★
6300 Hollywood Way
Orlando, FL 32819
☎ 407-503-3000
loewshotels.com/royal-pacific
-resort

LOCATION	4
ROOM QUALITY	86
COST ($=$50)	$ x 11
DAILY RESORT FEE	None

COMMUTING TIMES TO PARKS (in minutes):

MAGIC KINGDOM	21:45
EPCOT	17:15
ANIMAL KINGDOM	20:15
DHS	19:45

Loews Sapphire Falls Resort at Universal Orlando ★★★★
6601 Adventure Way
Orlando, FL 32819
☎ 407-503-5000
loewshotels.com/sapphire-falls
-resort

LOCATION	4
ROOM QUALITY	86
COST ($=$50)	$- x 8
DAILY RESORT FEE	None

COMMUTING TIMES TO PARKS (in minutes):

MAGIC KINGDOM	20:00
EPCOT	15:15
ANIMAL KINGDOM	15:15
DHS	17:45

Margaritaville Resort Orlando
8000 Fins Up Circle
Kissimmee, FL 34747
☎ 407-479-0950
tinyurl.com/margaritaville-fl

LOCATION	3
ROOM QUALITY	–
COST ($=$50)	$$$$$-
DAILY RESORT FEE	None

COMMUTING TIMES TO PARKS (in minutes):

MAGIC KINGDOM	20:00
EPCOT	15:00
ANIMAL KINGDOM	17:00
DHS	14:00

Marriott's Harbour Lake ★★★★½
7102 Grand Horizons Blvd.
Orlando, FL 32821
☎ 407-465-6100
tinyurl.com/harbourlake

LOCATION	2
ROOM QUALITY	94
COST ($=$50)	$$$$-
DAILY RESORT FEE	None

COMMUTING TIMES TO PARKS (in minutes):

MAGIC KINGDOM	15:00
EPCOT	12:45
ANIMAL KINGDOM	15:45
DHS	15:15

Meliá Orlando Celebration ★★★½
225 Celebration Pl
Celebration, FL 34747
☎ 407-964-7000
tinyurl.com/meliaorlando
celebration

LOCATION	3
ROOM QUALITY	82
COST ($=$50)	$$$+
DAILY RESORT FEE	$32

COMMUTING TIMES TO PARKS (in minutes):

MAGIC KINGDOM	18:00
EPCOT	13:30
ANIMAL KINGDOM	18:00
DHS	16:30

Mi Casa Hotel Orlando ★★★★½
9350 Turkey Lake Rd.
Orlando, FL 32819
☎ 407-351-5050
micasahotels.com

LOCATION	2
ROOM QUALITY	94
COST ($=$50)	$$+
DAILY RESORT FEE	$5

COMMUTING TIMES TO PARKS (in minutes):

MAGIC KINGDOM	14:45
EPCOT	10:00
ANIMAL KINGDOM	13:00
DHS	12:30

*Irlo Bronson Memorial Highway

Homewood Suites by Hilton Orlando Theme Parks ★★★★
6940 Westwood Blvd.
Orlando, FL 32821
☎ 407-778-5888
tinyurl.com/homewoodorl

LOCATION	1
ROOM QUALITY	87
COST ($=$50)	$$$–
DAILY RESORT FEE	None
COMMUTING TIMES TO PARKS (in minutes):	
MAGIC KINGDOM	18:00
EPCOT	12:00
ANIMAL KINGDOM	18:00
DHS	14:00

Homewood Suites by Hilton Orlando–International Drive/Convention Center ★★★★½
8745 International Dr.
Orlando, FL 32819
☎ 407-248-2232
tinyurl.com/homewoodidrive

LOCATION	1
ROOM QUALITY	93
COST ($=$50)	$$$
DAILY RESORT FEE	None
COMMUTING TIMES TO PARKS (in minutes):	
MAGIC KINGDOM	17:00
EPCOT	14:00
ANIMAL KINGDOM	13:00
DHS	14:00

Homewood Suites by Hilton Orlando–Nearest to Universal Studios ★★★★
5893 American Way
Orlando, FL 32819
☎ 407-226-0669
tinyurl.com/homewoodnearuni

LOCATION	1
ROOM QUALITY	87
COST ($=$50)	$$$
DAILY RESORT FEE	None
COMMUTING TIMES TO PARKS (in minutes):	
MAGIC KINGDOM	21:45
EPCOT	17:00
ANIMAL KINGDOM	20:00
DHS	19:30

La Quinta Inn & Suites by Wyndham Orlando Universal Area
5621 Major Blvd.
Orlando, FL 32819
☎ 407-313-3100
laquintaorlandomajorblvd.com

LOCATION	4
ROOM QUALITY	–
COST ($=$50)	$$
DAILY RESORT FEE	None
COMMUTING TIMES TO PARKS (in minutes):	
MAGIC KINGDOM	15:00
EPCOT	12:00
ANIMAL KINGDOM	18:00
DHS	11:00

Liki Tiki Village ★★★½
17777 Bali Blvd.
Winter Garden, FL 34787
☎ 407-239-5000
likitiki.com

LOCATION	3
ROOM QUALITY	77
COST ($=$50)	$$$$$
DAILY RESORT FEE	$30
COMMUTING TIMES TO PARKS (in minutes):	
MAGIC KINGDOM	18:00
EPCOT	13:15
ANIMAL KINGDOM	16:15
DHS	16:00

Loews Portofino Bay Hotel at Universal Orlando ★★★★½
5601 Universal Blvd.
Orlando, FL 32819
☎ 407-503-1000
loewshotels.com/portofino-bay-hotel

LOCATION	4
ROOM QUALITY	90
COST ($=$50)	$ x 12
DAILY RESORT FEE	None
COMMUTING TIMES TO PARKS (in minutes):	
MAGIC KINGDOM	09:00
EPCOT	08:45
ANIMAL KINGDOM	05:15
DHS	08:15

Marriott's Cypress Harbour Villas
11251 Harbour Villa Rd.
Orlando, FL 32821
☎ 407-238-1300
tinyurl.com/marriottchv

LOCATION	2
ROOM QUALITY	–
COST ($=$50)	$$$$$+
DAILY RESORT FEE	None
COMMUTING TIMES TO PARKS (in minutes):	
MAGIC KINGDOM	15:00
EPCOT	14:00
ANIMAL KINGDOM	16:00
DHS	14:00

Marriott's Imperial Palms Villas
8404 Vacation Way
Orlando, FL 32821
☎ 407-238-6200
tinyurl.com/marriottipv

LOCATION	2
ROOM QUALITY	–
COST ($=$50)	$+ x 7
DAILY RESORT FEE	None
COMMUTING TIMES TO PARKS (in minutes):	
MAGIC KINGDOM	15:00
EPCOT	13:00
ANIMAL KINGDOM	19:00
DHS	13:00

Marriott's Grande Vista ★★★★
5925 Avenida Vista
Orlando, FL 32821
☎ 407-238-7676
tinyurl.com/marriottsgrandevista

LOCATION	1
ROOM QUALITY	89
COST ($=$50)	$$$$
DAILY RESORT FEE	None
COMMUTING TIMES TO PARKS (in minutes):	
MAGIC KINGDOM	06:00
EPCOT	04:00
ANIMAL KINGDOM	06:00
DHS	04:00

Mystic Dunes Resort & Golf Club
(Diamond Resorts) ★★★★½
7600 Mystic Dunes Ln.
Celebration, FL 34747
☎ 407-396-1311
mystic-dunes-resort.com

LOCATION	3
ROOM QUALITY	90
COST ($=$50)	$$$–
DAILY RESORT FEE	$30
COMMUTING TIMES TO PARKS (in minutes):	
MAGIC KINGDOM	10:45
EPCOT	10:30
ANIMAL KINGDOM	07:45
DHS	10:00

Omni Orlando Resort at ChampionsGate ★★★★★
1500 Masters Blvd.
ChampionsGate, FL 33896
☎ 407-390-6664
tinyurl.com/omnichampionsgate

LOCATION	2
ROOM QUALITY	97
COST ($=$50)	$– x 7
DAILY RESORT FEE	$40
COMMUTING TIMES TO PARKS (in minutes):	
MAGIC KINGDOM	15:30
EPCOT	15:00
ANIMAL KINGDOM	15:00
DHS	14:30

Orlando World Center Marriott ★★★★★
8701 World Center Dr.
Orlando, FL 32821
☎ 407-239-4200
marriottworldcenter.com

LOCATION	2
ROOM QUALITY	97
COST ($=$50)	$– x 6
DAILY RESORT FEE	$42
COMMUTING TIMES TO PARKS (in minutes):	
MAGIC KINGDOM	09:45
EPCOT	05:00
ANIMAL KINGDOM	08:00
DHS	07:30

Hotels with no star rating did not have enough surveys to rate.

HOTEL INFORMATION TABLE *(continued)*

Parc Corniche Resort ★★★½
6300 Parc Corniche Dr.
Orlando, FL 32821
☎ 407-239-7100
parccorniche.com

LOCATION	1
ROOM QUALITY	80
COST ($=$50)	$- x 10
DAILY RESORT FEE	$30
COMMUTING TIMES TO PARKS *(in minutes):*	
MAGIC KINGDOM	21:00
EPCOT	18:00
ANIMAL KINGDOM	20:00
DHS	18:00

Parkway International Resort
★★★★
6200 Safari Trl.
Kissimmee, FL 34747
☎ 407-396-6600
parkwayresort.com

LOCATION	3
ROOM QUALITY	88
COST ($=$50)	$$$$-
DAILY RESORT FEE	$15
COMMUTING TIMES TO PARKS *(in minutes):*	
MAGIC KINGDOM	08:30
EPCOT	08:15
ANIMAL KINGDOM	06:15
DHS	07:45

Polynesian Isles Resort
(Diamond Resorts) ★★★★
3045 Polynesian Isles Blvd.
Kissimmee, FL 34746
☎ 407-396-1622
polynesianisle.com

LOCATION	3
ROOM QUALITY	88
COST ($=$50)	$$$$$+
DAILY RESORT FEE	$15
COMMUTING TIMES TO PARKS *(in minutes):*	
MAGIC KINGDOM	14:30
EPCOT	14:15
ANIMAL KINGDOM	12:30
DHS	14:00

The Ritz-Carlton Orlando, Grande Lakes ★★★★½
4012 Central Florida Pkwy.
Orlando, FL 32837
☎ 407-206-2400
ritzcarlton.com/en/hotels/florida/orlando

LOCATION	1
ROOM QUALITY	95
COST ($=$50)	$ x 17
DAILY RESORT FEE	$40
COMMUTING TIMES TO PARKS *(in minutes):*	
MAGIC KINGDOM	23:00
EPCOT	18:15
ANIMAL KINGDOM	21:30
DHS	20:45

Rodeway Inn Maingate West
7455 W. US 192*
Kissimmee, FL 34747
☎ 407-390-0197
tinyurl.com/rodewaymaingatewest

LOCATION	3
ROOM QUALITY	–
COST ($=$50)	$+
DAILY RESORT FEE	None
COMMUTING TIMES TO PARKS *(in minutes):*	
MAGIC KINGDOM	11:15
EPCOT	11:00
ANIMAL KINGDOM	09:15
DHS	10:30

Rosen Centre Hotel ★★★
9840 International Dr.
Orlando, FL 32819
☎ 407-996-9840
rosencentre.com

LOCATION	1
ROOM QUALITY	67
COST ($=$50)	$$$$+
DAILY RESORT FEE	None
COMMUTING TIMES TO PARKS *(in minutes):*	
MAGIC KINGDOM	19:45
EPCOT	15:15
ANIMAL KINGDOM	18:15
DHS	17:45

Shades of Green ★★★★½
1950 W. Magnolia Palm Dr.
Lake Buena Vista, FL 32830
☎ 407-824-3400
shadesofgreen.org

LOCATION	WDW
ROOM QUALITY	92
COST ($=$50)	$$$+
DAILY RESORT FEE	None
COMMUTING TIMES TO PARKS *(in minutes):*	
MAGIC KINGDOM	03:30
EPCOT	04:45
ANIMAL KINGDOM	09:30
DHS	06:15

Sheraton Vistana Resort Villas, Lake Buena Vista ★★★★
8800 Vistana Centre Dr.
Orlando, FL 32821
☎ 407-239-3100
tinyurl.com/sheratonresortlbv

LOCATION	2
ROOM QUALITY	88
COST ($=$50)	$$$$$
DAILY RESORT FEE	None
COMMUTING TIMES TO PARKS *(in minutes):*	
MAGIC KINGDOM	11:15
EPCOT	06:30
ANIMAL KINGDOM	09:30
DHS	09:00

Sheraton Vistana Villages Resort Villas, I-Drive/Orlando ★★★★½
12401 International Dr.
Orlando, FL 32821
☎ 407-238-5000
tinyurl.com/vistanavillagesresort

LOCATION	1
ROOM QUALITY	90
COST ($=$50)	$$$$$
DAILY RESORT FEE	None
COMMUTING TIMES TO PARKS *(in minutes):*	
MAGIC KINGDOM	11:15
EPCOT	06:30
ANIMAL KINGDOM	09:30
DHS	09:00

SpringHill Suites Orlando at Flamingo Crossings ★★★★
13279 Hartzog Rd.
Winter Garden, FL 34787
☎ 407-507-1200
tinyurl.com/fc-springhill

LOCATION	2
ROOM QUALITY	88
COST ($=$50)	$$$$+
DAILY RESORT FEE	None
COMMUTING TIMES TO PARKS *(in minutes):*	
MAGIC KINGDOM	22:00
EPCOT	09:00
ANIMAL KINGDOM	11:00
DHS	10:00

SpringHill Suites Orlando Lake Buena Vista South ★★★½
4991 Calypso Cay Way
Kissimmee, FL 34746
☎ 407-997-1300
tinyurl.com/springhillkiss

LOCATION	3
ROOM QUALITY	80
COST ($=$50)	$$$$
DAILY RESORT FEE	None
COMMUTING TIMES TO PARKS *(in minutes):*	
MAGIC KINGDOM	15:45
EPCOT	15:15
ANIMAL KINGDOM	14:15
DHS	13:30

Star Island Resort & Club ★★★½
5000 Avenue of the Stars
Kissimmee, FL 34746
☎ 407-997-8000
star-island.com

LOCATION	3
ROOM QUALITY	82
COST ($=$50)	$$$-
DAILY RESORT FEE	$15
COMMUTING TIMES TO PARKS *(in minutes):*	
MAGIC KINGDOM	18:00
EPCOT	17:00
ANIMAL KINGDOM	13:00
DHS	17:00

*Irlo Bronson Memorial Highway

Ramada by Wyndham Kissimmee Gateway ★★½
7470 W. US 192*
Kissimmee, FL 34747
☎ 407-396-4400
ramadagateway.com

LOCATION	3
ROOM QUALITY	57
COST ($=$50)	$$+
DAILY RESORT FEE	$12

COMMUTING TIMES TO PARKS
(in minutes):

MAGIC KINGDOM	26:00
EPCOT	11:00
ANIMAL KINGDOM	17:00
DHS	16:00

Residence Inn Near Universal Orlando ★★★★
5614 Major Blvd.
Orlando, FL 32819
☎ 407-313-1234
tinyurl.com/residenceinnuniversal orlando

LOCATION	1
ROOM QUALITY	87
COST ($=$50)	$$$$+
DAILY RESORT FEE	None

COMMUTING TIMES TO PARKS
(in minutes):

MAGIC KINGDOM	05:00
EPCOT	09:00
ANIMAL KINGDOM	09:00
DHS	07:00

Residence Inn Orlando Flamingo Crossings Town Center
2111 Flagler Ave.
Winter Garden, FL 34787
☎ 407-993-3233
tinyurl.com/resinnflamingo

LOCATION	2
ROOM QUALITY	–
COST ($=$50)	$$$+
DAILY RESORT FEE	None

COMMUTING TIMES TO PARKS
(in minutes):

MAGIC KINGDOM	18:00
EPCOT	14:15
ANIMAL KINGDOM	18:00
DHS	16:00

Rosen Inn at Pointe Orlando ★★★½
9000 International Dr.
Orlando, FL 32819
☎ 407-996-8585
roseninn9000.com

LOCATION	1
ROOM QUALITY	77
COST ($=$50)	$$$$–
DAILY RESORT FEE	None

COMMUTING TIMES TO PARKS
(in minutes):

MAGIC KINGDOM	22:15
EPCOT	17:30
ANIMAL KINGDOM	20:30
DHS	20:00

Rosen Plaza Hotel
9700 International Dr.
Orlando, FL 32819
☎ 407-996-9700
rosenplaza.com

LOCATION	1
ROOM QUALITY	–
COST ($=$50)	$+ x 6
DAILY RESORT FEE	None

COMMUTING TIMES TO PARKS
(in minutes):

MAGIC KINGDOM	20:45
EPCOT	16:15
ANIMAL KINGDOM	19:15
DHS	18:45

Rosen Shingle Creek ★★★½
9939 Universal Blvd.
Orlando, FL 32819
☎ 407-996-9939
rosenshinglecreek.com

LOCATION	1
ROOM QUALITY	80
COST ($=$50)	$ x 7
DAILY RESORT FEE	None

COMMUTING TIMES TO PARKS
(in minutes):

MAGIC KINGDOM	24:00
EPCOT	17:00
ANIMAL KINGDOM	16:00
DHS	14:00

Signia by Hilton Orlando Bonnet Creek ★★★★
14100 Bonnet Creek Resort Ln.
Orlando, FL 32821
☎ 407-597-3600
hiltonbonnetcreek.com

LOCATION	WDW
ROOM QUALITY	87
COST ($=$50)	$$$$+
DAILY RESORT FEE	$45

COMMUTING TIMES TO PARKS
(in minutes):

MAGIC KINGDOM	08:15
EPCOT	08:00
ANIMAL KINGDOM	04:30
DHS	07:30

Silver Lake Resort ★★★★
7751 Black Lake Rd.
Kissimmee, FL 34747
☎ 407-397-2828
silverlakeresort.com

LOCATION	3
ROOM QUALITY	87
COST ($=$50)	$$$$–
DAILY RESORT FEE	None

COMMUTING TIMES TO PARKS
(in minutes):

MAGIC KINGDOM	14:15
EPCOT	09:30
ANIMAL KINGDOM	12:30
DHS	12:00

Sonesta ES Suites Lake Buena Vista
8751 Suiteside Dr.
Orlando, FL 32836
☎ 407-238-0777
tinyurl.com/sonestalbv

LOCATION	2
ROOM QUALITY	–
COST ($=$50)	$$$$
DAILY RESORT FEE	None

COMMUTING TIMES TO PARKS
(in minutes):

MAGIC KINGDOM	18:00
EPCOT	16:00
ANIMAL KINGDOM	10:00
DHS	15:00

Star Wars: Galactic Starcruiser
(closing September 2023)
201 S. Studio Dr.
Lake Buena Vista, FL 32836
☎ 407-939-5277
tinyurl.com/galacticstarcruiser

LOCATION	WDW
ROOM QUALITY	83
COST ($=$50)	$ x 80
DAILY RESORT FEE	None

COMMUTING TIMES TO PARKS
(in minutes):

MAGIC KINGDOM	12:00
EPCOT	11:00
ANIMAL KINGDOM	12:00
DHS	08:00

Staybridge Suites Orlando at SeaWorld
6985 Sea Harbor Dr.
Orlando, FL 32821
☎ 407-917-9200
tinyurl.com/staybridgeseaworld

LOCATION	1
ROOM QUALITY	–
COST ($=$50)	$$$$+
DAILY RESORT FEE	None

COMMUTING TIMES TO PARKS
(in minutes):

MAGIC KINGDOM	15:00
EPCOT	12:00
ANIMAL KINGDOM	14:00
DHS	12:00

Staybridge Suites Royale Parc
5876 W. US 192*
Kissimmee, FL 34746
☎ 407-396-8040
tinyurl.com/staybridgeroyaleparc

LOCATION	3
ROOM QUALITY	–
COST ($=$50)	$$$+
DAILY RESORT FEE	$16

COMMUTING TIMES TO PARKS
(in minutes):

MAGIC KINGDOM	11:15
EPCOT	11:00
ANIMAL KINGDOM	09:15
DHS	10:30

Hotels with no star rating did not have enough surveys to rate.

HOTEL INFORMATION TABLE (continued)

TownePlace Suites Orlando at Flamingo Crossings ★★★★
13295 Hartzog Rd.
Winter Garden, FL 34787
☎ 407-507-1300
tinyurl.com/fc-towneplace

LOCATION	2
ROOM QUALITY	87
COST ($=$50)	$$$
DAILY RESORT FEE	None
COMMUTING TIMES TO PARKS (in minutes):	
MAGIC KINGDOM	18:00
EPCOT	16:00
ANIMAL KINGDOM	10:00
DHS	16:00

Treehouse Villas at Disney's Saratoga Springs Resort & Spa ★★★★
1960 Broadway
Lake Buena Vista, FL 32830
☎ 407-827-1100
tinyurl.com/saratogawdw

LOCATION	WDW
ROOM QUALITY	89
COST ($=$50)	$+ x 32
DAILY RESORT FEE	None
COMMUTING TIMES TO PARKS (in minutes):	
MAGIC KINGDOM	12:45
EPCOT	07:15
ANIMAL KINGDOM	16:45
DHS	12:30

Universal's Aventura Hotel ★★★★
6725 Adventura Way
Orlando, FL 32819
☎ 407-503-6000
loewshotels.com/universals-aventura-hotel

LOCATION	4
ROOM QUALITY	88
COST ($=$50)	$$$$$
DAILY RESORT FEE	None
COMMUTING TIMES TO PARKS (in minutes):	
MAGIC KINGDOM	20:00
EPCOT	15:00
ANIMAL KINGDOM	17:00
DHS	14:00

Vacation Village at Parkway ★★★★
2975 Arabian Nights Blvd.
Kissimmee, FL 34747
☎ 407-396-9086
tinyurl.com/vacation-village-pkwy

LOCATION	3
ROOM QUALITY	89
COST ($=$50)	$$$-
DAILY RESORT FEE	$30 (one-time)
COMMUTING TIMES TO PARKS (in minutes):	
MAGIC KINGDOM	08:30
EPCOT	08:15
ANIMAL KINGDOM	06:45
DHS	07:45

The Villas at Disney's Grand Floridian Resort & Spa ★★★★½
4401 Floridian Way
Lake Buena Vista, FL 32830
☎ 407-824-3000
tinyurl.com/grandfloridianvillas

LOCATION	WDW
ROOM QUALITY	93
COST ($=$50)	$- x 21
DAILY RESORT FEE	None
COMMUTING TIMES TO PARKS (in minutes):	
MAGIC KINGDOM	on monorail
EPCOT	04:45
ANIMAL KINGDOM	11:45
DHS	06:45

Waldorf Astoria Orlando ★★★★½
14200 Bonnet Creek Resort Ln.
Orlando, FL 32821
☎ 407-597-5500
waldorfastoriaorlando.com

LOCATION	WDW
ROOM QUALITY	90
COST ($=$50)	$ x 16
DAILY RESORT FEE	$45
COMMUTING TIMES TO PARKS (in minutes):	
MAGIC KINGDOM	08:00
EPCOT	06:00
ANIMAL KINGDOM	07:15
DHS	04:15

Westgate Lakes Resort & Spa ★★★★
9500 Turkey Lake Rd.
Orlando, FL 32819
☎ 407-345-0000
westgateresorts.com/lakes

LOCATION	2
ROOM QUALITY	89
COST ($=$50)	$$$$
DAILY RESORT FEE	$20
COMMUTING TIMES TO PARKS (in minutes):	
MAGIC KINGDOM	17:30
EPCOT	14:30
ANIMAL KINGDOM	19:15
DHS	18:00

Westgate Vacation Villas Resort ★★★★
7700 Westgate Blvd.
Kissimmee, FL 34747
☎ 407-239-0510
westgateresorts.com/vacation-villas

LOCATION	3
ROOM QUALITY	83
COST ($=$50)	$$$+
DAILY RESORT FEE	$20
COMMUTING TIMES TO PARKS (in minutes):	
MAGIC KINGDOM	08:45
EPCOT	08:30
ANIMAL KINGDOM	05:45
DHS	08:00

Wingate by Wyndham Universal Studios & Convention Center
5661 Windhover Dr.
Orlando, FL 32819
☎ 407-226-0900
wingateorlando.com

LOCATION	4
ROOM QUALITY	–
COST ($=$50)	$$$$-
DAILY RESORT FEE	None
COMMUTING TIMES TO PARKS (in minutes):	
MAGIC KINGDOM	21:00
EPCOT	16:00
ANIMAL KINGDOM	19:00
DHS	18:00

Wyndham Orlando Resort International Drive ★★★½
8001 International Dr.
Orlando, FL 32819
☎ 407-351-2420
wyndhamorlandoresort.com

LOCATION	1
ROOM QUALITY	77
COST ($=$50)	$$$+
DAILY RESORT FEE	$28
COMMUTING TIMES TO PARKS (in minutes):	
MAGIC KINGDOM	19:45
EPCOT	15:00
ANIMAL KINGDOM	18:15
DHS	17:30

*Irlo Bronson Memorial Highway

Universal's Cabana Bay Beach Resort ★★★½
6550 Adventure Way
Orlando, FL 32819
☎ 407-503-4000
loewshotels.com/cabana-bay
-hotel

LOCATION	4
ROOM QUALITY	82
COST ($=$50)	$$$$+
DAILY RESORT FEE	None
COMMUTING TIMES TO PARKS (in minutes):	
MAGIC KINGDOM	20:00
EPCOT	15:00
ANIMAL KINGDOM	17:00
DHS	14:00

Universal's Endless Summer Resort: Dockside Inn & Suites ★★★★
7125 Universal Blvd.
Orlando, FL 32819
☎ 407-503-8000
loewshotels.com/dockside-inn
-and-suites

LOCATION	4
ROOM QUALITY	85
COST ($=$50)	$$$+
DAILY RESORT FEE	None
COMMUTING TIMES TO PARKS (in minutes):	
MAGIC KINGDOM	19:00
EPCOT	17:00
ANIMAL KINGDOM	22:00
DHS	16:00

Universal's Endless Summer Resort: Surfside Inn & Suites ★★★★
7000 Universal Blvd.
Orlando, FL 32819
☎ 407-503-7000
loewshotels.com/surfside-inn
-and-suites

LOCATION	4
ROOM QUALITY	86
COST ($=$50)	$$$+
DAILY RESORT FEE	None
COMMUTING TIMES TO PARKS (in minutes):	
MAGIC KINGDOM	19:00
EPCOT	17:00
ANIMAL KINGDOM	22:00
DHS	16:00

Walt Disney World Dolphin ★★★★
1500 EPCOT Resorts Blvd.
Lake Buena Vista, FL 32830
☎ 407-934-4000
swandolphin.com

LOCATION	WDW
ROOM QUALITY	85
COST ($=$50)	$ x 6
DAILY RESORT FEE	$40
COMMUTING TIMES TO PARKS (in minutes):	
MAGIC KINGDOM	06:45
EPCOT	05:00
ANIMAL KINGDOM	06:15
DHS	04:00

Walt Disney World Swan ★★★★
1200 EPCOT Resorts Blvd.
Lake Buena Vista, FL 32830
☎ 407-934-3000
swandolphin.com

LOCATION	WDW
ROOM QUALITY	86
COST ($=$50)	$ x 6
DAILY RESORT FEE	$40
COMMUTING TIMES TO PARKS (in minutes):	
MAGIC KINGDOM	06:30
EPCOT	04:45
ANIMAL KINGDOM	06:15
DHS	04:00

Walt Disney World Swan Reserve ★★★★
1255 EPCOT Resorts Blvd.
Lake Buena Vista, FL 32830
☎ 407-934-3000
swandolphin.com

LOCATION	WDW
ROOM QUALITY	86
COST ($=$50)	$ x 8
DAILY RESORT FEE	$40
COMMUTING TIMES TO PARKS (in minutes):	
MAGIC KINGDOM	06:30
EPCOT	04:45
ANIMAL KINGDOM	06:15
DHS	04:00

WorldMark Orlando–Kingstown Reef
12000 International Dr.
Orlando, FL 38321
☎ 407-597-2550
tinyurl.com/wmokingstownreef

LOCATION	1
ROOM QUALITY	–
COST ($=$50)	$$$+
DAILY RESORT FEE	None
COMMUTING TIMES TO PARKS (in minutes):	
MAGIC KINGDOM	18:00
EPCOT	15:00
ANIMAL KINGDOM	21:00
DHS	15:00

Wyndham Garden Lake Buena Vista ★★★½
1850-B Hotel Plaza Blvd.
Lake Buena Vista, FL 32830
☎ 407-842-6644
wyndhamlakebuenavista.com

LOCATION	WDW
ROOM QUALITY	80
COST ($=$50)	$$$$–
DAILY RESORT FEE	$34
COMMUTING TIMES TO PARKS (in minutes):	
MAGIC KINGDOM	15:15
EPCOT	10:45
ANIMAL KINGDOM	14:45
DHS	12:15

Wyndham Grand Orlando Resort Bonnet Creek ★★★★★
14651 Chelonia Pkwy.
Orlando, FL 32821
☎ 407-390-2300
tinyurl.com/wyndhamgrand
bonnetcreek

LOCATION	WDW
ROOM QUALITY	96
COST ($=$50)	$ x 6
DAILY RESORT FEE	$28
COMMUTING TIMES TO PARKS (in minutes):	
MAGIC KINGDOM	18:00
EPCOT	08:00
ANIMAL KINGDOM	15:00
DHS	10:00

Hotels with no star rating did not have enough surveys to rate

DINING *in* AND *around* WALT DISNEY WORLD

READER SURVEYS *plus* EXPERT OPINIONS: *Our Approach to Dining*

WE'VE RECEIVED MORE THAN 220,000 SURVEYS about Walt Disney World restaurants in the past year, and over 1 million since 2018. We think that's more than Yelp and TripAdvisor *combined*.

What makes the *Unofficial Guide* different from Yelp and others is that we display those surveys alongside objective reviews written by culinary experts. With these critical analyses, you get a consistent evaluation of the entire range of Disney dining options from people who've tried every restaurant, kiosk, and food stand in the World. We (Bob and Len) weigh in occasionally too. Here's how to use the reader surveys and critical reviews together:

If a restaurant has earned ratings of 90% or better in our reader surveys and at least four stars (sit-down) or a B or better (counter-service) from our critics, make plans to visit. Chances are good that you'll enjoy your meal. In EPCOT, for example, France's counter-service **Les Halles Boulangerie–Pâtisserie** and Italy's sit-down **Via Napoli Ristorante e Pizzeria** both fit this profile.

In general, avoid restaurants with ratings of 80% or less in our reader surveys and either three stars or less (sit-down) or a C or lower (counter-service) from our critics. That said, you may need to bend this rule—for example, with in-demand, kid-friendly restaurants such as **Akershus Royal Banquet** Hall at EPCOT.

When reader ratings disagree with our critical analysis, check the review for an explanation. An example is **Takumi-Tei** at EPCOT's Japan Pavilion in World Showcase. The food quality, presentation, and service of their kaiseki makes this one of the five best restaurants in Walt Disney World. Its low ratings are entirely due to its $250-per-person price, well beyond what many theme park guests pay for Japanese food in their hometowns. But those hometown experiences are typically hibachi, which is like comparing Waffle House to Ruth's Chris. Readers from large cities who are comfortable paying $125-$150 per person for omakase sushi have much higher opinions of Takumi-Tei.

SURVEY RESULTS DEMYSTIFIED

FOR BOTH COUNTER-SERVICE and full-service restaurants, along with the restaurants mentioned in "Dining in Universal CityWalk" (see page 362), we list reader-survey results for each restaurant profiled, expressed as a percentage of positive (+) responses.

The average positive rating for all Disney counter-service restaurants is **88.5%** at a 95% confidence interval. If that sounds too technical, know this: In a nutshell it means these ratings are derived from highly accurate data that you can trust in deciding whether a restaurant is worth trying.

We use the following categories to provide context for the percentages:

OUR DINING SURVEY RATINGS SYSTEM		
CATEGORY	**COUNTER-SERVICE RESTAURANTS** *(average positive rating)*	**SIT-DOWN RESTAURANTS** *(average positive rating)*
EXCEPTIONAL	94% or higher	95% or higher
MUCH ABOVE AVERAGE	92%–94%	94%–95%
ABOVE AVERAGE	90%–92%	91%–93%
AVERAGE	87%–89%	89%–91%
BELOW AVERAGE	84%–87%	86%–89%
MUCH BELOW AVERAGE	79%–84%	81%–86%
DO NOT VISIT	78% or lower	80% or lower

DINING *in* WALT DISNEY WORLD

THIS SECTION AIMS TO HELP YOU FIND good food worth the effort of getting a reservation and the money it costs. More than 200 restaurants—including around 90 full-service establishments, around 30 of which are in the theme parks—operate within the World. These restaurants offer exceptional variety, serving everything from Moroccan lamb to Texas barbecue. Most are expensive, and many serve food that doesn't live up to the prices; nevertheless there are good choices to be found in every area of Walt Disney World.

Many guests explore restaurants outside Walt Disney World to expand their options. The choices are plentiful, and you'll save enough money to pay for a rental car or ride-hailing service. See pages 363–365 for our recommendations.

DINING OPTIONS AND EXPERIENCES

READER RATINGS FOR DISNEY RESTAURANTS have bounced back to pre-pandemic levels. Restaurants operated by third parties seem to be operating at very high levels: 5 of the top 10 sit-down restaurants in Walt Disney World are operated by third parties at Disney Springs.

The rest of this chapter offers detailed advice on how to find the best Disney dining experiences. Here are a couple of quick tips to keep in mind, regardless of where you decide to eat:

- Place your counter-service restaurant order 30–45 minutes before you want to eat; that will allow the restaurant enough time to prepare your food before you arrive, and it will reduce your wait. During busier times of the year, you may need to submit orders 1–2 hours in advance, just to be safe.
- Consider eating before noon or after 1 p.m., when it will be easier to find open tables at counter-service restaurants.

GETTING IT RIGHT

ALTHOUGH WE WORK HARD to be fair, objective, and accurate, many readers, like this one from Charleston, West Virginia, think we're overly critical of Disney dining:

> Get a life! It's crazy and unrealistic to be so snobbish about restaurants at a theme park. Considering the number of people Disney feeds each day, I think they do a darn good job. Also, you act so surprised that the food is expensive. Have you ever eaten at an airport? HELLO IN THERE? . . . Surprise, you're a captive! It's a theme park!

And a mom from Erie, Pennsylvania, strikes a practical note:

> Most of the food at Walt Disney World is OK. You pay more than you should, but it's more convenient to eat in Disney World than to try to find cheaper restaurants somewhere else.

As you may infer from these comments, researching and reviewing restaurants is no straightforward endeavor—to the contrary, it's fraught with peril and intrigue.

It's a Shill World: Disney and the Blogosphere

When it comes to dining reviews, we suspect that Disney plays favorites with blogs and social media influencers they know are likely to provide positive coverage. Most of these sites rely on ad views to make money, so drawing in readers with exclusive content is a quid pro quo. Thus, the sites' primary goals are (1) not to offend Disney and (2) to show lots of ads to lots of people. (Keep in mind the lesson learned from Facebook: If you're not paying for something online, you're probably the product being sold to advertisers.)

Be especially skeptical of online opening-night "reviews." Representatives from social media–driven sites show up to cover these events in droves; Disney, knowing this, stage-manages them with a gravitas worthy of a royal wedding, bringing in executive chefs to ensure perfection in everything from preparation to presentation.

This is unsustainable, of course. As soon as the social media posts go up, the menu changes to ensure profits, the chefs go back to their regular jobs, and the kitchen staff is left to figure things out on their own. It's highly unlikely that the lavish dishes showcased on Instagram will actually make it to the restaurant's diners each night.

The *Unofficial* Difference

How, then, do we go about presenting the best possible dining coverage? At the *Unofficial Guide,* we begin with highly qualified culinary experts and then balance their opinions with those of our readers—which, by the way, don't always coincide. (Likewise, the coauthors' assessments don't always agree with those of our dining experts.)

*un*official **TIP**
Our research team has eaten at every restaurant, kiosk, bar, cart, and food stand in Walt Disney World many times.

In the spirit of democracy, we encourage you to fill out our online reader survey at touringplans.com/walt-disney-world/survey. If you'd like to share your dining experiences in greater depth, we invite you to write us a letter or shoot us an email (see page 5).

WHERE TO FIND GOOD MEALS

THE BEST CONCENTRATIONS OF SIT-DOWN RESTAURANTS in Walt Disney World are found at **Disney's Animal Kingdom Lodge; Disney's Grand Floridian Resort & Spa;** the **Contemporary Resort;** and the **Disney Springs** dining, shopping, and entertainment complex.

Animal Kingdom Lodge boasts 3 of the top 5 sit-down restaurants in Walt Disney World: **Boma—Flavors of Africa** (No. 1 overall out of more than 110 sit-down restaurants), a beloved buffet favorite, and **Sanaa** (tied for No. 8), serving delicious African–Indian fusion dishes. A third sit-down restaurant at Animal Kingdom Lodge, **Jiko—The Cooking Place,** comes in just behind Sanaa.

The Grand Floridian houses the best restaurant in Walt Disney World: **Victoria & Albert's,** which won its 20th consecutive AAA Five Diamond Award in early 2020 and is almost certain to be reviewed by Michelin. The food is extraordinary, of course, as is the service. Beyond V&A's, you'll find the **Grand Floridian Cafe** and the **1900 Park Fare** character buffet (still closed at press time). Within walking distance of the Grand Flo is the **Polynesian Village Resort**'s **Kona Cafe,** with excellent breakfast options, and **'Ohana,** with family-style dining at breakfast and dinner; the **Contemporary Resort**'s **California Grill** (tied for No. 8 overall) is a short monorail ride away too. If dining is an important part of your Disney World vacation and these resorts are within your budget (and the restaurants have reopened), we suggest staying at one of them.

The next best concentration of restaurants is at the **Contemporary Resort.** Along with the California Grill, the resort has a sit-down restaurant called **Steakhouse 71** and character buffets at **Chef Mickey's.**

The counter-service **Contempo Cafe** is convenient for simple meals. If the Contemporary isn't an option, consider dining at Disney Springs.

Highlights at Disney Springs include **Chef Art Smith's Homecomin'** (No. 4), with excellent fried chicken, tasty cocktails, and luscious desserts. For seafood and steaks, try **The Boathouse** (No. 7). Disney Springs also has some of the World's top counter-service spots, including **The Polite Pig** barbecue joint (No. 3 in this category), **Earl of Sandwich** (tied for No. 8), and **Blaze Fast-Fire'd Pizza.**

Disney Springs is also home to two of our favorite tapas restaurants. **Wine Bar George** (tied for No. 8 sit-down restaurant overall) is run by a master sommelier who partnered with a chef to create a menu that pairs food and wine. It's the perfect choice for a glass or two and some small bites. Our other tapas favorite is **Jaleo** (No. 6 overall), from celebrity chef José Andrés. Jaleo's menu of modern Spanish dishes is extensive and affordable. We'd willingly start a fight over the last bite of patatas bravas. The Jamón Ibérico is the stuff of dreams.

If the dining at Disney Springs sounds good to you, consider a stay at **Disney's Saratoga Springs Resort & Spa.** Many of the buildings are a short walk to Disney Springs.

Finally, among the theme parks, the food in **Disney's Animal Kingdom** and **EPCOT** gets the highest marks.

DISNEY DINING 101

WALT DISNEY WORLD RESTAURANT CATEGORIES

IN GENERAL, food and beverage offerings at Walt Disney World are defined by service, price, and convenience:

FULL-SERVICE RESTAURANTS Full-service restaurants are in all Disney resorts (except the Value resorts and Port Orleans French Quarter), all major theme parks, and Disney Springs. Disney operates most of the restaurants in the theme parks and its hotels, while contractors or franchisees operate the rest. **Advance Dining Reservations** (see page 272) are recommended for all full-service restaurants.

CHARACTER MEALS Eleven Walt Disney World restaurants have Disney characters in attendance during meals. Five are buffets (see next section), and six offer either a family-style fixed menu (all tables get the same food) or a menu of limited choices. All have a separate kids' menu featuring dishes such as hot dogs, burgers, chicken nuggets, pizza, and macaroni and cheese.

BUFFETS AND FAMILY-STYLE RESTAURANTS Disney buffets are self-serve and all-you-care-to-eat, and they include separate kid-friendly offerings such as chicken nuggets, pizza, and fries. There's no less food at Disney's family-style restaurants, such as EPCOT's Garden Grill. There, your party will be provided with several platters stacked high with meats, vegetables, and salads. You can ask for more (or less) of any item. We've tried all of Disney's family-style restaurants, and we've been pleasantly surprised at the food quality and quantity at most of them.

Advance Dining Reservations are strongly recommended for character meals and recommended for all other restaurants. Most credit cards are accepted. An automatic 18% gratuity is added to the bill for parties of six or more, but when the tipping is at *your* discretion, a North Carolina reader urges generosity with waitstaff:

> *I've seen diners leave a dollar or two per person. I've also heard of people protesting Disney's prices by leaving a small tip or none at all. This is unacceptable—these servers keep your drinks full, keep your plates clean, and check on you constantly. They deserve at least 15%–18%. If you can't afford to tip, you shouldn't eat there.*

FOOD COURTS Featuring a number of counter-service eateries under one roof, food courts can be found at Disney's Moderate and Value resorts. If you're staying at one of these resorts, chances are you'll eat once or twice a day at your hotel's food court. As with its theme park restaurants, Disney has simplified and standardized its food court menus across all of its resorts. Reader satisfaction ratings have dropped considerably as a result—all but one of Disney's food courts (at Port Orleans French Quarter) are rated below average or worse in this year's surveys.

DISNEY RESORT FOOD COURTS: Reader-Survey Ratings		
RESORT	**FOOD COURT**	**POSITIVE RATING**
All-Star Movies	World Premier Food Court	79% (*Much Below Average*)
All-Star Music	Intermission Food Court	86% (*Below Average*)
All-Star Sports	End Zone Food Court	77% (*Do Not Visit*)
Art of Animation	Landscape of Flavors	82% (*Much Below Average*)
Caribbean Beach	Centertown Market	82% (*Much Below Average*)
Coronado Springs	El Mercado de Coronado Food Court	61% (*Do Not Visit*)
Fort Wilderness	P & J's Southern Takeout	73% (*Do Not Visit*)
Pop Century	Everything POP	84% (*Below Average*)
Port Orleans French Quarter	Sassagoula Floatworks & Food Factory	89% (*Average*)
Port Orleans Riverside	Riverside Mill Food Court	82% (*Much Below Average*)

The closest thing to a food court at the theme parks is **Sunshine Seasons** in EPCOT; see "Fast Casual" on the next page, and the full profile on page 303. Reservations are not available at these restaurants.

COUNTER SERVICE Counter-service fast food is plentiful in all the theme parks and at the BoardWalk and Disney Springs. You'll find hot dogs, hamburgers, chicken sandwiches, salads, and pizza almost everywhere. They're augmented by special items that relate to the park's theme or the part of the park you're touring. In EPCOT's Germany, for example, counter-service bratwurst and beer are sold; in Frontierland in the Magic Kingdom, vendors sell smoked turkey legs.

Ordering meals ahead of time through the My Disney Experience app is strongly suggested at all counter-service restaurants.

Most counter-service restaurants serve combo meals, but you can order any meal without the side to save some money. Counter-service prices are fairly consistent from park to park. You can expect to pay the same for your coffee or hot dog in Disney's Animal Kingdom as you would in Disney's Hollywood Studios (see table on page 297).

FAST CASUAL Somewhere between burgers and formal dining are the establishments in Disney's fast casual category, including two in the theme parks: **Satu'li Canteen** in the Animal Kingdom and **Sunshine Seasons** in EPCOT. These are also some of the highest-rated options in the parks.

VENDOR FOOD Vendors abound at the theme parks, Disney Springs, and the BoardWalk. Offerings include popcorn, ice-cream bars, churros, soft drinks, bottled water, and (in the theme parks) fresh fruit. Prices include tax; many vendors accept credit cards, charges to your room at a Disney resort, and the Disney Dining Plan (when it returns; see below). Others take cash only (look for a sign near the register).

DISNEY DINING PLANS

AS WE WERE GOING TO PRESS, Disney announced that the standard and quick-service dining plans will return in 2024. If you want to sign up for a prepaid dining plan, you must do so when you book your Disney resort room; thus, we typically cover the topic in Part 5, "Accommodations." Because further details had not yet been released at press time, our coverage in this book remains suspended. When available, updated information will be posted at tinyurl.com/wdwupdates.

ADVANCE DINING RESERVATIONS

GET THEME PARK RESERVATIONS, if required, before you make dining reservations. Having a dining reservation inside a theme park doesn't provide access to that park. For now, you still need a theme park reservation to get in (see pages 30 and 277).

You can make reservations for Disney's sit-down restaurants, including those in the theme parks, as you can at most sit-down restaurants in your hometown. See the table at right for specifics.

The main difference between most hometown restaurants and Disney's, however, is that hundreds of people are trying to get reservations at Disney's popular restaurants the instant they become available.

In fact, Disney's most popular restaurants can run out of reservations months in advance. Also, most Disney restaurants hold no tables at all—none—for walk-in guests. That means it's important to book your dining reservations as soon as you're able (typically 60 days before your visit). This section explains how it all works, and why.

Behind the Scenes at Advance Dining Reservations

Although they're called reservations, most dining reservations at Walt Disney World don't actually guarantee you a table at a specific time as they do at your typical hometown restaurant. Instead, Disney restaurants operate on what's known as a template system: Instead of an actual table, you're assigned a time slot. The number of slots available is based on the average length of time that guests occupy a table at a particular restaurant, adjusted for seasonality.

Here's a rough example of how it works: Let's say Coral Reef Restaurant has 40 tables for four and 8 tables for six, and that the average length of time for a family to be seated, order, eat, pay, and depart is 40 minutes. Add 5 minutes to bus the table, and the table is turning every 45 minutes. The restaurant then provides Disney's central dining-reservations system

ADVANCE DINING RESERVATIONS
The Official Line

YOU CAN RESERVE THE FOLLOWING up to 60 days in advance:

AFTERNOON TEA AND CHILDREN'S PROGRAMS* at the Grand Floridian Resort & Spa

ALL DISNEY TABLE-SERVICE RESTAURANTS and character-dining venues

FANTASMIC! **DINING PACKAGE** in Disney's Hollywood Studios

HOOP-DEE-DOO MUSICAL REVUE at Fort Wilderness Resort & Campground

OGA'S CANTINA at Star Wars: Galaxy's Edge, Disney's Hollywood Studios

Guests staying at Disney-owned resorts may make dining reservations for the entire length of their stay—up to 10 days—in a single booking up to 60 days in advance.

*Closed at press time; no reopening date announced

(**CDRS**) with a computer template of its capacity, along with the average amount of time the table is occupied. Disney uses CDRS to process reservations both online and by phone.

Thus, when you use the website to make Advance Dining Reservations for four people at 6:15 p.m., CDRS removes one table for four from its overall capacity for 45 minutes. The system template indicates that the table will be unavailable for reassignment until 7 p.m. (45 minutes later). And so it goes for all tables in the restaurant, each being subtracted from overall capacity for 45 minutes, then listed as available again, then assigned to other guests and subtracted again, and so on throughout the meal period.

CDRS tries to fill every time slot for every seat in the restaurant or come as close to filling every slot as possible; again, no seats are reserved for walk-ins. Templates are filled differently depending on the season and restaurant.

When you arrive at a restaurant with a reservation, your wait to be seated will usually be less than 20 minutes during peak hours and often less than 10. If you just show up unencumbered by a reservation, especially during busier seasons, expect to either wait 40–75 minutes or—more likely—be told that there are no tables available. You can sometimes get seated as a walk-in (see page 275), but don't count on it.

NO-SHOW PENALTIES Disney restaurants charge a no-show fee of $10–$25 per person (or $100 per person in the case of **Monsieur Paul** at EPCOT and **Victoria & Albert's** at the Grand Floridian). This has reduced the no-show rate to virtually zero, and these restaurants are booked every day according to their actual capacity. Note the following, however:

- Only one person needs to dine at the restaurant for Disney to consider your reservation fulfilled, even if you have a reservation for more people.
- You can cancel up to 2 hours before your reservation time.

The upside to the no-show fee is that it generally makes booking easier closer to the date of your visit, as the fee discourages tentative plans.

GETTING ADVANCE DINING RESERVATIONS AT POPULAR RESTAURANTS

TWO OF THE HARDEST RESERVATIONS TO GET in Walt Disney World these days are at EPCOT's **Space 220** and Hollywood Studios' **Oga's Cantina.** Why? The Studios is very popular because of the *Star*

Wars and *Toy Story* attractions, and Oga's Cantina's capacity is very limited. Likewise, Space 220 is, along with Coral Reef Restaurant, one of the most picturesque dining locations in the park. You'll have to put in some effort to secure an Advance Dining Reservation at these places, especially during busier times of year. Also, keep in mind that readers who've eaten at Space 220 rate it poorly.

The easiest and fastest way to get a reservation is to go to disney world.disney.go.com/dining starting at 5:45 a.m. Eastern time, a full hour before phone reservations open. If you live in California and you have to get up at 2:45 a.m. Pacific time to make a reservation, Disney couldn't care less: There's no limit to the number of hoops they can make you jump through if demand exceeds supply.

To familiarize yourself with how the site works, try it out a couple of days before you actually make reservations. Be sure to read the directions below for some time-saving keyboard shortcuts—every millisecond counts. You'll also save time by setting up a **My Disney Experience** account online (see page 29) before your 60-day booking window, making sure to enter any credit card information needed to guarantee your reservations.

Disney's website is usually within a few seconds of the official time as determined by the federal government, accessible online at time.gov. Using this site, synchronize your computer *to the second* the night before your 60-day window opens, if your computer hasn't synchronized automatically already.

Early on the morning on which you want to make reservations, take a few moments to select your date, time, and party size on Disney's dining reservations page. If you're looking for a specific kind of dining, such as character meals, use the page's filters to restrict the number of results returned to as few as possible; when the page returns results, you'll have less scrolling to find what you want, saving time.

Next, start trying the Disney website about 3 minutes before 5:45 a.m. Then click "search times." The results returned will tell you whether your restaurant has a table available.

Note that while you're typing, other guests are also trying to make reservations, so you want the transaction to go down as quickly as possible. Flexibility on your part counts—it's much harder to get seating for a large group, so consider breaking your group into numbers that can be accommodated at tables for four. Also make sure you have your credit card out where you can read it.

Advance Dining Reservations for **Cinderella's Royal Table**, other character meals, and the ***Fantasmic!* Dining Package** and the ***Hoop-Dee-Doo Musical Revue*** are actual reservations—that is, they require complete prepayment with a credit card at the time of the booking. The name on the booking can't be changed after the reservation is made. Reservations may be canceled, with the deposit refunded in full, by calling ☎ 407-WDW-DINE at least 48 hours before seating for these shows (versus 24 hours ahead for regular Advance Dining Reservations). Disney will work with you in the event of an emergency.

If you don't have access to a computer at 5:45 a.m. on the morning you need to make reservations, be ready to call ☎ 407-WDW-DINE at 6:45 a.m. Eastern time and follow the prompts to speak to a live person.

You may still get placed on hold if call volume is higher than usual, and you'll be an hour behind the early birds with computers. Still, you'll be well ahead of those who couldn't make it up before sunrise.

Note that when the Disney Dining Plan returns and you want to book a *Fantasmic!* package, Cinderella's Royal Table, or the *Hoop-Dee-Doo* dinner show, you may be better off reserving by phone anyway. The online system may not recognize your table-service credits, but you can book and pay with a credit card, then call ☎ 407-WDW-DINE after 6:45 a.m. and have them credit the charge for the meal back to your card; be aware that this can be a potential hassle if you get an uncooperative cast member. When you get to Walt Disney World, you'll use credits from your dining plan to "pay" for the meal. (Sometimes the online system has glitches and shows no availability; in this case, call after 6:45 a.m. to confirm if the online system is correct.)

NEVER, NEVER, NEVER, NEVER GIVE UP Not getting what you want the first time you try doesn't mean the end of the story. A mom from Cincinnati advises persistence in securing reservations:

> *I was crushed when I called and tried to reserve Chef Mickey's and couldn't. I decided not to give up and would go online once or twice a day to check reservations for Chef Mickey's and the other restaurants I wanted. It took me about a week, but sooner or later I ended up booking every single reservation I wanted except one.*

A woman from Franklin, Tennessee, agrees:

> *I started trying to get a reservation at Be Our Guest Restaurant about a month out from our vacation. By checking the website whenever I thought of it—morning, noon, and night—I ended up getting not only a lunch reservation but a dinner reservation!*

LAST-MINUTE DINING RESERVATIONS Because Advance Dining Reservations require a credit card, and because a fee is charged for failing to cancel in time, you can often score a last-minute reservation. Guests sometimes have to cancel their reservations due to sudden changes of plans, and as long as they cancel before midnight the day before, they won't be charged a no-show penalty (see page 273). So your best shot at picking up a canceled reservation is to repeatedly visit disneyworld.disney.go.com/dining as often as possible between 10 and 11 p.m.

***STILL* CAN'T GET A RESERVATION?** Go to the restaurant on the day you wish to dine, and try for a table as a walk-in. Yes, we've already told you this is a long shot—that said, you *may* be able to swing it between 2:30 and 4:30 p.m., the hours when most full-service restaurants are most likely to take walk-ins, if they do at all. Your chances of success increase during less-busy times of year or on cold or rainy days during busier seasons. If you don't mind eating late, see if you can get a table during the restaurant's last hour of serving.

Full-service restaurants in the theme parks can be hard-nosed about walk-ins: Even if you walk up and see that the restaurant isn't busy, you may still need to use Disney's app or visit Guest Services to make a reservation, as was this Fayetteville, Georgia, reader's experience:

> *We went to the Hollywood & Vine check-in podium at DHS to try for walk-in seating because it was an off time—3:30 p.m.—and*

THE REALITY OF GETTING LAST-MINUTE DINING RESERVATIONS

IF YOUR VACATION is more than 60 days out and you want to dine at a popular venue, following our advice below will get you the table you want more than 80% of the time.

The longer you wait, the more effort you'll have to put in to find a reservation. For example, if you're trying for an early breakfast at Be Our Guest (a restaurant we don't recommend) within the next seven days, your chance of finding any table the first time you check is less than 3%, based on our tests. But if you have the time and patience to visit Disney's website around 30 times over the next week—nope, not a typo—you have a 50–50 shot at snapping up a last-minute cancellation.

Besides Be Our Guest, the list below shows the restaurants where capacity and demand make finding a last-minute reservation more difficult. If you're planning a trip within the next 30 days, see table at right for our recommended alternatives.

- **AKERSHUS ROYAL BANQUET HALL** (*EPCOT*) Reservations are somewhat easier to get for lunch than dinner.
- **BEACHES & CREAM SODA SHOP** (*Beach Club*) It's not the food or the atmosphere—it's the limited seating.
- **THE BOATHOUSE** (*Disney Springs*) Highly rated by readers. Dinner reservations from 5–9 p.m. are the most difficult to get.
- **CHEF ART SMITH'S HOMECOMIN'** (*Disney Springs*) One of Disney Springs' best restaurants. Your options might be lunch, or dinner after 10 p.m.
- **CHEF MICKEY'S** (*Contemporary Resort*) The food isn't anything special, and neither is the venue. But the draws are the Disney characters and the service, both of which are great.
- **OGA'S CANTINA** (*Disney's Hollywood Studios*) Tiny capacity and photogenic drinks make this the hardest place to get into at the Studios.
- **SPACE 220** (*EPCOT*) The draw here is the setting, inside a simulated space station, rather than the food.
- **T-REX** (*Disney Springs*) A popular venue for kids because of the theming and dinosaurs. If you can't get a reservation here, join Landry's Select Club (landrysselect .com) to get priority access instead.

we could see that the restaurant was virtually empty. But we were turned away for lack of availability. So we walked to Guest Services, obtained a reservation there, walked back to the podium, and were immediately checked in.

Landing a reservation for Cinderella's Royal Table at dinner is somewhat easier than at lunch or breakfast, but the price is $79 for adults and $47 for children ages 3–9 during peak times of year (prices may vary seasonally by as much as $15–$20). Throw in tax and gratuity, and you're looking at around $320 for one meal for a family of four. But if you're unable to lock up a table for breakfast or lunch, a dinner reservation will at least get your kids inside the castle.

ALSO TRY OPENTABLE Several Disney World restaurants take reservations through the popular online-booking service **OpenTable** (open table.com; mobile app available for iOS and Android). The participating restaurants (subject to change) are listed in the table on page 278. If you're having trouble getting a dining reservation through the usual Disney channels, this option may be worth checking out. *A big bonus:* If you book through OpenTable, some restaurants won't subject you to the same no-show fee you'd have to pay through Disney if you missed your reservation without canceling. We should add, however, that OpenTable monitors no-shows and will chastise you by email if you fail to appear. Your account will be suspended if you no-show for

GOOD RESTAURANTS WITH LAST-MINUTE AVAILABILITY

IF YOU CAN'T GET A RESERVATION FOR	TRY ONE OF THESE INSTEAD
CINDERELLA'S ROYAL TABLE (Magic Kingdom) CHEF MICKEY'S (Contemporary) AKERSHUS ROYAL BANQUET HALL (EPCOT)	**Liberty Tree Tavern** (Magic Kingdom; no characters) serves comfort-food classics in an interesting early-American setting. If you suddenly have a hankering for turkey and stuffing in the middle of summer, this is the place to get it. **Grand Floridian Cafe** (Grand Floridian Resort; no characters) serves a limited menu of mostly comfort food. Its take on fried chicken is outstanding.
VICTORIA & ALBERT'S (Grand Floridian)	Our first choice for an adults' night out would be **Jiko—The Cooking Place,** at Animal Kingdom Lodge. It has excellent food and an extensive wine list. If Jiko isn't available, the Contemporary Resort's **California Grill** is highly rated but very loud at dinner.
VIA NAPOLI RISTORANTE E PIZZERIA (Italy/EPCOT)	In EPCOT, try **Teppan Edo** (Japan) or the **Rose & Crown Dining Room** (United Kingdom). Outside of EPCOT, try **Trattoria al Forno** (BoardWalk).
BOATHOUSE, RAGLAN ROAD, or CHEF ART SMITH'S HOMECOMIN' (all Disney Springs)	In Disney Springs, adults should try **Wine Bar George. Jaleo by José Andrés** (also Disney Springs) has a relatively large capacity, and excellent food.

four reservations within a year. Besides being the polite thing to do, it's a snap to cancel or change reservations on the website or app.

THEME PARK RESTAURANTS AND ADMISSION

MANY FIRST-TIME VISITORS to Walt Disney World are surprised when making their Advance Dining Reservations to learn that both admission to a theme park and theme park reservations (see page 30) are required to eat at restaurants inside of it. The lone exception is **Rain-forest Cafe** in Animal Kingdom, which can be entered from the parking lot just outside of the theme park; you must have admission and a park reservation, however, if you want to enter Animal Kingdom.

If you're booking a meal for a day when you weren't expecting to visit the parks, you'll need to check the restaurant's location to make sure it isn't in a theme park. Also, if you've visited a theme park earlier in the day that's different from the one in which your restaurant is located, you'll need to have purchased the **Park Hopper** option (page 375) in order to dine inside the second theme park.

DRESS

DRESS IS INFORMAL at most theme park restaurants, but Disney has a business casual dress code for some of its resort restaurants: khakis, slacks, or dress shorts with a collared shirt for men, and capris, skirts, dresses, and dress shorts for women; jeans may be worn by men and women if in good condition. Restaurants with this dress code are **Jiko— The Cooking Place** in Animal Kingdom Lodge, **Flying Fish** at the Board-Walk, **California Grill** at the Contemporary Resort, **Monsieur Paul** at EPCOT's France Pavilion, **Takumi-Tei** at EPCOT's Japan Pavilion, **Cítri-cos** and **Narcoossee's** at the Grand Floridian, **Yachtsman Steakhouse** at the Yacht Club Resort, **Todd English's Bluezoo** and **Shula's Steak House**

WDW RESTAURANTS BOOKABLE WITH OPENTABLE (subject to change)

BONNET CREEK

• **Bull & Bear Steakhouse** Waldorf Astoria Orlando

DISNEY RESORTS

• **Big River Grille & Brewing Works** BoardWalk • **Flying Fish** BoardWalk • **Toledo—Tapas, Steak & Seafood** Coronado Springs • **Jiko—The Cooking Place** Animal Kingdom Lodge–Jambo House

DISNEY SPRINGS

• **The Boathouse** The Landing • **City Works** West Side • **The Edison** Town Center • **Enzo's Hideaway, Maria & Enzo's Ristorante** The Landing • **Frontera Cocina** Town Center • **House of Blues** West Side • **Jaleo** West Side • **Morimoto Asia** The Landing • **Paddlefish** The Landing • **Paradiso 37** The Landing • **Planet Hollywood** Town Center • **Raglan Road Irish Pub & Restaurant** The Landing • **Splitsville Dining Room** West Side • **STK Steakhouse** The Landing • **Terralina Crafted Italian** The Landing • **Wine Bar George** The Landing • **Wolfgang Puck Bar & Grill** Town Center

DOLPHIN, SWAN, AND SWAN RESERVE

• **Amare** Swan Reserve • **Il Mulino New York** Swan • **Rosa Mexicano** Dolphin • **Shula's Steak House** Dolphin • **Todd English's Bluezoo** Dolphin

FORT WILDERNESS AREA

• **Plancha** and **Ravello** Four Seasons Resort Orlando

at the Dolphin, **Il Mulino** at the Swan, and **Topolino's Terrace** at the Riviera Resort. **Victoria & Albert's** at the Grand Floridian is the only Disney restaurant that requires men to wear a jacket to dinner (they'll provide one if needed).

FOOD ALLERGIES AND DIETARY NEEDS

IF YOU HAVE SPECIAL DIETARY NEEDS, make them known when you make reservations. For more information, see Part 8.

unofficial **TIP**
Be aware that there is a charge for canceling a meal with kosher or other special requests, to cover the extra cost of ordering the individual meal components.

A Phillipsburg, New Jersey, mom reports her family's experience:

My 6-year-old has many food allergies. When making my Advance Dining Reservations, I indicated these to the clerk. When we arrived at the restaurants, the staff was already aware of my child's allergies and assigned our table a chef who double-checked the list with us. The chefs were very nice and made my son feel very special.

A Milford, Pennsylvania, family advises patience:

Disney is great with allergies, but expect LOTS of waiting for someone to call a chef, wait for a chef, and wait for your food. Sit-down restaurants were actually faster than quick-service, which is ridiculous as there was always a line of allergy diners. There should be a separate kiosk or at least a call button so diners can call a chef themselves.

Healthful Food at Walt Disney World

Health-conscious choices such as fresh fruit are available at most fast-food counters and from vendors. Vegetarians, people who have diabetes, those requiring kosher meals, and anyone trying to eat healthfully should have no trouble finding something that meets their needs.

SIT-DOWN-RESTAURANT TIPS AND TRIC

BEFORE YOU BEGIN EATING your way through the W
to know a few things:

1. Theme park restaurants often rush their customers to make room fo
next group of diners. Dining at high speed may appeal to a family w
young, restless children, but for people wanting to relax, it can be more lik
eating in a pressure chamber than fine dining.

2. Disney restaurants have comparatively few tables for parties of two, and
servers are disinclined to seat two guests at larger tables. If you're a duo,
you might have to wait longer—sometimes much longer—to be seated.

3. At full-service Disney restaurants, an automatic gratuity of 18% is added to
your tab for parties of six or more—even at buffets where you serve yourself.

While the inflation-adjusted peak cost of a one-day theme park
ticket has increased about 175% since 2010, the average lunch entrée
price at Le Cellier has gone from around $22 to around $50—an
increase of 124%. For reference, the average meal cost in a US restaurant went up 51% during the same time, according to the Federal
Reserve Bank of St. Louis. This comment from a New Orleans mom
spells it out:

> *Disney keeps pushing prices up and up. For us, the sky is NOT the*
> *limit. We won't be back.*

Fortunately, you're not limited to dining in the World. See "Dining
Outside Walt Disney World," page 361.

MOBILE ORDERING

DISNEY STRONGLY RECOMMENDS mobile ordering at almost all
of its in-park counter-service restaurants. Using the My Disney Experience (MDE) app, you place an order, pay for your meal online, choose
a time to pick up your food, and notify the restaurant when you've
arrived for that pickup. The app will tell you when your food is ready.
Show that notification to a cast member, and you'll be directed to a
specific window or line to collect your food. Be sure to keep your app
updated to see the latest participating restaurants.

It can take restaurants 30 minutes or more to prepare your order
once it's placed, and it may take another 5–10 minutes to pick it up.
Plan to place your order 30–40 minutes before you want to eat during
most times of the year, or 1–2 hours in advance during the holidays.

If you're unable to access the MDE app or use mobile ordering,
speak with a cast member outside the restaurant. They'll usually provide a paper menu and individual access to a cashier for payment. You
may still have to wait to be served.

A Portsmouth, Rhode Island, family found that the mobile app
flaked on them:

> *We used mobile ordering once for Pinocchio Village Haus. The app*
> *said we would be notified when our order was ready, but we never*
> *got notice, and after waiting for 10–15 minutes, we went in and*
> *found our food had been ready the entire time and was now cold.*

Lesson learned: If your order seems to be running behind and you
haven't received an alert, check with a cast member right away.

TIME AND MONEY

...NE YOUR MEALS to counter-service fare, you
...ng food in the parks—not to mention the costs
... the table on page 297). Here are some ways to
...u spend hunting and gathering:

...e you arrive, either at a restaurant outside the World or
...dge or cooler in your room. This will save you a ton of time.

...akfast, buy vendor snacks in the parks, or bring your own.

...restaurants are busiest between 11:30 a.m. and 2:15 p.m. for
...ween 6 and 9 p.m. for dinner. Avoid trying to eat during these
...cially 12:30–1:30 p.m.

... Many counter-service restaurants sell cold sandwiches. Buy a cold lunch minus drinks before 11:30 a.m., and carry it in small plastic bags until you're ready to eat (within an hour or so of purchase). Ditto for dinner. Buy drinks at the appropriate time from any convenient vendor.

5. If you're short on time and the park is closing early, just stay until closing and eat dinner outside the World before returning to your hotel. If the park stays open late, eat dinner at about 4 or 4:30 p.m. at the restaurant of your choice. You should sneak in just ahead of the dinner crowd.

This Missouri mom shares her variations on our tips:

We arrived at WDW with our steel cooler well stocked with milk and sandwich fixings. I froze a block of ice in a milk bottle, and we replenished it daily with ice from the resort ice machine. [Note: Loose ice and dry ice are prohibited in coolers inside the theme parks and water parks.] We ate cereal, milk, and fruit each morning, with boxed juices.

Each child had a belt bag of his own, which he filled from a special box of goodies each day with things like packages of crackers and cheese and packets of peanuts and raisins. Each child also had a small, rectangular plastic water bottle that could hang on the belt. We filled these at water fountains before getting into lines.

We left the park before noon; ate sandwiches, chips, and soda in the room; and napped. We purchased our evening meal in the park at a counter-service eatery. We budgeted for both morning and evening snacks from a vendor but often didn't need them.

A Whiteland, Indiana, mom adds a tip of her own:

If you're traveling with younger kids, take a supply of small paper or plastic cups to split drinks, which are both huge and expensive.

CHARACTER DINING

CHARACTER DINING IS FOUND throughout Walt Disney World. At press time, 11 restaurants offer a chance to see Disney characters while you eat. There's enough demand for these character experiences that reservations for popular dining times can be hard to come by if you wait until a couple of weeks before your vacation to book.

What's more, if you want to book a character meal, you must provide Disney with a credit card number. Your card will be charged $10 per person if you don't show or if you cancel your reservation less than 24 hours in advance; you may, however, reschedule with no penalty. See "Getting Advance Dining Reservations at Popular Restaurants" (page 273) for the full story.

WHAT TO EXPECT

CHARACTER MEALS ARE BUSTLING AFFAIRS held in the largest full-service restaurants at the theme parks and on-property resorts, along with the Swan at Walt Disney World, select hotels in the Disney Springs Resort Area and Bonnet Creek Resort, and the Four Seasons.

Character breakfasts typically offer a fixed menu served family-style (in large skillets or platters at your table), buffet-style, or à la carte. The typical breakfast includes scrambled eggs; bacon and sausage; potato casserole; waffles, pancakes, or French toast; biscuits, rolls, or pastries; and fruit.

Character dinners range from buffets to family-style fixed menus to dishes ordered off the menu. Dinners, such as those at 1900 Park Fare at the Grand Floridian (closed at press time) and Akershus Royal Banquet Hall at EPCOT, separate the kids' fare from the grown-ups', though everyone is free to eat from both menus. Typically, the kids' menu includes burgers, hot dogs, pizza, fish sticks, chicken nuggets, macaroni and cheese, and peanut-butter-and-jelly sandwiches. Selections from the buffet and adult menu usually include prime rib or another carved meat, baked or broiled seafood, pasta, chicken, an ethnic dish or two, vegetables, potatoes, and salad.

At all meals, characters circulate around the room while you eat. During your meal, each of the three to five characters present will stop by your table, sign autographs, and pose for photos with your family. Characters move slowly, and it's unlikely you'll miss them when they swing by.

WHEN TO GO

ATTENDING A RESORT'S CHARACTER BREAKFAST usually prevents you from arriving at the theme parks in time for opening. Because early morning is best for touring and you don't want to burn daylight lingering over breakfast, we suggest the following strategies:

1. Go to a character dinner or lunch instead of breakfast. It will be a nice break.

2. Schedule the first seating for lunch, typically 11 or 11:30 a.m. Have a light snack such as cereal or bagels before you head to the parks for opening, hit the most popular attractions until 10:45–11:15 or thereabouts, and then head for lunch. That should keep you fueled until dinnertime, especially if you eat another light snack in the afternoon.

3. Go on arrival or departure day. The day you arrive and check in is good for a character dinner—not only is it a good way to ease into your trip, but it can also help your children get acquainted with how they'll encounter characters at a distance in the parks. Similarly, scheduling a character breakfast on checkout day, before you head for the airport or begin your drive home, is a nice way to cap off the trip.

4. Go on a rest day. If you plan to stay five or more days, you'll probably take a day or a half day off from touring to rest or do something else. These are perfect days for a character meal.

If you book an in-park character breakfast, schedule yours for the first seating if the park opens at 8 a.m. or later. You'll be admitted to the park before other guests (admission and park reservations are still required; see pages 30 and 277) through a special line at the turnstiles. Arrive early to be among the first parties seated.

HOW TO CHOOSE A CHARACTER MEAL

MANY READERS ASK FOR ADVICE about character meals. This question from a Waterloo, Iowa, mom is typical:

> Are all character meals pretty much the same or are some better than others? How should I go about choosing one?

In fact, some *are* better, sometimes much better. When we evaluate character meals, we look for the following:

1. THE CHARACTERS The meals feature a diverse assortment of characters. See our Character-Meal Hit Parade table on pages 284–285 to find out which characters are assigned to each meal. Most restaurants stick with the same characters; even so, check the lineup when you call to make your Advance Dining Reservations.

2. ATTENTION FROM THE CHARACTERS At all character meals, Disney characters circulate among diners. How much time a character spends in camera range of you and your children depends primarily on the ratio of characters to guests. The more characters and fewer guests, the better. Because many character-meal venues never fill to capacity, the character-to-guest ratios in our table have been adjusted to reflect an average attendance. Even so, there's quite a range. The best ratio of currently open restaurants is at Garden Grill and Topolino's Terrace, where there's about one character to every 46 guests.

The worst ratio is theoretically at the Swan resort's **Garden Grove,** where there could be as few as 1 character for every 198 guests. (*Note:* At press time it's open, but no characters visit.) We say *theoretically,* however, because in practice there are far fewer guests at Garden Grove than at character meals in Disney-owned resorts, and often more characters. (During one meal, some friends of ours were the only guests in the restaurant for breakfast and had to ask the characters to leave them alone so they could eat.)

A Jerseyville, Illinois, mom gives the characters high marks:

> Our 7-year-old daughter wanted to have dinner with Sleeping Beauty, so we scheduled a princess dinner in the Norway Pavilion. The princesses were so accessible and took their time with our child, answering questions and smiling for pictures. In fact, our daughter told us she had the best day of her life.

An Indiana mother of two relates the importance of keeping tabs on the characters:

> For character meals, take note of which characters are there when you arrive, and mentally check them off as they visit your table. If the last one or two seem slow to arrive, seek out the "character manager" and let him or her know ASAP.

3. THE SETTING Some character meals have exotic settings; for others, moving the event to an elementary-school cafeteria would be an improvement. Our table rates each meal's setting with the familiar scale of one (worst) to five (best) stars. The **Garden Grill Restaurant** in The Land in EPCOT deserves special mention. Garden Grill is a revolving restaurant overlooking several scenes from the Living with the Land boat ride. Also in EPCOT, the popular Princess Storybook Dining is held in the castlelike **Akershus Royal Banquet Hall.** Though **Chef Mickey's** at the Contemporary Resort is rather sterile in appearance, it affords a great view of the monorail running through the hotel. Themes and settings of the remaining character-meal venues, while apparent to adults, will be lost on most children.

4. THE FOOD Although some food served at character meals is quite good, most is just average. In variety, consistency, and quality, restaurants generally do a better job with lunch or dinner than breakfast. To help you sort everything out, we rate the food at each character meal in the Character-Meal Hit Parade table using a five-star scale.

Most restaurants currently offer a buffet or family-style service in which all hot items are served from the same pot or skillet. A Texas mom notes:

> *The family-style meals are much better for character dining—at a buffet, you're scared to leave your table in case you miss a character or other action.*

5. NOISE If you want to eat in peace, character meals are a bad choice. That said, some are much noisier than others. Our table gives you an idea of what to expect.

6. WHICH MEAL? Although breakfasts seem to be most popular, character lunches and dinners are usually more practical because they don't interfere with early-morning touring. During hot weather, a character lunch can be heavenly.

7. COST Dinners and lunches cost more than breakfasts. Meal prices vary considerably from the least expensive to the most expensive restaurant; they can also vary by as much as $15–$20 depending on the season. Breakfasts run about $42–$65 for adults and $27–$39 for kids ages 3–9. For character lunches and dinners, expect to pay around $55–$79 for adults and $36–$47 for kids. Little ones age 2 years and younger eat free.

8. ADVANCE DINING RESERVATIONS (See "Advance Dining Reservations: The Official Line," page 273, for details.) Though reservations are generally tough to get for in-demand restaurants, reservations for most character meals are easy to obtain even if you call only a couple of weeks before your trip, as long as you're not particular about the time you eat. **Akershus Royal Banquet Hall, Garden Grill** and **Topolino's Terrace** are another story—for these, you'll need our strategy (see page 273). If you don't get what you want at first, keep trying, advises a London mother of two:

> *When a booking window opens, many people overbook and then either get buyer's remorse or find alternative bookings and cancel. When my booking window first opened, I was able to book barely 20% of what I wanted, but within two to three weeks I had 100%.*

CHARACTER-MEAL HIT PARADE

1. AKERSHUS ROYAL BANQUET HALL   EPCOT

- **MEALS SERVED** Breakfast, lunch, dinner • **SETTING** ★★★★
- **CHARACTERS** 4–6 Disney princesses chosen from among Ariel, Belle, Jasmine, Snow White, Aurora, Mulan, and Cinderella
- **TYPE OF SERVICE** Buffet and menu (all you care to eat)
- **FOOD VARIETY & QUALITY** ★★★½ • **NOISE LEVEL** Loud
- **CHARACTER-GUEST RATIO** 1:54

2. ARTIST POINT   WILDERNESS LODGE

- **MEAL SERVED** Dinner • **SETTING** ★★★½
- **CHARACTERS** Snow White, Dopey, Grumpy, the Evil Queen
- **TYPE OF SERVICE** Fixed menu with several choices
- **FOOD VARIETY & QUALITY** ★★★★
- **NOISE LEVEL** Quiet • **CHARACTER-GUEST RATIO** 1:35

3. CAPE MAY CAFÉ   BEACH CLUB RESORT

- **MEAL SERVED** Breakfast • **SETTING** ★★★
- **CHARACTERS** Goofy, Donald, Minnie, Daisy
- **TYPE OF SERVICE** Buffet • **FOOD VARIETY & QUALITY** ★★½
- **NOISE LEVEL** Moderate • **CHARACTER-GUEST RATIO** 1:67

4. CHEF MICKEY'S   CONTEMPORARY RESORT

- **MEALS SERVED** Breakfast, dinner • **SETTING** ★★★
- **CHARACTERS** Mickey, Minnie, Donald, Goofy, Pluto
- **TYPE OF SERVICE** Buffet • **FOOD VARIETY & QUALITY** ★★★½
- **NOISE LEVEL** Very loud • **CHARACTER-GUEST RATIO** 1:56

5. CINDERELLA'S ROYAL TABLE   MAGIC KINGDOM

- **MEALS SERVED** Breakfast, lunch, dinner • **SETTING** ★★★★
- **CHARACTERS** Cinderella, Ariel, Aurora, Belle, Jasmine, Snow White, Fairy Godmother
- **TYPE OF SERVICE** Fixed menu • **FOOD VARIETY & QUALITY** ★★★
- **NOISE LEVEL** Quiet • **CHARACTER-GUEST RATIO** 1:26

6. THE CRYSTAL PALACE   MAGIC KINGDOM

- **MEALS SERVED** Breakfast, lunch, dinner • **SETTING** ★★★
- **CHARACTERS** Pooh, Eeyore, Piglet, Tigger • **TYPE OF SERVICE** Buffet
- **FOOD VARIETY & QUALITY** Breakfast ★★½ Lunch and dinner ★★★
- **NOISE LEVEL** Very loud
- **CHARACTER-GUEST RATIO** Breakfast, 1:67; lunch and dinner, 1:89

7. GARDEN GRILL RESTAURANT   EPCOT

- **MEAL SERVED** Lunch, dinner • **SETTING** ★★★★
- **CHARACTERS** Mickey, Pluto, Chip 'n' Dale • **TYPE OF SERVICE** Family-style
- **FOOD VARIETY & QUALITY** ★★★½ • **NOISE LEVEL** Very quiet
- **CHARACTER-GUEST RATIO** 1:46

Characters are subject to change, so check before you go.

9. CHECKING IT TWICE Disney occasionally shuffles the characters and theme of a character meal. If your little one's heart is set on Pooh and Piglet, getting Hook and Mr. Smee instead will just brand you forever as lame. Reconfirm all character-meal reservations three weeks or so before you leave home by calling ☎ 407-WDW-DINE (939-3463).

CHARACTER-MEAL HIT PARADE

8. GARDEN GROVE** SWAN

- MEALS SERVED Breakfast (Sat. and Sun.) • SETTING ★★½
- CHARACTERS Chip 'n' Dale, Goofy, Pluto • TYPE OF SERVICE Buffet
- FOOD VARIETY & QUALITY ★★½ • NOISE LEVEL Moderate
- CHARACTER-GUEST RATIO 1:198, but frequently much better

9. HOLLYWOOD & VINE DISNEY'S HOLLYWOOD STUDIOS

- MEALS SERVED Breakfast, lunch, and dinner • SETTING ★★½
- CHARACTERS *Breakfast:* Disney Junior characters
  Lunch and dinner: Minnie, Mickey, Goofy, Pluto, Donald (and sometimes Daisy)
- TYPE OF SERVICE Buffet • FOOD VARIETY & QUALITY ★★★
- NOISE LEVEL Moderate • CHARACTER-GUEST RATIO 1:71

10. 'OHANA POLYNESIAN VILLAGE RESORT

- MEAL SERVED Breakfast • SETTING ★★
- CHARACTERS Lilo and Stitch, Mickey, Pluto • TYPE OF SERVICE Family-style
- FOOD VARIETY & QUALITY ★★½ • NOISE LEVEL Loud
- CHARACTER-GUEST RATIO 1:57

11. 1900 PARK FARE* GRAND FLORIDIAN RESORT

- MEALS SERVED Breakfast, dinner • SETTING ★★★
- CHARACTERS *Breakfast:* Mary Poppins, Alice, Mad Hatter, Pooh, Tigger
  Dinner: Cinderella, Prince Charming, Lady Tremaine, the two stepsisters
- TYPE OF SERVICE Buffet
- FOOD VARIETY & QUALITY Breakfast ★★★ Dinner ★★★½
- NOISE LEVEL Moderate • CHARACTER-GUEST RATIO Breakfast, 1:54; dinner, 1:44

12. TUSKER HOUSE RESTAURANT DISNEY'S ANIMAL KINGDOM

- MEALS SERVED Breakfast, lunch, dinner • SETTING ★★★
- CHARACTERS Donald, Daisy, Mickey, Goofy, Pluto • TYPE OF SERVICE Fixed menu
- FOOD VARIETY & QUALITY ★★★ • NOISE LEVEL Very loud
- CHARACTER-GUEST RATIO 1:112

13. TOPOLINO'S TERRACE RIVIERA RESORT

- MEALS SERVED Breakfast • SETTING ★★★★
- CHARACTERS Mickey, Minnie, Donald, Daisy
- TYPE OF SERVICE Fixed menu • FOOD VARIETY & QUALITY ★★★★
- NOISE LEVEL Moderate • CHARACTER-GUEST RATIO 1:45

14. TRATTORIA AL FORNO** DISNEY'S BOARDWALK

- MEAL SERVED Breakfast • SETTING ★★★½
- CHARACTERS Rapunzel, Flynn Ryder, Ariel, Prince Eric
- TYPE OF SERVICE Fixed menu with several choices
- FOOD VARIETY & QUALITY ★★★½
- NOISE LEVEL Quiet • CHARACTER-GUEST RATIO 1:50

*Closed at press time   **Open but no characters at press time

10. "FRIENDS" Some character meals advertise a main character and a varying cast of "friends"—for example, "Pooh and friends," meaning Eeyore, Piglet, and Tigger, or some combination thereof, or "Mickey and friends" with some assortment chosen from among Minnie, Goofy, Pluto, Donald, Daisy, Chip, and Dale.

11. CINDY'S ROYAL RUSH Most character meals are leisurely affairs, and you can usually stay as long as you want. However, because Cinderella's Royal Table in the Magic Kingdom is in such high demand, the restaurant does everything short of prechewing your food to move you through, as this European mother of a 5-year-old can attest:

> We dined a lot, did three character meals and a few Signature restaurants, and every meal was awesome except for lunch with Cinderella. It was a rushed affair. We had barely sat down when the appetizers were thrown on our table, the princesses each spent just a few seconds with our daughter—almost no interaction—and the side dishes were cold. We were out of there within 40 minutes and felt very stressed. Considering the price, I cannot recommend it.

DISNEY DINING SUGGESTIONS

FOLLOWING ARE OUR SUGGESTIONS for dining at each of the major theme parks. If you want to try a full-service restaurant at one of the parks, be aware that the restaurants continue to serve after the park's official closing time.

THE MAGIC KINGDOM

OF THE PARK'S full-time full-service restaurants, the best are **Liberty Tree Tavern** in Liberty Square and the **Jungle Navigation Co. Ltd. Skipper Canteen** in Adventureland. Liberty Tree Tavern (92%/Above Average) serves standard American family-style meals for lunch and dinner, while Skipper Canteen (92%/Above Average) serves hearty food in a Jungle Cruise–themed environment.

The big draw at the pricey **Cinderella's Royal Table** (84%/Much Below Average) is the setting—the food is . . . not. **The Plaza Restaurant** (81%/Much Below Average) on Main Street serves passable meals at more moderate prices than the other sit-down restaurants.

unofficial **TIP**
All Magic Kingdom sit-down restaurants serve beer and wine with dinner.

The most in-demand restaurant in the Magic Kingdom is **Be Our Guest** (79%/Do Not Visit) in Fantasyland; unfortunately, the entire dining experience has declined substantially, even as the prices have increased. This woman from Hartland, Wisconsin, recalls that she was served attitude instead of food:

> I was unable to get a reservation for Be Our Guest. When I mentioned this to the cast member out front, she offered no suggestions, told me I couldn't go in just to look around, and said the fact that I couldn't get a reservation is "what makes it so special." In that moment, I just wanted to slap her.

We agree it's an especially poor value for the money. Likewise, quality at **The Crystal Palace** (82%/Much Below Average) has dropped. Likewise, avoid **Tony's Town Square** (82%/Much Below Average) on Main Street and (if it's open) **The Diamond Horseshoe** (73%/Do Not Visit)—these are among the worst restaurants in Walt Disney World.

- **Casey's Corner** Main Street, USA • **Columbia Harbour House** Liberty Square
- **Liberty Square Market** Liberty Square

Columbia Harbour House (91%/Above Average) is the best counter-service restaurant in the Magic Kingdom. Its menu focuses on seafood, with a tasty lobster roll, grilled salmon, and grilled shrimp all worth ordering, plus solid options for kids, vegans, and vegetarians. **Casey's Corner** (91%/Above Average), on Main Street, U.S.A., serves ballpark-style hot dogs and fries. It's one of the rare Disney restaurants to have substantially improved its food quality coming out of the pandemic. The highly-rated **Liberty Square Market** (93%/Much Above Average) also serves tasty hot dogs, plus pretzels and other snacks.

If these places don't do it for you, be prepared to make some compromises at the Magic Kingdom's other counter-service restaurants, all of which struggle to achieve average levels of quality. The best is probably **Pecos Bill Tall Tale Inn and Cafe** (86%/Below Average) in Frontierland, serving healthy portions of burgers and Tex-Mex. Avoid **Cosmic Ray's Starlight Cafe** (81%/Much Below Average) in Tomorrowland and, if it's open, **Tortuga Tavern** (75%/Do Not Visit) in Adventureland.

EPCOT

SINCE THE BEGINNING, dining has been an integral component of EPCOT's entertainment product. World Showcase has many more restaurants than attractions, and EPCOT has added bars, tapas-style eateries, and full-service restaurants faster than any park in memory. (See table on next page for a list of all the park's full-service restaurants.)

EPCOT runs food festival booths almost every day. Its annual **Food & Wine Festival** runs from late-July through mid-November; the **International Festival of the Holidays** begins a few days later. The **Festival of the Arts** follows that and lasts through late February, and then it's time for the **Flower & Garden Festival** from March through July.

While it's not the same as sitting inside a well-themed World Showcase pavilion, food booths have their pluses: There's a lot of variety, the food quality can be quite good, and it's generally faster than a full sit-down meal.

> *uno*fficial **TIP**
> EPCOT has 21 full-service restaurants: 3 in Future World and 18 in World Showcase. With a couple of exceptions, these are among the best restaurants at Walt Disney World, in or out of the theme parks.

For the most part, EPCOT's restaurants serve decent food, although World Showcase spots can be timid when it comes to delivering authentic representations of their host nations' cuisine—the "spicy" items in China are nowhere close to their domestic intensity, for example. While it's true that the less adventuresome diner can find steak and potatoes on virtually every menu, the same kitchens will happily serve up a more traditional preparation of any dish if you ask. (We've had wonderful experiences by asking for our food to be prepared the way the chefs would make it for themselves.)

An afternoon without dinner at World Showcase is like not having a date on the day of the prom. Each pavilion except the United States

RESTAURANTS IN EPCOT

WORLD DISCOVERY (formerly Future World)

The Seas with Nemo & Friends • Garden Grill Restaurant The
World Discovery

CASE

shus Royal Banquet Hall Norway • Biergarten Restaurant Germany • Chefs de
rance France • La Crêperie de Paris France • La Hacienda de San Angel Mexico
• Le Cellier Steakhouse Canada • Monsieur Paul France • Nine Dragons Restaurant
• China • Rose & Crown Dining Room United Kingdom • San Angel Inn Restaurante
Mexico • Spice Road Table Morocco • Takumi-Tei Japan • Teppan Edo Japan
• Tokyo Dining Japan • Tutto Gusto Wine Cellar Italy • Tutto Italia Ristorante Italy
• Via Napoli Ristorante e Pizzeria Italy

has a beautifully seductive ethnic restaurant. To tour these exotic settings and not partake is almost beyond the limits of willpower. Still, some restaurants are better than others.

EPCOT restaurants that combine attractive ambience and well-prepared food with good value are **Teppan Edo** in Japan (95%/Exceptional)—the No. 2–rated sit-down restaurant in Walt Disney World over the past year; **Via Napoli Ristorante e Pizzeria** in Italy (91%/Above Average); **Spice Road Table** in Morocco (91%/Above Average); **Garden Grill Restaurant** in The Land (90%/Average); and **Rose & Crown Dining Room** in the United Kingdom (89%/Average). Those that *don't* provide good value for the money include **San Angel Inn Restaurante** in Mexico (85%/Much Below Average); **Tutto Italia** in Italy (83%/Much Below Average); **Akershus Royal Banquet Hall** in Norway (79%/Do Not Visit); and **Monsieur Paul** in France (76%/Do Not Visit). Of course, some readers take issue with our assessments, as is the case with this Wilmington, North Carolina, couple:

> We disagree that Monsieur Paul is overpriced. A similar meal would fetch a similar price in any foodie town, such as New York or Miami; therefore, we'd call it "foodie priced." If you want overpriced food at Disney World, pay $12.50 for a turkey leg.

For the record, the last time we were served bisque at Monsieur Paul, it had sat long enough to form a skin. But the reader has a point—many readers from different parts of the country have different price expectations for high-quality meals, based on what they're used to paying in their hometowns. A reader we contacted about their experience at Japan's **Takumi-Tei** is used to paying $150 per person for good omakase sushi in Manhattan and said that the $250-per-person price at Takumi-Tei was in line with the experience and quality; another reader we contacted, from Wilmington, North Carolina, couldn't get past the cost, saying it was "Oprah money."

A Germantown, Tennessee, woman who ate at Via Napoli found the leisurely service uncharacteristic—and not in a good way:

> We waited 40 minutes for dessert, which we wouldn't have bothered to order had it not been included in our Candlelight Processional dining package. On one hand, this more closely resembled what we experienced on a trip to the actual country of Italy versus the typical in-and-out experience of WDW restaurants. On the other hand, I don't believe Via Napoli was particularly striving for authenticity—it was just bad service.

- Les Halles Boulangerie–Pâtisserie France • **Kringla Bakeri og Kafe** Norway
- **Tangierine Café** Morocco

Les Halles Boulangerie–Pâtisserie (93%/Much Above Average) in France is one of the highest-rated counter-service restaurants in Walt Disney World. It sells pastries, sandwiches, and quiches. The bread and pastries are made on-site, and the sandwiches are as close to actual French street food—in taste, portion size, *and* price—as you'll get anywhere in EPCOT. Another favorite is the grilled meats at Morocco's **Tangierine Café** (93%/Much Above Average).

In addition to these, we recommend the United Kingdom's **Rose & Crown Pub** (95%/Exceptional) for Guinness, Harp, and Bass beers, and the **Yorkshire County Fish Shop** (95%/Exceptional) for fresh fish-and-chips.

EPCOT FOOD FESTIVALS EPCOT hosts four major festivals per year. No matter what season or theme the festival has, food and drinks are the main draw. For each festival, EPCOT runs small, semipermanent, themed booths around World Showcase and Future World. The booths serve appetizer-size portions—and almost always beer and wine—that fit the stand's theme.

These festivals give EPCOT's chefs a chance to experiment with new ingredients and flavor combinations. The food quality is generally very good, and sometimes amazing: Chefs from the Canada Pavilion, for example, have produced an outstanding honey-mascarpone cheesecake made with local wildflower honey—one of the best desserts we've had anywhere in Walt Disney World. It was perfect, and small enough to eat on the way to our next pavilion.

Readers also rate the food quality of the booths at the Flower & Garden and Food & Wine festivals as above average. Many guest favorites return year after year. For this edition, we've compiled a list of the best food items you're likely to find at each EPCOT festival (see next page). Each list is organized as an appetizer/entrée/dessert tasting menu. Trying all the dishes in each grouping should cost between $50 and $75 per festival.

Drinking Around the World (Showcase)

A popular adult pastime in EPCOT is to make a complete circuit of World Showcase, sampling the alcoholic drinks native to each nation. Here's a list of the don't-miss places.

LA CAVA DEL TEQUILA, MEXICO (95%/Exceptional) Located inside the pyramid of the Mexico Pavilion, this is the best bar in Walt Disney World and one of the best tequila bars in the country. Its ever-changing menu includes more than 200 kinds of tequila and mezcal, several margaritas, and various light appetizers. On weekends and during special events such as the Food & Wine Festival, Cinco de Mayo, and National Tequila Day (July 24), expect a wait to get a drink.

Most days, La Cava has a tequila expert on hand to explain the different types and provide tasting notes. (Ask for Hilda or Humberto, both from Tequila in Jalisco, Mexico—tell them Len sent you.) If you happen to be in EPCOT during the fall Food & Wine Festival,

BEST FOOD ITEMS AT EACH EPCOT FESTIVAL

FESTIVAL OF THE ARTS (January–February)

• **Tomato Soup** with Pimento Cheese, Bacon, and Fried Green Tomato Grilled Cheese (Pop Eats) • **Cast Iron–Roasted P.E.I. Mussels** (Craftsman's Courtyard) • **Angry Crab** (Moderne) • **Carne Asada** (El Artista Hambriento) • **Red Wine–Braised Beef Short Rib** (Pastoral Palate) • **Decadent Valrhona Chocolate** (Deco Delights) • **House-Made Crispy Almond Phyllo Pockets** (Tangierine Café) • Anything from the **Deconstructed Dish** booth

FLOWER & GARDEN FESTIVAL (March–July)

• **Chilled Potato and Leek Soup "Vichyssoise"** (Farmer's Feast) • **Avocado Toast** with Marinated Toy Box Tomatoes on Toasted Ciabatta (BrunchCOT) • **Grilled Street Corn on the Cob** (Florida Fresh) • **Hummus Trio** (Tangierine Café) • **Creamy Shrimp Udon** with Spring Vegetables (Hanami) • **Orange Sesame Tempura Shrimp** with Orange Chile Sauce (Citrus Blossom) • **Taco Vampiro** (Jardin de Fiesta) • **Chargrilled Bison Ribeye** with Creamy Leek Fondue (Farmer's Feast) • **Fried Cinnamon Roll Bites** (Farmer's Feast) • **Bananas Foster Bread Pudding** (Magnolia Terrace) • **Florida Strawberry Shortcake** (Florida Fresh)

FOOD & WINE FESTIVAL (July–November)

• **Grilled Pork Lettuce Wraps** (The Swanky Saucy Swine) • **Impossible Burger Slider** (Earth Eats) • **Schinkennudeln** (ham, onion, and cheese casserole; Germany) • **Crispy Paneer** (India booth) • **Crispy Brussels Sprouts** (Brew-Wing at the Odyssey) • **Barbacoa Tostada** (Mexico) • **Pão de Queijo** (cheese bread; Brazil booth) • **Three-Cheese Beignet** (France) • **Apple Strudel** (Germany)

FESTIVAL OF THE HOLIDAYS (November–December)

• **Beef & Noodle Soup Bowl** (Shanghai Holiday Kitchen) • **New Year Celebration Soba** (Shi Wasu, Japan) • **Peanut Stew** or **Githeri** (Refreshment Outpost) • **Cheese Fondue** (Bavaria Holiday Kitchen) • **Potato Latkes** (L'Chaim!) • **Pork Schnitzel** (Bavaria Holiday Kitchen) • **Kālua Pork** (Mele Kalikimaka) • **Linzer Cookie** (Bavaria Holiday Kitchen) • **Blackened Catfish** (American Holiday Table)

sign up for a tequila tasting if they're offered. Done in small groups with flights of tequila, it will teach you how to appreciate this magical liquid that Len likens to "a hug, but from the inside." He regrets that many of his favorite La Cava stories are unsuitable for print.

CHOZA DE MARGARITA, MEXICO (92%/Much Above Average) The menu is limited—just four on-the-rocks and four frozen options, three beers, two nonalcoholic options, and small plates for snacking—but each item is intensely flavorful and delicious, making this a great spot to visit when La Cava del Tequila is full. The rocks margaritas are what we gravitate toward.

ROSE & CROWN PUB, UNITED KINGDOM (95%/Exceptional) It's a little brighter than many British pubs we've seen, but Rose & Crown serves a wide variety of ales, lagers, stouts, and ciders alongside traditional English pub fare such as fish-and-chips and sausage rolls. If you're wanting something stronger, the pub has Scotch whiskies and not-quite-in-the-UK Irish whiskeys. Service is cheerful and fast.

SAKE BARS, JAPAN (93%/Much Above Average) There are two sake bars in Japan: One is an outdoor kiosk on the walking path toward the back of the pavilion, and the other is a small counter tucked into the back of the first floor of the Mitsukoshi Department Store. Both have decent, affordable selections of sakes. The ones in the department store can be purchased from a shelf right next to the bar table. We're still amazed these haven't turned into a waterside bar.

WEINKELLER, GERMANY (92%/Much Above Average) Decorated with stone, dark woods, and heavy chandeliers, Weinkeller serves wines by the glass (around $9). If you love sweet white wines, this is the place to be. Selections usually include a couple of Rieslings, a Liebfraumilch, dessert wines, and ice wines. The bar has no seating and wasn't serving food at press time, but the wine pours are generous.

TUTTO GUSTO, ITALY (90%/Above Average) Tucked away on the left side of the pavilion, this small bar looks like the inside of a small home (or cave). With a wide selection of Italian wines, cheeses, and meats, it's perfect for snacking around the world.

DISNEY'S ANIMAL KINGDOM

ALONG WITH EPCOT, Disney's Animal Kingdom has the best dining options of any Disney theme park. The food isn't particularly exotic, and a lot of it is counter-service, but the quality is superior to that found in the Magic Kingdom and Disney's Hollywood Studios.

The park's *Avatar*-themed **Satu'li Canteen** (96%/Exceptional) is Disney's answer to Chipotle's rice bowls—you pick a base of starch, grain, or lettuce and then add a protein and garnishes. The nearby **Pongu Pongu Lounge** (95%/Exceptional) serves drinks inspired by *Avatar,* plus the best breakfast biscuits in Walt Disney World. If you need a drink and a place to gather yourself before venturing into Flight of Passage's multihour wait in line, stop at the **Nomad Lounge** (97%/Exceptional), which is on the way to Pandora from Discovery Island. The drinks here are well balanced and full of flavor, and the lounge's decor is pretty.

A Lodi, California, dad praises Satu'li Canteen:

Our favorite place to eat was, by far, Satu'li Canteen. I would honestly make a special trip just to eat there. First, the food was crazy good. Yes, they basically make a bowl of food and that's all they serve, but everything was so delicious I could mix and match my ingredients to create something new every time. Second, they make everything from scratch there on-site. I can't stress enough how important this was to us, especially considering that our son has special dietary needs.

Our choices for sit-down restaurants in the park include **Yak & Yeti Restaurant** (94%/Much Above Average) in Asia, serving familiar Asian and Indian dishes, and **Tusker House Restaurant** (89%/Average) in Africa, whose choices are much more interesting than most others at Disney. **Tiffins** (91%/Above Average) is too expensive for what you get for us to recommend. Also skip the **Rainforest Cafe** (82%/Much Below Average), which is among the lowest-rated Disney restaurants.

**AUTHORS' FAVORITE ANIMAL KINGDOM
COUNTER-SERVICE RESTAURANTS**

• Flame Tree Barbecue Discovery Island   • Harambe Market Africa
• Satu'li Canteen Pandora

Besides Satu'li Canteen, our two other favorite counter-service dining options in the park are **Flame Tree Barbecue** (95%/Exceptional), serving house-made barbecue at waterfront dining pavilions, and **Harambe Market** (94%/Exceptional) in Africa, serving rice bowls with chicken or ribs, plant-based "sausages," and salads.

DISNEY'S HOLLYWOOD STUDIOS

DINING QUALITY AT THE STUDIOS has improved but remains largely the same kinds of food you'll find at the Magic Kingdom. Two of the three highest-rated counter-service restaurants are in Galaxy's Edge. **Docking Bay 7 Food and Cargo** (91%/Above Average) serves chicken, ribs, and a vegetarian kefta, and **Ronto Roasters** (96%/Exceptional) serves a limited menu of sausage wraps. Along with these, **Woody's Lunch Box** (91%/Above Average) in Toy Story Land is also rated better than average, with very good sandwiches, including plant-based options. As far as the rest of the park goes, **ABC Commissary** (88%) and **Backlot Express** (87%) are Average.

If you're looking for something to beat the heat, **Baseline Taphouse** (98%/Exceptional) on Grand Avenue is the highest-rated bar in Walt Disney World. It's small and mostly unthemed, but service is quick, and there's a decent selection of beers, plus snacks.

Good sit-down dining remains a long-running weakness at the Studios. The only real option you have for a good meal is the upscale **Hollywood Brown Derby** (91%/Above Average), which serves well-prepared steaks, chicken, and fish. Our second recommendation would be the **50's Prime Time Café** (89%/Average), a sit-down restaurant where you sit in Mom's time-warp kitchen and scarf down meat loaf while watching clips of classic sitcoms. Beyond that, readers rate the experience of counter-service restaurants, packaged foods, popcorn, and booze higher than anything found in an actual restaurant.

What we think our reader surveys are saying here is that there are few restaurants in the Studios that combine good food, good service, an entertaining atmosphere, *and* reasonable prices; almost every place has at least one major flaw. Recent menu updates have improved the food quality at the **Sci-Fi Dine-In Theater** (84%/Much Below Average), where you eat in fun little cars at a simulated drive-in movie. You won't find a more entertaining restaurant in Walt Disney World. **Hollywood & Vine** (80%/Do Not Visit) features singing and dancing characters such as Minnie Mouse and friends at lunch and dinner; kids will love it, but there's no reason to go otherwise. For simple Italian food, including flatbread pizzas, **Mama Melrose's Ristorante Italiano** (84%/Much Below Average) is just OK; don't expect anything fancy. A new sit-down restaurant, **Roundup Rodeo BBQ** opened in early 2023.

AUTHORS' FAVORITE HOLLYWOOD STUDIOS COUNTER-SERVICE RESTAURANT

● **Docking Bay 7 Food and Cargo** Galaxy's Edge

Besides Docking Bay 7 and Ronto Roasters, other food options in **Star Wars: Galaxy's Edge** are a bar, a popcorn stand, and a "milk" stand. **Oga's Cantina** (85%/Below Average), reminiscent of the bar from *A New Hope*, serves exotic alcoholic and nonalcoholic cocktails. Oga's is the only Galaxy's Edge restaurant that offers reservations, but they're difficult to get. If you can't get a reservation, try walking up in the last hour the park is open.

The land's two outdoor stands are **Kat Saka's Kettle** (88%/Average), which offers multiflavored popcorn, and **Milk Stand** (87%/Average), which serves the films' famous blue and green milk. Both "milks" are actually vegan, made from coconut and rice. Neither is very good, but you can add shots to get you through the experience.

Our general advice when it comes to the Studios is to eat a good breakfast before you get to the park. For lunch and dinner, go with the cheapest acceptable snacks or counter-service options to avoid wasting your money. If you have time, consider a 20-minute walk to one of the EPCOT resort restaurants for a sit-down meal.

FULL-SERVICE DINING FOR FAMILIES WITH YOUNG CHILDREN

DISNEY RESTAURANTS OFFER an excellent (though expensive) opportunity to introduce young children to the variety and excitement of food from different cultures. No matter how for-

> **unofficial TIP**
> Look for the **Mickey Check** icon on healthy menu items such as fresh fruit and low-fat milk.

mal a restaurant appears, rest assured that the staff is accustomed to fidgety, impatient, and often boisterous children. **Chefs de France** in EPCOT may be the only French restaurant in the US where most patrons wear shorts and T-shirts and at least two dozen young diners are attired in basic black . . . mouse ears.

Almost all Disney restaurants offer kids' menus, and all have booster seats and high chairs. Servers understand how tough it is for children to sit still for an extended period, and they'll supply little ones with crackers and rolls and serve your dinner much faster than in comparable restaurants elsewhere. Reader letters suggest that being served too quickly is more common than waiting too long.

A Saratoga Springs, New York, dad says timing is key when dining with younger kids:

> As a family with three girls all under the age of 10, we quickly discovered that no sit-down restaurant is worth dragging the family to after 8 p.m. We ended up with at least two children sleeping on the chairs after ordering chicken nuggets for the second time that day. I would rather eat at a quick-service restaurant if it gets my family in bed by 9 p.m.

Good Restaurants for Children

Be Our Guest and **Jungle Navigation Co. Ltd. Skipper Canteen** are hot tickets in the **Magic Kingdom,** and reservations at both are often difficult to get. (The only character at Be Our Guest is the Beast.) Be Our Guest's quality is substandard, it's overpriced, and you shouldn't eat there. We think the most kid-friendly fare is served at **Liberty Tree Tavern** in Liberty Square.

In **EPCOT,** preschoolers most enjoy **Biergarten Restaurant** in Germany, **San Angel Inn** in Mexico, and **Coral Reef Restaurant** at The Seas with Nemo & Friends Pavilion in World Nature. Biergarten (91%/ Above Average) combines a rollicking and noisy atmosphere with tasty, mostly familiar foods, including rotisserie chicken. A German oompah band entertains guests at both lunch and dinner. San Angel Inn (85%/Much Below Average) is in the Mexico village marketplace. From the table, children can watch boats on the Gran Fiesta Tour drift beneath a smoking volcano. With a choice of quesadillas, tacos, and other familiar items, picky kids usually have no difficulty finding something to eat. Coral Reef (80%/Do Not Visit), with tables beside windows looking into The Seas' aquarium, offers a satisfying mealtime diversion for all ages. For those who don't eat fish, it also serves beef, chicken, and vegetarian options, although none are worth writing home about. Biergarten offers reasonable value, plus good food. San Angel Inn is overpriced, though the food is pretty good. Coral Reef is overpriced and serves unmemorable food.

The best full-service restaurant for kids in **Disney's Animal Kingdom** is **Yak & Yeti Restaurant.**

In **Disney's Hollywood Studios,** all ages enjoy the atmosphere and entertainment at **Hollywood & Vine, Sci-Fi Dine-In Theater Restaurant,** and **50's Prime Time Café.**

NOISE AT RESTAURANTS

RESTAURANTS ARE NOISY in and out of the World. A Palmyra, Pennsylvania, reader using the Disney Dining Plan shared this:

> We ate four times at Signature restaurants. The food was always good, and the check, with wine and tip, was always at least $150. However, the noise, especially at Le Cellier and Il Mulino, was overwhelming. WDW seems to have really skimped on the acoustics, even at Cítricos and the California Grill.

QUIET, ROMANTIC PLACES TO EAT

RESTAURANTS WITH GOOD FOOD and a couple-friendly ambience are rare in the theme parks. Only a handful of dining locales satisfy both requirements: an alfresco table at **Tutto Italia Ristorante,** the terraces at **Rose & Crown Dining Room** and **Teppan Edo,** and the Japanese-themed **Tokyo Dining,** all in EPCOT, and old-school-cool **Hollywood Brown Derby** in Disney's Hollywood Studios. Waterfront dining is available at **Narcoossee's** at the Grand Floridian.

unofficial **TIP**
The **California Grill** at the Contemporary Resort and **Topolino's Terrace** at the Riviera have the best views at Walt Disney World.

Victoria & Albert's at the Grand Floridian is the World's showcase gourmet restaurant; the current menu starts at $295 per person. Other good choices for couples include **Jiko—The Cooking Place** and **Sanaa** in Animal Kingdom Lodge, along with **Cítricos** at the Grand Floridian.

Eating later in the evening and choosing a restaurant we've mentioned will improve your chances for intimate dining; nevertheless, children—well behaved or otherwise—are everywhere at Walt Disney World, and there's no way to escape them. These honeymooners from Slidell, Louisiana, write:

> We made dinner reservations at some of the nicer Disney restaurants. We made sure to reserve past dinner hours, and we tried to stress that we were on our honeymoon. But in every restaurant we went to, we were seated next to large families. It's very difficult to enjoy a romantic dinner when there are small children crawling around under your table. Our suggestion: Seat couples without children together and families with kids elsewhere.

Meanwhile, a Canadian mom acknowledges that the upscale California Grill may not have been the best place to bring her little ones:

We ate dinner on our last night at the California Grill. It was wonderful, but it's not a great place to take your kids. We were there from 7 to 10 p.m., and it was just too much for them.

WALT DISNEY WORLD DINNER THEATERS

AS IS THE CASE WITH other Disney restaurant reservations, when you make a reservation for **Hoop-Dee-Doo Musical Revue** (the only dinner show currently offered), you'll receive a confirmation number and be told to pick up your tickets at the Guest Relations desk at a Disney hotel. Unlike regular Advance Dining Reservations, your seating times for dinner shows are guaranteed. Unless you cancel your tickets at least 48 hours before your reservation time, your credit card will still be charged the full amount. Dinner-show reservations can be made 60 days in advance; call ☎ 407-939-3463. It's worth noting that obtaining reservations for *Hoop-Dee-Doo* is a trick of the first order.

A couple from Bismarck, North Dakota, explains:

I'm glad we made our reservations so early. I was able to reserve space for us at the Hoop-Dee-Doo Musical Revue. *Disney seats you according to when you made your reservation. At* Hoop-Dee-Doo, *we had a front-center table. We were so close to the stage, we could see how many cavities the performers had!*

If you can't get reservations and want to see a show:

1. Call ☎407-939-3463 at 9 a.m. each morning while you're at Disney World to make a same-day reservation. There are two to three performances (depending on the show) each night, and for all showings combined, only 3–24 people total will be admitted with same-day reservations.

2. Arrive at the show 45 minutes before showtime (early and late shows are your best bets) and put your name on the standby list. If someone with reservations fails to show, you may be admitted.

Borrowing a page from Las Vegas shows where nearsighted old coots get charged extra to sit way up front, Disney offers tiered seating for *Hoop-Dee-Doo*. The best seats are in **Category 1**. Next comes **Category 2,** with seats off to the side or behind Category 1. Finally, **Category 3** seats are at the Orlando Greyhound station, where you watch the show on a coin-operated black-and-white TV. (Actually, they're farther still to the side or back, or on another level from the stage.) Good views can be had from almost all seats, so you can decide if sitting closer to the action is worth the extra bucks.

unofficial TIP
To make reservations for the **Hoop-Dee-Doo Musical Revue,** call as soon as you know the dates of your visit. The earlier you call, the better your seats will be.

Hoop-Dee-Doo Musical Revue

➕ 92% (Above Average)

Pioneer Hall, Fort Wilderness Campground ☎ 407-939-3463. **Showtimes** Nightly, 4, 6:15, and 8:30 p.m. **Cost** Category 1, $74 adults ($44 children ages 3–9); Category 2, $69 adults ($40 children); Category 3, $66 adults ($39 children). Prices include tax and gratuity. **Duration of show** 2 hours. **Discounts** Seasonal. **Type of seating** Tables of various sizes to fit the number in each party, set in an Old West–style dance hall.

Menu All-you-can-eat barbecue ribs, fried chicken, salad, baked beans, and cornbread; unlimited beer, wine, sangria, and soft drinks. Vegetarian, vegan, and gluten-free options available; mention dietary needs when making reservations. **Comments** Disney Dining Plan credits can be used for Category 2 and 3 seats but not Category 1.

DESCRIPTION AND COMMENTS *Hoop-Dee-Doo* is the longest-running dinner show at Walt Disney World and a nostalgic favorite for many families. If you've ever thought *Country Bear Jamboree* would benefit from free-flowing barbecue, beer, and wine, this is the show for you.

Audience participation includes sing-alongs, hand-clapping, and a finale where you may find yourself onstage. During the meal, the music continues (softly). The food itself is pretty good, and you can't complain about the portion sizes.

Give special consideration to transportation when planning your evening at Fort Wilderness; it'll take some time to get there and back. There is no parking at Pioneer Hall, which is accessible only by boat (the Magic Kingdom and the loop between Fort Wilderness, Wilderness Lodge, and the Contemporary), and the Fort Wilderness internal bus system. After the show, resort buses at the Pioneer Hall stop will take you back to your resort. The fastest option may be to take a **Disney Minnie Van** (page 423), which will drop you off as close as possible to the venue.

MORE READER COMMENTS ABOUT WALT DISNEY WORLD DINING

EATING IS A POPULAR TOPIC among *Unofficial Guide* readers. In addition to participating in our annual restaurant survey, many readers share their thoughts. The following comments are representative.

Here's a 13-year-old girl from Omaha, Nebraska, who doesn't get bent out of shape over one bad meal:

> *Honestly, when was the last time you came home from Disney World and said, "Gosh, my vacation really sucked because I ate at a bad restaurant?"*

From a reader in the United Kingdom:

> *We had the most fantastic meal at California Grill. Being central London–living foodie-types, we're very hard to please, but the meal there really was second to none.*

Sanaa, in the Kidani Village section of Animal Kingdom Lodge, really impressed an Ellicott City, Maryland, family:

> *Sanaa is a beautiful restaurant with delicious and inexpensive (for Disney) food that you can't find anywhere else in Walt Disney World. We had a fabulous adults-only evening here, but I would bring children too, for an early dinner overlooking the savanna.*

Speaking of expensive food, this Superior, Wisconsin, reader noticed a pricing trend:

> *All the food is similarly priced. For example, all the main dishes in the nicer restaurants are between $35 and $60 for the most part. There are some outliers, but I was trying to find a nice, reasonably priced restaurant, and I couldn't. This is also true for the counter-service places: The prices are all similar, so finding a good deal is difficult. I get that they have you stuck there and can force you to buy the food—but still.*

COST OF COUNTER-SERVICE FOOD

BAGEL OR MUFFIN	$5
BROWNIE	$5
BURRITO BOWL	$12
CAKE OR PIE	$6-$9
CEREAL WITH MILK	$5-$6
CHEESEBURGER WITH FRIES	$12-$14
CHICKEN BREAST SANDWICH	$12-$14
CHICKEN NUGGETS WITH FRIES	$11-$12
CHILDREN'S MEAL (various)	$8-$11
CHIPS	$4
COOKIE	$4-$8
FRIED-FISH BASKET WITH FRIES	$14-$16
FRIES	$5
FRUIT (whole)	$2-$4
FRUIT CUP/FRUIT SALAD	$6
HOT DOG	$10-$14
ICE CREAM/FROZEN NOVELTIES	$6-$13
NACHOS WITH CHEESE	$12
PB&J SANDWICH	$8 (kids' meal)-$11
PIZZA (personal)	$12
POPCORN	$5
PRETZEL	$8
SALAD (entrée)	$9-$12
SALAD (side)	$4
SMOKED TURKEY LEG	$12-$15
SOUP/CHILI	$5-$7
SUB/DELI SANDWICH	$12-$14
TACO SALAD	$11-$13
VEGGIE BURGER	$13

COST OF COUNTER-SERVICE DRINKS

DRINK	SMALL	LARGE
BEER	$9	$14
BOTTLED WATER	$4 (one size)	
COFFEE	$4 (one size)	
LATTE	$5	$6
FLOAT, MILKSHAKE, OR SUNDAE	$6	$12
FRUIT JUICE	$5	$7
HOT TEA AND COCOA	$4 (one size)	
MILK	$2 (one size)	
SOFT DRINKS, ICED TEA, AND LEMONADE	$4	$5

Each person on a Disney Dining Plan (returns 2024) gets a free mug, refillable at any Disney resort. If you're not on a dining plan, a refillable souvenir mug costs $20 including tax (free refills) at Disney resorts and around $12 at the water parks.

A Columbus, Ohio, mom loved the character meal at Chef Mickey's:

Our favorite character dinner was Chef Mickey's. The kids were comfortable there, and the characters really spent time with our family getting pictures, being silly, and having fun. It was a great experience for the whole family. Was the food above and beyond? Nah. But the look on my 4-year-old's face when she saw Mickey was amazing.

The following reader tried several character meals:

The Crystal Palace (Magic Kingdom) *A HUGE hit with my kids! We met Eeyore, Pooh, Tigger, and Piglet. The food was great too—lots of choices, and all done very well.*

Chef Mickey's (Contemporary Resort) *By far the best dining experience we had. And with it being Chef Mickey's, we of course got to meet Mickey, Minnie, Pluto, Goofy, and Donald. A must-do!*

Hollywood & Vine (Hollywood Studios) *We didn't care for this one at all—if it hadn't been for meeting the Disney Junior characters, we probably wouldn't have picked it. The food was subpar, but the worst was the seating and organization of the characters: Most of the tables were booths, which made it very hard for children to get in and out. There was no rhyme or reason to which way the characters were going, and the handlers were nowhere to be found.*

One mom in Columbia, South Carolina, was unimpressed with the character dinners:

Walt Disney World is becoming grossly overpriced. Major piece of advice: Unless your kids love character dining, skip ALL the sit-down restaurants.

And finally, Raglan Road at Disney Springs was a big hit with another mom of two, this one from Los Angeles:

Cannot say enough about this amazing Irish pub. The ambience, the food, and the entertainment were all absolutely top-notch.

COUNTER-SERVICE
Mini-Profiles

TO HELP YOU FIND TASTY FAST FOOD, we profile the counter-service restaurants in each theme park and Disney Springs. The restaurants are rated for quality, value, and portion size. All participated in the previous Disney Dining Plan, except where noted, though participating restaurants are subject to change when the plans return in 2024; check tinyurl.com/wdwupdates for the latest updates. Mobile ordering (see page 279) is required at almost all these restaurants. Value ratings range from A to F, as follows:

A	Exceptional value; a real bargain
B	Good value
C	Fair value; you get exactly what you pay for
D	Somewhat overpriced
F	Extremely overpriced

See page 267 for a rundown of how the reader-survey percentages break down.

THE MAGIC KINGDOM

Aloha Isle

QUALITY Excellent   VALUE B+   PORTION Medium   LOCATION Adventureland
READER-SURVEY RESPONSES ☉ 97% (Exceptional)

Selections Soft-serve, ice-cream floats, pineapple juice.

Comments Located next to *Walt Disney's Enchanted Tiki Room*. The pineapple Dole Whip soft-serve is a world-famous Disney theme park treat. Usually opens at 10 a.m.

Casey's Corner

QUALITY Good   VALUE C   PORTION Medium   LOCATION Main Street, U.S.A.
READER-SURVEY RESPONSES ☉ 91% (Above Average)

Selections Hot dogs, plant-based "sausage" dogs, corn dog nuggets, fries, chocolate silk pie.

Comments Casey's is producing the best hot dogs in Walt Disney World. The buns are properly steamed, and the quality rivals that of a good ballpark frank. Tied with Columbia Harbour House for best counter-service in the Magic Kingdom.

Columbia Harbour House

QUALITY Good   VALUE B+   PORTION Medium   LOCATION Liberty Square
READER-SURVEY RESPONSES ☉ 91% (Above Average)

Selections Eat light with the grilled salmon with rice, indulge with fried shrimp and battered fish, or split the difference with the lobster roll. Other choices: fried chicken, grilled shrimp, plant-based "crab" cake sandwich, salads, hush puppies, and a milkshake with a donut on top or strawberry yogurt for dessert. For kids: shrimp skewer or grilled salmon.

Comments Columbia Harbour House is tied with Casey's Corner as the highest-rated counter-service restaurant in the Magic Kingdom. The upstairs seating is far quieter than the seating downstairs.

Cosmic Ray's Starlight Cafe

QUALITY Fair-Poor   VALUE C−   PORTION Large   LOCATION Tomorrowland
READER-SURVEY RESPONSES ☉ 81% (Much Below Average)

Selections Burgers, hot dogs, Greek salad, chicken sandwich, chicken strips, hot dogs, Angus bacon cheeseburger, plant-based burger, chocolate Bundt cake for dessert. Kosher choices available on request.

Comments Cosmic Ray's is a crowded, high-volume restaurant where food quality and ambience are sacrificed in the name of just getting something to eat. The burgers' secret ingredient is indifference.

The Diamond Horseshoe *(seasonal)*

QUALITY Fair-Poor   VALUE D   PORTION Medium–Large   LOCATION Frontierland
READER-SURVEY RESPONSES ☉ 73% (Do Not Visit)

Selections All-you-care-to-eat roast turkey, pot roast, pork, veggies, stuffing, and mashed potatoes. A plant-based meat loaf is also available. Serves wine and beer.

Comments The Diamond Horseshoe is technically a table-service restaurant. We've stuck it here because it's open only sporadically and readers don't like it, even though it shares the same menu and kitchen with the highly rated Liberty Tree Tavern.

The Friar's Nook

QUALITY Good **VALUE** B **PORTION** Medium–Large **LOCATION** Fantasyland
READER-SURVEY RESPONSES ➕ 87% (Below Average)

Selections Hot dogs; burgers; bacon mac and cheese. Also serves a bacon, egg, and cheese breakfast croissant with potato tots.

Comments A good place for a snack, but it can be difficult to find seating, especially in the shade.

Gaston's Tavern

QUALITY Good **VALUE** C **PORTION** Medium **LOCATION** Fantasyland **READER-SURVEY RESPONSES** ➕ 94% (Much Above Average) **NOT ON DISNEY DINING PLAN**

Selections Ham-and-Swiss sandwich, turkey legs, cinnamon rolls, dome cakes, LeFou's Brew (frozen apple juice with toasted-marshmallow flavoring).

Comments Very popular throughout the day. The cinnamon rolls are roughly the size of a barge. Ask for extra icing with yours.

Golden Oak Outpost (seasonal)

QUALITY Fair **VALUE** C **PORTION** Medium **LOCATION** Frontierland
READER-SURVEY RESPONSES ➕ 85% (Below Average)

Selections Fried-fish sandwich, chicken strips, chili-cheese fries, chocolate chip cookies, bottled water and soft drinks.

Comments Bare-bones basic eats. The lemon-and-sweet-tea slushie will bring a smile to any Southerner's face.

Liberty Square Market

QUALITY Good **VALUE** C **PORTION** Medium **LOCATION** Liberty Square **READER-SURVEY RESPONSES** ➕ 93% (Much Above Average) **NOT ON DISNEY DINING PLAN**

Selections Tasty hot dogs, plus fruit and packaged drinks and snacks.

Comments There's seating nearby, but none of it is covered.

The Lunching Pad

QUALITY Fair **VALUE** C **PORTION** Medium **LOCATION** Tomorrowland
READER-SURVEY RESPONSES ➕ 86% (Below Average)

Selections Hot dogs, chicken strips, pretzels, and specialty frozen drinks.

Comments The frozen sodas (cola or blue raspberry) are a treat on hot days.

Main Street Bakery (Starbucks)

QUALITY Good **VALUE** B **PORTION** Medium **LOCATION** Main Street, U.S.A.
READER-SURVEY RESPONSES ➕ 92% (Much Above Average)

Selections Coffees, pastries, breakfast sandwiches.

Comments Extremely popular throughout the day, but the lines move fast.

Pecos Bill Tall Tale Inn and Cafe

QUALITY Good **VALUE** C **PORTION** Medium–Large **LOCATION** Frontierland
READER-SURVEY RESPONSES ➕ 86% (Below Average)

Selections Pork carnitas and chicken fajita platter with rice and beans; beef nachos; rice-and-veggie bowl; salad with or without chicken; burgers.

Comments Pecos Bill has taken a page from Chipotle. The fare is an improvement over the old burgers, but it's more expensive than and not quite as good as Chipotle's. The menu gets mixed reactions, like this one from a Mount Holly, New Jersey, reader:

We were less than impressed with the menu, though it was fine for staving off a "hanger" tantrum.

If you're ordering the tacos or fajitas, ask for extra toppings.

Pinocchio Village Haus

QUALITY Fair–Poor   VALUE D   PORTION Medium   LOCATION Fantasyland
READER-SURVEY RESPONSES ⊕ 82% (Much Below Average)

Selections Flatbread pizzas; chicken strips; fries; Caesar salad; kids' meal of pizza, chicken strips, or PB&J sandwich.

Comments Your only reason to eat here instead of at Columbia Harbour House (see above) or Casey's Corner (page 299) would be if you had an inexplicable hankering for a bland flatbread pizza.

Tomorrowland Terrace Restaurant *(seasonal)*

QUALITY Fair   VALUE C–   PORTION Medium-Large   LOCATION Tomorrowland
READER-SURVEY RESPONSES ⊕ 86% (Below Average)

Selections Varies.

Comments Rarely open. Doesn't have the kitchen space or equipment to do much more than turn out subpar food.

Tortuga Tavern *(seasonal)*

QUALITY Fair   VALUE B   PORTION Medium-Large   LOCATION Adventureland
READER-SURVEY RESPONSES ⊕ 75% (Do Not Visit)

Selections Chicken strips, burgers, and hot dogs.

Comments The eating area is large and shaded. Disney changes up the menu here from time to time—it's been Mexican and barbecue before. Still, the fact that it's not a full-time restaurant means it's not a priority for Disney to serve anything special here. Not worth your time or money.

EPCOT

L'Artisan des Glaces

QUALITY Excellent   VALUE C   PORTION Large   LOCATION France   READER-SURVEY RESPONSES ⊕ 94% (Much Above Average)   NOT ON DISNEY DINING PLAN

Selections Ice-cream flavors change but may include vanilla, chocolate, mint chocolate, coffee, coconut–white chocolate, cinnamon with caramelized pecans or apples, and candied peanut with chocolate–peanut butter fudge. The dairy-free sorbet flavors may include mango, strawberry, and piña colada. Over-21s can enjoy two scoops in a martini glass, topped with Grand Marnier, rum, or whipped cream–flavored vodka.

Comments L'Artisan des Glaces serves the best ice cream at Disney World. The coconut in our coconut–white chocolate was freshly shaved. The macaron ice-cream sandwich is a gift from heaven.

La Cantina de San Angel

QUALITY Good   VALUE B   PORTION Medium-Large   LOCATION Mexico
READER-SURVEY RESPONSES ⊕ 91% (Above Average)

Selections Tacos with seasoned beef, chicken, or shrimp; fried cheese empanada; grilled chicken with Mexican rice, corn, cascabel pepper sauce, and pickled onions; guacamole; churros; margaritas. For kids, chicken tacos, empanadas, chicken tenders, or mac and cheese.

Comments A popular spot for a quick meal, with 150 covered outdoor seats, some well shaded. When it's extra busy, the back of La Hacienda de San Angel's dining room is opened for air-conditioned seating.

Connections Cafe

QUALITY Fair   VALUE C   PORTION Large   LOCATION World Celebration
READER-SURVEY RESPONSES ⊕ 88% (Average)

Selections Burgers, pizza, and salads, with plant-based options.

Comments Spacious, bright, and cheerful seating areas, with open-kitchen views into the pizza-making process. Most of the food is average—there's only so much you can do with theme park burgers and pizza—but the General Tso Chicken Salad is pretty good.

Fife & Drum Tavern

QUALITY Fair	VALUE C	PORTION Large	LOCATION United States
READER-SURVEY RESPONSES ✪ 89% (Average)			

Selections Turkey legs, hot dogs, popcorn, soft-serve ice cream, slushies, beer, alcoholic lemonade, and root beer floats.

Comments Seating is available in and around the Regal Eagle Smokehouse, behind the Fife & Drum.

Les Halles Boulangerie–Pâtisserie

QUALITY Good	VALUE A	PORTION Small-Medium	LOCATION France
READER-SURVEY RESPONSES ✪ 93% (Much Above Average)			

Selections The beautiful deli–bakery case is stocked with goodies such as sandwiches (ham and cheese; Brie, cranberry, and apple), imported-cheese plates, quiches, soups, and delicate pastries.

Comments Les Halles is consistently rated as the No. 2 counter-service restaurant in EPCOT (behind Yorkshire County Fish Shop) and one of the best in the World. Breads and pastries are made on-site. For an authentic Parisian experience, grab a half baguette (ask for extra butter) and eat it while you walk around France. Usually crowded all day.

Katsura Grill

QUALITY Good	VALUE B	PORTION Small-Medium	LOCATION Japan
READER-SURVEY RESPONSES ✪ 84% (Below Average)			

Selections Basic sushi; udon noodle bowls (vegetarian or shrimp tempura); pork ramen; chicken, beef, or shrimp teriyaki; chicken curry; edamame; miso soup; yuzu tea cheesecake; teriyaki kids' plate; Kirin beer, sake, and plum wine.

Comments The food is just average, but this might be the loveliest spot to escape the EPCOT crowd and eat a quick meal outside.

Kringla Bakeri og Kafe

QUALITY Good-Excellent	VALUE B	PORTION Small-Medium	LOCATION Norway
READER-SURVEY RESPONSES ✪ 94% (Above Average)			

Selections Norwegian pastries and desserts, iced coffee, and imported beers and wines.

Comments Limited menu. The School Bread (a sweet roll filled with custard and dipped in coconut) is popular. Shaded outdoor seating.

Lotus Blossom Café

QUALITY Fair	VALUE C	PORTION Medium	LOCATION China
READER-SURVEY RESPONSES ✪ 81% (Much Below Average)			

Selections Pork and vegetable egg rolls, pot stickers, orange chicken, chicken fried rice, Mongolian beef with rice, caramel-ginger or lychee ice cream, plum wine, Tsingtao beer.

Comments The menu rarely changes, and the food remains a snooze. You'd be better off picking a random festival food booth.

Refreshment Outpost

QUALITY Good	VALUE B-	PORTION Small	LOCATION Between Germany and China
READER-SURVEY RESPONSES ✪ 91% (Above Average)			

Selections All-beef hot dogs, slushies, sodas, draft beer.

Comments The hot dogs here aren't bad at all, but there are plenty of better dining options within a few minutes' walk. Will often serve African dishes during the Food & Wine festival. If they're serving githeri (a Kenyan stew), it's worth stopping by.

Refreshment Port

QUALITY Good	VALUE B–	PORTION Medium	LOCATION Near Canada
READER-SURVEY RESPONSES ➊ 92% (Much Above Average)			

Selections Poutine, chicken nuggets, unusual alcoholic drinks, and beer.

Comments The menu hasn't changed in a while, which is atypical for this place.

Regal Eagle Smokehouse: Craft Drafts & Barbecue

QUALITY Good	VALUE B	PORTION Large	LOCATION United States
READER-SURVEY RESPONSES ➊ 91% (Above Average)			

Selections Regional barbecue specialties, including Memphis smoked ribs, Kansas City chicken, North Carolina chopped pork, and Texas brisket, plus burgers, salads, and vegetarian options. Usually serves at least four beers from around the country, plus hard ciders, wines, and specialty cocktails.

Comments Regal Eagle serves passable barbecue in hearty portions, with the Texas brisket (on garlic toast) being our favorite. If you're craving more, **The Polite Pig** at Disney Springs (see page 309) sets the standard in Walt Disney World.

Rose & Crown Pub

QUALITY Good	VALUE C+	PORTION Medium	LOCATION United Kingdom
READER-SURVEY RESPONSES ➊ 95% (Exceptional)		NOT ON DISNEY DINING PLAN	

Selections Fish-and-chips; Scotch egg; Guinness, Harp, and Bass beers, along with other spirits.

Comments Authentic British pub with ales, lagers, and stouts.

Sommerfest

QUALITY Fair	VALUE C	PORTION Medium	LOCATION Germany
READER-SURVEY RESPONSES ➊ 90% (Above Average)			

Selections Bratwurst, pretzel bread pudding, jumbo pretzel, cold beer.

Comments Tables are set up in the courtyard. Much of the food looks better than it tastes.

Sunshine Seasons

QUALITY Excellent	VALUE A	PORTION Medium	LOCATION The Land
READER-SURVEY RESPONSES ➊ 83% (Much Below Average)			

Selections Sunshine Seasons, a food court–like counter-service venue, consists of the following three areas: (1) wood-fired grills and rotisseries, with rotisserie chicken and wood-grilled fish with seasonal vegetables; (2) sandwiches, such as an amazing pulled pork and Cheddar on Texas toast, and a cheese flatbread option; and (3) the soup-and-salad shop, with soups made daily and unusual creations such as the Power Salad (quinoa, almonds, and chicken).

Comments We suspect the low reader ratings are due to long lines to get food and pay, not the food quality. Open for lunch and dinner.

Tangierine Café

QUALITY Good	VALUE B	PORTION Medium	LOCATION Morocco
READER-SURVEY RESPONSES ➊ 93% (Much Above Average)			

Selections Grilled kebabs, hummus, Moroccan wine and beer.

Comments One of the highest-rated restaurants in EPCOT pre-COVID, Tangi-erine Café was run by a third party that pulled out during the pandemic. Disney now runs the place and has drastically shrunk the menu. But the food remains much better than average, and it's a lovely place to dine.

Yorkshire County Fish Shop

QUALITY Good	VALUE B+	PORTION Medium	LOCATION United Kingdom
READER-SURVEY RESPONSES ➕ 95% (Exceptional)			

Selections Fish-and-chips, Bass Pale Ale draft, and Harp Lager.

Comments The highest-rated counter-service spot in EPCOT. There's usually a line for the crisp, hot fish-and-chips at this convenient fast-food window attached to the Rose & Crown Dining Room (see full-service profile on page 345). A tasty chicken-and-mushroom pie might be served during cooler months. Outdoor seating overlooks the lagoon.

DISNEY'S ANIMAL KINGDOM

Creature Comforts *(Starbucks)*

QUALITY Good	VALUE C	PORTION Small	LOCATION Discovery Island near Africa
READER-SURVEY RESPONSES ➕ 96% (Exceptional)			

Selections Coffee drinks and teas; sandwiches and pastries.

Comments The fare is largely the same as you'd find at any other Starbucks, plus the occasional Animal Kingdom–themed treat.

Flame Tree Barbecue

QUALITY Excellent	VALUE B-	PORTION Large	LOCATION Discovery Island
READER-SURVEY RESPONSES ➕ 95% (Exceptional)			

Selections St. Louis–style ribs; smoked half-chicken; ribs and chicken sampler; pulled-pork sandwich; smokehouse chicken salad; mac and cheese with smoked pulled pork; plant-based "sausage" sandwich; child's plate of baked chicken drumstick, hot dog, or PB&J; fries and onion rings; Safari Amber beer, Bud Light, frozen mango-raspberry coconut rum drink, wine.

Comments Along with Satu'li Canteen, one of the best counter-service spots in the park. Expanded outdoor seating provides more shaded space overlooking the water. One of our favorites for lunch.

Harambe Market

QUALITY Good	VALUE B	PORTION Large	LOCATION Africa
READER-SURVEY RESPONSES ➕ 94% (Much Above Average)			

Selections Grilled chicken or ribs served over rice and salad greens, salads, plant-based "sausage." Kids' selections include PB&J, chicken nuggets, and chicken and rice bowl.

Comments Plenty of shaded seating. Disney Imagineers modeled Harambe's marketplace setting after a typical real-life market in an African nation during the 1960s colonial era. We like the ribs and rice.

Kusafiri Coffee Shop and Bakery

QUALITY Good	VALUE B	PORTION Medium	LOCATION Africa
READER-SURVEY RESPONSES ➕ 92% (Above Average) NOT ON DISNEY DINING PLAN			

Selections Impossible empanadas with plant-based picadillo filling; flatbreads; breakfast pastries; pistachio-honey croissants; cookies; sausage, egg, and cheese biscuit; coffee; beer.

Comments The cinnamon roll is a favorite. Kosher items are available.

Pizzafari

QUALITY Fair   **VALUE** C   **PORTION** Medium   **LOCATION** Discovery Island
READER-SURVEY RESPONSES ➕ 78% (Do Not Visit)

Selections Chicken Parmesan sandwich; cheese, pepperoni, or sausage personal pizza; Caesar salad. For kids, mac and cheese, pasta with turkey marinara, cheese pizza, or PB&J. Cannoli cake for dessert.

Comments The pizza is profoundly unimpressive. One of the worst dining options in the park.

Restaurantosaurus

QUALITY Fair   **VALUE** C   **PORTION** Medium-Large   **LOCATION** DinoLand U.S.A.
READER-SURVEY RESPONSES ➕ 84% (Much Below Average)

Selections Angus bacon cheeseburger; chili-cheese hot dog; chicken sandwich; chicken nuggets; Cobb salad; breaded shrimp; plant-based spicy Southwestern burger; kids' chicken nuggets, cheeseburger, or PB&J.

Comments A wide variety of selections. There's plenty of seating, but it's divided into rooms, so make sure to agree on where everyone's going to sit. A hard-to-find lounge next door serves adult beverages.

Royal Anandapur Tea Company

QUALITY Good   **VALUE** B   **PORTION** Medium   **LOCATION** Asia   **READER-SURVEY RESPONSES** ➕ 92% (Much Above Average) NOT ON DISNEY DINING PLAN**

Selections Wide variety of hot and iced teas, hot chocolate, and coffees (fantastic frozen chai); lattes and espresso; pastries.

Comments Halfway between Expedition Everest and Kali River Rapids, this is the kind of small, eclectic, Animal Kingdom–specific food stand that you wish other parks had. Around 10 loose teas from Asia and Africa can be ordered hot or iced.

Satu'li Canteen

QUALITY Good   **VALUE** A   **PORTION** Medium   **LOCATION** Pandora
READER-SURVEY RESPONSES ➕ 96% (Exceptional)

Selections The signature item is the customizable bowl. Start with a base of salad, red and sweet potato hash, rice and beans, or whole grains and rice. Add wood-grilled chicken, slow-roasted beef, chili-garlic shrimp, or chili-spiced fried tofu, and finish with a choice of sauces. The menu also offers steamed "pods": bao buns with a cheeseburger filling, served with root-vegetable chips and crunchy vegetable slaw. The children's menu is similar to the one for adults.

Comments The top counter-service spot in the park. Breakfast is served seasonally here, but if it's not available, get the sausage, egg, and cheese biscuit next door at **Pongu Pongu.**

Yak & Yeti Local Food Cafes

QUALITY Fair   **VALUE** C   **PORTION** Large   **LOCATION** Asia
READER-SURVEY RESPONSES ➕ 91% (Above Average)

Selections Honey chicken with steamed rice, cheeseburger, teriyaki chicken salad, veggie tikka masala, Korean fried chicken sandwich, sweet-and-sour tempura shrimp, egg rolls, and fried rice. Kids' menu: chicken tenders, PB&J, or cheeseburger with carrot sticks and fresh fruit. Breakfast is American-style fare such as breakfast bowls and sausage-and-egg English muffins.

Comments For filling up when you're in a hurry. Expanded seating area behind the pickup windows.

DISNEY'S HOLLYWOOD STUDIOS
ABC Commissary

QUALITY Fair	VALUE D	PORTION Medium-Large	LOCATION Commissary Lane

READER-SURVEY RESPONSES ➕ 88% (Average)

Selections Pork carnitas or shrimp tacos, Buffalo chicken grilled cheese, Mediterranean salad with or without chicken, chicken club sandwich, plant-based burger, wine and beer. Some kosher.

Comments The Buffalo chicken grilled cheese and the shrimp tacos are the standout menu items.

Backlot Express

QUALITY Fair	VALUE C	PORTION Medium-Large	LOCATION Echo Lake

READER-SURVEY RESPONSES ➕ 87% (Average)

Selections One-third-pound Angus bacon cheeseburger, chicken strips, Cuban sandwich, Southwest salad, teriyaki chicken or tofu bowl.

Comments Fun props, some used in movies, decorate this spacious eatery.

Catalina Eddie's

QUALITY Fair	VALUE C	PORTION Medium-Large	LOCATION Sunset Boulevard

READER-SURVEY RESPONSES ➕ 76% (Do Not Visit)

Selections Cheese and pepperoni pizzas, Caesar salad with or without chicken. Kids' menu has the same pizzas.

Comments Almost anything in the park—even a lemon-and-water cleanse, for that matter—is a better option.

Docking Bay 7 Food and Cargo

QUALITY Excellent	VALUE A	PORTION Medium	LOCATION Galaxy's Edge

READER-SURVEY RESPONSES ➕ 91% (Above Average)

Selections Smoked Kaadu Ribs, named after the creature Jar Jar Binks rode in *Episode I* but actually pork, are cut vertically to give them an alien appearance, then glazed with a sticky-sweet sauce and served with down-home blueberry corn muffins. Endorian Tip Yip (chicken) is roasted on a salad or compressed into cubes, deep-fried, and served with mac and cheese and roasted vegetables. Vegans will rejoice at meatless menu items featuring Impossible Foods, while pescatarians can try the chilled Peka Tuna Poke.

Comments This is our choice for the best restaurant in Hollywood Studios. Most items here are above-average quality. The Tip Yip chicken is moist and flavorful, as are the vegetable kefta in the Felucian Garden Spread; the ribs, however, are difficult to eat. Also, if you have picky eaters in your crew, note that the kids' menu isn't particularly kid-friendly: In keeping with the idea that you're on an alien planet, many of the foods come in unfamiliar shapes and colors.

Dockside Diner

QUALITY Fair	VALUE C	PORTION Small-Medium	LOCATION Echo Lake

READER-SURVEY RESPONSES ➕ 84% (Below Average)

Selections Hot dogs with over-the-top toppings (the California BLTA Dog, for instance, is served with lettuce, tomato, bacon, avocado, mayo, and mustard aioli). Readers don't seem impressed, though.

Comments Limited seating at nearby picnic tables.

Fairfax Fare

QUALITY Fair	VALUE B	PORTION Medium-Large	LOCATION Sunset Boulevard

READER-SURVEY RESPONSES ➕ 83% (Much Below Average)

Selections Assorted hot dogs and a Chicago-style hot dog salad.

Comments This is the best dining option in the area of Sunset Boulevard near Tower of Terror and Rock 'n' Roller Coaster—but that's not to say it's good.

Milk Stand

QUALITY Fair	VALUE D	PORTION Small	LOCATION Galaxy's Edge
READER-SURVEY RESPONSES ✚ 87% (Average)			

Selections Frozen nondairy drinks, with or without alcohol.

Comments These plant-based beverages have the consistency of a smoothie. Green milk, as seen in *The Last Jedi,* has floral flavors, while the blue drink from *A New Hope* tastes of melon and pineapple. These "milks" are expensive, so if you *have* to try one, split it with a friend. The optional splash of booze—rum for blue milk, tequila for green—doesn't add anything but cost.

Oga's Cantina

QUALITY Fair	VALUE D	PORTION Medium	LOCATION Galaxy's Edge
READER-SURVEY RESPONSES ✚ 85% (Below Average)			

Selections Alcoholic and nonalcoholic cocktails; wine and beer; Batuu Bits snack and a sampler platter with cured and roasted meats, cheese, and pork cracklings.

Comments This cantina, overseen by alien proprietor Oga Garra, will instantly remind fans of the Mos Eisley watering hole from *A New Hope.* A droid DJ—actually a recycled Captain Rex from the original Star Tours—spins an original 1980s-style synth-pop soundtrack. Nine signature alcoholic cocktails are on the menu. Draft craft beers and private-label wines are also served, as are nonalcoholic drinks (try the frozen cookie-crowned Blue Bantha).

Oga's has stayed packed from the moment it opened. Disney makes online reservations available up to 60 days in advance (see page 272), so be ready at your 60-day mark to grab one. If you can't get in, try showing up in the last hour the park is open for a possible walk-up spot. The later the park is open, the better your chances of getting in.

PizzeRizzo

QUALITY Poor	VALUE D	PORTION Large	LOCATION Grand Avenue
READER-SURVEY RESPONSES ✚ 83% (Much Below Average)			

Selections Personal pizzas, meatball subs, and salads—none of them good. The too-doughy pizza's one accomplishment is that it manages to be both burned on top and underdone below.

Comments Rizzo's Deluxe Supreme Banquet Hall features an ongoing wedding reception, with a disco-heavy soundtrack. The upstairs decor might be the best part of the restaurant.

Ronto Roasters

QUALITY Good	VALUE B	PORTION Medium	LOCATION Galaxy's Edge
READER-SURVEY RESPONSES ✚ 96% (Exceptional)			

Selections Ronto Wrap (pita bread filled with roasted pork, grilled pork sausage, and slaw); pork rinds; nonalcoholic fruit punch. Breakfast wraps available too.

Comments A disgruntled smelting droid named 8D-J8 does the cooking, turning alien mystery meats on a rotating spit as they roast beneath a recycled podracing engine. The sandwiches are delicious and filling.

Rosie's All-American Cafe

QUALITY Fair	VALUE C	PORTION Medium	LOCATION Sunset Boulevard
READER-SURVEY RESPONSES ✚ 83% (Much Below Average)			

Selections Burgers, hot dogs, chicken nuggets, fries, plant-based "lobster" roll; child's chicken nuggets with a yogurt smoothie and fruit.

Comments A quick stop on the way to Tower of Terror or Rock 'n' Roller Coaster. It's close enough that you can hear the screams as you eat.

The Trolley Car Cafe (Starbucks)

QUALITY Good	VALUE B	PORTION Small	LOCATION Hollywood Boulevard
READER-SURVEY RESPONSES ➕ 92% (Much Above Average)			

Selections Coffee drinks and teas; breakfast sandwiches and pastries.

Comments Disney-themed Starbucks. The building is the real attraction: The pink-stucco Spanish Colonial exterior calls to mind Old Hollywood, and the industrial-style interior evokes a trolley-car switching station.

Woody's Lunch Box

QUALITY Excellent	VALUE A-	PORTION Medium-Large	LOCATION Toy Story Land
READER-SURVEY RESPONSES ➕ 91% (Above Average)			

Selections *Breakfast:* Lunch Box Tarts (think gourmet toaster pastries), breakfast bowl with scrambled eggs, potato barrels, and country gravy. *Lunch and dinner:* Sandwiches (barbecue brisket, smoked turkey, grilled three-cheese); tomato-basil soup; "totchos" (potato barrels smothered with chili, queso, and corn chips).

Comments Very limited seating and shade. Seasonal tarts are great.

DISNEY SPRINGS

Amorette's Patisserie

QUALITY Excellent	VALUE B	PORTION Small-Medium	LOCATION Town Center
READER-SURVEY RESPONSES ➕ 95% (Exceptional)			NOT ON DISNEY DINING PLAN

Selections Cakes and pastries made by talented Disney chefs; Disney-themed 11-layer dome cake; sandwiches; Champagne.

Comments Don't miss Amorette's Petit Cake, a smaller portion of its signature cake with 11 layers of red velvet and chocolate cakes, cherry and chocolate mousses, raspberry jelly, and Italian buttercream.

Blaze Fast-Fire'd Pizza

QUALITY Excellent	VALUE A	PORTION Large	LOCATION Town Center
READER-SURVEY RESPONSES ➕ 93% (Much Above Average)			

Selections Specialty and build-your-own 11-inch pizzas with a selection of 40-plus fresh toppings and sauces; salads.

Comments Each fast-fired pizza is prepared in around 3 minutes after you select your toppings, Chipotle-style. Ignore the long line outside—it moves very quickly. Go light on the toppings for best results.

Chicken Guy!

QUALITY Fair	VALUE C	PORTION Large	LOCATION Town Center
READER-SURVEY RESPONSES ➕ 87% (Average)			

Selections Fried chicken tenders, fries, mac and cheese.

Comments Chicken tenders and fries are the name of the game at Chicken Guy! (*Guy* refers to the restaurant's creator, celebrity chef Guy Fieri.) If you want to get adventurous, do it with the sauces, of which there are dozens. We think the food here is better than readers do.

Cookes of Dublin

QUALITY Fair-Good	VALUE C-	PORTION Medium-Large	LOCATION The Landing
READER-SURVEY RESPONSES ➕ 89% (Average)			

Selections Fried chicken tenders, burgers, fish-and-chips, and Irish cheese-and-bacon dip.

Comments Wait times can be on the high side, but even the pickiest eaters will like the excellent onion rings and chicken fingers.

D-Luxe Burger

QUALITY Good   **VALUE** C   **PORTION** Medium-Large   **LOCATION** Town Center
READER-SURVEY RESPONSES ● 87% (Average)

Selections Specialty burgers (The Southern, topped with a fried green tomato; veggie with mango salsa); hand-cut fries with a variety of dipping sauces (curry ketchup and garlic ranch are zesty and unique); gelato shakes (spiked and nonalcoholic).

Comments Burgers and fries take a little time, but the specialty options are worth the wait. Mobile ordering available.

Earl of Sandwich

QUALITY Good   **VALUE** B-   **PORTION** Small-Medium   **LOCATION** Marketplace
READER-SURVEY RESPONSES ● 94% (Exceptional)

Selections Sandwiches, salads, wraps, soups; brownies and cookies.

Comments There's always a long line here, but it tends to move quickly. The sandwiches, while tasty, aren't anything you can't find at your local deli. Nonetheless, Earl of Sandwich has been very highly rated by readers for many years.

Pepe by José Andrés

QUALITY Good   **VALUE** B   **PORTION** Small   **LOCATION** West Side
READER SURVEY RESPONSES Not enough to rate   **NOT ON DISNEY DINING PLAN**

Selections Spanish sandwiches such as bikinis (think an elevated grilled cheese), as well as gazpacho.

Comments Pepe is the first permanent location of José Andrés's popular food truck in Disney Springs.

Pizza Ponte

QUALITY Good   **VALUE** C   **PORTION** Medium   **LOCATION** The Landing
READER-SURVEY RESPONSES ● 82% (Much Below Average)

Selections Sandwiches, pizza by the slice, and Italian desserts such as cannoli and tiramisu.

Comments The platonic ideal of square pizza costs around $6 per slice and is found at Mama's Too at 105th and Broadway in Manhattan. Pizza Ponte isn't close to Mama's Too, but it's still above average even for New York. The prices (around $7–$8 per slice) are very high, but the slices are large. If you want to build your own pizza, head over to **Blaze Fast-Fire'd Pizza** (see page 308), where, for about the same price, you can get a small pie that generally serves two.

The Polite Pig

QUALITY Good-Excellent   **VALUE** A   **PORTION** Medium   **LOCATION** Town Center
READER-SURVEY RESPONSES ● 96% (Exceptional)

Selections Southern barbecue staples (pulled pork, ribs, smoked chicken); specialty veggie sides (barbecue cauliflower, grilled corn, whiskey-caramel Brussels sprouts); bourbon bar; cocktails and local beers on tap; homemade cakes and pies for dessert.

Comments A hybrid fast-casual/table-service restaurant, The Polite Pig offers a bit more than your standard quick-service spot. Barbecue smoked on-site is the name of the game, but the side dishes are not to be missed. Skip the sandwiches and split a few entrées (the pulled pork and ribs are our favorites) with sides; it's the best bang for your buck and offers a chance to try more of the outstanding appetizers (house-made giant pretzels, smoked wings) and delicious desserts.

Salt & Straw

QUALITY Excellent	VALUE A	PORTION Medium	LOCATION West Side
READER SURVEY RESPONSES ✪ 94% (Exceptional)			

Selections Gourmet flavors made by people who really care about ice cream.
Comments Along with familiar flavors based around chocolate and vanilla, our favorites include the strawberry honey balsamic with black pepper; the Arbequina olive oil; and the salted, malted chocolate chip cookie dough.

Starbucks

QUALITY Good	VALUE C	PORTION Small	LOCATION Marketplace
READER-SURVEY RESPONSES ✪ 95% (Exceptional)			

Selections Coffee drinks and teas; breakfast sandwiches and pastries.
Comments Rated highly by readers, but it's your typical Starbucks.

FULL-SERVICE RESTAURANTS
In Depth

THE PROFILES IN THIS SECTION allow you to quickly check the cuisine, location, star rating, cost range, quality rating, and value rating of every full-service restaurant at WDW. Reservations for full-service restaurants are strongly recommended.

The following profiles, including the reader ratings, reflect menus and prices as we went to press. The Disney Dining Plan information is based on the 2019 version of the plan and is subject to change when Disney brings back the standard and quick-service plans in 2024.

OVERALL RATING Ranging from one to five stars, this rating encompasses the entire dining experience: style, service, ambience, and food quality. Five stars is the highest rating attainable. Our star ratings don't correspond to those awarded by AAA, Mobil, Zagat, or other restaurant reviewers.

COST RANGE This tells you approximately how much you can expect to spend on a full-service entrée (not including appetizers, side dishes, soups and salads, desserts, drinks, and tips). Cost ranges are categorized as **inexpensive** (less than $15), **moderate** ($15–$25), or **expensive** ($25 and up).

QUALITY RATING Food quality is rated from one to five stars, five being the highest possible rating. The criteria are taste, freshness of ingredients, preparation, presentation, and the creativity of the food served. Price is no consideration.

VALUE RATING If, on the other hand, you're looking for both quality *and* value, then you should check this rating, which is also expressed as stars.

continued on page 315

WDW RESTAURANTS BY CUISINE

CUISINE	LOCATION	OVERALL RATING	COST	QUALITY RATING	VALUE RATING
AFRICAN					
BOMA—FLAVORS OF AFRICA	Animal Kingdom Lodge–Jambo House	★★★★½	Exp	★★★★	★★★★
JIKO—THE COOKING PLACE	Animal Kingdom Lodge–Jambo House	★★★★½	Exp	★★★★	★★½
SANAA	Animal Kingdom Villas–Kidani Village	★★★★	Exp	★★★★	★★★★
JUNGLE NAVIGATION CO. LTD. SKIPPER CANTEEN	Magic Kingdom	★★★½	Exp	★★★	★★★
TUSKER HOUSE RESTAURANT	Animal Kingdom	★★★	Exp	★★★	★★★
AMERICAN					
CHEF ART SMITH'S HOMECOMIN'	Disney Springs	★★★★	Mod	★★★★	★★★½
CÍTRICOS	Grand Floridian	★★★★	Exp	★★★★½	★★★
GEYSER POINT BAR & GRILL	Wilderness Lodge	★★★★	Mod	★★★½	★★★
THE HOLLYWOOD BROWN DERBY	DHS	★★★★	Exp	★★★★	★★★
CALIFORNIA GRILL	Contemporary	★★★½	Exp	★★★★	★★
GRAND FLORIDIAN CAFE	Grand Floridian	★★★½	Mod–Exp	★★★½	★★★½
LIBERTY TREE TAVERN	Magic Kingdom	★★★½	Exp	★★★	★★★
STORY BOOK DINING WITH SNOW WHITE AT ARTIST POINT	Wilderness Lodge	★★★½	Exp	★★★★	★★★½
TIFFINS	Animal Kingdom	★★★½	Exp	★★★½	★★½
ALE & COMPASS	Yacht Club	★★★	Mod	★★★	★★★
CAPE MAY CAFE	Beach Club	★★★	Exp	★★★	★★★
CINDERELLA'S ROYAL TABLE	Magic Kingdom	★★★	Exp	★★★	★★
CITY WORKS EATERY AND POUR HOUSE	Disney Springs	★★★	Mod	★★★	★★★
THE EDISON	Disney Springs	★★★	Exp	★★★½	★★★
50'S PRIME TIME CAFÉ	DHS	★★★	Mod	★★★	★★★
GARDEN GRILL RESTAURANT	EPCOT	★★★	Exp	★★★	★★★
HOUSE OF BLUES	Disney Springs	★★★	Mod	★★★½	★★★
OLIVIA'S CAFE	Old Key West	★★★	Exp	★★★	★★
THREE BRIDGES	Coronado Springs	★★★	Exp	★★★	★★½
TUSKER HOUSE	Animal Kingdom	★★★	Exp	★★★	★★★
WHISPERING CANYON CAFE	Wilderness Lodge	★★★	Exp	★★½	★★★★
WOLFGANG PUCK BAR & GRILL	Disney Springs	★★★	Exp	★★★	★★★
BE OUR GUEST RESTAURANT	Magic Kingdom	★★½	Exp	★★½	★★
BEACHES & CREAM SODA SHOP	Beach Club	★★½	Mod	★★½	★★
CHEF MICKEY'S	Contemporary	★★½	Exp	★★½	★★★

continued on next page

WDW RESTAURANTS BY CUISINE (continued)

CUISINE	LOCATION	OVERALL RATING	COST	QUALITY RATING	VALUE RATING
AMERICAN (continued)					
THE CRYSTAL PALACE	Magic Kingdom	★★½	Exp	★★½	★★★
HOLLYWOOD & VINE	DHS	★★½	Exp	★★	★★★
1900 PARK FARE*	Grand Floridian	★★½	Exp	★★★	★★★
PADDLEFISH	Disney Springs	★★½	Exp	★★★	★★½
RAINFOREST CAFE	Animal Kingdom and Disney Springs	★★½	Mod	★★	★★
SPACE 220	EPCOT	★★½	Exp	★★½	★★
SPLITSVILLE	Disney Springs	★★½	Mod	★★½	★★
BIG RIVER GRILLE & BREWING WORKS	BoardWalk	★★	Mod	★★	★★
BOATWRIGHT'S DINING HALL	Port Orleans Riverside	★★	Mod–Exp	★★	★★
THE FOUNTAIN	Dolphin	★★	Mod	★★	★★
GARDEN GROVE	Swan	★★	Mod	★★½	★★
THE PLAZA RESTAURANT	Magic Kingdom	★★	Mod	★★	★★
SCI-FI DINE-IN THEATER RESTAURANT	DHS	★★	Mod	★★½	★★
T-REX	Disney Springs	★★	Exp	★★	★★
TURF CLUB BAR & GRILL	Saratoga Springs	★★	Exp	★★½	★★
PLANET HOLLYWOOD	Disney Springs	★½	Mod	★★	★★
MAYA GRILL	Coronado Springs	★	Exp	★	★
ROUNDUP RODEO BBQ	Disney's Hollywood Studios	Too new to rate	Exp	Too new to rate	Too new to rate
TRAIL'S END*	Fort Wilderness	NA	Exp	NA	NA
BRITISH					
ROSE & CROWN DINING ROOM	EPCOT	★★★	Mod	★★★½	★★★
BUFFET					
BOMA—FLAVORS OF AFRICA	Animal Kingdom Lodge–Jambo House	★★★★½	Exp	★★★★	★★★★
BIERGARTEN	EPCOT	★★★	Exp	★★★	★★★★
CAPE MAY CAFE	Beach Club	★★★	Exp	★★★	★★★
THE CRYSTAL PALACE	Magic Kingdom	★★½	Exp	★★½	★★★
CHEF MICKEY'S	Contemporary	★★½	Exp	★★½	★★★
HOLLYWOOD & VINE	DHS	★★½	Exp	★★	★★★
1900 PARK FARE	Grand Floridian	★★½	Exp	★★★	★★★
AKERSHUS ROYAL BANQUET HALL	EPCOT	★★	Exp	★★	★★★★
CAJUN					
BOATWRIGHT'S DINING HALL	Port Orleans Riverside	★★	Mod–Exp	★★	★★
CHINESE					
NINE DRAGONS	EPCOT	★★★	Mod	★★★	★★½
COCKTAILS AND BAR BITES					
JOCK LINDSEY'S HANGAR BAR	Disney Springs	★★	Inexp	★★	★★

*Closed at press time

WDW RESTAURANTS BY CUISINE *(continued)*

CUISINE	LOCATION	OVERALL RATING	COST	QUALITY RATING	VALUE RATING
FRENCH					
TOPOLINO'S TERRACE	Riviera	★★★★	Exp	★★★★	★★★
LA CRÊPERIE DE PARIS	EPCOT	★★★½	Mod	★★★½	★★★★
MONSIEUR PAUL	EPCOT	★★★	Exp	★★★	★★★
BE OUR GUEST RESTAURANT	Magic Kingdom	★★½	Exp	★★½	★★
CHEFS DE FRANCE	EPCOT	★★½	Exp	★★½	★★★
GERMAN					
BIERGARTEN	EPCOT	★★★	Exp	★★★	★★★★
GOURMET					
VICTORIA & ALBERT'S	Grand Floridian	★★★★★	Exp	★★★★★	★★★★
INDIAN					
SANAA	Animal Kingdom Villas–Kidani Village	★★★★	Exp	★★★★	★★★★
IRISH					
RAGLAN ROAD	Disney Springs	★★★★	Exp	★★★★	★★★
ITALIAN					
TOPOLINO'S TERRACE	Riviera	★★★★	Exp	★★★★	★★★
VIA NAPOLI	EPCOT	★★★★	Exp	★★★½	★★★
TUTTO GUSTO WINE CELLAR	EPCOT	★★★½	Exp	★★½	★★★
IL MULINO	Swan	★★★	Exp	★★★	★★
TRATTORIA AL FORNO	BoardWalk	★★★	Mod	★★★½	★★
TUTTO ITALIA RISTORANTE	EPCOT	★★★	Exp	★★★★	★★
MAMA MELROSE'S RISTORANTE ITALIANO	DHS	★★½	Exp	★★★	★★
MARIA & ENZO'S RISTORANTE	Disney Springs	★★½	Exp	★★½	★★★
TERRALINA CRAFTED ITALIAN	Disney Springs	★★½	Exp	★★½	★★½
TONY'S TOWN SQUARE	Magic Kingdom	★★	Exp	★★	★★
JAPANESE/SUSHI					
TAKUMI-TEI	EPCOT	★★★★½	Exp	★★★★★	★★★½
KIMONOS	Swan	★★★★	Mod	★★★★	★★★
MORIMOTO ASIA	Disney Springs	★★★★	Exp	★★★★	★★★★
TEPPAN EDO	EPCOT	★★★½	Exp	★★★★	★★★
TOKYO DINING	EPCOT	★★★	Mod	★★★★	★★★
LATIN					
JUNGLE NAVIGATION CO. LTD. SKIPPER CANTEEN	Magic Kingdom	★★★½	Exp	★★★	★★★
PARADISO 37	Disney Springs	★★½	Exp	★★½	★★½
SEBASTIAN'S BISTRO	Caribbean Beach	★★	Exp	★★	★★½
MEDITERRANEAN					
CÍTRICOS	Grand Floridian	★★★★	Exp	★★★★½	★★★

continued on next page

WDW RESTAURANTS BY CUISINE *(continued)*

CUISINE	LOCATION	OVERALL RATING	COST	QUALITY RATING	VALUE RATING
MEXICAN					
LA HACIENDA DE SAN ANGEL	EPCOT	★★★★	Exp	★★★★	★★★½
FRONTERA COCINA	Disney Springs	★★★½	Exp	★★★½	★★★
SAN ANGEL INN RESTAURANTE	EPCOT	★★★	Exp	★★★	★★
MAYA GRILL	Coronado Springs	★	Exp	★	★
ROSA MEXICANO	Dolphin	Too new to rate			
MOROCCAN					
SPICE ROAD TABLE	EPCOT	★★★★	Inexp	★★★★	★★★
NORWEGIAN					
AKERSHUS ROYAL BANQUET HALL	EPCOT	★★	Exp	★★	★★★★
PAN-ASIAN/POLYNESIAN					
MORIMOTO ASIA	Disney Springs	★★★★	Exp	★★★★	★★★★
JUNGLE NAVIGATION CO. LTD. SKIPPER CANTEEN	Magic Kingdom	★★★½	Exp	★★★	★★★
TIFFINS	Animal Kingdom	★★★½	Exp	★★★½	★★½
KONA CAFE	Polynesian Village	★★★	Mod	★★★	★★★★
'OHANA	Polynesian Village	★★★	Exp	★★★½	★★★
TRADER SAM'S GROG GROTTO	Polynesian Village	★★★	Inexp	★★★	★★★
YAK & YETI RESTAURANT	Animal Kingdom	★★★	Exp	★★★	★★
SEAFOOD					
NARCOOSSEE'S	Grand Floridian	★★★★½	Exp	★★★½	★★
THE BOATHOUSE	Disney Springs	★★★½	Exp	★★★	★★
FLYING FISH	BoardWalk	★★★½	Exp	★★★	★★★
TODD ENGLISH'S BLUEZOO	Dolphin	★★★	Exp	★★★	★★
CORAL REEF RESTAURANT	EPCOT	★★½	Exp	★★	★★
PADDLEFISH	Disney Springs	★★½	Exp	★★★	★★½
SEBASTIAN'S BISTRO	Caribbean Beach	★★	Exp	★★	★★½
SPANISH/TAPAS					
JALEO BY JOSÉ ANDRÉS	Disney Springs	★★★★	Mod	★★★★	★★★★
TOLEDO	Coronado Springs	★★★½	Exp	★★★	★★½
THREE BRIDGES BAR & GRILL	Coronado Springs	★★★	Exp	★★★	★★½
STEAK					
LE CELLIER STEAKHOUSE	EPCOT	★★★★	Exp	★★★★	★★★½
SHULA'S STEAKHOUSE	Dolphin	★★★★	Exp	★★★★	★★
STEAKHOUSE 71	Contemporary	★★★★	Exp	★★★★	★★★½
STK ORLANDO	Disney Springs	★★★½	Exp	★★★★	★★½
YACHTSMAN STEAKHOUSE	Yacht Club	★★½	Exp	★★★½	★★
WINE/SMALL PLATES					
WINE BAR GEORGE	Disney Springs	★★★★	Mod–Exp	★★★★	★★★★

continued from page 310

PAYMENT All Walt Disney World restaurants take the following credit cards: American Express, Diners Club, Discover, Japan Credit Bureau, MasterCard, and Visa. And, unless otherwise noted, all are expected to accept the Disney Dining Plan, when it returns.

NEW IN 2023
Rosa Mexicano
Dolphin; ☎ 407-934-1609

SUMMARY AND COMMENTS Part of a national chain, this new Mexican spot replaces Fresh Mediterranean Market.

Roundup Rodeo BBQ
Toy Story Land, Disney's Hollywood Studios; ☎ 407-939-3463

SETTING AND ATMOSPHERE Opened in late March 2023, this colorfully themed sit-down barbecue place is located to the right of Slinky Dog Dash in Toy Story Land.

HOUSE SPECIALTIES Our picks are the fried pickles, the baked beans, the outstanding chicken (better than **Regal Eagle Smokehouse,** page 303), and our new do-it-yourself favorite: Throw some brisket, pepper jelly, and slaw on a biscuit. Our dessert pick is the Plant-Based Peach-Strawberry Pie with the frozen sweet tea. North Carolina barbecue fans will enjoy the vinegar base in many of the bites.

SUMMARY AND COMMENTS This is a very loud, very fun, well-themed meal that offers an enormous amount of decent (and some great) dishes.

FULL-SERVICE RESTAURANT PROFILES
Akershus Royal Banquet Hall   ★★

NORWEGIAN/BUFFET	EXPENSIVE	QUALITY ★★	VALUE ★★★★
READER-SURVEY RESPONSES ⊕ 79% (Do Not Visit)			

Norway, World Showcase, EPCOT; ☎ 407-939-3463

Reservations Required; a credit card is required to reserve. **Dining Plan credits** 1 per person, per meal. **When to go** Lunch or dinner. **Cost range** $63 (child $41). Prices vary seasonally; check before you go. **Service** ★★★★. **Friendliness** ★★★★. **Parking** EPCOT lot. **Bar** Full service. **Wine selection** Good. **Dress** Casual. **Disabled access** Yes. **Customers** Theme park guests. **Character breakfast** 8:30 a.m.–12:10 p.m. **Character lunch** 12:15–4:40 p.m. **Character dinner** 5:25–8:05 p.m.

SETTING AND ATMOSPHERE The inside of Akershus looks like every child's vision of a fairy-tale castle: high ceilings, stone archways, sumptuous purple carpets, regal banners flying. Disney's version is almost as ungodly expensive as the real thing, though, and you're apt to hear Norwegian spoken by your servers.

HOUSE SPECIALTIES Salads, Norwegian meatballs, grilled salmon, chicken and dumplings, lefse, mashed potatoes, green beans. *For kids:* Macaroni and cheese, corn dogs.

OTHER RECOMMENDATIONS Beer on tap, wine, aquavit cocktails.

SUMMARY AND COMMENTS Akershus has never been on our "you've gotta try this" list, but if you have kids who love the Disney princesses, they won't be disappointed. There was a time when the Scandinavian-style buffet was noteworthy, but these days all the attention in the kitchen goes to feeding families fast. As for the prices? You're paying for that princess face time.

Ale & Compass ★★★

AMERICAN	MODERATE	QUALITY ★★★	VALUE ★★★
READER-SURVEY RESPONSES ⊕ 90% (Average)			

Yacht Club Resort; ☎ 407-939-3463

Reservations Recommended. **Dining Plan credits** 1 per person, per meal. **When to go** Anytime. **Cost range** Breakfast buffet $23 per person; à la carte items $15–$35 for all meals **Service** ★★★½. **Friendliness** ★★★½. **Parking** Resort lot. **Bar** Full service. **Wine selection** Good. **Dress** Casual. **Disabled access** Yes. **Customers** EPCOT and hotel guests. **Breakfast** Daily, 7:30 a.m.–11 a.m. **Lunch** Daily, 11:45 a.m.–2 p.m. **Dinner** Daily, 5–9 p.m.

SETTING AND ATMOSPHERE The large dining room is polished and pretty in a generic way, but there's no theme to speak of.

HOUSE SPECIALTIES For dinner, start with the Cabernet-braised short ribs with roasted vegetables and end with the 12-layer chocolate cake. The pappardelle pasta is our second recommendation here.

OTHER RECOMMENDATIONS Breakfast selections include salted caramel-apple French toast, plus the usual eggs, bacon, pancakes, and waffles. Dinner features pastas, chicken, steaks, a bacon–Vermont Cheddar burger, and a seafood pot pie with shrimp, scallops, crab, and sustainable fish. Vegetarians have two full-fledged meal options: the Protein Bowl (with quinoa, vegan Italian "sausage," sweet potato, and Broccolini) and a pasta with mushrooms and other veggies.

SUMMARY AND COMMENTS The cuisine is advertised as "New England comfort food."

Beaches & Cream Soda Shop ★★½

AMERICAN	MODERATE	QUALITY ★★½	VALUE ★★
READER-SURVEY RESPONSES ⊕ 91% (Above Average)			

Beach Club Resort; ☎ 407-939-3463

Reservations Strongly recommended. **Dining Plan credits** 1 per person, per meal. **When to go** Lunch or dinner. **Cost range** $21–$29. **Service** ★★★. **Friendliness** ★★★★. **Parking** Hotel lot. **Bar** Beer, wine, hard floats. **Wine selection** Minimal. **Dress** Casual. **Disabled access** Yes. **Customers** Resort guests. **Hours** Daily, 11 a.m.–11 p.m.

SETTING AND ATMOSPHERE Casual eats and retro soda-fountain decor. Guests in bathing suits and flip-flops queue up for the burgers, sandwiches (Reuben, French dip, chicken), and piles of hot fries.

HOUSE SPECIALTIES Burgers and fries; chili and soup; hand-scooped ice cream, including the gargantuan $35 Kitchen Sink dessert, featuring five flavors of ice cream slathered with toppings.

OTHER RECOMMENDATIONS Root beer float.

SUMMARY AND COMMENTS Beaches & Cream is a hit with readers. We find the food just so-so. Seating is scarce during peak hours.

Be Our Guest Restaurant ★★½

FRENCH/AMERICAN	EXPENSIVE	QUALITY ★★½	VALUE ★★
READER-SURVEY RESPONSES ⊕ 79% (Do Not Visit)			

Fantasyland, Magic Kingdom; ☎ 407-939-3463

Reservations Strongly recommended. **Dining Plan credits** 1 quick-service credit per person, per meal for breakfast (not currently offered); 2 table-service credits per person, per meal for lunch and dinner. **When to go** Lunch or dinner. **Cost range** Prix fixe lunch and dinner $67 (child $39). **Service** ★★★. **Friendliness** ★★★★. **Parking** Magic Kingdom lot. **Bar** Wine and beer only. **Wine selection** Solid wine list with some French to match the restaurant's theme—from sparkling starters to a private-label wine sampler. A handful of popular California vintages are on the list as well. **Dress** Casual. **Disabled access** Yes. **Customers** Magic Kingdom guests. **Lunch** Daily, 10 a.m.–2:55 p.m. **Dinner** Daily, 3–10 p.m.

SETTING AND ATMOSPHERE Be Our Guest re-creates Beast's Castle from *Beauty & the Beast* with three themed rooms: the Grand Ballroom, the mysterious West Wing, and the pretty Castle Gallery. The rooms fill up fast, with a noise level to match the hordes (the restaurant has space for up to 550 seats). The lights are dimmed at lunch and dinner, which offers table service and a tad more serenity than breakfast (when offered).

HOUSE SPECIALTIES French onion soup or charcuterie plate appetizers, roasted pork tenderloin with seasonal vegetables as an entrée.

OTHER RECOMMENDATIONS Filet mignon with Robuchon potatoes; pan-seared scallops with risotto.

SUMMARY AND COMMENTS Be Our Guest has been the most popular restaurant in Walt Disney World since it opened in 2012. Disney has tried to meet that demand in several ways, most notably adding breakfast (not offered at press time) and switching to a common fixed-price menu for both lunch and dinner. These changes, especially the fixed-price menu, have steadily chipped away at Be Our Guest's survey ratings; it was Below Average for several years, according to readers, and now it's firmly in the Do Not Visit range. The menu is heavy and expensive, it lacks enough choices to justify the cost, and it takes far too long to finish the meal.

We've received quite a few reader comments about Be Our Guest with a common refrain of "just OK." First up, from Fletcher, North Carolina:

I got up early to snag this dinner reservation. The atmosphere was fun and unique, but the food really wasn't that special. I had the layered ratatouille, which was too salty. My son had experienced lamb for the first time at Boma the night before, so he ordered the roasted lamb. He was extremely disappointed by the portion size, which was really just a few bites. The Beast made several appearances during our meal, which was nice, but I felt the food should have been better.

A reader from Lincoln, Rhode Island, chimes in:

I was able to get reservations for Be Our Guest for breakfast and dinner. Unless you have to meet the Beast, skip dinner. While the food was good, the price for kids is ridiculous. And I don't know any kids who eat cheese in block form.

If you're looking for good food at comparable prices, **Liberty Tree Tavern** (page 337) or **Jungle Navigation Co. Ltd. Skipper Canteen** (page 335) is a better choice for lunch and dinner. For a fast, inexpensive breakfast, try **Main Street Bakery** (page 300). For a quick lunch, go to **Columbia Harbour House** (page 299), the highest-rated indoor restaurant in the Magic Kingdom.

Biergarten Restaurant ★★★

GERMAN/BUFFET	EXPENSIVE	QUALITY ★★★	VALUE ★★★★
READER-SURVEY RESPONSES ⊕ 91% (Above Average)			

Germany, World Showcase, EPCOT; ☎ 407-939-3463

Reservations Recommended. **Dining Plan credits** 1 per person, per meal. **When to go** Lunch or dinner. **Cost range** $49 (child $27). **Service** ★★★★. **Friendliness** ★★★★. **Parking** EPCOT lot. **Bar** Full service. **Wine selection** German. **Dress** Casual. **Disabled access** Yes. **Customers** Theme park guests. **Lunch** Daily, noon–3:55 p.m. **Dinner** Daily, 4–8 p.m.

SETTING AND ATMOSPHERE Biergarten is a German restaurant set inside a nighttime Teutonic town square. You're seated at long tables lined up in rows emanating like the moon's rays from a central dance floor and stage. A lederhosen-clad oompah band plays and encourages diners to sing along. Tables are not shared between families, and there's plenty of space between occupied tables.

HOUSE SPECIALTIES Schnitzel, potato salad, traditional German sausages, and homemade spaetzle.

OTHER RECOMMENDATIONS Rotisserie chicken, braised red cabbage, and German beer.

ENTERTAINMENT AND AMENITIES Oompah band and German dancers perform throughout the day.

SUMMARY AND COMMENTS The buffet is stacked with an astonishing amount of good-quality food. There are plenty of places in Walt Disney World where you could pay more for less. (If you leave here hungry, don't rule out tapeworms.) The lively 25-minute show (one every hour) and noisy dining room are part of the fun, especially for families. Kids seem to love the place.

Big River Grille & Brewing Works ★★

AMERICAN	MODERATE	QUALITY ★★	VALUE ★★
READER-SURVEY RESPONSES 75% ⊕ (Do Not Visit)			

BoardWalk; ☎ 407-751-1544

Reservations Recommended. **Dining Plan credits** 1 per person, per meal. **When to go** Lunch or dinner. **Cost range** $16-$32. **Service** ★★★. **Friendliness** ★★★★. **Parking** BoardWalk lot. **Bar** Full service. **Wine selection** Good. **Dress** Casual. **Disabled access** Yes. **Customers** Tourists. **Hours** Daily, 11 a.m.–10 p.m. (until 11 p.m. on Friday and Saturday).

SETTING AND ATMOSPHERE Situated for prime people-watching on Disney's BoardWalk, the outdoor tables fill up fast on a pretty day. A minimalist interior focuses on the craft beer made on the premises, with glass walls allowing you to see the process as ales and lagers are microbrewed. The place is small—it seems like the huge copper brewing tanks take up more room than the dining area.

HOUSE SPECIALTIES Beer-cheese soup, baby back ribs with honey-chipotle barbecue sauce.

SUMMARY AND COMMENTS The food is disappointing, but the popularity of craft beer makes Big River Grille a hot spot on the BoardWalk. House brews include a light lager, a robust ale, and seasonal choices.

The Boathouse ★★★½

SEAFOOD	EXPENSIVE	QUALITY ★★★	VALUE ★★
READER-SURVEY RESPONSES ⊕ 93% (Above Average)			

The Landing, Disney Springs; ☎ 407-939-BOAT (2628)

Reservations Strongly recommended. **Dining Plan credits** 2 per person, per meal. **When to go** Lunch or dinner. **Cost range** $27–$75 (child $11). **Service** ★★★★. **Friendliness** ★★★★. **Parking** Orange garage. **Bar** Full service. **Wine selection** Good. **Dress** Casual. **Disabled access** Yes. **Customers** Locals and Disney guests. **Hours** Daily, 11 a.m.–11 p.m. (until 11:30 p.m. on Friday and Saturday).

SETTING AND ATMOSPHERE The first things you notice about The Boathouse, on the waterfront at Disney Springs, are the vintage American Amphicars (amphibious autos produced in the 1960s) and the Italian water taxis floating next to the front door—the multimillion-dollar fleet of 19 features rare boats from private collectors, museums, and boat shows around the world. Take a ride in an Amphicar for $125 per car. The airy restaurant seats up to 600 in nautically themed dining rooms (two private), as well as outdoors. There are three bars, including one built over the water and attached to more than 300 feet of boardwalk and docks.

HOUSE SPECIALTIES The menu changes daily, but there's seafood of every sort: a raw bar with fresh oysters, tuna, and wild-caught shrimp; lobster; fish and shellfish, including Florida seasonal varieties; and jumbo lump crab cake. There's also filet mignon, as well as ice-cream pie for dessert.

SUMMARY AND COMMENTS If you're not quite sure where to eat in Disney Springs, then go to The Boathouse. Consistently good quality, especially with fresh seafood, made this restaurant the No. 2 highest-grossing independent restaurant in the United States in 2022, behind Komodo in Miami—but the average bill at Komodo was more than double that at The Boathouse. The restaurant does enough volume that it has proprietary lines of oysters and rib eyes. While seafood is the star, the steaks are top-notch as well. Along with **Chef Art Smith's Homecomin'** (see page 322) The Boathouse has the best service in Disney Springs.

A North Carolina family advises readers to save room—lots of room—for dessert:

By far the best meal was at The Boathouse in Disney Springs. Everyone's meal was superb—we all ordered seafood entrées. We had a mile-high ice-cream dessert designed to serve two. It was delicious and easily served all four of us.

Boatwright's Dining Hall ★★

AMERICAN/CAJUN   MODERATE-EXPENSIVE   QUALITY ★★   VALUE ★★
READER-SURVEY RESPONSES ➕ 83% (Much Below Average)

Port Orleans Resort–Riverside; ☎ 407-939-3463

Reservations Strongly recommended. **Dining Plan credits** 1 per person, per meal. **When to go** Early evening. **Cost range** $29–$43 (child $13–$14). **Service** ★★★★½. **Friendliness** ★★★★★. **Parking** Hotel lot. **Bar** Full service. **Wine selection** None. **Dress** Casual. **Disabled access** Yes. **Customers** Hotel guests. **Hours** Daily, 5–9 p.m.

SETTING AND ATMOSPHERE Situated between River Roost Lounge and Riverside Mill Food Court, just off of Port Orleans Riverside's lobby, Boatwright's features a simply appointed open dining room bathed in golden wood finishes, with diners feasting on New Orleans–inspired classics underneath a large boat skeleton. Always busy and a tad noisy, the restaurant serves dinner daily.

HOUSE SPECIALTIES The Mardi Gras pimento cheese fritters are the best appetizers. The best entrées are the shrimp and grits and the Nashville hot chicken (which isn't that hot).

OTHER RECOMMENDATIONS Blackened Prime Rib, slow-roasted and served with mashed potatoes and horseradish cream.

SUMMARY AND COMMENTS The kitchen struggles with consistency when the restaurant is full. Stick to the basics.

Boma—Flavors of Africa ★★★★½

AFRICAN/BUFFET   EXPENSIVE   QUALITY ★★★★   VALUE ★★★★
READER-SURVEY RESPONSES ➕ 96% (Exceptional)

Animal Kingdom Lodge & Villas–Jambo House; ☎ 407-939-3463

Reservations Strongly recommended. **Dining Plan credits** 1 per person, per meal. **When to go** Breakfast or dinner. **Cost range** Breakfast $25 (child $21), dinner $54 (child $32).

Service ★★★★½. **Friendliness** ★★★★. **Parking** Valet ($33) or hotel lot. **Bar** Full service. **Wine selection** All South African. **Dress** Casual. **Disabled access** Yes. **Customers** Hotel guests. **Breakfast** Daily, 7:30–11:30 a.m. **Dinner** Daily, 5–9:30 p.m.

SETTING AND ATMOSPHERE On the first floor of Animal Kingdom Lodge, Boma's huge dining room evokes an African marketplace, complete with thatched-roof ceilings. With so many tables and buffet dining stations, plus the massive open kitchen where guests can observe all the goings-on, the dining room can be loud during peak mealtimes. Still, large and small families alike find it welcoming.

HOUSE SPECIALTIES Boma's buffet takes guests to a culinary frontier full of rich flavors. Dishes represent regional cuisines from across Africa. Daily rotating entrées include carved African spice–crusted beef sirloin, whole-roasted salmon, and slow-roasted ribs. Side dishes include spiced sweet potatoes, couscous, peanut rice, and Zulu cabbage. Cold prepared salads are bursting with fresh produce, ranging in flavor from sweet and sour (watermelon rind) to savory (lentils and hearts of palm). Boma's signature dessert, the Zebra Dome—a thin layer of white cake supporting an orb of Amarula cream-liqueur mousse, smothered with white chocolate ganache and drizzled with dark chocolate—has a cult following.

OTHER RECOMMENDATIONS A varying selection of specialty soups—the carrot-ginger soup and Cape Malay lamb stew in particular are must-tries. Specialty dips and condiments such as Kalamata olive hummus, tamarind barbecue sauce, coriander chutney, and Masai Mara sauce (think a Kenyan pesto) will tickle taste buds as complements to any dish or bread. For breakfast, French toast bread pudding shines; made-to-order omelets and carved meats satisfy those in search of more-American options.

SUMMARY AND COMMENTS Boma is consistently rated as one of the best restaurants in Walt Disney World—it's as much an attraction at the Animal Kingdom Lodge as, well, the animals. The buffet includes fresh, seasonal, well-prepared offerings at each meal station. And the value, at both breakfast and dinner, is almost impossible to beat. Advance Dining Reservations are a must—walk-up tables here are few and far between.

California Grill ★★★½

AMERICAN	EXPENSIVE	QUALITY ★★★★	VALUE ★★
READER-SURVEY RESPONSES ✪ 93% (Above Average)			

Contemporary Resort; ☎ 407-939-3463

Reservations Strongly recommended. **Dining Plan credits** 2 per person, per meal. **When to go** During evening fireworks. **Cost range** Dinner $89 (child $39). **Service** ★★★★½. **Friendliness** ★★★★★. **Parking** Hotel lot. **Bar** Full service. **Wine selection** Fantastic. **Dress** Dressy casual. **Disabled access** Yes. **Customers** Hotel guests and locals. **Dinner** Daily, 5–10 p.m.

SETTING AND ATMOSPHERE California Grill remains one of the most popular choices for Disney dining, both for its remarkable view from the 15th floor of the Contemporary Resort and for its bustling open kitchen. It can be crowded and noisy, filled with families who want a view of the Magic Kingdom fireworks; book a table early or late for a quieter experience. A showstopping wine display features 1,600 bottles in a climate-controlled case just off the elevator. If you don't have a reservation, ask for a seat at the sushi bar, where you can order appetizers but not entrées, or the lounge, which serves the same menu as the restaurant.

HOUSE SPECIALTIES The 35-ounce rib eye is an additional $80 upcharge. However, (1) it's delicious, and (2) they'll let you keep the comically large bone if you ask. (The menu says "for two," but we're Ameri-*cans*, not Ameri-*can'ts*.) For starters, try the duck pizza and the braised beef wontons. Avoid the wild mushroom ravioli.

ENTERTAINMENT AND AMENITIES Magic Kingdom fireworks are the star of the show and can be observed from the terrace—but only guests with dining reservations may watch from the Contemporary Resort's 15th floor.

SUMMARY AND COMMENTS California Grill uses its $89-per-person fixed-price menu to discourage large groups from splitting one pizza and staying 3 hours to watch the fireworks. The problem is that the kitchen isn't consistent enough to deliver value for that kind of money.

Cape May Cafe ★★★

AMERICAN/BUFFET	EXPENSIVE	QUALITY ★★★	VALUE ★★★
READER-SURVEY RESPONSES ➕ 83% (Much Below Average)			

Beach Club Resort; ☎ 407-934-3358

Reservations Strongly recommended. **Dining Plan credits** 1 per person, per meal. **When to go** Breakfast or dinner. **Cost range** Breakfast $45 (child $29), dinner $46 (child $27). **Service** ★★★★★. **Friendliness** ★★★★★. **Parking** Hotel lot. **Bar** Full service. **Wine selection** Limited. **Dress** Casual. **Disabled access** Yes. **Customers** EPCOT and hotel guests. **Character breakfast** Daily, 7:30–11:30 a.m. **Dinner** Daily, 5–9 p.m.

SETTING AND ATMOSPHERE Just off the lobby at the Beach Club, Cape May Cafe features nautical New England decor in two dining rooms and lots of comfortable seating.

HOUSE SPECIALTIES Breakfast buffet includes made-to-order crepes and omelets, a carving station, and salted caramel "beach buns" for dessert. It might be the best breakfast in Walt Disney World for the money.

SUMMARY AND COMMENTS Breakfast is a character buffet with Mickey and friends. Cape May Café is a buffet for dinner too. Entrées include a seafood boil with shrimp and clams, a carving station, and snow crab legs, but none of it is memorable. Better dining options include **Ale & Compass** (page 316) at Yacht Club and **Trattoria al Forno** (page 356) at BoardWalk Inn.

Le Cellier Steakhouse ★★★★

STEAK	EXPENSIVE	QUALITY ★★★★	VALUE ★★★½
READER-SURVEY RESPONSES ➕ 91% (Above Average)			

Canada, World Showcase, EPCOT; ☎ 407-939-3463

Reservations Required. **Dining Plan credits** 2 per person, per meal. **When to go** Before 6 p.m. **Cost range** $34–$62 (child $11–$18). **Service** ★★★★. **Friendliness** ★★★★★. **Parking** EPCOT lot. **Bar** Full bar. **Wine selection** Canadian wines featured. **Dress** Casual. **Disabled access** Yes. **Customers** Theme park guests. **Lunch** Daily, noon–3:55 p.m. **Dinner** Daily, 4–9 p.m.

SETTING AND ATMOSPHERE Walk past the Canada Pavilion's pretty gardens into this small, darkened dining room, intended to evoke the look and feel of a wine cellar. Given the high prices, it doesn't feel upscale, with heavy wooden tables and no linens, but the crowd doesn't seem to mind—the steaks make up for lack of the ambience. Service is "cheerful Canadian," meaning servers apologize to *you* if you spill something on *them*.

HOUSE SPECIALTIES Appetizer charcuterie plate that comes with an edible beef-fat candle—the idea is that you use the melted fat as a spread; AAA Canadian filet mignon; Canadian Cheddar soup.

OTHER RECOMMENDATIONS For sides, share the mac and cheese, the loaded mashed potatoes, or the poutine. For dessert, try the warm pecan–brown butter tart. Excellent wine selection.

SUMMARY AND COMMENTS Le Cellier improved a couple of years ago and has maintained that quality. It's still expensive, but the steaks are perfectly seasoned and cooked, with a beautiful char. Service is unrushed—it's possible for a full dinner to take 2 hours, so plan accordingly. The menu is the same at lunch and dinner.

Chef Art Smith's Homecomin' ★★★★

AMERICAN	MODERATE	QUALITY ★★★★	VALUE ★★★½
READER-SURVEY RESPONSES ⊕ 94% (Much Above Average)			

The Landing, Disney Springs; ☎ 407-560-0100

Reservations Strongly recommended. **Dining Plan credits** 1 per person, per meal. **When to go** Brunch, lunch, or dinner. **Cost range** $19–$37 (child $10). **Service** ★★★★. **Friendliness** ★★★★. **Parking** Orange garage. **Bar** Full service. **Wine selection** Modest. **Dress** Casual. **Disabled access** Yes. **Customers** Disney guests and locals. **Lunch and dinner** Daily, 11 a.m.–11 p.m. **Brunch** Saturday–Sunday, 9 a.m.–12:55 p.m.

SETTING AND ATMOSPHERE Florida farm-style decor with a reclaimed-wood-and-mason-jar vibe. Dining room chairs are covered in faux-burlap sacks. Florida born and raised, Art Smith is Oprah Winfrey's former private chef and is well known for his appearances on *Top Chef Masters* and *Iron Chef America*.

HOUSE SPECIALTIES Fried chicken, optionally served with iced house-made doughnuts. The Thigh High Chicken Biscuits appetizer well may be one of the best food items on Disney property; be sure to check it out. The cocktails and desserts are fabulous.

OTHER RECOMMENDATIONS Beyond the fried chicken, the Art Burger is good; ask for the house-made pimento cheese instead of the menu's suggested slice of American. If you're from the South and live within driving distance of a barbecue restaurant, Art Smith's pork barbecue probably won't meet your standards (Len's favorite is Stamey's in Greensboro, North Carolina). Stick to the fried chicken and burgers and you'll be fine.

SUMMARY AND COMMENTS One of the best restaurants in Walt Disney World. If you can't get a table, try the bar.

Chef Mickey's ★★½

AMERICAN/BUFFET	EXPENSIVE	QUALITY ★★½	VALUE ★★★
READER-SURVEY RESPONSES ⊕ 83% (Much Below Average)			

Contemporary Resort; ☎ 407-939-3463

Reservations Required. **Dining Plan credits** 1 per person, per meal. **When to go** Breakfast. **Cost range** Breakfast $51 (child $33), dinner $62 (child $39). **Service** ★★★★. **Friendliness** ★★★★★. **Parking** Hotel lot. **Bar** Full service. **Wine selection** Fair. **Dress** Casual. **Disabled access** Yes. **Customers** Theme park guests. **Character breakfast** Daily, 7:30 a.m.–12:30 p.m. **Character dinner** Daily, 5–9:30 p.m.

SETTING AND ATMOSPHERE Can you say *madhouse*? This big, open dining room with the monorail whizzing by overhead (inside the hotel) is a cacophony of children's and parents' voices. The food is secondary—everyone's here to see Mickey and his pals.

HOUSE SPECIALTIES Banana-bread French toast, potato-cheese casserole with bacon and chives. At dinner, the gratin potato and farro wheat fried rice are better than average.

OTHER RECOMMENDATIONS Breakfast buffet offers standard options, such as eggs, Mickey waffles, and bacon.

ENTERTAINMENT AND AMENITIES Character sightings.

SUMMARY AND COMMENTS Both breakfast and dinner are buffets. Nothing on the dinner menu is as good as at EPCOT's **Garden Grill** or the Magic Kingdom's **Liberty Tree Tavern,** but you won't leave hungry, and the kids' choices will satisfy picky eaters. Best of all, nobody cares if the kids are loud.

Chefs de France ★★½

FRENCH	EXPENSIVE	QUALITY ★★½	VALUE ★★★
READER-SURVEY RESPONSES ✪ 85% (Much Below Average)			

France, World Showcase, EPCOT; ☎ 407-827-8709

Reservations Strongly recommended. **Dining Plan credits** 1 per person, per meal. **When to go** Lunch or dinner. **Cost range** $26–$41 (child $11–$13), prix-fixe meal $66. **Service** ★★★★★. **Friendliness** ★★★★★. **Parking** EPCOT lot. **Bar** Beer and cocktails. **Wine selection** Very good. **Dress** Casual. **Disabled access** Yes. **Customers** Theme park guests. **Lunch** Daily, noon–3 p.m. **Dinner** Daily, 4–8:55 p.m.

SETTING AND ATMOSPHERE It's like stepping into a busy bistro. The smells are delicious, with baguettes from the on-site bakery on every table. White cloth napkins and cushioned banquettes accentuate the classic bistro decor of the main dining room, where window tables make for fun people-watching on the World Showcase Promenade.

HOUSE SPECIALTIES Dishes inspired by the three French chefs for whom the restaurant is named: Paul Bocuse, Gaston Lenôtre, and Roger Vergé. The prix fixe menu features French onion soup with Gruyère for your appetizer and the Boeuf Bourguignon for your entrée.

OTHER RECOMMENDATIONS Ask your server for the vegetarian options.

SUMMARY AND COMMENTS The kitchen has struggled with the basics of food temperature and seasoning during our last couple of visits. The charcuterie plate isn't as good as the ones at Via Napoli or Le Cellier. Stick to the French onion soup and Boeuf Bourguignon.

Cinderella's Royal Table ★★★

AMERICAN	EXPENSIVE	QUALITY ★★★	VALUE ★★
READER-SURVEY RESPONSES ✪ 84% (Much Below Average)			

Cinderella Castle, Fantasyland, Magic Kingdom; ☎ 407-939-3463

Reservations Required; must prepay in full. **Dining Plan credits** 2 per person, per meal. **When to go** Early. **Cost range** Breakfast $65 (child $39), lunch and dinner $79 (child $47). Prices may vary seasonally; check before you go. **Service** ★★★★. **Friendliness** ★★★★. **Parking** Magic Kingdom lot. **Bar** Limited selection of sparkling wine by the glass and bottle. **Dress** Casual. **Disabled access** Yes. **Customers** Theme park guests. **Character breakfast** Daily, 8–10:15 a.m. **Character lunch** Daily, 11 a.m.–2:55 p.m. **Character dinner** Daily, 3–9 p.m.

SETTING AND ATMOSPHERE A spiffy medieval banquet hall in the middle of Fantasyland. While the food is tasty, it's more about experiencing a meal in Cinderella Castle. Cinderella makes an appearance at all three meals, with plenty of time for photos. Other princesses include some combination of Ariel, Aurora, Snow White, Jasmine, and Rapunzel.

HOUSE SPECIALTIES Lunch and dinner have the same entrée selections: beef or pork tenderloin, chicken thighs, fish, or a vegetarian pasta. For starters, try the charcuterie plate or the salad; for mains, the beef tenderloin comes with a Bordelaise sauce that should be sold by the bottle. Ask your server if you can sample each of the three desserts.

SUMMARY AND COMMENTS We think the food quality is better than average, despite the reader-survey ratings; plus, it's less expensive than it was before (but still pricey), and service is good. For more on reserving a spot at the Royal Table, see page 273.

Cítricos ★★★★

AMERICAN/MEDITERRANEAN	EXPENSIVE	QUALITY ★★★★½	VALUE ★★★
READER-SURVEY RESPONSES ➕ 92% (Above Average)			

Grand Floridian Resort & Spa; ☎ 407-939-3463

Reservations Required. **Dining Plan credits** 2 per person, per meal. **When to go** Dinner. **Cost range** $36–$59 (child $13–$19). **Service** ★★★★★. **Friendliness** ★★★★★. **Parking** Valet ($33); self-parking is deceptively far away. **Bar** Full service. **Wine selection** Very good. **Dress** Dressy casual. **Disabled access** Yes. **Customers** Hotel guests and locals. **Dinner** Daily, 5–9:30 p.m.

SETTING AND ATMOSPHERE Cítricos got a *Mary Poppins*–themed makeover before it reopened. The changes are subtle, and the restaurant feels upscale without being stuffy. The full-view show kitchen is still on display.

HOUSE SPECIALTIES The roulade of chicken belongs with rainbows and puppy dogs in the pantheon of things everyone should love. Other standouts: sweet corn bisque; strawberry salad; house-made pasta.

OTHER RECOMMENDATIONS For starters, try the pork belly with plantain croquette and salsa verde, or the smoked duck. The best dessert might be the orange blossom flan, a nice nod to the restaurant's name.

SUMMARY AND COMMENTS This is a really good choice for dinner, with enough availability that you'll have a decent chance to get in. Expect the menu to change often, and ask your server for their recommendations. If you can't get a reservation at **Victoria & Albert's** next door (see page 358), this is the next-best place we've eaten at the Grand Floridian.

City Works Eatery and Pour House ★★★

AMERICAN	MODERATE	QUALITY ★★★	VALUE ★★★
READER-SURVEY RESPONSES ➕ 85% (Much Below Average)			

West Side, Disney Springs; ☎ 407-801-3730

Reservations Accepted. **Dining Plan credits** Not accepted. **When to go** Brunch, lunch, or dinner. **Cost range** $19–$39 (child $10). **Service** ★★★★. **Friendliness** ★★★★. **Parking** Orange garage. **Bar** Full service. **Wine selection** Good. **Dress** Casual. **Disabled access** Yes. **Customers** Tourists. **Hours** Monday–Friday, 11 a.m.–10 p.m.; Saturday–Sunday, 10 a.m.–11 p.m.

SETTING AND ATMOSPHERE Indoor seating may be available; 17 outdoor seats can be very warm in the Florida sun.

HOUSE SPECIALTIES "A solid beer selection for brew nerds," says one of our resident beer experts. The fish tacos are a favorite.

SUMMARY AND COMMENTS City Works is a small chain of sports bars with an extensive list of beer taps. Its location near Cirque du Soleil means crowds before and after shows. Food is standard for sports bars, which explains the low reader ratings. The bar's strength is the beer selection.

Coral Reef Restaurant ★★½

SEAFOOD	EXPENSIVE	QUALITY ★★	VALUE ★★
READER-SURVEY RESPONSES ➕ 80% (Do Not Visit)			

The Seas with Nemo & Friends, World Nature, EPCOT; ☎ 407-939-3463

Reservations Required. **Dining Plan credits** 1 per person, per meal. **When to go** Lunch. **Cost range** $24–$36 (child $11–$14). **Service** ★★★★. **Friendliness** ★★★★. **Parking** EPCOT lot. **Bar** Full service. **Wine selection** Good. **Dress** Casual. **Disabled access** Yes. **Customers** Theme park guests. **Lunch** Daily, 11:30 a.m.–3:30 p.m. **Dinner** Daily, 3:45–8:30 p.m.

SETTING AND ATMOSPHERE Though the decor could use a face-lift, you can't beat the view in this darkened dining room, which faces one of the world's largest saltwater aquariums; tiered seating gives everyone a pretty good view of the multitude of fishes (and sometimes Mickey in a scuba suit). The ethereal entryway gives the impression that you're going under the sea; special light fixtures throw ripple patterns on the ceiling.

HOUSE SPECIALTIES The 10-ounce slow-roasted prime rib and the chocolate cake. For kids, grilled fish, steak, chicken, or shrimp.

SUMMARY AND COMMENTS Not the best restaurant in EPCOT by a long shot, but Coral Reef is a great escape from the Florida sun. Grab a souvenir fish guide and check out the more than 2,000 sea creatures that call this place home—but are probably not on the menu.

La Crêperie de Paris ★★★½

FRENCH	MODERATE	QUALITY ★★★½	VALUE ★★★★
READER-SURVEY RESPONSES ➕ 84% (Much Below Average)			

France, World Showcase, EPCOT; ☎ 407-939-3463

Reservations Strongly recommended. **Dining Plan credits** Not available. **When to go** Anytime. **Cost range** $17–$36 (child $15). **Service** ★★★★. **Friendliness** ★★★★. **Parking** EPCOT lot. **Bar** Full service. **Wine selection** Good. **Dress** Casual. **Disabled access** Yes. **Customers** Theme park guests. **Hours** 9:15 a.m.–8:50 p.m.

SETTING AND ATMOSPHERE Set behind most of the France Pavilion, on the walk to Remy's Ratatouille Adventure, La Crêperie de Paris looks from the outside like any streetside Parisian café. There's little theming inside—you could be anywhere from a Canadian poutine place to a nice Wendy's.

HOUSE SPECIALTIES Try the chèvre, spinach, and walnut savory crepe for dinner, with the banana-filled crepe for dessert. The fixed-price meal is a relative bargain for Walt Disney World.

SUMMARY AND COMMENTS Generous portions. A walk-up window is available. The below-average reader rating might indicate that it's a lot of folks' introduction to savory crepes; fish pancakes in Florida heat might not be for everyone.

The Crystal Palace ★★½

AMERICAN/BUFFET	EXPENSIVE	QUALITY ★★½	VALUE ★★★
READER-SURVEY RESPONSES ➕ 82% (Much Below Average)			

Main Street, U.S.A., Magic Kingdom; ☎ 407-939-3463

Reservations Required. **Dining Plan credits** 1 per person, per meal. **When to go** Lunch and dinner. **Cost range** Breakfast $45 (child $29), lunch and dinner $59 (child $38). Prices vary seasonally. **Service** ★★★. **Friendliness** ★★★★. **Parking** Magic Kingdom lot. **Bar** Wine and beer. **Dress** Casual. **Disabled access** Yes. **Customers** Park guests. **Character breakfast** Daily, 8–10:45 a.m. **Character lunch** Daily, 11:30 a.m.–2:55 p.m. **Character dinner** Daily, 3–10 p.m.

SETTING AND ATMOSPHERE A lunch visit to The Crystal Palace surrounds you with cool sunlight and decorative plants. The restaurant's white steel supports, arched ceilings, and glass roof (especially the atrium) are tributes to its namesake, built to house London's 1851 Great Exhibition—the first world's fair—and among the first structures to use plate glass in large quantities. The setting is less distinctive for dinner after dark.

HOUSE SPECIALTIES Nothing is very good.

SUMMARY AND COMMENTS The character meals have returned, with Pooh, Piglet, and friends at all meals. Despite the return of the buffet, the restaurant continues to have trouble maintaining its food quality. The fried chicken is greasy, and the prime rib is tough and overcooked. The best of the bunch might be the Southern Fried Cauliflower, but nobody should have to pay $59 for albino broccoli.

Reader ratings for The Crystal Palace remain low. For the same price, we recommend **Liberty Tree Tavern** (see page 337) in the Magic Kingdom or **Garden Grill Restaurant** (see page 328) in EPCOT instead.

The Edison ★★★

AMERICAN	EXPENSIVE	QUALITY ★★★½	VALUE ★★★
READER-SURVEY RESPONSES ➊ 81% (Much Below Average)			

The Landing, Disney Springs; ☎ 407-560-WATT (9288)

Reservations Recommended. **Dining Plan credits** 1 per person, per meal. **When to go** Dinner. **Cost range** $22-$43 (child $15). **Service** ★★★½. **Friendliness** ★★★★. **Parking** Orange garage. **Bar** Full service. **Wine selection** Good. **Dress** Casual. **Disabled access** Yes. **Customers** Tourists and locals on date night. **Hours** Sunday–Thursday, 11:30 a.m.–10:30 p.m. (until 11 p.m. on Friday and Saturday).

SETTING AND ATMOSPHERE The concept: a 1920s electric company with high ceilings and themed rooms. Clips of black-and-white movies are projected onto some of the walls. With its steampunk aesthetic and an abundance of gear imagery, the place has a distinct industrial vibe.

HOUSE SPECIALTIES The DB Clothesline Candied Bacon is the signature appetizer: four pieces of heavily smoked candied bacon and a few sprigs of rosemary clipped to a suspended string with clothespins. It's eminently Instagrammable—and that may be the entire point, because we don't know what the concept is supposed to be. The entrées are American comfort food: prime rib and burgers. The food is decent but pricey for what you get.

OTHER RECOMMENDATIONS Drinks are where The Edison shines. In addition to signature cocktails such as the Time Turner, made with Bacardi light rum, Campari, lime, pineapple, and orgeat (almond-flavored flower-water syrup), there are about 10 draft beers, along with bottled and canned beers and ciders; substantial wine offerings by the bottle and glass; a dozen vodkas; and almost as many varieties of gin, tequila, whiskey, and rum.

SUMMARY AND COMMENTS Beyond the bacon appetizer, we haven't identified a signature dish here, and it's not in the first or second tier of restaurants we'd recommend at Disney Springs. It's not bad for an after-dinner drink, but our experience in getting one is that service is terse.

50's Prime Time Café ★★★

AMERICAN	MODERATE	QUALITY ★★★	VALUE ★★★
READER-SURVEY RESPONSES ➊ 89% (Average)			

Echo Lake, Disney's Hollywood Studios; ☎ 407-939-3463

Reservations Strongly recommended. **Dining Plan credits** 1 per person, per meal. **When to go** Lunch or dinner. **Cost range** $17-$28 (child $12-$14). **Service** ★★★★★. **Friendliness** ★★★★★. **Parking** DHS lot. **Bar** Full service. **Wine selection** Good. **Dress** Casual. **Disabled access** Yes. **Customers** Theme park guests. **Lunch** Daily, 10:45 a.m.–3:55 p.m. **Dinner** Daily, 4–9 p.m.

SETTING AND ATMOSPHERE Dine in a 1950s kitchen stocked with antique fridges, laminate tabletops, sunburst clocks, and decoupage art. Black-and-white TVs play vintage sitcom clips while you wait for your entrées.

HOUSE SPECIALTIES Pot roast, fried chicken, meat loaf, plus a sampler platter with some of each; PB&J milkshake and other retro fare. Desserts are a strong point, with warm apple crisp and a chocolate–peanut butter layer cake being the highlights.

SUMMARY AND COMMENTS Though the restaurant is usually packed and noisy, the waitstaff makes it worthwhile, admonishing you just like Mom did to "take your elbows off the table!" and reminding you that "green beans are nature's French fries."

Flying Fish   ★★★½

SEAFOOD	EXPENSIVE	QUALITY ★★★	VALUE ★★★
READER-SURVEY RESPONSES ➕ 88% (Below Average)			

BoardWalk; ☎ 407-939-3463

Reservations Strongly recommended. **Dining Plan credits** 2 per person, per meal. **When to go** Dinner. **Cost range** $38-$59 (child $15-$24). **Service** ★★★★. **Friendliness** ★★★★★. **Parking** Valet ($33) or Boardwalk hotel lot. **Bar** Full service. **Wine selection** Extensive. **Dress** Dressy casual. **Disabled access** Yes. **Customers** Hotel guests; locals. **Dinner** Daily, 5–9:30 p.m.

SETTING AND ATMOSPHERE Situated at the heart of the BoardWalk, Flying Fish takes diners under the sea for an upscale modern seafood dinner enveloped by splashy blue–and–silver restaurant decor. The open kitchen and showcase bar entertain guests seated near the front of the bustling restaurant, with diners enjoying a more muted experience in the rear of the main dining room.

HOUSE SPECIALTIES Plancha-seared scallops with savory grits shines on the seafood-dominant menu, though landlubbers will be perfectly content with the filet mignon. Soup and salad, rotating frequently throughout every season, are solid ways to start any meal here, with both highlighting the freshest produce Florida has to offer. The house's specialty is probably the potato-wrapped red snapper, which has been on the menu through several iterations of chefs and management. Adroit bartenders craft specialty cocktails that pair with most meals, while a strong wine program complements every dish from start to finish.

OTHER RECOMMENDATIONS House fish specials are different every day and are accompanied by the freshest seasonal vegetables you can find at Walt Disney World.

SUMMARY AND COMMENTS The kitchen can sometimes force a slower-paced meal here.

The Fountain   ★★

AMERICAN	MODERATE	QUALITY ★★	VALUE ★★
READER-SURVEY RESPONSES ➕ 78% (Do Not Visit)			

Dolphin Resort; ☎ 407-934-1609

Reservations Not accepted. **Dining Plan credits** Not accepted. **When to go** Lunch or dinner. **Cost range** $12-$20 (child $13). **Service** ★★★★. **Friendliness** ★★★★. **Bar** Beer and wine only. **Wine selection** Limited. **Parking** Valet ($39) or hotel lot ($29), both free with validation. **Dress** Casual. **Disabled access** Yes. **Customers** Hotel guests. **Lunch and dinner** Daily, 11 a.m.–11 p.m.

SETTING AND ATMOSPHERE Informal soda-shop ambience.

HOUSE SPECIALTIES Hot dogs and burgers (including veggie and turkey burgers), milkshakes (we love the PB&J), and ice cream.

OTHER RECOMMENDATIONS Big salads, including seared salmon and chicken Caesar.

SUMMARY AND COMMENTS The Fountain is one of the Dolphin's few casual-dining spots, none of which get high marks from readers.

Frontera Cocina ★★★½

MEXICAN	EXPENSIVE	QUALITY ★★★½	VALUE ★★★
READER-SURVEY RESPONSES ⊕ 86% (Below Average)			

Town Center, Disney Springs; ☎ 407-939-3463

Reservations Strongly recommended. **Dining Plan credits** 1 per person, per meal. **When to go** Dinner. **Cost range** $20–$45 (children $10–$13). **Service** ★★★★. **Friendliness** ★★★★. **Parking** Disney Springs Lime garage. **Bar** Full service. **Wine selection** Modest. **Dress** Casual. **Disabled access** Yes. **Customers** Disney guests and locals. **Hours** Daily, 11 a.m.–11 p.m.

SETTING AND ATMOSPHERE Contrasting with the exterior's muted beige walls and white accents meant to evoke classic Florida waterfront architecture, bright pops of color from the centerpiece chandelier and bar accents highlight the sleek modern eatery's interior, made casual by exposed ductwork and cozy dark-wood furnishings. The open show kitchen and Wall of Fame shelves, packed with specialty liquors and wines, are bathed in natural sunlight from the large windows on nearly every wall, showcasing the springs and the patio from the back dining room.

HOUSE SPECIALTIES Tacos with carne asada or chipotle chicken, chicken enchiladas in red sauce, plantains, margaritas and specialty tequila flights.

OTHER RECOMMENDATIONS Guacamole, coconut-lime cuatro leches cake. The dessert menu is small; kids may be happier with a cupcake from nearby Sprinkles.

SUMMARY AND COMMENTS Ratings are improving. The menu often spotlights the flavors and ingredients of a particular region of Mexico. **Frontera Cocina To Go,** a walk-up window, serves two kinds of tacos, soft drinks, beer, and margaritas.

Garden Grill Restaurant ★★★

AMERICAN	EXPENSIVE	QUALITY ★★★	VALUE ★★★
READER-SURVEY RESPONSES ⊕ 90% (Average)			

The Land, World Nature, EPCOT; ☎ 407-939-3463

Reservations Required. **Dining Plan credits** 1 per person, per meal. **When to go** Anytime. **Cost range** $55 (child $36). Prices vary seasonally; check before you go. **Service** ★★★★. **Friendliness** ★★★★. **Parking** EPCOT lot. **Bar** Wine, beer, and mixed drinks. **Wine selection** Fair. **Dress** Casual. **Disabled access** Yes. **Customers** Theme park guests. **Character lunch** 11:30 a.m.–3:40 p.m. **Character dinner** 3:45–8 p.m.

SETTING AND ATMOSPHERE With the popular Soarin' Around the World attraction nearby, the all-you-can-eat Garden Grill stays busy, even though the concept and the dining room have grown rather dated. Even so, it's a classic: The floor revolves slowly as you peer down into the unseen side of scenes from Living with the Land, the Land Pavilion's ride-through attraction (see page 524). At about the time you finish a meal, you've revolved once, past scenes of a desert, a rainforest, and a farm—an otherwise hidden view of inside the farmhouse. The constant crowing of a "rooster" and dog barks are questionable highlights.

Much more exciting for kids are the Disney characters. Mickey, Chip 'n' Dale, Pluto, and others stop at each table for autographs and photos.

HOUSE SPECIALTIES Grilled beef with chimichurri, turkey breast with stuffing and gravy, BBQ ribs, mashed potatoes, veggies, and salads made with ingredients from The Land's greenhouses. Dessert is a berry shortcake with whipped cream. Plant-based options available on request.

ENTERTAINMENT AND AMENITIES The view. Character dining at both meals. Free nonalcoholic beverages included with meals.

SUMMARY AND COMMENTS The food quality is just OK. Nevertheless, readers really seem to like Garden Grill; we think the retro-Disney setting and the characters are at least as much of a draw as the food. If you can't get an Advance Dining Reservation for one of the other character meals, this place is worth checking out.

Garden Grove ★★

AMERICAN	MODERATE	QUALITY ★★½	VALUE ★★
READER-SURVEY RESPONSES ➊ 67% (Do Not Visit)			

Swan Resort; ☎ 407-934-1609

Reservations Recommended. **Dining Plan credits** Not accepted. **When to go** Breakfast or brunch. **Cost range** $16–$22 (child $11). **Service** ★★★. **Friendliness** ★★★. **Parking** Valet ($39) or hotel lot ($29), both free with validation. **Bar** Full service. **Wine selection** Good. **Dress** Casual. **Disabled access** Yes. **Customers** Hotel guests, some locals, tourists. **Hours** Daily, 7 a.m.–11:30 a.m.

SETTING AND ATMOSPHERE A spacious dining room features a 25-foot faux oak tree in the center. When it's open at night, the lights are dimmed and the oak tree is illuminated with lanterns and twinkling lights.

HOUSE SPECIALTIES Familiar breakfast combinations, including waffles, French toast, and eggs.

SUMMARY AND COMMENTS Garden Grove isn't worth a special trip if you aren't staying at the Swan. But the room is pretty, and the food is plentiful, if not highly rated.

Geyser Point Bar & Grill ★★★★

AMERICAN	MODERATE	QUALITY ★★★½	VALUE ★★★
READER-SURVEY RESPONSES ➊ 94% (Much Above Average)			

Wilderness Lodge & Boulder Ridge/Copper Creek Villas; ☎ 407-939-3463

Reservations Not accepted. **Dining Plan credits** 1 per person, per meal. **When to go** Lunch or dinner. **Cost range** $11–$21 (child $9). **Service** ★★★½. **Friendliness** ★★★★. **Parking** Valet ($44) or hotel lot. **Bar** Full service. **Customers** Hotel guests. **Wine selection** Fair. **Hours** 11 a.m.–11 p.m.

SETTING AND ATMOSPHERE Picturesque views of the resort's geyser and pool area along with Bay Lake. Geyser Point is a hybrid quick-service restaurant and table-service lounge, with both sharing the same lovely seating area. The main food offerings are counter service, but a substantial bar menu features imaginative drinks and hearty snacks.

HOUSE SPECIALTIES A step up from most standard quick-service fare, lighter lunch and dinner options include a turkey sandwich with cranberry mayo and an upgraded bison cheeseburger with Tillamook Cheddar and marionberry sauce that impresses without being stuffy or overpriced.

OTHER RECOMMENDATIONS The veggie-packed portobello salad can be ordered with salmon, chicken, or steak.

SUMMARY AND COMMENTS The quality of the food and the view of the resort area from any given table combine to create an upscale quick-service dining experience. Best of all, guests don't have to fuss with paper plates and trays of food in the busy dining area; orders are delivered to guests at their chosen tables on real dishes with nonplastic silverware (or neatly packaged in to-go containers, if desired).

This family from London thinks Geyser Point is worth a quick boat or bus ride from the Magic Kingdom:

We found Geyser Point to be a brilliant place for lunch after a morning in the Magic Kingdom. Although not air-conditioned, it was still cool and very relaxing, with nice views and comfortable chairs. Plus, it's quick-service, but you get waited on.

Grand Floridian Cafe ★★★½

AMERICAN   **MODERATE-EXPENSIVE**   **QUALITY ★★★½**   **VALUE ★★★½**
READER-SURVEY RESPONSES ➊ 89% (Average)

Grand Floridian Resort & Spa; ☎ 407-939-3463

Reservations Recommended. **Dining Plan credits** 1 per person, per meal. **When to go** Anytime. **Cost range** Breakfast and lunch $15–$28 (child $10–$13), dinner $21–$36 (child $11–$16). **Service ★★★★. Friendliness ★★★★. Parking** Valet ($33); self-parking is far away. **Bar** Full service. **Wine selection** Good. **Dress** Casual. **Disabled access** Yes. **Customers** Hotel guests. **Breakfast** Daily, 7:30–11 a.m. **Lunch** Daily, 11:05 a.m.–2 p.m. **Dinner** Daily, 5–9 p.m.

SETTING AND ATMOSPHERE Light and airy decor with lots of sunlight, servers dressed in Victorian costumes, and pretty views of the pool and courtyard. Open three meals a day for casual dining.

HOUSE SPECIALTIES The breakfast/lunch menu is extensive, ranging from eggs Benedict and buttermilk pancakes to tomato-and-feta quiche and miso-glazed salmon. Try the Signature Burger (with Brie, bacon-pepper jam, and roasted garlic aioli) or the buttermilk-fried chicken (which is outstanding) served with a waffle drizzled with sriracha honey. Dinner options include New York strip, vegetable curry with chicken or tofu, and fried chicken served with loaded mashed potatoes.

OTHER RECOMMENDATIONS Any dessert the kitchen recommends.

SUMMARY AND COMMENTS A quick place to grab a tasty bite in a pleasantly themed room.

La Hacienda de San Angel ★★★★

MEXICAN   **EXPENSIVE**   **QUALITY ★★★★**   **VALUE ★★★½**
READER-SURVEY RESPONSES ➊ 90% (Average)

Mexico, World Showcase, EPCOT; ☎ 407-939-3463

Reservations Required. **Dining Plan credits** 1 per person, per meal. **When to go** Dinner. **Cost range** $28–$54 (child $11). **Service ★★★★. Friendliness ★★★★★. Parking** EPCOT lot. **Bar** Full service. **Wine selection** Good. **Dress** Casual. **Disabled access** Yes. **Customers** Theme park guests. **Hours** Daily, 3 p.m.–park closing.

SETTING AND ATMOSPHERE Right along the waterfront in Mexico, La Hacienda is a primo spot for watching fireworks through the tall windows. The interior has authentic touches of Mexico in its lighting and decor.

HOUSE SPECIALTIES Excellent guacamole; queso fundido; carne asada–style New York strip; tenderloin fajitas with bacon, poblano and bell peppers, cheese, and salsa; and fried-shrimp tacos with chipotle-lime aioli.

OTHER RECOMMENDATIONS For starters, try the flautas—fried tortillas with potato, chipotle chicken, cheese, and ranchero sauce. The margaritas are the real deal—or just go for a flight of fine tequila.

SUMMARY AND COMMENTS The menu quality is first-rate. We think some patrons might be expecting tacos and burritos (those can be found at the **San Angel Inn Restaurante,** inside the pyramid; see page 346), rather than the more upscale menu on offer here. The Alambre de Res tenderloin fajitas are our favorite.

Hollywood & Vine   ★★½

AMERICAN/BUFFET   **EXPENSIVE**   **QUALITY ★★**   **VALUE ★★★**
READER-SURVEY RESPONSES ➕ 80% (Do Not Visit)

Echo Lake, Disney's Hollywood Studios; ☎ 407-939-3463

Reservations Strongly recommended. **Dining Plan credits** 1 per person, per meal. **When to go** Breakfast, lunch, or dinner. **Cost range** Breakfast $42 (child $27), lunch and dinner $59 (child $38). Prices may vary seasonally; check before you go. **Service ★★★★**. **Friendliness ★★★★★**. **Parking** DHS lot. **Bar** Full service. **Wine selection** Limited. **Dress** Casual. **Disabled access** Yes. **Customers** DHS guests. **Character breakfast** Daily, 8:30–10:30 a.m. **Character lunch** Daily, 11:30 a.m.–3:55 p.m. **Character dinner** Daily, 4–8 p.m.

SETTING AND ATMOSPHERE Just off Hollywood Boulevard, this 1940s-era diner has a sleek Art Deco design (think chrome and tile) that gets lost amid all the Disney-character frenzy. Breakfast includes characters from Disney Junior, such as Doc McStuffins and Fancy Nancy, while seasonal lunches and dinners feature Minnie, Mickey, Goofy, Pluto, and Donald (and sometimes Daisy), usually in holiday- or Hollywood-themed outfits.

HOUSE SPECIALTIES *Breakfast:* Caramel sticky buns. *Dinner:* Beef tenderloin, roasted chicken, mac and cheese with shrimp, or roasted pork. There's also a plant-based option, most recently a mushroom risotto.

SUMMARY AND COMMENTS The only value to be found here is at breakfast, especially if you have children who are fans of Disney Junior shows.

The Hollywood Brown Derby   ★★★★

AMERICAN   **EXPENSIVE**   **QUALITY ★★★★**   **VALUE ★★★**
READER-SURVEY RESPONSES ➕ 91% (Above Average)

Hollywood Boulevard, Disney's Hollywood Studios; ☎ 407-939-3463

Reservations Strongly recommended. **Dining Plan credits** 2 per person, per meal. **When to go** Early evening. **Cost range** $31–$49 (child $9–$17). **Service ★★★★★**. **Friendliness ★★★★★**. **Parking** DHS lot. **Bar** Full service. **Wine selection** Very good. **Dress** Casual. **Disabled access** Yes. **Customers** Theme park guests. **Lunch** Daily, 11 a.m.–3:55 p.m. **Dinner** Daily, 4–9 p.m.

SETTING AND ATMOSPHERE An oasis of civility in the middle of a theme park, this is a replica of the original Brown Derby on Vine Street in Hollywood (the Wilshire Boulevard Brown Derby was the one shaped like a hat). The sunken dining room has a certain elegance, with tuxedoed waiters, curved booths, and white linen. Tall palm trees in huge pots stand in the center of the room and reach for the high ceiling. Ask for a seat on the second-level gallery; it's much quieter and affords good people-watching in the hectic main space.

HOUSE SPECIALTIES Cobb salad (named for Bob Cobb, owner of the original restaurant); the famous grapefruit cake made from the original Brown Derby recipe. Kids' menu includes beef filet, a fish special, and grilled chicken.

OTHER RECOMMENDATIONS The menu varies and the kitchen is unusually adept with pork and lamb—we'd recommend those if available. Or try the chicken breast, which is prepared differently each season but is always solid.

SUMMARY AND COMMENTS The Brown Derby is one of the top theme park restaurants at Disney World. It's expensive, yes, but also a wonderful way to relax and regenerate. This reader from Montgomery, Alabama, recommends staying away from the entrées to save money:

I love The Hollywood Brown Derby. It's so nice to escape the parks, heat, and people in the refined, cool, quiet, and it doesn't have to cost much more than many other meals. I get the Cobb Salad, the lovely margarita flight, and the dessert trio.

If you don't have reservations, the patio lounge opens at 11 a.m. and is first come, first served, with a menu of small plates and cocktails, and it's a good place to have a drink and wait until your table is ready.

This reader from Hudson, New York, found the patio lounge a good venue for watching the Studios' live entertainment:

Our two favorite spots were the Nomad Lounge [see page 353] and the Brown Derby patio lounge! We sat just outside the door to the regular Brown Derby restaurant, so the air-conditioning from inside kept us cool midday in July. We also had a great view of the Star Wars show from our spot!

Drink choices are far more extensive than Disney's online menu might indicate and include various flights—martinis, margaritas, Champagnes, white and red wines, Scotches, and Grand Marnier vintages—along with wines by the bottle and by the glass, beer, and classic cocktails.

House of Blues Restaurant & Bar   ★★★

AMERICAN	MODERATE	QUALITY ★★★½	VALUE ★★★
READER-SURVEY RESPONSES	✚ 86% (Below Average)		

West Side, Disney Springs; ☎ 407-934-2583

Reservations Recommended. **Dining Plan credits** 1 per person, per meal. **When to go** Lunch or early dinner; weekend brunch. **Cost range** Brunch $13–$22, lunch and dinner $21–$34 (child $10). **Service** ★★★★. **Friendliness** ★★★. **Parking** Orange garage. **Bar** Full service. **Wine selection** Modest. **Dress** Casual. **Disabled access** Yes. **Customers** Blues lovers. **Brunch** Saturday–Sunday: 10 a.m.–1:55 p.m. **Lunch** Monday–Friday, 11:30 a.m.–3:55 p.m.; Saturday–Sunday, 2 p.m.–3:55 p.m. **Dinner** Daily, 4–11 p.m. (until 11:30 p.m. on Friday and Saturday).

SETTING AND ATMOSPHERE Adjacent to the Cirque du Soleil theater, House of Blues has a ramshackle look that's almost out of place in Disney Springs, but it's a solid stop for lunch or dinner before or after a show. A separate concert hall hosts great live music, along with a lively Sunday gospel brunch. A quick-service window (the Smokehouse), along with the outdoor bar and seating, draws passersby. But if you have time for a sit-down meal, the fabulous folk art in the restaurant is worth a look.

HOUSE SPECIALTIES Barbecue sandwiches (pulled pork and brisket), ribs, steaks, burgers, and shrimp and grits.

OTHER RECOMMENDATIONS Jambalaya and jalapeño cornbread.

SUMMARY AND COMMENTS Meat-centric menu on Disney Springs' West Side in a fun and casual setting.

Il Mulino   ★★★

ITALIAN	EXPENSIVE	QUALITY ★★★	VALUE ★★
READER-SURVEY RESPONSES	✚ 85% (Much Below Average)		

Swan Resort; ☎ 407-939-3463

Reservations Recommended. **Dining Plan credits** Not accepted. **When to go** Dinner. **Cost range** $25–$63 (child $12–$16). **Service** ★★★. **Friendliness** ★★★. **Parking** Valet ($39) or hotel lot ($29), both free with validation. **Bar** Full service. **Wine selection** Good. **Dress** Dressy casual. **Disabled access** Yes. **Customers** Mostly hotel guests and conventioneers. **Hours** Daily, 5–11 p.m.

SETTING AND ATMOSPHERE A spin-off of the acclaimed Manhattan restaurant, Il Mulino takes an upscale-casual, downtown New York approach to Italian cuisine, with family-style platters for sharing. An open kitchen creates a bustle. You can request private dining in one of the smaller rooms.

HOUSE SPECIALTIES The cuisine focuses on Italy's Abruzzo region, with hearty pastas and big cuts of meat. Try the spaghetti carbonara or the veal saltimbocca. The risottos are well made; the spaghetti with baby shrimp, scallops, clams, mussels, and calamari is also well made but is overpriced.

OTHER RECOMMENDATIONS Charcuterie, mussels in white wine, pizzas, sautéed jumbo shrimp, rib eye with sautéed spinach.

SUMMARY AND COMMENTS A predictable menu with a little bit of everything you would expect in a bustling Italian restaurant: pizza, pasta, meat, seafood. Il Mulino New York attracts conventioneers, so adventurous eaters may want to go elsewhere.

Jaleo by José Andrés ★★★★

SPANISH/TAPAS	MODERATE	QUALITY ★★★★	VALUE ★★★★
READER-SURVEY RESPONSES ⊕ 94% (Much Above Average)			

West Side, Disney Springs; ☎ 407-939-3463

Reservations Strongly recommended. **Dining Plan credits** 2 per person, per meal. **When to go** Dinner. **Cost range** Tapas $10–$30 (child $10–$14). **Service** ★★★★. **Friendliness** ★★★★. **Parking** Orange garage. **Bar** Full bar with emphasis on Spanish drinks and wines. **Dress** Casual. **Disabled access** Yes. **Customers** Locals and Disney resort guests. **Hours** Daily, 11:30 a.m.–11 p.m.

SETTING AND ATMOSPHERE Jaleo's entrance is an expansive, open space with tile mosaics and large-scale photo murals of iconic Spanish scenes on the walls. Warm colors from lighting in the kitchen and dining areas bathe the restaurant, reflecting off metal accents. The highlight is the paella pit and accompanying view into the kitchen—every time one of the massive paella dishes has finished cooking, the chefs ring a bell and the entire restaurant joins in the celebration.

HOUSE SPECIALTIES The restaurant serves Spain's famed Jamón Ibérico. A selection of Spanish cheeses and, of course, traditional pan de cristal con tomate are both good first courses. Garlic shrimp and grilled chicken with garlic sauce burst with flavor, highlighting incredibly fresh produce and tons of herbs (with rosemary and cilantro at the fore). Our table nearly came to blows fighting over the last morsels of patatas bravas—fried potatoes topped with spicy tomato sauce and aioli. The paella is decent. The kitchen seems reluctant to serve the socarrat—the intensely flavorful crispy rice at the bottom of the paella pan. To us that's like serving Thanksgiving turkey without the skin. Ask the waitstaff, though, and they'll bring you some.

OTHER RECOMMENDATIONS Drinks are on par with other Disney Springs restaurants in terms of pricing and quality: $12–$15 will get you a cocktail off Jaleo's varied drink menu, with beers in the $8–$9 range and a high-quality selection of vermouth. The wine menu is extensive, featuring a pretty nifty table at the front describing standard wine qualities and color-coding them on the subsequent menu.

SUMMARY AND COMMENTS This restaurant from celebrity chef José Andrés brings classic Spanish cuisine to Disney Springs' West Side neighborhood. We think Jaleo is one of the best restaurants in Disney Springs.

Jiko—The Cooking Place ★★★★½

AFRICAN/FUSION	EXPENSIVE	QUALITY ★★★★	VALUE ★★½
READER-SURVEY RESPONSES ⊕ 93% (Above Average)			

Animal Kingdom Lodge & Villas–Jambo House; ☎ 407-939-3463

Reservations Required. **Dining Plan credits** 2 per person, per meal. **When to go** Dinner. **Cost range** $38–$54 (child $10–$18). **Service** ★★★★★. **Friendliness** ★★★★★. **Parking** Valet ($33) or hotel lot. **Bar** Full bar. **Wine selection** All South African. **Dress** Dressy casual. **Disabled access** Yes. **Customers** Hotel guests and locals. **Hours** Daily, 5–9:30 p.m.

SETTING AND ATMOSPHERE Bathed in a perpetual sunset, with metal birds soaring around, the main dining room is warm and inviting, accented by the central *jiko* ("cooking place" in Swahili), where chefs prepare many of the appetizers featured on the restaurant's seasonally rotating menu in view of a few lucky diners. As you enter, stop to gaze at the wine room. The bottles on display represent just a sample of the massive wine selection—the largest collection of South African wines available in any North American restaurant.

HOUSE SPECIALTIES Guests flock to Jiko for several dishes, among them the braised wild-boar tenderloin appetizer, African spice–infused flatbreads, seafood tagine, and oak-grilled filet mignon with South African red-wine sauce and bobotie mac and cheese. The seasonally updated malva (mallow) pudding dessert highlights traditional African flavors on the sweet spectrum.

OTHER RECOMMENDATIONS Botswanan-style beef short ribs and Moroccan lamb shank bring on the spices, while luscious seasonal soups like the curried cauliflower bisque start any meal off on the right foot. For those in search of vegan and vegetarian options, Jiko stands out as one of the few Disney Signature restaurants to offer dedicated options that are both satisfying and flavorful. A large selection of specialty teas and Kenyan press-pot coffee complement the excellent dessert selections.

SUMMARY AND COMMENTS Tucked away in a quiet corner of Animal Kingdom Lodge, Jiko is one of the true hidden gems of fine dining in Walt Disney World. Superb service in a nonfussy atmosphere can be tough to pull off, but Jiko does that and more, welcoming guests into the cooking place for a meal packed with truly unique flavors. Families will enjoy the dining room's perpetual sunset, while solo diners or small parties may want to take advantage of the cooking place's seating for both dinner and a show.

Jiko has remained good for a long time, even through the pandemic and chef and staff changes. The experience of this reader from Columbia, Missouri, is typical:

Jiko was fabulous! My husband and I went on a date and ended up sitting next to a nice family who had two younger kids with them. They were a bit loud, but we didn't mind. Near the end of our meal, the server brought us two complimentary martinis at the manager's request because of the "noisy" table nearby. That was good service even though we weren't inconvenienced. In fact, we shared our martinis with them and had a great conversation!

Jock Lindsey's Hangar Bar ★★

COCKTAILS AND BAR BITES	INEXPENSIVE	QUALITY ★★	VALUE ★★
READER-SURVEY RESPONSES ✚ 93% (Above Average)			

The Landing, Disney Springs; ☎ 407-939-3463

Reservations Not accepted. **Dining Plan credits** Not accepted. **When to go** Anytime. **Cost range** Appetizers $10–$22, alcoholic drinks $13–$21. **Service** ★★★★. **Friendliness** ★★★★. **Parking** Disney Springs Lime garage. **Bar** Full service. **Wine selection** OK; beer selection is better. **Dress** Casual. **Disabled access** Yes. **Customers** Theme park guests. **Hours** Daily, noon–11 p.m. (until 11:30 p.m. on Friday and Saturday).

SETTING AND ATMOSPHERE The backstory: A 1940s-era hangar belonging to Indiana Jones's indefatigable pilot has been converted into a bar. Naturally, references to Indy and aviation suffuse the decor (a mammoth propeller dangling from the rafters, for example). Booths, tables, bar seating, and covered outdoor seating—all kid-friendly—are available.

HOUSE SPECIALTIES Readers are quite fond of Jock Lindsey's, but we're not impressed. The wings, tacos, and flatbreads, while fancifully named, are standard-issue bar grub: Air Pirate's Pretzels are, well, pretzels, and Snakebite Sliders are miniburgers that you could get at virtually any chain "neighborhood grill."

OTHER RECOMMENDATIONS Creative cocktails such as the Hovito Mojito, made with Barsol Quebranta Pisco (a Peruvian brandy), fresh lime, mint, simple syrup, and club soda, and the Bedtime Story, made with Absolut Mandarin vodka, Domaine de Canton ginger liqueur, hibiscus syrup, fresh lemon juice, and iced tea.

SUMMARY AND COMMENTS With such touches as a sign that advises ARTIFACTS NO LONGER TAKEN AS PAYMENT, Jock Lindsey's is long on gimmicks. That's not necessarily a bad thing if you're a movie buff, but the food and drinks take a back seat to the gimmickry.

Jungle Navigation Co. Ltd. Skipper Canteen ★★★½

AFRICAN/ASIAN/LATIN	EXPENSIVE	QUALITY ★★★	VALUE ★★★
READER-SURVEY RESPONSES ⊕ 92% (Above Average)			

Adventureland, Magic Kingdom; ☎ 407-939-3463

Reservations Strongly recommended. **Dining Plan credits** 1 per person, per meal. **When to go** Lunch or dinner. **Cost range** $21–$38 (child $11–$14). **Service** ★★★★. **Friendliness** ★★★★. **Parking** Magic Kingdom lot. **Bar** Limited selection of beer and wine. **Dress** Casual. **Disabled access** Yes. **Customers** Magic Kingdom guests. **Hours** Daily, 11:30 a.m.–9 p.m.

SETTING AND ATMOSPHERE Posited as the home of off-duty Jungle Cruise skippers, Skipper Canteen offers guests an oasis from the theme park, with three distinct dining rooms (and a boatload of corny jokes). The crew's mess hall features high ceilings, dark wooden fixtures, and souvenirs collected from the skippers' travels, all bathed in stained glass–tinted natural light. Behind a hidden bookcase (with highly amusing titles), guests can visit the secret meeting room of the Society of Explorers and Adventurers, filled with posh fixtures, maps, and a beautiful collection of butterflies. The Jungle Room completes the dining set, with intimate seating near intricately carved wood bookshelves and colorful stained glass lamps.

HOUSE SPECIALTIES The menu features flavors from several world cuisines, with Asian influences in the char siu pork (a house favorite) and Korean barbecue–inspired crispy fried chicken. Latin flavors make their way into the grilled steak with adobo, as well as the house-made corn pancakes topped with pork and avocado cream. The Kungaloosh! (chocolate cake with caramelized bananas) will close out any meal with a smile—and is the only dessert worth ordering here.

OTHER RECOMMENDATIONS Plant-based dining is well represented here, with an emphasis on vegetables instead of meat substitutes. Even the kids' menu satisfies across the board.

SUMMARY AND COMMENTS Skipper Canteen has fresh flavors and fine service. The menu decidedly doesn't cater to simpler tastes and aims higher than it can sometimes achieve, but any in-park restaurant that identifies its fish option as "not piranha" is OK in our book.

Kimonos ★★★★

JAPANESE	MODERATE	QUALITY ★★★★	VALUE ★★★
READER-SURVEY RESPONSES ✚ 85% (Much Below Average)			

Swan Resort; ☎ 407-934-1792

Reservations Not accepted. **Dining Plan credits** Not accepted. **When to go** Dinner. **Cost range** Sushi rolls and appetizers à la carte $6–$20. **Service** ★★★★★. **Friendliness** ★★★★★. **Parking** Valet or hotel lot; validated for customers. **Bar** Full service. **Wine selection** Very good. **Dress** Casual. **Disabled access** Yes. **Customers** Hotel guests and locals. **Hours** Daily, 5:30 p.m.–1 a.m.

SETTING AND ATMOSPHERE Sushi and nightly karaoke—what a combo! Go early if you want a zen experience with sushi and sake in the serene setting: dark teak tabletops and counters, tall pillars rising to bamboo rafters with rice-paper lanterns, and elegant kimonos that hang outstretched on the walls and between the dining sections. The chefs will greet you with a friendly welcome, and you'll be offered a hot towel to clean your hands.

HOUSE SPECIALTIES Both cooked and raw sushi and hot dishes. Classic rolls include California, tuna, and soft-shell crab; the Kimonos Roll features tuna, salmon, yellowtail, and wasabi mayo. Small plates include beef satay and chicken katsu.

SUMMARY AND COMMENTS The skill of the sushi artists is as much a joy to watch as is eating the wonderfully fresh creations; thus, we're puzzled by the low reader rating. Excellent sake choices. Karaoke starts at 9:30 p.m.

Kona Cafe ★★★

PAN-ASIAN/POLYNESIAN	MODERATE	QUALITY ★★★	VALUE ★★★★
READER-SURVEY RESPONSES ✚ 89% (Average)			

Polynesian Village Resort; ☎ 407-939-3463

Reservations Strongly recommended. **Dining Plan credits** 1 per person, per meal. **When to go** Anytime. **Cost range** Breakfast $15–$17 (child $6–$10), lunch $16–$29 (child $10–$12), dinner $16–$40 (child $10–$12). **Service** ★★★★. **Friendliness** ★★★★★. **Parking** Valet ($33) or hotel lot. **Bar** Full service. **Wine selection** OK. **Dress** Casual. **Disabled access** Yes. **Customers** Mostly hotel guests; some locals. **Breakfast** Daily, 7:30–11 a.m. **Lunch** Daily, 11:30 a.m.–2 p.m. **Dinner** Daily, 5–10 p.m.

SETTING AND ATMOSPHERE Kona Cafe is the Polynesian Village's coffee shop, open three meals a day. Right next to the monorail station, the casual, open dining room is an easy ride from the Magic Kingdom by boat (or take the monorail to the Transportation and Ticket Center and walk) should you want to escape the park for lunch or dinner.

HOUSE SPECIALTIES *Breakfast:* Tonga Toast (French toast with bananas) is the most requested dish. *Lunch:* Turkey banh mi, chicken stir-fry, noodle bowls with pork belly or vegetables, duck fried rice, and sushi rolls. *Dinner:* Sushi, tuna poke, Kona coffee–braised short rib.

OTHER RECOMMENDATIONS The kids' sushi makes for a great adult snack. Pot stickers. Desserts, served in small glasses, include Key lime, s'mores, tiramisu, banana, and coconut tapioca; Kona coffee served in a press pot.

SUMMARY AND COMMENTS The menu is themed to the island decor, and though the dining room isn't fancy by any stretch, the food is on a higher plane than your average java joint's.

Liberty Tree Tavern ★★★½

AMERICAN   **EXPENSIVE**   **QUALITY ★★★**   **VALUE ★★★**
READER-SURVEY RESPONSES ➕ **92% (Above Average)**

Liberty Square, Magic Kingdom; ☎ 407-939-3463

Reservations Strongly recommended. **Dining Plan credits** 1 per person, per meal. **When to go** Lunch or dinner. **Cost range** $39 (child $21). **Service ★★★★**. **Friendliness ★★★★**. **Parking** Magic Kingdom lot. **Bar** Limited selection of beer, wine, and hard cider. **Dress** Casual. **Disabled access** Yes. **Customers** Theme park guests. **Hours** Daily, 11 a.m.–9 p.m.

SETTING AND ATMOSPHERE With six rooms themed to key figures in early American history—Betsy Ross, Benjamin Franklin, Thomas Jefferson, John Paul Jones, Paul Revere, and George and Martha Washington—Liberty Tree Tavern feels like a quaint and cozy Colonial home. Appropriately creaky wooden staircases flank the central lobby, which can be quite busy.

HOUSE SPECIALTIES Most guests come (and return) to Liberty Tree for the All-You-Care-to-Enjoy Patriot's Platter, consisting of roasted turkey, carved pork roast, mashed potatoes, stuffing, seasonal vegetables, and house-made mac and cheese. Save room for the Ooey Gooey Toffee Cake.

OTHER RECOMMENDATIONS The Impossible Meatloaf, a plant-based dish served with mashed potatoes, seasonal vegetables, and mushroom gravy, is a tasty vegan option.

SUMMARY AND COMMENTS A solid standby for families in search of classic American fare, the tavern serves up high-quality food with good service at a quick pace—a luxury in the Magic Kingdom. It's popular for both lunch and dinner, so reservations can be hard to get but are worth the effort: Liberty Tree Tavern still ranks as one of the top meals inside this park.

Mama Melrose's Ristorante Italiano ★★½

ITALIAN   **EXPENSIVE**   **QUALITY ★★★**   **VALUE ★★**
READER-SURVEY RESPONSES ➕ **84% (Much Below Average)**

Grand Avenue, Disney's Hollywood Studios; ☎ 407-939-3463

Reservations Strongly recommended. **Dining Plan credits** 1 per person, per meal. **When to go** Lunch or dinner. **Cost range** $23–$36 (child $10–$11). **Service ★★★**. **Friendliness ★★★★★**. **Parking** DHS lot. **Bar** Full service. **Wine selection** Good. **Dress** Casual. **Disabled access** Yes. **Customers** Theme park guests. **Hours** Daily, 10:45 a.m.–9 p.m.

SETTING AND ATMOSPHERE Tucked at the back of Disney's Hollywood Studios, Mama Melrose's is easy to miss. This casual restaurant is inspired by red-sauce Italian joints as much as New York and LA movie scenes: twinkling lights, red vinyl booths, and grapevines hanging from the rafters. It's generally quiet unless it's peak season.

HOUSE SPECIALTIES Fresh mozzarella, campanelle with shrimp, flatbread "pizzas," seasonal pastas.

OTHER RECOMMENDATIONS Charred strip steak; tiramisu, Ghirardelli chocolate and cherry torte, and cannoli for dessert.

SUMMARY AND COMMENTS The food won't win any awards—the red sauce is a little heavy, for instance—but for family-style Italian, it's fine.

Maria & Enzo's Ristorante ★★½

ITALIAN   **EXPENSIVE**   **QUALITY ★★½**   **VALUE ★★★**
READER-SURVEY RESPONSES ➕ **73% (Do Not Visit)**

The Landing, Disney Springs; ☎ 407-939-3463

Reservations Recommended. **Dining Plan credits** 1 per person, per meal. **When to go** Dinner. **Cost range** Brunch $23–$52 (child $16), lunch $17–$23 (child $16), dinner $28–$52 (child $16). **Service** ★★★½. **Friendliness** ★★★★. **Parking** Orange garage. **Bar** Full service. **Wine selection** Extensive. **Dress** Casual. **Disabled access** Yes. **Customers** Theme park guests. **Brunch** Saturday–Sunday, 11:30 a.m.–3:30 p.m. **Lunch** Monday–Friday, 11:30 a.m.–3:30 p.m. **Dinner** Daily, 4–10 p.m.

SETTING AND ATMOSPHERE This trattoria is housed in an elegant Art Deco replica of a 1930s airline terminal. The airline motif is expertly rendered throughout, beginning with a Passenger Check-In where you'll meet your servers, who are clad in spiffy period flight-attendant uniforms. A smaller seating area called the First Class Lounge offers dining in a quieter setting.

HOUSE SPECIALTIES The extensive bar menu features aperitivi (including a Negroni), prosecco cocktails, and a variety of seasonal specialty drinks. The dishes consist primarily of Italian classics: appetizers such as polpettine (braised meatballs), fried calamari, and antipasti; pasta, steaks, and fish for the bulk of the entrées; and dessert mainstays, including cannoli, tarts, and gelato.

SUMMARY AND COMMENTS Excellent setting, mediocre food, high prices.

Maya Grill ★

MEXICAN/AMERICAN	EXPENSIVE	QUALITY ★	VALUE ★
READER-SURVEY RESPONSES 77% (Do Not Visit)			

Coronado Springs Resort; ☎ 407-939-3463

Reservations Strongly recommended. **Dining Plan credits** 1 per person, per meal. **When to go** Dinner. **Cost range** $19–$27 (child $11). **Service** ★★★. **Friendliness** ★★★. **Parking** Hotel lot (free). **Bar** Full service. **Wine selection** Fair. **Dress** Casual. **Disabled access** Yes. **Customers** Hotel guests. **Hours** Daily, 5–10 p.m.

SETTING AND ATMOSPHERE The dining room, which has long been in need of a redo, is intended to evoke the ancient world of the Maya, achieving "a harmony of fire, sun, and water." But the idea misses the mark. The kitchen is open to view—but so is the barren and starkly lit walkway outside.

HOUSE SPECIALTIES Tex-Mex and Nuevo Latino dinner fare, including a fajita skillet and slow-cooked pork with corn tortillas.

SUMMARY AND COMMENTS Located at the relatively overlooked Coronado Springs, Maya Grill is owned by the same folks who run the restaurants at the Mexico Pavilion in EPCOT. Those restaurants are rated highly, but execution falls short here. And $25 for fish tacos is expensive.

Monsieur Paul ★★★

FRENCH	EXPENSIVE	QUALITY ★★★	VALUE ★★★
READER-SURVEY RESPONSES ✚ 76% (Do Not Visit)			

France, World Showcase, EPCOT; ☎ 407-939-3463

Reservations Required; a $100 no-show fee applies if you fail to cancel at least 72 hours before your meal. **Dining Plan credits** 2 per person, per meal. **When to go** Late dinner. **Cost range** $195 fixed-price menu (child $13–$19). **Service** ★★★★. **Friendliness** ★★★★★. **Parking** EPCOT or BoardWalk lot; enter through the International Gateway. **Bar** Full service. **Wine selection** Good but pricey. **Dress** Dressy casual (no swimwear). **Disabled access** Elevator to second level. **Customers** Theme park guests. **Hours** Daily, 5:30–7:30 p.m.

SETTING AND ATMOSPHERE Light and modern, Monsieur Paul is tucked away at the France Pavilion, accessed by a stairway lined with photos of legendary chef Paul Bocuse, whose son, Jérôme, owns and runs this restaurant and Chefs de France. Request a table at the windows to watch the world go by on World Showcase Lagoon. Seats just 120.

HOUSE SPECIALTIES Chef Bocuse's black-truffle soup, black sea bass in potato "scales," and roasted duck.

SUMMARY AND COMMENTS Disney's moving a number of fancy restaurants to fixed-price menus, and Monsieur Paul is a casualty. For one thing, the food, while serviceable, doesn't live up to the price. And few people want to get dressed up, pay $160 for theme park admission, and then pay another $250 per person (including tax and tip) for a heavy nine-course dinner.

Morimoto Asia ★★★★

JAPANESE/PAN-ASIAN	EXPENSIVE	QUALITY ★★★★	VALUE ★★★★
READER-SURVEY RESPONSES ➕ 88% (Below Average)			

The Landing, Disney Springs; ☎ 407-939-6686

Reservations Recommended. **Dining Plan credits** 2 per person, per meal. **When to go** Lunch or dinner. **Cost range** $15-$59 (child $16). **Service** ★★★★. **Friendliness** ★★★★. **Parking** Disney Springs Lime garage. **Bar** Wine, beer, sake, cocktails. **Wine selection** Wide range by the glass or bottle. **Dress** Casual. **Disabled access** Yes. **Customers** Theme park guests and locals. **Lunch** Daily, 11:30-3:30 p.m. **Dinner** Daily, 4:30-10 p.m. (until 10:30 p.m. on Friday and Saturday).

SETTING AND ATMOSPHERE Orlando's version of a big-city club, with Japanese wood-tone highlights, Morimoto Asia expands beyond sushi and into a pan-Asian expedition, in most cases hitting the mark. Quirky takes on Chinese, Japanese, and Korean dishes join a substantial sushi menu from the kitchen and upstairs sushi bar, where Iron Chef Masaharu Morimoto makes frequent appearances. Fishing baskets and steel beads form the chandeliers, and a continuous white engineered-stone ribbon runs from the "secret" entrance to the Forbidden Lounge upstairs, creating the handrail, bar, and seating areas throughout the building and framing the glass-bottle lighting upstairs (a nod to the building's fictional beginnings as a bottling company). There are anime cartoons and graphic photographs throughout.

HOUSE SPECIALTIES Pork dim sum; 24-hour-marinated, house-carved Peking duck; orange chicken; Morimoto spare ribs; Korean buri bop; lo mein and ramen noodles; sushi rolls and sashimi.

SUMMARY AND COMMENTS Chef Morimoto is famously hands-on with this restaurant, and it's not uncommon to see him in the kitchen or behind the sushi counter. We think this is one of the top restaurants in Disney Springs. The food is both better and more expensive than at most hometown Asian restaurants. Our theory is that this may not be what some guests are expecting, hence the lower ratings. If you're ordering the Peking duck for yourself and the waitstaff says it serves two, the proper response is "Challenge accepted."

The outdoor terrace upstairs has what might be the best view of the Disney Springs lagoon, rising above the sometimes noisy crowd below. If you're in a hurry, the walk-up window outside and to the left of the entrance serves noodle bowls and other snacks. Prices at the walk-up window range from $7 to $16, and outdoor seating is available.

Narcoossee's ★★★★½

SEAFOOD	EXPENSIVE	QUALITY ★★★½	VALUE ★★
READER-SURVEY RESPONSES ➕ 90% (Average)			

Grand Floridian Resort & Spa; ☎ 407-939-3463

Reservations Required. **Dining Plan credits** 2 per person, per meal. **When to go** Early evening. **Cost range** $34–$59 (child $14–$17). **Service** ★★★★★. **Friendliness** ★★★★★. **Parking** Valet ($33); self-parking is deceptively far away. **Bar** Full service. **Wine selection** Good. **Dress** Dressy casual. **Disabled access** Yes. **Customers** Hotel guests and locals. **Hours** Daily, 5–9:30 p.m.

SETTING AND ATMOSPHERE Situated on the Seven Seas Lagoon at the far end of the Grand Floridian Resort, Narcoossee's has just completed an extended refurbishment. While we didn't get a chance to review it before press time, we expect the old two-level dining room to be replaced with a single floor and the décor to be updated throughout.

Nine Dragons Restaurant ★★★

CHINESE	MODERATE	QUALITY ★★★	VALUE ★★½
READER-SURVEY RESPONSES 85% (Much Below Average)			

China, World Showcase, EPCOT; ☎ 407-939-3463

Reservations Recommended. **Dining Plan credits** 1 per person, per meal. **When to go** Lunch or dinner. **Cost range** $18–$30 (child $9–$12). **Service** ★★★. **Friendliness** ★★★★. **Parking** EPCOT lot. **Bar** Full service. **Wine selection** Minimal. **Dress** Casual. **Disabled access** Yes. **Customers** Theme park guests. **Hours** Daily, noon–9 p.m.

SETTING AND ATMOSPHERE Nine Dragons' attractive interior—subdued wood tones, colorful lanterns, beautiful backlit glass sculptures from China—and efficient service create a respite from the bustle of World Showcase. Ask for a window seat for a view of passersby on the promenade.

HOUSE SPECIALTIES Crispy duck bao buns, honey-sesame chicken, salt-and-pepper shrimp.

OTHER RECOMMENDATIONS Stick to the appetizers and put the chili oil on everything. It's made in-house and should be sold as a souvenir.

SUMMARY AND COMMENTS You can usually get a table without a wait in the spacious dining room, and while Nine Dragons gets a bad rep for being pricey, we think the food and service are above average.

1900 Park Fare *(closed at press time)* ★★½

AMERICAN/BUFFET	EXPENSIVE	QUALITY ★★★	VALUE ★★★
READER-SURVEY RESPONSES* ● 91% (Much Above Average)			

Grand Floridian Resort & Spa; ☎ 407-939-3463

Ratings are from 2019 and will be updated when the restaurant reopens.

Reservations Strongly recommended. **Dining Plan credits** 1 per person, per meal. **When to go** Breakfast or dinner. **Cost range** Breakfast $45 (child $29), dinner $60 (child $39). **Service** ★★★★. **Friendliness** ★★★★. **Parking** Valet ($33); self-parking is deceptively far away. **Bar** Full service. **Wine selection** Limited. **Dress** Casual. **Disabled access** Yes. **Customers** Hotel and resort guests. **Character breakfast** Daily, 8–11:40 a.m. **Character dinner** Daily, 4–9 p.m.

SETTING AND ATMOSPHERE Everyone is here to see the Disney characters—the food and decor are afterthoughts, though the tables are set with linen and service is first-rate in the bright, cavernous, high-ceilinged room. An antique band organ, Big Bertha, periodically pumps out music to dine by.

HOUSE SPECIALTIES The buffet usually includes herb-crusted prime rib and Florida strawberry soup.

OTHER RECOMMENDATIONS A separate buffet for kids includes mac and cheese, pizza, chicken nuggets, and pasta.

ENTERTAINMENT AND AMENITIES Character dining with Mary Poppins, Pooh, Tigger, and Alice at breakfast, and Cinderella, Prince Charming, and others at dinner.

SUMMARY AND COMMENTS A good, relatively inexpensive choice for character dining but too bright and loud for adults without children.

'Ohana ★★★

POLYNESIAN	EXPENSIVE	QUALITY ★★★½	VALUE ★★★
READER-SURVEY RESPONSES ➕ 86% (Below Average)			

Polynesian Village Resort; ☎ 407-939-3463

Reservations Strongly recommended. **Dining Plan credits** 1 per person, per meal. **When to go** Breakfast or dinner. **Cost range** Breakfast $45 (child $29), dinner $59 (child $38). Prices vary seasonally; check before you go. **Service** ★★★★. **Friendliness** ★★★★★. **Parking** Hotel lot (free). **Bar** Full service. **Wine selection** Limited. **Dress** Casual. **Disabled access** Yes. **Customers** Resort guests. **Character breakfast** Daily, 7:30 a.m.–noon. **Dinner** Daily, 3:30–10 p.m.

SETTING AND ATMOSPHERE Columns of carved tiki gods support the raised thatched roof in the center of 'Ohana's main dining room, while the dining tables, arranged in rows, resemble long, segmented surfboards. Request a seat in the main dining room, where the fire pit is.

HOUSE SPECIALTIES There's no menu—your only option is to ask for vegan or vegetarian options. With that decided, the food starts arriving and doesn't stop until you've had enough. Breakfast, a character meal with Lilo, Stitch, Mickey, and Pluto, starts with seasonal fruit and pineapple-coconut "breakfast bread" (it's a Danish, really). Standard breakfast skillets include scrambled eggs, sausage, ham, potatoes, Mickey waffles, and biscuits; plant-based options are available too. At dinner, starters include honey-glazed chicken wings, fried pork dumplings, mixed green salads, and coconut-papaya scones and Cheddar-bacon biscuits. The main course features teriyaki beef, peel-and-eat shrimp, grilled chicken, noodles, and Broccolini, all placed on a lazy Susan in the center of the table.

SUMMARY AND COMMENTS *'Ohana* means "family," and *family-style* certainly applies to the portions—it's an astounding amount of food that just keeps coming. That's great if you've got a hungry crew, but be aware that the servers tend to bring out your food at warp speed. This reader from Rochester, Minnesota, noticed it first:

Our dinner felt very rushed. The food quality was as expected—it just seemed like we were being timed.

The reader has a point—your server will bring food out as fast as you can eat it.

If you're dining with little ones, 'Ohana is *fabulous*—when our kids were very young, we would've donated a kidney to any server who brought our food to the table that fast. If, however, you're a group of grown-ups looking for a relaxed meal, 'Ohana will probably feel more akin to competitive eating than dinner, unless you ask your server to space out your courses a bit.

Olivia's Cafe ★★★

AMERICAN	EXPENSIVE	QUALITY ★★★	VALUE ★★
READER-SURVEY RESPONSES ➕ 89% (Average)			

Old Key West Resort; ☎ 407-939-3463

Reservations Recommended. **Dining Plan credits** 1 per person, per meal. **When to go** Lunch. **Cost range** Lunch $15–$25 (child $9–$11), dinner $21–$37 (child $11–$13).

Service ★★★★. **Friendliness** ★★★★. **Parking** Hotel lot (free). **Bar** Full service. **Wine selection** Limited. **Dress** Casual. **Disabled access** Yes. **Customers** Resort guests. **Breakfast** Monday–Friday, 7:30–10:30 a.m. **Brunch** Daily, 7:30 a.m.–2 p.m. **Dinner** Daily, 5–9 p.m.

SETTING AND ATMOSPHERE Old Key West was the first Disney Vacation Club (DVC). Many DVC members consider Olivia's their home restaurant, and their photos decorate the walls. The decor is Disneyfied Key West, with pastels, mosaic-tile floors, potted palms, and tropical trees in the center of the room. Some outside seating looks out over the waterway. Tile, wood siding, and no tablecloths add up to one noisy dining room.

HOUSE SPECIALTIES *Brunch:* Banana-bread French toast, omelets, waffles, pancakes. *Dinner:* Slow-cooked prime rib, shrimp pasta, fried chicken.

OTHER RECOMMENDATIONS Catch of the day, tofu and coconut curry, banana-bread pudding sundae, Key lime tart.

SUMMARY AND COMMENTS Brunch might be worth a special trip here. Unless you're staying at Old Key West, you might not know Olivia's exists—all the more reason to visit. Service is super friendly, and the kitchen turns out tasty casual fare.

Paddlefish ★★½

AMERICAN/SEAFOOD	EXPENSIVE	QUALITY ★★★	VALUE ★★½
READER-SURVEY RESPONSES ⊕ 78% (Do Not Visit)			

The Landing, Disney Springs; ☎ 407-934-2628

Reservations Recommended. **Dining Plan credits** 2 per person, per meal. **When to go** Lunch or dinner. **Cost range** $14–$70 (child $9–$15). **Service** ★★★★½. **Friendliness** ★★★★★. **Parking** Disney Springs Lime garage. **Bar** Full service. **Wine selection** Good. **Dress** Casual. **Disabled access** Yes. **Customers** Park guests, locals, fans of seafood. **Hours** Daily, noon–11 p.m.

SETTING AND ATMOSPHERE Paddlefish has a modern aesthetic, making the stationary "steamship" seem more like a classy yacht than a classic paddleboat. Sleek design and muted colors inside don't distract from the views offered from the large picture windows at the sides and rear of the ship, overlooking her iconic paddlewheel. Outdoor seating on the first and third decks offers prime views of the area, but the true star of the restaurant is the rooftop bar, where you can enjoy an iconic Florida sunset with your cocktail.

HOUSE SPECIALTIES Crab guacamole. The crab fries (hand-cut and perfectly fried) are a solid choice for an appetizer if you're in search of fresh seafood. Ahi poke and ceviche will cool you down and tickle your palate on hot summer days. That said, we don't think the food is outstanding enough to justify the high prices.

OTHER RECOMMENDATIONS Our recommendation is to go somewhere else—**The Boathouse** (page 318), for example, or **Chef Art Smith's Homecomin'** (page 322) or **Morimoto Asia** (page 339). If you can't get in there, you can't go wrong with the lobster roll or the crab cakes here, but the house burger might be the best thing on the menu.

SUMMARY AND COMMENTS Readers apparently don't think much of Paddlefish, and we share the sentiment.

Paradiso 37 ★★½

GLOBAL	EXPENSIVE	QUALITY ★★½	VALUE ★★½
READER-SURVEY RESPONSES ⊕ 63% (Do Not Visit)			

The Landing, Disney Springs; ☎ 407-934-3700

Reservations Recommended. **Dining Plan credits** 1 per person, per meal. **When to go** Lunch or dinner. **Cost range** $22–$39 (child $14). **Service** ★★★. **Friendliness** ★★★★. **Parking** Disney Springs Lime garage. **Bar** Full service. **Wine selection** Limited. **Dress** Casual. **Disabled access** Yes. **Customers** Theme park guests, locals. **Hours** Daily, 11 a.m.–11 p.m. (until 11:30 p.m. on Friday and Saturday).

SETTING AND ATMOSPHERE Paradiso's outdoor seating is just as large as the inside's, with elevated terrace dining and a stage along the waterfront for live music performances. Those performances can get loud, so seating farther away is better. Ambience is festive and casual, with an open kitchen. The menu features dishes from North, Central, and South America. (The *37* in the name refers to the number of countries represented on the menu.)

HOUSE SPECIALTIES Argentinean skirt steak, Patagonian seared salmon, burgers, and the P37 Swirl, a margarita–sangria combo.

OTHER RECOMMENDATIONS Baja fish tacos.

SUMMARY AND COMMENTS Readers rate this as one of the worst restaurants in Walt Disney World. It must do an amazing bar business to stay in Disney Springs.

Planet Hollywood ★½

AMERICAN	MODERATE	QUALITY ★★	VALUE ★★
READER-SURVEY RESPONSES ⊕ 66% (Do Not Visit)			

Town Center, Disney Springs; ☎ 407-827-7827

Reservations Recommended. **Dining Plan credits** 1 per person, per meal. **When to go** Lunch or dinner. **Cost range** $19–$50 (child NA). **Service** ★★★. **Friendliness** ★★★. **Parking** Orange garage. **Bar** Full service. **Wine selection** Limited. **Dress** Casual. **Disabled access** Yes. **Customers** Tour groups, theme park guests. **Hours** Daily, 11:30 a.m.–11 p.m. (until 11:30 p.m. on Friday and Saturday).

SETTING AND ATMOSPHERE Wall projections and a house DJ take center stage in the typically loud and busy main dining room, but an outdoor patio offers seating with a view of Disney Springs in a much quieter atmosphere. Stargazers Lounge, outside on the ground-floor rear of the restaurant, features a colorful constellation of alcoholic concoctions.

HOUSE SPECIALTIES Thanks to celebrity chef Guy Fieri, over-the-top burgers, including a burger topped with bacon mac and cheese, reign supreme. The signature Chicken Crunch remains a solid option. L.A. Lasagna (fried pasta tubes stuffed with ricotta and Bolognese and topped with roasted garlic cream and tomato-basil sauces), St. Louis–style barbecue ribs served on a mini picnic table, and the High Roller appetizer sampler served on a (nonfunctioning) Ferris wheel round out the highlights of the all-day menu.

OTHER RECOMMENDATIONS Salads, nachos, pasta, and steak, much like what you'd find at your neighborhood chain restaurant, make up much of the menu. Highly decorated milkshakes and individual desserts in jars occupy the dessert menu.

SUMMARY AND COMMENTS With higher-quality food just a few steps away at **Chef Art Smith's Homecomin', Blaze Fast-Fire'd Pizza,** and **D-Luxe Burger,** we just don't think Planet Hollywood is worth your time or money.

The Plaza Restaurant ★★

AMERICAN	MODERATE	QUALITY ★★	VALUE ★★
READER-SURVEY RESPONSES ⊕ 81% (Much Below Average)			

Main Street, U.S.A., Magic Kingdom; ☎ 407-939-3463

Reservations Recommended. **Dining Plan credits** 1 per person, per meal. **When to go** Lunch or dinner. **Cost range** $20–$25 (child $10–$12). **Service** ★★★★. **Friendliness** ★★★★. **Parking** Magic Kingdom lot. **Bar** Wine and beer only. **Dress** Casual. **Disabled access** Yes. **Customers** Theme park guests. **Hours** Daily, 11 a.m.–9 p.m.

SETTING AND ATMOSPHERE The Plaza, a quaint and cozy spot tucked away on a side street at the end of Main Street as you head to Tomorrowland, adds Art Nouveau touches to Main Street's Victorian theme. Decor aside, it's air-conditioned heaven on a sweltering Florida day.

HOUSE SPECIALTIES Main Street Burger, the Plaza Restaurant Sundae.

OTHER RECOMMENDATIONS Chicken sandwich. For kids, grilled chicken strips, cheeseburger, PB&J.

SUMMARY AND COMMENTS The Plaza isn't fine dining, but it was one of the first restaurants in the Magic Kingdom when the park opened in 1971. So go and enjoy an old-fashioned indulgence like a hot-fudge sundae. Because it's a small space, reservations are strongly suggested.

Raglan Road Irish Pub & Restaurant ★★★★

IRISH	EXPENSIVE	QUALITY ★★★★	VALUE ★★★
READER-SURVEY RESPONSES ⊕ 93% (Above Average)			

The Landing, Disney Springs; ☎ 407-938-0300

Reservations Strongly recommended. **Dining Plan credits** 1 per person, per meal. **When to go** Monday–Saturday after 7 p.m. **Cost range** Brunch $17–$30 (child $8–$12), lunch and dinner $23–$38 (child $9–$12). **Service** ★★★½. **Friendliness** ★★★★★. **Parking** Disney Springs Lime garage. **Bar** Irish whiskeys and beers. **Wine selection** Better than a pub's but not extensive. **Dress** Casual. **Disabled access** Yes. **Customers** Tourists and locals. **Brunch** Saturday–Sunday, 9 a.m.–3 p.m. **Lunch** Monday–Friday, 11 a.m.–3 p.m. **Dinner** Daily, 3:05–11:30 p.m.

SETTING AND ATMOSPHERE Many of the elements of this pub, including the bars (there are four), were handcrafted from hardwoods in Ireland and sent to the United States for reassembly. The venue is huge by Irish-pub standards, but the dark polished-wood paneling, along with the snugs (small, private cubbyholes), preserves the feel of the traditional pub. The pentagonal main room sits beneath an impressive (but very unpublike) dome. In the middle of the room is a tall, tablelike platform that's accessible to Celtic dancers via a permanently attached short staircase. A modest bandstand is situated along the wall in front of a large pseudo-hearth. Branching from this cavernous domed center room are cozy dining areas and snugs.

HOUSE SPECIALTIES While you could order a burger, we recommend branching out and trying something different—say, the Worth the Wait beef sandwich (made with 12-hour braised beef, garlic aioli, mushrooms, onions, and Cheddar). And of course, the beer-battered fish-and-chips (gluten-free option available).

Brunch options include the whimsically named Now You're Talkin' Chicken Sandwich (buttermilk fried chicken breast with hot sauce and scallions); a vegan shepherd's pie; the Full Irish breakfast with Cheshire heritage pork Irish banger, bacon, black-and-white pudding, roasted tomato, mushrooms, fried eggs, and double-cooked chips; and Irish coffee.

ENTERTAINMENT AND AMENITIES Although you could consider a great selection of Irish lagers and stouts an amenity, the real draw here is the Celtic music. A talented band plays daily. Starting in the early evening with a couple of superb acoustic sets, the band sets up as the diners filter out and the pub crawlers settle in. Celtic dancers fill the stage and dance on the aforementioned table to some of the numbers.

SUMMARY AND COMMENTS A night in a good Irish pub, Raglan Road included, is a joyous and uplifting experience. As the Irish say, it'll set you right up. A quick fish-and-chips can be had around the corner at **Cookes of Dublin** (page 308) if you're in a hurry.

Rainforest Cafe ★★½

AMERICAN	MODERATE	QUALITY ★★	VALUE ★★
READER-SURVEY RESPONSES ➊ 82% (Much Below Average)			

Disney's Animal Kingdom; ☎ 407-938-9100
Marketplace, Disney Springs; ☎ 407-827-8500

Reservations Recommended. **Dining Plan credits** 1 per person, per meal. **When to go** After the lunch crunch, in late afternoon, and before dinner hour. **Cost range** $20–$43 (child $11). **Service** ★★★. **Friendliness** ★★★★. **Parking** Animal Kingdom lot or Disney Springs Marketplace lot. **Bar** Full bar. **Wine selection** Limited. **Dress** Casual. **Disabled access** Yes. **Customers** Theme park guests, tourists, locals. **Hours** *Disney's Animal Kingdom:* Daily, 8:30–7:30 p.m. *Disney Springs Marketplace:* Daily, 11 a.m.–10 p.m. (until 11:30 p.m. on Friday and Saturday).

SETTING AND ATMOSPHERE Even though it's always packed and there's usually a wait, families flock to this now-familiar restaurant for big plates of food served in a noisy dining room with lots to keep the kids entertained. The dining room looks like a jungle (imagine all the silk plants in the world tacked to the ceiling), complete with animatronic elephants, bats, and monkeys—not the most realistic we've seen. There's occasional thunder and even some rainfall. At the Disney Springs location, look for the giant volcano that can be seen, and heard, erupting all over the Marketplace; the smoke coming from the volcano is nonpolluting, in accordance with the restaurant's conservation theme.

HOUSE SPECIALTIES Spinach-and-artichoke dip, Caribbean coconut shrimp, burgers, ribs, brownie cake with ice cream.

ENTERTAINMENT AND AMENITIES If you're willing to pay to avoid the long wait, stop by the day before and buy a Landry's Select Club membership for $25 (you get a $25 Welcome Reward back for joining). Present your card on the day you want to dine, and you'll be seated much faster (and earn points and sometimes discounts).

SUMMARY AND COMMENTS We've never been impressed by the Rainforest Cafes. The shopping and the kid appeal must be the attractions—it certainly isn't the food (or service). But the semisecret entrance into Animal Kingdom, hidden past the Rainforest gift shop, might be the best reason for its existence.

Rose & Crown Dining Room ★★★

BRITISH	MODERATE	QUALITY ★★★½	VALUE ★★★
READER-SURVEY RESPONSES ➊ 89% (Average)			

United Kingdom, World Showcase, EPCOT; ☎ 407-939-3463

Reservations Strongly recommended. **Dining Plan credits** 1 per person, per meal. **When to go** Dinner. **Cost range** $22–$26 (child $15). **Service** ★★★★★. **Friendliness** ★★★★★. **Parking** EPCOT lot. **Bar** Full bar with Bass, Guinness, and Harp beers on tap. **Wine selection** Limited. **Dress** Casual. **Disabled access** Yes. **Customers** EPCOT guests. **Hours** Daily, 3:45–9 p.m.

SETTING AND ATMOSPHERE Pub in the front, dining room in the back. The pub hops with activity from open to close and has the look and feel of a traditional English watering hole: a large, cozy bar with rich wood appointments, beamed ceilings, and a hardwood floor. The adjoining dining room is rustic and simple.

HOUSE SPECIALTIES Fish-and-chips, bangers and mash (sausage and mashed potatoes), and shepherd's pie (the vegetarian version is delicious too), washed down with Bass ale.

OTHER RECOMMENDATIONS The Scotch egg (a hard-boiled egg with a deep-fried sausage coating) and the sticky toffee pudding for dessert.

SUMMARY AND COMMENTS The current menu is very limited (two appetizers, four entrées, and two desserts). At dinnertime, the Rose & Crown is packed with folks appropriating tables for the EPCOT fireworks. The food is good, so branch out and try something new—you can always get fish-and-chips at the adjacent walk-up window, the **Yorkshire County Fish Shop** (see page 304).

Sanaa ★★★★

AFRICAN/INDIAN	EXPENSIVE	QUALITY ★★★★	VALUE ★★★★
READER-SURVEY RESPONSES ✪ 93% (Above Average)			

Animal Kingdom Lodge & Villas–Kidani Village; ☎ 407-939-3463

Reservations Strongly recommended. **Dining Plan credits** 1 per person, per meal. **When to go** Lunch or dinner. **Cost range** Breakfast $10–$13 (child $8), lunch $20–$31 (child $11–$14), dinner $23–$36 (child $11–$13). **Service** ★★★★. **Friendliness** ★★★★. **Parking** Valet ($33) or hotel garage. **Bar** Full service. **Wine selection** Good. **Dress** Casual. **Disabled access** Yes. **Customers** Theme park guests, locals, Disney Vacation Club guests. **Quick-service breakfast** Daily, 7:30–11 a.m. (reservations not necessary). **Lunch** Daily, 11:30 a.m.–3 p.m. **Dinner** Daily, 5–9:30 p.m.

SETTING AND ATMOSPHERE A floor down from the Kidani Village lobby, Sanaa's casual dining room is inspired by African outdoor markets, with baskets, beads, and art on the walls. It's a cozy space, with 9-foot-tall windows that look out on the resort's savanna—giraffes, zebras, and other animals wander within yards of you as you dine.

HOUSE SPECIALTIES Starters include vegetable samosas and Indian-style breads (naan, onion kulcha, and paneer paratha) served with red-chile sambal, spicy jalapeño-lime pickle, coriander chutney, and cucumber raita. Entrées feature tandoori chicken, and plant-based options.

OTHER RECOMMENDATIONS African triple-chocolate mousse.

SUMMARY AND COMMENTS Sanaa (sah-NAH) is a favorite of Disney cast members and locals—the flavors are addicting. It's not as upscale as **Jiko— The Cooking Place,** the resort's fine-dining restaurant (page 333), offering instead a casual take on African–Indian fusion cuisine. Sanaa serves a quick-service version of breakfast in the morning. Selections include hot foods such as eggs, waffles, and bacon, as well as a limited array of grab-and-go cold foods.

San Angel Inn Restaurante ★★★

MEXICAN	EXPENSIVE	QUALITY ★★★	VALUE ★★
READER-SURVEY RESPONSES ✪ 85% (Much Below Average)			

Mexico, World Showcase, EPCOT; ☎ 407-939-3463

Reservations Strongly recommended. **Dining Plan credits** 1 per person, per meal. **When to go** Lunch or dinner. **Cost range** $18–$52 (child $11–$12). **Service** ★★★.

Friendliness ★★★. **Parking** EPCOT lot. **Bar** Full service. **Wine selection** Limited. **Dress** Casual. **Disabled access** Yes. **Customers** Theme park guests. **Hours** Daily, 11:30 a.m.–9 p.m.

SETTING AND ATMOSPHERE Step inside the Aztec pyramid in Mexico, navigate the busy marketplace, and end up at San Angel Inn, which overlooks a starry sky and the Gran Fiesta Tour boat ride. Its decor is inspired by the original San Angel Inn in Mexico City and is incredibly atmospheric—it really does feel like you're dining in an outdoor Mexican square.

HOUSE SPECIALTIES For appetizers try the queso fundido (melted cheese with flour tortillas).

OTHER RECOMMENDATIONS Ribeye tacos should please almost anyone. Vegetarians can try the huarache vegetariano—fried corn masa with pinto beans, grilled queso fresco, and salsa verde. If the chocolate "fiesta" pyramid is available for dessert, get that. Otherwise, have the sweet corn ice cream.

SUMMARY AND COMMENTS The prices may be steep (and that likely accounts for the low reader ratings), but the menu goes beyond the typical tacos and such, offering regional dishes that are difficult to find in the States. Request a waterside table overlooking the boat ride for more room and a slightly quieter evening. The dining room is a cool, quiet respite from the theme park—but you might need a flashlight to read the menu.

Sci-Fi Dine-In Theater Restaurant ★★

AMERICAN	MODERATE	QUALITY ★★½	VALUE ★★
READER-SURVEY RESPONSES ⊕ 84% (Much Below Average)			

Commissary Lane, Disney's Hollywood Studios; ☎ 407-939-3463

Reservations Strongly recommended. **Dining Plan credits** 1 per person, per meal. **When to go** Lunch or dinner. **Cost range** $19–$26 (child $11–$13). **Service** ★★★★★. **Friendliness** ★★★★★. **Parking** DHS lot. **Bar** Full service. **Wine selection** Limited. **Dress** Casual. **Disabled access** Yes. **Customers** Theme park guests. **Hours** Daily, 10:30 a.m.–9 p.m.

SETTING AND ATMOSPHERE Walk through the doors and into the back of a simulated soundstage, then round the corner into a stage set resembling a drive-in from the 1950s, with faux classic cars instead of tables. Hop in, order, and watch campy black-and-white clips. It's a hoot.

HOUSE SPECIALTIES The menu is the same at lunch and dinner, with sandwiches, burgers, and pasta.

OTHER RECOMMENDATIONS The milkshakes are expensive but worth it. Burgers are also expensive; the Feature Film Burger, with Cheddar, pork belly, and house-made mustard BBQ sauce on a brioche bun, is the best.

ENTERTAINMENT AND AMENITIES Clips of cartoons and vintage horror and sci-fi movies, such as *Attack of the 50 Foot Woman, Robot Monster,* and *The Blob.*

SUMMARY AND COMMENTS The kitsch is fun, but the food remains below average. Stick with simple fare like one of the burgers. Or just fill up on an appetizer and dessert.

Sebastian's Bistro ★★

LATIN/SEAFOOD	EXPENSIVE	QUALITY ★★	VALUE ★★½
READER-SURVEY RESPONSES ⊕ 88% (Below Average)			

Caribbean Beach Resort; ☎ 407-939-3463

Reservations Recommended. **Dining Plan credits** 1 per person, per meal. **When to go** Dinner. **Cost range** $29 (child $17). **Service** ★★★. **Friendliness** ★★★★. **Parking**

Hotel lot. **Bar** Full service. **Wine selection** Limited. **Dress** Casual. **Disabled access** Yes. **Customers** Hotel guests. **Hours** Daily, 4:30–9:30 p.m.

SETTING AND ATMOSPHERE Named after the crab in *The Little Mermaid*, Sebastian's is remarkably understated for a Disney restaurant. White walls and tables are offset by blue-and-white chairs in two rooms with vaulted ceilings and plenty of windows to let in the sun.

HOUSE SPECIALTIES This family-style menu includes Caribbean Pull-Apart Rolls (warm bread with guava butter and caramelized onion jam), oven-roasted citrus chicken, slow-cooked mojo pork, grilled flank steak, cilantro rice and beans, vegetable curry, Broccolini, and coconut-pineapple bread pudding with caramel sauce and vanilla ice cream. There's also a plant-based menu option. Overall, though, the food is pricey for what you get.

SUMMARY AND COMMENTS The pull-apart rolls are probably adding 10 points to Sebastian's reader surveys by themselves. But unless you have no other options, head over to the Riviera for better restaurants.

Shula's Steak House ★★★★

STEAK	EXPENSIVE	QUALITY ★★★★	VALUE ★★
READER-SURVEY RESPONSES ✪ 83% (Much Below Average)			

Dolphin Resort; ☎ 407-934-1362

Reservations Strongly recommended. **Dining Plan credits** Not accepted. **When to go** Dinner. **Cost range** $38–$75 (child $9–$14). *Note:* Everything is à la carte (that is, side dishes cost extra). **Service** ★★★★. **Friendliness** ★★★★. **Parking** Valet ($39) or hotel lot ($35), both free with validation. **Bar** Full service. **Wine selection** Good; expensive. **Dress** Dressy. **Disabled access** Yes. **Customers** Hotel guests and locals. **Hours** Daily, 5–11 p.m.

SETTING AND ATMOSPHERE Shula's feels more like a men's club than a resort restaurant: dark woods, even darker lighting, framed black-and-white photos of football players, and high prices that get passed on to expense accounts.

HOUSE SPECIALTIES In a word, meat—really expensive but very high-quality meat. Only certified Angus beef is served: filet mignon, New York strip, cowboy rib eye, and porterhouse (including a 24-ounce cut).

OTHER RECOMMENDATIONS New Orleans–style shrimp, catch of the day.

SUMMARY AND COMMENTS We had a fantastic rib eye here in early 2022—one of the best steaks we've had on Disney property in a long, long time. And then . . . reader ratings dropped by 10 points. We still think it's worth trying, however.

Space 220 ★★½

AMERICAN	EXPENSIVE	QUALITY ★★½	VALUE ★★
READER-SURVEY RESPONSES ✪ 77% (Do Not Visit)			

World Discovery, EPCOT; ☎ 407-939-3463

Reservations Strongly recommended. **Dining Plan credits** Not yet available. **When to go** Lunch or dinner. **Cost range** Lunch $55 (child $29), dinner $79 (child $29). **Service** ★★★★. **Friendliness** ★★★★. **Parking** EPCOT parking lot. **Bar** Full service. **Wine selection** Fair. **Dress** Casual. **Disabled access** Yes. **Customers** EPCOT guests. **Lunch** Daily, 11:30 a.m.–3:30 p.m. **Dinner** Daily, 4–8:40 p.m.

SETTING AND ATMOSPHERE The idea here is that you're transported from EPCOT to a space station high in orbit, where you dine in front of large windows (really computer screens) that show the earth, moon, and stars, and various passersby, while you dine. To complete the effects, your journey includes a ride on a "space elevator" up to and back from the space station. Besides the screens, it's a fairly generic, dark semicircle.

HOUSE SPECIALTIES The house's specialty is making disappointment a seasoning. Used liberally. On everything.

SUMMARY AND COMMENTS If there was a restaurant that represented modern EPCOT, it's Space 220: a hassle to get into, overpriced for what you get, and in need of new ideas. There's no possible way that a four-person dinner here is worth $320 before tax and tip. This place will only last as long as there are people interested in its theme.

Spice Road Table ★★★★

MOROCCAN	INEXPENSIVE	QUALITY ★★★★	VALUE ★★★
READER-SURVEY RESPONSES ➕ 91% (Above Average)			

Morocco, World Showcase, EPCOT; ☎ 407-939-3463

Reservations Recommended. **Dining Plan credits** 1 per person, per meal. **When to go** Anytime; great spot for nightly fireworks when offered. **Cost range** Small plates $9–$15. **Service** ★★★★★. **Friendliness** ★★★★★. **Parking** EPCOT lot. **Bar** Full service. **Wine selection** Good. **Dress** Casual. **Disabled access** Yes. **Customers** EPCOT guests. **Lunch** Daily, 11:30–3:30 p.m. **Dinner** Daily 3:45–9 p.m.

SETTING AND ATMOSPHERE A prime location for daytime people-watching and nighttime fireworks, Spice Road Table is situated directly along World Showcase Lagoon at the front of the Morocco Pavilion. The covered patio features excellent dining in plein air when Florida weather cooperates, and indoor seating provides colorful pops of modern Moroccan decor.

HOUSE SPECIALTIES Perfectly fried calamari and hummus fries stand out as favorites on the small-plates side of the menu.

OTHER RECOMMENDATIONS Lamb kefta with tzatziki offers a bit of punch and spice. Spiced shrimp and chicken may sound simple, but the accompanying sauces and sides elevate the otherwise pedestrian dish.

SUMMARY AND COMMENTS The food quality and service are both good at Spice Road Table. The appetizers and desserts pair excellently with the restaurant's extensive wine and cocktail lists. The service is attentive, and the casual atmosphere seems appropriate for the outdoor seating area and modern EPCOT.

Splitsville Dining Room ★★½

AMERICAN	MODERATE	QUALITY ★★½	VALUE ★★
READER-SURVEY RESPONSES ➕ 92% (Above Average)			

West Side, Disney Springs; ☎ 407-938-7467

Reservations Strongly recommended. **Dining Plan credits** 1 per person, per meal. **When to Go** Lunch or dinner. **Cost range** $17–$28 (child $8). **Service** ★★½. **Friendliness** ★★★. **Parking** Orange garage. **Bar** Full service. **Wine selection** Don't expect Lafite Rothschild. **Dress** Casual. **Disabled access** Yes. **Customers** Tourists. **Hours** Monday–Thursday, 11 a.m.–10 p.m.; Friday–Sunday, 10:30 a.m.–11 p.m.

SETTING AND ATMOSPHERE As part of a chain of combination restaurants and bowling alleys, Splitsville is loud, as you might expect, but there's plenty to see and room for rambunctious kids to roam while you wait for your food. Decor is vaguely midcentury modern, with Sputnik lamps and other space-age touches.

HOUSE SPECIALTIES The sushi—salmon, shrimp, tuna, crab, and various combinations thereof—is the best thing on the menu.

SUMMARY AND COMMENTS The menu is more spread out than a 7/10 split: burgers, pizza, seafood, Asian, and Mexican are represented, along with assorted bar food. Readers seem to love it, but the only thing we'd order again is the sushi.

Steakhouse 71 ★★★★

STEAK	EXPENSIVE	QUALITY ★★★★	VALUE ★★★½
READER-SURVEY RESPONSES ⊕ 90% (Average)			

Contemporary Resort; ☎ 407-939-3463

Reservations Recommended. **Dining Plan credits** Not available. **When to go** Anytime. **Cost range** Breakfast $13–$21 (child $11), brunch $13–$26, lunch $15–$26 (child $13–$15), dinner $24–$39 (child $13–$15). **Service** ★★★★. **Friendliness** ★★★★. **Parking** Contemporary Resort parking lot. **Bar** Full service. **Wine selection** Good. **Dress** Casual. **Disabled access** Yes. **Customers** Resort and theme park guests. **Breakfast** 7:30–11 a.m. **Lunch** 11:30 a.m.–2 p.m. **Dinner** 5–9 p.m.

SETTING AND ATMOSPHERE A midcentury modern vibe with bold colors and sleek (for Disney) design.

HOUSE SPECIALTIES For appetizers, the Fork & Knife Caesar Salad or the chef's "Bacon & Eggs"—maple-lacquered pork belly with smoky cheese grits and a poached egg. For mains, the Stack Burger is the go-to for those not sure what to order. Plant-forward folks should absolutely try Chef Nik's vegan take on Beef Wellington, which may be the best thing on the menu.

SUMMARY AND COMMENTS On the ground floor of the Contemporary Resort, Steakhouse 71 is designed to appeal to everyone. Thankfully, Disney didn't just go for the lowest common denominator here, and there are some pretty good dishes to be found.

STK Orlando ★★★½

STEAK	EXPENSIVE	QUALITY ★★★★	VALUE ★★½
READER-SURVEY RESPONSES ⊕ 74% (Do Not Visit)			

The Landing, Disney Springs; ☎ 407-917-7440 ·

Reservations Strongly recommended. **Dining Plan credits** 2 per person, per meal. **When to go** Weekend brunch and dinner. **Cost range** Brunch $24–$49, lunch $17–$49 (child $12–$18), dinner $50–$112 (child $12–$18). **Service** ★★★★. **Friendliness** ★★★★. **Parking** Orange garage. **Bar** Full service. **Wine selection** Not bad but not encyclopedic either. **Dress** Casual. **Disabled access** Yes. **Customers** Theme park guests. **Brunch** Saturday–Sunday, 11 a.m.–3 p.m. **Lunch** Monday–Friday, 11 a.m.–3 p.m. **Dinner** Daily, 4–10 p.m. (until 11 p.m. on Friday and Saturday).

SETTING AND ATMOSPHERE The turreted brick exterior, intended to evoke a turn-of-the-20th-century train station, couldn't be more different from the inside. A lower level houses a bar and seating area with a Las Vegas–ultralounge feel, complete with DJ and *lots* of noise. The quieter, less-glitzy upstairs has both indoor and outdoor seating.

HOUSE SPECIALTIES Steaks, ranging from a $49 filet mignon to a $112, 14-ounce dry-aged Delmonico. Sides include macaroni and cheese, sweet corn pudding, and Parmesan-truffle fries.

SUMMARY AND COMMENTS Since it opened, STK has been rated as one of the worst dining experiences in Disney World: The steaks are good but overpriced, and they're inexplicably accompanied by a club DJ playing loud music. In Disney Springs, we recommend **The Boathouse, Chef Art Smith's Homecomin', Jaleo, Wine Bar George,** or **Morimoto Asia** instead.

Story Book Dining with Snow White at Artist Point ★★★½

AMERICAN	EXPENSIVE	QUALITY ★★★★	VALUE ★★★½
READER SURVEY RESPONSES ⊕ 85% (Much Below Average)			

Wilderness Lodge & Boulder Ridge/Copper Creek Villas; ☎ 407-939-3463

Reservations Recommended. **Dining Plan credits** 1 per person, per meal. **When to go** Dinner. **Cost range** $65 (child $39). **Service** ★★★★★. **Friendliness** ★★★★★.

Parking Hotel lot. **Bar** Full service. **Wine selection** Decent array of reds and whites from the Pacific Northwest. **Dress** Dressy casual. **Disabled access** Yes. **Customers** Hotel guests. **Character dinner** Daily, 4–9 p.m.

SETTING AND ATMOSPHERE The understated Arts and Crafts decor takes cues from the Old Faithful Inn at Yellowstone National Park, with massive landscape paintings, heavy wooden tables, and cast-iron chandeliers.

HOUSE SPECIALTIES Appetizers include shrimp cocktail and mushroom bisque. Entrées include prime rib, pork shank, roast chicken, a fish dish, and a vegetarian option. For kids, there's grilled chicken, grilled fish, or prime rib. Despite the below-average reader ratings, we think the food is good.

SUMMARY AND COMMENTS Characters include Snow White, Dopey, Grumpy, and the Evil Queen—odd choices for a restaurant, as Snow White falls into a coma immediately after eating doctored food. (Apparently Disney's in on the joke, though, because there's a "Poison" Apple dessert.)

Takumi-Tei ★★★★½

JAPANESE	EXPENSIVE	QUALITY ★★★★★	VALUE ★★★½
READER-SURVEY RESPONSES	See Summary and Comments below		

Japan, World Showcase, EPCOT; ☎ 407-939-3463

Reservations Strongly recommended. **Dining Plan credits** 1 per person, per meal. **When to go** Dinner. **Cost range** $150 or $250 (child $100). **Service** ★★★★★. **Friendliness** ★★★★★. **Parking** EPCOT lot. **Bar** Full service. **Wine selection** Minimal. **Dress** Casual. **Disabled access** Yes. **Customers** EPCOT guests. **Hours** Thursday–Monday, 4:30–8 p.m.

SETTING AND ATMOSPHERE The decor celebrates five natural elements revered by Japanese craftsmen: water, wood, earth, stone, and washi (paper). (*Takumi-Tei* means "house of the artisan.") The private dining room, home to traditional kaiseki dining, features a custom waterfall that looks like it's flowing straight into the dining table.

HOUSE SPECIALTIES The fixed-price menu rotates seasonally to reflect the freshest and most seasonal produce at the chef's disposal. The Hama no Kani ("Crab on the Beach") appetizer playfully combines two different crab preparations with frisée, heirloom tomato, and pickled watermelon. A-5 Wagyu beef—the most prized in the world—anchors the main-course menu, and while it's a significant spend, it makes for a meal unlike any other.

OTHER RECOMMENDATIONS Sashimi and nigiri with the freshest fish you'll ever taste; specialty desserts tailor-made for Instagramming.

SUMMARY AND COMMENTS Filtering classical Japanese cookery through an upscale modern lens, Takumi-Tei treats diners to an indulgent retreat from the hustle and bustle of the theme park. So many readers confuse this with **Teppan Edo** (see below) that we're redoing our survey format to make it clear which restaurant is which. In the meantime, if you're comfortable spending $135–$175 per person on a good omakase sushi meal in your hometown, you'll love Takumi-Tei.

Teppan Edo ★★★½

JAPANESE	EXPENSIVE	QUALITY ★★★★	VALUE ★★★
READER-SURVEY RESPONSES	⊕ 95% (Exceptional)		

Japan, World Showcase, EPCOT; ☎ 407-939-3463

Reservations Strongly recommended. **Dining Plan credits** 1 per person, per meal. **When to go** Lunch or dinner. **Cost range** $26–$65 (child $18–$20). **Service** ★★★★★. **Friendliness** ★★★★★. **Parking** EPCOT lot. **Bar** Full service. **Wine selection** Limited. **Dress** Casual. **Disabled access** Via elevator. **Customers** EPCOT guests. **Hours** Daily, noon–9 p.m.

SETTING AND ATMOSPHERE Six Japanese dining rooms with grills on tables and entertaining chefs chopping, slicing, and dicing.

HOUSE SPECIALTIES Chicken, shrimp, beef, scallops, and Asian vegetables stir-fried on a teppanyaki grill by a knife-juggling chef.

ENTERTAINMENT AND AMENITIES Watching the teppanyaki chefs.

SUMMARY AND COMMENTS A popular dining option for families, Teppan Edo has been the highest-rated restaurant in EPCOT for three years. The food quality is comparable to what you'd get in a hometown teppan place. You'll get plenty to eat, and the starters include sushi, ribs, edamame, and miso soup. What's not to like?

Terralina Crafted Italian ★★½

ITALIAN	EXPENSIVE	QUALITY ★★½	VALUE ★★½
READER-SURVEY RESPONSES ⊕ 76% (Do Not Visit)			

The Landing, Disney Springs; ☎ 407-934-8888

Reservations Recommended. **Dining Plan credits** 1 per person, per meal. **When to go** Lunch or dinner. **Cost range** $17–$46 (child $8–$13). **Service** ★★★★. **Friendliness** ★★★★½. **Parking** Disney Springs Lime garage. **Bar** Full service. **Wine selection** Mostly Italian. **Dress** Casual. **Disabled access** Yes. **Customers** Disney Springs guests. **Hours** Daily, noon–11 p.m.

SETTING AND ATMOSPHERE "Italian Lake District" is the theme, with stonework, exposed wood beams, and warm colors. The waiting area has a fireplace and leather chairs; an even better place to wait is the open-air bar.

HOUSE SPECIALTIES Mozzarella-stuffed rice ball appetizer, gnocchi with pork ragù and shaved Parmesan, eggplant Parmesan, tiramisu for dessert.

SUMMARY AND COMMENTS If you're in the mood for really good Italian, you'll have to look outside of Disney Springs.

Three Bridges Bar & Grill at Villa del Lago ★★★

AMERICAN/SPANISH	EXPENSIVE	QUALITY ★★★	VALUE ★★½
READER-SURVEY RESPONSES ⊕ 91% (Above Average)			

Coronado Springs Resort; ☎ 407-939-3463

Reservations Not available. **Dining Plan credits** 1 per person, per meal. **When to go** Dinner. **Cost range** $16–$25 (child $11). **Service** ★★★½. **Friendliness** ★★★★. **Parking** Coronado Springs lot. **Bar** Full service. **Wine selection** Mostly Spanish. **Dress** Casual. **Disabled access** Yes. **Customers** Hotel guests. **Hours** Daily, 4:30 p.m.–midnight.

SETTING AND ATMOSPHERE At the crux of Coronado Springs Resort's three commuter bridges, this bar and grill floats in the middle of picturesque Lago Dorado, reflecting sunsets nightly and offering grand views of the complex's Gran Destino Tower. Lounge-style seating occupies half of the dining area, with a central bar and standard tables adjacent. Three Bridges is a happening spot even in the late afternoon.

HOUSE SPECIALTIES Stick to the basics: Szechuan peppercorn wings, Oaxaca cheese dip with chorizo, a fantastic house burger, ridiculously fresh tacos (with made-from-scratch tortillas). Portions aren't hefty, but they are enough to satisfy anyone looking to split a few snacks or grab a light meal. Specialty cocktails complement a hearty wine-and-beer selection.

OTHER RECOMMENDATIONS Hearty salads and harissa lamb chops are good main-dish choices.

SUMMARY AND COMMENTS Taking waterside dining to the next level, Three Bridges unites traditional bar fare with Spanish flair. Dishes are nicely executed and drinks are delightful at this beautiful island retreat.

Tiffins Restaurant ★★★½

AMERICAN/PAN-ASIAN **EXPENSIVE** **QUALITY ★★★½** **VALUE ★★½**
READER-SURVEY RESPONSES ⊕ 91% (Above Average)

Discovery Island, Animal Kingdom; ☎ 407-939-3463

Reservations Strongly recommended. **Dining Plan credits** 2 per person, per meal.
When to go Lunch or dinner. **Cost range** $37–$52 (child $12–$16). **Service ★★★★**.
Friendliness ★★★★★. **Parking** Animal Kingdom lot. **Bar** Full bar. **Wine selection**
Excellent. **Dress** Casual. **Disabled access** Yes. **Customers** Theme park guests. **Hours**
Daily, noon–7 p.m.

SETTING AND ATMOSPHERE Tiffins is tucked behind the Pizzafari counter-
service restaurant on a walking path to the land of Pandora. Inside are three
relatively small, quiet dining rooms, plus the **Nomad Lounge.** A wraparound
porch behind the dining rooms offers outdoor seating.

The decor is said to be inspired by the travel adventures of the Imagineers who built Animal Kingdom. You'll see artifacts from Asia and Africa
lining the walls of one room, and giant butterflies in another. The main dining room's centerpiece is carved-wood sculptures.

HOUSE SPECIALTIES Charred octopus and honey-glazed pork belly appetizers. For entrées, try the whole fried sustainable fish or butter chicken.

OTHER RECOMMENDATIONS Skip the bread service and desserts.

SUMMARY AND COMMENTS Despite the above-average reader ratings, we
think the food here is overpriced and not as good as it used to be. That
said, the Nomad Lounge next door is still an excellent place to relax with
a drink and some light bites.

Todd English's Bluezoo ★★★

SEAFOOD **EXPENSIVE** **QUALITY ★★★** **VALUE ★★**
READER-SURVEY RESPONSES ⊕ 83% (Much Below Average)

Dolphin Resort; ☎ 407-934-1609

Reservations Recommended. **Dining Plan credits** Not accepted. **When to go** Dinner.
Cost range $30–$57 (child $10–$12). **Service ★★★★**. **Friendliness ★★★**. **Parking**
Valet ($35) or hotel lot ($25), both free with validation. **Bar** Full service. **Wine selection** Excellent. **Dress** Dressy casual. **Disabled access** Yes. **Customers** Hotel guests,
locals. **Hours** Daily, 5–11 p.m.

SETTING AND ATMOSPHERE A lovely yet slightly cold dining room swathed
in blues with iridescent bubbles suspended from the lights. The name is
courtesy of celebrity chef Todd English's son, who as a young boy saw an
under-the-sea movie and said it looked like a "blue zoo." Open kitchen and
a unique circular rotisserie that makes the fish being grilled on it seem to
dance on the coals.

HOUSE SPECIALTIES Nightly fish selection (from the rotisserie), Angus filet.

OTHER RECOMMENDATIONS New England–style clam chowder with salt-
cured bacon, teppan-seared jumbo sea scallops.

SUMMARY AND COMMENTS You could fashion a good meal from just the
appetizers and desserts, which are above average.

Tokyo Dining ★★★

JAPANESE **MODERATE** **QUALITY ★★★★** **VALUE ★★★**
READER-SURVEY RESPONSES ⊕ 85% (Much Below Average)

Japan, World Showcase, EPCOT; ☎ 407-939-3463

Reservations Strongly recommended. **Dining Plan credits** 1 per person, per meal. **When to go** Lunch. **Cost range** $18–$30. **Service** ★★★★. **Friendliness** ★★★. **Parking** EPCOT lot. **Bar** Full service. **Wine selection** Limited. **Dress** Casual. **Disabled access** Yes. **Customers** Theme park guests. **Lunch** Daily, noon–3:45 p.m. **Dinner** Daily, 4–9 p.m.

SETTING AND ATMOSPHERE Gracious service and modern Asian decor distinguish this restaurant. There are no seats at the beautifully lit sushi bar, but the chefs are great entertainment for the entire dining room. Tables near the windows have a wonderful second-floor view of World Showcase.

HOUSE SPECIALTIES Sushi and sashimi.

SUMMARY AND COMMENTS The dining room is sleek; the sushi is super-fresh; and the overall experience is relaxing, congenial, and quintessentially Japanese. Prices have increased, though, and reader ratings have dropped as a result.

Toledo—Tapas, Steak & Seafood ★★★½

SPANISH	EXPENSIVE	QUALITY ★★★	VALUE ★★½
READER-SURVEY RESPONSES ✚ 77% (Do Not Visit)			

Gran Destino Tower, Coronado Springs Resort; ☎ 407-939-3463

Reservations Recommended. **Dining Plan credits** 1 per person, per meal. **When to go** Dinner. **Cost range** $29–$37 (child $11–$15). **Service** ★★★★. **Friendliness** ★★★★. **Parking** Hotel lot. **Bar** Full service. **Wine selection** Mostly Spanish. **Dress** Casual. **Disabled access** Yes. **Customers** Hotel guests. **Hours** Wednesday–Sunday, 5–10 p.m.

SETTING AND ATMOSPHERE High atop Gran Destino Tower, Toledo envelops diners in a Cubist cloud heaven, complete with color-changing ceiling and trees reaching to the sky right beside several tables. A showcase bar anchors one side of the restaurant, while an open tapas kitchen greets guests at the far end of the dining room. The real attraction, though, is the massive wall of windows, offering views of some of Walt Disney World's most popular attractions and nighttime spectaculars.

HOUSE SPECIALTIES None.

OTHER RECOMMENDATIONS Stick to the less expensive small plates and save your money for somewhere else. The blistered shishito peppers are more than enough to share.

SUMMARY AND COMMENTS **Jaleo by José Andrés** (page 333) has better food for less money. Toledo caters to resort guests and conventioneers (that is, people unwilling or unable to go elsewhere).

Tony's Town Square Restaurant ★★

ITALIAN	EXPENSIVE	QUALITY ★★	VALUE ★★
READER-SURVEY RESPONSES ✚ 82% (Much Below Average)			

Main Street, U.S.A., Magic Kingdom; ☎ 407-939-3463

Reservations Strongly recommended. **Dining Plan credits** 1 per person, per meal. **When to go** Late lunch or early dinner. **Cost range** $26–$36 (child $11–$12). **Service** ★★★★. **Friendliness** ★★★★★. **Parking** Magic Kingdom lot. **Bar** Limited selection of beer and wine. **Dress** Casual. **Disabled access** Yes. **Customers** Theme park guests. **Hours** Daily, 11:30 a.m.–9 p.m.

SETTING AND ATMOSPHERE Just inside the Magic Kingdom on Main Street, with a glass-windowed porch that's wonderful for watching the action outside, Tony's Town Square doesn't have good food, but it's a rite of passage for Disney fans—one *must* have a plate of spaghetti in the restaurant that commemorates *Lady and the Tramp*.

HOUSE SPECIALTIES Spaghetti with meatballs, shrimp fettuccine Alfredo, chicken parmigiana, butcher's steak.

SUMMARY AND COMMENTS Though it's consistently rated as one of the worst restaurants in the Magic Kingdom, Tony's does a decent job with simple pasta (multigrain and gluten-free options available).

Topolino's Terrace—Flavors of the Riviera ★★★★

FRENCH/ITALIAN   **EXPENSIVE**   **QUALITY ★★★★**   **VALUE ★★★**
READER-SURVEY RESPONSES ➕ 94% (Much Above Average)
Riviera Resort; ☎ 407-939-3463

Reservations Strongly recommended. **Dining Plan credits** 2 per person, per meal. **When to go** Breakfast or dinner. **Cost range** Breakfast $45 (child $27); dinner $32–$54 (child $10–$17). **Service** ★★★★½. **Friendliness** ★★★★★. **Parking** Hotel lot. **Bar** Full service. **Dress** Dressy casual. **Disabled access** Yes. **Customers** Hotel and other Disney guests. **Character breakfast** Daily, 7:30 a.m.–12:15 p.m. **Dinner** Daily, 5–9:30 p.m.

SETTING AND ATMOSPHERE The big feature of this rooftop restaurant is the fantastic view of EPCOT and Disney's Hollywood Studios, especially at night when those parks run their fireworks spectaculars. Beyond the windows, you'll find burgundy-and-cream carpets and dark wood tables and accents. In keeping with Disney's recent decorative trends, there's absolutely nothing here that's overtly tied to the Riviera.

HOUSE SPECIALTIES *Breakfast:* Sour cream waffle with roasted apples and orange-maple syrup; smoked salmon bagel. *Dinner:* French veal chop with potatoes; roasted eggplant with romesco sauce.

OTHER RECOMMENDATIONS Lobster linguini; rigatoni pasta with chicken, Broccolini, and wild mushrooms.

SUMMARY AND COMMENTS One of the most difficult reservations to get in Walt Disney World. There are seemingly no bad choices on this menu, and the service team is excellent. Breakfast features a parade of Disney characters including Mickey, Minnie, Donald, and Daisy.

Trader Sam's Grog Grotto ★★★

PAN-ASIAN   **INEXPENSIVE**   **QUALITY ★★★**   **VALUE ★★★**
READER-SURVEY RESPONSES ➕ 94% (Much Above Average)
Polynesian Village Resort; ☎ 407-939-3463

Reservations Not accepted. **Dining Plan credits** Not accepted. **When to go** Dinner. **Cost range** $10–$18 (small plates only). **Service** ★★★. **Friendliness** ★★★★. **Parking** Valet ($33) or hotel lot. **Bar** Full service. **Wine selection** Good. **Dress** Casual. **Disabled access** Yes. **Customers** Locals and Disney guests. **Hours** Daily, 3 p.m.–midnight (only guests age 21 and up are admitted after 8 p.m.).

SETTING AND ATMOSPHERE Off the Polynesian Village's main lobby and featuring views of the marina and Seven Seas Lagoon, this highly themed tiki bar has its own lore built in: It was started by Trader Sam, Adventureland's famous "head" salesman, who welcomes you to his enchanted South Seas hideaway to explore a menu of "magical tropical drinks and food."

HOUSE SPECIALTIES Cocktails are the stars, with names like Tahitian Torch and the over-the-top Uh-Oa! (Plantation Original Dark and Bacardi rums mixed with various fruit juices and served in a communal tiki bowl).

OTHER RECOMMENDATIONS Small plates include sushi, Kalua pork tacos, Thai chicken flatbread, and dumplings.

SUMMARY AND COMMENTS Trader Sam's is a hit with Disneyphiles, so get there early—there are just 50 seats inside and 80 on the patio.

Trattoria al Forno ★★★

ITALIAN	MODERATE	QUALITY ★★★½	VALUE ★★
READER-SURVEY RESPONSES ⊕ 90% (Average)			

BoardWalk; ☎ 407-939-3463

Reservations Strongly recommended. **Dining Plan credits** 1 per person, per meal. **When to go** Breakfast or dinner. **Cost range** Breakfast $13–$21 (child $7–$10), dinner $21–$39 (child $13–$16). **Service** ★★★. **Friendliness** ★★★★. **Parking** BoardWalk lot. **Bar** Full service. **Wine selection** Good; all Italian. **Dress** Casual. **Disabled access** Yes. **Customers** Locals, Disney guests. **Breakfast** Daily, 7:30–11:30 a.m. **Dinner** Monday–Saturday, 5–10 p.m.

SETTING AND ATMOSPHERE The space contains three dining areas, a private room, and an open kitchen for watching the action. Our favorite spots are the formal dining room, right in front of the kitchen, or a booth at the back.

HOUSE SPECIALTIES *Breakfast:* Poached egg over polenta with fennel sausage; pancakes; steak and eggs; breakfast pizza (scrambled eggs, bacon, ham, sausage, bell peppers, and cheese). *Dinner:* Rigatoni Bolognese, chicken parmigiana, tiramisu.

SUMMARY AND COMMENTS The kitchen makes mozzarella and fresh pasta daily. The wines represent Italy's major regions, with more than 30 available by the glass or quartino. The breakfast is one of the best on Disney property, even though the characters are temporarily unavailable.

T-REX ★★

AMERICAN	EXPENSIVE	QUALITY ★★	VALUE ★★
READER-SURVEY RESPONSES ⊕ 80% (Do Not Visit)			

Marketplace, Disney Springs; ☎ 407-828-8739

Reservations Strongly recommended. **Dining Plan credits** 1 per person, per meal. **When to go** Lunch or dinner. **Cost range** $20–$44 (child $11). **Service** ★★★. **Friendliness** ★★★. **Parking** Orange garage. **Bar** Full service. **Wine selection** Minimal. **Dress** Casual. **Disabled access** Yes. **Customers** Families. **Hours** Daily, 11 a.m.–11 p.m.

SETTING AND ATMOSPHERE Sensory overload in a cavernous dining room with life-size robotic dinosaurs, giant fish tanks, bubbling geysers, waterfalls, fossils in the bathrooms, and crystals in the walls. Volume: loud.

HOUSE SPECIALTY Megasaurus Burger.

SUMMARY AND COMMENTS Expect a wait unless there's an empty seat at the bar. But nobody's here just for the ordinary, overpriced food—it's nonstop "eatertainment," with kid-friendly food served in huge portions.

Turf Club Bar and Grill ★★

AMERICAN	EXPENSIVE	QUALITY ★★½	VALUE ★★
READER-SURVEY RESPONSES ⊕ 70% (Do Not Visit)			

Saratoga Springs Resort & Spa; ☎ 407-939-3463

Reservations Accepted. **Dining Plan credits** 1 per person, per meal. **When to go** Dinner. **Cost range** $24–$38 (child $11–$13). **Service** ★★★. **Friendliness** ★★★★. **Parking** Hotel lot. **Bar** Full service. **Wine selection** Good. **Dress** Casual. **Disabled access** Good. **Customers** Hotel guests. **Hours** Wednesday–Sunday, 4:30–9 p.m.

SETTING AND ATMOSPHERE When the weather is nice, ask for an outdoor table; you can spot golfers on the adjacent Lake Buena Vista Golf Course and look across the way to Disney Springs. Just off the lobby of Saratoga Springs Resort, the dining room is equestrian themed.

HOUSE SPECIALTY Slow-roasted 10-ounce prime rib.

OTHER RECOMMENDATIONS Pan-seared salmon.

SUMMARY AND COMMENTS Rarely crowded, but you'll find much better food at Disney Springs.

Tusker House Restaurant ★★★

AFRICAN/AMERICAN	EXPENSIVE	QUALITY ★★★	VALUE ★★★
READER-SURVEY RESPONSES ➕ 89% (Average)			

Africa, Animal Kingdom; ☎ 407-939-3463

Reservations Required. **Dining Plan credits** 1 per person, per meal. **When to go** Anytime. **Cost range** Breakfast $45 (child $29), lunch and dinner $59 (child $38). Prices may vary seasonally; check before you go. **Service** ★★★. **Friendliness** ★★★. **Parking** Animal Kingdom lot. **Bar** Full-service bar next door. **Dress** Casual. **Disabled access** Yes. **Customers** Theme park guests. **Character breakfast** Daily, 8–10:30 a.m. **Character lunch** Daily, 11 a.m.–3:30 p.m. **Character dinner** Daily, 3:35–7 p.m.

SETTING AND ATMOSPHERE Character meals feature Mickey, Donald, Daisy, and Goofy. The setting—inside the Harambe Village square—is plainer than promotional photos indicate, especially after dark. The food, however, is surprisingly good, with spices and taste combinations you won't find at other character-dining spots.

HOUSE SPECIALTIES Roast pork, beef, and chicken.

SUMMARY AND COMMENTS Tusker House appeals not just to kids but also to grown-ups who appreciate more interesting dishes. This mom from Campobello, South Carolina, is a fan:

We had a supergood meal at Tusker House, probably the best of the entire trip.

Tutto Gusto Wine Cellar ★★★½

ITALIAN	EXPENSIVE	QUALITY ★★½	VALUE ★★★
READER-SURVEY RESPONSES ➕ 90% (Average)			

Italy, World Showcase, EPCOT; ☎ 407-560-8040

Reservations Not accepted. **Dining Plan credits** Not accepted. **When to go** Dinner. **Cost range** $17–$42 (child $11). **Service** ★★★★. **Friendliness** ★★★½. **Parking** EPCOT lot. **Bar** Full service. **Wine selection** Large and diverse. **Dress** Casual. **Disabled access** Yes. **Customers** Theme park guests. **Hours** Daily, 12:30–9 p.m.

SETTING AND ATMOSPHERE Tutto Gusto is an intimate space with cozy fireplace-adjacent seating and unique wine-bottle chandeliers. Dark and cool as befits any wine cellar, it can be packed during the day with guests looking to cool off with a glass of one of 200-plus wines.

HOUSE SPECIALTIES Wine flights with three pours, plus quartinos and full bottles available for those wanting to settle in awhile. Shareable plates feature cheeses, charcuterie, marinated vegetables, and desserts. Kids can choose spaghetti, pizza, mozzarella sticks, or chicken tenders.

SUMMARY AND COMMENTS Tutto Gusto serves light fare and high-quality wines in a beautifully quaint space. The standing bar area typically has a shorter wait than for tables at peak times.

Tutto Italia Ristorante ★★★

ITALIAN	EXPENSIVE	QUALITY ★★★★	VALUE ★★
READER-SURVEY RESPONSES ➕ 83% (Much Below Average)			

Italy, World Showcase, EPCOT; ☎ 407-939-3463

Reservations Strongly recommended. **Dining Plan credits** 1 per person, per meal. **When to go** Midafternoon. **Cost range** $24–$42 (child $11). **Service** ★★★★. **Friendliness** ★★★★. **Parking** EPCOT lot. **Bar** Beer and wine only. **Wine selection** All Italian. **Dress** Casual. **Disabled access** Yes. **Customers** Theme park guests. **Hours** Daily, 12:30–9 p.m.

SETTING AND ATMOSPHERE Tutto Italia feels like a big restaurant in Rome or Milan, with murals of a piazza along the wall behind upholstered banquettes. It can get noisy—if the weather is nice, request an outside table.

HOUSE SPECIALTIES It's hard to identify anything as being done particularly well.

OTHER RECOMMENDATIONS Stick to the least-expensive menu items.

SUMMARY AND COMMENTS This *should* be one of the best Italian restaurants in Orlando, but it's not. Everything that happens inside Tutto Italia—from the cooking to the service—feels like it's done on autopilot. The food quality can't support the prices, even taking the "Disney bubble" cost premium into account: $34 for chicken parm is nearly double what you'd pay in many neighborhood Italian joints and 30% more expensive than in Manhattan. Everything here needs to be done better.

Via Napoli Ristorante e Pizzeria ★★★★

ITALIAN	EXPENSIVE	QUALITY ★★★½	VALUE ★★★
READER-SURVEY RESPONSES ➕ 91% (Above Average)			

Italy, World Showcase, EPCOT; ☎ 407-939-3463

Reservations Strongly recommended. **Dining Plan credits** 1 per person, per meal. **When to go** Lunch or dinner. **Cost range** Entrées $28–$40, individual pizzas $21–$26, pizzas (serves 2–5) $38–$55. **Service** ★★★★. **Friendliness** ★★★★. **Parking** EPCOT lot. **Bar** Beer and wine only. **Dress** Casual. **Disabled access** Yes. **Customers** Theme park guests. **Hours** Daily, 11:30 a.m.–9 p.m.

SETTING AND ATMOSPHERE Three big pizza ovens, named after the three active Italian volcanoes—Etna, Vesuvio, and Stromboli—are the stars of the show in this loud, cavernous dining room.

HOUSE SPECIALTIES The best pizza in Walt Disney World.

SUMMARY AND COMMENTS The Carciofi (artichokes, fontina, and truffle oil) and Quattro Formaggi (four-cheese) pies are our favorites. As we went to press, many of the servers were not Italian but from Orlando. The people who greet you, however, are Italian and beautiful.

Victoria & Albert's ★★★★★

GOURMET	EXPENSIVE	QUALITY ★★★★★	VALUE ★★★★
READER-SURVEY RESPONSES ➕ Not enough to rate			

Grand Floridian Resort & Spa; ☎ 407-939-3463

Reservations Required; call at least 60 days in advance to reserve; you must confirm special dietary needs by noon the day of your seating. A $100 no-show fee applies if you fail to cancel at least 5 days before your meal; if you cancel less than 24 hours before, you'll be charged the full price. **Dining Plan credits** Not accepted. **When to go** Dinner. **Cost range** Main dining room $295, Queen Victoria's Room $375, Chef's Table $425 (all menus fixed price; tax and gratuities extra). Optional wine pairings $200, nonalcoholic beverage pairings $110. **Service** ★★★★★. **Friendliness** ★★★★. **Parking** Valet (free); self-parking is deceptively far away. **Wine selection** 700 on the menu, 4,200 more in the cellar. **Dress** Jacket required for men, evening wear for women. **Disabled access** Yes. **Customers** Hotel guests, locals. **Hours** Open Tuesday–Saturday. Main dining room: 5:30–8:05 p.m. Queen Victoria's Room: 5:30–7 p.m. Chef's Table: 1 seating at 5:30 p.m. (Seating times may vary.) *Note:* No children under age 10 admitted except at Chef's Table.

SETTING AND ATMOSPHERE With just 14 tables in the main dining room, Queen Victoria's Room with seating for up to eight, and the eight-seat Chef's Table, this is the top dining experience at Walt Disney World. A consecutive winner of AAA's Five Diamond Award since 2000—the only restaurant in Central Florida so honored—Victoria & Albert's is lavish and expensive, with Frette linens, Riedel crystal, and Christofle silver.

HOUSE SPECIALTIES Chef Scott Hunnel's menu changes daily, but has included Minnesota elk tenderloin, Alaskan salmon, local free-range chicken, Florida sturgeon caviar, and Australian Kobe-style beef. Pastry chef Kristine Farmer's desserts are divine.

SUMMARY AND COMMENTS Hunnel (a James Beard Award nominee) and his team prepare modern American cuisine with the best of the best from around the world. The main dining room and Queen Victoria's Room are whisper-quiet, but the Chef's Table is convivial and relaxed.

V&A reopened in the fall of 2022 with a single, fixed-price menu and its usual excellent food and service. The vast majority of readers who rate the restaurant poorly do so on price. While V&A opened too late for consideration in that year's Michelin guide, we'd be surprised if it doesn't get a star or two in the next review.

Whispering Canyon Cafe ★★★

AMERICAN	EXPENSIVE	QUALITY ★★½	VALUE ★★★★
READER-SURVEY RESPONSES ✚ 86% (Below Average)			

Wilderness Lodge & Boulder Ridge/Copper Creek Villas; ☎ 407-939-3463

Reservations Strongly recommended. **Dining Plan credits** 1 per person, per meal. **When to go** Anytime. **Cost range** Breakfast $11–$26 (child $9–$11), lunch $11–$26 (child $9–$11), dinner $22–$38 (child $9–$11). **Service** ★★★★. **Friendliness** ★★★★. **Parking** Hotel lot. **Bar** Full service. **Wine selection** Limited. **Dress** Casual. **Disabled access** Yes. **Customers** Hotel guests. **Breakfast** Daily, 7:30–11:25 a.m. **Lunch** Daily, 11:30 a.m.–2 p.m. **Dinner** Daily, 5–10 p.m.

SETTING AND ATMOSPHERE A big, open dining room just off the lobby, with whimsical Wild West decor.

HOUSE SPECIALTIES For breakfast, the all-you-can-eat skillet offers bacon, sausage, scrambled eggs, waffles, and buttermilk biscuits and gravy. For lunch and dinner, a big skillet loaded with barbecue pulled pork or ribs, roasted chicken, mashed potatoes, green beans, and corn is a crowd-pleaser. Three other skillet options are also available at dinner.

SUMMARY AND COMMENTS The all-you-can-eat skillets give hungry folks their money's worth.

Wine Bar George ★★★★

WINE/SMALL PLATES	MODERATE-EXPENSIVE	QUALITY ★★★★	VALUE ★★★★
READER-SURVEY RESPONSES ✚ 93% (Above Average)			

The Landing, Disney Springs; ☎ 407-490-1800

Reservations Accepted. **Dining Plan credits** 1 per person, per meal. **When to go** Anytime. **Cost range** Brunch $17–$25, lunch $15–$19, dinner $28–$42, family-style entrées (serve 2 or more), $75–$76 (child $10). Small plates run $8–$18. The midrange for wines is around $40 per bottle, and many wines by the glass run $8–$17. **Service** ★★★★. **Friendliness** ★★★★. **Parking** Disney Springs Lime garage. **Bar** Full service. **Wine selection** Wide-ranging—more than 140 wines in all—with a focus on affordability. **Dress** Casual. **Disabled access** Yes. **Customers** Disney Springs guests. **Brunch** Saturday–Sunday, 10:30 a.m.–2 p.m. **Lunch** Monday–Friday, noon–2:55 p.m. **Dinner** Daily, 3–11 p.m. (until 11:30 p.m. on Friday and Saturday).

SETTING AND ATMOSPHERE Decor is spare and industrial: exposed air vents, concrete floors, brick walls, and lots of windows. The focus of the ground floor is the central bar, with an elevated wine rack and seating for around 18 people; a dozen 6-person high-tops and four 4-person tables are also available. It's noisy here even before you add alcohol, but the second floor is much quieter, and it has outdoor as well as indoor seating.

HOUSE SPECIALTIES Tapas-style small bites made for sharing—we like the saganaki (cheese set on fire!). Entrées are limited, but a few are made for two or more—try the family-style skirt steak with roasted potatoes and seasonal vegetables.

OTHER RECOMMENDATIONS Many of the wines are available by the ounce, the glass, and the bottle, letting you create your own inexpensive wine-flight theme.

SUMMARY AND COMMENTS One of the highest-rated restaurants in Walt Disney World. Owner and namesake George Miliotes is one of just 274 Master Sommeliers in the world. Miliotes is also committed to making great wines affordable: The wines we price-checked are offered at the industry-standard markup of two to three times the retail price, compared with several times that at other Disney restaurants.

The Basket, a counter-service window beneath the second-story terrace, serves European-style sandwiches, cheese, olives, hummus, charcuterie, cookies, and wines on tap—served to-go by the glass or carafe.

Wolfgang Puck Bar & Grill ★★★

AMERICAN	EXPENSIVE	QUALITY ★★★	VALUE ★★★
READER-SURVEY RESPONSES ✪ 84% (Much Below Average)			

Town Center, Disney Springs; ☎ 407-939-3463

Reservations Recommended. **Dining Plan credits** 1 per person, per meal. **When to go** Brunch, lunch, or dinner. **Cost range** Brunch $19–$62, lunch and dinner $18–$62. **Service ★★★★. Friendliness ★★★★. Parking** Orange garage. **Bar** Full service. **Dress** Casual. **Disabled access** Yes. **Customers** Locals and Disney resort guests. **Brunch** Saturday–Sunday, 10 a.m.–3 p.m. **Lunch** Monday–Friday, 11 a.m.–3 p.m. **Dinner** Daily, 3:05–10 p.m. (until 11 p.m. on Friday and Saturday).

SETTING AND ATMOSPHERE The decor—farmhouse chic meets brutalist modern architecture—melds the sleek style of the surrounding garage and over-the-top retail locations with the Florida-waterfront look of the rest of Town Center. An open kitchen draws the eye from the restaurant's front door, while exposed wood beams and a copper-accented pizza oven bring warmth to the restaurant's 250-seat interior, with an indoor bar offset from the main dining room. A slight outdoor seating area abuts one side of the restaurant's exterior, with the other side dedicated to a grab-and-go dessert and gelato window.

HOUSE SPECIALTIES The pizza is recommended. For dinner, the chicken Wiener schnitzel and roasted half chicken are both good.

OTHER RECOMMENDATIONS Nothing here is bad, but the meats are better than the pastas.

SUMMARY AND COMMENTS Not the flashiest restaurant, but it has good food at decent (for Disney) prices. It's also often easier to get into than other places in Disney Springs.

Yachtsman Steakhouse ★★½

STEAK	EXPENSIVE	QUALITY ★★★½	VALUE ★★
READER-SURVEY RESPONSES ✪ 86% (Below Average)			

Yacht Club Resort; ☎ 407-939-3463

Reservations Strongly recommended. **Dining Plan credits** 2 per person, per meal. **When to go** Dinner. **Cost range** $36–$59 (child $10–$13). *Note:* Everything is à la carte (that is, side dishes cost extra). **Service** ★★★★. **Friendliness** ★★★★. **Parking** Hotel lot. **Bar** Full service. **Wine selection** Very good. **Dress** Dressy casual. **Disabled access** Yes. **Customers** Hotel guests, locals. **Hours** Daily, 5–9:30 p.m.

SETTING AND ATMOSPHERE Wooden beams, white linens, and a view of the Yacht Club's sandy lagoon make Yachtsman feel light and airy rather than dark and masculine like the typical steakhouse. Beef is the star, of course, but there are other options on the menu.

HOUSE SPECIALTIES Bread service with roasted sweet garlic.

SUMMARY AND COMMENTS We've visited twice after Yachtsman reopened. Neither visit went well. The kitchen struggled with the basics of flavor and temperature. The prices are simply too high to accept for the quality of the food that's being produced here. Try **Shula's** over at the Dolphin instead.

Yak & Yeti Restaurant ★★★

PAN-ASIAN	EXPENSIVE	QUALITY ★★★	VALUE ★★
READER-SURVEY RESPONSES ✪ 94% (Much Above Average)			

Asia, Animal Kingdom; ☎ 407-939-3463

Reservations Strongly recommended. **Dining Plan credits** 1 per person, per meal. **When to go** Dinner. **Cost range** $21–$38 (child $11). **Service** ★★★★. **Friendliness** ★★★★. **Parking** Animal Kingdom lot. **Bar** Full service. **Wine selection** Limited. **Dress** Casual. **Disabled access** Yes. **Customers** Theme park guests. **Hours** Daily, 10:30 a.m.–6:50 p.m.

SETTING AND ATMOSPHERE A rustic two-story Nepalese inn—with seating for hundreds. Windows on the second floor overlook the Asia section of the theme park.

HOUSE SPECIALTIES Lo mein bowls, coconut shrimp, chicken tikka masala.

OTHER RECOMMENDATIONS Try the Korean fried chicken tenders or the firecracker shrimp.

SUMMARY AND COMMENTS The food isn't groundbreaking, but Yak & Yeti is one of the highest-rated sit-down restaurants in a theme park. Sitting at the bar with a Pink Himalayan cocktail and a basket of egg rolls is the perfect escape from Animal Kingdom madness. Note the early closing time.

DINING *outside*
WALT DISNEY WORLD

UNOFFICIAL GUIDE RESEARCHERS LOVE good food and invest a fair amount of time scouting new places to eat. And because food at Walt Disney World is so expensive, we (like you) have an economic incentive for finding palatable meals outside the World. Alas, the surrounding area isn't exactly a culinary mecca. If you thrive on the fare at fast food and chain restaurants (Denny's, Olive Garden, TGI Friday's, and the like), you'll be as happy as an alligator at a chicken farm. But if you're in the market for a superlative dining experience, you'll find the pickings outside the World of about the same quality as those inside, only less expensive. Plus, you'll find some ethnic cuisines that aren't represented in WDW restaurants.

Among specialty restaurants both in and out of the World, location and price will determine your choice. Our recommendations for specialty and ethnic fare served outside of the World are summarized in the table that starts on page 363.

IN OR OUT OF THE WORLD FOR THESE CUISINES?
AMERICAN Good selections both in and out of the World.
BARBECUE Better out of the World.
BUFFETS A toss-up—Disney buffets are expensive but offer excellent quality and variety. Out-of-World buffets aren't as upscale but are inexpensive.
CHINESE Better out of the World.
FRENCH Toss-up; good but expensive both in and out of the World.
GERMAN Passable but not great, in or out of the World.
ITALIAN Tie on quality; better value out of the World.
JAPANESE/SUSHI **Teppan Edo** in the Japan Pavilion in EPCOT is tops for teppanyaki (table grilling). For sushi and sashimi, try **Tokyo Dining,** also in Japan, or visit **Morimoto Asia** at Disney Springs.
MEXICAN **La Hacienda de San Angel** in EPCOT is good but expensive, with more affordable food right next door at the quick-service **La Cantina de San Angel.** For decent Tex-Mex, try **El Patron** outside the World.
MIDDLE EASTERN More choices and better value out of the World.
SEAFOOD Toss-up.
STEAK/PRIME RIB Try **The Boathouse** at Disney Springs or **The Capital Grille** on International Drive out of the World. For more-affordable but nevertheless delicious wads o' meat, try one of the **Black Angus** steakhouses on FL 535 in Lake Buena Vista, on International Drive, or on West Irlo Bronson Memorial Highway in Kissimmee.

Better restaurants outside the World cater primarily to adults. That's a plus, however, if you're looking to escape children or you want to eat in peace and quiet.

DINING IN UNIVERSAL CITYWALK

DINING AND SHOPPING are the focus at CityWalk, whose restaurants tend to cater more to adult tastes than the theme park restaurants do. Probably the best of the bunch is **Vivo,** but each restaurant has a couple of decent options if you know what to look for. One thing all of them have in common is noise: Your fussy toddler will have to fight to be heard in some of these places. Most restaurants at CityWalk and inside the parks use **Zomato** via universalorlando.com for online reservations, and you can make reservations for the other venues with **OpenTable** (see page 278).

ANTOJITOS (83%/Much Below Average) ☎ 407-224-2690; tinyurl.com /antojitosuniversal. The name means "little cravings," the Mexican equivalent of Spain's tapas, so it's only natural that the best dishes are the appetizers. Try the esquites, roasted corn on the cob with Cotija cheese and jalapeño mayo. Antojitos carries more than 200 tequila brands and makes a tasty margarita too.

BIGFIRE (85%/Much Below Average) ☎ 407-224-2074; tinyurl.com /bigfirecitywalk. The decor features blazing hearths and open fire pits—both odd choices given Orlando's infamous humidity. The "elevated American fare" focuses on steaks and freshwater fish wood-grilled over open flames.

continued on page 365

Where to Eat Outside Walt Disney World

AMERICAN

• **THE RAVENOUS PIG** 565 W. Fairbanks Ave., Winter Park; ☎ 407-628-2333; theravenouspig.com; moderate–expensive. Closed Monday. New American cuisine; award-winning menu changes seasonally. Online ordering and curbside pickup.

• **SEASONS 52** 7700 W. Sand Lake Road, Orlando; ☎ 407-354-5212; seasons52.com; moderate–expensive. Delicious, creative New American food that's low in fat and calories. Extensive wine list. Online ordering and curbside pickup.

• **SLATE** 8323 W. Sand Lake Road, Orlando; ☎ 407-500-7528; slateorlando.com; moderate–expensive. Combines intimacy and casual dining with greater success than many Restaurant Row establishments. Grab a quick bite from the extensive menu or try heartier fare from the copper-clad wood oven. Delivery via Grubhub.

BARBECUE

• **BUBBALOU'S BODACIOUS BAR-B-QUE** 5818 Conroy Road, Orlando (near Universal Orlando); ☎ 407-295-1212; bubbalous.com; inexpensive. Tender, smoky barbecue; tomato-based Killer Sauce. Online ordering. Delivery via DoorDash, Grubhub, and Uber Eats.

• **4 RIVERS SMOKEHOUSE** 874 W. Osceola Pkwy., Kissimmee, and six area locations; ☎ 844-474-8377; 4rsmokehouse.com; inexpensive. Closed Sunday. Award-winning brisket, plus fried okra, cheese grits, and collards. Outdoor seating available. Online ordering, curbside pickup, and drive-thru.

CARIBBEAN

• **BAHAMA BREEZE** 8849 International Dr., Orlando; ☎ 407-248-2499; 8735 Vineland Ave.; ☎ 407-938-9010; bahamabreeze.com; moderate. Chain-restaurant Caribbean fare from the owners of Olive Garden and LongHorn Steakhouse. Patio seating available. Use call-ahead seating to check wait time. Online ordering.

CUBAN/SPANISH

• **COLUMBIA** 649 Front St., Celebration; ☎ 407-566-1505; columbiarestaurant.com; moderate–expensive. Authentic Cuban and Spanish creations, including paella and the famous 1905 Salad. One of our favorite places in Celebration. Outdoor seating available.

• **CUBA LIBRE** 9101 International Dr. at Pointe Orlando; ☎ 407-226-1600, cubalibre restaurant.com; moderate. Upscale, like Columbia above, it specializes in ceviche, tapas, and classic Cuban main courses ranging from $20 to $32. Salsa dancing until 2 a.m. on Fridays and 2:30 a.m. on Saturdays.

• **HAVANA'S CAFÉ** 8544 Palm Pkwy., Orlando; ☎ 407-238-5333, havanascubancuisine .com; moderate. Authentic homemade Cuban cuisine and Bob and Len's personal favorite. We've had several Orlando-area Cuban Americans email us to say, "There's a hole-in-the-wall place on Palm Parkway you need to try," and they always mean Havana's. Reservations recommended. Outdoor seating available. Takeout available. Delivery via Uber Eats and Grubhub.

ETHIOPIAN

• **NILE ETHIOPIAN RESTAURANT** 7048 International Dr., Orlando; ☎ 407-354-0026; nileorlando.com; inexpensive–moderate. Authentic stews and delicious vegetarian dishes. Bob's favorite Orlando/WDW-area restaurant. Curbside pickup available. Delivery via Grubhub.

• **SELAM ETHIOPIAN & ERITREAN CUISINE** 5494 Central Florida Pkwy., Orlando; ☎ 407-778-3119; ethiopianrestaurantorlando.com; inexpensive–moderate. Closed Tuesday. The dishes here are a little spicier than the ones at Nile (see above). Specialties from Eritrea (Ethiopia's neighbor to the north) provide some nice variety. Outdoor seating available. Delivery via Grubhub, Uber Eats, and DoorDash.

GREEK

• **TAVERNA OPA ORLANDO** 9101 International Dr., Orlando; ☎ 407-351-8660; opaorlando.com; moderate. Try traditional Greek standouts like pastitsio, boureki, and moussaka, along with kebabs and seafood specialties cooked on a wood fire. Live entertainment many nights. Reservations available online or via OpenTable. Delivery via DoorDash and Uber Eats.

continued on next page

Where to Eat Outside Walt Disney World (continued)

INDIAN

- **TABLA CUISINE** 5847 Grand National Dr., Orlando; ☎ 407-248-9400; tablacuisine .com; moderate. Within the Clarion Inn on I-Drive, but don't let that keep you away from one of the better Indian restaurants in the area. The menu also includes Chinese and Thai dishes. Online ordering, curbside pickup, and delivery available.

ITALIAN

- **ANTHONY'S COAL FIRED PIZZA AND WINGS** 8031 Turkey Lake Road, Orlando; ☎ 407-363-9466; acfp.com; inexpensive. Pizzas, eggplant, wings, sandwiches, beer, and wine. Online wait list and ordering. Delivery via Uber Eats, but coal-fired pizza doesn't travel well.

- **BICE RISTORANTE ORLANDO** Loews Portofino Bay Hotel, Universal Orlando Resort, 5601 Universal Blvd., Orlando; ☎ 407-503-1415; bice-orlando.com; expensive. Authentic Italian and great wines. Excellent service—we've never had a bad meal here. Reservations required. Outdoor seating available.

- **PEPERONCINO CUCINA** 7988 Via Dellagio Way, Orlando; ☎ 407-440-2856; facebook.com/peperoncinoorlando; moderate. Calabrian chef Barbara Alfano runs a tight and authentic kitchen, creating pastas and wood-fired pizzas worthy of the name. Reservations available. Outdoor seating available. Delivery via Uber Eats.

JAPANESE/SUSHI

- **HANAMIZUKI** 8255 International Dr., Ste. 136, Orlando; ☎ 407-363-7200; hana mizuki.us; moderate–expensive. Pricey but authentic. Takeout available. Delivery via DoorDash, Grubhub, and Uber Eats.

- **NAGOYA SUSHI** 7600 Dr. Phillips Blvd., Ste. 66, in the very rear of The Marketplace at Dr. Phillips; ☎ 407-248-8558; nagoyasushi.com; moderate. Closed Monday. Small, intimate restaurant with great sushi and an extensive menu. Reservations available by phone or online. Takeout available. Delivery via DoorDash and Uber Eats.

LATIN

- **SOFRITO LATIN CAFE** 8607 Palm Pkwy., Orlando; ☎ 407-778-4205; sofritocafe .com; inexpensive. Located near the corner of FL 535 and Palm Parkway, Specializes in comfort foods from Argentina, Brazil, Chile, Colombia, Cuba, Dominican Republic, Peru, Puerto Rico, and Venezuela. Atmosphere is modern but sterile. The best play is to order takeout. Outdoor seating available. Delivery via DoorDash.

MEXICAN

- **EL PATRON** 12167 S. Apopka–Vineland Road, Orlando; ☎ 407-238-5300; elpatron orlando.com; moderate. Family-owned restaurant serving freshly prepared Mexican dishes. Full bar. Weekend brunch buffet and weekday lunch buffet, with the buffet now served by staff. Outdoor seating available. Online reservations, takeout, and delivery available. The all-you-can-eat Taco Tuesdays should be a national holiday.

- **EL TENAMPA MEXICAN RESTAURANT** 4565 W. Irlo Bronson Memorial Hwy., Kissimmee; ☎ 407-397-1981; inexpensive. Family-owned, with an extensive menu of authentic Mexican regional fare in a small, colorful room. Try their steak dish called Arrachera el Tenampa. Outdoor seating available. Takeout and delivery available. Delivery also via DoorDash and Grubhub.

MOROCCAN

- **MERGUEZ** 11951 International Dr., Orlando; ☎ 407-778-4343; merguezrestaurant .com; inexpensive. Bright, informal setting with adjacent alfresco option. Excellent and representative Moroccan specialties. Awesome bastillas and tagines. Couscous, following the Moroccan custom, is served on Friday only. No alcohol sold. Outdoor seating available. Takeout available. Delivery via Uber Eats.

PERUVIAN

- **EL INKA GRILL** 7600 Dr. Phillips Blvd., Orlando; ☎ 407-930-2810; elinkagrill.com; moderate. El Inka Grill features numerous ceviche and tiradito (raw fish marinated in citrus juice) preparations, including three ceviches that are grilled. Traditional Peruvian beef, fish, and chicken entrées run $17–$24, and most come with several sides. Portions are generous. Outdoor seating available. Takeout available. Delivery via DoorDash.

Where to Eat Outside Walt Disney World (continued)

SEAFOOD

- **CELEBRATION TOWN TAVERN** 721 Front St., Celebration; ☎ 407-566-2526; thecelebrationtowntavern.com; moderate. Popular hangout for locals, featuring New England–style seafood. Clam chowder and lobster rolls are big hits. Outdoor seating available. Takeout available.

STEAK

- **BULL & BEAR** Waldorf Astoria Orlando, 14200 Bonnet Creek Resort Ln.; ☎ 407-597-5413; bullandbearorlando.com; expensive. Closed Mondays; offers dinner only. Classic steakhouse with a clubby ambience. The fried chicken is life-affirming. Reservations via phone, website, or OpenTable.

- **THE CAPITAL GRILLE** Pointe Orlando, 9101 International Dr., Orlando; ☎ 407-370-4392; thecapitalgrille.com; expensive. Closed Sunday. Dry-aged steaks, good wine list, and classic decor. Curbside pickup available.

- **TEXAS DE BRAZIL** 5259 International Dr., Orlando; ☎ 407-355-0355; texasdebrazil .com; expensive. All you can eat in a Brazilian-style *churrascaria*. Filet mignon, sausage, pork, chicken, lamb, and more. Age 2 and under are free, ages 3–5 are $5, and ages 6–12 are half-price. Salad bar with 40-plus options temporarily unavailable, but salads are available to order. Takeout and delivery via website.

- **VITO'S CHOP HOUSE** 8633 International Dr., Orlando; ☎ 407-354-2467; vitoschop house.com; moderate. Offers dinner only. Upscale meatery with a taste of Tuscany. Specialty martini list, 850 wine selections, and a variety of cigars.

THAI

- **THAI SILK** 5532 International Dr., Orlando; ☎ 407-226-8997; thaisilkorlando.com; moderate. Acclaimed by Orlando dining critics for its authentic Thai dishes. Delicious vegetarian options; vegan and gluten-friendly options; impressive wine list. Takeout available. Delivery via DoorDash, Grubhub, Postmates, or Uber Eats.

- **THAI THANI** 11025 International Dr., Orlando; ☎ 407-239-9733; thaithani.net; moderate. Specializes in Thai duck dishes.

continued from page 362

BOB MARLEY—A TRIBUTE TO FREEDOM (Not enough surveys to rate) ☎ 407-224-3663; tinyurl.com/bobmarleyuniversal. Set in a replica of the singer's Jamaica home, the building is filled with memorabilia and photos showcasing his career and life. The Caribbean-inspired dishes—beef patties, yucca fries, oxtail stew, and such—aren't particularly memorable, but the laid-back atmosphere makes it worth a visit.

BUBBA GUMP SHRIMP CO. (84%/Much Below Average) ☎ 407-903-0044; bubbagump.com. A seafood-and-cocktails eatery, part of an international chain inspired by *Forrest Gump*. Shrimp and/or crab is in almost everything, with particular highlights being Mama Blue's shrimp gumbo and seafood hush pups.

THE COWFISH (89%/Average) ☎ 407-224-3663; tinyurl.com/thecow fishuniversal. An unusual combination of burger joint and sushi bar, The Cowfish is a small chain out of North Carolina that offers tasty food at reasonable prices. We like the burgers a bit more than the sushi. Try the crab Rangoon dip and the bacon coleslaw. The servers are friendly, but food delivery is painfully slow at peak times because the kitchen is undersized for the multistory dining rooms.

HARD ROCK CAFE (87%/Below Average) ☎ 407-351-7625; hardrock .com. The best meals we've had here have consisted of drinks and appetizers or desserts. The entrées—burgers, sandwiches, steaks, and such—aren't outstanding. More remarkable is the collection of music memorabilia, including a 1959 pink Cadillac revolving over the bar. It's the biggest such collection on display anywhere in the Hard Rock Cafe chain.

HOT DOG HALL OF FAME (69%/Do Not Visit) ☎ 407-224-3663; tinyurl .com/hotdoguniv. The menu is inspired by the food from baseball stadiums around the US—Kayem dogs from Boston, Sabretts from New York—served on bleacher seating with broadcasts of live and classic baseball games. Readers rate it the lowest of the CityWalk restaurants.

JIMMY BUFFETT'S MARGARITAVILLE (79%/Do Not Visit) ☎ 407-224-2155; margaritavilleorlando.com. At this boisterous tribute to the head Parrothead, the focal point is a volcano that spews margarita mix instead of lava. The food is Floridian–Caribbean, so expect lots of seafood, jerk seasoning, and Key lime pie. If you're not a Buffett fan, it isn't worth a special trip.

NBC SPORTS GRILL & BREW (82%/Much Below Average) ☎ 407-224-3663; tinyurl.com/nbcsportsgrilluniversal. With nearly 100 high-definition TVs, this is the go-to place at Universal to catch a game. The menu is surprisingly deep, with a large selection of burgers and beers (more than 100 beers, including one brewed exclusively for the restaurant).

PAT O'BRIEN'S (88%/Average) ☎ 407-224-2102; patobriens.com. Has been rated as one of the best CityWalk restaurants for several years, though it flies under the radar of many. Dueling pianos in the lounge, a full menu in the Courtyard Restaurant, those rum-filled Hurricanes throughout. Behind a facade that replicates the French Quarter original, Pat's offers NOLA classics (try the jambalaya) and massive sandwiches. The brick courtyard is a slice of the Big Easy, but noise levels are high during outdoor concerts nearby.

RED OVEN PIZZA BAKERY (89%/Average) ☎ 407-224-3663; tinyurl .com/redovenpizzabakery. Offers artisan pizza baked in a 900°F oven. Choose from white and red Neapolitan-style pies, made with San Marzano tomatoes, organic extra-virgin olive oil, buffalo mozzarella, fine-ground "00" flour, and filtered water. Pizzas run $14–$18 and serve two people.

TOOTHSOME CHOCOLATE EMPORIUM (84%/Much Below Average) ☎ 407-224-3663; tinyurl.com/toothsomekitchen. Candies, cakes, and ice-cream concoctions, plus steaks, salads, and sandwiches, served inside a whimsical Wonka-esque steampunk confectionery factory.

VIVO ITALIAN KITCHEN (88%/Average) ☎ 407-224-2318; tinyurl.com /vivoorl. CityWalk's second-highest-rated restaurant in our latest reader survey, and highly rated for a number of years prior. Surprisingly good house-made pasta (Squid Ink Seafood is outstanding), interesting cocktails, and a 2-pound cannoli for dessert. Sit by the open kitchen and watch the show.

A food court located on CityWalk's upper level offers serviceable quick bites: **Bread Box Handcrafted Sandwiches, BK Whopper Bar, Fusion Bistro Sushi and Sake Bar, Menchie's Frozen Yogurt, Moe's Southwest Grill,** and **Panda Express.**

STRONG WATER TAVERN (88%/Average) ☎ 888-503-5000; loews hotels.com/sapphire-falls-resort. Strong Water is at Universal's Sapphire Falls Resort, not CityWalk, but if you're a fan of rum and tasty tapas, it might be worth a trip. The menu features dozens of rums, mostly from the Caribbean, in individual glasses or regional flights. The Caribbean-influenced small-plates menu leans toward seafood but also includes chicken and beef at a quality better than you'd expect at a midpriced hotel. We're told all dishes are prepared on request from fresh ingredients.

BUFFETS AND MEAL DEALS OUTSIDE WALT DISNEY WORLD

BUFFETS, RESTAURANT SPECIALS, and discount dining abound in the area surrounding Walt Disney World, especially on US 192 (aka Irlo Bronson Memorial Highway) and along International Drive. Local visitor magazines, distributed free at non-Disney hotels and other places, are packed with advertisements and coupons for seafood feasts, Chinese buffets, Indian buffets, breakfast buffets, and a host of other specials. For a family trying to economize, some of the come-ons are mighty sweet. But are the places good? Is the food fresh, tasty, and appealing? Are the restaurants clean and inviting? Armed with little more than a roll of Tums, the *Unofficial* research team tried all the eateries that advertise heavily in the tourist magazines. Here's what we discovered. *Note:* To the best of our knowledge, the buffets in this section are still self-serve unless stated otherwise.

CHINESE SUPER BUFFETS If you've ever tried preparing Chinese food, especially a stir-fry, you know that split-second timing is required to avoid overcooking. It's no surprise, then, that Chinese dishes languishing on a buffet lose their freshness, texture, and flavor in a hurry.

Ichiban Buffet (5269 W. Irlo Bronson Memorial Highway; ☎ 407-396-6668; 5529 International Dr.; ☎ 407-930-8889; ichibanbuffet .com) and **Hokkaido Chinese and Japanese Buffet** (12173 S. Apopka–Vineland Road; ☎ 407-778-5188; 5737 W. Irlo Bronson Memorial Highway; ☎ 407-396-0669; hokkaidobuffetorlando.co) are the best choices in their genre. The two Hokkaido buffets are comparable, so select whichever is most convenient for you. And remember: Selections dry out the longer they sit, so seek out a popular buffet, where dishes are replenished frequently.

INDIAN BUFFETS Indian food works better on a buffet than Chinese food; in fact, it actually improves as the flavors marry. In the Disney World area, most Indian restaurants offer a buffet at lunch only—not too convenient if you're spending your day at the theme parks. If you're out shopping or taking a day off, these are worth trying: **Aashirwad Indian Cuisine** (7000 S. Kirkman Road, at the corner of International Drive; ☎ 407-370-9830; aashirwadrestaurant.com); **Ahmed Indian Restaurant** (11301 S. Orange Blossom Trail; ☎ 407-856-5970; ahmedrestaurant.com); and **Woodlands Pure Vegetarian Indian Cuisine** (6040 S. Orange Blossom Trail; ☎ 407-854-3330; woodlandsusa.com), which isn't a buffet and has a very large menu.

CHURRASCARIAS Several of these South American–style meat emporiums have sprung up along I-Drive. Our picks are **Café Mineiro** (6432 International Dr.; ☎ 407-248-2932; cafemineirosteakhouse.us/en), a Brazilian steakhouse north of Sand Lake Road, and **BoiBrazil Steakhouse** (5668 International Dr.; ☎ 407-354-0260; boibrazil.com). Both offer good food and good value. More expensive are the Argentinean churrasco specialties at **The Knife** (12501 FL 535; ☎ 321-395-4892; thekniferestaurant.com); be sure to try the sweetbreads, an Argentinean specialty rarely found in the United States. If you prefer chains, the pricey **Texas de Brazil** and **Fogo de Chão** also have locations in Orlando.

ITALIAN BUFFETS A relatively new buffet, **Oreganatta Italian Buffet** (6320 International Dr., Orlando; ☎ 407-985-4312) is advertising everywhere. It's a concept with a lot of potential, but our experience was disappointing. The average Cicis Pizza would do as well or better—and there are about half a dozen Cicis in the I-Drive, Kissimmee, and Lake Buena Vista areas.

SEAFOOD AND LOBSTER BUFFETS These affairs don't exactly fall under the category of inexpensive dining. The main draw (no pun intended) is all the lobster (and crab legs) you can eat. The problem is that, after a few minutes on the buffet line, lobsters make better tennis balls than dinner, so try to grab your lobster immediately after a fresh batch has been brought out. Because everyone's there for lobster and crab, it sometimes looks like the other buffet items have been out since the Carter administration.

Two lobster buffets are on I-Drive, and another two are on US 192 (Irlo Bronson Memorial Highway). All four do a reasonable job, but we prefer **Boston Lobster Feast** (7702 W. Irlo Bronson Memorial Highway, ☎ 407-768-1166; 6071 W. Irlo Bronson Memorial Highway, ☎ 407-396-2606; and 8731 International Dr., five blocks north of the Convention Center, ☎ 407-248-8606; bostonlobsterfeast.com). The I-Drive location is cavernous and noisy, which is why we prefer the 6071 Irlo Bronson location, where you can actually have a conversation over dinner. Dining is expensive at all three.

BREAKFAST AND ENTRÉE BUFFETS Most chain steakhouses in the area, including **Ponderosa** and **Golden Corral,** offer entrée buffets. All serve breakfast, lunch, and dinner. At lunch and dinner, you generally get the buffet when you buy an entrée; at breakfast you don't have to buy an entrée. As for the food, it's chain-restaurant quality but pretty good all the same. Prices are a bargain, and you can get in and out at lightning speed. In addition to the steakhouses, the WDW-area **Shoney's** also offers buffets. Local freebie visitor magazines are full of discount coupons for all the above restaurants.

Regarding hours, a New Hampshire reader notes the importance of checking the hours at breakfast buffets:

unofficial **TIP**
Most chain-restaurant breakfast buffets have a number of locations in the Disney World area, but their operating hours aren't always the same, so check online or call before you go.

You mention quite a few buffets for off-site dining, but it would have been nice to know their normal morning business hours. Some buffets (like Ponderosa) didn't open until 8 a.m. for breakfast. This is way too late if you're trying to get to the park for a 9 a.m. opening time.

DISNEY BUFFETS VS. OFF-SITE BUFFETS Most off-site buffets are long on selection but don't compare favorably with Disney's in terms of quality, setting, and ambience. If you're trying to save money, however, non-Disney buffets offer excellent value. Though some dishes may be below par, you should find enough that's palatable to put together a more than acceptable meal.

One outstanding exception to the above is the **Café Osceola** buffet at Rosen Shingle Creek Resort (9939 Universal Blvd., Orlando; ☎ 407-996-9939; rosenshinglecreek.com/dining). Café Osceola specializes in carved meats.

MEAL DEALS Discount coupons are available for a wide range of restaurants. **Sonny's Real Pit Bar-B-Q** is a meat eater's delight. Among its offerings, the Family Feast, $57 per family of four, includes pulled pork, plus chicken, ribs, barbecue beans, slaw, fries, corn bread, and tea. The closest Sonny's location to Walt Disney World and Universal is at 7423 S. Orange Blossom Trail in Orlando (☎ 407-859-7197; sonnysbbq.com). No coupons are available (or needed) for Sonny's, but they're available for other "meateries."

COUPONS Find discounts and two-for-one coupons for many of the restaurants mentioned in the free visitor guides available at most hotels outside Walt Disney World. **Visit Orlando** (☎ 407-363-5800; visitorlando.com) offers discounts and information on its website and by phone. In Kissimmee, visit the **Osceola County Welcome Center and History Museum** (4155 W. Vine St.; ☎ 407-396-8644; osceola history.org; open daily [except holidays], 10 a.m.–4 p.m.).

The Great Orlando Pizza Scam

Plenty of reputable local pizza joints deliver to hotels in and around the theme parks; many Disney and Universal resorts offer pizza delivery as well. But for a few years now, con artists have been distributing flyers advertising pizza delivery to hotel guests—they ask for your credit card number over the phone, but the pizza never arrives. Disregard any such flyers you find.

WALT DISNEY WORLD *with* KIDS

The **ECSTASY** *and the* **AGONY**

TRUE STORY: Bob was inspired to write the original *Unofficial Guide to Walt Disney World* after screwing up his family's first Disney trip. Len's didn't go any better.

It's safe to say that most of the *Guide,* and especially this chapter, is based on real-world experience: what we and our readers have learned by making every possible mistake in Walt Disney World. If you prepare the best you can and don't beat yourself up when something goes wrong, there will be moments of pure magic.

When it comes to Walt Disney World, parents and kids alike are likely to get revved up about a visit to this special place—all you have to do is watch a WDW commercial to see what we mean. But the reality of doing so, particularly during the summer, can be closer to agony than to ecstasy.

An Ohio mother who took her 5-year-old one summer recalls:

I felt so happy and excited before we went, but when I look back I think I should have had my head examined. The first day we went to the Magic Kingdom, it was packed. By 11 in the morning, we had walked so far and stood in so many lines that we were all exhausted. Kristy cried about going on anything that looked or even sounded scary and was frightened by all of the Disney characters (they're so big!) except Minnie and Snow White.

We got hungry about the same time as everyone else, but the lines for food were too long and my husband said we'd have to wait. By 1 in the afternoon, we were just plugging along, not seeing anything we were really interested in, but picking rides because the lines were short or because it was air-conditioned. At around 2:30, we finally got something to eat, but by then we were so hot and tired that it felt like we had worked in the yard all day. At the end, we were so P.O.'d and uncomfortable that we weren't having any fun.

Before you stiffen in denial, let us assure you that this family's experience is not unusual. Most young children are as picky about rides as they are about what they eat, and many preschoolers are intimidated by the Disney characters. Few humans (of any age) are mentally or physically equipped to march all day in a throng of 60,000-plus people in the Florida heat and humidity. And would it surprise you to learn that almost 60% of preschoolers said the thing they liked best about their Disney trip was the hotel swimming pool?

unofficial **TIP**
When considering a trip to Walt Disney World, think about whether your kids are old enough to enjoy what can be a very fun but taxing trip.

With good planning and a sense of humor, you'll be emailing us messages like this one from a Harrisburg, Pennsylvania, mom:

I knew it would be fun for my daughter, but what I didn't expect was just how much fun it would be for me.

REALITY TESTING: WHOSE DREAM IS IT?

REMEMBER WHEN YOU WERE A KID and you got that nifty remote-control car or collector Barbie for Christmas—the one you weren't allowed to play with? Did you wonder who the gift was really for? Ask yourself a similar question about your vacation to Walt Disney World. Whose dream are you trying to make come true: yours or your child's?

Young children are experts at reading their parents' emotions. When you ask, "Honey, how would you like to go to Disney World?" your child will respond more to your smile and enthusiasm than to any notion of what Disney World is all about. The younger the child, the more this holds true. From many preschoolers, you could elicit the same excitement by asking, "Sweetie, how would you like to go to Cambodia on a dogsled?"

So is your happy fantasy of introducing your child to Disney magic a pipe dream? Well, not necessarily—but you have to be open to reality testing. For example, would you increase the probability of a successful visit by waiting a year or two? Will your child have sufficient endurance and patience to cope with long lines and large crowds?

RECOMMENDATIONS FOR MAKING THE DREAM COME TRUE

WHEN YOU'RE PLANNING a Walt Disney World vacation with young children, consider the following:

AGE Although Disney World's color and festivity excite all children, and specific attractions delight toddlers and preschoolers, its entertainments are generally oriented to older kids and adults. Children should be a fairly mature 7 years old to *appreciate* the Magic Kingdom and Animal Kingdom, and a year or two older to get much out of EPCOT or Hollywood Studios.

Readers continually debate how old a child should be or the ideal age to go to Disney World. A Rockaway, New Jersey, mom writes:

> *Our hotel pool was the one and only thing our kids enjoyed. I had planned and saved for this trip for over a year, and I cried all week at the realization that our kids just wanted to swim.*

A Lawrenceville, Georgia, mother of two toddlers emphasizes the importance of maintaining your kids' regular schedule:

> *The first day, we tried your suggestion about an early start, so we woke the kids (ages 4 and 2) and hurried them to get going. BAD IDEA. This put them off-schedule for naps and meals the rest of the day.*

A Pennsylvania mom with two young kids recounts her experience:

> *Eighteen months is the absolute worst age to bring a child to Disney. They have no concept of waiting in lines, can't stand the heat, will not sit in a stroller, only want to be carried, and only want to go up and down the stairs outside of the attraction you want to ride. Expect lots of meltdowns, and good luck with the baby swap when they have to go to someone else. (Mom didn't get to do much.)*

WHEN TO VISIT Avoid the hot, crowded summer months, especially if you have preschoolers. Go in November (except Thanksgiving), early December, January, or February (except Mardi Gras and Presidents' Day). Or try October and May, which are hot but less crowded than summer. If your children can't afford to miss school, try late August, before school starts; crowds and hotel rates should be lower. We should warn you, however, that staff shortages (which reduce the number of guests an attraction can handle in a day), special festivals and events, and attraction breakdowns can combine to make the parks seem crowded irrespective of the time of year. Concerning ride breakdowns, a mom from Springville, Alabama, says:

> *We had a lot of rides with tech problems: Pirates of the Caribbean, Winnie the Pooh, Avatar Flight of Passage, Peter Pan's Flight, and Spaceship Earth. VERY frustrating. We spent over 3 hours in line just for Flight of Passage. It made other rides less fun when a ride would just stop in the middle and lose the magic.*

If you have children of varying ages and they're good students, take the older ones out of school and visit during the cooler, less congested off-season. Most readers who have tried this at various times agree. A New Hampshire parent writes:

> *I took my grade-school children out of school for a few days to go during a slow time and highly recommend it. We communicated with the teachers about a month before traveling to seek their preference for whether classwork and homework should be completed before, during, or after our trip. It's so much more enjoyable to be at Disney when your children can experience rides and attractions and all that is Disney rather than standing in line.*

There's another side to this story, and we've received some well-considered letters from parents and teachers who don't think taking kids out of school is such a hot idea. From a father in Fairfax, Virginia:

> My wife and I are disappointed that you seem to be encouraging families to take their children out of school to go to WDW. My wife is an eighth-grade teacher of chemistry and physics. She has parents pull their children, some honor-roll students, out of school for vacations, only to discover when they return that the students are unable to comprehend the material.

A Martinez, California, teacher offers a compelling analogy:

> There are a precious 180 days for us as teachers to instruct our students, and there are 185 days during the year for Disney World. I've seen countless students struggle to catch up the rest of the year due to a week of vacation. The analogy I use with my students' parents is that it's like walking out of a movie after watching the first 5 minutes, then returning for the last 5 minutes and trying to figure out what happened.

But a teacher from Penn Yan, New York, sees things differently:

> As a teacher and a parent, I disagree that it's horrible for a parent to take a child out for a vacation. If a parent takes the time to let us know that a child is going to be out, we help them get ready for upcoming homework the best we can. If the child is a good student, why shouldn't they go have a wonderful experience with their family?

If possible, ask your child's teacher for a list of topics they'll be covering while you're away. Have your child study these on the plane or in the car, during midday breaks, and at night before bed.

BUILD NAPS AND REST INTO YOUR ITINERARY By a wide margin, the thing most parents say they learned during their first Disney visit was the importance of daily breaks and naps.

unofficial **TIP**
If you must rent a car to make returning to your hotel practicable, do it.

Why? The parks and crowds can be huge, and inevitably someone is going to run out of steam. And when that someone isn't happy, nobody's happy. Pushing the tired or discontented beyond their capacity will spoil the day for them *and* you. Go back to your hotel midday to rest and relax, then return to the park (or hop to another) in the late afternoon or early evening.

A family from Texas underlines the importance of naps and rest:

> Probably the most important tip your guide gave us was going to the hotel to swim and regroup during the day. The parks became unbearable by noon—and so did my husband and boys. The hotel was an oasis that calmed our nerves! After about 3 hours of playtime, we headed out to a different park for dinner and a cool evening of fun.

Regarding naps, this mom doesn't mince words:

> Take the book's advice, get out of the park, and take the nap, take the nap, TAKE THE NAP!

A mom from Chicago offers a suggestion:

With small children, two days on, one day off is helpful. We did three park days in a row, with travel days on either end, and our third day was a waste for the 5-year-old—she was tired and sick of walking, and she and I ended up only doing a few rides while everyone else went off and had fun. If I'd thought through that, we would have made one of the travel days a park day and had a pool day in the middle.

Be prepared for someone to get tired and irritable. Call time-out when it happens, and trust your instincts: What would feel best—another ride, an ice-cream break, or going back to the room for a nap?

WHERE TO STAY If you're going to take midday breaks, you'll be making two trips per day to the theme parks, so you'll want to book a hotel that's within a 20-minute drive. This doesn't necessarily mean you have to lodge inside Disney World. Because the World is so geographically dispersed, many off-site hotels are closer to the parks than some Disney resorts (see our Hotel Information Table, pages 254–265, showing commuting times from Disney and non-Disney hotels).

If you want to stay in Walt Disney World, we recommend the **Polynesian Village & Villas, Grand Floridian & Villas,** or **Wilderness Lodge & Boulder Ridge/Copper Creek Villas** (in that order), if they fit your budget. The **Contemporary Resort, Bay Lake Tower, Polynesian Village & Villas,** and **Grand Floridian & Villas** are within walking distance of the Magic Kingdom; the downside is that they're expensive and the theming of some hotels may not appeal to kids.

For less expensive rooms, try **Port Orleans French Quarter.** The least expensive on-site rooms are at the **All-Star Resorts. All-Star Music** and **Art of Animation** also have two-room Family Suites that can sleep up to six and provide kitchenettes. Log cabins at **Fort Wilderness Resort & Campground,** along with the DVC resorts, are another option for families who need a little more space. Outside the World, check out our top hotels for families (see page 229), but know that many good options exist in addition to these.

BUILDING ENDURANCE Though most kids are active, their normal play usually doesn't condition them for the exertion required to tour a Disney park. Start family walks four to six weeks before your trip to get in shape. A mother from Wescosville, Pennsylvania, reports:

We had our 6-year-old begin walking with us a bit every day one month before leaving—when we arrived at Disney World, her little legs could carry her, and she had a lot of stamina.

From a Middletown, Delaware, mom:

You recommended walking for six weeks prior to the trip, but we began months in advance, just because. My husband lost 10 pounds, my daughter never once complained, and we met a lot of neighbors!

At the very least, run a little test, say a 6-mile walk or hike, to establish your family's baseline level of fitness. Be safe. Many find out the hard way that they're not as fit as they think. As a postscript, 6 miles is less ground than most cover in a Disney park.

SETTING LIMITS AND MAKING PLANS To avoid arguments and disappointments, establish guidelines for each day and get everybody committed. Include the following:

1. Wake-up time and breakfast plans
2. When to depart for the park and what to take with you
3. A policy for splitting the group or for staying together, and what to do if the group gets separated or someone is lost
4. What you want to see, including plans in the event that an attraction is closed or too crowded
5. A policy on what you can afford for snacks
6. How long you plan to tour in the morning and what time you'll return to your hotel to rest
7. When you'll return to the park and how late you'll stay
8. Dinner plans
9. A policy for buying souvenirs, including who pays (kids or parents)
10. Bedtimes

BE FLEXIBLE Any day at Disney World includes surprises, so be prepared to adjust your plan. Listen to your intuition.

MAINTAINING SOME SEMBLANCE OF ORDER AND DISCIPLINE

DISCIPLINE AND ORDER are more difficult to maintain when traveling than at home because everyone is, as a Boston mom puts it, "in and out"—in strange surroundings and out of the normal routine. For kids, it's hard to contain the excitement and anticipation that pop to the surface in the form of fidgety hyperactivity, nervous energy, and (sometimes) acting out. Confinement in a car, plane, or hotel room only exacerbates things.

Once you're in the theme parks, it doesn't get much better. There's more elbow room, but there are also crowds, overstimulation, heat, and miles of walking. All this, coupled with marginal or inadequate rest, can lead to meltdowns in the most harmonious of families.

Sound parenting and standards of discipline practiced at home, applied consistently, will suffice to handle most situations on vacation. Still, you need to study the hand you're dealt when traveling. For starters, aside from being jazzed and ablaze with adrenaline, your kids may believe that rules followed at home can be suspended when away from it. Parents may reinforce this misguided intuition by being overly lenient in the name of keeping the peace.

While select house rules—cleaning your plate, going to bed at a set time—can safely be relaxed on vacation, tossing your normal approach to discipline out the window can precipitate major misunderstanding and possibly disaster.

Kids, being kids, are likely to believe that a vacation to Walt Disney World is intended just for them—and that can dramatically increase their sense of shock and hurt when you have to correct them or tell them no. An incident that would hardly elicit a pouty lip at home could well escalate to tears or defiance when traveling. It's important before you depart on your trip, therefore, to discuss the ground rules with your children, and to explore their wants and expectations as well.

According to *Unofficial Guide* child psychologist Karen Turnbow, PhD, addressing behavioral problems on the road begins with a clear-cut disciplinary policy at home, based on the following key concepts:

1. LET EXPECTATIONS BE KNOWN Discuss what you expect from your children as far as complying with parental directives, treatment of siblings, resolution of disputes, schedules (including waking up and bedtime), manners, staying together, and who pays for what.

2. EXPLAIN THE CONSEQUENCES OF NONCOMPLIANCE Be clear and firm: "If you do X (or don't do X), this is what will happen."

3. GIVE THEM A WARNING You're dealing with excited, expectant children, not machines, so it's important to issue a warning before meting out discipline. And by *warning*, we mean just one—multiple warnings without consequences not only undermine your credibility but also effectively put your child in control of things.

4. FOLLOW-THROUGH A corollary to the above: If you say you're going to do something, *do it*. Children must understand that you mean what you say.

5. CONSISTENCY Random discipline encourages random behavior, which in turn translates to a near total loss of parental control. Long-term, both at home and on the road, your response to a given situation or transgression must be both predictable and reliable.

Active Listening and a Feeling Vocabulary

Whining, tantrums, defiance, and holding up the group aren't just things your kids do to drive you nuts; they're also methods your kids use to communicate with you. Taken at face value, a fit may *seem* to be about the ice cream you refused to buy little Beulah, but there's almost always something deeper bubbling just beneath the surface. And as often as not, the root cause is a need for attention. This need is so powerful in some kids that they willingly subject themselves to punishment to get that attention—even if it's negative.

Getting at the root causes of unwanted behaviors involves two important concepts. **Active listening** involves not only being alert to what a child says but also tuning in to the context in which it's said, to the words used and possible subtext, to the child's emotional state and body language, and even to what's *not*

> *unofficial* **TIP**
> Teaching your kids to tell you clearly what they want or need will help make the trip more enjoyable for everyone.

said. Similarly, helping children develop a **feeling vocabulary** involves teaching them to express their emotions in words, not tantrums. If you've ever heard a parent encourage a child to "use your words," that's what we mean.

Kids are almost never too young to start developing a feeling vocabulary. And helping them get in touch with—and to communicate—their emotions will stimulate you to focus on *your* feelings and mood states in a similar way. With persistence and effort, the whole family can achieve a vastly improved ability to communicate.

A Shelby, North Carolina, reader touts a resource for parents:

> *I use a therapy technique at work called the* **Alert Program** *that helps kids develop self-regulation skills, including a feeling vocabulary. The website (alertprogram.com) provides an explanation and additional resources [some for free, most for sale]. You can use many analogies to make it work, but an especially fun one is to use Disney characters: A child might feel like Winnie the Pooh if he's "just right," Tigger if he's hyper or needs a movement break, or Eeyore if he's feeling tired or sad.*

Dealing with Negative Behaviors

Until you and your child get the hang of active listening and a feeling vocabulary, you need to be careful not to become part of the problem —yelling, nagging, guilt-tripping, and getting physical only make things worse. Responding appropriately in a disciplinary situation requires thought and preparation, so keep the following in mind when your world blows up as you wait in line for Dumbo.

1. BE THE ADULT Most kids are practiced masters when it comes to pushing their parents' buttons. If you take the bait and respond with a tantrum of your own, you're no longer the adult in the room; worse, you suggest by your example that ranting and raving is acceptable behavior. No matter what happens, remind yourself, "I'm the adult here."

2. FREEZE THE ACTION Instead of responding to your kids' provocations in kind, and at a comparable maturity level, what you need to do is (to borrow a sports term) freeze the action. This usually means initiating a time-out (see "Frequent Acting Out," below). Find a place, preferably one that's private, to sit your child down, and refrain from talking until you've both cooled off.

3. SEPARATE THE CHILD FROM THE GROUP Let the rest of the family go eat or explore without you and the child, and arrange to meet up later. In addition to letting the others get on with their day, this relieves the child of the burden of being the focus of attention—and the object of the rest of the family's frustration.

4. REVIEW THE SITUATION AND TAKE ACTION If, as we've recommended, you've made your expectations clear, stated the consequences of not complying, and issued a warning, review the situation with the child and follow through with the discipline warranted.

5. FREQUENT ACTING OUT Tantrums, of course, aren't always one-off events—kids often learn through experience that acting out will get them what they want. By scolding, admonishing, threatening, or negotiating, you further draw out the cycle, prolong the behavior, and cede control of the situation to your child. What's more, many kids, cunning as they are, know that pitching a fit in public is embarrassing to you, ensuring that you're more likely to cave to their demands on vacation than you would be at home.

To break the cycle, you must learn to disengage. The best ways to do this are to ignore the behavior, remove yourself from the child's presence (or vice versa), or give the child a brief time-out. This takes discipline on your part, however: At first your child may ratchet up the tantrums until they realize you mean business.

A private place is ideal for a break, but it's not absolutely necessary. You can carve out space for one almost anywhere: on a theme park bench, in a park, in your car, in a restroom, or even on a sidewalk.

Finally, you can head off an impending meltdown by giving your child attention—the key motivator behind most tantrums—before things reach an explosive emotional pitch.

6. SALVAGE OPERATIONS Kids are full of surprises, and sometimes those surprises are, well, not good. What if your sweet precious pulls a stunt so beyond the pale that it threatens to derail your entire trip? In the case of one Ohio boy visiting Disney World with his family, his offense resulted in his being grounded more or less for life. For starters, his parents split up the group: One parent escorted the miscreant back to the hotel room, where he was effectively confined for the duration. That evening, Mom and Dad arranged for in-room sitters for the rest of the stay. Expensive? Yep, but better than ruining the vacation for everybody else.

In another case, a child acted out in the Magic Kingdom, though the offense was of a lesser order of magnitude. Because it was the family's last day at Disney World, the parents elected to place the misbehaver in time-out for the rest of their day in the park—one parent would monitor the culprit while the other parent and the siblings enjoyed the attractions. At agreed-upon times, the parents would switch places.

WHAT KIDS LIKE BEST IN WALT DISNEY WORLD

WHEN IT COMES TO DISNEY WORLD, what kids want is often different from what parents want: Children consistently name their hotel's pool as their favorite vacation activity, for example. Likewise, children prefer vastly different attractions in Disney's theme parks.

Elon University has offered a psychology class called "The Science of Happiness at Disney," taught by Alexis Franzese, PhD. Each student chooses a research topic that explores how Walt Disney World makes its guests happy. One student's research question asked whether boys and girls equally enjoyed meeting the Disney princesses (the short answer is yes). While looking at our reader-survey responses for this, however, we noticed something else: Kids prefer almost any character greeting, parade, or fireworks show over any ride in Walt Disney World.

The table below lists the 10 most popular attractions in the Magic Kingdom for preschool and grade-school kids from 2019 to the present. (Using these dates allows us to compensate for when character greetings were closed during the pandemic.) The only two rides that appeared in the top 10 for preschoolers are **Dumbo** and **Buzz Lightyear.** In fact, 17 of the top 20 attractions were parades, fireworks, or character greetings (the third ride was **The Magic Carpets of Aladdin**).

Grade-school kids enjoy Disney's thrill rides more, but 7 of their 10 favorite attractions were also parades, fireworks, and character greetings. While the touring plans in this edition include character greetings

KIDS' FAVORITE MAGIC KINGDOM ATTRACTIONS (2019–present)		
RANK	**PRESCHOOL**	**GRADE SCHOOL**
1	Meet Mickey Mouse at Town Square Theater	Evening fireworks
2	Pete's Silly Sideshow meet and greet	Seven Dwarfs Mine Train
3	Meet Tiana at Princess Fairytale Hall	Halloween/Christmas fireworks
4	Halloween/Christmas parades	Big Thunder Mountain Railroad
5	Meet Tinker Bell at Town Square Theater	Halloween/Christmas parades
6	Afternoon parade	Meet Mickey Mouse at Town Square Theater
7	Halloween/Christmas fireworks	Meet Tiana at Princess Fairytale Hall
8	Dumbo the Flying Elephant	Meet Cinderella at Princess Fairytale Hall
9	Meet Ariel at Her Grotto	Pete's Silly Sideshow meet and greet
10	Buzz Lightyear's Space Ranger Spin	Meet Tinker Bell at Town Square Theater

and parades, keep these survey results in mind if you don't expect to use a touring plan. Each theme park chapter contains an updated list of age-group favorites too. (For more on the Disney characters, see page 398.)

ABOUT THE *UNOFFICIAL GUIDE* TOURING PLANS

CHILDREN HAVE A SPECIAL SKILL for wreaking havoc on a schedule. During one trip with daughter Hannah, Len is certain that she entered Peter Pan's Flight wearing two shoes, but she came out with one. It took half an hour to find replacements, and their carefully crafted touring plan required seat-of-the-pants updating. This specific incident led us to change our Lines app.

If you're following a touring plan on the Lines app and something unexpected happens, just click "Optimize" when you're ready to get started again. Lines will redo your touring plan from that moment forward, based on current crowd conditions and Genie+ and Individual Lightning Lane availability. (See page 23 for more information on Lines.)

If you're following a paper-based touring plan, here's what to expect regarding some common sources of interruptions:

1. CHARACTER GREETINGS CAN SLOW DOWN THE TOURING PLANS. Lines at character greetings can be as long as those for major attractions. Consider using Genie+ (see page 60) for any character greetings that are offered.

2. OUR TOURING PLANS CALL FOR VISITING ATTRACTIONS IN A CERTAIN ORDER, OFTEN SKIPPING ATTRACTIONS ALONG THE WAY. Children don't like to skip *anything*! If something catches their eye, they want to see it right then and there. Some can be persuaded to skip attractions if parents explain their plans in advance, but other kids flip out at skipping something, particularly in Fantasyland. A mom from Charleston, South Carolina, writes:

> We didn't have much trouble following the touring plans at Hollywood Studios and EPCOT. The Magic Kingdom plan, on the other hand, turned out to be a train wreck. While we were on Dumbo, my 5-year-old saw eight dozen other things in Storybook Circus she wanted to do. Long story short: After Dumbo, there was no getting her out of there.

A mother of two from Burlington, Vermont, adds:

> My kids were very curious about the castle because we had read Cinderella at home. Whenever I wanted to leave Fantasyland, I would just say, "Let's go to the castle and see if Cinderella is there." Once we got as far as the front door to the castle, it was no problem going out to the Central Plaza and then to another land.

3. IF YOU'RE USING A STROLLER, YOU WON'T BE ABLE TO TAKE IT INTO ATTRACTIONS OR ONTO RIDES. It takes time to park and retrieve a stroller outside each attraction. Also, cast members will often move and rearrange strollers to make space, which adds to the time it takes to find yours later.

Magic Kingdom visitors often use the park's **Walt Disney World Railroad** to save on walking. The railroad, however, permits only folded strollers on board. If you're renting a Disney stroller, allow time to remove your stuff from it before boarding, and allow time at your destination to get another stroller. Read more stroller advice on page 383.

OTHER CONSIDERATIONS FOR KIDS

OVERHEATING, SUNBURN, AND DEHYDRATION are the most common problems of younger children at Walt Disney World. Carry and use sunscreen. Apply it on children in strollers, even if the stroller has a canopy. To avoid overheating, stop for rest regularly—say, in the shade, or in a restaurant or at a show with air-conditioning. Carry bottles of water (refillable bottles with screw caps are sold in all major parks for about $5; bottled water is $4).

BLISTERS AND SORE FEET are the next most common problem that First Aid treats. In addition to wearing comfortable shoes, bring along blister bandages if you or your children are susceptible to blisters. These bandages (also available at First Aid in more shapes than you can imagine) offer excellent protection, stick well, and won't sweat off. Remember that a preschooler may not say anything about a blister until it has already formed, so keep an eye on things during the day. See page 453 for more on blister prevention.

GLASSES AND SUNGLASSES If your kids (or you) wear them, attach a strap or string to the frames so the glasses will stay on during rides and can hang from the child's neck while indoors. Check Lost and Found (page 452) if they go missing.

THINGS YOU FORGOT OR RAN OUT OF The theme parks and Disney Springs sell raingear, diapers, baby formula, sunburn treatments, memory cards, and other sundries. The water parks sell towels and disposable waterproof cameras. If you don't see something you need, ask if it's in stock.

RUNNING OUT OF STEAM When Bob was preparing to hike from the Colorado River to the rim of the Grand Canyon—a 5,000-foot ascent—a park ranger advised him to mix an electrolyte-replacement powder into his water and eat an energy-boosting snack at least twice every hour. While there's not much ascending to do at Walt Disney World, battling heat, humidity, and crowds contributes to poop-out, especially with kids in the mix. Limiting calorie consumption to mealtimes just won't cut it, as this wise grandma points out:

Children who get cranky during a visit often do so from all that time and energy expended without food. Feed them! A snack at any price goes a long way toward keeping little ones happy and parents sane!

A mom from Blountville, Tennessee, says kids aren't the only ones who need an energy boost:

I offered my kid a snack every hour or so because I wanted to prevent hunger meltdowns. I also brought almonds for my husband and made him eat a snack when the kids did.

As you walk through the parks, keep these words from Len's therapist in mind: "If you hate everyone else, you probably need to eat. If you hate yourself, you probably need to sleep."

WILD THINGS Alligators can be found in almost all bodies of water in Florida, including those at Disney World. Though attacks are very rare, adults and especially kids may become targets while swimming, wading, or sitting near the water's edge. Alligators are most active when feeding in the late afternoon and evening. If you happen to see a gator in a nonthreatening situation, put as much space between you and it as possible, and keep kids close by. (In case you're wondering, alligators can run 11 mph but only for a short distance.)

BABY CARE

IN EACH OF THE MAJOR THEME PARKS, the **First Aid** and **Baby Care Centers** are located next to each other. In the **Magic Kingdom,** they're at the end of Main Street on the left, by Casey's Corner and The Crystal Palace. At **EPCOT,** they're on the World Showcase side of Odyssey Center. In **Animal Kingdom,** they're in Discovery Island, on the left just before you cross the bridge to Africa, near Creature Comforts. In **Hollywood Studios,** they're at Guest Relations inside the main entrance.

Everything necessary for changing diapers, preparing formula, and warming bottles and food is available at the Baby Care Centers. A small shop at each center sells diapers, wipes, baby food, and other things you may need. Rockers and special chairs for nursing mothers are provided. Dads are welcome, too, and can use most services; in addition, many of the men's restrooms in the major parks have changing stations.

If your baby is on formula, this Wisconsin mom has a handy tip:

We got hot water from the food vendors and mixed the formula as needed. It eliminated having to keep bottles cold and then warm them up.

Infants and toddlers are allowed in any attraction that doesn't have minimum height or age restrictions. But as a Minneapolis mom reports, some attractions are better for babies than others:

Theater and boat rides are easier for babies. Rides where there's a bar that comes down are doable, but harder—Peter Pan was our first encounter with this type of ride, and we had barely gotten situated when I realized my son might fall out of my grasp.

The same mom also advises:

We used a baby sling on our trip, and it was great when standing in lines—much better than a stroller, which you have to park before getting in line (and navigate through crowds).

NURSING Let us state unequivocally that nursing mothers are free to feed their babies whenever and wherever in Walt Disney World they choose. A Georgia mom, not sure that all nursing mothers understand this, writes:

Women have the right to nurse in public without being criticized. It's not necessary to sit through all of The Hall of Presidents to feed your child.

A Lake Charles, Louisiana, mom is more blunt:

Don't tell me that men who will do almost anything to see a boob will faint dead away at the sight of a nursing mother's breast. Ladies, feed your babies and tell the prudes to get over themselves!

FIRST AID If your child (or you) needs minor medical attention, go to a **First Aid Center.** Staffed by registered nurses, the centers treat everything from paper cuts to allergic reactions in addition to sunburns and blisters. Basic over-the-counter meds are often available free in small quantities too.

STROLLERS

THE NEED FOR STROLLERS at Walt Disney World is a hot topic among families with kids. Some parents, in fact, don't realize just how important strollers are until they take their first trip to the World.

Walt Disney World Stroller Policy

The size limit for strollers in the theme parks is **31 inches wide by 52 inches long.** Stroller wagons, both pull and push models, are prohibited.

Strollers for Older Kids

It's not just the parents of babies and toddlers who rent strollers in the parks: Many parents tell us that they use them with kids who are well past needing them at home. If that seems odd, consider that a typical day in the parks requires at least a few miles of walking, which most kids don't do regularly (see "Building Endurance," page 375). A New Lenox, Illinois, family advocates this approach:

> If your kids are 8 or under, rent strollers for all of them! My husband suggested getting a stroller for our 6-year-old and the two "babies" (ages 3 and 4). We plowed through crowds, and the kids didn't get nearly as tired since they could be seated whenever they wanted.

Other readers, like this Toronto mom, bristle at the thought:

> Stop recommending that parents get strollers for kids over the age of 5. Kids who are in school can easily walk. I've never seen so many big kids in strollers in my life.

A mom from Chicago recalls:

> It seemed like everyone under 8 and over 60 was being pushed around, making it much harder for us—especially our 5- and 7-year-olds—to navigate on foot.

You have three options for using a stroller in Walt Disney World: renting or buying from Disney, bringing your own, or renting from a third party. We discuss the pros and cons of each option next.

DISNEY RENTS STROLLERS at all four WDW theme parks and at Disney Springs, and improved stroller models were introduced in 2021. To see what these strollers look like, Google "rental strollers at Walt Disney World." A single stroller costs $15 per day with no deposit, $13 per day for multiday rental; double strollers cost $31 per day with no deposit, $27 per day for multiday rental; note that stroller rentals at Disney Springs require a $100 credit card deposit. Strollers are welcome at Blizzard Beach and Typhoon Lagoon, but no rentals are available.

With multiday rentals, you can skip the rental line completely after your first visit—simply head over to the stroller-pickup area, present your receipt, and you'll be wheeling out of there in no time. If you rent a stroller in the Magic Kingdom and you decide to go to EPCOT,

Disney's Animal Kingdom, or Disney's Hollywood Studios, just turn in your Magic Kingdom stroller and present your receipt at the next park. You'll be issued another stroller at no additional charge.

Note that you can rent a stroller in advance; this allows you to bypass the payment line and go straight to the pickup line. Disney resort guests can pay ahead at their resort's gift shop, so hang on to your receipts.

Pick up strollers at the **Magic Kingdom** entrance; to the left of **EPCOT**'s Entrance Plaza and at EPCOT's International Gateway; and at **Oscar's Super Service,** just inside the entrance of **Disney's Hollywood Studios**. In **Animal Kingdom,** they're at **Garden Gate Gifts,** to the right just inside the entrance. Returning a stroller is a breeze—you can ditch it anywhere in the park when you get ready to leave.

Disney's strollers might be too large for infants and many toddlers. If you still want to rent one, bring pillows, cushions, or rolled towels to buttress your child in. Because the strollers are large, they also provide a convenient place to stow water and snacks.

If you go to your hotel for a break and intend to return to the park, leave your rental in the stroller-parking area near the park entrance, marking it with something personal like a bandanna. When you return, your stroller will be waiting.

YOU CAN BUY A STROLLER at Walt Disney World too. Most Disney parks and hotels stock the highly rated **Kolcraft Cloud** model for around

$60 (available at Walmart and online for $35 and at kolcraft.com for $52). The lightweight, collapsible Cloud has an overhead canopy for sun and rain protection, plus a mesh storage basket below the seat.

BRINGING YOUR OWN STROLLER is another option. Be aware, though, that only collapsible strollers are allowed on monorails, the Walt Disney World Railroad, parking trams, and buses.

This Secaucus, New Jersey, mom meticulously lays out the pros and cons of bringing your own stroller:

> **If your child is under age 2, bring your own stroller.** *Without one, you have to go all the way from your car to the Transportation and Ticket Center to the monorail (or ferry) to the stroller rental with your child, a diaper bag, and your own stuff in tow. But that's not half as bad as doing it in reverse on your way out, when you're exhausted, you now have purchases to carry, and the toddler who might have walked in wants to be carried out.*
>
> **WDW strollers are simply too large for most children under age 2** *to be comfortable in without significant padding, and despite being so big, they have no place to store purchases.*
>
> **If your child is past needing a diaper bag, the WDW strollers are a pretty good deal.** *They're especially good for children ages 4–6 who no longer need a stroller at home but who won't make it walking all day.*
>
> **If your child is 2 or 3, it's a toss-up.** *If you're a type-A mom like me who carries extra clothes, snacks, toys, diapers, etc., just in case, you've probably found a stroller that suits your needs and you'll be miserable with the WDW kind. If you're a type-B "we can get everything we need at the park" mom, then you'll probably be tickled with the WDW strollers.*

An Oklahoma mom found that bringing her own stroller was a hassle all around:

> *It's much easier to rent a stroller in the park. The one we brought was nearly impossible to get on the buses and was a hassle at the airport. I remember feeling dread when a bus pulled up—people look at you like you have a cage full of chickens.*

If you're bringing your own stroller to save money, you're flying, and you're checking the stroller as luggage, see if the airline's luggage fees outweigh the cost of renting or buying in Orlando.

THIRD-PARTY RENTAL OPTIONS Because Disney's stroller rentals are generally expensive, a number of Orlando rental companies have sprung up that undercut Disney's prices, provide more comfortable strollers, and deliver them to your hotel or offer pickup and drop-off at the Orlando airport. Most of the larger companies offer the same stroller models (the Baby Jogger City Mini Single, for example), so the primary differences between the companies are price and service.

Regarding service, Disney no longer allows stroller companies to drop off and pick up at a Disney hotel without the guest being physically present. Guests must meet the delivery driver for all stroller and scooter rentals. The three companies reviewed below are part of the **Disney Featured Stroller Provider** program.

unofficial **TIP**
Always ask any stroller company if you have to be present when the stroller is delivered.

We had mom and TouringPlans.com writer **Angela Dahlgren** rent strollers from different companies, use them in the parks, then return them. Her evaluations cover the overall experience, from the ease with which the stroller was rented to the delivery of the stroller, its condition upon arrival, usability in the parks, and the return process.

Kingdom Strollers (☎ 407-271-5301; kingdomstrollers.com) came in first on Angela's list, getting top marks for its website's ease of use, along with stroller selection, condition, and overall customer service. The stroller she rented was much easier to use than Disney's standard model, had more storage, and had an easier-to-use braking system. A rental of one to three nights costs $59; four to seven nights is $80. That's a five-day break-even point for choosing Kingdom Strollers over Disney's strollers.

Angela also recommends **Orlando Stroller Rentals**, LLC (☎ 800-281-0884; orlandostrollerrentals.com), which has similar prices ($65 for one to three nights and $86 for four to seven nights) and an excellent website that allows you to easily compare the features of the different strollers.

STROLLER WARS Sometimes strollers will disappear while you're enjoying a ride or watching a show. Disney staff will often rearrange strollers parked outside an attraction. This may be done to tidy up or to clear a walkway. Don't assume that your stroller is stolen because it isn't where you left it. It may be neatly arranged a few feet away—or perhaps more than a few feet away, as this Skokie, Illinois, dad reports:

> *unofficial* **TIP**
> Do **not** try to lock your stroller to a fence, post, or anything else at WDW.

> *More than once, our stroller was moved out of visible distance from the original spot. On one occasion, it was moved to a completely different stroller-parking area near another ride, and no sign or cast member was around to advise where. We had to track a cast member down to find out where it had been moved.*

Sometimes, however, strollers are taken by mistake or ripped off by people too lazy to rent their own. Don't be alarmed if your rental disappears: You won't have to buy it, and you'll be issued a new one at no charge. But while replacing a stroller is free, it's inconvenient. We heard from one Minnesota family who complained that their stroller was taken six times in one day at EPCOT and five times in a day in Hollywood Studios—even with free replacements, petty larceny on this scale represents a lot of wasted time.

Through our own experiments and readers' suggestions, we've developed a technique for hanging on to a rented stroller: Affix something personal but expendable to the handle. We tried several items and concluded that a bright, inexpensive scarf or bandanna tied to the handle works well as identification.

A multigenerational family from Utah went a step further and made their stroller difficult to heist:

> *We decorated our stroller with electrical tape to make it stand out, and my son added a small cowbell to make it clang if moved.*

A St. Louis dad pleads for tidiness:

Please tell people not to leave food and drinks in a stroller when dropping it off. The stroller parking lots turned into buffets for crows and squirrels, which is gross.

LOST CHILDREN

ALTHOUGH IT'S AMAZINGLY EASY to lose a child (or two) in the theme parks, it usually isn't a serious problem: Disney employees are schooled in handling the situation. If you lose a child, let a cast member know, and then check at the **Baby Care Center** (see page 382 for locations in each theme park) and at **City Hall** in the Magic Kingdom, where lost-children logs are kept. Paging isn't used except in an emergency, but a bulletin can be issued throughout the park(s) via internal communications. If a Disney employee encounters a lost child, they will take the child immediately to the park's Baby Care Center.

Sew a label onto each child's shirt that states his or her name, your name, the name of your hotel, and your phone number. You can also purchase custom iron-on labels, write the information on a strip of masking tape, or attach a MagicBand to the child's clothing.

An easier and trendier option is a temporary tattoo with the child's name and your phone number. Unlike labels, ID bracelets, or wristbands, the tattoos can't fall off or get lost. They last about two weeks, won't wash or sweat off, and are not irritating to the skin. Purchase online from **SafetyTat** (safetytat.com). Special tattoos are available for children with food allergies, hearing impairments, and autism spectrum disorder.

unofficial **TIP**
Children under age 14 must be accompanied by someone age 14 or older when entering Disney World's theme parks and water parks.

A Kingston, Washington, reader recommends recording vital info for each child on a plastic key tag or luggage tag and affixing it to the child's shoe. This reader also snaps a photo of the kids each morning to document what they're wearing. A Rockville, Maryland, mom shared a strategy one step short of a cattle brand:

Traveling with a 3-year-old, I was very anxious about losing him, so I wrote my cell phone number on his leg with a permanent marker. I felt much more confident that he'd get back to me quickly if he became lost.

Another way to keep track of your family is to buy each person a Disney "uniform"—in this case, the same brightly and distinctively colored T-shirt. A Yuma, Arizona, family tried this with great success:

We all got the same shirts (bright red) so that we could easily spot each other in case of separation (VERY easy to do). It was a lifesaver when our 18-month-old decided to get out of the stroller and wander off. No matter what precautions you may try, it seems there are always opportunities to lose a child, but the recognizable shirts helped tremendously.

HOW KIDS GET LOST

CHILDREN GET SEPARATED FROM THEIR PARENTS every day at Disney World under similar (and predictable) circumstances:

1. PREOCCUPIED SOLO PARENT The party's only adult is preoccupied with something like buying refreshments, reading a map, or using the restroom. Junior is there one second, gone the next.

2. THE HIDDEN EXIT Sometimes parents wait on the sidelines while two or more children experience a ride together. Parents expect the kids to exit in one place, but the youngsters pop out elsewhere. Exits from some attractions are distant from entrances. Know exactly where your children will emerge before you allow them to ride by themselves.

3. AFTER THE SHOW At the end of many shows and rides, a Disney staffer announces, "Check for personal belongings and take small children by the hand." When dozens, if not hundreds, of people leave an attraction simultaneously, it's easy for parents to lose their children unless they have direct contact.

4. POTTY PROBLEMS Mom tells 6-year-old Tommy, "I'll be sitting on this bench when you come out of the restroom." Three possibilities: One, Tommy exits through a different door and becomes disoriented (Mom may not know there's another door). Two, Mom decides she will also use the restroom, and Tommy emerges to find her gone. Three, Mom pokes around in a shop while keeping an eye on the bench but misses Tommy when he comes out.

If you can't find a companion- or family-accessible restroom, make sure there's only one exit. One specific restroom in the Magic Kingdom, on a passageway between Frontierland and Adventureland, is the all-time worst for disorienting visitors. Children and adults alike have walked in from the Adventureland side and walked out on the Frontierland side (and vice versa). Adults realize quickly that something is wrong, but kids sometimes fail to recognize the problem.

Designate an easy-to-remember meeting spot, and provide clear instructions: "I'll meet you by this flagpole. If you get out first, stay right here." Have your child repeat the directions back to you. When children are too young to leave alone, sometimes you have to think outside the box, as our Rockville, Maryland, mom did:

> It was very scary at times to be alone with children who had just turned 1 and 2. At Epcot, I left my kids with a WDW employee outside of the restroom because [I didn't think] the stroller would fit inside with me. I later found that most WDW bathrooms can accommodate a front-and-back double stroller inside the handicapped stall.

5. PARADES There are many parades and shows at which the audience stands. Children tend to jockey for a better view. By moving a little this way and that, the child quickly puts distance between you and him before either of you notices.

6. MASS MOVEMENTS Be on guard when huge crowds disperse after a fireworks presentation or parade, or at park closing. With thousands of people at once in an area, it's very easy to get separated from a child or others in your party. Use extra caution after the evening parade and fireworks, or any other day-capping event. Plan where to meet in case you get separated.

7. CHARACTER ENCOUNTERS When the Disney characters appear, children can slip out of sight, even at a meet and greet or character meal.

8. GETTING LOST IN ANIMAL KINGDOM It's especially easy to lose a child in this theme park, particularly at The Oasis entryway, on the Maharajah Jungle Trek, and on the Gorilla Falls Exploration Trail. Mom and Dad will stop to observe an animal; Junior stays close for a minute or so and then, losing patience, wanders to the exhibit's other side or to a different exhibit. Especially in the multipath Oasis, locating a lost child can be maddening, as a Safety Harbor, Florida, mother describes:

> *Manny wandered off in the paths that lead to the jungle village while we were looking at a bird. It reminded me of losing somebody in the supermarket, when you run back and forth looking down each aisle but can't find the person you're looking for because they're running around too. I was nutso before we even got to the first ride.*

DISNEY, KIDS, *and* SCARY STUFF

DISNEY RIDES AND SHOWS are adventures with universal themes: good and evil, death, beauty and ugliness, fellowship and enmity. As you sample the attractions at Walt Disney World, you'll transcend the spinning and bouncing of midway rides to encounter thought-provoking and emotionally powerful entertainment.

unofficial **TIP**
If your child has difficulty coping with the ghouls of The Haunted Mansion, then think twice about exposing him to battle scenes in Star Tours at the Studios or the carnivorous prehistoric predators in Dinosaur at Animal Kingdom.

The endings are happy ones, but given Disney's gift for special effects, these adventures often intimidate and occasionally scare young children. There are attractions with menacing witches, burning towns, skeletons, and ghouls popping out of their graves—all done with humor, provided you're old enough to understand the joke.

You can reliably predict that Walt Disney World will, at one time or another, send a young child into system overload. Be sensitive, alert, and prepared for almost anything, even behavior that is out of character for your child. Most children take Disney's more macabre trappings in stride, and others are easily comforted by an arm around the shoulder or a squeeze of the hand. Parents who know that their children tend to become upset should take it slow and easy, sampling benign adventures like the Jungle Cruise, gauging reactions, and discussing with the children how they feel about what they've seen.

Sometimes young children will try to rise above their anxiety in an effort to please their parents or siblings. This doesn't necessarily indicate mastery of fear, much less enjoyment. If your child leaves a ride in apparently good shape, ask if she'd like to go on it again—not necessarily now, but sometime. Her response should tell you all you need to know.

Evaluating children's capacity to handle the visual and tactile effects of Walt Disney World requires patience and understanding. If your child balks at or is frightened by a ride, respond

continued on page 392

SMALL-CHILD FRIGHT-POTENTIAL TABLE

THIS QUICK REFERENCE identifies attractions to be wary of if you have kids ages 3–7. Younger children are more likely to be frightened than older ones. Attractions not listed aren't frightening in any respect.

The Magic Kingdom

ADVENTURELAND

- **JUNGLE CRUISE** Moderately intense; some macabre sights. A good test attraction.
- **THE MAGIC CARPETS OF ALADDIN** Could scare kids who don't like heights if you raise your ride vehicle high in the air.
- **PIRATES OF THE CARIBBEAN** Slightly intimidating queuing area; intense boat ride with gruesome (though humorously presented) sights and a short, unexpected slide.
- **SWISS FAMILY TREEHOUSE** Anyone who's afraid of heights may want to skip it.
- *WALT DISNEY'S ENCHANTED TIKI ROOM* A thunderstorm, loud volume level, and simulated explosions frighten some preschoolers.

FRONTIERLAND

- **BIG THUNDER MOUNTAIN RAILROAD*** Visually intimidating from outside, with moderately intense visual effects. The roller coaster is wild enough to frighten many adults, particularly seniors.
- **FRONTIERLAND SHOOTIN' ARCADE** Frightening to kids who are scared of guns.
- **TIANA'S BAYOU ADVENTURE*** *(formerly Splash Mountain; opens 2024)* Visually intimidating from the outside, the ride culminates in a 52-foot plunge down a steep chute.
- **TOM SAWYER ISLAND AND FORT LANGHORN** Some very young children are intimidated by dark walk-through tunnels that can be easily avoided.

LIBERTY SQUARE

- **THE HAUNTED MANSION** The name alone raises anxiety, as do the sounds and sights of the waiting area. Intense attraction with humorously presented macabre sights. The ride itself is gentle.

FANTASYLAND

- **THE BARNSTORMER*** May frighten some preschoolers.
- **DUMBO THE FLYING ELEPHANT** Could scare kids who are afraid of heights if you raise your ride vehicle high in the air.
- **MAD TEA PARTY** Midway-type ride; can induce motion sickness in all ages.
- **THE MANY ADVENTURES OF WINNIE THE POOH** Frightens a few preschoolers.
- **SEVEN DWARFS MINE TRAIN*** May frighten some preschoolers.
- **UNDER THE SEA: JOURNEY OF THE LITTLE MERMAID** Animatronic octopus frightens some preschoolers.

TOMORROWLAND

- **ASTRO ORBITER** Visually intimidating from the waiting area, but relatively tame.
- **BUZZ LIGHTYEAR'S SPACE RANGER SPIN** May frighten some preschoolers.
- *MONSTERS, INC. LAUGH FLOOR* May frighten some preschoolers.
- **SPACE MOUNTAIN*** Very intense roller coaster in the dark; the Magic Kingdom's wildest ride and a scary coaster by any standard.
- **TOMORROWLAND SPEEDWAY*** The noise of the waiting area slightly intimidates preschoolers; otherwise, not frightening.
- **TRON LIGHTCYCLE/RUN*** Intense outdoor coaster.

EPCOT

FUTURE WORLD

- **GUARDIANS OF THE GALAXY: COSMIC REWIND*** Intense coaster in the dark.
- **JOURNEY INTO IMAGINATION WITH FIGMENT** Loud noises and unexpected flashing lights startle younger children.

*Rider Switch option provided (see page 396)

SMALL-CHILD FRIGHT-POTENTIAL TABLE (continued)

EPCOT (continued)

FUTURE WORLD (continued)

- **SOARIN' AROUND THE WORLD*** May frighten kids age 7 and under, or anyone with a fear of heights. Otherwise mellow.
- **MISSION: SPACE*** Extremely intense space-simulation ride that has been known to frighten guests of all ages.
- **THE SEAS WITH NEMO & FRIENDS** Sweet but may frighten toddlers.
- **SPACESHIP EARTH** Dark, imposing presentation intimidates a few preschoolers.
- **TEST TRACK*** Intense thrill ride that may frighten guests of any age.

WORLD SHOWCASE

- **FROZEN EVER AFTER*** Small drop at the end could scare little ones.
- **REMY'S RATATOUILLE ADVENTURE** May frighten some preschoolers.

Disney's Animal Kingdom

DISCOVERY ISLAND

- *AWAKENINGS* This nighttime show's shadows, sounds, and projections may frighten kids 5 years and younger.
- **THE TREE OF LIFE / *IT'S TOUGH TO BE A BUG!*** Intense and loud, with special effects that startle viewers of all ages and potentially terrify little kids.

AFRICA

- *FESTIVAL OF THE LION KING* A bit loud, but otherwise not frightening.
- **KILIMANJARO SAFARIS** The proximity of the animals can make a few young children anxious.

ASIA

- **EXPEDITION EVEREST*** Can frighten guests of all ages.
- *FEATHERED FRIENDS IN FLIGHT* Swooping birds may frighten a few small children.
- **KALI RIVER RAPIDS*** Potentially frightening and certainly wet for guests of all ages.
- **MAHARAJAH JUNGLE TREK** Some children may balk at the bat exhibit.

DINOLAND U.S.A.

- **DINOSAUR*** High-tech thrill ride rattles riders of all ages.
- **TRICERATOP SPIN** This midway-type ride frightens only a handful of younger kids.

PANDORA—THE WORLD OF AVATAR

- **AVATAR FLIGHT OF PASSAGE*** May frighten kids age 7 and younger, those with claustrophobia or a fear of heights, or those who are prone to motion sickness.
- **NA'VI RIVER JOURNEY*** Dark ride with imposing animatronic figures frightens some preschoolers.

Disney's Hollywood Studios

SUNSET BOULEVARD

- *FANTASMIC!* Terrifies some preschoolers.
- **ROCK 'N' ROLLER COASTER*** The wildest coaster at Walt Disney World. May frighten guests of any age.
- **THE TWILIGHT ZONE TOWER OF TERROR*** Visually intimidating to young kids; contains intense and realistic special effects. The plummeting elevator at the end frightens many adults as well as kids.

*Rider Switch option provided (see page 396)

continued on next page

SMALL-CHILD FRIGHT-POTENTIAL TABLE *(continued)*
Disney's Hollywood Studios *(continued)*

ECHO LAKE

- *INDIANA JONES EPIC STUNT SPECTACULAR!* An intense show with powerful special effects, including explosions, but young kids generally handle it well.
- *STAR TOURS—THE ADVENTURES CONTINUE** Extremely intense visually for all ages; too intense for kids under age 8.

GRAND AVENUE

- *MUPPET-VISION 3-D* Intense and loud, but not frightening.

HOLLYWOOD BOULEVARD

- *MICKEY AND MINNIE'S RUNAWAY RAILWAY* Track ride with wild twists and turns but benign visuals. May scare kids 6 and under.

TOY STORY LAND

- *ALIEN SWIRLING SAUCERS** Can induce motion sickness in riders of all ages.
- *SLINKY DOG DASH** Mild first roller coaster for most kids. May frighten preschoolers.
- *TOY STORY MANIA!* Dark ride that may frighten some preschoolers.

STAR WARS: GALAXY'S EDGE

- *MILLENNIUM FALCON:* SMUGGLERS RUN* Intense visual effects and movement.
- *STAR WARS: RISE OF THE RESISTANCE* Intense visual effects and movement for all ages.

*Rider Switch option provided (see page 396)

continued from page 389

compassionately—make clear that it's all right to be scared and that you won't think any less of your child for not wanting to ride.

What you definitely *don't* want to do is compound a child's fear and distress by coercing, belittling, or guilt-tripping, nor should you tolerate taunting or bullying from the child's siblings. A New York City psychologist speaks out on pressuring kids to ride:

> *I felt ethically torn watching parents force their children to go on rides they didn't want to ride. The Disney staff were more than willing to organize a parental swap to save these children from such abuse!*

THE FRIGHT FACTOR

WHILE EACH YOUNGSTER IS DIFFERENT, following are seven attraction elements that alone or combined could push a child's buttons and indicate that a certain attraction isn't age appropriate for that child:

1. THE NAME It's only natural that young children will be apprehensive about something called, say, The Haunted Mansion or The Twilight Zone Tower of Terror.

2. THE VISUAL IMPACT OF THE RIDE FROM OUTSIDE Tiana's Bayou Adventure (opens 2024), the Tower of Terror, and Big Thunder Mountain Railroad look scary enough to give adults second thoughts, and they terrify many little kids. A Utah grandma reports the following:

> At 5 years old, my granddaughter was willing to go on almost every-thing. The problem was with the preliminary introductions to The Haunted Mansion and the Tower of Terror. Walking through and learning the stories before the actual rides were what frightened her and made her opt out without going in. The rides themselves wouldn't have been bad—she loved Splash Mountain [now Tiana's Bayou Adventure] and Big Thunder Mountain, but she could SEE those before entering.

3. THE VISUAL IMPACT OF THE INDOOR-QUEUING AREA The caves at Pirates of the Caribbean and the dungeons and "stretch rooms" of The Haunted Mansion can frighten kids.

4. THE INTENSITY Some attractions inundate the senses with sights, sounds, movements, and even smells. Animal Kingdom's *It's Tough to Be a Bug!* show, for example, combines loud sounds, lights, smoke, and animatronic insects with 3-D cinematography to create a total sensory experience. A Johnston, Iowa, mom describes it well:

> The 3-D and 4-D experiences are way too scary for even a very brave 5-year-old girl. The shows that blew things on her, shot smells in the air, had bugs flying, etc., scared the bejesus out of her. We escorted her crying from It's Tough to Be a Bug! and Mickey's PhilharMagic.

A Gloucester, Massachusetts, mom had an on-the-spot solution:

> My 3½-year-old was afraid of The Haunted Mansion. We just pulled his hat over his face and quietly talked to him while we rode.

5. THE VISUAL IMPACT OF THE ATTRACTION Sights in various attrac-tions range from falling boulders to lurking buzzards, from grazing dinosaurs to waltzing ghosts. What one child calmly absorbs may scare the pants off another who's the same age.

6. THE DARKNESS Many Walt Disney World attractions operate indoors in the dark, which can be scary. A child who gets frightened on one dark ride (such as The Haunted Mansion) may be unwilling to try others.

7. THE PHYSICAL EXPERIENCE Some rides are wild enough to cause motion sickness, wrench backs, and discombobulate guests of any age.

A BIT OF PREPARATION

WE RECEIVE MANY TIPS from parents telling how they prepared their young children for the Disney experience. Common strategies include reading Disney books and watching Disney videos. A Lexington, Ken-tucky, mom suggests watching videos of the theme parks on **YouTube:**

> My timid 7-year-old daughter and I watched ride and show videos on YouTube, and we cut out all the ones that looked too scary.

You can also watch Walt Disney World specials produced by Dis-ney and others on Disney+, Netflix, and YouTube.

ATTRACTION AND RIDE RESTRICTIONS

THE MAGIC KINGDOM

The Barnstormer* 35″ minimum height

Big Thunder Mountain Railroad* 40″ minimum height

Seven Dwarfs Mine Train* 38″ minimum height

Space Mountain* 44″ minimum height

Tiana's Bayou Adventure *(formerly Splash Mountain)* * 40″ minimum height

Tomorrowland Speedway* 32″ minimum height to ride, 54″ to drive unassisted

Tron Lightcycle/Run* 48″ minimum height

EPCOT

Guardians of the Galaxy: Cosmic Rewind* 42″ minimum height

Mission: Space* 40″ minimum height (Green); 44″ minimum height (Orange)

Soarin' Around the World* 40″ minimum height

Test Track* 40″ minimum height

DISNEY'S ANIMAL KINGDOM

Avatar Flight of Passage* 44″ minimum height

Dinosaur* 40″ minimum height

Expedition Everest* 44″ minimum height

Kali River Rapids* 38″ minimum height

DISNEY'S HOLLYWOOD STUDIOS

Alien Swirling Saucers* 32″ minimum height

Millennium Falcon:* Smugglers Run 38″ minimum height

Rock 'n' Roller Coaster* 48″ minimum height

Slinky Dog Dash* 38″ minimum height

Star Tours—The Adventures Continue* 40″ minimum height

Star Wars: Rise of the Resistance 40″ minimum height

The Twilight Zone Tower of Terror* 40″ minimum height

DISNEY SPRINGS

Marketplace Carousel 42″ minimum height

BLIZZARD BEACH WATER PARK

Chairlift 32″ minimum height

Downhill Double Dipper 48″ minimum height

Slush Gusher* 48″ minimum height

Summit Plummet 48″ minimum height

T-Bar *(in Ski Patrol Training Camp)* 60″ maximum height

Tike's Peak children's area 48″ maximum height

TYPHOON LAGOON WATER PARK

Bay Slides 60″ minimum height

Crush 'n' Gusher 48″ minimum height

Humunga Kowabunga 48″ minimum height

Ketchakiddee Creek 48″ maximum height

Wave Pool *Adult supervision required*

*Rider Switch option provided (see page 396)

ATTRACTIONS THAT EAT ADULTS

YOU MAY SPEND SO MUCH ENERGY worrying about the kids that you forget to take care of yourself. The attractions in the table below can cause motion sickness or other issues for older kids and adults.

POTENTIALLY PROBLEMATIC ATTRACTIONS FOR GROWN-UPS
THE MAGIC KINGDOM
• Mad Tea Party • Big Thunder Mountain Railroad • Tiana's Bayou Adventure (formerly Splash Mountain) • Space Mountain • Tron Lightcycle/Run
EPCOT
• Guardians of the Galaxy: Cosmic Rewind • Mission: Space • Test Track
DISNEY'S ANIMAL KINGDOM
• Expedition Everest • Kali River Rapids • Dinosaur • Avatar Flight of Passage
DISNEY'S HOLLYWOOD STUDIOS
• Star Tours—The Adventures Continue • Rock 'n' Roller Coaster • The Twilight Zone Tower of Terror • *Millennium Falcon:* Smugglers Run • Star Wars: Rise of the Resistance

A WORD ABOUT HEIGHT REQUIREMENTS

A NUMBER OF ATTRACTIONS REQUIRE children to meet minimum height and age requirements (see opposite page). All Appeal by Age attraction ratings for preschoolers in the theme park chapters assume that the kids surveyed were tall enough to ride. All rides, regardless of height requirements, state that children under the age of 7 must have someone age 14 or older ride with them.

If you have children who don't meet the posted requirements, you have several options, including Rider Switch (see page 396). If those kids are resentful of their taller (or older) siblings who do qualify to ride, a mom from Virginia has some good advice:

> Our petite 5-year-old, to her outrage, was left out while our 8-year-old went on Splash Mountain [now Tiana's Bayou Adventure] and Big Thunder Mountain with Grandma and Granddad, and the nearby alternatives weren't helpful (too long a line for rafts to Tom Sawyer Island, etc.). The best areas had a nearby playground or other quick attractions near the rides with height requirements, like The Boneyard near Dinosaur at Animal Kingdom.

Another tip: Ask the cast member stationed at the entrance to the height-restricted attraction how long the wait will be. Now tack on 5 minutes of riding time to the wait time, then add 5 or so minutes for the riders to exit and reach your agreed-upon meeting point. This way you'll have a better sense of whether the kids who are too short to ride (and their supervising adults) will have time to do other stuff while the tall-enough members of your group experience the attraction.

Our guess is that even with the long line for the rafts, this mom would've had sufficient time to take her daughter to Tom Sawyer Island while the siblings rode Splash Mountain and Big Thunder Mountain Railroad with the grandparents. For sure, she had time to tour the Swiss Family Treehouse in adjacent Adventureland.

WAITING-LINE STRATEGIES *for* YOUNG CHILDREN

CHILDREN HOLD UP BETTER THROUGH THE DAY if you limit the time they spend in lines. Arriving early and using our touring plans are two ways to greatly reduce waiting. Here are other ways to reduce stress for children:

1. RIDER SWITCH (AKA SWITCHING OFF OR RIDER SWAP) Several attractions have minimum height and/or age requirements. Some couples with children too small or too young forgo these attractions, while others take turns riding. Missing some of Disney's best rides is an unnecessary sacrifice, and waiting in line twice for the same ride is a tremendous waste of time. Disney's solution to this problem is a system called Rider Switch. There must be at least two adults for this to work. Here's how to do it:

1. Adults and kids wait in line together.
2. When you approach the queue, tell the first ride attendant you see that you want to use Rider Switch.
3. The cast member will divide the group into those riding first and those riding second—that is, the nonriding child and up to three supervising adults.
4. The first group will enter the ride.
5. The cast member will scan the MagicBand or ticket of the adult riding second, who then waits with the nonriding child in a designated spot near the ride entrance.
6. When the first group returns, that adult takes over watching the nonriding child while the other adult returns to the Alternate Access line.
7. The cast member will scan the second group's MagicBands/tickets again, after which the group enters the ride's Alternate Access line.
8. The entire group reunites after the second group finishes the ride.

Rider Switch passes—which are digital entitlements scanned into your MagicBand or ticket—must be used on the same day they're issued. Guests may hold no more than one Rider Switch pass at a time—a pass must be redeemed before another one can be issued.

Cast members administering Rider Switch are very accommodating, as a Natick, Massachusetts, family attests:

At both Universal and Disney, the cast members were really nice about Rider Switch. If your child changes their mind at the last minute, no problem, and if they then decide they want to ride after the first part of the group has ridden, they let the full group ride together. I thought that was very nice and added needed flexibility. After all, it is hard to know two months in advance if your 8-year-old is up for the "mountains"!

2. LINE GAMES Anticipate that children will get restless in line, and plan activities to reduce the stress and boredom. In the morning, have waiting children discuss what they want to see and do during the day. Later, watch for and count Disney characters or play simple games such as 20 Questions. Games requiring pen and paper are impractical in a fast-moving line, but waiting in the holding area of a theater attraction is a different story—here, tic-tac-toe, hangman, drawing, and coloring can make the time fly.

ATTRACTIONS WHERE RIDER SWITCH IS USED
MAGIC KINGDOM
• The Barnstormer • Big Thunder Mountain Railroad • Seven Dwarfs Mine Train • Space Mountain • Tiana's Bayou Adventure *(formerly Splash Mountain, opens 2024)* • Tomorrowland Speedway • Tron Lightcycle/Run
EPCOT
• Frozen Ever After • Guardians of the Galaxy: Cosmic Rewind • Mission: Space • Soarin' Around the World • Test Track
DISNEY'S ANIMAL KINGDOM
• Avatar Flight of Passage • Dinosaur • Expedition Everest • Kali River Rapids • Na'vi River Journey
DISNEY'S HOLLYWOOD STUDIOS
• Alien Swirling Saucers • *Millennium Falcon:* Smugglers Run • Rock 'n' Roller Coaster • Slinky Dog Dash • Star Tours—The Adventures Continue • The Twilight Zone Tower of Terror

A Springfield, Ohio, mom reports on an unexpected but welcome assist from her brother:

I have a bachelor brother who joined my 5-, 7-, and 9-year-olds and me for vacation. Pat surprised all of us with a bunch of plastic animal noses he had in his hip pack. When the kids got restless or cranky in line, he'd turn away and pull out a pig nose or a parrot nose or something. When he turned back around with the nose on, the kids would majorly crack up.

A Waco, Texas, dad broke out the bubbly:

I took bubbles along with us. My boys loved them and so did the other children waiting in line. (I bought wedding-size bottles that would fit into everyone's fanny pack.)

We can confirm that the bubble thing has caught on big all over the theme parks.

3. PHONE FUN If games and coloring are likely to induce eye rolls, load some age-appropriate games on your or your kids' phones. For suggestions beyond Angry Birds and Candy Crush, do a search for "best iPhone/Android games for kids" or something similar. Be aware, however, that some games that are free to download and play may have add-ons that cost extra—to prevent a surprise on your credit card bill, Google "block in-app purchases on iOS/Android."

4. LAST-MINUTE COLD FEET If your young child gets cold feet while you're waiting to board a ride where Rider Switch isn't offered, you can usually arrange a switch-off with the loading attendant. (This happens frequently in Pirates of the Caribbean's dungeon waiting area.) If you reach the boarding area and someone is unhappy, just tell an attendant that you've changed your mind and you'll be shown the way out.

5. "THROW YOURSELF ON THE GRENADE, MILDRED!" For saintly, long-suffering parents who are determined to sacrifice themselves on behalf of their kids, we provide the opposite of a waiting-line strategy: the Magic Kingdom one-day touring plan called the **Dumbo-or-Die-in-a-Day Touring Plan for Parents with Small Children** (see page 717–718). Don't let the cutesy name fool you: This plan guarantees that you'll go home battered and exhausted. On the upside, it's cheaper than a $4,000 VIP tour—and it really works. Anyone under age 8 will love it!

The DISNEY CHARACTERS

THE LONGEST LEN HAS EVER WAITED in line at a theme park was 5 hours, with daughter Hannah to meet Anna and Elsa from *Frozen*. ("I've had relationships that didn't last that long," he muses.) Spontaneous group parenting took over, with adults taking turns buying food and drinks and running bathroom breaks for each other's kids.

But the thing that surprised Len most was how excited Anna was to see Hannah at the end of that 5-hour wait. Displaying the energy of a squirrel fed Cuban coffee, Anna jumped and danced around Hannah, hugging and talking to her as if it was Anna who'd been waiting to see her.

Hannah cried. Len cried. It was great.

Len's experience is repeated every day throughout Walt Disney World by cast members determined to be the Disney characters they're dressed as. We receive hundreds of reader comments telling us how much these cast members enhanced their theme park experience. This email from a Wisconsin mom is representative:

> *I can't say enough about the characters and how they react to the children and just people in general. They are highly trained in people skills and just add an extra dimension to the park.*

As we mention on page 379, meeting the Disney characters is one of the highest-rated activities among all age groups who visit Walt Disney World. To those who love them, the characters in Disney's films and TV shows are as real as family or friends; never mind that they were drawn by an animator or generated by a computer.

By extension, the theme park personifications of the Disney characters are just as real: It's not a guy in a mouse costume but Mickey himself; she's not a cast member in a sequined fish tail but Ariel, Princess of Atlantica. Meeting a Disney character is an encounter with a real celebrity—a memory to be treasured.

MEETING THE CHARACTERS

DISNEY MAKES ITS MOST POPULAR CHARACTERS available in dedicated meet-and-greet venues in each theme park (see table 401) and at Disney Deluxe resorts that host character meals (see "Character Meals," page 402). As a mom from Little Rock, Arkansas, notes, this has mostly eliminated the likelihood of bumping into characters spontaneously as you walk around the parks:

> *We were disappointed in Disney's system of character greetings. You must find the schedule and wait in line to meet any characters. I miss the days when they would just appear—we once saw Jafar walking through Adventureland all by himself! Now they're completely scheduled, so you have to plan your visit and queue up with all the other visitors. I can't tell you how many times we tried to get in line only to be told the line was closed.*

Some characters who don't have dedicated spaces appear only in parades or stage shows, and still others appear only in a location consistent with their starring role. The Fairy Godmother, for example, is often near Cinderella Castle in Fantasyland, while Buzz Lightyear appears close to his eponymous attraction in Tomorrowland. Characters may visit the Disney resorts and water parks and occasionally appear at Disney Springs.

A Brooklyn, New York, dad was surprised at how much time his family was willing to spend meeting characters:

> *The characters are now available practically all day long at different locations, according to a fixed schedule, which our son was old enough to read. We spent more time standing in line for autographs than we did for the most popular rides!*

PREPARING YOUR CHILDREN TO MEET CHARACTERS There are two kinds of Disney characters: **fur characters,** whose costumes include face-covering headpieces (including animal characters and humanlike characters such as Captain Hook), and **face characters,** who wear no mask or headpiece, such as the Disney princesses and princes, Aladdin, Mary Poppins, and the like.

Only face characters speak. Because cast members couldn't possibly imitate the furs' distinctive cinema voices, it's more effective for them to be silent. Nonetheless, fur characters are warm and responsive, and they communicate effectively with gestures. Most of the furs are quite large; a few, like Buzz Lightyear, are huge. Small children don't expect this, and preschoolers especially can be intimidated.

On first encounter, don't thrust your child at the character; rather, allow the little one to deal with this big thing from whatever distance feels safe. If two adults are present, one should stay near the youngster while the other approaches the character and demonstrates that it's safe and friendly.

Be aware that some character costumes are quite cumbersome and make it hard for the cast members inside to see well. (Eyeholes are frequently placed in the mouth of the costume or even on the neck or chest.) Children who approach the character from the back or side may not be noticed, even if the child touches the character. It's possible in this situation for the character to accidentally step on the child or knock him down.

A child should approach a character from the front, but occasionally not even this works—Donald and Daisy, for example, have to peer around their bills. If a character appears to be ignoring your child, the character's handler will get its attention.

It's OK for your child to touch, pat, or hug the character. Understanding the unpredictability of children, the character will keep his feet still, particularly refraining from moving backward or sideways.

Most characters will pose for pictures or sign autographs, but note that costumes can make it difficult to wield a normal pen. Buzz Lightyear, in fact, can't sign autographs at all but sometimes uses a stamp; in any case, he's always glad to pose for photos.

Character-Greeting Venues

Walt Disney World has numerous character-greeting locations. The table on pages 401–402 lists them by park and character. *Note:* Characters are subject to change, so check before you head to the parks.

During these meet and greets, characters often engage in dialogue appropriate to their story lines, which catches many people by surprise. Here's a letter from a Hamilton, Ohio, mom who didn't catch Cinderella's concern for missing footwear:

> We went to Princess Fairytale Hall to meet a couple of princesses. Rapunzel was very cool and chatty, but Cinderella was another story. While the 6-year-old was waiting for a picture, I sat the 1-year-old on the floor so I could reach for my camera. All of a sudden, Cinderella goes ballistic, yelling in the most un-princesslike voice, "Oh no, the little princess MUST have shoes! The little princess CANNOT be in the castle without shoes!" I'm like, "Listen, Cindy, the little princess can't walk yet, so she doesn't have shoes. Just smile for the picture and we'll be on our way."

Characters in the parks will also know about the park's attractions that involve them, as this Canadian mom found out:

> Immediately after watching Mickey's PhilharMagic, my daughter was so worried about Donald smashing through a wall [on film as part of the show] that we had to drop what we were going to do and stand in line just so she could kiss Donald and make sure he was OK. Fortunately, Donald knew what she was talking about and played along with the doctoring.

These parents, also from Canada, discovered their 3-year-old's depth of feeling for the Seven Dwarfs—one in particular:

> We got in line early for the dwarfs (her favorites) at 5:50 p.m., waited almost 2 hours before her turn in line . . . and then she wouldn't

WDW CHARACTER-GREETING VENUES

Magic Kingdom

MICKEY AND HIS POSSE

• **Daisy, Donald, Goofy, Minnie, and Pluto** Pete's Silly Sideshow • **Mickey** Town Square Theater

DISNEY ROYALTY *(Princesses, Princes, Suitors, and Such)*

• **Aladdin and Jasmine** Adventureland • **Anna and Elsa** On float during the Festival of Fantasy Parade and in *Mickey's Royal Friendship Faire* stage show • **Ariel** Ariel's Grotto • **Belle** *Enchanted Tales with Belle* • **Cinderella, Elena of Avalor, Rapunzel, and Tiana** Princess Fairytale Hall • Gaston Fountain outside Gaston's Tavern • **Merida** Fairytale Garden • Snow White Next to City Hall • **The Tremaines and Fairy Godmother** In Fantasyland near Cinderella's Castle

FAIRIES

• **Tinker Bell and Friends** Town Square Theater

MISCELLANEOUS

• **Alice** (*Alice in Wonderland*) Mad Tea Party • **Buzz Lightyear** (*Toy Story*) Tomorrowland • **Captain Jack Sparrow** (*Pirates of the Caribbean*) Adventureland • **Chip 'n' Dale** Storybook Circus/Fantasyland • **Country Bears** Frontierland • **Mary Poppins** Liberty Square • **Peter Pan** Fantasyland next to Peter Pan's Flight • **Pooh and Tigger** Fantasyland by The Many Adventures of Winnie the Pooh • **Stitch** (*Lilo & Stitch*) Tomorrowland

EPCOT

MICKEY AND HIS POSSE

• **Daisy** World Showcase Plaza • **Donald** Mexico, at the Mexico Pavilion • **Mickey** Disney & Pixar Short Film Festival

DISNEY ROYALTY

• **Anna and Elsa** Norway • **Aurora** France gazebo • **Belle** France • **Jasmine** Morocco • **Mulan** China • **Snow White** Germany

MISCELLANEOUS

• **Alice, Mary Poppins, and** (on rare occasions) **Bert** United Kingdom • **Winnie the Pooh** Lawn between the Imagination! and Land Pavilions • **Joy** (*Inside Out*) Near the Imagination! Pavilion

Disney's Animal Kingdom

MICKEY AND HIS POSSE

• **Daisy** DinoLand U.S.A., Lower Cretaceous Trail • **Donald** DinoLand U.S.A., Celebration Welcome Center • **Goofy and Pluto** Near main entrance • **Mickey and Minnie** Adventurers Outpost on Discovery Island

DISNEY ROYALTY

• **Pocahontas** Discovery Island at Character Landing

MISCELLANEOUS

• **Chip 'n' Dale** DinoLand U.S.A., Upper Cretaceous Trail • **Flik** (*A Bug's Life*) Discovery Island across from Creature Comforts • **Kevin** (*Up*) Discovery Island and near *Feathered Friends in Flight* • **Launchpad McQuack** DinoLand U.S.A., Aerial Adventure Base • **Russell** (*Up*) Discovery Island (**Dug** may appear randomly) • **Scrooge McDuck** DinoLand U.S.A., near Restaurantosaurus

Disney's Hollywood Studios

MICKEY AND HIS POSSE

• **Chip 'n' Dale** Grand Avenue • **Daisy and Donald** Near park entrance • **Goofy** Grand Avenue across from BaseLine Tap House • **Minnie and Sorcerer Mickey** Red Carpet Dreams on Commissary Lane • **Pluto** Animation Courtyard

Characters are subject to change.

WDW CHARACTER-GREETING VENUES (continued)

DISNEY CHANNEL STARS

- **Doc McStuffins and Friends** Animation Courtyard near *Disney Junior Play and Dance!* • **Vampirina** Animation Courtyard

MISCELLANEOUS

- **Buzz, Jessie, Woody, and Green Army Men** (*Toy Story*) Toy Story Land
- **Chewbacca, Darth Vader, and BB-8** (*Star Wars*) Star Wars Launch Bay
- **Cruz Ramirez** (*Cars*) Lightning McQueen's Racing Academy • **Olaf** (*Frozen*) Celebrity Spotlight in Echo Lake • **Stormtroopers** (*Star Wars*) Animation Courtyard

Blizzard Beach Water Park

- **Goofy** Appears seasonally, usually from spring break until Labor Day, at park entrance

Typhoon Lagoon Water Park

- **Lilo and Stitch** Singapore Sal's near the park entrance. They meet in the spring and summer months on a rotational basis.

Characters are subject to change.

leave. She insisted on hugging and interacting with every dwarf; she squeezed herself between the seven of them and avoided our attempts to grab her and pull her away. We eventually snagged her as she was screaming "GRUMPY! YOU HAVE TO BE HAPPY! BE HAPPY, GRUMPY!" at the top of her lungs.

CHARACTER MEALS

DISNEY CHARACTERS APPEAR at meals served in full-service restaurants at the theme parks and Deluxe resorts, among other locations. For more information, see page 400. At press time, character-dining experiences were available only at

- **Artist Point** Wilderness Lodge Resort (page 350)
- **Akershus Royal Banquet Hall** Norway, World Showcase, EPCOT (page 315)
- **Cape May Cafe** Beach Club Resort (page 321)
- **Chef Mickey's** Contemporary Resort (page 322)
- **The Crystal Palace** Magic Kingdom (page 325)
- **Garden Grill Restaurant** EPCOT (page 328)
- **Hollywood & Vine** Disney's Hollywood Studios (page 331)
- **'Ohana** Polynesian Resort (page 341)
- **Topolino's Terrace—Flavors of the Riviera** Rivera Resort (page 355)
- **Tusker House Restaurant** Animal Kingdom (page 357)

CHILDCARE

IN-ROOM BABYSITTING Kid's Nite Out (☎ 877-761-3580; kidsniteout .com) provides in-room and in-park childcare in the Walt Disney World/ Universal area. Base hourly rates (4-hour mini-

unofficial **TIP**
Childcare is unavailable at Walt Disney World resort hotels.

mum) are $30 for one child and $3 per hour for each additional child, plus a $15 travel fee. Sitters are security-checked, bonded, and trained in CPR. See the website for additional services and fees.

SPECIAL KIDS' PROGRAMS

FREE ACTIVITIES

MANY DISNEY DELUXE AND DVC RESORTS offer a continuous slate of free kids' activities from early morning through the evening, from storytelling and cookie decorating to hands-on activities themed to the resort. (Many of these activities are outdoors too.) These programs offer an inexpensive alternative to the theme parks on your first or last day of travel, or whenever parents need a quiet break by the pool.

BIRTHDAYS *and* SPECIAL OCCASIONS

WHEN YOU CHECK IN TO A HOTEL or restaurant, Disney cast members will generally ask if you're celebrating something special, such as a birthday or anniversary. A Lombard, Illinois, mom put the word out and was glad she did:

> *My daughter was turning 5 while we were there; our hotel asked me who her favorite character was and did the rest. We came back to our room on her birthday and there were helium balloons, a card, and a Cinderella photo autographed in ink! When we entered the Magic Kingdom, we received an "It's My Birthday Today" pin (FREE!), and at the restaurant she got a huge cupcake with whipped cream, sprinkles, and a candle. IT PAYS TO ASK!*

PART 8

TIPS *for* VARIED CIRCUMSTANCES

KEY QUESTIONS ANSWERED IN THIS CHAPTER

- How do Disney theme parks accommodate people with disabilities? *(see below)*
- What is Disney's Disability Access Service? *(see opposite page)*
- Can I use a wheelchair or electric scooter in the parks and resorts? *(pages 407)*
- How do Disney restaurants handle dietary restrictions? *(pages 408)*
- What should seniors know about visiting Walt Disney World? *(pages 412)*
- Can I get married in Walt Disney World? *(pages 417)*

WALT DISNEY WORLD *for* GUESTS *with* DISABILITIES

DISNEY WORLD IS EXCEPTIONALLY ACCOMMODATING to guests with physical challenges. If you have a disability, Disney is well prepared to meet your needs.

DISNEY RESORTS

IF YOU'LL BE STAYING AT A DISNEY RESORT, let the reservation agent know of any special needs you have when you book your room. The following equipment, services, and facilities are available at most Disney hotels; note that not all hotels offer all items.

- Accessible vanities
- Bed and bathroom rails
- Braille on signs and elevators
- Closed-captioned TVs
- Double peepholes in doors
- Handheld showerheads
- Knock and phone alerts
- Lowered beds
- Phone amplifiers
- Portable commodes
- Refrigerators
- Roll-in showers
- Rubber bed padding
- Shower benches
- Strobe-light smoke detectors
- TTYs
- Wheelchairs for temporary use
- Widened bathroom doors

SERVICE ANIMALS

DISNEY WELCOMES DOGS AND MINIATURE HORSES that are trained to assist guests with disabilities. Service animals are permitted in most locations in all Disney resorts and theme parks, although they may not be admitted on certain theme park rides. Check disneyworld .disney.go.com/guest-services/service-animals for more information.

IN THE THEME PARKS

EACH THEME PARK OFFERS a free booklet describing services and accommodations for guests with disabilities at tinyurl.com/disabilities guide. You can also obtain these pamphlets when you enter the parks, at resort front desks, and at wheelchair-rental locations inside the parks. For specific requests, call ☎ 407-560-2547 (voice). When the recorded menu comes up, press *1*. Limit your questions and requests to those regarding your disability; address other questions to ☎ 407-824-4321 or 407-827-5141 (TTY).

DISNEY'S DISABILITY ACCESS SERVICE (DAS)

DISNEY'S DISABILITY ACCESS SERVICE is designed to accommodate guests who can't wait in regular standby lines. Among its benefits is the complimentary access to the (much shorter) Lightning Lane lines at popular attractions. We strongly suggest registering online between 2 and 30 days in advance of your trip (see tinyurl.com/wdw-das) for a video chat with a Disney representative, who'll help get everything set up. Alternatively, you can register on the day of your visit at the **Guest Relations** window of the first theme park you enter.

You only need to sign up once every 60 days, and the service carries over to each subsequent park you visit. The process is explained below. For clarity, we'll refer to the person signing up for the DAS service as the DAS enrollee. *Note:* Guests whose disability requires only a wheelchair or mobility vehicle do not need the DAS.

PREPARATION Before you sign up, make sure you have either the MagicBands, park tickets, or My Disney Experience emails of everyone in your group. All your group's MagicBands/tickets will be linked to the DAS—this comes in handy in situations we'll describe below. The DAS is good for parties of up to six people. For parties of more than six, check with Guest Relations.

SIGNING UP FOR DAS At your video chat or Guest Relations, you'll be asked to present identification and describe the enrollee's limitations. You don't have to provide documentation of a specific condition; rather, what Disney is looking for is a description of how the condition affects the enrollee in the parks. The goal is to determine the right level of assistance, not to obligate you to prove that the enrollee qualifies. The enrollee must be present during this call or visit.

Be as detailed as possible in describing limitations. For instance, if your child has autism spectrum disorder and has trouble waiting in long lines or has sensory issues such as sensitivity to noise, let the cast member know each of these things specifically.

The DAS also requires a photograph. Pictures are taken with an iPad (the cast member will come to you if you can't make it up to the counter). If the DAS is for a child, you may use either the child's photo or substitute your own. Finally, you must check a box that says you agree to be bound by Disney's DAS rules. While this seems like a formality, this Disney travel agent notes that nothing happens until you click:

> *Make sure readers know to follow down through the directions and click on "Accept Terms and Conditions." This is really important, and they won't help you if you don't accept them, so do this before you start the chat.*

Once you're registered, the interview process gets rave reviews:

> *I signed up for DAS this morning, and the process was really easy. The whole thing took less than an hour, and I was able to prebook all the rides I wanted.*
>
> —A reader from Greenwich, Connecticut

DAS ADVANCE This feature allows you to select two attractions to visit on each day of your trip. For example, if you say you're visiting EPCOT on the Tuesday of your trip, then at some point before Tuesday, you'll be able to pick two attractions in EPCOT to visit using the Lightning Lane. You'll see these DAS Advance reservations in My Disney Experience too. As with Genie+, you'll get a 1-hour return window during which you can come back and ride those selected attractions. And unlike the regular Genie+ and Individual Lightning Lane programs (page 60), DAS lets you reride these attractions via Lightning Lane on the same day.

This dad loved the DAS Advance selections:

> *The DAS Advance selections are a life-saver for those that need it. I don't know what we would have done without DAS and being able to effectively stay one ride ahead of the crowds. I was very impressed that all rides were available—we could have used DAS for Rise of the Resistance if we had wanted to.*

USING DAS ON THE DAY OF YOUR VISIT The DAS may be used at any attraction or character-greeting venue with a queue. Anyone with a linked MagicBand or ticket can present it outside the attraction; if the standby wait time is less than 15 minutes, you'll usually be escorted through the standby entrance or the Alternate Access/Lightning Lane entrance. If the standby time is higher, a cast member will provide a time for you to return to ride—again, this is entered into MDE.

The return time will be the current wait time minus 10 minutes—if, say, you get to Seven Dwarfs Mine Train at 12:20 p.m. and the standby time is 40 minutes, your return time will be 30 minutes later, at 12:50 p.m. You may return at the specified time or anytime thereafter. The DAS enrollee must also return to ride. When you return, the enrollee's MagicBand will be scanned first, followed by those of the other members of the group. The whole group will use the Lightning Lane or Alternate Access line.

Make sure everyone enrolled in the DAS wants to ride the same rides. Because they're effectively Genie+ or Individual Lightning Lane reservations, people in your group who want another reservation instead of DAS will still be constrained by the "when can I get a next reservation" rules of Genie+ and ILL. Here's some advice from a large family with different tastes in rides:

A word of warning—only add to your DAS selection if you're sure you or others in your party will be riding that ride. If someone backs out, MDE doesn't easily let you cancel their inclusion immediately. MDE will think some of your party won't be eligible for a "next" DAS selection because they haven't used their most recent one. And if you do book a future one with the eligible party members, there's no way of adding the remaining party later without going to Guest Relations. It made me think twice before booking so I wouldn't have to stop by Guest Relations every time I needed help clearing up the past ride they didn't use.

After your first two DAS Advance selections, you can hold one DAS return time at a time. However, you can also use Genie+ (where offered), Individual Lightning Lane, boarding groups, and the DAS at the same time. *Tip:* Bring an extra battery for your phone.

WHAT HAPPENS IF I'M LATE FOR THE RETURN WINDOW? In most circumstances, Disney cast members grant a lot of leeway when it comes to using your DAS even after the return window has closed. Let's say your return window is 12:50–1:50 p.m. Even if you show up at 2:30 p.m., most cast members are likely to allow you to ride. (If not, wait 15 minutes for another cast member to staff the line, and try again.)

WHEELCHAIRS AND ELECTRIC VEHICLES

GUESTS WITH LIMITED MOBILITY may rent wheelchairs, three-wheeled electric conveyance vehicles (ECVs, also known as scooters), and electric standing vehicles (ESVs). These give nonambulatory guests tremendous freedom and mobility. Most rides, shows, attractions, restrooms, and restaurants accommodate them. If you are in a park and need assistance, go to Guest Relations.

Wheelchairs rent for $12 per day, or $10 per day for multiday rentals. Rentals are available at all Walt Disney World theme parks (see Parts 11–14 for specific locations) and at Disney Springs. ECVs and ESVs cost $50 per day, plus a $20 refundable deposit ($100 refundable deposit at Disney Springs and the water parks). Wheelchairs are available for rent at the water parks and Disney Springs for $12 per day with a refundable $100 deposit.

Your rental deposit slip is good for a replacement wheelchair in any park during the same day. You can rent a chair in the Magic Kingdom in the morning, return it, go to any other park, present your deposit slip, and get another chair at no additional charge.

Apple Scooter (☎ 321-726-6837, applescooter.com) rents scooters with a wide variety of options, and is by far the least expensive choice for rentals of three or more days. **Buena Vista Scooters** (☎ 407-331-9147, buenavistascooters.com) also rents scooters with many options but is much more expensive. Both companies include free delivery to and pickup from your Disney resort. You'll need to be present for delivery and pickup, however.

All Disney lots have close-in parking for visitors with disabilities; request directions when you pay your parking fee. Most (but not all) rides, shows, restrooms, and restaurants accommodate wheelchairs, as do monorails and buses, as outlined on the next page.

Even if an attraction doesn't accommodate wheelchairs, ECVs, or ESVs, nonambulatory guests may ride if they can transfer from their wheelchair to the ride's vehicle. Disney staff, however, aren't trained or permitted to assist with transfers—guests must be able to board the ride unassisted or have a member of their party assist them. Either way, members of the nonambulatory guest's party will be permitted to ride with the guest.

Because the waiting areas of most attractions won't accommodate wheelchairs, nonambulatory guests and their parties should ask a cast member for boarding instructions as soon as they arrive at an attraction entrance.

Disabled guests and their families give Disney high marks for accessibility and sensitivity. An Arlington, Virginia, woman writes:

My mom has mobility problems, and she was worried about getting around. Disney supplied a free wheelchair, every bus had kneeling steps for wheelchair users, and the cast members sprang into action when they saw us coming.

Much of the Disney transportation system is accessible. Monorails can be accessed by ramp or elevator, the Skyliner has special gondolas for wheelchairs and scooters, and all bus routes are served by vehicles with wheelchair lifts, though unusually wide or long wheelchairs (or motorized chairs) may not fit the lift. Watercraft accommodations for wheelchairs are iffier.

A large number of Disney hotel guests use scooters (ECVs). This affects commuting times by bus, as each Disney bus can accommodate only two scooters or wheelchairs. A Minneapolis woman touring with her parents shared her experience:

I was stunned by the number of scooters this year. My parents each had one, and several times they had to wait to find a bus that had available space for scooters or wheelchairs. If people needing a scooter can make it to the bus stop on foot, they'd be better off waiting until they get to the park and renting a scooter there.

If you plan to use a wheelchair or scooter while visiting **Wilderness Lodge & Villas, Fort Wilderness Resort & Campground,** or an **EPCOT** resort, call ☎ 407-560-2547 (voice) for the latest information on watercraft accessibility.

Food and merchandise locations at theme parks, Disney Springs, and hotels are generally accessible, but some fast-food queues and shop aisles are too narrow for wheelchairs. At these locations, ask a cast member or member of your party for assistance.

A scooter user from Riverside, California, shares her experience:

Had a great time! It wasn't easy using a scooter, though. Stores and restaurants have little room for a scooter to maneuver—I kept getting boxed in by people or had to back out of areas that had no turnaround space.

DIETARY RESTRICTIONS AND ALLERGIES

WALT DISNEY WORLD works hard to accommodate special dietary needs. When you make a dining reservation online or by phone, you'll be asked about food allergies and the like. When you arrive at table-service restaurants and buffets, alert the host or hostess and your server.

Almost all Walt Disney World restaurants have dedicated allergy-friendly menus available upon request. The menus cover most people and offer a variety of food as diverse as the standard menu. For example, the Magic Kingdom's **Cosmic Ray's Starlight Cafe** offers at least 14 entrées for guests with seafood, nut, grain, egg, dairy, and soy allergies, as well as for Jewish guests who keep kosher.

Also, Disney chefs at many sit-down restaurants have adapted their dishes so that almost anyone with a common allergy can order off the standard menu. At **Narcoossee's,** for example, every item on the standard menu has been adapted to the allergy menu. **Touring Plans.com** also maintains a list of Disney World restaurant menus, including most special offerings and prices—look for the words *allergy friendly* on the menu list at tinyurl.com/allergymenuswdw. For more information, email special.diets@disneyworld.com or visit tinyurl.com/wdwspecialdiets.

An Idaho mom and her teenage daughter found Disney restaurants very responsive to their dietary needs:

> *My daughter and I both have a gluten allergy. I have never felt so well cared for and safe eating anywhere else in the world. From our resort (both the food court and Boatwright's) to every single quick-service or sit-down restaurant, we had several choices, and we never waited longer than 8 minutes for our special orders.*

To request kosher meals at table-service restaurants, call ☎ 407-824-1391 24 hours in advance. All Disney menus have vegetarian options; most can be made vegan without your having to talk to the chef, but vegetarians, vegans, and pescatarians should still speak up when making dining reservations.

Those with special diets *and* a sweet tooth should try the vegan, gluten-free, and kosher treats from **Erin McKenna's Bakery NYC,** with locations at Disney Springs and many Disney hotel food courts (they also deliver to the Disney area). Besides sweets, the bakery does a tasty line of savory breads from time to time. You can also order special-occasion cakes and baked goods (☎ 407-938-9044; erinmckennas bakery.com).

MEDICATIONS

FOR GUESTS WHO EXPERIENCE ALLERGIC REACTIONS that can be severe or life-threatening, Disney provides epinephrine injectors (**EpiPens**) at **First Aid Centers** and other locations throughout the parks (check your park guide maps for locations). Nurses and emergency responders are trained in EpiPen use, but guests with known conditions should always travel with their own supplies.

CBD PRODUCTS In 2019, a 69-year-old grandmother from Tennessee was arrested at a Magic Kingdom security checkpoint for possession of CBD (cannabidiol) oil, which her doctor had prescribed to treat arthritis pain. The charges against her were later dropped, but the incident highlighted a major discrepancy between federal and then-current Florida law. Federal law permits the production and sale of hemp-derived CBD products containing 0.3% THC or less, but at the time of the woman's arrest, these products were subject to the same restrictions as medical marijuana in Florida. A state law that removed these restrictions went into effect July 1, 2019. Disney guests should verify that their products' THC content falls within legal limits.

VISUALLY IMPAIRED, DEAF, OR HARD-OF-HEARING GUESTS

GUEST RELATIONS PROVIDES FREE **assistive-technology devices** to guests who are visually impaired, deaf, or hard-of-hearing ($25 refundable deposit, depending on the device). Sight-impaired guests can customize the given information (such as architectural details, restroom locations, and descriptions of attractions and restaurants) through an interactive audio menu that is guided by a GPS in the device. For deaf or hard-of-hearing guests, amplified audio and closed-captioning for attractions can be loaded into the same device.

Braille guidebooks are available from Guest Relations at all parks ($25 refundable deposit), and **Braille menus** are available at some theme park restaurants. Some rides provide **closed-captioning;** many theater attractions provide **reflective captioning.**

Disney provides **sign language interpretations** of live shows at the theme parks on certain designated days of the week:

- **MAGIC KINGDOM** Mondays and Thursdays
- **EPCOT** Fridays
- **DISNEY'S ANIMAL KINGDOM** Saturdays and Tuesdays
- **DISNEY'S HOLLYWOOD STUDIOS** Sundays and Wednesdays

Get confirmation of the interpreted-performance schedule a minimum of one week in advance by calling Disney World information at ☎ 407-824-4321 (voice) or 407-827-5141 (TTY). You'll be contacted before your visit with a schedule of the interpreted performances.

NONAPPARENT DISABILITIES

WE RECEIVE MANY LETTERS FROM READERS whose traveling companion or child requires special assistance but who, unlike a person in a wheelchair, is not visibly disabled. Autism, for example, can make it very difficult or impossible for someone to wait in line for more than a few minutes or in queues surrounded by a crowd. A trip to Disney World can be nonetheless positive and rewarding for guests who are on the autism spectrum. And while any Disney vacation requires planning, a little extra effort to accommodate the affected person will pay large dividends. Disney's guide for guests with cognitive disabilities can be downloaded at tinyurl.com/wdwcognitiveguide. (At press time, the guide hadn't been updated since 2021, but other than references to FastPass+ that should be Genie+, the information appears current.) For a ride-by-ride chart of the sights, sounds, smells, and experiences you'll encounter on each ride, see tinyurl.com/wdw cognitivematrix. For information on **Disney's Disability Access Service** (**DAS**), which accommodates guests with nonapparent disabilities, see page 405.

WALT DISNEY WORLD
for LARGER GUESTS

YOU'VE JUST SPENT A SMALL FORTUNE for your vacation. If you're a person of size, you don't want to worry about whether you're going to have trouble fitting in the ride vehicles. Fortunately, Walt Disney World realizes that its guests come in all shapes and sizes and is quite accommodating. **Deb Wills** and **Debra Martin Koma,** experts on Walt Disney World travel for people with physical challenges, offer the following suggestions.

- You'll be on your feet for hours at a time, so wear comfortable, broken-in shoes. If you feel a blister starting to form, take care of it quickly. (Each theme park has a **First Aid Center** stocked with bandages and other necessities. For more on blister prevention, see page 453.)

- If you're prone to chafing, consider bringing an antifriction product designed to control or eliminate rubbing (**Body Glide** is a well-known brand). You can find this and similar products at most pharmacies and sporting-goods stores.

- In restaurants, look for chairs without arms. Check with a dining host if you don't see one.

- Request a resort hotel room with a king-size bed. The good sleep you'll get will be worth it.

- Attractions have different kinds of vehicles and seating. Some have bench seats, while others have individual seats; some have overhead harnesses, while others have seat belts or lap bars. Learn what type of seating or vehicle each attraction has before you go so you know what to expect (check out tinyurl.com/allears-ride-gallery for details). If the attraction has a seat belt, pull it all the way out before you sit down to make it easier to strap yourself in. Note that some attractions have seat-belt extenders—ask a cast member about these.

- Front seats (such as those on Rock 'n' Roller Coaster and Test Track) often have more legroom; they don't on Space Mountain, however.

- Several attractions offer a sample ride vehicle for you to try before you get in line. These can be found at **Tron Lightcycle/Run** in the Magic Kingdom, **Test Track** in Epcot, **Avatar Flight of Passage** and **Expedition Everest** in Animal Kingdom, and **Star Wars: Rise of the Resistance** and **Rock 'n' Roller Coaster** in Disney's Hollywood Studios. Ask a cast member if the test seats aren't immediately visible.

Sometimes it isn't largeness in general but your particular build that can present a problem when it comes to ride vehicles. For example, Tron's leg restraints don't accommodate all guests with large calves, regardless of torso size. Likewise, a Connecticut reader relates her experience in Animal Kingdom:

Since I was a very young girl, I've dreamed of riding on a dragon, so I was extremely excited about the chance to experience Avatar Flight of Passage in Pandora. Unfortunately, though I was able to mount the ride's motorcycle-like seat without difficulty, the safety braces that came up behind would not lock due to my particular dimensions. The cast member in charge of checking the safeties was very kind and did try to coach me into a better fit, but in the end I had to get out and leave the ride as my husband and son looked on. I was absolutely mortified, though I was graciously offered two additional ride reservations as compensation.

Fast-forward to the next day at Disney's Hollywood Studios. I was determined not to repeat the experience, so when the time came to ride the Rock 'n' Roller Coaster, I asked if there were sample seats and restraints I could try before entering the line. I was ushered backstage by a cast member and was able to try out the exact seating configuration with success.

WALT DISNEY WORLD *for* SENIORS

SENIOR CITIZENS have much the same problems and concerns as all Disney visitors ("Is Space Mountain too rough? How much walking is there? Can I stop aging forever by turning to the Dark Side?"). Older guests do, however, get into predicaments caused by touring with younger people. Pressured by their grandchildren to endure a frantic pace, many seniors concentrate on surviving Disney World rather than enjoying it. Seniors must either set the pace or dispatch the young folks to tour on their own.

An older reader in Alabaster, Alabama, writes:

Being a senior is not for wussies, particularly at Walt Disney World. Things that used to be easy take a lot of effort, and sometimes your brain has to wait for your body to catch up. Half the time, your grandchildren treat you like a crumbling ruin; then they turn around and trick you into getting on a roller coaster in the dark. Seniors must be alert and not trust anyone—not their children, not the Disney people, and especially not their grandchildren. Don't follow along blindly like a lamb to the slaughter. He who hesitates is launched!

Most seniors we interview enjoy the World much more when they tour with folks their own age. If, however, you're considering visiting with your grandchildren, we recommend making an exploratory visit without them first; this way, it'll be easier to establish limits, maintain control, and set a comfortable pace later on. Similarly, to get a sense of what kinds of problems might materialize, take the grandkids to a local theme park or fair before you extend the Walt Disney World invitation.

If you're *determined* to take the grandkids, carefully read the sections of this book that discuss family touring. (*Hint:* The Dumbo-or-Die-in-a-Day Touring Plan has been known to bring grown-ups of all ages to their knees.)

When it comes to attractions, we feel that personal taste should trump age. We hate to see seniors pass up a full-blown adventure like Rise of the Resistance just because it's a so-called thrill ride—it gets its appeal more from the music and visual effects than from the thrill of the ride. Use our theme park attraction profiles to help you make informed decisions.

GETTING AROUND

MANY SENIORS LIKE TO WALK, but a 7-hour visit to a theme park includes 4–10 miles on foot. Consider renting a wheelchair or mobility vehicle (see page 407).

LOOK OUT FOR STROLLERS! Given the number of wheeled vehicles, pedestrians, and tight spaces, mishaps are inevitable. A middle-aged couple from Brunswick, Maine, lobbies for a temporary ban:

As an over-45 couple, we couldn't believe the number and sizes of strollers and those ubiquitous scooters. You had to be constantly vigilant or you would have your foot run over or path slowed down. One day a week, in one theme park, there should be a "no wheels" day.

A reader named Linda (no hometown given) would certainly agree:

We were appalled by the Stroller Brigades. We are seniors, and twice I was actually hit—not bumped—by strollers that were guided by people on their phones racing to get somewhere. Once I was hit hard enough that a cast member actually came over. I don't know what the solution is, but there should be some kind of limit to the size of these things. This was such a serious issue for us that we very well may not go back.

In response to the concerns of readers like Linda, Disney limits stroller sizes to **31 inches wide by 52 inches long.**

TIMING YOUR VISIT

RETIREES SHOULD MAKE THE MOST of their flexible schedules and go to Walt Disney World in the fall or spring (excluding holiday weeks), when the weather is nicest and the crowds are comparatively thinner. Crowds are also generally sparse from late January through early February. See page 32 for more information.

LODGING

IF YOU CAN AFFORD IT, STAY IN WALT DISNEY WORLD. Rooms are among the Orlando–Kissimmee area's nicest, and transportation is always available to any Disney destination at no additional cost.

Disney hotels reserve rooms close to restaurants and transportation for guests of any age who can't tolerate much walking. They also provide golf carts to pick up and deliver guests at their rooms. Service can vary dramatically depending on the time of day and the number of guests requesting carts. At check-in time (around 3 p.m. for regular hotels, 4 p.m. for DVC), for example, the wait for a ride can be as long as 40 minutes.

Here are four good reasons to consider staying at a Walt Disney World resort:

1. The quality of the properties is consistently above average.
2. Staying in the World guarantees transportation when you need it. Disney buses run about every 20 minutes. (If you miss the last bus, though, you may need to call an Uber, Lyft, or taxi.)
3. You get free parking at the major theme parks.
4. You get extra time in the theme parks, with lower crowds.

Walt Disney World hotels are spread out—it's easy to avoid most stairs, but it's often a long hike to your room from parking lots or bus stops. Seniors intending to spend more time in Epcot and Hollywood Studios than in the Magic Kingdom or Animal Kingdom should consider the **BoardWalk Inn & Villas, Dolphin, Swan, Swan Reserve,** or **Yacht & Beach Club Resorts.**

The **Contemporary Resort** and **Bay Lake Tower** are good choices for seniors who want to be on the monorail system. So are the **Grand Floridian** and the **Polynesian Village,** though they cover many acres, necessitating a lot of walking. For a restful, rustic feeling, choose **Wilderness Lodge & Boulder Ridge/Copper Creek Villas.**

If you want a kitchen and the comforts of home, book **Animal Kingdom Villas, Beach Club Villas, BoardWalk Villas, Grand Floridian Villas, Old Key West Resort, Polynesian Villas & Bungalows, Riviera,** or **Saratoga Springs.** If you enjoy watching birds and animals, try **Animal Kingdom Lodge & Villas.** Try **Saratoga Springs** for golf.

RVers will find pleasant surroundings at **The Campsites at Disney's Fort Wilderness Resort.** Several independent campgrounds are within 30 minutes of Walt Disney World; see campflorida.com/regions/central-florida for listings. They're not as nice, but they cost less.

TRANSPORTATION

ROADS IN DISNEY WORLD CAN BE DAUNTING. Armed with a decent sense of direction and a great sense of humor, however, even the most timid driver can get around. Plus, you don't have to be zip code–specific to use GPS on your smartphone—if you want to go to EPCOT for example, entering "EPCOT" or "EPCOT parking" will get the job done. (See page 441 for GPS information for each theme park.)

Parking for guests with disabilities is available near each theme park's entrance; toll-plaza attendants will provide a dashboard ticket and direct you to the reserved spaces. Disney requires that you be recognized officially as disabled to use this parking, but temporarily disabled persons are also permitted access.

DINING

EAT BREAKFAST AT YOUR HOTEL RESTAURANT or have juice and rolls in your room. Carry snacks in a fanny pack supplemented by fresh or dried fruit, fruit juice, and soft drinks purchased from vendors. Make Advance Dining Reservations for lunch before noon to avoid the crowds. Follow with an early dinner and be out of the restaurants, ready for evening touring and fireworks (if available), long before the main crowd even thinks about dinner.

WALT DISNEY WORLD *for* INTERNATIONAL VISITORS

AS OF MARCH 10, 2023, the United States rescinded its requirement that visitors from China, Hong Kong, and Macau be vaccinated before entering the country. Visitors from these countries no longer need to get tested, show a negative test result, or show documentation of recovery from COVID-19 prior to boarding a flight to the U.S. See tinyurl.com/usentrycovid for the latest requirements.

A mom from Menorca, Spain, offers advice to readers who are making the long haul to Walt Disney World:

> *You cannot predict how the time difference is going to affect you or the little people. Coming from Spain, we were looking at a 9-hour flight from the UK and a 6-hour time difference, and we spent our first few days in a haze after trying to do too much too soon.*

Londoner and *Unofficial* friend Andrew Dakoutros sent us this grab bag of tips and advice for other Disney-bound Brits:

> *(1) Jellyrolls [the piano bar at Disney's BoardWalk] doesn't accept UK driving licences as ID for entry [they accept passports]; (2) many MouseSavers codes [see page 31] can't be used from the UK; (3) the Twinings tea at The Tea Caddy at EPCOT doesn't taste as good as in London.*
>
> *Additionally, you need to emphasise how hot Florida is and the importance of sunscreen. Most Britons holiday in Spain or Greece, where the sun is nowhere near as strong.*

TRANSLATION SERVICES A wireless device called **Ears to the World** provides synchronized narration in French, German, Japanese, Portuguese, or Spanish for more than 30 attractions in the theme parks. The wireless, lightweight headsets provide real-time translation and are available for a $25 refundable deposit at Guest Relations in all parks.

WALT DISNEY WORLD *for* PREGNANT GUESTS

WHEN IT COMES TO VISITING DISNEY WORLD while pregnant, the authors, alas, have no wisdom of their own to impart. Enter **Debbie Grubbs,** a Colorado reader. During her fifth month of pregnancy, she waddled intrepidly all over the World, compiling observations and tips for expectant moms that she shares below.

MAGIC KINGDOM Splash Mountain *[now Tiana's Bayou Adventure] is a no-go, obviously, due to the drop—or so I thought. It turns out that the seat configuration in the logs has more to do with it than the drop. The seats are made so that your knees are higher than your rear, compressing the abdomen (when it's this large). This is potentially harmful to the baby.*

Big Thunder Mountain Railroad *is also out of the question. It's just not a good idea to ride roller coasters when pregnant.*

Mad Tea Party *may be OK if you don't spin the cups. We didn't ride this one because my doctor advised me to skip rides with centrifugal [or centripetal] force.* **Dumbo** *in Fantasyland and the* **Astro Orbiter** *in Tomorrowland are OK, though.*

Space Mountain *is one of my favorite rides . . . but a roller coaster nonetheless.*

Tomorrowland Speedway *isn't recommended due to the amount of rear-ending by overzealous younger drivers.*

We also think Debbie would have had to pass on **Seven Dwarfs Mine Train** and its swinging cars, as well as **Tron Lightcycle/Run.**

ANIMAL KINGDOM Dinosaur *is very jerky and should be avoided.*

We think Debbie would've avoided **Expedition Everest** too. **Na'vi River Journey** at Pandora might be fine, but **Avatar Flight of Passage** is probably too much.

EPCOT Mission: Space, Test Track, *and* Guardians of the Galaxy: Cosmic Rewind *are restricted, as are all simulator rides; they're way too rough and jerky. [Nonmoving seats are available in some simulation attractions—ask a cast member.]* **Soarin'** *is fine.*

HOLLYWOOD STUDIOS Tower of Terror *is out of the question for the drop alone, and* **Star Tours** *is restricted because it's a simulator.* **Rock 'n' Roller Coaster** *is clearly off-limits. In Toy Story Land,* **Slinky Dog Dash** *(the beginner coaster) is out, as are the* **Alien Swirling Saucers.**

Millennium Falcon: **Smugglers Run** *at Star Wars: Galaxy's Edge is a no-go, and possibly* **Star Wars: Rise of the Resistance** *for its reentry segment at the end.* **Mickey and Minnie's Runaway Railway** *might be doable—there's one scene where the ride vehicle shakes side to side while you're doing the mambo (we're not making this up, we swear).*

WATER PARKS Slides *are off-limits, but not the* **wave pools** *and* **floating creeks** *(great for getting the weight off your feet).*

A mother of three from Bethesda, Maryland, adds:

Go to a golf shop and buy one of those walking sticks with a seat attached to it—I would've been a goner without one. They're lightweight and easy to carry. Also, a support garment (such as a BellyBra) is a must for relieving pressure on your lower back.

A Branchburg, New Jersey, woman advises:

Moms-to-be should be really mindful of the temperature, staying hydrated, and having realistic expectations for how much you'll be able to do. We averaged 5–7 miles of walking per day during our trip, which may have been a bit too much for me (I was six months pregnant at the time). Once the temperatures started approaching 90, I found it difficult to catch my breath and my feet began to swell. A midday nap or swim break was 100% required—I tried to skip it on a few days, and I was miserable as a result. I was most frustrated at EPCOT, where most of the headliner attractions are restricted for pregnant guests.

MORE TIPS FOR MOMS-TO-BE

IN ADDITION TO OUR READERS' TIPS, here are a few of ours:

1. Discuss your Disney World plans with your OB-GYN before your trip.
2. Start walking at home to build up your stamina for walking in the parks. Once in the World, however, try to use in-park transportation when you can so that you're not having to walk all the time.
3. While there have been no confirmed cases of the Zika virus in the Orlando area to date, there have been a small number of cases in other parts of Florida, including one case in Osceola County, where Celebration and Kissimmee are located. You may want to carry insect repellent. Visitors who are or may become pregnant may want to take extra precautions.

WALT DISNEY WORLD
for SINGLES

DISNEY WORLD IS GREAT FOR SINGLES. It's safe, clean, and low-pressure. Safety and comfort are unsurpassed, especially for women traveling alone. Parking lots are well lit and constantly patrolled.

If you're looking for a place to relax without being hit on, Walt Disney World is perfect. The bars, lounges, and nightclubs are among the most laid-back and friendly you're likely to find. Between the BoardWalk and Disney Springs, nightlife abounds; virtually every type of entertainment is available at a reasonable price. If you overimbibe and you're a Disney resort guest, Disney buses will return you safely to your hotel.

See "Tips for Going Solo," on the next page, for more ways to enjoy Walt Disney World on your own.

WALT DISNEY WORLD
for COUPLES

MANY COUPLES THINK Walt Disney World is strictly for kids. Not so, an Evans City, Pennsylvania, woman attests:

> *I have many friends who think I was crazy to travel to Walt Disney World without my children (ages 9 and 12). I absolutely loved it! Instead of rushing from thrill ride to thrill ride, we were able to slow down and enjoy all of the amazing details that make WDW the incredibly special place that it is. It is an entirely different experience, but equally magical.*

WEDDINGS, COMMITMENT CEREMONIES, AND VOW RENEWALS

SO MANY COUPLES TIE THE KNOT or honeymoon in the World that Disney has a dedicated department to help arrange the day of your dreams. **Disney's Fairy Tale Weddings & Honeymoons** (☎ 321-939-4610; disneyweddings.com) offers a range of ceremony venues and services, plus honeymoon planning and registries.

You are responsible for obtaining an officiant and a marriage certificate. Disney maintains a list of officiants from which you can choose, or you can bring your own—if you do, the officiant counts as one of your guests.

*un*official **TIP**
Contact Disney as soon as you have a date in mind for your event—popular dates may not be available on short notice. If you wish to hold your ceremony inside a theme park, you're restricted to very early in the morning or late at night, when the park is closed to guests.

LEGALITIES

TO MARRY IN THE WORLD, you need a marriage license ($94), issued at any Florida county courthouse. Florida residents must complete a 4-hour premarital counseling session to marry less than 3 days after applying for their license; completing the course reduces the license fee to $61. There is no waiting period for residents of other states; all

TIPS FOR GOING SOLO

TRAVELING BY YOURSELF doesn't mean you can't have a great time at Disney World. **Deb Wills,** creator of the all-things-Disney website AllEars.net, offers this advice.

- One of the best parts about traveling solo is that you can be your own boss. Sleep in, have leisurely morning coffee on the balcony, relax by the pool . . . or not. If you'd rather get up and go early, who's to stop you?

- Put some spontaneity into your day. If you're taking Disney transportation, get on the first park bus that arrives.

- Get on the resort monorail (not the Express!) at the Magic Kingdom, and visit each of the resorts it stops at. Each resort has its own theme and character, with lots to see and explore.

- Did you know you can walk through the queues and view the preshows of the thrill rides even if you don't ride? Wander through at your own pace, then tell the cast member before boarding that you don't wish to ride. You'll be shown to a nearby exit.

- If you *do* want to experience the thrill rides, take advantage of the single-rider lines (when available) for the Rock 'n' Roller Coaster, Expedition Everest, *Millennium Falcon: Smugglers Run,* and Test Track. They can cut your wait time significantly.

- If you encounter folks taking photos of each other, ask if they'd like to be in one photo, then offer to snap the picture. This is a great way to make friends.

- Get your favorite Disney snack, find a bench, and people-watch. You'll be amazed at what you see: the honeymooning couple wearing bride-and-groom mouse ears, toddlers seeing Mickey and the characters for the first time, grandparents smiling indulgently as their grandchildren smear ice cream all over their faces. If you're missing the smiles of your own children, buy a couple of balloons and give them away. You'll help make the kids near you very, very happy.

weddings must occur within 60 days of getting the license. Blood tests aren't required, but both parties must present valid identification and their Social Security numbers. Finally, if you're widowed or divorced, you must also present a certified copy of the deceased spouse's death certificate or your divorce decree.

HONEYMOONS AND HONEYMOON REGISTRIES

HONEYMOON PACKAGES are adaptations of regular Walt Disney World travel packages, though you may purchase add-ons such as flowers and in-room gifts to make your trip more special. Some couples who honeymoon at Walt Disney World create a registry that allows friends and family to bestow gifts of tours, spa packages, special dinners, and the like. For more information on Disney honeymoon registries, visit disney.honeymoonwishes.com.

CELEBRATE . . . EVERYTHING!

DISNEY WORLD IS ALL ABOUT CELEBRATING—marriages, birthdays, anniversaries, the works—but only if you let somebody know. A St. Louis newlywed offers this advice:

If you're celebrating, ask for Celebration Buttons when you check into your hotel or at any park's Guest Relations, then WEAR THEM! Cast members regularly congratulated us, and I'm relatively certain we were seated at better tables for dinner based solely on our buttons.

- Learn how some of the magic is created. Take a behind-the-scenes tour or one of the Deluxe hotel tours if they're offered.

- Visit Animal Kingdom Lodge and relax at an animal-viewing area. Find an animal keeper; they'll gladly discuss care of the wild animals at the resort.

- Don't hesitate to strike up conversations with cast members or guests in line with you. International cast members in EPCOT's World Showcase will be happy to share stories about their homelands.

- Enjoy a leisurely shopping adventure around the World. Some stores (**Arribas Brothers** in Disney Springs and **Mitsukoshi Department Store** in the Japan Pavilion at World Showcase) have really neat displays and exhibits.

- Go to a restaurant you've always wanted to try but your picky eater has always declined. You don't have to order a full meal; try several appetizers or, better yet, just dessert.

- Special fun can be had at a character meal (no waiting in long lines). Which one has characters you love? Make an early or late reservation for fewer people and more character time. The Garden Grill in The Land, for example, is a hidden gem!

- Check the calendar for special events. The annual Flower & Garden Festival has lots of eye candy that you can enjoy at your own pace.

- Use common sense about your personal security. I feel very comfortable and safe traveling alone at Walt Disney World and have done so many times, but I still don't do things that I wouldn't do at home (like announce to anyone listening that I'm traveling solo). If you aren't comfortable walking to your room alone, ask at the front desk for a security escort. Use extra caution in the parking lots at night, just as you would at home.

TIPS FOR VISITORS WHO NEED "ADULT TIME"

AS WE'VE NOTED, WALT DISNEY WORLD is a great destination for adults traveling without kids, either as solos, couples, or groups of friends. The self-contained Disney universe, with its easy transportation, security, and variety of dining, drinking, and entertainment options, makes it a fabulous place to vacation without children (don't tell ours!).

Naturally, anyone who visits The Most Magical Place on Earth is well advised to be prepared to see children—lots of them. Indeed, it would be naive to think otherwise. But that doesn't mean that you need to be around the little tykes every minute. Here are some tips.

- **Dine late.** Most families will try to eat dinner before 8 p.m. Have a late lunch and try for a reservation closer to the last seating at your restaurant. The exceptions to this are California Grill and Topolino's Terrace, where many people (families or not) will try to time their meals around the fireworks in the Magic Kingdom, EPCOT, and Disney's Hollywood Studios.

- **Dine at Victoria & Albert's.** V&A is the only on-property restaurant that bans guests under age 10 (except at the Chef's Table). Pricey? Yes. Worth it? You bet.

- **Go to the spa.**

- **Linger in World Showcase.** We could spend hours poring over the details of the World Showcase pavilions. Favorites include the Bijutsu-kan Gallery in Japan and the Gallery of Arts and History in Morocco.

- **Really take in the trails of Animal Kingdom.** The animal trails in Asia, Africa, and Discovery Island are peaceful and beautiful.

- **Stay up late.** Take a tip from Tom Bricker, a friend of this book, and don't leave the park until well past closing. There's something magical about having all of Main Street or Sunset Boulevard to yourself with the lights and background music still playing. Make sure you don't miss the last bus to your resort, though, if you didn't drive.

- **Take a tour.** Many Walt Disney World tours have an age limit for how young a guest can be to experience them.
- **Spend the morning at the pool.** Most families hit the parks in the morning and come back to their hotels around lunch. Do the opposite and pretend the lifeguard is your personal cabana boy or girl.
- **See page 119** for a list of the quietest rooms at Walt Disney World, or use the TouringPlans.com hotel room finder (touringplans.com/walt-disney-world/room -finder) to scope out the quietest rooms at any Disney resort.

ROMANTIC GETAWAYS

NOT ALL DISNEY HOTELS lend themselves to a couple's getaway: Some are too family-oriented, while others swarm with conventioneers. For romantic (though expensive) lodging, we recommend **Animal Kingdom Lodge & Villas, Bay Lake Tower** at the Contemporary, **BoardWalk Inn & Villas, Grand Floridian Resort & Spa** and its **Villas, Polynesian Village & Villas,** the **Riviera, Wilderness Lodge & Villas,** and the **Yacht & Beach Club Resorts.** The Alligator Bayou section at **Port Orleans Riverside,** a Disney Moderate resort, also has secluded rooms.

ODDS *and* ENDS

SMOKING All Walt Disney World theme parks and water parks, along with the ESPN Wide World of Sports Complex, are smoke-free—*smoking is allowed only outside of the park entrances.* Disney resort guests may smoke only in designated areas; smoking in your room or on your balcony is prohibited.

For a full list of places where smoking is permitted, see disneyworld .disney.go.com/guest-services/designated-smoking-areas.

LOOSE ICE AND DRY ICE are prohibited in coolers inside the theme parks and water parks. Reusable ice packs are permitted.

FRIENDS OF BILL W. For information on **Alcoholics Anonymous** meetings in the area, visit osceolacountyintergroup.org. For information on **Al-Anon** and **Alateen** meetings, visit al-anonorlando.org.

ARRIVING *and* GETTING AROUND

GETTING *to* WALT DISNEY WORLD

FROM ORLANDO INTERNATIONAL AIRPORT (MCO)

YOU HAVE SEVERAL OPTIONS for getting from MCO to Disney World. Because most readers stay at a Disney hotel, we cover the **Mears Connect** bus service first, followed by towncar services, ride-hailing apps, and car rentals. Driving directions conclude this section.

Getting Between Orlando International Airport and Walt Disney World

Until 2022, Disney offered a free bus shuttle, called **Magical Express,** between Orlando International Airport (MCO) and Disney's hotels. With that service discontinued, several alternatives are available.

Behind the scenes, Disney's Magical Express was operated by Mears Transportation, which also runs taxi, towncar, and shuttle services throughout Central Florida. Shortly after Disney announced it was discontinuing Magical Express, Mears announced a similar bus service, called **Mears Connect** (☎ 407-422-4561; mearsconnect.com), that runs between MCO and Walt Disney World–area hotels. With Mears Connect's introduction, Mears has discontinued its older shuttle service from the airport to Disney's hotels.

Mears Connect comes in two flavors: Standard and Express. **Standard** works almost exactly like Magical Express, with shared bus

ORLANDO AIRPORT-TO-DISNEY RESORT TRANSPORTATION OPTIONS
RIDE-HAILING APP (LYFT, UBER)
ROUND-TRIP PRICE • $80–$160 plus gratuity (up to 3 adults)
PROS • Possibly the cheapest option for 3 or 4 people • Direct service to your resort
CONS • Price varies considerably based on demand • May be hard to find cars with child seats • Car quality ranges from basic to luxurious
MEARS CONNECT
ROUND-TRIP PRICE • *Standard:* $32/adult, $27/child plus small gratuity • *Express:* $500 for up to 4 adults
PROS • Cheapest option for 1 or 2 people • Mears ran Magical Express for years, so they know what they're doing • Child seats available
CONS • Standard is longest transportation time of any option • Standard service may drop off passengers at other resorts before yours • Express service is expensive
TOWNCAR SERVICE
ROUND-TRIP PRICE • $236 plus gratuity (up to 4 adults)
PROS • Likely the fastest way to get to your resort • Direct service to your resort • Child seats available • Driver will meet at baggage claim and assist with luggage
CONS • More expensive than other options

service between the airport and Disney's hotels, including the non-Disney-owned Disney Springs and Bonnet Creek hotels, plus the Four Seasons, Shades of Green, Swan, Swan Reserve, and Dolphin. Pricing is $32 per adult and $27 per child, round-trip; one-way fares are half that. As with Magical Express, the bus may drop off passengers at other hotels before you get to yours. If you're traveling alone or with one other adult and you don't mind the wait to drop off other guests at their resorts, Standard is the cheapest option to get between your hotel and Walt Disney World. The **Express** option will take you (and possibly other groups) directly to your hotel. The one-way cost is $250 for up to four people, then $55 for each additional passenger.

Towncar Service

If you're concerned about finding a ride using an app or having to wait on other people to fill a bus to your destination, a towncar service might be your best bet. **Happy Limousine** (☎ 407-856-1280; happylimo.com) provides towncar, minivan, and limo service between MCO (and Sanford International Airport) and Disney World–area hotels. Child seats and boosters are available, as are wheelchair-accessible options. One-way trips start at $118 for a 4-person luxury SUV or 5-person minivan, and $160 for a 10-person transit van.

One advantage of a towncar is that the driver will meet you at baggage claim with a placard showing your name and will assist with your luggage. Another advantage is that towncar services generally don't use surge pricing, so you know in advance how much your transportation will cost. Towncar services are probably the best choice for groups of five or more; the direct service to your hotel and the convenience of having your driver meet you at baggage claim probably more than make up for the cost increase between Mears Connect Standard and a towncar.

Ride-Hailing Apps

We generally recommend **Lyft** and **Uber** over taxis and shuttle services. They're often significantly less expensive, and while you can't pick the specific car you'll get, it's rare that we're in one and find ourselves think-ing a taxi or shuttle van would've been cleaner or more comfortable.

Both services are cheaper than taxis when commuting within the World. On a recent trip from Saratoga Springs Resort to the Magic Kingdom via Fort Wilderness, for example, we paid $12, while the return taxi ride along the same route, in the same traffic, was $25.

Lyft and Uber can also pick you up and drop you off at the airport. The pickup location is on MCO's second level, where baggage claim is and where passengers are currently picked up by family and friends.

The cost of a one-way ride from the airport varies greatly depend-ing on the number of people in your party, the kind of car you request, and the time of day you need to travel. A basic Uber or Lyft vehicle for up to three people in the middle of the day runs around $40, plus gra-tuity. The same ride can be $80 or more at 5 p.m. because of demand. Likewise, a vehicle with room for five costs around $55 midday but more during peak times. Fancy cars, such as Uber Black or Lyft Pre-mier, cost $80–$90 one-way, about the same as a towncar service. We prefer Lyft over Uber.

A Washington, D.C., reader found Uber a welcome alternative to Disney's bus service:

> *My first night at EPCOT, the bus line was so long—and so stalled— that I decided it made more sense to shell out for an Uber than to wait another hour to get back to my hotel; likewise at other busy times throughout the World. It was money well spent—less than rent-ing a car for a week.*

And from an Indianapolis couple:

> *If you're using a touring plan to make the most of your day and time is tight, we can't recommend Uber enough. We used the monorail and buses during the day and evening, but when it came to making it to our breakfast reservations and getting to Animal Kingdom for rope drop, Uber was immediately our first choice vs. losing sleep to get to the bus stop early. We never waited for a car for longer than 4 min-utes, and the drivers were friendly and quick.*

DISNEY MINNIE VANS Disney's own ride-hailing service, developed in partnership with Lyft, uses the Lyft app to summon a car driven by a Disney cast member. Minnie Vans operate only within Walt Disney World and can't be used to get between Disney and the airport, Uni-versal, or anywhere else outside of property.

Minnie Vans—which are painted red with white dots—might be marginally nicer than some Lyfts we've been in. But Minnie Vans cost roughly three times as much as a standard Lyft. And because there are relatively few of them, you may wait longer to be picked up.

Taxis

Taxis carry four to eight passengers, depending on vehicle type. Rates vary according to distance. If your hotel is in the World, your fare will be about $70–$82, plus tip. For the US 192 Maingate area, it will cost about $55. To International Drive or downtown Orlando, expect to pay in the neighborhood of $50–$70.

Mears (see page 421) provides local cab service, shuttle service, and an exclusive partnership with Uber called **Uber Taxi.** Using the Uber app, customers can book Mears taxis just as they would regular Uber rides. Mears says Uber Taxi is intended to offer the convenience of Uber to customers who prefer and trust a traditional taxi service over a ride-hailing app.

Renting a Car

Readers staying in Walt Disney World ask us frequently if they'll need a car. If your plans don't include regular visits to restaurants, attractions, or other destinations outside Disney World, then the answer is a qualified no. If you want (or need) a car, the good news is that Orlando is one of the least-expensive car-rental markets in the US, averaging under $44 per day. As we went to press, the lowest price for a weekly rental we could find for mid-2023 was $40 per day for a car at the airport, or $62 per day if you schlep your family and luggage to and from an off-site company via shuttle.

> *unofficial* **TIP**
> MCO's new terminal C holds an intermodal facility that includes commuter and intercity rail stations, plus rental car, taxi, shuttle, and public bus operations.

That said, take into account the thoughts of this reader from Washington State:

> *We rented a car and were glad we did. With a car, we could drive to the grocery store to restock our snack supply. It also came in handy for our night out.*

A dad from Avon Lake, Ohio, adds:

> *Although we stayed at the Grand Floridian, we found the monorail convenient only for the Magic Kingdom. Of the six nights we stayed, we used our car five days.*

An Ann Arbor, Michigan, mother of three shares her experience:

> *During our stay it was almost impossible to get into any of the Disney restaurants. Purely out of desperation, we rented a car so we could eat outside WDW. We had no problem finding good places to eat at a fraction of what you'd pay inside.*

PLAN TO RENT A CAR IF

1. Your hotel is outside Walt Disney World.
2. Your hotel is in the World but you want to eat someplace other than the theme parks and your hotel.
3. You plan to return to your hotel for naps or swimming during the day.
4. You plan to visit other area theme parks or water parks (including Disney's).

At **MCO,** all car-rental counters are on **level 1** of the main terminal (with terminals A and B). Level 1 is also where you can catch a courtesy shuttle to an off-site rental location.

Orlando is the largest rental-car market in the world. At last count, 36 companies vie for your business. Ten—**Alamo, Avis, Budget, Dollar, Enterprise, Hertz, National, Payless, SixT,** and **Thrifty**—have counters at terminals A, B, and C. **Fox** and 25 other companies have locations near the airport and provide courtesy shuttles outside the Arrivals level at all terminals.

We prefer renting inside the airport for the following reasons:

1. You can complete your paperwork while you wait for your checked luggage to arrive at baggage claim.
2. It's just a short walk to the garage to pick up your car.
3. The extra time and effort it takes to use the shuttle usually isn't worth the money saved, especially when you're traveling with kids.

If you rent on-site, you'll return your car to the garage adjacent to the terminal where your airline is located. If you return your car to the wrong garage, you'll have to haul your luggage from one side of the airport to the other to reach your check-in.

Most rental companies charge about $5–$8 a gallon to fill the gas tank. If you plan to drive a lot, prepay for a fill-up so you can return the car empty, or fill up at the **7-11** on airport property at 10505 Jeff Fuqua Blvd.

HOW ORLANDO RENTAL-CAR COMPANIES STACK UP When it comes to renting a car, most *Unofficial Guide* readers are looking for the following, as reflected in the table on the next page:

1. Quick, courteous, and efficient processing on pickup
2. A nice, well-maintained, late-model automobile
3. A car that is clean and odor-free
4. Quick, courteous, and efficient processing on return
5. If applicable, an efficient shuttle between the rental agency and airport

On a 0 (worst) to 100 (best) scale, the table shows how readers rate the Orlando operations of each company. Companies not listed didn't get enough surveys to analyze; we strongly recommend renting from a company listed in the table. To participate in our survey, visit touringplans.com/walt-disney-world/survey.

National Car Rental was named the top rental company for the 13th time in the past 14 years. If you prioritize service and car condition as much as getting a good deal, go with National. **Alamo,** the only other winner in the last 13 years, is almost always in the top two. **Turo** is new to the list—let us know your experience if you rent from them. They're off-site, so they must be doing something right to be ranked this high.

Most companies, in fact, deliver consistently good cars and service. If budget is a top priority, we're comfortable recommending any company in the top five that has the lowest price. In general, cars from less-expensive companies tend to have higher miles and fewer amenities, such as backup cameras and satellite navigation or radio (one even had crank-up windows).

Readers complain most about the hassle of off-site shuttles and the paperwork involved in picking up cars at the off-site locations. At **Fox,** be prepared for the staff to assume you're going to steal the car; the voluminous paperwork is to help the bounty hunters find you. Also, the pace is slow at **SixT,** even if the line is short—we suspect most of their customers are visiting from outside the US and the staff needs time to review differences in rental policies, insurance coverage, electronic tolls, and the like. Both companies' people are fantastic at what they do.

INSURANCE AND FEES Car renters should know what their auto insurance does and doesn't cover. If you have the slightest question

RENTAL COMPANY	Pickup Efficiency	Condition of Car	Cleanliness of Car	Return Efficiency	Overall Rating	Survey Rank
NATIONAL	96	94	97	91	94	1
TURO	94	91	94	87	91	2 (tie)
ALAMO	92	91	94	87	91	2 (tie)
ENTERPRISE	90	89	93	87	90	4
HERTZ	85	88	92	87	88	5
SIXT	84	92	94	80	88	6
AVERAGE	83	89	91	84	87	NA
AVIS	81	86	88	81	84	7
THRIFTY	71	88	89	84	83	8 (tie)
FOX	78	85	86	82	83	8 (tie)
BUDGET	70	84	87	82	81	10 (tie)
DOLLAR	71	87	88	75	81	10 (tie)

Note: For any car-rental agency not shown, we didn't receive enough survey responses to analyze.

about your coverage, call your agent. A corollary discussion pertains to added coverage from your credit card company if the rental fee is charged on the card. Usually, credit card coverage picks up deductibles and some ancillary charges that your auto-insurance policy doesn't cover. The tune is the same, however: Make sure you understand what is and isn't covered.

A 6%–7% sales tax, a $2.50-per-day airport-facility surcharge, and a vehicle-license-recovery fee of 45¢ to $2.02 per day will be added to your rental car bill. Some companies, including Alamo, add fees for tire and battery wear, plus other cryptic fees. Luckily, you can rent a car at your hotel on the day you actually need it.

OUR BEST RENTAL-CAR DISCOUNT TIP We've saved hundreds of dollars over the past couple of years with a website called **AutoSlash** (autoslash.com), which does two things very well:

1. If you haven't yet rented a car, Autoslash will help you find the lowest rates available, using every discount you're eligible for.

2. If you've already rented a car, tell AutoSlash the details, and it'll search continuously for a lower rate. If a lower rate turns up, AutoSlash will email you a link to rebook.

AutoSlash frequently finds multiple low-price deals through **Priceline**. In those cases, AutoSlash will list the car type, rental company, and price for every deal available. Use our list of the best rental companies, above, to weed out the ones that don't appeal to you, and book the cheapest one that does.

TOLLS If you're flying into Orlando and plan on driving extensively, consider picking up a **Visitor Toll Pass** (visitortollpass.com) when you arrive at the airport. You'll pick up a small Toll Pass device from a vending machine at terminal A on level 1 and link it to your credit card. The Toll Pass hangs from your rearview mirror, pays tolls automatically, and allows you to use the electronic toll and express lanes throughout Florida. If the Visitor Toll Pass program isn't working, you can pick up a regular toll transponder at most grocery stores and drugstores, such as Publix and CVS.

Interstate 4

Regardless of how you navigate to Orlando, you'll almost certainly drive on I-4, its busiest highway and one that demands a great deal of a driver's concentration. I-4 in Orlando is under more or less constant construction: A new four-year project will add lanes and interchanges starting in 2023 between Exits 58 (Champions Gate) and 67 (Osceola Parkway, leading to EPCOT and Disney Springs).

WDW EXITS OFF I-4 East to west (in the direction of Orlando to Tampa), five I-4 exits serve Walt Disney World:

Exit 68 (FL 535/Lake Buena Vista) primarily serves the Disney Springs Resort Area and Disney Springs, including the Marketplace and the West Side. It also serves non-Disney hotels with a Lake Buena Vista address. This exit puts you on a road with lots of traffic signals, especially near I-4. A construction project to improve the I-4 exit here began in late 2021. Avoid this area unless you're headed to one of the preceding destinations.

Exit 67 (FL 536/EPCOT/Disney Springs) delivers you to a four-lane expressway into the heart of Disney World. It's the fastest and most convenient way for westbound travelers to access almost all Disney destinations except Animal Kingdom and ESPN Wide World of Sports Complex. Be alert for road construction through 2027.

Exit 65 (Osceola Parkway) is the best exit for westbound travelers to access Disney's Animal Kingdom, Animal Kingdom Lodge, Pop Century Resort, Art of Animation Resort, the All-Star Resorts, and the ESPN Wide World of Sports Complex. Expect road construction through 2027.

Exit 64 (US 192/Magic Kingdom) is the best route for eastbound travelers to access all Disney destinations. If eastbound traffic is heavy, get off at **Exit 62** instead. Expect road construction through 2027.

Exit 62 (Disney World/Celebration) is the first Disney exit you'll encounter heading east. This four-lane, controlled-access highway connects to the Walt Disney World Maingate. Accessing Disney World via the next exit, **Exit 64,** also routes you through the main entrance. Expect road construction through 2027.

I-4 DELAYS I-4 can be a mess anywhere from Tampa to Daytona. The greatest congestion is between the Universal Orlando–International Drive area and downtown Orlando, but the section to the southwest serving the Disney World exits can become a choke point at almost any time of day.

If you're going from Walt Disney World toward Orlando (east), the jam usually breaks up after you pass the FL 535 exit, but it gets congested again near Universal Orlando and northeast due to construction. As you head west toward Tampa, traffic eases up after the US 192 interchange.

If you're considering a hotel on or near I-Drive, try to find one toward the southern end. If I-4 traffic becomes intolerable, it's pretty easy to commute from the Universal Orlando–International Drive area to Walt Disney World on (1) **Turkey Lake Road,** connecting to Palm Parkway and FL 535 on the northwest side of I-4; (2) the southernmost section of **I-Drive,** connecting to FL 536 on the southeast side of the interstate; or (3) **Daryl Carter Parkway,** which bridges I-4 just

I-4 & Walt Disney World Area

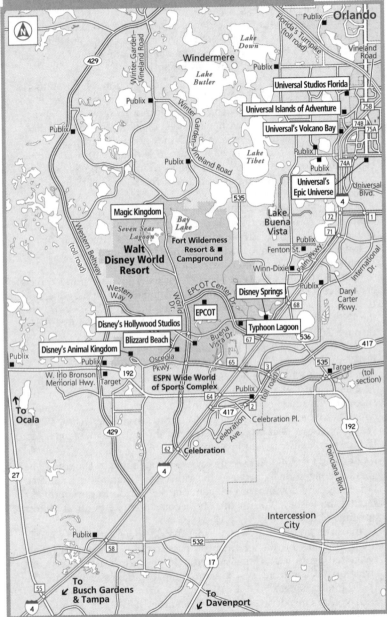

northeast of FL 535, connecting Palm Parkway and International Drive near the Orlando International Premium Outlets.

AVOIDING THE I-4 BLUES Many GPS apps and newer GPS units will automatically reroute you around delays from construction and traffic issues. For those without GPS, we provide the following alternative routes. Before you take any of these detours, however, use the websites below to verify whether the construction zones are still active.

If you're driving at low-traffic times, you might prefer to deal with I-4 construction rather than make a detour. During the day (6 a.m.–10 p.m.), most projects try to keep all lanes open, though traffic sometimes slows to a crawl (as it does in the WDW area even when no work is going on). From 10 p.m. to 6 a.m., however, there may be lane closures.

*un*official **TIP**
FL 417, aka the **Central Florida GreeneWay,** is a toll road, so make sure you have about $5 in cash or change to pay the toll.

Real-time road conditions are available online at the **Interstate 4 Exit Information Guide** (i4exit guide.com/i-4-traffic), and the **FDOT Interactive Project Map** (data .fdot.gov/road/projects) shows all active construction projects in Florida. Information about construction in Orlando and the tourist areas is available at **Central Florida Roads** (cflroads.com). For info about and current conditions on area toll roads, visit the website for the **Central Florida Expressway Authority** (cfxway.com).

Traveling southwest on I-4, we recommend going around Orlando on FL 417/Central Florida GreeneWay (a toll road) and taking Exit 3 onto West Osceola Parkway into Walt Disney World. In addition to construction in Orlando and the Disney World area, there might also be construction between Daytona and DeLand. To avoid this part of I-4, take Exit 260C from southbound I-95 onto US 92 West, and turn south (left) onto US 17. When you hit I-4, take it west a short distance to FL 417, and bypass Orlando to the east.

From I-95 southbound, take Exit 260C onto US 92 westbound; then turn south (left) onto US 17. When you hit I-4, take it west a short distance to FL 417; bypass Orlando to the east, taking Exit 3 onto West Osceola Parkway and then into Walt Disney World.

From I-95 northbound, take Exit 249 onto FL 44 West toward DeLand. At I-4, go southwest, exiting onto Saxon Boulevard. Take Saxon Boulevard west to US 17, and turn south (left). When you hit I-4 again, take it west a short distance to FL 417. Take FL 417, and bypass Orlando to the east.

From MCO, exit the airport on Jeff Fuqua Boulevard and proceed south to the FL 417/Central Florida GreeneWay toll road. Turn right up the ramp and take FL 417 northwest. Take Exit 3 onto West Osceola Parkway and follow it to Walt Disney World.

From Sanford International Airport, take East Airport Boulevard west to the FL 417/Central Florida GreeneWay toll road and bypass Orlando to the east, taking Exit 3 onto West Osceola Parkway and continuing to Walt Disney World.

From Miami, Fort Lauderdale, and southeastern Florida, head north on Florida's Turnpike to Exit 249/Osceola Parkway West and follow the signs.

From Tampa and southwest Florida, take I-75 northbound to I-4; then drive east on I-4, take Exit 64 onto US 192 West and follow the signs.

ALTERNATIVE AIRPORTS

A SHORT DISTANCE northeast of Orlando is **Sanford International Airport** (**SFB;** orlandosanfordairport.com). Small, convenient, and easily accessible, it's low-hassle compared with the huge MCO and its block-long security-checkpoint lines.

The primary domestic carrier at SFB is **Allegiant Air** (☎ 702-505-8888; allegiantair.com), with service throughout the East Coast and the Midwest. **Sun Country** (☎ 651-905-2737; suncountry.com) also serves SFB and dozens of US cities. Two low-cost Canadian airlines also serve Sanford: **Flair Airlines** (flyflair.com) offers service between Canada and four other US cities, and **Swoop** (flyswoop.com) offers flights to Sanford from November through April, with twice-weekly return flights to Canada. An Uber or Lyft from Sanford to Disney property will run you $70–$150 or more one-way.

A reader from Roanoke, Virginia, uses Sanford frequently, writing:

> *The 45-minute drive to WDW is more than made up for by avoiding the chaos at Orlando International, and it's stress-free.*

This couple from White Township, New Jersey, prefers flying into Tampa instead:

> *Flying from Newark to Tampa instead of Orlando saves us money and our sanity. It means significantly lower fares, fewer children on the plane, and shorter security lines.*

Be aware, however, that it's a 77-mile drive from Tampa International Airport to the Magic Kingdom—about an hour and 15 minutes.

HOW *to* TRAVEL *around the* WORLD (or, The *Real* Mr. Toad's Wild Ride)

TRYING TO COMMUTE around Walt Disney World can be frustrating, simply because of the number of transportation options available. To get between many points, your options include cars, boats, monorails, and elevated gondolas, plus walking.

Between any two points in Walt Disney World, there's almost always a free transportation option available. Some of the free options are slow enough, however, that paying for an alternative option often makes more sense. We'll walk you through those options right after some orientation.

FINDING YOUR WAY

WALT DISNEY WORLD IS HUGE—about the size of San Francisco. As with any big city, it's easy to get lost here. The easiest way to orient yourself is to think in terms of five major clusters:

1. **The Magic Kingdom area** encompasses all hotels and theme parks around Seven Seas Lagoon. This includes the Magic Kingdom; hotels connected by the monorail; Shades of Green resort; and the Palm, Magnolia, and Oak Trail Golf Courses.

2. **The Bay Lake area** includes developments on and around Bay Lake: Wilderness Lodge & Villas, Fort Wilderness campground, and the Four Seasons Resort Orlando and Tranquilo Golf Club.

3. **The EPCOT area** contains EPCOT and its resort hotels, Disney's Hollywood Studios, the BoardWalk, ESPN Wide World of Sports, Pop Century Resort,

Art of Animation Resort, Caribbean Beach Resort, Riviera Resort, and Star Wars: Galactic Starcruiser.

4. **The Disney Springs area** includes Disney Springs; Typhoon Lagoon water park; Lake Buena Vista Golf Course; the Disney Springs Resort Area; and the Port Orleans, Saratoga Springs, and Old Key West resorts.

5. **The Animal Kingdom area** includes Disney's Animal Kingdom, Animal Kingdom Lodge & Villas, the All-Star Resorts, Coronado Springs Resort and Blizzard Beach water park.

The following section covers how to get around Walt Disney World using the Disney transportation system. Tips using non-Disney hotel shuttles and for driving yourself begin on page 439.

THE DISNEY TRANSPORTATION SYSTEM (DTS)

THE DISNEY TRANSPORTATION SYSTEM is large, diversified, and generally efficient, but sometimes it's overwhelmed, particularly at park opening and closing. If you could always be assured of getting on a bus, boat, monorail, or gondola at these critical times, we'd advise you to leave your car at home. In reality, delays are unavoidable when huge crowds want to go somewhere at once. In addition, some destinations are served directly, while many others require one or more transfers. Finally, it's sometimes difficult to figure out how Disney's various methods of transportation interconnect.

The DTS is a "hub and spoke" system. Hubs include the **Transportation and Ticket Center** (**TTC**), **Disney Springs,** and all four major **theme parks** (from about an hour before official opening time to 1 hour after closing). With some exceptions, direct service is available from Disney resorts to the major theme parks and Disney Springs, as well as between parks.

unofficial **TIP**
If a hotel offers boat or monorail service, its bus service will be limited— you'll have to transfer at a hub for many destinations.

If you're staying at a Magic Kingdom resort that's served by the monorail (**Contemporary** and **Bay Lake Tower, Grand Floridian & Villas, Polynesian Village & Villas**), you'll be able to commute efficiently to the Magic Kingdom. If you want to visit EPCOT, you must take the monorail to the TTC and transfer to the EPCOT monorail. (Guests at the Polynesian Village & Villas can eliminate the transfer by walking 5–10 minutes to the TTC and catching the direct monorail to EPCOT.)

If you're staying at an EPCOT resort (**BoardWalk Inn & Villas, Dolphin, Swan, Swan Reserve, Yacht & Beach Club Resorts**), you can walk or commute by boat to EPCOT's International Gateway (rear) entrance. Although direct buses link EPCOT resorts to the Magic Kingdom and Disney's Animal Kingdom, there's no direct bus to EPCOT's main entrance or Disney's Hollywood Studios. To reach the Studios from the EPCOT resorts, you must take a boat or the Skyliner, or walk. Note that the Swan, Swan Reserve, and Dolphin use Mears Transportation, not Disney, for bus service—if you're headed to the Magic Kingdom, Mears will drop you off at the TTC, while Disney buses will drop you off at the park entrance. Walk over to the Yacht Club bus stop when you want to go to the Magic Kingdom.

The **Caribbean Beach, Pop Century, Art of Animation, Saratoga Springs, Port Orleans, Coronado Springs, Old Key West, Animal Kingdom**

Lodge & Villas, and **All-Star** resorts offer direct buses to all theme parks (though Pop and Animation may provide only the Skyliner to EPCOT and Hollywood Studios during slower times of the year). The rub is that you must sometimes walk a long way to bus stops or endure more than a half dozen additional pickups before actually heading for the park(s). Commuting in the morning from these resorts is generally easy, though you may have to ride standing. Returning in the evening, however, can be a different story. **Shades of Green** runs frequent shuttles from the resort to the TTC, where guests can transfer to their final destinations.

Hotels of the **Disney Springs Resort Area** (**DSRA**) provide shuttle service through an independent company. The DSRA shuttles constitute a negative for guests at these hotels—the service is simply substandard. Before you book a DSRA hotel, check the nature and frequency of its shuttles.

Guests staying at **Fort Wilderness Resort & Campground** must use its buses to reach boat landings or the Settlement Depot and Reception Outpost bus stops. From these points, guests can travel directly by boat to the Magic Kingdom or by bus to other destinations. Except for going to the Magic Kingdom, the best way for Fort Wilderness guests to commute is in their own car.

The Disney Transportation System vs. Driving Your Own Car

To help you assess your transportation options, we've developed a table comparing the approximate commuting times from Disney resorts to various Walt Disney World destinations, using Disney transportation or your own car (see pages 434–435). The table represents more than 600,000 data points collected for this edition, all in 2022 and 2023. It includes bus, monorail, and boat options—the Skyliner system has its own table.

DISNEY TRANSPORTATION The times listed in the table in the "Disney System" columns represent an average-case and worst-case scenario. For example, if you want to go from the All-Star Resorts to the Magic Kingdom, the table indicates the times as "33 (50)." The first number, 33, indicates how many minutes your commute will take on an average day. It assumes that buses arrive every 20 minutes (see "Walt Disney World Bus Service," 433), your average wait is half of that, there are no major traffic delays, and everything else is as usual. It represents the average time we observed during our research of the transportation system. For the pessimists, the number in parentheses (50) indicates the maximum trip times—the longest it should take for the next bus to show up, load, and get you to your destination. Use this to plan for contingencies. (*Example:* The bus is pulling away as you arrive at the stop, and you must wait around 20 minutes for the next one. Once en route, the bus hits every red light on the way to the Magic Kingdom.)

Bus schedules are also adjusted based on demand and fuel costs. By far the biggest influence on your travel time between two points on the DTS is the amount of time you have to wait for your bus to arrive. Once you hop on your bus, the travel time is pretty consistent—barring any unusual traffic problems—but your time waiting for the bus can vary greatly. Most cast members will tell you that buses run every 20 minutes. Our data indicates they run slightly more often: about every 19 minutes. The mode (the most common transportation time) for a bus between any two points is 28 minutes—that's been consistent for a couple of years. Also, the maximum bus travel time between any two destinations is frequently 50 minutes. That's either a policy that Disney works really hard to enforce ("never make a guest wait more than 50 minutes to get to a destination") or something in the data feed ("never show a total transportation time above 50 minutes"). Service at the Value and Moderate resorts is about the same as at Deluxe resorts, something we were a bit surprised to see.

Walt Disney World Bus Service

Note: For an up-to-date look at what time buses start running at each resort, visit tinyurl.com/wdw -bus-times.

unofficial **TIP**
If your Disney resort doesn't have direct bus service to the water parks, use Uber, Lyft, or a taxi instead.

Each Disney bus has an illuminated panel above its windshield that flashes the bus's destination. Theme parks also have designated waiting areas for each Disney destination. To catch the bus to the Old Key West Resort from Disney's Hollywood Studios, for example, go to the bus stop and wait in the area designated for passengers going that resort. At the resorts, go to any bus stop and wait for the bus displaying your destination on the illuminated panel; the **My Disney Experience** app (see page 31) displays the approximate arrival time of the next bus to your destination. Directions to Disney destinations are available at check-in or at your hotel's Guest Relations desk. Guest Relations can also answer questions about the transportation system.

Service from resorts to major theme parks is fairly direct. You may have intermediate stops, but you won't have to transfer. Service to the water parks and other Disney resorts almost always requires transfers or extra stops.

Travel between your Disney hotel and the water parks can be tricky. To travel between your Disney hotel and Blizzard Beach, you must transfer at the Animal Kingdom. Traveling between your Disney hotel and **Typhoon Lagoon** will probably also require a stop (and possibly a bus transfer) at Disney Springs; if you're unlucky, this round-trip journey takes 2–3 hours per day. Our advice is to ask your hotel if direct service is available; if not, use a ride-hailing app.

The fastest way to commute among resorts by bus is to take a bus from your resort to one of the major theme parks and then transfer to a bus for your resort destination. This works, of course, only when the parks are open—actually, from 1 hour before the park opens for Early Theme Park Entry (ETPE) until 1 hour after closing. (Disney buses stop taking passengers *to* the theme parks when they close, but they'll take passengers *from* the parks for an hour afterward.) If the park is open late for Extended Evening Theme Park Hours, buses will continue to run for an hour after the end of that.

continued on page 436

COMMUTING TIMES BY CAR VS. THE

Average MAXIMUM time in minutes from	to MAGIC KINGDOM		to EPCOT		to DHS	
	YOUR CAR	**DISNEY SYSTEM**	**YOUR CAR**	**DISNEY SYSTEM**	**YOUR CAR**	**DISNEY SYSTEM**
ALL-STAR RESORTS	37 (47)	33 (50)	18 (23)	27 (50)	16 (20)	29 (49)
ANIMAL KINGDOM	37 (48)	26 (44)	16 (17)	38 (49)	16 (17)	24 (34)
ANIMAL KINGDOM LODGE & VILLAS	39 (50)	32 (44)	19 (21)	32 (45)	18 (19)	34 (50)
ART OF ANIMATION RESORT	40 (51)	33 (49)	23 (28)	27 (50)	20 (24)	34 (50)
BEACH CLUB RESORT & VILLAS	36 (46)	32 (49)	16 (21)	29 (36*)	14 (18)	29 (41*)
BLIZZARD BEACH	36 (46)	28 (39)	18 (23)	—	18 (22)	39 (54)
BOARDWALK INN & VILLAS	36 (46)	30 (46)	16 (21)	29 (46*)	14 (18)	23 (49*)
CARIBBEAN BEACH AND RIVIERA	37 (47)	31 (49)	18 (23)	***	15 (19)	***
CONTEMPORARY- BAY LAKE	—	—	21 (26)	36 (49)	23 (27)	31 (49)
CORONADO SPRINGS	37 (47)	39 (44)	18 (23)	39 (45)	16 (20)	31 (44)
DHS	36 (46)	25 (35)	19 (24)	25 (35)	—	—
DISNEY SPRINGS	Bus service only back to your Disney resort					
DISNEY SPRINGS RESORT AREA	41 (51)	69 (91)	21 (26)	47 (62)	20 (24)	45 (60)
DOLPHIN	35 (45)	33 (65)	15 (20)	16 (44*)	15 (19)	16 (42*)
EPCOT	36 (46)	26 (37)	—	—	19 (23)	21 (30)
FORT WILDERNESS	37 (47)	28 (50)	18 (23)	34 (51*)	19 (23)	34 (50)
GRAND FLORIDIAN & VILLAS	—	—	18 (23)	38 (50*)	20 (24)	33 (50)
MAGIC KINGDOM	—	—	26 (39)	33 (45)	22 (29)	24 (34)
OLD KEY WEST	36 (46)	29 (50)	18 (23)	30 (50)	18 (22)	30 (50)
POLYNESIAN VILLAGE	—	—	17 (22)	33 (43**)	19 (23)	31 (50)
POP CENTURY RESORT	40 (51)	32 (50)	23 (28)	***	20 (24)	***
PORT ORLEANS FRENCH QUARTER	37 (47)	32 (50)	19 (24)	29 (50)	19 (23)	32 (50)
PORT ORLEANS RIVERSIDE	38 (48)	34 (50)	20 (25)	29 (50)	20 (24)	32 (50)
RIVIERA RESORT	37 (47)	32 (50)	18 (23)	***	15 (19)	***
SARATOGA SPRINGS	38 (48)	28 (49)	18 (23)	31 (47)	20 (24)	31 (47)
SHADES OF GREEN	28 (36)	35 (49)	18 (23)	33 (45)	20 (24)	20 (28)
STAR WARS: GALACTIC STARCRUISER	35 (46)	NA	20 (25)	NA	10 (13)	NA
SWAN/SWAN RESERVE	35 (45)	24 (61)	15 (20)	18 (42*)	15 (19)	14 (33*)
TREEHOUSE VILLAS (SARATOGA SPRINGS)	37 (47)	28 (49)	18 (23)	31 (47)	19 (23)	31 (47)
TYPHOON LAGOON	37 (47)	41 (56)	18 (23)	51 (70)	15 (19)	62 (85)
WILDERNESS LODGE	—	24 (63)	20 (25)	27 (50)	22 (26)	30 (50)
YACHT CLUB	36 (46)	33 (65)	16 (21)	16 (40*)	14 (18)	15 (35*)

Note: Before 4 p.m., all transportation between the theme parks and Disney Springs requires a transfer at a nearby resort. After 4 p.m., buses run directly from the theme parks to Disney Springs. There are no buses from Disney Springs directly to the theme parks.

† Driving time vs. time on DTS. Driving times include time in your car, stops to pay tolls, time to park, and any transfers on Disney trams and monorails.

DISNEY TRANSPORTATION SYSTEM†

to ANIMAL KINGDOM		to TYPHOON LAGOON		to DISNEY SPRINGS		to BLIZZARD BEACH	
YOUR CAR	DISNEY SYSTEM	YOUR CAR	DISNEY SYSTEM	YOUR CAR	DISNEY SYSTEM	YOUR CAR	DISNEY SYSTEM
11 (12)	26 (49)	12 (13)	27 (63)	13 (14)	31 (50)	6 (7)	26 (46)
—	—	17 (19)	65 (83)	19 (21)	—	10 (13)	41 (50)
9 (10)	26 (50)	19 (21)	26 (67)	22 (24)	33 (50)	11 (14)	23 (50)
14 (16)	29 (50)	12 (14)	19 (59)	15 (16)	22 (49)	10 (12)	29 (50)
17 (18)	31 (49)	9 (10)	23 (59)	10 (11)	32 (50)	12 (13)	22 (60)
10 (13)	—	13 (14)	80 (103)	14 (15)	—	—	—
17 (18)	33 (50)	9 (10)	25 (59)	10 (11)	31 (49)	12 (13)	22 (58)
17 (18)	32 (50)	6 (7)	23 (59)	7 (8)	31 (40)	12 (13)	25 (61)
20 (21)	35 (50)	17 (18)	27 (63)	16 (17)	34 (49)	15 (16)	25 (62)
11 (12)	32 (49)	12 (13)	6 (54)	13 (14)	28 (49)	6 (7)	30 (46)
16 (17)	20 (30)	8 (9)	77 (99)	9 (10)		11 (12)	56 (71)
Bus service only back to your Disney resort							
21 (22)	48 (64)	9 (10)	26 (29)	6 (7)	—	16 (17)	66 (81)
16 (17)	36 (60)	10 (11)	21 (61)	11 (12)	25 (62)	11 (12)	22 (57)
16 (17)	33 (48)	12 (13)	50 (62)	13 (14)	—	11 (12)	51 (65)
29 (25)	35 (50)	10 (11)	26 (62)	11 (12)	33 (50)	19 (20)	30 (60)
18 (19)	34 (50)	15 (16)	26 (67)	16 (17)	33 (50)	13 (14)	24 (61)
17 (18)	45 (63)	23 (31)	59 (75)	27 (36)	—	12 (13)	61 (77)
19 (20)	28 (50)	8 (9)	20 (57)	9 (10)	32 (49)	14 (15)	20 (56)
17 (18)	32 (50)	14 (15)	25 (63)	15 (16)	32 (50)	12 (13)	18 (57)
14 (16)	30 (49)	12 (14)	23 (57)	15 (16)	32 (50)	10 (12)	20 (61)
19 (20)	28 (50)	9 (10)	20 (55)	10 (11)	29 (50)	14 (15)	23 (60)
20 (21)	30 (71)	10 (11)	19 (56)	11 (12)	31 (46)	15 (16)	24 (64)
15 (18)	29 (50)	5 (7)	24 (60)	7 (8)	28 (50)	10 (12)	25 (60)
21 (22)	28 (50)	9 (10)	23 (61)	6 (7)	36 (50)	16 (17)	24 (63)
18 (19)	22 (33)	15 (16)	59 (75)	18 (20)	57 (83)	13 (14)	50 (64)
15 (17)	NA	15 (17)	NA	16 (17)	30 (60)	NA	24 (58)
16 (17)	35 (60)	10 (11)	21 (60)	11 (12)	24 (60)	11 (12)	21 (56)
17 (19)	28 (50)	9 (10)	22 (59)	6 (7)	36 (60)	13 (14)	24 (59)
20 (21)	28 (40)	—	—	8 (9)	—	15 (16)	55 (70)
20 (21)	32 (50)	17 (18)	28 (64)	18 (19)	33 (50)	15 (16)	24 (60)
17 (18)	31 (46)	8 (10)	24 (58)	10 (12)	31 (40)	12 (13)	21 (57)

 * This hotel is within walking distance of EPCOT; time given is for boat transportation to the International Gateway (EPCOT's rear entrance).

 ** By foot to Transportation and Ticket Center and then by EPCOT monorail

 *** Not enough data to calculate

continued from page 433

If you're trying to commute to another resort for a late dinner during the off-season, when parks close early, you'll have to transfer at **Disney Springs**—which Disney, in its transportation instructions, lists somewhat disingenuously as the transfer point for *all* resort-to-resort commuting, hoping you'll stop and drop some dough en route. If the theme park buses are running, though, proceed to the park closest to your resort, and then transfer to the bus going to the resort where you'll be dining.

Despite what Disney's official schedule says, bus service to the parks begins about 90 minutes before official park opening, which is 60 minutes before ETPE (that is, buses will start running around **7 a.m.** on days when ETPE is at 8 a.m. and official park opening is 9 a.m.). Generally, buses run every 20–25 minutes. Buses to all four parks deliver you to the park entrance (except, as noted above, buses from the Swan, Dolphin, and Swan Reserve to the Magic Kingdom).

To be on hand for ETPE, catch direct buses to the parks 60–90 minutes before official park opening. If you must transfer to reach your park, such as at Fort Wilderness, leave 15–20 minutes earlier.

For your return bus trip in the evening, leave the park 40–60 minutes before closing to avoid the rush. If you're caught in the exodus, you may be inconvenienced, but you won't be stranded.

As you may have noticed by now, this book is replete with reader complaints about Disney's bus service. From an Ohio mom:

> *WDW needs to do something about the buses to and from the parks. They are the WORST! Slow, infrequent, and too small. Thank goodness we rented a car. We drove everywhere after taking the terrible buses three times—zipped in and out and got around quickly.*

A Massillon, Ohio, family thinks Disney should work on its bus-tracking technology:

> *Several times at Saratoga Springs, we had to wait 45 minutes or more for a bus. Often two buses for the same park will arrive back-to-back, and then you may need to wait 45 minutes until they come again. They need to track how the buses are spaced—maybe have some buses close by that can jump in when needed, or track them with GPS.*

A reader who stayed at Port Orleans reports:

> *The DTS was wildly erratic, but we were lucky more often than not. For every time we had to wait half an hour at the bus stop, there were two or three times with no wait at all.*

If you're planning on riding a bus from **Port Orleans Riverside** to a park around opening time, the **West or North bus stop** may be your best option. These are the first stops on the route, and the bus is sometimes full or standing-room-only before it gets to all the stops. Likewise, here are the first bus pickup points for Disney resorts with multiple bus stops:

- **CARIBBEAN BEACH** Martinique
- **OLD KEY WEST** Peninsular Road
- **SARATOGA SPRINGS** The Grandstand
- **CORONADO SPRINGS** Gran Destino
- **PORT ORLEANS RIVERSIDE** West Depot

As is the case elsewhere in Walt Disney World, bus service at Disney Springs is a crapshoot. This reader found himself in bus hell:

I budgeted an hour for the return trip from Disney Springs to Animal Kingdom Lodge on the morning of our departure, and I STILL found myself on the phone with Magical Express [since discontinued] 30 minutes before our bus was supposed to leave for the airport, asking when the next bus after that would leave Animal Kingdom Lodge. We barely made the backup bus. This was not a magical ending to my vacation.

NOT ALL HUBS ARE CREATED EQUAL All major theme parks, Disney Springs, and the TTC are hubs on the bus system. If your route requires you to transfer at a hub, transfer at the closest park or the TTC, except at park closing. Avoid Disney Springs as a transfer point—traffic around there slows everything to a crawl.

Except at Fort Wilderness, no buses run between the TTC and the Disney resorts. If you're commuting from resort to resort, you must transfer at Disney Springs or one of the major theme parks during park operating hours. If you're parked at the TTC and you want to travel to a Disney resort, go to the right of the Magic Kingdom entrance to catch a bus to your destination.

Walt Disney World Monorail Service

Picture the monorail system as three loops. **Loop A** is an express route that runs counterclockwise connecting the Magic Kingdom with the TTC. **Loop B** runs clockwise alongside Loop A, making all stops, with service to (in order) the TTC, Polynesian Village & Villas, Grand Floridian & Villas, the Magic Kingdom, Contemporary Resort and Bay Lake Tower, and back to the TTC. The long **Loop C** dips southeast, connecting the TTC with EPCOT. The hub for all loops is the TTC (where you usually park to visit the Magic Kingdom).

The monorail that serves the **Magic Kingdom** resorts usually starts running an hour or so before official park opening. If you're staying at a Magic Kingdom resort and you wish to be among the first into the park for Early Theme Park Entry when official opening is 9 a.m., board the monorail at these times:

- **FROM CONTEMPORARY RESORT AND BAY LAKE TOWER** 7:45–8 a.m.
- **FROM POLYNESIAN VILLAGE & VILLAS** 7:50–8:05 a.m.
- **FROM GRAND FLORIDIAN & VILLAS** 8–8:10 a.m.

If you're a day guest, you'll be allowed on the monorail at the TTC between 8:15 and 8:30 a.m. when official opening is 9 a.m. If you want to board earlier, walk from the TTC to the Polynesian Village Resort and board there.

If you bought Disney's Park Hopper pass, you might think that means you can flit among the parks; alas, it's more complicated. For example, you can't go directly from the Magic Kingdom to EPCOT— you must catch the express monorail (Loop A) to the TTC and then transfer to the Loop C monorail to EPCOT. If lines to board either monorail are short, you can usually reach EPCOT in 30–40 minutes, but if you want to go to EPCOT for dinner (as many do) and you're leaving the Magic Kingdom in late afternoon, you may have to wait 30 minutes or longer to board the Loop A monorail. This delay boosts your commuting time to 50–60 minutes.

Disney frequently changes the monorail's operating hours to allow for daytime inspection of the track and vehicles. Rain and lightning, which happen frequently in Orlando, will also stop the monorails, as this reader from Saginaw, Michigan found out:

> It would have helped to know that monorails shut down during thunderstorms and lightning. We got stuck at EPCOT trying to get back to our Magic Kingdom hotel at the end of the night due to a thunderstorm. There were thousands of people drenched with nowhere to go for hours. Had we known there was no bus service back, we would not have gambled with even a slight chance of rain.

When the monorail is closed, Disney is supposed to provide bus or boat transportation to get you where you're going. As the reader above notes, that's not always the case. If this happens to you, your best bet is a ride-hailing app or taxi. If you're going to book an expensive monorail resort, first call the resort and inquire about monorail maintenance or construction that might impact its operation. Phone numbers for the resorts can be found on pages 40–41.

Walt Disney World Boat Service

Boats are a popular, third transportation option between some theme parks and resorts, as a reader from Ames, Iowa, reminds us:

> We stayed at Port Orleans French Quarter in December and took the ferry to Disney Springs several times. We also did a self-guided resort Christmas-decorations tour and had fun taking different boats around the Magic Kingdom and EPCOT resorts. These ferries were a much more pleasant option than buses for most legs of that tour.

The table shows the routes served by boats. Note that most routes stop at several resorts and that service may be suspended during thunderstorms. Wheelchairs and scooters are permitted; strollers must be folded before you board and stowed while you're on the boat. Most routes run from about 45 minutes before park opening to 45 minutes after park closing.

WALT DISNEY WORLD BOAT ROUTES *(round-trip)*
Magic Kingdom → Fort Wilderness → Magic Kingdom
Magic Kingdom → Grand Floridian Resort & Villas → Polynesian Village → Magic Kingdom
Fort Wilderness Campground → Wilderness Lodge → Contemporary Resort → Fort Wilderness ***Note:*** Walk or take the monorail from the Contemporary to the Magic Kingdom.
EPCOT → Boardwalk Inn & Villas → Beach Club → Yacht Club → Swan → Dolphin → EPCOT
Disney's Hollywood Studios → Boardwalk Inn & Villas → Beach Club Resort & Villas → Yacht Club → Swan → Dolphin → Disney's Hollywood Studios
Disney Springs → Saratoga Springs → Old Key West → Disney Springs
Disney Springs → Port Orleans French Quarter → Port Orleans Riverside → Disney Springs

SKYLINER TRAVEL TIMES *(in minutes)*					
	POP CENTURY/ ART OF ANIMATION	CARIBBEAN BEACH	EPCOT	HOLLYWOOD STUDIOS	RIVIERA RESORT
POP CENTURY/ ART OF ANIMATION	—	9-18 (3)	31-45 (15)	22-40 (10)	19-37 (7)
CARIBBEAN BEACH RESORT	9-18 (3)	—	18-27 (12)	13-22 (7)	10-19 (4)
EPCOT	28-37 (15)	22 (12)	—	35-44 (19)	18 (8)
HOLLYWOOD STUDIOS	26-35 (10)	17 (7)	35-44 (19)	—	27-36 (11)
RIVIERA RESORT	16-25 (10)	7 (4)	11 (8)	20-29 (14)	—

Disney Skyliner

This elevated, ski lift–like Skyliner connects the **Art of Animation, Pop Century, Caribbean Beach,** and **Riviera Resorts** with **Disney's Hollywood Studios** and **EPCOT**'s International Gateway. The Skyliner routes have been added to our Walt Disney World overview map on pages 14–15 and to the maps for the above Disney resorts in Part 5.

Each gondola holds about 10 guests, though it's rare for guests in different groups to share one. **Caribbean Beach Resort** serves as the hub for all Skyliner routes; Disney runs Caribbean Beach's internal buses between the Skyliner station and guest rooms at the resort.

As fans of both multimodal transportation and Disney, we like the Skyliner. Our big initial concern was that the gondolas lacked air-conditioning. However, their 17-mph speed and good ventilation keep passengers cool even on very warm days.

Our one minor gripe is that riders have to get off the gondolas at the Caribbean Beach hub, then reboard another line to get to the Studios, EPCOT, the Riviera, or Pop Century and the Art of Animation (AOA). Anyone who's ever had to change trains in a major metropolitan city's subway hub, however, will take this in stride.

The table above shows typical point-to-point transportation times between any two Skyliner stations. The first pair of numbers is the average trip time assuming normal crowds, and the number in parentheses is the trip time assuming no crowds.

For example, the time to get from the Pop Century/AOA station to EPCOT reads "31–45 (15)." Thus, you should expect the trip to EPCOT to take 31–45 minutes from the time you arrive at the Pop/AOA station. The actual time in transit will be about 15 minutes, and the rest of the time will be spent waiting to board.

The table uses the following estimates for the time it takes to board at these stations:

- **CARIBBEAN BEACH RESORT** 6-15 minutes
- **DISNEY'S HOLLYWOOD STUDIOS** 10 minutes
- **POP CENTURY/ART OF ANIMATION RESORTS** 6-15 minutes
- **EPCOT** 10 minutes
- **RIVIERA RESORT** 3 minutes

During off-peak hours, your times may be much shorter.

DRIVING TO AND AROUND WALT DISNEY WORLD

THE VAST MAJORITY of *Unofficial Guide* readers who drive to Orlando use GPS to get where they're going, either through their phone, their car, or a dedicated device. All GPS units and apps made in the last few years recognize location names such as Magic Kingdom and Pop Century. If you have an older unit, use the addresses in the table at right for the theme parks and in Part 5, "Accommodations" for hotels.

The best GPS apps will get traffic updates and route you around delays. Our favorite is **Waze,** which provides real-time traffic updates along with navigation. **TomTom** GPS units do the same using an accessory cable that picks up traffic signals from HD radio broadcasts.

If you're driving without GPS, print out directions to Walt Disney World from **Google Maps** (maps.google.com) before you leave home; then, once you're in Orlando, use the overview maps in Part One (see pages 12–15) and in this chapter to find your way around. If you want to go primitive, the rental-car companies have free maps available (we like **Alamo Rent a Car**'s Walt Disney World road map, also available at the front desk or concierge desk of any Disney resort). Use Disney's road signs as a supplement to any option.

GPS Names and Addresses for the Theme Parks

Google Maps gives correct directions for the addresses and/or names shown in the table at right. Disney's road signs also direct you to parking as you get close. Some apps' driving directions to the Magic Kingdom will try to route you to a backstage area near Space Mountain. If this happens, follow the signs to the Magic Kingdom parking lot, or pull into the nearest Disney resort and ask for directions.

Driving to and from the Theme Parks

1. PARKING LOT LOCATIONS The **Animal Kingdom, EPCOT,** and **DHS** lots are adjacent to each park's entrance; the **Magic Kingdom** lot is adjacent to the TTC. From the TTC, take a ferry, monorail, or bus to the park's entrance (the bus is often fastest). Electronic displays will show you the estimated transit times for the ferry and monorail.

2. PAYING TO PARK Disney resort guests and Annual Pass holders park free; all others pay. If you paid to park and you move your car later that day, show your receipt and you won't have to pay again at the new lot. The daily parking rate for motorcycles and standard cars is $25; a preferred parking option, with spots closer to the park entrances, costs $45–$50 per day.

3. REMEMBERING WHERE YOUR CAR IS PARKED Jot down, text, or take a phone picture of the section and row where you've parked. If you're driving a rental, note the license-plate number.

4. HOW LONG IT TAKES TO PARK AND GET TO THE PARK ENTRANCE At the **Magic Kingdom,** it'll take 35–50 minutes to get to the TTC; go through the security screening; board a monorail, ferry, or bus; and reach the park entrance. Add another 20 minutes if you haven't purchased your park admission in advance. At **EPCOT** and **Animal Kingdom,** figure about 15–20 minutes to pay, park, walk, or ride to the entrance and get through the security screening. At Disney's Hollywood Studios, allow 15–20 minutes, and see the following note.

5. GETTING TO DISNEY'S HOLLYWOOD STUDIOS FROM POP CENTURY AND ART OF ANIMATION If the line to use the **Skyliner** is more than

DESTINATION PARKING LOT	NAME TO LOOK FOR IN GPS	ADDRESS
MAGIC KINGDOM	"Magic Kingdom Park" or "Magic Kingdom Toll Plaza" works better than the address.	3450 World Dr. Winter Garden, FL 34787
EPCOT	"EPCOT" (but not "EPCOT Parking Lot")	200 EPCOT Center Dr. Lake Buena Vista, FL 32830
ANIMAL KINGDOM	"Animal Kingdom" or "Disney's Animal Kingdom Theme Park"	2901 Osceola Pkwy. Lake Buena Vista, FL 32380
DHS	Try "Disney's Hollywood Studios-South Studio Drive" before using the address.	351 S. Studio Dr. Lake Buena Vista, FL 32830
BLIZZARD BEACH	"Blizzard Beach" should get you close, but the address works better.	1534 Blizzard Beach Dr. Lake Buena Vista, FL 32830
TYPHOON LAGOON	"Typhoon Lagoon" should work better than the address.	1145 E. Buena Vista Dr. Lake Buena Vista, FL 32830
DISNEY SPRINGS	"Disney Springs" should give a list of all parking lots to choose from.	1530 E. Buena Vista Dr. Lake Buena Vista, FL 32830

30 minutes, consider using Uber, Lyft, or a taxi. Note that Disney also offers bus service between the two resorts and Hollywood Studios during busier times of year.

6. COMMUTING FROM PARK TO PARK Using Disney transportation or your car, allow 45–60 minutes one-way, entrance to entrance. If you plan to park-hop, leave your car in the lot of the park where you'll finish the day.

7. LEAVING THE PARK AT THE END OF THE DAY If you stay at a park until closing, expect the parking-lot trams, monorails, gondolas, and ferries to be mobbed. (The Magic Kingdom has wait-time displays showing the lines for the monorail and ferry.) If the tram is taking too long, walk to your car or walk to the first stop on the tram route, and wait there for a tram. When someone gets off, you can get on.

8. DINNER AND A QUICK EXIT One way to beat closing crowds in the Magic Kingdom is to arrange reservations for dinner at the **Contemporary Resort.** When you leave the Magic Kingdom for dinner, move your car from the TTC lot to the Contemporary lot. After dinner, walk (8–10 minutes) or take the monorail back to the Magic Kingdom. When the park closes and everyone else is fighting to board the monorail or ferry, you can stroll back to the Contemporary, claim your car, and get on your way. Use the same strategy in Epcot by arranging a reservation at an EPCOT resort. When the park closes after the fireworks, exit via the International Gateway and walk to the resort where you parked.

9. CAR TROUBLE Parking lots have security patrols; if you have a dead battery or minor automotive problem, they can help. For more-serious trouble, go to the **Car Care Center** (☎ 407-824-0976), near the Magic Kingdom parking lot. Prices for most services are comparable to those at home. The facility stays busy, so expect to have to leave your car unless the fix is simple. Hours are Monday–Friday, 7 a.m.–7 p.m.; Saturday, 7:30 a.m.–2 p.m.; and closed Sunday.

10. SCORING A GREAT PARKING SPOT If you arrive at a park after noon or move your car from park to park, check for available parking spaces close to the park entrance; these will have been vacated

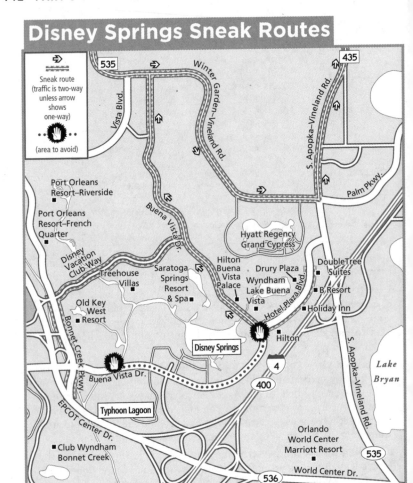

Disney Springs Sneak Routes

by early guests who've left. Instead of following signs or being directed by staff to a distant space, drive straight to the front and start hunting, or use the approach of this Coopersburg, Pennsylvania, couple:

> *After leaving EPCOT for lunch, we returned to find a fullish parking lot. We were unhappy because we had left a third-row parking spot. My husband told the attendant that we had left just an hour ago and that there were lots of spaces up front. Without a word of protest, he waved us to the front and we got our same spot back!*

Speeders Beware

Orange County law enforcement's jurisdiction extends to Disney's roads. Many readers have written us surprised after receiving citations, assuming they'd be let off with a warning at worst. Remember, it's a speed limit, not a speed suggestion.

I-Drive Area Sneak Routes

↗ **East to Downtown Orlando**

Universal Orlando

Universal's Volcano Bay

Orlando International Premium Outlets

Peregrine Ave.
Windhover Dr.
Vineland Rd.
Florida's Turnpike (toll road)
Tom Williams Way
Major Blvd.
Caravan Ct.
Oak Ridge Rd.
W. Oak Ridge Rd.
Universal Blvd.
Turkey Lake Rd.
Adventure Way
Hollywood Way
American Way
Grand National Dr.
International Dr.
Del Verde Way
Kirkman Rd.
Carrier Dr.
Canada Ave.
Sand Lake Rd.
Jamaican Ct.
Austrian Ct.
Austrian Row
International Dr.
Samoan Ct.
Pointe Plaza Ave.
Universal Blvd.
Official Visitor Center
Universal's Epic Universe
Orange County Convention Center
Destination Pkwy.
Hawaiian Ct.
Aquatica
Beachline Expy. (toll road)
To Orlando → International Airport
West to Walt Disney World Resort & Tampa
Westwood Blvd.
Sea Harbor Dr.
International Dr.
SeaWorld Orlando
Discovery Cove
Central Florida Pkwy.

Avoid this intersection

sneak route (two-way traffic)

International Drive (area to avoid)

bridge or overpass

toll road

I-4 Exits

77 Florida's Turnpike
75A E Universal Studios/ International Dr.
75AB W FL 435 N/S
75B E Kirkman Rd.
74B Universal
74A Sand Lake Rd.
72 FL 528 (Beachline Expy.)
71 Central Florida Pkwy.

Sneak Routes

We're constantly looking for ways to avoid traffic snarls. If you have a GPS that will route you around traffic delays, use that. If not, try these sneak routes we've discovered.

US 192–Kissimmee Resort Area Sneak Routes

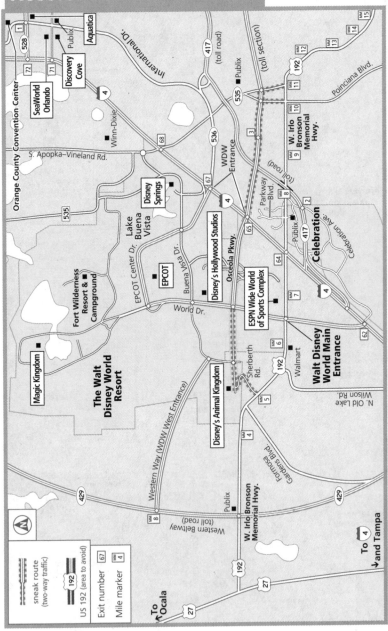

US 192 (IRLO BRONSON MEMORIAL HIGHWAY) Traffic on US 192 runs east–west south of Walt Disney World. The road is divided into east and west sections—west is from I-4 to Kissimmee, and east is from

I-4 Sneak Routes

I-4 east to US 27. Traffic is bad both ways. If your hotel is along the west section, you can bypass most of the traffic by driving north on **International Drive** or **Poinciana Boulevard** (a right turn if you're driving on US 192 in the direction of I-4) and accessing **Osceola Parkway**, a four-lane toll road that dead-ends in Disney World. If your hotel is on the east side, take US 192 to **Sherberth Road** at mile marker 5 and turn north to enter the World near Animal Kingdom.

DISNEY SPRINGS The 3-mile stretch of **Buena Vista Drive** from Coronado Springs Resort to Disney Springs has 15 traffic signals—about one every 1,000 feet—making it a major traffic bottleneck from late afternoon through late evening. And it's not just around Disney Springs: Buena Vista Drive is one of Walt Disney World's most important roads, connecting the hotels of the Disney Springs Resort Area (DSRA), EPCOT, Disney's Hollywood Studios, the Magic Kingdom, Disney's Animal Kingdom, and Typhoon Lagoon.

The good news is that if you're coming by car from I-4 or on foot from the DSRA, it's easy to get to Disney Springs. Westbound **I-4** offers three exits to Disney Springs, including a direct exit to the Disney Springs parking garages—take **Exit 67** for EPCOT/Disney Springs. Guests staying at a DSRA hotel will find convenient pedestrian bridges linking Disney Springs to Hotel Plaza Boulevard and Buena Vista Drive.

Coming from the theme parks, you can bypass the mess by taking **I-4** or alternatively by looping around on **Bonnet Creek Parkway** and **Disney Vacation Club Way.** If you're going back to an EPCOT or Magic Kingdom resort from Disney Springs, it may be faster to take I-4 West and follow the signs back to Disney property.

WESTBOUND EXIT 68 CONSTRUCTION A new off-ramp at Exit 68 is being constructed for westbound I-4 traffic to get to Disney Springs. This should open in 2024.

I-4 Expect heavy traffic and possible westbound delays from about 7 to 9:30 a.m.; eastbound toward Orlando, expect heavy traffic from 4 to 7 p.m. If you want to avoid I-4 altogether, check out our I-4 Sneak Routes map, on page 445.

INTERNATIONAL DRIVE The I-Drive area is by far the most difficult to navigate without long traffic delays. Most hotels on I-Drive are between **Kirkman Road** to the north and **FL 417 (Central Florida GreeneWay)** to the south. Between Kirkman Road and FL 417, three major roads cross I-Drive: From north to south on I-Drive (in the direction of Disney World), the first is **Universal Boulevard.** Next is **Sand Lake Road (FL 482),** pretty squarely in the middle of the hotel district. Finally, the **Beachline Expressway (FL 528)** connects I-4 and the airport.

The southern third of I-Drive can be accessed via **Central Florida Parkway,** which connects I-4 and Palm Parkway with the SeaWorld area of I-Drive, and by **Daryl Carter Parkway,** which connects Palm Parkway with the Orlando Vineland Premium Outlets.

I-Drive is a mess for a number of reasons: scarcity of left-turn lanes; long, multidirectional traffic signals; and, most critically, limited access to westbound I-4 (toward Disney). From the Orange County Convention Center south to the Beachline Expressway and FL 417/Central Florida GreeneWay, getting on westbound I-4 is easy, but in the stretch where the hotels are concentrated (from Kirkman to about a mile south of Sand Lake), the only way most visitors know to access I-4 westbound is to slog through the gridlock of the I-Drive–Sand Lake Road intersection en route to the I-4–Sand Lake Road interchange.

Since this is about as much fun as a root canal, the object is to access I-4 westbound without getting on Sand Lake Road. If your hotel is north of Sand Lake, access **Kirkman Road** by going north on I-Drive (in the opposite direction of the heaviest traffic) to Kirkman Road and turning left, or by cutting over to Kirkman via eastbound **Carrier Drive.** In either case, take Kirkman north over I-4 and make a U-turn at the first traffic signal (at the entrance to Universal Orlando). This puts you directly onto a westbound I-4 ramp. You can also go north on **Universal Boulevard,** which parallels I-Drive to the east; after you cross I-4 onto Universal property, stay left and follow the signs through two left turns to I-4—the signs are small, so stay alert.

If your hotel is south of Sand Lake Road but north of Austrian Court, use **Austrian Row** to cut over to Universal Boulevard. Turn right (south) on Universal and continue until you intersect the **Beachline Expressway (FL 528);** then take the Beachline west to I-4 (no toll).

TAKING A SHUTTLE BUS FROM YOUR OUT-OF-THE-WORLD HOTEL

MANY INDEPENDENT HOTELS and motels near Disney World provide trams and buses. They're fairly carefree, depositing you near theme park entrances and saving you parking fees. The rub is that they might not get you there as early as you desire (a critical point if you take our touring advice) or be available when you wish to return to your lodging.

unofficial **TIP**
Warning: Most shuttles don't add vehicles at park opening or closing. In the morning, you may not get a seat.

Some shuttles go directly to Walt Disney World, while others stop at other hotels en route. This can be a problem if your hotel is the second or third stop on the route. During periods of high demand, buses frequently fill up at the first stop, leaving little or no room for passengers at subsequent stops. Before booking, ask how many hotels are on the route and the sequence of the stops.

The different hotels are often so close together that you can easily walk to the first hotel on the route and board there. Similarly, if there's a large hotel nearby, it might have its own bus service that's more efficient; use that instead of the service provided by your hotel. Most out-of-the-World shuttles work on a fixed schedule instead of arriving and departing somewhat randomly like the Disney buses. Knowing exactly when a bus will depart makes it easier to plan your day.

A multigenerational family from Seattle share their experience:

> We stayed at a hotel off-site and it was fine, but I think next time we'll stay in the World. The shuttles weren't all that convenient or frequent, so we ended up taking taxis more than we thought we would.

A woman from Carlisle, Pennsylvania, adds this:

> I much prefer staying at a Disney resort so that I can use Disney transportation, but because the person I was traveling with booked the room, I reluctantly stayed off-site. The room and breakfast service were fine. The shuttle to and from the park, however, was not ideal. The only shuttles to the park were at 8:45 a.m. to EPCOT and 9:45 a.m. to the TTC, and the only shuttles back to the resort were 9 p.m. from the TTC and 10 p.m. from EPCOT. We had to call Uber to take us to Disney Springs.

At closing or during a hard rain, more people will be waiting for the shuttle than it can hold, and some will be left behind. Most shuttles return for stranded guests, but guests might have to wait 20 minutes to more than an hour.

unofficial **TIP**
If you want to go from resort to resort or almost anywhere else, you'll have to transfer at a bus hub.

If you're depending on non-Disney shuttles, leave the park at least 45 minutes before closing. If you stay until closing and you don't want the hassle of the shuttle, take Uber, Lyft, or a taxi; cab stands are located at the TTC and near the Bus Information buildings at Disney's Hollywood Studios. If no cabs are on hand, a cast member will call one for you. If you're leaving the Magic Kingdom at closing, it's easier to take the monorail to a hotel and hail a cab from there rather than at the TTC.

DEPARTING FROM ORLANDO INTERNATIONAL AIRPORT (MCO)

IF YOU'RE USING **Mears Connect** (page 421), your bus will depart your hotel 3–4 hours before your flight, depending on how busy the airport is expected to be.

DRIVING Plan on leaving for the airport 2–3 hours before your flight, depending on whether you have to return a rental car, the route you take, and whether you have TSA PreCheck for security lines.

It takes about 35 minutes and around $5 in small bills and quarters to drive from Walt Disney World to MCO along the FL 417 or FL 528 toll roads. The same trip on I-4, FL 482 East, and Jeff Fuqua Boulevard is free but averages 50–60 minutes with traffic, and there's a greater chance it'll take longer.

If you're returning a rental car, allow an extra 20 minutes to complete that process for on-site car rental companies; allow an extra 60 minutes to return a car to an off-site company and catch the airport shuttle to the terminal.

MCO handled over 50 million passengers in 2022. It's not unusual to see lines from the checkpoints snaking out of the terminal and into the main shopping corridor and food court. A number of passengers have reported missing their flights even when they arrived at the airport 90 minutes before departure. System improvements have alleviated some, but by no means all, of the congestion. Most waits to clear security average 20 minutes or less, compared with 55 minutes or longer before the improvements.

Waits in the **TSA PreCheck** lines are almost always 5 minutes or less. If you fly frequently, PreCheck (tsa.gov/precheck) is good for five years and costs $78 per person. We wouldn't fly without it.

ELECTRIC-VEHICLE CHARGING

ECO-FRIENDLY READER Craig from Canada wrote us with this list of charging stations in and around the World.

In Walt Disney World

- **Animal Kingdom Parking Lot (2 chargers)** Follow the path to disabled parking, turn left after the shelter, go to the end of the row, and then double back.

- **Coronado Springs Resort (3 chargers)** In the parking lot adjacent to Gran Destino Tower
- **Disney's Fort Wilderness Resort** Campsites have 110V outlets plus 30-amp RV outlets
- **Disney's Hollywood Studios Parking Lot (2 chargers)** Just east of the main park entrance and northwest of the lots
- **Disney's Riviera Resort (1 charger)** West parking lot
- **Disney Springs Grapefruit Garage (2 chargers)** Level 3
- **Disney Springs Lime Garage (2 chargers)** Top level
- **Disney Springs Orange Garage (2 chargers)** Level 5
- **Disney's Wilderness Lodge (1 charger)** Halfway down the first row, near the taxi stand
- **EPCOT Parking Lot** At the front of the Journey lot
- **Shades of Green (1 generic charger plus 2 Tesla Destination Chargers)** Valet parking only
- **Transportation and Ticket Center (3 chargers)** Follow the blue lines on the right lane after paying for parking.

Tesla Superchargers (Off-Property)

- **Applebee's (10 chargers)** 6290 W. Irlo Bronson Memorial Hwy., just behind the restaurant
- **Wawa (6 chargers)** 7940 W. Irlo Bronson Memorial Hwy.

Craig adds, "There are Level 2 (midspeed) chargers in various places around Disney property; all are run by **ChargePoint** (chargepoint.com). Each charging station has two J-1772 charging ports to accommodate two cars at a time per station."

Finally, check **PlugShare** (plugshare.com) for the locations of other chargers near Walt Disney World.

BARE NECESSITIES

MONEY, *Etc.*

CREDIT CARDS, MOBILE PAYMENTS, AND DISNEY GIFT CARDS

CREDIT CARDS ACCEPTED throughout Disney World are **American Express, Diners Club, Discover, Japan Credit Bureau, MasterCard**, and **Visa.** If you have one of these cards linked to an iPhone 6 or newer, you can use **Apple Pay** as well. **Disney Gift Cards** can be used at most Disney-owned and -operated stores and restaurants, and for recreational activities, tickets, and parking (see disneygiftcard.com).

unofficial **TIP**
Note that a handful of places around WDW take only cash. We recommend carrying $20 or so for incidentals just in case.

If you're staying at a Disney-owned resort, a **MagicBand** (see page 81) or your room key can be linked to the credit card you'll put on file for incidental hotel charges. This lets you use your MagicBand (or room key) as you would a credit card at most Disney-owned stores and restaurants on-property. This is useful if you're covering the expenses of others in your group, such as responsible teens or young adults, who won't be with you all the time, don't have their own credit cards, and don't want to carry cash.

BANKING SERVICES

AT THE THEME PARKS, banking is limited to ATMs, which are marked on park maps and are plentiful throughout Walt Disney World; most MasterCard, Visa, Discover, Cirrus, Plus, Star, and Honor cards are also accepted. To get cash with an American Express card, you must sign an agreement with Amex before your trip. ATMs are also at every Disney resort and throughout Disney Springs.

CURRENCY EXCHANGE

IN THE MAGIC KINGDOM, it's at **Guest Relations** in City Hall, on Main Street, U.S.A., at the park entrance. In EPCOT, it's at Guest Relations on the west side of the EPCOT Entrance Plaza. In the Studios or Animal Kingdom, exchange your euros, kroner, or zloty at Guest Relations to the left of the entrance turnstiles. Disney Springs' Guest Relations location is at the Welcome Center. Finally, all Disney resorts can do currency exchange at their front desks.

IN-PARK ISSUES

CELL PHONES

BRING YOUR PHONE CABLE and wall plug to the parks. Your phone will likely get a lot of use in the parks, either from guiding you around or entertaining you during waits in line. You'll probably want to increase your phone's screen brightness, too, for easier reading in the glaring Florida sun. All of that will drain your phone's battery faster than normal.

We strongly recommend investing in an external battery pack or battery case. We're fans of **Mophie** and **New Trent** batteries; both are available at online retailers such as Amazon.

Charging stations are located near the *Tangled*-themed restrooms in Fantasyland in the Magic Kingdom; they're built into the faux-wood posts near the seating area. Also try the seating area behind Big Top Treats in Storybook Circus or the shopping area at the exit to Space Mountain. In EPCOT, look for outlets upstairs at The Land; near the restrooms at The Seas; and outside at Norway and Morocco.

Be aware that on very busy days, the park's cell towers and Wi-Fi may be overwhelmed, making it difficult to send or receive calls, texts, or data. A woman from Leawood, Kansas, spells out the problem:

In our group, we were using three different carriers, and we all had problems sending and receiving texts and making calls.

A Kennesaw, Georgia, woman adds:

I found the Wi-Fi horrible in all the parks. Dropped out continually, drained my battery, and wasn't strong enough to run Disney's own app. Very disappointing.

RAIN

LEN'S TWIN SISTER, LINDA, notes that when it comes to theme parks, "rain culls the weak from the herd." (She's the competitive one.) So go to the parks even in bad weather. Besides lighter crowds, most of the attractions and waiting areas are under cover. And rain showers, especially during warmer months, are short.

unofficial **TIP**
Raingear isn't always displayed in shops, so ask for it if you don't see it.

Ponchos and umbrellas cost about $13. Ponchos sold at Walt Disney World are made of clear plastic, so picking out somebody in your party on a rainy day can be tricky. Amazon sells an inexpensive orange poncho that will make your family pumpkin-colored beacons in a plastic-covered sea of humanity.

A Wilmington, North Carolina, mom thinks good raingear is worth the investment:

> We're outdoor-sports people, so we have good raincoats. It rained every day on this trip, driving many people out of the parks and leaving others looking miserable. Meanwhile, we hardly noticed the rain from inside our high-end jackets.

Some unusually heavy rain precipitated (no pun intended) dozens of reader suggestions for dealing with soggy days. The best came from this Memphis, Tennessee, mom:

1. Raingear should include ponchos and umbrellas. When rain isn't beating down on your ponchoed head, it's easier to ignore.

2. If you're using a stroller, bring a plastic sheet or an extra poncho to protect it from rain. (Ponchos cover Disney's single strollers only.) Carry a towel in a plastic bag to wipe off your stroller after experiencing an attraction during a rainfall.

One *Unofficial Guide* researcher advises, "Wear a baseball cap under the poncho hood. Without it, the hood never covers your head properly, and your face always gets wet."

LOST AND FOUND

IF YOU LOSE (OR FIND) something in the Magic Kingdom, go to **City Hall.** In Epcot, Lost and Found is behind Spaceship Earth. In Disney's Hollywood Studios, it's at **Hollywood Boulevard Guest Relations,** and in Disney's Animal Kingdom, it's at **Guest Relations** at the main entrance. If you discover that you've lost something 24 hours or more after you've left the parks, call ☎ 407-824-4245 (for all parks). The central Lost and Found is on the east side of the Transportation and Ticket Center. You can also report lost items at disneyworld.com/lostandfound.

It's unusual for readers to send us tips about Lost and Found, but a mom from Indianapolis sent two! Here's the first:

> If you lose something on a ride and it has medication in it, Disney cast members will shut down the ride for 45 seconds to try to retrieve it. If they can't find it or it didn't contain meds, you have to come back to Lost and Found for it at the end of the day.

LOST MAGICBANDS AND TICKETS Duplicates can be made, usually at no cost, at Guest Relations at any theme park or resort. A replacement fee may be charged depending on your situation.

Lost tickets are the subject of the second tip from our mom above:

> If you've got plastic tickets, write down or take a picture of the serial numbers on the back. This way, a cast member can look up when the ticket was last used, giving you an idea of where it was lost.

LOST CARS Don't forget where you parked—snap a picture with your phone or camera, send yourself a text or email, or write down your section and row.

MEDICAL MATTERS

HEADACHE RELIEF Aspirin and other sundries are sold at the **Emporium** on Main Street, U.S.A., in the Magic Kingdom (behind the counter—you have to ask); at most retail shops in EPCOT's Future World and World Showcase, Disney's Hollywood Studios, and Disney's Animal Kingdom; and at each Disney resort's gift shop.

ILLNESSES REQUIRING MEDICAL ATTENTION For the locations of the **First Aid Centers** in the theme parks, please see the "Services" sidebar of each theme park chapter. Guests who use the service are generally very positive about it. This Hickory, North Carolina, reader's experience is representative:

> We visited First Aid a time or two in the parks (my wife needed her blood pressure checked because she was worried about the heat and her pregnancy). We found trained medical staff, no wait, and all the friendliness and knowledge you would expect from Disney.

Off-property, there's an **Advent Health Centra Care** walk-in clinic at 12500 S. Apopka–Vineland Road (☎ 407-934-CARE [2273]; open 24 hours. They also do COVID testing (☎ 407-938-0650).

A North Carolina family had a good experience at **Buena Vista Urgent Care** (8216 World Center Drive, Suite D; ☎ 407-465-1110):

> We started day one needing medical care for our son, who has asthma and had developed croup. We found great care at Buena Vista Urgent Care. We waited 20 minutes, and then we were off to the parks.

The Medical Concierge (☎ 855-932-5252; themedicalconcierge .com) has board-certified physicians on call 24-7 to make in-person visits to your hotel room, including administering COVID tests. Walk-in clinics are also available.

DOCS (Doctors on Call Service; ☎ 407-399-DOCS [3627]; doctors oncallservice.com) also offers 24-hour house-call service. The physicians are either board-certified or board-eligible. A father of two from O'Fallon, Illinois, gives them a thumbs-up:

> My wife's cold developed into an ear infection that required medical attention, and DOCS was able to respond in 40 minutes. The doctor had medicine with him and was very professional and friendly.

Another option for house or video calls is **Physician Room Service** (☎ 407-238-2000; physicianroomservice.com). Like the others, they're staffed by board-certified doctors.

DENTAL NEEDS Call **Celebration Dental Group** (☎ 407-566-2222).

PRESCRIPTION MEDICINE Three drugstores located nearby are **CVS** (8242 World Center Drive; ☎ 407-239-1442), **Walgreens** (12100 S. Apopka–Vineland Road; ☎ 407-238-0600), and **Turner Drugs** (1530 Celebration Blvd., Ste. 105A; ☎ 407-828-8125; turnerdrugs celebration.com).

PREVENT BLISTERS IN FIVE EASY STEPS

1. PREPARE You can easily cover 5–12 miles a day at the parks, so get your feet and legs into shape before you leave home. Start with short walks around the neighborhood. Increase your distance gradually until you can do 6 miles without needing CPR.

2. PAY ATTENTION During your training program, your feet will tell you if you're wearing the right shoes. Choose well-constructed, broken-in running or hiking shoes. If you feel a hot spot coming on, chances are a blister isn't far behind. The most common sites for blisters are heels, toes, and balls of feet. If you develop a hot spot in the same place every time you walk, cover it with a blister bandage (such as Johnson & Johnson) or cushion before you set out.

Don't wear sandals, flip-flops, or slip-ons in the theme parks. Even if your feet don't blister, they'll get stepped on by other guests or run over by strollers.

3. SOCK IT UP Good socks are as important as good shoes. When you walk, your feet sweat, and the moisture only increases friction. To counteract friction, wear socks made from material such as Smartwool or CoolMax, which wicks perspiration away from your feet (Smartwool socks come in varying thicknesses). To further combat moisture, dust your feet with antifungal powder.

4. DON'T BE A HERO Take care of foot problems the minute you notice them. Carry a small foot-emergency kit with gauze, antibiotic ointment, disinfectant, moleskin or blister bandages, scissors, a sewing pin or something else sharp (to drain blisters), and rubbing alcohol to sterilize the pin. Extra socks and foot powder are optional.

If carrying all of that sounds like too much, stop by a park **First Aid Center** as soon as you notice a hot spot forming on your foot.

5. CHECK THE KIDS Children might not say anything about blisters forming until it's too late. Stop several times a day and check their feet. If you find a blister, either treat it using the kit you're carrying, or stop by a First Aid Center.

LODGING A COMPLAINT WITH DISNEY

COMPLAINING ABOUT A LEAKY FAUCET or not having enough towels is pretty straightforward, and you'll usually find Disney folks highly responsive. But for a complaint that goes beyond an on-site manager's ability to resolve, don't expect much—if anything.

Disney's unresponsiveness in fielding complaints is one of our readers' foremost gripes. A Providence, Rhode Island, dad's remarks are typical:

> It's all warm fuzzies and big smiles until you have a problem—then everybody plays hide-and-seek. The only thing you know for sure is it's never the responsibility of the Disney person you're talking to.

A Portland, Maine, reader sums it up in classic New England style:

> Lodging a complaint with Disney is like shouting at a brick.

Disney prefers to receive complaints in writing. Address your letter to **Walt Disney World Guest Communications** at PO Box 10040, Lake Buena Vista, FL 32830-0040, or email wdw.guest.communications @disneyworld.com.

Be aware, though, that by the time you get home and draft a letter, it's often too late to correct the problem. And although Disney would have you believe they're a touchy-feely lot, they generally won't make things right for you after the fact. You *may* receive an acknowledgment of the nonapology sort ("we're sorry you *felt* inconvenienced"), but don't count on them actually offering to fix anything—even if you decide to take it up with Bob Iger himself.

If you're *really* steamed, you could fire off a letter to the ***Orlando Sentinel*** (633 N. Orange Ave., Orlando, FL 32801-1349; insight@orlando sentinel.com) or perhaps contact the consumer-affairs reporter for one of the Orlando TV stations.

SERVICES

PHOTOPASS AND MEMORY MAKER

FOR YEARS NOW, Walt Disney World has employed roving bands of photographers to take photos of guests as part of its **PhotoPass** service; guests may purchase these photos online. Use the **My Disney Experience** (**MDE**) app to find the specific locations of PhotoPass photographers on the day of your visit.

Individual PhotoPass images can be purchased at disneyphotopass .com. Current prices range from around $18 for a digital download to around $22 for an 8-by-10-inch print. You can also buy personalized photo products such as mugs and smartphone cases.

Photographs are also sold in a package called **Memory Maker** (see disneyworld.disney.go.com/memory-maker) that includes not only PhotoPass pictures but also photos and videos taken by automated cameras on theme park rides (for the full list, see the next page). Memory Maker costs $169 when purchased at least three days before your trip or $199 when purchased in the park. If you're planning to spend just one day in a park, you can buy a **Memory Maker One Day Entitlement** ($69), available exclusively through the MDE app. Disney Annual Pass holders can download photos at no charge.

unofficial **TIP**
On its face, Memory Maker is a better deal than paying by the photo, but only if you know you want to buy lots of photos. You'll have to make the call regarding which option is best for your budget.

Because PhotoPass and Memory Maker are linked to your MDE account (see page 28), you can also see the photos of friends and family you've linked to there. Here's how to get started:

1. Find a PhotoPass photographer to take your first picture. Photographers roam throughout the theme parks and water parks, including near park entrances, in restaurants (and during character meals), and around iconic attractions such as The Twilight Zone Tower of Terror.

2. The photographer will scan your RFID ticket, MagicBand, or (coming soon) your phone. This links your pictures to your MDE account. Onboard ride-photo systems should automatically detect your MagicBand and link the photos to your account.

3. Visit the MDE website within 45 days of your trip to view your photos. You can add decorative borders and short captions to your pictures, too, as well as share photos online.

In some areas, such as the Test Track postshow, Disney has replaced live photographers with automated cameras that capture your photos at select posing stations. Like the photos taken by live photographers, these images will be linked to your MDE account. If you're already logged in to MDE, your purchase will be automatically linked to your account. If not, you'll be asked to do so (or sign up for MDE) to complete the purchase. Photos taken on the following rides will be automatically linked to your MDE account:

THE MAGIC KINGDOM • Big Thunder Mountain Railroad • Buzz Lightyear's Space Ranger Spin • *Enchanted Tales with Belle* • Pirates of the Caribbean • Seven Dwarfs Mine Train • Space Mountain • Tiana's Bayou Adventure (formerly Splash Mountain; opens 2024)	
EPCOT • Frozen Ever After • Test Track	
DISNEY'S ANIMAL KINGDOM • Dinosaur • Expedition Everest	
DISNEY'S HOLLYWOOD STUDIOS • Rock 'n' Roller Coaster • Slinky Dog Dash • The Twilight Zone Tower of Terror	

You can download Memory Maker photos as many times as you want, subject to a few restrictions: First, if you prepurchase the package, you must do so at least three days before your trip in order to have all of your photos included. If you prepurchase fewer than three days before you arrive, you'll have to buy separately any photos taken during that three-day window. Next, Disney will store your photos for 45 days, so you'll need to download them promptly once you return home (you can also pay for extra time). Finally, once you've downloaded the first photo, you have 30 days to download the rest. Disney grants you a limited license to reproduce Memory Maker photos for your personal use.

Because any two families can share a Memory Maker package via MDE, folks in the *Unofficial Guide* online community often split the cost with others traveling around the same time. It's a great way to get your photos at half price. Visit tinyurl.com/share-memory-maker to find a partner on our discussion boards.

We get a lot of reader comments about PhotoPass and Memory Maker, most of them positive. From a Loveland, Ohio, mom:

> *The PhotoPass option is awesome and so easy. Everywhere we went, we would find Disney photographers and we got a lot of great pictures, which is nice since usually when you are on vacation you have part of your family missing as he/she is taking the photo.*

These honeymooners from Cambridge, Massachusetts, give Memory Maker a thumbs-up:

> *My wife talked me into getting Memory Maker, and we both ended up happy with the memories captured. Not having to carry a camera around was very convenient, especially when we went on water rides. Another advantage was having access to all the on-ride photos and videos—the Tower of Terror video alone made the purchase worth it.*

A Silver Spring, Maryland, dad got an unexpected disappointment:

> *I advance-purchased Memory Maker largely because we were planning several character meals, under the apparently incorrect assumption that photographers would be there. There was no sign of any photographer at any of the four character meals we did.*

Disney has installed multiple automatic cameras at character meal and greeting venues. These cameras capture numerous moments throughout the meal or meet and greet and offer guests a variety of character photos.

Tip: Call ahead of your WDW visit to verify whether photographers will be on hand at a particular character meal, and then check again closer to your trip. Participating venues change from time to time, and we've seen conflicting/inconsistent information on otherwise reliable Disney websites—including Disney's own.

In addition to the in-park photographers, there is now a Memory Maker station at **Disney Springs.** There are no characters, but if you want a photographer to take a few snaps of your family, stop by. This can be a quick alternative to a formal posed photo session, and as a bonus, the pictures will be included in your existing photo package.

PET CARE

ACROSS FROM THE PORT ORLEANS RESORTS, the plush **Best Friends Pet Care** accommodates up to 270 dogs in its Doggy Village, which has standard and luxury suites, some with private outdoor patios and play yards; the Kitty City pavilion houses up to 24 cats in two- and four-story cat condos. There's also a separate area just for birds and "pocket pets" such as hamsters. Encompassing more than 17,000 square feet of air-conditioned indoor space plus 10,000 square feet of covered outdoor runs and play areas, the resort is open to both on-site and off-site guests. We sent Rosie, the *Unofficial Guide* research poodle, and it went great. The staff even emailed us photos of her during her stay. For more information, call ☎ 877-4-WDW-PETS (877-493-9738) or visit bestfriendspetcare.com. (*Note:* Pet parents must provide written proof of current vaccinations from a vet, either at check-in or by fax at 203-840-5207.)

In addition, dogs are welcome at four hotels on Disney property: **Art of Animation, Port Orleans Riverside, Fort Wilderness Resort & Campground,** and the **Yacht Club.** Additional fees of $50–$75 per night apply, along with a host of human- and animal-conduct rules; inquire when making your hotel reservation. This dog-accommodating policy was poorly received by many readers, including this one:

> *I refuse to pay $400 to sleep in a bed where a dog previously slept.*

That said, we still haven't seen a single complaint regarding dogs at Disney hotels in all the reader surveys we've received since the policy was enacted.

EXCUSE ME, BUT WHERE CAN I FIND . . .

RELIGIOUS SERVICES IN THE WALT DISNEY WORLD AREA? Visit allears .net/btp/church.htm for a partial list.

SOMEPLACE TO PUT ALL THESE PACKAGES? Lockers are located on the right side of the entrance to the Magic Kingdom; to the right of Spaceship Earth in EPCOT, at the International Gateway; to the right of the entrance in DHS; and to the left of the entrance in Animal Kingdom. The cost is $10 per day for small lockers and $12 per day for large lockers at the theme parks. Lockers at the water parks cost $10 for small and $15 for large. Jumbo lockers, in EPCOT and the Magic Kingdom only, cost $15 per day. All lockers are now keyless.

Package Pickup remains temporarily suspended as of early 2023; when it's running, it's located near each theme park's entrance and closes 2 hours before the parks do (EPCOT has two Package Pickups, near the Future World and International Gateway entrances). Ask the salesperson to send your purchases to Package Pickup; when you leave the park, they'll be waiting for you. If you're staying at a Disney resort, you can also have packages delivered to your resort's gift shop for pickup the following day. If you're leaving within 24 hours, though, take them with you or use the in-park pickup location.

If you live in the United States, the gift shop at your Disney resort will ship your items to you via standard ground shipping. We're told that the maximum shipping cost is $40, so now is the time to buy souvenirs in bulk.

GROCERY STORES THAT DELIVER? If you don't have a car or you're too slothful to drive, you have a couple of options.

Amazon Prime members can use **Amazon Pantry** to order prepackaged items, from boxed cereals and snacks to coffee, sunscreen, aspirin, and diapers, at very competitive prices and have them delivered to your resort. If you're looking for fresh foods, along with beer and wine, **Garden Grocer** (gardengrocer.com) will shop for you and deliver your groceries.

The best way to compile your Garden Grocer order is on the website before you leave home—they even offer discounts for ordering 60, 30, or 15 days ahead. Delivery arrangements are per your instructions. If you're staying at a hotel where they deliver, you can arrange for your groceries (including alcohol) to be left with Bell Services. If there's something you want that you don't see on the website, click "Request an Item" and they'll try to find it for you. If you prefer to order by phone, call ☎ 866-855-4350.

For orders of less than $200 (before tax), a $14 delivery fee applies; for orders of $200 or more, delivery is free. Same-day delivery (before 10 a.m.) costs $30, and next-day delivery is $20. Orders canceled or modified without proper notice are subject to restocking fees; check the website for details.

As of this writing, Garden Grocer doesn't deliver to the Swan, Swan Reserve, or Dolphin; delivery to Disney's EPCOT resorts may be limited to afternoon. All Disney hotels have refrigerators to store perishable goods, and you don't need to be present to accept the delivery. Finally, note that Garden Grocer's delivery schedule may fill completely around holidays, at which point they'll stop accepting orders.

WINE, BEER, AND LIQUOR? In Florida, wine and beer are sold in grocery stores; for the stronger stuff, you'll have to go to a state-licensed liquor store. The best range of booze in the Disney area is sold at **ABC Fine Wine & Spirits,** less than a mile north of the Crossroads shopping center (11951 S. Apopka–Vineland Road; ☎ 407-239-0775). We also like **Publix Liquors** in the Water Tower Shoppes (29 Blake Blvd., Celebration; ☎ 321-939-3109).

KEY QUESTIONS ANSWERED IN THIS CHAPTER

OVERVIEW

OPENED IN 1971, the Magic Kingdom was the first of Walt Disney World's four theme parks, much of it built by the same people who built Disneyland in California almost two decades prior. The crown jewel of the World's parks, the Magic Kingdom is what springs to most people's mind when they think of Disney World. Its attractions, such as Cinderella Castle, Pirates of the Caribbean, and Haunted Mansion, have helped set the standard for theme park attractions the world over.

ARRIVING

FROM INSIDE WALT DISNEY WORLD If you're staying at the **Contemporary, Bay Lake Tower, Grand Floridian Resort,** or **Polynesian Village,** you can commute to the Magic Kingdom by monorail (guests at the first three can walk to the park more quickly). If you're staying at **Wilderness Lodge & Boulder Ridge/Copper Creek Villas** or **Fort Wilderness Resort & Campground,** you can take a boat or bus. (Note that monorails and boats don't run when lightning is in the area; Disney

continued on page 462

The Magic Kingdom

G+ Offers Genie+

ILL Offers Individual Lightning Lane

Counter-Service Restaurants

- **A.** Aloha Isle
- **B.** Casey's Corner 👍
- **C.** Columbia Harbour House 👍
- **D.** Cosmic Ray's Starlight Cafe
- **E.** The Diamond Horseshoe *(seasonal)*
- **F.** The Friar's Nook
- **G.** Gaston's Tavern
- **H.** Golden Oak Outpost *(seasonal)*
- **I.** Liberty Square Market
- **J.** The Lunching Pad
- **K.** Main Street Bakery *(Starbucks)* 👍
- **L.** Pecos Bill Tall Tale Inn and Cafe
- **M.** Pinocchio Village Haus
- **N.** Tomorrowland Terrace Restaurant *(seasonal)*
- **O.** Tortuga Tavern *(seasonal)*

Table-Service Restaurants

- **AA.** Be Our Guest Restaurant
- **BB.** Cinderella's Royal Table
- **CC.** The Crystal Palace
- **DD.** Jungle Navigation Co. Ltd. Skipper Canteen 👍
- **EE.** Liberty Tree Tavern 👍
- **FF.** The Plaza Restaurant
- **GG.** Tony's Town Square Restaurant

First Aid Center · *Happily Ever After* Viewing Area
Restrooms · Recommended Dining · ········ Parade Route · ☑ Not To Be Missed

Fantasyland

Tomorrowland

Walkway to Resort Buses

Attractions

1. Ariel's Grotto G+
2. Astro Orbiter
3. The Barnstormer G+
4. Big Thunder Mountain Railroad ☑ G+
5. Buzz Lightyear's Space Ranger Spin ☑ G+
6. Casey Jr. Splash 'N' Soak Station
7. *Country Bear Jamboree*
8. Dumbo the Flying Elephant G+
9. *Enchanted Tales with Belle* G+
10. Frontierland Shootin' Arcade

11. *The Hall of Presidents*
12. The Haunted Mansion ☑ G+
13. *It's a Small World* G+
14. Jungle Cruise G+
15. *Liberty Belle* Riverboat
16. Mad Tea Party G+
17. The Magic Carpets of Aladdin G+
18. The Many Adventures of Winnie the Pooh G+
19. Meet Merida at Fairytale Garden ☑
20. *Mickey's PhilharMagic* ☑ G+
21. *Monsters, Inc. Laugh Floor* G+
22. Peter Pan's Flight ☑ G+
23. Pete's Silly Sideshow
24. A Pirate's Adventure: Treasures of the Seven Seas ☑
25. Pirates of the Caribbean ☑ G+
26. Prince Charming Regal Carrousel
27. Princess Fairytale Hall Meet and Greets ☑ G+
28. Seven Dwarfs Mine Train ☑ ILL
29. Space Mountain ☑ G+
30. Tiana's Bayou Adventure *(opens 2024)* ☑ G+
31. Swiss Family Treehouse
32. Tom Sawyer Island and Fort Langhorn
33. Tomorrowland Speedway G+
34. Tomorrowland Transit Authority PeopleMover ☑
35. Town Square Theater Meet and Greets ☑ G+
36. Tron Lightcycle/Run ☑ ILL
37. Under the Sea: Journey of the Little Mermaid G+
38. *Walt Disney's Carousel of Progress*
39. *Walt Disney's Enchanted Tiki Room*
40. WDW Railroad *(multiple stations)*

continued from page 459

will provide bus service instead.) Guests at other Walt Disney World resorts can reach the park by bus. All Disney lodging guests, regardless of conveyance, are deposited at the park's entrance, bypassing the Transportation and Ticket Center (TTC).

DRIVING If you're thinking about driving to the Magic Kingdom, consider having a taxi or ride-hailing service drop you off at either the **Contemporary** or the **Grand Floridian Resort** instead, especially if you are arriving after park opening; it may cost slightly more than parking at the Magic Kingdom, but it's significantly faster. Otherwise, you'll encounter lines to pay for parking, to board trams (or walk) to take you to the TTC, to get through security, or to get on a monorail or ferry to take you to the park. All of this can take an hour or more on busy days.

unofficial **TIP**
Getting dropped off at the Contemporary or Grand Floridian saves off-site guests the daily $25 Magic Kingdom parking fee and virtually all the waiting.

Have your driver go past the hotel entrance and drop you off in the far corner; from here, it's a short walk to the park, and lines at the security checkpoint there are much shorter. When you're ready to leave, just head to the Contemporary or Grand Floridian and hail a ride, making sure to wait in front of the hotel. You'll avoid the morning hassle in reverse.

This mom from Salt Lake City found using a ride-hailing app a big time-saver:

We used Lyft to go to and from the parks every day. It was SO convenient and much quicker than using Disney buses. The tip to get dropped off at the Contemporary to go to the Magic Kingdom was a lifesaver. Saved us so much time, especially in marathon traffic one Saturday morning. And getting picked up there to go to the hotel at night was seamless.

We've published this tip for a few years now, and it generally works pretty well. On very busy days, though, the security detail at the Contemporary or Grand Floridian may deny access to people being dropped off at those hotels. If security balks, there's nothing stopping your Uber driver from dropping you off on the street corner of the Contemporary's parking lot that's closest to the Magic Kingdom or at any of the alternate (and unstaffed) entrances to the Grand Floridian parking lot.

If driving is unavoidable (see page 441 for GPS names and addresses) and you're bringing a stroller, a Ridgewood, New Jersey, family recommends the ferry (which starts operating 30–90 minutes before official park opening):

The ferry to the Magic Kingdom is a must if you're using a stroller. You can drive the stroller right onto the ferry and then just head to the back to be the first ones off when it docks.

MAGIC KINGDOM OPENING PROCEDURES (ROPE DROP)

ARRIVING AT THE MAGIC KINGDOM **30–60 minutes before official opening** ensures the shortest possible waits for rides.

On-site guests who want to take advantage of Early Theme Park Entry (see page 36) should arrive at the park entrance 60 minutes before official opening (that is, 30 minutes before Early Entry) on all days. Off-site guests (who aren't eligible for Early Theme Park Entry) should arrive 30 minutes before official opening on all days.

Once in the park, you'll find most of the rides in Fantasyland and Tomorrowland running. Rides in Adventureland, Frontierland, and Liberty Square may start operations closer to the park's official opening time.

Main Street's larger shops, such as the **Emporium,** will be open when you're admitted into the park, in case you need sunscreen, ponchos, or aspirin. **The Main Street Bakery (Starbucks)** will also be open for coffee and breakfast items.

Upon entering the park, most guests head for one of the headliners: Seven Dwarfs Mine Train in Fantasyland attracts families with small children, and Tron Lightcycle/Run opens in Tomorrowland

unofficial **TIP**
Rope drop refers to cast members using a length of rope to hold back crowds until the park opens. After the rope is dropped—or rewound, to be precise—crowds race-walk to their first rides.

pulls in teens and adults. Big Thunder Mountain in Frontierland is also a top destination. When Tiana's Bayou Adventure opens in Frontierland in 2024, it should be the biggest draw in the park for families with older children, along with many teens and adults.

GETTING ORIENTED

IN THE MAGIC KINGDOM, **stroller, wheelchair, ECV/ESV rentals,** and **locker rentals** are on the right, just inside the entrance. On your left as you enter **Main Street, U.S.A.,** is **City Hall,** the center for information, lost and found, guided tours, and entertainment schedules.

Be sure to pick up a **guide map** at the park entrance or at City Hall. It shows all attractions, shops, and eating places; provides information about first aid, baby care, and assistance for the disabled; and provides tips for good photos. It also lists times for the day's special events, live entertainment, Disney-character parades, and concerts if they're offered; plus, it tells you when and where to find Disney characters.

The guide map is supplemented by a daily entertainment schedule, the *Times Guide.* In addition to performance times, the *Times Guide* contains info on Disney-character appearances and what Disney calls **Special Hours,** or operating hours for attractions and restaurants that

NOT TO BE MISSED IN THE MAGIC KINGDOM
ADVENTURELAND • Pirates of the Caribbean
FANTASYLAND • Character meet and greets (various) • Peter Pan's Flight • Seven Dwarfs Mine Train
FRONTIERLAND • Big Thunder Mountain Railroad • Tiana's Bayou Adventure *(opens 2024)*
LIBERTY SQUARE • The Haunted Mansion
MAIN STREET, U.S.A. • Meet Mickey Mouse at Town Square Theater
PARADES AND FIREWORKS • Festival of Fantasy afternoon parade • *Happily Ever After* fireworks • Holiday parades and fireworks (seasonal)
TOMORROWLAND • Buzz Lightyear's Space Ranger Spin • Space Mountain • Tron Lightcycle/Run

MAGIC KINGDOM SERVICES

MOST PARK SERVICES are centered on Main Street, U.S.A., including

Baby Care Center Next to The Crystal Palace, left around the Central Plaza (toward Adventureland)

Banking Services ATMs underneath the Main Street railroad station

Cell Phone Charging Space Mountain exit and behind Big Top Treats in Storybook Circus. Can drop at City Hall with cord for charging.

First Aid Center Next to The Crystal Palace, left around the Central Plaza (toward Adventureland)

Live Entertainment and Parade Information In the *Times Guide*, available at City Hall, at the railroad-station end of Main Street

Lost and Found City Hall

Lost Persons City Hall

Storage Lockers Inside the turnstiles, to the right as you face the train station

Walt Disney World and Local Attraction Information City Hall

Wheelchair, ECV/ESV, and Stroller Rentals Inside turnstiles at right as you face the train station

open late or close early. The **My Disney Experience** app (see page 31) contains this information too, but, in a rare triumph of analog over digital, it's faster to use the *Times Guide*.

unofficial **TIP**
Because Cinderella Castle is so large, designate a very specific meeting spot, such as the entrance to Cinderella's Royal Table restaurant at the rear of the castle.

Main Street, U.S.A., ends at the **Central Plaza,** from which branch the entrances to five other "lands": (clockwise from the left) **Adventureland, Frontierland, Liberty Square, Fantasyland,** and **Tomorrowland.**

Cinderella Castle, at the entrance to Fantasyland, is the Magic Kingdom's visual anchor. The castle is an excellent meeting place if your group decides to split up or gets separated.

FAVORITE ATTRACTIONS BY AGE GROUP

INCLUDING RIDES, SHOWS, PARADES, fireworks, and street performers, there are almost 80 individual attractions in the Magic Kingdom. The table on the opposite page lists the 10 most popular attractions by age group.

Parades and fireworks appear in the top 10 for every age group. Character greetings are especially popular with preschool and gradeschool children, and meeting Mickey Mouse ranked in the top 20 park experiences for every age group.

These attractions form the core of our Magic Kingdom touring plans. If you're looking for step-by-step instructions on where to go and when, start with these (see page 504). Most of the attractions listed here offer Lightning Lane to reduce waits in line (see next section).

ATTRACTION RATINGS The attractions profiled in this book have two sets of ratings: an overall rating next to the attraction's name, which reflects the authors' impressions, and reader ratings broken down by age group. Both use a five-star scale, with five stars being best.

Appeal by Age ratings are rounded to the nearest half-star. To help place them in context, we also provide a label, such as Above Average, showing how that attraction stacks up to others in the park. Labels are assigned using the attraction's average number of reader ratings and incorporate a 95% confidence interval (sort of like a margin of error), similar to our restaurant ratings (see page 267). As with

MAGIC KINGDOM MOST POPULAR ATTRACTIONS BY AGE GROUP

PRESCHOOL	GRADE SCHOOL	TEENS	YOUNG ADULTS	OVER 30	SENIORS
Meet Mickey Mouse at Town Square Theater	Happily Ever After fireworks	Big Thunder Mountain Railroad	Big Thunder Mountain Railroad	Pirates of the Caribbean	Pirates of the Caribbean
Meet Donald and Goofy at Pete's Silly Sideshow	Seven Dwarfs Mine Train	Pirates of the Caribbean	The Haunted Mansion	The Haunted Mansion	The Haunted Mansion
Tiana Princess Meet and Greet	Halloween/Christmas fireworks	The Haunted Mansion	Pirates of the Caribbean	Big Thunder Mountain Railroad	Big Thunder Mountain Railroad
Halloween/Christmas parades	Big Thunder Mountain Railroad	Space Mountain	Space Mountain	Seven Dwarfs Mine Train	Tomorrowland Transit Authority PeopleMover
Tinker Bell Meet and Greet	Halloween/Christmas parades	Seven Dwarfs Mine Train	Seven Dwarfs Mine Train	Space Mountain	Mickey's PhilharMagic
Festival of Fantasy parade	Meet Mickey Mouse at Town Square Theater	Happily Ever After fireworks	Happily Ever After fireworks	Tomorrowland Transit Authority PeopleMover	Walt Disney's Carousel of Progress
Halloween/Christmas fireworks	Tiana Princess Meet and Greet	Halloween/Christmas parades	Halloween/Christmas parades	Festival of Fantasy parade	Happily Ever After fireworks
Dumbo the Flying Elephant	Cinderella Princess Meet and Greet	Buzz Lightyear's Space Ranger Spin	Festival of Fantasy parade	Mickey's PhilharMagic	Monsters, Inc. Laugh Floor
Ariel Meet and Greet	Meet Donald and Goofy at Pete's Silly Sideshow	Festival of Fantasy parade	Meet Donald and Goofy at Pete's Silly Sideshow	Happily Ever After fireworks	The Hall of Presidents
Buzz Lightyear's Space Ranger Spin	Tinker Bell Meet and Greet	Mad Tea Party	Buzz Lightyear's Space Ranger Spin	Halloween/Christmas parades	Halloween/Christmas parades

Not enough surveys for Tron Lightcycle/Run at press time.

restaurants, the authors' ratings for attractions don't always jibe with readers' ratings.

The average reader ratings for all Magic Kingdom attractions by age group are as follows, based on the 92,000 attraction ratings we received over the past year:

PRESCHOOL	GRADE SCHOOL	TEENS	YOUNG ADULTS	OVER 30	SENIORS
3.9 stars	4.1 stars	3.8 stars	3.8 stars	4.1 stars	3.9 stars

GENIE+, INDIVIDUAL LIGHTNING LANE, AND THE TOURING PLANS

NOTE: See page 60 for detailed information and strategy suggestions for Genie+ and Individual Lightning Lane.

The big questions for this edition are

1. Are Genie+ and Individual Lightning Lane worth paying for in the Magic Kingdom?

2. If they're worth the cost, which attractions benefit most?

3. How can you avoid paying for Individual Lightning Lane?

4. How do Genie+ and Individual Lightning Lane work with the touring plans?

GENIE+ AND INDIVIDUAL LIGHTNING LANE (ILL) RESERVATIONS IN THE MAGIC KINGDOM
ADVENTURELAND • Jungle Cruise • The Magic Carpets of Aladdin • Pirates of the Caribbean
FANTASYLAND • The Barnstormer • Dumbo the Flying Elephant • It's a Small World • Mad Tea Party • The Many Adventures of Winnie the Pooh • *Mickey's PhilharMagic* • Peter Pan's Flight • Meet Tiana and Cinderella at Princess Fairytale Hall • Seven Dwarfs Mine Train *(ILL)* • Under the Sea: Journey of the Little Mermaid
FRONTIERLAND • Big Thunder Mountain Railroad • Tiana's Bayou Adventure *(formerly Splash Mountain; opens 2024)*
LIBERTY SQUARE • The Haunted Mansion
MAIN STREET, U.S.A. • Festival of Fantasy Parade • Meet Mickey Mouse at Town Square Theater
TOMORROWLAND • Buzz Lightyear's Space Ranger Spin • *Monsters, Inc. Laugh Floor* • Space Mountain • Tomorrowland Speedway • Tron Lightcycle/Run *(ILL)*

We think Tiana's Bayou Adventure will be ILL only when it opens.

Are Genie+ and Individual Lightning Lane Worth Paying For in the Magic Kingdom?

The Magic Kingdom might be the easiest park to recommend using Genie+ for. We think Genie+ is worth the cost here if you meet any of these criteria:

- You'll arrive at the park after Early Theme Park Entry begins (that is, you won't be at the park as soon as it opens). This includes off-site guests (who aren't eligible for Early Theme Park Entry) and on-site guests who want to sleep in.
- You won't be using a touring plan.
- You're visiting during anything other than the slowest times of the year.

The other consideration with Genie+ is the number of Genie+ ride reservations you'll be able to get in a given day. Under the old Fast-Pass+ system, we think the vast majority of guests used five or fewer FastPasses per day in the Magic Kingdom. Below we break down how much time we think you can save using Genie+ with a touring plan, based on different assumptions about how many Genie+ reservations it's possible to obtain in a day.

The **Typical Use** scenario assumes you'll be able to obtain Genie+ reservations for three attractions in your touring plan, provided you haven't already experienced those rides, the reservations don't conflict with any meals or breaks you've already planned, and the standby lines are long enough to justify obtaining the reservation. The **Optimistic Use** scenario assumes all the preceding *and* that Genie+ reservations are available at almost exactly the pace at which you'll visit the attractions. The **Perfect Use** scenario assumes you're able to get

ESTIMATED TIME SAVINGS USING A TOURING PLAN WITH GENIE+ FOR VARIOUS CROWD LEVELS			
CROWD LEVEL	**TYPICAL USE (3 RESERVATIONS PER DAY)**	**OPTIMISTIC USE (5 RESERVATIONS PER DAY)**	**PERFECT USE (8 RESERVATIONS PER DAY)**
Low	20 minutes saved	40 minutes saved	65 minutes saved
Medium	40 minutes saved	80 minutes saved	130 minutes saved
High	60 minutes saved	100 minutes saved	170 minutes saved

ATTRACTION	LOW ATTENDANCE	MODERATE ATTENDANCE	HIGH ATTENDANCE
WHEN GENIE+ AND INDIVIDUAL LIGHTNING LANE RESERVATIONS RUN OUT BY ATTENDANCE LEVEL			
The Barnstormer	10 p.m.	10 p.m.	10 p.m.
Big Thunder Mountain Railroad	10 p.m.	10 p.m.	9 p.m.
Buzz Lightyear's Space Ranger Spin	10 p.m.	10 p.m.	10 p.m.
Dumbo the Flying Elephant	10 p.m.	10 p.m.	10 p.m.
Festival of Fantasy Parade	2 p.m.	2 p.m.	2 p.m.
The Haunted Mansion	10 p.m.	10 p.m.	8 p.m.
It's a Small World	10 p.m.	10 p.m.	10 p.m.
Jungle Cruise	10 p.m.	9 p.m.	5 p.m.
Mad Tea Party	9 p.m.	10 p.m.	10 p.m.
The Magic Carpets of Aladdin	10 p.m.	10 p.m.	10 p.m.
The Many Adventures of Winnie the Pooh	10 p.m.	10 p.m.	10 p.m.
Meet Cinderella at Princess Fairytale Hall	8 p.m.	7 p.m.	5 p.m.
Meet Mickey Mouse at Town Square Theater	8 p.m.	6 p.m.	6 p.m.
Meet Tiana at Princess Fairytale Hall	8 p.m.	8 p.m.	6 p.m.
Mickey's PhilharMagic	10 p.m.	10 p.m.	10 p.m.
Monsters, Inc. Laugh Floor	10 p.m.	10 p.m.	11 p.m.
Peter Pan's Flight	9 p.m.	7 p.m.	5 p.m.
Pirates of the Caribbean	10 p.m.	10 p.m.	10 p.m.
Seven Dwarfs Mine Train (*ILL*)	9 p.m.	8 p.m.	3 p.m.
Space Mountain	10 p.m.	10 p.m.	6 p.m.
Tomorrowland Speedway	10 p.m.	10 p.m.	10 p.m.
Under the Sea: Journey of the Little Mermaid	10 p.m.	10 p.m.	10 p.m.

LOW ATTENDANCE Crowd levels 1–3 on the TouringPlans.com crowd calendar

MODERATE ATTENDANCE Crowd levels 4–7   **HIGH ATTENDANCE** Crowd levels 8–10

At press time, Tron Lightcycle/Run did not yet have enough data to analyze, and Tiana's Bayou Adventure had not opened.

Genie+ reservations, one-by-one, with a nearly immediate return time, for every eligible ride on your touring plan. We think that's exceedingly unlikely to happen; we mention it here to estimate the upper limit on what might be possible. Finally, remember that Seven Dwarfs Mine Train and Tron Lightcycle/Run are not part of Genie+; there's a separate cost to use Lightning Lane with those attractions.

Which Attractions Benefit Most from Genie+ and Individual Lightning Lane?

For Genie+, the table on the next page shows the attractions that might benefit most from using Genie+, based on the data we've collected since launch. The chart does *not* assume use of a touring plan.

Whether Individual Lightning Lanes will be worth the cost will depend on what Disney's charging for them and how that lines up with your personal time-versus-money spectrum.

MAGIC KINGDOM ATTRACTIONS THAT BENEFIT MOST FROM GENIE+ AND INDIVIDUAL LIGHTNING LANE (ILL) *(Highest Priority to Lowest)*			
ATTRACTION	**AVG. TIME IN LINE SAVED (IN MINUTES)**	**ATTRACTION**	**AVG. TIME IN LINE SAVED (IN MINUTES)**
Seven Dwarfs Mine Train (*ILL*)	53	Under the Sea: Journey of the Little Mermaid	19
Peter Pan's Flight	52	It's a Small World	19
Space Mountain	42	The Barnstormer	18
Jungle Cruise	36	Dumbo the Flying Elephant	17
Meet Mickey Mouse at Town Square Theater	34	Princess Fairytale Hall Meet and Greets	16
Big Thunder Mountain Railroad	30	Tomorrowland Speedway	10
Buzz Lightyear's Space Ranger Spin	25	Mad Tea Party	9
The Haunted Mansion	23	The Magic Carpets of Aladdin	8
Pirates of the Caribbean	21	Monsters, Inc. Laugh Floor	0
The Many Adventures of Winnie the Pooh	20	Mickey's PhilharMagic	0

At press time, Tron Lightcycle/Run did not yet have enough data to analyze, and Tiana's Bayou Adventure had not opened.

When Do Genie+ and Individual Lightning Lane Reservations Run Out in the Magic Kingdom?

The table on the previous page shows the approximate time at which the Magic Kingdom's attractions run out of Genie+ or Individual Lightning Lane capacity, by crowd level. Use this table in conjunction with the "Attractions That Benefit Most" table, above, to determine which reservations to get first.

How Can You Avoid Paying for Individual Lightning Lane?

There are a few strategies to avoid paying for Individual Lightning Lane. Each of them involves another cost:

1. Stay at a Disney resort, use Early Theme Park Entry over multiple days, and head to each attraction as soon as the park opens. For new attractions, such as Tron, this is likely to be the strategy recommended by our touring plan software.
2. Stay at a Disney Deluxe or DVC resort and visit the attractions during Extended Theme Park Hours.
3. Visit the attraction during an After Hours event or the Halloween or Christmas parties.

Clearly, Disney has thought hard about how to force consumers into an explicit time-versus-money calculation with these attractions.

How Do Genie+ and Individual Lightning Lane Work with the Touring Plans?

FOR INDIVIDUAL LIGHTNING LANE First, obtain an Individual Lightning Lane return time from My Disney Experience. Next:

If you're using one of the touring plans from this book, follow the plan step by step until it's time to use your reservation. Suspend the touring plan while riding the attraction, then pick up the plan where you left off. If the plan recommends visiting the attraction before or after your return time, skip that step.

If you're using our free touring plan software, enter the reservation return time into the software. The software will organize your plan so that you return to the attraction at your designated return time.

FOR GENIE+ If you're using one of our touring plans, keep track of the next two or three steps in your plan as you go through the park. In Genie+, get the first available reservation for any of those three attractions, and fit that return-time window into the plan. For example, suppose the next three steps in your touring plan are Jungle Cruise, Pirates of the Caribbean, and Big Thunder Mountain Railroad. You check Genie+ for the next available return time for those three attractions, and the return times are 10:45 a.m. for Big Thunder, 11 a.m. for Jungle Cruise, and 11:30 a.m. for Pirates. You'd select Big Thunder because it's the next available return time from among those three. Once in line for Big Thunder, check Genie+ availability for the next three attractions in your plan. If none of the next three steps in your plan participate in Genie+, then get a reservation for the next attraction in your plan that participates in Genie+.

If you're using our touring plan software, the software will recommend which attraction to obtain a Genie+ reservation for next by analyzing your touring plan, the current Genie+ reservation distribution rate, and likely wait times for the rest of the day. When you obtain that reservation, simply enter the return time into the software, and the software will redo your touring plan to use it.

DINING IN THE MAGIC KINGDOM

HERE'S A QUICK RECAP of the Magic Kingdom's major restaurants, rated by readers from highest to lowest. See Part 6 for details.

MAGIC KINGDOM RESTAURANT REFRESHER
COUNTER SERVICE
• **Aloha Isle** (➕ 97%/Exceptional), Adventureland
• **Gaston's Tavern** (➕ 94%/Much Above Average), Fantasyland
• **Liberty Square Market** (➕ 93%/Much Above Average), Liberty Square
• **Main Street Bakery (Starbucks)** (➕ 92%/Much Above Average), Main Street, U.S.A.
• **Casey's Corner** (➕ 91%/Above Average), Main Street, U.S.A.
• **Columbia Harbour House** (➕ 91%/Above Average), Liberty Square
FULL SERVICE
• **Jungle Navigation Co. Ltd. Skipper Canteen** (➕ 92%/Above Average), Adventureland
• **Liberty Tree Tavern** (➕ 92%/Above Average), Liberty Square

Restaurants not shown are rated as average or below.

MAIN STREET, U.S.A.

YOU'LL BEGIN AND END YOUR VISIT on Main Street, U.S.A., which closes 30 minutes–1 hour after the rest of the park. A Disneyfied version of a turn-of-the-20th-century small-town American thoroughfare, Main Street is lined with shops, character-greeting venues, places to eat, City Hall, and a fire station displaying an old fire engine. In the morning, horse-drawn trolleys, fire engines, and horseless carriages transport visitors along Main Street to the

Central Plaza. In the afternoon, artists in Main Street's glassware shop perform live glass blowing and sculpting.

The circular area around the Central Plaza is a paved, landscaped viewing spot for the large crowds that watch the parades and evening fireworks, when they're offered. To disperse heavy crowds during these events, the areas behind the shops on either side of Main Street can become pedestrian walkways on which guests can exit and enter the park.

unofficial **TIP**
The pedestrian walkway most frequently used during parades and fireworks runs from just past **Tony's Town Square Restaurant** to the Tomorrowland side of **The Plaza Restaurant;** the other runs from near the **First Aid Center,** next to The Crystal Palace, to the Main Street fire station (**Engine Co. 71**), near City Hall on Main Street.

The **Walt Disney World Railroad** (see below) stops at Main Street Station; get on to tour the park or ride to Frontierland or Fantasyland. It's not faster than walking, but it's easier on the feet.

KEY TO ABBREVIATIONS In the attraction profiles that follow, each star rating is accompanied by a category label in parentheses (see page 464). **E** means **Exceptional, MAA** means **Much Above Average, AA** means **Above Average, A** means **Average, BA** means **Below Average,** and **MBA** means **Much Below Average.**

Town Square Theater Meet and Greets: Mickey Mouse, Tinker Bell and Friends ★★★★

PRESCHOOL ★★★★½ (MAA)	GRADE SCHOOL ★★★★½ (MAA)	TEENS ★★★★ (AA)
YOUNG ADULTS ★★★★ (AA)	OVER 30 ★★★★ (AA)	SENIORS ★★★★ (AA)

What it is Character-greeting venue. **Scope and scale** Minor attraction. **When to go** Before 10 a.m. or after 4 p.m. **Comment** Mickey and the fairies have 2 separate queues, requiring 2 separate waits in line. **Duration of experience** 2 minutes per character. **Probable waiting time** 30 minutes. **Queue speed** Slow. **ECV/wheelchair access** May remain in wheelchair. **Participates in Genie+** Likely in the near future. **Early Theme Park Entry** No. **Extended Evening Hours** No.

DESCRIPTION AND COMMENTS Children and teenagers rate character greetings among the highest of any Disney attractions, and there's no bigger celebrity than Mickey Mouse. Meet Mickey throughout the day at the Town Square Theater on Main Street, to your right as you enter the park. Tinker Bell and her Pixie Hollow friends were not available at press time but should return in 2023.

TOURING TIPS Lines tend to recede after dinner. If Genie+ isn't available, our touring plans frequently put meeting Mickey as the first step in the day. He usually starts greeting guests at official opening time, even if you're let in early.

Transportation Rides

DESCRIPTION AND COMMENTS Trolleys, buses, and the like.
TOURING TIPS Will save you a walk to the Central Plaza. Not worth a wait.

Walt Disney World Railroad ★★★

PRESCHOOL ★★★½ (MAA)	GRADE SCHOOL ★★★★ (A)	TEENS ★★½ (BA)
YOUNG ADULTS ★★★★ (A)	OVER 30 ★★★★½ (AA)	SENIORS ★★★★½ (AA)

What it is Scenic railroad ride around the perimeter of the Magic Kingdom; provides transportation to Frontierland and Fantasyland. **Scope and scale** Minor attraction. **When to go** Anytime. **Comment** Main Street is usually the least congested station.

Duration of ride About 20 minutes for a complete circuit. **Average wait in line per 100 people ahead of you** 8 minutes; assumes 2 or more trains operating. **Loading speed** Moderate. **ECV/wheelchair access** Guests must transfer from ECV to provided wheelchair. **Participates in Genie+** No. **Early Theme Park Entry** No. **Extended Evening Hours** No.

DESCRIPTION AND COMMENTS Take a relaxing ride around the perimeter of the Magic Kingdom aboard a real steam-powered locomotive, with stops in Frontierland and Fantasyland. Views from the train include a peek into each land except Adventureland (where you're apt to see more of the behind-the-scenes infrastructure). The most scenic part of the tour is between the Frontierland and Main Street, U.S.A., stations. If you're in Frontierland and headed out of the park, it's a nice way to end your visit.

TOURING TIPS We suggest saving the train until after you have seen the featured attractions, or use it when you need transportation. On busy days, lines form at the Frontierland station but rarely at the Main Street station. Wheelchair access is available at the Frontierland and Fantasyland stations.

Only folded strollers are permitted on the train, so you can't board with your rented Disney stroller. You can, however, obtain a replacement at your destination (keep your stroller name card and rental receipt with you).

A dad from Green Pond, New Jersey, points out that all stations are not equal:

Tell your readers that if they ride the railroad they should go to the Main Street station. We tried to get on [at another station], and it was a zoo—there were people shoving past other people and rolling over other people with strollers and wheelchairs. The Main Street station is much more organized, efficient, and relaxing because of the extra cast members working there.

Finally, note that the railroad shuts down immediately before and during parades and fireworks; check your park guide map or *Times Guide* for times. Needless to say, this is not the time to get in line.

ADVENTURELAND

ADVENTURELAND IS THE FIRST land to the left of Main Street, U.S.A. It combines an African-safari theme with a tropical island atmosphere. Some of Adventureland's attractions are theme park classics. They're also among the oldest in the park, so crowds don't usually build here until late morning.

Jungle Cruise ★★★½

PRESCHOOL ★★★★ (MBA)   GRADE SCHOOL ★★★★ (MBA)   TEENS ★★★½ (BA)
YOUNG ADULTS ★★★★ (BA)   OVER 30 ★★★★ (BA)   SENIORS ★★★★ (A)

What it is Outdoor safari-themed boat ride. **Scope and scale** Major attraction. **When to go** Before 10:30 a.m., during the last 2 hours before closing, or use Genie+. **Duration of ride** 8–9 minutes. **Average wait in line per 100 people ahead of you** 3½ minutes; assumes 10 boats operating. **Loading speed** Moderate. **ECV/wheelchair access** May remain in ECV/wheelchair and wait for specially configured boats. **Participates in Genie+** Yes. **Early Theme Park Entry** No. **Extended Evening Hours** No.

DESCRIPTION AND COMMENTS Jungle Cruise is an outdoor group boat ride through some of the world's best-known simulated tropical waterways. You'll pass through forest and jungle populated entirely by animatronic animals (some hostile) and natives.

Jungle Cruise was the park's signature ride when it opened at Disneyland. With the advent of modern, highly themed, *real* zoo environments such as Animal Kingdom, the Magic Kingdom's version would surely have faded into obscurity were it not for one thing: The skippers tell jokes. OK, *jokes* is a stretch—the skippers do *the* cheesiest, most groan-inducing stand-up you've ever heard. If you dig that sort of thing, it's glorious. If not, heed this Pelham, Alabama, reader's warning:

Jungle Cruise severely needs an update. Our tour guide indulged in annoying comedy to make up for the lack of excitement. I would rather have been eaten by the animatronic hippos.

This reader's prayers have partially been answered: Disney updated the Jungle Cruise's scenery and jokes in 2021. The puns remain.

The best Jungle Cruise experience we've ever had began with all the passengers agreeing beforehand to laugh enthusiastically at whatever jokes we heard. It took about two puns for the skipper to catch on and play along. The ride ended with us chanting the skipper's name during thunderous applause, to which the skipper said, "Is this what unconditional love feels like? Take that, Mom and Dad!"

TOURING TIPS We think the ride is better at night.

The Magic Carpets of Aladdin ★★½

PRESCHOOL ★★★★½ (MAA)	**GRADE SCHOOL ★★★★** (BA)	**TEENS ★★★** (BA)
YOUNG ADULTS ★★★ (MBA)	**OVER 30 ★★★** (MBA)	**SENIORS ★★★** (MBA)

What it is Elaborate midway ride. **Scope and scale** Minor attraction. **When to go** Before 11 a.m. or after 7 p.m. **Duration of ride** 1½ minutes. **Average wait in line per 100 people ahead of you** 16 minutes. **Loading speed** Slow. **ECV/wheelchair access** Must transfer from ECV to provided wheelchair. **Participates in Genie+** Yes. **Early Theme Park Entry** No. **Extended Evening Hours** Yes.

DESCRIPTION AND COMMENTS This spinning midway ride is like Dumbo with magic carpets instead of elephants. A spitting camel sprays jets of water on carpet riders. Riders can maneuver their carpets up and down and side to side to avoid the water. The front seat controls vehicle height, while the back seat controls tilt—if you let the kids sit up front, prepare to get wet!

TOURING TIPS Like Dumbo, this ride has great eye appeal but an extremely slow loading time. Try to get younger kids on during the first 30 minutes the park is open, or try just before park closing.

A Pirate's Adventure: Treasure of the Seven Seas ★★★½

PRESCHOOL ★★★★½ (A)	**GRADE SCHOOL ★★★★½** (A)	**TEENS ★★★★** (A)
YOUNG ADULTS ★★★★ (A)	**OVER 30 ★★★★½** (A)	**SENIORS ★★★★** (A)

What it is Interactive game. **Scope and scale** Diversion. **When to go** Noon–6 p.m. **Duration of experience** About 20 minutes to play the entire game. **ECV/wheelchair access** May remain in ECV/wheelchair. **Participates in Genie+** No. **Early Theme Park Entry** No. **Extended Evening Hours** No.

DESCRIPTION AND COMMENTS A Pirate's Adventure features interactive areas with physical props and narrations that lead guests through a quest to help Captain Jack Sparrow find lost treasure, all within Adventureland.

Guests begin their journey at The Crow's Nest. Your group of up to six people chooses a leader; the leader's MagicBand (or ticket or talisman) activates a video screen that assigns the group to one of five different missions. Your group is given a map and sent off to your first location.

Once at the location, the leader of the party touches the talisman to the symbol at the station, and the animation begins. Each adventure has four or five stops throughout Adventureland; each stop contains 30–45 seconds of activity. No strategy or action is required: Simply watch what unfolds on the screen, get your next destination, and head off.

We like how well each station integrates into its surroundings and how the stations' artifacts and props tie together the attraction and movie story lines. If you're not yet convinced to play, stand in Adventureland and watch the faces of the kids playing when they do something that triggers smoke, noise, or other effects.

A Maryland mom writes:

The very best thing we did with our 4-year-old was A Pirate's Adventure. It was incredible. We did all five scavenger hunts, and it took 2 hours—our most fun 2 hours at the park! It's high-tech, magical, imaginative, active, and individualized. And you can keep the beautiful maps!

And from a New York City reader:

Our girls (age 9) had a blast and were eager to complete all five stages of the journey. The maps were a fun challenge for them: easy enough to be fun but challenging enough to give them a sense that they were accomplishing something—and the surprises at each stage were lots of fun for all of us. The only caution I would add is that you should try to take part when there aren't too many other people participating. Waiting in line behind another group took the fun out of finding a stop.

TOURING TIPS Not a must if time is tight.

Pirates of the Caribbean ★★★★

PRESCHOOL ★★★½ (MBA)	GRADE SCHOOL ★★★★ (A)	TEENS ★★★★½ (MAA)
YOUNG ADULTS ★★★★½ (MAA)	OVER 30 ★★★★½ (MAA)	SENIORS ★★★★½ (MAA)

What it is Indoor pirate-themed boat ride. **Scope and scale** Headliner. **When to go** Before 11 a.m., after 7 p.m., or use Genie+. **Comment** Frightens some children. **Duration of ride** About 7½ minutes. **Average wait in line per 100 people ahead of you** 3 minutes; assumes 1 Genie+ line, 1 standby line. **Loading speed** Fast. **ECV/wheelchair access** Must transfer from ECV to provided wheelchair and then from wheelchair to boat. **Participates in Genie+** Yes. **Early Theme Park Entry** No. **Extended Evening Hours** Yes.

DESCRIPTION AND COMMENTS An indoor cruise through a series of sets that depict a pirate raid on an island settlement, from bombardment of the fortress to ransacking after the victory. Arguably one of the most influential theme park attractions ever created, the Magic Kingdom's version retains the elaborate queuing area, grand scale, and detailed scenes that have awed audiences since its debut in Disneyland in 1967.

As one of the theme park's most popular rides, Pirates is scrutinized and revised often. The successful *Pirates of the Caribbean* movies have boosted the ride's popularity, and guests' demands led to the addition of animatronic figures of Captain Jack Sparrow and Captain Barbossa in scenes. The latest refresh changes a scene of raiders auctioning off women to an auction of captured townsfolk's luxury possessions and chickens, led by a gun-wielding female pirate.

The cumulative effect of these additions, however, makes the ride's narrative confusing and self-contradicting. For example, while you might believe that your boat is floating past these scenes at a specific point in time, the appearance of Jack Sparrow in multiple places means that you're also in different timelines. And it's nonsense to suggest that these pirates will bombard a town, torture its inhabitants, and pillage everything in sight, but will stop all of that for an auction that determines the correct market price for chickens. The new scene just doesn't make sense in the context of the rest of the ride.

TOURING TIPS Engineered to move large crowds in a hurry, Pirates is a good attraction to see in the late afternoon.

Swiss Family Treehouse ★★★

PRESCHOOL ★★★½ (BA) **GRADE SCHOOL ★★★½ (MBA)** **TEENS ★★★ (MBA)**
YOUNG ADULTS ★★★ (MBA) **OVER 30 ★★★½ (MBA)** **SENIORS ★★★½ (MBA)**

What it is Outdoor walk-through treehouse. **Scope and scale** Minor attraction. **When to go** Anytime. **Comment** Requires climbing a lot of stairs. **Duration of tour** 10–15 minutes. **Probable waiting time** None most days, 10 minutes tops. **ECV/wheelchair access** Must be ambulatory. **Participates in Genie+** No. **Early Theme Park Entry** No. **Extended Evening Hours** Yes.

DESCRIPTION AND COMMENTS An immense replica of the Swiss Family Robinson's arboreal abode. With its multiple stories and mechanical wizardry, it's the queen of all treehouses.

TOURING TIPS A self-guided walk-through tour involves a lot of stairs up and down, but no ropes, ladders, or anything fancy. Lookie-loos or people stopping to rest sometimes create bottlenecks that slow things down. Visit in late afternoon or early evening if you're on a one-day tour, or in the morning of your second day.

Walt Disney's Enchanted Tiki Room ★★★

PRESCHOOL ★★★★ (MBA) **GRADE SCHOOL ★★★½ (MBA)** **TEENS ★★★ (MBA)**
YOUNG ADULTS ★★★½ (MBA) **OVER 30 ★★★★ (BA)** **SENIORS ★★★★ (A)**

What it is Audio-Animatronic Pacific Island musical-theater show. **Scope and scale** Minor attraction. **When to go** Before 11 a.m. or after 3:30 p.m. **Comment** Frightens some preschoolers. **Duration of presentation** 15½ minutes. **Preshow entertainment** Talking birds. **Probable waiting time** 15 minutes. **ECV/wheelchair access** May remain in ECV/wheelchair. **Participates in Genie+** No. **Early Theme Park Entry** No. **Extended Evening Hours** Yes.

DESCRIPTION AND COMMENTS This show, conceived by Walt Disney, stars four singing, wisecracking mechanical parrots: José, Fritz, Michael, and Pierre. The quartet performs songs arranged in styles from the 1940s to the 1960s, accompanied by dozens of other birds, plants, and tikis that come to life all around you.

The show was an engineering marvel when it opened in Disneyland in 1963. We suspect most millennials regard it as lame. It remains a favorite of many, including us, who enjoy the period-appropriate musical references and, frankly, Walt's idea of a building full of animatronic birds.

Readers such as this mom of three from Coleman, Michigan, caution that the attraction may frighten some younger kids:

The Tiki Room *show was very scary, with a thunder-and-lightning storm and a loud volcano. Can't Disney do anything without scaring young children?*

TOURING TIPS Usually not too crowded. We go in the late afternoon, when we appreciate sitting in air-conditioned comfort with our brains in park.

FRONTIERLAND

THIS "LAND" FOLLOWS ADVENTURELAND as you move clockwise around the Magic Kingdom. Frontierland's focus is on 1800s America, with stockade-type structures and pioneer trappings. If you start at Big Thunder Mountain and walk toward The Haunted Mansion in Liberty Square, you'll also be walking back in time: The different rides and buildings represent distinct eras in US history, from the settling of the frontier through the California gold rush to the early-19th-century South.

Big Thunder Mountain Railroad ★★★★

PRESCHOOL ★★★★ (BA) GRADE SCHOOL ★★★★½ (MAA) TEENS ★★★★½ (MAA)
YOUNG ADULTS ★★★★½ (MAA) OVER 30 ★★★★½ (MAA) SENIORS ★★★★½ (A)

What it is Western mining–themed roller coaster. **Scope and scale** Headliner. **When to go** Before 10 a.m. or in the hour before closing, or use Genie+. **Comments** Must be 40" to ride; Rider Switch option provided (see page 396). **Duration of ride** About 3½ minutes. **Average wait in line per 100 people ahead of you** 2½ minutes; assumes 5 trains operating. **Loading speed** Moderate-fast. **ECV/wheelchair access** Must transfer to the ride vehicle. **Participates in Genie+** Yes. **Early Theme Park Entry** No. **Extended Evening Hours** Yes.

DESCRIPTION AND COMMENTS Every age group from grade-schoolers through seniors rates Big Thunder as the best roller coaster in the Magic Kingdom (we'll see if that holds up with Tron open). The idea is that you're on a runaway mine train careening through a gold rush frontier town. Big Thunder contains first-rate examples of Disney creativity: a realistic mining town, colorful caverns, and an earthquake, all humorously animated with swinging possums, smart-aleck buzzards, and the like. Ride it after dark if you can. Seats in the back offer the best experience.

In terms of intensity, we put this coaster at about a 5 on a scary scale of 10—it has tight turns rather than big hills or drops, and no loops or upside-down parts. Because it's outdoors and kids can see most of the ride, it's a better introduction to "real" roller coasters for young children than Space Mountain; we'd recommend it if your kids enjoyed Seven Dwarfs Mine Train.

TOURING TIPS Nearby **Tiana's Bayou Adventure** (see 477) will affect traffic flow to Big Thunder Mountain Railroad—guests who ride one usually ride both. This will translate to large crowds in Frontierland all day and long waits for Big Thunder. Once Tiana's opens, your two-day schedule should have Tron, Big Thunder, and Tiana's on one day, and Seven Dwarfs and Space Mountain on the other. A good one-day schedule with Tiana's open might be (1) Tron, (2) Big Thunder, (3) Tiana's Bayou Adventure, and in the evening (4) Space Mountain and (5) Seven Dwarfs Mine Train.

A Midwestern mom offers this tip to families with kids too short to ride:

If you're rider-swapping on Thunder Mountain or [Tiana's Bayou Adventure] and have young kids to entertain, there's a fantastic little playground nearby where you can pass the time. It's completely covered and near the restrooms too! It's next to [Tiana's Bayou Adventure], under the train tracks.

Guests experience Disney attractions differently. Consider this letter from a woman in Brookline, Massachusetts:

Being older and having limited time, my friend and I confined our activities to attractions rated as four or five stars for seniors. Because of your recommendation, we waited an hour to board Big Thunder Mountain Railroad, which you rated a 5 on a scary scale of 10. After living through 3½ minutes of pure terror, I will rate it a 15. We were so busy holding on and screaming and even praying for our safety that we didn't see any falling rocks, a mining town, or an earthquake.

A Vermont woman feels there's more to consider about Big Thunder than being scared:

Big Thunder Mountain Railroad rates high on the lose-your-lunch meter. One more sharp turn and the kids in front of me would have needed a dip in the Rivers of America!

Country Bear Jamboree ★★★½

| PRESCHOOL ★★★★ (BA) | GRADE SCHOOL ★★★½ (MBA) | TEENS ★★★ (MBA) |
| YOUNG ADULTS ★★★ (MBA) | OVER 30 ★★★½ (MBA) | SENIORS ★★★★ (BA) |

What it is Corny Audio-Animatronic hoedown. **Scope and scale** Minor attraction. **When to go** Anytime. **Duration of presentation** 11 minutes. **Preshow entertainment** None. **Probable waiting time** Not terribly popular but has a comparatively small capacity. Waiting time between noon and 5:30 p.m. on a busy day will average 11–22 minutes. **ECV/wheelchair access** May remain in wheelchair. **Participates in Genie+** No. **Early Theme Park Entry** No. **Extended Evening Hours** Yes.

DESCRIPTION AND COMMENTS A charming cast of animatronic bears sings and stomps through a series of country and Western songs. On the plus side, it's an air-conditioned refuge on hot days, and the remix of "The Ballad of Davy Crockett" and "Ole Slew Foot" is genius. However, the *Jamboree* has run for so long that the geriatric bears are a step away from assisted living.

Reader comments tend to echo a desire for something new. From a Sandy Hook, Connecticut, mom:

I know they consider it a classic, and kids always seem to love it, but could they PLEASE update it after half a century?

A woman from Carmel, Indiana, put her experience in succinct perspective:

Here is a half hour of my life that I can never get back.

But a Mississippi dad defends the show:

In my 30s I considered Country Bear Jamboree *hokey and lame, yet I thoroughly enjoyed my daughter's intense love of it at ages 3 and 8 on previous trips. This time, at age 54, I sat up fairly close with my wife and loved it—we even sang along! Of course, this was partly to embarrass my now-16-year-old daughter, who sat hunched down in the very last row. She says we have creeping senility, but I told her, "Just wait till you bring your kids!"*

TOURING TIPS On hot and rainy days and during peak seasons, the *Jamboree* draws large crowds from midmorning on.

Frontierland Shootin' Arcade ★½

| PRESCHOOL ★★★ (MBA) | GRADE SCHOOL ★★★★ (BA) | TEENS ★★★½ (BA) |
| YOUNG ADULTS ★★★ (MBA) | OVER 30 ★★★½ (MBA) | SENIORS ★★★★ (BA) |

What it is Electronic shooting gallery. **Scope and scale** Diversion. **When to go** Anytime. **ECV/wheelchair access** May remain in ECV/wheelchair. **Participates in Genie+** No. **Early Theme Park Entry** Yes. **Extended Evening Hours** Yes.

DESCRIPTION AND COMMENTS At press time, the Frontierland Shootin' Arcade remained free to play. Each shot is followed by a short delay before the next shot can be taken—this prevents small children from accidentally using all 35 shots in 5 seconds. Despite the arcade's low overall rating, many Unofficial Guide staff gladly stop here when they visit the World. It's a small bit of you're-in-control interactivity in a park with a lot of sitting and watching.

TOURING TIPS Skip it if time is tight. The fun is entirely in the shootin'—no prizes can be won.

Tiana's Bayou Adventure
(formerly Splash Mountain; opens 2024)

What it is Indoor–outdoor water-flume adventure. **Scope and scale** Super-headliner. **When to go** During warm weather: as soon as the park opens, during afternoon or evening parades, just before closing, or use Genie+/Individual Lightning Lane. **Comments** Must be 40″ to ride; Rider Switch option provided (see page 396). Many preschoolers will be too short to ride; others freak out when they see it from the waiting line. Among preschoolers who actually ride, however, most should love it. **Duration of ride** About 10 minutes. **Average wait in line per 100 people ahead of you** 3½ minutes; assumes ride is operating at full capacity. **Loading speed** Moderate. **ECV/wheelchair access** Must transfer to the ride vehicle; transfer device available. **Participates in Genie+** (Likely Individual Lightning Lane when it opens). **Early Theme Park Entry** No. **Extended Evening Hours** Yes.

DESCRIPTION AND COMMENTS Tiana's Bayou Adventure is a welcome retheming of Frontierland's controversial Splash Mountain ride to the characters and story of Disney's 2009 film *The Princess and the Frog*. At press time, Disney's only details around the new story is that it follows Tiana's expansion of her culinary empire, from restaurant to farms, salt mines, and cooking schools. We're reasonably sure however, that since it's a retheming, Tiana's should retain all of Splash Mountain's architecture, including its pacing, small drops, and big drop near the end.

Disney is retheming both this Splash Mountain and the one in Disneyland to Tiana's Bayou Adventure. From a thematic perspective, the Disneyland version is straightforward: Tiana's is adjacent to The Haunted Mansion, which is in New Orleans Square. Since Tiana's story also takes place in New Orleans and there's no specific chronology associated with The Haunted Mansion, Tiana's post-1927 timeline fits in just fine. It'll be interesting to see how Disney fits Tiana into a Frontierland that doesn't exist after 1890.

TOURING TIPS If you ride in the front seat, you'll almost certainly get wet; riders elsewhere get at least splashed. Since you don't know which seat you'll be assigned, go prepared. On a cool day, carry a plastic garbage bag and tear holes in the bottom and sides to make a water-resistant (not waterproof) sack dress (tuck the bag under your bum). Or store a change of clothes, including footwear, in one of the park's rental lockers.

Leave your camera or phone with a nonriding member of your group, or wrap it in plastic. For any attraction where there's a distinct possibility of getting soaked, wear Tevas or some other type of waterproof sandal, and change back to regular shoes after the ride.

The scariest part of this adventure ride is the steep chute you see when standing in line. The drop looks worse than it is; nonetheless, many children freak out when they see it. A mom from Grand Rapids, Michigan, recalls her kids' rather unique reaction:

We discovered after the fact that our children thought they would go under water after the big drop, so they tried to hold their breath throughout the ride in preparation. They were too preoccupied with that to enjoy the clever story.

Tom Sawyer Island and Fort Langhorn ★★★

PRESCHOOL ★★★★ (A)	GRADE SCHOOL ★★★★ (A)	TEENS ★★½ (BA)
YOUNG ADULTS ★★★½ (MBA)	OVER 30 ★★★½ (MBA)	SENIORS ★★★½ (MBA)

What it is Outdoor walk-through exhibit and rustic playground. **Scope and scale** Minor attraction. **When to go** Midmorning–late afternoon. **Comments** Closes at dusk. Great for rambunctious kids. **ECV/wheelchair access** Must be ambulatory. **Participates in Genie+** No. **Early Theme Park Entry** No. **Extended Evening Hours** No.

DESCRIPTION AND COMMENTS Tom Sawyer Island is a getaway within the park. It has hills to climb; a cave, windmill, and pioneer stockade (Fort Langhorn) to explore; a tipsy barrel bridge to cross; and paths to follow. You can watch riverboats chug past. It's a delight for adults and a godsend for children who want to cut loose after being closely supervised all day.

TOURING TIPS Tom Sawyer Island is underrated—we think it's one of the Magic Kingdom's better-conceived attractions. Kids revel in its frontier atmosphere, and it's a must for families with children ages 5–15. If your group is made up of adults, visit on your second day or on your first day after you've seen the attractions you most wanted to see.

Although kids could spend a whole day here, plan on at least 40 minutes. Access is by raft from Frontierland; two rafts operate simultaneously, and while the trip itself is pretty efficient, you may have to stand in line to board both ways.

A St. Clair Shores, Michigan, family made an unplanned visit:

My 5-year-old son needed to run off some energy, so we veered from the touring plan and took the raft to Tom Sawyer Island. I thought it was a playground (we never bothered to head there before), but it was the coolest area to explore for our whole family! Very few people were there, which meant I got amazing pictures of my kids without strangers in the background, and the buildings, tunnels, and fort were so fun to explore! My kids asked to go back here the next day, and we did!

Walt Disney World Railroad

DESCRIPTION AND COMMENTS Stops in Frontierland on its circuit of the park. See the description on page 470 for additional details.

TOURING TIPS Pleasant, feet-saving link to Main Street and Fantasyland, but the Frontierland station is more congested than those stations.

LIBERTY SQUARE

LIBERTY SQUARE re-creates the United States at the time of the Revolutionary War. The architecture is Federal and Colonial. The **Liberty Tree,** a live oak more than 150 years old, lends dignity and grace to the patriotic setting.

The Hall of Presidents ★★★

PRESCHOOL ★★½ (MBA)*	GRADE SCHOOL ★★★ (MBA)*	TEENS ★★★ (MBA)*
YOUNG ADULTS ★★★½ (MBA)	OVER 30 ★★★★ (A)	SENIORS ★★★★½ (MAA)

This is the lowest-rated Magic Kingdom attraction among preschoolers, grade-schoolers, and teens.

What it is Audio-Animatronic historical theater presentation. **Scope and scale** Minor attraction. **When to go** Anytime. **Duration of presentation** Almost 23 minutes. **Preshow entertainment** None. **Probable waiting time** About 15 minutes. It would be exceptionally unusual not to be admitted to the next show. **ECV/wheelchair access** May remain in wheelchair. **Participates in Genie+** No. **Early Theme Park Entry** No. **Extended Evening Hours** No.

DESCRIPTION AND COMMENTS *The Hall of Presidents* combines a wide-screen theater presentation of key highlights and milestones in the political history of the United States with a short stage show featuring life-size animatronic replicas of every US president. The figures' physical resemblances and costumes are masterful.

Abraham Lincoln and George Washington have speaking roles, and President Joseph R. Biden recites the oath of office. Regardless of who speaks, the inspirational, patriotic tone is a constant. For that reason, foreign visitors rate the show lower than Americans do.

We've always had a high opinion of *The Hall of Presidents*. The current version of the show, however, reiterates so many of the same social and political points as EPCOT's *The American Adventure* that it's probably not worthwhile to see both. Of the two, *The American Adventure* is better.

We receive a lot of comments from readers who get more than entertainment from it. A young mother in Marion, Ohio, advises:

The Hall of Presidents is a great place to breast-feed!

And a woman in St. Louis writes:

We always go when my husband gets cranky so he can take a nice nap.

TOURING TIPS The *Hall's* latest addition is President Biden. Over the last decade or so, it's become commonplace for some members of the audience to cheer or jeer, according to their political affiliation, as the current president and his contemporaries are named. These partisan displays are divisive and not in keeping with the show's positive message, but they aren't likely to go away—so skip *The Hall of Presidents* if you'd rather not be reminded of politics on vacation.

The Haunted Mansion ★★★★½

PRESCHOOL ★★★ (MBA)	GRADE SCHOOL ★★★★ (MBA)	TEENS ★★★★½ (MAA)
YOUNG ADULTS ★★★★½ (MAA)	OVER 30 ★★★★½ (MAA)	SENIORS ★★★★½ (MAA)

What it is Haunted-house dark ride. **Scope and scale** Major attraction. **When to go** Before 11 a.m. or during the last 2 hours before closing. **Comment** Frightens some very young children. **Duration of ride** 7-minute ride plus a 1½-minute preshow. **Average wait in line per 100 people ahead of you** 2½ minutes; assumes both "stretch rooms" operating. **Loading speed** Fast. **ECV/wheelchair access** Must transfer to the ride vehicle. **Participates in Genie+** Yes. **Early Theme Park Entry** No. **Extended Evening Hours** Yes.

DESCRIPTION AND COMMENTS Only slightly scarier than a whoopee cushion, The Haunted Mansion—which opened with the rest of Walt Disney World in 1971—proves that top-notch special effects don't always require 21st-century technology. "Doom Buggies" on a conveyor belt transport you through the house from parlor to attic, then through a graveyard. The effects change tone with the setting: Those found in the house are generally spooky, while the graveyard effects, such as a ghostly opera singer wearing a Viking helmet, are for laughs. Some kids get anxious about what they think they'll see, but almost nobody actually gets scared.

Eve Zibart, a veteran journalist and the author of several *Unofficial Guides*, ranks The Haunted Mansion among her favorite Disney attractions:

This is one of the best attractions in the Magic Kingdom, jam-packed with visual puns, special effects, hidden Mickeys, and lovely Victorian-spooky sets. It's not scary except in the sweetest of ways, and it will remind you of the days before ghost stories gave way to slasher flicks.

A Temple, Texas, mom isn't convinced when we say it isn't scary:

You say the actual sights aren't really frightening—but what isn't frightening about a hanging corpse, a coffin escapee, and an axe-wielding skeleton bride?

A mom from Victoria, British Columbia, wishes that teens would shut their pieholes:

My 4-year-old daughter loved Space Mountain, but The Haunted Mansion really scared her. Our experience was that teenagers deliberately scream and pretend to be scared on this ride. This scares the crap out of the little ones.

Interactive elements in the left side of the outdoor queue ensure that guests have something to occupy them when lines are long. Features include a music-playing monument and a ship captain's tomb that squirts water.

TOURING TIPS Lines here ebb and flow more than those at most other Magic Kingdom hot spots because the Mansion is near *The Hall of Presidents* and the *Liberty Belle* Riverboat. These two attractions disgorge hundreds of guests when each show or ride ends, and many of these folks head straight for the Mansion. If you can't go before 11:30 a.m. or in the last 2 hours the park is open, try to slip in around dinner.

When admitted to the Mansion, you'll first enter a foyer with a fireplace, then be guided quickly into a second preshow room with wood paneling, and four paintings above you. Keeping close to the wall, find the wall panel with a small, red light at about eye level, and stand with your back to that panel while you watch the preshow.

Liberty Belle Riverboat ★★½

PRESCHOOL ★★½ (BA)	**GRADE SCHOOL ★★★** (MBA)	**TEENS ★★★** (BA)
YOUNG ADULTS ★★½ (BA)	**OVER 30 ★★★½** (MBA)	**SENIORS ★★★★** (A)

What it is Scenic boat ride. **Scope and scale** Minor attraction. **When to go** Anytime. **Duration of ride** About 16 minutes. **Average wait to board** 10–14 minutes. **ECV/wheelchair access** May remain in ECV/wheelchair. **Participates in Genie+** No. **Early Theme Park Entry** No. **Extended Evening Hours** No.

DESCRIPTION AND COMMENTS This large paddle-wheel riverboat navigates the waters around Tom Sawyer Island and Fort Langhorn, passing settler cabins, old mining paraphernalia, an American Indian village, and a small menagerie of animatronic wildlife. A beautiful craft, the *Liberty Belle* provides a lofty perspective of Frontierland and Liberty Square.

TOURING TIPS The riverboat, which departs roughly every half hour, is a good attraction for the busy middle of the day. If you encounter huge crowds, chances are that the attraction has been inundated by guests coming from a just-concluded performance of *The Hall of Presidents*. If it's hot outside, find a spot in the shade on the bottom deck.

FANTASYLAND

FANTASYLAND IS THE ENCHANTED HEART of the Magic Kingdom, spread gracefully like a miniature Alpine village beneath the steepled towers of **Cinderella Castle.**

Fantasyland is divided into three distinct sections. Directly behind Cinderella Castle and set upon a snowcapped mountain is **Beast's Castle,** part of a *Beauty and the Beast*–themed area. Most of this section holds dining and shopping, such as **Be Our Guest Restaurant** (reviewed in Part 6); **Gaston's Tavern,** a small quick-service restaurant; and a gift shop. The far-right corner of Fantasyland—including **Dumbo, The Barnstormer** kiddie coaster, and the Fantasyland train station—is called **Storybook Circus** as an homage to Disney's *Dumbo* films. A covered seating area with plush chairs, electrical outlets, and USB phone chargers is located behind **Big Top Souvenirs.**

The middle of Fantasyland holds the headliner, **Seven Dwarfs Mine Train,** and a secondary attraction, **Under the Sea: Journey of the Little Mermaid.** The placement of these two attractions allows good traffic flow either to the left (toward Beast's Castle) for dining, to the right for attractions geared to smaller children, or back to the original part of Fantasyland for Disney classics such as **Peter Pan's Flight** and **The Many Adventures of Winnie the Pooh.**

The original section, behind Cinderella Castle, holds an antique carousel, *Mickey's PhilharMagic,* and the popular **Princess Fairytale Hall** meet and greet. Finally, when nature calls, don't miss the *Tangled-***themed restrooms and outdoor seating**, near Peter Pan's Flight.

Ariel's Grotto ★★★

**PRESCHOOL ★★★★½ (MAA) GRADE SCHOOL ★★★★ (AA) TEENS ★★★★ (A)
YOUNG ADULTS ★★★★ (A) OVER 30 ★★★★ (MBA) SENIORS ★★★★ (A)**

What it is Character-greeting venue. **Scope and scale** Minor attraction. **When to go** Before 10:30 a.m. or during the last 2 hours before closing. **Duration of experience** About 30–90 seconds. **Probable waiting time** 45 minutes. **Queue speed** Slow. **ECV/wheelchair access** May remain in wheelchair. **Participates in Genie+** Yes. **Early Theme Park Entry** No. **Extended Evening Hours** No.

DESCRIPTION AND COMMENTS This is Ariel's home turf, next to her signature ride (see page 489). In the base of the seaside cliffs under Prince Eric's Castle, Ariel greets guests from a seashell throne.

An older couple from San Antonio didn't find what they were expecting at the Grotto:

The description on the park map reads, "Visit Ariel and all her treasures," which led us to believe it was some sort of walk-through gallery. Curious, we were ushered into Ariel's Treasure Room. Imagine our surprise when we saw a young woman dressed only in a clamshell bra and a fish tail. When we told her we weren't interested in a photo opportunity—I could just imagine having a picture of a scantily clad woman on my desk—she looked hurt and said, "You don't want a picture of me?"

TOURING TIPS The Grotto may close an hour before the rest of the park. The greeting area is set up almost as if to encourage guests to linger on purpose, which keeps the line long. The queue isn't air-conditioned.

The Barnstormer ★★

**PRESCHOOL ★★★★½ (AA) GRADE SCHOOL ★★★★ (MBA) TEENS ★★★ (MBA)
YOUNG ADULTS ★★★ (MBA) OVER 30 ★★★ (MBA) SENIORS ★★★ (MBA)**

What it is Small roller coaster. **Scope and scale** Minor attraction. **When to go** Before 11 a.m., during parades, or in the 2 hours before closing. **Comment** Must be 35" to ride.

Duration of ride 53 seconds. **Average wait in line per 100 people ahead of you** 7 minutes. **Loading speed** Slow. **ECV/wheelchair access** Must transfer to the ride vehicle. **Participates in Genie+** Yes. **Early Theme Park Entry** Yes. **Extended Evening Hours** Yes.

DESCRIPTION AND COMMENTS The Barnstormer is a dinky little coaster with a brief but zippy ride. Of the 53 seconds the ride is in motion, 32 seconds are consumed by leaving the loading area, being ratcheted up the first hill, and braking into the off-loading area. The actual time you spend careering around the track: 21 seconds.

A Westport, Connecticut, reader warns adults that the ride may not be as tame as it looks:

A nightmare that should have gone in your "Eats Adults" section. It looked so innocent—nothing hidden in the dark, over quickly—but it took me hours to stop feeling nauseated.

Though the reader's point is well taken, we think The Barnstormer is a good introduction to roller coasters, one that can help your kids step up to more-adventuresome rides. (**Seven Dwarfs Mine Train** would be next.)

TOURING TIPS The cars are too small for most adults and tend to whiplash taller people. Parties without children should skip this one. Because the ride draws in kids visually and aurally, it subjects families to slow-moving lines. If The Barnstormer is high on your children's hit parade, try to ride within the first 2 hours that Fantasyland is open.

A Cary, North Carolina, mom offers a heads-up for solo parents:

There are some fussy rules for riding The Barnstormer. Each of the ride cars holds only two people, and every child under 7 must be accompanied by [someone age 14 or older]. That means a single parent can't take two small children on the ride alone—you either need to rustle up another adult [or older child] to help or skip it entirely.

Casey Jr. Splash 'N' Soak Station ★★★

PRESCHOOL ★★★½ (MAA)	GRADE SCHOOL ★★★★ (AA)	TEENS ★★½ (MBA)
YOUNG ADULTS ★★ (MBA)	OVER 30 ★★½ (MBA)	SENIORS ★★½ (BA)

What it is Elaborate water-play area. **Scope and scale** Diversion. **When to go** When it's hot. **ECV/wheelchair access** May remain in wheelchair. **Participates in Genie+** No. **Early Theme Park Entry** No. **Extended Evening Hours** No.

DESCRIPTION AND COMMENTS Casey Jr., the circus train from *Dumbo*, plays host to an absolutely drenching experience outside the Fantasyland Train Station in the Storybook Circus area. A cadre of captive circus beasts sprays water on kids and hapless parents.

TOURING TIPS Puts all other theme park splash areas to soaking shame—bring a change of clothes and a big towel. Note that it doesn't run during cooler weather.

Dumbo the Flying Elephant ★★½

PRESCHOOL ★★★½ (MAA)	GRADE SCHOOL ★★★★ (MBA)	TEENS ★★★ (MBA)
YOUNG ADULTS ★★★ (MBA)	OVER 30 ★★★½ (MBA)	SENIORS ★★½ (BA)

What it is Disneyfied midway ride. **Scope and scale** Minor attraction. **When to go** Before 11 a.m. or after 6 p.m. **Duration of ride** 1½ minutes. **Average wait in line per 100 people ahead of you** 10 minutes. **Loading speed** Slow. **ECV/wheelchair access** Must transfer to the ride vehicle. **Participates in Genie+** Yes. **Early Theme Park Entry** Yes. **Extended Evening Hours** Yes.

DESCRIPTION AND COMMENTS A sweet, happy children's ride based on the lovable flying pachyderm. Parents and kids sit in small fiberglass elephants mounted on long metal arms, which spin around a central axis. Controls inside each vehicle allow you to raise the arm, making you spin higher off the ground. Despite being little different from rides at state fairs and carnivals in parking lots, Dumbo is the favorite Magic Kingdom attraction of many younger children. Wait times average less than 30 minutes.

TOURING TIPS If Dumbo is essential to your child's happiness, ride after dinner; not only are the crowds smaller at night, but the lighting and effects make the ride much prettier then. Or you can try to ride following the afternoon parade, if it's performed.

If you want to ride twice with a minimal wait, have two adults get in line on the same side of Dumbo, and allow between 32 and 64 people to get between the first adult and child and the second adult. Pass the child to the second adult when the first ride is over.

Enchanted Tales with Belle ★★★★

PRESCHOOL ★★★½ (MAA)   **GRADE SCHOOL** ★★★★ (AA)   **TEENS** ★★½ (MBA)
YOUNG ADULTS ★★★½ (MBA)   **OVER 30** ★★★½ (MBA)   **SENIORS** ★★★½ (BA)

What it is Interactive live character show. **Scope and scale** Minor attraction. **When to go** First or last 2 hours the park is open. **Duration of presentation** Approximately 20 minutes. **Preshow entertainment** A walk through Maurice's cottage and workshop. **Probable waiting time** 30 minutes. **Queue speed** Slow. **ECV/wheelchair access** Must transfer from ECV to provided wheelchair. **Participates in Genie+** No. **Early Theme Park Entry** No. **Extended Evening Hours** No.

DESCRIPTION AND COMMENTS This multiscene *Beauty and the Beast* experience begins in the cottage and workshop of Belle's father, Maurice, which is filled with odd gadgets, mementos from his daughter's younger days, and a magic mirror.

Soon enough, the room gets dark and the mirror begins to sparkle. With magic and some really good carpentry skills, the mirror turns into a full-size doorway, through which guests enter into a wardrobe room. Once in the wardrobe room, the attraction's premise is explained: You're supposed to reenact the story of *Beauty and the Beast* for Belle on her birthday, and guests are chosen to act out key parts in the play.

Once the parts are cast, everyone walks into the castle's library and takes a seat. Cast members explain how the play will take place and introduce Belle, who gives a short speech about how thrilled she is for everyone to be there. The play is acted out within a few minutes, and all of the actors get a chance to take photos with Belle and receive a small bookmark as a memento.

During our visits, only guests who were chosen to act in the play got to take photos with Belle. Those so chosen received a separate Memory Maker card for their photos.

Enchanted Tales with Belle is surely the prettiest and most elaborate meet-and-greet station in Walt Disney World. For the relative few who get to act in the play, it's also a chance to interact with Belle in a way that isn't possible in other character encounters. Sure, you may have a 30-minute wait for a 20-minute play, but it's the best thing of its kind in Orlando—your kids will love it.

An enthusiastic review from an Austin, Texas, mom:

Enchanted Tales with Belle *surprised us with how well it was done. My husband was a knight, my daughter was Mrs. Potts, and my son was silverware. It was so much fun, and the kids were so proud.*

TOURING TIPS Because the line moves slowly, see *Enchanted Tales* early in the morning or try to visit during the last 2 hours the park is open.

It's a Small World ★★★½

PRESCHOOL ★★★½ (MAA)   GRADE SCHOOL ★★★★ (MBA)   TEENS ★★★ (MBA)
YOUNG ADULTS ★★★½ (MBA)   OVER 30 ★★★★ (BA)   SENIORS ★★★★ (BA)

What it is World harmony–themed indoor boat ride. **Scope and scale** Major attraction. **When to go** Before 11 a.m. or after 7 p.m. **Duration of ride** About 11 minutes. **Average wait in line per 100 people ahead of you** 3½ minutes; assumes busy conditions with 30 or more boats operating. **Loading speed** Fast. **ECV/wheelchair access** Must transfer from ECV to provided wheelchair. **Participates in Genie+** Yes. **Early Theme Park Entry** Yes. **Extended Evening Hours** Yes.

DESCRIPTION AND COMMENTS Happy and upbeat to an almost unsettling degree, It's a Small World is guaranteed *not* to leave you asking, "How'd that song go again?" Small boats carry you on a tour around the world, with singing and dancing dolls showcasing the dress and culture of each nation represented. One of Disney's oldest entertainment offerings, Small World first unleashed its mind-numbing theme song and lethal cuteness at the 1964 New York World's Fair; the original exhibit was moved to Disneyland afterward, and a duplicate was created for Disney World when it opened in 1971.

Almost everyone enjoys It's a Small World—the first time, anyway. It stands, however, with *Enchanted Tiki Room,* and *Country Bear Jamboree* as monuments to a bygone age of entertainment.

A reader from Campbellton, New Brunswick, offers these handy tips for coping with the maddening repetition of the theme song:

If, like me, you can't stand It's a Small World but get dragged on anyway, (1) ask to sit at the back of the boat, then (2) once you're in the building, pull out your iPhone and headphones and blast some heavy metal. You'd be amazed at how different and deceptively funny the ride becomes!

TOURING TIPS If you wear a hearing aid, *turn it off.*

Mad Tea Party ★★

PRESCHOOL ★★★★½ (MAA)   GRADE SCHOOL ★★★★½ (AA)   TEENS ★★★★ (AA)
YOUNG ADULTS ★★★★ (BA)   OVER 30 ★★★½ (MBA)   SENIORS ★★★ (MBA)

What it is Midway-style spinning ride. **Scope and scale** Minor attraction. **When to go** Before 11 a.m. or after 5 p.m. **Comment** The teacup spins faster when you turn the wheel in the center. We're not sure if that's a good thing or not. **Duration of ride** 1½ minutes. **Average wait in line per 100 people ahead of you** 7½ minutes. **Loading speed** Slow. **ECV/wheelchair access** Must transfer to the ride vehicle; transfer device available. **Participates in Genie+** Yes. **Early Theme Park Entry** Yes. **Extended Evening Hours** Yes.

Motion Sickness

DESCRIPTION AND COMMENTS Riders whirl feverishly in big teacups. *Alice in Wonderland*'s Mad Hatter provides the theme. Teens like to lure adults onto the teacups and then turn the wheel in the middle—making the cup spin faster—until the adults are plastered helplessly against the sides and on the verge of tossing their tacos. Don't even *consider* getting on this thing with any person younger than 21. Against our better judgment, here's a tip from a reader we've dubbed Melba the Human Centrifuge:

If you want to spin your teacup, don't put more than three people in one cup.

TOURING TIPS Mad Tea Party is notoriously slow-loading. Ride on the morning of your second day if your schedule is more relaxed.

The Many Adventures of Winnie the Pooh ★★★½

PRESCHOOL ★★★½ (MAA) **GRADE SCHOOL ★★★★** (MBA) **TEENS ★★★** (MBA)
YOUNG ADULTS ★★★½ (MBA) **OVER 30 ★★★½** (MBA) **SENIORS ★★★★** (MBA)

What it is Indoor track ride. **Scope and scale** Minor attraction. **When to go** Before 10 a.m. or in last hour park is open. **Duration of ride** About 4 minutes. **Average wait in line per 100 people ahead of you** 4 minutes. **Loading speed** Moderate. **ECV/wheelchair access** Must transfer from ECV to provided wheelchair. **Participates in Genie+** Yes. **Early Theme Park Entry** Yes. **Extended Evening Hours** Yes.

DESCRIPTION AND COMMENTS Ride a Hunny Pot through the pages of a huge picture book into the Hundred Acre Wood, where you encounter Pooh, Piglet, Eeyore, Owl, Rabbit, Tigger, Kanga, and Roo as they contend with a blustery day. There's even a dream sequence with Heffalumps and Woozles.

A 30-something couple from Lexington, Massachusetts, thinks Pooh has plenty to offer adults:

The attention to detail and special effects make it worth seeing even if you don't have children in your party. The Pooh dream sequence was great!

A Richmond, Indiana, mom loved Pooh's interactive queue:

The queue for The Many Adventures of Winnie the Pooh was amazing! There were so many things for little kids to do, and consequently fewer meltdowns! I wish there were more queues like that.

TOURING TIPS Sunny, happy, and upbeat, Pooh is a good choice if you have small children and you're touring over two or more days.

Meet Merida at Fairytale Garden ★★★½

PRESCHOOL ★★★★½ (MAA) **GRADE SCHOOL ★★★★** (A) **TEENS ★★★½** (MBA)
YOUNG ADULTS ★★★½ (MBA) **OVER 30 ★★★½** (MBA) **SENIORS ★★★★** (A)

What it is Storytelling session plus character meet and greet. **Scope and scale** Diversion. **When to go** Check *Times Guide* for schedule. **Duration of presentation** About 10 minutes. **Probable waiting time** 30 minutes. **Queue speed** Slow. **ECV/wheelchair access** May remain in wheelchair. **Participates in Genie+** No. **Early Theme Park Entry** No. **Extended Evening Hours** No.

DESCRIPTION AND COMMENTS Merida, the flame-haired Scottish princess from *Brave,* greets guests in Fairytale Garden, in front of Cinderella Castle on the Tomorrowland side, between the castle and Cosmic Ray's Starlight Cafe.

A mom from Shelby, North Carolina, saw red here and liked it:

Many of the princesses give red-lipstick kisses, which delighted both of my children!

TOURING TIPS Princess meet and greets tend to be exceedingly popular, so expect long lines. If meeting Merida is a must-do, get in line about 15 minutes before the next performance.

Mickey's PhilharMagic ★★★★

PRESCHOOL ★★★★ (A) **GRADE SCHOOL ★★★★½** (AA) **TEENS ★★★★** (A)
YOUNG ADULTS ★★★★ (A) **OVER 30 ★★★½** (A) **SENIORS ★★★★½** (AA)

What it is 3-D movie. **Scope and scale** Major attraction. **When to go** Anytime. **Duration of presentation** About 12 minutes. **Probable waiting time** 20–30 minutes. **ECV/wheelchair access** May remain in wheelchair. **Participates in Genie+** Yes. **Early Theme Park Entry** Yes. **Extended Evening Hours** Yes.

DESCRIPTION AND COMMENTS *Mickey's PhilharMagic* is a 3-D film with an odd collection of Disney characters, mixing Mickey and Donald with Simba and Ariel as well as Jasmine, Aladdin, and characters from *Coco*.

Presented in a theater large enough to accommodate a 150-foot-wide screen—huge by 3-D standards—the movie is augmented by an arsenal of special effects built into the theater. The plot involves Mickey, as the conductor of the *PhilharMagic,* leaving the theater to solve a mystery. In his absence, Donald attempts to take charge, with disastrous results.

Brilliantly conceived, furiously paced, and laugh-out-loud funny, *Mickey's PhilharMagic* will leave you grinning. And where other Disney 3-D movies are loud, in-your-face affairs, this one is softer and cuddlier. Things pop out of the screen, but they're really not scary. It's the rare child who's frightened—but there are always exceptions, as was the case with the 3-year-old child of this North Carolina mom:

Our family found PhilharMagic *way too violent (what seemed like minutes on end of Donald getting the crap kicked out of him by various musical instruments). I had to haul my screaming child out of the theater and submit to a therapeutic carousel ride afterwards.*

Happily, an Oregon mom has an easy way to nip the willies in the bud:

My advice to parents is simply to have their kids not wear the 3-D glasses. We took my daughter's off, and she began giggling and having a good time.

TOURING TIPS One of the rare Disney attractions that is both rated highly and has short waits. Provides a nice midday air-conditioning break.

Peter Pan's Flight ★★★★

| PRESCHOOL ★★★★½ (AA) | GRADE SCHOOL ★★★★ (A) | TEENS ★★★½ (MBA) |
| YOUNG ADULTS ★★★★ (MBA) | OVER 30 ★★★★ (A) | SENIORS ★★★★½ (AA) |

What it is Indoor track ride. **Scope and scale** Minor attraction. **When to go** First or last 30 minutes the park is open. **Duration of ride** A little more than 3 minutes. **Average wait in line per 100 people ahead of you** 5½ minutes. **Loading speed** Moderate–slow. **ECV/wheelchair access** Must be ambulatory. **Participates in Genie+** Yes. **Early Theme Park Entry** Yes. **Extended Evening Hours** Yes.

DESCRIPTION AND COMMENTS Peter Pan's Flight is superbly designed and absolutely delightful, combining beloved characters, beautiful effects, and charming music. The ride begins in the Darling family's house before embarking on a relaxing trip in a "flying pirate ship" over old London and then to Never Land, where Peter saves Wendy from walking the plank and Captain Hook rehearses for *Dancing with the Stars* on the snout of the ubiquitous crocodile. Nothing here will frighten young children.

A themed queue has air-conditioning and features a walk through the Darlings' street and home, where you'll see family portraits and various rooms, play a few games, and get sprinkled with a bit of (virtual) pixie dust.

TOURING TIPS Count on long lines all day. Fortunately, the queue runs under the roof of the building, out of direct sun and rain, and has tons of art and interactive games to help pass the time. Ride in the first 30 minutes the park is open, during a parade, or just before the park closes. Along with Jungle Cruise, Peter Pan's Flight is one of the most helpful Genie+ reservations you can get in the Magic Kingdom.

Pete's Silly Sideshow ★★★½

| PRESCHOOL ★★★★★ (E) | GRADE SCHOOL ★★★★½ (E) | TEENS ★★★ (A) |
| YOUNG ADULTS ★★★½ (A) | OVER 30 ★★★★ (A) | SENIORS ★★★★ (A) |

What it is Character-greeting venue. **Scope and scale** Minor attraction. **When to go** Before 11 a.m. or during the last 2 hours before closing. **Duration of experience** 3 minutes per character. **Probable waiting time** Under 30 minutes each side. **Queue speed** Slow. **ECV/wheelchair access** May remain in wheelchair. **Participates in Genie+** No. **Early Theme Park Entry** No. **Extended Evening Hours** No.

DESCRIPTION AND COMMENTS Pete's Silly Sideshow is a circus-themed character-greeting area. The characters' costumes are distinct from the ones normally worn around the parks. Characters include Goofy as The Great Goofini, Donald Duck as The Astounding Donaldo, Daisy Duck as Madame Daisy Fortuna, and Minnie Mouse as Minnie Magnifique.

TOURING TIPS Pete's may open 1 hour later than the rest of the park (10 a.m. is common) and usually closes at the same time as the first evening fireworks show. The queue is indoors and air-conditioned. There's one queue for Goofy and Donald and a second queue for Minnie and Daisy; you can meet two characters at once, but you have to line up twice to meet all four.

Prince Charming Regal Carrousel ★★★

PRESCHOOL ★★★★½ (MAA) **GRADE SCHOOL ★★★★ (BA)** **TEENS ★★★½ (MBA)**
YOUNG ADULTS ★★★½ (MBA) **OVER 30 ★★★½ (MBA)** **SENIORS ★★★½ (MBA)**

What it is Merry-go-round. **Scope and scale** Minor attraction. **When to go** Anytime. **Duration of ride** About 2 minutes. **Average wait in line per 100 people ahead of you** 5 minutes. **Loading speed** Slow. **ECV/wheelchair access** Must transfer from ECV to provided wheelchair. **Participates in Genie+** No. **Early Theme Park Entry** Yes. **Extended Evening Hours** Yes.

DESCRIPTION AND COMMENTS One of the most elaborate and beautiful merry-go-rounds you'll ever have the pleasure of seeing, especially when its lights are on.

TOURING TIPS Unless young children in your party insist on riding, appreciate the carousel from the sidelines—while lovely to look at, it loads and unloads very slowly.

Princess Fairytale Hall ★★★

PRESCHOOL ★★★★½ (MAA) **GRADE SCHOOL ★★★★½ (MAA)** **TEENS ★★★½ (A)**
YOUNG ADULTS ★★★★ (A) **OVER 30 ★★★★ (A)** **SENIORS ★★★★ (A)**

What it is Character-greeting venue. **Scope and scale** Minor attraction. **When to go** Before 10:30 a.m. or after 4 p.m. **Duration of experience** 7–10 minutes (estimated). **Probable waiting time** Under 50 minutes (estimated). **Queue speed** Slow. **ECV/wheelchair access** May remain in wheelchair. **Participates in Genie+** Yes. **Early Theme Park Entry** No. **Extended Evening Hours** No.

DESCRIPTION AND COMMENTS Fairytale Hall is Princess Central in the Magic Kingdom. Inside are two greeting venues, with each holding a small reception area for two princesses. Thus, there are four princesses meeting and greeting at any time, and you can see two of them at once. Signs outside the entrance tell you which line leads to which princess pair and how long the wait will be. Tiana usually leads one side, typically paired with Rapunzel. Cinderella and Elena of Avalor (a Disney Channel character) are the usual pair on the other.

Around 5–10 guests at a time are admitted to each greeting area, where there's plenty of time for small talk and a photo with each princess. Enough time is given to each family, in fact, that we ran out of things to say to Rapunzel before we shuffled quietly along.

TOURING TIPS These lines can be substantial when new princesses are introduced. If your kids love princesses, even the B-list ones, get Fairytale Hall out of the way first thing, or use Genie+.

Seven Dwarfs Mine Train ★★★★

PRESCHOOL ★★★★ (A)   GRADE SCHOOL ★★★★½ (MAA)   TEENS ★★★★½ (MAA)
YOUNG ADULTS ★★★★½ (MAA)   OVER 30 ★★★★½ (MAA)   SENIORS ★★★★ (AA)

What it is Indoor-outdoor roller coaster. **Scope and scale** Headliner. **When to go** As soon as the park opens. **Comment** Must be 38″ to ride. **Duration of ride** About 2 minutes. **Average wait in line per 100 people ahead of you** About 4½ minutes. **Loading speed** Fast. **ECV/wheelchair access** Must transfer to the ride vehicle. **Participates in Genie+** No (it offers Individual Lightning Lane). **Early Theme Park Entry** Yes. **Extended Evening Hours** Yes.

DESCRIPTION AND COMMENTS Seven Dwarfs Mine Train lies somewhere between The Barnstormer and Big Thunder Mountain Railroad—that is, it's geared to older grade-school kids who've been on amusement park rides before. There are no loops, inversions, or rolls in the track, and no massive hills or steep drops; rather, your ride vehicle's seats swing side-to-side as you go through turns. And—what a coincidence!—Disney has designed a curvy track with steep turns. An elaborate indoor section shows the Seven Dwarfs' underground mining operation.

The exterior design includes waterfalls, forests, and landscaping and is meant to join together all of the various Fantasyland locations surrounding it. The swinging effect is more noticeable the farther back you're seated in the train.

The Mine Train generates a lot of reader comments. First, from a Rhode Island couple:

We give high marks to Seven Dwarfs Mine Train. It's faster than it looks in videos, and the animatronics are top-notch. Much like Big Thunder and [Tiana's Bayou Adventure], this ride is even better at night!

A Chester, Virginia, mom offers a little cost-benefit analysis:

Seven Dwarfs Mine Train was a great ride but not worth a 90-minute wait.

A mom from Horsham, Pennsylvania, felt let down:

Our family's rating is two stars at most. The detail and activities in line were great, and I thought the animation of the characters' faces was amazing. But we were all sadly disappointed in the ride—it's over so quickly that it really isn't worth your time.

A woman from White City, Saskatchewan, was particularly irked:

One-and-a-half hours of my time for one-and-a-half minutes of disappointment.

Finally, from a Philadelphia reader:

The Guide is correct in calling the Seven Dwarfs Mine Train underwhelming, but we found it was much, much better at night. The lighting and track layout combined to make the ride feel a little faster, and it was generally more enjoyable. I see no reason to ride it in daylight again.

TOURING TIPS If you have children who might be interested in riding this but not Space Mountain, then head for Seven Dwarfs as soon as the park opens. Try Big Thunder Mountain or Tiana's Bayou Adventure (when it opens) next, depending on how well they do here.

See our Tiana's Bayou Adventure touring tips on page 477 for advice on how to see Seven Dwarfs Mine Train and the Magic Kingdom's other headliners as quickly as possible.

Under the Sea: Journey of the Little Mermaid ★★★

PRESCHOOL ★★★★½ (MAA) GRADE SCHOOL ★★★★ (MBA) TEENS ★★★½ (MBA)
YOUNG ADULTS ★★★ (MBA) OVER 30 ★★★½ (MBA) SENIORS ★★★★ (MBA)

What it is Dark ride retelling the film's story. **Scope and scale** Major attraction. **When to go** Before 10:30 a.m. or during the last 2 hours before closing. **Duration of ride** About 5½ minutes. **Average wait in line per 100 people ahead of you** 3 minutes. **Loading speed** Fast. **ECV/wheelchair access** Must transfer from ECV to provided wheelchair. **Participates in Genie+** Yes. **Early Theme Park Entry** Yes. **Extended Evening Hours** Yes.

DESCRIPTION AND COMMENTS Under the Sea takes riders through almost a dozen scenes retelling the story of *The Little Mermaid,* with animatronics, video effects, and a vibrant 3-D set the size of a small theater.

Guests board a clamshell-shaped ride vehicle running along a continuously moving track (similar to The Haunted Mansion's), then the ride "descends under water," past Ariel's grotto and on to King Triton's undersea kingdom. The most detailed animatronic is of Ursula, the octopus, and she's a beauty. Other scenes hit the film's highlights, including Ariel meeting Prince Eric, her deal with Ursula to become human, and, of course, the couple's happy ending.

The attraction's exterior is attractive, with detailed rock work, water, and story elements. Our favorite effect is a "hidden Mickey" that's created through a special alignment of the sun's shadow and the rock work, and only at noon on November 18, Mickey's birthday.

This ride isn't Disney's most ambitious: Most of the effects throughout are simple and unimaginative—for example, starfish that only spin or lobsters that simply turn left and right. Also, virtually the entire second half of the story is condensed into a handful of small scenes crammed together at the end, as if the budget ran out before the ride could be finished properly.

TOURING TIPS Expect moderate waits most of the day. If you can, ride early in the morning or late at night.

Walt Disney World Railroad

DESCRIPTION AND COMMENTS The railroad stops in Fantasyland on its circle tour of the park. The leg from Fantasyland to Main Street, U.S.A., is the most scenic of the entire loop. See the description under Main Street, U.S.A. (page 470), for additional details.

TOURING TIPS Pleasant, feet-saving link to Main Street and Frontierland . . . but so crowded in the afternoon during times of peak attendance that you'll almost certainly find it faster to walk anywhere in the park.

TOMORROWLAND

AT VARIOUS POINTS IN ITS HISTORY, Tomorrowland's attractions presented life's possibilities in adventures ranging from the modern-day (If You Had Wings' round-the-world travel in the 1970s) to the distant future (Mission to Mars). The problem that stymied Disney repeatedly: The future came faster and looked different than they'd envisioned.

Today, Tomorrowland's theme makes the least sense of any area's in any Disney park. Its current attractions are based on gas-powered race cars, rocket travel (two rides), a look back at 20th-century technology, a ride with aliens, a comedy show with monsters, and a motorcycle race inside a computer. It's not so much a vision of the future as it is a collection of attractions that don't fit anywhere else in the park.

Astro Orbiter ★★

PRESCHOOL ★★★ (BA)	**GRADE SCHOOL ★★★★** (MBA)	**TEENS ★★★** (BA)
YOUNG ADULTS ★★★ (MBA)	**OVER 30 ★★★** (MBA)	**SENIORS ★★½** (MBA)

What it is Retro-style rockets revolving around a central axis. **Scope and scale** Minor attraction. **When to go** Before 11 a.m. or in the last hour before closing. **Comment** Not as innocuous as it appears. **Average wait in line per 100 people ahead of you** 13½ minutes. **Loading speed** Slow. **ECV/wheelchair access** Must transfer to the ride vehicle. **Participates in Genie+** No. **Early Theme Park Entry** Yes. **Extended Evening Hours** Yes.

DESCRIPTION AND COMMENTS Though visually appealing, the Astro Orbiter is at heart a slow-loading carnival ride: The fat little rocket ships simply fly in circles, albeit circles on a three-story platform above Tomorrowland. The best thing about the Astro Orbiter is the nice view when you're aloft.

TOURING TIPS Expendable on any schedule. If you ride with preschoolers, seat them first. The Astro Orbiter flies higher and faster than Dumbo and frightens some young children. It also apparently messes with some adults. A mother from Lev HaSharon, Israel, writes:

It was a nightmare—I was able to sit through all the "Mountains," the "Tours," and the like without my stomach reacting even a little, but after Astro Orbiter I thought I would be finished for the rest of the day. Very quickly I realized that my only chance for survival was to pick a point on the toe of my shoe and stare at it (and certainly not lift my eyes out of the "jet") until the ride was over. My 4-year-old was my copilot; she loved it (go figure), and she had us up high the whole time.

Buzz Lightyear's Space Ranger Spin ★★★★

PRESCHOOL ★★★★ (A)	**GRADE SCHOOL ★★★★½** (MAA)	**TEENS ★★★★** (MAA)
YOUNG ADULTS ★★★★ (A)	**OVER 30 ★★★★** (BA)	**SENIORS ★★★★** (A)

What it is Whimsical space-themed indoor ride. **Scope and scale** Minor attraction. **When to go** First or last hour the park is open. **Duration of ride** About 4½ minutes. **Average wait in line per 100 people ahead of you** 3 minutes. **Loading speed** Fast. **ECV/wheelchair access** Must transfer from ECV to provided wheelchair. **Participates in Genie+** Yes. **Early Theme Park Entry** Yes. **Extended Evening Hours** Yes.

DESCRIPTION AND COMMENTS This indoor attraction is based on the space-commando character Buzz Lightyear from the *Toy Story* film series; the marginal story line has you and Buzz trying to save the universe from the evil Emperor Zurg. You spin your car and shoot simulated laser cannons at Zurg and his minions. The first room's mechanical claw and red robot contain high-value targets, so aim for these.

TOURING TIPS Each car is equipped with two laser cannons and two score-keeping displays, enabling you to compete with your riding partner. A joystick allows you to spin the car to line up the various targets. Each time you pull the trigger, you release a red laser beam that you can see hitting or missing the target.

Most folks spend their first ride learning how to use the equipment (keep the trigger depressed instead of firing individual shots—you get an automatic 100 points every few seconds even without aiming) and figuring out how the targets work. On the next ride, you'll be surprised by how much better you do. If you're hopeless at games of skill, check out our tips at tinyurl.com/buzzfortheunskilled.

Many *Unofficial* readers praise Buzz Lightyear. Some, in fact, spend several hours on it, riding again and again. The following comment from a Snow Hill, Maryland, dad is representative:

Buzz Lightyear was so much fun it can't be legal! We hit it first on early-entry day and rode it 10 times without stopping. The kids had fun, but it was Dad who spun himself silly trying to shoot the Z's.

Experience Buzz after riding Space Mountain first thing in the morning or in the last hour the park is open.

Monsters, Inc. Laugh Floor ★★★

PRESCHOOL ★★★★ (MBA) GRADE SCHOOL ★★★★½ (AA) TEENS ★★★★ (AA) YOUNG ADULTS ★★★★ (AA) OVER 30 ★★★★ (AA) SENIORS ★★★★½ (A)

What it is Interactive animated comedy show. **Scope and scale** Major attraction. **When to go** Anytime. **Comment** Audience members may be asked to participate in skits. **Duration of presentation** About 15 minutes. **ECV/wheelchair access** May remain in wheelchair. **Participates in Genie+** Yes. **Early Theme Park Entry** No. **Extended Evening Hours** Yes.

DESCRIPTION AND COMMENTS In Disney-Pixar's *Monsters, Inc.,* children's screams could be converted to electricity, which was used to power a town inhabited by monsters. During the film, the monsters discovered that kids' laughter worked even better as an energy source, so in this attraction they've set up a comedy club to capture as many laughs as possible.

Mike Wazowski, the one-eyed green monster, emcees the club's three comedy acts. Each act consists of an animated monster (most aren't seen in the film) trying out various bad puns and knock-knock jokes. Using technological wizardry, behind-the-scenes Disney employees voice the characters and often interact with audience members during the skits. As with any comedy show, some performers are funny and some are not, but Disney has shown a willingness to experiment with new routines and jokes.

A Sioux Falls, South Dakota, mom is a big fan:

Laugh Floor was great—it's amazing how the characters interact with the audience. I got picked on twice without trying. Plus, kids can text jokes to Roz.

TOURING TIPS The theater holds several hundred people, so there's no need to rush here first thing in the morning. Try to arrive late in the morning after you've visited other Tomorrowland attractions, or after the afternoon parade when guests start leaving the park.

Space Mountain ★★★★

PRESCHOOL ★★½* (MBA) GRADE SCHOOL ★★★★½ (MAA) TEENS ★★★★½ (E) YOUNG ADULTS ★★★★½ (MAA) OVER 30 ★★★★½ (MAA) SENIORS ★★★★ (MBA)

*Some preschoolers love Space Mountain; others are terrified by it.

What it is Roller coaster in the dark. **Scope and scale** Super-headliner. **When to go** When the park opens or in the last hour the park is open. **Comments** Great fun—much wilder than Big Thunder Mountain Railroad. Must be 44″ to ride; Rider Switch option provided (see page 396). **Duration of ride** Almost 3 minutes. **Average wait in line per 100 people ahead of you** 3 minutes; assumes 2 tracks, dispatching at 21-second intervals. **Loading speed** Moderate–fast. **ECV/wheelchair access** Must transfer from ECV to provided wheelchair and then from wheelchair to the ride vehicle. **Participates in Genie+** Yes. **Early Theme Park Entry** Yes. **Extended Evening Hours** Yes.

DESCRIPTION AND COMMENTS Totally enclosed in a mammoth futuristic structure, Space Mountain has always been one of the Magic Kingdom's most popular attractions. The theme is a space flight through dark recesses of the galaxy. Effects are superb, and the ride is the fastest and wildest in the Magic Kingdom: much zippier than Big Thunder Mountain Railroad but much tamer than Tron Lightcycle/Run next door, Rock 'n' Roller Coaster in Hollywood Studios, or Expedition Everest in Animal Kingdom.

Motion Sickness

Roller-coaster aficionados will tell you (correctly) that Space Mountain is a designer version of the Wild Mouse, a midway ride that's been around for more than 70 years. There are no long drops or swooping hills as there are on a traditional coaster—only quick, unexpected turns and small drops. Disney's contribution essentially was to add a space theme to the Wild Mouse and put it in the dark. People who can handle a fairly wild coaster ride will take Space Mountain in stride. What sets Space Mountain apart is that darkness. Half the fun is not knowing where the car will go next.

An Elburn, Illinois, reader recommends bracing yourself—literally:

They should require you to wear a neck brace on Space Mountain. That ride is painful.

TOURING TIPS Most guests head to Tron Lightcycle/Run first, then visit Space Mountain. See our comments for Tiana's Bayou Adventure (page 477) for advice on how to see Space Mountain and the park's other coasters most quickly over one or two days. Parents touring with children too small to ride can take advantage of **Rider Switch** (page 396).

Seats are one behind another, as opposed to side by side, which means that parents can't sit next to their kids who meet the height requirement but who might get scared.

If you don't catch Space Mountain first thing in the morning, try again during the hour before closing.

Tomorrowland Speedway ★★

| PRESCHOOL ★★★★½ (AA) | GRADE SCHOOL ★★★★ (A) | TEENS ★★★½ (MBA) |
| YOUNG ADULTS ★★★ (MBA) | OVER 30 ★★★ (MBA) | SENIORS ★★½ (MBA) |

What it is Drive-'em-yourself minicars. **Scope and scale** Minor attraction. **When to go** Before 10 a.m. or during the last 2 hours before closing. **Comment** Kids must be 54" tall to drive unassisted, 32" with a person age 14 or older. **Duration of ride** About 4¼ minutes. **Average wait in line per 100 people ahead of you** 4½ minutes; assumes 285-car turnover every 20 minutes. **Loading speed** Slow. **ECV/wheelchair access** Must transfer to the ride vehicle; transfer device available. **Participates in Genie+** Yes. **Early Theme Park Entry** Yes. **Extended Evening Hours** Yes.

DESCRIPTION AND COMMENTS An elaborate miniature raceway with gas-powered cars that travel up to 7 mph. The raceway, with its sleek cars and racing noises, is quite alluring. The cars poke along on a guide rail, leaving drivers little to do, but teens and many adults still enjoy it.

Motion Sickness

TOURING TIPS This ride is visually appealing, and the 9-and-under set loves it (adults, not so much). If your child is too short to drive, ride along and allow them to steer the car while you work the foot pedal.

A mom from North Billerica, Massachusetts, writes:

I was truly amazed by the number of adults in line—the only reason I could think of for that would be an insane desire to go on absolutely every ride at Disney World. The cars aren't a whole lot of fun, and they tend to pile up at the end, so it takes almost as long to get off as it did to get on.

A dad from Pleasantville, New York, had this to say:

This is one attraction I wish they would replace with something better. It's boring and it smells bad.

The line for the speedway snakes across a pedestrian bridge to the ride's loading areas. For a shorter wait, turn right off the bridge, then head to the first loading area rather than continuing to the second one.

Tomorrowland Transit Authority PeopleMover ★★★½

PRESCHOOL ★★★★ (A)   **GRADE SCHOOL ★★★★ (BA)**   **TEENS ★★★★ (A)**
YOUNG ADULTS ★★★★ (A)   **OVER 30 ★★★★½ (MAA)**   **SENIORS ★★★★½ (MAA)**

What it is Scenic tour of Tomorrowland. **Scope and scale** Minor attraction. **When to go** Anytime, but especially during hot, crowded times of day (11:30 a.m.–4:30 p.m.). **Comment** A good way to check out the line at Space Mountain and Tron. **Duration of ride** 10 minutes. **Average wait in line per 100 people ahead of you** 1½ minutes; assumes 39 trains operating. **Loading speed** Fast. **ECV/wheelchair access** Must be ambulatory. **Participates in Genie+** No. **Early Theme Park Entry** Yes. **Extended Evening Hours** Yes.

DESCRIPTION AND COMMENTS Tramlike cars, a once-unique prototype of a linear induction–powered mass-transit system, carry riders on a leisurely tour of Tomorrowland, including a peek inside Space Mountain.

A Delafield, Wisconsin, family offers only the faintest of praise:

Tomorrowland is best at night. With the lights, it turns boring rides like the PeopleMover into something less boring.

TOURING TIPS A relaxing ride where lines move quickly. It's a good choice during busier times of day.

Tron Lightcycle/Run ★★★★

NOT ENOUGH SURVEYS TO RATE

What it is Elevated, high-speed indoor-outdoor roller coaster. **Scope and scale** Super-headliner. **When to go** As soon as the park opens, using Early Theme Park Entry if possible, or the last hour the park is open. **Comment** Estimated 48″ minimum height requirement. **Duration of ride** 1 minute. **Average wait in line per 100 people ahead of you** About 3½ minutes. **Loading speed** Fast. **ECV/wheelchair access** Must transfer from wheelchair. **Participates in Genie+** No (it offers Individual Lightning Lane). **Early Theme Park Entry** Yes. **Extended Evening Hours** Yes.

DESCRIPTION AND COMMENTS Riders sit as if on a motorcycle while they rocket past scenes that simulate being inside a computer (and one with neon lighting at that). The ride vehicles are set up as 14 semidetached lightcycles, with seven rows of two cycles each. Riders must lean forward slightly to hold onto the cycle's handlebars. Once seated and out of the ride's loading zone, riders are launched like a catapult into the ride's first set of turns. An impressive set of video effects surrounds the rider through most of the journey.

Tron is most similar to the Rock 'n' Roller Coaster in Hollywood Studios (see page 586), which is also a catapult-launched indoor coaster. Tron is by far the most intense coaster in the Magic Kingdom, although it doesn't have any loops or inversions. If Seven Dwarfs Mine Train or Big Thunder Mountain give you pause, skip Tron.

As a high-speed thrill ride, Tron has safety restraints that may not fit every body type. Disney has two solutions for this: (1) a more traditional, seated car at the end of the motorcycle-like train of ride vehicles and (2) a test vehicle with test restraints, located just before you enter the ride's main building. If the restraints seem balky, ask to sit in the seated car.

TOURING TIPS Tron is one of the Magic Kingdom's hottest rides. Expect hundreds of guests to head straight for it as soon as the park opens. If you're an off-site guest, it's possible that a thousand or more people will already be in line before you arrive. Likewise, expect Individual Lightning Lane reservations for Tron to sell out daily within minutes of being offered.

If you're staying on-site, your best bet for riding with minimal waits is to arrive at the Magic Kingdom at least an hour before official opening. As soon as you're admitted into the park for Early Theme Park Entry, head for Tomorrowland and ride Tron. Once you're done, ride Space Mountain nearby if the wait is 15 minutes or less.

If Early Theme Park Entry isn't an option, try Tron in the last hour the park is open, or during lunch or dinner. Expect long waits almost anytime. Tron had a virtual queue (see page 60) in place when it opened. Check Disney's website to see if it's still using one before you go.

BOARDING GROUPS These function like mandatory Genie+ reservations without a specific return time. You obtain a boarding group for everyone in your party through the My Disney Experience (MDE) app at exactly 7 a.m. or exactly 1 p.m. on the day of your Magic Kingdom visit. If you're successful, you'll get a boarding group number. Once you have a boarding group, MDE will tell you which boarding groups are currently eligible to ride (for example, "Groups 40–45 now boarding") or give you a rough estimate of how long your wait will be to ride. If your phone is set up to receive alerts from MDE, you'll also get one when your group is ready. Disney is reasonably flexible if you're doing something else, such as eating lunch, when your boarding group is called—showing up late shouldn't be a problem unless the ride is about to close.

Through 2023, you and everyone in your group must have a park reservation (see page 30) for the park in which the attraction is located, on the day you attempt to get a boarding group. That is, if you're trying to get a boarding group at the Magic Kingdom, you can't start at another park, hop to the Magic Kingdom, and get a boarding group.

The good news is you don't have to be in the park (or even in Florida) to request a boarding group at 7 a.m. The bad news is that you must be in the park to request a boarding group at 1 p.m. Further, for newly opened rides, all boarding groups will be snapped up within a few seconds of 7 a.m., so there's no room for delay or error. And that's a problem because neither MDE not Disney's Wi-Fi are completely reliable either.

We tested the network speed and reliability of Disney's Wi-Fi in locations around Hollywood Studios, as well as on T-Mobile's cellular network, to see how fast we could connect to MDE servers. Disney's Wi-Fi speeds were two to nine times faster than our cellular network. However, Disney's Wi-Fi was much less reliable than our cell service. See tinyurl.com/rotr -networks for more details on our tests.

The fast but unreliable nature of Disney's Wi-Fi means you should have as many people as possible try to obtain boarding groups for your entire party at 7 a.m. and at 1 p.m. If you're in the park, half of you should be on Disney's Wi-Fi and half should be on a cellular network.

Even if you're able to submit a boarding group request exactly at 7 a.m. or 1 p.m., the flood of requests from thousands of other people is enough to overwhelm the MDE computers. It's common to have MDE respond to your request with a message like "Oh no! Something went wrong!" By the time you've received the error and resent your request, all boarding groups are likely to be taken.

Disney's implementation of boarding groups is essentially a lottery—some people win and some people lose, through no fault of their own. And because the process fails for hundreds of people every morning, Disney is unlikely to do anything to make it up to you.

Disney's second supply of boarding groups, handed out at 1 p.m., is generally considered a "backup" batch that gets used only if the attraction has run reliably and on time throughout the day.

Walt Disney's Carousel of Progress ★★★

PRESCHOOL ★★★ (MBA)   GRADE SCHOOL ★★★½ (MBA)   TEENS ★★★½ (MBA)
YOUNG ADULTS ★★★★ (BA)   OVER 30 ★★★★ (A)   SENIORS ★★★★½ (AA)

What it is Audio-Animatronic theater show. **Scope and scale** Major attraction. **When to go** Anytime. **Duration of presentation** 21 minutes. **Preshow entertainment** Documentary on the attraction's long history. **Probable waiting time** Less than 10 minutes. **ECV/wheelchair access** May remain in wheelchair. **Participates in Genie+** No. **Early Theme Park Entry** Yes. **Extended Evening Hours** No.

DESCRIPTION AND COMMENTS *Carousel of Progress* is a four-act play offering a nostalgic look at how electricity and technology changed the lives of an animatronic family during the 20th century. General Electric sponsored the first version of the show for the 1964 World's Fair in New York, in keeping with the fair's theme of progress.

The first scene is set around 1900 (our research indicates Thursday, February 14, 1901, on a farm outside Arkansas City, Kansas); the second, around 1927; and the third, in the late 1940s. The fourth scene is allegedly contemporary, but references to laser discs and car phones are not-so-subtle clues that the script hasn't been refreshed in over 25 years.

Although the last scene needs updating, *Carousel of Progress* is the only attraction in the park that displays Walt's optimistic vision of a better future through technology and industry. If you're interested in the man behind the mouse, this show is a must-see.

TOURING TIPS The show handles big crowds effectively and is a good choice during busier times of day. Because of its age, it seems to have more operational glitches than most attractions, so you may be subjected to the same dialogue and songs several times. Think of it as extra time in the AC.

MAGIC KINGDOM ENTERTAINMENT

LIVE ENTERTAINMENT

FOR SPECIFIC EVENTS the day you visit, check the schedule in the My Disney Experience app or in the *Times Guide,* available along with the guide map. Walt Disney World live-entertainment guru Steve Soares usually posts the Magic Kingdom's performance schedule about a week in advance at wdwent.com.

CHARACTER CAVALCADES In lieu of large parades during the pandemic, Disney began running a series of small one- or two-float cavalcades throughout the day, usually starting about an hour after the park opens. The cavalcade route is the same as the parade route: from

unofficial **TIP**
Note: If you're short on time, it's impossible to see both Magic Kingdom feature attractions and live performances.

Frontierland near Tiana's Bayou Adventure, through Liberty Square, then around the central hub and down Main Street, U.S.A. One cavalcade includes Pixar characters, and another has Mickey, Minnie, and friends. Seasonal cavalcades for Halloween and Christmas are also represented. Check the My Disney Experience app for times.

FLAG RETREAT At 5 p.m. daily at Town Square (the Walt Disney World Railroad end of Main Street). Sometimes performed with large college marching bands, sometimes with a smaller Disney band.

FIREWORKS AND OTHER NIGHTTIME ENTERTAINMENT

LIKE ITS PARADES, the Magic Kingdom's dazzling nighttime spectaculars are highly rated and not to be missed.

BAY LAKE AND SEVEN SEAS LAGOON ELECTRICAL WATER PAGEANT ★★★★ Usually performed at nightfall (8:50 at the Polynesian Village Resort, 9 at the Grand Floridian Resort, and 10:15 at the Contemporary Resort) on Seven Seas Lagoon and Bay Lake, this is one of our favorites among the Disney extras, but you must leave the Magic Kingdom to view it. The pageant is a stunning electric-light show aboard small barges and set to nifty electronic music. Leave the Magic Kingdom and take the monorail to the Polynesian Village, the Grand Floridian, or the Contemporary.

HAPPILY EVER AFTER **FIREWORKS SHOW** ★★★★½ This multisensory show of fireworks, music, and video projections on the theme of Happily Ever After is one of the highest-rated attractions in Walt Disney World, across all age groups.

Happily, the show is not just about princesses and romance but also includes messages about work and determination as part of a path to fulfillment. Images projected onto the castle include snippets from the usual suspects of *Frozen* and *Cinderella,* as well as *Hunchback of Notre Dame, Monsters, Inc., Cars,* and *Wreck-It Ralph,* among others. *Happily Ever After*'s fireworks can be enjoyed from outside the park. However, due to the strong integration of the castle projections into the performance, be aware that you'll be missing a substantial portion of the show if you're not viewing from the Main Street area inside the Magic Kingdom.

TINKER BELL'S FLIGHT Look for this quintessentially Disney special effect in the sky above Cinderella Castle during *Enchantment* when the park is open late.

Fireworks Dessert Parties and Cruises

FIREWORKS DESSERT PARTIES Disney reserves the **Plaza Gardens** and **Tomorrowland Terrace** restaurant for three paid fireworks-viewing opportunities:

1. **Happily Ever After Pre-Party** begins approximately 90 minutes before the show. It costs $99 per adult and $59 per child. You'll be served desserts, beer, wine, and sodas until just before the fireworks begin, when you'll be escorted to a special, standing-room-only viewing spot.

2. **Happily Ever After Fireworks Dessert Parties** run before, during, and after the show inside the Tomorrowland Terrace. They cost $114 per adult and $69 per child. Note that the view of the castle is blocked at many seats, and the sound quality is poor inside the all-concrete echo chamber of Tomorrowland Terrace. The big advantage here is that you get actual seats for the show.

3. **Happily Ever After Post-Party** You'll be escorted to a special, standing-room-only viewing location approximately 30 minutes before the fireworks begin. After the fireworks, you'll be admitted to the Tomorrowland Terrace for desserts, beer, wine, and sodas, for the next hour. The cost is $99 per adult and $59 per child.

Reservations can be made 60 days in advance online or by calling ☎ 407-WDW-DINE (939-3463).

A St. Louis reader who went to the dessert party declared it "meh":

We did the fireworks dessert party at Tomorrowland Terrace against my better judgment. While the vantage point was pretty good and the desserts were tasty, it was definitely not worth the price.

FIREWORKS CRUISE For a different view, you can watch the fireworks from Seven Seas Lagoon aboard a pontoon boat. The cost is $425 (including tax) for up to 10 people. Chips, soda, and water are provided; sandwiches and more-substantial food items may be arranged through reservations. Your Disney captain will take you for a little cruise and then position the boat in a perfect place to watch the fireworks. (A major indirect benefit of the charter is that you can enjoy the fireworks without fighting the mob afterward.)

Because this is a private charter, only your group will be aboard. Life jackets are provided, but wearing them is at your discretion. To reserve a charter, call ☎ 407-WDW-PLAY (939-7529) at exactly 7 a.m. Eastern time about 180 days before the day you want to cruise. Because the Disney reservations system counts days in a somewhat atypical manner, we recommend that you phone about 185 days out to have a Disney agent specify the exact morning to call for reservations.

FERRYTALE FIREWORKS: A SPARKLING DESSERT CRUISE Another option for seeing the evening fireworks at an extra cost. Guests board a ferry at the TTC for desserts, souvenir glasses, and a view of the fireworks. This event includes alcoholic beverages for the adults; unlike the pontoon cruise, it's not a private charter. Pricing is $99 for adults and $69 for children. Reserve at ☎ 407-939-3463 or online at disney world.disney.go.com (search for "Ferrytale Fireworks").

VIEWING (AND EXIT) STRATEGIES FOR PARADES AND FIREWORKS

Vantage Points for Parades

Note: *Even though there isn't a regular evening parade right now, the following advice is still generally useful for* Happily Ever After *and the nighttime parades and fireworks held during special events (see previous section), which follow a similar schedule.*

Magic Kingdom parades usually begin in **Frontierland** by Tiana's Bayou Adventure and follow the waterfront through **Liberty Square.** From there, they cross the bridge to the **Central Plaza,** circle around it, then head down **Main Street.** A quick circle of **Town Square,** follows before they head off-stage behind the Main Street fire station.

Because most spectators pack Main Street and the Central Plaza, we recommend watching the parade from **Liberty Square** or **Frontierland** instead. Great vantage points that are frequently overlooked are

1. **Sleepy Hollow snack-and-beverage shop, immediately to your right as you cross the bridge into Liberty Square.** If you arrive early, buy refreshments and claim a table closest to the rail. You'll have a perfect view of the parade as it crosses Liberty Square Bridge.

2. **The pathway on the Liberty Square side of the moat from Sleepy Hollow snack-and-beverage shop to Cinderella Castle.** Any point along the way offers an unobstructed view as the parade crosses Liberty Square Bridge.

3. **The covered walkway between Liberty Tree Tavern and the Diamond Horseshoe Saloon.** This elevated vantage point is perfect (particularly on rainy days) and usually goes unnoticed until just before the parade starts.

4. **Elevated platforms in front of the Frontierland Shootin' Arcade, Frontier Trading Post, and the building with the sign reading** FRONTIER MERCANTILE. These spots usually get picked off 10–12 minutes before parade time.

5. **Benches on the perimeter of the Central Plaza, between the entrances to Liberty Square and Adventureland,** offer a comfortable resting place and an unobstructed (though somewhat distant) view of the parade as it crosses Liberty Square Bridge.

6. **Liberty Square and Frontierland dockside areas;** spots here usually go early.

7. **The porch of Tony's Town Square Restaurant,** on Main Street, provides an elevated viewing platform and an easy exit path when the fireworks are over.

Assuming it starts in Frontierland, the parade takes 16–20 minutes to reach Main Street.

On evenings when the parade runs twice, the first draws a huge crowd, siphoning guests from attractions. Many guests leave the park after the early parade, and many more depart following the fireworks (which are scheduled on the hour between the two parades).

Vantage Points for Fireworks

As noted on page 496, the nightly fireworks show includes a dazzling video-projection display on the front of Cinderella Castle and down Main Street, U.S.A. The best viewing spots for the entire presentation are **between the Central Plaza and the castle,** offering up-close views of the castle projections.

The next-best spots are in **Plaza Gardens East and West** nearest the castle. These gardens are specifically constructed for fireworks viewing. We prefer Plaza Gardens East (the same side of the park as Tomorrowland) because the configuration of light/audio poles is slightly less obtrusive when you're viewing the castle.

If those spots are already taken, your next-best alternatives are on Main Street, where you'll get to see the (smaller) projections closer. Watching from the train-station end of Main Street is the easiest way to facilitate a quick departure, but you won't recognize most of the castle's images.

If we're staying in the park and trying to avoid the crowds on Main Street, our two favorite spots to see just the fireworks are as follows:

1. **In Fantasyland between Seven Dwarfs Mine Train and Enchanted Tales with Belle.** Some of the minor fireworks that float above the castle will be behind you, but all of the major effects will be right in front of you.

2. **On the bridge between the Central Plaza and Tomorrowland.** A few trees block some of the castle, but if Tinker Bell does her fireworks flight from the castle, she'll fly directly over this area.

Leaving the Park Before or During Parades

If you're trying to exit the park just before or during the parade, you'll need to walk down the east side of Main Street, U.S.A., to get out of the park, or use the Tomorrowland Main Street passageways (see next page) if they're open. (If you're facing the train station, with Cinderella Castle behind you, east is on your left.) The parade route cuts off the central and west walking paths of Main Street and their access to the park exits.

Leaving the Park After Evening Parades and Fireworks

With armies of guests leaving the park after evening parades and fireworks, the Disney transportation system (buses, ferries, and monorail) gets overwhelmed, causing long waits in boarding areas. (Similar situations often occur during the special holiday parades and fireworks, when they're offered.)

> *un**official* **TIP**
> Digital displays at the Magic Kingdom exit show the wait to board the monorails and ferry—take the one with the shorter line.

A mom from Kresgeville, Pennsylvania, recounts:

> *Our family of five made the mistake of going to the Magic Kingdom the Saturday night before Columbus Day to watch the parade and fireworks. Afterwards, we lingered at The Crystal Palace to wait for the crowds to lessen, but it was no use. We started walking toward the gates and soon became trapped by the throng, not able to go forward or back. Our group became separated, and it became a nightmare. We left the park at 10:30 p.m. and didn't get back to the Polynesian Village (less than a mile away) until after midnight. Even if they were to raise Walt Disney himself from cryogenic sleep and parade him down Main Street, I'll never go to the Magic Kingdom on a Saturday night again!*

An Oklahoma City dad offers this advice:

> *un**official* **TIP**
> Be aware that the railroad doesn't run during parades because the floats must cross the tracks when entering or exiting the parade route in Frontierland.

> *Never, never leave the Magic Kingdom just after the evening fireworks. Go for another ride—no lines because everyone else is trying to get out!*

Congestion persists from the end of the early evening parade (if it's performed) until closing time. Most folks watch the early parade and then the fireworks a few minutes later. If you're parked at the Transportation and Ticket Center (TTC) and are intent on beating the crowd, view the early parade from the Town Square end of Main Street, leaving the park as soon as the parade ends.

Here's what happened to a family from Cape Coral, Florida:

> *We tried to leave the park before the parade began, but Main Street was already packed, and we didn't see any way to get out of the park—we were stuck. In addition, it was impossible to move across the street, and even the shops were so crowded it was virtually impossible to maneuver a stroller through them to get close to the entrance.*

If you don't have a stroller (or are willing to forgo the return refund for rental strollers), catch the **Walt Disney World Railroad** in **Frontierland** and ride to the park exit at Main Street. Again, don't cut it too close—the train stops running for the parade.

MAIN STREET PASSAGEWAYS The Magic Kingdom has two pedestrian walkways behind the shops on either side of Main Street, U.S.A., specifically for guests who want to get in or out of the park without walking down the middle of Main Street. If you're on the Tomorrowland side of the park, look for a passageway that runs from between **The Plaza Restaurant** and **Tomorrowland Terrace,** back behind the east side of Main Street, to **Tony's Town Square Restaurant** near the park exit. If you're on the Adventureland side of the park, the passageway runs from the **First Aid** area to the **Main Street Fire Station** near the park exit.

unofficial **TIP**
Instead of walking outside, you can cut through the Main Street shops—they have interior doors that let you pass from one shop to the next.

However, these passageways aren't used every night, so there's no guarantee that they'll be available.

If the passageways aren't open and you're on the Tomorrowland side of the park, here's how to exit during a parade: Cut through Tomorrowland Terrace and then work your way down Main Street until you're past the Main Street Bakery (Starbucks) and have crossed a small cul-de-sac. Bear left into the side door of that corner shop. Work your way from shop to shop until you reach Town Square—easy, because people will be outside watching the parade. Then, at Town Square, bear left to reach the train station and park exit.

Note: This won't work if you're on the Adventureland side of the park. You can make your way through **Casey's Corner** to Main Street and then work your way through the shops, but when you pop out of the **Emporium** at Town Square, you'll be trapped by the parade. As soon as the last float passes, however, you can bolt for the exit.

If your car is parked at the TTC lot, you could also just watch the early parade and then leave before the fireworks show starts. Line up for the ferry; one will depart about every 8–10 minutes. Try to catch the ferry that will be crossing Seven Seas Lagoon while the fireworks show is in progress. The best vantage point is on the top deck to the right of the pilothouse as you face the Magic Kingdom—the sight of fireworks silhouetting the castle and reflecting off the lagoon is unforgettable.

While there's no guarantee that a ferry will load and depart within 3 or 4 minutes of the fireworks, your chances are about 50–50 of timing it just right. If you're in the front of the line for the ferry and don't want to board the boat that's loading, stop at the gate and let people pass you. You'll be the first to board the next boat.

Strollers, wheelchairs, and ECVs make navigating crowds even more difficult. If you have one of these, or if you're staying at a Disney hotel that is not served by the monorail and you have to depend on Disney transportation, watch the early parade and fireworks; then enjoy the attractions until about 20–25 minutes before the late parade is scheduled to begin. Then leave the park using one of the strategies listed previously, and catch the Disney bus or boat back to your hotel.

MAGIC KINGDOM HARD-TICKET EVENTS

THE MAGIC KINGDOM HOSTS several **holiday-themed after-hours events** from mid-August through December. Celebrating Halloween and Christmas, they require separate paid admission and can sell out. Space doesn't permit us to cover them with more than a brief mention in the book (see "The Walt Disney World Calendar," pages 39–42). That said, ride wait times during these events are as low as they can be, making them a plausible alternative to, say, paying for a second day (and another hotel night) to finish seeing the Magic Kingdom. But we provide full details, including photos, best days to go, touring advice, and more, at **TouringPlans.com:** Go to blog.touringplans.com and search "Halloween party" and "Christmas party."

TRAFFIC PATTERNS *in* *the* MAGIC KINGDOM

WHEN WE RESEARCH THE MAGIC KINGDOM, we study its traffic patterns, asking:

1. WHICH SECTIONS OF THE PARK AND WHICH ATTRACTIONS DO GUESTS VISIT FIRST? When the park opens, guest traffic is heaviest going to Fantasyland and Tomorrowland, followed by Frontierland. Seven Dwarfs Mine Train pulls people into the back reaches of the park, while Tron Lightcycle/Run pulls people to the right. When it opens, Tiana's Bayou Adventure in Frontierland will draw large crowds as well.

2. HOW LONG DOES IT TAKE FOR THE PARK TO FILL UP? HOW ARE THE VISITORS DISPERSED IN THE PARK? A surge of early birds arrives before or around opening time but are quickly dispersed throughout the empty park. After the initial wave is absorbed, there's a lull lasting about an hour after opening. Then the park is inundated for about 2 hours, peaking between 10 a.m. and noon. Arrivals continue in a steady but diminishing stream until around 2 p.m. The lines we sampled were longest between 1 and 2 p.m., indicating more arrivals than departures into the early afternoon. For touring purposes, most attractions develop long lines between 10 and 11:30 a.m.

unofficial **TIP**
As the park fills up, visitors head for the top attractions before lines get long. This, more than anything else, determines morning traffic patterns.

From late morning until early afternoon, guests are equally distributed among all the lands. However, guests concentrate in **Fantasyland, Liberty Square,** and **Frontierland** in late afternoon, with a decrease of visitors in Adventureland and Tomorrowland. Adventureland's **Jungle Cruise** and **Space Mountain** continue to be crowded, but most other attractions in those lands are readily accessible.

3. HOW DO MOST VISITORS TOUR THE PARK? Many **first-time visitors** are guided by friends or relatives familiar with the Magic Kingdom; these tours may or may not follow an orderly sequence. First-timers without personal guides tend to be more orderly in their touring, but they also tend to be drawn to Cinderella Castle upon entering the park, and thus they begin their rotation from Fantasyland. **Repeat visitors** usually head straight to their favorite attractions.

4. WILL GOING LEFT (OR RIGHT) HELP AVOID CROWDS? We tested a frequent claim that most people turn right into Tomorrowland and tour the Magic Kingdom counterclockwise. We found the claim to be baseless. Neither do most people turn left and start in Adventureland.

Here's why: Magic Kingdom headliner attractions are located intentionally at opposite points around the park to distribute crowds evenly: **Space Mountain** and **Tron** on the east side, **Tiana's Bayou Adventure** (opens 2024) and **Big Thunder Mountain Railroad** on the west, **Seven Dwarfs Mine Train** to the north, and so on.

If, therefore, you were to start touring by heading left, you'd have low crowds in Adventureland and moderate crowds in Frontierland— but by the time you got to Fantasyland and Tomorrowland, you'd run into the largest crowds of the day. A similar scenario would await you if you started by bearing right into Tomorrowland: packed crowds in the rest of the lands you visit.

Avoiding the biggest crowds in the Magic Kingdom, then, requires the following:

1. Knowing which attractions to visit, and when.
2. Knowing how to make the best use of Genie+ and Individual Lightning Lane (if you're willing to pay for them).
3. Being willing to cross the park to save time.

5. HOW DO SPECIAL EVENTS, SUCH AS PARADES AND LIVE SHOWS, AFFECT TRAFFIC PATTERNS? Parades pull huge numbers of guests away from attractions and provide a window of opportunity for experiencing the more popular attractions with less of a wait. (Character cavalcades don't have this effect.) Castle Forecourt Stage shows also attract crowds but only slightly affect lines.

6. WHAT ARE THE TRAFFIC PATTERNS NEAR AND AT CLOSING TIME? On our sample days, in busy times and off-season at the park, departures outnumbered arrivals beginning in midafternoon. Many visitors left in late afternoon as dinnertime approached. When the park closed early, guests departed steadily during the 2 hours before closing, with a huge exodus at closing. When the park closed late, the exodus began immediately after the early-evening parade and fireworks, with a second mass departure after the late parade, continuing until closing.

Because Main Street and transportation services remain open after the other five lands close, crowds at closing mainly congregate on Main Street and at the monorail-, ferry-, and bus-boarding areas. In the hour before closing, the other five lands are normally not crowded.

To get a complete view of actual traffic patterns while you're in the park, use our mobile app, **Lines.** It gives you current wait times as well as estimates in half-hour increments for today and tomorrow. A quick glance shows how traffic patterns affect wait times throughout the day.

MAGIC KINGDOM TOURING PLANS

STARTING ON PAGE 713, our step-by-step touring plans are field-tested for seeing *as much as possible* in one day with a minimum of

STARTING ON PAGE 713,

time wasted in lines. They're designed to help you avoid crowds and bottlenecks on days of moderate to heavy attendance. You should understand, however, that there's more to see in the Magic Kingdom than can be experienced in one day.

On days of lighter attendance (see "Selecting the Time of Year for Your Visit," page 32), our plans will save you time but won't be as critical to successful touring as on busier days.

Each Magic Kingdom touring plan has two versions: one for Disney resort guests and one for off-site guests; the former uses Early Theme Park Entry to minimize waits in line. Because Early Entry means thousands of guests will already be in lines and on rides before off-site guests set foot in the park, the touring strategy for off-site guests must be different. Even with a perfect touring plan, Early Entry means off-site guests may wait up to an hour more in lines per day in the Magic Kingdom.

*un***official TIP**
Don't worry that other people will be following the touring plans, rendering them useless. Fewer than 4 in every 100 people in the park will have been exposed to this info.

The touring plans do *not* require you to use Genie+ or Individual Lightning Lane. If you opt for either (or both) of these offerings, simply tell our free touring plan software which reservation times you have, and the software will adjust the plan.

CHOOSING THE APPROPRIATE TOURING PLAN

WE PRESENT FOUR MAGIC KINGDOM touring plans:

- One-Day Touring Plan for Adults
- One-Day Touring Plan for Parents with Small Children
- Dumbo-or-Die-in-a-Day Touring Plan for Parents with Small Children
- Two-Day Touring Plan for Adults

If you have two days (or two mornings) in the Magic Kingdom, the **Two-Day Touring Plan** is *by far* the most relaxed and efficient. It takes advantage of early morning, when lines are short and the park hasn't filled with guests. This plan works well year-round and eliminates much of the extra walking required by the one-day plans. No matter when the park closes, our two-day plan guarantees the most efficient touring and the least time in lines. The plan is perfect for guests who wish to sample both the attractions and the atmosphere of the Magic Kingdom.

If you have just a single day to visit but you want to see as much as possible, then use the **One-Day Touring Plan for Adults.** Yes, it's a bear, but it gives you maximum bang for your buck.

If you have children younger than age 8, choose the **One-Day Touring Plan for Parents with Small Children.** A compromise that blends the preferences of younger children with those of older siblings and adults, this plan includes many children's rides in Fantasyland but omits the more intense rides and other attractions that may frighten young children or are off-limits because of height requirements. You could also use the One-Day Touring Plan for Adults, and take advantage of **Rider Switch,** whereby children accompany adults to the loading area of a ride with age and height requirements but don't board (see page 396).

*un***official TIP**
Rider Switch allows adults to enjoy the more adventurous attractions while keeping the group together.

The **Dumbo-or-Die-in-a-Day Touring Plan for Parents with Small Children** is designed for parents who are happy to self-sacrificially stand around, sweat, wipe noses, pay for stuff, and watch the kids enjoy themselves. **You'll love it!**

"Not a Touring Plan" Touring Plans

For the type-B reader, these touring plans (see page 710) avoid detailed step-by-step strategies for saving every last minute in line. To paraphrase one of our favorite movies, they're more guidelines than actual rules. Use them to avoid the longest waits in line while having maximum flexibility to see whatever interests you in a particular part of the park.

For the Magic Kingdom, these "not" touring plans include advice for adults and parents with one day in the park, for anyone with two days, and for anyone with an afternoon and a full day to tour.

Two-Day Touring Plan for Families with Small Children

If you have young children and are looking for a two-day itinerary, combine the **Magic Kingdom One-Day Touring Plan for Parents with Small Children** with the second day of the **Magic Kingdom Two-Day Touring Plan**.

Alternate Two-Day Touring Plan: Sleep In on Day Two

Many of us enjoy an early start in the Magic Kingdom on one day, followed by a second day with a lazy sleep-in morning, resuming your touring in the afternoon and/or evening. If this appeals to you, use the **Magic Kingdom One-Day Touring Plan for Adults** or the **Magic Kingdom One-Day Touring Plan for Parents with Small Children** on your early day. Stick to the plan for as long as it feels comfortable (many folks leave after the afternoon parade). On the second day, pick up where you left off. Customize the rest of the plan to incorporate parades, fireworks, and other live performances according to your preferences.

TOURING PLAN COMPANIONS

WE'VE CONSOLIDATED A GREAT DEAL of information about the theme parks in the Touring Plan Companions, which start on page 737, just after the touring plans. Like the plans, the companions are designed to clip out and take with you to the park. The Touring Plan Companions recap key information: the best times to visit each attraction, the authors' ratings, attraction height requirements and fright potential, and quick-reference info on dining and places to take a break.

THE SINGLE-DAY TOURING CONUNDRUM

TOURING THE MAGIC KINGDOM in one day is complicated by two facts:

1. The park's average day is shorter than it was a few years ago.
2. The premier attractions are at opposite ends of the park.

Tiana's Bayou Adventure (when it opens) and **Big Thunder Mountain Railroad** are in Frontierland, **Space Mountain** and **Tron** are in **Tomorrowland,** and **Seven Dwarfs Mine Train** is in the top center. It's virtually impossible to ride all five without encountering lines at one or another.

If, for example, you hit Tron and Space Mountain right as the park opens, you won't have too bad of a wait, but by the time you get to Fantasyland, the line for Seven Dwarfs Mine Train will already be substantial. Likewise, you can ride Seven Dwarfs without a problem first thing in the morning, but by the time you get to Tomorrowland, Space Mountain and Tron will already have fair-size lines. See our Tiana's Bayou Adventure Description and Comments on page 477 for our recommended one- and two-day strategies for these attractions.

PRELIMINARY INSTRUCTIONS FOR USING THE TOURING PLANS

BECOME FAMILIAR WITH THE MAGIC KINGDOM'S **opening procedures** (see page 462). On days of moderate to heavy attendance, follow your chosen touring plan exactly, deviating from it only as follows:

1. **When you're not interested in an attraction in the plan.** Simply skip it and proceed to the next attraction.
2. **When you encounter a very long line at an attraction.** In this case, skip to the next attraction and try again later at the one with the line.

Before You Go

1. Call ☎ 407-824-4321 or check disneyworld.disney.go.com the day before you go to verify official opening time.
2. Purchase admission before you arrive.
3. Get familiar with park-opening procedures (see above), and reread the plan you've chosen so you know what you're likely to encounter.
4. At 7 a.m. on the day of your visit, make Genie+ and/or Individual Lightning Lane reservations if you bought them.

MAGIC KINGDOM TOURING PLANS AT A GLANCE

Magic Kingdom One-Day Touring Plan for Adults
(pages 713–714)

FOR Adults without young children.

ASSUMES Willingness to experience all major rides (including roller coasters) and shows that were operating at press time. Does not assume the use of Genie+ or Individual Lightning Lane.

THIS PLAN INCLUDES THE ATTRACTIONS we think best represent the Magic Kingdom, from its newest roller coasters to those created by Walt Disney himself. It requires a lot of walking and some backtracking to avoid lines. Extra walking and morning hustling will spare you hours of standing in line. How far you get depends on how quickly you move from ride to ride, how many times you rest or eat, how quickly the park fills, and what time the park closes.

Magic Kingdom One-Day Touring Plan For Parents with Small Children *(pages 715–716)*

FOR Parents with children younger than age 8.

ASSUMES Periodic stops for rest, restrooms, and refreshments.

THIS PLAN INCLUDES the park's highest-rated attractions for younger children, plus many of the ones for adults and older kids. It also includes the evening fireworks.

The plan has a slower pace, with plenty of free time throughout the day. If more time is needed, though, the overall ratings of It's a Small World and The Many Adventures of Winnie the Pooh make them the most expendable in the plan.

Magic Kingdom Dumbo-or-Die-in-a-Day Touring Plan for Parents with Small Children   *(pages 717–718)*

FOR Adults compelled to devote every waking moment to the pleasure and entertainment of their young children; rich people who are paying someone else to do the same.

ASSUMES Frequent stops for rest, restrooms, and refreshments.

NAME ASIDE, this plan is no joke, y'all. Whether you're loving, masochistic, selfless, or just unhinged, this itinerary will provide a youngster with about as perfect a day as is possible in the Magic Kingdom. Families using this plan should review the Magic Kingdom attractions in our **Small-Child Fright-Potential Table** in Part 7 (pages 390–392).

Magic Kingdom Two-Day Touring Plan for Adults   *(pages 719–720)*

FOR Those wishing to spread their Magic Kingdom visit over two days.

ASSUMES Willingness to experience all major rides and shows.

THIS TWO-DAY TOURING PLAN takes advantage of early-morning touring. Each day, you should complete the structured part of the plan by about 4 p.m. This leaves plenty of time for live entertainment, or time for a break back at your hotel before deciding what to do in the evening.

█ OVERVIEW

WALT DISNEY'S ORIGINAL 1960s-era vision for EPCOT was a complete rethinking of the American city. Back then, **EPCOT** was an acronym meaning "Experimental Prototype Community of Tomorrow." Among Walt's ideas for future city living were self-driving electric cars, prefab solar-powered homes electronically connected to a network of information services; and an entire city center enclosed in a giant air-conditioned dome.

After Walt Disney died in 1966, the people who took over his company considered his ideas too risky to implement. When EPCOT Center finally opened at Walt Disney World 16 years later, it was a theme park with a split personality: Half of it—called **Future World**—was based on a futuristic, semi-educational, "better living through technology" look at the world, while the other half—**World Showcase**—was a kind of permanent world's fair (another of Walt's passions).

IS EPCOT WORTH VISITING IN 2023?

EPCOT REMAINS THE DISNEY WORLD theme park most in need of refurbishment. The good news: It's happening, albeit slowly, and in fits and starts.

continued on page 510

EPCOT

Attractions

1. *The American Adventure* ☑
2. *Awesome Planet*
3. *Canada Far and Wide*
4. Club Cool
5. Disney and Pixar Short Film Festival G+
6. *Frozen Ever After* ☑ G+
7. Gran Fiesta Tour Starring the Three Caballeros
8. Guardians of the Galaxy: Cosmic Rewind ☑ ILL
9. *Impressions de France/ Beauty and the Beast Sing-Along*
10. Journey into Imagination with Figment G+
11. Journey of Water, Inspired by Moana
12. Living with the Land ☑ G+
13. Mission: Space ☑ G+
14. *Reflections of China*
15. Remy's Ratatouille Adventure ☑ G+
16. SeaBase ☑
17. The Seas with Nemo & Friends G+
18. Meet Anna and Elsa at Royal Sommerhus
19. Soarin' Around the World ☑ G+
20. Spaceship Earth ☑ G+
21. Test Track ☑ G+
22. *Turtle Talk with Crush* ☑ G+

G+ Offers Genie+

ILL Offers Individual Lightning Lane

☑ Not To Be Missed

👍 Recommended Dining

➕ First Aid Center

✳ Fireworks Top Viewing Spot

🚻 Restrooms

Germany

United States

Italy

Japan

America Gardens Theatre

Morocco

World Showcase Lagoon

France

International Gateway Entrance

United Kingdom

Walkway to EPCOT Resorts & Disney's Hollywood Studios

Canada

World Showplace Events Pavilion

Imagination!

World Nature

The Land

Table-Service Restaurants

AA. Akershus Royal Banquet Hall
BB. Biergarten Restaurant
CC. Le Cellier Steakhouse
DD. Chefs de France
EE. Coral Reef Restaurant
FF. La Crêperie de Paris

GG. Garden Grill Restaurant
HH. La Hacienda de San Angel
II. Monsieur Paul
(closed at press time)
JJ. Nine Dragons Restaurant
KK. Restaurant Marrakesh
(closed at press time)
LL. Rose & Crown Dining
Room 👍
MM. San Angel Inn Restaurante
NN. Space 220
OO. Spice Road Table
PP. Takumi-Tei
QQ. Teppan Edo 👍
RR. Tokyo Dining 👍
SS. Tutto Gusto Wine Cellar
TT. Tutto Italia Ristorante 👍
UU. Via Napoli Ristorante e
Pizzeria

Counter-Service Restaurants

A. L'Artisan des Glaces 👍
B. La Cantina de San Angel
C. Connections Cafe
D. La Crêperie de Paris
E. Fife & Drum Tavern
F. Les Halles Boulangerie–
Pâtisserie 👍
G. Katsura Grill
H. Kringla Bakeri og Kafe
I. Lotus Blossom Café
J. Refreshment Outpost
K. Refreshment Port
L. Regal Eagle Smokehouse
M. Rose & Crown Pub
N. Sommerfest
O. Sunshine Seasons 👍
P. Tangierine Café 👍
Q. Yorkshire County Fish Shop

continued from page 506

Two new headliner attractions have opened in the past few years: The **Guardians of the Galaxy: Cosmic Rewind** roller coaster opened in 2022, and **Remy's Ratatouille Adventure,** a family-friendly ride through a French kitchen, opened in World Showcase's France Pavilion in 2021. An all-new fireworks show should debut sometime in late 2023 or 2024.

NOT TO BE MISSED IN EPCOT
FUTURE WORLD • Guardians of the Galaxy: Cosmic Rewind • Living with the Land • Mission: Space • SeaBase • Soarin' Around the World • Spaceship Earth • Test Track • *Turtle Talk with Crush*
WORLD SHOWCASE • *The American Adventure* • Frozen Ever After • Japan and Mexico Pavilions • Meet Anna and Elsa at Royal Sommerhus • Remy's Ratatouille Adventure

NAME CHANGES

IN 2019 DISNEY ANNOUNCED that the front half of EPCOT—Future World—would be subdivided into three "lands." **World Discovery** covers the east side of Future World, formerly known as Future World East, including the Test Track, Mission: Space, and Guardians of the Galaxy Pavilions. **World Nature** incorporates attractions in what was formerly known as Future World West, including the Imagination!, Land, and Seas Pavilions. The central part of Future World, including Spaceship Earth, is now known as **World Celebration.** The World Showcase Pavilion will keep its name.

We'll use the older term "Future World" to generally refer to the half of the park that isn't World Showcase, and we'll use the new land names when discussing those specific sections of Future World.

ARRIVING

ENTRANCES EPCOT has two entrances. The larger one is in Future World, at the front of the park, and it's the one you'll use if you arrive by car, bus, or monorail. The other, the **International Gateway** (**IG**), is in the rear of the park, between the France and United Kingdom in World Showcase. The Future World entrance can handle more people and is closer to headliner rides such as Guardians of the Galaxy, Soarin' Around the World, and Test Track, while the IG entrance will put you closer to Remy's Ratatouille Adventure, which is important if you're touring with small children.

unofficial **TIP**
Arriving at EPCOT 30-60 minutes before official opening ensures the shortest possible waits for rides.

This Sacramento, California, reader suggests using the IG entrance:

The IG entrance is convenient for getting into EPCOT first thing in the morning. We entered by boat from the Dolphin and were met inside the gate by cast members who helped us set up our ride reservations for the day.

ARRIVING FROM INSIDE DISNEY WORLD If you're staying at an EPCOT resort, it will take you about 20–30 minutes to walk the mile or so from your hotel to the IG and then from there to Future World. **Boat**

EPCOT SERVICES

EPCOT'S SERVICE FACILITIES, most located in Future World, include
Baby Care Center On the World Showcase side of the Odyssey Center
Banking Services ATMs outside the main entrance, on the Future World bridge, and in World Showcase at the US Pavilion and International Gateway entrance
Cell Phone Charging Outlets available in The Seas with Nemo & Friends Pavilion, upstairs near the women's restroom; in The Land Pavilion, upstairs near Garden Grill; and possibly a few open outlets in the Test Track postshow, depending on how displays are arranged
Dining Reservations At Guest Relations, to the left of Spaceship Earth, or through the My Disney Experience app
First Aid Center On the World Showcase side of the Odyssey Center, next door to the Baby Care Center
Live-Entertainment Information In the *Times Guide,* available at Guest Relations
Lost and Found At the main entrance at the gift shop or Guest Relations
Lost Persons At Guest Relations and the Baby Care Center
Walt Disney World and Local Attraction Information At Guest Relations
Wheelchair, ECV, ESV, and Stroller Rentals Inside the main entrance and to the left, toward the rear of the Entrance Plaza; also at the International Gateway entrance

service is also available from the EPCOT resorts to the IG. It's also about a 10- to 20-minute ride (20–40 minutes with crowds) on the **Skyliner** (see page 439), which links the IG with Disney's Hollywood Studios and Disney's Caribbean Beach, Riviera, Pop Century, and Art of Animation Resorts. Add another 5–8 minutes to walk to Future World from the IG.

DRIVING Arriving by car is easy and direct (see page 441 for GPS names and addresses). EPCOT has its own parking lot, and unlike the Magic Kingdom, doesn't require you to take a monorail or ferry to reach the park entrance. Take a tram or walk from the parking lot to the front gate. Monorail service connects EPCOT with the Magic Kingdom (transfer required), the Magic Kingdom resorts (transfer required), and the Transportation and Ticket Center.

If you want to drive and use the IG entrance, you'll need to pay for parking at the resorts closest to EPCOT: the **Swan, Dolphin,** or **Swan Reserve.** It may be cheaper and/or easier to use a ride-hailing app.

EPCOT OPENING PROCEDURES (ROPE DROP)

FUTURE WORLD AND WORLD SHOWCASE both typically open at 9 a.m. and close at 9 p.m. On-site guests who want to take advantage of Early Theme Park Entry (see page 36) should arrive 60 minutes before official opening (that is, 30 minutes before Early Entry) on all days. Off-site guests (who aren't eligible for Early Theme Park Entry) should arrive 30 minutes before official opening on all days.

WHICH EPCOT ENTRANCE SHOULD YOU USE? The IG is about 10 minutes closer to the family-friendly **Remy's Ratatouille Adventure,** located in World Showcase's France Pavilion, than the Future World entrance is, and that's a huge head start. But if the rat ride isn't a priority, then enter at Future World instead for easier access to **Soarin' Around the World, Test Track,** and **Guardians of the Galaxy: Cosmic Rewind.**

GETTING ORIENTED

EPCOT'S THEMED AREAS are markedly different: World Showcase features the landmarks, cuisine, and culture of almost a dozen nations and is meant to be a sort of permanent World's Fair. Future World is in flux: Its older attractions examine where mankind has come from and where it's going, while its newer attractions are themed to Disney's make-believe universe of characters.

Navigating EPCOT is unlike getting around in the Magic Kingdom, where nearly every "land" is discrete and visually distinct from its neighbors—for example, Liberty Square and Main Street, U.S.A.

EPCOT, by contrast, is visually open. And while it might seem odd to see a Japanese pagoda and the Eiffel Tower on the same horizon, getting around is fairly simple. An exception is Future World, where construction walls hide (for now) everything on its east and west sides.

The park's architectural anchor is **Spaceship Earth,** a shiny 180-foot geosphere that's visible from almost everywhere in the park. Like Cinderella Castle in the Magic Kingdom, Spaceship Earth can help you keep track of where you are in EPCOT. But it's in a high-traffic area and isn't centrally located, so it's not a good meeting place.

Any World Showcase pavilion makes a good meeting place, but specifics matter. Each pavilion is a town in miniature, with buildings, gardens, and plazas. So instead of just saying "Let's meet in Japan," pick a specific place—for instance, the sidewalk side of the pagoda.

FAVORITE ATTRACTIONS BY AGE GROUP

EPCOT'S LINEUP INCLUDES more than 50 attractions, shows, live performers, and festival and seasonal entertainment. The table on the opposite page shows the park's 10 most popular attractions by age group. EPCOT's live entertainers are popular across all age groups. Those should be part of your day in EPCOT as they're available and convenient to your schedule. The average reader ratings for all EPCOT attractions by age group are as follows, based on the 70,000 attraction ratings we received over the past 18 months:

PRESCHOOL	GRADE SCHOOL	TEENS	YOUNG ADULTS	OVER 30	SENIORS
3.9 stars	3.8 stars	3.8 stars	3.9 stars	4.0 stars	3.8 stars

RIDER SWITCH IN EPCOT At all Disney parks, select attractions allow one parent to ride while the other stays with a nonriding child. The parents then switch roles so that the other can ride using the Alternate Access line. (See page 396 for complete details.)

unofficial **TIP**
If you plan to use Rider Switch in EPCOT, plan for extra time in line for the second rider.

In EPCOT, however, long waits in the Alternate Access line may complicate Rider Switch, requiring families to spend inordinate amounts of time in line so that both parents can ride. A Tulsa, Oklahoma, dad of one elaborates:

Rider Switch worked out really well on every ride in every park except EPCOT. The Alternate Access lines plus ride times for Soarin' Around the World (30 minutes), Mission: Space (30 minutes),

EPCOT MOST POPULAR ATTRACTIONS BY AGE GROUP

PRESCHOOL	GRADE SCHOOL	TEENS	YOUNG ADULTS	OVER 30	SENIORS
Frozen Ever After	Soarin' Around the World	Guardians of the Galaxy	Guardians of the Galaxy	Guardians of the Galaxy	Soarin' Around the World
The Seas with Nemo and Friends	Remy's Ratatouille Adventure	Soarin' Around the World	Soarin' Around the World	Soarin' Around the World	Remy's Ratatouille Adventure
The Seas Main Tank and Exhibits	Frozen Ever After	Remy's Ratatouille Adventure	Remy's Ratatouille Adventure	Remy's Ratatouille Adventure	Spaceship Earth
Turtle Talk with Crush	Test Track	Test Track	Test Track	Test Track	Living with the Land
Meet Anna and Elsa at Royal Sommerhus	Guardians of the Galaxy	Club Cool	Mexico Pavilion	Mexico Pavilion	Test Track
Remy's Ratatouille Adventure	The Seas Main Tank and Exhibits	Japan Pavilion	Spaceship Earth	France Pavilion	France Pavilion
Soarin' Around the World	*Turtle Talk with Crush*	Mission: Space (Orange)	Living with the Land	Voices of Liberty	United Kingdom Pavilion
Gran Fiesta Tour	Club Cool	The Seas Main Tank and Exhibits	Frozen Ever After	Spaceship Earth	*The American Adventure*
Journey into Imagination with Figment	Meet Anna and Elsa at Royal Sommerhus	Mexico Pavilion	The Seas Main Tank and Exhibits	Living with the Land	Voices of Liberty
Test Track	Spaceship Earth	France Pavilion	Mission: Space (Orange)	The Seas Main Tank and Exhibits	Frozen Ever After

and Test Track (45 minutes) were so long that it made Rider Switch very frustrating.

GENIE+, INDIVIDUAL LIGHTNING LANE, AND THE TOURING PLANS

DISNEY'S GENIE+ ride reservation system is offered at 12 EPCOT attractions, with two designated as Individual Lightning Lane:

GENIE+ AND INDIVIDUAL LIGHTNING LANE (ILL) SELECTIONS IN EPCOT
FUTURE WORLD • Disney and Pixar Short Film Festival • Guardians of the Galaxy: Cosmic Rewind (*ILL*) • Journey into Imagination with Figment • Living with the Land • Mission: Space • The Seas with Nemo & Friends • Soarin' Around the World • Spaceship Earth • Test Track • *Turtle Talk with Crush*
WORLD SHOWCASE • Frozen Ever After • Remy's Ratatouille Adventure

It was easy for us to recommend using Disney's old FastPass+ system with our touring plans because it was free to use and behaved predictably. Neither is true with Genie+. So the four big questions for this edition are as follows:

1. Is Genie+ worth paying for in EPCOT?
2. If it's worth the cost, which attractions benefit most from Genie+ or Individual Lightning Lane?
3. How can you avoid paying for Individual Lightning Lane?
4. How do Genie+ and Individual Lightning Lane work with the touring plans?

Are Genie+ and Individual Lightning Lane Worth Paying For in EPCOT?

We think so, provided you meet any of these three criteria:

- You'll be arriving at EPCOT after Early Theme Park Entry begins (that is, you won't be at the park as soon as it opens). This includes off-site guests who aren't eligible for Early Entry and on-site guests who want to sleep in.
- You won't be using a touring plan.
- You're visiting during a holiday, spring break, or another peak season.

Regardless of the time of year you visit, arriving at park opening should allow you to see at least one of EPCOT's headliner attractions without significant waits. Because just 11 attractions participate in Genie+ , it's unlikely you'd need more than five to seven ride reservations per day. On days of heavy attendance, though, you'll be competing with lots of other people for reservations, which pushes out return times and limits how many reservations you can obtain. The table below shows how much time we estimate you'll be able to save using Genie+ with one of our touring plans, at three different crowd and Genie+ usage levels (see page 466 for an explanation of the usage levels):

ESTIMATED TIME SAVINGS USING A TOURING PLAN WITH GENIE+ FOR VARIOUS CROWD LEVELS			
CROWD LEVEL	TYPICAL USE (3 GENIE+ RESERVATIONS PER DAY)	OPTIMISTIC USE (5 GENIE+ RESERVATIONS PER DAY)	PERFECT USE (7 GENIE+ RESERVATIONS PER DAY)
Low	50 minutes saved	85 minutes saved	110 minutes saved
Moderate	70 minutes saved	115 minutes saved	150 minutes saved
High	90 minutes saved	135 minutes saved	170 minutes saved

Which EPCOT Attractions Benefit Most from Genie+ and Individual Lightning Lane?

The table below shows the top attractions that might benefit most from using Genie+, based on current wait times and historical Genie+ wait times. Regarding Individual Lightning Lane, we think Guardians of the Galaxy is not worth the cost.

EPCOT ATTRACTIONS THAT BENEFIT MOST FROM GENIE+ AND INDIVIDUAL LIGHTNING LANE *(Highest Priority to Lowest)*			
ATTRACTION	AVG. TIME IN LINE SAVED (IN MINUTES)	ATTRACTION	AVG. TIME IN LINE SAVED (IN MINUTES)
Remy's Ratatouille Adventure	70	Mission: Space (Orange/Green)	23/9
Frozen Ever After	53	Spaceship Earth	15
Test Track	43	Living with the Land	9
Soarin' Around the World	30	Journey into Imagination with Figment	2
The Seas with Nemo and Friends	23	Turtle Talk with Crush	2

WHEN GENIE+ AND INDIVIDUAL LIGHTNING LANE RESERVATIONS RUN OUT BY ATTENDANCE LEVEL			
ATTRACTION	**LOW ATTENDANCE**	**MODERATE ATTENDANCE**	**HIGH ATTENDANCE**
Disney and Pixar Short Film Festival	Available	Available	Available
Frozen Ever After	6 p.m.	2 p.m.	Noon
Guardians of the Galaxy: Cosmic Rewind	5 p.m.	Noon	9 a.m.
Journey into Imagination with Figment	8 p.m.	9 p.m.	9 p.m.
Living with the Land	8 p.m.	9 p.m.	9 p.m.
Mission: Space	8 p.m.	9 p.m.	9 p.m.
Remy's Ratatouille Adventure	Noon	11 a.m.	10 a.m.
The Seas with Nemo and Friends	8 p.m.	9 p.m.	9 p.m.
Soarin' Around the World	8 p.m.	9 p.m.	9 p.m.
Spaceship Earth	8 p.m.	9 p.m.	9 p.m.
Test Track	2 p.m.	Noon	11 a.m.
Turtle Talk with Crush	8 p.m.	9 p.m.	9 p.m.

AVAILABLE Attractions rarely run out of reservations at this crowd level.
LOW ATTENDANCE Crowd levels 1–3 on the TouringPlans.com crowd calendar
MODERATE ATTENDANCE Crowd levels 4–7
HIGH ATTENDANCE Crowd levels 8–10

Attractions closed for more than two years are not shown.

When Do Genie+ and Individual Lightning Lane Reservations Run Out in EPCOT?

The table above shows the approximate time at which EPCOT attractions run out of Genie+ or Individual Lightning Lane capacity, by crowd level. Use this table along with the "Which Attractions Benefit Most" table above to determine which reservations to get first.

How Can You Avoid Paying for Individual Lightning Lane?

There are a couple of strategies, although each entails spending money somewhere else.

1. Stay at any Disney resort, use Early Theme Park Entry over multiple days, and head to each attraction as soon as the park opens. For popular attractions such as Guardians of the Galaxy: Cosmic Rewind, this is likely to be the strategy recommended by our touring plan software.

2. Stay at a Disney Deluxe or DVC/DDV resort, and visit the attractions during Extended Theme Park Hours.

How Do Genie+ and Individual Lightning Lane Work with the Touring Plans?

See our corresponding advice for the Magic Kingdom on page 468.

DINING IN EPCOT

ON THE NEXT PAGE, you'll find a recap of EPCOT's top restaurants, rated by readers starting with the highest. There are too many EPCOT restaurants rated average or better to list here. See Part 6 for details.

EPCOT RESTAURANT REFRESHER

COUNTER SERVICE	FULL SERVICE
Yorkshire County Fish Shop (⊕ 95%/Exceptional) United Kingdom, World Showcase	**Teppan Edo** (L, D) (⊕ 95%/Exceptional) Japan, World Showcase
Kringla Bakeri og Kafe (⊕ 94%/Much Above Average) Norway, World Showcase	**Biergarten Restaurant** (L, D) (⊕ 91%/Above Average) Germany, World Showcase
L'Artisan des Glaces (⊕ 94%/Much Above Average) France, World Showcase	**Le Cellier Steakhouse** (L, D) (⊕ 91%/Above Average) Canada, World Showcase
Les Halles Boulangerie–Pâtisserie (⊕ 93%/Much Above Average) France, World Showcase	**Spice Road Table** (L, D) (⊕ 91%/Above Average) Morocco, World Showcase
Tangierine Café (⊕ 93%/Much Above Average) Morocco, World Showcase	**Via Napoli Ristorante e Pizzeria** (L, D) (⊕ 91%/Above Average) Italy, World Showcase
La Cantina de San Angel (⊕ 91%/Above Average) Mexico, World Showcase	**La Hacienda de San Angel** (D) (⊕ 90%/Average) Mexico, World Showcase
Regal Eagle Smokehouse (⊕ 91%/Above Average) United States, World Showcase	**Garden Grill Restaurant** (L, D) (⊕ 90%/Average) The Land, World Nature
	Rose & Crown Dining Room (L, D) (⊕ 89%/Average) United Kingdom, World Showcase

FUTURE WORLD

IMMENSE, GLEAMING FUTURISTIC STRUCTURES define the first themed area just beyond EPCOT's main entrance. Broad thoroughfares are punctuated with billowing fountains, all reflected in shiny space-age facades. Front and center is the **Spaceship Earth** geosphere. Pavilions to the east are dedicated to mankind's technological achievements; those to the west celebrate human imagination and the natural world.

WORLD DISCOVERY, WORLD CELEBRATION, AND WORLD NATURE

FUTURE WORLD CONSISTS OF THESE three main "lands." Attractions are grouped together in pavilions within these areas, but it's not clear how they relate to their names. For example, the pavilion dedicated to imagination is in World Nature, while the pavilion dedicated to space is in World Discovery, and the pavilion covering human communication is in World Celebration. If you think that's confusing, Disney also insists that Guardians of the Galaxy, located in the front of the park between attractions in World Discovery and World Celebration, and nearly three-tenths of a mile from the Mexico Pavilion, is part of World Showcase. Balderdash!

We lead off the next section with the pavilions and attractions in World Discovery, then World Celebration, and then World Nature.

KEY TO ABBREVIATIONS In the attraction profiles that follow, each star rating is accompanied by a category label in parentheses (see page 464). **E** means **Exceptional, MAA** means **Much Above Average, AA** means **Above Average, A** means **Average, BA** means **Below Average,** and **MBA** means **Much Below Average.**

Guardians of the Galaxy: Cosmic Rewind *(World Discovery)*
★★★★

PRESCHOOL ★★½ (BA)   **GRADE SCHOOL** ★★★★½ (MAA)   **SENIORS** ★★★★ (A)
TEENS, YOUNG ADULTS, AND OVER 30 ★★★★★ (E)

What it is Massive indoor roller coaster. **Scope and scale** Super-headliner. **When to go** As soon as the park opens, using Early Theme Park Entry if it's open. **Comments** 42″ minimum height requirement. Audio descriptions and assistive-listening devices are available. **ECV/wheelchair access** Must transfer to the ride vehicle. **Participates in Genie+** No (it offers Individual Lightning Lane). **Early Theme Park Entry** No. **Extended Evening Hours** Yes.

Motion Sickness

DESCRIPTION AND COMMENTS Guardians of the Galaxy is one of the highest-rated attractions in Walt Disney World. The premise of the ride is that it's EPCOT's newest World Showcase pavilion, with a twist: You're not visiting another country—you're visiting another planet: Xandar.

You'll start your interplanetary voyage at the Guardians of the Galaxy building near EPCOT's front entrance, in World Discovery. If you're using the standby queue, you'll be directed to doors on the left side of the entrance. If you're using Lightning Lane, you'll enter the pavilion through doors on your right. As at other attractions, you'll skip a lot of the preshow elements by using the Lightning Lane, but none of what you're missing is needed for the attraction.

Once inside, the preshow area looks like a cross between EPCOT's Test Track Pavilion and Animal Kingdom's Dinosaur: lots of walkways curved around various display items that explain the history and culture of Xandar and introduce the *Guardians of the Galaxy* cast for those who haven't seen the movies.

The queue is set up to incorporate several holding areas—small rooms through which guests are "pulsed" through in regular intervals. The idea is that by switching you from lines to rooms to lines again, you'll feel better about the wait than if you were just in one long, uninterrupted line.

Eventually, you make it to the final preshow room, where the ride's actual plot is revealed. Like most modern Disney rides (Rise of the Resistance, *Millennium Falcon:* Smugglers Run, Mickey and Minnie's Runaway Railway, Remy's Ratatouille Adventure), Guardians of the Galaxy uses the all-too-predictable "and then something went wrong" trope. In this case, the thing-going-wrong is a villain stealing a very important power supply.

Actor Terry Crews delivers the bad news about the power supply—and let us say that his acting is one of the highlights of the ride. If we ever detect an asteroid hurtling toward Earth, we want Terry Crews to break the news. He tells you to join the Guardians of the Galaxy to get the power supply back. (There are a couple of other neat show elements in this scene: One will be familiar to anyone who's been on the Haunted Mansion; the other will be familiar to anyone who's seen *Mickey's PhilharMagic* or Avatar Flight of Passage.)

From there you enter the ride's loading area. It's a large room with loading platforms to your left and your right. Both sides are otherwise identical, and having two distinct loading areas allows faster ride dispatches. That keeps wait times lower.

The ride begins with a familiar ride element: a backwards launch, very, very similar to the one in Expedition Everest over in Animal Kingdom. Then, at the exact moment you're supposed to enter deep space, your ride vehicle turns around to face forward.

This might be the best effect in the entire ride. Disney's programmed the ride vehicle to spin and tilt down just a bit as you enter a massive room, pitch black other than some simulated stars and planets. On our first ride, we felt like we were floating in space—an actual "wow!" moment.

Much of the rest of the ride felt similar to Rock 'n' Roller Coaster: lots of tight turns past a few scenic objects and a rock-and-roll soundtrack to accompany your ride (songs at Guardians include A Flock of Seagulls' "I Ran," Blondie's "One Way or Another," and Earth, Wind, and Fire's "September"). Guardians of the Galaxy's ride track doesn't have the loops or inversions that Rock 'n' Roller Coaster has, though.

The ride ends with the Guardians' mission succeeding. The whole onboard ride experience takes just under 3 minutes. That potentially gives Guardians an hourly capacity of around 2,500–2,800 riders per hour, which is very good.

TOURING TIPS Guardians of the Galaxy is one of EPCOT's three thrill rides. Disney calls it a "family thrill ride." In practice, this means it's about as intense as Space Mountain or Expedition Everest.

At press time, Guardians of the Galaxy was requiring guests to obtain a boarding group reservation to ride or pay to ride using Individual Lightning Lane (that is, you can't just show up and wait in a standby line). Boarding groups were available at 7 a.m. and 1 p.m. for all guests, with a special 6 p.m. boarding group for guests staying at Disney Deluxe and DVC resorts on nights when EPCOT hosted Extended Evening Theme Park Hours. See page 494 of our coverage of **Tron Lightcycle/Run** for an explanation of how boarding groups work and how to obtain a boarding group reservation.

We're surprised that Guardians still uses boarding groups more than a year after opening. We're certain (certain!) it's not to restrict ride access so that guests who can't get a boarding group but really want to ride have to pay for Individual Lightning Lane—because that would be *wrong*.

Mission: Space *(World Discovery)*   ★★★½

PRESCHOOL ★★★½ (BA/Green) GRADE SCHOOL ★★★★ (A/Both) TEENS ★★★★ (AA/Orange)
YOUNG ADULTS ★★★★ (A/Orange) OVER 30 ★★★½ (A/Both) SENIORS ★★★½ (BA/Green)

What it is Space-flight simulator ride. **Scope and scale** Super-headliner. **When to go** Before noon or after 6 p.m. **Comments** Orange version not recommended for pregnant guests or anyone prone to motion sickness or claustrophobia; must be 40" to ride Green, the gentler nonspinning version, and 44" to ride the Orange version. **Duration of ride** About 5 minutes plus preshow. **Average wait in line per 100 people ahead of you** 4 minutes. **Loading speed** Moderate–fast. **ECV/wheelchair access** Must transfer to the ride vehicle. **Participates in Genie+** Yes. **Early Theme Park Entry** Yes. **Extended Evening Hours** Yes.

DESCRIPTION AND COMMENTS Mission: Space was created as a centrifuge-based space simulator that spins riders around a central axis to simulate the g-forces of rocket liftoff and, eventually, a moment of weightlessness. It was one of the most popular rides at Disney World until two guests died after riding it in 2005 and 2006. While neither death was linked directly to the attraction, the negative publicity caused many guests to skip it entirely. In response, Disney added a tamer nonspinning version.

Even before you walk into the building, you're asked whether you want your ride with or without spin. Choose the spinning version and you're on

DISNEY DISH WITH JIM HILL

TAKING WALT OFF HIS PEDESTAL A statue of Walt Disney is being created for EPCOT, but unlike the one in the Magic Kingdom, this one is being designed so that it's far closer to the ground and easier to get to. By placing Walt on an open set of steps, he'll be accessible to anyone carrying a camera or packing an iPhone—perfect for up-close selfies.

the **Orange** team; the **Green** team trains on the no-spin side. Either way, you're immediately handed the appropriate "launch ticket" containing the first of myriad warnings, as this *Unofficial Guide* reader discovered:

I chose the more intense version and was handed the Orange launch ticket to read. Basically, it explained that if I had ever had a tonsillectomy or even a mild case of pattern baldness, I should take the less intense ride.

Mission: Space's Orange version is a journey to Mars. The Green version, which takes you orbiting around Earth, is comparatively smooth and mild enough for first-time astronauts.

This San Antonio reader says you don't give up much by choosing the Green option:

I am 65 and have ridden the Orange version a number of times. On our latest trip, we went on the Orange version again and felt a little uncomfortable. My wife suggested that we try the Green version, which I mistakenly believed was some sort of boring mission-control exercise where we would sit behind a computer. The Green version gave us a great experience, including the feeling of lift-off and zero gravity, without the nausea.

A Nashville, Tennessee, reader tried both versions:

I felt the Green was a little lacking, but then Orange was more than I was expecting—the g-force made me want to puke.

Guests for both versions enter the International Space Training Center, where they're introduced to the deep-space exploration program and then divided into groups for flight training. After orientation, they're strapped into space capsules for a simulated flight, where, of course, the unexpected happens. Each capsule accommodates a crew consisting of a group commander, a pilot, a navigator, and an engineer, with a guest in each role. The crews' execution of their respective responsibilities has no effect on the outcome of the flight.

The capsules are small, and both ride versions are amazingly realistic. The nonspinning (Green) version doesn't subject your body to g-forces, but it does bounce and toss you around in a manner roughly comparable to other Disney motion simulators. A Bradenton, Florida, mom found motion sickness to be the least of her problems:

I'd like to see warnings here about claustrophobia—I had no clue until the capsule closed that it would be so tight in there. I went into full panic mode.

TOURING TIPS We're told that the posted wait time for the Orange version is always higher than the Green one to give those on the fence about riding a nudge toward trying the tamer version.

Hit the john before you get in line—you'll think your bladder really has been to Mars and back before you get out of this one.

Few things delight our readers more than kibitzing about rides that can make you vomit, and Mission: Space is at the top of this particular heap. From a Yakima, Washington, reader:

Mission: Space is awesome. Quite a few people we spoke to didn't ride because they were intimidated by the warnings about motion sickness.

If all else fails, each simulator has motion-sickness bags.

A woman from Lisbon, Connecticut, used Mission: Space as her own personal relationship lab:

We now understand why husbands and wives will probably never go to space together, after I (the "navigator") pushed his (the "pilot's") button during the flight. I couldn't help being a backseat driver—we could have crashed!

A space-themed restaurant, **Space 220,** opened between Mission: Space and Test Track in 2021 (see page 348). Its "dine on a space station" theme includes video displays of Earth from orbit.

TEST TRACK PAVILION *(World Discovery)*

SPONSORED BY CHEVROLET, this pavilion (the last on the left before World Showcase) consists of the **Test Track** ride and **Inside Track,** a collection of transportation-themed exhibits and multimedia presentations. All age groups except preschoolers rate Test Track highly. Grade-schoolers, teens, and young adults rate Inside Track as Above Average. Many readers say Test Track "is one big commercial" for Chevrolet. We agree that the promotional hype is more heavy-handed here than in most other sponsored attractions. But Test Track is nonetheless one of the most creatively conceived attractions in Disney World.

Test Track ★★★★

PRESCHOOL ★★★★ (A)　GRADE SCHOOL ★★★½ (MAA)　TEENS ★★★★½ (MAA)
YOUNG ADULTS ★★★★½ (MAA)　OVER 30 ★★★★½ (MAA)　SENIORS ★★★★½ (MAA)

What it is Auto-test-track simulator ride. **Scope and scale** Super-headliner. **When to go** The first 30 minutes the park is open or just before closing, or use the single-rider line (if offered). **Comment** Must be 40" to ride. **Duration of ride** About 4 minutes. **Average wait in line per 100 people ahead of you** 4½ minutes. **Loading speed** Moderate–fast. **ECV/wheelchair access** Must transfer to the ride vehicle. **Participates in Genie+** Yes. **Early Theme Park Entry** Yes. **Extended Evening Hours** Yes.

DESCRIPTION AND COMMENTS Test Track takes guests through the process of designing a new vehicle and then "testing" their car in a high-speed drive through and around the pavilion.

As they enter the pavilion, guests pass displays of sleek, futuristic concept cars and glossy video screens where engineers discuss the work of car design and consumers explain the characteristics of their perfect car.

After hearing about auto design, guests are admitted into the Chevrolet Design Center to create their own concept car. Using a large touchscreen interface (think a giant iPad), groups of up to three guests drag their fingers to design their car's body, engine, wheels, trim, and color. The computer screen reflects each design decision's impact on the car's capability, efficiency, responsiveness, and power. (For example, designing a large truck with a huge V-8 engine increases the car's capability and power but drastically reduces its efficiency.) The entire creative experience takes 5–8 minutes.

Next, guests board a six-seat ride vehicle attached to a track on the ground for a "drive" through Chevrolet's test track. The idea here is that guests are taking part in a computer simulation designed to test their vehicle's performance characteristics. The tests include braking maneuvers, cornering, and acceleration, culminating in a spin around the outside of the pavilion at speeds of up to 65 mph.

The ride visuals are sleek and eye-catching, but trying to understand them as a coherent story is fruitless. At various points during the ride, video screens show the virtual cars designed by the guests in your vehicle and a status update on how the vehicle's tests are progressing. Most guests figure out quickly that absolutely nothing in their car's design has any effect whatsoever on their ride experience.

Test Track's postshow area continues the design process by allowing guests to create commercials for their concept cars. Farther into the pavilion are displays of actual Chevys, many of which you can sit in.

TOURING TIPS Test Track breaks down more often than almost any other ride in Walt Disney World—it's down for about 2 hours per day, on average. It's also one of the attractions most likely to be down at park opening. Ask a cast member whether it's operating before you trek to this corner of Future World.

When it's working properly, it's one of the park's better attractions—but for this London, Ontario, mom, such instances never materialized:

Test Track breaks down more than any ride I've ever seen. We went back there over and over again, got in line, and then had to get out.

A repeat visitor from East Aurora, New York, suggests that all is not lost when the ride malfunctions:

If the ride breaks down, tell a cast member. They'll most likely give you a slip that allows you to skip the line and ride again. This happened to us twice during the busiest time of the year, and we rode again with no problem.

Because most groups are unwilling to split up, the **single-rider line** is usually much shorter than the regular standby line.

Club Cool *(World Celebration)*

PRESCHOOL ★★★½ (MBA) **GRADE SCHOOL** ★★★★½ (MAA) **TEENS** ★★★★½ (MAA)
YOUNG ADULTS ★★★★ (AA) **OVER 30** ★★★★ (AA) **SENIORS** ★★★★ (A)

DESCRIPTION AND COMMENTS Attached to the Creations Shop in the center of Future World, this Coca-Cola–sponsored retail space/soda fountain provides free unlimited samples of soft drinks from around the world. Some of the flavors will taste strange to Americans (such as bitter-tasting **Beverly** from Italy). Past selections have included supersweet **Inca Kola** from Peru, apricot-and-passion fruit–flavored **VegitaBeta** from Japan, and raspberry-flavored **Sparletta Sparberry** from Zimbabwe. Perhaps because it's free and indoors, most age groups rate Club Cool higher than most EPCOT attractions.

TOURING TIPS Club Cool can get crowded, so you may have to wait a bit before dispensing your drink during busier times. But because there's not much else to do here, people don't usually spend a lot of time inside. Don't come in expecting to fill a Big Gulp–size cup with free soda—the machines dispense just an ounce or two at a time. Finally, watch out for sticky floors.

Spaceship Earth *(World Celebration)*   ★★★★

PRESCHOOL ★★★½ (MBA) **GRADE SCHOOL** ★★★★ (A) **TEENS** ★★★½ (BA)
YOUNG ADULTS ★★★★ (AA) **OVER 30** ★★★★ (MAA) **SENIORS** ★★★½ (AA)

What it is Educational dark ride through past, present, and future. **Scope and scale** Headliner. **When to go** Before noon or after 4 p.m. **Comment** If lines are long when you arrive, try again after 4 p.m. **Duration of ride** About 16 minutes. **Average wait in**

line per 100 people ahead of you 3 minutes. **Loading speed** Fast. **ECV/wheelchair access** Must transfer from ECV to provided wheelchair and then from wheelchair to the ride vehicle. **Participates in Genie+** Yes. **Early Theme Park Entry** Yes. **Extended Evening Hours** Yes.

DESCRIPTION AND COMMENTS EPCOT's signature landmark, Spaceship Earth spirals through an 18-story geosphere, taking visitors past animatronic scenes depicting humankind's developments in communications, from cave painting to printing to television to space communications and computer networks. The ride shows an amazing use of the geosphere's interior.

Interactive screens in the vehicles let you customize the ending animated video. A postshow area with games and interactive exhibits rounds out the attraction.

TOURING TIPS Because it's located near EPCOT's main entrance, Spaceship Earth attracts arriving guests soon after the park opens. Your time is better spent on other Future World attractions, such as Soarin' Around the World, Test Track, or Guardians of the Galaxy. Wait times at Spaceship Earth usually fall after 4 p.m., so one option is to see it on the way out of the park. Finally, Spaceship Earth averages around 50 minutes of downtime per day. Before you hike over to it, ask a cast member if it's running.

IMAGINATION! PAVILION (World Nature)

THIS MULTI-ATTRACTION PAVILION is on the south side of World Nature. Outside are an "upside-down" waterfall and one of our favorite Future World landmarks: a fountain that "hops" over the heads of unsuspecting passersby. We recommend touring here in the early afternoon; see individual attractions for specifics.

Disney & Pixar Short Film Festival ★★½

NOT ENOUGH SURVEYS TO RATE

What it is Short movies and trailers for Disney and Pixar films. **Scope and scale** Diversion. **When to go** Hardly ever. **Duration of presentation** About 20 minutes. **Probable waiting time** About 13 minutes. **ECV/wheelchair access** May remain in wheelchair. **Participates in Genie+** Yes. **Early Theme Park Entry** No. **Extended Evening Hours** No.

DESCRIPTION AND COMMENTS This theater screens three 3-D shorts—Pixar's *Feast* and *Piper* and Disney's *Get a Horse*—all of which can be easily found online. The only reason to go here is to get out of the sun (or rain) and sit in the air-conditioning for a few minutes. Very few *Unofficial Guide* readers go here to watch the films.

The Film Festival building often hosts a Mickey Mouse meet and greet.

TOURING TIPS Rarely crowded. Not a good reason to buy Genie+. Not worth your time or money.

Journey into Imagination with Figment ★★½

PRESCHOOL ★★★★ (A)   GRADE SCHOOL ★★★★ (MBA)   TEENS ★★★ (MBA)
YOUNG ADULTS ★★★ (MBA)   OVER 30 ★★★ (MBA)   SENIORS ★★★½ (MBA)

Note: For attractions that we get more than 1,000 surveys annually, Journey into Imagination is the lowest-rated attraction in Walt Disney World.

What it is Fantasy-adventure dark ride. **Scope and scale** Major-attraction wannabe. **When to go** Anytime. **Duration of ride** About 6 minutes. **Average wait in line per 100 people ahead of you** 2 minutes. **Loading speed** Fast. **ECV/wheelchair access**

May remain in wheelchair. **Participates in Genie+** Yes. **Early Theme Park Entry** No. **Extended Evening Hours** No.

DESCRIPTION AND COMMENTS The story takes you on a tour of the Imagination Institute, a research lab dedicated to studying human imagination. Sometimes you're a passive observer and sometimes you're a test subject as the ride provides a glimpse of the fictitious lab's inner workings. Stimulating all your senses and then some, it hits you with optical illusions, a room that defies gravity, and other brain teasers. All along the way, Figment (a purple dragon) makes surprise appearances. After the ride, you can adjourn to a sparse interactive-exhibit area.

Reader responses to Figment and company are pretty consistent—and negative. It's one of the lowest-rated attractions in EPCOT. From a Franklin, Tennessee, family of three:

Journey into Imagination should be experienced only if you're a HUGE Figment fan. We, on the other hand, hated it.

TOURING TIPS You can enjoy the interactive postshow exhibit without taking the ride, so save it for later in the day. Skip this one if time is short.

Journey of Water, Inspired by Moana
(World Nature; opens late 2023)

DESCRIPTION AND COMMENTS A walk-through attraction built to simulate the lush landscapes of waterfalls and streams, this attraction sits—appropriately—on the walk from the center of Future World to The Seas with Nemo & Friends Pavilion. It can be toured at any time.

THE LAND PAVILION (World Nature)

THIS HUGE THEMED PAVILION contains three attractions and two restaurants. When The Land was built, its emphasis was on farming, but it now focuses on the environment.

This is a good place to grab a fast-food lunch. If you're coming here to see the attractions, however, stay away during mealtimes. Be forewarned that strollers aren't allowed inside the pavilion—those with babes in arms might want to bring an infant carrier.

Awesome Planet   ★★½

NOT ENOUGH SURVEYS TO RATE

Likely one of the lowest-rated attractions in EPCOT by most age groups.

What it is Indoor film about the environment. **Scope and scale** Minor attraction. **When to go** Anytime, but save it for later in the day. **Comments** The film is on the pavilion's upper level. **Duration of presentation** About 15 minutes. **Probable waiting time** 10 minutes. **ECV/wheelchair access** May remain in wheelchair. **Participates in Genie+** No. **Early Theme Park Entry** No. **Extended Evening Hours** No.

DESCRIPTION AND COMMENTS *Awesome Planet* is a gorgeous short film that comprehensively covers the planet's animals and biomes alike. To its credit as a multinational corporation, Disney has always presented the best scientific theories of the time in its public presentations on everything from the relationship between biodiversity and evolution, to dinosaur extinction, to how the solar system and universe were formed. The beginning of *Awesome Planet* continues this, with a fantastic clip about the Giant Impact Hypothesis, which suggests that the earth and moon were formed by a collision of the early Earth and a planet about the size of Mars.

Where the film falls short is that the script has narrator Ty Burrell mimicking his role as real estate agent Phil Dunphy from the ABC-Disney TV show *Modern Family*. The film's premise is that you're looking for a planet to buy and Phil is walking you through the benefits of Earth—including, yes, use of the phrase "location, location, location."

TOURING TIPS The theater is large enough to accommodate everyone who wants to see the film, at any time of year.

Living with the Land ★★★★

PRESCHOOL ★★★½ (MBA) GRADE SCHOOL ★★★½ (MBA) TEENS ★★★½ (MBA)
YOUNG ADULTS ★★★★ (A) OVER 30 ★★★★ (AA) SENIORS ★★★★½ (MAA)

What it is Indoor boat ride chronicling the past, present, and future of farming and agriculture in the United States. **Scope and scale** Major attraction. **When to go** Before noon or after 3 p.m. **Comments** Go early and save other Land attractions (except for Soarin') for later in the day. The ride is on the pavilion's lower level. **Duration of ride** About 14 minutes. **Average wait in line per 100 people ahead of you** 3 minutes; assumes 15 boats operating. **Loading speed** Moderate. **ECV/wheelchair access** Must transfer from ECV to provided wheelchair. **Participates in Genie+** Yes. **Early Theme Park Entry** No. **Extended Evening Hours** No.

DESCRIPTION AND COMMENTS The boat ride takes you through swamps, past inhospitable farm environments, and through a futuristic greenhouse where real crops are grown using the latest agricultural technologies. The greenhouse exhibits change constantly: Along with familiar fruits and grains such as tomatoes, corn, and rice, recent plantings include Mickey-shaped pumpkins, hot peppers, Malabar nuts, pandan, caimito, and amaranth. This produce is used in restaurants throughout Walt Disney World.

Many EPCOT guests assume that Living with the Land will be too dry and educational for their tastes. A woman from Houston writes:

I had a bad attitude about Living with the Land—I just didn't think I was up for a movie about wheat farming. Wow, was I surprised!

TOURING TIPS See this attraction before the lunch crowd hits The Land's restaurants or after 3 p.m. If you have a special interest in the agricultural techniques being demonstrated, take the **Behind the Seeds at EPCOT** tour.

Soarin' Around the World ★★★★½

PRESCHOOL ★★★★ (A) GRADE SCHOOL ★★★★½ (MAA) TEENS ★★★★½ (MAA)
YOUNG ADULTS ★★★★½ (MAA) OVER 30 ★★★★½ (MAA) SENIORS ★★★★★ (E)

What it is Flight simulator ride. **Scope and scale** Super-headliner. **When to go** First 2 hours the park is open or between 4 p.m. and park closing. **Comments** Entrance on the lower level of the Land Pavilion. May induce motion sickness; must be 40" to ride; Rider Switch option provided (see page 396). **Duration of ride** 5½ minutes. **Average wait in line per 100 people ahead of you** 4 minutes; assumes 3 concourses operating. **Loading speed** Moderate. **ECV/wheelchair access** Must transfer to the ride vehicle. **Participates in Genie+** Yes. **Early Theme Park Entry** Yes. **Extended Evening Hours** Yes.

Motion Sickness

DESCRIPTION AND COMMENTS Soarin' Around the World is a thrill ride for all ages, as exhilarating as a hawk on the wing and as mellow as swinging in a hammock. If you've ever experienced flying dreams, you'll have a sense of how Soarin' feels.

Once you enter the main theater, you're secured in a seat not unlike those on inverted roller coasters. Then the rows of seats swing into position, making you feel as if the floor has dropped away, and you're suspended with your legs dangling. Thus hung out to dry, you embark on a simulated hang-glider tour, with IMAX-quality images projected all around you and with the flight simulator moving in sync with the movie. The images are well chosen and drop-dead beautiful. Special effects include wind, sound, and even smell. The ride itself is thrilling but perfectly smooth.

The film glides around the globe, from the Matterhorn and an Arctic glacier to the Taj Mahal and the Great Wall of China. The visuals are stunningly sharp thanks to laser IMAX projectors, and computer-animated animals create clever transitions. However, the film's display of vertical landmarks appears comically distorted from seats on the left or right side of the screen. To avoid this, once you're directed to one of the three concourses, politely request to wait an extra cycle for seats in row B1 for an ideal view.

Soarin' is a must for guests of any age who meet the height requirement—and yes, there are Seniors who absolutely love it. A Lewiston, Maine, dad gives it a hearty thumbs-up:

Soarin' is amazing! Even if the "trip around the world" doesn't make a lot of sense, it's still stunning.

If heights make you nervous, you may have reservations, as did this North Carolina mom:

Soarin' was VERY cool, but also on the scary side for people who are afraid of heights or who don't like that unsteady feeling. While we were "soaring" up, I was fine, but when we were going down, I had to keep telling myself, "This is only an illusion. I cannot fall out. This is only an illusion . . ."

TOURING TIPS Soarin' Around the World, Test Track, Remy's Ratatouille Adventure, and Guardians of the Galaxy: Cosmic Rewind take some crowd pressure off all four corners of the park. Keep in mind, however, that Test Track and Guardians serve up a little too much thrill for some guests. Soarin', conversely, is an almost-perfect ride for any age. For that reason, it's near the top of the hit parade. See it in the first 2 hours the park is open or between 4 p.m. and park closing.

THE SEAS WITH NEMO & FRIENDS PAVILION
(World Nature)

FEATURING CHARACTERS from Disney/Pixar's *Finding Nemo* and *Finding Dory,* The Seas encompasses what was once one of America's top marine aquariums, a ride that tunnels through the aquarium, an interactive animated film, and a number of walk-through exhibits. The exhibits need updating, but the tank alone makes the pavilion a must-visit.

SeaBase (The Seas Main Tank and Exhibits) ★★★½

PRESCHOOL ★★★★½ (MAA) GRADE SCHOOL ★★★★½ (MAA)   TEENS ★★★★ (A)
YOUNG ADULTS ★★★★ (A)   OVER 30 ★★★★ (A)   SENIORS ★★★★ (A)

What it is A huge saltwater aquarium, plus exhibits on oceanography, ocean ecology, and sea life. **Scope and scale** Major attraction. **When to go** Before 12:30 p.m. or after 5 p.m., especially when it gets dark early. **Comment** Watch for tank feeding times at 10 a.m. and 3:30 p.m. **Average wait in line per 100 people ahead of you** 3½ minutes. **Loading speed** Fast. **ECV/wheelchair access** May remain in wheelchair. **Participates in Genie+** No. **Early Theme Park Entry** Yes. **Extended Evening Hours** Yes.

DESCRIPTION AND COMMENTS SeaBase is among Future World's most ambitious offerings, housed in a 200-foot-diameter, 27-foot-deep main tank containing fish, marine mammals, and crustaceans in a simulation of an ocean ecosystem. Visitors can watch the activity through 8-inch-thick windows below the surface (including some at the **Coral Reef Restaurant**). Upon entering, you're directed to the loading area for **The Seas with Nemo & Friends** (see next profile), an attraction that conveys you via a plexiglass tunnel through SeaBase's main tank. You disembark at **SeaBase Alpha,** where you can enjoy the other attractions.

About two-thirds of the main aquarium is home to reef species, including sharks, rays, and a number of fish that you've seen in quiet repose on your dinner plate. The other third, separated by an inconspicuous divider, houses bottlenose dolphins and sea turtles. As you face the main aquarium, the most glare-free viewing windows for the dolphins are on the ground floor to the left by the escalators. For the reef species, it's the same floor on the right by the escalators. Stay as long as you like.

TOURING TIPS Experience the ride and *Turtle Talk* by lunchtime before the park gets crowded, saving the excellent exhibits for later. If you see a cast member standing near the tank's windows, ask them what kind of fish you're looking at and whether they have names.

SeaBase is usually less crowded during the evening, making it a perfect time to have large swaths of the aquarium to yourself.

If the wait for Nemo is too long, head straight for the exhibits by going through the pavilion's exit, around back, and to the left of the main entrance.

The Seas with Nemo & Friends ★★★

PRESCHOOL ★★★½ (MAA)	GRADE SCHOOL ★★★★ (BA)	TEENS ★★★ (MBA)
YOUNG ADULTS ★★★½ (MBA)	OVER 30 ★★★½ (MBA)	SENIORS ★★★½ (MBA)

What it is Ride through a tunnel in SeaBase's main tank. **Scope and scale** Major attraction. **When to go** After 2 pm. **Duration of ride** 4 minutes. **Average wait in line per 100 people ahead of you** 3½ minutes. **Loading speed** Fast. **ECV/wheelchair access** Must transfer to the ride vehicle. **Participates in Genie+** Yes. **Early Theme Park Entry** Yes. **Extended Evening Hours** Yes.

DESCRIPTION AND COMMENTS This high-tech ride features characters from the animated hit *Finding Nemo*. The ride likewise deposits you at the heart of the pavilion, where the exhibits, *Turtle Talk with Crush,* and viewing platforms for the main SeaBase aquarium are.

Upon entering the Seas pavilion, you're given the option of experiencing the ride or proceeding directly to the SeaBase exhibit area. If you choose the ride, you'll be ushered to its loading area, where you'll be made comfortable in a "clamobile" for your journey through the aquarium. The attraction features technology that makes it seem like the animated characters are swimming with live fish. Almost immediately you meet Mr. Ray and his class and learn that Nemo is missing. The remainder of the odyssey consists of finding Nemo with the help of Dory, Bruce, Marlin, Squirt, and Crush. Unlike the film, however, the ride ends with a musical finale.

A mom from Asheville, North Carolina, thinks we underestimate the fright factor:

The Seas with Nemo & Friends is scary—sharks, jellyfish, and anglerfish, along with growling, and so on. My 8-year-old hated it!

TOURING TIPS The later you ride, the better (ditto for *Turtle Talk with Crush;* see next profile).

Turtle Talk with Crush ★★★★

PRESCHOOL ★★★★½ (MAA)	GRADE SCHOOL ★★★★½ (MAA)	TEENS ★★★½ (BA)
YOUNG ADULTS ★★★★ (A)	OVER 30 ★★★★ (A)	SENIORS ★★★★ (A)

What it is Interactive animated film. **Scope and scale** Minor attraction. **When to go** After 3 p.m. **Duration of presentation** 15 minutes. **Preshow entertainment** None. **Probable waiting time** 10–20 minutes. **ECV/wheelchair access** May remain in wheelchair. **Participates in Genie+** Yes. **Early Theme Park Entry** No. **Extended Evening Hours** No.

DESCRIPTION AND COMMENTS *Turtle Talk with Crush* is an interactive theater show starring the 153-year-old surfer-dude turtle from *Finding Nemo* and Dory (the blue tang) and other characters from *Finding Dory.*

Although it starts like a typical Disney-theme-park movie, *Turtle Talk* quickly turns into a surprise interactive encounter as the on-screen Crush begins to have actual conversations with guests in the audience. Real-time computer graphics are used to accurately move Crush's mouth when forming words, and he's voiced by a guy who went to the Jeff Spicoli School of Diction.

A mom from Henderson, Colorado, has a crush on Crush:

Turtle Talk with Crush is a must-see. Our 4-year-old was picked out of the crowd by Crush, and we were just amazed by the technology. It was adorable and enjoyed by everyone from Grammy and Papa to the 4-year-old!

TOURING TIPS It's unusual to wait more than one or two shows to get in. If you find long lines at park opening, try back after 3 p.m. when more of the crowd has moved on to World Showcase.

WORLD SHOWCASE

EPCOT'S OTHER THEMED AREA, World Showcase, is an ongoing world's fair encircling a picturesque 40-acre lagoon. The cuisine, culture, history, and architecture of almost a dozen countries (and one pretend kingdom) are permanently displayed in individual national pavilions spaced along a 1.2-mile promenade. The pavilions replicate familiar landmarks and present representative street scenes from the host countries.

World Showcase has some of the most beautiful gardens anywhere in the United States. In Germany, France, the United Kingdom, Canada, and, to a lesser extent, China, they're sometimes tucked away and out of sight on the World Showcase Promenade. They're best appreciated during the day, as a Clio, Michigan, woman explains:

Visit World Showcase in the daylight in order to view the beautiful gardens. We were sorry we didn't do this because we were following the guide and riding rides that we could have done later in the dark.

In addition to the gardens, World Showcase's live entertainers are some of the most highly rated attractions in EPCOT, for all age groups. The following reviews call out those that are especially popular. Check the *Times Guide* for performances and schedules.

Some kids find the World Showcase pavilions and live entertainment boring, so to make it more interesting, most EPCOT retail shops sell **Passport Kits** for about $15. Each kit contains a blank "passport" and stamps for every World Showcase country. As kids accompany their folks to each country, they tear out the appropriate stamp and stick it in the passport. Disney has built a lot of profit into this little product, but guests—namely, parents—don't seem to mind the cost.

As this dad from Birmingham, Alabama, relates, the Passport Kit helps get the kids through World Showcase with a minimum of impatience, whining, and tantrums:

Adding stamps from the EPCOT countries was the only way I was able to see all the displays with cheerful children.

Children also enjoy **Kidcot Fun Stops,** which are usually nothing more than a large table set up somewhere in each pavilion. Tables are staffed by Disney cast members who hand out free souvenirs, such as postcards or stamps, from the host country.

A mom from Billerica, Massachusetts, is a fan of the Fun Stops:

The Kidcot project at EPCOT was amazing! Our 2- and 5-year-olds loved collecting stamps.

An adult version of passport-stamp collecting, **Drinking Around the World** (see page 289) is enthusiastically endorsed by a woman from party-hearty New Orleans:

We drank a beer in each country at EPCOT—Dad was the designated driver—and posed for photos in each, and it quickly became hilarious, as were the progression-of-drunkenness photos that followed.

There's another side to Drinking Around the World, though, and this dad from New Hampshire states it forcefully:

Although Disney might not be actively pushing alcohol consumption in World Showcase, they were very obviously not policing it either when we visited. I like to drink and I love a good party, but time and place are important. I know it's a huge moneymaker for Disney, but if it gets any worse than it was this year, I can see where families would start taking their vacations elsewhere—there was nothing fun or relaxing about it. This year folks were either way too drunk or having to do battle to protect their families from those who were.

A reader from New York City agrees:

I had not been to EPCOT since 2018, and I was wholly unprepared for the HERDS OF DRUNK PEOPLE circling World Showcase in the evening. I counted at least five groups of 10+ people, in matching shirts that said stuff like "Let's Get Sheet-Faced," behaving very irresponsibly, acting out, and generally causing misery for people around them.

We avoid EPCOT on the opening weekends of all of the park's festivals for this reason.

World Showcase also offers some of the most diverse and interesting shopping in Walt Disney World. See Part 17 for details.

DuckTales World Showcase Adventure ★★★★

NOT ENOUGH SURVEYS TO RATE

What it is Interactive scavenger hunt in select World Showcase pavilions. **Scope and scale** Minor attraction. **When to go** Anytime. **Duration of presentation** Allow 30 minutes per adventure. **Preshow entertainment** None. **Probable waiting time** None. **ECV/Wheelchair access** May remain in wheelchair.

DESCRIPTION AND COMMENTS In DuckTales World Showcase Adventure, you help Scrooge McDuck find valuable artifacts located in and around select World Showcase pavilions. DuckTales requires a smartphone and the Play Disney Parks app to play; download it before you leave home.

Once you arrive at a pavilion, you'll be assigned a "mission" to find an artifact. Your phone's video and audio provide various clues to help solve a set of simple puzzles necessary to find the artifacts. As you discover each clue, you'll find special effects, such as talking statues and flaming lanterns, that physically animate some of the story you're following. Don't be surprised if people around you ask, "How did you make that happen?"

Playing the game is completely free, and we've found 35 "missions"—more than enough to fill an entire day at EPCOT. Beyond that, DuckTales makes static World Showcase pavilions more interactive and kid-friendly. The adventures have simple clues and fast pacing. Some have you speaking with cast members who give small rewards for solving the puzzles. Our kids would happily spend an entire afternoon in World Showcase playing this game and eating snacks along the way. Don't be surprised if, having completed one pavilion's missions, your child wants to do more.

DuckTales is the latest iteration of World Showcase scavenger hunt-style games. Previous versions were Agent P's World Showcase Adventure and Kim Possible World Showcase Adventure. All were well liked by those who played. This Tucker, Georgia, mother of a 7-year-old is a fan:

My daughter and I thoroughly enjoyed [DuckTales] World Showcase Adventure. The interactivity was clever and exciting, plus NO LINES!

TOURING TIPS A Granger, Indiana, mom discovered a practical dimension to DuckTales:

If it's raining, do the adventure in Mexico—it's all inside, and by the time you're done, the rain usually is too.

A Massillon, Ohio, mom advises that the game, while lots of fun, can take longer to play than you might think:

Our 9- and 6-year-olds really enjoyed the game, but it took way longer than the 25 minutes we were told (at least for the UK, the country we chose). It ended up being fine, but people should be aware.

WORLD SHOWCASE PAVILIONS

MOVING CLOCKWISE AROUND **World Showcase Promenade,** here are the nations represented and their attractions.

For World Showcase, we list Appeal by Age ratings not just for the attractions but for the pavilions themselves. In addition to rides and films, they offer peaceful gardens; unique architecture; interesting places to eat, drink, and rest; top-notch live entertainment; and more. Note that not every pavilion has a dedicated attraction.

MEXICO PAVILION

PRESCHOOL ★★★½ (BA)	GRADE SCHOOL ★★★★ (BA)	TEENS ★★★★ (A)
YOUNG ADULTS ★★★★½ (AA)	OVER 30 ★★★★½ (AA)	SENIORS ★★★★ (A)

PRE-COLUMBIAN PYRAMIDS dominate Mexico's architecture. One pyramid forms the pavilion's facade; the other overlooks the restaurant and plaza alongside the **Gran Fiesta Tour** indoor boat ride.

Readers rate Mexico as one of the best pavilions in World Showcase. The village scene inside the pavilion is beautiful and exquisitely detailed. A retail shop occupies most of the left half of the inner pavilion, while Mexico's **Kidcot Fun Stop** is in the first entryway inside the pyramid. On the opposite side of the main floor is **La Cava del Tequila,** a bar serving more than 200 tequilas, as well as cocktails, Mexican beer, wine, and mescal.

The pyramids contain many authentic and valuable artifacts. Take the time to stop and see these treasures.

Gran Fiesta Tour Starring the Three Caballeros ★★½

| PRESCHOOL ★★★★ (AA) | GRADE SCHOOL ★★★½ (BA) | TEENS ★★★½ (BA) |
| YOUNG ADULTS ★★★½ (MBA) | OVER 30 ★★★½ (MBA) | SENIORS ★★★½ (MBA) |

What it is Scenic indoor boat ride. **Scope and scale** Minor attraction. **When to go** Before noon or after 5 p.m. **Duration of ride** About 7 minutes (plus 1½-minute wait to disembark). **Average wait in line per 100 people ahead of you** 4½ minutes; assumes 16 boats in operation. **Loading speed** Moderate. **ECV/wheelchair access** Must transfer from ECV to provided wheelchair. **Participates in Genie+** No. **Early Theme Park Entry** No. **Extended Evening Hours** Yes.

DESCRIPTION AND COMMENTS The Gran Fiesta Tour incorporates animated versions of Donald Duck, José Carioca, and Panchito—an avian singing group called The Three Caballeros, from Disney's 1944 film of the same name—to spice up what's basically a slower-paced, Mexican-style It's a Small World.

The story line has the Caballeros scheduled to perform at a fiesta when Donald suddenly goes missing; large video screens show him enjoying Mexico's sights and sounds while José and Panchito try to track him down. Everyone is reunited in time for a rousing concert near the end of the ride.

At the risk of sounding like the Disney geeks we are, we must point out that Panchito is technically the only Mexican Caballero—José Carioca is from Brazil and Donald is from Burbank. In any case, more of the ride's visuals seem to be on the left side of the boat, so have small children sit nearer the left to keep their attention, and listen for Donald's humorous monologue as you wait to disembark at the end of the ride.

A Fanwood, New Jersey, reader feels the ride is culturally insensitive:

The Gran Fiesta Tour was dreadful. If the idea was to rid the ride of derogatory Mexican stereotypes, the designers woefully missed the mark.

A Wilmington, Delaware, woman blames Gran Fiesta Tour's lack of pizzazz on . . . who else?

Donald Duck has ruined even the minimal value of the Mexico ride.

TOURING TIPS If the line looks longer than 5 minutes, grab a margarita (or several!) at **La Cava del Tequila** and stagger back in 15.

"NORWAY" PAVILION

| PRESCHOOL ★★★½ (BA) | GRADE SCHOOL ★★★★ (A) | TEENS ★★★½ (BA) |
| YOUNG ADULTS ★★★½ (BA) | OVER 30 ★★★★ (BA) | SENIORS ★★★★ (BA) |

THIS PAVILION (note the scare quotes) encapsulates both everything we love about EPCOT and everything we hate about corporate Disney. Parts of the pavilion—that is, those based on the actual country of Norway—are complex, beautiful, and diverse. Highlights include replicas of the 14th-century **Akershus Castle** in Oslo; a miniature version of a **stave church** built in 1212 in Gol (go inside—the doors open!); and other buildings that accurately represent traditional Scandinavian architecture. We were even inspired to visit actual Norway specifically because of how great this pavilion *used* to be.

For years after it was built, however, EPCOT's Norway sat in a state of mostly benign neglect. The boat ride, Maelstrom, was a relatively short and lightly themed float-through of the country's history. The postride film was imbued with the same tired "our spirit is our people" platitudes that are repeated, in one way or another, in every World Showcase presentation ever made. But at least it was about a real country, at a real point in time.

All of that changed in 2013 when Disney released *Frozen*, set in the mythical Scandinavian-ish kingdom of Arendelle. In an unprecedented (and, we hope, never repeated) move, Disney replaced two World Showcase attractions about a real country—Norway—with a boat ride about a fictional place in an animated movie.

Yes, we get that a hit like *Frozen* comes along only once every 20 years and that Disney has to make hay while the sun shines. But when it comes to EPCOT, putting a make-believe kingdom in the middle of World Showcase trivializes the *theme* in *theme park*.

Frozen Ever After ★★★★

PRESCHOOL ★★★½ (MAA)	GRADE SCHOOL ★★★★½ (MAA)	TEENS ★★★½ (MBA)
YOUNG ADULTS ★★★★ (A)	OVER 30 ★★★★ (A)	SENIORS ★★★★ (A)

What it is Indoor boat ride and Disney film–shilling tool. **Scope and scale** Major attraction. **When to go** Before noon or after 7 p.m. **Duration of ride** Almost 5 minutes. **Average wait in line per 100 people ahead of you** 4 minutes; assumes 12–13 boats operating. **Loading speed** Fast. **ECV/wheelchair access** Must transfer to the ride vehicle. **Participates in Genie+** Yes. **Early Theme Park Entry** Yes. **Extended Evening Hours** Yes.

DESCRIPTION AND COMMENTS The premise of this nice boat ride through the pretend kingdom of Arendelle is that you've arrived in time for the Winter in Summer celebration, in which Elsa will use her magical powers to make it snow during the hottest part of the year. Nearly every character from the film is represented, from Olaf the snowman to Sven the reindeer, along with much of the soundtrack's songs with brand-new lyrics.

Be aware that there's a short, mild section where you're propelled backward for a few seconds, followed by a short downhill and small splash that most kids should take in stride. The ride's detailed sets are augmented with digital projection mapping and more than a dozen animatronics sporting video-screen faces (like Seven Dwarfs Mine Train) and demonstrating some of the most spookily sophisticated movements we've ever seen; watch the fluidity of Elsa's wrists and elbows during the pivotal "Let It Go" scene, and weep for a future of robotic massage parlors.

TOURING TIPS Along with Soarin' Around the World, Test Track, Remy's Ratatouille Adventure, and Guardians of the Galaxy, Frozen Ever After is one of the attractions that most guests head to first.

The ride experiences more breakdowns than most Walt Disney World attractions—it's down for about an hour per day on average. If you plan to see Frozen Ever After first thing in the morning, ask a cast member if it's running before you hike all the way to Norway.

The opening of Remy's Ratatouille Adventure has diverted a large portion of the park-opening crowd away from Frozen. Many guests take the long way from France to Future World by stopping at Frozen after Remy.

Meet Anna and Elsa at Royal Sommerhus ★★★★

PRESCHOOL ★★★★½ (MAA)	GRADE SCHOOL ★★★★½ (MAA)	TEENS ★★★½ (BA)
YOUNG ADULTS ★★★★ (A)	OVER 30 ★★★★ (A)	SENIORS ★★★½ (BA)

What it is Meet and greet with the famous *Frozen* princesses. **Scope and scale** Minor attraction. **When to go** At opening, at lunch or dinner, or in the last hour the park is open. **Duration of experience** About 3 minutes. **Probable waiting time** 15–25 minutes. **ECV/wheelchair access** May remain in wheelchair. **Participates in Genie+** No. **Early Theme Park Entry** No. **Extended Evening Hours** No.

DESCRIPTION AND COMMENTS Royal Sommerhus is a character-greeting venue for Anna and Elsa. While *Frozen* was set in a fictional kingdom instead of Norway, we grudgingly concede that the meet and greet features traditional Norwegian architecture and crafts. Having visited Norway, we think Disney did a decent job when it comes to authenticity.

TOURING TIPS During times of peak meet and greet, Royal Sommerhus has multiple rooms with multiple Annas and Elsas receiving guests. If you're visiting World Showcase in the afternoon, waits tend to be shortest around lunchtime (12:30-ish), 4 p.m., and 6–7 p.m.

CHINA PAVILION

PRESCHOOL ★★½ (MBA)   **GRADE SCHOOL** ★★★½ (MBA)   **TEENS** ★★★★ (A)
YOUNG ADULTS ★★★½ (BA)   **OVER 30** ★★★★ (A)   **SENIORS** ★★★½ (A)

A HALF-SIZE REPLICA of the **Temple of Heaven** in Beijing identifies this pavilion. Gardens and reflecting ponds simulate those found in Suzhou, and an art gallery features a lotus-blossom gate and formal saddle roofline. The pavilion also hosts exhibits on Chinese history and culture. Past exhibits have covered everything from China's Indigenous peoples to the layout of Hong Kong Disneyland.

Reflections of China   ★★★½

PRESCHOOL Not enough to rate **GRADE SCHOOL** ★★★½ (MBA) **TEENS** ★★★ (MBA)
YOUNG ADULTS ★★★½ (BA)   **OVER 30** ★★★½ (BA)   **SENIORS** ★★★★ (BA)

What it is Film about the Chinese people and culture. **Scope and scale** Minor attraction. **When to go** Anytime. **Comment** Audience stands throughout performance. **Duration of presentation** About 14 minutes. **Preshow entertainment** None. **Probable waiting time** 10 minutes. **ECV/wheelchair access** May remain in wheelchair. **Participates in Genie+** No. **Early Theme Park Entry** No. **Extended Evening Hours** No.

DESCRIPTION AND COMMENTS Pass through the Hall of Prayer for Good Harvest to view this Circle-Vision 360° film. Warm and appealing (albeit politically sanitized), it's a brilliant introduction to the people and natural beauty of China. We think the film's relatively low marks are due to the theater's lack of seats, not its cinematic quality.

TOURING TIPS The film can usually be enjoyed anytime without much waiting.

GERMANY PAVILION

PRESCHOOL ★★★ (MBA)   **GRADE SCHOOL** ★★★½ (MBA)   **TEENS** ★★★★ (A)
YOUNG ADULTS ★★★★ (A)   **OVER 30** ★★★★ (AA)   **SENIORS** ★★★★ (A)

DOMINATED BY A CLOCK TOWER with boy and girl figures and a fountain depicting St. George's victory over the dragon, the pavilion's *platz* (plaza) is encircled by buildings in traditional architectural styles. The main attraction is **Biergarten Restaurant,** which serves rib-sticking German food and beer (see page 317). Yodeling, folk dancing, and oompah-band music are part of the festivities.

The biggest draw in Germany may be **Karamell-Küche** ("Caramel Kitchen"), offering small caramel-covered sweets, including apples and cupcakes. We love coming here for a midday snack to tide us over until dinner. Check out the large and elaborate model railroad just beyond the restrooms as you walk from Germany toward Italy.

Live entertainment here is **Oktoberfest Musikanten,** who hold the stage down during meals inside the Biergarten.

Germany is pleasant and festive, so tour anytime.

ITALY PAVILION

PRESCHOOL ★★★ (MBA)	GRADE SCHOOL ★★★½ (MBA)	TEENS ★★★½ (BA)
YOUNG ADULTS ★★★★ (A)	OVER 30 ★★★★ (BA)	SENIORS ★★★★ (BA)

THE ENTRANCE TO ITALY is marked by an 83-foot-tall campanile (bell tower) modeled after the tower in St. Mark's Square in Venice. Left of the campanile is a replica of the 14th-century Doge's Palace, also in the famous square. The pavilion has a waterfront on the lagoon where gondolas are tied to striped moorings.

Streets and courtyards in Italy are among the most realistic in World Showcase. **Via Napoli** has some of the best pizza in Walt Disney World; **Tutto Gusto Wine Cellar** serves small plates along with libations. Because there's no film or ride, you can tour Italy at any hour.

UNITED STATES PAVILION

PRESCHOOL ★★½ (MBA)	GRADE SCHOOL ★★★ (MBA)	TEENS ★★★ (MBA)
YOUNG ADULTS ★★★½ (BA)	OVER 30 ★★★½ (BA)	SENIORS ★★★★ (AA)

THE UNITED STATES PAVILION consists of a decent barbecue place (the horribly named **Regal Eagle**), a preshow gallery of rotating exhibits on American history (the **American Heritage Gallery**), and a patriotic show called *The American Adventure.*

The **Voices of Liberty** is a skilled and popular singing group that performs all-American and Disney classics either inside the pavilion or at the America Gardens Theatre stage opposite the pavilion. All age groups from Teens on up rate the performances highly.

The American Adventure ★★★★

PRESCHOOL ★★ (MBA)	GRADE SCHOOL ★★★ (MBA)	TEENS ★★★ (MBA)
YOUNG ADULTS ★★★½ (BA)	OVER 30 ★★★★ (A)	SENIORS ★★★★½ (MAA)

What it is Mixed-media and Audio-Animatronic theater presentation on US history. **Scope and scale** Headliner. **When to go** Anytime. **Duration of presentation** About 29 minutes. **Preshow entertainment** Voices of Liberty vocal group. **Probable waiting time** 25 minutes. **ECV/wheelchair access** May remain in wheelchair. **Participates in Genie+** No. **Early Theme Park Entry** No. **Extended Evening Hours** No.

DESCRIPTION AND COMMENTS *The American Adventure* demonstrates how good Disney theater presentations can be, but it's not without its shortcomings. Housed in an imposing brick structure reminiscent of Colonial Philadelphia, the 29-minute show is a stirring, albeit sanitized, rendition of American history, narrated by an animatronic Mark Twain (who carries a burning cigar) and Ben Franklin. Behind a stage almost half the size of a football field is a 72-foot rear-projection screen on which motion picture images are interwoven with onstage action.

The production arouses patriotic emotion in some viewers but drowsiness in others. A man from Fort Lauderdale, Florida, writes:

I saw The American Adventure about 10 years ago and snoozed through it. I tried it again and it was still ponderous. I'll try it again in 10 years.

The American Adventure's scale is both its strength and its weakness: It takes a lot of time and money to mount a presentation this big, which explains why no new stage scenes have been added or updated since the show opened more than 40 years ago. In the meantime, our understanding of America's history and its role in the world has evolved, but the show hasn't kept pace: Topics such as racism, gender equality, labor relations, and the environment are treated as solved problems instead of the ongoing challenges they are. This Erie, Pennsylvania, couple resented what they saw as Disney's squeaky-clean take on American history:

The American Adventure glosses over America's dark points. For example, it neatly cuts out the audio about who bombed Pearl Harbor (in EPCOT, after all, Japan is right next door). Why not focus on the natural beauty of America, its ethnic diversity, its contributions to world society?

The American Adventure's ratings have fallen steadily in young adult and teen demographics, and younger kids have never liked it that much. We know it'll be expensive and time-consuming, and that Disney will get criticized no matter how it does it, but it's time to update this attraction.

TOURING TIPS *The American Adventure* is (still) Disney's best patriotic attraction, but it isn't hard to get into: Because of the theater's large capacity, it's highly unusual not to be admitted to the next performance.

JAPAN PAVILION

PRESCHOOL ★★★ (MBA)   **GRADE SCHOOL** ★★★★ (A)   **TEENS** ★★★★½ (MAA)
YOUNG ADULTS ★★★★ (AA)   **OVER 30** ★★★★ (AA)   **SENIORS** ★★★★½ (AA)

A FIVE-STORY, BLUE-ROOFED PAGODA, inspired by an eighth-century shrine in Nara, sets this pavilion apart. A hill garden behind it features waterfalls, rocks, flowers, lanterns, paths, and rustic bridges. On the right as you face the entrance, a building inspired by the ceremonial and coronation hall at Kyoto's Imperial Palace contains restaurants and a branch of Japan's **Mitsukoshi** department store (in business since 1673). Through the center entrance and to the left, **Bijutsu-kan Gallery** exhibits colorful displays on Japanese pop culture. Recent subjects have included everything from comics to *kawaii,* Japan's "culture of cute."

Japan blends simplicity, architectural grandeur, and natural beauty. Tour anytime. The second floor of the Japan pavilion is also a decent viewing spot for EPCOT's fireworks show.

MOROCCO PAVILION

PRESCHOOL Not enough surveys to rate   **GRADE SCHOOL** ★★★½ (BA)   **TEENS** ★★★½ (BA)
YOUNG ADULTS ★★★★ (A)   **OVER 30** ★★★★ (A)   **SENIORS** ★★★★ (A)

A BUSTLING MARKET, WINDING STREETS, lofty minarets, and stuccoed archways re-create the romance and intrigue of Marrakesh and Casablanca. The pavilion also has a museum of Moorish art and three restaurants, one of which was (still) closed at press time. Of the restaurants that are open, the counter-service **Tangierine Café** is one of the highest-rated restaurants in EPCOT. A Northfield, Minnesota, mother of two exploring Morocco found, of all things, peace and quiet:

We found an awesome resting place in Morocco—an empty air-conditioned gallery with padded benches. No one came in during the 15 minutes that we rested, which was quite a difference from the rest of the park! Look for the red doors on your left when you enter.

Morocco is Len's favorite World Showcase pavilion. In particular, the open-air courtyard just past the archway on the left is a peaceful gem of design. This pavilion has neither a ride nor a theater. Tour anytime.

FRANCE PAVILION

PRESCHOOL ★★★½ (MBA)   **GRADE SCHOOL** ★★★½ (MBA)   **TEENS** ★★★★ (A)
YOUNG ADULTS ★★★★ (A)   **OVER 30** ★★★★½ (MAA)   **SENIORS** ★★★★½ (MAA)

A REPLICA OF THE EIFFEL TOWER is, *naturellement,* this pavilion's centerpiece. The restaurants, along with the bakery and ice-cream shop, are very popular. The pavilion hosts two films: a ***Beauty and the Beast*-themed sing-along show,** which plays from park opening to 6 p.m., in the same theater as ***Impressions de France,*** which plays from 6:30 p.m. to just before park closing.

Beauty and the Beast Sing-Along   ★★

PRESCHOOL ★★★★ (A)   **GRADE SCHOOL** ★★★★ (A)   **TEENS** ★★ (MBA)
YOUNG ADULTS ★★★½ (MBA)   **OVER 30** ★★★½ (BA)   **SENIORS** ★★★★ (BA)

What it is Film retelling of the story, with singing. **Scope and scale** Minor attraction. **When to go** 11 a.m.–6 p.m. **Duration of presentation** About 15 minutes. **Preshow entertainment** None. **Probable waiting time** 15 minutes. **ECV/wheelchair access** May remain in wheelchair. **Participates in Genie+** No. **Early Theme Park Entry** Yes. **Extended Evening Hours** Yes.

DESCRIPTION AND COMMENTS This is the third current Walt Disney World attraction to tell the *Beauty and the Beast* story, along with the Magic Kingdom's *Enchanted Tales with Belle* and Hollywood Studios' *Beauty and the Beast—Live on Stage.* It's also the lowest-rated version, lacking the intimate charm of *Enchanted Tales* and the production value of *Live on Stage.*

For this show, Disney's script writers threw a small twist into the original *Beauty* story, presumably to entice people who have seen the other, better attractions to give this one a chance. That twist is that LeFou, Gaston's sidekick during the film, was secretly working behind the scenes to bring Belle and Beast together. Extra animation scenes were created to tell this (tiny) part of the story, and these scenes serve as glue between clips from the original movie.

Speaking of the original movie, this new idea of LeFou as matchmaker doesn't add up. For one thing, LeFou is the one who tries to persuade angry villagers that Belle's father is crazy, and it's that assembled mob that Gaston leads to kill Beast. If Disney wants us to believe that LeFou was a genius and that attempted homicide was all part of his plan, they're going to need a better script than this.

What's even more confusing is that Mrs. Potts starts the film by saying that this is the true story of Beauty and the Beast, leaving viewers wondering whether everything they thought they knew was wrong or if Angela Lansbury is lying.

Sadly, Disney doesn't take advantage of the full 200-degree screen—the entire film plays on just one of the five screens that can be used.

TOURING TIPS The film rarely plays to full theaters; see it anytime.

Impressions de France ★★★½

PRESCHOOL, GRADE SCHOOL, TEENS, AND YOUNG ADULTS Not enough surveys to rate
OVER 30 ★★★★ (A)   SENIORS ★★★★½ (AA)

What it is Film essay on France and its people. **Scope and scale** Diversion. **When to go** 6:30-8.45 p.m. **Duration of presentation** About 18 minutes. **Preshow entertainment** None. **Probable waiting time** 15 minutes (at suggested times). **ECV/wheelchair access** May remain in wheelchair. **Participates in Genie+** No. **Early Theme Park Entry** No. **Extended Evening Hours** No.

DESCRIPTION AND COMMENTS *Impressions de France* is an 18-minute movie with beautiful scenery, beautiful music, beautiful people, and beautiful towns, all projected over 200 degrees onto five screens. Unlike at China and Canada, the audience sits to view the film.

While we think this is the best film in World Showcase, it was outdated way before the Notre Dame fire in the spring of 2019. Disney needs to update the film or put it out of its misery.

TOURING TIPS Usually begins on the half hour. France's streets are small and become congested when visitors queue for the film.

Remy's Ratatouille Adventure ★★★★

PRESCHOOL ★★★★ (A)   ALL OTHER AGE GROUPS ★★★★½ (MAA)

What it is Indoor dark ride. **Scope and scale** Major attraction. **When to go** As soon as the park opens. **Duration of ride** About 4½ minutes. **Average wait in line per 100 people ahead of you** About 3 minutes; assumes hourly capacity of around 2,200 riders. **Loading speed** Moderate. **ECV/wheelchair access** Must transfer to the ride vehicle. **Participates in Genie+** Yes. **Early Theme Park Entry** Yes. **Extended Evening Hours** Yes.

DESCRIPTION AND COMMENTS In Remy's Ratatouille Adventure, you're shrunk to the size of a rat and whisked through Paris for a quick retelling of the *Ratatouille* film's story. As one of Remy's vermin pals, you watch him ascend from a rodent with a dream to become one of Paris's most celebrated chefs running his own kitchen.

Remy's storytelling combines 3-D films on room-size screens with large, detailed ride-through sets that include water and heat effects. Along with the ride and film, Remy's building and show scenes feature more three-dimensional depth than we expected, adding to the illusion you're in Paris.

A couple of frenetic scenes, such as one in which Remy is chased with a cleaver, may frighten small children.

TOURING TIPS Remy's was the first all-new major attraction in World Showcase since 1988. It's family-friendly, with good theming and a lead character who's as lovable as any disease vector could hope to be.

The one big issue with Remy is that the ride experiences about an hour of downtime per day. Because it's located in a far corner of the park, check that it's running before making the hike over to ride.

Your best bet to experience Remy without paying for Lightning Lane is to arrive at EPCOT's International Gateway entrance about an hour before opening. (If you're driving, park at one of the EPCOT resorts—the Swan and Dolphin are the closest, but note that parking is $35 a day versus $25 at the other resorts.) That gives you a 10-minute head start on folks walking from the park's front entrance. Before walking over, ask a cast member if Remy is operating. If it is, ride as soon as the park opens. If you have small children, head next to Frozen Ever After in Norway, about 0.5 mile either way around World Showcase. After experiencing Frozen, you'll have completed two of the park's five headliner rides, with Guardians of the Galaxy, Test Track, and Soarin' Around the World remaining.

UNITED KINGDOM PAVILION

PRESCHOOL Not enough surveys to rate **GRADE SCHOOL** ★★★½ (MBA) **TEENS** ★★★★ (A)
YOUNG ADULTS ★★★★ (A) **OVER 30** ★★★★ (A) **SENIORS** ★★★★ (A)

A HODGEPODGE OF PERIOD ARCHITECTURE attempts to depict Britain's urban and rural sides. One street alone has a thatched-roof cottage, a four-story Tudor half-timber building, a pre-Georgian plaster building, a formal Palladian facade of dressed stone, and a city square with a Hyde Park bandstand (whew!). The pavilion consists mostly of shops. The **Rose & Crown Pub** and **Rose & Crown Dining Room** offer dining on the water side of the promenade. For fish and chips to go, try **Yorkshire County Fish Shop.** Reservations aren't required for the Rose & Crown Pub, making it a nice place to stop for a beer.

There are no attractions here, so it's possible to tour anytime. We prefer to visit when the house band plays sets of British rock classics, generally between 3 and 8 p.m. daily. The cover of "You Really Got Me" is more Eddie Van Halen than Dave Davies, but Zeppelin's "Immigrant Song" rocks.

CANADA PAVILION

PRESCHOOL Not enough surveys to rate **OVER 30** ★★★★ (BA) **SENIORS** ★★★★ (BA)
GRADE SCHOOL, TEENS, AND YOUNG ADULTS ★★★½ (MBA)

THE DIVERSITY OF CANADA—cultural, natural, and architectural—is reflected in this large, impressive pavilion. Thirty-foot-tall totem poles embellish a native village at the foot of a replica of a magnificent château-style hotel. **Le Cellier Steakhouse** is on Canada's lower level (see page 321 for our review).

Canada Far and Wide ★★★½

PRESCHOOL Not enough surveys to rate **GRADE SCHOOL AND TEENS** ★★★ (MBA)
YOUNG ADULTS ★★★½ (BA) **OVER 30** ★★★½ (BA) **SENIORS** ★★★★ (A)

What it is Film essay on Canada and its people. **Scope and scale** Major attraction. **When to go** Anytime. **Comment** Audience stands. **Duration of presentation** About 14 minutes. **Preshow entertainment** None. **Probable waiting time** 9 minutes. **ECV/ wheelchair access** May remain in wheelchair. **Participates in Genie+** No. **Early Theme Park Entry** No. **Extended Evening Hours** No.

DESCRIPTION AND COMMENTS The third film shown in this pavilion since EPCOT opened, *Canada Far and Wide* is the best one yet. It combines all of the visual majesty that you'd want in a 360-degree film with a faster, more modern script that works its way from one end of the country to the other. As in the previous films, Montreal, Calgary, and Vancouver get their own segments (some of which have been repurposed from the old films). *Far and Wide* has additional clips of Canada's capital, Ottawa, and specifically mentions its three territories—Yukon, Northwest Territories, and Nunavut—and highlights their Indigenous peoples and cultures.

TOURING TIPS This large-capacity attraction (guests who are able must stand) gets moderate late-morning attendance, as Canada is the first pavilion encountered as you travel counterclockwise around World Showcase Lagoon. The film's theater is closed during some food festivals, so check the *Times Guide* before walking over to see it.

EPCOT ENTERTAINMENT

LIVE ENTERTAINMENT IN EPCOT is more diverse than in the Magic Kingdom. In World Showcase, it reflects the nations represented. Future World provides a perfect setting for new and experimental offerings. Offerings on the day you visit can be found in the EPCOT guide map, often supplemented by a *Times Guide*. WDW live-entertainment guru Steve Soares usually posts EPCOT's performance schedule about a week in advance at wdwent.com. Here are some of the venues, performers, and performances you'll encounter:

AMERICA GARDENS THEATRE This large amphitheater, near the US Pavilion, faces World Showcase Lagoon. It hosts pop and oldies musical acts throughout much of the year, EPCOT's popular **Candlelight Processional** for the Christmas holidays, and sometimes the **Voices of Liberty** (see below).

AROUND WORLD SHOWCASE Impromptu performances take place in and around the pavilions. Among the acts are a strolling mariachi group in Mexico; a juggler in Italy; a singing group (Voices of Liberty) at the US Pavilion; acrobats in China; traditional songs, drums, and dances in Japan; more traditional music in Morocco and the UK pub; and a band in Canada. Performances occur about every half hour.

Live entertainment in World Showcase exceeded the expectations of this Ayden, North Carolina, reader:

My husband and I loved the Japanese drumming and the Chinese acrobats. These performances were much more indicative of foreign cultures than the rides.

A Vero Beach, Florida, couple love Voices of Liberty:

Voices of Liberty is one of our favorite acts. Their period costuming, rousing folk and patriotic songs, incredible a cappella sound, and heartwarming spirit bring forth a huge, sincere response from the audience.

Note that Disney changes up Voices of Liberty's song set seasonally. When they're not in the US Pavilion, their repertoire consists of tunes from Disney movies—including, yes, "Let It Go."

IN FUTURE WORLD The **JAMMitors,** a musical crew of drumming janitors, work near the front entrance and around the rest of Future World, according to the daily entertainment schedule.

EPCOT Forever ★★★½

NOT ENOUGH SURVEYS TO RATE

DESCRIPTION AND COMMENTS Despite its name, *EPCOT Forever* is a temporary show put in place when Disney's big-budget extravaganza *Harmonious* flopped so badly that audiences left the park early rather than spend money while waiting to see it. Disney has said a new show is in the works, but neither details nor a specific start date were available at press time.

EPCOT Forever celebrates the history of EPCOT's classic attractions through their music. If you're a fan of EPCOT, you'll enjoy hearing "Veggie,

Veggie, Fruit, Fruit" one more time. Everyone else will wonder why you're crying to a song about good nutrition. But as someone who listened to 1991's *The Official Album of Disneyland and Walt Disney World* so much while writing his master's thesis that he can't play it anymore, Len would like to point out that Disney's selling nostalgia because it's out of other ideas.

TOURING TIPS Fireworks dining packages let you see the show at the **Rose & Crown Dining Room** in the United Kingdom. Check-in for dinner starts 45 minutes before the show begins, meaning your meal should end around the same time the show ends. The fixed-price dinner is $89 per adult and $39 per child. Reservations are strongly encouraged.

VIEWING (AND EXIT) STRATEGIES FOR EPCOT'S FIREWORKS

AS NOTED ABOVE, EPCOT is developing a new, permanent fireworks show to replace *Harmonious*. One of *Harmonious*' many flaws was that it couldn't be viewed properly from anywhere except two spots around World Showcase Lagoon. In contrast, all previous EPCOT shows had at least decent views from all around the lagoon. We're going to assume Disney's learned a lesson from *Harmonious* and that the next show will be viewable from all around the lagoon.

The best viewing location for fireworks is in **Showcase Plaza**—the area where Future World meets World Showcase—between the Disney Traders and Port of Entry shops.

The best place for viewing fireworks on World Showcase Lagoon is around Japan. Come early—at least 90 minutes before the show—and relax with a cold drink or snack while you wait for the show.

A woman from Pasadena, California, nailed down a seat but missed the relaxation:

> Stake out a prime site for the fireworks at least an hour and a half ahead—and be prepared to defend it. We got a lakeside table at Cantina de San Angel at 6:30 p.m.; unfortunately, we had to put up with troops of people asking us to share our table and trying to wedge themselves between our table and the fence.

La Hacienda de San Angel in Mexico, the **Rose & Crown Pub** in the United Kingdom, and **Spice Road Table** in Morocco also offer lagoon views. The views at Spice Road Table are better than those at the other restaurants. If you want to combine dinner at these sit-down locations with viewing the show, make a reservation for about 1 hour and 15 minutes before showtime. Report a few minutes early for your seating, and tell the host that you want a table outside where you can watch the show. Our experience is that the staff will bend over backward to accommodate you.

Because most guests run for the exits after a presentation and islands in the southern (US Pavilion) half of the lagoon block the view from some places, the most popular spectator positions are along the **northern waterfront,** from Norway and Mexico to Canada and the United Kingdom. Although this half of the lagoon offers good views, you must usually claim a spot 60–100 minutes before the show begins.

For those who are late finishing dinner or don't want to spend an hour or more standing by a rail, here are some good viewing spots along the **southern perimeter** (moving counterclockwise from the

United Kingdom to Germany) that often go unnoticed until 10–30 minutes before showtime:

1. **International Gateway Island** The pedestrian bridge across the canal near the International Gateway spans an island that offers great viewing. This island normally fills 30 minutes or more before showtime.

2. **Second-Floor (Restaurant-Level) Deck of the Mitsukoshi Building in Japan** An Asian arch slightly blocks your sight line, but this covered deck offers a great vantage point, especially if the weather is iffy. Only La Hacienda de San Angel in Mexico is more protected. If you take up a position on the Mitsukoshi deck and find the wind blowing directly at you, you can be reasonably sure that the smoke from the fireworks won't be far behind. May be reserved by Disney for private viewings.

3. **Gondola Landing at Italy** An elaborate waterfront promenade offers decent viewing of all but the central barge images. Claim a spot at least 30 minutes before showtime.

4. **Boat Dock Opposite Germany** Another good vantage point, the dock generally fills 30 minutes before the show. Note that this area may be exposed to more smoke from the fireworks because of EPCOT's prevailing winds.

5. **Waterfront Promenade by Germany** Views are good from the 90-foot-long lagoonside walkway between Germany and China.

None of these viewing locations are reservable (except by Disney), and the best spots get snapped up early on busy nights. Most nights, you can still find an acceptable vantage point 15–30 minutes before the show. Don't position yourself under a tree, an awning, or anything that blocks your overhead view.

A New Yorker who staked out his turf well in advance made this suggestion for staying comfortable until showtime:

Your excellent guide also served as a seat cushion while I waited seated on the ground. Please make future editions even thicker for greater comfort.

Getting Out of EPCOT After the Fireworks

EPCOT's fireworks show ends the day—when it's over, everyone leaves at once. It's important, then, to not only decide how quickly you want to flee the park after the show but also to pick a vantage point that will help you do that most efficiently.

The **Skyliner** gondola system connects EPCOT with Disney's Hollywood Studios as well as the **Caribbean Beach, Riviera, Pop Century, and Art of Animation Resorts.** EPCOT's Skyliner station is just beyond the International Gateway exit. Waits can be half an hour or more on busy nights. Also note that the Skyliner doesn't operate during thunderstorms or when lightning is in the area.

If you're staying at (or you parked at) an EPCOT resort (**Swan, Dolphin, Swan Reserve, Yacht & Beach Club Resorts,** or **BoardWalk Inn & Villas**), watch the show from somewhere on the southern (**US Pavilion**) half of World Showcase Lagoon, then leave through the **International Gateway** between France and the United Kingdom. You can walk or take a boat back to your hotel from the International Gateway.

If you're staying at any other Disney hotel and you don't have a car, the fastest way home is to join the mass exodus through **the main Future World gate** after the show and catch a bus or the monorail.

Those who've left a car parked in the EPCOT lot have a stickier situation. To beat the crowds, find a viewing spot at **the end of World**

Showcase Lagoon nearest Future World (and the exits). Leave as soon as the show wraps up, trying to exit ahead of the crowd (noting that thousands of people will be doing the same thing).

If you want a good vantage point **between Mexico and Canada** on the northern end of the lagoon, stake out your spot 60–100 minutes before the show (45–90 minutes during less-busy periods). Otherwise, you may squander more time holding your spot before the show than you would if you watched from the less-congested southern end of the lagoon and took your chances with the crowd upon departure.

More groups get separated and more kids get lost following the evening fireworks than at any other time. In summer, you'll be walking in a throng of up to 30,000 people. If you're heading for the parking lot, anticipate this congestion and pick a spot in the main EPCOT entrance area where you can meet if someone gets separated from the group. We recommend the **flower beds just behind Spaceship Earth.**

For those with a car, the hardest part is reaching the parking lot: Once you've made it there, you're more or less home free. If you've paid close attention to where you parked, consider skipping the tram and walking. But if you do, watch your children closely and hang on to them for all they're worth—the parking lot can get dicey at this time of night, with hundreds of moving cars.

This Salt Lake City mom hailed a ride out of Dodge, um, EPCOT:

We watched the fireworks from the bridge at the International Gateway by the United Kingdom; then we just walked straight to the BoardWalk Inn and got a ride from Lyft. It took us 10 minutes from leaving the fireworks to getting to our ride to getting dropped off at our hotel. Super convenient, and we didn't have to leave with the 30,000 people exiting EPCOT in the front of the park!

TRAFFIC PATTERNS *in* EPCOT

WITH REMY'S RATATOUILLE ADVENTURE and Guardians of the Galaxy open, crowds head for two opposite ends of EPCOT when it opens. Frozen Ever After in Norway is the second stop for many of the guests who headed to Remy first, while guests who headed to Guardians disperse among the other attractions in Future World, with Test Track the closest headliner.

EPCOT TOURING PLAN

TOURING EPCOT is much more strenuous than touring the other theme parks. EPCOT requires about twice as much walking and, unlike the Magic Kingdom, has no effective in-park transportation—wherever you want to go, it's always quicker to walk.

Our **One-Day Touring Plan** will help you avoid crowds and bottlenecks on days of moderate to heavy attendance, but it can't shorten the distance you have to cover. (Wear comfortable shoes.) On days of lighter attendance, when crowds aren't a critical factor, the touring plan will help you organize your day.

The plan packs as much as possible into one long day and requires a lot of hustle and stamina. It has two versions: one for Disney resort guests and one for off-site guests; the former uses Early Theme Park Entry to minimize waits in line. Because Early Entry means thousands of guests will already be in lines and on rides before off-site guests set foot in the park, the touring strategy for off-site guests must necessarily be different. The plan does not assume use of Genie+ or Individual Lightning Lane. If you opt for either (or both) of these, just use our free touring plan software to enter your return times.

To convert the one-day plan to a two-day plan, see the attractions on the east side of the park on one day, and those on the west side on the other. Alternatively, tour Future World's attractions on one day and World Showcase's on the other. That strategy has a couple of disadvantages: One is that Future World has three headliner attractions, while World Showcase has one; the second is that World Showcase has better restaurant choices for dinner.

"Not a Touring Plan" Touring Plans

For the type-B reader, these touring plans (see page 710) dispense with detailed step-by-step strategies for saving every last minute in line. For EPCOT, these "not" touring plans include advice for adults and parents with one day in the park, for anyone with two days, and for anyone with an afternoon and a full day to tour.

PRELIMINARY INSTRUCTIONS FOR USING THE TOURING PLANS

BECOME FAMILIAR WITH EPCOT'S **opening procedures** (see page 511). On days of moderate to heavy attendance, follow the touring plan exactly, deviating from it only as follows:

1. **When you're not interested in an attraction in the plan.** Simply skip it and proceed to the next attraction.

2. **When you encounter a very long line at an attraction.** In this case, skip to the next attraction and try again later at the one with the line.

Before You Go

1. Call ☎ 407-824-4321 or check the day before you go to verify the official opening time.

2. Make reservations at the EPCOT full-service restaurant(s) of your choice 60 days before your visit.

3. At 7 a.m. on the day of your visit, make Genie+ and/or Individual Lightning Lane reservations if you bought them.

EPCOT TOURING PLAN AT A GLANCE
EPCOT One-Day Touring Plan   *(pages 721–722)*

FOR Adults and children age 8 or older.
ASSUMES Willingness to experience all major rides and shows.

THIS PLAN INCLUDES **Frozen Ever After, Guardians of the Galaxy: Cosmic Rewind, Remy's Ratatouille Adventure, Soarin' Around the World,** and **Test Track.**

PART 13

DISNEY'S ANIMAL KINGDOM

KEY QUESTIONS ANSWERED IN THIS CHAPTER

- How do I get to Animal Kingdom? *(pages 545 and 548)*
- How does park opening (rope drop) work? *(pages 548–549)*
- What are the don't-miss rides? *(page 549)*
- What's the best way to use Genie+ and Individual Lightning Lane in Animal Kingdom? *(pages 550–552)*
- How do I ride Avatar Flight of Passage with a minimal wait in line? *(pages 569–5...*

OVERVIEW

WITH ITS LUSH FLORA, winding streams, meandering paths, and exotic settings, Disney's Animal Kingdom is stunningly beautiful. The

*un*official **TIP**
Disney's Animal Kingdom is four times the size of the Magic Kingdom and almost twice the size of EPCOT, but most of it is accessible only on guided tours or as part of attractions.

landscaping alone conjures images of rainforest, veldt, and formal gardens. Soothing, mysterious, and exciting, every vista is a feast for the eyes. Add to this loveliness a population of some 1,700 animals, replicas of Africa's and Asia's most intriguing architecture, and a singular array of attractions, and you have Disney's most distinctive theme park.

Six "lands" comprise Animal Kingdom (**Africa, Asia, Discovery Island, DinoLand U.S.A., The Oasis,** and **Pandora— The World of Avatar**) but it offers relatively few attractions in its 500 acres: eight rides, several walk-through exhibits, an indoor theater, three amphitheaters, a conservation exhibit, and a children's playground.

Once upon a time, Disney's idea of animals in theme parks was limited to cartoon characters and Audio-Animatronic figures. But 84 miles away in Tampa, **Busch Gardens** had been slowly building on a successful combination of natural-habitat zoological exhibits and thrill rides.

There's nothing like competition to make Disney change its tune. Disney went public with its plans for Animal Kingdom in 1995, and the park opened in 1998.

Even if Disney largely copied its recipe from Busch Gardens, Animal Kingdom serves up more than its share of innovations. For starters, there's lots of space, allowing for sweeping vistas worthy of *National Geographic* or the Discovery Channel. Then there are the enclosures—natural in appearance, with few or no apparent barriers between you and the animals. The operative word, of course, is *apparent:* That flimsy stand of bamboo separating you from a gorilla is actually a neatly disguised set of steel rods embedded in concrete.

Animal Kingdom gets mixed reviews from readers. The animal exhibits, along with the architecture and the landscaping, consistently draw praise, but guests also complain about the park's layout—in particular, the necessity of backtracking through Discovery Island to reach the themed areas—as well as its congested walkways and lack of shade.

Yet in spite of its weaknesses, Animal Kingdom works. It's a place to linger in, to savor. Of course, Disney, with its crowds, lines, and regimentation, has conditioned guests to do just the opposite of that; nevertheless, many visitors understand instinctively that Animal Kingdom must be approached differently from, say, the Magic Kingdom.

A mother of three (ages 5, 7, and 9) from Hampton Bays, New York, writes:

> To enjoy Animal Kingdom, you must have the right attitude. It's an educational experience, not a thrill park. We spoke to a cast member who played games with the kids—my daughter found a drawer full of butterflies, and the boys located a hidden ostrich egg and lion skull.

We agree: Animal Kingdom's best features are its animals, nature trails, and cast members. The **Wilderness Explorers** scavenger hunt (see page 556) ties together all of the park's best elements, and it's part of our Animal Kingdom touring plan described on pages 572–573. It's a lot of fun to play, and you just might learn something along the way.

Pandora—The World of Avatar is Animal Kingdom's newest land, themed to the James Cameron films. Pandora has two attractions: **Avatar Flight of Passage,** a state-of-the-art flight simulator, and **Na'vi River Journey,** a slow-moving boat ride through colorful forests and swamps. Readers rate Flight of Passage as one of the best attractions at any Disney *or* Universal theme park in the United States.

*un*official **TIP**
If you want to beat the lines in Pandora, arrive well before opening or wait until the last hour the park is open.

ARRIVING

FROM INSIDE WALT DISNEY WORLD, Disney buses are the only free option for getting to Animal Kingdom from on-property resorts, but service from many resorts is erratic.

DRIVING Animal Kingdom is in the southwest corner of Walt Disney World; from I-4, take **Exit 65** for Osceola Parkway. (For GPS address, see page 441.) **Animal Kingdom Lodge** is about a mile from the park on its west side; **Blizzard Beach** water park, **Coronado Springs Resort,** and the **All-Star Resorts** are also in the vicinity.

continued on page 548

Disney's Animal Kingdom

Restrooms

First Aid Center

G+   Offers Genie+

ILL   Offers Individual
      Lightning Lane

Recommended Dining

Not To Be Missed

Attractions

1. The Animation Experience at Conservation Station G+
2. Avatar Flight of Passage ☑ ILL
3. The Boneyard
4. Conservation Station and Affection Section
5. Dinosaur ☑ G+
6. Expedition Everest ☑ G+
7. *Feathered Friends in Flight* ☑ G+
8. *Festival of the Lion King* ☑ G+
9. *Finding Nemo: The Big Blue . . . and Beyond!* G+
10. Gorilla Falls Exploration Trail
11. Kali River Rapids G+
12. Kilimanjaro Safaris ☑ G+
13. Maharajah Jungle Trek
14. Meet Favorite Disney Pals at Adventurers Outpost G+
15. Na'vi River Journey ☑ G+
16. Tree of Life ☑ / *Awakenings/ It's Tough to Be a Bug!* G+
17. TriceraTop Spin
18. Valley of Mo'ara
19. Wilderness Explorers ☑
20. Wildlife Express Train

Rafiki's Planet Watch

Asia

DinoLand U.S.A.

Counter-Service Restaurants

A. Creature Comforts *(Starbucks)* 👍
B. Flame Tree Barbecue 👍
C. Harambe Market 👍
D. Kusafiri Coffee Shop & Bakery 👍
E. Pizzafari
F. Pongu Pongu
G. Restaurantosaurus
H. Royal Anandapur Tea Company 👍
I. Satu'li Canteen 👍
J. Thirsty River Bar & Trek Snacks
K. Yak & Yeti Local Food Cafes 👍

Table-Service Restaurants

AA. Nomad Lounge
BB. Rainforest Cafe
CC. Tiffins 👍
DD. Tusker House Restaurant 👍
EE. Yak & Yeti Restaurant 👍

ANIMAL KINGDOM SERVICES

MOST PARK SERVICES are inside the main entrance and on Discovery Island, including

Baby Care Center On Discovery Island

Banking Services ATMs at the main entrance, by the turnstiles, and near Dinosaur in DinoLand U.S.A.

Cell Phone Charging Outlets available at Pizzafari, Restaurantosaurus, Tusker House, and Conservation Station

Entertainment Information In the *Times Guide,* available at Guest Relations

First Aid Center On Discovery Island

Guest Relations/Information Inside the main entrance to the left

Lost and Found Inside the main entrance to the left

Lost Persons Can be reported at Guest Relations and the Baby Care Center

Magic Bands Just inside the main entrance at Garden Gate Gifts, in Africa at Mombasa Marketplace, and at other retail shops throughout the park

Storage Lockers Inside the main entrance to the left

Wheelchair, ECV/ESV (Scooter), and Stroller Rentals Inside the main entrance, to the right

continued from page 545

Animal Kingdom has its own vast paid parking lot with close-in parking for guests with disabilities. Disney usually opens the parking lot about an hour before official park opening. Once parked, you can walk or catch a tram to the entrance.

ANIMAL KINGDOM OPENING PROCEDURES (ROPE DROP)

ANIMAL KINGDOM is usually the first Disney World park to open in the morning, and the first to close. Expect it to open at 8 a.m. daily, and possibly earlier during holidays and other times of peak attendance.

Disney resort guests eligible for Early Theme Park Entry should arrive at the entrance 60 minutes before official opening (30 minutes before Early Entry). Off-site guests (who are not eligible for Early Entry) should arrive 30 minutes before official opening.

unofficial **TIP**
During summer and holidays, your best chance to avoid a long wait in line at Avatar Flight of Passage (without paying for Individual Lightning Lane) is to stay at a Disney hotel and arrive at the Animal Kingdom entrance 1 hour before official opening.

Once you're in the park, you'll usually find all of Pandora, along with *It's Tough to be a Bug!,* **Expedition Everest, Dinosaur,** and **TriceraTop Spin,** already open.

Avatar Flight of Passage remains among the hottest tickets in all of Walt Disney World. As a result, Animal Kingdom adjusts its opening procedures based on crowd levels, catching some guests by surprise. Here's what a Fort Wayne, Indiana, reader experienced while trying to beat the morning crush:

> We arrived at 7:20 expecting to be in the crowd for rope drop, but the crowd had already been admitted and we immediately had a 90-minute wait—before 7:40 a.m.—for Avatar Flight of Passage.

Because the park has relatively few attractions, most guests who arrive at park opening have left the park by midafternoon. The lack of attractions also means Animal Kingdom can get swamped from mid-morning to early afternoon during holidays.

During slower or colder periods, the park may delay opening its secondary attractions: **Kali River Rapids** and **Maharajah Jungle Trek** in Asia, as well as **The Boneyard** in DinoLand U.S.A. The **Wildlife Express Train** and **Conservation Station** may either open late or remain closed for the day.

unofficial **TIP**
To confirm the official park-opening time, check online the night before you go. To stay abreast of ride closures, delays, and the like, also check the daily *Times Guide,* the My Disney Experience app, and/or our app, **Lines.**

GETTING ORIENTED

AT THE ENTRANCE PLAZA, the security checkpoint and ticket kiosks are in front of the main entrance. To your right, before the turnstiles, is an ATM. After you pass through the turnstiles, **wheelchair and stroller rentals** are to your right. **Guest Relations** is to the left. Nearby are **restrooms and lockers.** Beyond the entrance plaza, you enter **The Oasis,** a lush green network of converging pathways winding through a landscape punctuated with streams, waterfalls, and misty glades and inhabited by what Disney calls "colorful and unusual animals."

Animal Kingdom is arranged somewhat like the Magic Kingdom, in a hub-and-spoke configuration. Similar to Main Street, U.S.A., The Oasis funnels visitors to **Discovery Island.** Dominated by the park's central icon—the 14-story hand-carved **Tree of Life**—Discovery Island is the park's retail and dining center. From here, guests fan out to access the themed areas: **Africa, Asia, DinoLand U.S.A.,** and **Pandora.** Discovery Island also hosts a theater attraction in the Tree of Life and several short nature trails. You should be able to take in all of Animal Kingdom in one day—but we encourage you to take your time.

NOT TO BE MISSED IN ANIMAL KINGDOM
DISCOVERY ISLAND • Tree of Life/*Awakenings* • Wilderness Explorers
AFRICA • *Festival of the Lion King* • Kilimanjaro Safaris
ASIA • Expedition Everest • *Feathered Friends in Flight*
DINOLAND U.S.A. • Dinosaur • *Finding Nemo: The Big Blue . . . and Beyond!*
PANDORA—THE WORLD OF AVATAR • Avatar Flight of Passage

FAVORITE ATTRACTIONS BY AGE GROUP

ANIMAL KINGDOM HAS ABOUT TWO DOZEN RIDES, shows, live performers, and seasonal entertainment. The table on page 551 shows the park's most popular attractions by age group. All groups except preschoolers and seniors put **Avatar Flight of Passage** as their No. 1, and all but preschoolers include **Kilimanjaro Safaris** and **Expedition Everest** in their top attractions. Every age group's list includes at least one animal-centered attraction.

The average reader ratings for all Animal Kingdom attractions by age group are as follows, based on the 41,000 attraction ratings we received over the past year:

PRESCHOOL	GRADE SCHOOL	TEENS	YOUNG ADULTS	OVER 30	SENIORS
3.6 stars	4.1 stars	3.8 stars	3.8 stars	4.1 stars	4.0 stars

GENIE+ AND INDIVIDUAL LIGHTNING LANE (ILL) SELECTIONS IN ANIMAL KINGDOM		
AFRICA • Kilimanjaro Safaris • The Animation Experience at Conservation Station • *Festival of the Lion King*		
ASIA • Expedition Everest • *Feathered Friends in Flight* • Kali River Rapids		
DINOLAND U.S.A. • Dinosaur • *Finding Nemo: The Big Blue . . . and Beyond!*		
DISCOVERY ISLAND • *It's Tough to Be a Bug!* • Meet Favorite Disney Pals at Adventurers Outpost		
PANDORA—THE WORLD OF AVATAR • Avatar Flight of Passage (*ILL*) • Na'vi River Journey		

GENIE+, INDIVIDUAL LIGHTNING LANE, AND THE TOURING PLANS

AS A REMINDER, the big questions for these programs are:

1. Is Genie+ worth paying for in Animal Kingdom?
2. If worth the cost, which attractions benefit most from Genie+ and Individual Lightning Lane?
3. How can you avoid paying for Individual Lightning Lane?
4. How do Genie+ and Individual Lightning Lane work with the touring plans?

Is Genie+ Worth Paying For in Animal Kingdom?

We think Genie+ is worth the cost if you meet any of these criteria:

- You'll arrive at the park after Early Theme Park Entry begins (that is, you won't be at the park as soon as it opens). This includes off-site guests (who aren't eligible for Early Theme Park Entry) and on-site guests who want to sleep in.
- You won't be using a touring plan.
- You're visiting during a holiday, spring break, or other peak season.

Regardless of the time of year you visit, arriving at park opening should allow you to see at least two headliner attractions without significant waits. Since only 11 Animal Kingdom attractions participate in Genie+, it's unlikely you'd need more than three or four reservations per day. On days of heavy attendance, though, the lack of attractions means you'll be competing with lots of people, which pushes out return times and limits how many you can obtain. Below, we break down how much time we think you can save using Genie+ with a touring plan, based on different assumptions about how many reservations it's possible to obtain in a day. See page 466–467 for more on the different usage levels.

ESTIMATED TIME SAVINGS USING A TOURING PLAN WITH GENIE+ FOR VARIOUS CROWD LEVELS			
CROWD LEVEL	**TYPICAL USE (2 GENIE+ RESERVATIONS PER DAY)**	**OPTIMISTIC USE (4 GENIE+ RESERVATIONS PER DAY)**	**PERFECT USE (6 GENIE+ RESERVATIONS PER DAY)**
Low	40 minutes saved	60 minutes saved	90 minutes saved
Moderate	55 minutes saved	95 minutes saved	125 minutes saved
High	70 minutes saved	110 minutes saved	45 minutes saved

Which Attractions Benefit Most from Genie+ and Individual Lightning Lane?

The table at right shows the top attractions that benefit most from using Genie+ and Individual Lightning Lane, based on historical wait times over the past year.

ANIMAL KINGDOM MOST POPULAR ATTRACTIONS BY AGE GROUP

PRESCHOOL	GRADE SCHOOL	TEENS	YOUNG ADULTS	OVER 30	SENIORS
Kilimanjaro Safaris	Kilimanjaro Safaris	Avatar Flight of Passage	Avatar Flight of Passage	Avatar Flight of Passage	Kilimanjaro Safaris
Meet Favorite Disney Pals at Adventurers Outpost	Avatar Flight of Passage	Expedition Everest	Expedition Everest	Kilimanjaro Safaris	Avatar Flight of Passage
Festival of the Lion King	Expedition Everest	Kilimanjaro Safaris	Kilimanjaro Safaris	Expedition Everest	*Festival of the Lion King*
The Boneyard	Kali River Rapids	*Feathered Friends in Flight*	*Festival of the Lion King*	*Festival of the Lion King*	Gorilla Falls Exploration Trail
TriceraTop Spin	*Festival of the Lion King*	Dinosaur	Gorilla Falls Exploration Trail	*Feathered Friends in Flight*	Expedition Everest
Finding Nemo: The Big Blue . . . and Beyond	The Boneyard	Kali River Rapids	*Feathered Friends in Flight*	*Finding Nemo: The Big Blue . . .and Beyond*	Maharajah Jungle Trek
Wilderness Explorers	*Feathered Friends in Flight*	*Festival of the Lion King*	Dinosaur	The Animation Experience at Conservation Station	*Feathered Friends in Flight*
Na'vi River Journey	*Finding Nemo: The Big Blue . . . and Beyond*	Gorilla Falls Exploration Trail	Kali River Rapids	Tree of Life/ Awakenings	Tree of Life/ Awakenings
Gorilla Falls Exploration Trail	Wilderness Explorers	Maharajah Jungle Trek	Maharajah Jungle Trek	*Winged Encounters— The Kingdom Takes Flight*	Na'vi River Journey
Kali River Rapids	Meet Favorite Disney Pals at Adventurers Outpost	*Finding Nemo: The Big Blue . . . and Beyond*	*Finding Nemo: The Big Blue . . . and Beyond*	Various live entertainment acts	*It's Tough to Be a Bug*

Regarding Individual Lightning Lane, we think Flight of Passage is worth the cost. As for Genie+, it only seems to be useful at a handful of attractions, most notably Na'vi River Journey and Kilimanjaro Safaris. These two should be your priorities.

ANIMAL KINGDOM ATTRACTIONS THAT BENEFIT MOST FROM GENIE+ AND INDIVIDUAL LIGHTNING LANE (ILL)
(Highest Priority to Lowest)

ATTRACTION	AVERAGE TIME IN LINE SAVED (IN MINUTES)
Avatar Flight of Passage (*ILL*)	92
Kilimanjaro Safaris	47
Na'vi River journey	46
Kali River Rapids	41 (summer)
Expedition Everest	33
Meet Favorite Disney Pals at Adventurers Outpost	17
Dinosaur	15

Note: We haven't observed any time savings using Genie+ at the Animal Kingdom's live shows, *It's Tough to Be a Bug!*, or The Animation Experience at Conservation Station.

When Do Genie+ and Individual Lightning Lane Reservations Run Out in Animal Kingdom?

The table below shows the approximate time at which Animal Kingdom's attractions run out of Genie+ or Individual Lightning Lane capacity, by crowd level. Use this table in conjunction with the "Which Attractions Benefit Most" table, on the previous page, to determine which reservations to get first.

WHEN GENIE+ AND INDIVIDUAL LIGHTNING LANE (ILL) RESERVATIONS RUN OUT BY ATTENDANCE LEVEL			
ATTRACTION	**LOW ATTENDANCE**	**MODERATE ATTENDANCE**	**HIGH ATTENDANCE**
The Animation Experience at Conservation Station	Available	Available	Available
Avatar Flight of Passage (*ILL*)	2 p.m.	10 a.m.	8 a.m.
Festival of the Lion King	Available	Available	Available
Dinosaur	7–8 p.m.	7–8 p.m.	6 p.m.
Expedition Everest	7 p.m.	7 p.m.	7 p.m.
Feathered Friends in Flight	Available	Available	Available
It's Tough to Be a Bug!	Available	Available	Available
Kali River Rapids	7–8 p.m.	7–8 p.m.	7–8 p.m.
Kilimanjaro Safaris	4 p.m.	4 p.m.	1–2 p.m.
Na'vi River Journey	6 p.m.	5 p.m.	2 p.m.

AVAILABLE Attractions rarely run out of reservations at this crowd level.
LOW ATTENDANCE Crowd levels 1–3 on the TouringPlans crowd calendar
MODERATE ATTENDANCE Crowd levels 4–7
HIGH ATTENDANCE Crowd levels 8–10

Attractions closed for more than two years are not shown.

How Can You Avoid Paying for Individual Lightning Lane?

Animal Kingdom doesn't participate in Disney's Extended Evening Theme Park Hours program, so your best option to see Flight of Passage is to stay at a Disney resort and use Early Theme Park Entry: Head to Flight of Passage as soon as the park opens.

How Do Genie+ and Individual Lightning Lane Work with the Touring Plans?

See our advice for the Magic Kingdom on pages 468–469.

DINING IN ANIMAL KINGDOM

ON THE OPPOSITE PAGE IS A QUICK RECAP of Animal Kingdom's top restaurants, rated by readers, starting with the highest rated. See Part 6 for details.

The OASIS

THOUGH THE FUNCTIONAL PURPOSE of The Oasis is the same as that of Main Street, U.S.A., in the Magic Kingdom—that is, to direct guests to the center of the park—it also serves as what Disney

ANIMAL KINGDOM RESTAURANT REFRESHER

COUNTER SERVICE	FULL SERVICE
Satu'li Canteen (● 96%/Exceptional), Pandora	Yak & Yeti Restaurant (● 94%/Much Above Average), Asia
Creature Comforts (Starbucks) (● 96%/Exceptional), Discovery island	Tiffins (● 91%/Above Average), Discovery Island
Flame Tree Barbecue (● 95%/Exceptional), Discovery Island	Tusker House Restaurant (● 89%/Average), Africa
Harambe Market (● 94%/Much Above Average), Africa	
Royal Anandapur Tea Company (● 92%/Much Above Average), Asia	
Kusafiri Coffee Shop and Bakery (● 92%/Above Average), Africa	
Yak & Yeti Local Food Cafes (● 91%/Above Average), Asia	

Restaurants not shown are rated as below average.

calls a transitional experience. In plain English, this means that it sets the stage and gets you in the right mood for enjoying Disney's Animal Kingdom. The minute you pass through the turnstiles, however, you'll know that this isn't just another central hub.

Rather than consisting of a single broad thoroughfare, The Oasis encompasses multiple paths. Whereas Main Street, Hollywood Boulevard at the Studios, and the Future World entrance plaza in Epcot direct you like an arrow straight into the heart of their respective parks, The Oasis immediately envelops you in an environment replete with choices. Nothing obvious clues you in to where you're going. Instead, you'll find a lush, green, canopied landscape dotted with streams, grottoes, and waterfalls.

The zoological exhibits in The Oasis are representative of those throughout Animal Kingdom. A sign identifies the animal(s) in each exhibit, but be aware that there's no guarantee they'll be immediately visible. Because most of the habitats are large and provide their occupants ample terrain in which to hide, you must linger and concentrate, looking for small movements in the vegetation. When you do spot the animal, you may make out only a shadowy figure, or perhaps only a leg or a tail.

The Oasis is a place to savor and appreciate—if you're used to blitzing at warp speed to queue up for the big attractions, plan to spend some time here, on your way in or out of the park. The Oasis usually closes 30–60 minutes after the rest of Animal Kingdom.

DISCOVERY ISLAND

DISCOVERY ISLAND COMBINES TROPICAL GREENERY with whimsical equatorial African architecture. Connected to the other lands by bridges, the island is the hub from which guests can access the park's various themed areas. A village is arrayed in a crescent around the base of Animal Kingdom's iconic landmark, the **Tree of Life.** Towering 14 stories above the village, it's this park's version of Cinderella Castle or Spaceship Earth. Flanked by pools, meadows, and exotic gardens populated by a diversity of birds and animals, the Tree of Life houses a theater attraction inspired by Disney/Pixar's *A Bug's Life.*

As you enter Discovery Island over the bridge from The Oasis and the park entrance, you'll see the Tree of Life directly ahead, at 12 o'clock. The bridge to **Asia** is to the right at 2 o'clock, with the bridge to **DinoLand U.S.A.** at roughly 4 o'clock. The bridge connecting The Oasis to Discovery Island is at 6 o'clock, the bridge to **Pandora—The World of Avatar** is at 8 o'clock, and the bridge to **Africa** is at 11 o'clock.

Discovery Island is also the park's central headquarters for shopping and services. Here you'll find the **First Aid** and **Baby Care Centers.** For Disney merchandise, try **Island Mercantile.** Counter-service food and snacks are available, as is upscale full-service dining at **Tiffins.**

KEY TO ABBREVIATIONS In the attraction profiles that follow, each star rating is accompanied by a category label in parentheses (see page 464). E means **Exceptional,** MAA means **Much Above Average,** AA means **Above Average,** A means **Average,** BA means **Below Average,** and MBA means **Much Below Average.**

Discovery Island Trails

PRESCHOOL ★★★★ (A)	GRADE SCHOOL ★★★★ (A)	TEENS ★★★★ (B)
YOUNG ADULTS ★★★★ (A)	OVER 30 ★★★★ (A)	SENIORS ★★★★ (A)

What it is Scenic walking trails. **Scope and scale** Diversion. **When to go** Anytime. **ECV/wheelchair access** May remain in wheelchair. **Participates in Genie+** No. **Early Theme Park Entry** Yes. **Extended Evening Hours** No.

DESCRIPTION AND COMMENTS Winding behind the Tree of Life, a network of walking trails offers around a dozen animal-viewing opportunities, from otters and tortoises to lemurs, storks, and porcupines. One end of the path begins just before the bridge from Discovery Island to Africa, on the right side of the walkway; the other is to the right of the entrance to the Tree of Life. In addition to the animals, you'll find verdant landscaping, waterfalls, and quiet spots to sit and reflect on your relationship with nature. Or nap. As we think Henry David Thoreau once said, "Not until we have dozed do we begin to understand ourselves."

Meet Favorite Disney Pals at Adventurers Outpost ★★★½

PRESCHOOL ★★★★★ (E)	GRADE SCHOOL ★★★★½ (AA)	TEENS ★★★★ (A)
YOUNG ADULTS ★★★★ (A)	OVER 30 ★★★★ (AA)	SENIORS ★★★★½ (AA)

What it is Character-greeting venue. **Scope and scale** Minor attraction. **When to go** First thing in the morning or after 5 p.m. **Duration of experience** About 2 minutes. **Probable waiting time** About 20 minutes. **Queue speed** Fast. **ECV/wheelchair access** May remain in wheelchair. **Participates in Genie+** Yes. **Early Theme Park Entry** No. **Extended Evening Hours** No.

DESCRIPTION AND COMMENTS An indoor, air-conditioned greeting location for Mickey and Minnie, Adventurers Outpost is decorated with photos and other memorabilia from the Mouses' world travels.

TOURING TIPS The Outpost has two greeting rooms with two identical sets of characters, so lines move fairly quickly.

Tree of Life ★★★★½ / It's Tough to Be a Bug! ★★★ / Awakenings ★★★★

It's Tough to Be a Bug!

PRESCHOOL ★★★ (MBA)　GRADE SCHOOL ★★★½ (MBA)　TEENS ★★★½ (MBA)
YOUNG ADULTS ★★★½ (MBA)　OVER 30 ★★★½ (MBA)　SENIORS ★★★★ (BA)

Awakenings

PRESCHOOL ★★★★ (A)　GRADE SCHOOL ★★★★ (A)　TEENS ★★★★ (A)
YOUNG ADULTS ★★★★ (A)　OVER 30 ★★★★½ (A)　SENIORS ★★★★½ (AA)

What it is 3-D theater show (*It's Tough to Be a Bug!*)/nighttime projection show (*Awakenings*). **Scope and scale** Major attraction. **When to go** Anytime. **Comment** The theater is inside the tree. **Duration of presentation** About 8 minutes (*It's Tough to Be a Bug!*)/3 minutes (*Awakenings*). **Probable waiting time** Under 20 minutes. **ECV/wheelchair access** May remain in wheelchair. **Participates in Genie+** Yes (*It's Tough to Be a Bug!*)/no (*Awakenings*). **Early Theme Park Entry** Yes. **Extended Evening Hours** No.

DESCRIPTION AND COMMENTS The Tree of Life, apart from its size, is a work of art—the most visually compelling structure in any Disney theme park. Although it's magnificent from afar, it's not until you get up close that you can truly appreciate the tree's rich detail. What appears from a distance to be ancient, gnarled bark is, in fact, hundreds of carvings depicting all manner of wildlife, each integrated seamlessly into the trunk, roots, and limbs of the tree. Look for these carvings on the front left side of the tree, along the Discovery Island walkway to Africa.

In sharp contrast to the grandeur of the tree is the subject of the attraction housed within its trunk. Called ***It's Tough to Be a Bug!***, this humorous, intense 3-D presentation is about the difficulties of being small and creepy-crawly. The show is similar to *Mickey's PhilharMagic* in the Magic Kingdom in that it combines a 3-D film with an arsenal of tactile and visual special effects. But where *Mickey's PhilharMagic* stars familiar Disney characters in zany situations, *It's Tough to Be a Bug!* can do a number on anybody, young or old, who's squeamish about insects. A mom of two from Williamsville, New York, shared this experience:

It's Tough to Be a Bug! was my girls' first Disney experience, and almost their last. The story line was difficult to follow—all they were aware of was the torture of sitting in a darkened theater being overrun with bugs. A constant stream of parents headed to the exits with terrorized children. Those who were left behind were screaming and crying as well. The 11-year-old refused to talk for 20 minutes after the fiasco, and the 3½-year-old wanted to go home. Not back to the hotel, but **home.**

From a Louisville, Kentucky, reader:

My 12-year-old son and I laughed at the comments from concerned parents about It's Tough to Be a Bug!, *so we thought it would be fun to [go to the show to] watch families leave early with crying kids. Our particular show didn't disappoint, even in ways beyond my expectation—as the show progressed, my son became eerily quiet. In fact, only a matter of time later, I found him hunkered under his seat after he saw and "felt" the bugs coming at him. Needless to say, he was a good sport, and we were able to put it behind him after spending several hours with the on-site child psychologist. (Just kidding!)*

The Tree of Life also hosts **Awakenings,** a child-friendly nighttime show projected onto the tree's trunk and canopy. Shown several times a night (when the park is open late), *Awakenings* combines digital video projections with music and special effects. Several shows have been created; in each, special projection effects make it appear that some animals carved into the tree trunk have come alive. Other special effects happen in the leaves and branches. We rate *Awakenings* as not to be missed.

TOURING TIPS *It's Tough to Be a Bug!* is rarely crowded even on the busiest days. Go in the morning after the Pandora attractions, Kilimanjaro Safaris, Kali River Rapids, Expedition Everest, and Dinosaur. If you miss it in the morning, try again late afternoon (or skip it for a nap—every age group rates it as below average). The best viewing spots for *Awakenings* are directly in front of the tree on Discovery Island, across from Island Mercantile.

Wilderness Explorers ★★★★

PRESCHOOL ★★★★½ (A)	**GRADE SCHOOL ★★★★½ (AA)**	**TEENS ★★★½ (BA)**
YOUNG ADULTS ★★★½ (A)	**OVER 30 ★★★★ (BA)**	**SENIORS ★★★★ (BA)**

What it is Parkwide scavenger hunt and puzzle-solving adventure game. **Scope and scale** Diversion. **When to go** Sign up first thing in the morning and complete activities throughout the day. **Comment** Collecting more than 25 badges takes 3–5 hours, which can be done over several days. **ECV/wheelchair access** May remain in wheelchair. **Participates in Genie+** No. **Early Theme Park Entry** No. **Extended Evening Hours** No.

DESCRIPTION AND COMMENTS Walt Disney World offers several interactive games in its theme parks, and Wilderness Explorers is the best of the bunch—a scavenger hunt based on Russell's Scout-like troop from the movie *Up.* Players earn "badges" (stickers given out by cast members) for completing predefined activities throughout the park. For example, to earn the Gorilla Badge, you walk the Gorilla Falls Exploration Trail to observe how the primates behave, then mimic that behavior back to a cast member to show what you've seen.

Sign up near the bridge from The Oasis to Discovery Island. You'll be given an instruction book and a map showing the park location for each badge to be earned.

Cast members have been specially trained for this game and can tailor the activities based on the age of the child playing: Small children might get an explanation about what deforestation means, for example, while older kids may have to figure out why tigers have stripes. It's tons of fun for kids and adults, and we play it often when we're in the park.

The Wilderness Explorers program is a big hit with kids, as a Melbourne, Australia, mom relates:

Wilderness Explorers was the highlight of my son's day. Much time is spent collecting badges, but it is well worth the investment of time!

TOURING TIPS Activities are spread throughout the park, including areas to which many guests never venture. You have to ride specific attractions to earn certain badges, so visiting those at our suggested times will save time.

■ AFRICA

THE LARGEST OF ANIMAL KINGDOM'S LANDS, Africa is entered through **Harambe,** a Disneyfied take on a modern rural African town. A market is equipped with modern cash registers, and dining options consist of a sit-down buffet, a few counter-service options, and snack stands. What distinguishes Harambe is its understatement: It's most definitely (and realistically) *not* hyperstylized. The buildings, while interesting, are architecturally simple. Though better maintained and more idealized than the real McCoy, Disney's Harambe would be a lot more at home in Kenya than the Magic Kingdom's Main Street would be in Missouri.

Harambe serves as the gateway to Animal Kingdom's largest and most ambitious zoological exhibit: the African veldt habitat. Guests access the veldt via the **Kilimanjaro Safaris** attraction, at the end of Harambe's main drag near the fat-trunked baobab tree. Harambe is also the departure point for the train to **Rafiki's Planet Watch** and **Conservation Station** (the park's veterinary headquarters), as well as the home of *Festival of the Lion King,* a long-running live show performed in its own theater. A walkway by the theater connects Africa with Pandora.

Festival of the Lion King ★★★★

PRESCHOOL ★★★½ (MAA)   GRADE SCHOOL ★★★★½ (MAA)   TEENS ★★★★ (AA)
YOUNG ADULTS ★★★★½ (MAA)   OVER 30 ★★★★½ (MAA)   SENIORS ★★★★½ (MAA)

What it is Theater-in-the-round stage show. **Scope and scale** Major attraction. **When to go** Before 11 a.m. or after 4 p.m. Check your park map or *Times Guide* for showtimes. **Duration of presentation** 30 minutes. **Preshow entertainment** None. **When to arrive** 20-30 minutes before showtime. **ECV/wheelchair access** May remain in wheelchair. **Participates in Genie+** Yes. **Early Theme Park Entry** No. **Extended Evening Hours** No.

DESCRIPTION AND COMMENTS Inspired by the Disney animated feature, *Festival of the Lion King* is part stage show and part parade; the theater is behind and to the left of Tusker House Restaurant. Guests sit in four sets of bleachers surrounding the stage and organized into cheering sections, which are called on to make elephant, warthog, giraffe, and lion noises. (You won't be alone if you don't know what a giraffe or warthog sounds like.) There's a great deal of strutting around and a lot of singing and dancing. By our count, every tune from *The Lion King* is belted out—some more than once. If you didn't know the words to the songs before the show, you definitely will after.

Some readers think *Lion King*'s sound system could be turned down a bit, as this reader from Yardville, New Jersey says:

The acoustics at Festival of the Lion King *were terrible to the point where you could not understand what the singers were saying.*

Unofficial Guide readers are almost unanimous in their praise of *Festival of the Lion King.* This letter from a Naples, Florida, mom is typical:

Festival of the Lion King *was the best thing we experienced at Animal Kingdom. The singers, dancers, fire twirlers, acrobats, and sets were spectacular.*

TOURING TIPS *Festival of the Lion King* is a big draw, so try to see the first show in the morning or one of the last two shows at night. For midday performances, you'll need to queue up at least 20–30 minutes before showtime; to minimize waiting in the hot sun, don't hop in line until cast members give the word. The bleachers can make viewing difficult for shorter folks—if you have small children or short adults in your party, snag a seat higher up. Despite its popularity, using Genie+ here doesn't save much time.

Gorilla Falls Exploration Trail ★★★★

| PRESCHOOL ★★★★ (A) | GRADE SCHOOL ★★★★ (A) | TEENS ★★★★ (A) |
| YOUNG ADULTS ★★★★½ (AA) | OVER 30 ★★★★ (A) | SENIORS ★★★★½ (AA) |

What it is Walk-through zoological exhibit. **Scope and scale** Major attraction. **When to go** Before or after Kilimanjaro Safaris. Also check the *Times Guide* for early off-season closures. **Duration of tour** About 20–25 minutes. **ECV/wheelchair access** May remain in wheelchair. **Participates in Genie+** No. **Early Theme Park Entry** No. **Extended Evening Hours** No.

DESCRIPTION AND COMMENTS As the trail winds between the domain of two troops of lowland gorillas, it's hard to see what, if anything, separates you from the primates. Also on the trail is a hippo pool with an underwater viewing area, plus a naked-mole-rat exhibit. A highlight is an exotic-bird aviary so craftily designed that you can barely tell you're in an enclosure.

TOURING TIPS The Gorilla Falls Exploration Trail is lush, beautiful, and filled with people much of the time. Guests exiting Kilimanjaro Safaris can choose between returning to Harambe or walking the Gorilla Falls Exploration Trail. Many opt for the trail. Thus, when the Safaris are operating at full tilt, it spews hundreds of guests every couple of minutes onto the Exploration Trail.

The trail's hours are cut during fall and winter, closing as early as 4:30 p.m. Check the *Times Guide* for the schedule.

Kilimanjaro Safaris ★★★★★

| PRESCHOOL ★★★★½ (MAA) | GRADE SCHOOL ★★★★½ (MAA) | TEENS ★★★★½ (MAA) |
| YOUNG ADULTS ★★★★½ (MAA) | OVER 30 ★★★★½ (MAA) | SENIORS ★★★★★ (E) |

What it is Simulated ride through an African wildlife reservation. **Scope and scale** Super-headliner. **When to go** As soon as the park opens or after 3 p.m. **Duration of ride** About 20 minutes. **Average wait in line per 100 people ahead of you** 4 minutes; assumes full-capacity operation with 18-second dispatch interval. **Loading speed** Fast. **ECV/wheelchair access** Must transfer from ECV to provided wheelchair. **Participates in Genie+** Yes. **Early Theme Park Entry** No. **Extended Evening Hours** No.

DESCRIPTION AND COMMENTS As Animal Kingdom's premier zoological attraction, Kilimanjaro Safaris offers an exceptionally realistic, albeit brief, imitation of an actual African photo safari. Thirty-two guests at a time board tall, open vehicles and are dispatched into a simulated African veldt habitat. Animals such as zebras, wildebeests, impalas, Thomson's gazelles, giraffes, and even rhinos roam apparently free, while predators such as lions, as well as potentially dangerous large animals like hippos, are separated from both prey and guests by all-but-invisible, natural-appearing barriers. Although the animals have more than 100 acres of savanna, woodland, streams, and rocky hills to call home, careful placement of watering holes, forage, and salt licks ensures that the critters are hanging out by the road when safari vehicles roll by.

Having traveled in Kenya and Tanzania, I (Bob) can tell you that Disney has done an amazing job of replicating the sub-Saharan East African landscape. As on a real African safari, what animals you see, and how many, is pretty much a matter of luck. We've experienced Kilimanjaro Safaris more than 100 times and had a different experience on each trip.

Before the pandemic, Animal Kingdom offered a **nighttime version** of Kilimanjaro Safaris. We think it's a long shot to return. If it's offered, do it after you've experienced the daytime version.

TOURING TIPS Kilimanjaro Safaris is one of Animal Kingdom's busiest attractions, along with Expedition Everest and the two Pandora attractions. From a touring standpoint, this is a good thing: By distributing guests evenly throughout the park, those other attractions make it unnecessary to run to Kilimanjaro Safaris first thing in the morning. Waits for Kilimanjaro Safaris diminish around midafternoon, sometimes as early as 3 p.m. but more commonly somewhat later.

If you want to take photos, note that the vehicle isn't guaranteed to stop at a given location. Drivers try their best to accommodate guests and stop when big animals come into view, but be prepared to snap at any time. As for the ride, it's not that rough.

RAFIKI'S PLANET WATCH

NOT A TRUE "LAND" in scope or scale, this section of Animal Kingdom—named for a beloved character from *The Lion King*—consists of **Conservation Station** (the animal-care center), the petting zoo, and environmental exhibits, all accessible from Harambe via the **Wildlife Express Train.** Rafiki's Planet Watch may operate seasonally.

The Animation Experience at Conservation Station   ★★★

PRESCHOOL, GRADE SCHOOL, TEENS, AND YOUNG ADULTS Not enough surveys to rate
OVER 30 ★★★★½ (MAA)   **SENIORS** ★★★★½ (MAA)

What it is Character-drawing class. **Scope and scale** Minor attraction. **When to go** Check *Times Guide* for hours. **Comments** Accessible only by the Wildlife Express Train. Fun but out of place in this theme park. **Participates in Genie+** Yes. **Early Theme Park Entry** No. **Extended Evening Hours** No.

DESCRIPTION AND COMMENTS This experience provides insight into the history of Disney animation and gives participants of any skill level a chance to draw Disney characters with the help of an instructor, using real-life animals as inspiration.

TOURING TIPS The Animation Experience is in a remote section of the park, so crowds shouldn't be large during the early and late part of the day. Only use Genie+ here if you're out of other things to use it on. Board the Wildlife Express Train 40 minutes prior to the experience start time.

Conservation Station and Affection Section   ★★★

PRESCHOOL Not enough surveys to rate   **GRADE SCHOOL** ★★★★ (A)   **TEENS** ★★★ (MBA)
YOUNG ADULTS ★★★ (MBA)   **OVER 30** ★★★½ (BA)   **SENIORS** ★★★½ (BA)

What it is Behind-the-scenes educational exhibit and petting zoo. **Scope and scale** Minor attraction. **When to go** Anytime. **Comments** Opens later and closes earlier than the rest of the park. Check *Times Guide* for hours. Accessible only by the Wildlife Express Train. **Probable waiting time** None. **ECV/wheelchair access** May remain in wheelchair. **Participates in Genie+** No. **Early Theme Park Entry** No. **Extended Evening Hours** No.

DESCRIPTION AND COMMENTS Conservation Station is Animal Kingdom's veterinary and conservation headquarters. Here guests can meet wildlife experts, learn about the behind-the-scenes operations of the park, and observe ongoing projects. Conservation Station also serves as a rehabilitation center for injured animals and a nursery for recently born (or hatched) critters.

While there are several permanent exhibits, including Affection Section (an animal-petting area), what you see at Conservation Station will largely depend on what's going on when you arrive. On most days when we've visited, there isn't enough happening to justify waiting in line twice (coming and going) for the train.

Most of our readers agree that Conservation Station isn't worth the hassle. A Tinley Park, Illinois, mom writes:

Skip Conservation Station. Between the train ride to get to it and being there, we wasted a precious 1½ hours!

A Denver family had a better experience:

We really enjoyed Conservation Station. We saw a 13-foot python eating a rat!

And a reader from Kent, England, was amused by both the goings-on and the other guests:

The most memorable part of Animal Kingdom for me was watching a veterinary surgeon and his team at Conservation Station perform an operation on a rat snake that had inadvertently swallowed a golf ball, presumably believing it to be an egg! This operation caused at least one onlooker to pass out.

TOURING TIPS Because Conservation Station is so removed from the rest of the park, you won't see it unless you take the train. Conservation Station typically opens 90 minutes after the rest of the park and closes an hour or more earlier.

Wildlife Express Train ★★

PRESCHOOL ★★★★ (A)	**GRADE SCHOOL** ★★★½ (BA)	**TEENS** ★★★ (MBA)
YOUNG ADULTS ★★★½ (MBA)	**OVER 30** ★★★½ (MBA)	**SENIORS** ★★★★ (BA)

What it is Scenic railroad ride to Rafiki's Planet Watch and Conservation Station. **Scope and scale** Minor attraction. **When to go** Anytime. **Comments** Opens 90 minutes after rest of park; last train departs at 4:30 p.m. **Duration of ride** About 7 minutes one-way. **Average wait in line per 100 people ahead of you** 9 minutes. **Loading speed** Moderate. **ECV/wheelchair access** May remain in wheelchair. **Participates in Genie+** No. **Early Theme Park Entry** No. **Extended Evening Hours** No.

DESCRIPTION AND COMMENTS This ride snakes behind the African wildlife reserve as it makes its loop connecting Harambe to Rafiki's Planet Watch and Conservation Station. En route, you see the nighttime enclosures for the animals that populate Kilimanjaro Safaris. Similarly, returning to Harambe, you see the backstage areas of Asia. Regardless of which direction you're heading, the sights aren't especially stimulating.

TOURING TIPS Most guests who head to Conservation Station do so after experiencing Kilimanjaro Safaris and the Gorilla Falls Exploration Trail. Thus, the train begins to get crowded between 10 and 11 a.m.

ASIA

CROSSING THE BRIDGE from Discovery Island, you enter Asia through the village of **Anandapur,** a veritable collage of themes inspired by the architecture and ruins of India, Indonesia, Nepal, and Thailand. Situated near the bank of the Discovery River and surrounded by lush vegetation, Anandapur provides access to a gibbon exhibit and Asia's two feature attractions: the **Kali River Rapids** raft ride and **Expedition Everest.**

Expedition Everest—yep, a mountain and, at 200 feet, the tallest in Florida—is a super-headliner roller coaster. You board an old mountain railway destined for the base camp of Mount Everest and end up racing both forward and backward through caverns and frigid canyons en route to paying a social call on none other than the Abominable Snowman.

Expedition Everest ★★★★½

PRESCHOOL ★★½ (MBA)   GRADE SCHOOL ★★★★½ (MAA)   TEENS ★★★★★ (E)
YOUNG ADULTS ★★★★★ (E)   OVER 30 ★★★★½ (MAA)   SENIORS ★★★★½ (AA)

What it is High-speed outdoor roller coaster through Nepalese mountain village. **Scope and scale** Super-headliner. **When to go** First or last hour the park is open. **Comments** Must be 44" to ride; Rider Switch option provided (see page 396); has single-rider line. **Duration of ride** 4 minutes. **Average wait in line per 100 people ahead of you** 4 minutes; assumes 2 tracks operating. **Loading speed** Moderate-fast. **ECV/wheelchair access** Must transfer to the ride vehicle. **Participates in Genie+** Yes. **Early Theme Park Entry** Yes. **Extended Evening Hours** No.

Motion Sickness

DESCRIPTION AND COMMENTS Expedition Everest is the only true roller coaster in Animal Kingdom. Your journey begins in an elaborate waiting area modeled after a Nepalese village; then you board an old train headed for the base camp of Mount Everest. Notes from previous expeditions are posted throughout the waiting area, some with cryptic observations regarding a mysterious creature said to guard the mountain. These ominous signs are ignored (as if you have a choice!), resulting in a high-speed encounter with the Abominable Snowman himself.

The ride consists of tight turns (some while traveling backward), hills, and dips but no loops or inversions. From your departure at the loading station through your first high-speed descent, you'll see some of the most spectacular panoramas in Walt Disney World: On a clear day, you can see Coronado Springs Resort, EPCOT's Spaceship Earth, and possibly downtown Orlando. But look quickly because you're immediately propelled, projectile-like, through the inner and outer reaches of the mountain. The final drop and last few turns are among Disney's very best coaster effects.

Disney bills Expedition Everest as a "family thrill ride"—more akin to Big Thunder Mountain Railroad than Rock 'n' Roller Coaster—but it's an exciting experience nonetheless, and as is typical of a super-headliner attraction, it generates lots of reader comments. A Seattle family of four gives Expedition Everest a thumbs-up:

Expedition Everest is tremendous. It has enough surprises and runaway speed to make it one of the more enjoyable thrill rides in the whole Orlando area.

A Macon, Georgia, teen successfully recruited Grandma to ride:

Expedition Everest was so smooooth! I went right out and brought my granny back to ride it. She didn't throw up or anything!

TOURING TIPS Everest averages over an hour of downtime per day, so check before walking over just to ride it. A touring strategy that doesn't require much backtracking is to start with Dinosaur, then see Expedition Everest and Kali River Rapids as part of a counterclockwise tour of the park.

Expedition Everest reaches a top speed of around 50 mph, about twice that of Space Mountain, so expect to see the usual safety warnings for health. Ask to be seated up front—the first few rows offer the best front-seat experience of any Disney coaster, indoor or outdoor. Also, note the animal poop on display in the Lightning Lane if you use it—a deliberate attempt at verisimilitude, or did Disney run out of money for ride props and use whatever they could find?

Feathered Friends in Flight ★★★★

What it is Stadium show about birds. **Scope and scale** Major attraction. **When to go** Anytime. **Special comment** Performance times listed in park map and *Times Guide*. **Duration of presentation** 30 minutes. **Preshow entertainment** None. **When to arrive** 10–15 minutes before showtime. **ECV/wheelchair access** May remain in wheelchair. **Participates in Genie+** Yes. **Early Theme Park Entry** No. **Extended Evening Hours** No.

DESCRIPTION AND COMMENTS Asia's theater has presented a show featuring live birds for years. *Feathered Friends in Flight* is the best, and highest-rated, version ever. The show's hosts are some of Disney's animal trainers, who explain different bird species' habitats and characteristics. A number of species are represented, with plenty more flying overhead. The show is fast-paced, informative, and entertaining for everyone. In many ways the show is a model of how other shows in the park might work. We rate it as not to be missed.

Like its predecessor, *Feathered Friends* focuses on the birds' natural talents and characteristics, which far surpass any tricks they might have learned from humans—don't expect parrots riding bikes or cockatoos playing tiny pianos. A reader from Brattleboro, Vermont, found the birds extremely compelling:

The birds are thrilling, and we especially appreciated the fact that their antics were not the results of training against the grain but actual survival techniques that the birds use in the wild.

TOURING TIPS *Feathered Friends* plays at the stadium near the bridge on the walkway into Asia. Though the stadium is covered, it's not air-conditioned; therefore, early-morning and late-afternoon performances are more comfortable. To play it safe, arrive at the stadium about 10–15 minutes before showtime.

Kali River Rapids ★★★½

PRESCHOOL ★★★★ (A)	GRADE SCHOOL ★★★★½ (MAA)	TEENS ★★★★ (AA)
YOUNG ADULTS ★★★★ (A)	OVER 30 ★★★★ (A)	SENIORS ★★★★ (BA)

What it is Whitewater raft ride. **Scope and scale** Headliner. **When to go** Before 11 a.m. or the last hour the park is open. **Comments** You're likely to get wet; may open 30 minutes after the rest of the park and close early on off-peak or cold days; must be 38" to ride; Rider Switch option provided (see page 396). **Duration of ride** About 5 minutes. **Average wait in line per 100 people ahead of you** 5 minutes. **Loading speed** Moderate. **ECV/wheelchair access** Must transfer to the ride vehicle; transfer device available. **Participates in Genie+** Yes. **Early Theme Park Entry** No. **Extended Evening Hours** No.

Wet

DESCRIPTION AND COMMENTS Kali River Rapids is an unguided trip in a circular rubber raft down an artificial river; each raft has a top-mounted platform that seats 12 people. The raft essentially floats free in the current and is washed downstream through rapids and waves. Because the "river" is fairly wide, with various currents, eddies, and obstacles, each trip is different and exciting.

What distinguishes Kali River Rapids from other theme park raft rides is Disney's trademark attention to visual detail. Whereas some raft rides are just an unadorned plunge down a concrete ditch, Kali River Rapids flows through a dense rainforest and past waterfalls, temple ruins, and bamboo thickets, emerging into a cleared area where greedy loggers have ravaged the forest, and finally drifting back under the tropical canopy as the river cycles back to Anandapur. Along the way, your raft runs a gauntlet of raging cataracts, logjams, and other dangers.

The queuing area, which winds through an ancient Southeast Asian temple, is one of the most striking and visually interesting settings of any Disney attraction; the sights on the raft trip itself are also first-class.

That said, Kali River Rapids is marginal in two important respects: First, you get only about 3½ minutes on the water, and second . . . well, it's a weenie ride. Sure, you get wet, but the drops and rapids aren't all that exciting, as this Kansas family points out:

It was boiling hot, so we were happy about the prospect of being drenched. At the end, we all looked at each other and said, "Is that IT?" We couldn't believe we'd stood in line, sweating half to death, for 75 minutes just for that.

TOURING TIPS Kali River Rapids is hugely popular on hot summer days. Ride before 11 a.m. or during the last hour the park is open.

Disney has toned down the amount of water splashed at you during the ride. While you won't get totally soaked, you'll still get pretty wet; therefore, we recommend wearing shorts and sport sandals (such as Tevas) to the park, as well as bringing along a jumbo trash bag *plus* a smaller plastic bag. Before you board, punch a hole in the big bag for your head. *Note:* You'll stay drier if you don't cut holes for your arms; the downside is that it'll make fastening your seat belt awkward, so it's your call. If you're wearing closed shoes and socks, take them off, put your shoes back on minus the socks, and then wrap the smaller bag around your shoes. If you're worried about mussing your coiffure, bring a third bag for your head.

A Shaker Heights, Ohio, family who donned our *couture de garbage* discovered that staying dry on Kali River Rapids is not without its social costs:

Cast members and the other people in our raft looked at us like we'd just beamed down from Mars. (One cast member asked if we needed wet suits and snorkels.) Plus, we didn't cut arm holes in our trash bags because we thought we'd stay drier that way—once we sat down, though, we couldn't fasten our seat belts. After a lot of wiggling and adjusting and helping each other, we finally got belted in, and off we went, looking like sacks of fertilizer with heads poking out. Very embarrassing, but we stayed nice and dry.

A family from Humble, Texas, who rode early in the morning on a cool day, shares this:

We didn't read your precautions for Kali River Rapids until after we rode. The 6-year-old and Mom were COMPLETELY drenched—so much so that we had to leave the park and go back to our room at Port Orleans to change clothes. Since the temperature was around 60 degrees that morning, we were pretty miserable by the time we got back to our room. Needless to say, our schedule was shot by then.

Riding later in the day would have been a better option in this case.

Kali River Rapids offers free 2-hour locker rentals to the left of the attraction entrance, near the restrooms. Store a change of dry clothes here or, alternatively, wear as little as the law and Disney will allow. If you're wearing closed shoes, prop up your feet above the bottom of the raft—slogging around in wet shoes is a surefire ticket to Blisterville.

Maharajah Jungle Trek ★★★★

PRESCHOOL ★★★★ (A)	**GRADE SCHOOL ★★★★ (A)**	**TEENS ★★★★ (A)**
YOUNG ADULTS ★★★★ (A)	**OVER 30 ★★★★ (A)**	**SENIORS ★★★★½ (A)**

What it is Walk-through zoological exhibit. **Scope and scale** Headliner. **When to go** Anytime it's open. **Comment** May open later and close earlier than rest of park. **Duration of tour** About 20–30 minutes. **ECV/wheelchair access** May remain in wheelchair. **Participates in Genie+** No. **Early Theme Park Entry** No. **Extended Evening Hours** No.

DESCRIPTION AND COMMENTS This walk is similar to the Gorilla Falls Exploration Trail (page 558) but with a Southeast Asian setting. Animals you might see range from Komodo dragons to Malayan flying foxes. Next is a cave with fruit bats. Ruins of the maharajah's palace provide the setting for Bengal tigers. From the top of a parapet in the palace you can view a herd of blackbuck antelope and Asian deer. The trek concludes with an aviary.

Labyrinthine, overgrown, and elaborately detailed, the ruins would be a compelling attraction even without the animals. Look for a plaster triptych just after the tiger exhibit that shows (right to left) a parable about man living in harmony with nature. Throw in a few bats, bucks, and Bengals, and you're in for a treat. Most readers, like this Washington, D.C., couple, agree:

The Maharajah Jungle Trek was absolutely amazing. We were able to see all the animals, which were awake by that time (9:30 a.m.), including the elusive tigers. The part of the trek with the birds was fabulous; you could spot hundreds, some of which were eating on the ground a mere 3 feet away from us.

TOURING TIPS The Maharajah Jungle Trek doesn't get as jammed up as the Gorilla Falls Exploration Trail and is a good choice for midday touring when most other attractions are crowded. The downside, of course, is that the exhibit showcases tigers, bats, and other creatures that might not be very active in the heat of the day. Finally, the Jungle Trek's operating hours may be shorter than the park's, especially during fall and winter, so check your *Times Guide* for the latest information.

DINOLAND U.S.A.

THIS MOST TYPICALLY DISNEY of Animal Kingdom's lands crosses an anthropological dig with a quirky roadside attraction. Accessible via the bridge from Discovery Island, DinoLand U.S.A. is home to a children's play area, a nature trail, a 1,500-seat amphitheater, and **Dinosaur,** one of Animal Kingdom's three thrill rides.

Also in DinoLand are a couple of natural-history exhibits, including **Dino-Sue,** an exact replica of the largest, most complete *Tyrannosaurus rex* skeleton discovered to date (the original, discovered in 1990, is displayed in Chicago). Named for fossil hunter Sue Hendrickson, the skeleton is 40 feet long and 13 feet tall. Dino-Sue doesn't dance, sing, or whistle, but she will get your attention nonetheless.

The Boneyard ★★★½

PRESCHOOL ★★★★½ (MAA)	GRADE SCHOOL ★★★★½ (MAA)	TEENS ★★½ (MBA)
YOUNG ADULTS ★★ (MBA)	OVER 30 ★★★ (MBA)	SENIORS ★★½ (MBA)

What it is Elaborate playground. **Scope and scale** Diversion. **When to go** Anytime. **Comment** Opens 1 hour after rest of park. **Duration of experience** Varies. **Probable waiting time** None. **ECV/wheelchair access** May remain in wheelchair. **Participates in Genie+** No. **Early Theme Park Entry** No. **Extended Evening Hours** No.

DESCRIPTION AND COMMENTS With an open-air "dig site" as its centerpiece, this elaborately themed playground appeals to kids age 10 and younger but is visually appealing to all ages. Decorated with dinosaur skeletons, the "dig site" is a sand pit where kids can scrounge for bones and fossils. There's also a ropes course, as well as slides, swings, climbing areas, and caves to play in.

TOURING TIPS Not the most pristine of Disney attractions, but certainly one where younger kids will want to spend some time. Aside from being dirty (or at least sandy), The Boneyard gets mighty hot in the Florida sun, so keep your kids well hydrated, and drag them into the shade from time to time. Try to save this until after you've experienced the main attractions.

Because The Boneyard is so close to the center of the park, it's easy to drop in whenever your kids get antsy. While the little ones clamber around on giant femurs and ribs, you can sip a tall cool one in the shade.

As a Michigan family attests, kids love The Boneyard:

The highlight for our kids was The Boneyard, especially the dig site. They just kept digging and digging to uncover the bones of the woolly mammoth.

Be aware, however, that The Boneyard rambles over about 0.5 acre and is has multiple stories, making it easy to lose sight of a small child. Fortunately, there's only one entrance and exit. A mother of two from Stillwater, Minnesota, found the playground too large for her liking:

If you're a parent who likes to have your eyes on your kids at all times, you won't like The Boneyard. Kids climb to the top of the slides; then you can't see them and you don't know what chute they'll be exiting from.

From the mother of a 3-year-old:

If your child is quite young, make sure you have two people in The Boneyard—one to help them up all the stairs, the other to stay at the bottom and watch them as they exit the slide. By the time you get from the top of the structure to the bottom, they're off who-knows-where getting into mischief of one kind or another without adult supervision.

Dinosaur ★★★★

PRESCHOOL ★★★ (MBA)	**GRADE SCHOOL ★★★★** (A)	**TEENS ★★★★** (A)
YOUNG ADULTS ★★★★ (A)	**OVER 30 ★★★★** (A)	**SENIORS ★★★½** (MBA)

What it is Motion-simulator dark ride. **Scope and scale** Headliner. **When to go** Before 10:30 a.m. or after 4 p.m. **Comment** Must be 40″ to ride; Rider Switch option provided (see page 396). **Duration of ride** 3½ minutes. **Average wait in line per 100 people ahead of you** 3 minutes; assumes full-capacity operation with 18-second dispatch interval. **Loading speed** Fast. **ECV/wheelchair access** Must transfer to the ride vehicle. **Participates in Genie+** Yes. **Early Theme Park Entry** Yes. **Extended Evening Hours** No.

DESCRIPTION AND COMMENTS Dinosaur is a combination track ride and motion simulator. In addition to moving along a cleverly hidden track, the ride vehicle also bucks and pitches (the simulator part) in sync with the visuals and special effects.

The plot has you traveling back in time on a mission of rescue and conservation. Your objective: to haul back a living dinosaur before the species becomes extinct. Whoever is operating the clock, however, cuts it a little close, and you arrive on the prehistoric scene just as a giant asteroid is hurtling toward Earth. General mayhem ensues as you evade carnivorous predators, catch Barney, and get out before the asteroid hits.

Dinosaur serves up nonstop action from beginning to end, with brilliant visual effects. Elaborate even by Disney standards, the tense, frenetic ride is embellished by the entire Imagineering arsenal of high-tech gimmickry.

A mother from Kansasville, Wisconsin, liked Dinosaur a lot:

Dinosaur is the best ride at WDW. Our group of 10, ranging in age from 65 (grandma) to 8 (grandson), immediately—and unanimously!—got back in line after finishing.

That said, the menacing dinosaurs, along with the overall intensity of the experience, make Dinosaur a no-go for younger kids, as this Michigan family discovered:

Our 7-year-old son withstood every ride Disney threw at him, from Space Mountain to Tower of Terror. Dinosaur, however, did him in. By the end, he was riding with his head down, scared to look around.

TOURING TIPS Disney situated Dinosaur in such a remote corner of the park that you have to poke around to find it. This, in conjunction with the overwhelming popularity of Pandora's rides, along with Kilimanjaro Safaris and Expedition Everest, makes Dinosaur the easiest headliner attraction at Walt Disney World to get on. Lines should be relatively light through midmorning. A decent strategy for avoiding backtracking and long waits is to start a counterclockwise tour of the park here, saving Pandora's attractions for last. Dinosaur averages around 45 minutes per day of downtime, however, so check that it's running before walking over.

Theater in the Wild / *Finding Nemo: The Big Blue . . . and Beyond!*

PRESCHOOL ★★★★½ (MAA)	**GRADE SCHOOL ★★★★½** (MAA)	**TEENS ★★★★** (AA)
YOUNG ADULTS ★★★★ (A)	**OVER 30 ★★★★½** (AA)	**SENIORS ★★★★** (A)

What it is Enclosed venue for live stage shows. **Scope and scale** Major attraction. **When to go** Anytime. **Comment** Check your park map or *Times Guide* for showtimes. **Duration of presentation** About 24 minutes. **When to arrive** 30 minutes before showtime. **ECV/wheelchair access** May remain in wheelchair. **Participates in Genie+** Yes. **Early Theme Park Entry** No. **Extended Evening Hours** No.

DESCRIPTION AND COMMENTS Along with *Festival of the Lion King, Finding Nemo* is arguably the most elaborate live show in any Disney World theme park. Incorporating dancing, special effects, and sophisticated digital backdrops of the undersea world, it features onstage human performers retelling Nemo's story with colorful, larger-than-life puppets. To be fair, *puppets* doesn't adequately convey the size or detail of these props, many of which are as big as a car and require two people to manipulate. The current show is a revamped, shorter version of the original's almost 35 minute run time.

TOURING TIPS To get a seat, show up 20–25 minutes in advance. Access to the theater is via a relatively narrow pedestrian path—if you arrive as the previous show is letting out, you'll feel like a salmon swimming upstream. Rarely a good use of Genie+.

TriceraTop Spin ★★

PRESCHOOL ★★★★½ (MAA)	**GRADE SCHOOL ★★★★** (BA)	**TEENS ★★★** (MBA)
YOUNG ADULTS ★★★ (MBA)	**OVER 30 ★★★** (MBA)	**SENIORS ★★★** (MBA)

What it is Hub-and-spoke midway ride. **Scope and scale** Minor attraction. **When to go** Before noon or after 3 p.m. **Duration of ride** 1½ minutes. **Probable wait in line per 100 people ahead of you** 10 minutes. **Loading speed** Slow. **ECV/wheelchair access** Must transfer from ECV to provided wheelchair. **Participates in Genie+** No. **Early Theme Park Entry** Yes. **Extended Evening Hours** No.

DESCRIPTION AND COMMENTS Another Dumbo-like ride for young children. Here you spin around a central hub until a dinosaur pops out of the top of the hub.

TOURING TIPS Come back later if the wait exceeds 20 minutes.

■ PANDORA—*The World of Avatar*

IN AN ATTEMPT TO COUNTER Universal Orlando's Harry Potter lands that opened in 2010 and 2014, Disney signed director James Cameron to a theme park development deal in 2011 based on his blockbuster 2009 film *Avatar.* It was a smart decision. Pandora's headliner attraction, **Avatar Flight of Passage,** opened as (and is still) one of the highest-rated attractions in any Disney or Universal theme park in the United States. In addition, Pandora boasts an awe-inspiringly immersive setting, officially called the **Valley of Mo'ara.** *Unofficial Guide* readers rate this themed environment among the top 20 attractions in Animal Kingdom.

In the *Avatar* universe, Pandora is a planetary moon in a star system 4.3 light-years from Earth. But rather than tie this Pandora to *Avatar* characters or story lines, Disney chose to set the scene a generation after the events in the first movie: The Indigenous Na'vi have made peace with the humans who had exploited Pandora for its natural resources, and Pandora is now an ecotourism destination and a center for scientific research.

What Disney has built in Pandora is a world more beautiful than nature produces on its own. The colors are more vibrant, the sounds more alive, the landscaping entirely more interesting, and the details more, well, *detailed* than what you can probably see out your window right now. It's intersected by perfectly placed waterfalls, and in the middle of it all is a giant floating mountain.

The exquisite detail extends to the ride queues. The one for Na'vi River Journey showcases the weaving skills of Pandora's Indigenous peoples, while the seemingly endless line for Avatar Flight of Passage wends through cave dwellings, nocturnal jungle scenes, and high-tech laboratories on its way to the ride itself.

Avatar Flight of Passage ★★★★½

PRESCHOOL ★★★ (MBA)	GRADE SCHOOL ★★★★½ (MAA)	TEENS ★★★★★ (E)
YOUNG ADULTS ★★★★★ (E)	OVER 30 ★★★★★ (E)	SENIORS ★★★★½ (MAA)

What it is Flight simulator. **Scope and scale** Super-headliner. **When to go** As soon as the park opens or after 3 p.m. **Comments** One of Disney's most advanced rides; must be 44" to ride. **Duration of ride** About 6 minutes. **Average wait in line per 100 people ahead of you** About 5 minutes. **Loading speed** Moderate. **ECV/ wheelchair access** Must transfer from ECV to provided wheelchair and then from wheelchair to the ride vehicle; transfer device available. **Participates in Genie+** No (it offers Individual Lightning Lane). **Early Theme Park Entry** Yes. **Extended Evening Hours** No.

DESCRIPTION AND COMMENTS Avatar Flight of Passage is one of the most technologically advanced rides Disney has ever produced: a flight simulator in which you hop on the back of a winged, dragonlike Pandora banshee for a spin to take in the planet's scenery.

Your journey begins with a long walk from the base of Pandora, up an inclined path, and into abandoned cave dwellings. Wall paintings and markings inside the caves tell the story of the Na'vi. From there, you walk through jungle and more rocks to reach the research laboratory of the humans who have settled on Pandora and are studying the planet's wildlife.

The laboratory's star exhibit is a Na'vi avatar that is lying in suspended animation. Encased in a giant water-filled tube, the sleeping apparition floats gently, its rest briefly interrupted by a finger twitch or leg movement. (People we've toured with have described it as either mesmerizing or vaguely unsettling.)

Once through the queue, you're brought to a 16-person chamber to prepare for your flight. A video explains the concept of an avatar: a way to project your consciousness onto another being—in this case a Na'vi riding astride a banshee—and feel everything it feels. Your preparation includes a "parasite decontamination procedure" and other quasi-scientific processes, mainly to help pass the time until your ride vehicles are ready.

When it's time to ride, you're led into a small room holding what looks like 16 stationary bicycles without pedals. You're handed 3-D goggles and told to approach the "bike," swing one leg over, mount it, and scoot as far forward as you can. Once you're seated, padded restraints are deployed along your calves and lower back, ensuring that you don't fall off during your flight. (The snugness of the restraints, coupled with the somewhat confined space holding the vehicles, makes some claustrophobic guests exit before riding.)

Then the room goes dark, there's a flash of light, and suddenly your brain is "linked" to the Na'vi surfing a banshee. You swoop up and down, left and right, on this flying dragon, going over the Pandora plains, through the mountains, and across its seas, all through a high-definition video projected onto a giant screen in front of you. As you fly, airbags at your legs inflate and deflate to simulate the banshee's breathing below you.

The flying effects are very well done. You can turn your head almost 90 degrees either way, and about 45 degrees up and down, to survey the Pandora landscape. Riders toward the middle of the room (seats 4–8 in one group and 9–12 in the other) have, we think, better range of vision.

The technology at work here is similar to that used at EPCOT's Soarin' Around the World, with the individual "bikes" replacing the grouped seats. Likewise, the ebb and flow of the flight reminds us of the Soarin' film's pacing, right down to the finale over the beach. The video is clear and well synchronized with the ride vehicles, and we've heard very few reports of motion sickness—which is unusual for screen-based motion simulators.

The word *rave* hardly does justice to how Flight of Passage has been received. First, from an Indiana family of four:

Our favorite ride in all of Walt Disney World is Avatar Flight of Passage. The experience is magical. It really does feel like you're flying because of the wind, smells, and movement of the banshee. A lot of people compare it to Soarin', but after riding Flight of Passage first, Soarin' was a letdown.

An Edmonton, Alberta, couple had this to say:

Flight of Passage is one of the best rides we've ever been on. We would gladly wait 3 hours to ride this. A MUST-DO!

And from a Freehold, New Jersey, mom:

From the "breathing" ride vehicle to the unbelievable visuals to (my favorite) the wafting aromas, this ride is absolutely amazing. I love Forbidden Journey at Universal, but aside from Hogwarts Castle being a better queueing area, the Avatar ride is by far superior.

Flight of Passage is super, provided you can ride. A tall Oklahoman who couldn't complains:

I am 6'6", and I was too tall to ride. Two other individuals from my pod were also too tall/large. Very disappointing, and Disney did not handle it very well.

TOURING TIPS Flight of Passage is the first ride most people head for in Animal Kingdom. The good news is that when the park opens by 8 a.m., most guests leave well before closing. Thus, lines for Flight of Passage drop considerably near park closing. A Napa, California, reader recounts a very typical experience:

We did rope drop at Animal Kingdom during spring break on a day with park opening at 7 a.m. for resort guests. By 6:30 a.m., the line to get in was out in the parking lot. It's also kinda stressful with everyone bumping into each other trying to get to Flight of Passage.

Park opening is erratic at Animal Kingdom for several reasons, but it's mainly a matter of safety and traffic control. To forestall a mob at the entrance—and a Pamplona-like stampede to Pandora—Disney modulates the crowds as they arrive, ushering guests safely into a queue. Making crowd control even more critical is the fact that Animal Kingdom's walkways are the narrowest in all of the Disney World parks, which can create choke points.

If you intend to be among the first in the park:

1. Check online or call ☎ 407-824-4321 the night before your visit to confirm official park-opening time.

2. Disney resort guests should arrive 60 minutes before official opening; off-site guests should arrive 30 minutes before official opening.

3. If you're staying on-site, use Disney transportation; Disney's buses get into the parking lot before cars. If you're driving, consider a cab or use Uber or Lyft rather than driving yourself—this way you won't get stuck waiting to pay for parking.

4. Have your admission in hand, thus avoiding the ticket booth.

5. Look for a turnstile that seems to be processing people quickly and smoothly.

6. If you need to use the restroom, use the facilities to the left of the park entrance. Disney has a process for letting you rejoin your party in the queue later on if you need to take a bathroom break, but it's not nearly as convenient as getting that out of the way first thing.

If you can't arrive at park opening or stay until closing, we think purchasing Individual Lightning Lane for Flight of Passage is worth the cost.

Na'vi River Journey ★★★½

PRESCHOOL ★★★★ (A)	**GRADE SCHOOL ★★★★** (BA)	**TEENS ★★★½** (MBA)
YOUNG ADULTS ★★★½ (MBA)	**OVER 30 ★★★½** (BA)	**SENIORS ★★★★** (BA)

What it is Boat ride. **Scope and scale** Headliner. **When to go** Before 9:30 a.m. or during the last 2 hours before closing. **Comments** Very pretty but needs a plot; no height requirement. **Duration of ride** 5 minutes. **Average wait in line per 100 people ahead of you** About 5 minutes. **Loading speed** Moderate. **ECV/wheelchair access** Must transfer to the ride vehicle; transfer device available. **Participates in Genie+** Yes. **Early Theme Park Entry** Yes. **Extended Evening Hours** No.

DESCRIPTION AND COMMENTS Na'vi River Journey is a 4½-minute boat ride through the Pandora jungle. You begin by boarding one of two small, hewn rafts joined together. Each raft has two rows of seats, so four people go in each boat. That might seem small, but it's likely a nod to authenticity: The Na'vi are unlikely to have invented technology like fiberglass to make larger vessels like those in, say, It's a Small World.

Off you go into the nighttime jungle, past glowing plants and exotic animals. To create these, Disney has used traditional 3-D sets for the flora, coupled with video screens showing the movement of the fauna. These video screens are semitransparent, though. What's past them are more screens, with background scenes that also move. That means you're seeing action in the foreground and background simultaneously, all surrounded by densely packed landscaping.

Another bit of technology put to great use is video projection mapping like that used in the Magic Kingdom's nighttime shows. Here it's used to project three-dimensional bugs crawling on tree trunks in one of the middle scenes.

The big star, however, is displayed in the ride's culminating scene: the Shaman of Songs, the most lifelike animatronic figure Disney has ever created. The shaman's arms move with astonishing grace—we certainly don't know any real people who are that coordinated. Yet another nice touch: The shaman sings off-key rather than professionally pitch-perfect.

The main problem with Na'vi River Journey has to do with storytelling: You go into it not knowing anything about the character, and not enough story unfolds during the ride to get you excited about meeting the shaman.

TOURING TIPS It's not worth waiting longer than 30 minutes (the queue only has enough shade to cover maybe 30 minutes' worth of guests).

ANIMAL KINGDOM ENTERTAINMENT

ANIMAL ENCOUNTERS Throughout the day, Animal Kingdom staff members conduct impromptu short lectures on specific animals at the park. Look for a cast member in safari garb holding a bird, reptile, or small mammal.

Winged Encounters—The Kingdom Takes Flight, a small, interactive event featuring macaws and their handlers, takes place on Discovery Island in front of the Tree of Life. Guests can talk to the animals' trainers and see the birds fly around the middle of the park.

CHARACTER CAVALCADES In place of parades and other live entertainment, small boats whisk Disney characters on the waterway around Discovery Island, each to its own soundtrack. Characters include Chip 'n' Dale, Donald and characters from *DuckTales,* Pocahontas, the *Lion King* cast, and Mickey Mouse. The characters don't appear at specific times, but they appear regularly starting about an hour after park opening. The spot where you can see the characters closest is under the bridge on the walkway between Pandora and Africa.

DONALD'S DINO-BASH! ★★½ Regular character greetings are a welcome addition to DinoLand U.S.A. In this case, Donald has discovered that birds are evolutionary descendants of dinosaurs, so he's brought out his friends to celebrate. Characters usually appear intermittently starting at 10 a.m. as follows: **Chip 'n' Dale** across from TriceraTop Spin until 4:30 p.m.; **Daisy, Donald,** and **Goofy** until 7 p.m. at Chester and Hester's Dino-Rama; and **Launchpad McQuack** and **Scrooge McDuck** at The Boneyard until 5 p.m. Because the venues are outdoors, the Dino-Bash may shut down temporarily if it's raining.

*un*official **TIP**
Donald's Dino-Bash was still closed at press time, but we expect it to return.

STREET PERFORMERS The park's most popular live performers are found in Africa (page 556), including the **Tam Tam Drummers of Harambe** (★★★★) and a harp-playing act called **Kora Tinga Tinga** (★★★★). The **Harambe Village Acrobats** (★★★★) dance, vault, and climb through sets around the Dawa Bar. Over on Discovery Island, the **Viva Gaia Street Band** (★★★★) plays high-energy music across from Flame Tree Barbecue.

Far and away the most intriguing of these performers, though, is a stilt walker named **DiVine** (★★★★). Bedecked in foliage and luxuriant vines, she blends so completely with Animal Kingdom's dense flora that you don't notice her until she moves. We've seen guests standing less than a foot away gasp in amazement as DiVine brushes them with a leafy tendril. Found near the park entrance or on the path between Asia and Africa, DiVine is a must-see. You can also find her on YouTube (search "DiVine Disney's Animal Kingdom").

TRAFFIC PATTERNS
in ANIMAL KINGDOM

THE PARK'S MAIN DRAWS are the **Pandora** attractions, **Kilimanjaro Safaris** in Africa, and **Expedition Everest** in Asia.

During busy times of year, guests will start lining up outside the Animal Kingdom entrance 30 minutes to an hour before opening to be close to the front of the standby line for Flight of Passage. Plan on arriving 45–60 minutes before park opening.

Pandora, the Safaris, and Everest are at opposite sides of the park, which allows for even guest distribution. Waits at Dinosaur remain low until 10:30 or 11 a.m. Likewise, crowds don't peak at Expedition Everest until about an hour after park opening, and even later than that at Kali River Rapids. As the day wears on, guests who've experienced the headliners turn their attention to other rides, animal exhibits, and shows, further distributing crowds across the entire park.

unofficial **TIP**
Wait times at the Pandora attractions often peak in the 2 hours after park opening. Less popular attractions generally don't get high traffic until 11 a.m.

Many guests who arrive at opening will leave after having completed their tour of the park by late afternoon. Wait times at the headliners historically dip as the afternoon wears on, usually bottoming out between 3 and 6 p.m. If evening hours return to the Animal Kingdom, crowds will pick back up after sunset for the nighttime Kilimanjaro Safaris and for Pandora's attractions as guests stay to see the land's "bioluminescent" landscaping.

Our mobile app, **Lines,** gives you current wait times and future estimates in half-hour increments for the day of and the day after your visit.

ANIMAL KINGDOM
TOURING PLAN

OUR ANIMAL KINGDOM TOURING PLAN has two versions: one for Disney resort guests and one for off-site guests; the former uses Early Theme Park Entry (see page 36) to minimize waits in line. Because Early Entry means thousands of guests will already be in lines and on rides before off-site guests set foot in the park, the touring strategy for off-site guests must necessarily be different.

The plan does not assume use of Genie+ or Individual Lightning Lane. If you opt for either (or both) of these, just use our free touring plan software to enter your return times.

"Not a Touring Plan" Touring Plans

For the type-B reader, these "not" touring plans (see page 710) dispense with detailed step-by-step strategies for saving every last minute in line.

For Animal Kingdom, these plans include advice for adults and parents with one day to tour the park, arriving either at park opening or later in the morning.

PRELIMINARY INSTRUCTIONS FOR USING THE TOURING PLAN

BECOME FAMILIAR WITH Animal Kingdom's **opening procedures** (see page 548). On days of moderate to heavy attendance, follow the touring plan exactly, deviating from it only as follows:

1. **When you're not interested in an attraction in the plan.** Simply skip it and proceed to the next attraction.

2. **When you encounter a very long line at an attraction.** In this case, skip to the next attraction and try again later at the one with the line.

Before You Go

1. Call ☎ 407-824-4321 or check online the day before you go to verify opening time.

2. Make reservations at the Animal Kingdom full-service restaurant(s) of your choice 60 days before your visit.

ANIMAL KINGDOM TOURING PLAN AT A GLANCE

Disney's Animal Kingdom One-Day Touring Plan (pages 723–724)

THIS TOURING PLAN ASSUMES a willingness to experience all major rides and shows. If you have children under age 8, refer to the **Small-Child Fright-Potential Table** on pages 390–392.

DISNEY'S HOLLYWOOD STUDIOS

OVERVIEW

DISNEY'S HOLLYWOOD STUDIOS has added two new lands and five new rides in the past six years. **Toy Story Land** opened in 2018 with two new child-friendly rides. The other land, **Star Wars: Galaxy's Edge,** opened in 2019 with two cutting-edge rides geared to older kids, teens, and adults. And the Studios launched the family-friendly ride **Mickey & Minnie's Runaway Railway** in early 2020 to rave reviews.

WHO SHOULD SEE THE STUDIOS

SEVERAL OF THE STUDIOS' latest rides are among Disney's best and most popular for older children, teens, and adults. Star Wars: Rise of the Resistance is arguably the best ride Disney has made in decades, while Mickey and Minnie's Runaway Railway is so immersive, colorful, and full of Mickey's personality that it's impossible not to come out with a smile on your face.

Parents with small children may want to opt for a second day in the Magic Kingdom or Animal Kingdom rather than visit the Studios. The Studios has just four child-friendly rides; three musicals (one of them not worth your time); a Muppets film and *Indiana Jones*–themed stunt show, both 35 years old; a handful of character greetings; and two walk-through exhibits unlikely to appeal to most small children.

PARK RESERVATIONS WARNING

THE STUDIOS HAS LIMITED CAPACITY, as well as many of Walt Disney World's most popular attractions, so getting park reservations for it is more difficult than for the other three parks. Our suggestion is to obtain reservations, if they're required (see page 30), as soon as you know your travel dates. If you're an Annual Pass holder not staying at a Disney resort, make reservations at least 30 days in advance.

ARRIVING

ARRIVING FROM INSIDE DISNEY WORLD If you're staying at an EPCOT resort, it'll take you 20–30 minutes to walk the mile or so from your hotel to the Studios' entrance. **Boat service** is also available from the EPCOT resorts to the Studios, and it's about a 20-minute ride on the **Skyliner** system (see page 439), which links EPCOT's International Gateway with Hollywood Studios and Disney's Caribbean Beach, Riviera, Pop Century, and Art of Animation Resorts. In addition to the Skyliner, Disney may offer bus service to the Studios from these hotels on days with high attendance. Guests at other Disney resorts access DHS by **bus**.

Guests at Pop Century and Art of Animation will need to head for the Skyliner up to 2 hours before official opening. While the ride is free, that's not a great use of time. A better option is to use Disney's bus service (if available) or a ride-hailing app.

DRIVING The DHS parking lot is located next to the park (for GPS names and addresses, see page 441). The parking lots open about an hour before official park opening. Take a tram or walk from the parking lot to the front gate. There can be traffic delays in the morning while everyone waits for the lot to open.

DHS OPENING PROCEDURES (ROPE DROP)

ALL RIDES WILL BEGIN OPERATION as soon as guests are admitted into the park. Shows normally begin running an hour or more after the rest of the park. Disney resort guests wishing to use Early Theme Park Entry should arrive at the Studios entrance 60 minutes before official opening on off-peak days and 90 minutes before official opening on days with high attendance. Off-site guests (who are not eligible for Early Entry) should arrive 30 minutes before official opening on all days.

HOW MUCH TIME TO ALLOCATE

DEPENDING ON WHEN YOU ARRIVE, the time of year you tour, and how big a *Star Wars* fan you are, a comprehensive tour of the park takes 8–10 hours with lunch and breaks. Allow more time if you want to enjoy the lightsaber- or droid-building experiences in Galaxy's Edge. At press time, the Studios did not participate in Extended Evening Theme Park Hours but did offer after-hours events.

continued on page 578

Disney's Hollywood Studios

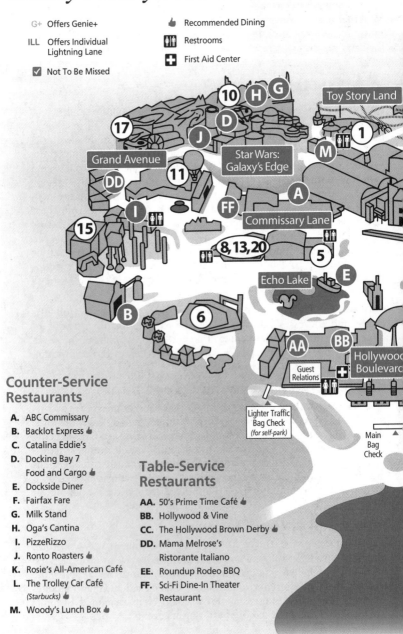

G+ Offers Genie+

ILL Offers Individual
Lightning Lane

☑ Not To Be Missed

👍 Recommended Dining

🚻 Restrooms

➕ First Aid Center

Toy Story Land

Grand Avenue

Star Wars:
Galaxy's Edge

Commissary Lane

Echo Lake

Hollywood
Boulevard

Guest
Relations

Lighter Traffic
Bag Check
(for self-park)

Main
Bag
Check

Counter-Service Restaurants

A. ABC Commissary
B. Backlot Express 👍
C. Catalina Eddie's
D. Docking Bay 7
   Food and Cargo 👍
E. Dockside Diner
F. Fairfax Fare
G. Milk Stand
H. Oga's Cantina
I. PizzeRizzo
J. Ronto Roasters 👍
K. Rosie's All-American Café
L. The Trolley Car Café
   (Starbucks) 👍
M. Woody's Lunch Box 👍

Table-Service Restaurants

AA. 50's Prime Time Café 👍
BB. Hollywood & Vine
CC. The Hollywood Brown Derby 👍
DD. Mama Melrose's
   Ristorante Italiano
EE. Roundup Rodeo BBQ
FF. Sci-Fi Dine-In Theater
   Restaurant

Attractions

1. Alien Swirling Saucers G+
2. *Beauty and the Beast—Live on Stage/* Theater of the Stars G+
3. *Disney Junior Play and Dance!* G+
4. *Fantasmic!* ☑
5. *For the First Time in Forever: A Frozen Sing-Along Celebration* G+
6. *Indiana Jones Epic Stunt Spectacular!* G+
7. *Lightning McQueen's Racing Academy*
8. Meet Olaf at Celebrity Spotlight ☑ G+
9. Mickey and Minnie's Runaway Railway ☑ ILL G+
10. *Millennium Falcon:* Smugglers Run ☑ G+
11. *Muppet-Vision 3-D* G+
12. Rock 'n' Roller Coaster Starring Aerosmith ☑ G+
13. See Disney Stars at *Red Carpet Dreams* ☑
14. Slinky Dog Dash ☑ G+
15. Star Tours—The Adventures Continue ☑ G+
16. Star Wars Launch Bay
17. Star Wars: Rise of the Resistance ☑ ILL
18. Toy Story Mania! ☑ G+
19. The Twilight Zone Tower of Terror ☑ G+
20. *Vacation Fun* at Mickey Shorts Theater
21. *Walt Disney Presents*

continued from page 575

HOLLYWOOD STUDIOS SERVICES

MOST PARK SERVICES are on Hollywood Boulevard, including

Baby Care Center At Guest Relations; baby food and other necessities also available at Oscar's Super Service, on the right just inside the park

Banking Services ATM on the right just inside the park

Cell Phone Charging Outlets in the Hollywood Brown Derby lobby, inside Backlot Express, and near the restrooms next to Toy Story Mania!

ECV/Scooter Rentals At Package Pickup, outside and to the left of the park entrance

First Aid Center At Guest Relations

Live Entertainment and Character Information In the *Times Guide,* available at Guest Relations

Lockers On the right just inside the park

Lost and Found At Guest Relations

Lost Persons Report at Guest Relations/Baby Care Center

Magic Bands At The Darkroom on the right side of Hollywood Boulevard as you enter the park, just past Oscar's Super Service

Wheelchair and Stroller Rentals To the right of the entrance, at Oscar's Super Service

GETTING ORIENTED

ON YOUR LEFT AS YOU ENTER, **Guest Relations** serves as the Studios' headquarters and information center. Go there to pick up a park map or entertainment schedule (***Times Guide***), to report lost persons, or to access the **Baby Care Center.** To the right of the entrance are **locker, stroller, and wheelchair rentals; Package Pickup;** and **Lost and Found.**

As in the Magic Kingdom, you enter the park and then pass down a main street. In this case, it's the **Hollywood Boulevard** of the 1930s and '40s. At the end is a replica of the iconic **Grauman's Chinese Theatre,** home of **Mickey & Minnie's Runaway Railway.**

As you face the Chinese Theatre, two themed areas, **Sunset Boulevard** and **Animation Courtyard,** branch off Hollywood Boulevard to the right. Branching left off Hollywood Boulevard is **Echo Lake.** Beyond that, **Grand Avenue** holds *Muppet-Vision 3-D* and **Mama Melrose's,** a full-service Italian restaurant.

Toy Story Land's attractions are located behind the Chinese Theatre and to the left of Animation Courtyard. Finally, **Star Wars: Galaxy's Edge** is in the upper-left corner of the park, accessible from Grand Avenue and Toy Story Land.

NOT TO BE MISSED IN DISNEY'S HOLLYWOOD STUDIOS

HOLLYWOOD AND SUNSET BOULEVARDS • *Fantasmic!* • Mickey and Minnie's Runaway Railway • Rock 'n' Roller Coaster • The Twilight Zone Tower of Terror

ECHO LAKE • Star Tours—The Adventures Continue • Meet Olaf at Celebrity Spotlight • *For the First Time in Forever: A Frozen Sing-Along Celebration*

COMMISSARY LANE • Meet Mickey and Minnie at *Red Carpet Dreams*

TOY STORY LAND • Slinky Dog Dash • Toy Story Mania!

STAR WARS: GALAXY'S EDGE • *Millennium Falcon:* Smugglers Run • Star Wars: Rise of the Resistance

		DISNEY'S HOLLYWOOD STUDIOS MOST POPULAR ATTRACTIONS BY AGE GROUP			
PRESCHOOL	GRADE SCHOOL	TEENS	YOUNG ADULTS	OVER 30	SENIORS
Mickey and Minnie's Runaway Railway	Toy Story Mania!	Star Wars: Rise of the Resistance	Star Wars: Rise of the Resistance	Star Wars: Rise of the Resistance	Mickey and Minnie's Runaway Railway
Toy Story Mania!	Mickey and Minnie's Runaway Railway	Rock 'n' Roller Coaster	Rock 'n' Roller Coaster	Toy Story Mania!	Toy Story Mania!
Alien Swirling Saucers	Star Wars: Rise of the Resistance	Toy Story Mania!	The Twilight Zone Tower of Terror	Mickey and Minnie's Runaway Railway	Star Wars: Rise of the Resistance
For the First Time in Forever	Slinky Dog Dash	Millennium Falcon: Smugglers Run	Millennium Falcon: Smugglers Run	Millennium Falcon: Smugglers Run	Slinky Dog Dash
Meet Olaf at Celebrity Spotlight	Millennium Falcon: Smugglers Run	Mickey and Minnie's Runaway Railway	Slinky Dog Dash	Slinky Dog Dash	The Twilight Zone Tower of Terror
Disney Junior Play and Dance!	Star Tours— The Adventures Continue	Slinky Dog Dash	Mickey and Minnie's Runaway Railway	Rock 'n' Roller Coaster	For the First Time in Forever
Beauty & the Beast—Live on Stage	Rock 'n' Roller Coaster	The Twilight Zone Tower of Terror	Fantasmic!	The Twilight Zone Tower of Terror	Beauty & the Beast—Live on Stage
Slinky Dog Dash	For the First Time in Forever	Fantasmic!	Star Tours— The Adventures Continue	For the First Time in Forever	Walt Disney Presents: One Man's Dream
Muppet-Vision 3-D	Meet Olaf at Celebrity Spotlight	Star Tours— The Adventures Continue	Muppet-Vision 3-D	Fantasmic!	Fantasmic!
Lightning McQueen's Racing Academy	Fantasmic!	Indiana Jones Epic Stunt Spectacular!	Indiana Jones Epic Stunt Spectacular!	Star Wars Launch Bay: Meet Chewbacca	Millennium Falcon: Smugglers Run

Attractions closed more than 2 years are not shown.

FAVORITE ATTRACTIONS BY AGE GROUP

THE TABLE ABOVE shows the park's 10 most popular attractions by age group. Below are the average ratings for DHS attractions, by age group, for the 50,000 attraction ratings we received in the past year:

PRESCHOOL	GRADE SCHOOL	TEENS	YOUNG ADULTS	OVER 30	SENIORS
3.8 stars	4.0 stars	3.9 stars	3.9 stars	4.2 stars	4.2 stars

GENIE+, INDIVIDUAL LIGHTNING LANE, AND THE TOURING PLANS

THE BIG QUESTIONS, as always, are

1. Is Genie+ worth paying for in Disney's Hollywood Studios?
2. If it's worth the cost, which attractions benefit most from Genie+ or Individual Lightning Lane?
3. How can you avoid paying for Individual Lightning Lane?
4. How do Genie+ and Individual Lightning Lane work with the touring plans?

GENIE+ AND INDIVIDUAL LIGHTNING LANE (ILL) SELECTIONS IN DHS
ANIMATION COURTYARD • *Disney Junior Play and Dance!*
ECHO LAKE • *For the First Time in Forever—A Frozen Sing-Along Celebration* • *Indiana Jones Epic Stunt Spectacular!* • Meet Olaf at Celebrity Spotlight • Star Tours—The Adventures Continue
GALAXY'S EDGE • *Millennium Falcon:* Smugglers Run • Star Wars: Rise of the Resistance *(ILL)*
GRAND AVENUE • *Muppet-Vision 3-D*
HOLLYWOOD BOULEVARD • Mickey and Minnie's Runaway Railway
SUNSET BOULEVARD • *Beauty & the Beast—Live on Stage* • Rock 'n' Roller Coaster Starring Aerosmith • The Twilight Zone Tower of Terror
TOY STORY LAND • Alien Swirling Saucers • Slinky Dog Dash • Toy Story Mania!

Some character greetings were not offered with Genie+ and Lightning Lane at press time. We expect them to be added.

Is Genie+ Worth Paying For in Disney's Hollywood Studios?

Along with the Magic Kingdom, the Studios might be the easiest park to recommend Genie+ for, especially if you meet any of these criteria:

- You'll arrive at the park after Early Theme Park Entry begins (that is, you won't be at the park as soon as it opens). This includes off-site guests who aren't eligible for Early Theme Park Entry and on-site guests who want to sleep in.
- You won't be using a touring plan.
- You're visiting during a day of moderate or high crowds

Regardless of the time of year you visit, arriving at park opening should allow you to see one or two of the Studios' headliners without significant waits. Since only 13 attractions participate in Genie+/Individual Lightning Lane, you'll be competing with lots of people for reservations, which pushes out return times and limits how many you can obtain. Below we break down how much time we think you can save using Genie+ with a touring plan, based on different assumptions about how many reservations it's possible to obtain in a day. See pages 466–467 for more on the usage levels.

ESTIMATED TIME SAVINGS USING A TOURING PLAN WITH GENIE+ FOR VARIOUS CROWD LEVELS			
CROWD LEVEL	**TYPICAL USE (3 RESERVATIONS PER DAY)**	**OPTIMISTIC USE (5 RESERVATIONS PER DAY)**	**PERFECT USE (8 RESERVATIONS PER DAY)**
Low	50 minutes saved	80 minutes saved	120 minutes saved
Medium	80 minutes saved	100 minutes saved	140 minutes saved
High	100 minutes saved	150 minutes saved	210 minutes saved

Which Attractions Benefit Most from Genie+ and Individual Lightning Lane?

For Genie+, the table on the opposite page (top) shows the attractions that might benefit most from using Genie+, based on current wait times and historical Genie+/Individual Lightning Lane data. Attractions are listed in descending order of priority.

DHS ATTRACTIONS THAT BENEFIT MOST FROM GENIE+ AND INDIVIDUAL LIGHTNING LANE (ILL) *(Highest Priority to Lowest)*	
ATTRACTION	**AVERAGE TIME IN LINE SAVED (IN MINUTES)**
The Twilight Zone Tower of Terror	84
Star Wars: Rise of the Resistance (ILL)	70
Slinky Dog Dash	68
Millennium Falcon: Smugglers Run	53
Rock 'n' Roller Coaster Starring Aerosmith	52
Toy Story Mania!	49
Mickey and Minnie's Runaway Railway	42
Alien Swirling Saucers	17
Star Tours—The Adventures Continue	15

At press time, we had not seen evidence that Genie+ reduces waits at shows.

When Do Genie+ and Individual Lightning Lane Reservations Run Out in DHS?

The table below shows the approximate time at which the Studios' attractions run out of Genie+ or Individual Lightning Lane capacity, by crowd level. Use this table along with the "Attractions That Benefit Most" table, above, to determine which reservations to get first.

WHEN GENIE+ AND INDIVIDUAL LIGHTNING LANE (ILL) RESERVATIONS RUN OUT BY ATTENDANCE LEVEL			
ATTRACTION	**LOW ATTENDANCE**	**MODERATE ATTENDANCE**	**HIGH ATTENDANCE**
Alien Swirling Saucers	8 p.m.	8 p.m.	8 p.m.
Beauty & the Beast—Live on Stage	Available	Available	5 p.m.
Disney Junior Play and Dance!	Available	Available	5 p.m.
For the First Time in Forever	Available	Available	7 p.m.
Indiana Jones Epic Stunt Spectacular!	Available	6 p.m.	5 p.m.
Meet Olaf at Celebrity Spotlight	5 p.m.	5 p.m.	5 p.m.
Mickey and Minnie's Runaway Railway	8 p.m.	8 p.m.	8 p.m.
Millennium Falcon: Smugglers Run	8 p.m.	8 p.m.	8 p.m.
Muppet-Vision 3-D	Available	Available	Available
Star Wars: Rise of the Resistance (*ILL*)	8 a.m.	7 a.m.	7 a.m.
Rock 'n' Roller Coaster	8 p.m.	7 p.m.	4 p.m.
Slinky Dog Dash	1 p.m.	1 p.m.	1 p.m.
Star Tours—The Adventures Continue	8 p.m.	8 p.m.	8 p.m.
Toy Story Mania!	8 p.m.	8 p.m.	8 p.m.
The Twilight Zone Tower of Terror	1 p.m.	1 p.m.	1 p.m.

AVAILABLE Attractions rarely run out of reservations at this crowd level.
LOW ATTENDANCE Crowd levels 1–3 on the TouringPlans crowd calendar
MODERATE ATTENDANCE Crowd levels 4–7
HIGH ATTENDANCE Crowd levels 8–10
Attractions closed for more than two years are not shown.

How Can You Avoid Paying for Individual Lightning Lane?

The easiest way to avoid paying for Individual Lightning Lane at Rise of the Resistance is to be at the park for Early Theme Park Entry, then head for Rise as soon as you enter the park. Note that Rise of the Resistance averages almost 2 hours of downtime per day. Ask a cast member if it's running before you head over there.

How do Genie+ and Individual Lightning Lane Work with the Touring Plans?

See our advice for the Magic Kingdom on pages 468–469.

DINING IN DISNEY'S HOLLYWOOD STUDIOS

HERE'S A QUICK RECAP of the Studios' top restaurants, rated by readers from highest to lowest. See Part 6 for details.

DHS RESTAURANT REFRESHER	
COUNTER SERVICE	**FULL SERVICE**
Ronto Roasters (➕ 96%/Exceptional), Galaxy's Edge	**The Hollywood Brown Derby** (➕ 91%/Above Average), Hollywood Boulevard
The Trolley Car Cafe (Starbucks) (➕ 92%/Much Above Average), Sunset Boulevard	
Docking Bay 7 Food and Cargo (➕ 91%/Above Average), Galaxy's Edge	**50's Prime Time Cafe** (➕ 89%/Average), Echo Lake
Woody's Lunch Box (➕ 91%/Above Average), Toy Story Land	
ABC Commissary (➕ 88%/Average), Commissary Lane	

Roundup Rodeo BBQ didn't have enough surveys at press time. Other restaurants not shown are average or below.

DISNEY'S HOLLYWOOD STUDIOS ATTRACTIONS

HOLLYWOOD BOULEVARD

THIS PALM-LINED THOROUGHFARE re-creates Tinseltown's main drag during the Golden Age of Hollywood. Most of the Studios' service facilities are located here, interspersed with eateries and shops. The merchandise sold here includes everything from Disney trademark items to movie-related souvenirs.

SUNSET BOULEVARD

EVOKING THE GLAMOUR OF THE 1940s, Sunset Boulevard—the first right off Hollywood Boulevard—provides another venue for dining, shopping, and street entertainment.

KEY TO ABBREVIATIONS In the attraction profiles that follow, each star rating is accompanied by a category label in parentheses (see page 464). E means **Exceptional**, MAA means **Much Above Average**, AA means **Above Average**, A means **Average**, BA means **Below Average**, and MBA means **Much Below Average**.

Beauty & the Beast—Live on Stage / Theater of the Stars ★★★★

PRESCHOOL ★★★★½ (AA)	GRADE SCHOOL ★★★★ (BA)	TEENS ★★★½ (MBA)
YOUNG ADULTS ★★★★ (BA)	OVER 30 ★★★★ (A)	SENIORS ★★★★½ (AA)

What it is Live Hollywood-style musical with Disney characters, performed in an open-air theater. **Scope and scale** Major attraction. **When to go** Anytime, but not as hot after sunset. **Comment** Check *Times Guide* for showtimes. **Duration of presentation** 25 minutes. **Preshow entertainment** None. **When to arrive** 25–35 minutes in advance. **ECV/wheelchair access** May remain in wheelchair. **Participates in Genie+** Yes. **Early Theme Park Entry** No. **Extended Evening Hours** No.

DESCRIPTION AND COMMENTS The long-running *Beauty & the Beast* show combines a shortened (but complete) retelling of the story with all of the major musical numbers, with tons of characters and good set decoration. The theater affords a clear field of vision from almost every seat. Best of all, a canopy protects the audience from the Florida sun (or rain), but the theater still gets mighty hot in the summer.

TOURING TIPS *Beauty & the Beast* usually runs from midmorning to around 5 p.m. The show is popular, so you should arrive 25–35 minutes early to get a good seat. If you can't make it in time, look for overflow seating outside: Two sets of bleachers offer perfect views of the stage. The seating isn't covered, though, so drink plenty of water and use sun protection as needed.

Fantasmic! ★★★★½

PRESCHOOL ★★★★ (A)	GRADE SCHOOL ★★★★½ (AA)	TEENS ★★★★½ (AA)
YOUNG ADULTS ★★★★½ (AA)	OVER 30 ★★★★½ (AA)	SENIORS ★★★★½ (AA)

What it is Mixed-media nighttime spectacular. **Scope and scale** Super-headliner. **When to go** Check *Times Guide* for schedule; if 2 shows are offered, the second will be less crowded. **Comment** One of Disney's best nighttime events. **Duration of presentation** 25 minutes. **Probable waiting time** 50–90 minutes for a seat, 35–40 minutes for standing room. **ECV/wheelchair access** May remain in wheelchair. **Participates in Genie+** No. **Early Theme Park Entry** No. **Extended Evening Hours** No.

DESCRIPTION AND COMMENTS Off Sunset Boulevard behind the Tower of Terror, this mixed-media show is staged on an island opposite the 7,900-seat Hollywood Hills Amphitheater. By far the largest theater facility ever created by Disney, it can accommodate an additional 2,000 standing guests for an audience of nearly 10,000.

Fantasmic! is one of the most innovative outdoor spectacles we've seen at any theme park. Starring Mickey Mouse in his role as the Sorcerer's Apprentice from *Fantasia,* the production uses lasers, images projected on a shroud of mist, fireworks, lighting effects, and music in combinations so stunning you can scarcely believe what you're seeing. The theme is simple: good versus evil. The plot gets lost in all the special effects at times, but no matter: It's the spectacle, not the story line, that's powerful.

A Pearland, Texas, mom found *Fantasmic!* too intense for her young child:

Fantasmic! should come with a warning. The larger-than-life laser visages, loud and ominous music, and thundering explosions sent hordes of parents with screaming children fleeing for the exits.

We don't receive many reports of young children being terrified by *Fantasmic!*, but the reader's point is well taken. Spend some time preparing your kids for what they will see. You can mitigate the fright factor somewhat by sitting back a bit. Also, hang on to your kids after the show, and give them instructions for regrouping should you get separated.

TOURING TIPS During busier times of the year, *Fantasmic!* is presented one or more times most evenings, but Disney is known to change the schedule, so check before you go. *Fantasmic!* is to the Studios what *Enchantment* is to the Magic Kingdom: While it's hard to imagine a 10,000-person amphitheater running out of space, that's exactly what happens almost every time the show is staged. On evenings when there are two shows, the second will always be less crowded. If you attend the first (or only) scheduled performance, then arrive at least an hour in advance; if you opt for the second, arrive 50 minutes early.

A Cross Junction, Virginia, woman offers this planning tip:

Buy deli sandwiches outside the park, pack them with snacks and water, and get an early seat.

A multigenerational family from Barrie, Ontario, makes this suggestion for guests who are short on nature's upholstery:

Bring pillows or towels to sit on. We were sitting on those benches from 6 p.m. for the 7:30 show, and boy, did our rears hurt by the end!

Rain and wind sometimes cause *Fantasmic!* to be canceled; unfortunately, Disney usually doesn't make a final ruling about whether to proceed or cancel until just before showtime. We've seen guests wait stoically for over an hour with no assurance that their patience and sacrifice will be rewarded. In any case, we don't recommend arriving more than 20 minutes before showtime on rainy or especially windy nights. On nights like these, pursue your own agenda until 10–20 minutes or so before showtime; then head to the stadium to see what happens.

Our own researcher David, a dad of two, notes that the Magic Kingdom's Halloween and Christmas parties affect *Fantasmic!* crowds:

As a kid-friendly nighttime show, Fantasmic! *is a hot mess on nights when the Magic Kingdom closes early.*

When this happens, plan to arrive about 90 minutes before the show to ensure good seats.

A veteran of both Disneyland and Walt Disney World notes:

Disneyland's [crowd-control] cast members push throngs of guests through the park like clockwork, even when it's bursting at the seams. At Disney World, it's basically every man for himself as the cast members retreat, leaving very tired, very cranky guests to duke it out. Such is the case at Fantasmic!—*thankfully, a backstage corridor was open for a quick reroute, but the presence of cast members was rare.*

Finally, a couple from Alberta, Canada, sums things up:

For a show so deservedly hyped, I would hope that WDW finds ways to make seeing it less stressful.

FANTASMIC! DINING PACKAGE If you're planning to eat at any of the park's sit-down restaurants, you can obtain a voucher for the members of your dining party to enter *Fantasmic!* via a special entrance and sit in a reserved section. This saves you 30–90 minutes of waiting in the regular line to be admitted. If you know you're going to eat at one of these restaurants, the dining package is a better way to see *Fantasmic!* than lining up in advance.

You must call ☎ 407-WDW-DINE (939-3463) up to 60 days in advance and request the package for the night you want to see the show. *Note:* This is a real reservation, not an Advance Reservation, and it must be guaranteed with a credit card at the time of booking. There's no additional charge for the package itself, but there is a $10-per-person charge for canceling with less than 48 hours' notice.

Fixed-price menus are included in the package; prices listed below are the most recent available for adults and kids ages 3–9:

- **50's Prime Time Cafe:** Lunch and dinner $51 (child $22)
- **Hollywood & Vine:** Breakfast $54 (child $36), lunch and dinner $71 (child $47)
- **The Hollywood Brown Derby:** Lunch and dinner $73 (child $29)
- **Mama Melrose's Ristorante Italiano:** Lunch and dinner $43 (child $18)
- **Sci-Fi Dine-In Theater Restaurant:** Lunch and dinner $49 (child $22)

Nonalcoholic drinks are included; tax, tips, and park admission are not. Prices may vary seasonally, so call ☎ 407-WDW-DINE (939-3463) to confirm.

You'll receive your vouchers at the restaurant during your meal; if you're eating dinner, you'll need to arrive no later than 2½ hours before showtime. Then, about half an hour before the show, you'll report to the Highlands Gate on Sunset Boulevard, between Theater of the Stars and the Once Upon a Time store. A cast member will collect your vouchers and escort you to the reserved-seating section of the amphitheater. Although you're required to arrive early, you can be seated immediately. The reserved seats are in the center of the stadium; you won't have assigned seats—it's first come, first served—so arrive early for the best choice. If *Fantasmic!* is canceled due to weather or other circumstances, you'll get a voucher for another performance within five days.

Weather notwithstanding, a Waldorf, Maryland, couple thinks the dining package is the only way to go:

> We booked dinner at Hollywood & Vine, got our passes for the package, and waltzed on into the show. We felt like VIPs, and it was so relaxing to see the show without the rush of the crowds.

Lightning McQueen's Racing Academy ★★½

PRESCHOOL ★★★★ (A)	GRADE SCHOOL ★★★½ (BA)	TEENS ★★★ (BA)
YOUNG ADULTS ★★★½ (BA)	OVER 30 ★★★ (MBA)	SENIORS ★★★½ (MBA)

What it is Wide-screen movie of Lightning McQueen's racing tips. **Scope and scale** Minor attraction. **When to go** Anytime. **Duration of presentation** Continuous 10 minutes. **Preshow entertainment** None. **ECV/wheelchair access** May remain in wheelchair. **Participates in Genie+** No. **Early Theme Park Entry** No. **Extended Evening Hours** No.

DESCRIPTION AND COMMENTS This theater show features *Cars* superstars Lightning McQueen, Cruz Ramirez, and Tow Mater. While the last two appear only on the massive wraparound screen, Lightning McQueen is front and center as a full-size animatronic.

The show starts slowly, with Lightning explaining why he developed a racing academy, but it becomes impressive once the simulation starts. Using the huge screens, Lightning mimes racing as a track flies by around you. As usual, things don't go quite as planned when an old adversary shows up, but it's all settled by a race, of course.

For a relatively short show, the visuals and the wonderfully subtle movements of Lightning on the stage make this a worthwhile stop in Disney's Hollywood Studios.

TOURING TIPS Added to increase the park's capacity, *Lightning McQueen's Racing Academy* is located in one of the most remote corners of DHS: past the end of Sunset Boulevard, then past the end of the Rock 'n' Roller Coaster plaza. Because it's hard to find and requires backtracking to get anywhere else, it's rarely crowded. A photo opportunity with Cruz Ramirez is outside the show.

Mickey and Minnie's Runaway Railway ★★★★

PRESCHOOL ★★★★½ (AA)	GRADE SCHOOL ★★★★½ (AA)	TEENS ★★★★½ (AA)
YOUNG ADULTS ★★★★½ (AA)	OVER 30 ★★★★½ (AA)	SENIORS ★★★★½ (AA)

What it is Indoor dark ride through the new Mickey Mouse cartoon universe. **Scope and scale** Headliner. **When to go** As soon as the park is open or in the last hour before park closing. **Duration of ride** 5 minutes. **Average wait in line per 100 people ahead of you** 4 minutes; assumes all trains operating. **Loading speed** Moderate. **ECV/wheelchair access** Must transfer to ride vehicle. **Participates in Genie+** Yes. **Early Theme Park Entry** Yes. **Extended Evening Hours** No.

DESCRIPTION AND COMMENTS Disney restarted regular production of Mickey Mouse cartoons in 2013. Mostly written and directed by Paul Rudish, these 7-minute vignettes—more than 100 have been made so far—are minor masterpieces of storytelling, animation, and humor; Mickey and Minnie sport a 1930s look, complete with "pie eyes." In settings across the world, and sometimes in languages other than English, the Mouses, Goofy, Donald, and the rest of the gang embark on crazy adventures that always seem to end up just fine. If you haven't seen them yet, plan on binge-watching them with your kids (they're all on YouTube and Disney+).

Runaway Railway places you in the center of one of those cartoons. The premise is that you're on an out-of-control railroad car, courtesy of Goofy. You careen, gently, through 10 large cartoon show scenes, from tropical islands to cities to out-of-control factories. In each scene, Mickey and Minnie attempt to save you from disaster, with mixed results.

In each scene, Disney uses a mix of traditional, three-dimensional painted sets and the latest in video projection technology to show movement and special effects. It's all done very well, and there are so many things to see on either side of the ride that it's impossible to catch everything in one or two rides. In case you're wanting more, the **Mickey Shorts Theater,** near *Indiana Jones Epic Stunt Spectacular!* at Echo Lake, shows a montage of the new cartoons too.

TOURING TIPS Runaway Railway is the Studios' sleeper hit of the decade, so expect long lines throughout the day. Your best bet is to get in line as soon as the park opens or late in the afternoon.

Rock 'n' Roller Coaster Starring Aerosmith ★★★★

PRESCHOOL NA	GRADE SCHOOL ★★★★½ (MBA)	TEENS ★★★★★ (E)
YOUNG ADULTS ★★★★★ (E)	OVER 30 ★★★★½ (MBA)	SENIORS ★★★★ (BA)

What it is Rock music–themed roller coaster. **Scope and scale** Headliner. **When to go** First 30 minutes the park is open or after 4 p.m. **Comments** Must be 48" to ride; Rider Switch option provided (see page 396). **Duration of ride** Almost 1½ minutes. **Average wait in line per 100 people ahead of you** 2½ minutes; assumes all trains operating. **Loading speed** Moderate-fast. **ECV/wheelchair access** Must transfer from ECV to provided wheelchair and then from wheelchair to ride vehicle; transfer device available. **Participates in Genie+** Yes. **Early Theme Park Entry** Yes. **Extended Evening Hours** Yes.

Motion Sickness

DESCRIPTION AND COMMENTS Way wilder than Space Mountain or Big Thunder Mountain Railroad in the Magic Kingdom, Rock 'n' Roller Coaster is made for fans of high-speed thrill rides. Although the presence of Aerosmith and the synchronized music add measurably to the experience, the ride itself is what you're here for. Its loops, corkscrews, and drops make Space Mountain seem like It's a Small World. What really makes this metal coaster unusual, however, is that first, it's in the dark (like Space Mountain but with Southern California nighttime scenes), and second, you are launched up the first hill like a jet off a carrier deck. By the time you crest the hill, you'll have gone from 0 to 57 mph in less than 3 seconds. When you enter the first loop, you'll be pulling almost 5 g's—2 more than astronauts experienced at liftoff on a space shuttle.

Reader opinions of Rock 'n' Roller Coaster are predictably mixed, and invariably colored by how the reader feels about roller coasters. First, from a mother of two from High Mills, New York:

You can't warn people enough about Rock 'n' Roller Coaster. My daughter and I refused to go on it at all. My 9-year-old son, who had no problems with any ride, including Tower of Terror, went on with my husband and came off so shaken he was "done for" the rest of the day. My husband just closed his eyes and hoped for the best.

From a Longmont, Colorado, dad:

The first 15 seconds are spectacular. I've never experienced anything like the initial take-off.

From an Australian couple who traveled a long way to ride a coaster:

My wife and I are definitely not roller-coaster people. However, we found Rock 'n' Roller Coaster quite exhilarating—and because it's dark, we didn't always realize that we were being thrown upside down. We rode it twice!

As we went to press, Rock 'n' Roller Coaster was undergoing a lengthy refurbishment. It's possible Disney chooses another band to helm this ride.

TOURING TIPS Rock 'n' Roller Coaster is not for everyone—if Space Mountain or Big Thunder pushes your limits, skip it. The attractions in Galaxy's Edge, along with Slinky Dog Dash and Mickey & Minnie's Runaway Railway, draw crowds away from Rock 'n' Roller Coaster. If you can't ride first thing in the morning, waits after 4 p.m. should be manageable.

The Twilight Zone Tower of Terror ★★★★★

PRESCHOOL ★★½ (MBA) **GRADE SCHOOL** ★★★★ (MBA) **TEENS** ★★★★★ (MAA)
YOUNG ADULTS ★★★★★ (MAA) **OVER 30** ★★★★½ (MAA) **SENIORS** ★★★★ (AA)

What it is Sci-fi–themed indoor thrill ride. **Scope and scale** Super-headliner. **When to go** First 30 minutes the park is open or after 4 p.m. **Comments** Must be 40" to ride; Rider Switch option provided (see page 396). **Duration of ride** About 4 minutes plus preshow. **Average wait in line per 100 people ahead of you** 4 minutes; assumes all elevators operating at full capacity. **Loading speed** Moderate. **ECV/wheelchair access** Must transfer from ECV to provided wheelchair and then to ride vehicle. **Participates in Genie+** Yes. **Early Theme Park Entry** Yes. **Extended Evening Hours** No.

DESCRIPTION AND COMMENTS The Tower of Terror is a different species of Disney thrill ride, though it borrows elements of The Haunted Mansion in the Magic Kingdom. The story is that you're touring a once-famous Hollywood hotel gone to ruin. As at Star Tours, the queuing area here immerses guests in the adventure as they pass through the hotel's once-opulent public rooms. From the lobby, guests are escorted into the hotel's library, where *Twilight Zone* creator Rod Serling, speaking from an old black-and-white TV, greets them and introduces the plot.

The Tower of Terror is a whopper, at 13 stories tall. Breaking tradition in terms of visually isolating themed areas, it lets you see the entire Studios from atop the tower . . . but you have to look quick.

The ride vehicle, one of the hotel's service elevators, takes guests to see the haunted hostelry. The tour begins innocuously, but at about the fifth floor things get pretty weird. Guests are subjected to a full range of eerie effects as they cross into the Twilight Zone. The sudden drops and ascents begin when your ride vehicle travels horizontally across the building, into a second elevator shaft. There are several different lift-and-drop sequences that are selected randomly, making the attraction faster and keeping you guessing about when, how far, and how many times the elevator will fall.

A senior from the United Kingdom tried the Tower of Terror and liked it very much:

I was thankful I had read your review of the Tower of Terror, or I certainly would have avoided it. As you say, it's so full of magnificent detail that it's worth riding even if you don't fancy the drops involved.

A Washington state reader thinks the randomness is a net negative:

The last time I rode the Tower of Terror was almost 20 years ago, and I remember a HUGE drop initially. This time it was just kind of up-down, up-down, up-up-down. Bummer.

The Tower has great potential for terrifying young children and rattling more-mature visitors. If you have teenagers in your party, use them as experimental probes: If they report back that they really, really liked the Tower of Terror, run as fast as you can in the opposite direction.

TOURING TIPS The attractions in Galaxy's Edge, along with Slinky Dog Dash and Mickey & Minnie's Runaway Railway, draw crowds away from Tower of Terror. If you can't ride first thing in the morning, waits should be shorter in the last hour the park is open.

To save time once you're inside the queuing area, when you enter the library waiting room, stand in the far back corner across from the door where you entered and at the opposite end of the room from the TV. When the doors to the loading area open, you'll be the first admitted.

If you have young children (or anyone) who are apprehensive about this attraction, ask the attendant about **Rider Switch** (see page 396).

ECHO LAKE

THIS MINIATURE LAKE near the middle of the Studios, to the left of Hollywood Boulevard, pays homage to its real-life California counterpart, which served as the backdrop to many early motion pictures.

For the First Time in Forever: A Frozen Sing-Along Celebration ★★★½

PRESCHOOL ★★★½ (MAA)	GRADE SCHOOL ★★★★½ (AA)	TEENS ★★★★ (BA)
YOUNG ADULTS ★★★★ (BA)	OVER 30 ★★★★½ (AA)	SENIORS ★★★★½ (A)

What it is Sing-along stage show retelling the story of the 2013 film *Frozen*, with appearances by Anna and Elsa. **Scope and scale** Minor attraction. **When to go** Check the park map or *Times Guide* for showtimes. **Duration of presentation** 30 minutes. **When to arrive** 25 minutes before showtime. **ECV/wheelchair access** May remain in wheelchair. **Participates in Genie+** Yes. **Early Theme Park Entry** No. **Extended Evening Hours** No.

DESCRIPTION AND COMMENTS This 30-minute musical recap of the chilly Disney hit includes songs from the original movie and a visit from Anna and Elsa. Scenes from the movie, projected on a drive-in-size screen in the background, provide continuity and bring those who haven't seen the film up to speed. Live performers, including two "royal historians" and several supporting characters from *Frozen,* retell the story with corny and sometimes punchy humor.

Most of the show unfolds at a leisurely pace, but the ending is presented in a nanosecond, leaving much of the audience stupefied. Of course, the finale features Anna and Elsa and another rousing belting of "Let It Go." If you're a fan of the movie, you probably won't care about the weak points. And even if you're not a fan, you'll enjoy the show's spirit as well as that of a theater full of enraptured kids. Yes, it's contagious.

Most readers really like the sing-along, including this mom from Houston:

I'm glad we didn't skip it, because it was a total hoot—my husband and I loved it, and it turned out to be the highlight of our DHS visit! When we got home, my husband and 9-year-old son, neither of whom had seen the movie before, watched Frozen *with my daughter.*

But a Connecticut reader was less impressed:

The sing-along was extremely disappointing—most of the time, you're just watching scenes from the movie.

TOURING TIPS The indoor theater is one of Disney World's largest and most comfortable, with excellent sight lines from every seat. Crowd management when entering the theater is a little confusing, but once you're inside it sorts itself out.

Indiana Jones Epic Stunt Spectacular!   ★★★½

PRESCHOOL ★★★½ (MBA)	GRADE SCHOOL ★★★★ (A)	TEENS ★★★½ (BA)
YOUNG ADULTS ★★★★ (A)	OVER 30 ★★★★ (A)	SENIORS ★★★★½ (AA)

What it is Movie-stunt demonstration and action show. **Scope and scale** Headliner. **When to go** First two shows or last show. **Comment** Performance times posted on a sign at the entrance to the theater. **Duration of presentation** 30 minutes. **When to arrive** 20–30 minutes before showtime. **ECV/wheelchair access** May remain in wheelchair. **Participates in Genie+** Yes. **Early Theme Park Entry** No. **Extended Evening Hours** No.

DESCRIPTION AND COMMENTS Educational though somewhat unevenly paced, this popular production showcases professional stuntpeople who offer behind-the-scenes demonstrations of their craft. Sets, props, and special effects are very elaborate.

TOURING TIPS The Stunt Theater holds 2,000 people; capacity audiences are possible. The first performance is always the easiest to see. If the first show is at 11 a.m. or earlier, you can usually walk in, even if you arrive 5 minutes late. For the second performance, show up about 15–20 minutes ahead of time; for the third and subsequent shows, arrive 20–30 minutes early. If you plan to tour during late afternoon and evening, attend the last performance of the day. To beat the crowd out of the stadium, sit on the far right (as you face the staging area) and near the top.

Meet Disney Stars at *Red Carpet Dreams*   ★★★★

PRESCHOOL ★★★★½ (AA)	GRADE SCHOOL ★★★★½ (AA)	TEENS ★★★★ (A)
YOUNG ADULTS ★★★★ (A)	OVER 30 ★★★★ (A)	SENIORS ★★★★ (A)

What it is Character-greeting venue. **Scope and scale** Diversion. **When to go** First or last hour the park is open or during mealtimes. **Duration of experience** About 2 minutes. **Comments** Everybody loves Mickey and Minnie; not to be missed. **Average wait in line per 100 people ahead of you** 60 minutes. **Queue speed** Slow. **ECV/wheelchair access** May remain in wheelchair. **Participates in Genie+** No. **Early Theme Park Entry** No. **Extended Evening Hours** No.

DESCRIPTION AND COMMENTS This is the venue for meeting Mickey and Minnie Mouse in Disney's Hollywood Studios. The idea is that you're visiting while the two are working on Minnie's latest films. Minnie's greeting area is the set of her latest film, a musical blockbuster. Mickey's dressed as the Sorcerer's Apprentice from *Fantasia*.

TOURING TIPS The meet-and-greet entrance is found on Commissary Lane, between the entrance to the ABC Commissary and the entrance to the Sci-Fi Dine-In Theater. Long lines form once the park is full but drop considerably during lunch and dinner.

Meet Olaf at Celebrity Spotlight ★★★½

PRESCHOOL ★★★★½ (MAA)	**GRADE SCHOOL ★★★★½ (MAA)**	**TEENS ★★★★ (A)**
YOUNG ADULTS NA	**OVER 30 ★★★★ (A)**	**SENIORS ★★★★ (A)**

What it is Character-greeting venue. **Scope and scale** Diversion. **When to go** First or last hour the park is open or during mealtimes. **Duration of experience** About 2 minutes. **Average wait in line per 100 people ahead of you** 60 minutes. **Queue speed** Slow. **ECV/wheelchair access** May remain in wheelchair. **Participates in Genie+** Yes. **Early Theme Park Entry** No. **Extended Evening Hours** No.

DESCRIPTION AND COMMENTS Resist the urge to sing–ask your kids, "Do you want to meet a snowman?" Though this is a low-frills photo shoot, Olaf puts forth a ton of effort.

TOURING TIPS Wait-in-line times are lowest during lunch and after 4 p.m.

Star Tours—The Adventures Continue ★★★½

PRESCHOOL ★★★½ (BA)	**GRADE SCHOOL ★★★★½ (AA)**	**TEENS ★★★★ (A)**
YOUNG ADULTS ★★★★ (A)	**OVER 30 ★★★★ (A)**	**SENIORS ★★★★ (A)**

What it is Indoor space-flight-simulation ride. **Scope and scale** Major attraction. **When to go** During lunch or after 4 p.m. **Comments** Expectant mothers and anyone prone to motion sickness should not ride. Too intense for many children younger than age 8; must be 40" to ride; Rider Switch option available (see page 396). **Duration of ride** About 7 minutes. **Average wait in line per 100 people ahead of you** 5 minutes; assumes all simulators operating. **Loading speed** Moderate-fast. **ECV/wheelchair access** Must transfer from ECV to provided wheelchair and then from wheelchair to ride vehicle. **Participates in Genie+** Yes. **Early Theme Park Entry** Yes. **Extended Evening Hours** No.

Motion Sickness

DESCRIPTION AND COMMENTS Based on the *Star Wars* saga, this was Disney's first modern simulator ride. Guests ride in a flight simulator modeled after those used for training pilots and astronauts, experiencing dips, turns, twists, and climbs. The ride film, projected in high-definition 3-D, has more than 50 combinations of opening and ending scenes, including clips from *The Force Awakens*. You could ride Star Tours all day without seeing the same scenes twice. The downside to Star Tours is that it's not in Galaxy's Edge.

TOURING TIPS Wait-in-line times are lowest during lunch and after 4 p.m.

Vacation Fun at Mickey Shorts Theater ★★★½

PRESCHOOL NA	**GRADE SCHOOL ★★★★ (A)**	**TEENS ★★★★ (A)**
YOUNG ADULTS ★★★½ (BA)	**OVER 30 ★★★★ (A)**	**SENIORS ★★★½ (BA)**

What it is Cartoon featuring Mickey Mouse. **Scope and scale** Diversion. **When to go** Anytime. **Duration of presentation** 10 minutes. **Preshow entertainment** None. **Probable waiting time** 9 minutes. **ECV/wheelchair access** May remain in wheelchair. **Participates in Genie+** No. **Early Theme Park Entry** No. **Extended Evening Hours** No.

DESCRIPTION AND COMMENTS The Mickey Shorts Theater shows a new 10-minute Mickey Mouse cartoon called *Vacation Fun,* which combines clips from several of the newest and best Mickey Mouse cartoons. If you've seen *Couple Sweaters, O Sole Minnie, Amore Motore,* or *Potatoland,* you'll recognize the scenes. If you loved Mickey & Minnie's Runaway Railway, here's your chance to see more of the new-style cartoons. And if you've not yet seen the new cartoons, this is the place to get familiar with them.

TOURING TIPS Even if you've seen some of the clips, the theater is large, comfortable, and air-conditioned—perfect for a short break on a hot day.

GRAND AVENUE

THIS THEMED AREA has just one attraction, two restaurants, and a bar. The street sets serve as a pedestrian thoroughfare to Galaxy's Edge.

Muppet-Vision 3-D ★★★★

| PRESCHOOL ★★★★ (A) | GRADE SCHOOL ★★★★ (MBA) | TEENS ★★★½ (MBA) |
| YOUNG ADULTS ★★★★ (MBA) | OVER 30 ★★★★ (MBA) | SENIORS ★★★★ (A) |

What it is 3-D movie starring the Muppets. **Scope and scale** Major attraction. **When to go** Anytime. **Duration of presentation** 17 minutes. **Preshow entertainment** The Muppets on TV. **Probable waiting time** 15 minutes. **ECV/wheelchair access** May remain in wheelchair. **Participates in Genie+** Yes. **Early Theme Park Entry** No. **Extended Evening Hours** No.

DESCRIPTION AND COMMENTS *Muppet-Vision 3-D* provides a total sensory experience, with wacky 3-D action augmented by auditory, visual, and tactile special effects. If you're tired and hot, this zany show will make you feel brand-new. Arrive early to enjoy the hilarious video preshow. Although the film hasn't been updated in decades and we've seen it dozens of times, the comedic timing and dialog still makes us laugh.

A New Brunswick, Canada, reader thinks the Muppets are heaven-sent:

I think Muppet-Vision 3-D is a godsend for five reasons: (1) It NEVER has a line (even on our visit on New Year's Day!). (2) Everyone ages 1–100 gives the show high marks. (3) Between the preshow and the movie, it's half an hour of sitting comfortably in an air-conditioned theater. (4) Between the live actors and animatronics, it's so much more than just another silly 3-D movie. (5) IT'S THE MUPPETS!

TOURING TIPS Waits generally peak around lunchtime, and it's unusual to find a wait longer than one show. If you do encounter a long line, try again later. Rarely a good use of Genie+.

PIXAR PLACE

THE TINY DEAD-END STREET on the way to Toy Story Land holds a few food stands. The street is rarely used, so it's a good place to find shade and relax.

TOY STORY LAND

THE 11-ACRE Toy Story Land opened in 2018. The idea behind it is that you've been shrunk to the size of a toy and placed in Andy's backyard, where you get to play with other toys he's set up.

Toy Story Land's attractions are designed to appeal to young children. This is a great thing that DHS has needed more of for years (and still does), but because two of the rides have relatively low capacity, you should expect long waits throughout the day.

Toy Story Land is one of two ways to access Galaxy's Edge, the other being **Grand Avenue** (see 591).

Alien Swirling Saucers ★★½

PRESCHOOL ★★★★½ (MAA)	**GRADE SCHOOL ★★★★ (MBA)**	**TEENS ★★★ (MBA)**
YOUNG ADULTS ★★★½ (MBA)	**OVER 30 ★★★½ (MBA)**	**SENIORS ★★★½ (MBA)**

What it is Spinning car ride. **Scope and scale** Minor attraction. **When to go** First 30 minutes the park is open or after 3 p.m. **Comment** Must be 32" to ride. **Duration of ride** 3 minutes. **Average wait in line per 100 people ahead of you** 10 minutes. **Loading speed** Slow. **ECV/wheelchair access** Must transfer to ride vehicle. **Participates in Genie+** Yes. **Early Theme Park Entry** Yes. **Extended Evening Hours** No.

DESCRIPTION AND COMMENTS Alien Swirling Saucers is themed around *Toy Story*'s vending-machine aliens and their obsession with The Claw. About a dozen ride cars move, whiplike, in an elongated figure-eight around three circular tracks embedded in the ground. The ride experience is actually much milder than the Magic Kingdom's Mad Tea Party.

TOURING TIPS For the shortest waits, ride during the first 30 minutes or last hour the park is open. Consider skipping the Saucers if the wait exceeds 20 minutes.

Slinky Dog Dash ★★★★

PRESCHOOL ★★★★ (AA)	**GRADE SCHOOL ★★★★½ (MAA)**	**TEENS ★★★★½ (MAA)**
YOUNG ADULTS ★★★★½ (MAA)	**OVER 30 ★★★★½ (MAA)**	**SENIORS ★★★★½ (AA)**

What it is Mild outdoor roller coaster. **Scope and scale** Major attraction. **When to go** As soon as the park opens or just before closing. **Comment** Must be 38" to ride. **Duration of ride** 2 minutes. **Average wait in line per 100 people ahead of you** 4 minutes. **Loading speed** Moderate. **ECV/wheelchair access** Must transfer from ECV to provided wheelchair and then from wheelchair to ride vehicle. **Participates in Genie+** Yes. **Early Theme Park Entry** Yes. **Extended Evening Hours** No.

DESCRIPTION AND COMMENTS Slinky Dog Dash is a long outdoor children's roller coaster designed to look as if Andy built it out of Tinkertoys. The trains are themed to *Toy Story*'s Slinky Dog, complete with bobbing tail. As for intensity, it's something along the lines of the Magic Kingdom's Barnstormer or Seven Dwarfs Mine Train—lots of turns, dips, and hills but no loops or high-speed curves—and not nearly as rough as Big Thunder Mountain Railroad. For adults, it's more fun than you might expect, but not worth a very long wait.

TOURING TIPS Slinky Dog Dash gets crowded as soon as the park opens and stays that way all day. Visit at park opening or right before the park closes. The ride does not run during thunderstorms or when lightning is in the area, though it does run in light rain.

Toy Story Mania! ★★★★½

ALL AGE GROUPS ★★★★½ (MAA)

What it is 3-D ride through indoor shooting gallery. **Scope and scale** Headliner. **When to go** At park opening or after 4:30 p.m. **Duration of ride** About 6½ minutes. **Average wait in line per 100 people ahead of you** 4½ minutes. **Loading speed** Fast. **ECV/**

wheelchair access Must transfer from ECV to provided wheelchair. **Participates in Genie+** Yes. **Early Theme Park Entry** Yes. **Extended Evening Hours** No.

DESCRIPTION AND COMMENTS Toy Story Mania! ushered in a new generation of Disney attraction: the virtual 3-D dark ride. Conceptually, it's an interactive shooting gallery much like **Buzz Lightyear's Space Ranger Spin** (see page 490), but in Toy Story Mania!, your ride vehicle passes through a totally virtual midway, with booths offering such games as ring tossing and ball throwing. You use a cannon on your vehicle to play as you move from booth to booth. Unlike the laser guns in Buzz Lightyear, though, the pull-string cannons in Toy Story Mania! take advantage of CGI technology to toss rings, shoot balls, and even throw eggs and pies. Each booth is manned by a *Toy Story* character who's right beside you in 3-D glory, cheering you on. In addition to 3-D imagery, you experience vehicle motion, wind, and water spray.

The ride begins with a training round, then continues through a number of "real" games in which you compete against your riding mate. The technology has the ability to self-adjust the level of difficulty, and there are plenty of easy targets for small children to reach. *Tip:* Let the string retract all the way back into the cannon before pulling it again.

TOURING TIPS Toy Story Mania! is one of the most reliable rides in the park. As such, it's often the first spot guests go to when Slinky Dog Dash is down. If you find yourself behind a large crowd, come back in an hour or try Genie+.

ANIMATION COURTYARD

THIS AREA IS TO THE RIGHT of Mickey & Minnie's Runaway Railway in the middle of the park. It holds a large theater used for live stage shows (one was closed at press time), a walk-through display of *Star Wars* movie props, and several character-greeting locations.

Disney Junior Play and Dance!   ★★

PRESCHOOL ★★★★½ (MAA)	GRADE SCHOOL ★★★★ (A)	TEENS NA
YOUNG ADULTS NA	OVER 30 ★★★½ (MBA)	SENIORS NA

What it is Live show for preschool children. **Scope and scale** Minor attraction. **When to go** Check *Times Guide* for showtimes. **Comment** Audience sits on the floor. **Duration of presentation** 25 minutes. **When to arrive** 20–30 minutes before showtime. **ECV/wheelchair access** May remain in wheelchair. **Participates in Genie+** Yes. **Early Theme Park Entry** No. **Extended Evening Hours** No.

DESCRIPTION AND COMMENTS This high-energy music-and-videos show features characters from Disney Channel's *The Lion Guard, Doc McStuffins,* and *Vampirina,* along with Mickey Mouse. A simple narrative serves as the platform for all the singing, dancing, and audience participation.

Play and Dance! includes the Disney characters plus a DJ who rally the kids as if this were a CrossFit class for preschoolers. The audience sits on the floor so that kids can spontaneously erupt into motion when the mood strikes. *Note:* They do, and it does. There's also plenty of room, which helps.

TOURING TIPS Staged in a huge building on the right side of the courtyard. Get here around 25 minutes before showtime, pick a spot on the floor, and chill until the action begins.

Star Wars Launch Bay ★★★
Exhibits

PRESCHOOL NA	GRADE SCHOOL ★★★★ (MBA)	TEENS ★★★★ (BA)
YOUNG ADULTS ★★★★ (BA)	OVER 30 ★★★★ (MBA)	SENIORS ★★★★ (BA)

Character Greetings

ALL AGE GROUPS ★ ★ ★ ½ (MAA)

What it is Displays of a few *Star Wars* movie models and props and character greetings. **Scope and scale** Diversion. **When to go** Anytime. **Comment** There are separate lines for each character greeting. **Probable waiting time** 20–30 minutes each for the character greetings. **ECV/wheelchair access** May remain in wheelchair. **Participates in Genie+** No. **Early Theme Park Entry** No. **Extended Evening Hours** No.

DESCRIPTION AND COMMENTS Launch Bay opened when the Studios needed more things for guests to do while new rides were being built; now it's essentially a walk-through commercial for the latest *Star Wars* films. There are a few interesting models on display for the serious fan to admire, but the real draw is the character greetings.

Three characters hold court, currently Chewbacca, Darth Vader, and BB-8. Waits in line for Chewie and Vader usually run about 20–30 minutes.

TOURING TIPS Visit anytime.

Walt Disney Presents   ★ ★ ★

PRESCHOOL NA	**GRADE SCHOOL ★ ★ ★ ½ (MBA)**	**TEENS ★ ★ ★ ½ (MBA)**
YOUNG ADULTS ★ ★ ★ ★ (BA)	**OVER 30 ★ ★ ★ ★ (BA)**	**SENIORS ★ ★ ★ ★ ½ (A)**

What it is Disney-memorabilia collection plus a short film about Walt Disney. **Scope and scale** Minor attraction. **When to go** Anytime. **Duration of presentation** 25 minutes. **Preshow entertainment** Disney memorabilia. **Probable waiting time** For the film, 7 minutes. **ECV/wheelchair access** May remain in wheelchair. **Participates in Genie+** No. **Early Theme Park Entry** No. **Extended Evening Hours** No.

DESCRIPTION AND COMMENTS *Walt Disney Presents* consists of an exhibit area showcasing Disney memorabilia and recordings, followed by a film about Walt Disney's life and achievements, narrated by Julie Andrews. On display are various innovations in animation developed by Disney, along with models and plans for Disney World and other Disney theme parks.

TOURING TIPS Every minute spent among these extraordinary artifacts will enhance your visit, taking you back to a time when the creativity and vision that created the park you're in were personified by one struggling entrepreneur. The standard film is sometimes replaced with previews of current Disney movies.

STAR WARS: GALAXY'S EDGE

STAR WARS HAS SO MANY DEDICATED FANS that the Jedi Code constitutes a government-recognized religion in several countries, including tax-exempt status in the United States.

In 2015, Disney announced its plans for Galaxy's Edge, arguably the biggest bet made on their US theme parks since EPCOT in 1982. Two virtually identical 14-acre versions were built, the other at Disneyland; together they're rumored to have cost more than $2 billion. By way of comparison, Disney bought the entire *Star Wars* franchise for $4 billion, and building the entire 500-acre Animal Kingdom cost $1.5 billion in today's dollars when it opened in 1998.

Disney's goal with Galaxy's Edge was to redefine the entire theme park experience. It put more money, technology, and storytelling effort into this one project than it had put into anything in a long, long time. Disney incorporated the *Star Wars* alphabet of Aurebesh to spell out signage. Disney cast members were provided background stories about their lives in Galaxy's Edge and used invented terminology and idioms in conversation with guests: "Hello!" became "Bright suns!" and restrooms were called "refreshers."

Fans couldn't wait to experience Galaxy's Edge: Disney's CEO Bob Iger joked that the entire marketing campaign for the land would consist of him tweeting, "It's open."

The expectations were impossible to live up to. The first ride to open in Galaxy's Edge was *Millennium Falcon:* Smugglers Run, to mixed reviews. The land itself, while looking reasonably like a *Star Wars* planet's outpost, lacks visual elements such as movement and water found in Pandora and the Wizarding Worlds. Guests didn't appreciate having to navigate the land's language idioms when all they wanted was directions to the nearest bathroom. Most cast members have abandoned their stories and verbiage. And while Rise of the Resistance is the best ride Disney has built in decades, it exhibits more operational delays and problems than almost any other Disney World ride. Its unsteady operation, coupled with its incredible popularity, means long lines throughout the day.

Perhaps the biggest gamble with the land was Disney's decision to place Galaxy's Edge at a specific time in the *Star Wars* canon: in the third trilogy, between *The Last Jedi* and *Rise of Skywalker.* That means the land doesn't have any characters from the original trilogy, such as Luke Skywalker, Han Solo, Obi-Wan Kenobi, Princess Leia, or Darth Vader (though Disney has added characters from the hit Disney+ series *The Mandalorian*). Disney's thinking here was that the land would be future-proof, able to host new stories and new characters that are written into subsequent films in the *Star Wars* franchise. And the problem, of course, is that not only do those stories or characters not exist yet, but most *Star Wars* fans love the characters from the original three films most.

THE LAND Galaxy's Edge is an outpost in the village of Black Spire Outpost, on the planet of Batuu. Formerly a busy trading port and waypoint before the invention of light speed–capable transportation, it's now a dusty backwater filled with bounty hunters, smugglers, and those who make a living by not being recognized. As if that weren't enough, members of the Resistance and the First Order live in and around the town in an uneasy coexistence.

Galaxy's Edge has two access points: on **Grand Avenue** and in **Toy Story Land.** Entering through Grand Avenue puts you in the middle of the Resistance's encampment, while the side closest to Toy Story Land is controlled by the First Order.

Galaxy's Edge Attractions

Millennium Falcon: Smugglers Run ★★★★

PRESCHOOL ★★½ (BA)	GRADE SCHOOL ★★★★½ (AA)	TEENS ★★★★½ (AA)
YOUNG ADULTS ★★★★½ (AA)	OVER 30 ★★★★½ (AA)	SENIORS ★★★★ (A)

What it is Interactive simulator ride. **Scope and scale** Super-headliner. **When to go** As soon as it opens or after 6 p.m. **Comments** Could've been great; 38" height requirement; Rider Switch option available (see page 396). **Duration of ride** 4½ minutes. **Average wait in line per 100 people ahead of you** 3½ minutes. **Loading speed**

Moderate–fast. **ECV/wheelchair access** Must transfer to ride vehicle. **Participates in Genie+** Yes. **Early Theme Park Entry** Yes. **Extended Evening Hours** No.

DESCRIPTION AND COMMENTS Smugglers Run lets guests fly Han Solo's *Millennium Falcon*, the "fastest hunk of junk in the galaxy." Guests approaching the attraction will see a life-size *Millennium Falcon* parked outside the spaceport, periodically venting gas as technicians tinker with the temperamental craft. (You can look at the replica, but you can't walk under or touch it.)

To board, you're recruited by Hondo Ohnaka, an animatronic pirate who has cut a deal with Chewbacca to use the *Falcon* for some sketchy transportation business. After ascending to a second-story catwalk with wraparound views of the ship, visitors enter Ohnaka's command center, where Hondo explains the mission, while the *Falcon* can be seen on a video screen preparing for launch. Ohnaka is one of Disney's most advanced animatronics, with electric motors capable of 50 functions, and his movements are eerily fluid.

At this point, you enter the *Falcon* through an umbilical bridge and are assigned to a flight crew of up to six people. While awaiting your turn, you can relax in the ship's instantly recognizable main hold, complete with a holographic chess board from the movies.

When the time arrives, your flight crew walks down the ship's curving corridors and appears to enter the *Falcon*'s one and only cockpit, thanks to a patented carousel system that keeps the small simulator cabins hidden from each other. Your mission has you stealing supplies from the First Order to sell on the black market. Each rider is assigned his or her own station: a pilot and copilot up front to steer around obstacles and activate the hyperdrive, two gunners in the middle to shoot down enemy fighters, and a pair of engineers in the rear to repair the ship when the pilots and gunners mess up. Computer-generated scenery is projected on an ultra-HD dome outside the windshield. By far, the best role is that of pilot.

What separates this ride from other simulators (such as Star Tours) are 200 buttons, switches, and levers in the cockpit, each of which does something when activated: Watch for indicator rings to illuminate around certain controls, cluing you in to the correct moment to punch them.

Another difference between Smugglers Run and other simulators is that the video screens displaying the action aren't attached to the ride vehicle. This not only allows for a more realistic display of the action but also reduces the potential for motion sickness.

At the end of the day, however, in spite of the amount of money, time, and technology that Disney has invested in this attraction, the Smugglers Run ride experience is a disappointment. Seats for the gunners and

---

DISNEY DISH WITH JIM HILL

MINI *MILLENNIUM* One of the worst-kept secrets in Galaxy's Edge is that there's a mini version of the *Millennium Falcon* on the full-size *Millennium Falcon*. To see it, stand facing the *Falcon* straight on, with the entrance to Smugglers Run on your left. Locate the cockpit (the round circle thing with glass windows) on the left side of the *Falcon*. Directly under that is a dark-gray grated exhaust that leads down to a set of two pipes that head right. Follow those pipes until you see what looks like a boxed radiator. Directly in front of that radiator is the mini *Millennium Falcon*.

engineers are situated far enough back from the video screens that it's like watching a drive-in movie through a tunnel. Worse, the controls for those four seats are mounted at a 90-degree angle from the action on-screen: If you're in one of these seats, you can either look at the screen or the controls you're supposed to be working—but not both. It's so hard to work the controls, in fact, that we gave up halfway through our rides.

The experience for the pilots is no better—one pilot controls left and right movements while the other, inexplicably, controls up and down. The real *Millennium Falcon* doesn't work this way, and nobody with any sense would design actual controls like this.

Terrible ergonomics are only part of the problem, though. *Star Wars* fans have known since 1977 exactly how the *Falcon*'s guns and gunners are supposed to look and work. What Disney has built here captures none of that—the thrill of combat has been reduced to push-button data entry. It's an inexcusable design compromise, one that undercuts the entire land's claim at realism.

Finally, the script that our rides followed was so comically predictable that it actively distracted from the experience. If you've ever been on any other Disney simulator, say, Star Tours or Mission: Space, you'll recognize the exact same plot points, at the exact same pace.

The *Millennium Falcon* enjoys a beloved, unique place in American cinema. We think it deserved better. That said, opinions among the *Unofficial* team aren't uniform: Seth Kubersky, coauthor of *The Unofficial Guide to Disneyland,* describes it as "a four-star ride in a five-star wrapper."

TOURING TIPS Disney's posted wait time for this ride might be the most accurate estimate of how long you'll actually wait than any other major ride in Walt Disney World. Wait times here drop off after 6 p.m. Ride early in the morning, immediately after Rise of the Resistance, or use Genie+.

Star Wars: Rise of the Resistance   ★★★★★

PRESCHOOL ★★★½ (BA)   GRADE SCHOOL ★★★★½ (E)   TEENS ★★★★★ (E)
YOUNG ADULTS ★★★★★ (E)   OVER 30 ★★★★★ (E)   SENIORS ★★★★½ (E)

Note: Rise of the Resistance is the highest-rated attraction in any Disney or Universal theme park in the United States.

What it is Next-generation dark ride. **Scope and scale** Super-headliner. **When to go** When your boarding group is called. **Comments** Get a boarding group on the My Disney Experience app at exactly 7 a.m. or 1 p.m. on the day of your visit; not to be missed; 40" height requirement; Rider Switch option available (see page 396). **Duration of ride** About 25 minutes with all preshows; about 5 minutes for ride. **Average wait in line per 100 people ahead of you** 4 minutes. **Loading speed** Moderate-fast. **ECV/wheelchair access** Must transfer to ride vehicle. **Participates in Genie+** No (it offers Individual Lightning Lane). **Early Theme Park Entry** Yes. **Extended Evening Hours** No.

Motion Sickness

DESCRIPTION AND COMMENTS A mobile Resistance gun turret tucked into a scrubland forest marks the entrance to the most epic indoor dark ride in Disney theme park history. Rise of the Resistance is an innovative attempt to integrate at least four different ride experiences—trackless vehicles, a motion simulator, walk-through environments, and even an elevator drop—into Disney's longest attraction ever.

The adventure begins as you explore the Resistance military outpost, laser-carved out of ancient stone. An animatronic BB-8 rolls in, accompanied by a hologram of Rey, who recruits you to strike a blow against the First Order. Fifty guests at a time exit the briefing room to board a standing-room-only shuttlecraft piloted by Nien Nunb from *Return of the Jedi.* As the ship breaks orbit, you can feel the rumble and see Poe

Dameron accompanying you in his X-Wing, until a Star Destroyer snags you in its tractor beam and sucks you into its belly.

When the doors to your shuttlecraft reopen, you've been convincingly transported into an enormous hangar, complete with 50 Stormtroopers, TIE Fighters, and a 100-foot-wide bay window looking into outer space. Cast members clad as First Order officers brusquely herd captive guests into holding rooms to await their interrogation by black-clad baddie Kylo Ren.

Before long, you're making a break for it in an eight-passenger (two four-seat rows) troop transport with an animatronic droid as your driver; the car is capable of traveling without a fixed track and simulating movement. The ride blends dozens of robotic characters and enormous sets with video projections to create some of the most overwhelming environments ever seen in an indoor ride. One sequence sends you between the legs of two towering AT-ATs while dodging laser fire from legions of Stormtroopers, while another puts you face-to-face with the Solo-slaying Ren. In the epic finale, you'll survive an escape pod's dramatic crash back to Batuu, a heart-stopping multistory plunge enhanced by digital projections. The drop at the end isn't quite as intense as the one on the Tower of Terror—but don't underestimate its ability to loosen your lunch.

TOURING TIPS We think Rise of the Resistance is the best ride Disney has produced in decades. It's the most popular ride in the park, and the most complex ride Disney has ever made. That complexity makes it prone to breakdowns—daily, on average, and sometimes more than once.

The best way to experience Rise of the Resistance without a long wait is to stay at a Disney resort and use Early Theme Park Entry to get in line as soon as the park opens. Alternatively, purchasing Individual Lightning Lane reservations will save you more time here than on any other ride in Walt Disney World.

Galaxy's Edge Shopping, Dining, and More

SHOPPING Outside of the area's two headliner rides, **Batuu** boasts a Marrakech-esque marketplace of shops selling unique in-universe merchandise, some of which are practically attractions themselves. None of the items for sale bear the standard *Star Wars* or Disney logos, to maintain the illusion that everything on offer was actually crafted by and for the Black Spire Outpost villagers.

unofficial **TIP**
Costumes are forbidden at Galaxy's Edge for guests age 14 and older.

At **Savi's Workshop,** small groups are led by "Gatherers" through the process of building their own lightsabers, from picking a colorful kyber crystal to selecting customizable handles. The cost of this experience is around $266; reservations via Disney's website or app are strongly recommended, and you pay when you make the reservation. (A small number of same-day reservations might be available for spots starting 2 hours from reservation time.) Despite the steep price tag, it's one of the best things we experienced in Galaxy's Edge: The finished lightsaber feels substantial, balanced, and elegant in your hands. We'd do it again.

If you want to build a lightsaber of your own, make park reservations (if required; see page 30) and reservations for Savi's up to 60 days in advance. You can proudly pair your saber with a screen-accurate Jedi tunic ensemble from **Black Spire Outfitters**—but you may wear it only outside of Galaxy's Edge.

At **Droid Depot,** you can pick robot parts off of conveyor belts to build your own pint-size R-series or BB-series droid, which will then communicate with its counterparts around the land; preassembled droids, including a chatty C-3PO and a DJ R3X Bluetooth speaker, are also available. Reservations for Droid Depot can be made 60 days in advance and are strongly recommended.

DINING When you get hungry, you'll find that just as much attention has gone into the food and drink at Galaxy's Edge as everything else; even the Coca-Cola sodas come in unique spherical bottles emblazoned in Aurebesh, the *Star Wars* alphabet. There's no sit-down service, but Galaxy's Edge has the two highest-rated counter-service restaurants in the park: Rustle up galactic food-truck grub from **Docking Bay 7,** or grab a sausage grilled under a Podracer engine at **Ronto Roasters.** Wash it down with a cold glass of (nondairy) blue or green milk from the **Milk Stand. Oga's Cantina** pours exclusive adult drinks, from Spice Runner cider to Jet Juice cocktails; reservations are strongly recommended. See pages 306–308 for detailed reviews of these four venues.

INTERACTIVITY IN GALAXY'S EDGE Perhaps the most intriguing elements of Galaxy's Edge are its experiments in live interaction, both digital and analog. Live performers, actor-controlled creature puppets, and roving droids can engage with guests and selected souvenirs. Characters include Rey, Chewbacca, Kylo Ren, and various Stormtroopers.

THE HOTEL In 2022, Disney opened a themed hotel, called **Star Wars: Galactic Starcruiser,** connected to Galaxy's Edge. The immersive, two-day live-action role-playing experience was lauded by guests who participated; however, the steep price tag (starting at $4,800 for two people) may have proven prohibitively expensive for many would-be guests. Disney has announced the *Halcyon* will make its last "voyage" in September 2023. Read more on page 196.

GALAXY'S EDGE TOURING TIPS Make park reservations for Hollywood Studios (if required; see page 30) as soon as you know your travel dates. Obtain Individual Lightning Lane reservations for Rise of the Resistance at 7 a.m.

Ride *Millennium Falcon:* Smugglers Run early in the morning, after you've experienced Slinky Dog Dash, or try riding during the last hour the park is open.

Save shopping and dining for after you've done the rides. Make reservations for Savi's Workshop, the Droid Depot, and Oga's Cantina 60 days before your visit.

DISNEY'S HOLLYWOOD STUDIOS ENTERTAINMENT

IN ADDITION TO THE SHOWS and performances profiled earlier in this chapter, the Studios offers the following. Check your *Times Guide* for showtimes.

BEACONS OF MAGIC Started in 2021, *Beacons of Magic* is a new show projected onto Sunset Boulevard's Twilight Zone Tower of Terror. It runs approximately every 15 minutes starting at dusk. When it starts, the Tower's exterior walls are bathed in bright, shimmering projections. Look closely—the best views are on Sunset and by the Tower of Terror entrance—and you'll see hotel guests dancing in the windows.

CHARACTER GREETINGS Chip 'n' Dale (as Rescue Rangers) can often be found in Echo Lake next to the *Indiana Jones* stunt show from around 10 a.m. to 5 p.m. *Toy Story* characters appear in Toy Story Land from around noon until dinnertime. Sully from *Monsters, Inc.* often appears inside the *Walt Disney Presents* theater.

WONDERFUL WORLD OF ANIMATION This 12-minute nighttime projection show displayed on the front of the Grauman's Chinese Theater (home of Mickey and Minnie's Runaway Railway) shows classic clips from Disney and the studios it has acquired. It's not the best (or sec-ond-, third- or fourth-best) projection show Disney has done, but it's a nice way to end the evening, if you're around, and can be a low-hassle substitute for seeing *Fantasmic!*

DISNEY'S HOLLYWOOD STUDIOS TOURING PLAN

OUR HOLLYWOOD STUDIOS TOURING PLAN (see pages 725– 728) has two versions: one for Disney resort guests and one for off-site guests; the plan for on-site guests uses Early Theme Park Entry (see page 36) to minimize waits in line. Because Early Entry means thousands of guests will already be in lines and on rides before off-site guests set foot in the park, the touring strategy for off-site guests must necessarily be different.

Our Hollywood Studios touring plan for this edition does *not* assume the use of Genie+ or Individual Lightning Lane. If you opt for these, just use our free touring plan software to adjust the plan.

UNIVERSAL ORLANDO

OVERVIEW

UNIVERSAL ORLANDO is a complete destination resort: A system of roads and two multistory parking facilities is connected by moving sidewalks to **CityWalk,** a shopping, dining, and nighttime-entertainment complex that also serves as a gateway to **Universal Studios Florida (USF)** and **Universal Islands of Adventure (IOA)** theme parks, as well as **Universal's Volcano Bay** water park (see "The Water Parks," page 640, for a description). And **Universal's Epic Universe,** a new park surrounded by more hotels, is currently rising on an expansion campus several miles to the south.

LODGING AT UNIVERSAL ORLANDO

UNIVERSAL HAS EIGHT RESORT HOTELS. The 750-room **Loews Portofino Bay Hotel** is a gorgeous property set on an artificial bay and themed like an Italian coastal town. The 650-room **Hard Rock Hotel** is an ultracool "Hotel California" replica, and the 1,000-room, Polynesian-themed **Loews Royal Pacific Resort** is sumptuously decorated and richly appointed. These three resorts are on the pricey side, but guests get free Universal Express Unlimited passes for the length of their stay, including check-in and checkout day (see page 606 for details).

The retro-style **Cabana Bay Beach Resort,** Universal's largest hotel, has 2,200 moderate- and value-priced rooms, plus amenities (bowling

continued on page 604

Universal Orlando

To Tampa &
Walt Disney
← World

Turkey Lake Road

Hollywood Way

Universal's
Cabana Bay
Beach Resort

**Universal's
Volcano Bay**

Loews Sapphire
Falls Resort

**Universal
Islands of
Adventure**

Universal's
Aventura Hotel

4

main
entrance

Universal's Endless Summer
Resort—Surfside Inn & Suites

Loews Royal Pacific Resort

**Universal
CityWalk**

Universal Blvd.

400
4

Universal's Endless Summer
Resort—Dockside Inn & Suites

Hollywood Way

400
4

parking garage

435

American Way

435

Grand National Dr.

4

continued from page 601

alley, lazy river) not seen at comparable Disney resorts. **Loews Sapphire Falls Resort** has a Caribbean theme and is priced between the Royal Pacific and Cabana Bay Beach Resorts.

A sixth hotel, **Universal's Aventura Hotel,** is adjacent to Loews Sapphire Falls Resort. The 16-story tower has 600 rooms, including 13 Kids' Suites, along with a food hall showcasing five cuisines and Universal's first rooftop bar and grill with a view of Volcano Bay. The seaside-themed **Endless Summer Resort,** just off Universal's main campus on the former Wet 'n Wild water-park property, includes both **Surfside Inn** and **Dockside Inn;** combined, the duo offers 2,800 value-priced rooms (including 1,450 two-bedroom suites).

Bus service is available from Endless Summer, while Aventura and Cabana Bay connect to the rest of the resort via shuttle buses and walking paths; the other four hotels also offer water-taxi service. All hotel guests get Early Park Admission to The Wizarding World of Harry Potter (one or both theme parks, depending on the season) and Volcano Bay up to 1 hour before the general public.

ARRIVING AT UNIVERSAL ORLANDO

THE UNIVERSAL ORLANDO COMPLEX can be accessed from eastbound I-4 by taking **Exit 75A** and turning left at the top of the ramp onto Universal Boulevard. Traveling westbound on I-4, use **Exit 74B** and then turn right onto Hollywood Way. Entrances are also off **Kirkman Road** to the east, **Turkey Lake Road** to the north, and **Vineland Road** to the west. **Universal Boulevard** connects the International Drive area to Universal via an overpass bridging I-4. Turkey Lake and Vineland Roads are good alternatives when I-4 is gridlocked.

unofficial **TIP**

If you want to ensure you arrive at Universal Orlando before park opening, we advise using a ride-hailing app.

Once on-site, you'll be directed to park in one of two multitiered parking garages. Parking runs $30 for cars and $40 for RVs. Prime parking is $60 ($50 during slower seasons), and valet is $75 ($40 after 6 p.m.; $30 for under 2 hours; not valid on select event nights). From the garages, (sometimes) moving sidewalks deliver you to Universal CityWalk; it takes about 8–20 minutes to get from the garages to the parks. From CityWalk, you can access the main entrances of both USF and IOA. Volcano Bay guests park on the bottom level of the same garages and are shuttled to the water park. Parking is free for everyone after 6 p.m. (after midnight during Halloween Horror Nights).

If you don't have your own car, **Mears** (☎ 407-422-2222; mearstransportation.com) operates taxis and luxury cars that will take you from Walt Disney World to Universal Orlando for about $50–$75 each way. Better yet, use a **ride-hailing app;** at the day's end, an Uber-branded pickup area awaits on the parking garage's roof, but you can save a service fee by using Lyft to depart.

unofficial **TIP**

MouseSavers offers a convenient list of current ticket prices at Universal Orlando. Access the list at tinyurl.com/uordeals. All prices include tax.

Universal offers one- to five-day tickets for one or two theme parks; adding Volcano Bay to a multiday ticket costs $43–$65, depending on length, and upgrading from one-park-per-day to Park-to-Park access costs \$59–\$74. Single and multiday tickets are date-specific, and prices can vary by up to \$50 per day, depending on the date you select during purchase for its first use. Flexible-date tickets are also available for \$6–\$13 per day more than the cost of the most expensive equivalent date-specific passes. Examine Universal's ticket calendar carefully: In certain seasons, you may save money by buying multiday passes with start dates a few days before your arrival. All multiday tickets expire five to eight days after their first use, depending on pass type and length. Universal also sells a range of two- and three-park annual passes, some of which include sizable discounts on hotels, food, and merchandise. Children ages 3–9 are charged \$5 less than adults on single-day tickets and \$10 less on multiday passes; there's no kids' discount on annual passes. Unlike Walt Disney World, Universal Orlando does not require advance reservations to visit its parks, although the turnstiles may temporarily close on rare occasions when the capacity limit is reached; on-site hotel guests, those with date-specific tickets, and reentering guests are granted priority admission over

UNIVERSAL ORLANDO ADMISSIONS *(prices include tax)*		
TICKET TYPE	**ADULTS**	**CHILDREN (ages 3-9)**
1-Day Single-Park (USF/IOA)	$116-$169	$111-$164
1-Day Volcano Bay	$85-$90	$65-$85
1-Day Park-to-Park (USF/IOA)	$175-$228	$169-$223
2-Day Single-Park (USF/IOA)	$230-$330	$219-$320
2-Day Park-to-Park (USF/IOA)	$294-$394	$283-$383
2-Day Park-to-Park (USF/IOA/VB)	$337-$431	$326-$421
3-Day Single-Park (USF/IOA)	$258-$359	$247-$348
3-Day Single-Park (USF/IOA/VB)	$300-$396	$290-$386
3-Day Park-to-Park (USF/IOA)	$322-$423	$311-$412
3-Day Park-to-Park (USF/IOA/VB)	$364-$460	$354-$449
4-Day Single-Park (USF/IOA)	$278-$373	$267-$362
4-Day Single-Park (USF/IOA/VB)	$331-$420	$321-$410
4-Day Park-to-Park (USF/IOA)	$347-$442	$337-$432
4-Day Park-to-Park (USF/IOA/VB)	$400-$490	$390-$479
5-Day Single-Park (USF/IOA)	$293-$387	$282-$376
5-Day Single-Park (USF/IOA/VB)	$357-$445	$346-$435
5-Day Park-to-Park (USF/IOA)	$367-$461	$357-$450
5-Day Park-to-Park (USF/IOA/VB)	$431-$520	$420-$509
2-Park Seasonal Annual Pass	$453	$453
2-Park Power Annual Pass	$506	$506
2-Park Preferred Annual Pass	$671	$671
2-Park Premier Annual Pass	$964	$964
3-Park Seasonal Annual Pass	$559	$559
3-Park Power Annual Pass	$623	$623
3-Park Preferred Annual Pass	$788	$788
3-Park Premier Annual Pass	$1,166	$1,166

multiday-ticket holders and annual-pass holders if the parks approach their capacity limit.

The prices in the table on page 605 are what you'll pay at Universal's website, including 6.5% sales tax. Buy your passes in advance at ☎ 800-711-0080 or universalorlando.com, or through Universal Orlando's official mobile app for iOS or Android.

Be sure to check Universal Orlando's website for seasonal deals and specials. You will pay $20 more than the online price by buying your multiday tickets at the gate. Consider using an online ticket wholesaler such as **Tripster** (☎ 888-590-5910; tripster.com) or **Orlando Ticket Connection** (☎ 855-473-7987; orlandoticketconnection.com). All tickets are brand-new. Vendors will provide you with electronic tickets just like Universal does.

The main Universal Orlando information line is ☎ 407-363-8000; the website is universalorlando.com. Reach **Guest Services** at ☎ 407-224-4233. To file a report with **Lost and Found**, visit tinyurl.com/uor lostandfound.

UNIVERSAL EXPRESS

SIMILAR TO DISNEY WORLD'S LIGHTNING LANE, Universal Express is a system whereby any guest can "skip the line" and experience an attraction via a special queue with little or no waiting. While Disney's system requires scheduling your ride reservation hours ahead of time, Universal Express involves no planning; you simply visit any eligible operating attraction whenever you choose, with no return-time window required. Universal Express costs more per day than Disney's Genie+ and Individual Lightning Lane options but is much easier and more efficient to use.

Unlimited Universal Express access at the two theme parks is a complimentary perk (valued at $138 per person, per day) for guests at Universal's top three hotels: **Hard Rock, Portofino Bay,** and **Royal Pacific.** Guests may use the Express lines all day long simply by flashing the pass they get at check-in. This perk far surpasses any benefit accorded to guests of Disney resorts and is especially valuable during peak season.

Day guests, along with guests staying at **Cabana Bay, Sapphire Falls, Endless Summer,** and **Aventura,** can buy Universal Express passes for the theme parks for an extra $96–$372 (depending on the season), which provides line-jumping privileges at each Universal Express attraction at a given park. You can buy Universal Express for one or both theme parks and for either single (one ride only on each participating attraction) or unlimited use.

unofficial **TIP**
If you use Universal Express, be careful not to lose your pass. We recommend bringing a lanyard (or buying one from Universal for $14 and up) so you can wear the pass around your neck.

Universal Express at **Volcano Bay** is not free for hotel guests but can be purchased by anyone for $21–$160, depending on the season and included slides.

More than 90% of rides and shows are covered by Universal Express, a much higher percentage than those covered by Genie+ at Walt Disney World; the notable exceptions are **Pteranodon Flyers** and (for now) **Hagrid's Magical Creatures Motorbike Adventure** at IOA.

You can also buy Universal Express at the theme parks' ticket windows, just outside the front gates, but it's faster to buy inside. Express passes are sold at most gift shops; Express is also available up to eight months in advance at universalorlando.com and through Universal's mobile app. You'll need to know when you plan on using it, though, because prices vary depending on the date.

IS UNIVERSAL EXPRESS WORTH IT? It depends on when you visit, hours of park operation, and crowd levels. If you want to sleep in and arrive at a park after opening, Express is an effective, albeit expensive, way to avoid long lines at the headliner attractions, especially during holidays and busy times.

If, however, you arrive 30 minutes before park opening and you use our Universal touring plans (see pages 729–734), you should experience the lowest possible waits at both parks. We encourage you to try the touring plans first, but if the waits for rides become intolerable, you can always buy Express in the parks.

VIRTUAL LINES

AT CERTAIN TIMES, SELECT ATTRACTIONS and special events may offer—or even require—the use of Virtual Line reservations instead of the standard standby queue. These 30-minute timed-return windows can be secured for free using Universal's mobile app; upon redemption, guests should be able to board the ride or enter the experience after a modest wait. You must be on Universal property and signed in to the app to claim a spot in a Virtual Line, but you don't have to be inside the parks or register an admission ticket. The lineup of participating attractions can change daily (or hourly) based on attendance, and additional return times may be released throughout the day, so recheck the website periodically. At press time, Virtual Line was offered only for seasonal experiences (like Mardi Gras float riding and Grinchmas meet and greets), but it has been implemented on peak days at Hagrid's Magical Motorbike Adventure. Guests with Universal Express passes don't need a return time to use Express at participating attractions.

SINGLE-RIDER LINES

SEVERAL ATTRACTIONS HAVE THIS LINE for guests riding alone. As Universal employees will tell you, it's often just as fast as the Express line—it will decrease your wait and leave more time for repeating rides or just bumming around. Note, though, that some queues (particularly at Forbidden Journey and Escape from Gringotts) are attractions in themselves and deserve to be experienced during your first ride. Single-rider queues are most efficient on attractions with four-person seats; rides with two-by-two seating (such as VelociCoaster and Hagrid's) provide minimal advantage and are sometimes slower than standby.

LOCKERS

UNIVERSAL ENFORCES A MANDATORY locker system at its big thrill rides. On most rides, all bags, purses, and other objects too large to be secured in a pocket must be placed in a locker. A "no loose items" policy is strictly enforced at **The Incredible Hulk Coaster, Jurassic World VelociCoaster,** and **Hollywood Rip Ride Rockit.** At these rides, guests must pass through an airport-style security screening to ensure that no phones, keys, or even spare change enters the boarding area.

unofficial **TIP**

You must scan your park ticket before receiving a locker number or retrieving your valuables from a locker, so keep your pass with you while you ride.

Small lockers at these attractions are free to use for an amount of time that depends on the length of the standby line. If the line is 30 minutes, for example, and the ride itself is 10 minutes, you get 40 minutes plus a small cushion of about 15 minutes. If you need to stow something larger than a small purse or fanny pack, larger lockers are available for a fee. The small mandatory lockers then cost $3 for each half hour after the free period, with a $20 maximum; large lockers cost $2 while you ride and then $3 for each additional half hour, up to $20.

Adjacent to IOA's soaking water rides are optional lockers that cost $4–$5 for the first 90 minutes and $3 for each additional hour, up to $20. And at the front of each park are paid all-day lockers in standard and family sizes for $10–$15; these can be opened and relocked with your park ticket as many times as you like.

UNIVERSAL DINING PROGRAMS

CHARACTER DINING A weekly character breakfast with *Despicable Me*'s Minions is offered at **The Tahitian Room** at Royal Pacific Resort on Saturdays ($37 adults, $22 kids ages 3–9, plus tip), and a Marvel Super Hero dinner is held at **Cafe 4** in IOA Thursday–Sunday ($56 adults, $31 kids ages 3–9, plus tip). For information and reservations, call ☎ 407-224-3663.

COVID *tip*

The *Despicable Me* character breakfast was still suspended at press time.

A character breakfast is also held during the holiday season at IOA with The Grinch ($45 adults, $29 kids ages 3–9, plus tip). After purchasing your dining experience online, you must call ☎ 407-224-7554 up to 24 hours before arriving to confirm your table. Separate theme park admission is required.

COCA-COLA FREESTYLE SOUVENIR CUP This perk entitles you to a souvenir sipper cup with one day of unlimited fountain soft drinks at all participating Coca-Cola Freestyle locations at both USF and IOA. Cost is $19 for one cup or $15 each for three or more. The price includes the first day of refills; each additional day costs $12.

UNIVERSAL, KIDS, AND SCARY STUFF

THOUGH THERE'S PLENTY FOR YOUNGER CHILDREN to enjoy at the Universal Orlando parks, most major attractions can potentially make kids under age 8 wig out.

At **Universal Studios Florida**, forget **Fast & Furious: Supercharged, Hollywood Rip Ride Rockit, Men in Black Alien Attack, Revenge of the Mummy, The Simpsons Ride,** and **Transformers: The Ride—3D.** The first part of the **E.T. Adventure** ride is a little intense for a few preschoolers, but the end is all happiness and harmony.

Although these are billed as family rides, both **Hogwarts Express** trains running between the two parks have some scary visuals, as does **Harry Potter and the Escape from Gringotts.** Interestingly, very few families report problems with *Universal Orlando's Horror Make-Up Show.* Anything we haven't listed here is probably a safe bet.

At **Universal Islands of Adventure,** watch out for **The Amazing Adventures of Spider-Man, Doctor Doom's Fearfall, Hagrid's Magical Creatures Motorbike Adventure, Harry Potter and the Forbidden Journey, The Incredible Hulk Coaster, Jurassic Park River Adventure,** and **Jurassic World VelociCoaster. Skull Island: Reign of Kong** is visually and psychologically intense; it may be too much for little ones. **Popeye & Bluto's Bilge-Rat Barges** is wet and wild, but most younger kids handle it pretty well. **Dudley Do-Right's Ripsaw Falls** is a toss-up, to be considered only if your kids really like water-flume rides. No other attractions should pose a problem.

At **Volcano Bay,** the **Ko'okiri Body Plunge** and **Kala and Tai Nui Serpentine Body Slides** feature a fall through a drop door before you plunge down twisting, winding tubes. The **Puihi and Honu Round Raft Rides** and the **Ohyah and Ohno Drop Slides** are also not for the faint of heart.

CHILD SWAP Universal's Child Swap is similar to Disney's Rider Switch (see page 396), but it's superior in several respects. The entire family goes through the whole line together before being split into riding and nonriding groups near the loading platform. The nonriding parent and child(ren) wait in a designated room, usually with some sort of entertainment (for example, Forbidden Journey at IOA shows the first 20 minutes of *Harry Potter and the Sorcerer's Stone* on a loop), a place to sit down, and sometimes restrooms with changing tables. At any theme park, the best tip we can give is to ask the greeter in front of the attraction what you're supposed to do.

UNIVERSAL CITYWALK

AT CITYWALK you'll find a variety of restaurants, clubs, and shops; outdoor entertainment; a concert hall (**Hard Rock Live**); the **Hollywood Drive-In** minigolf course; and the **Universal Cinemark** movie theater. There are also a number of combination restaurants and clubs; open to families with kids until 9 p.m., many of these offer live entertainment.

Eye-catching eateries include **Bigfire,** specializing in wood-grilled meats; the **Toothsome Chocolate Emporium & Savory Feast Kitchen,** a sweets shop and restaurant in a 19th-century-inspired steampunk building; and **Voodoo Doughnut,** an Oregon chain that bakes dozens of over-the-top varieties. For more dining options, see page 362.

Entertainment options include **CityWalk's Rising Star,** a karaoke joint where singers are backed by a live band; reggae at **Bob Marley—A Tribute to Freedom;** a **Pat O'Brien's** dueling-pianos club; **Fat Tuesday,** specializing in New Orleans–style daiquiris; a **Hard Rock Cafe** and **Hard Rock Live** concert venue; **Jimmy Buffett's Margaritaville;** and the **Red Coconut Club,** a two-story retro cocktail lounge that gets a new kitschy theme each season. No cover charges are required to visit the clubs. For details, call Universal CityWalk information at ☎ 407-224-2691.

Universal's Great Movie Escape (☎ 407-224-8463) offers hour-long interactive adventures inspired by *Back to the Future* and *Jurassic World* for up to eight guests ($48–$69 per person, ages 3 and up). Each takes you through eight highly themed environments, filled with special effects and cinematic Easter eggs. Whether you solve the puzzles quickly or get completely stumped, you'll still progress through your adventure at roughly the same pace, making this accessible for novices but unsatisfying for escape room veterans.

CityWalk is open daily, 8 a.m.–midnight (it closes at 1 or 2 a.m. during peak seasons). Parking, located in the same garages that serve the theme parks, is free after 6 p.m. If you're staying at a Universal resort, it's a short walk, but water taxis and buses are also available to transport you to CityWalk. Call ☎ 407-224-FOOD (3663) or visit tinyurl.com/unidinres for dinner reservations.

UNIVERSAL ISLANDS *of* ADVENTURE

OPENED IN 1999, ISLANDS OF ADVENTURE is a direct competitor of Disney's Magic Kingdom, the most-visited theme park in the world. IOA has kid-friendly rides and cartoon characters (like Fantasyland), thrill rides in a sci-fi city (like Tomorrowland), and a jungle river with robot creatures (like Adventureland). Its layout—a central entry corridor leading to a ring of connected lands—even mimics the classic Disney model, with one major exception: Instead of a hub and castle in the center, Universal built a large lagoon, with estuaries separating the park's thematically diverse "islands" (actually peninsulas).

*un*official **TIP**
Due to a smaller pool of reader data for Universal Orlando versus the Disney parks, we provide only basic appeal-by-age reader-survey ratings for the attractions in this chapter.

In 2007 Universal made a very bold bet: securing the rights to build a *Harry Potter*–themed area within IOA. Universal went all-out to create a setting and attractions designed to be the envy of the industry. The **Wizarding World of Harry Potter-Hogsmeade** opened at IOA in 2010 and was an immediate hit. In summer 2019, IOA opened **Hagrid's Magical Creatures Motorbike Adventure**, and the **Jurassic World VelociCoaster** opened in 2021.

NOT TO BE MISSED AT UNIVERSAL ISLANDS OF ADVENTURE
• The Amazing Adventures of Spider-Man • Hagrid's Magical Creatures Motorbike Adventure • Harry Potter and the Forbidden Journey • Hogwarts Express–Hogsmeade Station • The Incredible Hulk Coaster • Jurassic Park River Adventure • Jurassic World VelociCoaster • Popeye & Bluto's Bilge-Rat Barges • Skull Island: Reign of Kong

GETTING ORIENTED AT ISLANDS OF ADVENTURE

BOTH UNIVERSAL THEME PARKS are accessed from Universal CityWalk. Crossing CityWalk from the parking garages, bear left to Universal Islands of Adventure or right to Universal Studios Florida.

Islands of Adventure is arranged much like EPCOT's World Showcase—in a large circle surrounding a lake—but its themed areas are self-contained "lands" reminiscent of those in the Magic Kingdom.

Port of Entry is where you'll find Guest Services, lockers, stroller and wheelchair rentals, ATMs, lost and found, and shopping. From Port of Entry, moving clockwise around the lagoon, you first access **Marvel Super Hero Island;** then **Toon Lagoon, Skull Island, Jurassic Park, The Wizarding World of Harry Potter–Hogsmeade,** and **The Lost Continent;** and finally **Seuss Landing.**

unofficial **TIP**
Consider yourself warned: Several attractions at Islands of Adventure will drench you to the bone.

ISLANDS OF ADVENTURE ATTRACTIONS

MARVEL SUPER HERO ISLAND

WITH ITS FUTURISTIC DESIGN and comic book signage, Marvel Super Hero Island offers attractions themed to Marvel Comics characters.

The Amazing Adventures of Spider-Man ★★★★★

| PRESCHOOL ★★★½ | GRADE SCHOOL ★★★★½ | TEENS ★★★★½ |
| YOUNG ADULTS ★★★★½ | OVER 30 ★★★★ | SENIORS ★★★★ |

What it is Indoor adventure simulator ride based on Spider-Man. **Scope and scale** Super-headliner. **When to go** During the first 40 minutes the park is open. **Comments** Single-rider line available; must be 40″ to ride. **Duration of ride** 4½ minutes. **Loading speed** Fast. **Universal Express** Yes.

DESCRIPTION AND COMMENTS The Amazing Adventures of Spider-Man combines moving ride vehicles, 3-D film, and live action. It's frenetic, fluid, and considered by many to be the best theme park attraction on the planet.

Motion Sickness

The story line is that you're a reporter for the *Daily Bugle* (where Peter Parker, aka Spider-Man, works as a mild-mannered photographer) when it's discovered that evildoers have stolen—we're not making this up—the Statue of Liberty. You're drafted on the spot by your cantankerous editor to get the story. After speeding around and being thrust into a battle between good and evil, you experience a 400-foot "sensory drop" from a skyscraper all the way to the pavement. Spidey is less frantic than the similar Transformers ride at USF and features more dialogue and humor.

TOURING TIPS If you were on hand for Early Park Admission, ride after experiencing The Wizarding World and Skull Island: Reign of Kong. If you skip the Wizarding World, ride after Hulk.

Doctor Doom's Fearfall ★★★

| PRESCHOOL ★½ | GRADE SCHOOL ★★★½ | TEENS ★★★★ |
| YOUNG ADULTS ★★★½ | OVER 30 ★★★½ | SENIORS ★★★ |

What it is Vertical ascent and free fall. **Scope and scale** Major attraction. **When to go** First 40 minutes the park is open or after 3 p.m. **Comments** Single-rider line available; must be 52″ to ride. **Duration of ride** 40 seconds. **Loading speed** Slow. **Universal Express** Yes.

DESCRIPTION AND COMMENTS Here you're strapped into a seat with your feet dangling, blasted 200 feet up in the air, and then allowed to partially free-fall back down. The scariest part of the ride by far is the apprehension

continued on page 614

Universal Islands of Adventure

Attractions

1. The Amazing Adventures
   of Spider-Man UX ☑
2. Camp Jurassic
3. Caro-Seuss-el UX
4. The Cat in the Hat UX
5. Doctor Doom's Fearfall UX
6. Dudley Do-Right's Ripsaw Falls UX
7. Flight of the Hippogriff UX
8. Hagrid's Magical Creatures
   Motorbike Adventure ☑
9. Harry Potter and the Forbidden Journey UX ☑
10. The High in the Sky Seuss Trolley Train Ride! UX
11. Hogwarts Express–Hogsmeade Station UX ☑
12. If I Ran The Zoo
13. The Incredible Hulk Coaster UX ☑
14. Jurassic Park Discovery Center
15. Jurassic Park River Adventure UX ☑

16. Jurassic World VelociCoaster UX ☑
17. Me Ship, *The Olive*
18. Ollivanders
19. One Fish, Two Fish, Red Fish, Blue Fish UX
20. Popeye & Bluto's Bilge-Rat Barges UX ☑

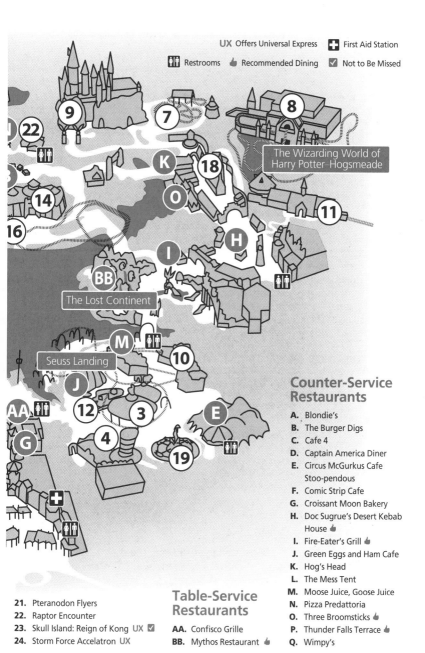

UX Offers Universal Express   ✚ First Aid Station

🚻 Restrooms   👍 Recommended Dining   ☑ Not to Be Missed

The Wizarding World of Harry Potter–Hogsmeade

The Lost Continent

Seuss Landing

Counter-Service Restaurants

A. Blondie's
B. The Burger Digs
C. Cafe 4
D. Captain America Diner
E. Circus McGurkus Cafe Stoo-pendous
F. Comic Strip Cafe
G. Croissant Moon Bakery
H. Doc Sugrue's Desert Kebab House 👍
I. Fire-Eater's Grill 👍
J. Green Eggs and Ham Cafe
K. Hog's Head
L. The Mess Tent
M. Moose Juice, Goose Juice
N. Pizza Predattoria
O. Three Broomsticks 👍
P. Thunder Falls Terrace 👍
Q. Wimpy's

21. Pteranodon Flyers
22. Raptor Encounter
23. Skull Island: Reign of Kong UX ☑
24. Storm Force Accelatron UX

Table-Service Restaurants

AA. Confisco Grille
BB. Mythos Restaurant 👍

continued from page 609

that builds as you sit, strapped in, waiting for the ride to launch; blasting up and falling down are actually pleasant.

TOURING TIPS We've seen glaciers that move faster than the line here. If you want a shorter wait, be on hand at park opening or try after 3 p.m.

The Incredible Hulk Coaster ★★★★½

| PRESCHOOL ★ | GRADE SCHOOL ★★★★½ | TEENS ★★★★★ |
| YOUNG ADULTS ★★★★★ | OVER 30 ★★★★½ | SENIORS ★★★★ |

What it is Roller coaster. **Scope and scale** Super-headliner. **When to go** During the first 40 minutes the park is open or after 3 p.m. **Comments** Single-rider line available; must be 54" to ride. **Duration of ride** 2¼ minutes. **Loading speed** Moderate. **Universal Express** Yes.

DESCRIPTION AND COMMENTS The Hulk is one of the best coasters in Florida, providing a ride comparable to Kumba at Busch Gardens. You'll be shot like a cannonball from 0 to 40 mph in 2 seconds; then you'll be flung upside down 100 feet off the ground. Then it's a mere six rollovers, punctuated by two plunges into holes in the ground, before you're allowed to get out and throw up.

TOURING TIPS Ride first thing, or immediately after you've enjoyed early entry at the Potter attractions; otherwise, wait until late afternoon. Mandatory free lockers are provided for stowing phones and other unsecured objects. There's a separate line inside the boarding station for those who want to ride in the first row.

Storm Force Accelatron ★★½

| PRESCHOOL ★★★★ | GRADE SCHOOL ★★★½ | TEENS ★★★½ |
| YOUNG ADULTS ★★★½ | OVER 30 ★★★ | SENIORS ★★★ |

What it is Covered spinning ride. **Scope and scale** Minor attraction. **When to go** Anytime. **Duration of ride** 1½ minutes. **Loading speed** Slow. **Universal Express** Yes.

DESCRIPTION AND COMMENTS Storm Force is a spiffed-up version of Disney's nausea-inducing Mad Tea Party. A story line loosely ties this midway-type ride to Marvel Super Hero Island, but it offers no useful advice on keeping your lunch down.

TOURING TIPS The ride is typically a walk-on; the wait rarely tops 20 minutes.

TOON LAGOON

WHIMSICAL AND GAILY COLORED, this land translates cartoons into real buildings and settings. **Comic Strip Lane,** the main street of Toon Lagoon, is the domain of Beetle Bailey, Blondie, and Dagwood—among other characters that your kids have probably never heard of.

Dudley Do-Right's Ripsaw Falls ★★★½

| PRESCHOOL ★½ | GRADE SCHOOL ★★★★½ | TEENS ★★★★½ |
| YOUNG ADULTS ★★★★ | OVER 30 ★★★★ | SENIORS ★★★★ |

What it is Flume ride. **Scope and scale** Headliner. **When to go** Before 11 a.m. **Comment** Must be 44" to ride. **Duration of ride** 5 minutes. **Loading speed** Moderate. **Universal Express** Yes.

DESCRIPTION AND COMMENTS Inspired by characters from the *Rocky and Bullwinkle* cartoons, this ride features Canadian Mountie

Dudley Do-Right as he tries to save his girlfriend, Nell Fenwick, from the nefarious Snidely Whiplash. Story line aside, it's a flume ride with the inevitable big drop at the end.

TOURING TIPS Make no mistake—this ride *will* get you wet, though not as soaked as Popeye. Ride the Ripsaw Falls after you've experienced the Marvel Super Hero rides and Skull Island: Reign of Kong.

Me Ship, *The Olive* ★★★

| PRESCHOOL ★★★★½ | GRADE SCHOOL ★★★★ | TEENS ★★★ |
| YOUNG ADULTS ★★½ | OVER 30 ★★★ | SENIORS ★★★½ |

What it is Interactive playground for kids. **Scope and scale** Minor attraction. **When to go** Anytime. **Universal Express** No.

DESCRIPTION AND COMMENTS *The Olive* is Popeye's three-story boat come to life as an interactive playground. Younger kids can scramble around in Swee'Pea's Playpen, while older sibs shoot water cannons at riders trying to survive the adjacent Bilge-Rat Barges.

TOURING TIPS If you're into the big rides, save this for later in the day.

Popeye & Bluto's Bilge-Rat Barges ★★★★

| PRESCHOOL ★★★ | GRADE SCHOOL ★★★★½ | TEENS ★★★★½ |
| YOUNG ADULTS ★★★★½ | OVER 30 ★★★★½ | SENIORS ★★★★ |

What it is Whitewater raft ride. **Scope and scale** Headliner. **When to go** Before 11 a.m. **Comment** Must be 42" to ride. **Duration of ride** 4½ minutes. **Loading speed** Moderate. **Universal Express** Yes.

Wet

DESCRIPTION AND COMMENTS This family raft ride is engineered to ensure that everyone gets drenched. The rapids are rougher and more interesting, and the ride longer, than Animal Kingdom's Kali River Rapids, but Disney wins for theming hands-down.

TOURING TIPS You'll get a lot wetter from the knees down on this ride, so use your poncho or garbage bag, and ride barefoot with your britches rolled up. This ride often opens an hour after the rest of the park. Experience the barges in the morning after the Marvel Super Hero attractions and Dudley Do-Right.

SKULL ISLAND

THIS IS BOTH AN ATTRACTION and an entire "island" unto itself, between Dudley Do-Right's Ripsaw Falls and Thunder Falls Terrace.

Skull Island: Reign of Kong ★★★★

| PRESCHOOL ★★★ | GRADE SCHOOL ★★★½ | TEENS ★★★★ |
| YOUNG ADULTS ★★★★ | OVER 30 ★★★★ | SENIORS ★★★★ |

What it is Indoor-outdoor truck safari with 3-D effects. **Scope and scale** Super-headliner. **When to go** Immediately after park opening or just before closing. **Comments** Single-rider line available; must be 34" to ride. Probably not a good choice for little ones. **Duration of ride** About 6 minutes; 4 minutes when exterior is bypassed in inclement weather. **Loading speed** Fast. **Universal Express** Yes.

DESCRIPTION AND COMMENTS Skull Island: Reign of Kong is an original adventure set in the 1930s, casting guests as jungle explorers with the 8th Wonder Expedition Company. The spooky queue experience features an ancient temple inhabited by lifelike animatronic figures that may startle the unwitting.

Your transportation is an oversize open-sided "expedition vehicle" helmed by one of five animatronic tour guides. You pass through a maze of caves, where you're swiftly assaulted by prehistoric bats, bugs, and beasties brought to gruesome life through a combination of detailed physical effects and razor-sharp 3-D screens. You're then thrust into the center of a battle between vicious V-Rex dinosaurs and the big ape himself. Just when you think it's all over, you'll have one last face-to-face encounter with the "eighth wonder of the world," only this time in the fur-covered flesh.

TOURING TIPS Skull Island is epic in every sense—including its lines. Ride early in the morning or immediately following the Hogsmeade attractions if you're using Early Park Admission. Finally, riders who are afraid of the dark, insects, or man-eating monsters may want to forgo the monkey.

JURASSIC PARK

JURASSIC PARK, with its *Jurassic World* follow-up trilogy, is a Steven Spielberg film franchise about a fictitious theme park with real dinosaurs. Jurassic Park at IOA is a real theme park (or at least a section of one) with *fictitious* dinosaurs. A bridge from The Lost Continent allows guests to bypass Hogsmeade on busy days and head directly to the Jurassic World VelociCoaster.

Camp Jurassic ★★★½

PRESCHOOL ★★★★½	GRADE SCHOOL ★★★★½	TEENS ★★★
YOUNG ADULTS ★★★	OVER 30 ★★★	SENIORS ★★★

What it is Kids' play area. **Scope and scale** Minor attraction. **When to go** Anytime. **Universal Express** No.

DESCRIPTION AND COMMENTS One of the best theme park playgrounds you'll find anywhere. A sort of dinosaur-themed Tom Sawyer Island minus the rafts, it allows kids to explore lava pits, caves, mines, and a rainforest. It's big enough for many kids to spend a solid hour just running around.

TOURING TIPS Camp Jurassic will fire the imaginations of the under-13 set—if you don't impose a time limit on the exploration, you could be here awhile.

Jurassic Park Discovery Center ★★½

PRESCHOOL ★★★★	GRADE SCHOOL ★★★★	TEENS ★★★
YOUNG ADULTS ★★★½	OVER 30 ★★★	SENIORS ★★★

What it is Interactive natural-history exhibit. **Scope and scale** Minor attraction. **When to go** Anytime. **Universal Express** Yes.

DESCRIPTION AND COMMENTS This interactive educational exhibit mixes fiction from *Jurassic Park,* such as using fossil DNA to bring dinosaurs to life, with various skeletal remains and other paleontological displays. The best exhibit here lets guests watch an animatronic raptor being hatched, with a young witness getting to name the newborn.

TOURING TIPS The lower level of the Discovery Center also doubles as a post-ride gift shop and oversize locker area for the VelociCoaster, but all of the exhibits are still accessible. Tour after seeing the park's major rides and attractions, or on your second day in the park. Most folks can digest this exhibit in 10–15 minutes.

Jurassic Park River Adventure ★★★★

PRESCHOOL ★★★	GRADE SCHOOL ★★★★	TEENS ★★★★
YOUNG ADULTS ★★★★	OVER 30 ★★★★	SENIORS ★★★★

What it is Indoor–outdoor river-raft adventure ride based on the *Jurassic Park* movies. **Scope and scale** Headliner. **When to go** Before 11 a.m. **Comments** Must be 42" to ride; single-rider line available. **Duration of ride** 6½ minutes. **Loading speed** Fast. **Universal Express** Yes.

Wet

DESCRIPTION AND COMMENTS Guests board boats for a water tour of Jurassic Park. Everything is tranquil as the tour begins, but the tour boat is then accidentally diverted into Jurassic Park's maintenance facilities. Here, the boat and its riders are menaced by an assortment of hungry meat-eaters. At the climactic moment, the boat and its passengers escape by plummeting over an 85-foot drop.

TOURING TIPS Though the boats make a huge splash at the bottom of the drop, you can stay relatively dry if you sit in an interior seat. Because Jurassic Park River Adventure is situated next to The Wizarding World of Harry Potter–Hogsmeade, the boat will experience heavy crowds earlier in the day. Try to ride before 11 a.m. Unless your kids are fairly hardy, wait a year or two before you spring the River Adventure on them.

Jurassic World VelociCoaster ★★★★★

PRESCHOOL ★	GRADE SCHOOL ★★★★	TEENS ★★★★★
YOUNG ADULTS ★★★★★	OVER 30 ★★★★★	SENIORS ★★★★

What it is Roller coaster. **Scope and scale** Super-headliner. **When to go** After Hagrid's during Early Entry, late morning, or just before closing. **Comment** Must be 51" to ride; single-rider line available. **Duration of ride** About 2 minutes. **Loading speed** Medium-fast. **Universal Express** Yes.

DESCRIPTION AND COMMENTS Universal Orlando's most extreme roller coaster to date features queue cameos from *Jurassic World* actors Chris Pratt (as Owen Grady), Bryce Dallas Howard (as Claire Dearing), and B. D. Wong (as Dr. Henry Wu), who are offering guests tours of the maximum-security paddocks where Blue the velociraptor and her carnivorous pals camp out. What could possibly go wrong?

Riders board 24-passenger trains to experience two high-speed launches, an 80-degree dive down a towering 155-foot-tall "top hat," and close encounters with realistic rockwork and sculpted dinosaurs. With a top speed of 70 mph and an astounding 12 moments of out-of-your-seat air time (including a first-of-its-kind zero-g inverted stall), VelociCoaster is one of the most intense scream machines in town (if not on earth), delivering nonstop adrenaline from the first burst of acceleration until you hit the final brake run. Thankfully, the restraints rest comfortably across your hips and upper thighs, holding you securely as you're flung helplessly through the finale's heart-stopping "Mosasaurus roll" above the lagoon. (Loose-fitting eyeglasses or face masks may not be so lucky.) Other roller coasters may have a taller drop or greater maximum velocity, but nothing else strings together so many exhilarating elements into 4,700 feet of relentlessly paced track.

TOURING TIPS VelociCoaster quickly overtook The Incredible Hulk Coaster as the favorite ride of hard-core thrill junkies, but Hagrid's at Hogsmeade continues to attract bigger crowds because it's accessible to a wider range of guests. If you can't be among the first riders of the day during early entry, try to hit VelociCoaster in late morning after experiencing the other top attractions. Otherwise, make it your last ride of the night; it's even scarier in the dark.

Unlike at The Incredible Hulk Coaster or Rip Ride Rockit, you can hold onto your cell phone, wallet, and other items until just before boarding, when you can stash them in lockers for retrieval immediately after the ride.

Pteranodon Flyers ★★★

| PRESCHOOL ★★★★½ | GRADE SCHOOL ★★★★ | TEENS ★★★ |
| YOUNG ADULTS ★★½ | OVER 30 ★★★ | SENIORS ★★ |

What it is Suspended kiddie coaster. **Scope and scale** Minor attraction. **When to go** In the first or last 30 minutes of the day. **Comment** Adults and older children must be accompanied by a child 36"–56" tall. **Duration of ride** 1¼ minutes. **Loading speed** More sluggish than a hog in quicksand. **Universal Express** No.

DESCRIPTION AND COMMENTS This ride swings you along a track that passes over a small part of Jurassic Park. The queue moves at a glacial pace, and the ride itself lasts barely 75 seconds, but you get a gorgeous view of the island's greenery, and the swinging cars deliver a surprisingly satisfying snap as they negotiate the track's curves.

TOURING TIPS We don't think Pteranodon Flyers is worth a long wait, and Universal Express isn't valid on the attraction. If your children insist on riding and abject bribery fails to sway them, get in line as quickly as possible after the park opens.

Raptor Encounter ★★★½

| PRESCHOOL ★★★½ | GRADE SCHOOL ★★★★ | TEENS ★★★★½ |
| YOUNG ADULTS ★★★★½ | OVER 30 ★★★★½ | SENIORS ★★★★½ |

What it is Photo op with lifelike dinosaur. **Scope and scale** Minor attraction. **When to go** Before noon. **Duration of encounter** About a minute. **Queue speed** Slowish. **Universal Express** No.

DESCRIPTION AND COMMENTS Blue from *Jurassic World*, IOA's semitame velociraptor star (actually an amazingly realistic puppet), makes regular appearances in her paddock next to the River Adventure. A game warden briefs one family at a time regarding proper safety procedures—convey calm assurance, move in slowly, don't smell like meat—before they step up for a photo. Selfies are encouraged; just don't be surprised if the dino snaps when you say, "Smile!"

TOURING TIPS The Raptor Encounter is quite popular, so ask a team member stationed outside the paddock entrance approximately how long your wait will be before queuing. When the full-grown dino needs a break, an adorable handheld baby velociraptor may take her place.

unofficial **TIP**
The only restrooms in The Wizarding World at IOA, labeled PUBLIC CONVENIENCES, are in the middle of Hogsmeade. Remember where they are—especially if you're planning to ride Forbidden Journey and are prone to motion sickness.

THE WIZARDING WORLD OF HARRY POTTER-HOGSMEADE

IN 2007, UNIVERSAL INKED A DEAL with Warner Bros. Entertainment to create an immersive *Harry Potter*-themed environment based on the best-selling books by J. K. Rowling and the companion movies from Warner Bros.

Depicted in winter, the village of **Hogsmeade** is rendered in exquisite detail: The stone cottages and shops have steep slate roofs; bowed, multipaned windows; gables; and tall, crooked chimneys.

Wizarding World-Hogsmeade Attractions

Flight of the Hippogriff ★★★

| PRESCHOOL ★★★★ | GRADE SCHOOL ★★★★ | TEENS ★★★½ |
| YOUNG ADULTS ★★★½ | OVER 30 ★★★½ | SENIORS ★★★½ |

What it is Kids' roller coaster. **Scope and scale** Minor attraction. **When to go** First 90 minutes the park is open or after 4 p.m. **Comment** Must be 36" to ride. **Duration of ride** 1 minute. **Loading speed** Slow. **Universal Express** Yes.

DESCRIPTION AND COMMENTS Below and to the right of Hogwarts Castle, next to Hagrid's Hut, the Hippogriff is short and sweet but not worth much of a wait. Potter nerds will want to ride to see Hagrid's Hut and a charming animatronic of Buckbeak.

TOURING TIPS Have your kids ride soon after the park opens or in the late afternoon while older sibs enjoy other Wizarding World attractions.

Hagrid's Magical Creatures Motorbike Adventure
★★★★★

| PRESCHOOL ★★ | GRADE SCHOOL ★★★★½ | TEENS ★★★★★ |
| YOUNG ADULTS ★★★★★ | OVER 30 ★★★★★ | SENIORS ★★★★½ |

What it is Indoor-outdoor roller coaster. **Scope and scale** Super-headliner. **When to go** First thing during Early Park Admission, around midday, or after sunset. **Comments** Single-rider line occasionally available; must be 48" to ride. **Duration of ride** About 3 minutes. **Loading speed** Medium. **Universal Express** No (uses Virtual Line).

DESCRIPTION AND COMMENTS This family-friendly thrill ride is a highly themed roller coaster without huge hills or upside-down loops. Instead, it focuses on thrilling launches through forested terrain during outdoor segments, as well as close encounters with animatronic creatures inside and between the ride's indoor buildings.

Guests board 14-passenger trains inspired by Hagrid's motorcycle and sidecar for an adventure that includes a vertical climb leading into a backward helix, followed by a free-fall drop into darkness. Fantastical creatures and familiar figures from the Potter world make appearances during your experience, such as the flying Ford Anglia, Fluffy the three-headed dog, and old Hagrid himself (an impressively lifelike animatronic).

If you think Universal's attractions are too dependent on video screens and simulated movement, Hagrid comes to the rescue with richly detailed scenery, spectacular practical effects, and accelerated air time that's exhilarating but not too extreme for tweens and parents to enjoy together. While the coaster's 50-mph top speed might not sound terribly swift, it feels far faster when you're navigating ground-hugging twists and turns through a grove of 1,200 real trees. Hagrid's is the best "story coaster" in the park, and a strong contender for the best ride at Universal Orlando.

TOURING TIPS The ride receives a huge rush of guests every morning at Early Entry rope drop and often experiences a delayed opening; standby waits are shortest at lunchtime and in the early evening, and the effects look best after dark.

Hagrid's doesn't currently offer Universal Express access but may in the future. A single-rider queue is sometimes available when Virtual Line is not active, but it doesn't save that much time. The sidecar sits lower than the cycle but closer to the effects, so every rider gets a good view. Larger guests (40-inch waists and above) should test the sample seats before lining up and then request a motorbike seat, which affords a little more breathing room than a cramped sidecar.

Harry Potter and the Forbidden Journey
★★★★★

| PRESCHOOL ★★ | GRADE SCHOOL ★★★★½ | TEENS ★★★★½ |
| YOUNG ADULTS ★★★★½ | OVER 30 ★★★★½ | SENIORS ★★★★ |

What it is Motion-simulator dark ride. **Scope and scale** Super-headliner. **When to go** At the end of Early Entry hour, or in the last hours before closing. **Comments** Single-rider line available; must be 48″ to ride. **Duration of ride** 4¼ minutes. **Loading speed** Fast. **Universal Express** Yes.

Motion Sickness

DESCRIPTION AND COMMENTS This dark ride provides the only opportunity at Universal Orlando to come in contact with Harry Potter, Ron Weasley, Hermione Granger, and Dumbledore as portrayed by the original actors. Half of the attraction is a series of preshows that sets the stage for the main event.

After entering through the castle dungeons, you ascend through the greenhouse into a multistory gallery of magically moving portraits, then proceed to Dumbledore's office, where the chief wizard (a realistic Musion EyeLiner hologram) appears on a balcony and welcomes you to Hogwarts. After his welcoming remarks, Dumbledore dispatches you to the Defence Against the Dark Arts classroom, where Harry, Ron, and Hermione pop out from beneath an invisibility cloak and invite you to a Quidditch match.

All of this leads to the Room of Requirement. Here, you board a four-passenger bench attached to the end of a Kuka robotic arm, which can be programmed to replicate all the sensations of flying, including broad swoops, steep dives, sharp turns, sudden stops, and fast acceleration. The ride vehicle moves you through a series of alternating sets and domes where scenes are projected all around you. The movement of the Kuka arm is synchronized to create the motion that corresponds to what's happening in the set or film. When everything works correctly, it's mind-blowing: You'll soar over Hogwarts Castle, narrowly evade an attacking dragon, spar with the Whomping Willow, get tossed into a Quidditch match, and fight off Dementors inside the Chamber of Secrets.

unofficial **TIP**

Parents: Because the seats on the benches are compartmentalized, kids can't see or touch Mom or Dad if they get frightened.

TOURING TIPS Try not to ride on an empty stomach if possible. If you start getting queasy, fix your gaze on your feet and try to exclude as much from your peripheral vision as possible.

Each bench has modified seats at either end for larger guests; try the test seat outside the entrance before queueing to make sure you'll fit.

At Forbidden Journey, the wait in the single-rider line (when available) can be as much as one-tenth the wait in the standby line. You'll miss much of the interior of the castle, though.

Hogwarts Express ★★★★½

PRESCHOOL ★★★★½ GRADE SCHOOL ★★★★½ TEENS ★★★★½
YOUNG ADULTS ★★★★½ OVER 30 ★★★★½ SENIORS ★★★★½

What it is Transportation attraction. **Scope and scale** Headliner. **When to go** Immediately after park opening until midafternoon. **Comment** Park-to-Park Ticket required to ride. Single-park tickets can be upgraded at Guest Services or at either train station. **Duration of ride** 4 minutes. **Loading speed** Moderate. **Universal Express** Yes.

DESCRIPTION AND COMMENTS See page 635 for a full review.

TOURING TIPS Waits in line are usually less than 20 minutes through the morning but can build later in the day, so ride before midafternoon if experiencing the train is important.

Ollivanders ★★★★

PRESCHOOL ★★★★ GRADE SCHOOL ★★★★½ TEENS ★★★★½
YOUNG ADULTS ★★★★½ OVER 30 ★★★★ SENIORS ★★★★½

What it is Combination wizarding demonstration and shopping op. **Scope and scale** Minor attraction. **When to go** In the first or last 30 minutes of the day. **Comments** Audience stands; identical to USF's version but with a much slower line. **Duration of show** 6 minutes. **Universal Express** No.

DESCRIPTION AND COMMENTS Next to the Owl Post is Ollivanders, offering the same wand-choosing ceremony as the Diagon Alley attraction of the same name (see page 635). It's great fun, but the tiny shop can accommodate only a handful of guests at a time. After the show, the whole group is dispatched to the Owl Post and Dervish and Banges to buy stuff. An interactive wand, which triggers special effects hidden inside shop windows throughout Hogsmeade and Diagon Alley, costs $67.

TOURING TIPS Because of the shop's very low capacity, long waits for the show at Ollivanders can form. If you need to see this show and you can't go to the USF Ollivanders, go first thing in the morning or as late as possible. If you just want to buy a wand, enter the store directly rather than waiting for the show; you can also buy wands at an outdoor cart near the *Frog Choir* stage, or in the large gift shop near the park's entrance, usually with little to no wait.

Wizarding World Entertainment

Nearly every retail space sports some sort of animatronic or special-effects surprise. At **Dervish and Banges,** for example, the fearsome *Monster Book of Monsters* rattles and snarls at you as Nimbus 2001 brooms strain at their tethers overhead. And at the **Hog's Head** pub, the titular porcine part, mounted behind the bar, similarly thrashes and growls. Hog's Head also serves The Wizarding World's signature non-alcoholic brew, Butterbeer.

Roughly across the street from the pub, you'll find benches in the shade at the **Owlery,** next to the **Owl Post,** where you can have snail mail stamped with a Hogsmeade postmark before dropping it off for delivery (an Orlando postmark will also be applied by the real USPS).

Street entertainment at the Forbidden Journey end of Hogsmeade includes the ***Frog Choir*** (★★★), composed of four singers, two of whom are holding large amphibian puppets sitting on pillows, and the ***Triwizard Spirit Rally*** (★★★), showcasing dancing and martial arts. Performances run about 6–15 minutes.

On select evenings, the **Nighttime Lights at Hogwarts Castle** show (★★★½) brings the Forbidden Journey facade to life with video projections synchronized to the films' scores. Best viewing is from in front of the *Frog Choir* stage or on the bridge to Jurassic Park. The 10-minute show is repeated several times from sunset to park closing; the first showing is the most crowded, so stay for the last. During the Halloween and holiday seasons, special ***Dark Arts*** and ***Magic of Christmas*** versions are shown.

THE LOST CONTINENT

THIS AREA IS A MIX of Silk Road bazaar and ancient ruins, with Greco-Moroccan accents. This entire area is slated for redevelopment; for now, its only attraction is the **Mystic Fountain,** an interactive talking fountain with an attitude—keep your umbrella handy.

SEUSS LANDING

THIS 10-ACRE THEMED AREA is based on Dr. Seuss' famous children's books. The buildings and attractions display a whimsical, brightly colored cartoon style with exaggerated features and rounded lines. Seuss Landing has four rides; an interactive play area called **If I Ran the Zoo,** populated by Seuss creatures; and *Oh! the Stories You'll Hear!* (★★★), a live musical show featuring the Lorax, the Cat in the Hat, and other beloved characters.

Caro-Seuss-el ★★★

| PRESCHOOL ★★★½ | GRADE SCHOOL ★★★½ | TEENS ★★★ |
| YOUNG ADULTS ★★★ | OVER 30 ★★★ | SENIORS ★★★½ |

What it is Merry-go-round. **Scope and scale** Minor attraction. **When to go** Anytime. **Comment** The ride is outside but is covered. **Duration of ride** 2 minutes. **Loading speed** Slow. **Universal Express** Yes.

DESCRIPTION AND COMMENTS Totally outrageous, this full-scale, 56-mount merry-go-round is made up entirely of Dr. Seuss characters.

TOURING TIPS Waits usually aren't too long, even in the middle of the day.

The Cat in the Hat ★★★½

| PRESCHOOL ★★★★½ | GRADE SCHOOL ★★★★ | TEENS ★★★ |
| YOUNG ADULTS ★★★ | OVER 30 ★★★½ | SENIORS ★★★★ |

What it is Indoor cartoon dark ride. **Scope and scale** Major attraction. **When to go** Before 11:30 a.m. or after 4 p.m. **Comment** Must be 36″ to ride. **Duration of ride** 3½ minutes. **Loading speed** Moderate. **Universal Express** Yes.

DESCRIPTION AND COMMENTS Guests ride on "couches" through 18 different sets inhabited by animatronic Seuss characters, including The Cat in the Hat, Thing 1 and Thing 2, and the beleaguered goldfish who tries to maintain order in the midst of bedlam.

TOURING TIPS Fun for all ages. Try to ride early or late in the day.

The High in the Sky Seuss Trolley Train Ride!
★★★½

| PRESCHOOL ★★★★½ | GRADE SCHOOL ★★★½ | TEENS ★★★ |
| YOUNG ADULTS ★★★ | OVER 30 ★★★½ | SENIORS ★★★★ |

What it is Elevated train. **Scope and scale** Major attraction. **When to go** Before 11:30 a.m. or just before closing. **Comment** Oddly, kids must be 40″ to ride. **Duration of ride** 3½ minutes. **Loading speed** Molasses. **Universal Express** Yes.

DESCRIPTION AND COMMENTS Trains putter along elevated tracks while a voice reads one of four Dr. Seuss stories over the train's speakers. As each train makes its way through Seuss Landing, it passes a series of animatronic characters that are part of the story being told. A strangely stringent minimum height requirement means that many in the Trolley's target demographic are too short to ride.

TOURING TIPS The trains are small, fitting about 20 people, and the loading speed is glacial. Ride at the end of the day or first thing in the morning.

If I Ran the Zoo ★★★

| PRESCHOOL ★★★★½ | GRADE SCHOOL ★★★★ | TEENS ★★½ |
| YOUNG ADULTS ★★½ | OVER 30 ★★★½ | SENIORS ★★★½ |

What it is Interactive play area and outdoor maze. **Scope and scale** Diversion. **When to go** Anytime. **Comment** Kids may get wet. **Universal Express** No.

DESCRIPTION AND COMMENTS This Dr. Seuss–themed play area is filled with the fantastic animals and gizmos from the beloved author's stories.

TOURING TIPS Tour anytime. Note that much of the play area is unshaded—bring cold drinks, hats, and sunscreen for the little ones.

One Fish, Two Fish, Red Fish, Blue Fish ★★★

| PRESCHOOL ★★★★½ | GRADE SCHOOL ★★★★★ | TEENS ★★★ |
| YOUNG ADULTS ★★★ | OVER 30 ★★★½ | SENIORS ★★★½ |

What it is Wet version of Dumbo the Flying Elephant. **Scope and scale** Minor attraction. **When to go** Before 10 a.m. **Comment** Plan on getting wet. **Duration of ride** 2 minutes. **Loading speed** Slow. **Universal Express** Yes.

DESCRIPTION AND COMMENTS Imagine the Magic Kingdom's Dumbo ride with Dr. Seuss–style fish instead of elephants, and you have half the story here—the other half involves another opportunity to get soaked. Guests steer their fish up or down 15 feet in the air while traveling in circles and trying to avoid streams of water projected from "squirt posts."

Wet

TOURING TIPS You'll get wetter on this thing than at a full-immersion baptism. Lines can build in the afternoon, so try to ride early, while you'll still have time to dry off.

DINING AT UNIVERSAL ISLANDS OF ADVENTURE

OF IOA'S DINING OPTIONS, we like **Three Broomsticks,** The Wizarding World of Harry Potter's counter-service restaurant, which serves Boston Market–style rotisserie chicken plus fish-and-chips, shepherd's pie, and barbecue ribs; a similar menu (minus the Potter theming and crowds) is available at **Thunder Falls Terrace** in Jurassic Park. The **Hog's Head** pub, attached to Three Broomsticks, serves beer, wine, mixed drinks, and the obligatory Butterbeer. We're also fond of the gyros at **Fire Eater's Grill** and the kabobs at **Doc Sugrue's.**

unofficial **TIP**
Vendors besides Hog's Head also sell Butterbeer, but the wait at the pub is generally 10 minutes or less, versus half an hour or more elsewhere.

IOA has two sit-down restaurants: **Confisco Grille,** in Port of Entry, and **Mythos Restaurant,** in The Lost Continent. Confisco is fine for appetizers, sandwiches, and drinks. Despite its Hellenic-sounding name, Mythos isn't really a Greek restaurant; it offers spanakopita and souvlaki, but it also serves something for everyone, including Italian risotto, Thai noodles, and Japanese sushi rolls, plus steaks and burgers. That said, some of the entrées (such as the cranberry-crusted pork and the pan-seared salmon) are excellent, and the prices are similar to quick-service.

ISLANDS OF ADVENTURE TOURING PLANS
Decisions, Decisions

When it comes to touring IOA efficiently in a single day, you have two basic choices:

1. If you're intent on experiencing The Wizarding World first thing during Early Park Admission, be at the turnstiles at least 30–60 minutes before

park opening. Once admitted, hurry to Hogsmeade and ride **Hagrid's Magical Creatures Motorbike Adventure,** followed by **VelociCoaster** (or **Flight of the Hippogriff**) and then **Forbidden Journey.** Next head to other must-experience attractions before the park gets crowded. The catch? Ride difficulties could have you stuck in a long line while crowds—and more lines—spread to other areas of the park.

2. If you don't have Early Park Admission privileges at IOA, we recommend skipping Potterville first thing. Instead, try to grab a Virtual Line reservation for Hagrid's (if available) while enjoying other attractions in the meantime, starting at **Marvel Super Hero Island** and then heading for **Skull Island.** The Wizarding World usually clears out in the afternoon, and its queues are often empty in the last hour, even on busy days, meaning you can ride Forbidden Journey with a minimal wait if you get in line shortly before closing time.

Universal Orlando Highlights One-Day, Two-Park Touring Plan *(pages 729–732)*

THIS PLAN IS FOR GUESTS with park-to-park tickets who wish to see the highlights of USF and IOA in a single day. We offer one version that starts and finishes in Universal Studios Florida (page 729) and another that begins and ends in Islands of Adventure (page 731); both highlight the resort's top headliners, but they include alternate second-tier attractions in the afternoon. If your focus is on Diagon Alley, pick the version that starts in USF; visitors prioritizing VelociCoaster or Hagrid's should select the one starting in IOA. The plans use Hogwarts Express to get from one park to the other and back again; you can walk back for the return leg if the line is too long. Both plans include lunch and dinner. During holiday periods, you may need to substitute a quick-service snack for one or both meals to fit in all of the plan's attractions.

Universal Islands of Adventure One-Day Touring Plan *(page 733)*

THIS TOURING PLAN is for guests without Park-to-Park Tickets and is appropriate for groups of all sizes and ages. It includes thrill rides that may induce motion sickness or get you wet. If the plan calls for you to experience an attraction that doesn't interest you, simply skip it and go to the next step. If you have young children in your party, customize the plan to fit their needs and take advantage of Child Swap at thrill rides.

UNIVERSAL STUDIOS FLORIDA

UNIVERSAL STUDIOS FLORIDA OPENED IN JUNE 1990. At the time, it was almost four times the size of Disney's Hollywood Studios, and much more of the facility was accessible to visitors.

USF is laid out in a *P* configuration, with the rounded part of the *P* sticking out disproportionately from the stem. Beyond the main entrance, a wide boulevard stretches past several shows and rides to the park's New York area. Branching off this pedestrian thoroughfare to the right are four streets that access other areas of the park and intersect a promenade circling a large lake.

The park is divided into eight areas: **Hollywood, Production Central, New York, San Francisco, The Wizarding World of Harry Potter–Diagon**

NOT TO BE MISSED AT UNIVERSAL STUDIOS FLORIDA

• *The Bourne Stuntacular* • Harry Potter and the Escape from Gringotts • Hogwarts Express–King's Cross Station • Men in Black Alien Attack • Ollivanders • Revenge of the Mummy • The Simpsons Ride • Transformers: The Ride 3D • *Universal Orlando's Horror Make-Up Show*

Alley, World Expo, Springfield: Home of the Simpsons, and **KidZone** (closed at press time for a DreamWorks makeover). Because most USF attractions aren't thematically integrated into the areas of the park in which they reside, we present them alphabetically rather than by area, with the exception of The Wizarding World.

USF offers all standard services and amenities, including stroller and wheelchair rentals, lockers, baby-care facilities, car assistance, a quiet room for guests who need a sensory break, and foreign-language assistance. Most of the park is accessible to guests with disabilities, and TDDs are available for those who are deaf or hard of hearing. Almost all services are in the **Front Lot,** located just inside the main entrance.

HOW MUCH TIME TO ALLOCATE

TOURING UNIVERSAL STUDIOS FLORIDA, including one meal and a visit to Diagon Alley, takes about 10–12 hours. Some theater attractions don't schedule performances until 11 a.m. or later. This means that early in the day, park guests are all concentrated among the limited number of attractions in operation.

You won't have to worry about any of this if you use our USF touring plan (see page 733). We'll keep you a step ahead of the crowd and make sure any given attraction is running by the time you get there.

UNIVERSAL STUDIOS FLORIDA ATTRACTIONS

Animal Actors on Location! ★★★½

| PRESCHOOL ★★★★ | GRADE SCHOOL ★★★★½ | TEENS ★★★½ |
| YOUNG ADULTS ★★★½ | OVER 30 ★★★★ | SENIORS ★★★★ |

What it is Animal tricks and comedy show. **Scope and scale** Major attraction. **When to go** After you've experienced all rides. **Duration of show** 25 minutes. **Universal Express** Yes.

DESCRIPTION AND COMMENTS This show integrates video segments with live sketches, jokes, and animal tricks performed onstage. Live animals, some of which are veterans of TV and movies (and many of which were rescued from shelters), take part, and kids are invited to participate.

TOURING TIPS Sit in the center of the stadium about halfway up for the best chance to be picked. Check the entertainment schedule for showtimes.

The Bourne Stuntacular ★★★★½

| PRESCHOOL ★★ | GRADE SCHOOL ★★★★ | TEENS ★★★★½ |
| YOUNG ADULTS ★★★★½ | OVER 30 ★★★★½ | SENIORS ★★★★ |

What it is Live-action stunt show. **Scope and scale** Headliner. **When to go** Scheduled showtimes; after you've experienced all rides. **Duration of show** 25 minutes. **Universal Express** Yes.

continued on page 628

Universal Studios Florida

Attractions

1. *Animal Actors on Location!* UX
2. *The Bourne Stuntacular* UX ☑
3. Despicable Me Minion Mayhem UX
4. DreamWorks KidZone Playgrounds UX
5. DreamWorks KidZone Trollercoaster UX
6. Fast & Furious: Supercharged UX
7. E.T. Adventure UX
8. Harry Potter and the Escape from Gringotts UX ☑
9. Hogwarts Express–King's Cross Station UX ☑
10. Hollywood Rip Ride Rockit UX
`11. Kang & Kodos' Twirl 'n' Hurl UX
12. Men in Black Alien Attack UX ☑
13. Ollivanders ☑

14. Race Through New York Starring Jimmy Fallon UX
15. Revenge of the Mummy UX ☑
16. The Simpsons Ride UX ☑
17. Transformers: The Ride–3D UX ☑
18. *Universal Orlando's Horror Make-Up Show* UX ☑
19. Villain-Con Minion Blast UX

UX Offers Universal Express · ✚ First Aid Station · 👫 Restrooms
👍 Recommended Dining · ☑ Not to Be Missed · - - - Parade Route

The Wizarding World of Harry Potter–Diagon Alley

San Francisco

The Embarcadero

London Waterfront

Springfield, U.S.A.: Home of the Simpsons

World Expo

DreamWorks KidZone *(opens 2024)*

Table-Service Restaurants

AA. Finnegan's Bar & Grill
BB. Lombard's Seafood Grille

Counter-Service Restaurants

A. Bumblebee Man's Taco Truck
B. Central Park Crepes
C. Chez Alcatraz
D. Duff Brewery
E. Fast Food Boulevard 👍
F. Florean Fortescue's Ice-Cream Parlour 👍
G. Fountain of Fair Fortune

H. The Hopping Pot
I. KidZone Pizza Company *(seasonal)*
J. Leaky Cauldron 👍
K. London Taxi Hut
L. Louie's Italian Restaurant
M. Mel's Drive-In
N. Minion Cafe
O. Moe's Tavern
P. Richter's Burger Co.
Q. San Francisco Pastry Company
R. Schwab's Pharmacy *(seasonal)*
S. Today Cafe 👍

continued from page 625

DESCRIPTION AND COMMENTS This replacement for the revered *Terminator 2: 3-D* show once again blurs the line between stage and screen, blending flesh-and-blood stunt actors and automated moving props—including full-size vehicles and buildings—against a massive 130-foot-wide LED display. You don't need to know the first thing about Matt Damon's amnesiac assassin to enjoy watching Jason Bourne battle bad guys across Moroccan rooftops or dangle beneath a helicopter flying above the streets of Dubai. Fast-paced, faithful to the film franchise, and filled with showstopping special effects, this is easily the best stunt show in Orlando.

TOURING TIPS Performances start about every 45 minutes, but the theater tends to fill up, so arrive at least 15 minutes early. Seats in the front row are great for fight-choreography aficionados, but we prefer the view of the screen from the rear. The *Stuntacular* features earsplitting gunfire and brutal violence (including choke holds) but no blood or guts.

Despicable Me Minion Mayhem ★★★½

PRESCHOOL ★★★★ **GRADE SCHOOL** ★★★★½ **TEENS** ★★★★
YOUNG ADULTS ★★★★ **OVER 30** ★★★★ **SENIORS** ★★★★

What it is Motion-simulator ride. **Scope and scale** Major attraction. **When to go** Within 30 minutes of park opening or after 4 p.m. **Comment** Expect *long* waits in line. **Duration of ride** 5 minutes. **Loading speed** Moderate-slow. **Universal Express** Yes.

Motion Sickness

DESCRIPTION AND COMMENTS This ride involves high-tech motion simulators moving and reacting in sync with a cartoon projected onto an IMAX-like high-definition screen. The story line combines elements from the animated movie *Despicable Me,* starring Gru, the archvillain, along with his adopted daughters and his diminutive yellow Minions. During the queue and preshow, you visit Gru's house and are then ushered into his lab, where you're turned into a Minion. Guests disembark the ride into a disco party with a Minion meet and greet before making the obligatory exit through the gift shop.

TOURING TIPS Despicable Me Minion Mayhem is unfortunately situated at the very front of the park, within a few yards of the turnstiles. As a result, and because it's a popular attraction, long lines develop as soon as the park opens. If you're among the first to enter and the wait is 20 minutes or less, get in line for Despicable Me; then ride Hollywood Rip Ride Rockit. But if the line for Villain-Con followed by Despicable Me exceeds 20 minutes, try late afternoon or the hour before the park closes. Stationary seating is available for those prone to motion sickness and for children less than 40 inches tall.

DreamWorks KidZone Playgrounds *(opens 2024)*

PRESCHOOL ★★★★★ **GRADE SCHOOL** ★★★★ **TEENS** ★★½
YOUNG ADULTS ★★ **OVER 30** ★★½ **SENIORS** ★★

What it is Interactive playground. **Scope and scale** Minor attraction. **When to go** Anytime. **Comment** The place for rambunctious kids.

DESCRIPTION AND COMMENTS Universal's long-in-the-tooth KidZone playgrounds themed to Fievel and Curious George were gutted in 2023 and replaced with more-modern playscapes based on DreamWorks Animation franchises such as *Shrek* and *Kung Fu Panda*. Since Universal is obsessed with wet stuff, there are innumerable spigots, pipes, and opportunities to get splashed. Kids who want to stay dry can mess around in the foam-ball playground, also equipped with chutes, tubes, and ball blasters.

TOURING TIPS Visit after you've experienced all the major attractions.

DreamWorks KidZone TrollerCoaster *(opens 2024)* ★★½

PRESCHOOL ★★★★½   **GRADE SCHOOL** ★★★★   **TEENS** ★★★
YOUNG ADULTS ★★★   **OVER 30** ★★★   **SENIORS** ★★★½

What it is Kids' roller coaster. **Scope and scale** Minor attraction. **When to go** Anytime. **Comments** Must be 36" to ride; children 36"–48" must be accompanied by a supervising companion. **Duration of ride** 1 minute. **Loading speed** *Slooow.* **Universal Express** Yes.

DESCRIPTION AND COMMENTS This new kiddie coaster is virtually identical to the Magic Kingdom's Barnstormer: It's small enough for little ones to enjoy but sturdy enough for adults, though its moderate speed might unnerve some younger kids (note the height requirement). The entire ride lasts about a minute, and at least 20 of those 60 seconds are spent cranking the train up the first (and only) lift hill. Originally themed to Woody Woodpecker, this ride was retained and renamed after *Trolls* during the renovation of KidZone that's also scheduled to introduce new DreamWorks-based playgrounds and character encounters in 2024.

TOURING TIPS Visit after you've experienced the major attractions. If your young child has never before experienced a roller coaster, this would be an appropriate first attempt.

E.T. Adventure ★★★½

PRESCHOOL ★★★★   **GRADE SCHOOL** ★★★½   **TEENS** ★★★
YOUNG ADULTS ★★★½   **OVER 30** ★★★½   **SENIORS** ★★★★

What it is Indoor adventure ride based on the beloved movie. **Scope and scale** Major attraction. **When to go** Within 30 minutes of ride opening or late afternoon. **Comment** Must be 34" to ride. **Duration of ride** 4½ minutes. **Loading speed** Moderate. **Universal Express** Yes.

DESCRIPTION AND COMMENTS Board a bicycle-like conveyance to escape with E.T., The Extra-Terrestrial, from earthly law enforcement officials and journey to his home planet. Concerning the latter, where E.T. is reunited with family and friends, Len likens it to *The Wizard of Oz*'s Technicolor scene, only reenacted with a cave full of naked mole rats. (C'mon, Len, where's the love?) Even so, E.T. is one of Universal's only family-friendly dark rides that relies on sets and robotics instead of screens, so we hope it sticks around for a long time to come.

TOURING TIPS Most preschoolers and grade-school children love E.T. Ride in the morning or late afternoon. On peak days, a time-saving single-rider line is occasionally opened.

Fast & Furious: Supercharged ★★★

PRESCHOOL ★★   **GRADE SCHOOL** ★★★   **TEENS** ★★★
YOUNG ADULTS ★★★   **OVER 30** ★★½   **SENIORS** ★★½

What it is Car chase 3-D motion simulator. **Scope and scale** Headliner. **When to go** After experiencing the other headliners. **Comments** Single-rider line available; must be 40" to ride. **Duration of ride** 5 minutes. **Loading speed** Fast. **Universal Express** Yes.

DESCRIPTION AND COMMENTS Inspired by the $5 billion box office behemoth that is Universal's *Fast & Furious* franchise, Fast & Furious: Supercharged begins in an industrial warehouse–themed queue; here, you can check out some of the high-performance cars showcased in the films. Two preshows, in which live hosts interact awkwardly with recorded clips of Jordana Brewster (Mia) and Chris "Ludacris" Bridges (Tej), establish the backstory for anyone who hasn't seen the nine-and-counting films.

After boarding specially designed tramlike "party buses," you're taken to an underground club, where a postrace rave is in full swing until the feds crash the party in search of a crucial crime witness who's hiding among the guests. Lead characters Dom Toretto (played by Vin Diesel), Luke Hobbs (Dwayne "The Rock" Johnson), Letty Ortiz (Michelle Rodriguez), and Roman Pearce (Tyrese Gibson) appear in holographic form to rescue you from Owen Shaw (Luke Evans), the bad guy from *Fast & Furious 6*. In the attraction's climax, a 360-degree projection tunnel with hydraulic platforms, 400-foot-long screens, and 4K projectors makes it seem as if your ride vehicle is in the middle of a high-stakes car chase, speeding at 100-plus mph through a West Coast urban jungle.

Fast & Furious: Supercharged is similar to Skull Island: Reign of Kong at IOA, but without the immersive 3-D or impressive animatronics. The dialogue and visual effects are shockingly cheesy, even by theme park standards—Len considers this a feature, not a bug—but it all goes by in such a nitro-fueled blur that it may not matter to fans of the flicks.

TOURING TIPS The best views are from the center-right seats in the first bus—stay to the left if the queue splits before the loading dock. Though less scary than the King Kong ride, Supercharged has a slightly higher height requirement; luckily, the slot-car-racing game in the Child Swap room may be more fun than the actual attraction.

Hollywood Rip Ride Rockit ★★★★

What it is High-tech roller coaster. **Scope and scale** Headliner. **When to go** The first hour after park opening or late afternoon. **Comments** Single-rider line available; must be 51" to ride. **Duration of ride** 2½ minutes. **Loading speed** Moderate. **Universal Express** Yes.

Motion Sickness

DESCRIPTION AND COMMENTS A sit-down X-Car coaster, Rip Ride Rockit runs on a 3,800-foot steel track, with a maximum height of 167 feet and a top speed of 65 mph. You ascend—vertically—at 11 feet per second to crest the 17-story-tall first hill, the second-highest point reached by any roller coaster in Orlando (only SeaWorld's Mako is higher). The drop is almost vertical, too, and launches you into Double Take, a 136-foot-tall loop inversion in which you begin on the inside of the loop, twist to the outside at the top (so you're upright), and then twist back inside the loop for the descent. You next hurtle into a stretch of track shaped like a musical treble clef, followed by a spiraling negative-gravity maneuver: You feel like you're in a corkscrew inversion, but you never actually go upside down.

Like Rock 'n' Roller Coaster in Hollywood Studios, this coaster has a musical soundtrack. With Rip Ride Rockit, however, you get to choose the genre of music you want to hear as you ride: classic rock, country, disco, pop, or rap. When it's all over, Universal sells photos and a DVD of your ride that intercuts stock coaster footage with clips of you screaming.

The "Triple R" has become increasingly bumpy over the years, subjecting you to lots of side-to-side jarring. A Wisconsin reader warns:

I've ridden coasters over 400 feet tall and with speeds in excess of 120 mph, but I've never ridden one as rough as Rip Ride Rockit. With the beating my head and neck took, I'll never ride it again.

TOURING TIPS Because the ride is so close to the USF entrance, it's a crowd magnet. Your only chance to ride without a long wait is to be one of the first to enter the park when it opens.

Kang & Kodos' Twirl 'n' Hurl ★★★

| PRESCHOOL ★★★★ | GRADE SCHOOL ★★★½ | TEENS ★★★ |
| YOUNG ADULTS ★★★ | OVER 30 ★★★ | SENIORS ★★★ |

What it is Spinning ride. **Scope and scale** Minor attraction. **When to go** Before 11 a.m. or whenever there are 50 people or fewer in line. **Comment** Rarely has long lines but loads slowly. **Duration of ride** 1½ minutes. **Loading speed** Slow. **Universal Express** Yes

DESCRIPTION AND COMMENTS The Twirl 'n' Hurl is Dumbo with Bart Simpson's sense of humor. Tentacled aliens Kang and Kodos hold pictures of *Simpsons* characters; you make the characters speak and spin by steering your craft to the proper altitude. All the while, Kang exhorts you (loudly) to destroy Springfield while haughtily insulting humans. Preschoolers enjoy the ride; older kids love the snarky narration.

TOURING TIPS Twirl 'n' Hurl rarely attracts long lines, but slow loading speeds ensure a long wait. It usually opens at 10 a.m., so try to ride before 11. If you want to enjoy the jokes without the wait, you can easily hear them from the sidelines.

Men in Black Alien Attack ★★★★

| PRESCHOOL ★★★ | GRADE SCHOOL ★★★★ | TEENS ★★★★ |
| YOUNG ADULTS ★★★★ | OVER 30 ★★★★ | SENIORS ★★★★ |

What it is Interactive dark thrill ride. **Scope and scale** Headliner. **When to go** During the first 2 hours the park is open or anytime using the single-rider line. **Comments** Single-rider line available; must be 42" to ride. **Duration of ride** 4½ minutes. **Loading speed** Moderate–fast. **Universal Express** Yes

Motion Sickness

DESCRIPTION AND COMMENTS In this ride based on the movie of the same name, you volunteer as a Men in Black (MIB) trainee. MIB Chief Zed briefs you on the finer points of alien-spotting and familiarizes you with your training vehicle and your weapon, an alien "zapper." Then you load up and are dispatched on an innocuous training mission that immediately deteriorates into a situation where only you are in a position to prevent aliens from taking over the universe.

If you saw the movie, you understand that the aliens are mostly giant bugs and that zapping them makes them explode into myriad gooey body parts. Thus, the meat of the ride (no pun intended) consists of careening around Manhattan in your MIB vehicle and shooting aliens.

TOURING TIPS Each of the 120 or so alien figures has sensors that activate special effects and respond to your zapper—aim for the eyes and keep shooting until the alien's eyes turn red. Targets above you score the most points; look for aliens behind second-story windows. To avoid a long wait, ride during the first 2 hours the park is open, or try the single-rider line if you don't mind splitting your group.

Race Through New York Starring Jimmy Fallon ★★★½

| PRESCHOOL ★★★½ | GRADE SCHOOL ★★★★ | TEENS ★★★★ |
| YOUNG ADULTS ★★★½ | OVER 30 ★★★½ | SENIORS ★★★½ |

What it is Comedic 3-D simulator ride. **Scope and scale** Headliner. **When to go** First 2 hours of the day. **Comments** Must be 40" to ride. **Duration of ride** 4 minutes. **Loading speed** Moderate. **Universal Express** Yes

DESCRIPTION AND COMMENTS Race Through New York is housed in a replica of NBC's historic offices at 30 Rockefeller Plaza (30 Rock) in Manhattan.

Once inside, you're directed up to a fancy lounge outfitted with sofas and touchscreen tables with video games inspired by *The Tonight Show Starring Jimmy Fallon*. The main attractions, however, are live appearances by two *Tonight Show* regulars: the Ragtime Gals, a male vocal quintet that performs tongue-in-cheek barbershop interpretations of pop hits, and Hashtag the Panda, a goofy dancer in an animal costume.

Soon it's time to make your way to Jimmy Fallon's studio. The Roots, Fallon's house band, rap the safety instructions before you enter a 72-seat theater with a large screen; here, you don 3-D glasses and race against Fallon in his souped-up "Tonight Rider" roadster. Starting at the *Tonight Show* studio, the competition sends you careening through the streets and subways of New York and eventually to, yes, the moon.

The preshow areas get a lot of points, and the ride itself has some of the sharpest visuals and smoothest movement in the Universal repertoire. But it breaks no new technical ground for the genre, and it relies on guests recognizing Fallon's stable of characters (like Ew! Girl and Tight Pants Man) for its jokes—which grow stale after several viewings.

TOURING TIPS Walk-ins are usually allowed during the first and last hours of the day.

Revenge of the Mummy ★★★★½

PRESCHOOL ★½	**GRADE SCHOOL** ★★★½	**TEENS** ★★★★½
YOUNG ADULTS ★★★★½	**OVER 30** ★★★★½	**SENIORS** ★★★★

What it is Combination dark ride/roller coaster. **Scope and scale** Headliner. **When to go** First 2 hours the park is open or after 4 p.m. **Comments** Single-rider line available; must be 48" to ride. **Duration of ride** 3 minutes. **Loading speed** Moderate. **Universal Express** Yes

Motion Sickness

DESCRIPTION AND COMMENTS In this ride based on the *Mummy* flicks, you fight off "deadly curses and vengeful creatures" while you fly through Egyptian tombs and other spooky places on a high-tech roller coaster. The special effects (refurbished in 2022) range from video effects and animatronics to lighting and enough fire-spewing gas vents to roast a chicken.

The ride begins slowly, passing through various chambers, including one where flesh-eating scarab beetles descend on you. Suddenly your vehicle stops, then drops backward and rotates. The next thing you know, you're shot at high speed up the first hill of the roller coaster. Though it's a wild ride by anyone's definition, the emphasis remains as much on the visuals, robotics, and special effects as on the ride itself.

TOURING TIPS The singles line is often faster than Universal Express.

While most grade-schoolers we surveyed who were plucky enough to ride the Mummy like it, one dad feels we underestimate the fright factor:

My second-grader (who wasn't scared at all on Space Mountain) was terrified during this ride and cried afterward. Even I thought it was quite scary, and other adults on our ride echoed the same.

The Simpsons Ride ★★★★

PRESCHOOL ★★½	**GRADE SCHOOL** ★★★★	**TEENS** ★★★½
YOUNG ADULTS ★★★½	**OVER 30** ★★★½	**SENIORS** ★★★½

Motion Sickness

What it is Mega-simulator ride. **Scope and scale** Headliner. **When to go** First 2 hours the park is open or after 4 p.m. **Comments** Must be 40" to ride; not recommended for pregnant guests or anyone prone to motion sickness. **Duration of ride** 4½ minutes, plus preshow. **Loading speed** Moderate. **Universal Express** Yes

DESCRIPTION AND COMMENTS This ride is similar to Despicable Me Minion Mayhem and Disney's Hollywood Studios' Star Tours, but it has a larger screen like that of Soarin' Around the World in EPCOT.

Two preshows have *Simpsons* characters speaking sequentially on different video screens in the queue; their comments help define the characters for guests who are unfamiliar with the TV show. The story line has the conniving Sideshow Bob secretly arriving at Krustyland amusement park and plotting his revenge on Krusty the Clown and Bart, who once revealed that Sideshow Bob had committed a crime for which he'd framed Krusty. Sideshow Bob gets even by making things go wrong with the attractions that the Simpsons (and you) are riding.

TOURING TIPS Like the TV show on which it's based, The Simpsons Ride has a definite edge—some parents, in fact, may find the humor a little crass for younger kids. Because the screen is a giant curved dome, sitting outside the central sweet spot may worsen motion sickness. For the best experience, ask the attendant at the bottom of the ramps for Level 2; then ask the next attendant you see for Room 6.

Transformers: The Ride—3D ★★★★

| PRESCHOOL ★★★ | GRADE SCHOOL ★★★★ | TEENS ★★★★ |
| YOUNG ADULTS ★★★★ | OVER 30 ★★★★ | SENIORS ★★★½ |

What it is Multisensory 3-D dark ride. **Scope and scale** Super-headliner. **When to go** First hour the park is open or after 4 p.m. **Comments** Single-rider line available; must be 40" to ride. **Duration of ride** 4½ minutes. **Loading speed** Moderate-fast. **Universal Express** Yes

Motion Sickness

DESCRIPTION AND COMMENTS Hasbro's Transformers—those toy robots from the 1980s that you turned and twisted into trucks and planes—have been, er, transformed into director Michael Bay's blockbuster movie franchise and then into a theme park attraction. The story line: Decepticon baddies are after the Allspark, source of cybernetic sentience. Your job is to safeguard the shard with the help of your Autobot allies, Optimus Prime and Bumblebee.

The plot amounts to little more than a giant game of keep-away, and the uninitiated will likely be unable to tell one meteoric mass of metal from another, but you'll be too dazzled by the debris whizzing by to notice. Transformers: The Ride—3D is very intense and immersive, but it doesn't hold up as well after repeated rides as The Amazing Adventures of Spider-Man, whose humor, heart, and moving props it lacks.

TOURING TIPS This ride draws crowds—your only solace is that the ones at The Wizarding World of Harry Potter–Diagon Alley are even larger. The single-rider line moves faster, but it closes when it gets backed up. Front-row seats may be too close to the screen for you to focus on the action.

Universal Orlando's Horror Make-Up Show ★★★★½

| PRESCHOOL ★★ | GRADE SCHOOL ★★★½ | TEENS ★★★★ |
| YOUNG ADULTS ★★★★ | OVER 30 ★★★★ | SENIORS ★★★★½ |

What it is Theater presentation on the art of movie makeup. **Scope and scale** Major attraction. **When to go** At scheduled showtimes and after you've experienced all rides. **Comment** May frighten some young children. **Duration of show** 25 minutes. **Universal Express** Yes

DESCRIPTION AND COMMENTS This show is a lively, well-paced look at how makeup artists create film monsters, realistic wounds, severed limbs, and other assorted grossness. Its humor and tongue-in-cheek style transcend the gruesome effects, and most folks (including preschoolers) take the blood and guts in stride.

TOURING TIPS Look for the second-story windows to the left of the marquee for a touching tribute to victims of the 2016 Pulse nightclub tragedy.

Villain-Con Minion Blast

TOO NEW TO RATE

What it is Stand-up shooting gallery meets moving sidewalk. **Scope and scale** Major attraction. **When to go** Immediately upon park opening or late afternoon. **Duration of ride** Not open at press time. **Loading speed** Expected to be fast. **Universal Express** Yes

DESCRIPTION AND COMMENTS Universal's second Minions-themed attraction, which opened in the summer of 2023, lets aspiring evildoers compete to join the Vicious 6 (as introduced in the second Minions movie) by causing mayhem with handheld blasters. Unlike Buzz Lightyear or Men In Black, there's no ride vehicle; rather, guests stand on a moving walkway that can navigate corners, gliding like luggage on an airport conveyor belt past physical sets and projection screens that react to your shots.

TOURING TIPS Like its Minion Mayhem sibling across the street, Villain-Con's location near the park's entrance dooms it to draw large crowds all day. Make it your first stop if you're present at rope drop, or try after 4 p.m. Use the Universal mobile app to track your scores.

THE WIZARDING WORLD OF HARRY POTTER–DIAGON ALLEY

SECRETED BEHIND A LONDON STREET FACADE featuring **Grimmauld Place** and **Wyndham's Theatre,** Diagon Alley is accessed through a secluded entrance. As in the *Harry Potter* books and films, the unmarked portal is concealed within a magical brick wall that is ordinarily reserved for wizards and the like. The endless procession of Muggles in tank tops and flip-flops will leave little doubt where that entryway is, however.

Wizarding World–Diagon Alley Attractions

Harry Potter and the Escape from Gringotts ★★★★★

| PRESCHOOL ★★½ | GRADE SCHOOL ★★★★½ | TEENS ★★★★½ |
| YOUNG ADULTS ★★★★★ | OVER 30 ★★★★½ | SENIORS ★★★★½ |

What it is Super-high-tech 3-D dark ride with roller-coaster elements. **Scope and scale** Super-headliner. **When to go** Immediately after park opening or just before closing. **Comments** Single-rider line available; must be 42″ to ride. **Duration of ride** 4½ minutes. **Loading speed** Moderate–fast. **Universal Express** Yes

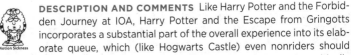

Motion Sickness

DESCRIPTION AND COMMENTS Like Harry Potter and the Forbidden Journey at IOA, Harry Potter and the Escape from Gringotts incorporates a substantial part of the overall experience into its elaborate queue, which (like Hogwarts Castle) even nonriders should experience. You enter through the bank's lobby, where you're critically appraised by glowering animatronic goblins before visiting with Bill Weasley, Ron's curse-breaking big brother. Then you take a simulated 9-mile plunge into the earth aboard an "elevator" with a bouncing floor and ceiling projections. All this is before you pick up your 3-D goggles and then ascend a spiral staircase into the stalactite-festooned boarding cave where your vault cart awaits.

Escape from Gringotts merges Revenge of the Mummy's indoor-coaster aspects with The Amazing Adventures of Spider-Man's seamless integration of high-resolution 3-D film and massive sculptural sets while adding a few new tricks, such as independently rotating cars and motion-simulator bases built into the track. The result is a ride that combines favorite innovations from its predecessors in an exhilarating new way, making it one of the greatest themed thrill attractions of all time.

As far as physical thrills go, Gringotts falls somewhere between Disney's Seven Dwarfs Mine Train and Space Mountain, with only one short (albeit unique) drop and no upside-down flips.

TOURING TIPS If you're a Universal resort guest and you qualify for Early Park Admission, take advantage of it, or use Universal Express or the single-rider line (which bypasses all preshows). Otherwise, try the attraction around lunchtime or in the late afternoon; wait times usually peak after opening but become reasonable later in the day. Note that you must leave your bags in a free locker.

Hogwarts Express ★★★★½

PRESCHOOL ★★★★½   GRADE SCHOOL ★★★★½   TEENS ★★★★½
YOUNG ADULTS ★★★★½   OVER 30 ★★★★½   SENIORS ★★★★½

What it is Transportation attraction. **Scope and scale** Headliner. **When to go** Late morning or just before park closing. **Comment** Requires a Park-to-Park Ticket to ride. **Duration of ride** 4 minutes. **Loading speed** Moderate. **Universal Express** Yes

DESCRIPTION AND COMMENTS As in the Harry Potter novels and films, Diagon Alley at USF is connected to Hogsmeade at IOA by the Hogwarts Express train. The counterpart to Hogsmeade Station in IOA is USF's King's Cross station, located a few doors down from Diagon Alley's hidden entrance. (*Note:* King's Cross has a separate entrance and exit from Diagon Alley—you can't go directly between them without crossing through the London Waterfront.)

The passage to Platform 9¾, from which Hogwarts students depart on their way to school, is concealed from Muggles by a seemingly solid brick wall, through which you'll witness guests ahead of you dematerializing. The train itself looks authentic to the nth degree, from the billowing steam to the brass fixtures and upholstery in your eight-passenger private cabin.

Along your one-way journey, moving images projected beyond the windows of the car simulate the streets of London and the Scottish countryside rolling past. You experience a different presentation coming and going; plus, there are surprise appearances by secondary characters (Fred and George Weasley, Hagrid) and threats en route (Dementors, licorice spiders), augmented by sound effects in the cars.

TOURING TIPS You must have a valid Park-to-Park Ticket to ride; disembarking passengers must enter the second park and, if desired, queue again for their return trip. You'll be allowed (nay, encouraged) to upgrade your 1-Park Base Ticket at the station entrance. If the posted wait is more than 15 minutes, it's typically quicker to walk to the other Wizarding World than to take the train.

Ollivanders ★★★★

PRESCHOOL ★★★½   GRADE SCHOOL ★★★★½   TEENS ★★★★½
YOUNG ADULTS ★★★★½   OVER 30 ★★★★   SENIORS ★★★★

What it is Combination wizarding demonstration and shopping op. **Scope and scale** Major attraction. **When to go** After riding Harry Potter and the Escape from Gringotts. **Comment** No seating is provided. **Duration of show** 6 minutes. **Universal Express** No

DESCRIPTION AND COMMENTS Unlike the branch location in Hogsmeade (see page 620), the Diagon Alley Ollivanders is in its rightful location per the books, and in much larger digs. The shop has multiple separate choosing chambers, where wands choose a wizard (rather than vice versa).

TOURING TIPS Check out the self-sweeping broom (shades of *Fantasia*) while waiting for the show. If your young 'un is selected to test-drive a wand, be forewarned that you'll have to buy it if you want to take it home. Ollivanders may distribute free return-time reservations when the standby wait becomes excessive; these can all be claimed by midmorning on busy days. Ask an employee at the attraction entrance for details.

Wizarding World Entertainment

Take a moment to spot **Kreacher** (the house elf regularly peers from a second-story window above 12 Grimmauld Place) and chat with the **Knight Bus conductor** and his Jamaican-accented shrunken head. Look down the alley to the rounded facade of **Gringotts Wizarding Bank,** where a 40-foot fire-breathing Ukrainian Ironbelly dragon (as seen in *Harry Potter and the Deathly Hallows: Part 2*) perches atop the dome.

To the right of Escape from Gringotts is **Carkitt Market,** a canopy-covered plaza where short live shows are staged every half hour or so. *Celestina Warbeck and the Banshees* (★★★½) showcases the swinging sorceress, who sings jazzy tunes by Alan Zachary and Michael Weiner (the songwriting team behind Broadway's *First Date*), while *Tales of Beedle the Bard* (★★★½) recounts the Three Brothers fable from *Deathly Hallows* with puppets crafted by Michael Curry (*Festival of the Lion King, Finding Nemo—The Musical*).

Intersecting Diagon Alley near the Leaky Cauldron is **Knockturn Alley,** a labyrinth of passageways where the *Harry Potter* bad guys hang out. A covered walk-through area with a projected sky creating perpetual night, it features spooky special effects in the faux shop windows (don't miss the creeping tattoos and crawling spiders).

UNIVERSAL STUDIOS FLORIDA ENTERTAINMENT

IN ADDITION TO THE SHOWS profiled earlier, USF offers a range of street entertainment. Costumed comic-book and cartoon characters, along with movie star look-alikes, roam the park for photo ops. When **DreamWorks KidZone** opens in 2024, it will offer a dance party and photo op with characters from *Shrek, Kung Fu Panda, Trolls,* and other DreamWorks films. The Universal app notes times and places for character greetings and shows.

The Blues Brothers Show (★★★½) is a 12-minute R&B concert held in the New York area, featuring Jake and Elwood performing hit songs from the classic 1980 movie musical. The concert is a great pick-me-up, and the short run time keeps the energy high. **Marilyn Monroe and the Diamond Bellas** (★★½) perform a 4-minute song-and-dance routine in front of the Macy's facade in New York; **Sing It!** (★★★) is an a cappella "competition" on Delancey Street loosely inspired by the riff-off scene in *Pitch Perfect;* ¡Vamos!—Báilalo (★★★½), a 15-minute, high-energy Latin dance show inspired by *West Side Story* and *In The Heights,* takes over the intersection outside Finnegan's; and the **Beat Builders** (★★★) are a *Stomp*-style quartet of beefy guys who drum on the scaffolding outside Louie's Italian Restaurant.

Universal's Superstar Parade concluded its run in 2022, with no daily replacement announced at press time, but seasonal parades are still held during the popular Mardi Gras and holiday events. Parades begin at the Esoteric Pictures gate in Hollywood between the *Horror Make-Up Show* and Cafe La Bamba. They turn left onto Hollywood Boulevard, then make a hard right near the park entrance onto Plaza of the Stars past Despicable Me Minion Mayhem, and head to New York. From there, they turn right and proceed along 5th Avenue past Revenge of the Mummy, then take a right at Louie's Italian Restaurant and follow the waterfront past Transformers: The Ride—3D and Mel's Drive-In before disappearing backstage through the gate where they entered. The best viewing spots are along **5th Avenue,** on the front steps of the faux buildings in New York.

Universal Orlando's Cinematic Celebration, USF's big nighttime spectacular, also ended in 2023; a new lagoon show (rumored to involve drones) is reportedly under development. The former show's lights and fountains have also been used for seasonal shows during Halloween Horror Nights. The terraced **Central Park,** across the lagoon from San Francisco, is the primary viewing location for these shows, with additional viewing between Mel's Drive-In and Transformers: The Ride—3D, and near Duff Brewery. No reservations are required, and you should be able to get a good view by arriving about 15 minutes before showtime.

DINING AT UNIVERSAL STUDIOS FLORIDA

SPRINGFIELD: HOME OF THE SIMPSONS has a number of wacky *Simpsons*-inspired eateries: **Krusty Burger, The Frying Dutchman** for seafood, **Cletus' Chicken Shack, Luigi's Pizza, Lard Lad Donuts, Lisa's Teahouse of Horror, Bumblebee Man's Taco Truck, Duff Brewery,** and **Moe's Tavern.** The portions are large, and the quality is good.

The best quick-service food in USF is served at the **Leaky Cauldron.** Diagon Alley's flagship restaurant serves authentically hearty British pub fare such as bangers and mash (sausages and mashed potatoes), cottage pie, toad-in-the-hole, Guinness stew, and a ploughman's platter of Scotch eggs and imported cheeses that serves two. When you're done, head over to **Florean Fortescue's Ice-Cream Parlour** and cap off your meal with some delicious Butterbeer ice cream. For a lighter option, we like the salads and sandwiches at **Today Cafe.**

USF's two sit-down restaurants are **Finnegan's Bar and Grill,** in New York, and **Lombard's Seafood Grille,** in San Francisco. Finnegan's serves burgers and wings as well as fish-and-chips and other takes on Irish cuisine. Lombard's is the better restaurant, but it's not in the same league (in terms of price or quality) as, say, DHS's Hollywood Brown Derby.

UNIVERSAL STUDIOS FLORIDA TOURING PLANS

WHEN EARLY PARK ADMISSION IS IN EFFECT, USF admits resort guests 1 hour before the general public, with the turnstiles opening up to 75 minutes before the official opening time. Arrive at least 30 minutes before early entry starts; during peak season, we recommend showing up on the very first boat or bus from your hotel. If you're a day guest visiting on a busy Early Park Admission day, Diagon Alley may already be packed when you arrive.

Even when Early Park Admission isn't offered at USF, all guests may enter Diagon Alley from the front gates up to 15 minutes before park opening, and early guests departing IOA will arrive via Hogwarts Express a little after that, though Harry Potter and the Escape from Gringotts doesn't begin operating until near official opening time.

Universal Orlando Highlights One-Day, Two-Park Touring Plan *(pages 729–732)*

See page 624 for the description of this plan.

Universal Studios Florida One-Day Touring Plan *(page 734)*

This plan is for guests without Park-to-Park Tickets and includes every recommended attraction at USF. If a ride or show is listed that you don't want to experience, skip that step and proceed to the next. Move quickly from attraction to attraction, and if possible, hold off on lunch until after experiencing at least six rides.

UNIVERSAL'S EPIC UNIVERSE: *A Preview*

ON AUGUST 1, 2019, Universal officially announced construction of its second resort campus, **Universal's Epic Universe.** Construction is well underway on more than 750 acres acquired by Universal near the Orange County Convention Center, about a 12-minute drive south of the current resort. Concept art and construction permit filings (as unearthed by Alicia Stella of **Orlando ParkStop** (orlandoparkstop.com) reveal a celestially inspired central hub with fountain-filled lagoons, surrounded by two hotels—the 500-room **Helios Grand** attached to the rear of the hub, as well as two 750-room hotels, **Stella Nova** and **Terra Luna,** across the street from the campus—multiple shops and restaurants, and at least four highly themed "lands":

SUPER NINTENDO WORLD The first featured franchise officially confirmed for the new park is Super Nintendo World, based on the 1980s Super Mario Bros. video games. The multilevel land, which guests access via a green "warp pipe" tunnel, is built around the imposing fortress housing **Mario Kart: Bowser's Challenge,** an interactive dark ride that uses augmented-reality goggles to put riders inside the racing games. The land will also include a *Donkey Kong Country*–themed indoor–outdoor roller coaster, which uses an innovative cantilevered design to make your mine cart appear to fly over gaps in the track; the family-friendly **Yoshi's Adventure,** with colorful dinosaurs that slowly traverse an elevated track past animated scenes; and interactive games that can be activated with optional Power-Up wristbands that connect to a smartphone app. Of course, there will also be meet and greets with Mario, Luigi, Princess Peach, and Toad, along with exclusive merchandise stores and food that's too kawaii (cute) to eat.

HOW TO TRAIN YOUR DRAGON—ISLE OF BERK DreamWorks' Isle of Berk looks to be the most densely packed land in Epic Universe, with multiple attractions and eateries woven around a whimsical waterfront, all encircled by an Intamin launched steel roller coaster (think a tamer version of VelociCoaster). Other highlights include a water-blasting interactive boat adventure, a pair of passenger-controlled spinning rides, and an indoor stage show starring massive dragon puppets. Elaborate play areas, shops, and character encounters themed to Hiccup's hometown round out this land's roster.

THE WIZARDING WORLD OF HARRY POTTER Universal's third—and presumably final—Wizarding World will re-create the streets of Paris from the *Fantastic Beasts* spin-off film series, as well as the Ministry of Magic in London, as seen in the original *Harry Potter* films. Guests will enter the British side through Floo Network fireplaces and board an attraction that combines moving vehicles with video projections to simulate the ministry's signature enchanted elevators. There will also be a theater show where you can witness wizards dueling, with bolts of actual electricity arcing between them.

UNIVERSAL'S CLASSIC MONSTERS The legendary fiends from Universal's vintage black-and-white fright flicks finally get their due with the first-ever theme park land dedicated to the monsters made famous by Lon Chaney (*The Hunchback of Notre Dame* and *Phantom of the Opera*), Boris Karloff (*Frankenstein*), Elsa Lanchester (*The Bride of Frankenstein*), and Bela Lugosi (*Dracula*). A rustic Bavarian village surrounds the Gothic manor of Dr. Victor Frankenstein, where brave guests are strapped onto a Kuka robotic arm (similar to that used in Harry Potter and the Forbidden Journey) for hair-raising encounters with Frankenstein's monster and his bride, Count Dracula, and other iconic boogeypersons.

A second attraction inside the land is a werewolf-inspired spinning launched roller coaster.

In addition to the attractions inside the four lands, the expansive hub itself will be home to a water-based nighttime spectacular, along with several rides, including a fanciful carousel and a dual-track, space-themed launched roller coaster made by Mack Rides that will be the longest and fastest thrill ride in the park. Each land is isolated from the others, with no direct access except through the hub, potentially allowing certain areas to limit capacity. You may not even need a physical ticket to traverse the new campus because Universal has patented touchless technology to replace traditional turnstiles. (Of course, all of these plans are speculative and subject to change.)

Originally anticipated to open in 2023, Epic Universe was delayed when the pandemic began, but construction resumed as of March 3, 2021; an exact opening date has not been officially announced, but the theme park is on track to be operational by summer 2025.

The WATER PARKS

YOU'RE SOAKING *in* IT!

DISNEY AND UNIVERSAL operate water parks alongside their Orlando theme parks. Disney's water parks are **Blizzard Beach** and **Typhoon Lagoon,** and Universal's is **Volcano Bay.**

Disney's and Universal's water parks are much larger and more elaborately themed than the local or regional water parks you may have visited. Almost all the waterslides, wave pools, and lazy rivers at these parks are larger and longer than those at local and regional water parks too.

COST One day of admission to either of Disney's water parks costs around $73 for adults and $68 for kids, including tax. Peak season is late May–late September. If you visit outside of that window, Disney offers a discount of around $5 per ticket.

If you buy your Walt Disney World admission tickets before leaving home and you're considering the **Water Park and Sports (WPS)** add-on (see page 75), you might want to wait until you arrive and have some degree of certainty about the weather during your stay. You can add the WPS option at any Disney resort or Guest Relations window at the theme parks. This is true regardless of whether you purchased your Base Tickets separately or as part of a package. Also note that if you're planning to visit only one theme park per day and you're planning only one day to visit a water park, buying separate water-park admission is almost always cheaper than buying the **Park Hopper Plus** add-on (see page 75).

Admission to Volcano Bay (including tax) costs $85–$91 per adult ($80–$85 for kids ages 3–9) for one day or $26–$65 as an upgrade to any multiday ticket.

GETTING THERE Disney provides regular daily bus service between its resorts and water parks. Likewise, Universal runs shuttle buses between most of its resort hotels and Volcano Bay; Universal's Aventura and Cabana Bay hotels are adjacent to Volcano Bay, so walking is usually faster. Disney's bus service might route you through other hotels or Disney Springs, though, and when it does, it takes a while to get there. If you're staying at a Disney hotel and don't have a car, a ride-hailing app or taxi is the best way to get to Disney's water parks.

The best way to get to the water parks from off-site is to drive. At Disney's water parks, parking is free and close by; Universal's parking fee is $27 (including tax), and you'll take a shuttle from the parking structure to the water park. If you don't have a car, then a ride-hailing service, taxi, or shuttle can drop you off at the park entrance.

WHEN TO GO

DISNEY AND UNIVERSAL generally open their water parks every day of the year. Orlando-area temperatures can vary from the high 40s to the low 80s during December, January, and February. When it's warmer out, these off-season months can serve up a dandy water-park experience, as this Batavia, Ohio, reader confirms:

> *unofficial* **TIP**
> If your schedule is flexible, a good time to visit the water parks is midafternoon to late in the day, when the weather has cleared after a storm.

> *Going to Blizzard Beach in December was the best decision ever! They told us at the entrance that if the park didn't reach 100—yes, I said 100—people by noon, they would be closing. I guess they got to 101, because it stayed open but was virtually empty. There was no wait for anything all day! In June we waited in line for an hour for Summit Plummet, but in December it was just the amount of time it took to walk up the stairs. We had the enormous wave pool to ourselves. We did everything in the entire park and ate lunch in less than 3 hours. It was perfect. The weather was slightly chilly at 71°F and overcast with very light rain, but the water was heated, so we were fine.*

We've had experiences similar to this reader's: We visited Volcano Bay on a Saturday in September when the daily high temperature was "only" 72°F. So few people were in the park with us that we were able to count all of them. We never encountered a line longer than 10 people for any slide.

That said, the water parks may close if the daytime high temperatures dip much below 60°F or so. If you're visiting during late fall, winter, or early spring and temperatures are low, check the park's website before you visit.

AVOIDING LINES The best way to avoid standing in lines is to visit the water parks when they're least crowded. Our research over many weeks in the parks indicates that tourists, not locals, make up most visitors on any given day. And because weekends are popular travel days, the water parks tend to be less crowded then. In fact, of the weekend days we evaluated, the parks never reached full capacity;

during the week, Thursday had the most closures for capacity, and both parks closed at least once every other weekday. Therefore, we recommend going on a Monday or Friday.

A mom from Manlius, New York, describes what *crowded* means:

> We visited Typhoon Lagoon, arriving before opening so we could stake out a shady spot. The kids loved it until the lines got long (11 a.m.–noon), but I hated it. It made Coney Island seem like a deserted island in the Bahamas. Floating on Castaway Creek was really unpleasant. Whirling around in a chlorinated concrete ditch with some stranger's feet in my face, periodically getting squirted by water guns, passing under cascades of cold water, and getting hung up by the crowd is not at all relaxing for me. My husband and I then decided to bob in the Surf Pool. After about 10 minutes of being tossed around like corks in boiling water, we sought the peace of our shady little territory—which in our absence had become much, much smaller.

A visitor from Middletown, New York, had a somewhat better experience at the same park:

> On our second trip to Typhoon Lagoon, we dispensed with the locker rental (having planned to stay for only the morning, when it was least crowded), and at park opening we just took right off for the Storm Slides before the masses arrived—it was perfect! We must have ridden the slides at least five times before any kind of line built up, and then we were also able to ride the tube and raft rides (Keelhaul and Mayday Falls) in a similar uncrowded, quick fashion because everyone else was busy getting their lockers!

When Typhoon Lagoon or Blizzard Beach reopens after inclement weather has passed, you almost have a whole park to yourself.

WHICH WATER PARK TO VISIT?

WE ASK *UNOFFICIAL GUIDE* READERS to rate water-park attractions, just as they do those at the theme parks. Taken in aggregate, readers rank **Volcano Bay** first, with **Blizzard Beach** and **Typhoon Lagoon** tied for second.

Volcano Bay's big advantage is that it's open up to 3 hours more per day than Disney's water parks, including later closings. If you're looking for the best choice for a diverse group, Blizzard Beach is probably your best bet because it's rated first or second by every age group. A couple from Woodridge, Illinois, agrees:

> If you have time to go to only one water park, definitely go to Blizzard Beach. It seems like they took everything from Typhoon Lagoon and made it better and faster. Summit Plummet was awesome—a total rush. The toboggan and bobsled rides were exciting—the bobsled really throws you around. The family tube ride was really good—much better and longer than the one at Typhoon Lagoon.

A hungry reader from Aberdeen, New Jersey, notes that Blizzard Beach's dining options are lacking:

> At Blizzard Beach, there's only one main place to get food (most of the other spots are more for snacks). At lunchtime, it took almost 45 minutes to get some sandwiches and drinks.

Finally, a mother of four from Winchester, Virginia, gives her opinion on choosing between Typhoon Lagoon and Blizzard Beach:

At Blizzard Beach, the family raft ride is great, but the kids' area is poorly designed. As a parent, when you walk your child to the top of a slide or the tube ride, they're lost to your vision as they go down because of the fake snowdrifts. There are no direct ways down to the end of the slides, so little ones are left standing unsupervised while parents scramble down from the top. The Typhoon Lagoon kids' area is far superior in design.

That said, Disney may open only one water park per day, throughout the year. If you're intent on visiting a specific water park, check Disney's website for its operating status before purchasing tickets.

PLANNING YOUR DAY *at the* WATER PARKS

DISNEY WATER PARKS are almost as large and elaborate as the major theme parks. You must be prepared for a lot of walking, exercise, sun, and jostling crowds. If your group really loves the water, schedule your visit early in your vacation. If you go at the beginning of your stay, you'll have more flexibility if you want to return.

To have a great day and beat the crowds, consider:

1. GETTING INFORMATION Call ☎ 407-WDW-MAGIC (939-6244) or check disneyworld.disney.go.com the night before to verify when the park opens.

2. TO PICNIC OR NOT TO PICNIC Decide whether you want to carry a picnic lunch. Guests are permitted to take lunches and beverage coolers into the parks, but alcoholic beverages, glass containers, and loose ice and dry ice are prohibited; reusable ice packs are permitted. Only one cooler per family is allowed. The in-park food is comparable to fast food, but the prices are a bit high.

3. GETTING STARTED If you're going to Blizzard Beach or Typhoon Lagoon, get up early and have breakfast. If you have a car, drive instead of taking a Disney bus. If you don't have a car, ask a cast member at your hotel if direct bus service is available to the water park. If it is, take the bus; if not, take an Uber, Lyft, or taxi instead. Either way, plan to arrive at the park 40 minutes before opening.

4. FOLLOW A GOOD TOURING PLAN We have two touring plans designed to help you avoid crowds and bottlenecks at Disney water

MOST POPULAR WATER PARKS BY AGE GROUP					
PRESCHOOL	**GRADE SCHOOL**	**TEENS**	**YOUNG ADULTS**	**OVER 30**	**SENIORS**
Blizzard Beach	Blizzard Beach	Volcano Bay	Typhoon Lagoon	Volcano Bay	Typhoon Lagoon
Typhoon Lagoon	Typhoon Lagoon	Blizzard Beach	Blizzard Beach	Blizzard Beach	Blizzard Beach
Volcano Bay	Volcano Bay	Typhoon Lagoon	Volcano Bay	Typhoon Lagoon	Volcano Bay

parks (see pages 735 and 736). If you're attending on a day of moderate to heavy attendance (see the Crowd Calendar at **TouringPlans .com**), consider using one of these tested plans. More touring plans are also available on the website.

5. ATTIRE Wear your swimsuit under shorts and a T-shirt so you don't need to use lockers or dressing rooms. Be advised that it's extremely common for those wearing two-piece swimsuits to accidentally part company with one of the pieces on the slides. Both the paths and beach sand get incredibly hot during the summer, so some form of foot protection is a must. Socks will do in a pinch, but water socks or sandals that strap to your feet are best. Shops in the parks sell sandals, Reef Runners, and other protective footwear that can be worn in and out of the water.

6. WHAT TO BRING You'll need a towel, sunscreen, and money. If you don't have towels, they can be rented for $2 each. Sunscreen is available in all park shops. Because wallets and purses get in the way, lock them in your car's trunk, or leave them at your hotel. Carry your Disney resort ID (if you have one) and enough money for the day in a plastic bag or other waterproof container, or use your MagicBand to pay for things.

Though nowhere is completely safe, we felt comfortable hiding our plastic money bags in our cooler. Nobody disturbed our stuff, and our cash was much easier to reach than if we'd stashed it in a locker across the park. If you're carrying a wad or you worry about money anyway, rent the locker.

A Canadian reader suggests the following option if you don't feel totally comfortable stashing your valuables in a locker, a cooler, or the like:

> As our admission was from an all-inclusive ticket [not a MagicBand], I was concerned about our passes being stolen or lost, yet I didn't want the hassle of a locker. I discovered that the gift shop sells water-resistant plastic boxes (with strings to go around your neck) in two sizes for around $5, with the smallest being just big enough for passes, credit cards, and a bit of money. I would've spent nearly as much on a locker rental, so I was able to enjoy the rest of the day with peace of mind.

Finally, a limited number of **wheelchairs** are available for rent for $12 per day with a $100 refundable deposit. Personal flotation devices (life jackets) can be rented for free with a refundable deposit.

7. WHAT NOT TO BRING Personal swim gear (fins, masks, rafts, and the like) isn't allowed. Everything you need is provided or available to rent. If you forgot your swimsuit, you can buy one.

8. ADMISSION Buy your admission in advance or about 45 minutes before official opening. Guests staying five or more days should consider the **Park Hopper Plus** add-on (see page 75), which provides admission to either Blizzard Beach or Typhoon Lagoon.

9. LOCKERS Rental lockers are $10 per day for a standard size and $15 per day for a large (lockers are keyless). Standard-size lockers are roomy enough for one person or a couple, but a family will generally need a large locker. Though you can access your locker freely all day, not all lockers are conveniently located.

Getting a locker at Blizzard Beach or Typhoon Lagoon is truly competitive. When the gates open, guests race to the locker-rental desk. The rental procedure is somewhat slow; if you aren't among the first in line, you can waste a lot of time waiting. We recommend skipping the locker. Carry a MagicBand or only as much cash as you'll need for the day in a watertight container that you can stash in your cooler. Ditto for personal items, including watches and eyeglasses.

10. TUBES for bobbing on the waves, floating in the creeks, and riding the tube slides are available for free.

11. GETTING SETTLED Establish your base for the day. There are many beautiful sunning and lounging spots scattered throughout both Disney water parks—arrive early and you can almost have your pick.

The breeze is best along the beaches of the surf pools at Blizzard Beach and Typhoon Lagoon. At Typhoon Lagoon, if there are children younger than age 6 in your party, choose an area to the left of Mount Mayday (ship on top) near the children's swimming area.

Also available are flat lounges (nonadjustable) and chairs (better for reading), shelters for guests who prefer shade, picnic tables, and a few hammocks. If you have money to burn, private cabanas are available at both water parks for up to six guests. Called **Polar Patios** at Blizzard Beach and **Beachcomber Shacks** at Typhoon Lagoon, they come outfitted with lounge chairs, tables, towels, private lockers, a refillable drink mug, and an attendant who'll be at your beck and call. Available by reservation at ☎ 407-WDW-PLAY (939-7529), the cabanas run from around $373 to $506, depending on the season.

We think the best spectator sport at Typhoon Lagoon is the body-surfing in the Surf Pool—it's second only to being out on the waves yourself. With this in mind, position yourself to have an unobstructed view of the waves.

12. A WORD ABOUT THE SLIDES Waterslides come in many shapes and sizes. Some are steep and vertical, and some are long and undulating. Some resemble corkscrews, while others imitate the pool-and-drop nature of whitewater

unofficial **TIP**
When lines for the slides become intolerable, head for the surf or wave pool or the tube-floating streams.

streams. Depending on the slide, swimmers ride mats, inner tubes, or rafts. With body slides, swimmers slosh to the bottom on the seat of their pants.

Though Typhoon Lagoon and Blizzard Beach are huge parks with many slides, they're overwhelmed almost daily by armies of guests. If your main reason for going to Typhoon Lagoon or Blizzard Beach is the slides and you hate long lines, be among the first guests to enter the park. Go directly to the slides, and ride as many times as you can before the park fills.

For maximum speed on a body slide, cross your legs at the ankles, and cross your arms over your chest. When you take off, arch your back so almost all your weight is on your shoulder blades and heels (the less contact with the surface, the less resistance). Steer by shifting most of your upper-body weight onto one shoulder blade. For top speed on turns, weight the shoulder blade on the outside of each curve. If you want to go slowly, distribute your weight equally, as if you were lying

SOGGY TIPS FROM A WATER-LOVING FAMILY

A Bow, New Hampshire, family who are evidently working on a PhD in Disney water parks were kind enough to share their knowledge.

IF YOU'RE GOING TO THE WATER PARKS, **train on your StairMaster** prior to going, especially if you visit Blizzard Beach. For Runoff Rapids, you climb 125 stairs (yes, I counted). Imagine doing that three times in a row, trying to keep up with kids who want to go down the slide multiple times. In addition, there are at least (and here, I'm guessing) 300 stairs if you choose the Alpine Path instead of the chairlift to get to Summit Plummet. At Typhoon Lagoon, each slide, except Miss Adventure Falls, has about 60 steps, so at either park you have quite a bit of stairs to climb or go down.

We were at Blizzard Beach 15 minutes before park opening in late August, and we felt that this was plenty of time to beat the crowds. We noticed crowds building [about an hour after opening]. If you are there at park opening, **stash your things as quickly as possible while you take the chairlift to Summit Plummet.** We were first in line for the chairlift, and we were at the top with no lines. The chairlift is definitely faster if you are one of the first in line, and you won't get winded from walking the Alpine Path. However, if you arrive later in the day, the line for the chairlift builds, and you'll be left having to climb the Alpine Path—great if you're in shape, but not so much if you're not!

Check the closing time of the water parks if you plan on arriving in late afternoon. When Typhoon Lagoon closed at 8 p.m. and we arrived shortly after 2 p.m., lines tended to thin out by 4 p.m. However, when we tried that same tactic (arriving in the afternoon) when Typhoon Lagoon closed at 6 p.m., we noticed that the lines were still long, and it seemed like the crowd wasn't thinning at all. On those days, we wished that we had been there for park opening and left when crowds started to build.

We enjoyed the water parks, but **we only stayed about 3 hours max.** Though the water parks are big (as in spread out), there weren't enough attractions to keep us there the entire day. Yes, they have slides, but not as many as I expected a Disney park to have. When lines started to build, it became less fun to wait 15-plus minutes for a slide that takes less than 2 minutes to go down. Also,

on your back in bed. For curving slides, maximize speed by hitting the entrance to each curve high and exiting the curve low.

Some slides and rapids have a minimum height requirement. Riders for **Humunga Kowabunga** at Typhoon Lagoon and for **Slush Gusher** and **Summit Plummet** at Blizzard Beach, for example, must be 4 feet tall. You shouldn't ride if you are pregnant or have back problems or other health difficulties.

13. LAZY RIVERS Each of the water parks we cover here offers a lazy river. These long, tranquil inner-tube floats give you the illusion that the less popular attractions, such as the lazy river, got really busy, and there were hardly any tubes to be found.

Water shoes or water sandals are a good bet in the water parks, as the paths can get really hot in the summer, and only a few water jets are near the pathways to keep them cool. However, on some slides (such as the body slides), water shoes aren't allowed, so stash your water shoes at the base of the path where you exit, and grab them on your way out.

Some of the slides at Blizzard Beach, such as the **Downhill Double Dipper**, take FOREVER in line because you're waiting for a tube to make it from the pool up the conveyor belt to the slide stairs. Once the tube finally arrives, you still have to wait for both parties to go down together and to exit the pool. This process takes a long time. If this slide is important to you, make it one of the first things you do. The toboggan rides can also take a while because there is no clear system of who can take the mat when it finally arrives at the top (two mat rides are at the top of the mat conveyor belt: **Toboggan Racers** and **Snow Stormers**).

Some of the slides aren't very comfortable. At Typhoon Lagoon, the **Humunga Kowabunga** should be called the Wedgie Maker. Also, if your family will be going to both water parks (like we did), I suggest **skipping Gangplank Falls at Typhoon Lagoon and doing Teamboat Springs at Blizzard Beach instead.** Not only is Teamboat Springs a LOT longer than Gangplank Falls, but it's also more fun.

The wave pools at both parks are very different. At Typhoon Lagoon, it's "The Wave" pool—as in, there's only one HUGE wave that you can try to bodysurf (good luck with that!). At Blizzard Beach, it's more like "The Waves" pool, where waves are put out at a continual rate, at all times, like a gentle rocking motion, and there are tubes you can use. Typhoon Lagoon has no flotation devices of any kind because, well, they'd be dangerous to everyone involved.

If you have something electronic like a smartphone or tablet that you need to stay dry at the water parks, **buy a waterproof container BEFORE you go.** The water parks sell only water-resistant containers, and even though the one we bought didn't seem to leak, it would have given us more peace of mind to have a waterproof bag/container.

you're doing something while you're being sedentary. Disney's flow ever so slowly around the entire park, through caves, beneath waterfalls, past gardens, and under bridges, offering a relaxing alternative to touring a park on foot. Lazy rivers can be reached from several put-in and take-out points. There are never lines; just wade into the creek and plop into one of the tubes floating by. Ride the current all the way around, or get out at any exit. It takes 30–35 minutes to float the full circuit.

14. BAD WEATHER Thunderstorms are common in Florida. On summer afternoons, storms can occur daily. Water parks close during a storm. Most storms, however, are short-lived, allowing the parks to resume normal operations. If a storm is severe and prolonged, it can cause a great deal of inconvenience: In addition to the park's closing, guests compete aggressively for shelter, and Disney resort guests may have to joust for seats on a bus back to the hotel.

You should monitor the local weather forecast the day before you go, checking again in the morning before leaving for the water park. Scattered thundershowers are no big deal, but moving storm fronts are to be avoided.

15. ENDURANCE The water parks are large and require almost as much walking as one of the theme parks. Add to this wave surfing, swimming, and all the climbing required to reach the slides, and you'll be pooped by day's end. Unless you spend your hours like a lizard on a rock, don't expect to return to the hotel with much energy. Consider something low-key for the evening. You'll probably want to hit the hay early.

16. LOST CHILDREN AND LOST ADULTS It's easier to lose a child or become separated from your party at one of the water parks than it is at a major theme park. Upon arrival, pick a very specific place to meet should you get separated. If you split up on purpose, set times for checking in. Lost-children stations at the water parks are so out of the way that neither you nor your lost child will find them without help from a Disney cast member. Explain to your children how to recognize cast members (by their distinctive name tags) and how to ask for help.

WATER-PARK TOURING PLANS

ONE-DAY TOURING PLANS for Typhoon Lagoon and Blizzard Beach can be found on pages 735 and 736, respectively. These plans are for parents with small children; touring plans for adults, along with our online reader survey, are available at **TouringPlans.com.** We'd love to hear from families who have tried these plans.

The plans presented here include all the slides, flumes, and rides appropriate for kids in both parks. Having brought our own children to these parks, we've also included tips on which slides to try first in case this is your child's first water-park experience. For example, at **Typhoon Lagoon** we suggest the family whitewater raft ride **Miss Adventure Falls** as the first attraction. If your child enjoys that, we list **Gangplank Falls** and then **Keelhaul Falls** as the next steps up in water-slides. If that seems a bit much, however, the touring plan recommends the **Ketchakiddee Creek** play area as an alternative.

BLIZZARD BEACH

unofficial **TIP**
Picnic areas are scattered around the park, as are pleasant places for sunbathing.

BLIZZARD BEACH IS DISNEY'S more unusual water-adventure park, and it arrived with its own legend. The story goes that an entrepreneur tried to open a ski resort in Florida during a particularly savage winter. Alas, the snow melted; the palm trees grew back; and all that remained of the ski resort was its alpine lodge, the ski lifts, and, of course, the mountain. Plunging off the mountain are ski slopes and bobsled runs transformed into waterslides. Visitors to Blizzard Beach catch the thaw—icicles drip and patches of snow remain. The melting snow has formed a lagoon (wave pool), which is fed by gushing mountain streams.

Both Disney water parks are distinguished by their landscaping and the attention paid to executing their themes. As you enter Blizzard Beach, you face the mountain. Coming off the highest peak and bisecting the area at the mountain's base are two long slides. To the left of the slides is the wave pool. To the right are the children's swimming area and the ski lift. Surrounding the layout like a moat is a tranquil stream for floating in tubes.

unofficial **TIP**
If you're into slides, Blizzard Beach is tops among the Disney water parks.

On either side of the highest peak are tube, raft, and body slides. Including the two slides coming off the peak, Blizzard Beach has 19 slides. Among them are **Summit Plummet,** Disney World's longest speed slide, which begins with a 120-foot free fall, and the **Teamboat Springs** 1,200-foot-long water-bobsled run.

One reader reports that the Blizzard Beach slides picked her husband's pocket:

> *Our family absolutely loved Summit Plummet, but it claimed all four of our park passes/room-key cards as its victims. My husband had the four cards in an exterior pocket of his swimsuit, secured closed by Velcro AND a snap. But after doing Summit Plummet and Slush*

Blizzard Beach

Attractions

1. Chairlift
2. Cross Country Creek
3. Downhill Double Dipper
4. Melt-Away Bay
5. Runoff Rapids
6. Ski Patrol Training Camp
7. Slush Gusher
8. Snow Stormers
9. Summit Plummet
10. Teamboat Springs
11. Tike's Peak
12. Toboggan Racers

Restaurants

A. Avalunch
B. Cooling Hut
C. Frostbite Freddy's
D. Lottawatta Lodge
E. Polar Pub
F. Warming Hut

 Restrooms

Gusher twice apiece and Teamboat Springs once, he looked down, noticed the pocket flapping open, and found all four cards missing! So we had to cancel all the cards (they had charging privileges) and couldn't purchase any food or drinks while we were there (we didn't bring any cash because we planned to charge with our cards)!

We've worn MagicBands at the water parks, and they're much more secure. The point is that anything in your pockets—cash, keys, and the like—may come out. A couple from Bowie, Maryland, came away with battle scars:

BLIZZARD BEACH ATTRACTIONS

CHAIRLIFT UP MOUNT GUSHMORE **Height requirement: 32".** Great ride even if you go up just for the view. When the park is packed, use the singles line.

CROSS COUNTRY CREEK **No height requirement.** Lazy river circling the park; grab a tube.

DOWNHILL DOUBLE DIPPER **Height requirement: 48".** Side-by-side tube-racing slides. At 25 mph, the tube zooms through water curtains and free falls. It's a lot of fun, but it's rough.

MELT-AWAY BAY **No height requirement.** Wave pool with gentle, bobbing waves. Great for younger swimmers.

RUNOFF RAPIDS **No height requirement.** Three corkscrew tube slides to choose from. The center slide is for solo raft rides; the other two slides offer one- or two-person tubes. The dark, enclosed tube gives you the feeling of being flushed down the john.

SKI PATROL TRAINING CAMP **Height requirement: 60" for T-Bar.** Place for preteens to train for the big rides.

SLUSH GUSHER **Height requirement: 48".** 90-foot double-humped slide. Cling to those swimsuit tops and hang on for your lives.

SNOW STORMERS **No height requirement.** Consists of three mat-slide flumes; down you go on your belly.

SUMMIT PLUMMET **Height requirement: 48".** 120-foot free fall at 60 mph. Needless to say, this ride is very intense. Make sure your child knows what to expect; being over 48" tall doesn't guarantee an enjoyable experience. If you think you'd enjoy being washed out of a 12th-floor window during a heavy rain, then this slide is for you.

TEAMBOAT SPRINGS **No height requirement.** 1,200-foot group whitewater raft flume. Wonderful ride for the whole family.

TIKE'S PEAK **Height requirement: 48" and under only.** Kid-size version of Blizzard Beach. Recently rethemed to Disney's *Frozen* films. This is the place for little ones.

TOBOGGAN RACERS **No height requirement.** Eight-lane race course. You go down the flume on a mat. Less intense than Snow Stormers.

Summit Plummet gave me a bunch of bruises. Even my husband hurt for a few days. It wasn't a fun ride. Basically, you drop until you hit the slide, and that is why everyone comes off rubbing their butts. They say you go 60 mph on a 120-foot drop. I'll never do it again.

For our money, the most exciting and interesting slides are the **Slush Gusher** and **Teamboat Springs,** on the front right of the mountain, and **Runoff Rapids,** on the back side of the mountain. Slush Gusher is an undulating speed slide that we consider as exciting as the more vertical Summit Plummet but not as bone-jarring. On Teamboat Springs, you ride in a round raft that looks like a children's blow-up wading pool.

Runoff Rapids is accessible from a path that winds around the far-left bottom of the mountain. The rapids consist of three corkscrew tube slides, one of which is enclosed and dark. As at Teamboat Springs, you'll go much faster on a two- or three-person tube than on a one-person tube. If you lean so that you enter curves high and come out low, you'll really fly. Because we like to steer the tube and go fast, we much prefer the open slides (where we can see) to the dark, enclosed tube. We thought crashing through the pitch-dark tube felt disturbingly like being flushed down a toilet.

The **Snow Stormers** mat slides, on the front of the mountain, are fun but not as fast or as interesting as Runoff Rapids or **Downhill**

Double Dipper, on the far left front. **Toboggan Racers,** at the front and center of the mountain, consists of eight parallel slides where riders are dispatched in heats to race to the bottom. The ride itself is no big deal, and the time needed to get everybody lined up ensures that you'll wait extra-long to ride. A faster, more exciting race venue can be found on the side-by-side slides of the undulating Downhill Double Dipper. Competitors here can reach speeds of up to 25 mph.

unofficial **TIP**
Blizzard Beach fills early during hotter months. To stake out a nice sunning spot and to enjoy the slides without long waits, arrive at least 35 minutes before the official opening time (check disneyworld. disney.go.com the night before you go).

A ski lift carries guests to the mountaintop (you can also walk up), where they can choose from **Summit Plummet, Slush Gusher,** or **Teamboat Springs.** For all other slides at Blizzard Beach, the only way to reach the top is on foot. If you're among the first in the park and don't have to wait to ride, the ski lift is fun and provides a bird's-eye view of the park. After riding once to satisfy your curiosity, however, you're better off taking the stairs to the top. The following attractions have a minimum height requirement of 48 inches: **Slush Gusher, Summit Plummet,** and **Downhill Double Dipper.**

The wave pool, called **Melt-Away Bay,** has gentle, bobbing waves. The float creek, **Cross Country Creek,** circles the park, passing through the mountain. The children's areas (**Tike's Peak** and **Ski Patrol Training Camp**) are creatively designed, nicely isolated, and—like the rest of the park—visually interesting. Tike's Peak was rethemed in 2022 with characters from Disney's *Frozen.*

The layout of Blizzard Beach (and Typhoon Lagoon, described next) is a bit convoluted. With slides on both the front and back of the mountain, it isn't always easy to find a path leading to where you want to go.

At the ski resort's now-converted base area are shops; counter-service food; restrooms; and tube, towel, and locker rentals. Blizzard Beach has its own parking lot but no lodging, though Disney's All-Star and Coronado Springs Resorts are almost within walking distance.

TYPHOON LAGOON

TYPHOON LAGOON is comparable in size to Blizzard Beach. The park has 15 waterslides, some as long as 420 feet, and two streams. Most of the slides drop from the top of a 100-foot-tall artificial mountain. Landscaping and a typhoon-aftermath theme add interest and a sense of adventure to the wet rides.

Guests enter Typhoon Lagoon through a misty rainforest and then emerge in a ramshackle tropical town where the park's concessions and services are situated. Special sets make every ride an odyssey as swimmers encounter bat caves, lagoons and pools, spinning rocks, formations of dinosaur bones, and many other imponderables.

Typhoon Lagoon has its own parking lot. Disney resort guests can commute to the water park on Disney buses.

If you indulge in all features of Typhoon Lagoon, admission is a fair value. If you go primarily for the slides, you'll have just 2 early-morning hours to enjoy them before the wait becomes prohibitive.

Typhoon Lagoon provides water adventure for all ages. Activity pools for young children and families feature geysers, tame slides, bubble jets, and fountains. For the older and more adventurous are the enclosed **Humunga Kowabunga** speed slides; the corkscrew **Storm Slides;** and three whitewater raft rides: **Gangplank Falls, Keelhaul Falls,** and **Mayday Falls. Crush 'n' Gusher,** billed as a water roller coaster, consists of a series of flumes and spillways that course through an abandoned tropical fruit–processing plant. It features tubes that hold one or two people, and you can choose from three routes—Banana Blaster, Coconut Crusher, and Pineapple Plunger—ranging from 410 to 420 feet long. Only Crush 'n' Gusher and the Humunga Kowabunga speed slides (where you can hit 30 mph) have a minimum height requirement of 48 inches.

A Waterloo, Ontario, mom found Typhoon Lagoon more strenuous than she'd anticipated:

I wish I'd been prepared for the fact that we'd have to haul the tubes up the stairs of Crush 'n' Gusher. My daughter was not strong enough to carry hers, so I had to lug them up by myself. I was exhausted by the end of the day, and my arms ached for a couple of days afterward. Had I known that was the case, I would have started lifting weights several months before our trip in preparation!

A New Jersey reader agreed:

Thumbs WAY DOWN to the designer who made several places in the queue for Storm Slides where the stairs go down, then back up, then back down, then up again—leading to all guests walking UP extra needless fights of stairs. BOO!

Those of you who share the sentiments of the readers quoted above will appreciate Typhoon Lagoon's **Miss Adventure Falls,** near Crush 'n' Gusher. Riders hop into a circular, four-person raft at the bottom of the slide, then ride a conveyor belt up to the top in about a minute. (The conveyor belt is, let's be honest, not a bad shiatsu massage for your butt.) Though the rafts hold four, the ride works just as well for singles and couples.

The queuing area at the bottom of the conveyor is inadequate, making for major jam-ups on busy days. Because the attraction is suitable for all ages, expect big crowds and long waits unless you ride just after park opening.

Those looking for a more relaxing experience will also enjoy the meandering, 2,000-foot-long **Castaway Creek,** which floats tubers through hidden grottoes and rainforests. And, of course, sunbathers will always find plenty to doze in. Typhoon Lagoon's **Surf Pool** is the world's largest inland surf facility, with waves up to 6 feet high (enough, so Disney says, to "encompass an ocean liner").

SURF POOL

WHILE BLIZZARD BEACH AND VOLCANO BAY have wave pools, Typhoon Lagoon has a Surf Pool. Most people will encounter larger waves here than they have in the ocean. The surf machine puts out a wave about every 90 seconds (just about how long it takes to get back

Typhoon Lagoon

Attractions

1. Bay Slides
2. Castaway Creek
3. Crush 'n' Gusher
4. Gangplank Falls
5. Humunga Kowabunga
6. Keelhaul Falls
7. Ketchakiddee Creek
8. Mayday Falls
9. Miss Adventure Falls

10. Storm Slides
11. Surf Pool

Restaurants

A. Leaning Palms
B. Lowtide Lou's
C. Snack Shack
D. Typhoon Tilly's

👫 Restrooms

in position if you caught the previous wave). Perfectly formed and ideal for riding, each wave is about 5–6 feet from trough to crest. Before you join the fray, watch two or three waves from shore. Because each wave breaks in almost the same spot, you can get a feel for position and timing. Observing other surfers is also helpful.

The best way to ride the waves is to swim about three-fourths of the way to the wall at the wave-machine end of the pool. When the waves come—trust us, you'll feel and hear them—swim vigorously toward the beach and try to position yourself one-half to three-fourths of a body length below the breaking crest. The waves are so perfectly

TYPHOON LAGOON ATTRACTIONS

BAY SLIDES **Height requirement: 60″ and under only.** Miniature two-slide version of Storm Slides, specifically designed for small children. The kids splash down into a far corner of the Surf Pool.

CASTAWAY CREEK **No height requirement.** Half-mile lazy river in a tropical setting with cool mists, waterfalls, and a tunnel through Mount Mayday. Wonderful!

CRUSH 'N' GUSHER **Height requirement: 48″.** Water roller coaster where you can choose from three slides—Banana Blaster, Coconut Crusher, and Pineapple Plunger—ranging from 410 to 420 feet long. This thriller leaves you wondering what exactly happened, if you make it down in one piece, that is; it's not for the faint of heart. If your kids are new to water-park rides, this is not the place to break them in, even if they're tall enough to ride.

GANGPLANK FALLS **No height requirement.** Whitewater raft flume in a four-person tube.

HUMUNGA KOWABUNGA **Height requirement: 48″.** Speed slides that hit 30 mph. A five-story drop in the dark rattles even the most courageous rider. We recommend doing this one in a one-piece swimsuit.

KEELHAUL FALLS **No height requirement.** Fast whitewater ride in a single-person tube.

KETCHAKIDDEE CREEK **Height requirement: 48″ and under only.** Toddlers and pre-schoolers love this area reserved only for them. Say "splish-splash" and have lots of fun.

MAYDAY FALLS **No height requirement.** Wild single-person tube ride. *Hang on!*

MISS ADVENTURE FALLS **No height requirement.** Gentle family raft ride down a well-themed slide.

STORM SLIDES **No height requirement.** Three body slides plunge down and through Mount Mayday.

SURF POOL **No height requirement.** World's largest inland surf facility, with waves up to 6 feet high. Adult supervision required. Surfing lessons may be offered (see below for details).

engineered that they'll either carry you forward or bypass you. Unlike ocean waves, though, they won't slam you down.

A teenage girl from Urbana, Illinois, notes that the primary hazard in the Surf Pool is colliding with other surfers and swimmers:

The Surf Pool was nice, except I kept landing on really hairy guys when the big waves came.

A Gate City, Virginia, mom was caught off-guard by the size and power of the waves:

I had forgotten how violent the wave pool is at Typhoon Lagoon. Thinking I'd be able to hold on to two young(ish) nephews is a mistake I made only once before getting them back to shallower water.

> **unofficial TIP**
> Personal flotation devices (life jackets) can be rented for free with a refundable deposit.

As noted earlier, complimentary life jackets are available at the parks' entrances.

A reader from Somerset, New Jersey, alerted us to another problem:

Typhoon Lagoon is a great family water park—our unexpected favorite. However, please tell your readers not to sit on the bottom of the wave pool—I got a horrible scratch/raspberry and saw about five others with similar injuries. The waves are stronger than they look.

The best way to avoid collisions while surfing is to paddle out far enough that you'll be at the top of the wave as it breaks. This tactic eliminates the possibility of anyone landing on you from above and ensures maximum forward visibility. A corollary to this: The worst place to swim is where the wave actually breaks. You'll look up to see a 6-foot wall of water carrying eight dozen screaming surfers bearing down on you. This is the time to remember every submarine movie you've ever seen: *Dive! Dive! Dive!*

Either in the early morning before the park opens or in the evening after the park closes (hours vary), you can take **surfing lessons,** with an actual surfboard (lessons were suspended at press time). Practice waves range from 3 to 6 feet tall; most students are first-timers. The cost is $199 per person for 2½ hours, including tax; minimum age is 8, and classes are limited to 12 guests. Equipment is provided, but park admission is not included. For details, and to see if lessons are being offered, call ☎ 407-WDW-PLAY (939-7529).

AFTER HOURS EVENTS As we went to press, Disney was holding After Hours events at Typhoon Lagoon during summer months, from roughly mid-May through early September. Usually staged on Saturday from 8–11 p.m., with ticket holders admitted into the park at 6 p.m., these events include access to all of the park's major rides and slides. Tickets cost $80 for adults and $75 for children.

UNIVERSAL'S VOLCANO BAY

UNIVERSAL'S WATER PARK (universalorlando.com/web/en/us/theme -parks/volcano-bay), Volcano Bay, on Universal Orlando property next to Cabana Bay Beach Resort, features a scenic, man-made mountain and a colorful atmosphere that goes toe-to-toe with those of Typhoon Lagoon and Blizzard Beach. The thrill, scope, and diversity of its 18 attractions make Volcano Bay an excellent alternative to the Disney swimming parks.

There is no guest parking at Volcano Bay itself; visitors will park in the same parking garages as other Universal theme park guests and pay the same rates (see page 604). Special shuttle buses transport guests along dedicated lanes to the front gate of Volcano Bay, which is also accessible on a walking path from the neighboring **Cabana Bay Beach Resort** and **Aventura Hotel.**

unofficial **TIP**
Don't try to park at Cabana Bay or Aventura if you're not staying there—you'll get hit with a $45/day fee.

Buy your tickets at the Volcano Bay bus stop inside the parking structure, at any on-site hotel, at the park entrance, or at universal orlando.com. Buying your ticket and setting up an online account in advance will greatly speed your entry into the park. The park opens at 10 a.m. (9 a.m. in the summer, with 30–60 minutes of early admission daily for all on-site hotel guests) and stays open as late as 9 p.m. during the summer. Disney water parks typically close by 6 or 7 p.m., but Volcano Bay was designed for nighttime operation, with special lighting effects activated after sunset.

Universal Orlando describes Volcano Bay's 28 acres as "a lush tropical oasis that unfolds before you, instantly transporting you to a little-known Pacific Isle." The park's icon, visible to passing cars on

I-4, is a colossal volcano rising above a pristine beach, with majestic waterfalls transforming into blazing lava by night.

Universal also replaced queues with **Virtual Lines** and built conveyor belts for all the rafts. Every visitor is issued a waterproof **TapuTapu** wristband that you use to claim your place in the Virtual Lines, as well as reserve and open lockers and make payments throughout the park when the band is linked to your credit card (with a secure PIN) using the Universal Orlando website or app. The TapuTapu bands also trigger special effects throughout Volcano Bay, such as controlling streams of water in **Tot Tiki Reef** or shooting water cannons at other guests who are enjoying the **Kopiko Wai Winding River.**

Tap your TapuTapu band against a tiki totem outside a ride, and you'll be given an approximate time before you can return; your wait may be shorter than expected if other guests skip their return times, or it could be longer if the attraction temporarily closes due to weather or technical problems. You can hold a reservation for just one ride at a time, and TapuTapu will alert you when it's time to return with a minimal wait. Note that you can't get in another Virtual Line until you use or cancel your first ride.

In theory, this system allows guests to enjoy the wave pool and lazy river instead of standing in hot queues, but peak days can be plagued by multihour waits for most of the slides, with some popular attractions completely filling up for the day by midday. **Universal Express** passes can be purchased online or inside the park on select days; they start at $21 per person for one use per ride. Your best bet is to arrive as early as possible and secure a spot on **Krakatau Aqua Coaster,** followed by **Honu, Ko'okiri Body Plunge,** and **Puihi,** in that order. Also look for slides advertising RIDE NOW during early and late hours; you can hop on without losing your place in a Virtual Line.

VOLCANO BAY AT A GLANCE

VOLCANO BAY IS DIVIDED into four primary areas (lands), each with a unique theme, but because all the areas sport the same lush South Seas scenery, it's impossible to tell where one section ends and another begins without a map.

The park's theme is based on the fictional story of the Waturi, an ancient Polynesian people who set out on outrigger canoes to find a new home. The Waturi visited many islands, drawing elements from each culture, until they caught sight of the legendary fish Kunuku playing in the waves of Volcano Bay and settled there.

In practical terms, the park looks like an upscale resort in the South Pacific, with lush palm trees, tiki carvings, and thatched cabanas; as long as you're at ground level, you'd hardly guess there's a busy interstate only yards away. The Waturi legend also influenced the names of most of the attractions, but that's about as far as the theming goes on the slides—don't expect any indoor scenes or dark ride–style effects.

Guests enter the park at **Wave Village,** which is dominated by the **Waturi Beach** multidirectional wave pool and the **Reef** leisure pool. Paths from there lead clockwise to **Rainforest Village,** housing the park's densest collection of thrill rides, including **TeAwa the Fearless River,** and **River Village,** which features family-friendly attractions like the **Kopiko**

Universal's Volcano Bay

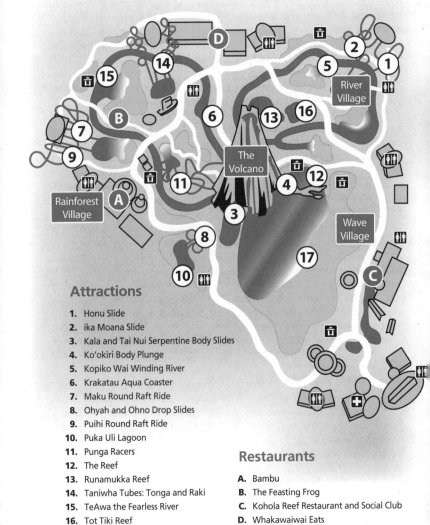

Attractions

1. Honu Slide
2. ika Moana Slide
3. Kala and Tai Nui Serpentine Body Slides
4. Ko'okiri Body Plunge
5. Kopiko Wai Winding River
6. Krakatau Aqua Coaster
7. Maku Round Raft Ride
8. Ohyah and Ohno Drop Slides
9. Puihi Round Raft Ride
10. Puka Uli Lagoon
11. Punga Racers
12. The Reef
13. Runamukka Reef
14. Taniwha Tubes: Tonga and Raki
15. TeAwa the Fearless River
16. Tot Tiki Reef
17. Waturi Beach

Restaurants

A. Bambu
B. The Feasting Frog
C. Kohola Reef Restaurant and Social Club
D. Whakawaiwai Eats

First Aid Station   Restrooms   Cabanas

Wai lazy river. The heart of the park is its namesake volcano: 200-foot
Krakatau, home to the signature **Krakatau Aqua Coaster** as well as three
drop-capsule body slides, plus hidden caverns with cascading waterfalls
and special effects triggered by your TapuTapu band.

VOLCANO BAY ATTRACTIONS

RAINFOREST VILLAGE

KALA AND TA NUI SERPENTINE BODY SLIDES **Height requirement: 48".** After falling through a drop door, two riders go down 124-foot body slides simultaneously. Their paths cross several times as they hurtle down translucent intertwining tubes. The green side is like the VelociCoaster of slides: It starts fast and somehow gets faster as it goes.

MAKU AND PUIHI ROUND RAFT RIDES **Height requirement: 42", 48" if riding alone.** *Maku* and *Puihi* mean "wet" and "wild," and that's no exaggeration. North America's first "saucer ride," the six-person Maku raft plunges riders through bowl-like formations before depositing them in a pool surrounded by erupting geysers. Puihi is the far more frightening slide of the pair: A six-person raft launches down into a dark, winding tunnel before shooting up a banked curve; riders glimpse the highway below and momentarily experience zero gravity before sliding back down.

OHYAH AND OHNO DROP SLIDES **Height requirement: 48".** Two short but intense twisting slides that launch guests 4 and 6 feet above the water at the end; the Ohno slide is the taller of the two.

PUKA ULI LAGOON **No height requirement.** Tranquil leisure pool.

PUNGA RACERS **Height requirement: 42".** Guests go feet-first down four side-by-side body slides, passing through "underwater sea caves" (enclosed plastic tubes).

TANIWHA TUBES **Height requirement: 42", 48" if riding alone.** One tower sports four Easter Island–inspired waterslides with rafts for single or double riders. Along the way, tiki statues make sure that you don't stay dry. The slides are similar but not identical—bear left to the green Tonga slides with more-open sections if you get claustrophobic.

TEAWA THE FEARLESS RIVER **Height requirement: 42", 48" if riding alone.** Guests hang tight in their flotation vests amid roaring whitewater rapids as they surf beneath the slides inside Krakatau. If you're looking for a lazy river, this ain't it!

RIVER VILLAGE

HONU AND IKA MOANA SLIDES **Height requirement: Ika Moana, 42"; Honu, 42," or 48" if riding alone.** Honu and Ika Moana are two separate slides attached to the same tower, where guests board multiperson, animal-themed rafts (a sea turtle and a whale, respectively) before speeding down into a pool. Honu is a blue raft slide that sends you vertically up two giant sloped walls before sliding back down—it's the scariest group ride in the park. Ika Moana is a much gentler journey in and out of twisting green tunnels.

KO'OKIRI BODY PLUNGE **Height requirement: 48".** This 125-foot slide features a drop door with a 70-degree-angle descent straight through the heart of the mountain. Drumbeats building up to the drop get your heart pounding, but the plunge itself is over before you have time to scream.

KOPIKO WAI WINDING RIVER **No height requirement.** A gentle lazy river that passes through the park's landscape and into the volcano's hidden caves.

KRAKATAU AQUA COASTER **Height requirement: 42", 48" if riding alone.** Guests board a specially designed canoe that seats up to four. The ride uses linear induction motor technology, which launches the canoe uphill as well as downhill as you twist and turn around the volcano's blown-out interior. It's similar to Crush 'n' Gusher at Typhoon Lagoon, but far longer and more thrilling. Krakatau is the park's most popular ride, so get your TapuTapu reservation as early as possible.

RUNAMUKKA REEF **For children under 54" tall.** A three-story water playground for older children inspired by the coral reef, featuring twisting slides, sprinklers, and more.

TOT TIKI REEF **For children under 48" tall.** A toddler play area with spraying Maori fountains, slides, and a kid-size volcano.

WAVE VILLAGE

THE REEF **No height requirement.** Leisure pool with calm waters and its own waterfall. Relax and watch braver souls shoot down the Ko'okiri Body Plunge.

WATURI BEACH **Children under 48" must wear a lift vest.** Features a multidirectional wave pool, situated at the foot of Krakatau Lagoon and fed by waterfalls cascading off the volcano's peak.

Each area of the park offers amenities such as concierge locations and lockers ($10–$20 for all-day access). The themed restaurants and bars throughout Volcano Bay are particularly noteworthy, far exceeding what we've come to expect from water-park grub, with light, refreshing meals perfect for a day at the beach. Caribbean and island-inspired foods are on the menu, and even the less adventurous fare like pizza and hot dogs has been upgraded with flatbread crusts and pretzel buns.

At **Bambu,** in Rainforest Village, we love the quinoa-edamame burger, topped with roasted shiitake mushrooms, lettuce, tomato, and sriracha mayo, with a side of fries. Also at Rainforest Village is **The Feasting Frog;** try the tacos or poke tuna, both served with plantain chips. At River Village, **Whakawaiwai Eats** is home to the Hawaiian Pizza, with caramelized pineapple, diced ham, and pickled jalapeños. In Wave Village, at **Kohola Reef Restaurant and Social Club,** the slow-smoked glazed ribs, served with mango slaw and fries, don't disappoint. For dessert, try the chocolate lava cake. **Dancing Dragons Boat Bar** (Rainforest Village) and **Kunuku Boat Bar** (Wave Village) serve a variety of signature cocktails, but these are far too sugary for our taste. Stick with the locally brewed Volcano Blossom beer instead.

You can upgrade your visit with reserved padded loungers ($32–$159 per pair), 6-person cabanas ($170–$585), or 16-person Family Suite cabanas ($320–$640); all prices depend on the date. While they're not a necessity, we recommend the private loungers for their included shade canopy, locking storage box, and attendant to deliver food and drinks. The cabanas get all that, plus towel service, free fruit and bottled water, and a private kiosk for making TapuTapu reservations.

Volcano Bay offers a good variety of activities. If you can adjust your attraction-riding expectations to fit TapuTapu's quirks and relax into the park's immersive atmosphere, Volcano Bay is an enjoyable way to spend a day outside the theme parks.

DISNEY SPRINGS, SHOPPING, *and* NIGHTLIFE

A DISNEY WORLD VACATION isn't just theme parks and attractions: If you want to shop, see live entertainment, or just let loose in the evening, this chapter is for you.

Walt Disney World has a huge outdoor mall complex with restaurants, shopping, and theaters, so guests of its hotels and theme parks never need to spend money outside its borders. This chapter covers that complex, called **Disney Springs.** In addition, it explores the best **shopping** in the theme parks and nearby in Orlando. Finally, it lists the great **nightlife** options at the Disney resorts and elsewhere in the World.

DISNEY SPRINGS

ARRIVING AT DISNEY SPRINGS

BY CAR Guests driving to Disney Springs will take Buena Vista Drive from Disney property, and Hotel Plaza Boulevard from the Disney Springs resorts and FL 535. I-4 westbound offers direct access to the complex via Exit 67. There are three parking garages and four surface lots. The **Lime** garage serves The Landing, Town Center, and Marketplace areas of Disney Springs. The **Orange** garage is closest to the West Side, the AMC 16 movie theater, and Planet Hollywood. The third garage,

continued on page 664

Disney Springs

Disney's Saratoga Springs Resort & Spa

Strawberry Parking Lot

Lake Buena Vista

water taxi

water taxi

West Side Dock

water taxi

The Landing Dock

29

10

E

D

12

West Side

13

8

17

11

16

A

34

24

18

35

31

37

3

15

B

14

4 6 1 7 5

25

Parking

H

2

9

C

58

55

Orange Garage

41 50 59

WEST SIDE Shopping

1. Disney's Candy Cauldron
2. DisneyStyle
3. M&Ms Store
4. Pelé Soccer
5. Star Wars Galactic Outpost
6. Sunglass Icon
7. Super Hero Headquarters

WEST SIDE Dining

8. City Works Eatery & Pour House
9. Everglazed Donuts & Cold Brew
10. Food Trucks at Exposition Park
11. House of Blues Restaurant & Bar
12. The Smokehouse
13. Jaleo/Pepe by José Andrés
14. Salt & Straw
15. Splitsville
16. Starbucks
17. Summer House on the Lake (opening 2023)

THE LANDING Shopping

18. The Art of Shaving
19. Chapel Hats
20. Group 1: Erwin Pearl, Oakley, Sanuk, Savannah Bee Company
21. Havaianas

THE LANDING Dining

22. The Boathouse
23. Chef Art Smith's Homecomin'
24. The Edison
25. Enzo's Hideaway
26. Erin McKenna's Bakery NYC
27. The Ganachery
28. Gideon's Bakehouse
29. Jock Lindsey's Hangar Bar
30. Joffrey's Coffee & Tea
31. Maria & Enzo's
32. Morimoto Asia/ Morimoto Street Food
33. Paddlefish
34. Paradiso 37
35. Pizza Ponte
36. Raglan Road/ Cookes of Dublin
37. STK Orlando
38. Terralina Crafted Italian
39. Vivoli il Gelato
40. Wine Bar George

TOWN CENTER Shopping

41. Coca-Cola Store
42. Group 1: American Threads, Johnston & Murphy, Tommy Bahama, Fit2Run
43. Group 2: Columbia, Everything but Water, Free People, Johnny Was, Kate Spade New York, Lilly Pulitzer, Sperry, Sugarboo, Vera Bradley
44. Group 3: Coach, MAC, Jo Malone
45. Group 4: Lacoste, Luxury of Time
46. Group 5: Lovepop, Ron Jon Surf Shop, Sephora, Shore, Stance, Superdry
47. Group 6: Levi's, Orlando Harley-Davidson, TUMI, Volcom
48. Group 7: Alex and Ani, Anthropologie, Ever After Jewelry Co., Fabletics, Francesca's, Kendra Scott, lululemon, Melissa Clube, L'Occitane en Provence, Rustic Cuff, Under Armour, UNOde50

49. Group 8: Edward Beiner, Na Hoku, Pandora
50. Sundries
51. Uniqlo
52. Zara

TOWN CENTER Dining
53. Amorette's Patisserie
54. Blaze Fast-Fire'd Pizza
55. Chicken Guy
56. D-Luxe Burger
57. Frontera Cocina
58. Planet Hollywood
59. The Polite Pig
60. Sprinkles
61. Wolfgang Puck Bar & Grill

MARKETPLACE Shopping
62. Bibbidi Bobbidi Boutique
63. Build-a-Dino/Dino Store

64. Disney's Days of Christmas
65. Disney's Pin Traders
66. Group 1: Arribas Brothers, Basin, Ghirardelli Soda Fountain & Chocolate Shop, Marketplace Co-Op, Tren-D
67. Group 2: Goofy's Candy Co., Star Wars Trading Post, Swings N' Things,
68. Group 3: The Art of Disney, Disney's Wonderful World of Memories
69. The Lego Store
70. Once Upon a Toy
71. PhotoPass Studio
72. The Spice & Tea Exchange
73. World of Disney

MARKETPLACE Dining
74. The Daily Poutine
75. Earl of Sandwich

76. Rainforest Cafe
77. Starbucks
78. T-REX

Entertainment and Attractions
A. Aerophile
B. AMC Disney Springs 24/ MacGuffins
C. AMC Disney Springs 24 Dine-In Theatres
D. Cirque du Soleil
E. House of Blues
F. Marketplace Carousel
G. Marketplace Train Express
H. Splitsville Luxury Lanes
I. Vintage Amphicar & Italian Water Taxi Tours

continued from page 661

Grapefruit, sits opposite the Lime garage on the other side of Buena Vista Drive. It is connected to Disney Springs via a raised walkway. There is no charge to park in the garages.

An LED display on each level of the garages indicates how many open spaces there are on each level. As a rule, the lower levels fill up first, with more open spaces available on each successive level up. The Orange garage can be reached directly from westbound I-4 via Exit 67. All three garage entrances are accessed from Buena Vista Drive.

Most guests will enter the garages on Level 3. You'll want to navigate down to Level 2, where all guests are funneled through security. Otherwise, park as close to the center of the level you're on and walk down to the security checkpoint. There's also "preferred" parking available in the Lemon and Mango parking lots for $20. We're not sure why you'd pay this much to park, but, hey, it's there if you can't find a spot and you're desperate. All other parking is free.

BY DISNEY TRANSPORTATION All Disney resorts and theme parks offer **bus transportation** to Disney Springs; some bus routes also include a pickup or drop-off at **Typhoon Lagoon.** The Disney bus area is centrally located between the Orange and Lime garages. **Saratoga Springs, Old Key West,** and the **Port Orleans Resorts** offer boat transportation to the Disney Springs dock at The Landing.

BY TAXI/RIDE-HAILING APP Drop-off and pickup are at the **Cirque du Soleil** theater on the far west side of Disney Springs and at the far east side of the Marketplace.

ON FOOT Saratoga Springs Resort has walking paths to the West Side and Marketplace. Guests staying at hotels in the **Disney Springs Resort Area** (see page 201) can walk to Disney Springs on walkways and pedestrian bridges to avoid traffic.

GETTING ORIENTED

DISNEY SPRINGS IS DIVIDED INTO FOUR AREAS, each with its own theme. **Marketplace,** on the east side of Disney Springs, is the most Disney and the most kid-friendly, with the **World of Disney** store and many activities for children. It has a small carousel and mini-train rides for a nominal fee. A free splash area is great for cooling down, and free concerts take place across from World of Disney in the amphitheater.

The Landing is the waterfront section of Disney Springs. Open, winding paths offer sweeping views of the water and Saratoga Springs as you walk between the Marketplace and West Side.

The third area is the Old Florida–style **Town Center,** which has most of the well-known retail outposts of Disney Springs (**Zara** and **Uniqlo** are the largest). If you've ever found yourself at Pirates of the Caribbean and thought, "What this place needs is a Wetzel's Pretzels," you'll love shopping here. Town Center sits between The Landing and the parking lot.

On the **West Side,** a Disney-themed **Cirque du Soleil** production named *Drawn to Life* opened in 2021. **Jaleo by José Andrés** (page 333), an **AMC** multiplex theater, the **Splitsville** bowling lanes, and **Starbucks** are the biggest draws.

DISNEY SPRINGS SHOPPING AT A GLANCE

Marketplace

BIBBIDI BOBBIDI BOUTIQUE (*remains closed; the Magic Kingdom location is open*) Located at the far eastern end of the Disney Springs Marketplace next to Once Upon a Toy, BBB is a salon for kids ages 3–12 that will give princess hopefuls a royal makeover that includes so much hair spray that we suspect the place has an ozone hole hovering over it. Packages range from $107 to above $500 plus tip. While we may balk a bit that there's no PhD Princess or Med School Maiden package, we can't deny how popular the experience is with both the kids getting the makeovers and their parents. Photo packages, a Knight Package (for the brothers who have to sit around waiting for the princesses), and other add-ons are available for an extra charge.

Reservations can be made up to 60 days in advance (70 days for Disney resort guests); call ☎ 407-939-7895 for information or reservations. Allow 30 minutes–1 hour for the whole makeover.

DISNEY'S DAYS OF CHRISTMAS This shop is just plain fun, with hundreds of holiday decorations, from ornaments to stockings to stuffed animals wearing their Christmas best. We especially like the station for ornament personalization. There's also a section dedicated to *The Nightmare Before Christmas*.

GOOFY'S CANDY CO. An interactive show kitchen with lots of sweets. Enjoy create-your-own pretzel rods, marshmallows, and candy apples.

THE LEGO STORE This is an ideal rest stop for parents, and you don't even have to go inside the store. A hands-on outdoor play area has bins of Legos that the kids can go crazy with while Mom and Dad take a break. Inside is all the latest Lego paraphernalia. Photo ops with life-size Disney characters surround the shop.

MARKETPLACE CO-OP The Co-op is loved among Disney fans for its six pop-up-style retail experiences within one shop. Areas include **Bowes Signature Candles** (candles, diffusers, and oils), **Disney Centerpiece** (home and kitchen items), **D-Tech on Demand** (custom electronics accessories), **Superhero Showcase** (superhero goods), and **Disney Tails** (Disney-themed pet accessories).

ONCE UPON A TOY This is the place to find toy sets and a huge selection of plush; it's also the best place for books, video games, and other media. All the Disney franchises, from the Pixar titles to Marvel and *Star Wars,* are well represented here. We also appreciate that Once Upon a Toy is far less crowded than World of Disney.

THE SPICE AND TEA EXCHANGE Carries flavored salts and sugars, teas, and spice mixes. You can also purchase wines and cookbooks.

TREN-D A fun, hip, urban-inspired boutique for women, with fashion apparel and accessories, plus exclusive items from cutting-edge designers and Disney merchandise you won't find anywhere else.

*un*official **TIP**
At **Ghirardelli Soda Fountain & Chocolate Shop,** you can smell the chocolate when you walk in. Chocolate souvenirs abound, but treat yourself to a "world famous" sundae topped with hot fudge made daily at the shop. The line for ice cream often winds out the door—it's that good.

WORLD OF DISNEY With the largest selection of Disney merchandise on-site or anywhere else, World of Disney can get oppressively crowded at night. It has a little bit of everything. On especially busy days, you may be required to make reservations to enter. If so, signage in front of the store will provide instructions on how to do so.

Town Center

AMORETTE'S PATISSERIE Beautiful cakes and pastries; Disney character–themed cakes, large and small, that you won't see anywhere else; and Champagne by the glass. Amorette's will deliver a cake to your Disney Springs restaurant for special occasions with 72 hours notice. *Note:* They don't deliver outside of Disney Springs.

COCA-COLA STORE Not a must-visit unless you're just really obsessed with Coke, but the roof deck has a bar and views of Disney Springs.

JO MALONE Perfumes, candles, and other scented lifestyle items.

KATE SPADE NEW YORK What sets this location apart from the one at your local mall is that it often has Disney-themed bags and accessories you can otherwise find only online.

LILLY PULITZER Bright, fun prints for the country club and sorority girl sets. Sadly, there are no exclusive Disney Lilly prints here—a missed opportunity, if you ask us.

PANDORA The jewelry retailer has an agreement with Walt Disney World that includes another shop on Main Street, U.S.A., and sponsorship of the evening fireworks at Magic Kingdom. Many Disney-exclusive charms sell out quickly.

SUPERDRY Fun casual wear for teens and young adults. We can't put our finger on why we like Superdry, but we do.

TOMMY BAHAMA One of the few shops at Disney Springs with a decent selection of casual menswear. Also has a nice selection of swimwear for both men and women.

UNIQLO Fast fashion along with a nice selection of exclusive Disney apparel. Uniqlo is handy if you need to buy basics such as socks, underwear, and T-shirts.

VERA BRADLEY The ubiquitous quilted bags with a fanatical following. You'll find both Disney-exclusive and mainline prints here.

The Landing

THE ART OF SHAVING Sells shaving gear and offers men's barber and shaving services, including a haircut.

THE GANACHERY Exquisite handmade chocolates in gourmet flavor combinations. This is a Disney-run shop. The candy may be more pricey than you're expecting, but the quality is solid. Makes a nice late-night treat in your hotel room.

GIDEON'S BAKEHOUSE This bakery and coffee shop serves cookies that weigh almost half a pound, admirably attempting to redefine the phrase *single serving*. Expect a line of at least an hour most of the day. Tell an employee you want to join the virtual queue instead, and they'll text you when you're allowed to enter.

JOFFREY'S COFFEE & TEA COMPANY You can purchase leaves to take home or enjoy a hot or cold tea at the counter. Very pleasant and less hectic than Starbucks for your beverage needs.

You'll also find a variety of kiosks selling everything from wind chimes to yo-yos as you walk through The Landing.

Disney Springs West Side

DISNEY'S CANDY CAULDRON Watch as gooey treats are made in the open kitchen. Dipped candy apples (befitting the Snow White–Evil Queen theme) are the specialty of the house. There is also a decent selection of bulk candies.

EVERGLAZED DONUTS & COLD BREW In addition to cold-brew coffee, Everglazed also serves camera-ready doughnuts topped with fruit cereal, s'mores, and peanut butter cups.

M&M'S A large store selling everyone's favorite melt-in-your-mouth chocolates in every flavor imaginable, along with clothing, mugs, and other merchandise.

SALT & STRAW A premium-ice-cream parlor with excellent traditional and unusual flavors. Highly recommended.

STAR WARS GALACTIC OUTPOST A large selection of *Star Wars* souvenirs, from T-shirts to Stormtrooper helmets. See page 598 for more on *Star Wars* swag.

BARS AND NIGHTLIFE AT DISNEY SPRINGS

DISNEY SPRINGS IS A POPULAR DESTINATION after dark for folks who aren't ready to be in for the night but don't want to burn park admission for just a few hours in the evening. You'll find street entertainment, including singers, musicians, and performance artists spread throughout Disney Springs (it sometimes feels like they're spaced such that as soon as one is out of earshot, you can hear the next one). There's even more entertainment at many of the restaurants, including bands and singers at **Splitsville Dining Room** (page 349) and **House of Blues** (pages 332 and 674) and music and Irish dancers at **Raglan Road Irish Pub & Restaurant** (page 334).

Some of our favorite places to grab a drink are at Disney Springs. The aforementioned Raglan Road has multiple bars and a fantastic menu of appetizers. **Wine Bar George** (page 359) and **Jaleo by José Andrés** (page 333) have excellent drinks and tasty small-plate menus. **Morimoto Asia** (page 339) and **The Boathouse** (page 318) both have bars worth a visit. Reader ratings for **Enzo's Hideaway, The Edison,** and **STK Orlando** are so low that we can't recommend them.

TAKE IT ON THE RUN, BABY

FOR AN EVENING OF DRINKING and strolling, Disney Springs has you covered. Starting with the **AmphiBar** outside the entrance to **The Boathouse,** the restaurants quickly figured out that there was a market for cocktails to go. Find Guinness outside **Raglan Road** and margaritas at **Frontera Cocina** and **Dockside Margaritas.**

MAGIC KINGDOM SHOPPING SAMPLER	
I WANT...	**FIND IT AT...**
• One-stop shopping	• **The Emporium,** Main Street
• Candy, pastries, fudge	• **Main Street Confectionery,** Main Street • **Big Top Souvenirs,** Fantasyland
• Disney art and collectibles	• **Main Street Cinema,** Main Street
• Holiday decor	• **Olde Christmas Shoppe,** Liberty Square
• Memory cards and batteries	• **Box Office Gifts,** Main Street
• Personalized mouse ears	• **Box Office Gifts,** Main Street • **Fantasy Faire,** Fantasyland
• Princess wear	• **The Emporium,** Main Street
• Tech gifts	• **Space Mountain Gift Shop,** Tomorrowland
• Women's jewelry, handbags, accessories	• **Main Street Jewelers** (has a **Pandora** shop)

SHOPPING *in* WALT DISNEY WORLD *and* ORLANDO

WE ALMOST TITLED THIS SECTION "Exit Through the Gift Shop," but that would've been a cliché (and Banksy beat us to it). Retail is a huge revenue source for Disney. If you enjoy shopping, we recommend setting aside some time and money to do so. And even if you don't enjoy it, you may be traveling with someone who does.

SHOPPING AT DISNEY WORLD

EACH THEME PARK has at least one major retail space, several minor ones, and space attached to most attractions. While we occasionally bemoan the homogenization of the merchandise selection, this does mean that if something catches your eye, you'll most likely see it again. Ditto for sale prices. Pricing is consistent throughout the resorts, and an item on sale in one location will be the same price at all locations.

See the following pages for a quick-reference guide to which theme park shops carry what you're looking for.

EPCOT Shopping

Retail is a huge part of the **World Showcase** experience in EPCOT, much more so than in the other theme parks. This is one of the few times on your vacation that you won't be able to say "I'll see it again later" if something catches your eye. With a selection that ranges from affordable trinkets to Mikimoto pearls, the shops in World Showcase have something for everyone. Walking clockwise, you'll find the following:

★ **MEXICO** Probably the most immersive shopping experience in all of World Showcase, **Plaza de los Amigos** is a re-creation of a Mexican shopping village at dusk. You'll find all manner of sombreros, Day of the Dead items, Oaxacan carved wooden animals, and blankets. Along the side of the shopping area is **La Princesa de Cristal,** with crystal jewelry and trinkets, and another shop with leather items, women's dresses and blouses, and other accessories. If you need a break from

EPCOT SHOPPING SAMPLER	
I WANT . . .	**FIND IT AT . . .**
• One-stop shopping	• **Creations Shop,** World Celebration
• Disney art and collectibles	• **The Art of Disney,** United States Pavilion
• Disney comics and books	• **ImageWorks,** Imagination! Pavilion
• Eco-friendly gifts	• **Outpost,** World Showcase
• Kitchen supplies and decor	• **Port of Entry,** World Showcase
• Memory cards and batteries	• **Camera Center,** World Celebration
• Personalized mouse ears	• **Creations Shop,** World Celebration
• Princess wear	• **The Wandering Reindeer,** Norway Pavilion
• Tech gifts	• **Creations Shop and Camera Center,** World Celebration

shopping, the **San Angel Inn Restaurante** (page 346) and *Unofficial* favorite watering hole **La Cava del Tequila** (page 289) are located just off the shopping area.

★ **NORWAY The Fjording** is a series of small shopping galleries with popular imports such as trolls (from $15) and wooden Christmas ornaments (from $5). Other hard-to-find imports include Scandinavian foods and candies, Laila perfume and body lotion, and Helly Hansen and Dale of Norway clothing, including thick woolen sweaters. You'll also find all things *Frozen* here.

★ **CHINA** This pavilion features one of our favorite shops, piled with such imports as real silk kimonos, cloisonné, and thick silk rugs. **House of Good Fortune** is more like a rambling department store than a shop. You'll find everything here, from silk fans to $4,000 jade sculptures to antique furniture. The silk dresses and robes are competitively priced in the $100 range. Darling handbags are $10 and up, and silk ties are around $20. We always admire the handwoven pure-silk carpets, starting around $300 for a 2-foot rug and topping out around $2,500 for a 4-by-8-foot rug. The prices are comparable to what you'd pay in a retail shop—if you could find one that imports carpets like these.

Village Traders, a shop between China and Germany, sells beautiful, handmade African woodcarvings. Another specialty here is bead jewelry, crafted in Uganda from repurposed Disney paper products such as old handout guides.

★ **GERMANY** Shops interconnect on both sides of the cobblestoned central plaza and purvey an impressive collection of imports. Tiny **Das Kaufhaus** stocks a nice selection of Adidas sportswear. Next door is **Volkskunst,** where the walls are covered with Schneider cuckoo clocks and the shelves are stocked with limited-edition steins and glassware. Next is **Der Teddybär,** featuring Engel-Puppen dolls and Steiff plush toys, among other delights for children. Across the plaza, **Kunstarbeit in Kristall** carries a fabulous collection of Swarovski crystal, including pins, glassware, and Arribas Brothers collectibles (check out the limited-edition $37,500 replica of Cinderella Castle, blinged out with

DISNEY'S ANIMAL KINGDOM SHOPPING SAMPLER	
I WANT . . .	**FIND IT AT . . .**
• One-stop shopping	• **Discovery Trading Company,** Discovery Island
• African souvenirs	• **Mombasa Marketplace,** Harambe, Africa
• Dinosaur kitsch and toys	• **Chester and Hester's Dinosaur Treasures,** DinoLand U.S.A.
• Memory cards and batteries	• **Island Mercantile,** Discovery Island
• Personalized mouse ears	• **Island Mercantile,** Discovery Island
• African wines, cookbooks, and Flame Tree barbecue sauce	• **Zuri's Sweets Shop,** Africa
• My own shoulder-top banshee or glowing Pandora merch	• **Windtraders,** Pandora—The World of Avatar

more than 20,000 Swarovski crystals). Next is the **Weinkeller,** with nearly 300 varieties of German wine. Step through the door to **Die Weihnachts Ecke,** where Christmas ornaments and handmade nutcrackers are on display year-round. Anyone with a sweet tooth will go crazy just smelling the most delicious store in Germany's lineup, **Karamell-Küche.** Treats are made in-house with Werther's Original caramel, from caramel apples to cookies and candies made or drizzled with caramel. You'll also find an impressive selection of Werther's Original candies.

★ **ITALY Il Bel Cristallo** showcases sportswear, Bulgari and Emilio Pucci fragrances, Murano figurines, elaborate Venetian masks, and a small selection of Christmas decorations in the back room.

★ **JAPAN** An outpost of the country's 300-year-old **Mitsukoshi Department Store** stretches along one entire side of the Japan Pavilion. Kid-friendly merchandise (Hello Kitty, Naruto, and Yu-Gi-Oh! are often seen) fills the front, with kimonos, slippers, handbags, and lots more at the back. Mitsukoshi's expanded culinary display includes a sake-tasting bar, along with chopsticks, pretty rice bowls, a large variety of teas and teapots, and imported snacks. The selection of products related to anime is great as well. Tourists line up for an oyster that is

TIPS FOR AVOIDING BUYER'S REMORSE
1. Know ahead of time how much things cost. Many theme park items are available at disneystore.com.
2. Be specific. Disney collecting can spiral out of control if you don't narrow your focus. Pick a character or movie you love, and stick to that.
3. Don't buy dated merchandise. That Walt Disney World 2024 T-shirt you buy to commemorate your vacation is going to look awfully silly on January 1, 2024. There's a reason this stuff is the No. 1 seller at Disney outlets.
4. The local big-box stores will have a selection of low-priced Disney and Universal souvenirs. Look for them at the front of the stores.
5. Don't fall for limited editions. If they make 2,000 of something, is it really limited?
6. Wait. Don't make your purchases until you've been to more than one shop.
7. Consider purchasing comestibles as souvenirs. There's no buyer's remorse if you consume the evidence.
8. Some of the best things in life are free. Consider our favorite freebies at Walt Disney World (see 672) and skip the cash register.

DISNEY'S HOLLYWOOD STUDIOS SHOPPING SAMPLER	
I WANT . . .	**FIND IT AT . . .**
• One-stop shopping	• **Mickey's of Hollywood,** Hollywood Boulevard
• Holiday decor	• **It's a Wonderful Shop,** Streets of America
• Magic Bands and other Disney gifts	• **The Darkroom,** Hollywood Boulevard
• Personalized mouse ears	• **Legends of Hollywood,** Sunset Boulevard
• Princess wear	• **Legends of Hollywood,** Sunset Boulevard
• Clothes and accessories tied to Disney's current marketing promotion	• **Keystone Clothiers,** Hollywood Boulevard
• Women's jewelry, handbags, and accessories	• **Keystone Clothiers,** Hollywood Boulevard
• *Star Wars* souvenirs	• **Black Spire Outfitters,** Galaxy's Edge

guaranteed to have a pearl in its shell (pearls are polished for you by the salesperson).

★ **MOROCCO** Several shops wend through this pavilion, although many remain closed: **Tangier Traders** sells traditional Moroccan clothing, shoes, and fezzes; **The Brass Bazaar** features brass, of course, and ceramic and wooden kitchenware (not dishwasher safe); and **Casablanca Carpets** offers a wide variety of Moroccan rugs, as well as decorative pieces such as abstract-shaped lamps, sequined pillows, and incense holders.

★ **FRANCE** The courtyard at the France Pavilion has some *merveilleux* shopping opportunities. A dedicated Guerlain shop, **La Signature,** offers cosmetics and fragrances from the French house. **Plume et Palette** has fragrances, cosmetics, and women's accessories from Christian Dior, Givenchy, Kenzo, Le Tanneur, and Thierry Mugler, to name a few.

Find wines and kitchen goods, including a Champagne-tasting counter, at **Les Vins de Chefs de France** and **L'Esprit de la Provence,** which are connecting shops. And finally, at the back of the pavilion, **Souvenirs de France** sells a smattering of everything French, from berets and Eiffel Tower models to T-shirts and language books.

★ **UNITED KINGDOM** A handful of interesting imports from across the pond are scattered throughout half a dozen small shops. **The Toy Soldier** stocks costumes, books, and plush toys featuring English characters from favorite films and television shows, such as *Dr. Who* and *Downton Abbey,* as well as British rock and roll–themed items, including Beatles merchandise. You'll find plenty of Alice in Wonderland, Peter Pan, and Winnie the Pooh merchandise too. Stop at **The Crown & Crest** to look up your family name in the coat-of-arms book, and the shop will create your family's insignia in a beautiful frame of your choice. At the adjacent **Sportsman's Shoppe,** you'll find plenty of football (soccer) apparel, balls, and books.

Across the street, you'll find **The Queen's Table,** a gift shop with UK-themed clothing, glassware, and more. **Lords and Ladies,** a quaint store, offers lotions, soaps, scarves, jewelry, and perfume from the United Kingdom. **The Tea Caddy** stocks Twinings tea, biscuits (cookies to us Yanks), and candy.

★ **CANADA** There's not much shopping here, but **Northwest Mercantile** has a wide selection of merchandise, including NHL jerseys, T-shirts, sweatshirts, aprons, and pajamas. Bottles of ice wine and maple syrup make nice souvenirs for foodies.

Our Favorite Free Souvenirs from Walt Disney World

CELEBRATION BUTTONS Just married? Just graduated? Just happy to be nominated? There's a button for that.

KIDCOT FUN STOPS Sometimes the best souvenir is the one you get for free (or at least it's a good line to tell your kids).

BIRTHDAY TREATS Be sure to mention any special occasions you're celebrating when you check in for your meal at a full-service restaurant. You may get a surprise dessert.

STICKERS Cast members give out so many of these, we're afraid there might be an adhesive shortage.

TRANSPORTATION TRADING CARDS Did you know that monorail and bus drivers have trading cards to give out?

TOILETRIES We may or may not have hoards of Disney resort shampoos, bath gels, and soaps in our own homes.

If you realize on your flight home that you forgot to buy mouse ears for your niece, don't worry. **ShopDisney** online (shopdisney.com) has a dedicated section of parks merchandise.

SHOPPING OUTSIDE DISNEY WORLD

Upscale Shopping

The Mall at Millenia is anchored by **Bloomingdale's, Macy's,** and **Neiman Marcus.** You'll find designer boutiques, such as **Burberry, Chanel, Gucci, Hermès, Louis Vuitton,** and **Salvatore Ferragamo.** Millenia also has the closest **Apple Store** to Universal or Walt Disney World. The mall isn't entirely high-end, however, with fast-fashion staples such as **H&M** and **Forever 21,** as well as the usual suspects, including **Gap, Victoria's Secret,** and **J.Crew.** Visit mallatmillenia.com for a full directory.

Midscale Shopping

The Florida Mall is home to **Dillard's, JCPenney, Macy's,** and **Sears.** Apart from the anchors and high-end designer shops, it has many of the same stores as The Mall at Millenia. Visit simon.com/mall/the -florida-mall.

Outlet Shopping

If you think the crowds at the parks are overwhelming, then you'll want to avoid the two **Orlando Premium Outlets** (premiumoutlets .com/outlet/orlando-vineland) at International Drive and Vineland Avenue. Tourists arrive here by the busload, and the experience will leave you questioning everything from consumer culture to your own judgment in dropping by. For the theme park visitor, the only redeeming aspect of these two malls is the **Disney Character Warehouse** (there are locations at both outlets).

Disney Shopping Outside of Walt Disney World

The Disney outlet at Vineland is about twice the size of the location on I-Drive. To get an idea of what you'll find there, check out Derek Burgan's past **"The Magic, The Memories, and Merch!"** entries on the **TouringPlans.com** blog (blog.touringplans.com/author/derek), in which he gives the scoop on what Disney made too much of.

Fans seeking one-of-a-kind souvenirs, including costumes, props, and local art, should check out **TD Collectibles** (☎ 407-347-0670; tdcollectibles.net).

Orlando International Airport has three Disney shops, one at each terminal, for purchases you need to make on the way home. The shops are fairly large and well themed for what they are; plus, they're run by Disney. They're good spots to kill time while you wait for your flight.

NIGHTLIFE *at* WALT DISNEY WORLD RESORTS

unofficial TIP
Nightlife doesn't just mean stuff for the olds to do. There are plenty of kid-friendly activities after dark for the young ones. Check your resort's recreation schedule for campfires, movies on the beach or at the pool, and more.

DISNEY'S BOARDWALK OFFERS two adult-oriented venues, Jellyrolls and Atlantic Dance Hall. **Jellyrolls** is a dueling-piano bar that's open 7 p.m.–2 a.m. nightly (cover charge applies). It's one of the few 21-and-up places you'll find at Walt Disney World. The entertainment is outstanding here. Across from Jellyrolls is **Atlantic Dance Hall**. It's often booked for private events, but on weekends it's generally open in the evenings (and has free admission). The house DJ spins everything from '70s disco to top 40 and EDM. Like Jellyrolls, Atlantic Dance Hall is 21-and-up.

At Coronado Springs, you'll find **Rix Sports Bar & Grill**. It usually isn't busy unless there's a convention at the resort. Other Walt Disney World resort bars with live entertainment are **Scat Cat's Club** at Port Orleans French Quarter and **River Roost** at Port Orleans Riverside.

Trader Sam's Grog Grotto (inspired by the bar at the Disneyland Hotel in California) at the Polynesian Village is a delight. If you've ever found yourself at the *Enchanted Tiki Room* and thought to yourself, "You know, booze would really make this better," this is your place. See page 355 for a detailed review.

Our favorite nightspot at Walt Disney World, **Top of the World** at Bay Lake Tower, is for Disney Vacation Club members and their guests. If you're a member, or you can talk one into letting you in, try to stay after the Magic Kingdom fireworks—the view and setting are outstanding.

Free Concerts at Walt Disney World

EPCOT INTERNATIONAL FESTIVAL OF THE ARTS This festival takes place in January and February and includes concerts at the America Gardens Theatre. The Disney on Broadway series is often featured.

GARDEN ROCKS Held during the International Flower & Garden Festival in the spring, this series features acts from the 1960s onward.

Many bands are more or less in their original lineup, while others have one member from a more famous group.

EAT TO THE BEAT For this concert series, classic and once-in-the-news acts accompany your trip around the World Showcase during the fall International Food & Wine Festival. Featured artists tend to be from the 1980s and later.

House of Blues

Type of show Live concerts with an emphasis on rock and blues. **Tickets and information** ☎ 407-934-BLUE (2583); houseofblues.com/orlando. You can also purchase tickets in person at the Box Office Tuesday–Thursday, noon–7 p.m., and after noon on show days. **Nights of lowest attendance** Monday and Tuesday. **Usual showtimes** Between 7 and 9:30 p.m., depending on who's performing.

DESCRIPTION AND COMMENTS Developed by Blues Brother Dan Aykroyd, House of Blues consists of a restaurant and blues bar, as well as a concert hall. The restaurant is one of the few late-night dining options in Walt Disney World. Live music cranks up every night at 10:30 p.m. in the restaurant and blues bar, but even before then, the joint is way beyond 110 decibels. The music hall next door features concerts by an eclectic array of musicians and groups. Genres have included gospel, blues, funk, ska, dance, salsa, rap, zydeco, hard rock, groove rock, and reggae.

TOURING TIPS Ticket prices vary from night to night according to the fame and drawing power of the featured band. They ranged from $19 to $95 in early 2023, with the higher-cost tickets for better-known performers.

The music hall is set up like a nightclub, with tables and barstools for only about 150 people and standing room for a whopping 1,850. The tables and stools are first come, first served, with doors opening an hour before showtime on weekdays and 90 minutes before showtime on weekends. Shows are all ages unless otherwise indicated.

READERS' QUESTIONS *and* COMMENTS

READERS' QUESTIONS *to the* AUTHORS

FOLLOWING ARE SOME FREQUENTLY ASKED QUESTIONS and comments from *Unofficial Guide* readers.

When you do your research, are you admitted to the parks for free? Does Disney know you're there?

We pay regular admission, and usually Disney doesn't know we're on-site. We pay for our own meals and lodging, both in and out of Walt Disney World.

How often is *The Unofficial Guide* revised?

We publish a new edition in hard copy and e-book formats once a year, with at least one reprint and e-update to account for changes at the theme parks. (Take it from us: The only constant at Walt Disney World is change.)

Where can I find out what's changed at Walt Disney World in between published editions of *The Unofficial Guide*?

We post important information online at **TouringPlans.com.**

Do you write each new edition from scratch?

Nope. When it comes to a destination the size of Walt Disney World, it's hard enough to keep up with what's new. Moreover, we put a lot of effort into communicating the most useful information in the clearest possible language. If an attraction or hotel hasn't changed, we try not to tinker with its coverage for the sake of freshening the prose.

I've never read any other *Unofficial Guides*. Are they all as critical as this one?

What some readers perceive as critical we see as objective and constructive. Our job is to prepare you for the best and worst of Walt Disney World. As it happens, some folks are very passionate about what one reader calls "the inherent goodness of Disney." These readers might be more comfortable with press releases or the *Official Guide* than with the strong consumer viewpoint represented in our guide. That said, some readers take us to task for being overly *positive*.

How many people have you surveyed for your age-group ratings regarding the attractions?

Since the first *Unofficial Guide* was published in 1985, we've interviewed or surveyed **more than 725,000** Walt Disney World patrons.

Do you stay in Walt Disney World? If not, where?

We stay at Walt Disney World lodging properties quite often. Since we began writing about Walt Disney World in 1982, we've stayed at all the Disney resorts and more than 100 different properties in various locations around Orlando, Lake Buena Vista, and Kissimmee.

Bob, what's your favorite Florida attraction?

What attracts me (as opposed to my favorite attraction) is **Juniper Springs,** a stunningly beautiful stream about 1½ hours north of Orlando in the Ocala National Forest. Winding through palm, cypress, and live oak trees, it's more exotic than the Jungle Cruise and is alive with birds, turtles, and alligators. Originating in a limestone aquifer, the crystal-clear water erupts from the ground and begins a 10-mile journey to the stream's mouth at Lake George. Put in at the Juniper Springs Recreation Area on FL 40, 36 miles east of Ocala. The 7-mile trip to the FL 19 bridge takes about 4½ hours. Canoe rentals and shuttle service are available at the recreation area. Call ☎ 352-625-3147 for more information.

▌ READERS' COMMENTS

A WOMAN FROM SUWANEE, GEORGIA, offers a suggestion for the perfect Disney vacation:

> *Your book made our trip a much more successful one. It also frustrated our male adults, who erroneously believed this was a trip for their enjoyment. We followed your advice to get up early and see as much as possible before an early lunch. But the men refused to go back to the hotel for a nap and a meal outside the park, so we fought the crowds until 3 or 4 p.m., by which time everyone was exhausted and cranky. My mother and I decided our next trip will include your guidebook and the children—but no men!*

A Midwestern mom loved getting in the game, writing:

> *It was a thrill for me to be at the official park opening—to hear the music and announcements, then hurry with the throngs to the first ride. It was so exciting! My husband teased me for days about running over old ladies and little children—I didn't run! I was* speed-walking!

A woman from Mount Gretna, Pennsylvania, had some questions about theme park attire:

> *I don't believe there was a section that addressed whether or not you could wear dresses on the rides. Quite a few amusement parks have*

security straps or bars that come up between one's knees, making it very difficult and immodest to wear dresses or skirts. Many women want to wear dresses for convenience, comfort, or cultural/religious convictions. I was concerned as I was packing whether this would limit any rides I could get on. I was quite pleased that it did not.

An Atlanta reader relates the story of a dirty bird and a solicitous cast member:

While riding Splash Mountain, a teenage boy in our boat had brought a poncho (smart move), and he took it off before we got out of the boat . . . just in time for a bird to poop on him. He went to buy a shirt in the gift shop, and when the cast member found out what had happened, he gave the kid a free shirt. I thought that was very nice!

A Columbia, Missouri, woman offers advice for wives with anxious husbands:

A smartphone is the best thing in the world for keeping your husband busy in line. As long as mine had that phone, he could check email, check dinner plans, and take and send pictures of the kids to family back home. He never complained about waiting in line, ever.

A Denver reader bursts our bubble (hey, we thought we were Disney's favorites):

WDW cast members have an interesting reaction to the Guide. *With the book in hand, we got an almost vampire-vs.-holy-water reaction from one cast member (who then asked if he could take a quick peek).*

From an exhausted mother:

Make sure moms are prepared for the fact that their kids will throw tantrums . . . and so will their husbands. Disney is a magical, wonderful thing, but it was also the most exhausting thing I have ever done. It required more patience than I've needed so far as a parent.

From an opinionated Georgia family of four:

My 13-year-old son's one-word description of Space Mountain: "Awesome." My husband's one-word description: "Hell." My 10-year-old's best comment: "Here's a Disney motto no one talks about: 'Bleed 'em dry.'" My 13-year-old's best comment, as I was trying to get everyone to stop and pose in front of the topiaries: "Keep movin', Mom! There's no time for memories!"

A Somerville, Alabama, woman is succinct if nothing else:

Everything, other than my husband, was perfect.

The weather is always, um, a hot topic with *Unofficial Guide* readers. First from a Poulsbo, Washington, reader:

Holy hell, the Florida humidity is NO JOKE!

From a woman who is more receptive after a couple of drinks:

We found (as an adult couple) that arriving early and leaving the parks for an afternoon drink or three in the monorail resorts was our saving grace! It also allowed my husband to convince me to go on more of the roller coasters!

And so it goes . . .

UNDERSTANDING DISNEY WORLD ATTRACTIONS

TO DEVELOP AN EFFICIENT TOURING PLAN, it's necessary to understand how the rides and shows are designed and function. Let's examine both.

CUT YOUR TIME IN LINE *by* UNDERSTANDING *the* RIDES

WALT DISNEY WORLD HAS MANY TYPES OF RIDES. Some, such as **Pirates of the Caribbean** in the Magic Kingdom, can carry more than 3,000 people an hour. At the other extreme, **TriceraTop Spin** in Animal Kingdom can handle only around 500 an hour. Most rides fall somewhere in between. Many factors figure into how long you'll wait to experience a ride: its popularity; how it loads and unloads; how many people can ride at once; how many **units** (ride vehicles, such as cars, rockets, boats, and flying elephants) are in service at a time; and how many cast members are available to operate the ride.

The Ride's Popularity

Newer rides, such as **Tron Lightcycle/Run** in the Magic Kingdom, attract a lot of people, as do such longtime favorites as Animal Kingdom's **Expedition Everest.** If a ride is popular, you need to know how it operates in order to determine the best time to ride. But a ride need not be especially popular to generate long lines; in some cases, such lines are due not to a ride's popularity but to poor traffic engineering. This is the case at the **Mad Tea Party** and **The Barnstormer** in Fantasyland (among others). Both rides serve only a small percentage of any day's attendance in the Magic Kingdom, yet because they take so long to load and unload, long lines form regardless.

How the Ride Loads and Unloads

Some rides never stop—they're like conveyor belts that go around and around. These are **continuous loaders.** Examples include **The Haunted Mansion** and **Under the Sea: Journey of the Little Mermaid** in the Magic

Kingdom, along with **Spaceship Earth** in EPCOT. The number of people who can be moved through in an hour depends on how many units are on the conveyor. The Haunted Mansion and Spaceship Earth have lots of units on the conveyor; consequently, both of these rides can move more than 2,000 people an hour.

Other rides are **interval loaders.** Units are unloaded, loaded, and dispatched at set intervals (sometimes controlled manually, sometimes by computer). **Space Mountain** in Tomorrowland is an interval loader: It has two tracks (the ride has been duplicated in the same facility). Each track can run as many as 14 space capsules, released at 36-, 26-, or 21-second intervals. (The bigger the crowd, the shorter the interval.)

In one kind of interval loader, empty units, as in **Space Mountain**'s space capsules, return to where they reload. In a second kind, such as **Tiana's Bayou Adventure,** one group of riders enters the vehicle while the previous group departs. Rides of the latter type are referred to as **in-and-out interval loaders.** As a boat docks, those who have just completed their ride exit to the left; at almost the same time, those waiting to ride enter the boat from the right. The reloaded boat is released to the dispatch point a few yards down the line, where it's launched according to the interval being used.

Interval loaders of both types can be very efficient people-movers if (1) the dispatch (launch) interval is relatively short and (2) the ride can accommodate many units at a time. Because many boats can float through **Pirates of the Caribbean** at one time and the dispatch interval is short, almost 3,000 people can see this attraction each hour.

The least efficient rides, in terms of traffic engineering, are **cycle rides,** also called **stop-and-go rides.** Those waiting to ride change places with those who have just ridden. Unlike in-and-out interval loaders, cycle rides shut down during loading and unloading. While one boat is loading and unloading in **It's a Small World** (an interval loader), many other boats are advancing through the ride. But when **Dumbo** (a cycle ride) touches down, the whole ride is at a standstill until the next flight launches (ditto **Prince Charming Regal Carrousel** and the **Mad Tea Party**).

With cycle rides, the time in motion is **ride time,** and the time the ride idles while loading and unloading is **load time.** Load time plus ride time equals **cycle time,** or the time from the start of one run of the ride to the start of the next. The only cycle rides in Disney World are in the Magic Kingdom and Animal Kingdom.

Number of People That Can Ride at a Time

This figure is the **system capacity.** The greater the carrying capacity of a ride (all other things being equal), the more visitors it can accommodate per hour. Some rides can increase capacity by adding extra units as crowds build; others, such as the **Astro Orbiter** in Tomorrowland, have a fixed capacity (it's impossible to add more rockets).

Number of Units in Service at a Given Time

On some rides (mostly cycle rides), the number of units operating at one time is fixed. There are always 32 flying elephants at **Dumbo** and 90 horses on **Prince Charming Regal Carrousel.** There's no way to increase the capacity of such rides by adding units. On a busy day, the only way to carry more people each hour on a fixed-unit cycle ride is to shorten the loading time or decrease the ride time.

The bottom line: On a busy day for a cycle ride, you'll wait longer and possibly be rewarded with a shorter ride. This is why we steer you away from cycle rides unless you're willing to ride them early in the morning or late at night. These are the cycle rides:

- **MAGIC KINGDOM** Astro Orbiter, The Barnstormer, Dumbo the Flying Elephant, Mad Tea Party, The Magic Carpets of Aladdin, Prince Charming Regal Carrousel
- **DISNEY'S ANIMAL KINGDOM** TriceraTop Spin

Many other rides throughout Walt Disney World can increase their capacity by adding units as crowds build. For example, if attendance is light, **Big Thunder Mountain Railroad** in Frontierland can start the day by running only one of its five mine trains from one of two available loading platforms. If lines build, the other platform is opened and more mine trains are placed into operation. At capacity, the five trains can carry about 2,400 people an hour. Likewise, **Star Tours** in Disney's Hollywood Studios can increase its capacity by using all its simulators, and the **Gran Fiesta Tour** boat ride at Mexico in EPCOT can add more boats. Sometimes a long queue will disappear almost instantly when new units are brought online. When an interval loader places more units into operation, it usually shortens the dispatch intervals, allowing more units to be dispatched more often.

Number of Cast Members Available to Operate the Ride

Adding cast members to a ride can allow more units to operate or additional loading or holding areas to open. In the Magic Kingdom, **Pirates of the Caribbean** and **It's a Small World** can run two waiting lines and loading zones. **The Haunted Mansion** has a 1½-minute preshow staged in a "stretch room." On busy days, a second stretch room can be activated, permitting a more continuous flow of visitors to the actual loading area.

Additional staff makes a world of difference to some cycle rides. Often, the **Mad Tea Party** has only one attendant. This person alone must clear visitors from the ride just completed, admit and seat visitors for the upcoming ride, check that each teacup is secured, return to the control panel, issue instructions to the riders, and, finally, activate the ride (whew!). A second attendant divides these responsibilities and cuts loading time by 25%–50%.

CUT YOUR TIME IN LINE *by* UNDERSTANDING *the* SHOWS

THE FEATURED ATTRACTIONS at Walt Disney World also include theater presentations. While they aren't as complex as rides, understanding them from a traffic-engineering standpoint may save you touring time as well.

Most theater attractions operate in three phases:

1. Guests are in the theater viewing the presentation.
2. Guests who have passed through the turnstile wait in a holding area or lobby. They will be admitted to the theater as soon as the show in progress concludes. Several attractions offer a preshow in their lobby to entertain guests until they're admitted to the main show. Examples include *Walt Disney's Enchanted Tiki Room* in the Magic Kingdom and *Muppet-Vision 3-D* in Hollywood Studios.
3. A line waits outside. Guests in line enter the lobby when there's room and will ultimately move into the theater.

The theater's capacity, the presentation's popularity, and park attendance all determine how long the lines will be at a show. Except for holidays and other days of heavy attendance, the longest wait for a show usually doesn't exceed the length of a single performance. Because almost all theater attractions run continuously, stopping only long enough for the previous audience to leave and the waiting audience to enter, a performance will be in progress when you arrive. For example, the **Canada Far and Wide** movie at EPCOT's Canada Pavilion in World Showcase lasts 14 minutes; your longest wait under normal circumstances is about 14 minutes if you arrive just after the show has begun.

ACCOMMODATIONS INDEX

Note: Page numbers in **bold** indicate a resort's main entry.

See also the Restaurant Index on pages 687–689 and the Subject Index on pages 690–709.

See also the Restaurant Index on pages 687–689 and the Subject Index on pages 690–709.

See also the Restaurant Index on pages 687-689 and the Subject Index on pages 690-709.

See also the Restaurant Index on pages 687-689 and the Subject Index on pages 690-709.

RESTAURANT INDEX

Note: Page numbers in **bold** indicate a restaurant's main entry.

See also the Accommodations Index on pages 682-686 and the Subject Index on pages 690-709.

See also the Accommodations Index on pages 682–686 and the Subject Index on pages 690–709.

See also the Accommodations Index on pages 682-686 and the Subject Index on pages 690-709.

SUBJECT INDEX

See also the Accommodations Index on pages 682–686 and the Restaurant Index on pages 687–689.

See also the Accommodations Index on pages 682–686 and the Restaurant Index on pages 687–689.

See also the Accommodations Index on pages 682-686 and the Restaurant Index on pages 687-689.

See also the Accommodations Index on pages 682-686 and the Restaurant Index on pages 687-689.

See also the Accommodations Index on pages 682–686 and the Restaurant Index on pages 687–689.

See also the Accommodations Index on pages 682–686 and the Restaurant Index on pages 687–689.

See also the Accommodations Index on pages 682-686 and the Restaurant Index on pages 687-689.

See also the Accommodations Index on pages 682–686 and the Restaurant Index on pages 687–689.

See also the Accommodations Index on pages 682-686 and the Restaurant Index on pages 687-689.

See also the Accommodations Index on pages 682-686 and the Restaurant Index on pages 687-689.

See also the Accommodations Index on pages 682–686 and the Restaurant Index on pages 687–689.

See also the Accommodations Index on pages 682-686 and the Restaurant Index on pages 687-689.

See also the Accommodations Index on pages 682-686 and the Restaurant Index on pages 687-689.

TOURING PLANS

"Not a Touring Plan" TOURING PLANS

FOR ALL PLANS, make theme park reservations (if they're required; see page 30) as soon as you know your travel dates.

MAGIC KINGDOM

FOR ALL GUESTS If Tron Lightcycle/Run is using boarding groups, obtain one as soon as they're available. If you're willing to purchase Individual Lightning Lane for Seven Dwarfs Mine Train (and Tron), do so as early as possible. If using Genie+, get the first available reservation for Big Thunder Mountain Railroad, Jungle Cruise, Peter Pan's Flight, or Space Mountain. Fit that return-time window into the plan. If none of those are available in Genie+, then get the earliest reservation for the first attraction in the plan that does have reservations available. Throughout the day, continue obtaining the earliest available Genie+ reservation for any of the next few attractions you're visiting.

FOR ALL GUESTS USING EARLY ENTRY Arrive at the Magic Kingdom entrance 40 minutes–1 hour before official opening. If Tron is using boarding groups, obtain one before you arrive.

FOR ALL OFF-SITE GUESTS ARRIVING AT OFFICIAL OPENING Arrive at the park entrance 30–60 minutes before official opening. If Tron is using boarding groups, obtain one before you arrive.

FOR PARENTS WITH ONE DAY TO TOUR AND USING EARLY ENTRY See Fantasyland first, starting with Seven Dwarfs Mine Train and then Peter Pan's Flight. See Frontierland, then Adventureland. Consider a midday break at the hotel if the park is open past 8 p.m. Then tour Tomorrowland and Liberty Square.

FOR PARENTS WITH ONE DAY TO TOUR AND ARRIVING AT OFFICIAL OPENING Begin a clockwise tour of the park in Fantasyland, skipping Seven Dwarfs Mine Train and Peter Pan's Flight. After Fantasyland, tour Tomorrowland, then Adventureland. Experience Seven Dwarfs Mine

Train and Peter Pan's Flight in the late afternoon or evening, or use Genie+/Individual Lightning Lane.

FOR ADULTS WITH ONE DAY TO TOUR AND USING EARLY ENTRY Ride Tron first, then see the rest of Tomorrowland. Tour the headliner attractions in Frontierland and Adventureland next, saving shows for the middle of the day. Tour Liberty Square around dinner. End the day with Fantasyland, saving Seven Dwarfs Mine Train and Peter Pan's Flight for as late as possible, or use Genie+/Individual Lightning Lane.

FOR ADULTS WITH ONE DAY TO TOUR AND ARRIVING AT OFFICIAL OPENING Start touring in Frontierland, then tour Adventureland and Liberty Square. Visit Fantasyland in the late afternoon and Tomorrowland after dinner.

FOR PARENTS AND ADULTS WITH TWO DAYS TO TOUR AND USING EARLY ENTRY On Day One, tour Fantasyland's headliner rides first, starting with Seven Dwarfs Mine Train. Tour Frontierland next, then Liberty Square. Finish up with Fantasyland's secondary rides. Start Day Two in Tomorrowland, then tour Adventureland and Liberty Square.

FOR PARENTS AND ADULTS WITH TWO DAYS TO TOUR AND ARRIVING AT OFFICIAL OPENING On Day One, tour Frontierland first, then Liberty Square. Finish with Peter Pan's Flight and Seven Dwarfs Mine Train in Fantasyland. Start Day Two in Adventureland, and then see Tomorrowland.

FOR PARENTS AND ADULTS WITH AN AFTERNOON AND A FULL DAY For the afternoon, tour Frontierland and Tomorrowland. On your full day of touring, see Fantasyland, Liberty Square, and Adventureland.

EPCOT

FOR ALL GUESTS If Disney is using boarding groups at Guardians of the Galaxy, obtain one as soon as they're available on the day of your visit. If you're willing to purchase Individual Lightning Lane for Guardians, do so as soon as possible on the day of your visit. Likewise, if you're using Genie+, obtain the earliest possible reservation for Remy's or Test Track. If those aren't available, get the earliest possible Genie+ reservation for any of the first few attractions in the plan. Throughout the day, continue obtaining the earliest available Genie+ reservation for any of the next few attractions you're visiting.

FOR ALL GUESTS USING EARLY ENTRY Enter EPCOT at the main entrance and ride Guardians of the Galaxy as soon as the park opens. Tour World Discovery, then World Nature, then World Celebration. Begin a clockwise tour of World Showcase starting with Mexico. For dinner, snack at the food booths in World Showcase. Finish the day with a ride on Remy's in France and a viewing of the fireworks.

FOR ALL GUESTS ARRIVING AT OFFICIAL PARK OPENING Enter EPCOT at the International Gateway entrance and ride Remy's in France as soon as you're admitted to the park. Tour to World Nature, then visit World Discovery and World Celebration. Begin a counterclockwise tour of World Showcase at Mexico. For dinner, snack at the food booths in World Showcase, and finish the day with a viewing of the fireworks.

DISNEY'S ANIMAL KINGDOM

FOR ALL GUESTS If you're willing to purchase Individual Lightning Lane for Avatar Flight of Passage, do so as soon as possible on the day of your visit. Likewise, if you're using Genie+, obtain the earliest possible reservation for either Na'vi River Journey or Kilimanjaro Safaris. If those aren't available, get the earliest possible Genie+ reservation for any of the first few attractions in the plan. Throughout the day, continue obtaining the earliest available Genie+ reservation for any of the next few attractions you're visiting.

FOR PARENTS AND ADULTS USING EARLY ENTRY Begin a land-by-land, counterclockwise tour of the park, starting at Dinosaur in DinoLand. Work in shows like *Feathered Friends in Flight* as you near them. If the park is open past dark, eat dinner, then end the night with *Awakenings* at the Tree of Life and a tour of the Valley of Mo'ara in Pandora.

FOR PARENTS AND ADULTS ARRIVING AT OFFICIAL PARK OPENING Begin a land-by-land, counterclockwise tour of the park starting at Kilimanjaro Safaris in Africa. Work in shows like *Feathered Friends in Flight* as you near them. Save the attractions in Pandora for last. If the park is open past dark, eat dinner, then end the night with *Awakenings* at the Tree of Life and a tour of the Valley of Mo'ara in Pandora.

FOR PARENTS AND ADULTS ARRIVING IN LATE MORNING Begin a clockwise tour of the park, starting in Africa and saving Pandora for last. If the park is open past dark, eat dinner, then end the night with *Awakenings* at the Tree of Life and a tour of the Valley of Mo'ara in Pandora.

DISNEY'S HOLLYWOOD STUDIOS

FOR ALL GUESTS If you're willing to purchase Individual Lightning Lane for Star Wars: Rise of the Resistance, do so as soon as possible on the day of your visit. Likewise, if you're using Genie+, obtain the earliest possible reservation for either Slinky Dog Dash, *Millennium Falcon: Smugglers Run*, Rock 'n' Roller Coaster, or Toy Story Mania! Throughout the day, continue to obtain the earliest available Genie+ reservation for any of the next few attractions you're visiting.

FOR GROUPS WITH OLDER CHILDREN, TEENS, AND ADULTS USING EARLY ENTRY Ride Rise of the Resistance as soon as you're admitted into the park. Next, begin a clockwise tour of the Studios in Toy Story Land, then head back to Galaxy's Edge. Try the attractions on Sunset Boulevard after lunch. Ride Mickey and Minnie's Runaway Railway later in the day, when crowds start to thin. Use Individual Lightning Lane and/or Genie+ as described above.

FOR ADULTS ARRIVING AROUND LUNCHTIME Begin a clockwise tour of the park in Galaxy's Edge, then visit the attractions on Sunset Boulevard. Ride Mickey and Minnie's Runaway Railway in midafternoon, and save Toy Story Land for last, when crowds have started to thin. Get in line for Rise of the Resistance during the last 2 hours the park is open. Use Individual Lightning Lane and/or Genie+ as described above.

The Magic Kingdom

MAGIC KINGDOM EARLY ENTRY ONE-DAY TOURING PLAN FOR ADULTS

If they're required, make park reservations for the Magic Kingdom as soon as you know your travel dates. If Tron is using boarding groups, sign up as early as possible on the day of your visit.

1. Arrive at the Magic Kingdom entrance 40 minutes before official opening on days of normal attendance, and 1 hour before official opening during holidays and busy times. Get guide maps and *Times Guide* while waiting to enter the park.

2. As soon as the park opens, ride Tron Lightcycle/Run in Tomorrowland.

3. Ride Space Mountain.

4. Try Buzz Lightyear's Space Ranger Spin.

5. Ride The Many Adventures of Winnie the Pooh in Fantasyland.

6. Tour The Haunted Mansion in Liberty Square.

7. Take the It's a Small World boat ride in Fantasyland.

8. Experience Pirates of the Caribbean in Adventureland. Order lunch using mobile ordering while in line. The closest nearby spot is Pecos Bill's, in Frontierland.

9. Eat lunch.

10. In Adventureland, take the Jungle Cruise.

11. Experience *Walt Disney's Enchanted Tiki Room.*

12. See the *Country Bear Jamboree* around the corner in Frontierland.

13. Ride Big Thunder Mountain Railroad.

14. See *Mickey's PhilharMagic* in Fantasyland.

15. Take Peter Pan's Flight in Fantasyland.

16. See *Enchanted Tales with Belle* or ride Under the Sea: Journey of the Little Mermaid, both in Fantasyland.

17. Ride Seven Dwarfs Mine Train.

18. Ride the Tomorrowland Transit Authority PeopleMover.

19. If time permits, see *Walt Disney's Carousel of Progress* in Tomorrowland.

20. If time permits, meet Mickey Mouse at Town Square Theater.

21. If time permits, revisit favorite attractions, try new ones, or tour the park.

22. See the *Happily Ever After* fireworks show.

To use Genie+ with this plan: The most useful Genie+ reservations for this plan are for Peter Pan's Flight, Space Mountain, and Jungle Cruise. Get the first available reservation for any of those, and fit that return-time window into the plan. Once you're able to get your next Genie+ reservation, look for the earliest return time for any of the next few attractions in the plan. **If using Individual Lightning Lane,** try to get a reservation for Tron Lightcycle/Run with a return time as close to park opening as possible and a Seven Dwarfs Mine Train reservation for anytime after 5 p.m.

See **tinyurl.com/free-tplans** to customize this plan at no charge, including the attractions and your walking speed, plus real-time updates while you're in the park.

The Magic Kingdom

MAGIC KINGDOM NON–EARLY-ENTRY ONE-DAY TOURING PLAN FOR ADULTS

If they're required, make park reservations for the Magic Kingdom as soon as you know your travel dates. If Tron is using boarding groups, sign up as early as possible on the day of your visit.

1. Arrive at the entrance 30 minutes before official opening on days of normal attendance and 1 hour before official opening during holidays and busy times. Get guide maps and *Times Guide* while waiting to enter the park.

2. As soon as you're admitted to the park, take the Jungle Cruise in Adventureland.

3. Ride Big Thunder Mountain Railroad in Frontierland.

4. Experience Pirates of the Caribbean in Adventureland.

5. Tour The Haunted Mansion in Liberty Square.

6. In Fantasyland, ride It's a Small World. While in line, use mobile ordering to order lunch. The best spot nearby is the Columbia Harbour House in Liberty Square.

7. Eat lunch.

8. See *Mickey's PhilharMagic*.

9. Ride Under the Sea: Journey of the Little Mermaid.

10. See *Walt Disney's Carousel of Progress* in Tomorrowland.

11. Ride the Tomorrowland Transit Authority PeopleMover.

12. Ride Buzz Lightyear's Space Ranger Spin.

13. Ride Tron Lightcycle/Run during the afternoon parade.

14. Ride Space Mountain.

15. Ride The Many Adventures of Winnie the Pooh in Fantasyland.

16. Experience Seven Dwarfs Mine Train.

17. Take Peter Pan's Flight in Fantasyland.

18. See *Walt Disney's Enchanted Tiki Room*. While in line, order dinner using mobile ordering. The best nearby spot is Pecos Bill's Tall Tale Inn & Cafe, in Frontierland.

19. See the *Country Bear Jamboree*.

20. If time permits, revisit favorite attractions, try new ones, or tour the park.

23. See the *Happily Ever After* fireworks show.

To use Genie+ with this plan: The most useful Genie+ reservations for this plan are for Big Thunder Mountain Railroad, Peter Pan's Flight, and Space Mountain. Get the first available reservation for any of those, and fit that return-time window into the plan. Once you're able to get your next Genie+ reservation, look for the earliest return time for any of the next few attractions in the plan. **If using Individual Lightning Lane,** try to get a reservation for Tron Lightcycle/Run with a return time as close to park opening as possible and a Seven Dwarfs Mine Train reservation for anytime after 5 p.m.

See **tinyurl.com/free-tplans** to customize this plan at no charge, including the attractions and your walking speed, plus real-time updates while you're in the park.

The Magic Kingdom

MAGIC KINGDOM EARLY-ENTRY ONE-DAY
TOURING PLAN FOR PARENTS WITH SMALL CHILDREN

Review the Small-Child Fright-Potential Table on pages 390–392. Attractions shown should be suitable for most children ages 5 and up. If they're required, make park reservations for the Magic Kingdom as soon as you know your travel dates. Interrupt the plan for meals, rest, and a cocktail or two.

1. Arrive at the entrance 40 minutes before official opening on days of normal attendance, and 1 hour before official opening during holidays and busy times. Get guide maps and *Times Guide* while waiting to enter the park.

2. As soon as the park opens, head toward the right-hand side of Cinderella Castle and follow the path to Seven Dwarfs Mine Train in Fantasyland. Ride.

3. Take Peter Pan's Flight.

4. Ride The Many Adventures of Winnie the Pooh.

5. Ride Prince Charming Regal Carrousel.

6. Meet the characters at Pete's Silly Sideshow.

7. Try the It's a Small World boat ride. Use mobile ordering to order lunch while in line. The best nearby spot is Columbia Harbour House in Liberty Square.

8. Eat lunch.

9. In Fantasyland, ride Dumbo the Flying Elephant.

10. Try The Barnstormer.

11. Ride Under the Sea: Journey of the Little Mermaid.

12. Give the Mad Tea Party a whirl.

13. See *Mickey's PhilharMagic.*

14. Catch the afternoon parade from Liberty Square.

15. Meet princesses at Princess Fairytale Hall.

16. See *Enchanted Tales with Belle* or meet Ariel at her grotto.

17. Take a spin on the Tomorrowland Speedway in Tomorrowland.

18. Ride Buzz Lightyear's Space Ranger Spin.

19. See *Monsters, Inc. Laugh Floor.*

20. If time permits, ride The Magic Carpets of Aladdin in Adventureland.

21. Meet Mickey Mouse at Town Square Theater on Main Street, U.S.A.

22. If time permits, revisit favorite attractions, try new ones, or tour the park.

23. Eat dinner.

24. See the *Happily Ever After* fireworks show.

To use Genie+ with this plan: The most useful Genie+ reservations for this plan are for Peter Pan's Flight (by a wide margin), then the Mickey Mouse meet and greet, Buzz Lightyear, and The Many Adventures of Winnie the Pooh. Get the first available reservation for any of those, and fit that return-time window into the plan. Once you're able to get your next Genie+ reservation, look for the earliest return time for any of the next few attractions in the plan. **Individual Lightning Lane** reservations shouldn't be needed for Seven Dwarfs Mine Train. If using it, try to get a reservation for around the park's official opening time.

See **tinyurl.com/free-tplans** to customize this plan at no charge, including the attractions and your walking speed, plus real-time updates while you're in the park.

The Magic Kingdom

MAGIC KINGDOM NON–EARLY–ENTRY ONE-DAY TOURING PLAN FOR PARENTS WITH SMALL CHILDREN

Review the Small-Child Fright-Potential Table on pages 390–392. If they're required, make park reservations for the Magic Kingdom as soon as you know your travel dates. Interrupt the plan for meals and rest.

1. Arrive at the Magic Kingdom entrance 30 minutes before official opening on days of normal attendance, and 1 hour before official opening during holidays and busy times. Get guide maps and *Times Guide* while waiting to enter the park.

2. As soon as the park opens, head to Fantasyland and ride The Many Adventures of Winnie the Pooh.

3. Give the Mad Tea Party a whirl.

4. Try The Barnstormer.

5. Ride Dumbo the Flying Elephant.

6. Meet some characters at Pete's Silly Sideshow.

7. Ride Under the Sea: Journey of the Little Mermaid.

8. Try the It's a Small World boat ride. Use mobile ordering to order lunch while in line. The best nearby dining location is Columbia Harbour House in Liberty Square.

9. Eat lunch.

10. See *Mickey's PhilharMagic*.

11. Meet princesses at Princess Fairytale Hall.

12. Ride The Magic Carpets of Aladdin in Adventureland.

13. Catch the afternoon parade from Frontierland.

14. Take the raft over to Tom Sawyer Island in Frontierland.

15. See *Monsters, Inc. Laugh Floor* in Tomorrowland.

16. Take a spin on the Tomorrowland Speedway.

17. Ride Buzz Lightyear's Space Ranger Spin. Use mobile ordering to order dinner while in line. The best nearby location is Cosmic Ray's in Tomorrowland.

18. Eat dinner.

19. Ride Seven Dwarfs Mine Train in Fantasyland.

20. Take Peter Pan's Flight.

21. If time permits, meet Mickey Mouse at Town Square Theater.

22. If time permits, revisit favorite attractions, try new ones, or tour the park.

23. See the *Happily Ever After* fireworks show.

To use Genie+ with this plan: The most useful Genie+ reservations for this plan are for Peter Pan's Flight (by a wide margin) and then the Mickey Mouse meet and greet, Buzz Lightyear, and The Many Adventures of Winnie the Pooh. Get the first available reservation for any of those, and fit that return-time window into the plan. Once you're able to get your next Genie+ reservation, look for the earliest return time for any of the next few attractions in the plan. **If using Individual Lightning Lane,** try to get a Seven Dwarfs Mine Train reservation for around noon or later.

See **tinyurl.com/free-tplans** to customize this plan at no charge, including the attractions and your walking speed, plus real-time updates while you're in the park.

The Magic Kingdom

MAGIC KINGDOM EARLY-ENTRY DUMBO-OR-DIE-IN-A-DAY TOURING PLAN FOR PARENTS WITH SMALL CHILDREN

Review the Small-Child Fright-Potential Table on pages 390–392. If they're required, make park reservations for the Magic Kingdom as soon as you know your travel dates. Interrupt the plan for meals and rest.

1. Arrive at the entrance 40 minutes before official opening on days of normal attendance, and 1 hour before official opening during holidays and busy times. Get guide maps and *Times Guide* while waiting to enter the park.
2. As soon as the park opens, ride Seven Dwarfs Mine Train in Fantasyland.
3. Take Peter Pan's Flight.
4. Tour The Haunted Mansion in Liberty Square.
5. Take the Jungle Cruise in Adventureland.
6. Experience Pirates of the Caribbean.
7. Ride The Magic Carpets of Aladdin.
8. Take the It's a Small World boat ride. While in line, use mobile ordering to order lunch. The closest good spot is Columbia Harbour House in Liberty Square.
9. Eat lunch.
10. Take the raft over to Tom Sawyer Island in Frontierland.
11. See *Mickey's PhilharMagic* in Fantasyland.
12. Meet princesses at Princess Fairytale Hall.
13. Ride Under the Sea: Journey of the Little Mermaid.
14. Meet the characters at Pete's Silly Sideshow.
15. Try The Barnstormer.
16. Ride Dumbo the Flying Elephant twice.
17. Ride The Many Adventures of Winnie the Pooh.
18. Try Buzz Lightyear's Space Ranger Spin in Tomorrowland. While in line, use mobile ordering to order dinner. The closest spot is Cosmic Ray's Starlight Cafe.
19. Eat dinner.
20. Meet Mickey Mouse at Town Square Theater.
21. If time permits, see *Monsters, Inc. Laugh Floor* in Tomorrowland.
22. Take a spin on the Tomorrowland Speedway.
23. Circle back to any skipped attractions, or revisit favorites.
24. See the *Happily Ever After* fireworks show.

To use Genie+ with this plan: The most useful Genie+ reservations for this plan are for Jungle Cruise, the Mickey Mouse meet and greet, The Magic Carpets of Aladdin, and then Buzz Lightyear. Get the first available reservation for any of those, and fit that return-time window into the plan. Once you're able to get your next Genie+ reservation, look for the earliest return time for any of the next few attractions in the plan. **Individual Lightning Lane** reservations shouldn't be needed for Seven Dwarfs Mine Train.

See **tinyurl.com/free-tplans** to customize this plan at no charge, including the attractions and your walking speed, plus real-time updates while you're in the park.

The Magic Kingdom

MAGIC KINGDOM NON–EARLY-ENTRY DUMBO-OR-DIE-IN-A-DAY TOURING PLAN FOR PARENTS WITH SMALL CHILDREN

Review the Small-Child Fright-Potential Table on pages 390–392. If they're required, make park reservations as soon as you know your travel dates. Interrupt the plan for meals and rest.

1. Arrive at the entrance 30 minutes before official opening on days of normal attendance, and 1 hour before official opening during holidays and busy times. Get guide maps and *Times Guide* while waiting to enter the park.
2. As soon as you're admitted to the park, take the Jungle Cruise in Adventureland.
3. Ride The Magic Carpets of Aladdin.
4. Experience Pirates of the Caribbean.
5. Tour The Haunted Mansion in Liberty Square.
6. See *Mickey's PhilharMagic* in Fantasyland.
7. Take the It's a Small World boat ride. While in line, use mobile ordering to order lunch. The best spot nearby is Columbia Harbour House in Liberty Square.
8. Eat lunch.
9. Take the raft over to Tom Sawyer Island in Frontierland.
10. Take the Walt Disney World Railroad from Frontierland to Fantasyland.
11. In Fantasyland, try The Barnstormer.
12. Meet the characters at Pete's Silly Sideshow.
13. Ride Dumbo the Flying Elephant twice.
14. Ride The Many Adventures of Winnie the Pooh.
15. Ride Under the Sea: Journey of the Little Mermaid.
16. Meet princesses at Princess Fairytale Hall.
17. Take a spin on the Tomorrowland Speedway. While in line, use mobile ordering to order dinner. The closest spot is Cosmic Ray's Starlight Cafe.
18. Eat dinner.
19. Try Buzz Lightyear's Space Ranger Spin in Tomorrowland.
20. Ride Seven Dwarfs Mine Train in Fantasyland.
21. Take Peter Pan's Flight.
22. If time permits, meet Mickey Mouse at Town Square Theater.
23. If time permits, see *Monsters, Inc. Laugh Floor* in Tomorrowland.
24. Circle back to any skipped attractions, or revisit favorites.
25. See the *Happily Ever After* fireworks show.

To use Genie+ with this plan: The most useful Genie+ reservations for this plan are for Peter Pan's Flight (by a wide margin), the Mickey Mouse meet and greet, and then Buzz Lightyear and The Haunted Mansion. Get the first available reservation for any of those, and fit that return-time window into the plan. Once you're able to get your next Genie+ reservation, look for the earliest return time for any of the next few attractions in the plan. **If using Individual Lightning Lane,** try to get a Seven Dwarfs Mine Train reservation for around 10:30 a.m.

See tinyurl.com/free-tplans to customize this plan at no charge, including the attractions and your walking speed, plus real-time updates while you're in the park.

The Magic Kingdom

MAGIC KINGDOM EARLY-ENTRY TWO-DAY
TOURING PLAN FOR ADULTS: DAY ONE

If they're required, make park reservations for the Magic Kingdom as soon as you know your travel dates. Interrupt the plan for meals and rest.

1. Arrive at the entrance 40 minutes before official opening on days of normal attendance, and 1 hour before official opening during holidays and busy times. Get guide maps and *Times Guide* while waiting to enter the park.

2. As soon as the park opens, ride Seven Dwarfs Mine Train in Fantasyland.

3. Ride Peter Pan's Flight.

4. In Frontierland, ride Big Thunder Mountain Railroad.

5. In Liberty Square, ride The Haunted Mansion.

6. Ride It's a Small World in Fantasyland.

7. See *Mickey's PhilharMagic*.

8. See *The Hall of Presidents* in Liberty Square. Order lunch using mobile ordering. The best nearby spot is Columbia Harbour House, next door.

9. Eat lunch.

10. Explore Tom Sawyer Island in Frontierland.

11. Work in a viewing of *Country Bear Jamboree* in Frontierland.

12. Revisit any favorite or skipped attractions.

13. If time permits, see the *Happily Ever After* fireworks show.

To use Genie+ with this plan: The most useful Genie+ reservations in the Magic Kingdom are for Peter Pan's Flight, Big Thunder Mountain, and Pirates of the Caribbean. Get the first available reservation for either of those, and fit that return-time window into the plan. Once you're able to get your next Genie+ reservation, look for the earliest return time for any of the next few attractions in the plan. **Individual Lightning Lane** reservations shouldn't be needed for Seven Dwarfs Mine Train.

See **tinyurl.com/free-tplans** to customize this plan at no charge, including the attractions and your walking speed, plus real-time updates while you're in the park.

The Magic Kingdom

MAGIC KINGDOM EARLY-ENTRY TWO-DAY
TOURING PLAN FOR ADULTS: DAY TWO

If they're required, make park reservations for the Magic Kingdom as soon as you know your travel dates. Interrupt the plan for meals and rest.

1. Arrive at the entrance 40 minutes before official opening on days of normal attendance, and 1 hour before official opening during holidays and busy times. Get guide maps and *Times Guide* while waiting to enter the park.
2. As soon as the park opens, ride Tron Lightcycle/Run in Tomorrowland.
3. Ride Space Mountain.
4. Ride Buzz Lightyear's Space Ranger Spin.
5. In Adventureland, take the Jungle Cruise.
6. See *Walt Disney's Enchanted Tiki Room.* Use mobile ordering to order lunch.
7. Eat lunch.

8. Tour the Swiss Family Treehouse.
9. Ride the Tomorrowland Transit Authority PeopleMover in Tomorrowland.
10. See *Walt Disney's Carousel of Progress.*
11. See *Monsters, Inc. Laugh Floor* if time permits.
12. See the afternoon parade from Main Street, U.S.A., near the train station.
13. Meet Mickey Mouse at Town Square Theater.
14. Revisit any favorite attractions or tour the rest of the park.
15. If you've not already done so, see the *Happily Ever After* fireworks show.

To use Genie+ with this plan: The most useful Genie+ reservations in the Magic Kingdom are for Space Mountain, Jungle Cruise, and Buzz Lightyear. Get the first available reservation for either of those, and fit that return-time window into the plan. Once you're able to get your next Genie+ reservation, look for the earliest return time for any of the next few attractions in the plan. **Individual Lightning Lane** reservations shouldn't be needed for Tron. If Tron isn't open, then Individual Lightning Lane reservations shouldn't be needed for Seven Dwarfs Mine Train either.

See **tinyurl.com/free-tplans** to customize this plan at no charge, including the attractions and your walking speed, plus real-time updates while you're in the park.

EPCOT EARLY-ENTRY ONE-DAY TOURING PLAN

If they're required, make park reservations as soon as you know your travel dates. If Guardians of the Galaxy: Cosmic Rewind is using boarding groups (see page 59), obtain a reservation at 7 a.m. or 1 p.m. on the day of your visit, and interrupt the plan when it's time to ride.

1. Arrive at EPCOT's main entrance 50 minutes before official opening (70 minutes on busy days and holidays). Get guide maps and *Times Guide*.

2. If it's not using boarding groups, ride Guardians of the Galaxy: Cosmic Rewind in World Discovery as soon as the park opens.

3. Ride Soarin' Around the World at the Land Pavilion in World Nature.

4. Ask a cast member if Test Track is operating. If yes, ride Test Track in World Discovery. Use the single-rider line if it's open and your group is willing.

5. If your group includes teens, ride Mission: Space in World Discovery and skip Living with the Land in step 7.

6. Ride Spaceship Earth in World Celebration.

7. Ride Living with the Land in the Land Pavilion in World Nature. Skip it if you have teens, to save time.

8. Eat a light, late lunch. Sunshine Seasons in The Land is the closest, best option.

9. Tour SeaBase (The Seas main tank and exhibits).

10. Walk through the Moana–Journey of Water exhibit.

11. Begin a tour of World Showcase at Mexico. Skip the boat ride to save time.

12. Tour the Norway Pavilion and ride Frozen Ever After.

13. See the China Pavilion. Skip the film—it's not rated highly by any age group.

14. Check out the Germany Pavilion.

15. Tour the Italy Pavilion.

16. See *The American Adventure*.

17. Tour the Japan Pavilion and exhibits.

18. Tour the Morocco Pavilion and exhibits.

19. In France, ride Remy's Ratatouille Adventure. To save time, skip the film shown elsewhere in the pavilion.

20. Tour the Canada Pavilion and see *Canada Far and Wide*.

21. See the fireworks show. Good viewing locations should be available around the Mexico Pavilion; in front of World Showcase where it meets Future World; and between Canada and France.

To use Genie+ with this plan: The most useful Genie+ reservations for this plan are for Remy's Ratatouille Adventure, Frozen Ever After, Test Track, and Soarin' Around the World (in that order). Get the first available reservation for one of those, and fit that return-time window into the plan. Once you're able to get your next Genie+ reservation, look for the earliest return time for any of the next few attractions in the plan. **If using Individual Lightning Lane,** try to get a Guardians reservation for as close to park opening as possible.

See **tinyurl.com/free-tplans** to customize this plan at no charge, including the attractions and your walking speed, plus real-time updates while you're in the park.

EPCOT

EPCOT NON-EARLY-ENTRY ONE-DAY TOURING PLAN

If they're required, make park reservations as soon as you know your travel dates. If Guardians of the Galaxy: Cosmic Rewind is using boarding groups (see page 59), obtain a reservation at 7 a.m. on the day of your visit and interrupt the plan when it's time to ride.

1. Arrive at EPCOT's main entrance 30 minutes before official opening (50 minutes on busy days and holidays). Get guide maps and *Times Guide*.

2. As soon as the park opens, ride Soarin' Around the World in World Nature.

3. Ask a cast member if Test Track is operating. If yes, ride Test Track in World Discovery. Use the single-rider line if it's open and your group is willing.

4. If your group includes teens, ride Mission: Space in World Discovery and skip Living with the Land in step 6.

5. Ride Spaceship Earth in World Celebration.

6. Ride Living with the Land at the Land Pavilion in World Nature. If you have teens, skip it to save time.

7. Eat a light, late lunch. Sunshine Seasons in The Land is the closest, best option.

8. Tour SeaBase (The Seas main tank and exhibits).

9. Walk through Moana—Journey of Water.

10. Begin a tour of World Showcase at Mexico. Skip the boat ride to save time.

11. Tour Norway and ride Frozen Ever After.

12. See the China Pavilion. Skip the film—it's not rated highly by any age group.

13. Check out the Germany Pavilion.

14. Tour the Italy Pavilion.

15. See *The American Adventure*.

16. Tour the Japan Pavilion and exhibits.

17. Tour the Morocco Pavilion and exhibits.

18. In France, ride Remy's Ratatouille Adventure. To save time, skip the film shown elsewhere in the pavilion.

19. If you have more than 2 hours before the park closes, tour the Canada Pavilion (19a) and see *Canada Far and Wide*. Otherwise, skip Canada and ride Guardians of the Galaxy (19b).

20. Return to World Discovery and ride Guardians of the Galaxy if you've not already done so.

21. See the evening fireworks. Good viewing locations should be available around the Mexico Pavilion; in front of World Showcase where it meets Future World; and between Canada and France.

To use Genie+ with this plan: The most useful Genie+ reservations for this plan are for Remy's Ratatouille Adventure, Frozen Ever After, Test Track, and Soarin' Around the World (in that order). Get the first available reservation for one of those, and fit that return-time window into the plan. Once you're able to get your next Genie+ reservation, look for the earliest return time for any of the next few attractions in the plan. If using Individual Lightning Lane, try to get a Guardians reservation for before noon—it'll save you a walk back from World Showcase later.

See **tinyurl.com/free-tplans** to customize this plan at no charge, including the attractions and your walking speed, plus real-time updates while you're in the park.

Disney's Animal Kingdom

ANIMAL KINGDOM EARLY-ENTRY ONE-DAY TOURING PLAN

If they're required, make park reservations for Animal Kingdom as soon as you know your travel dates.

1. Arrive at the main entrance 50 minutes before official opening on days of normal attendance (70 minutes during holidays and busy times). Follow cast member instructions to line up for Avatar Flight of Passage. Get guide maps and *Times Guide* while waiting to enter.
2. Ride Avatar Flight of Passage (**2a**), then Na'vi River Journey (**2b**) in Pandora.
3. Sign up for Wilderness Explorers on the bridge from Discovery Island to The Oasis, on your way to Asia. Play a few games as you tour the park.
4. Ride Expedition Everest in Asia.
5. Ride Dinosaur in Dinoland U.S.A.
6. Walk the Maharajah Jungle Trek. Use mobile ordering to order lunch. The best restaurants in the park are Satu'li Canteen in Pandora and Flame Tree Barbecue on Discovery Island.
7. Eat lunch.
8. Work in the next showing of *Festival of the Lion King* in Africa around the next two steps.
9. Take the Kilimanjaro Safaris tour in Africa.
10. Walk the Gorilla Falls Exploration Trail.
11. See *Feathered Friends in Flight* in Asia.
12. Get wet on Kali River Rapids in Asia, if temperatures permit.
13. Tour the Discovery Island Trails and any other animal exhibits that interest you.
14. See *Finding Nemo: The Big Blue . . . and Beyond!* in DinoLand U.S.A.

If the park is open past dark:

15. Eat dinner in the park.
16. See *Awakenings* at the Tree of Life. Check *Times Guide* for start time.
17. Tour the Valley of Mo'ara in Pandora.

To use Genie+ with this plan: The most useful Genie+ reservations for this plan are for Na'vi River Journey and Kilimanjaro Safaris, then Expedition Everest and (during summer) Kali River Rapids. Get the first available reservation for one of those, and fit that return-time window into the plan. Once you're able to get your next Genie+ reservation, look for the earliest return time for any of the next few attractions in the plan. **If using Individual Lightning Lane,** you shouldn't need one for Flight of Passage.

See **tinyurl.com/free-tplans** to customize this plan at no charge, including the attractions and your walking speed, plus real-time updates while you're in the park.

Disney's Animal Kingdom

ANIMAL KINGDOM NON-EARLY-ENTRY ONE-DAY TOURING PLAN

If they're required, make park reservations for Animal Kingdom as soon as you know your travel dates.

1. Arrive at the main entrance 30 minutes before official opening on days of normal attendance (50 minutes during holidays and busy times). Follow cast member instructions to line up for Avatar Flight of Passage. Get guide maps and *Times Guide* while waiting to enter the park.

2. As soon as you're admitted into the park, take the Kilimanjaro Safaris tour in Africa.

3. Get wet on Kali River Rapids in Asia, if temperatures permit.

4. Ride Expedition Everest.

5. Ride Dinosaur in DinoLand U.S.A. Use mobile ordering to order lunch in advance. The best restaurants in the park are Satu'li Canteen in Pandora and Flame Tree Barbecue on Discovery Island.

6. Eat lunch. On your way to lunch, sign up for Wilderness Explorers on the bridge from Discovery Island to The Oasis. Play a few games as you tour the rest of the park.

7. Walk the Maharajah Jungle Trek.

8. See *Feathered Friends in Flight* in Asia.

9. Walk the Gorilla Falls Exploration Trail.

10. See *Festival of the Lion King.*

11. Tour the Discovery Island Trails and any other animal exhibits that interest you.

12. Ride Avatar Flight of Passage in Pandora.

13. Take the Na'vi River Journey boat ride.

14. If it's open, see *Finding Nemo: The Big Blue . . . and Beyond!* in DinoLand U.S.A.

If the park is open past dark:

15. Eat dinner in the park.

16. See *Awakenings* at the Tree of Life. Check *Times Guide* for start time.

17. Tour the Valley of Mo'ara in Pandora.

To use Genie+ with this plan: The most useful Genie+ reservations for this plan are for Na'vi River Journey and Kilimanjaro Safaris, then Expedition Everest and (during summer) Kali River Rapids. Get the first available reservation for one of those and fit that return-time window into the plan. Once you're able to get your next Genie+ reservation, look for the earliest return time for any of the next few attractions in the plan. **If using Individual Lightning Lane,** obtain a reservation for Flight of Passage for around 4 p.m.

See **tinyurl.com/free-tplans** to customize this plan at no charge, including the attractions and your walking speed, plus real-time updates while you're in the park.

Disney's Hollywood Studios

DHS EARLY-ENTRY ONE-DAY TOURING PLAN

If they're required, make park reservations for the Studios as soon as you know your travel dates. Make reservations 60 days in advance for Savi's Workshop, the Droid Depot, and Oga's Cantina; check tinyurl.com/dhs-swge before your trip to get the latest information.

1. Check official park hours the night before your visit, and plan to arrive 50 minutes before official park opening on non-peak days (70 minutes during holidays and other busy times).
2. Ride Star Wars: Rise of the Resistance in Galaxy's Edge as soon as the park opens.
3. Ride *Millennium Falcon:* Smugglers Run.
4. Ride Toy Story Mania!
5. See *Muppet-Vision 3-D.*
6. Experience Star Tours—The Adventures Continue in Echo Lake.
7. Work in a showing of *For the First Time in Forever* around the next two steps. Use mobile ordering to order lunch. The best spot nearby is Docking Bay 7 in Galaxy's Edge.
8. Eat lunch.
9. Try Mickey and Minnie's Runaway Railway on Hollywood Boulevard.

10. Work in *Beauty and The Beast—Live on Stage* around the next two steps.
11. Ride the Rock 'n' Roller Coaster on Sunset Boulevard.
12. Ride The Twilight Zone Tower of Terror.
13. See *Walt Disney Presents* in Animation Courtyard. If you have small children, try *Disney Junior Play and Dance!*, also in Animation Courtyard, instead.
14. Ride Slinky Dog Dash in Toy Story Land.
15. Explore the rest of Galaxy's Edge.
16. Meet Mickey and Minnie at *Red Carpet Dreams.*
17. Meet Olaf at Celebrity Spotlight.
18. See the Mickey Mouse film *Vacation Fun* in Echo Lake.
19. See the *Indiana Jones Epic Stunt Spectacular!*
20. See the evening fireworks and/or *Fantasmic!*

(continued on next page)

To use Genie+ with this plan: The most useful Genie+ reservations for this plan are for Slinky Dog Dash, Tower of Terror, *Millennium Falcon:* Smugglers Run, and Rock 'n' Roller Coaster. (During summers and holidays, almost any Genie+ reservation except Star Tours will save time.) Get the first available reservation for one of those, and fit that return-time window into the plan. Once you're able to get your next Genie+ reservation, look for the earliest return time for any of the next few attractions in the plan. **If using Individual Lightning Lane,** you shouldn't need one for Rise of the Resistance.

See **tinyurl.com/free-tplans** to customize this plan at no charge, including the attractions and your walking speed, plus real-time updates while you're in the park.

Disney's Hollywood Studios

DHS NON-EARLY-ENTRY ONE-DAY TOURING PLAN

If they're required, make park reservations for the Studios as soon as you know your travel dates.
If Rise of the Resistance is using boarding groups, obtain one at exactly 7 a.m. on the day of your visit,
or try again at 1 p.m. Stop the touring plan when your boarding group is called.
Make reservations 60 days in advance for Savi's Workshop, the Droid Depot, and Oga's Cantina;
check tinyurl.com/dhs-swge before your trip to get the latest information.

1. Check official park hours the night before your visit, and plan to arrive 50 minutes before official park opening (70 minutes during holidays and other busy times.)
2. As soon as you're admitted into the park, ride *Millennium Falcon: Smugglers Run* in Galaxy's Edge.
3. See *Muppet-Vision 3-D* in Grand Avenue.
4. Experience Star Tours—The Adventures Continue in Echo Lake.
5. Work in a showing of *For the First Time in Forever* around the next few steps. Use mobile ordering to order lunch. The best spot nearby is Docking Bay 7 in Galaxy's Edge.
6. Eat lunch.
7. Ride Toy Story Mania! in Toy Story Land.
8. Try Mickey and Minnie's Runaway Railway on Hollywood Boulevard.
9. Work in *Beauty and the Beast—Live on Stage* around the next two steps.
10. Ride Rock 'n' Roller Coaster.
11. Ride The Twilight Zone Tower of Terror.
12. See *Walt Disney Presents* in Animation Courtyard. If you have small children, try *Disney Junior Play and Dance*, also in Animation Courtyard, instead.
13. Ride Slinky Dog Dash in Toy Story Land.
14. Meet Mickey and Minnie at Red Carpet Dreams.
15. Meet Olaf at Celebrity Spotlight.
16. See *Vacation Fun* in Echo Lake.
17. Ride Star Wars: Rise of the Resistance and explore the remainder of Galaxy's Edge.
18. See the *Indiana Jones Epic Stunt Spectacular!*
19. See the evening fireworks and/or *Fantasmic!*

(continued on next page)

To use Genie+ with this plan: The most useful Genie+ reservations for this plan are for Slinky Dog Dash, Tower of Terror, *Millennium Falcon:* Smugglers Run, and Rock 'n' Roller Coaster. (During summers and holidays, almost any Genie+ reservation except Star Tours will save time.) Get the first available reservation for one of those, and fit that return-time window into the plan. Once you're able to get your next Genie+ reservation, look for the earliest return time for any of the next few attractions in the plan. **If using Individual Lightning Lane,** try to obtain one for Rise of the Resistance for around 5 p.m.

See **tinyurl.com/free-tplans** to customize this plan at no charge, including the attractions and your walking speed, plus real-time updates while you're in the park.

Universal Studios Florida

UNIVERSAL ORLANDO HIGHLIGHTS
ONE-DAY/TWO-PARK TOURING PLAN: PART ONE
(Assumes: 1-Day Park-to-Park Ticket)

1. Buy admission in advance. Call ☎ 407-363-8000 or visit universalorlando.com the day before for the official opening time.

2. Arrive at USF 90–120 minutes before the official opening time if Early Park Admission is offered and you're eligible, or 30–45 minutes before opening if you're a day guest. Check Universal's app for daily showtimes. *Alternative:* If only IOA is open for Early Park Admission and you're eligible, arrive at IOA 90–120 minutes before official opening. Ride Hagrid's Magical Creatures Motorbike Adventure (**2a**), followed by Jurassic World VelociCoaster (**2b**) or Flight of the Hippogriff (**2c**). Then take the first Hogwarts Express (**2d**) of the morning to USF, and continue at the next step. (See next page for the map of steps 2a–2d.)

3. Early-entry guests should head to Diagon Alley to visit Ollivanders (**3a**) and ride Harry Potter and the Escape from Gringotts (**3b**). If Gringotts isn't operating, enjoy the rest of Diagon Alley but don't get in line.

4. Return to the front of the park to ride Despicable Me Minion Mayhem. Day guests should begin here.

5. Ride Hollywood Rip Ride Rockit.

6. Experience Transformers: The Ride 3-D in Production Central.

7. Ride Revenge of the Mummy in New York.

8. Ride Race Through New York Starring Jimmy Fallon if the standby wait is short.

9. Ride Men in Black Alien Attack in World Expo.

10. Experience The Simpsons Ride in Springfield.

11. Ride E.T. Adventure in Woody Woodpecker's KidZone.

12. Ride Hogwarts Express to IOA. Have your park-to-park ticket ready.

Tour Islands of Adventure using Part Two of this plan (see next page); then return to USF and resume at step 23 below.

23. See *Universal Orlando's Horror Make-Up Show* (**23a**) and/or *The Bourne Stuntacular* (**23b**) according to the daily entertainment schedule.

24. Chat with the Knight Bus conductor outside of Diagon Alley. Also look for Kreacher in the window of 12 Grimmauld Place and dial MAGIC (62442) in the red phone booth.

25. See *Celestina Warbeck and the Banshees* or *Tales of Beedle the Bard* in Diagon Alley.

26. See the wand ceremony at Ollivanders, and buy a wand if you wish.

27. Eat dinner at the Leaky Cauldron.

28. Tour Diagon Alley. Browse the shops, explore the dark recesses of Knockturn Alley, and discover the interactive effects.

29. Ride Harry Potter and the Escape from Gringotts.

30. If scheduled, watch *Universal Orlando's Cinematic Celebration* from Central Park (between Hollywood and KidZone).

(continued on next page)

Universal Islands of Adventure

UNIVERSAL ORLANDO HIGHLIGHTS
ONE-DAY/TWO-PARK TOURING PLAN: PART TWO

(continued from previous page)

13. Break for lunch. We suggest Fire Eater's Grill in Lost Continent (13a) for a quicker meal or Mythos (13b) for sit-down dining.

14. Ride The Cat in the Hat in Seuss Landing.

15. Ride The Incredible Hulk Coaster on Marvel Super Hero Island.

16. Ride The Amazing Adventures of Spider-Man.

17. Ride Skull Island: Reign of Kong.

18. Take the Jurassic Park River Adventure.

19. Ride the Jurassic World VelociCoaster.

20. Ride Harry Potter and the Forbidden Journey.

21. Experience Hagrid's Magical Creatures Motorbike Adventure.

22. Return to USF via Hogwarts Express, or walk back to the other park if the posted wait exceeds 20 minutes.

Resume Part One starting with step 23 (see previous page).

Universal Islands of Adventure

ALTERNATE UNIVERSAL ORLANDO HIGHLIGHTS
ONE-DAY/TWO-PARK TOURING PLAN: PART ONE

(Assumes: 1-Day Park-to-Park Ticket)

1. Buy admission in advance. Call ☎ 407-363-8000 or visit universalorlando.com the day before for the official opening time.

2. Arrive at IOA 90–120 minutes before the official opening time if Early Park Admission is offered and you're eligible, or 30–45 minutes before opening if you're a day guest. Check Universal's app for daily showtimes.

3. Early-entry guests should ride Hagrid's Magical Creatures Motorbike Adventure in Hogsmeade only if they are at the front of the pack.

4. Early-entry guests may ride the Jurassic World VelociCoaster (**4a**) or Flight of the Hippogriff (**4b**), followed by Harry Potter and the Forbidden Journey (**4c**), if at least 15 minutes remain in early entry.

5. Guests without early entry should first ride The Incredible Hulk Coaster.

6. Ride The Amazing Adventures of Spider-Man. Day guests should start with Spider-Man (**6a**), followed by Skull Island: Reign of Kong (**6b**). Early-entry guests may ride Reign of Kong (**6b**) on their way to Spider-Man (**6a**) while walking from Jurassic Park. Both early-entry and day guests continue as follows.

7. Take the Jurassic Park River Adventure.

8. Meet Blue at the Raptor Encounter.

9. Ride Hogwarts Express to USF. Have your park-to-park ticket ready.

Tour Universal Studios Florida using Part Two of this plan (see next page); then return to IOA and resume at step 21 below.

21. Chat with the Mystic Fountain.

22. Experience The High in the Sky Seuss Trolley Train Ride! in Seuss Landing.

23. Experience The Cat in the Hat.

24. In Marvel Super Hero Island, ride Doctor Doom's Fearfall.

25. Ride Storm Force Accelatron.

26. Ride The Incredible Hulk Coaster (**26a**) or Jurassic World VelociCoaster (**26b**), whichever one you did not ride earlier.

27. Eat dinner at Thunder Falls Terrace (**27a**) in Jurassic Park or Three Broomsticks (**27b**) in Hogsmeade.

28. See the Frog Choir or *Triwizard Spirit Rally* on the stage outside Hogwarts Castle.

29. See the wand ceremony at Ollivanders and buy a wand, if you wish.

30. Ride Flight of the Hippogriff (if you haven't).

31. Ride Harry Potter and the Forbidden Journey.

32. Ride Hagrid's Magical Creatures Motorbike Adventure in Hogsmeade after sunset, if possible.

33. Watch the last Hogwarts Castle light show of the night (if scheduled) or revisit attractions.

(continued on next page)

Universal Studios Florida

ALTERNATE UNIVERSAL ORLANDO HIGHLIGHTS
ONE-DAY/TWO-PARK TOURING PLAN: **PART TWO**

(continued from previous page)

10. Enter Diagon Alley and ride Harry Potter and the Escape from Gringotts.

11. Ride Men in Black Alien Attack in World Expo.

12. Experience The Simpsons Ride in Springfield.

13. Ride E.T. Adventure in Woody Woodpecker's KidZone.

14. Break for lunch at Simpsons' Fast Food Boulevard (**14a**) or Today Cafe (**14b**) near the front of the park.

15. See *Universal Orlando's Horror Make-Up Show* (**15a**) or *The Bourne Stuntacular* (**15b**) according to the entertainment schedule.

16. Experience Transformers: The Ride—3-D in Production Central.

17. Ride Hollywood Rip Ride Rockit.

18. Ride Race Through New York Starring Jimmy Fallon if the standby wait is short.

19. Ride Revenge of the Mummy in New York.

20. Take a look around Diagon Alley before returning to IOA via Hogwarts Express, or walk back to the other park if the posted wait exceeds 20 minutes.

Resume Part One starting with step 21 (see previous page).

Universal Studios Florida

UNIVERSAL STUDIOS FLORIDA ONE-DAY TOURING PLAN

1. Buy admission in advance. Call ☎ 407-363-8000 or visit universalorlando.com the day before for the official opening time.

2. Arrive at USF 90-120 minutes before the official opening time if Early Park Admission is offered and you're eligible, or 30-45 minutes before opening if you're a day guest. Check Universal's app for daily showtimes.

3. Early-entry guests should visit Ollivanders (**3a**) and ride Harry Potter and the Escape from Gringotts (**3b**). If Gringotts isn't operating, enjoy the rest of Diagon Alley but don't get in line.

4. Before early entry ends, ride Despicable Me Minion Mayhem. Day guests should begin their tour here.

5. Ride Hollywood Rip Ride Rockit.

6. Experience Transformers: The Ride—3-D.

7. Ride Revenge of the Mummy in New York.

8. Ride Race Through New York Starring Jimmy Fallon.

9. Experience Men in Black Alien Attack in World Expo.

10. Ride The Simpsons Ride in Springfield.

11. Try Kang & Kodos' Twirl 'n' Hurl.

12. Ride E.T. Adventure in Woody Woodpecker's KidZone.

13. Eat lunch at Fast Food Boulevard.

14. Work in *Animal Actors on Location!* around lunch, according to the daily entertainment schedule.

15. See *Universal Orlando's Horror Make-Up Show* (**15a**) and *The Bourne Stuntacular* (**15b**) according to the daily entertainment schedule.

16. Chat with the Knight Bus conductor and his shrunken head outside of Diagon Alley. Also look for Kreacher in the window of 12 Grimmauld Place, and dial MAGIC (62442) in the red phone booth.

17. See *Celestina Warbeck and the Banshees*.

18. See the wand ceremony at Ollivanders, and buy a wand if you wish.

19. See *Tales of Beedle the Bard*.

20. Tour Diagon Alley. Browse the shops, explore the dark recesses of Knockturn Alley, and discover the interactive effects. If you're hungry, try the Leaky Cauldron or Florean Fortescue's Ice-Cream Parlour.

21. Ride Harry Potter and the Escape from Gringotts.

22. Revisit favorite attractions, if time permits.

23. If it's scheduled, watch *Universal Orlando's Cinematic Celebration* from Central Park (between Hollywood and Woody Woodpecker's KidZone).

Universal Islands of Adventure

UNIVERSAL'S ISLANDS OF ADVENTURE ONE-DAY TOURING PLAN

1. Buy admission in advance. Call ☎ 407-363-8000 or visit universalorlando.com the day before for the official opening time.

2. Arrive 90–120 minutes before opening if Early Park Admission is offered and you're eligible, or 30–45 minutes before opening if you're a day guest. Check Universal's app for showtimes, and check vltest.universal orlando.com for Virtual Line reservations for Hagrid's Magical Creatures Motorbike Adventure starting at official park opening; if available, deviate from this plan when it's your turn, and return to it after riding.

3. Early-entry guests should ride Hagrid's Magical Creatures Motorbike Adventure only if they are at the front of the pack.

4. Early-entry guests may ride VelociCoaster (4a) or Flight of the Hippogriff (4b), followed by Harry Potter and the Forbidden Journey (4c), if at least 15 minutes remain in early entry.

5. Guests without early entry should first ride The Incredible Hulk Coaster.

6. Ride The Amazing Adventures of Spider-Man. Day guests should start with Spider-Man (6a), followed by Skull Island: Reign of Kong (6b). Early-entry guests may ride Reign of Kong (6b) on their way to Spider-Man (6a) while walking from Jurassic Park. Both early-entry and day guests continue as follows.

7. Take the Jurassic Park River Adventure. Leave your belongings in a pay locker here through the next two rides.

8. Ride Dudley Do-Right's Ripsaw Falls.

9. Ride Popeye & Bluto's Bilge-Rat Barges. Retrieve your property from Jurassic Park.

10. Experience The Cat in the Hat.

11. Experience The High in the Sky Seuss Trolley Train Ride!

12. Eat lunch. A good sit-down choice is Mythos. Make reservations at zomato.com.

13. Explore the Jurassic Park Discovery Center.

14. Meet Blue at the Raptor Encounter.

15. Watch the Frog Choir or *Triwizard Spirit Rally* on the stage outside Hogwarts Castle.

16. See the wand ceremony at Ollivanders, and buy a wand if you wish.

17. See the other show on the stage outside Hogwarts Castle, time permitting.

18. Chat with the Mystic Fountain.

19. See *Poseidon's Fury*.

20. Enjoy the Caro-Seuss-el.

21. Ride One Fish, Two Fish, Red Fish, Blue Fish.

22. Ride Doctor Doom's Fearfall.

23. Ride Storm Force Accelatron.

24. Ride The Incredible Hulk Coaster (24a) or Jurassic World VelociCoaster (24b).

25. Have dinner at Three Broomsticks.

26. Ride Flight of the Hippogriff (if you haven't).

27. Ride Harry Potter and the Forbidden Journey (if you haven't).

28. Ride Hagrid's Magical Creatures Motorbike Adventure, after sunset if possible.

29. Watch the last Hogwarts Castle light show (if scheduled), or revisit any favorite attractions.

Typhoon Lagoon

TYPHOON LAGOON ONE-DAY TOURING PLAN
FOR PARENTS WITH SMALL CHILDREN

1. Arrive at the park entrance 30 minutes before opening. Take care of locker and towel rentals at Singapore Sal's, to your right after you've walked along the winding entrance path and emerged into the park. Find a spot to stow the remainder of your gear, noting any nearby landmarks to help you find your way back.

2. Ride Miss Adventure Falls as many times as you like.

3. Ride Gangplank Falls as many times as you like.

4. If your kids enjoyed Gangplank Falls, try Keelhaul Falls if it seems appropriate.

5. Enjoy the Ketchakiddee Creek kids' play area.

6. Grab some tubes and ride Castaway Creek. A complete circuit takes 20–25 minutes.

7. Swim in the Surf Pool as long as you like.

8. Ride the Bay Slides in the Surf Pool.

9. Repeat your favorite attractions as desired.

Blizzard Beach

BLIZZARD BEACH ONE-DAY TOURING PLAN
FOR PARENTS WITH SMALL CHILDREN

1. Arrive at the park entrance 30 minutes before opening. Take care of locker and towel rentals at Lottawatta Lodge, to your left as you enter the park. Find a spot to stow the remainder of your gear, noting any nearby landmarks to help you find your way back.
2. Take the chairlift up Mount Gushmore to the Green Slope. *Note:* It might be faster—though more tiring—to walk to the top.
3. Raft down Teamboat Springs. Repeat as much as you like while the park is still uncrowded.

4. If your kids are up for it, try the Toboggan Racers.
5. If the kids enjoyed the Toboggan Racers, try the Snow Stormers next.
6. Visit the Ski Patrol Training Camp.
7. Visit Tike's Peak.
8. Grab some tubes and go floating in Cross Country Creek.
9. Swim in Melt-Away Bay's Wave Pool for as long as you like.

MAGIC KINGDOM Touring Plan Companion

Attraction | Recommended Visitation Times | Authors' Rating

Astro Orbiter | Before 11 a.m. or during the last hour before closing | ★★

The Barnstormer (*Genie+*) | Before 11 a.m., during parades, or during the last 2 hours before closing | ★★

Big Thunder Mountain Railroad (*Genie+*) | Before 10 a.m. or during the last hour before closing, or use Genie+ | ★★★★ *Comments* 40" minimum height; pregnant guests should not ride

Buzz Lightyear's Space Ranger Spin (*Genie+*) | First or last hour the park is open | ★★★★

Casey Jr. Splash 'N' Soak Station | When it's hot | ★★★

Country Bear Jamboree | Anytime | ★★★½

Dumbo the Flying Elephant (*Genie+*) | Before 11 a.m. or after 6 p.m. | ★★½

Enchanted Tales with Belle | First or last 2 hours the park is open | ★★★★

Frontierland Shootin' Arcade | Anytime | ★½

The Hall of Presidents | Anytime | ★★★

The Haunted Mansion (*Genie+*) | Before 11 a.m. or during the last 2 hours before closing | ★★★★½ *Comment* Fright potential

It's a Small World (*Genie+*) | Before 11 a.m. or after 7 p.m. | ★★★½

Jungle Cruise (*Genie+*) | Before 10:30 a.m. or during the last 2 hours before closing, or use Genie+ | ★★★½

Liberty Belle Riverboat | Anytime | ★★½

Mad Tea Party (*Genie+*) | Before 11 a.m. or after 5 p.m. | ★★ | *Comments* Pregnant guests should not ride; motion sickness potential

The Magic Carpets of Aladdin (*Genie+*) | Before 11 a.m. or after 7 p.m. | ★★½

The Many Adventures of Winnie the Pooh (*Genie+*) | Before 10 a.m. or during the last hour before closing ★★★½

Meet Ariel at Her Grotto (*Genie+*) | Before 10:30 a.m. or during the last 2 hours before closing | ★★★

Meet Merida at Fairytale Garden | Check *Times Guide* for schedule | ★★★½

Mickey's PhilharMagic (*Genie+*) | Anytime | ★★★★

Monsters, Inc. Laugh Floor (*Genie+*) | Anytime | ★★★

Peter Pan's Flight (*Genie+*) | First or last 30 minutes the park is open | ★★★★

Pete's Silly Sideshow | Before 11 a.m. or during the last 2 hours before closing | ★★★½

A Pirate's Adventure: Treasure of the Seven Seas | Noon–6 p.m. | ★★★½

Pirates of the Caribbean (*Genie+*) | Before 11 a.m., after 7 p.m., or use Genie+ | ★★★★

Prince Charming Regal Carrousel | Anytime | ★★★

Princess Fairytale Hall Meet and Greets (*Genie+*) | Before 10:30 a.m. or after 4 p.m. | ★★★

Seven Dwarfs Mine Train (*ILL*) | At park opening | ★★★★

Space Mountain (*Genie+*) | At park opening or during the last hour before closing | ★★★★ *Comments* Fright and motion sickness potential; 44" minimum height; pregnant guests should not ride

Swiss Family Treehouse | Anytime | ★★★ | *Comment* Fright potential due to height

Tiana's Bayou Adventure (*formerly Splash Moutain; opens 2024; likely ILL*) | *During warm weather:* as soon as the park opens,
during afternoon or evening parades, just before closing, or use Genie+ or ILL (whichever is offered) | *Comments* 40" minimum height; pregnant guests should not ride; you'll get wet

Tom Sawyer Island and Fort Langhorn | Midmorning–late afternoon | ★★★

Tomorrowland Speedway (*Genie+*) | Before 10 a.m. or during the last 2 hours before closing | ★★ *Comments* 54" minimum height requirement for kids to drive unassisted; motion sickness potential

Tomorrowland Transit Authority PeopleMover | Anytime, but especially during hot, crowded times of day (11:30 a.m.–4:30 p.m.) | ★★★½

Town Square Theater Meet and Greets (*Genie+*) | Before 10 a.m. or after 4 p.m. | ★★★★

Tron Lightcycle/Run (*ILL*) | As soon as the park opens, using Early Theme Park Entry if possible, or during the last hour before closing | ★★★★

Under the Sea: Journey of the Little Mermaid (*Genie+*) | Before 10:30 a.m. or during the last 2 hours before closing | ★★★

Walt Disney's Carousel of Progress | Anytime | ★★★

Walt Disney's Enchanted Tiki Room | Before 11 a.m. or after 3:30 p.m. | ★★★

Walt Disney World Railroad | Anytime | ★★★

DINING INFORMATION Counter Service

Restaurant | Location | Quality | Value | Selections

Aloha Isle | Adventureland | Excellent | B+ | Soft-serve, ice-cream floats, pineapple juice

Casey's Corner | Main Street, U.S.A. | Good | C | Hot dogs, plant-based "sausage" dogs, corn dog nuggets, fries, chocolate silk pie

Columbia Harbour House | Liberty Square | Good | B+ | Grilled salmon with rice, fried fish and shrimp, lobster roll, fried chicken, plant-based "crab" cake sandwich, grilled shrimp, salads, hush puppies, milkshake; kids' menu

DINING INFORMATION Counter Service *(continued)*

Cosmic Ray's Starlight Cafe | Tomorrowland | Fair-Poor | C– | Burgers, hot dogs, Greek salad, chicken sandwich, chicken strips, hot dogs, bacon cheeseburger, plant-based burger, chocolate Bundt cake; some kosher

The Diamond Horseshoe *(seasonal)* | Frontierland | Fair-poor | D | All-you-care-to-eat roast turkey, pot roast, pork, veggies, stuffing, and mashed potatoes; Impossible meat loaf; wine and beer

The Friar's Nook | Fantasyland | Good | B | Hot dogs; bacon mac and cheese; bacon, egg, and cheese breakfast croissant with potato tots

Gaston's Tavern | Fantasyland | Good | C | Ham-and-Swiss sandwich, turkey legs, cinnamon rolls, dome cakes, LeFou's Brew (frozen apple juice with toasted-marshmallow flavoring)

Golden Oak Outpost *(seasonal)* | Frontierland | Fair | C | Fried-fish sandwich, chicken strips, chili-cheese fries, chocolate chip cookies, bottled water and soft drinks

Liberty Square Market | Liberty Square | Good | C | Hot dogs, fresh fruit, packaged drinks and snacks

The Lunching Pad | Tomorrowland | Fair | C | Hot dogs, chicken strips, pretzels, specialty frozen drinks

Main Street Bakery (Starbucks) | Main Street, U.S.A. | Good | B | Coffees, pastries, breakfast sandwiches

Pecos Bill Tall Tale Inn and Cafe | Frontierland | Good | C | Pork carnitas and chicken fajita platter, nachos, rice bowl with veggies, salad with or without chicken, burgers, strawberry-limeade slush, shortcake, doughnut holes, yogurt

Pinocchio Village Haus | Fantasyland | Fair-Poor | D | Flatbread pizzas, chicken strips, fries, Caesar salad, kids' menu

Tomorrowland Terrace Restaurant *(seasonal)* | Tomorrowland | Fair | C– | Varies

Tortuga Tavern *(seasonal)* | Adventureland | Fair | B | Chicken strips, burgers, hot dogs

DINING INFORMATION Full Service

Restaurant | Meals Served | Location | Price | Quality | Value | Selections

Be Our Guest Restaurant | L-D | Fantasyland | Expensive | ★★★½ | ★★ | Breakfast, when offered, is counter service. *Lunch and dinner:* French onion soup or charcuterie plate appetizers, pork tenderloin with seasonal vegetables, filet mignon with Robuchon potatoes, pan-seared scallops with risotto

Cinderella's Royal Table | L-D | Fantasyland | Expensive | ★★★ | ★★ | *Breakfast:* Eggs, bacon, sausage, pastries, shrimp and grits, quiche, French toast, beef tenderloin frittata. *Lunch and dinner:* Jumbo-shrimp, salad, and braised-beef appetizers; beef tenderloin with house-made steak sauce, grilled marinated chicken thigh, vegetarian gnocchi, sustainable fish; chocolate mouse, cheesecake, and coffee pot de crème for dessert

The Crystal Palace | B-L-D | Main Street, U.S.A. | Expensive | ★★½ | ★★★ | Buffet with fried chicken, prime rib, Southern Fried Cauliflower, seasonal salads; character meals

Jungle Navigation Co. Ltd. Skipper Canteen | L-D | Adventureland | Expensive | ★★★ | ★★★ | Char siu pork, Korean barbecue–inspired crispy fried chicken, grilled steak with adobo, corn pancakes with pork and avocado cream; chocolate cake with caramelized bananas; plant-based options; kids' menu

Liberty Tree Tavern | L-D | Liberty Square | Expensive | ★★★ | ★★★ | All-you-can-eat platter with roasted turkey, pork roast, mashed potatoes, stuffing, vegetables, and mac and cheese; Impossible Meatloaf; toffee cake

The Plaza Restaurant | L-D | Main Street, U.S.A. | Moderate | ★★ | ★★ | Old-fashioned diner and ice-cream shop fare: burger, chicken sandwich, sundae; kids' menu; wine and beer only

Tony's Town Square Restaurant | L-D | Main Street, U.S.A. | Expensive | ★★★ | ★★ | Pasta (gluten-free and multigrain options available), shrimp fettuccine Alfredo, chicken parmigiana, butcher's steak

Advance Reservations are recommended for most Magic Kingdom full-service restaurants;
call ☎ 407-WDW-DINE (939-3463) or visit disneyworld.disney.go.com/reservations/dining.

GOOD REST AREAS IN THE MAGIC KINGDOM

Back of Storybook Circus, between Big Top Treats and the train station | Fantasyland | Covered plush seating with electrical outlets and USB phone-charging stations

Covered porch with rocking chairs on Tom Sawyer Island | Frontierland | Across the water from the *Liberty Belle* Riverboat dock; bring refreshments from Frontierland; closes at sunset

Cul-de-sac | Main Street, U.S.A. | Between the china shop and Main Street's Starbucks on the right side of the street as you face the castle; refreshments nearby

Picnic tables | Fantasyland | Near the *Tangled*-themed restrooms, between Peter Pan's Flight and The Haunted Mansion; outdoors but has phone-charging stations

Quiet seating area | Tomorrowland | Near restrooms on the right as you approach Space Mountain. Near building to the right of Space Mountain's entrance, near the trees, there's a covered seating area farther back in that corridor; refreshments nearby

Second floor of train station | Main Street, U.S.A. | Refreshments nearby; crowded during fireworks and parades

Upstairs at Columbia Harbour House | Liberty Square | Grab a beverage and relax upstairs; restrooms available

EPCOT Touring Plan Companion

Attraction | Location | Recommended Visitation Times | Authors' Rating

The American Adventure | United States, World Showcase | Anytime | ★★★★

Awesome Planet | The Land, World Nature | Anytime, but save it for later in the day | ★★½

Beauty and the Beast Sing-Along | France, World Showcase | 11 a.m.–6 p.m. | ★★

Canada Far and Wide | Canada, World Showcase | Anytime | ★★★½

Disney & Pixar Short Film Festival (*Genie+*) | Imagination! Pavilion, World Nature | Hardly ever | ★★½

Duck Tales World Showcase Adventure | World Showcase | Anytime | ★★★★

Frozen Ever After (*Genie+*) | Norway, World Showcase | Before noon or after 7 p.m. | ★★★★

Gran Fiesta Tour Starring the Three Caballeros | Mexico, World Showcase | Before noon or after 5 p.m. | ★★½

Guardians of the Galaxy: Cosmic Rewind (*ILL*) | World Discovery | As soon as the park opens, using Early Theme Park Entry if possible. | *Comments* Estimated 42" minimum height; motion sickness potential. | ★★★★

Impressions de France | France, World Showcase | 6:30–8:45 p.m. | ★★★½

Journey into Imagination with Figment (*Genie+*) | Imagination! Pavilion, World Nature | Anytime | ★★½

Living with the Land (*Genie+*) | The Land, World Nature | Before noon or after 3 p.m. | ★★★★

Meet Anna and Elsa at Royal Sommerhus | Norway, World Showcase | At park opening, at lunch or dinner, or during the last hour the park is open | ★★★★

Mission: Space (*Genie+*) | World Discovery | Before noon or after 6 p.m. | ★★★½ | *Comments* Orange version not recommended for pregnant guests or anyone prone to motion sickness or claustrophobia; 40" height requirement for the Green version and 44" height requirement for the Orange version

Reflections of China | China, World Showcase | Anytime | ★★★½

Remy's Ratatouille Adventure (*Genie+*) | France, World Showcase | At park opening. | *Comment* Single-rider line may be available | ★★★★

SeaBase (The Seas Main Tank and Exhibits) | The Seas, World Nature | Before 12:30 p.m. or after 5 p.m., especially when it gets dark early | ★★★½

The Seas with Nemo & Friends (*Genie+*) | The Seas, World Nature | After 2 p.m. | ★★★

Soarin' Around the World (*Genie+*) | The Land, World Nature | First 2 hours the park is open or between 4 p.m. and park closing | ★★★★½ | *Comments* 40" minimum height; motion sickness potential

Spaceship Earth (*Genie+*) | World Celebration | Before noon or after 4 p.m. | ★★★★

Test Track (*Genie+*) | World Discovery | First 30 minutes the park is open or just before closing, or use the single-rider line (if offered) | ★★★★ *Comments* 40" minimum height; pregnant guests should not ride; breaks down frequently

Turtle Talk with Crush (*Genie+*) | The Seas, World Nature | After 3 p.m. | ★★★★

DINING INFORMATION Counter Service

Restaurant | Location | Quality | Value | Selections

L'Artisan des Glaces | France, World Showcase | Excellent | C | Gourmet ice creams and dairy-free sorbets

La Cantina de San Angel | Mexico, World Showcase | Good | B | Tacos; fried cheese empanada; grilled chicken with Mexican rice, corn, and pickled onions; guacamole; churros; margaritas; kids' menu

Connections Cafe | World Celebration | Fair | C | Burgers, pizza, salads, plant-based options

Fife & Drum Tavern | United States, World Showcase | Fair | C | Turkey legs, hot dogs, popcorn, soft-serve ice cream, slushies, beer, alcoholic lemonade, root beer floats

Les Halles Boulangerie–Pâtisserie | France, World Showcase | Good | A | Sandwiches (ham and cheese; Brie, cranberry, and apple), imported-cheese plates, quiches, soups, pastries

Katsura Grill | Japan, World Showcase | Good | B | Sushi; udon noodle bowls; chicken, beef, or shrimp teriyaki; ramen; edamame; miso soup; yuzu tea cheesecake; Kirin beer, sake, plum wine; kids' plate

Kringla Bakeri og Kafe | Norway, World Showcase | Good–Excellent | B | Norwegian pastries and desserts, iced coffee, imported beers and wines

Lotus Blossom Café | China, World Showcase | Fair | C | Egg rolls, pot stickers, orange chicken, chicken fried rice, Mongolian beef with rice, caramel-ginger or lychee ice cream; plum wine, Tsingtao beer

Refreshment Outpost | Between Germany and China, World Showcase | Good | B- | All-beef hot dogs; slushies, soda, draft beer

Refreshment Port | Near Canada, World Showcase | Good | B- | Poutine, chicken nuggets; unusual alcoholic drinks, beer

Regal Eagle Smokehouse: Craft Drafts & Barbecue | United States, World Showcase | Good | B | Regional barbecue specialties, burgers, salads, vegetarian options; beer, hard cider, wine, and specialty cocktails

Rose & Crown Pub | UK, World Showcase | Good | C+ | Fish-and-chips, Scotch egg; beer and spirits

Sommerfest | Germany, World Showcase | Fair | C | Bratwurst, pretzel bread pudding, jumbo pretzel; beer

Sunshine Seasons | The Land, World Nature | Excellent | A | Rotisserie and wood-fired meats and fish; salads, sandwiches; soups

Tangierine Café | Morocco, World Showcase | Good | B | Kebabs; hummus; Moroccan wine and beer

Yorkshire County Fish Shop | United Kingdom, World Showcase | Good | B+ | Fish-and-chips, draft ale

DINING INFORMATION Full Service

Restaurant | Meals Served | Location | Price | Quality | Value | Selections

Akershus Royal Banquet Hall | L-D | Norway, World Showcase | Expensive | ★★ | ★★★★ | *Dinner:* Salad with lingonberry vinaigrette, Norwegian meatballs, grilled salmon, chicken and dumplings, lefse, mashed potatoes, green beans; kids' menu; full bar; character meal

Biergarten Restaurant | L-D | Germany, World Showcase | Expensive | ★★ | ★★★★ | Traditional German sausages, potato salad, homemade spaetzle, roast chicken, braised red cabbage; full bar

Le Cellier Steakhouse | L-D | Canada, World Showcase | Expensive | ★★★★ | ★★★½ | Charcuterie plate appetizer with edible beef-fat candle, Canadian Cheddar soup, steak, mac and cheese, loaded mashed potatoes, poutine, warm pecan–brown butter tart; full bar and Canadian wines

Chefs de France | L-D | France, World Showcase | Expensive | ★★★ | ★★★ | Boeuf Bourguignon, French onion soup topped with Gruyère; vegetarian options; beer, wine, cocktails

Coral Reef Restaurant | L-D | The Seas, Future World | Expensive | ★★ | ★★ | Steak and seafood; chocolate cake; full bar

La Crêperie de Paris | B-L-D | France, World Showcase | Moderate | ★★★½ | ★★★★ | Cuisine from the Brittany region of France: chèvre, spinach, and walnut savory crepe, banana-filled dessert crepe

Garden Grill Restaurant | L-D | The Land, World Nature | Expensive | ★★★ | ★★★ | Grilled beef with chimichurri, turkey breast with stuffing and gravy, BBQ ribs, mashed potatoes, veggies, salads; berry shortcake; plant-based options; kids' menu; wine, beer, and mixed drinks; character meals

La Hacienda de San Angel | D | Mexico, World Showcase | Expensive | ★★★★ | ★★★½ | Flautas appetizer, queso fundido, guacamole, carne asada–style NY strip, fried-shrimp tacos, tenderloin fajitas; full bar with margaritas and specialty tequilas

Monsieur Paul | D | France, World Showcase | Expensive | ★★★½ | ★★★ | Black-truffle soup, black sea bass in potato "scales," roasted duck; kids' menu; full bar

Nine Dragons Restaurant | L-D | China, World Showcase | Moderate | ★★★ | ★★½ | Crispy duck bao buns, honey-sesame chicken, salt-and-pepper shrimp; full bar

Rose & Crown Dining Room | L-D | United Kingdom, World Showcase | Moderate | ★★★½ | ★★ | Fish-and-chips, bangers and mash, shepherd's pie (with vegetarian option), Scotch egg; sticky toffee pudding; full bar

San Angel Inn Restaurante | L-D | Mexico, World Showcase | | ★★★ | ★★ | Queso fundido appetizer, rib eye tacos, vegetarian huarache; chocolate "fiesta" pyramid, sweet corn ice cream; full bar

Space 220 | L-D | World Discovery | Expensive | ★★★ | ★★ | Seared tuna, burger, vegetarian stuffed shells, chicken breast with potato gratin, spaghetti with shrimp, miso-glazed salmon, salads; Burrata, fried cauliflower, and fried calamari appetizers; kids' menu; dessert drinks; full bar

Spice Road Table | L-D | Morocco, World Showcase | Expensive | ★★★★ | ★★★ | Mediterranean-style small plates including fried calamari and hummus fries, lamb kefta, spiced shrimp and chicken; full bar

Takumi-Tei | D | Japan, World Showcase | Expensive | ★★★★ | ★★★½ | Frequently changing menu showcasing traditional Japanese kaiseki cuisine: crab appetizer, Wagyu beef, sushi; full bar

Teppan Edo | L-D | Japan, World Showcase | Expensive | ★★★★ | ★★★ | Chicken, shrimp, beef, scallops, and veggies stir-fried on teppanyaki grill; full bar

Tokyo Dining | L-D | Japan, World Showcase | Moderate | ★★★★ | ★★★ | Sushi and sashimi; full bar

Tutto Gusto Wine Cellar | D | Italy, World Showcase | Expensive | ★★★★ | ★★★ | Shareable plates with cheeses, charcuterie, and marinated vegetables; tiramisu, gelato, sorbet, torta di ricotta, cannoli; kids' menu; wine flights

Tutto Italia Ristorante | L-D | Italy, World Showcase | Expensive | ★★★★ | ★★ | Pasta, steak, salmon, chicken, fried calamari; torta di ricotta, tiramisu, cannoli, gelato; wine flights

Via Napoli Ristorante e Pizzeria | L-D | Italy, World Showcase | Expensive | ★★★½ | ★★★ | Wood-fired pizzas, pastas, beef filet, Mediterranean sea bass, chicken Parmesan; tiramisu, panna cotta, Torta Della Nonna, cheesecake; kids' menu; beer and wine

Advance Reservations recommended for most EPCOT full-service restaurants; call ☎ 407-WDW-DINE (939-3463) or visit disneyworld.disney.go.com/reservations/dining.

GOOD REST AREAS IN EPCOT

Benches | Mexico, World Showcase | Inside the pavilion against the inside of the wall that forms the walking ramps to the retail space; air-conditioned

Benches | The Seas, World Nature | Air-conditioned

Japan gardens | Japan, World Showcase | To the left of Katsura Grill, a set of tables overlooking a lovely garden and koi pond; outdoors but shaded, with refreshments nearby

Rotunda and lobby | United States, World Showcase | Ample room; air-conditioned; refreshments nearby; usually quiet

UK Rose Garden benches | United Kingdom, World Showcase | A small town square and manicured gardens behind the pavilion

DISNEY'S ANIMAL KINGDOM Touring Plan Companion

Attraction | Recommended Visitation Times | Authors' Rating

The Animation Experience at Conservation Station (*Genie+*) | Check *Times Guide* for hours | ★★★

Avatar Flight of Passage (*ILL*) | At park opening or after 3 p.m. | ★★★★½ | *Comments* 44" minimum height; pregnant guests should not ride

The Boneyard | Anytime; opens 1 hour after rest of park | ★★★½

Conservation Station and Affection Section | Anytime | ★★★

Dinosaur (*Genie+*) | Before 10:30 a.m. or after 4 p.m. | ★★★★ | *Comments* Fright potential; 40" minimum height; pregnant guests should not ride

Expedition Everest (*Genie+*) | First or last hour the park is open | ★★★★½ | *Comments* 44" minimum height; motion sickness potential; pregnant guests should not ride; single-rider line available

Finding Nemo: The Big Blue . . . and Beyond! / Theater in the Wild (*Genie+*) | Anytime

Feathered Friends in Flight (*Genie+*) | Anytime | ★★★★

Festival of the Lion King (*Genie+*) | Before 11 a.m. or after 4 p.m.; check *Times Guide* for showtimes | ★★★★

Gorilla Falls Exploration Trail | Before or after Kilimanjaro Safaris; check *Times Guide* for off-season closures | ★★★★

Kali River Rapids (*Genie+*) | Before 11 a.m. or last hour the park is open | ★★★½ | *Comments* You'll get wet; 38" minimum height; pregnant guests should note that the ride is bouncy

Kilimanjaro Safaris (*Genie+*) | At park opening or after 3 p.m. | ★★★★★

Maharajah Jungle Trek | Anytime it's open; may open later and close earlier than rest of park | ★★★★

Meet Favorite Disney Pals at Adventurers Outpost (*Genie+*) | First thing in the morning or after 5 p.m. | ★★★½

Na'vi River Journey (*Genie+*) | Before 9:30 a.m. or during the last 2 hours before closing | ★★★½

The Oasis | Anytime | NA

Tree of Life ★★★★½ / *Awakenings* ★★★★ / *It's Tough to Be a Bug!* ★★★ (*Genie+*) | Anytime | *Comment* Fright potential for *It's Tough to Be a Bug!*

TriceraTop Spin | Before noon or after 3 p.m. | ★★

Wilderness Explorers | Sign up first thing in the morning and complete activities throughout the day. | ★★★★

Wildlife Express Train | Anytime | ★★

DINING INFORMATION Counter Service

Restaurant | Location | Quality | Value | Selections

Creature Comforts (Starbucks) | Discovery Island near Africa | Good | C | Coffee and espresso drinks, teas, sandwiches, pastries

Flame Tree Barbecue | Discovery Island | Excellent | B- | Pulled-pork sandwich, ribs, smoked half-chicken, smokehouse chicken salad, mac and cheese with smoked pulled pork, plant-based "sausage" sandwich, fries and onion rings; child's plate of baked chicken drumstick, hot dog, or PB&J sandwich; beer, frozen rum drink, wine

Harambe Market | Africa | Good | B | Grilled chicken or ribs served over rice and salad greens; salads; plant-based "sausage"; kids' menu

Kusafiri Coffee Shop and Bakery | Africa | Good | B | Impossible empanadas; flatbreads; croissants, cinnamon rolls and other pastries; sausage, egg, and cheese biscuit; cookies; coffee and beer; some kosher

Pizzafari | Discovery Island | Fair | C | Chicken Parmesan sandwich; cheese, pepperoni, and sausage personal pizzas; Caesar salad; kids' menu; cannoli cake

Restaurantosaurus | DinoLand U.S.A. | Fair | C | Burgers, chili-cheese hot dog, chicken sandwich, chicken nuggets, Cobb salad, breaded shrimp, plant-based Southwestern burger; kids' menu

Royal Anandapur Tea Company | Asia | Good | B | Hot and iced teas, hot chocolate, coffee and espresso drinks, frozen chai, pastries

Satu'li Canteen | Pandora | Good | A | Customizable bowls with chicken, beef, shrimp, or fried tofu; steamed "pods" (stuffed bao buns); kids' menu

Yak & Yeti Local Food Cafes | Asia | Fair | C | Honey chicken with steamed rice, cheeseburger, teriyaki chicken salad, vegetable tikka masala, Korean fried-chicken sandwich, tempura shrimp, egg rolls, fried rice; kids' menu; American-style breakfast fare

DINING INFORMATION Full Service

Restaurant | Meals Served | Location | Price | Quality | Value | Selections

Rainforest Cafe | B-L-D | Park entrance | Moderate | ★★ | ★★ | Spinach-and-artichoke dip, coconut shrimp, burgers, ribs; brownie cake with ice cream; full bar

Tiffins | L-D | Discovery Island | Expensive | ★★★★ | ★★★ | Charred octopus and honey-glazed pork belly appetizers, whole fried sustainable fish, butter chicken; full bar

DINING INFORMATION Full Service *(continued)*

Tusker House Restaurant | B–L–D | Africa | Expensive | ★★★ | ★★★ | Roast pork, beef, and chicken; character meals; full bar next door

Yak & Yeti Restaurant | L–D | Asia | Expensive | ★★½ | ★★ | Lo mein noodle bowls, coconut shrimp, chicken tikka masala, Korean fried-chicken tenders, firecracker shrimp; full bar

Advance Reservations recommended for most Animal Kingdom full-service restaurants; call ☎ 407-WDW-DINE (939-3463) *or visit* disneyworld.disney.go.com/reservations/dining.

GOOD REST AREAS IN DISNEY'S ANIMAL KINGDOM

Gazebo behind Flame Tree Barbecue | Discovery Island | Follow the path toward the water, along the left side of Flame Tree Barbecue; gazebo has ceiling fans

Outdoor covered benches near exit from Dinosaur | DinoLand U.S.A. | Gazebo-like structure with nearby water fountain

Seating area adjacent to Dawa Bar | Africa | Refreshments nearby; outdoors and can be noisy from street performers

Walkway between Africa and Asia | Plenty of shaded rest spots, some overlooking streams; refreshments nearby; a favorite of *Unofficial Guide* researchers

DISNEY'S HOLLYWOOD STUDIOS Touring Plan Companion

Attraction | Recommended Visitation Times | Authors' Rating

Alien Swirling Saucers (*Genie+*) | First 30 minutes the park is open or after 3 p.m. | ★★½ |
Comment 32" minimum height requirement; motion sickness potential

Beauty and the Beast—Live on Stage / Theater of the Stars (*Genie+*) | Anytime, but not as hot after
sunset | ★★★★

Disney Junior Play and Dance! (*Genie+*) | Check *Times Guide* for schedule | ★★

Fantasmic! | Check *Times Guide*; if 2 shows are offered, the second will be less crowded | ★★★★½

For the First Time in Forever: A Frozen Sing-Along Celebration (*Genie+*) | Check *Times Guide* for
showtimes | ★★★½

Indiana Jones Epic Stunt Spectacular! (*Genie+*) | First 2 shows or last show | ★★★½

Lightning McQueen's Racing Academy | Anytime | ★★½

Meet Disney Stars at Red Carpet Dreams | First or last hour the park is open or during mealtimes |
★★★★

Meet Olaf at Celebrity Spotlight | First or last hour the park is open or during mealtimes | ★★★½

Mickey and Minnie's Runaway Railway (*Genie+*) | At opening or during the last hour before closing |
★★★★

Millennium Falcon: Smugglers Run (*Genie+*) | At opening or after 6 p.m. | ★★★★ |
Comments 38" minimum height; pregnant guests should not ride; motion sickness potential;
single-rider line available

Muppet-Vision 3-D (*Genie+*) | Anytime | ★★★★

Rock 'n' Roller Coaster Starring Aerosmith (*Genie+*) | First 30 minutes the park is open or after 4 p.m. |
★★★★ | Comments 48" minimum height requirement; pregnant guests should not ride; motion
sickness potential; single-rider line available

Slinky Dog Dash (*Genie+*) | At opening or just before closing | ★★★★ | Comment 38" minimum height

Star Tours—The Adventures Continue (*Genie+*) | During lunch or after 4 p.m. | ★★★½ |
Comments Fright potential; 40" minimum height requirement; pregnant guests should not ride;
motion sickness potential

Star Wars Launch Bay | Check *Times Guide* for showtimes | ★★★

Star Wars: Rise of the Resistance (*ILL*) | When your boarding group is called. Get a boarding group on
the My Disney Experience app at exactly 7 a.m. or 1 p.m. on the day of your visit | ★★★★★ |
Comments 40" minimum height; pregnant guests should not ride; motion sickness potential

Toy Story Mania! (*Genie+*) | At opening or after 4:30 p.m. | ★★★★½

The Twilight Zone Tower of Terror (*Genie+*) | First 30 minutes the park is open or after 4 p.m. |
★★★★★ | Comments 40" minimum height requirement; pregnant guests should not ride

Vacation Fun at Mickey Shorts Theater | Anytime | ★★★½

Walt Disney Presents | Anytime | ★★★

DINING INFORMATION Counter Service

Restaurant | Location | Quality | Value | Selections

ABC Commissary | Commissary Lane | Fair | D | Pork carnitas or shrimp tacos, Buffalo chicken grilled
cheese, Mediterranean salad (vegetarian option available), chicken club sandwich, plant-based burger;
kids' menu; some kosher; wine and beer

Backlot Express | Echo Lake | Fair | C | Angus bacon cheeseburger, chicken strips, Cuban sandwich,
Southwest salad, teriyaki chicken or tofu bowl

Catalina Eddie's | Sunset Boulevard | Fair | C | Cheese and pepperoni pizzas, Caesar salad with or without
chicken; kids' menu

Docking Bay 7 Food and Cargo | Galaxy's Edge | Excellent | A | Smoked ribs served with blueberry corn
muffins, roasted chicken served on salad greens or with mac and cheese and roasted veggies, tuna poke;
vegan menu

Dockside Diner | Echo Lake | Fair | C | Shrimp salad roll, chicken salad roll, smoked fish dip

Fairfax Fare | Sunset Boulevard | Fair | B | Assorted hot dogs, Chicago-style hot dog salad

Milk Stand | Galaxy's Edge | Fair | D | Frozen nondairy drinks, with or without alcohol

Oga's Cantina | Galaxy's Edge | Fair | D | Batuu Bits snack mix; sampler platter with cured and roasted
meats, cheese, and pork cracklings; alcoholic and nonalcoholic cocktails; wine and beer |
Comment Online reservations available

PizzeRizzo | Grand Avenue | Poor | D | Personal pizzas, meatball subs, salads | Comment Not recommended

Ronto Roasters | Galaxy's Edge | Good | B | Pita wrap filled with roast pork, grilled pork sausage, and slaw;
pork rinds; nonalcoholic fruit punch; breakfast wraps

Rosie's All-American Cafe | Hollywood Boulevard | Fair | C | Burgers, hot dogs, chicken nuggets, fries,
plant-based "lobster" roll; child's chicken nuggets with a yogurt smoothie and fruit

The Trolley Car Cafe (Starbucks) | Hollywood Boulevard | Good | B | Coffee and espresso drinks, tea,
breakfast sandwiches, pastries

DINING INFORMATION Counter Service (continued)

Woody's Lunch Box | Toy Story Land | Excellent | A– | *Breakfast:* Lunch Box Tarts; breakfast bowl with scrambled eggs, potato barrels, and country gravy *Lunch and dinner:* Sandwiches (barbecue brisket, smoked turkey, grilled three cheese), tomato-basil soup, "totchos" (potato barrels with chili, queso, and corn chips)

DINING INFORMATION Full Service

Restaurant | Meals Served | Location | Price | Quality | Value | Selections

50's Prime Time Cafe | L-D | Echo Lake | Moderate | ★★★ | ★★★ | Pot roast, meat loaf, fried chicken, PB&J milkshake, warm apple crisp, chocolate–peanut butter layer cake; full bar

Hollywood & Vine | B-L-D | Echo Lake | Expensive | ★★★ | ★★★ | *Breakfast:* Caramel sticky buns *Dinner:* Beef tenderloin, roast chicken, mac and cheese with shrimp, roast pork, plant-based option; character breakfast; full bar

The Hollywood Brown Derby | L-D | Hollywood Boulevard | Expensive | ★★★★ | ★★★ | Cobb Salad (named after the owner of the original restaurant), pork, lamb, chicken breast; grapefruit cake; kids' menu. Patio lounge serves cocktails and small plates.

Mama Melrose's Ristorante Italiano | L-D | Grand Avenue | Expensive | ★★★ | ★★ | Seasonal pastas, fresh mozzarella, campanelle with shrimp, flatbread "pizzas," charred strip steak; tiramisu, chocolate-and-cherry torte, cannoli; full bar

Sci-Fi Dine-In Theater Restaurant | L-D | Commissary Lane | Moderate | ★★½ | ★★ | Sandwiches, burgers (plant-based option available), pasta; shakes and sundaes; kids' menu; full bar

Advance Reservations recommended for DHS full-service restaurants; call ☎ 407-WDW-DINE (939-3463) *or visit* disneyworld.disney.go.com/reservations/dining.

GOOD REST AREAS IN DISNEY'S HOLLYWOOD STUDIOS

Animation Building | Animation Courtyard | Benches in and around Star Wars Launch Bay; refreshments nearby

Benches along Echo Lake | Some shaded; refreshments nearby

Covered seating behind Sunshine Day Bar | Sunset Boulevard | Refreshments nearby; ample seating

Tune-In Lounge | Echo Lake, next to 50's Prime Time Cafe | Air-conditioned bar; nonalcoholic drinks and food from the cafe also available (thanks to Matt Hochberg of studioscentral.com for this tip)

UNOFFICIAL GUIDE USE #37
DEAD WEIGHT TO KEEP YOU GROUNDED DURING HURRICANES.